Caribbean Freedom

Economy and Society from Emancipation to the Present

A STUDENT READER

Editors:

Hilary Beckles and Verene Shepherd

 Markus Weiner Publishers, Princeton

 James Curry Publishers, London

 Ian Randle Publishers, Kingston, Jamaica

For Gordon Lewis, Neville Hall and Walter Rodney

First American Edition, 1996
©1993 Hilary McD. Beckles and Verene Shepherd

For information write to:

Markus Wiener Publishers
114 Jefferson Road, Princeton, NJ 08540

Ian Randle Publishers Limited,
206 Old Hope Road, Kingston 6, Jamaica.

James Curry Publishers
54b Thornhill Square, Islington, London, N1 1BE

United States Library of Congress Cataloging-In Publication Data
Caribbean Freedom: Society and Economy from Emancipation to the Present
Originally published: Kingston, Jamaica: I. Randle Publishers;
London: J. Curry Publishers, 1993.
Includes bibliographical references
ISBN 1-55876-128-4
1. Caribbean Area - Social conditions. 2. Caribbean Area -
Economic conditions.
3. Caribbean Area - Politics and government
I Beckles, Hilary, 1995
II Shepherd, Verene A.
HN 192.C37 1996
95-52867
301 09729-dc20

National Library of Jamaica Cataloguing in Publication Data
I. Beckles, Hilary
II Shepherd, Verene A.
Caribbean Freedom: Economy and Society from Emancipation to the Present
ISBN 976-8100-17-6

British Cataloguing in Publication Data
I. Beckles, Hilary McD
II Shepherd, Verene A.
Caribbean Freedom: Economy and Society from Emancipation to the Present
972.9
ISBN 0-85255-711-6

Printed in The United States of America on acid-free paper

CONTENTS

PREFACE

Our American colleagues in particular, have long demonstrated that Readers occupy an important niche in the literature that supports the teaching of defined courses and area studies. Clearly these collections are **not** intended (though they may be misused) as substitutes for monographs, journal articles and textbooks. Rather, editors expect them to be used in conjunction with complete units of literature as a means of highlighting the major perspectives, themes and interpretations that dominate the monograph and journal literature. Therefore, when they are well organized, and when students recognize their supplementary role, they become valuable guides for students (and teachers) to the current state of research and to the major debates between scholars. In these ways they can contribute significantly to teaching and learning by introducing students to important aspects of scholarship.

In Caribbean history, there is a special need for such aids. Increasingly over the last twenty years, important new research has been published but, as one would expect, most of this research remains relatively inaccessible to students because it exists in monographs and learned journals, many of which are chronically in short supply. To aggravate the problem, there is not yet available either a university-level general history or textbooks which provide comprehensive coverage and reflect a full appreciation of the current state of research. Until,

therefore, a good general history is finally published or quality textbooks are produced, this Reader, like its companion volume, **Caribbean Slave Society and Economy**, must play the dual role of outlining the contours of the subject and of pointing out the major interpretations and debates.

Certain complexities in subject matter as well as some aspects of the historiography make a Post-Slavery Reader particularly essential. While Caribbean history of the sixteenth to eighteenth centuries may be said to possess obvious unifying themes in European colonization, the plantation, and African enslavement, the post-slavery experience does not display a similar coherence. Adjustment to Emancipation and modernization do not adequately capture the great variety of developments in different territories and sub-regions during the post-slavery period. At the same time, as one would expect, research and writing in recent and current history have not been the exclusive domain of historians. Social scientists of all stripes have contributed to the historical literature to a larger degree than they have done for any earlier period. Because it is vital that students (and teachers) should not overlook these contributions, the Reader's role as a guide must also be interpretive and historiographical: calling attention to the variety of experience, and identifying all the major contributors and contributions to the literature.

W.K. Marshall

INTRODUCTION

The Caribbean region was first within the Atlantic colonial complex to experience a general emancipation of slaves and to build a society upon the premise of universal citizenry. It was also in the Caribbean that slaves, unlike their counterparts elsewhere, achieved their freedom by revolutionary self-liberation. These events took place between 1791 and 1804 in the French colony of St. Dominigue which occupied the western portion of the island of Hispaniola. After a protracted and bloody war, slaves and their free black and coloured allies, overthrew the planters' regime, took control of government, and declared the abolition of slavery. In 1804, the victors took these measures to their logical conclusion by proclaiming the end of the colonial relation and the establishment of the Independent Republic of Haiti. The impact of these developments upon the Caribbean was profound. In effect, they signalled the beginning of the end of slavery and colonial rule.

Subsequent struggles for Caribbean freedom, both in terms of internal social relations and the termination of the colonial status, were not often characterized by armed warfare, but reflected an amplification and extension of similar conceptual processes witnessed within Haiti. In general, these developments embrace three broad themes: first, the drawn out disintegration of the heterogeneous, but institutionally unifying slave systems (completed in 1886 with abolition in Cuba); second, the immediate attempts by resident social groups and imperial agencies to accept and adjust to refashioned socio-economic and political arrangements; third, the maturity of nationalist consciousness in which politically confident creoles asserted their autonomy and ontology in terms of constitutional and cultural independence.

Several generations of historical researchers have analyzed and assessed these remarkable events and processes and have illustrated the manner in which they constituted the foundations on which the structures of Caribbean civilization rest. On the whole, the historiography has been conceptually contentious, but empirically rich and intellectually gripping. The 'nature' of emancipation has received considerable attention, not surprisingly, since interpretations of contemporary society and economy rest to a great extent upon perceptions of what actually transpired at the onset of 'freedom'.

No matter how emancipation is conceived, dichotomous models based upon variables of fundamental continuity and change emerge, seeking generally to problematize the idea that it was in the final instance a revolutionary measure. With the benefit of hindsight, former slave owners and their respective imperial support groups, could conclude that the potential for radical transformation was considerably diminished once measures to curb the freedom of blacks by retaining control of government proved effective. Former slaves, however, did ultimately recognize that emancipation legislation did transform the nature of their lives in such drastic ways that conditionalities and constraints apart, the break with the past was so deep and irretrievable, that altogether it constituted a revolutionary experience.

Emancipation as a process, rather than an event, however, remained 'in action' well into the matured years of the first generation of those born within it. Experiences, of course, varied across the region, but it is now understood that patterns of historical change in individual territories were determined to a considerable degree by those features endemic to the slavery period.

The 'new beginning' then, could very well be conceived as a logical state in the unfolding of colonial relations. The resort to draconian labour laws in Haiti in 1826, for example, which were designed to secure and discipline workers for large-scale production, set the precedent for the entire region during the subsequent fifty years. This development illustrated clearly that the role of labour as a factor of production within the economics of emancipation, and the rights and expectations of labourers as 'citizens' within the politics of freedom, proved contradictory. As a result, political conflict (occasionally characterized by armed struggle) between traditional owners of the means of production on the one hand, and the continuing disenfranchised majority on the other, constituted the principal dialectical force that shaped the nature of the post-slavery period.

Since emancipation as an event did not produce any immediate success in the area of redressing major imbalances, such as extreme inequality in wealth distribution, and minority ethnic domination of political institutions, conflict over the use of state power, ownership and possession of land, and terms and conditions on the labour market, also remained endemic. That the emancipated should pursue the political franchise and ownership of land, in themselves directly related, with as much tenacity as their determination to receive a reasonable wage and honourable working conditions, should be interpreted as constituting proof of the broad-based nature of their expectations of freedom. Attempt by the ruling class to keep them marginal to both the electoral process and resource ownership should not be seen as separate and distinct from efforts to depress wage levels and maintain slave-like working conditions by means of the mass reduction of servile labour and the imposition of various systems of rent extraction.

Certainly, the crisis of profitability in the dominant sugar plantation sector of English colonies brought into sharper focus the necessity for social welfare policies and the role of gender in the division of labour. The relationship between sex, work and wage levels within the context of diminishing returns on capital indicated without a doubt that patriarchy had not only remained intact, but had strengthened ideologically and institutionally. Reforms, then, were few and had to be hard fought for. As a result, the ending of the nineteenth century witnessed the survival of many of the features evident at its beginning, some of which were clearly anachronistic.

During the 1920s and 1930s Caribbean people engaged in a range of political actions, violent and non-violent, against the legacies of the slave order long abolished in most places. Workers of all racial groups demanded economic justice within the market economy, racial equality within social life, political freedom within a democratic ethos, as well as an end to the abuses of empire and colonial domination. These were years of momentous transformation. In general, agitators called for the removal of the surviving elements of the nineteenth century world, and proposed instead rapid modernization in the areas of political liberalization, economic diversification and the right to social mobility and justice. These demands were reflected in the teachings and visions of Cuban José Martí at the end of the nineteenth century and Jamaican Marcus Garvey at the beginning of the twentieth century; both emphasized the need to struggle for West Indian nationhood, political independence, and social justice.

In the inter-war period, the pace of events moved rapidly. The call for industrialization, constitutional independence and socialist reforms became the order of the day. In most places these developments were accompanied by a cultural renaissance that emerged from, and dialectically reinforced, nationalist sensibilities and redefined ideological parameters. In turn, the Caribbean was forced to come to terms with the militancy of American imperialist aggression as relationships with Europe were being reconfigured. Euro-American imperialist responses to the Cuban revolution in 1959 brought back memories of what had transpired in Haiti at the beginning to the nineteenth century; while the 'black power movement' of the 1960s and 1970s sought to reaffirm the basic correctness of the grand Haitian ideological stance. Together, they indicate the inability of colonizing mentalities to see the Caribbean as a civilisation with the legitimate right to fashion its own destiny.

This book, then, seeks to address these various themes, and to reflect the general trends and specific focuses of Caribbean historiography. As editors, we have sought to be as comprehensive as possible, not only in thematic coverage, but also in terms of our presentation of the Caribbean as an historically unified world. In this regard, our hope is that we have correctly located and captured the epistomological concerns of authors whose work we have selected, and in few instances, edited.

The historiographical contour we followed does not evade those areas not rich in literature and polemics. Rather, we sought to identify both the high and low ground of research and writing, and to give even and equal treatment whenever possible. We are fully aware that our principal task is to present a teaching manual for students and tutors alike who function within the contexts of universities, colleges and upper levels of high schools. For this reason, some themes are given an in-depth treatment on a territorial basis, rather than a general survey. This methodological diversity, we hope, will enhance the volume's overall usefulness.

It is our wish, also that users will eventually agree that the book constitutes a reasonable representation of the general historiographic condition. If it facilitates their wish to follow through various themes and ideas outlined in volume one (which covers the slavery period) then half of our mission is complete.

Finally, we have sought to come as close as possible to the 'present'—given, of course, historians' rather peculiar interpretation of the term. Currently, the most immediate striking feature of the region's anxieties is the almost universal attempt of governments to wrestle with the fiscal and monetary policies of global financial institutions upon which they have grown increasingly dependent for economic viability; the most visible of which is the International Monetary Fund (IMF). In light of this reality, and given the quest for freedom and sovereignty so endemic within the Caribbean world, we decided to conclude with an assessment of the 1984 anti-IMF peoples' revolt in the Dominican Republic. This mass political action, we believe, for reasons that are indicated by the principal historical themes presented, and which might become clearer in the future, is the most fitting place to end the 'present'.

Hilary McD Beckles
Verene A. Shepherd

Acknowledgements

The Editors and Publishers are grateful to the authors and original publishers for their gracious permission to reproduce their work in this volume. Listed below are the original publication details.

Expectations of a New Beginning

Mats Lundhal, 'Toussaint L'ouverture and the War Economy of St. Dominique 1796–1802'. Reprinted by permission from the sixth issue, number two of *Slavery and Abolition* published by Frank Cass & Company Limited, 11 Gainsborough Road, London E11, England. Copyright Frank Cass & Co. Ltd.

Woodville Marshall, 'We be wise to many more things': Blacks' Hopes and Expectations of Emancipation. *Social and Economic Studies,* Institute of Social and Economic Research U.W.I. Mona Kingston, Jamaica No:17, 1968

Rebecca Scott, 'Former Slaves: Responses to Emancipation in Cuba' from *Slave Emancipation in Cuba: The Transition to Free Labor 1860–1899* pp. 227–240. Princeton University Press, Princeton New Jersey. The Editors thank the author for permission to change the title from the original ''Former Slaves''.

William Green, 'The Creolization of Caribbean History: The Emancipation Era and a Critique of the Dialectical Analysis'. Reprinted by permission from the fourteenth issue, number three of *Journal of Imperial and Commonwealth History* published by Frank Cass and Company Limited, 11 Gainsborough Road, London E11, England. Copyright Frank Cass and Co. Ltd.

Emancipation in Action

Robert LaCerte, 'The Evolution of Land and Labor in the Haitian Revolution 1791–1820', *The Americas Vol. XXXIV No. 4* pp. 449–459. Academy of American Franciscan History, Washington, D.C.

Swithin Wilmot 'Emancipation in Action: Workers and Wage Conflict in Jamaica 1838–1848' *Jamaica Journal Vol. 19 No. 3 1986* pp. 55–61.

Douglas Hall 'The Flight from the Estates Reconsidered: The British West Indies, 1838–1842' *Journal of Caribbean History Vol. 10/11 1978* pp. 7–24.

Woodville Marshall 'Metayage in the Sugar Industry of the British Windward Islands, 1838–1865' *Jamaica Historical Review Vol. 5, 1965.*

Rosamunde Renard 'Labour Relations in Post-Slavery Martinique and Guadeloupe' unpublished paper.

Peasants and Planters

Sidney Mintz 'The Origins of Reconstituted Peasantries' in Mintz: *Caribbean Transformations,* Johns Hopkins University Press, Baltimore Md. 1974 pp. 146–156.

Woodville Marshall 'Notes on Peasant Development in the West Indies since 1838' *Social and Economic Studies, Vol. 17 1968* pp. 1–14.

Nigel Bolland 'Systems of Domination after Slavery: The Control of Land and Labour in the British West Indies after 1838' *Comparative Studies in Society and History Vol. 23 No. 4 1981* pp. 591–619.

Howard Johnson 'The Share System in Nineteenth Century Bahamas' Reprinted by permission from the fifth issue of *Slavery and Abolition* published by Frank Cass and Company Limited, 11 Gainsborough Road, London E11, England. Copyright Frank Cass and Co. Ltd.

Immigrants and Indentured Labourers

Mary Turner 'Chinese Contract Labor in Cuba 1847–1874' *Caribbean Studies Vol. 14 No. 2 1974* pp. 66–81.

Keith Laurence 'The Evolution of Long-term Labour Contracts in Trinidad and British Guiana 1834–1863' *Jamaica Historical Review Vol. 5 1965.*

Brian Moore 'The Social Impact of Portuguese Immigrants into British Guiana after Emancipation' *Buletin de Estudios Latinoamericanos y del Caribe Vol. 19 1975* pp. 3–15.

Rosamunde Renard 'Immigration and Indentureship in the French West Indies, 1848–1870'. Unpublished paper.

Government, Political Control and Popular Revolt

Roy Augier 'Before and After 1865' *New World Quarterly Vol. 2 No. 2 1965.*

George Belle 'The Abortive Revolution of 1876 in Barbados' *Journal of Caribbean History Vol. 18 1984* pp. 1–32.

Michael Craton 'Continuity not Change: The incidence of Unrest among Ex-slaves in the British West Indies 1838–1876' Reprinted by permission from the ninth issue number two of *Slavery and Abolition* published by Frank Cass and Company Limited, 11 Gainsborough Road, London E11, England. Copyright Frank Cass & Co. Ltd.

Kusha Haraksingh 'Control and Resistance Among Overseas Indian Workers: A Study of Labour on the Sugar Plantations of Trinidad, 1875–1917' *Journal of Caribbean History Vol. 14 1981* pp. 1–17.

Women and Gender

Janet Momsen 'Gender Roles in Caribbean Agricultural Labour' in Malcolm Cross and Gad Heuman (eds.) *Labour in the Caribbean*; Macmillan Publishers, London 1988 pp. 141–158.

Rhoda Reddock 'Indian Women and Indentureship in Trinidad and Tobago, 1845–1917' *Caribbean Quarterly Vol. 32 No. 3/4, 1986* pp. 27–49.

Sidney Mintz 'Black Women, Economic Roles and Cultural Traditions' in Filomena Steady (ed.) *The Black Woman Cross-culturally*, Schenkman Publishing Co., Cambridge Mass. 1981.

Verene Shepherd 'Emancipation through Servitude: Aspects of the Condition of Indian Women in Jamaica 1845–1945' *Bulletin of the Society for the Study of Labour History No. 53 Vol. 3 1988* pp. 13–19.

David Trotman 'Women and Crime in Late 19th Century Trinidad' *Caribbean Quarterly Vol. 30 number 3/4 1984* pp. 60–72.

Social Policy and Class Formation

Carl Campbell 'Social and Economic Obstacles to the Development of Popular Education in post-Emancipation Jamaica 1834–1865' *Journal of Caribbean History Vol. 1 1970* pp. 57–72.

Keith Laurence 'The Development of Medical Services in Trinidad and British Guiana 1841–1873' *Jamaica Historical Review Vol. 4 1964*.

Bridget Brereton 'The Development of an Identity: The Negro Middle Class of Trinidad in the later 19th Century'. Paper presented to the Association of Caribbean Historians Conference 1974.

Patrick Bryan 'The Black Middle Class in 19th Century Jamaica' extracted from P. Bryan *The Jamaican People 1880–1902*, Macmillan, London 1991.

M. K. Bacchus 'Consensus and Conflict over the Provision of Elementary Education' in M. K. Bacchus: *Education as and For Legitimacy: Developments in West Indian Education between 1846 and 1895*; Centre for International Education and Development, University of Alberta.

The Sugar Industry: Crisis and Adjustments

Philip Curtin 'The British Sugar Duties and West Indian Prosperity' *Journal of Economic History XIV, 1954* pp. 157–164.

Richard Lobdell 'Patterns of Investment and Credit in the British West Indian Sugar Industry 1838–1897' *Journal of Caribbean History Vol. 4 1972* pp. 31–53.

Manuel Moreno Fraginals 'Plantations in the Caribbean: Cuba, Puerto Rico and the Dominican Republic in the Late Nineteenth Century' in Fraginals *et al* (eds.) *Between Slavery and Free Labor: The Spanish-speaking Caribbean in the Nineteenth Century*. Johns Hopkins University Press, Baltimore 1985 pp. 3–21.

Eric Williams 'American Capitalism and the Caribbean Economy' From *Columbus to Castro: The History of the Caribbean 1492–1969*, Andre Deutsch, London 1970 pp. 419–442.

The Labour Movement: Decolonization and Democracy

Walter Rodney 'The Ruimveldt Riots: Demerara British Guiana 1905' in Rodney: *A History of the Guianese Working People 1881–1905* Johns Hopkins University Press, Baltimore 1981 pp. 190–200.

Tony Martin 'Marcus Garvey the Caribbean and the Struggle for Black Jamaican Nationhood' in Martin: *The Pan-African Connection: From Slavery to Garvey and Beyond*, Schenkman Pub. Co., Cambridge 1983 pp. 59–62 and 111–131.

Richard Hart 'Labour Rebellions of the 1930s' in Cross and Heuman (eds.) *Labour in the Caribbean*, Macmillan, London.

W. Arthur Lewis 'The 1930s Social Revolution' in Lewis: *Labour in the West Indies: The Birth of a Workers Movement*; Fabian Society, London 1938.

Economic Diversification and Transformation

Havelock Brewster and Clyde Thomas 'Industrialization of the English Speaking West Indies' from Brewster and Thomas: *The Dynamics of West Indian Economic Integration* Institute of Social and Economic Research, Kingston 1967 pp. 58–76.

Kari Levitt and Lloyd Best 'Character of the Caribbean Economy' from George Beckford (ed.)

Caribbean Economy Institute of Social and Economic Research, Kingston 1975 pp. 34–61.

James L. Dietz 'Operation Bootstrap and Economic Change in Puerto Rico' from Dietz: *Economic History of Puerto Rico: Institutional Change and Capitalist Development* Princeton University Press, New Jersey 1986 pp. 240–267.

Cornelius Ch. Goslinga 'The Industrialization of the Netherlands West Indies' from Goslinga: *The Dutch in the Caribbean and in Suriname, 1791–1942* Van Gorcum, 1990 pp. 574–595.

Political and Economic Integration

Guy Lasserre and Albert Mabilau 'The French Antilles and their status as Overseas Departments' in Emanuel De Kadt (ed.) *Patterns of Foreign Influence in the Caribbean* Oxford University Press 1972 pp. 82–102.

Elizabeth Wallace 'The Break-up of the British West Indies Federation' from Wallace: *The British Caribbean: From the Decline of Colonization to the end of Federation* University of Toronto Press, Toronto 1977 pp. 192–227.

W. Andrew Axline 'From Carifta to CARICOM: Deepening Caribbean Integration' from Axline: *Caribbean Integration: The Politics of Regionalism* Nicols Press, N.Y. 1979 pp. 110–127.

Gordon Lewis 'American Colonial Integration of Puerto Rico' from Lewis: *Notes on the Puerto Rico Revolution*, Monthly Review Press, New York 1974 pp. 13–27.

Independence, Nationhood and Identity

Hilary Beckles 'Divided to the Vein: The Problem of Race, Colour and Class Conflict in Haitian Nation-Building 1804–1820' Unpublished paper.

Jaime Suchlicki 'The Political Ideology of José Martí' *Caribbean Studies Vol. 6 No. 1 1966* pp. 25–36.

Gordon Lewis 'The Challenge of Independence in the British Caribbean' from Lewis: *The Growth of the Modern West Indies* Monthly Review Press, New York pp. 387–401.

Rex Nettleford 'Race Identity and Independence in Jamaica' from Nettleford: *Identity Race and Protest in Jamaica* William Morrow, New York 1972 pp. 137–156.

Hilary Beckles 'Independence and the Social Crisis of Nationalism in Barbados' unpublished paper.

Protest, Socialism and Revolution

Ramon Edwards Ruiz 'Cuba: The Making of a Revolution' University of Massachusetts Press 1968 pp. 153–169.

Herman L. Bennett 'The Black Power February Revolution in Trinidad' from Franklin Knight and Colin Palmer: *The Modern Caribbean*, University of North Carolina Press, Chapel Hill 1989 pp. 129–146.

Jorge Heine 'Grenada: A Revolution Aborted' in Jorge Heine (ed.) *A Revolution Aborted: The Lessons of Grenada* University of Pittsburgh Press 1991 pp. 3–26.

James Ferguson 'Pain and Protest: The 1984 Anti-IMF Revolt in the Dominican Republic' in Ferguson: *Dominican Republic: Beyond the Lighthouse* Latin American Bureau, London 1992 pp. 93–110.

SECTION ONE
Expectations of a New Beginning

No other set of events in Caribbean History has generated as much debate as the general slave emancipations between 1794 and 1886. The wide-ranging and intensive nature of discussions reflect the widely differing opinions and expectations of those affected.

Broadly speaking, it is possible to identify four distinct groups that participated in the emancipation process; the slaves, their owners, emancipation lobbyists, and the imperial governments. On the ground, the day to day development of the process most concerned the future of slaves and their owners. The latter group expressed the view that freed slaves would engage in a wide range of hostile and generally uncooperative actions, which explains in part their fears for the security of their lives, social standing, and economic enterprises.

The expectations of the emancipated, however, were for redefinitions and social legitimization of their rights as human beings, control over their time and labour, greater opportunity to accumulate economic resources, and open access to social and political institutions. Former slave-owners indicated that blacks expected far too much from their new status, while blacks insisted that on the whole they were entirely moderate in their demands and aspirations.

These essays, especially those by Scott and Marshall, indicate that the realization of the blacks' hopes and expectations depended considerably upon the arrangements for emancipation made between slave-owners and imperial governments. Only in the case of Haiti did blacks resolve these matters amongst themselves, recreating socio-economic arrangements that reflected almost entirely internal needs and possibilities. Elsewhere, according to Green, the nature of the process was defined and determined principally by those who had created the system in the first place, and whose interests were in the maintenance of some of its critical features.

These essays, furthermore, reflect the wide range of expectations and experiences across the region. Lundahl examines the social development of the Haitian experience, while Marshall and Green assess the principal features of the British experience. Scott, in examining the Spanish Caribbean process, presents an analysis of emancipation patterns in Cuba. Together, they illustrate the articulations and expectations of former slaves, property owners, and imperial governments, and demonstrate the manner in which events were ultimately shaped between these groups.

Toussaint L'Ouverture and the War Economy of Saint-Dominigue, 1796–1802

Mats Lundahl*

The Haitian revolution against the French broke out in 1791. From 1796 to 1801 all foreign powers involved in the revolutionary wars, French, British and Spanish, were defeated by the Haitian forces under Toussaint L'Ouverture. Both Saint Dominigue in the west and Santo Domingo in the east fell to Toussaint's troops. In 1798, he was sovereign in the north and in the west. Two years later, by defeating the mulatto general Rigaud in a civil war, he added the south to his territory and in 1801 the Spanish part of the island was occupied.[1] His constitution issued on 16 July 1801, made him *gouverneur-général-à-vie* with power to name his successor.

The year 1801, however, did not constitute the endpoint of the wars of independence, but merely a pause. The situation facing the revolutionaries was an uneasy one. The return of a French invasion army under the command of Napoleon's brother-in-law, General Leclerc, was imminent, and both the British and the Spanish were generally hostile, having been defeated by the Haitians and fearing the spread of the slave uprising to their own colonies as well. In addition, relations between the Haitians themselves were becoming increasingly tense. Many of the mulatto *anciens libres* had been property owners (including slaves) during the colonial period and had a stake in the maintenance of slavery (which had been abolished by the French in 1793), and were therefore regarded with scepticism by the mass of ex-slaves. What were later to become the social classes of free Haiti had begun to take shape, partly along colour lines, partly along cultural, religious and economic ones.

The most important threat, however, was posed by the impending French return. The war between Britain and France could not continue forever, and as soon as this war was over Napoleon could be expected to strike against the Saint-Dominigue rebels. 'Occupied with his European campaigns, Bonaparte never lost sight of San Domingo, as he never lost sight of anything. His officers presented plan after plan, but the British fleet and the unknown strength of the blacks prevented action'[2]. Yet, it was only a matter of time before Bonaparte would turn his attention to the Western Hemisphere.

A successful French return to Saint-Dominigue would by necessity imply the return of the plantations to their former owners as well as the re-installation of slavery. The Haitians would once more be the property of the French planters. That the French aimed to restore slavery is evident from official correspondence. Thus, the First Consul in a letter to the Minister of Marine, Decrès, on 7 August 1807 wrote: 'Everything must be prepared for the restoration of slavery. This is not only the opinion of the metropolis, but is also the view of England and other European Powers'.[3] This, the Haitian revolutionaries sensed, and a return to the abominable conditions of slavery was an outcome they wanted to avoid at all costs. The threat came not only from the French; in the longer run other European powers were also posing a problem. According to Ralph Korngold, 'even if this immediate danger [of a French return] had not existed, what reason was there to believe that the slave-owning Powers surrounding them would leave the Haitian Negroes in peace once they had reverted to ancestral ways? To remain free, they must be strong.'[4]

In the present essay we will be concerned with how these military requirements determined the economic system set up by Toussaint, and then in particular with the shaping of the agricultural sector. We will begin by determining the probable economic goals held by Toussaint and contrast these with the state of agriculture around 1795. In the second section the choice of system as determined by relative transaction costs is analyzed. The third and fourth parts describe the chosen system and the change in it as a result of an uprising in 1801. Finally, an evaluation of the results of Toussaint's agricultural policies is offered.

*Department of Economics, University of Lund, Sweden.

Toussaint's Economic Objectives

The consolidation of the military gains and a successful defence against invasion were ultimately completely dependent on the strength of the Haitian army. Without an army capable of resisting the French, the final conquest of freedom and independence would never take place. A strong army, however, was available only at the cost of huge expenditure. In particular, arms and other necessary supplies had to be procured abroad. On 6 November 1798, Toussaint wrote to President John Adams of the United States to re-establish the commercial relations between that country and Saint-Dominigue which had been broken earlier the same year as a result of growing tension between France and the United States. He was successful in his endeavours. Trade was gradually reopened, and it was to a large extent due to the supplies and war material procured out of the revenues from the U.S. trade that Toussaint was able to defeat his rival for power, the mulatto general André Rigaud, in the 1800 civil war.[5] 'The black leader had shown canny statesmanship in winning the friendly cooperation of the president of the United States, John Adams. The ships that Adams sent enabled Toussaint not only to defeat Rigaud but to achieve independence from France in all but name', summarizes James Leyburn.[6] Through American mediation a favourable treaty was also signed with England.[7]

A report by a French official on 30 December 1800 estimates that 30,000 muskets plus huge quantities of ammunition had been imported from Britain and the United States.[8] The following year, 4.5 million francs were expended on the army and an unknown amount was used for acquiring military supplies in the United States. At the time of Toussaint's death, different Philadelphia banking institutions contained deposits in his name of more than 6 million francs destined to secure purchases of war material.[9]

The need to strengthen the army created a very strong need for public revenue in general and for foreign exchange in particular. Public finances became one of Toussaint's most central preoccupations. To the needs generated by defense requirements we may, however, also add a second source of demand for government revenues — one created by the need to avoid discord and tension within the dominant coalition of generals and other high officers in the army. Unity had to be maintained, or the coalition would split and break up, which in turn would constitute a severe threat to independence and freedom itself. In 1800, a report from the French Minister of Marine to the Consuls, based upon reports from French government agents, stated that

the greatest discord reigns between Toussaint L'ouverture and the different generals under his orders. General Moyse is on very bad terms with his uncle; he has even a desire to supplant him. Dessalines apparently enjoys Toussaint Louverture's chief confidence, but may shortly form a new party different from that of Moyse. In such an event, Maurepas, inclined to revolt like the others, would be ready to join Dessalines. Christophe is excessively discontented with Toussaint Louverture, and the white inhabitants would be for him ... The rivalries of Generals Moyse and Dessalines presage new storms for the colony. Toussaint holds them only by hopes of higher command and greater wealth.[10]

Other reports paint a similar picture.[11]

Thus, taken together, the two objectives of Toussaint's administration: maintaining freedom and independence on the one hand and keeping the upper ranks of the army satisfied on the other, makes it realistic to portray his supreme economic goal as being that of maximizing revenue, with special emphasis on foreign exchange. In the following, we will base the analysis on this assumption.

Government revenues were highly dependent on agricultural production. Sugar had been the most important colonial export product, followed by coffee, cotton and indigo. This fact created tremendous difficulties for Toussaint. The uprising against the French had broken out in 1791. Four years later, the colonial economy was completely in shambles. Much of the capital stock, in particular the sophisticated irrigation works, had been destroyed during the revolutionary turmoils, and most of the labour force was gone. In 1796, the British historian of the West Indies, Bryan Edwards, estimated that as a result of the wars 300,000 people had died.[12] Another estimate, made two years later by the French staff general Becker, claims that by the fall of that year two-thirds of the whites, one-fourth of the mulattoes and one-third of the blacks had either perished or fled.[13] Using Moreau de Saint-Méry's figures for the 1789 population,[14] this points to a population decline in the order of 185,000 people. While the Edwards figure is a heavy exaggeration, Becker's estimate is a reasonable one. In 1805, a census was taken which showed that the Haitian population had declined by some 140,000 people since the outbreak of the wars of liberation.[15]

Thus, many agricultural workers had either been killed during the wars or had (far less frequently) left the country. Of at least equal importance was the fact that the character of agriculture had changed in such a fashion as to leave the traditional export crops virtually without hands to tend them.

Already during the colonial period, an important part of the cultivation took place on plots that the slaves had been given for their subsistence. Although the provision plots never sufficed to provide all the food that the slaves required,[16] resulting in the necessity of imports, many of the colonialists found themselves being dependent on purchases of produce grown by the slaves on these plots. What Gerald Murray has termed an 'economy within an economy'[17] had been created.

When the uprising against the French broke out, no more than three out of ten adult males ever participated in the organized fighting forces.[18] The remainder either disappeared into the inaccessible mountains as *marrons*, attempting to eke out an existence at the very margin of society (or completely outside it), or stayed on the plantations but did not cultivate export crops. The wars caused a strain on the food supply. It was no longer possible to import food. Consequently the population of Saint-Dominigue to an increasing extent became dependent on what could be produced within the country; effectively, it became dependent on an expansion of the 'economy within the economy'. Plantation owners and overseers now became conciliatory vis-à-vis the slaves and allowed them to expand vastly their work on the provision plots, to secure the food supply and to make certain that the slaves did not run off to join the revolutionary forces. From the point of the view of the slaves as well this made excellent sense,

making more secure their possession of the plots on which they had been accustomed to grow provisions, simultaneously expanding their cash-cropping and animal raising activities to respond energetically to a social situation in which they had more economic leeway and to a market which had drastically altered in their favour.[19]

The consequences of this for export production can only be described as abysmal. If the amount exported of the four most important export products in 1789 is assigned an index number of 100, coffee exports were down to a figure of 2.8 in 1795, sugar was down even more, to 1.2, and cotton and indigo exports had fallen to a mere 0.7 and 0.5 percent, respectively, of their former levels.[20] In other words, export agriculture was virtually dead. The economy had become a closed one, based on subsistence production and production for limited, fragmented domestic markets.

Small Farms or Plantations?

An export agriculture in ruins constituted a completely unacceptable situation for Toussaint.

Although food production continued to be a necessity, new life had to be injected into the export branch. The problem was to find the most suitable set of property rights, the one maximizing the flow of foreign exchange from agriculture into the government treasury. Here, Toussaint could do either of two things: accept that the colonial plantations were a thing of the past and that agriculture in Saint-Dominigue was in the middle of a spontaneous process of reorganization along free smallholder lines and revive export production in this system, or go back to a plantation-based system.

The choice between these two alternatives was determined by their relative transaction costs. The smallholder alternative presented very high collection costs. If the ex-slaves were allowed to determine freely where they wanted to establish their residence, the creation of a system with a large number of scattered production units had to be expected. To wring government revenues out of such an arrangement would require either a method of gathering produce from all these units, via a network of market-places where some of the produce could be taxed away, a system for direct government procurement, or a system whereby foreign exchange earned by private exporters could be taxed.

Under the first two alternatives, collection and transport costs would be high, both because the produce had to be measured and its quality examined and because communications were in bad shape and means of transportation were lacking. To transport goods to the markets was difficult, because most horses, mules, oxen and carriages formerly belonging to the plantations had been requisitioned by the army. In 1799, large quantities of coffee from the districts of Petit Goâve, Grand Goâve, Miragoâne and Léogane could not be exported owing to lack of transport facilities.[21] With private exporters there would almost certainly be a problem of tax evasion. In all three cases a bureaucracy handling the collection of the taxes would be necessary, which in turn would give rise to a principal-agent problem on a fairly wide scale. Authority would have to be delegated to regional and local government agents who could not necessarily be trusted not to dissipate government revenues.[22] To prevent this, yet more bureaucrats would be necessary to supervise the lower levels. A complete bureaucratic hierarchy would have to be established.

The smallholder alternative also entailed heavy costs for creating the right output mix, with a sufficiently high share being devoted to export goods. During the wars the relative price of export and food crops had changed in favour of the latter,[23] and to this, considerations of risk and uncertainty in a war situation had to be added. Food crops could always be consumed by the producers if the export markets were cut off, whereas a coffee or sugar-producing peasant would be dependent on incomes derived from his marketed surplus as well as on the market system for foodstuffs to ensure that his family's needs were met. Thus, the smallholder producers would somehow have to be shifted partially away from food crops and towards production of export goods instead, to the extent that was needed to build the military strength of the country. No such system existed but would have to be created.

Thirdly, the smallholder system did not automatically bring about the distribution of income that was desirable from the point of view of keeping the dominant coalition of high army officers intact. With many small separate production units, and incomes accruing to independent peasants, a mechanism for redistributing incomes would have to be devised. Not only would the peasants have to be taxed, but the proceeds from this taxation would have to be channelled into the pockets of the leading individuals.[24]

Putting these three types of transaction costs together, we discover yet a fourth set of costs, one which was due to the need for creating the administrative apparatus for collection, measurement, incentive creation and redistribution. From the foregoing, it should be clear that even if such a machinery had existed in the country, costs would still have been high. The problem was, however, compounded by the fact that it did not exist. It had to be created, and virtually from scratch at that. The wars had driven out or killed the French administrative cadre. Virtually the entire experienced bureaucracy that the Saint-Dominigue colony had possessed was gone. Of course, lower-level functionaries were comparatively easy to replace, and there was no lack of people with agricultural and commercial experience among, for example, the *affranchis*, but once the step was taken to the levels where more organizational talent and planning experience was needed, a tremendous gap between demand and supply had been opened — one which would have been extremely costly to close at short notice, with a French invasion imminent.

Thus, the transaction costs connected with making a smallholder system produce foreign exchange to the desired extent were exceedingly high. Turning to the restoration of the plantation system, we face a different set of costs. It would be less costly to create incentives for export production. This was to a large extent a result of technological factors. Large units were much better suited to the production of sugar for example. With the technology of the day, the optimum size of the

crushing mill was fairly large, and this in turn conditioned the size of the necessary labour force.[25] Thus, the large estates were able to produce sugar much more profitably than the smallholdings. The income distribution problem would also have been solved. Putting the plantations directly into the hands of the politically important people would make the redistribution problem simply disappear, provided only that labour to man the plantations could be obtained. The collection costs, finally, would be substantially lower than under the smallholder system, because the number of production units in a *grande culture* system would be lower. With all these three problems being reduced, the need for a trained bureaucracy would be correspondingly reduced.

Other costs would be incurred instead. The measurement and collection costs related to the exchanges that would have to take place in produce markets or via a state procurement system in the smallholder system would, with a plantation system, be internalized within the production unit. There would be no scope for disagreements regarding measurements and many exchanges would simply disappear. However, a factor market problem would show up instead. Plantation workers were organized in gangs or teams which gave rise to certain economies of scale.[26] When team labour is used, the type of measurement problems which lead to shirking arise.[27] On the one hand, it is difficult to measure how much effort each worker puts into every hour worked and, on the other, it is hard to decide exactly how the individual worker's labour is related to the quality and quantity of output. Thus, determination of the wage to be paid either has to take place on the basis of imperfect proxies like the number of hours worked, or, if the free rider problem is to be avoided, a monitoring system must be used.

A monitoring system must fulfil at least two essential functions. Assuming that all individuals are 'classifiable into various categories on a scale from extremely cooperative to extremely adverse', it should ensure that '(i) the negative results imposed on others by those in the negative tail of the distribution are minimized, and (ii) the incentive for persons to adopt behaviour as exemplified by those in the adverse tail is minimized.'[28]

Monitored plantation work in gangs was something which the ex-slaves despised profoundly. With the technology of the time it was inevitable that work efforts had to be greatly increased during the harvest period in the case of sugar, the plantation crop *par préférence*. Added to this was all the work that had to be performed outside the peak periods. The resemblance with slavery was striking.

In spite of the costs of the plantation system, the choice was an easy one for Toussaint. The transaction costs related to the smallholder system were much higher, so high that they were practically prohibitive. Thus, he had to opt for the plantation system. 'He knew the natural wealth of Santo Domingo; he knew how his race could endure forced labour; lastly he knew that could he but wring sufficient wealth from these two factors, he might hold the loyalty of his greedy generals and buy the products of the civilized world.'[29]

Plantation Revival

To this end, Toussaint employed a *fermage* system which had its origins in the system invented by the French civil commissioner, Sonthonax, in the northern part of the country after the abolition of slavery in 1793.[30] The system as developed under Sonthonax's administration had not produced many positive results, but this, it seems, was basically because its principles had not been adhered to in practice.[31] Later on, the same system had been employed by the French general Laveaux in 1794 and by Henry Christophe and his French adviser, Colonel Vincent, also in the north, beginning in 1797.[32] These attempts had been far more successful, since the control had been better. 'Christophe, always enthusiastic for tidiness and industry, was soon establishing, overlooking and enforcing the new projects throughout the district under his control; and within eighteen months the sugar produced on one plantation had increased almost tenfold.[33]

Under this system, which was put to general use by Toussaint, the usufruct rights to the land were redistributed. A number of former mulatto *affranchis* were allowed to keep their properties, although after Toussaint's defeat of the mulatto general Rigaud in the south in 1800, black officers took over in some cases. Whites who had supported Toussaint's regime were also assured of their rights, and Toussaint even went so far as to encourage the return of French planters who had fled the country. In the main, however, the plantations, especially those abandoned by their former owners, had been taken over by the state and let to army officers — senior, high-ranking ones — as well as to deserving public officials and other members of the emerging black elite that was beginning to establish its claims on the national patrimony.[34] At the time of Leclerc's expedition to Haiti in 1802, the *général-habitant* system, in which the top army officers rented vast estates from the state, appears to have been in more or less general use across Saint-Dominigue.[35]

The plantations were to be held together. The spontaneous trend towards a society of smallholders had to be broken. As Paul Moral had noted, it is possible that beginning in the year 1800 certain cultivators who had somehow escaped the reconstruction of large estates proceeded, alone or together, to buy parts of the former estates.[36] To put an end to such practices, a decree was issued in 1801 which explicitly prohibited sales and purchases of land without a special permit and the notaries were instructed not to issue any such permits unless the transaction in question was one involving at least 50 carreaux, and this only if the would-be purchaser could prove that he possessed enough resources to develop the land.[37]

The system paid handsomely for those who were allowed to benefit from it. Hugh Cathart, British vice-agent in Port-au-Prince, reported in 1799 that Henry Christophe was believed to be worth almost 250,000 dollars[38] and Dessalines rented some thirty sugar plantations each of which gave him around 100,000 francs per year.[39] Toussaint himself owned various coffee plantations and other real estate besides. His nephew, General Moyse, was reputedly offered 20,000 piasters per month by a merchant company for the right to use farms that he possessed in the north.[40] Thus, the system produced enough for the strategic sectors to prove viable. 'The military commanders waxed rich. They became *nègres dorés*.'[41]

Keeping the plantations together was, however, not enough to make the system work. The most difficult problem, by far, was that of procuring the necessary labour and making this labour work hard enough. The 1801 constitution stated that 'The colony, being essentially agrarian, must not suffer the slightest interruption of work in its cultures.'[42] The ex-slaves, on the other hand, knew what a return to plantation labour would mean for them and preferred to work on the provision plots.

Drastic measures had to be taken. Toussaint's constitution authorized the governor, Toussaint himself, to undertake all necessary measures to increase the labour force by the introduction of slaves from Africa, who would be free citizens once they had landed in Saint-Dominigue.[43] However, the backbone of his system was that of putting the Haitian ex-slaves back to plantation work. This took place in a couple of steps. In a decree concerning agricultural work, dated 12 October 1800, he expressed in *very* strong terms: '. . . since I *absolutely* want that my proclamation be fully and completely carried out and that the abuses that have spread on the plantations immediately come to an end, *I order very determinately* the following . . .'[44] The agricultural workers were given eight days to return to their plantations. Every person who did not enlist in the army or who could not prove that he possessed a legitimate trade was by definition an agricultural worker. Severe penalties were meted out for those who helped agricultural workers to hide from the authorities. The workers were forbidden to leave the plantations to which they had been assigned unless equipped with a legal permit. A rural police was created which was to run *vagabonds* down and return illegally escaped workers to the plantations.[45]

On the plantations, the work was organized in a military fashion. The decree directed that 'Managers, foremen and cultivators must conduct themselves as if they were officers, non-commissioned officers and soldiers.'[46] Generals and other officers were made responsible directly to Toussaint himself.[47] 'The despotism of the sugar plantation was fused with that of the bureaucracy in an attempt to make the whole colony a huge plantation, with generals and colonels functioning as managers', writes Henri Cauvin.[48] The entire island was divided into districts under military commanders who besides defence and internal security were also made responsible for agricultural production.[49] The plantations themselves were considered military units and were administered as such. The same type of discipline and the same type of penalties were employed for agricultural workers as for soldiers in the army. No vagrancy was tolerated. The worker who ran away from a plantation was dragged before a court martial, exactly as a soldier who had left his post, and received the same punishment.[50] *Marronage* was fought intensively.[51] For Toussaint, *marron* and *vagabond* were synonyms. Both were considered bandits and received exactly the same treatment, being pursued by the rural police force. The work itself was closely monitored. The use of the whip — the instrument of the slave owners — was explicitly prohibited, but *cocomacacs* (clubs) appear to have been employed when the need arose.[52]

At any rate, stern discipline was maintained. It was rumoured that when faced with an inspection by Dessalines, who was military commander of the west and in charge of the south as well, ten agricultural workers would do more work and cultivate more land than thirty slaves during the colonial period.[53] The ultimate guarantee, however, lay in Toussaint himself. The provisions stating that the military were responsible to him in person were not empty words. Toussaint incessantly monitored his subordinates and would frequently strike in the most unexpected places:

Nobody ever knew what he was doing: if he was leaving, whither he was going, whence he was coming. He had hundreds of thoroughbred horses scattered in stables all over the country, and he habitually covered 125 miles a day, riding far in advance of his guards and arriving at his destination alone or with one or two well-mounted attendants. The inspection of agriculture, commerce, fortifications, Municipalities, schools, even the distribution of prizes to successful scholars — he was tireless in performing these duties all over the country, and none knew when and where the Governor would appear. He deliberately cultivated this mysteriousness.[54]

He was known to have advisers, but all authority was concentrated in his own person, and he paid attention to the smallest details himself, both in working them out and in checking that they had been carried out.[55]

Toussaint understood perfectly well that he had to economize on scarce administrative talent. With the civil administration largely disappeared, only the military remained who could conceivably undertake the pressing task of restoring plantation agriculture. The stern discipline inflicted on the workers minimized the direct supervision costs. The rules laid down left no doubt as to what the desirable behaviour was, and deviations from this behaviour were punished. Toussaint, however, also proceeded to simplify rules to cut down on transaction costs. The value of the *gourde* (the currency) was equalized across the country. Export and import duties were fixed. All property was uniformly taxed and everything manufactured to be consumed within the country was charged with the same duty. With fewer and uniform taxes and duties prevailing, the number of officials needed to administer the system was reduced. The scope for arbitrary practices was circumscribed and an increased consciousness of the amount of taxes that the taxpayers had to pay was created.[56] (There were some exceptions in taxation, mainly in the reduction of import duties on prime necessities to a lower percentage than the general one.) Together, discipline and uniformity contributed to keeping transaction costs to a minimum.

Toussaint did not rely exclusively on militarily imposed discipline, but in various ways attempted to create a deliberate ideology which was to further his cause. Central in this ideology was the role of agriculture as the generator of wealth and welfare and as the ultimate guarantee for freedom and independence from France. In his decree of 12 October 1800 on cultivation, the paramount importance of agriculture was heavily stressed: 'Citizens, you all know that agriculture is the most important support of governments, because it foments commerce, wealth and abundance, makes crafts and industry be born, because it gives occupation to all hands, thus being the mechanism of all states.'[57] This slogan was preached time and again. In a letter to the Directory of the French Republic he wrote in 1797:

Feeling the necessity of favoring agriculture, the only thing that may give Saint Dominigue back its old splendour and its old products, I do not cease . . . preaching the love of work to my brethren, making them dedicate themselves entirely to cultivating the soil.[58]

Moyse's Rebellion.
Changes in the System

Toussaint did not tolerate any questioning of the system, and possibly it was this insistence on the large-scale plantation system which triggered off the uprising led by his nephew Moyse. The causes of this uprising are to a large extent unknown, or at least contradictory. According to Korngold, the main cause was that Moyse was opposed to Toussaint's constitution, which he thought was an unnecessary provocation of the French, but this discontent could not have given him the necessary popular following.[59] Therefore, Moyse instead chose to build his platform on the plantation issue, and in particular on the forced labour component. C.L.R. James, on the other hand, gives the Moyse uprising an interpretation in terms of class, or rather, colour struggles. According to James, the ex-slaves in the province of the North, where Moyse was in charge, objected to working for white planters and Moyse sympathized with the labourers.[60] An economic reason may also have influenced Moyse. Toussaint had for some time been complaining about declining output from the plantations of the north where Moyse was in charge.[61]

Outwardly, at least, a central role was played by Moyse's professed program of breaking up the large estates and distributing the land to junior officers, common soldiers and workers instead of letting the higher military ranks monopolize the land. Needless to say, such a program appealed to the interests of the common worker. In addition, Moyse refused to institute the rigid discipline which Toussaint's system called for on the plantations in the north:

Whatever my old uncle may do, I will not be the hangman of my own colour. He urges me on in the name of the interests of France, but I notice that these same interests are always those of the whites; — and I shall never love the whites till they have given me back the eye that they put out in battle.[62]

Whatever the 'real' causes behind Moyse's uprising may have been (it is not easy to reconcile his professed views on land tenure with the fact that he owned important properties himself), threats like these to the plantation system were in themselves severe enough to call forth strong repression. An insurrection had been triggered in the north. Several hundred whites had been massacred before Toussaint managed to put the uprising down and have Moyse shot in the fall of 1801.

The immediate result of Moyse's uprising was to make Toussaint issue a new decree on agriculture, one which imposed an even more rigid discipline on the cultivators than before. He began by punishing those who had participated in the uprising: 'In the districts of the insurrection he shot without mercy. He lined up the labourers and spoke to them in turn; and on the basis of a stumbling answer or uncertainty decided who should be shot.'[63] Thereafter, on 25 November 1801, he issued a proclamation which bound the workers even harder to the plantations than the decree of the previous year. Everybody was required to carry a passport and such a passport would be issued only to those who could be proved to have an occupation. Persons found without a passport would simply be put to work in agriculture. Furthermore, soldiers were forbidden to visit plantations unless they did so to see their parents, and then only for short periods. Those found to be instigating disorders would be sentenced to hard work for six months, carrying a weight attached to the foot by a chain. Managers and foremen were made responsible for carrying out the proclamation under pain of imprisonment.[64]

The Performance of the System

How did Toussaint's system perform? We have already found that it produced enough to keep the central group of army officers together. After Toussaint's consolidation of power, the only manifestation of discontent was the one we have already referred to, that of General Moyse. The rest kept in line without making any attempts to break their ties with Toussaint. The system obviously also produced enough to consolidate the military strength of the army. The Haitians were not to prove an easy prey for Leclerc and the French invasion army, and this would hardly have been the case without Toussaint's deliberate efforts to strengthen the Haitian power of resistance.

Thus, no doubt, the economic system created by Toussaint served the ruler well in that it contributed efficiently to the attainment of both his goals. Whether it was the best system from the point of view of the future economic development of the country is a slightly meaningless question. The system was designed to revive the export economy during a period of considerable outside stress. Either the country could arm itself sufficiently, or freedom would soon be lost, and economic growth and development would then again be a matter of interest only for the returning French planters, while the masses would be put back into slavery. The only reasonable economic criterion against which to judge the success of the system is thus whether it successfully revived export agriculture or not.

This, it did. We recall from the foregoing that in 1795 export agriculture was virtually dead. Toussaint had to start from scratch. The odds he had to fight against were tremendous. Tadeusz Lepkowski has summarized the general state of destruction in the country around 1800:

The state in which the cities of the North found themselves was lamentable as late as 1800. To the east of Cap-Haitien at the end of 1800 only a small part of the sugar plantations had been reconstructed. The cattle was lacking. The labour force, which had been seriously diminished, could not carry out the immense quantity of work which was necessary. The situation was similar in some regions of the West. The canals and irrigation works which had not been repaired for ten years did not fulfill their functions in any convenient manner, which necessarily had a negative influence on the production of dry regions. To top off, the West in 1800 was hit by natural disasters. The inundations broke the canals and destroyed the irrigation works. Up to the epoch of the war for control of the South, that province indicated a rapid reconstruction after the destruction of the years 1792–1798 and a considerable production. But the bloody fratricidal fights (1799–1800) changed the situation completely. Thus, both Rigaud, who, when retreating, destroyed the entire country, and Toussaint's troops, who burned and killed, contributed to undermining seriously the economic potential of the South and especially that of its eastern part and of the border regions of the West.[65]

The reconstruction work was not allowed to go on without interruptions. Furthermore, it was not allowed to continue for any long period of time altogether. If only the territory of Saint-Dominigue is considered (and not the Spanish part of the island) Toussaint's experiment lasted from one and a half years in the South to four to six years in the west and north.[66] Still, according to Leyburn, 'the return of prosperity between 1799 and 1802 was amazing'.[67] Leyburn's words must be interpreted as valid mainly for export agriculture, but there things were changed in a hurry. Sir James Barskett (basing his account on a contemporary writer, James Stephens),[68] reported in 1818 that

The effects of these regulations were soon visible throughout the country. So great was the progress of agriculture from the time of their adoption, that, notwithstanding the ravages of nearly ten years' war, and other impediments which retarded its improvement, the land produced in the next crop full one-third of the quantity of sugar and coffee which it had ever before yielded in its most prosperous season.[69]

Other contemporary witnesses were of the same opinion.[70] If we turn to export figures, we find that in 1801 and 1802 much lost ground had been recovered, although there still was a long way to go. Thus, in the former year, the volume of sugar exported was 13% of its 1789 level, coffee was up to 57%, and cotton to 35%, although indigo had fallen to a mere 0.10% of the pre-revolutionary quantity.[71] The following year, with the exception of coffee, performance was even better: sugar 38%, coffee 45%, cotton 58% and indigo 4%.[72] Thus, given the extremely adverse circumstances under which Toussaint had to operate, it cannot be denied that the system turned out to be remarkably efficient.[73]

Conclusion

The economic system set up by Toussaint was completely conditioned by the needs of a war economy. The Haitians were fighting to liberate themselves from French sovereignty, but to reach this goal it was necessary to import weapons and war materials of different kinds from abroad in a situation where export agriculture was almost dead. A revitalization of this sector was urgently needed.

During the wars, a smallholder agriculture had emerged spontaneously, but this type of agricultural organization could produce export crops only at extremely high transaction costs. Therefore, Toussaint chose to go back to plantation agriculture, to a system which derived directly from the colonial period and which had much in common with slavery. This system, which was built on a military organization of production, allowed export agriculture to be revived at a critical moment of the Haitian revolution. Without it, the rebels would never have succeeded.

Toussaint was arrested by the French on 7 June 1802, and was immediately shipped to France where he died in the prison of Fort Joux in the Jura Mountains on 7 April, the following year. However, his work was continued. Toussaint's successor, Jean-Jacques Dessalines, the first head of state of independent Haiti, employed the same agricultural system for the same reasons as Toussaint.[74] Toussaint's formula had proved viable in that it allowed export incomes to be created when the need for such incomes was desperate.

Notes

1. For an overview of the war events, see e.g. James (1963), Ott (1973), or Geggus (1982).
2. James (1963), p. 270.
3. Quoted by Korngold (1945), p. 163.
4. Ibid., p. 164.

5. Montague (1940), pp. 35–41, Logan (1941), Chapters 2–4 and Turnier (1955), Chapter 2, give a detailed account of the negotiations between Toussaint and the United States.
6. Leyburn (1966), p. 27.
7. Ibid.; Turnier (1955), p. 46; Ott (1963), pp. 109–10.
8. Quoted by Stoddard (1914), p. 290.
9. Korngold (1945), p. 167.
10. Quoted by Stoddard (1914), p. 289–90.
11. Ibid., p. 290. Note, however, the statement by Brown (1837), p. 28: 'All his generals trembled before him, and even the ferocious Dessalines could not look him in the face . . .'
12. Edwards (1796), p. 257.
13. Quoted by Stoddard (1914), pp. 288–9.
14. Moreau de Saint-Méry (1958), p. 28: 40,000 whites, 28,000 gens de couleur or affranchis (freed slaves and their descendants) and 452,000 slaves. The figure 185,000 assumes that all affranchis were mulattoes and that all slaves were black, which is of course not true. This is of minor importance for the order of magnitude, however.
15. Leyburn (1966), p. 33. The census figures must be regarded as a crude measure only.
16. Murray (1977), p. 48.
17. Ibid., p. 49.
18. Ibid., pp. 56–7.
19. Ibid., p. 61.
20. Lepkowski (1968), p. 75.
21. Turnier (1955), p. 61.
22. This problem is dealt with by Jensen and Meckling (1976).
23. Murray (1977), pp. 57–65.
24. With free peasants, it would not have been possible to resort to a system whereby the land was distributed to private landowners who thereafter could lease that land to tenants. The loss of manpower had made marginal land a free good in Haiti. It was always possible for a free man to get hold of land at zero cost. Hence, there was no reason for him to pay rent on marginal land. (For details regarding this, see Lundahl (1985).
25. Lundahl (1979), pp. 257–8.
26. Cf. ibid., pp. 110–14 and Lundahl (1983), pp. 215–17, for a discussion of the advantages of team labour in the Haitian context.
27. Alchian and Demsetz (1972), North (1981), pp. 37–8.
28. Dahlman (1980), p. 213.
29. Stoddard (1914), p. 291.
30. Thébaud (1967), pp. 17–19.
31. Lepkowski (1968), pp. 71–2.
32. Ott (1973), pp. 130–1.
33. Cole (1970), p. 51.
34. Lepkowski (1968), pp. 78–9.
35. Moral (1961), p. 22. 1 carreau = 1.29 hectares. Cf., however, Thébaud (1967), pp. 23–4, where it is indicated that most of the land would have been in private hands in 1801. Thébaud's figures are, however, difficult to interpret. It is not clear where the estates rented from the state come in.
36. Moral (1961), p. 21.
37. Ibid., Korngold (1945), p. 164.
38. Cole (1970), p. 67.
39. Lepkowski (1968), p. 79.
40. Moral (1961), p. 22.
41. Korngold (1945), p. 165.
42. Quoted by Mackenzie (1830), p. 293.
43. James (1963), p. 265, Buch (1965),p. 125.
44. Buch (1975), p. 127.
45. Korngold (1945), p. 165, Lepkowski (1968), p. 77, Buch (1976), p.128.
46. Korngold (1945), p. 165.
47. Buch (1976), p. 128.
48. Cauvin (1977), p. 123.
49. James (1963), p. 242.
50. Buch (1976), p. 128.
51. According to Gabriel Debien, in certain districts in the north there were more marrons in 1800 than during the colonial period (Debien (1962), p. 161).
52. Korngold (1945), p. 166.
53. Lacroix (1819), p. 47.
54. James (1963), p. 249.
55. Ibid., p. 255.
56. Ibid., p. 245.
57. Quoted by Moral (1961), p. 18.
58. Quoted by Lepkowski (1968), note, p. 77.
59. Korngold (1945), pp. 180–1.
60. James (1963), p. 279.
61. Cole (1970), p. 71.
62. Lacroix (1819), p. 49.
63. James (1963), p. 279.
64. Buch (1976), pp. 131–2, James (1963), p. 279.
65. Lepkowski (1968), pp. 81–2.
66. Ibid., p. 76.
67. Leyburn (1966), p. 27.
68. Korngold (1945), p. 161.
69. Barskett (1818), p. 203.
70. Cf. Korngold (1945), pp. 160–1.
71. Lepkowski (1968), p. 83.
72. Franklin (1828), p. 322. The year is not given, but Leyburn (1966), p. 320, indicates 1802. The reason for the low coffee value is presumably explained by the 1802 figures which include the months of French administration (after the landing of Leclerc). Since coffee was produced to a large extent in the mountains which were not subjugated by the French, the figure fell (Lundahl (1979), p. 262).
73. The judgement passed by Robert Rotberg and Christopher Clague that Leyburn 'may be correct . . . if he means that any production above a subsistence level was remarkable considering the tribulations that the colony had endured' (Rotberg & Clague (1971), p. 50) is simply not fair.
74. Dessalines' system is dealt with in Lundahl (1984).

Bibliography

Alchian, Armen A. & Demsetz, Harold (1972), 'Production, Information Costs and Economic Organization', American Economic Review, vol. 62.
Barskett, James (1818), History of the Island of St. Domingo, from its First Discovery by Columbus to the Present Period. London.
Brown, Jonathan (1837), The History and Present Condition of St. Domingo, Vol 2. Philadelphia.
Buch, Hans Christoph (1976), Die Scheidung von San Domingo. Wie die Negersklaven von Haiti Robespierre beim Wort nahmen. Berlin.
Cauvin, Henri (1977), 'The Haitian Economy: A Case Study of Underdevelopment', Ph.D. thesis, New School for Social Research. New York.
Cole, Hubert (1970), Christophe, King of Haiti. New York.
Dahlman, Carl J. (1980), The Open Field System and Beyond. A Property Rights Analysis of an Economic Institution. Cambridge.
Debien, Gabriel (1962), Plantations et esclaves à Saint-Domingue. Dakar.
Edwards, Bryan (1796), An Historical Survey of the French Colony in the Island of St. Domingo. London.
Franklin, James (1828), The Present State of Hayti (Saint Domingo) with Remarks on its Agriculture, Commerce, Laws, Religion, Finance and Population, etc. etc. London.

Geggus, David (1982), *Slavery, War, and Revolution: The British Occupation of Saint Domingue, 1793–1798*. Oxford.

James, C.L.R. (1963), *The Black Jacobins. Toussaint L'ouverture and the San Domingo Revolution*, second edition. New York.

Jensen, M. & Meckling, W. (1976), 'Theory of the Firm: Managerial Behavior, Agency Costs and Ownership Structure', *Journal of Financial Economics*, vol. 3.

Korngold, Ralph (1945), *Citizen Toussaint*. London.

Lacroix, François-Joseph-Pamphile de (1819), *Mémoirs pour servir à l'histoire de la révolution de Saint-Domingue*, Vol. 2. Paris.

Lepkowski, Tadeusz (1968), *Haití*. Tomo I. La Habana.

Leyburn, James G. (1966), *The Haitian People*, second edition. New Haven.

Logan, Rayford W. (1941), *Diplomatic Relations of the United States with Haiti 1776–1891*. Chapel Hill.

Lundahl, Mats (1979), *Peasants and Poverty: A Study of Haiti*. London and New York.

Lundahl, Mats (1983), *The Haitian Economy, Man, Land and Markets*. London and Canberra.

Lundahl, Mats (1984), 'Defense and Distribution: Agricultural Policy in Haiti during the Reign of Jean-Jacques Dessalines, 1804–1806', *Scandinavian Economic History Review*, vol. 32.

Lundahl, Mats (1985), 'Government and Inefficiency in the Haitian Economy: The Nineteenth Century Legacy', in: Michael B. Connolly & John McDermott (eds.), *The Economics of the Caribbean Basin*. New York.

Mackenzie, Charles (1830), *Notes on Haiti, Made during a Residence in That Republic*, Vol. 2. London.

Montague, Ludwell Lee (1940), *Haiti and the United States 1714–1938*. Durham.

Moral, Paul (1961), *Le Paysan haïtien (Etude sur la vie rural en Haïti)*. Paris.

Moreau de Saint-Méry, Médéric-Louis-Elie (1958), *Description topografique, physique, civile, politique et historique de la partie française de l'isle Saint-Domingue*, New edition. Paris.

Murray, Gerald F. (1977), 'The Evolution of Haitian Peasant Land Tenure: A Case Study in Agrarian Adaptation to Population Growth', Ph.D. thesis, Columbia University. New York.

North, Douglass C. (1981), *Structure and Change in Economic History*. New York and London.

Ott, Thomas O. (1973), *The Haitian Revolution 1789–1804*. Knoxville.

Rotberg, Robert I. with Clague, Christopher K. (1971), *Haiti: The Politics of Squalor*. Boston.

Stoddard, T. Lothrop (1914), *The French Revolution in San Domingo*. Boston.

Thébaud, Schiller (1967), 'L'évolution de la structure agraire d'Haiti de 1804 à nos jours', Ph.D. thesis, Université de Paris.

Turnier, Alain (1955), *Les Etats-Unis et le marché haïtien*. Washington D.C.

'We be wise to many more tings':
Blacks' Hopes and Expectations of Emancipation

Woodville K. Marshall

My little talk has two titles: the one advertised. 'Blacks' Hopes and Expectations of Emancipation', and the one I prefer. 'We be wise to many more things'. This second title needs a little explanation. When in 1837 James A. Thome and J. Horace Kimball, two American abolitionists, were interviewing apprentices in Williamfield, Jamaica about 'the wrongs and hardships' of the Apprenticeship, they were told in full and rich detail about the harassments which masters visited on apprentices and about the obstacles which they wilfully erected against church attendance. One tearful old man reflected on that experience in this way:

I declare to you, massa, if de Lord spare we to be free, we be much more (re)ligious — *we be wise to many more tings;* we be better Christians; because we have all de Sunday for to go to meeting. But now de holy time taken up in work for we food.

I chose that title because of the ideas that were being expressed; even if we discount the apparent religious fervour, we can clearly hear a commitment to the exercise of *rational and informed choices* when legal constraints on use of labour time were finally removed.

The legislation which ended slavery hinted at momentous, probably revolutionary changes in Caribbean society. It transformed the legal status of more than 80% of the population by abolishing the legal oddity of property in persons and by substituting equality for all before law. It altered the labour base of the community by substituting a wage labour system for unpaid slave labour. It outlined the basis for the existence of a greatly enlarged community of free persons by removing that legal authority which had enabled a small minority to exercise virtually arbitrary power over the activities and even lives of the large majority. But it is not that obvious that radical changes or a revolution did immediately take place. If we are to find a transforming process in social relations, in cultural activity, in consciousness, we must go beyond the legislation and examine the actions and

choices of people; we must consider the hopes, expectations and perceptions which informed choices and responses in the post-slavery situation.

The role and activity of the blacks are crucial in all this, because of their previous relations with the dominant groups, because of the widespread and persistent doubts held by the elite groups about their ability to function as effective members of a free community. I am, therefore, suggesting that one perspective from which we should view the post-slavery experience must be the extent to which blacks' expectations were matched by their realization.

My main contention is that even after 150 years, the historical literature seems unclear about the nature and range of blacks' hopes and expectations of emancipation; therefore, we cannot fully understand how these expectations and the action they inspired affected the contours of post-slavery development. More important, this vagueness tends to obscure the extent to which frustration of expectations may have affected the consciousness and action of blacks in decades after the ending of slavery, which is another way of saying that important features of our historical experience may not yet be fully in focus.

I cannot hope in this talk to correct this apparent distortion. But what I shall try to do is this: relying on the work of those few historians (notably Phillip Curtin, Sid Mintz, G.K. Lewis, Monica Schuler, Edward Brathwaite and Barry Higman) who have in varying degrees called attention to the range and complexity of the slaves' activities and belief systems and to the continuities in the blacks' experience, I shall try to outline the range and nature of blacks' hopes and expectations and speculate about the significance of these for post-slavery developments *particularly during the first generation of freedom.*

Blacks' Hopes and Expectations in the Literature

Blacks' hopes and expectations of emancipation do not figure prominently in the literature. Often these are not even made explicit, and have to be deduced from discussion of the performance of wage labour systems and of the plantation-based economy. But both the direct and the implied statements about expectations suggest that these were very few in number, consisting in the main of the ex-slaves' attitudes to residence and regular wage labour on the plantation. In the older literature (of the 19th century) these are presented as the natural and inevitable characteristics of the 'lazy nigger', fatally corrupted for regular wage labour by the experience of slavery. Blacks, in this formulation (the subhuman black), envisaged emancipation as freedom from regular labour, and intended to perform the barest minimum needed to satisfy their simple needs. In the more extreme versions, blacks intended to secede from the centres of civilization (the plantation) so that they could gratify their animal wants by 'liming' and feasting under the mango and breadfruit trees or alongside the pumpkin vine. This racialist statement of expectations is most luridly expressed in the works of Thomas Carlyle, Anthony Trollope and J.A. Froude; but it finds a muted echo in the (modern?) work of W.A. Green when he writes that 'the needs of the former slaves could be easily satisfied' (p 188).

Later writers show slightly greater sophistication. They agree that blacks intended to remain in society and expected to exercise *choice* in employment and residence, but they disagree about *when* they intended to exercise that choice and *where* exactly they expected to locate themselves. One variation (the foolish black), popularized by Rawle Farley, Augier *et al*, Bill Riviere, and, for that reason, favoured by our undergraduates and school children, holds that the blacks, with vivid recollection of their slavery experience, were determined to immediately decamp from the plantations, the scene of their former degradation. In short, they wanted independence, but the plantation symbolized slavery. This formulation is attractive because it is simple and symmetrical, linking revulsion against slavery with the persistence of resistance against it. But it is vague about the nature of the 'independence' that was being sought, and it largely ignores the realities of the blacks' existence and their views about it. Throughout slavery, blacks had to a large degree fed themselves, had built and maintained houses, nurtured families, established kin networks in *particular locations* — in short, they had devised and executed survival strategies to the extent that it might be said that they had fashioned 'an alternative lifestyle' based mainly on the provision ground and huckstering. Therefore, as Sturge and Harvey recognized, they were always manifesting 'intelligence of mind, a firmness and self-reliance'. Such people would not

have been disposed towards suicidal gestures, to an exchange of their considerable investment in provision ground on the plantation for a spot in the bush, if such spots were indeed available. Blacks did leave plantations in some territories in significant numbers, particularly after 1842, but this 'flight' clearly occurred *when* workers and employers failed to agree on the terms and conditions of employment and tenancy, and *where* land for small scale agricultural activity was available.

The other main variation (the limited black) suggests that blacks hoped and intended to remain in plantation residence and employment; that they had a clear preference for this location because of kinship ties and their deep involvement in the provision ground/marketing complex developed during slavery; that they intended to accept wage labour contracts if these seemed equitable, but they would consider leaving the plantations if they were confronted by high rents, by insecure tenure, by low wages. This version (most clearly expressed by Douglas Hall) is persuasive because it stresses continuities and deliberate choices, and because it seems to accord with blacks' responses after the ending of slavery. But it has the weakness of apparently circumscribing the blacks' hopes and expectations to relationships with the plantation, by not exploring in detail what these choices may have entailed. Therefore, there is a suggestion in such a version that the blacks had a limited view of themselves and of the desirable social relationship, that they may have been incapable of acting *fully* as thinking, feeling individuals.

Such a skimpy treatment of blacks' hopes and expectations in the literature is somewhat surprising in light of the remarkable proliferation of writing in Caribbean History, particularly on slavery, in the last 20 or 25 years. The question must therefore arise: is this deficiency in the literature due to a paucity of evidence on blacks' hopes and expectations, or is it due to a persisting bias and/or perspective on the part of historians, or is it due to a combination of the two?

Superficially, the direct evidence of the nature of blacks' hopes and expectations of emancipation hardly exists. They left no extended written records of their thoughts and feelings (memoirs, letters); Oral History had not yet been invented; and contemporary commentators seldom bothered to interview them, no doubt convinced that they had little of importance to say or that whatever they might say was already obvious. Closer scrutiny reveals, however, that the evidential base, while not very extensive, is not as slender as it might at first appear. In the first place, some blacks made speeches, composed addresses and wrote petitions on the occasion of full emancipation and during the industrial disputes that occurred between August 1838 and 1844. Some of these speeches were published in newspapers; some of the addresses and petitions have been preserved in the archives. Secondly, a few interviews were conducted, in 1837, by itinerant abolitionists. While the interviews were unstructured and, naturally, tell us more about the concerns of the interviewers than about blacks' perceptions, yet they do give voice to some blacks and provide some hints about the nature of their perceptions. Thirdly, missionaries and stipendiary magistrates, because of their close and constant contact with blacks, acting often as self-appointed spokesmen and intermediaries, were well placed to hear and interpret blacks' hopes and expectations. Close and critical study of their regular reports will therefore reveal some of what they absorbed in the contact situation. Finally, when the content of these fragments are linked with blacks' actions before *and* just after full emancipation, the historian can make plausible deductions about the range and nature of those hopes and expectations.

But to arrive at this point is to assume that the historian has a particular angle of vision. However, this does not seem to be the case for many of the historians of post-slavery. Whether they wrote in the 19th century or more recently, they seem to share the staple concept of Caribbean societies. That is, that the importance, even the existence of these communities, is inseparable from the production of certain export staples; that the efficient means of creating a marketable surplus is the plantation; that the peasant option (that 'simple condition of society') is not viable because it could never generate acceptable levels of public amenities and therefore could not guarantee civilization and modernization; and that the role of the blacks is forever *determined* — to provide cheap and regular labour to the plantation. From this perspective, then, there is a tendency to impute hopes and expectations rather than to verify the existence of them. In effect, a partial depersonalization of the blacks is both perpetrated and perpetuated.

Range and Nature of Blacks' Hopes and Expectations

What I offer are mainly derived from what blacks did during slavery, from what blacks said or were reported to have said about their future during the Apprenticeship which seemed to have bearing on their intentions and from what they did and said particularly during conflict situations in the first years of full freedom. By allowing the blacks to speak, we may alter the perspective; by examining the interplay between statement and action, we may start to unlock their consciousness.

The interviews conducted by the travelling abolitionists. Sturge and Harvey, Thome and Kimball, and the few surviving speeches and addresses made and written around 1 August 1838 yield little direct evidence on the specifics of these hopes and expectations. We find in these interviews and speeches an indication that no flight from plantation residence and labour is contemplated, that children will be educated, and old and infirm relatives maintained. But, mainly, we discover that there is a sense that emancipation would make a great change in blacks' lives ('a good massa a very good 'ting, but freedom is still better!'), that they were proud and grateful to have reached that stage ('on the day that freedom came, they were as happy as though they just been going to heaven'); that recollection of injustices practised against them and a consciousness of rights would dispose them to a jealous defence of their new status. William Kerr of Falmouth, Jamaica summed up much of this on 1 August 1838:

We bless God, we bless the Queen, we bless the governor, we bless the people of England for the joy we have. Let me remember that we been on sugar estate from sunrise a morning till eight o'clock at night; the rain falling, the sun shining, we was in it all. Many of we own colour behind we, and many before; we get whip, our wives get beat like a dog before we face, and if we speak we get the same; they put we in shackle; but thank you heavenly Father we not slave again!

Similar sentiments, expressed less colourfully through the medium of a professional petition-writer, came from a group of twenty-nine (29) Barbadian apprentices in a formal address to Governor MacGregor:

With the greatest deference to your Excellency, we the undersigned, late Apprenticed labourers, beg leave to approach you, to return to your Excellency and the Legislative Body of the island, our warmest thanks for the speedy deliverance from our Great oppression, Assuring your Excellency *it will be our constant duty to Guard against future Tyranny and Oppression.* The joyful day has at last arrived and to you we are bound to acknowledge our gratitude for your interest and exertions to rid us of the Galling Yoke . . .

Action by blacks during the Apprenticeship gives some clearer indications of how blacks expected their lives to be altered. Disappointed that the emancipation apparently promised by the Abolition of Slavery Act of 1833 had not come, and continually harassed by masters who attempted by various legal and illegal contrivances to reduce that small portion of 'free time' which the Abolition Act had decreed, apprentices in general took action to protect their small corner of freedom and to defend their rights to customary allowances. In the process they began to outline their perception of full freedom.

In the first place, they displayed clear notions about the role of law, and argued for equality before the law. Though their experience with the newly appointed Special Magistrates may have convinced them that those 'military magistrates' were a new species of driver who seldom dispensed justice, yet they took their complaints to their courts. Though they were mainly defendants rather than complainants, more adjudged guilty rather than innocent, yet they seemed to accept the courts' legitimacy. They complained that 'there was no law now', but they were not alienated. Intuitively, they recognized that access to justice was an attribute of citizenship, that the presence of paid magistrates marked a qualitative change in their status, that law was the foundation of free society. Hear another Jamaican apprentice:

We could never live widout de law; we must have some law when we free. In other countries where dey are free, don't dey have de law? Wouldn't dey shoot one another if they didn't have law?

Secondly, they asserted control over the labour time at their disposal. They refused to apprentice the free children (those under age six in 1834), and they were 'particular' about the use of their free time (the quarter of the work week that they could dispose of as they wished). Clearly they set such store by the free children's new status that they were not prepared to participate in any scheme for their maintenance by planters which would imperil it. Their free time was clearly treated as a valuable asset to be invested where it brought the greatest material or psychological return. Some of it was sold to employers who often needed it desperately during the crop season, but much of it was withheld, either as protest against masters' harassment, or for employment in provision ground cultivation and huckstering. This action affected levels of labour supply and sugar production (a drop of about 10%, but not in Barbados) and therefore confirmed many planters' fears about the likely consequence of full emancipation. But, more to the point, this re-allocation of labour time was a clear hint of intentions for the future.

Thirdly, many apprentices sought to insure the permanence of their freedom through self-purchase even though the Apprenticeship was known to be a temporary condition. Remarkably, the incidence of self-purchase rose *after* the date for the termination of Apprenticeship was announced. Apparently, many blacks did not care for what looked like the Queen's charity; they wanted instead the respectability that freedman status might bring, the satisfaction that flowed from successful self-help activity, the guarantee of the legally executed 'free paper' which might be proof against changes in official emancipation policy. This suggests that blacks had concluded that freedom could be a temporary state unless vigorously defended, and they should trust no other agency but themselves to maintain its existence.

As in Apprenticeship, so in full freedom: blacks were quick to respond to (or invent) rumours of a return to slavery whenever policies they found distasteful or perplexing were pursued by employers or government. On several such occasions between 1838 and 1845, labourers in Barbados, Trinidad, St. Lucia and Dominica quickly downed tools and/ or decamped into the woods, or offered violence to those who executed the policies complained against.

For example, many labourers in Barbados, particularly at Haynesfield in St. John and at Salters in St. George, refused during the first weeks of August 1838 to accept general contracts of hiring (yearly contracts) and conditional tenancy because, according to the Police Inspector, they had been told that if 'they turned out for work so soon after emancipation, they would forfeit their freedom, and incur a further apprenticeship of six or seven years'. Similar rumours were reported in early 1840 when the Revised Masters and Servants Act (the located Labourers Act) came into force.

Fourthly, blacks sought freedom to practice religion. Strictly speaking, this issue was as old as African slavery itself. Planters, fearing what they could not understand (ancestor worship [duppies]) or penetrate (the complex kinship structure and the secret societies which sustained the religious rituals), and intent on exercising total control over their property in persons, had from the beginning of slavery waged a relentless campaign (through punitive legislation and exemplary punishment) against those vestiges of African religious practices which had survived the crossing and the dispersion of communities. By the 1830s, the campaign had long since succeeded in driving underground most of the practices and rituals associated with Obeah and Myalism; but, by then, troubling aspects of the issue of religious freedom had re-surfaced in a new guise. This was the establishment of the Mission Churches, the blacks' enthusiastic participation in them, and the religious syncretism which they made possible.

This development was as troubling to planters as African religious practices had been because they saw in the Mission Church elements disruptive of plantation routines and subversive of existing social arrangements. Moreover, the Mission Church seemed to be an open conspiracy between the enemies of the slave system (at home and abroad) to hasten emancipation in some form or fashion. But persistent efforts to check the spread of the contagion had foundered on the power of the humanitarian lobby in the metropole. Indeed, that lobby was powerful enough to secure the extension of a species of religious toleration to these colonies by the 1820s — a toleration that was marked by the formal opening of the Anglican Church to slaves by the 1820s.

This did not mean, however, that planter hostility was dissipated or that blacks were permitted easy access to missionaries and their churches. The 1820s and 1830s were marked in Guyana, Barbados and Jamaica by a virulent white backlash against missionary activity in the aftermath of the 1823 and 1831 slave rebellions. So, with missionaries being perceived as nurturing the violent opponents of slavery, religious freedom could not be taken for granted by blacks.

From the blacks' perspective, the issue was important for at least three reasons. First, the Mission Church was probably, after the Sunday market, the most important institution in their lives, because it provided recreation, fellowship, solace, the rudiments of education, and leadership opportunities. Second, this Mission Church provided a legal and respectable means by which they could consolidate or re-constitute what anthropologists call a 'culture focus' — 'those aspects of the life of the people which hold the greatest interest for them'. The blacks' culture focus featured religion but, as already indicated, that focus had been weakened by the planters' curbs on their religious and cultural practices. Now, under the cover of the Mission Church, it was possible for a black religious revival to take place — a religious revival with at least three features —

(a) the obvious, conversion to Christianity;
(b) also obvious, the reinterpretation of Christianity in the light of surviving religious beliefs to produce syncretized religious forms, the Afro-Christian cults, mainly symbolized by the Native or Black Baptists (spirit possession, the leader system);
(c) not so obvious, the revival and extension of re-constituted African religious forms — Myalism, Kumina, etc. — often functioning as a part of the Mission Church and clearly contributing to syncretism.

Third, black involvement in new churches, whether they were Mission or Afro-Christian, was often the expression of *political* activity. Missionaries, particularly the Baptist and Methodist, were perceived by slaves (and by planters) as abolitionist in sympathy if not in action, and the conclusion was easily drawn that, through their contact with their London headquarters, they were quietly working with other abolitionists for the ending of slavery. Slaves therefore may have viewed their association with missionaries as providing themselves with a *respectable* political leadership, a leadership which, because of its social status and metropolitan contacts, could not be easily lopped off, even though viewed as subversive. At the same time, the Afro-Christian cults were clearly associated with resistance to the status quo — in their songs ('take force with force'), in their liturgy, in their leadership and organization of slave rebellion. Both these points are supported by action after the ending of slavery. Baptist missionaries in Jamaica went into formal politics at the ending of slavery — campaigning for voter registration among blacks and fielding candidates in elections. Afro-Christian cults maintained their revolutionary attitudes and ideology after the ending of slavery; and it was they (Native Baptists in Jamaica, Wilderness People in St. Vincent) who were in the forefront of the direct challenges to the conservative social and political order during the first generation of freedom; and it was these groups which have remained the *political* refuges of lower status and disadvantaged groups.

The point is that blacks would have seen emancipation as removing all obstruction to Christian worship, as probably giving full legitimacy to the Afro-Christian cults, and as possibly providing opportunities for a revival and extension of the African religious practices that had been criminalized by their masters. Moreover, they may also have seen an opportunity in emancipation for an extension of their Africa-derived festivals with their 'lascivious' dance and 'most rude and monotonous' music, an opportunity to stage these entertainments where they wished to do so and not only when they were permitted to, as had happened during slavery. But, ironically enough, it was the missionaries, the blacks' defenders and protectors, who had by now become the chief scourge of all 'heathenish practices'.

Most of the specifics about blacks' hopes and expectations of emancipation can be derived, however, from the action which was stimulated by the establishment of the wage labour system. That action was a militant industrial action, 'a spirit of insubordination', which occurred particularly in August/September 1838 and again in 1841–4 when efforts were made by planters to impose conditional tenancy, to reduce wages and to vary the conditions of employment. Blacks at these times insisted on negotiation, withdrew their labour, virtually barricaded themselves on the provision grounds they occupied on the estates, and forced the governors to send magistrates to meet with them, or to appear in person, or to despatch the military. For example, the strikers at Salters declared during the first two weeks of August 1838 that, despite threats of ejection, they would remain on the estate because 'they had been born' on its soil; that, though troops from Gun Hill were being summoned, they would die rather than yield.

The hopes and expectations which can be deduced from these episodes naturally interconnect — but they may be considered separately for ease of analysis.

Freedom of Movement

Blacks clearly expected that the forced immobilization of slavery and Apprenticeship, symbolized by 'pass laws', would disappear and that they would be free to take their persons, their skills and labour to whatever location they chose. This was indicated by a significant urban drift the first months of full freedom in which many skilled and semi-skilled plantation workers participated; by the re-location of several agricultural workers inside territories, no doubt to re-establish family connections and to exploit differentials in wage levels; by significant migration from low wage areas (Barbados, Leewards and Windwards) to high wage areas (Trinidad, British Guiana), a migration particularly from the Windwards, that managed to evade the 'madly iniquitous' curbs that were placed upon it.

Consolidation of Family

Blacks during the Apprenticeship had indicated that they expected emancipation to facilitate consolidation of family by permitting the reconstitution of units that had suffered forced separation and by enabling heads of households to redistribute domestic responsibilities and to allocate family labour. Sturge and Harvey expected that labour population after emancipation would be reduced mainly by 'the gradual, voluntary withdrawal of women from regular field labour, to domestic duties'. This issue was prominent in the bargaining over the conditions of wage labour. Blacks generally insisted that women and children should work a shorter week than the men. Clearly this was done mainly to maximize the family effort in the provision grounds and local market; the women, as hucksters, insisted on additional time to prepare for market; and the children, when not at school, could

increase the domestic labour supply. But, in addition, blacks, as stipendiary magistrates noted, set some store by the comforts of 'home' which partial relief from plantation labour could provide.

'Just' and 'Equitable' Wages

Blacks had clear views about the desirable level of wages, and employers' refusal to meet their wishes as well as employers' attempts to effect unilateral wage reductions provoked intense and prolonged resistance. This was particularly evident in Jamaica in 1838–9 and 1841, in the Windward Islands. in August 1838, in Guyana in January 1842, in Trinidad in 1843, where strikes lasted for three weeks and longer. Blacks' notions of a just and equitable wage rate at emancipation was based on the level of wages paid for free time during the Apprenticeship, on the value that masters and magistrates during Apprenticeship had commonly placed on the unexpired portion of their labour times, and on the cost of basic necessities; and it was obvious to them that employers' offers were often 30% to 50% below the acceptable minimum. Later attempts (in 1841–4) to reduce wages by 25% to 50% in an already tense industrial climate only sharpened antagonisms and gave additional point to their calculations of the just wage. The Jamaican, William Allen put the point forcefully in September 1841:

De Busha all hab five to six horse, dem lib well, nyam belly full; lib na good house; we lib na hut . . . we pay half a dollar rent; den dem want to gib we shilling a day. Tell me now, how much lef fa ya when week out? No half a dollar lef fe you? Den wha fa we buy fish? Den wuh fe we gib parson? De Busha get ten shilling a day; dem want to rob we . . . Unoo will take one shilling a day? (No, No, from audience) Well, den (s)tick out fe good pay and see if dem no oblige and bound fe gee what we ax a day.

Loose Labour Arrangements

Generally, there was a distinct preference for uncontracted employment, for task work and job work. This reflected blacks' intention to control their time and pursue their own interests. What these loose arrangements could provide was maximum flexibility; the opportunity to seek cash when that supplement was required; the opportunity to plan the allocation of time and labour between plantation work, their own provision grounds, the market, or other employment; the opportunity to maximize earnings from plantation labour. All this was evident in the high degree of absenteeism of the resident labour force and in the prolonged opposition blacks offered, particularly in Barbados, Jamaica and Windward Islands, to contracts of general hiring, to implied contracts, and to conditional tenancy.

Easy Access to Provision Grounds

There had been clear indications during the Apprenticeship, in the preference blacks gave to provision ground cultivation in the allocation of their free time and in their increased attention to the cultivation of these grounds and to repair of their houses, particularly during the last months of the Apprenticeship that, far from contemplating flight from the plantation, they may have been preparing for a long siege. Such an intention became plain in the first weeks of full freedom and again in 1841–4. In many territories, resident labourers used their huts and grounds as a sort of strike fund to maintain themselves while they fought their employers' attempts either to impose high rents or conditional tenancy or to dispossess them. Such a posture, backed by firm repulse of police who tried to eject them or by claims that the Queen had given them the huts and grounds, suggested that blacks may have adopted a moral economy, were asserting a claim, based on long settlement and investment of labour, to possession of portions of their employers' property.

The base for these attitudes is obvious enough. Cultivation of provision grounds and gardens, the marketing of surplus produce, and the freedom to dispose of the returns from this transaction had together constituted the slaves' main independent activity and their chief adaptation to slavery. Established and maintained by the slaves themselves, this provision ground/marketing complex had, in many territories, become a sort of survival economy, dominating the exchange of locally produced food and handicrafts, deeply affecting the circulation of money, and providing the means by which slaves could improve their standard of living. For all these reasons, it could be argued that blacks came to identify their participation in own-account activities with the expression of their humanity and, possibly, with freedom. Therefore, they looked to the day when they could so rearrange their time that they could give priority to those activities that had transformed their lives, and the main area for the prosecution of these own-account activities was the provision ground.

To sum up, this evidence of the range and nature of blacks' hopes and expectations confirm the conclusions of Philip Curtin and Monica Schuler. Blacks hoped that emancipation would provide the opportunity for them to *take full control of their own lives*, to lay a completely new base for the society. They hoped to realize the revolutionary potential of the legislation to abolish slavery by extending those social, cultural and economic values and institutions which they had 'cultivated zealously' during slavery, particularly those relating to the nuclear family, the provision ground/marketing complex, the re-interpretation of African/Christian cosmology. So, their revolutionary ideology and programme were clearly anchored in their experience and in their sense of what had become a derided and emasculated ancestral culture. Unlike many of their descendants, they clearly had no intention of turning their backs on Africa and on what they had achieved during slavery.

Fate of the 'Revolution'

The revolution hardly got started. Blacks, as their militant industrial action clearly demonstrates, did attempt during the first years of full freedom to realize their hopes and expectations; but, within ten years, a planter counter-revolution had successfully blocked most of the embryonic programme and had rendered precarious the existence of those institutions on which blacks had hoped to build. The details which illustrate the blacks' failure to fashion the type of emancipation they wanted have been fully described (by Adamson, Mandle and Walter Rodney, Brian Moore, Donald Wood, Bridget Brereton and David Trotman, Philip Curtin, Douglas Hall, W.A. Green and Hugh Tinker). Therefore, only a bare outline should be necessary in order to bring into focus the question why this happened.

The blacks' hope for a form of economic self-sufficiency, based on the exploitation of the best available labour market and on a range of own-account activities, was frustrated by a thick web of restrictions on mobility, tenancy, occupational differentiation, squatting, use of plantation property; and by the depressed wages and limited opportunities for plantation labour that mass immigration produced. The provision ground/marketing complex, while it survived, could not fulfil its potential; it was put under severe pressure by planters' successful assertion of their right of possession of the provision grounds and by the necessity forced on blacks to seek substitutes or to drastically reduce the labour time they could devote to the cultivation of these grounds. The 'encircled' peasantry that emerged as a result was certainly *not* the development that blacks had envisaged.

Social institutions and amenities hardly fared better. While the process of the consolidation of family units probably proceeded, economic pressures ensured that family labour had to be directed outward rather than toward a family farm. Justice in the courts remained elusive because the counter-revolution returned the planter-Justices of the Peace to pivotal roles in judicial administration. Public amenities barely deserved the name. While government accepted responsibility for their extension, the funding was so meagre and irregular that the situation in areas like health care and relief of the poor and infirm was probably worse than in the days of slavery. Education was perhaps an exception. While the newly established facilities catered only to a small fraction of the population, they represented a great increase in opportunities for the acquisition of literacy. But this was probably a mixed blessing. The European content of education and the limited access to it weakened the cultural focus of those who were exposed to it, and sharpened divisions along class lines among the blacks.

Blacks' cultural expression encountered, as before, suppression and marginalization. Legal restrictions, where before none or few existed, were placed on a range of blacks' recreational/cultural activities. Equally important, that alliance between blacks and missionaries, which had created possibilities for the full legitimization of Afro-Christian cults, broke down. The blacks identified missionaries with the attack on aspects of their culture and objected to their support for wage reduction. Missionaries identified involvement in the Africa-related festivals and rituals as the cause of the 'back-sliding' of their black converts. The result was that blacks seceded from mission churches and schools, and Afro-Creole religions and cultural beliefs and practices received a new lease on life. But this now meant that all those activities formerly centered on the mission churches lost any vestige of 'respectability' because the white missionaries clearly distanced themselves from them. This impacted as well on blacks' formal political activity. Shorn of the respectable leadership provided by European missionaries and possessing few leaders of their own, blacks' political activity in the generation after emancipation was mainly underground, extra-legal or messianic — activity in the Afro-Christian sects, participation in religious revivals, involvement in rebellion.

Why all this happened is fairly obvious. In the first place, emancipation was a *managed operation*, managed in the sense that it was emancipation from the top, an action that was not intended by those who officially sponsored it to have fundamental social or economic consequences. This is clearly illustrated by the price that the British Government was prepared to pay to the West Indians (absentee and local) for their agreement *not* to oppose the emancipation measure. The price was

the $20m in compensation and the unstated promise to leave most of the details of implementation of the change to the colonial governments. This clearly gave the planters considerable latitude in framing the enabling legislation and in structuring the new arrangements to suit their interests. The British Government's action can be therefore roughly equated with appointing the mongoose to look after the chickens; and we have to assume that the implications of the action were understood before the action was taken.

Secondly, emancipation from the top naturally limited blacks' room for manoeuvre. The power equation was against them, and they could not break it unless they were prepared to deploy superior power, and nothing they said or did suggests that they thought in these terms. It was planters' power at the local level, backed by the acquiescence of the metropole, which created conditions for successful counter-revolution. It was the power of the control of the economy, it was the power of decision-making in the legislature, it was the power derived from full access to the state apparatus.

Thirdly, blacks had no powerful allies in their quest to take control of their lives. Neither those who sponsored the emancipation measure (the abolitionists), nor those who framed and approved it (the British Cabinet and Parliament), nor those who claimed to have prepared the slaves for emancipation (the missionaries) shared the blacks' perceptions of emancipation. All of them shared the staple view of West Indian colonies, and while some of the planters' labour recruitment strategies did not win their support, they generally agreed with the planters that the blacks' notions of the desirable economic arrangements were incompatible with the effective functioning and development of plantation-based communities.

Finally, the blacks' analysis of the situation was probably incomplete. It took little account of some elements of the politics — the distribution of power, the presence/absence of allies, the likely responses of planters, their own ability to deal with those responses. Perhaps, then, it may be suggested that, in spite of their 'two hundred years war' against slavery, blacks preferred to avoid direct confrontation and hope that mainly passive pressure would bring the structural adjustments that they sought.

Significance of Blacks' Hopes and Expectations

Blacks' failure to realize most of their hopes and expectations produced deep frustration, resentment and even demoralization. By the 1860s and 1870s when the combined effects of the planter counter-revolution and intermittent depression in export markets were clearly reflected in rising levels of unemployment, in rising food costs and falling wages, one can detect a strong current of anger in what they say and do. That anger remained submerged for most of the time, but it seeped through petitions and memorials and folk songs and in what Edward Braithwaite calls Nation Language. Some of it was channelled into emigration and into religious fervour like the Great Revival in Jamaica of 1860–66; and some of it clearly erupted in riots and disturbances like the Guerre Negre in Dominica (1844), the Angel Gabriel Riots of Guyana (1856), the Vox Populi Riots of St. Vincent (1862), the Morant Bay Disturbances (1865), the Belmanna Riots of Tobago (1876), the Confederation Riots of Barbados (1876). The point is that blacks, whatever the state of their consciousness at full emancipation, established positive correlations between their depressed or disadvantaged condition and action by authorities (planter or government), between their protest action and a sense of injury committed on them. Some of them, like the protestors at Stony Gut in 1865, even articulated their grievances in terms of 'oppression' since emancipation. In short, though they had failed to realize their hopes and expectations, they did not resign themselves to their fate. They protested, if only sporadically and indirectly; and their protests therefore serve as constant reminders of what they wanted to achieve and of the extent of unfinished business connected with emancipation.

What they wanted to achieve identifies a clear theme in our historical experience. That is, the basic continuity in culture, between the institutions and values of our past and those of our present. And the point should not be obscured because blacks were prevented from building on the foundations that they themselves had partly developed and partly inherited. Sometimes out of sight and often near the wrong side of the law, some of them sustained some of those institutions which carried the continuities — Obeah, Myal and Shango, Kumina and Cumfa, Jonkonnnu and Goombay, Carnival. At another level, that of speech and story, music and song, the protest itself helped to establish the continuity. Groups in later generations — Spiritual Baptists, Rastafari, Black Power — have built on these foundations, sometimes without fully recognizing that continuity.

To that first generation of adults in freedom, it was painfully obvious that emancipation was unfinished business, unfinished because, by the 1860s and 1870s, many of them had been returned to a dependence on the plantation and to a standard of living not far removed from the slavery that many of them had known. Hopefully, political developments over the last 30 or 40 years have ensured that the part of the agenda which dealt with material conditions of existence has been tidied up. But there is still unfinished business — unfinished business for the historian because he/she is not consciously involved in perpetuating 'selective memory', it is the business of integrating all the elements of our past, particularly those that have been criminalized and submerged, so that the *long* continuities can be clearly identified and preserved. And then hopefully we all will be wise to many more things.

Former Slaves:
Responses to Emancipation in Cuba

Rebecca Scott

The locks had been taken off the barracones *and the workers themselves had cut windows in the walls for ventilation. There was no longer any effort to prevent people from escaping, none of that. By this time all the blacks were free. They called it freedom, but I am witness to the fact that the horrors continued.*

— Esteban Montejo[1]

Cuban plantation slaves achieved legal freedom through a variety of mechanisms including war, self-purchase, individual manumission, litigation, and government decree. Their responses to that freedom also varied widely, ranging from a decision to leave the plantation world entirely, to a persistence in dependence on the old estates. Their different efforts to make something of their new freedom, however, did not simply fall along a continuum from passivity to activity, or from peacefulness to violence, or from plantation to peasantry. Rather they involved a mixture of such features, within the limitations imposed by the economic and political system, as well as by direct coercion.

Examination of the fate of former slaves is made difficult by a change in the nature of surviving sources. It is an irony of nineteenth century social history that slaves societies, while legally denying the slave's individuality, left written traces of that individuality in lawsuits, complaints, registers, and account books; while the nominally free societies that followed, in which employer and worker were tied primarily by the exchange of a wage, often left sparser records of the lives of individual workers. This is not surprising, for master and slave were entangled in each other's lives in multiple ways and committed to each other over long periods of time, while employer and worker were often linked only by anonymous and ephemeral ties. The lack of records, however explicable, poses a problem for the construction of a portrait of post-emancipation society, and one must rely disproportionately heavily on inference from statistical sources and on the inevitably subjective observations of contemporaries. (While the records of the Juntas de Patronato are in some ways comparable to those

of the United States Freedmen's Bureau in their reflection of the process of emancipation, they cannot provide a similar portrait of the free labour system, for they end with full emancipation).

With these limitations in mind, it is possible to sketch out the options that former plantation slaves faced, dividing them into rough categories. A freedman or freedwoman might: (1) remain on the plantation, move to another plantation, or join a labour gang to work in sugar by the day or by the task; (2) undertake the growing of sugar as a *colono*; (3) seek to achieve a certain distance from the plantation through a family division of labour or through part-time wage labour and part-time cultivation; or (4) migrate out of the sugar regions, either to the city, the hills, or the more open land of the east. Of course, not all of these options were available to every slave, and the degree of access to different alternatives varied both geographically and across time.

Wage Labour

Returning to, or remaining on, the plantation as an agricultural worker often meant continuing the same kind of labour under the same direction, that one had experienced as a slave. It might also mean living in the same dwelling. Esteban Montejo, the idiosyncratic and individualistic former slave whose oral 'autobiography' was compiled in the mid-twentieth century, looked backed upon this with a certain disdain:

The blacks who worked at Purio had almost all been slaves. They were used to life in the *barracón*, so they did not even go out to eat. When lunch-time came they same with dinner. They did not go out at night. They were afraid of people, and said they would get lost.[2]

For such freedmen and freedwomen, the major changes in their work lives would be the receipt of wages and some shifts in living conditions. Young children could be withdrawn from field work and women might choose when to offer their labour for a wage and when to work at domestic tasks. Family life could be constituted or re-constituted, though under the stress of heavy and often insecure labour for the parents. Many of the male labourers on estates nonetheless remained at least legally unmarried, continuing the pattern of a community of single males living in barracks within the plantation. This pattern now incorporated white immigrants as well as former slaves, however, and differed in its intensity from the prison-like concentrations of male slaves that had existed during the earlier booms in the sugar industry.[3]

Rather than remain on their old estates, some former slaves joined *cuadrillas* or work gangs. Planters had become familiar with contract labour gangs through their experience with Chinese labourers and seem readily to have adopted *cuadrillas* of other workmen after slavery. Some observers criticized this trend, pointing out that employers had to pay an intermediary, the contractor, and might also find workers abandoning one gang for another that paid higher wages. Records of payments to *cuadrillas* are nonetheless frequent in the account books of the immediate post-emancipation period.[4]

It is virtually impossible in retrospect to penetrate these gangs and determine their internal organization. They may have been under the strict control of the contractor, or they may have exhibited some of the internal democracy that has been attributed to comparable work squads in parts of the United States in the years immediately after emancipation.[5] The most that can be said is that they moved the former slave one step away from the estate's own overseer and tied his fate in part to the other members of the gang.

Whether hired individually or as part of a *cuadrilla*, workers received rations similar to those issued under slavery; rice, beans or chickpeas, and *tasajo* (jerked beef), with occasional fresh meat when an old ox was slaughtered, supplemented by *viandas* (starchy vegetables and edible roots such as *boniato, malanga, ñame*, etc.) and cornmeal. Some estates apparently also issued bread, pork, *aguardiente* (sugar cane brandy), codfish, olive oil, and lard to their employees. One *colonia* manager asserted that he provided coffee, oil, bacon, and spices in addition to basic rations, and cabbage, tomatoes and turnips during the winter.[6] The food

a worker actually received seems to have depended in part on the category of work being performed and sometimes on race as well. The American consul in Cienfuegos wrote in 1884:

The owner of one of the largest plantations in the island, which during the crop season employs about five hundred persons, tells me that by cooking for them, which he does by steam, he is enabled to feed the skilled labourers at 33 cents a day, the unskilled white labourers at 22 cents a day, and to feed the unskilled negro labourers at 16 cents a day. A distinction is usually though not always drawn between white and negro labourers of the same class.[7]

There was no guarantee that the food supplied would even consistently conform to the familiar description of *tasajo* and rice. In the records of the *ingenio* San Fernando toward the end of 1890, one finds that the rations, which had consisted primarily of *tasajo* and rice, suddenly contained less *tasajo*, and on November 17 the *tasajo* disappeared altogether. From then until January 11, 1891, the *raciones para braceros* consisted only of rice, lard, and coffee. While it is possible that during this period fresh meat may have been substituted for dried, it is unlikely, as there is no record of any substitution, nor had the *zafra*, the traditional occasion for slaughtering an animal, begun.[8]

On some estates workers could now exercise a degree of freedom in food preparation, obtaining permission from their overseer to collect their food uncooked and prepare it in their rooms. Receiving one's rations uncooked could also be a burden, however. An article in *El Productor* in 1889 reported that in Trinidad cutters and loaders of cane were paid eighteen pesos monthly and food, but that they had to pay three pesos to whoever cooked it for them, they had no time to cook it for themselves since they worked from 4:00 A.M. to 11:00 A.M., and from 12:00 noon to 7:00 P.M.[9]

The work itself continued much as before. 'One passed the hours in the fields and it seemed as though the time never ended. It went on and on until it left one exhausted', reported Montejo.[10] That the rhythm of work had changed little was also attested to by planters. An article in the official publication of the Cuban Planters' Association in 1888 described a worker's day on a plantation or cane farm *(colonia)* as beginning with a 2:00 A.M. rising, followed by work until 11:00 A.M., a break for lunch, and then work from 1:00 to 6:00 P.M.[11] The manager of a large American-owned *colonia*, founded in 1889, gave much the same picture of conditions for his work force of 350 during the *zafra* and 150 during the 'dead time', though he cited 4:00 A.M. as the rising time.[12]

Within a plantation, work fell into different categories. Both employers and employees had opinions about the desirability of various jobs and the appropriate kind of worker for them. P.M. Beal, the *colonia* manager cited earlier, expressed a preference for Canary Islanders and Spaniards for 'stowing cane on the cars, plowing, ditching, road repairing, and railroad work.' But he argued that, for 'cane cutting, carting, planting, and cultivating, native labour — in particular negro labour — is preferable, because, being experts, the work progresses more rapidly, the cane plant suffers less injury, resulting in more remunerative returns, and its life is prolonged, which is a big item to the farmer'. Another employer concurred: 'One negro in cutting cane can do as much as two of any other class'.[13] Freedmen themselves preferred some types of work over others. An observer in the Sancti Spíritus region reported in 1882 that when *libertos* returned to work on the *ingenios*, they chose the task of *machetero* (cane-cutter) over that of *alzador* (loader).[14]

Interestingly, specific tasks had different overtones in Cuba and in Puerto Rico, where emancipation had taken place some years before. In Cuba, ditching, for example, was not a highly skilled job and was likely to be given to new immigrants. In Puerto Rico, because of the importance of irrigation, ditching was a skilled and relatively prestigious job within field labour. Many ditchers there are reported to have been *libertos*, trained under slavery, and their descendants. Indeed, in the case of Puerto Rico, *libertos* were apparently crucial in a variety of skilled sectors within the sugar industry in the years immediately following emancipation, and employers sought them for both field and factory labour.[15]

Prior to abolition, some Cuban planters had imagined that an apartheid-like distinction between black agricultural workers and white factory workers would emerge after slavery. Indeed, they had seen this as part of a strategy for rapid development of the sugar industry.[16] One modern historian has asserted that such a division did exist and that the industrial work in the new *centrales* was performed exclusively by whites. Those who had been slaves on estates absorbed into *centrales*, he argues, ceased working in the processing of sugar and were employed exclusively in the agricultural tasks of cane growing and harvesting.[17]

The evidence on this point, however, seems inconclusive. If a sharp ethnic distinction between the agricultural and the manufacturing sectors were emerging in the 1890s, one would expect to find evidence of it on estates like Soledad, the modern *central* owned by Edwin Atkins. In a set of comments on the estate workers, the manager of Sole-dad, L.F. Hughes, did not address the question directly, but he did describe his work force as it stood in March 1898, the last month of crop time. Of the 1,600 men employed, there were 'from 150 to 200 Chinamen [sic]; of the balance of the labourers probably there were more negroes than Spanish, with the white Cubans in a distinct minority'. He went on to generalize about the different categories of workers: the Chinese he saw as steady but weak, the blacks and the Canary Islanders as the best labour, and so on. But particularly revealing is his comment that 'The white men are mainly employed as stevedores in the batey, though they are also good labourers in the field'. He did not single them out as mill workers.[18]

There may well have been a concentration of blacks in field work and whites in mill work, but several factors militated against absolute segregation. First, many Spanish immigrants were rural workers, some specifically imported for the harvest. One would expect most of them to be assigned to the field or the millyard where demand for seasonal unskilled and semi-skilled labour was high. Second, some former slaves undoubtedly possessed skills that were of value in the mill, particularly if they remained in residence on the estate and could be expected to be available year after year.[19]

The differentiation that the American consul had noted in 1884 between black and white 'unskilled' workers seems to have diminished in importance, while others grew. In the same way that there had been distinctions under slavery between indentured and free Chinese, and between owned and rented slaves, a distinction was now made between the categories of permanent and temporary worker. Esteban Montejo described the options for individual agricultural wage labourers in Santa Clara: one could sign on as a fixed labourer, contracted for several months, or one could work free-lance, agreeing on a price for weeding or clearing a specific area of land. Montejo viewed the free-lancers as having more autonomy because they were able to pace their own work, subject only to approval of the final job, and he described them as 'muy vivos' (very sharp). But they also were transient, lodged in the smallest rooms of the barracón (to which they did not bring women, Montejo noted), and obliged to move on if they ran out of money before there was more task work to be done.[20]

Even among those who worked regularly for wages on a single estate, there were further distinctions. On the plantation cited by Montejo, in order to receive one's pay in cash one had to go to the office and collect it from the *mayordomo*. Montejo preferred to collect his pay half in cash, half in credit from the storekeeper, in order to avoid going to the office to be 'looked up and down'. Others had no choice about dealing with the plantation store. The *Revista de Agricultura* in 1889 reported that one group of workers in the Trinidad area of Santa Clara province planned to emigrate because their wages were low and because they were obliged to buy in the stores established by the plantation owners.[21]

During the early states of the ending of slavery wages had generally been calculated to include maintenance, and rations were issued to most workers. On the *ingenio* Nueva Teresa in the late 1870s and early 1880s, for example, many wage workers signed on agreeing to take their meals with the appropriate group on the plantation: slaves, Asians, or white employees.[22] As the transition to wage labour advanced, workers (such as those in the *cuadrillas* of Chinese) took on more of the responsibility for their own maintenance, or transfered it to contractors, and the role of the plantation store changed. Instead of merely issuing rations, it sold goods. Purchases there on credit could thus take the place of some of the cash wage. Once emancipation was complete, the role of the store changed again. In place of cash payments, many planters issued *vales* or tokens good only at the store.[23] Others simply maintained an account for each worker and subtracted his or her purchases from the final payroll. Their motives seem to have included concern to limit mobility, desire to confine expenditures to the estate, and response to a lack of coinage.

The records of the plantation store at the *ingenio* Natividad in Sancti Spíritus reveal a wide variation in the degree to which its workers contracted debts with the store. Some never bought anything at the store; indeed eighteen out of thirty-two workers on one such list kept the amount they purchased below one peso. Others bought considerably more, though the only ones actually to exceed their cash wages were a *capataz* (foreman) and one temporary worker.[24] Rather than revealing an entire work force held by debt and credit, the *ingenio* Natividad presents a more complex picture. Those workers who grew enough for their own subsistence or who dealt with outside markets might avoid becoming indebted to their employers. Those who lacked resources or mobility or who preferred to avoid the *mayordomo* might deal extensively with company stores.

Factors beyond individual idiosyncrasy determined these differences. For some — perhaps particularly those who had struggled to purchase their freedom — refusing to deal with the company store could be an assertion of self-respect.[25] Temporary workers without either family or provision plots would probably be more likely to deal with the stores. On estates where payment was given in scrip, however, workers had little choice. An investigation carried out in 1883 in the sugar zone of Guanajayabo apparently revealed that within five days after the payment of monthly wages, 90% of the money paid out had returned to the estate through the *tienda mixta*.[26] This pattern of keeping wages almost entirely within the plantation may well have been uncharacteristic, but government authorities estimated in 1888 that hundreds of Cuban *ingenios* were issuing wages in *fichas*. They also cited reports of workers trying to use the plantation scrip at town stores.[27]

In areas where the demand for labour exceeded the supply, workers sometimes turned credit to their own advantage, extracting an initial payment prior to signing on. This obviously was a risky business, since it could lead to lasting debt. For temporary workers who left before their term was up, however, it meant an effective increase in wages. Thus employers were likely to be hostile to the extension of credit when they could not be sure of continued control over the workers. Articles in the Liberal Press of Sancti Spíritus inveighed against workers who asked for advances to purchase goods to give to their families and then did not work or return the advance.[28] The Junta de Agricultura of Santa Clara in 1881 went so far as to claim that one could not find workers unless one extended advances, which were often not repaid. However, a newspaper article reporting this complaint expressed some scepticism about the claim and denied that the phenomenon was extensive.[29]

The problem of credit was, from the point of view of masters, part of the more general one of ensuring the continuity of labour. Another article written in Sancti Spíritus complained of workers who left the plantations to go to town and participate in the *parrandas*, putting music and sociability above labour.[30] (The *parranda* was a party or gathering of singers and musicians for improvisations, and in Sancti Spíritus it was apparently likely to be an interracial gathering.)[31] The *Revista de Agricultura* in 1888 echoed this plaint, saying that there were too many holidays during the harvest and that workers left at crucial times in order to go to town for the festivities.[32]

The editors of *La Propaganda* in Sancti Spíritus and of the *Revista* in Havana professed to believe in freedom of movement. In an ominous passage, however, an author for La Propaganda wrote that while it would be regrettable if the government were forced to introduce a system of *cartillas* (workbooks) for rural workers, as had been done for domestic servants, if this happened it would be the fault of the workers themselves, who had made ill use of their individual guarantees. The author called on workers to fulfill their obligations and forsake their immoderate desire for entertainment in order to aid the reconstruction of the country. 'Entertainment as a habit degrades; work always ennobles,' he intoned.[33] The *Revista de Agricultura* was more cautious, calling only for a limit on the number of fiestas permitted and for restrictions on cockfighting.[34] For one *colono* quoted in a newspaper article, musical instruments themselves came to symbolize workers' unwillingness to labour steadily. Significantly, the instruments he cited were the drum and the accordion — one African, one European.[35]

For more conservative observers, what was at issue was the social order itself. An article in the journal of a local 'artistic and literary society' criticized workers' belief that they did not have to tolerate instructions when they were performing their tasks, and attributed this flaw to 'an exaggerated concept of one's own personality'. Workers, the author argued, had to understand that they were part of one class in society, and that because of their position they were dependent on another. Their spirit of independence would have to be 'harmonized' with their subordination. Though the article did not mention freedmen specifically, some of the perceived 'exaggerated concept of one's own personality' may have been an expression of autonomy by former slaves reacting to orders from their former masters. At the same time, the author's critique of this autonomy reflected a more generalized concept of hierarchy, applicable to whites as well as blacks.[36]

In addition to exhorting the rural working class to be deferential and work harder, employers tried to exercise control directly through the wage system. One *ingenio*, for example, advertised a 'good wage' for field workers — sixty cents per one hundred *arrobas* cut and loaded, thirty cents per day charged for food — but noted that pay would be given only after a month's work and that no advances would be issued.[37] Both the amount and the manner of payment on plantations varied widely according to the relationship of supply and demand across geographical areas and between seasons, the nature of production in each region, and the strategies of employers and workers.

In Trinidad, a severely depressed region in the province of Santa Clara that contained *ingenios* producing *mascabado* sugar but no *centrales*, monthly wages for day labourers did not go above nine or ten pesos during the summer of 1888; they had been ten to fourteen a few months earlier.[38] In Cienfuegos, which was undergoing development, a worker in 1888 might expect fourteen to seventeen pesos in gold, including maintenance, and some fresh meat. In Sagua, wages were twelve to fourteen pesos, with worse food. In Matanzas, where there were numerous former slaves, pay was thirty-five to forty pesos a month in depreciated bills (around half the value of gold) and maintenance was not included.[39]

An *informe* from the Sociedad Económica de Amigos del País, issued just before the abolition of the *patronato*, had estimated wages at from forty to seventy cents a day, or ten to eighteen pesos per month. The Círculo de Hacendados at the same time estimated a range of fifteen to twenty pesos per month without maintenance in 'dead time', twenty-five to forty during the *zafra*. This latter estimate probably included some specialized workers.[40] In practice, pay varied widely, even on the same plantation. In July 1889, monthly pay to the over two hundred *braceros* working on the *ingenio* Natividad in Sancti Spíritus ranged roughly from nine pesos for some cane haulers to thirty for some cane cutters. Most tasks earned around fifteen to twenty pesos.[41]

Wages were at roughly similar levels in the 1890s. One manager cited an average for field labourers during the summer months of seventeen pesos, although higher amounts (twenty-six pesos) were paid to cane cutters and cane loaders during crop time.[42] The *ingenio* Natividad recorded wage rates of twelve to twenty-six pesos to *braceros* during the *zafra* of 1895–1896.[43] The American-owned Soledad *central* in Santa Clara province reported paying from fourteen to twenty pesos Spanish gold in 1895.[44]

This cataloguing of general wage levels in different regions is not intended as a precise statement of the wages earned by former slaves who remained on plantations. If tied to a plantation store, they could find their real purchasing power as well as their freedom much reduced; if hired only part of the year, or part of each month, their income was correspondingly lower. The point is that the wages paid to the freedmen and freedwomen were certainly higher than the wages paid to Chinese and other contract labourers in the 1870s, but they were not markedly higher than wages paid to free workers in the 1870s. Planters' total expenditures on wages had risen sharply with the shift of workers into the wage-earning sector, but the wages paid to individual workers had not.

Planters seeking subsidized immigration or laws restricting workers' rights tended to speak in terms of a 'scarcity' of workers, but other observers noticed that in absolute numbers there was not a general 'labour shortage'. José Quintin Suzarte wrote in 1881 that there was in fact an abundance of *braceros*, and that they would have to reduce their 'pretenciones' when faced with competition from the work forces of those plantations that had gone out of business, from released soldiers, from urban workers displaced by released soldiers, and from freed *patrocinados*.[45]

Nonetheless, as in virtually all post-emancipation societies, planters in Cuba complained that former slaves spent too much time in leisure. Indeed, former slaves did at times choose to place domestic labour, the cultivation of food crops, and companionship with friends and family above the endless hoeing, cutting and lifting of cane. But observers also noted that workers migrated in search of higher pay, and shifted from one estate or gang to another in pursuit of better wages. In such cases, there was no denying former slaves' responsiveness to monetary incentives. The 'labour shortage' bemoaned by planters should thus be seen in the context of employers' desire for an expansion of the total work force to drive down the cost of labour and their unwillingness or inability to offer higher wages. One planter, recalling the nineties, wrote simply that 'planters, who were very poor, due to the low price of sugar and the excessive taxation, could not afford to employ all the labourers that presented themselves'.[46] Under these circumstances, the leisure of some former slaves was an enforced one.

Whatever the fears of employers, it is clear that abolition did not trigger a catastrophic flight of former slaves from plantation labour, thus crippling production. Although levels of sugar production in the 1880s were below those of the peak years of the 1870s (when prices were higher), they did not plummet, but remained comparable to earlier figures, averaging just 8% below the amounts for the previous decade. In the 1890s they began to climb again, and reached the unprecedented one million ton mark by 1892 (see Table 1). While technical innovations and the attraction of new workers accounted for some of the recovery, former slaves of necessity provided much of the labour.

Table 1. Cuban Sugar Production, 1870–1894

Year	Metric Tons	Year	Metric Tons	Year	Metric Tons
1870	702,974	1878	553,364	1887	707,442
1871	609,660	1879	775,368	1888	662,758
1872	772,068	1880	618,654	1889	569,367
1873	742,843	1881	580,894	1890	636,239
1874	768,672	1882	620,565	1891	807,742
1875	750,062	1883	601,426	1892	1,000,797
1876	626,082	1884	626,477	1893	945,035
1877	516,268	1885	628,990	1894	1,110,991
		1886	657,290		

SOURCE: Manuel Moreno Fraginals, *El ingenio: complejo económico social cubano del azúcar*, 3 vols. (Havana: Editorial de Ciencias Sociales, 1978) 3:37–39.

Notes

1. Miguel Barnet, **Biographia de un cimmaron**, (Havana: Instituto de Etnologia y Folklore, Academia de Ciencias de Cuba, 1966), p. 62.
2. Ibid., p. 64. The reliability of the Montejo memoir as a historical source is open to some question, given its format and its very recent compilation. It seems best to view it as reflective of individual attitudes and recollections, rather than as a source for evidence on matters requiring strict chronology or precision.
3. On the shift in female participation in the labour force, see 'Report by Consul Pierce, Cienfuegos', in U.S. Cong., House, *Labour in America, Asia, Africa, Australasia, and Polynesia*, 48th Cong., 2nd Sess., 1884–1885, House Exec. Doc. no. 54, vol. 26, pp. 255–56; and Statement by P.M. Beal, manager of Colonia Guabairo', in Robert P. Porter, **Appendix to the report on the commercial and industrial condition of the island of Cuba** (Washington, D.C.: Government Printing Office, 1899).
4. See 'La Cuestión de brazos', in *El Espanol: Diario Político de la Tarde*, Jan. 5, 1886. For payments to *cuadrillas* in the 1890s, see, for example, Cuadernos con relación de los contratos de tiro de cana y otros, APSS, Valle-Iznaga, leg. 7, exp. 19.
5. For observations on work squads in the U.S., I am grateful to Gerald Jaynes, personal communication, 1984.
6. On food, see Barnet, *Biografía*, pp. 63–64; 'Report by Consul Pierce', p. 254; and U.S. War Dept. **Report on the Census is**: U.S. War Department, **Report on the Census of Cuba, 1899**, (Washington D.C.: Government Printing Office, 1900).
7. 'Report by Consul Pierce', p. 254.
8. Archivo Provincial de Sancti Spiritus (hereafter APSS), Valle-Iznaga, leg. 24.
9. See Barnett, *Biografía*, p. 64, and *El Productor*, Havana (Feb. 7, 1889).
10. Barnet, *Bibiografia*.
11. Cited in Julio Le Riverend, 'Raices del 24 de Febrero: La economía y la sociedad cubanas de 1878 a 1895', *Cuba Socialista* 5 (Feb. 1965): 8.
12. U.S. War Dept., *Report on the Census*, pp. 531–32.
13. Porter, *Appendix to the Report*, pp. 253, 267.
14. 'Macheteros y alzadores', *La Propaganda Periodico Liberal*, Sancti Spiritus.
15. On ditchers, see Sidney W. Mintz, **Caribbean Transformations** (Chicago: Aldine Publishing Co., 1974), p. 114. On the role of **libertos** in the Puerto Rican sugar industry, see Andres Ramos Mattei, 'El liberto en el regimen de trabajo azucarero de Puerto Rico, 1870–1880', in Andres Ramos Mattei, (ed.) **Azucar y esclavitud** (San Juan: Universidad de Puerto Rico, 1982), pp. 91–124.
16. See Francisco Feliciano Ibanez, **Observaciones sobre la utilidad y conveniencia del establecimiento en esta isla de grandes ingenios centrales** (Havana: Imprenta y Litografia Obispo 27, 1880). He argues that . . . etc. (see article).
17. Manuel Moreno Fraginals, **El token azucarero cubano** (Havana: Museo Numismatico de Cuba, n.d.), p. 151.
18. Porter, *Appendix to the Report*, p. 267.
19. Walter Rodney singles out the category of 'pan-boilers' as a group of Creole Africans in the Guianese sugar industry whose skills were essential to the factory, and argues that they were able to gain some autonomy as a result. It is difficult to determine whether former slaves in Cuba held a comparable position prior to the introduction of fully mechanized controls on the vacuum pans. If they did, their importance would have been an inhibition to segregation within the factory. See Walter Rodney, *A History of the*

Guyanese Working People, 1881–1905 (Baltimore: The Johns Hopkins University Press, 1981), p. 161.

20. Barnett, *Bibiografía,* pp. 65–66.

21. Ibid., pp. 67–68. The *Revista* article is cited in LeRiverend, 'Raices'. p. 10. For a general discussion of plantation stores, see Moreno, 'El Token'.

22. See the account books of the *ingenio* Nuevas Teresa, Archivo Nacional de Cuba, Havana, Miscelanea de Libros, 11245, 10879.

23. Moreno, 'El token'.

24. Negocios 1857–1896, APSS, Valle-Iznaga, leg. 7, exp. 19.

25. For such sentiments expressed by a Puerto Rican sugar cane worker in the twentieth century, see Sidney W. Mintz, *Worker in the Cane: A Puerto Rican Life History* [New Haven: Yale University Press, 1960), p. 142.

26. Moreno, 'El token', pp. 154–55.

27. See the letter from the alcalde of Guara to the governor of Havana, Sept. 18, 1888, in Expediente . . . sobre el pago de jornales a braceros en forma de fichas que representan valor estimativo, Archivo Nacional de Cuba, Miscelanea de Expedientes, leg. 4330, exp. AH.

28. 'Trabajadores', *La Propaganda* (Feb. 26, 1882), and 'Hacendados y trabajadores', ibid., (Dec. 1, 1884).

29. *El Eco de Cuba* (Jan. 15, 1881). For a general discussion of debt and peonage see Arnold J. Bauer, 'Rural Workers in Spanish America: Problems of Peonage and Oppression', *Hispanic American Historical Review* 59 (Feb. 1979): 34–63.

30. *La Propaganda* (Feb. 26, 1882).

31. Personal Communication from Edelmiro Bonachea Jiménez, Director Provincial de Cultura, Sancti Spíritus, May 1979.

32. 'Las Fiestas en los campos', *Revista de Agricultura* 8 (Sept. 2, 1888): 385.

33. 'Trabajadores', *La Propaganda* (Feb. 26. 1882).

34. 'Las Fiestas en los campos'.

35. *La Propaganda* (May 17, 1885).

36. *La Fraternidad,* Sancti Spíritus (Aug. 17, 1890). One could go a step further and argue that employers' attitudes were in part a legacy of Iberian seigneurialism, reinforced by the institution of slavery. To demonstrate this convincingly, however, would require a tracing of elite ideology and its roots that is well beyond the scope of this study. For a discussion of Cuban slavery that employs the concept of seigneurialism, see Robert Louis Paquette, 'The Conspiracy of La Escalera: Colonial Society & Politics in Cuba in the Age of Revolution', Ph.D., Univ. of Rochester, 1982).

37. *La Propaganda* (March 26, 1882).

38. *Revista de Agricultura* 8 (Sept. 16, 1888): 142, and 8 (July 8, 1888): 279.

39. *Revista de Agricultura* 8 (July 8, 1888): 279.

40. Informe, Sociedad Económica de Amigos del País, Aug. 22, 1886, and Informe, Círculo de Hacendados, Aug. 7, 1886, Archivo Historico National, Madrid, Ultramar, leg. 280, exp. 610.

41. Relación de pagos, Natividad, July 31, 1889, APSS, Valle-Iznaga, leg. 7, exp. 13.

42. U.S. War Dept., *Report on the Census,* p. 531.

43. APSS, Valle-Iznaga, leg. 7, exp. 19.

44. Porter, *Appendix to the Report,* p. 268.

45. José Quintín Suzarte, *Estudios sobre la cuestion económica de la isla de cuba* (Havana: Miguel de Villa, 1881), p. 66.

46. Porter, *Appendix to the Report,* p. 263.

The Creolization of Caribbean History: The Emancipation Era and a Critique of Dialectical Analysis

William A. Green

History is the servant of present needs. Every historiographer appreciates that contemporary evaluations of the past are predicated upon currently esteemed values. The questions we ask shape the histories we produce, and, of course, our questions reflect our values. Empire is no longer esteemed. Colonial nationalism and the struggle of third world peoples for genuine independence are. For most of this century, the history of the British West Indies was written from an imperial perspective. Decolonization changed that. In recent decades, infant Caribbean states, seeking independent identities and new collective concepts of community, have attempted to differentiate themselves from their former imperial overlords. Historians and social scientists have strongly supported that endeavour. In 1955, Philip Curtin observed that West Indian history could be written from either of two perspectives: as an extension of the British experience, or as the history of separate societies possessing distinctive lives of their own.[1] His *Two Jamaicas* was a deliberate attempt to steer the latter course. Some years later, Sidney Mintz urged an assembly of scholars studying West Indian integration 'to specify those characteristics of the area ... that give it particularity and commonality — to discover what is authentically Caribbean.'[2] By the time of the publication of Edward Brathwaite's *The Development of Creole Society in Jamaica, 1770–1820* (1971), the creolization of West Indian history was well under way.

For Mintz and Brathwaite, creolization involved the identification of people, whatever their place of origin or racial composition, with the island societies in which they lived. Brathwaite insisted that by 1820 Jamaica had developed a distinctive culture that was neither British nor West African, but part of a broad New World complex.[3] Arguing that Europeans as well as Africans underwent significant cultural change in the West Indies, he shifted his historical centre of gravity from London to the Caribbean, from concentration on the complex requirements of empire to emphasis on the slow evolution of a self-conscious Caribbean society.[4]

Since Brathwaite's pioneering study, historians writing in the creole genre have increasingly focused their attention on one element of the Caribbean population: the labouring people, slave and ex-slave. The abiding theme of this work is black resistance to white domination. Intermittent acts of insurrection have received special attention, but many scholars now agree that endemic resistance to the white power structure was a fundamental feature of black West Indian culture.[5] By emphasizing the incessant struggle of an under-class, this orientation to Caribbean history has generated a pantheon of new national heroes whose historic exploits are thought to affirm creole traditions and express the legitimate aspirations of island peoples. Creolization has also occasioned increasing interest in dialectical analysis as a vehicle for studying the Caribbean past.

Although creolization and dialectical analysis may appear to be highly compatible, they possess different methodological properties. The former represents a particular perspective. Like all subjective perspectives in history, it carries certain risks. At its best, it will inspire greater appreciation for the internal evolution of island cultures without neglecting the importance of wider imperial relationships. At its worst, it will provide little more than the flip side of an older imperial history, ignoring global issues and blurring metropolitan distinctions while concentrating exclusively on indigenous colonial struggles.

Dialectical analysis represents more than a special perspective. It is a methodological procedure by which data are selected, classified and interpreted in accordance with a specific theory of historical change. In a world divided between rich nations and poor where the language of partisan politics is commonly expressed in the idiom of class and exploitation, a dualistic concept of struggle that pits have against have-nots, whites against blacks, and planters against plantation workers may seem to offer an eminently plausible and straightforward approach to colonial history. Despite its attractive simplicity, however, the dialectic is a blunt and imperfect instrument for pursuing Caribbean history in the nineteenth century. Because it emphasizes duality, it cannot accommodate the extraordinary plurality of Caribbean society without artificially fusing groups that possessed little conscious identity on a comprehensive range of societal issues. Even if it were possible to divide that society into neatly antagonistic camps, the dialectic would have to contend with an overriding third force — the imperial government — which intruded upon local problems and mediated between conflicting Caribbean factions. A dialectical conflict model for the post-emancipation West Indies conceals the extent to which all elements of the population, whatever their antagonisms, were locked in a painful but symbiotic set of economic relationships from which they could not escape without enduring even greater social and material hardships. That relationship pivoted on the plantations, particularly sugar plantations. It was a troubled relationship, and it was rendered more troubled by international economic forces which were hostile to Caribbean interests and beyond the power of Caribbean people — white or black — to control.

I

It is important to identify as succinctly as possible the salient characteristics of the dialectical approach as it has appeared in recent Caribbean historiography. By dialectic, I mean the bipolar concept that two broadly encompassing and antagonistic phenomena dominate social interaction. This orientation can readily be illustrated by reference to the work of two scholars, Peter Wilson and Monica Schuler. Wilson, an anthropologist, attempts to demonstrate that a relentless struggle has long persisted between two value systems in the Caribbean. Europeans, he argues, brought their own system to the islands, providing a constellation of formal institutional structures that stratified society into social classes based on privilege. *Inequality* was its basic principle. An alternative system — what Wilson calls a counter-principle as well as an authentic structural principle — arose among the subordinated people for whom metropolitan values offered no satisfaction. This latter system was and remains *aggressively egalitarian*. It rejects stratification; it assesses people's worth in terms of their conduct towards others; and it tolerates, even encourages, actions calculated to nullify or undermine the well-being, psychic or

material, of those who strive for upward social mobility. Most West Indians, Wilson asserts, have never embraced a European value system. It is, therefore, unreasonable and unfair to measure Caribbean society with metropolitan yardsticks. West Indian society must be studied on its own terms, not as a 'pathetic or exotic imitation' of European society. The Caribbean, Wilson concludes, 'provides us with what is possibly the clearest instance in history of a dialectical social system'.[6]

Wilson's bipolar socio-cultural analysis is complemented by Monica Schuler's studies of Pan-African cosmology. Africans and their Caribbean descendants shared a cosmological view which assumed that events in this world were caused by human action. Evil intruded upon the life of man through the sin of sorcery. People who experienced exceptional good fortune were suspected of practicing sorcery, of enhancing their fortunes at the expense of the community. Because of this, the religious rituals of Afro-Caribbean people were calculated, Schuler argues, to protect the community from the misfortunes imposed by sorcerers. She extends this argument to encompass black-white relationships, insisting that blacks believed their enslavement and oppression to have resulted from sorcery. Having perceived their oppressors as sorcerers, they could not accept bondage, nor indeed could they accept other more subtle forms of oppression when slavery ended. In sum, the religious beliefs central to every aspect of Afro-Caribbean society provided a powerful and perpetual source of resistance to European values and to European domination.[7] This resistance manifested itself in several ways. First, it evoked a fierce independence. Second, it occasioned a philosophical, even sentimental, attachment to the land. The land confirmed the freedman's identity; it provided him solidarity with the community and security against economic vicissitudes.[8]

Wilson and Schuler posit a fundamental conflict between dominant Europeans and slaves/freedmen — in other words, between the land monopolizing, labour-tyrannizing white oligarchy and the assertively independent freedmen with their propensity to possess the land. Nigel Bolland endorses this view. In what may be the most forceful advocacy to date of the dialectical approach to West Indian history, Bolland, also an anthropologist, contends that emancipation merely perpetuated the struggle between incompatible groups, between the ex-slaves who sought new forms of freedom and their former masters who sought new methods of coercion. Our task, he argues, is to define the emancipation period in terms of the 'survival and improved living standards of the former slaves', not 'in terms of the survival of the plantations and the prosperity of the planters'.[9]

For the dialectician, the issue is clear-cut. The well-being of the freedmen is pitted against the well-being of those who owned and managed the principal colonial industry. The conflict is expressed in terms of survival: the survival of former slaves versus the survival of the plantations. Moreover, the struggle assumes a moral cast. For too long, we are told, the history of the Caribbean has been written from the top down; it must now be assessed from the bottom up, and our sympathies must reside with those who have struggled from the underside of Caribbean life. Historians should not assume that sugar plantations and sugar planters were permanent fixtures of Caribbean society. Their continued presence was neither necessary nor desirable, nor was it in the best interests of the emancipated people.

II

In challenging the dialectical approach, one need not minimize the conflicts that persisted between planters and freedmen. They were profound, and they were aggravated by historical and cultural antagonisms. But sugar planters and sugar plantations were not expendable in the post-emancipation Caribbean any more than sugar, bauxite, or tourism have been expendable in the twentieth century. Sugar estates, however, unloved, provided a vital and irreplaceable source of income, direct and indirect, for the ex-slaves. Although freedmen clashed with planters over working relationships, they were no more inclined to shut down the sugar economy as a whole than coal miners have been to close mines, despite the onerous nature of both forms of labour and the varied grievances which cane workers and miners have felt towards management. Imperial historians have consistently taken this view. For them, the paramount institutional issue in the emancipation era was not whether the plantations should survive but upon what terms they should survive. Imperial historians have considered it a matter of certitude that the formal legislative abolition of slavery could only have proceeded in England on the premise that the plantations should survive.[10]

Their reasons are simple. In the 1830s, Caribbean plantations were more than social or economic units. They were the organizing principle for West Indian society. No metropolitan group — neither the British government nor the abolitionists nor people having commercial interests in the colonies — could contemplate, let alone favour, eliminating plantations as a part of the emancipation process. Plantations concentrated populations for the religious harvest of missionaries; they provided markets for merchants and pen-keepers; they offered employment for a variety of artisans and domestics; and they gave life, through multiple economic linkages, to ancillary businesses in the towns. Lowland plantations kept the roads and bridges open for coffee and cocoa producers as well as for small farmers in the highlands. The staple exports of the plantations purchased refined imports, few of which could be produced in the colonies. Shopping generated by export commerce created port-side employment while encouraging a minor coasting trade. In every sense, plantations formed a skeletal system for the Caribbean colonies, albeit a system thoroughly in accord with metropolitan values. For imperial historians, then, the principal issue in the post-emancipation Caribbean was not whether the planters and plantations would continue to exist but the role they would play and the influence they would wield.[11]

In order to evaluate the relative merits of these conflicting approaches, it is imperative to ask a difficult hypothetical question. What might have befallen Caribbean society had the plantation economy been dismantled?[12] Historians have rarely addressed this question directly, partly because it requires speculative counterfactual and comparative analysis.[13] By not confronting it, however, scholars have permitted themselves the unreal luxury of freely criticizing the post-emancipation planter elite for a variety of political, social, and economic misdemeanours without concurrently examining what the full implications of a wholesale withdrawal of the planting faction might have been.[14]

Emancipation history is uniformly written in the tragic style. The high expectations of ex-slaves and abolitionists as well as the guarded hopes of planters, merchants and the British government were all dashed, it would appear, in the decades after 1834. By the late 1860s most freedmen were extremely poor and only slightly more Europeanized than they had been in the 1830s. Small colonial economies were struggling desperately; the Jamaican sugar industry was a fragment of its former size; and the plantation systems of Trinidad and British Guiana were being held together by Indian indentured labour. In the wake of Morant Bay, the old legislative system was giving way to authoritarian Crown Colony governments.

Such misfortunes have evoked keen interest in apportioning blame. In the process of apportionment, many writers have assumed a 'soft' or quasi-dialectical orientation — that is, they have posited a bipolar struggle between planters and freedmen without making an explicit or consistent commitment to the dialectical form. These writers blame

Caribbean misfortunes on the planter elite, citing their mismanagement of labour relations, their obstinate attachment to King Sugar, and their stubborn resistance to new techniques, new technology and alternative cash crops.[15] Unlike affirmative dialecticians such as Wilson or Bolland who emphasize fundamental incompatibilities within West Indian society, these less theoretically explicit quasi-dialecticians lament the failure of the planter elite to set things right after emancipation. Theirs is the history of missed opportunities. Had the planters only been more reformist, more farsighted and innovative, they could have won the loyalty of freedmen, launched successful economic enterprises and established harmonious industrial relations. A society that might have achieved reasonable consensus in both structural and functional terms was doomed to perpetual dissension by callous and irresponsible planter malfeasance.

There are grounds for arguing that neither the 'hard' nor the 'soft' dialectical approach is satisfactory. As a body, planters were not as resistant to new technology or to commercial innovation as these writers assert.[16] Old animosities, the burdensome nature of plantation service, and the severe constraints imposed by international forces upon the production of all export crops made it highly unlikely that genuinely harmonious industrial relations could long be sustained in the British West Indies. Despite conflicts between management and labour in agriculture, a period of positive economic relations did occur in the aftermath of emancipation. This positive development was not shattered by incompatibilities inherent in the social structure of the Caribbean, but by external imperial action involving sugar tariffs.

The old image of the slothful, hide-bound and technologically backward West Indian planter dies hard, but it is, nevertheless, a regrettable stereotype that sorely misrepresents the prodigious efforts of many energetic, modernizing agriculturalists in the emancipation era. Having addressed this problem elsewhere,[17] I will confine my discussion to one disturbing tendency among contemporary historians. It has become commonplace for writers to lecture planters retrospectively on proper agrarian and business tactics, suggesting simple remedial measures which, if the planters had only adopted them, could have reduced the colonists' onerous economic problems and enhanced industrial harmony. It is often asserted, for example, that the planters' inordinate attachment to sugar prevented them from seizing the positive opportunities offered by alternative cash crops.[18] A leading Caribbean scholar declared that the Windward planters were remiss in not shifting their attention to vegetables

or to stock rearing or to minor staples such as cotton, coffee, cocoa, rice, nuts and fresh fruit.[19]

What, in fact, were the commercial prospects of these alternative cash crops after emancipation? The production of low-cost, high-volume slave-grown cotton in the American South rendered any hope of significant commercial competition from the free-labour British West Indies ludicrous. In Berbice alone, 111 plantations abandoned cotton production in the 15 years after 1809.[20] Coffee was equally unpromising. Between 1832 and 1847, 465 Jamaican coffee plantations ceased cultivation.[21] In British Guiana, where coffee had once been a major export staple, the crop was disappearing. Dominica continued to ship some coffee, but the home market had been captured, in large part, by Ceylonese growers.[22] Cocoa was produced in northern Trinidad, but Spain, not Britain, was the principal European importer. Tariff and navigation laws were a monumental obstacle to trade with Spain. The international price of cocoa was less than half what it had been in the 1820s, and Trinidad's cocoa planters were utterly prostrate.[23] Rice offered no better prospects, and the successful long-distance marketing of fresh fruit would have to await refrigeration and swifter seagoing transport. In fact, the appeal of alternative staples in the decade after emancipation turns out to be a mirage.[24]

This example helps to illustrate the continuing importance of a viable sugar industry to all elements of the West Indian population. Despite the depressing prospects of alternative staples, Windward Islanders could have exported fruits, vegetables, nuts and livestock to other West Indian locations. But if all the former sugar colonies had become exporters of fruits, vegetables and stock, which colony would have needed any other colony's products? An inter-island trade in foodstuffs and stock could *only* have prospered if some of the islands continued to maintain staple exporting economies of significant proportions.[25]

In the Windwards area, it was Trinidad that preserved an active sugar culture throughout the emancipation period. This was done at great cost, particularly in immigration. But what cost would that island and others in the Windward chain have borne if Trinidad had not retained an estate economy? The freedmen of Trinidad who lived in independent villages and supplied foodstuffs to functioning estates would have lost an irreplaceable market. Thousands of Windward Islanders who travelled seasonally to Trinidad to sell provisions and earn comparatively high wages in the cane fields would have found no sales and no supplementary income.[26] British Guiana is a more urgent case. Although the sugar industry survived there at very heavy social cost, there can be little doubt that the coastal lowlands inhabited by nearly the whole population of the colony would have been swallowed by the sea had the organizing presence of the plantations been removed.[27]

No modern historian is likely to express much fondness for the nineteenth-century sugar plantation, but it is perfectly legitimate to have serious reservations as to whether the general demise of plantations in the emancipation period would have had positive short or long-term consequences for any element of Caribbean society. Admittedly we have limited comparative bases for judgement on this issue. In the few British islands where sugar production was abandoned or virtually abandoned (Montserrat, for example), the population remained within easy geographical range of colonies where estate economies survived. This provided the local population access to seasonal wage labour as well as to markets for their surplus provisions.

In the Caribbean, only Haiti experienced the thorough dismantling of an oligarchic colonial sugar culture. Even there, comparisons with the British situation are strained since perpetual warfare ravaged the Haitian infrastructure between 1790 and 1804. Although successive Haitian leaders — Toussaint, Dessalines and Christophe — attempted, sometimes brutally, to revive plantations by using the forced labour of ex-slaves, their efforts failed. By 1820, the tiny state was swiftly retreating into a stagnant, utterly impoverished, peasant economy, largely isolated from the rest of the world.[28] One need not suppose that the systematic ruination of plantation structures in the British colonies would have produced the same appalling results that befell Haiti. Freedmen in Jamaica and the British islands participated in the small-scale export of coffee, pimento and minor crops to a greater extent, it appears, than Haitians.[29] But the fact that both Toussaint, a humane and philosophical leader, and Dessalines, the brutalized former field slave who blissfully executed whites, should have deemed it essential, even at the expense of forced labour, to preserve plantation institutions and a staple export economy is significant. It suggests that despite either the colour or the cultural origins of those who ruled in the Caribbean the social benefit derived from retaining plantation structures was thought to exceed the social costs entailed.

Without minimizing the tensions evident in post-emancipation industrial relations, it is not far-fetched to consider the first years after emancipation, particularly the early 1840s, as a kind of golden age for Caribbean working people — to the extent, that is, that Caribbean working people have ever enjoyed a golden age. Employment was abundant; wages were relatively high; and collective actions calculated to preserve pay levels and enhance the terms of work generally succeeded.[30] Except in Barbados and a few other islands or sections of islands where population density was uncommonly high, freedmen were able to acquire their own land. None of this was achieved without struggle, but reports from missionaries, magistrates, abolitionists, planters and governors uniformly declared that freedmen were enjoying more leisure, luxuries and access to freehold property than the working people of England.[31]

This relative comfort and independence was achieved at considerable cost to the plantations. Quality of husbandry, regularity of work and efficiency of operations declined on most estates. Productivity fell, and many of the weakest plantations were abandoned or sold off in multiple plots to freedmen.[32] Despite angry complaints by planters, the most aggressive among them tightened their belts, reorganized estate routines and introduced labour-saving equipment. If life in the colonies was not placid (it hardly ever had been), a *modus operandi* was established between planters and freedmen in the early 1840s by which both, in the main, secured their most important objectives without entirely negating opportunities for the other.[33] The West Indies were not consensual societies, but neither were they societies in which the best interest of the underclass would be served by the ruin of the elite. In spite of apparent incompatibilities, West Indians were locked together in a painful symbiotic embrace, the victims of a troubled past and an increasingly hostile world economy from which they could not escape without compounding their hardships.

It is incumbent, then, upon scholars who treat the history of the emancipation era in terms of a dialectical encounter between the Afro- and Euro-Caribbean sectors to demonstrate how the long-term quality of life and material well-being of the descendants of slaves would have been enhanced had the alleged incompatibilities operating within West Indian society produced the wholesale demolition of the plantation system. In effect, we need some thorough counter-factual argumentation. It is not enough simply to indicate that life in the sugar colonies was harsh and limiting, that working people suffered greatly, or that plantations were run fundamentally in the interests of European capitalists. It is entirely possible that without a viable plantation structure, Caribbean life would have been substantially harsher and more limiting.

III

It is worth noting that many imperial historians with no commitment to dialectical analysis have, like Peter Wilson, perceived duality in the cultural fabric of the West Indian colonies. The perspective of these historians differs radically from that of Wilson, however. As a rule, they have analyzed cultural tension in terms of an enlightened and complex culture struggling to subdue an unenlightened and primitive one in exceedingly difficult circumstances. The appropriateness of this struggle has seemed so obvious to them that the encounter of cultures within the Caribbean itself has never been placed at the centre of their analysis. Instead, primary attention has been given to conflicts arising within the dominant culture and to strategies employed to extend enlightened principles. To the extent that there was a particular slave culture, it was not deemed worthy of significant, let alone equal, attention. Instead, it was viewed as something which had to be subdued. What was important was the process by which it was subdued. Current writers in the creole genre, especially those committed to dialectical analysis, deplore this attitude and elevate Afro-Caribbean culture to a position of equality in a bipolar struggle. In doing so, they strongly differentiate the island people from their former imperial overlords and intensify Caribbean self-awareness. This has enormous value in modern political terms. Does it have merit in historical terms?

Any attempt to answer this question immediately involves the historian in a range of further considerations. How homogenous was Afro-Caribbean culture in the emancipation period? Was resistance to a Euro-Caribbean value system as strong or universal as scholars like Wilson and Schuler suggest? Where and how does one draw the line between one cultural nexus and the other? Did not the cultural composition of Afro-Caribbean peoples vary widely from one island to another, even from one part of a large island to another?

Mintz and Price perceive the process of creolization among Afro-Caribbean peoples as one of rapid and sustained adaptation to the colonial power structure, to a new economic regime, to an alien language and to a multitude of social conventions dictated very largely by the dominant European elite.[34] The pace at which this adaptation occurred depended in some degree upon the African composition of existing slave populations and the density and character of the local European population. This varied widely in the British colonies. As Higman has shown, African-born slaves in Barbados amounted to scarcely more than 10% of any adult age group in 1817 whereas in Jamaica they accounted for a majority of slaves over the age of 25.[35] One is bound to conclude that Afro-Caribbean peoples were differentiated along a cul-

tural continuum extending from 'liberated Africans' deposited in the islands by the Royal Navy to creoles with African forebears who had largely adopted the habits and values of white colonists. Maroons, though also an adaptive people, would have to be placed at the African end of that continuum.

In Jamaica, Cudgoe and Nanny, Sam Sharpe, Paul Bogle and George William Gordon have each, in their separate ways, become national heroes. Although their individual cultural characteristics varied widely, they all offered profound resistance to the British at critical moments in Jamaican history. It must be recalled, however, that the descendants of Cudgoe and Nanny were by no means allies to the Sharpes and Bogles of nineteenth-century Jamaica. Maroons helped the British capture rebels and runaways, and the Eastern Maroons poured out of their mountain villages to assist the Queen's forces during the Morant Bay crisis. Sam Sharpe may have led the most dangerous rebellion in the history of Jamaican slavery, but at the height of the Christmas fighting in 1831–32 slaves at Mesopotamia estate, living adjacent to the strife, rejected overtures to join the insurrection. They gave information to authorities on the activities of insurrectionaries, and, with their masters away from the estate hunting rebels, they started taking crops without white supervision.[36]

The historical record continuously confronts us with behaviour that defies the notion of perpetual resistance or of universal Afro-Caribbean solidarity. The common relationship between masters and bondsmen in any slave society may be a dialectical one, but, as Stanley Elkins argued many years ago,[37] slavery, like all forms of tyranny, produces varied responses that require subtle and discriminatory analysis. Not all West Indians who might be classified within an Afro-Caribbean culture group were defiant; not all were slaves. Some were slave-owners; still others hunted runaways under formal alliance with Europeans.

When full emancipation arrived in 1838, the allure of the dominant culture was high, if by no means overwhelming. Missionaries gloried in overflowing chapels and expressed immense gratification that so many ex-slaves formalized sexual unions through Christian marriage.[38] By 1840, free children were being enrolled in great numbers in the many schools erected by parliamentary subsidy. It was a buoyant time. Prosperity was unprecedented, and hope for a more bounteous future was widespread. Why was this buoyancy not sustained? For one thing, adherence to the dominant culture offered no dramatic or immediate uplift in social status. Social cleavages in the West Indies were deep; they were not based exclusively on cultural affiliations;[39] nor were they easily or quickly altered. More importantly, the sugar colonies were economically devastated during the mid–1840s. The relative prosperity that characterized those communities in the early years of the decade began to wane by 1845, and in 1846 the Sugar Duties Act, the imperial equivalent of the abolition of the corn laws, provided an economic *coup de grâce* by forcing British colonial sugar to compete on equal terms with non-British slave labour sugar in the home market. With the exception of Barbadians, free labour growers could not meet that competition. Between 1844 and 1854, 314 sugar plantations in Jamaica alone, almost half the total, ceased production.[40] Banks failed throughout the islands; money was unavailable to pay taxes, or wages, or to support public services, however minimal. Merchant houses collapsed as regularly as estates; cholera arrived in the islands in 1850; influenza followed. Missionaries lost their flocks, and ex-slaves, incapable of sustaining the style of life enjoyed during the first years of freedom, pulled away from the Euro-Caribbean sector. Chronology is important here. This socio-cultural withdrawal did not occur in the first blush of freedom. The slow process of estrangement was vastly accelerated by a paralyzing economic disaster.

IV

It is precisely such developments that must give pause to historians advocating a dialectical model. Having identified a bipolar struggle between Afro-Caribbean people and the Euro-Caribbean oligarchy, they are compelled to acknowledge that the terms of that struggle were constantly being altered by forces external to it. It would be futile to argue that such external forces were in league with either the Afro-Caribbean culture group or the planter elite. No vested interest suffered more grievous blows to its power and influence than the Caribbean plantocracy between 1807 and 1846. The abolition of the international slave trade, the abolition of the inter-colonial transfer of slaves, slave registration, the amelioration of slavery in the 1820s, the Emancipation Act, and the Sugar Duties Act — all these and others had been foisted on the West Indian planters against their will, breaking their economic power, and rendering them by the mid-nineteenth century an utterly spent force. When slavery died, Colonial Office policy was calculated to trim the sails of West Indian oligarchs without actually destroying them.[41] A separate magistracy responsible to London was established throughout the sugar colonies to adjudicate civil and criminal actions involving ex-slaves, and planter appeals for immigration from Africa and

Asia had to await imperial approval. These external controls and intrusions on the colonial oligarchy affected the life of the colonies at every level. Some blows were struck by missionaries, abolitionists and colonial officials, others by metropolitan capitalists or their representatives in Parliament in opposition to those same missionaries and abolitionists.[42] Such externally initiated changes cannot be integrated into a bipolar analysis of conflicting Caribbean groups without massively distorting the dialectical framework.

To the extent that conflict existed between planters and ex-slaves after emancipation, the loyalties of Europeans were scattered. Abolitionists and missionaries generally, but not invariably, allied with freedmen, business interests with the planters. The imperial government, particularly the Colonial Office, viewed itself as a responsible arbiter standing between conflicting private parties, delimiting the exercise of both the planter's power and the freedmen's liberty, honouring abolitionists and missionaries in some cases while denouncing their excesses in others. Successive ministers at the Colonial Office believed the worst fate that might befall the colonies, saving the re-establishment of a system of coerced labour, would be the demolition of the plantation structure. Modern proponents of dialectical analysis might view this solicitousness for plantations as evidence that the imperial government was solidly in the camp of the planters. But neither the planters nor the government in London believed that to be true. Why would the metropolitan government have rushed to the defence of an oligarchy whose power it had deliberately and systematically broken? In fact, the Colonial Office constituted a third force in Caribbean affairs, standing between the colonial oligarchy and the emancipated population. By any calculation, three such powerful and distinct forces cannot easily be accommodated by dialectical analysis.

By concentrating upon a division between Euro- and Afro-Caribbean groups, between the oppressors and the oppressed in the post-emancipation West Indies, dialecticians blur important distinctions. Where do abolitionists stand in a bipolar analysis? Abolitionists were implacable enemies of the planters. With unremitting intensity, they harassed and weakened the planters, but they did not want the plantations destroyed. In fact, they wanted the British West Indies to export more sugar after emancipation than before. Should such objectives cast them among the oppressors of emancipated people? They cared nothing for planters' profits, but they were profoundly committed to achieving the abolition of the slave trade and the emancipation of slavery in every part of the Atlantic world. Abolitionists believed that the failure of the sugar economy in the free British West Indies would deter slave-holders in North America, Cuba, and Brazil from proceeding toward emancipation. Such a failure, they believed, would vindicate pro-slavery forces throughout the hemisphere and ensure the continuation of the Atlantic slave trade.

Where does one locate the middle groups in Caribbean society in the dialectical process? Even if we place minor merchants, artisans, penkeepers, cocoa and coffee planters, or conceivably, small farmers within the ambit of the dominant Euro-Caribbean sector, we must be prepared to acknowledge that substantial friction prevailed between them and the leading oligarchs. Social position in the West Indian colonies did not depend on economic or cultural factors alone. Race was fundamental. In any dialectical division of Caribbean peoples during the emancipation era, West Indians of mixed ancestry would have occupied positions on both sides. But does this division adequately explain the position they held or the sentiments and aspirations they expressed? Before emancipation, free coloured people constituted a separate legal category, and traditional West Indian usage favoured slaves or freedmen of light skin in both the workplace and the bedroom. Judgments based on somatic properties pervaded *every* level of West Indian society, and so great is the evidence of distinctions by colour that scores of historians — including those, like Brathwaite, who advocate creolization — have divided Caribbean society into its component colour groups for the purpose of analysis.

In one respect, people of colour were the most creole of West Indians since their capacity to identify strongly with either their metropolitan or their African origins was blunted by their possession of mixed ancestry. At the same time, the hierarchical nature of Caribbean society, based very largely on distinctions of race, inexorably drew them towards the European sector, enabling the most successful among them to aspire to reasonable levels of wealth and influence while permitting the least successful to condescend towards people of darker complexion. In the emancipation era, West Indian society was not polarized. It was rigidly tripartite, and the intensity of racial feeling at the frontier of each social tier may have been greater after emancipation than in the days of slavery when such distinctions were reinforced by statute.[43] People of colour constituted the middle category, and their middleness was so apparent that the term 'middle class' was used to designate a racial, not an economic, cohort.[44]

Scholars of the emancipation era who deal in detail with the affairs of people of colour are beset by distinctions, some of them extremely petty, involving discriminatory practices which were calculated to exalt the status of one person or group over another. Other distinctions are significant and affect the growth and development of Caribbean government and economy. For example, influential people of colour in Jamaica wanted to preserve both the plantation economy and a white planter elite whose presence would continue to afford European cultural influences to the society at large.[45] People of colour were terribly concerned to retain balance in the social system. They resented white superiority, but they feared the example of Haiti. Their collective goal was to strengthen their own social role while steering a delicate course between two extremes.[46] While favouring plantations, coloured colonists viewed with satisfaction some wastage in the plantation economy, knowing that depressed white proprietors might sell off estates at low rates, enabling them to increase their share of colonial property. With few exceptions, people of colour also favoured the preservation of the old legislative system in the expectation that they would fall heir to its rewards. Any analysis of the emancipation era that blurs or neglects distinctions based on colour will distort colonial history. Historians need to confine their conceptual views of the past to those expressed by people who lived in the past. But to impose analytical structures on the emancipation period which may not be recognizable to persons who lived, thought and took daily decisions in that time is to place history entirely at the service of philosophy, politics or some other immediately felt need.

V

This is, perhaps, the principal objection to a dialectic approach. It narrows West Indian history and neglects its multiple subtleties, its richness and variation. If, in the past, imperial historians have erred by ignoring the depth and tenacity of Afro-Caribbean culture, the proponents of dialectical analysis err by superimposing on the West Indies an analytical structure that fails to accommodate the kaleidoscopic diversity of human motives and forces that influenced the course of life in the western tropics. The inherent logic of the dialectic is to emphasize the operation of two conflicting forces. Once this scheme is imposed on the historical landscape, it becomes difficult for a researcher to avoid fitting his data into preconceived packages. In the emancipation era, the data will not readily fit. Caribbean struggles were multi-faceted, diverse, inter-regional, even intercontinental; they involved differing culture groups, racial groups, economic groups, political, religious, philanthropic and administrative groups whose loyalties and alliances shifted as issues and circumstances changed.

Whatever one may think of the debates surrounding M.G. Smith's concept of the plural society,[47] pluralism is surely a much more appropriate orientation to the emancipation period than dialectical polarization. In the sense that Smith used history (though not thoroughly) as a vehicle for defining the nature of Caribbean society in the 1950s and 1960s, so too historians can probe the emancipation era with a pluralist orientation — one that is reasonably well-founded on earlier studies — and build their own theory of social interaction and historical change through inductive reasoning based on evidence drawn from both sides of the Atlantic.[48]

The abiding strength of history written from an older imperial standpoint is that individual colonies are viewed in global perspective. In the nineteenth century, everyone perceived the West Indian colonies as dependencies of the Mother Country, likely to remain dependencies for all foreseeable time. This assumption was pervasive at every social level. Although, in the late twentieth century, it is important to recognize that colonials of every complexion were becoming progressively creolized, laying down the embryonic cultural roots of future island nations, the major decisions that governed West Indian affairs, producing the sharpest twists and turns in Caribbean life, were made beyond those islands. They occurred for a variety of reasons, some of which had as much to do with domestic pressures in the metropole and with far-flung imperial problems as with circumstances prevailing in the West Indies themselves.[49] Does this mean that history written from an imperial viewpoint is superior to history written from the creole perspective? The answer to this is both yes and no: yes, in so far as imperial history comprehends a wider panorama and therefore places small island colonies in appropriate world context; no, in so far as it all too often ignores the underside of life in the Caribbean colonies themselves.

Creolization is capable of repairing this latter deficiency, but if it becomes wedded to the dialectic, it will do so only at significant cost. All historians are fallible, not just in the errors they make but in the limitations of their patience, range of vision, and capacity to devote time to research. It is too much to hope that scholars who are dedicated to ascertaining what is 'authentically Caribbean' and who choose to structure their work in terms of dialectical encounter between Afro- and Euro-Caribbean culture groups will, in practice, embrace the full range of metropolitan and global influences that shook the sugar islands. It is in the nature of dialectical analysis to focus on the internal tensions in a society. This may be tolerable for the study of societies having limited interaction with a wider world, but it is not tolerable for the British West Indies where society was profoundly, perpetually and inescapably shaped by forces external to it.

West Indian life was replete with ambivalence, and the pre-eminent object of ambivalent feeling was the plantation. Demanding, oppressive, laden with bitter memories, yet remarkably fragile,[50] the plantation was for many people an object of genuine hatred. At the same time it was the only institutional vehicle by which West Indians living in the emancipation period could be linked to the rest of the world, by which they could share a knowledge of that world, and by which they could hope to consume its goods in any volume. If the plantations were unloved, they were, nevertheless, in some manner or degree, considered indispensable by almost all contemporary parties, even in a grudging way by freedmen themselves.[51] The disposition of the plantations is a central issue for all scholars of the emancipation era. Dialecticians who perceive the plantation mainly as an evil medium for oppression consider its destruction to be commensurate with the promotion of liberty and well-being among the labouring people. This line of argument embodies an implied counter-claim — that the colonies would have been better off without plantations. Such counter-factual assumptions must be pursued to their logical conclusions so that the full consequences of a demolition of the sugar industry and its multiple ancillary institutions can be fathomed.

Perhaps the most effective way for us to contemplate such consequences is to bring the dialecticians' concept of struggle between Afro- and Euro-Caribbean forces into our own time. Peter Wilson does this by asking whether West Indians in the late twentieth century should not reject metropolitan values and all the institutional paraphernalia which those values entail. He concludes that they should. Rejecting metropolitan values and institutions is, in his view, the only avenue to a genuine West Indian identity. Of course, as Wilson observes, such action would require revamping an educational system that fosters Euro-North American values, one that currently produces civil servants, physicians, lawyers, professors and businessmen. New priorities would have to be identified, pride of place affirmed, oral culture revived, and the verbal talents of the people cultivated. Wilson's position is passionate and polemical.[52] But where does it lead us? Or, more appropriately, where would it lead those who reside in the anglophone Caribbean? Should West Indians — indeed, could West Indians — turn inward and cultivate a separate and indigenous value system in a fast-shrinking and cosmopolitan world in which the language of cosmopolitanism is European — or Euro-North American? Would such action offer any real prospect that public life or individual well-being in the former British colonies would be improved? Would West Indians themselves, if confronted by this alternative, embrace it no matter how much they might despise sugar plantations, bauxite mines or North American tourism? Would such an experiment be worth the risk? Could the islands ever recover their current position, however troubled, if such action proved disastrous? Could any Caribbean government entertain such ideas? In sum, does Wilson's formula — the ultimate product of dialectical analysis — make sense in the real world?

If, indeed, it does not make sense for the twentieth century, why should we employ the logic of his vision and the tools of his analysis for the nineteenth century? Wilson's question (should metropolitan values and their institutional accompaniments be rejected by modern West Indians?) is, in historical terms, the equivalent of asking should the plantations have been dismantled in the aftermath of slavery? When historians respond to the latter question by asking whether such action might have benefited working people, or whether freedmen in the 1840s might have embraced such a course, they are confronting the past with the same species of question we must ask of Wilson's formula for the modern Caribbean. In both cases, the answers seem clear. Dismantling the institutional structures of Euro-Caribbean or metropolitan origin makes no greater sense today than it did 140 years ago, even to ordinary labouring people who may have (or may have had) little fondness for them. The risks are too great, the benefits too vague. In the real world, then and now, such action cannot be entertained by responsible governments. In effect, for Caribbean history and society, the dialectic mode of analysis leads inexorably to an intellectual cul-de-sac.

Historians of the British Empire have traditionally examined the process of emancipation as a problem in imperial administration. Although that approach was, and remains, a viable avenue of historical inquiry, it offers little comfort to West Indian nationalists who seek to establish an historical matrix for newly independent island nations. Creolization has satisfied their needs and extended the scope of West Indian history. But creolization is in danger of going awry. It is time we considered the wisdom of disengaging it from the dialectic.

Notes

1. Philip D. Curtin, *Two Jamaicas: The Role of Ideas in a Tropical Colony 1830–1865* (Cambridge, MA. 1955), x.

2. Sidney W. Mintz, 'Caribbean Nationhood in Anthropological Perspective', in *Caribbean Integration: Papers on Social, Political, and Economic Integration*, edited by S. Lewis and T.G. Mathews (Rio Piedras, 1967), 141.

3. Edward Brathwaite, *The Development of Creole Society in Jamaica 1770–1820* (Oxford, 1971), xii–xvi.

4. It is to the credit of both Brathwaite and Curtin that in emphasizing the Caribbean experience they did not neglect the imperial connection. Curtin's preface to *Two Jamaicas* remains a model statement on historical perspectives towards the Caribbean in the nineteenth century.

5. The literature on resistance is ably summarized by Hilary McD. Beckles, 'The 200 Years War: Slave Resistance in the British West Indies: An Overview of the Historiography', *The Jamaican Historical Review*, XIII (1982), 1–10. This issue of the JHR is devoted almost entirely to the theme of resistance, principally during the 1830s. Michael Craton's *Testing the Chains: Resistance to Slavery in the British West Indies* (Ithaca, 1982) is clearly within the prevailing ideological mainstream. The book is dedicated to the late Walter Rodney, whose final work, *A History of the Guyanese Working People, 1881–1905* (Baltimore, 1981), reflects this theme. This is the emphasis of Richard Hart's recent *Slaves Who Abolished Slavery* (Kingston, 1980), though the project of his book was initiated many years ago. Monica Schuler's *'Alas, Alas, Kongo': A Social History of Indentured African Immigration into Jamaica, 1841–1865* (Baltimore, 1980) emphasises resistance to the dominant political-economic apparatus of Jamaican society among post-emancipation arrivals from West Africa. A brief work, Lucille Mathurin's *The Rebel Woman in the British West Indies During Slavery* (Kingston, 1975), indicates the extent to which the message of resistance, stridently presented, has penetrated historical literature addressed to a more general audience.

6. Peter J. Wilson, *Crab Antics: The Social Anthropology of English-speaking Negro Societies of the Caribbean* (New Haven and London, 1973), 219. Although Wilson is most critical of those who approach West Indian society in terms of a single value system, he also challenges the plural society concept in so far as it advocates a symbiotic rather than dialectic relationship between social groups.

7. Monica Schuler, 'Afro-American Slave Culture', in *Roots and Branches: Current Directions in Slave Studies*, edited by Michael Craton, *Historical Reflections*, VI (1979), 131–4. Schuler's argument dovetails with that of Wilson in that it affirms the egalitarian nature of the indigenous value system, so egalitarian that the community attempts to pull down anyone who threatens to rise above his peers in the same way that crabs confined in a barrel pull back those who threaten to crawl out (hence the title of Wilson's book, *Crab Antics*).

8. Even today, Wilson believes, long-suffering Caribbean peoples have only the land and one another with which to identify: 'In belonging to a place and in regarding a place as belonging to him, the individual gains a sense of identity that gives him social validity, a sense of belonging with rather than to others'. Wilson, *Crab Antics*, 224. In an interesting passage, Wilson writes, 'Slaves carried in the Middle Passage have probably come as near as any human being to having their sense of place denied. Only the Jews have been put through a similar mass experience, and one need only mention the magnetic power of Israel to appreciate the importance of this sentiment of belonging associated with land . . . Until such time as a Caribbean culture is recognized with pride by the people themselves, much of the burden of their identity must be placed on land' (pp. 224–5).

9. O. Nigel Bolland, 'Systems of Domination after Slavery: The Control of Land and Labor in the British West Indies

after 1838', *Comparative Studies in Society and History* 23 (1981), 592–3.

10. See, for example, the works of William Law Mathieson, *British Slavery and Its Abolition, 1828–38* (London, 1926) and *British Slave Emancipation* (London, 1932); G.R. Mellor, *British Imperial Trusteeship, 1783–1850* (London, 1951); W.P. Morrell, *British Colonial Policy in the Age of Peel and Russell* (Oxford, 1930); D.J. Murray, *The West Indies and the Development of Colonial Government, 1801–1834* (Oxford, 1965); and most recently, William A. Green, *British Slave Emancipation: The Sugar Colonies and the Great Experiment, 1830–1865* (Oxford, 1976).

11. In contemporary debate, this approach has a significant political liability. It is, in the main, the view of the Caribbean colonies taken by authorities in the British cabinet and the Colonial Office during the emancipation period. Historians who subscribe to a similar point of view are vulnerable to accusations that they are reactionary and anti-nationalist, that they see the world through nineteenth-century glasses, or that they are latter-day apologists for the Colonial Office.

12. Such dismantling is what Eric Williams would appear to have preferred. In criticizing abolitionists, he declared that it 'never dawned on them that the Negro's freedom could only be nominal if the *sugar plantation was allowed to endure'* (my emphasis), *Capitalism and Slavery,* (New York, 1966, Capricorn edn), 191.

13. Academic literature currently offers numerous analyses of the plantation as an institution or of the plantation in relation to its component households (see, for example, the various articles, with bibliographies, in *Review*, VII, 2(1983)), but it avoids direct encounter with this question.

14. This is particularly the case among authors writing on British Guiana where the geographical setting imposed a severe handicap on peasant agriculture and the international economic situation discouraged crops other than sugar. This point is made more fully in my reviews of Alan Adamson's, *Sugar Without Slaves: Political Economy of British Guiana* in the *Business History Review*, 47 (1973) and of Walter Rodney's, *A History of the Guyanese Working People, 1881–1905* in *The Journal of Interdisciplinary History*, XIV (1984).

15. See, for example, Curtin's *Two Jamaicas* and Woodville Marshall, 'Social and Economic Problems in the Windward Islands, 1838–65', in F.M. Andic and T.G. Mathews (eds.), *The Caribbean in Transition: Papers on Social, Political, and Economic Development* (Rio Piedras, 1965), 234–7.

16. Douglas Hall's *Free Jamaica 1838–1865: An Economic History* (New Haven, 1959) took strong exception to Curtin's *Two Jamaicas* on this line of argument. Hall's *Five of the Leewards, 1834–1870* (Barbados, 1971) also provides a balanced view of the planters' efforts and of the complex nature of the business and management problems they faced after 1834.

17. W.A. Green, 'The Planter Class and British West Indian Sugar Productions, Before and After Emancipation', *The Economic History Review*, XXVI (1973), 454–63; 'The Apprenticeship in British Guiana, 1834–1838', *Caribbean Studies*, IX (1969), 45–6; *British Slave Emancipation*, 203–18.

18. There is a secondary line of criticism which upbraids planters for excessive attachment to the vertical system of plantation management and a rejection of cane farming or sharecropping. If one reads such work as Ralph Shlomowitz's 'Plantation and Smallholdings: Comparative Perspective from the World Cotton and Sugar Cane Economies, 1865–1939', *Agricultural History*, 58 (1984), from the perspective of the mid-nineteenth century Caribbean, it becomes clear that in a competitive international economy, management structures other than the vertical plan would have confronted increasing difficulty in attracting the capital required to preserve an export trade.

19. Marshall, 'Social and Economic Problems in the Windward Islands', 237.

20. Adamson, *Sugar Without Slaves: The Political Economy of British Guiana, 1838–1904* (New Haven, 1972), 25.

21. Report of a committee of the Jamaica Assembly, enclosed in Public Record Office, C.E. Grey to Earl Grey, 7 Feb. 1848, Colonial Office 137/295 no. 17 (hereafter, PRO, CO).

22. *Parliamentary Papers*, 1847–48 (184), XXIII — Part 2, evidence of Alexander Geddes. It must be appreciated that planters could not immediately abandon one staple and commence exporting another. There was, for example, an extended period between the planting and maturing of coffee trees. One was not inclined to make rash crop adjustments until the commercial viability of the new crop was clearly established, particularly in view of the indebtedness common to planters throughout the Lesser Antilles.

23. The painful circumstances attending cocoa production are evident in a Memorial of the Cocoa Planters, enclosed in MacLeod to Stanley, 10 June 1842, PRO, CO 295/136 no. 62. In 1844, Henry Taylor, chief clerk in the West India department, observed that 'the Cocoa Plantations are deserted'. Minute by Taylor, enclosed in Macleod to Stanley, 6 July 1844, PRO, CO 295/143 no. 53.

24. World markets for many minor staples, including such spices as ginger and arrowroot grown in the Windwards, were limited, and any large-scale shift by Caribbean planters into those crops risked flooding the market and depressing prices. This happened with arrowroot. St. Vincent increased its output of arrowroot from 300,000 to 490,000 lb. between 1847 and 1851, but during that period the price fell from 3s.6d. per lb. to 6d. See John Davy, *The West Indies, Before and After Slave Emancipation* (London, 1854), 187–8.

25. The same logic applies to the intra-island trade of the larger islands. When plantations failed in north-eastern Jamaica, peasant farmers of the region were compelled to rely for the sale of their products on the surviving sugar estates of Trelawny.

26. By 1860 about 2,000 people were migrating annually from the Windwards to Trinidad to earn wages on the plantations. In Trinidad, it was determined that for every two immigrants taken on to an estate, an additional creole labourer could be hired. Because the sugar industry expanded in Trinidad under the immigration system, wages remained relatively high and the market for the surplus provisions of local peasants continued to be vigorous. Report of Committee of Council, 7 Feb. 1860, enclosed in Keate to Newcastle, 9 Feb. 1860, PRO, CO 295/208, no. 24. That the income of peasant cultivators often exceeded that of estate workers is no evidence that peasant economies in the West Indies would have been preferable to plantation economies. The earnings of peasants depended to a considerable extent upon their marketing their goods to people employed on estates or in enterprises ancillary to the staple industry. Without estates, those markets would have largely disappeared.

27. The coastal region of Guyana lies below sea level. Free villages established in that region had little success in preserving the elaborate network of dykes and drains needed to protect the land from the sea and to allow inland water to escape. Surface water accumulated and could not gain exit, and commonly the peasants' houses and grounds were awash. All authors on Guyana are conscious of this problem. See, for example, Alan H. Adamson, *Sugar Without Slaves*, 59–60.

28. Robert I. Rotberg, *Haiti: The Politics of Squalor* (Boston, 1971), 48–50, 54, 58–9, 62–4.

29. Writing on Jamaica, W.G. Sewell declared, 'They [peas-ants] come to the towns and villages with one, two, six, or a dozen bags [of coffee], and in this way a cargo is made up for foreign ports', *The Ordeal of Free Labor in the British West Indies* (New York, 1862), 221.

30. In St. Mary's parish, Jamaica, the attempt of planters to reduce wages in 1842 produced a successful strike. Report of W. Marlton, Stipendiary Magistrate, CO 137/263, no. 6. There were several attempts to lower wages in Trinidad, 1842–45, all of which failed. Donald Wood, *Trinidad in Transition: The Years After Slavery* (London, 1968), 54. The tough labour code introduced by planters in British Guiana in 1842 failed in the face of the workers' com-bined efforts. Light to Stanley, 21 Jan. 1842, PRO, CO 111/189, no. 18.

31. Stipendiary magistrates in Jamaica commented on the freedmen's possession of fine horses and elegant clothing. Report of Hall Pringle, PRO, CO 137/248, no. 50. When questioned by a parlimentary committee whether the labourers of Jamaica were not better off than working peo-ple in England, William Knibb, Baptist missionary and long-standing enemy of the planters, answered, 'decid-edly'. *Parliamentary Papers*, 1842 (479), XII, Select Committee on the West India Colonies, 6275. Travelling abolitionist John Gurney was shocked to discover the amount of money in the hands of labourers. See his, *A Winter in the West Indies, Described in Familiar Letters to Henry Clay, of Kentucky* (London, 1840), 103–4. In Demerara, a stipendiary magistrate called the peasants indisputably better off than 'the happiest and best paid labourers in the most fertile districts of England'. *Parli-mentary Papers*, 1842 (551), XII, Appendix 23, 463. Mis-sionaries were generally concerned about the freedmen's pursuit of material wealth. No one questioned that freed-men were vastly better off than the labouring poor of Ire-land. Arriving in Jamaica after an illustrious career in India, Governor Sir Charles Metcalfe referred to the local peasantry as among the most comfortable and independent in the world. Metcalfe to Russell, 30 March 1840, PRO, CO 137/248, no. 50.

32. In Jamaica, the abandonment of sugar estates was less dra-matic than that of coffee properties. The 465 coffee plan-tations abandoned between 1832 and 1847 gave freedmen access to mountain land while reducing their ability to earn money through wage payments on lowland sugar properties. Report of a Committee of the Jamaica Assem-bly, enclosed in C.E. Grey to Earl Grey, 7 Feb. 1848, PRO, CO 137/295, no. 17.

33. Admittedly, such generalizations are difficult in the Carib-bean. The degree to which this was the case varied, of course, from one colony to another.

34. Sidney W. Mintz and Richard Price, *An Anthropological Approach to the Afro-American Past: A Caribbean Per-spective* (Philadelphia, 1976), 4–19.

35. B.W. Higman, *Slave Populations of the British Caribbean* (Baltimore and London, 1984), 130.

36. Richard S. Dunn, 'Dreadful Idlers' in the Cane Field: The Slave Labor Pattern on a Jamaican Sugar Estate, 1762–1831' (unpublished paper, delivered at Conference on Capitalism and Slavery, Bellagio, Italy, May 1984), 8. Mary Turner indicates that a Scottish missionary wit-nessed similar acts of fidelity in Hanover, though she observes that these were clearly the exception, not the rule. Mary Turner, *Slaves and Missionaries: The Disinte-gration of Jamaican Slave Society, 1787–1834*, (Urbana, 1982), 159. Turner's fine work shows that virtually every slave in Jamaica deplored his servitude but that the atti-tude of the slave community towards whites was marked by a substantial degree of ambivalence, not unmitigated malice.

37. *Slavery: A Problem in American Institutional and Intellec-tual Life* (Chicago, 1959).

38. For evidence on Jamaica, Anton V. Long, *Jamaica and the New Order, 1827–47* (Mona, Jamaica, 1956), 6, Appendix D. For Barbados, Robert H. Schomburgk, *His-tory of Barbados* (London, 1848), 89.

39. The importance of race is enormous, as I shall argue. Interestingly, this is not only the case in the colonial Car-ibbean. It is very evident in the history of Haiti as well. See, for example, David Nicholls, *From Dessalines to Duvalier: Race, Colour, and National Independence in Haiti* (Cambridge, 1979), Chapters 2 and 3.

40. Douglas Hall, *Free Jamaica 1838–1865: An Economic History* (New Haven, 1959), 82.

41. For an analysis of the work of the most prominent perma-nent member of the Colonial Office in this period, see William A. Green, 'James Stephen and British West India Policy, 1834–1847', *Caribbean Studies*, XIII (1974), 33–56.

42. C. Duncan Rice, 'Humanity Sold for Sugar!' The British Abolitionist Response to Free Trade in Slave Grown Sugar', *Historical Journal*, XIV (1970), 402–18.

43. This is the view of David Lowenthal. See his *West Indian Societies* (New York, 1951), 26–7. Strict juridical catego-ries did not apply in all islands. It was the case in Barba-dos and Jamaica, for example, but not in St. Kitts or Gre-nada. Edward L. Cox, *Free Coloreds in the Slave Societies of St. Kitts and Grenada, 1763–1833* (Knoxville, Tenn., 1984), 152; Jerome S. Handler, *The Unappropri-ated People: Freedom in the Slave Society of Barbados* (Baltimore and London, 1974), 72–81; Gad J. Heuman, 'White over Brown over Black: The Free Coloureds in Jamaican Society during Slavery and after Emancipation', *The Journal of Caribbean History*, 14 (1981), 46–7.

44. Douglas Hall described Jamaican society in terms of an isosceles triangle. The apex represented the position of whites; the small middle section that of people of colour; the great base, the place of blacks. The three segments were separated by rigid lines so that the poorest white could not, regardless of his baseness, fall below his base line. One enjoyed social mobility only within one's own colour segment. See Hall's 'Jamaica', in David W. Cohen and Jack P. Greene (eds.), *Neither Slave Nor Free: Freed-men of African Descent in the Slave Societies of the New World* (Baltimore, 1972), 195. This position is reinforced by Gad J. Heuman. After emancipation, he writes, a few 'brown men enjoyed a privileged status, while most of the free coloreds remained excluded from white society'. Between browns and blacks, hostility appears to have increased. See his *Between Black and White. Race, Poli-tics, and the Free Coloreds in Jamaica, 1792–1865* (West-port, CT, 1981), 77.

45. Heuman, *Between Black and White,* 193.

46. This political posture has evoked very different responses among recent writers on the Jamaican coloureds. Mavis Campbell is intensely critical of Edward Jordan, the lead-ing coloured politician in Jamaica in the mid-century, for what she perceives as his collaboration with planter ele-ments and betrayal of blacks. See her *The Dynamics of Change in a Slave Society: A Sociopolitical History of the Free Coloreds of Jamaica, 1800–1865* (Cranbury, NJ., 1976), 239–48, 293–4, 367–8. Heuman offers a much more sympathetic view. His analysis of political action in nineteenth-century Jamaica is undertaken more in terms of the perspective and prejudices that motivated contempo-rary actors than in terms of what might satisfy a twentieth-century temperament.

47. *The Plural Society in the British West Indies* (Berkeley, 1965).

48. The proposition that historians should liberate themselves from social science theorists and formulate their own

social theory has been strongly advocated in Gareth Sted-man Jones, 'From Historical Sociology to Theoretical History', *British Journal of Sociology,* 27 (1976), 295–305.

49. One cannot, for example, appreciate the political dynamics of the early termination of apprenticeship without understanding something of Lord Brougham's alienation from the Whig leadership, nor can one evaluate the failure of the Melbourne government to suspend the Jamaican constitution without knowing something of the earlier Canadian constitutional imbroglio.

50. In his *The Negro in the Caribbean* (Washington, 1942), Eric Williams called the sugar plantation an agricultural autocrat. It was, indeed, a hard master, yet for all its size and capacity to oppress, the nineteenth-century sugar estate was, commercially, a fragile institution. After emancipation, estates that folded, folded for good. Sugar culture was labour-intensive; it imposed exceptional demands during the crop and manufacturing season; and it demanded careful husbandry and meticulous handling in the industrial process. If the sugar estate could not command dependable labour at critical periods of the year, if it was not served with reasonable care, efficiency and regularity, it could not hope to survive in a competitive world environment.

51. Looking back over the history of the Leewards in the emancipation era, Douglas Hall wrote the following: 'The ex-slaves and their descendants . . . were not in principle opposed either to estate-agriculture or to large landowners as such . . . For them too, the coming and the going of the ships brought excitement, work and wages, and new things in the shops to spend the wages on. And they, too, knew that the ships sometimes brought other things as well as goods: governors, for example, who sometimes acted on their behalf, and stipendiary magistrates, and, above all, the British Act abolishing slavery. They had no wish to model themselves on English labour; but even more positively, they had no wish to be cut off from Britain, from the Queen from whom, as they understood the thing, freedom and justice came'. *Five of the Leewards,* 146.

52. Wilson, *Crab Antics.* His final chapter, entitled 'A Polemic By Way of Conclusion', incorporates these views. Although I have singled out Wilson's orientation for criticism, his book is one of the most absorbing pieces I have read in the last decade and should be examined widely by Caribbean scholars.

SECTION TWO
Emancipation in Action

Plantation slavery had been a system of labour exploitation as well as a mode of racial domination that formed the basis of caste/white ruling class power. This group controlled the means of production and dominated the socio-political life of the colonies. The abolition of slavery, therefore, raised fundamental questions about what system of economic organization and set of social relations would replace those which had previously existed.

In reality, emancipation outside Haiti, did not immediately usher in any profound changes in economic ownership. It certainly destroyed forever a way of life based upon the ownership of human beings and substituted the relations of free labour for those of slavery. However, former slave-owners continued to frustrate the process of freedom by impeding the freed people's bid for economic independence by means of a wide range of legal and extra-legal constraints. They retained political power and many shaped aspects of the process of transition from slavery to free labour.

The articles in this section support the view that emancipation was only partially successful in that socio-economic and political relationships between former slaves and former slave-owners retained many elements of the old order. Marshall explores some of the strategies devised by ruling elites to control the 'making of freedom' process, and to contain responses of ex-slaves who were perceived as harbouring excessive demands that were hostile to the productive enterprise. In the plantation societies of Jamaica, and those in the French West Indies, Wilmot and Renard show respectively that emancipation resulted in a bitter conflict over labour use and political power as proprietors and their representatives tried to coerce ex-slaves to labour under familiar terms. In Haiti, according to Lacerte, Toussaint resorted to rigorous police measures to insure that the ex-slaves would return to the plantations. He pursued a conciliatory policy toward former landowners and sought to tie white planters and former slaves in a new relationship of interdependence. The attempts to revive the plantation system was resisted by the ex-slaves who had come to identify the labour associated with it, with their former condition, and the ownership of property with freedom. Though Dessalines reversed Toussaint's former conciliatory policy toward white landowners, nationalizing their property, he still resorted to intensive agriculture and a severe regulation of labour — both of which continued to antagonize the ex-slaves.

In the British colonies, full emancipation was delayed and most colonies (Antigua was a notable exception) implemented an apprenticeship system. Marshall, Wilmot and Hall show that this period, 1834–38, was conflict-ridden as planters sought to maintain coercive measures to control labour. The presence of the Stipendiary Magistrates did little to smooth labour relations. Apprentices on sugar estates, coffee plantations and livestock farms (pens in Jamaica) successfully agitated for the end of Apprenticeship before its stipulated end in 1840; and when labour relations failed to improve significantly, and as conflicts over wages, rents, hours of work and access to provision grounds intensified, workers' adopted an independent stance in relation to the estates.

One technique adopted by ex-slaves to achieve social liberty was to abandon the plantation and resettle outside the range of its immediate socio-economic reach. Hall indicates, however, that this option was not as popular in the British West Indies as was at first thought. It appears, he adds, that ex-slaves preferred to stay on estates and struggle for rights and liberties by confronting proprietors with a complex set of bargaining demands.

The Evolution of Land and Labour in the Haitian Revolution, 1791–1820

Robert K. LaCerte

Between 1791 when the Haitian revolution began, and the death of Henri Christophe in 1820, important economic changes occurred in Haiti which transformed one of the most prosperous plantation economies in the New World into a republic of peasant proprietors. While the political history of the revolution has received a moderate amount of attention, the economic and social changes which accompanied it have been poorly understood. It is the purpose of this study to focus on the internal developments which were occurring in an irresistible way to bring about a peasant economy and to delineate the responses of a variety of governments, both French and Haitian to try to halt these changes.

First, a few words about the nature of landholding and the extent of the prosperity of the old colony of Saint-Domingue. At the height of its economic development (1788–89) there were 8,000 plantations held as leases obtained from the French royal governors and the Intendants. Of these, 793 were given over to sugar, 3,154 to indigo, 3,117 to coffee, and 789 to cotton. Other properties produced cacao, mixed crops, and food.[1] The colonial trade with France brought in an average of 280,000,000 francs, occupied 750 ships, and employed 80,000 sailors. In 1788 over 163,405,221 pounds of sugar, 68,000,000 pounds of coffee, and lesser amounts of cotton and indigo were exported from Saint-Domingue.[2] Its total production was nearly one and a half times that of the British West Indies.[3]

The population of the colony consisted of 405,564 slaves, 40,000 whites, and 28,000 affranchis (freedmen) who were largely mulattos.[4] This last group had benefited from Colbert's Code Noir of 1685, which had given them the same rights and privileges of those born free, by acquiring one-third of the plantations and one-quarter of the slaves. They raised coffee and cotton, rarely sugar, and their properties were located mostly in the western and southern provinces.[5]

The thirteen year struggle which followed the insurrection of 1791 destroyed much of the sugar industry which was located in the exposed plains. It also reduced the population by nearly one-half.[6] Attempts to reconstruct the colonial economy were carried out by the French, who expected to hold on to the colony; and by various Haitian leaders as well, in order to find the necessary exports to pay for the arms needed to preserve their independence. The revival of the plantation system, however, was resisted by the ex-slaves who had come to identify the labour associated with it with their former condition and the ownership of property with freedom. They could only be made to work through the use of force; a situation which neither the French, the black, nor the mulatto leaders, who succeeded each other in power, could hope to maintain for very long.

The slaves had freed themselves in 1791; an act which received the sanction of the French commissioner, Felicite Leger Sonthonax, in his decree of August 29, 1793.[7] Sonthonax led a commission sent over by the French Convention in 1792 to administer the colony. His purpose in issuing the decree was to gain the support of the blacks in order to keep Saint-Domingue from falling completely into the hands of the British who were then at war with France and who had already seized much of the western and southern coasts. He discovered, however, that he was forced to reconcile the new freedom with an economic system whose prosperity was geared to slavery. His solution was that of the *cultivateur portionnaire:* a system which sought to tie labour to the plantation through annual contracts, but which also provided for payment in the form of one-quarter of the annual produce.[8] Hours and conditions of labour were regulated and represented a modification of the slave regime in that they provided for longer periods of rest. A certain degree of freedom was allowed by permitting the field workers to choose which planters they would be willing to contract with. Thus, the freedom of the ex-slaves was recognized but it was defined as freedom to work. This formula was the prototype for a series of similar plans which sought to counter the radicalism of the blacks who were intent on working for themselves on their own land.

A second member of the French commission, Etienne Polvorel, developed a different approach for solving the labour problem. He argued that the property which had belonged to the planters who had either fled to Jamaica or welcomed the British invasion should be sequestered by the government, and then distributed to the blacks who fought in the armies of the French republic.[9] Thus, the ownership of land would have been a reward for military service. This radical suggestion was not applied for some time because of the opposition of Sonthonax, Toussaint Louverture, General Charles Leclerc, and Christophe who were all wedded to the idea of resurrecting the colonial economy. It surfaced again, however, and became the basis for the land reforms of Alexander Pétion in 1809. Polvorel's position was closer to the emerging economic reality. In a letter to Sonthonax of October 3, 1793, he pointed out the absurdity of the use of forced labour: 'Can you expect Africans to resume work by giving them liberty unless you first give them land, and by so doing create an incentive to labour which they did not possess before?'[10] Their desire for land antedated the revolution whose outbreak simply accelerated a movement to parcelize the plantations which had begun on the coffee estates. Tadeusz Lepkowski, the Polish Latin Americanist, argues that an alternative economic system of small, privately owned properties given over to subsistence crops had developed among fugitive slaves (*marrons*) in the mountains.[11] While this could have been the case, the evidence is hard to come by. In the one instance where we do have a good knowledge of an economic system run by *marrons* it appears that their leader, Goman, demanded forced labour on common land rather than permit individually owned properties.[12] Lepkowski is on safer ground when he points to the small plots on which the planters allowed the slaves to raise food for themselves as a source of peasant proprietorship.

A closer link between freedom and landownership can be found on the plantation. After 1770 the custom of manumitting slaves unofficially grew, because of the high taxes involved in getting the sanction of the colonial government which tried to discourage the practice. These *libertes de savannes* continued to live on the plantation where they were alloted a piece of land larger than that assigned to the slaves as kitchen gardens.[13] The land was never legally alienated by the planter, but the *libertes* came to consider it theirs and even passed it on to their children who saw themselves as free. This type of manummission was usually a reward for devoted service; Toussaint being the most famous

case. Their number increased and was actually larger than that of the *affranchis* before the outbreak of the revolution.

Coffee estates were also run differently than sugar plantations. Slave gangs were not necessary for looking after and harvesting the coffee crop. This work gradually fell to slave families who came to regard the section of coffee trees assigned to them as their property. The abandonment of many plantations by the whites during the revolution, especially in the western part of the colony, opened the way for a parcelization of these lands by the blacks. Moreover, some planters sold portions of these estates to their field workers who purchased the land collectively and then subdivided it. Thus, the link between freedom and landownership was forged on the plantation. Polvorel realized this and urged the government to recognize and regulate the emerging agrarian order. The French administrators, and Toussaint as well, sought to reverse this process. You could not have a dual economy consisting of peasant proprietors raising coffee and agricultural produce while continuing forced labour on the sugar plantations, and the latter could not be broken up and still be viable. Therefore, the labour policy devised by Sonthonax received the approval of the Directory when its special agent, General Hedouville, endorsed it in his decree of July 27, 1789. He developed it further by insisting on three year contracts, required that the ex-slaves be forced to accept contracts, allowed planters to reclaim their former workers, and called for a rural police to enforce this regulation. He did, however, continue the practice of paying one-quarter of the produce.[14]

The French, dependent as they were on a black army, could not have hoped to carry out this scheme. It was left to Toussaint, who believed that only a severe agrarian regime could restore the colony, to do so. He sought to end the parcelization of estates by annulling the sales of land made to the field workers. On May 7, 1801, he prohibited the sale of parcels of less than fifty *carreaux*; a stipulation which made it impossible for the ex-slaves to acquire land legally.[15] Toussaint also invited the planters to return from abroad. His goal was a political one: dominion status within the French empire with himself as governor-general. Toussaint believed that the limited freedom achieved by the slaves in the revolution could only be secured by a black elite in command of the army with the economic cooperation of the white planters. The latter alone possessed the capital and technical skills needed to insure the prosperity and, therefore, the continued survival of a new society which was wholly radical for its time. It was an experiment, so Toussaint hoped, which could only be realized within an empire committed to its revolutionary goals.

His policy received greater definition in the Constitution of 1801.[16] Here, Toussaint sought to tie the white planters and their former slaves in a new relationship of interdependence. Blacks were bound to the plantation and not a word was said about contracts. Instead, the new organic law stated that the smallest interruption of the daily routine would not be tolerated. Movement from one plantation to another was prohibited. On the other hand, the planter was defined as a father who was responsible for the welfare of his field workers, corporal punishment was abolished, and prompt payment of one-quarter of the crop was required. This arrangement required balancing two opposite social interests without doing injury to either. It was a policy which the ex-slaves rejected. They rebelled in September 1801, under the leadership of Moise Louverture who demanded that the land be divided among the blacks. Toussaint crushed the rebellion and resorted to rigorous police measures to ensure that the field workers would return to the plantations.

From an economic point of view the new policy was a success. Sugar exports rose from a low of 1,750,387 pounds in 1795 to a high of 18,535,112 pounds in 1801.[17] Coffee exports also increased in the same time period from 2,228,270 pounds to 43,420,270 pounds.

The invasion of Saint-Domingue by a French army led by General Leclerc ended Toussaint's hopes for an autonomous black society living within the context of an important European state. Moreover, it upset the agrarian system created by him, especially in the mountainous areas of the colony which fell into the hands of black guerillas who fought Leclerc. The latter did manage to consolidate his hold in the plains where he continued the policy of forced labour. He succeeded in raising sugar exports to 53,400,000 pounds, but coffee exports declined to 34,000,000 pounds.[18] The French, however, could not develop the economy further because they lacked both labour and capital. Since Leclerc had arrived with a European army there was no further need to tolerate the existence of black troops, and his staff felt that the security and the economic prosperity of the colony necessitated that they be disarmed and returned to the plantations.[19] They also recommended that Africans be introduced into Saint-Domingue. There were problems, however, since the cost of bringing the level of economic productivity up to what it had been in 1789, by rebuilding most of the sugar plantations, was estimated at between 64,600,000 and 100,000,000 livres.[20] Added to this was the cost of an additional 202,782 blacks at

2,000 livres each which came to 405,564,000 livres. The total expenditure necessary to re-establish the old colony to its full productive capacity came to well over half a billion livres. The planters did not have this kind of capital while French investors had better opportunities for less risky financial ventures at home.

There were also objections to paying one-quarter of the produce to the field workers. In the circumstances in which the planters found themselves of having to repair machinery, replace labour and animals, and import necessities from France it was difficult for them to implement this part of the rural code.[21]

The cost of resurrecting the colony and preserving it for France was, therefore, prohibitive. Toussaint had succeeded in achieving a certain level of prosperity only by alienating the blacks. Leclerc was not able to continue the policy of forced labour in the face of increasing resistance while at the same time his European troops were being decimated by yellow fever.

A full scale revolt broke out on October 13, 1802. Slavery had been re-established on Guadaloupe in August, and fears that Saint-Domingue would be next led the black and mulatto leaseholders, the soldiers who were being disarmed and returned to the plantations, and the field workers to rebel. It was led by the mulatto officers Petion and Clervaux who were later joined by Jean-Jacques Dessalines and Christophe. The rebellion succeeded and General Donatien Rochambeau, Leclerc's successor, capitulated on November 10, 1803. Haiti became an independent country on January 1, 1804. The war caused considerable devastation. After 1804 sugar exports declined dramatically, but coffee managed to hold its own.[22] Dessalines, soon to become the first emperor of Haiti, chose to continue Toussaint's labour policy for military reasons. The preservation of independence meant maintaining an army of 49,500 men and a navy of 3,000.[23] He also had to buy arms and ammunition from American traders in order to conquer the eastern half of the island and eliminate the French bridgehead at Santo Domingo. He resorted to intensive agriculture and a severe regulation of labour to make up for the lack of capital needed to resurrect the plantations. Just what Dessalines' ultimate plans were for solving the land question is a debatable point. The evidence is strong that he sought to preserve the large plantation, but there is also some indication that he was not against a more democratic form of landownership. He warned those who had seized emigre properties that he meant to redistribute the land among the poor blacks in an equitable fashion.[24]

An important effect of the end of French rule was the emergence of two rival aristocracies. The black Louverture generals challenged the *affranchis* for the political and economic control of Haiti. The mulattos had benefited from the French defeat by taking over many of the plantations of the *emigres*. These properties had either been sold or willed to them, but there had been outright seizures as well.[25] The proclamation of independence had abolished the leases granted by the colonial authorities. Dessalines now insisted on nationalizing all the land which had formerly been held by the French and placing it under his new Administration of State Properties. This agency was charged with encouraging agriculture and centralizing the production of sugar.[26] The integration of the plantations into the public domain annulled the recent advantages of the mulattos. A decree of February 7, 1804, abolished the gifts and sales of land by the *emigres* to the Haitians.[27] It was followed by a second decree in July which called for a verification of land titles to determine ownership.[28] The director of State Properties, Joseph B. Inginac, carried out an effective investigation of these titles and confiscated 562 plantations in the west. The result of this vigorous investigation, and the threat of carrying it into the mulatto dominated south, caused an uprising which resulted in Dessalines' assassination on October 7, 1806.

A civil war ensued between the rival elites which divided Haiti into a kingdom in the north under Christophe and a republic in the west and south led by Petion. Christophe was a very successful monarch. He continued the pattern of large landholding granting concessions of between 400–500 *carreaux* to his nobles.[29] He also followed the labour policy developed by Toussaint. Work discipline was enforced by a specially trained corps of 4,000 Dahomeians.[30] Christophe diversified the economy of his kingdom with the addition of cereals and cattle to sugar and coffee, but the latter remained the chief export. Some of the profits were reinvested in the sugar plantations, and there was a revival of sugar exports.[31] Technical assistance came from English philanthropists who sent over mechanics and agricultural experts. In return the English received extensive commercial advantages.[32]

The republican Senate was also bent on preserving the large plantations. A law of February 9, 1807, restored the properties confiscated by Dessalines.[33] Sugar, molasses, syrup, and rum were freed of export duties in order to stimulate production while coffee continued to be subjected to these duties.[34] Petion had argued for a wider distribution of land, but his proposal was rejected as inimical to mulatto interests. Nevertheless, the Senate found

that it was impossible to deprive the blacks, who made up the largest part of the population of the west, of the land which they had appropriated. The law of April 20, 1807, guaranteed proprietorship to anyone regardless of the amount of land held as long as it was cultivated.[35] This was a concession to the peasants who had already divided up some of the coffee estates, but at the same time the law sought to stem the growth of small-holdings by prohibiting the sale of land of less than 10 *carreaux*. In order to further strengthen the plantation system, an elaborate rural code was added which was a modified version of Toussaint's formula. it returned to annual contracts and allowed the field workers to choose for whom they would work. The president was enjoined to round up vagabonds, who were mostly veterans and soldiers, and return them to the plantations. The experiment failed. Blacks deserted and productivity, along with the government's revenues, declined. The republic suffered a series of deficits between 1808 and 1812.[36]

Pétion sought to solve the problem of getting labour to remain on the plantation by raising the field worker's share from one-quarter to one-half.[37] This experiment was resented by the elite who feared that the base of their social and political dominance would be undermined if Pétion gave in to the blacks' demand for land. Matters came to a head in 1809 and the president, with the support of a largely black army, dissolved the Senate. As a dictator, he was now in a position to carry out a land reform and end the long and fruitless experience with forced labour. His goal was not to destroy the position of his class, but to strengthen it by reconciling the black majority to mulatto rule. The alternative was a caste war from which only Christophe would benefit.

The decree of December 30, 1809, gave land to the veterans of the wars of independence in accordance with their rank.[38]

Colonels	25 *carreaux*
Battalion chiefs	15 *carreaux*
Captains to Second Lieutenants	5 *carreaux*

It was followed in 1814 by a second distribution of land to all officers below the rank of colonel.[39] Other laws distributed land to hospital personnel and government employees in lieu of unpaid salaries.[40] Petion also gave land away to individuals on occasion.[41]

Exactly how much land was distributed is difficult to say because adequate statistics are lacking. One Haitian scholar, writing in 1888, estimated that 76,000 *carreaux* were distributed among 2,322 civil and military officers.[42] Only 134 of them received entire plantations. The remaining 2,188 got grants of 35, 30, 25, and 20 *carreaux*. They formed an intermediate class of landholders beneath whom were 6,000 soldiers who received grants of 5 *carreaux*. Moreover, many large estates were further subdivided by sale. Unable to secure labour, the mulatto elite either sold or abandoned the land to the blacks and moved into cities where they found government posts or went into commerce. An unfortunate side effect was the separation of the black countryside from the mulatto dominated towns; a situation which perpetuated the caste system into the twentieth century.

In the north, Christophe was forced by Petion's example to follow suit. In 1819 he distributed grants of land from one to twenty *carreaux* to his soldiers.[43] After his death the division of land was accelerated, but it never completely destroyed the large estate in this region.

The evolution of land and labour during the Haitian revolution was characterized by a search for some way to recombine the factors of production in order to resurrect the plantation. The market for sugar and coffee existed especially in the United States. By 1825 American merchants dominated trade with Haiti.[44] It was not a lack of markets which frustrated Toussaint and others, but the failure to secure capital, labour and technical expertise. Haitian leaders resorted to intensive labour to make up the difference. This was steadily resisted by the ex-slaves, but they were unable to have their way completely until after the death of Dessalines. It was then that the attempt was made by the mulatto elite to turn the plantation into a hacienda; the seeds of which were already present in Toussaint's policy of turning the master-slave relationship into one where affective ties would prevail. The hacienda system, however, succeeded where labour did not possess an economic alternative. This was not the case in Haiti where the blacks had begun to cut up the coffee estates in the last years of the colonial period. This process had been halted by Toussaint, Dessalines, and Christophe, but it gained momentum in Petion's republic where the mulattos were too few and too dependent on a black army to prevent it. By meeting the demands of the ex-slaves, Petion decided the agrarian future of Haiti. He had cut the Gordian knot and ended the long history of experimentation with landholding systems. A Frenchman, Lepelletier de Saint-Remy, wrote in 1846 that through successive parcelizations of the plantations, Petion had republicanized the soil.[45] By settling the land question, he also gave Haiti nearly twenty-five years of relative peace. But the first black republic emerged from the long wars of independence as a society of peasant proprietors given over to a subsistence economy except for coffee whose cultivation made Haiti dependent on a single export crop. This in turn placed the new nation in an adverse competitive position with the better capitalized Brazilian coffee planters and ensured its economic decline.

Notes

1. *Observations sur la necessite et les moyens de recouvrer et restaurer la colonie francaise de Saint-Domingue, 23 octobre 1801.* University of Florida, *Rochambeau Papers.* No 81. Also the account of the Intendant Barbe de Marbois for 1789 cited in Beauvais de Lespinasse, *Histoire des affranchis de Saint-Domingue* (Paris, 1882), 299.
2. British Museum, *Liverpool Papers*, Add. 38349–354.
3. Alfred de Laujon, *Souvenirs et voyages* (2 vols.; Paris, 1835), II, 102.
4. L. E. Moreau de Saint-Méry, *Description . . . , de la partie française de l'île de Saint-Dominique* (2 vols.; Philadelphia, 1797), I, 102.
5. Raymond Renaud, *Le Régime foncier en Haiti* (Paris, 1934), 75.
6. *Precis d'un recueil d'observations sur la colonie de Saint-Dominigue presenté au Général en chef Leclerc, 14 Avril 1802, Rochambeau Papers,* No. 229.
7. Victor Schoelcher, *Vie de Toussaint Louverture* (Paris, 1889), 78.
8. Decree cited in Beaubrun Ardouin, *Etudes sur l'histoire d'Haiti* (II vols., 2d ed., Port-au-Prince, 1958), II, 50–51.
9. *Ibid.,* 48–49.
10. Cited in Ralph Korngold, *Citizen Toussaint* (New York, 1965), 94.
11. Tadeusz Lepkowski, *Haiti* (2 vols; Havana, n.d.), I, 59.
12. *Instructions adresées par le President d'Haiti au général de division Bazelais, 8 mars 1914.* Linstant de Pradines, *Recueil général des lois et actes du gouvernement d'Haiti* (8 vols.; Paris, 1888), II, 245. Hereinafter cited as *Recueil.*
13. Gabriel Debien, 'Les affranchisements aux antilles francaises aux XVII et XVIII siecles,' *Anuario de estudos americanos,* XXIII (1967), 1194–1197.
14. *Arreté concernant la police des habitations et les obligations réciproques des proprietaires ou fermiers et des cultivateurs, 24 juillet 1798, Rochambeau Papers,* no. 47.
15. *Rapport de la commission sur la cultivation, 13 juin 1802, Rochambeau Papers,* No. 492. Paul Moral, *Le Paysan haitien* (Paris, 1961), 13. A *carreau* is equal to 3.1/3 acres.
16. Louis-Joseph Janvier, *Les Constitutions d'Haiti* (Paris, 1886), 10–11.
17. Commnications received at the Foreign Office, on the subject of the foreign and domestic trade, agriculture, populations, industry, legislation, and civilization of Hayti. 1826 to 1828. *British and Foreign State Papers,* XVI, 711. Lepkowski, I. 75, 83.
18. James G. Leyburn, *The Haitian People* (New Haven, 1966), 320.
19. *Rapport de la commission, 13 juin 1802, Rochambeau Papers,* No. 492.
20. *Opinion de Charles Malenfant sur les colonies, Rochambeau Papers,* No. 103. *Precis d'un recueil . . , . sur la colonie, 14 avril 1802, Rochambeau Papers,* No. 229.
21. *Quelques reflexions sur le quart des cultivateurs, 7 juin 1802. Rochambeau Papers,* No. 469.
22. Statistics for the period between 1804 and 1818, except for a few years during Christophe's reign, are not to be found. But by 1818 sugar exports had declined to 1,896,449 pounds and went down even further to 2,020 in 1825. Coffee also fell to 20,280,589 pounds in 1818 but rose again to 36,034,300 pounds in 1825. Leyburn, 320.

23. Thomas Madiou, *Histoire d'Haiti* (4 vols., 2ed; Port-au-Prince, 1922), III, 110.
24. *Ibid.*, 220.
25. *L'etat des habitations que tient a ferme le chef de brigade nerette, 14 janvier 1803. Christophe Dieudonne, chef de brigade, au general Rochambeau, 18 janvier 1803, Rochambeau Papers,* Nos. 1513, 1532.
26. *Recueil.*
27. *Ibid.*
28. Moral, 29.
29. Duracine Vaval, 'Le roi d' Haiti Henri Christophe,' *Revue de la societe Haitienne d'histoire, de geographie et de geologie* (juin, 1931), II, 10.
30. Pamphile de Lacroix, *Mémoires pour servir a l'histoire de la révolution de Saint-Dominigue* (2 vols.: Paris, 1820), I, 286.
31. Coffee exports rose from 5,608,253 pounds in 1806 to 10,232,910 pounds in 1810 and fluctuated between these two figures until the end of the reign. Sugar exports rose from 522,229 pounds in 1810 to 6,221,167 pounds in 1815, declined, and remained steady at between two to three million pounds. Communications received at the Foreign Office, on the subject of . . . Hayti, 1826–1828, *British and Foreign State Papers,* XVI, 792.
32. Pamphile de Lacroix, I, 269.
33. *Recueil,* I,206–207.
34. Ardouin, VII, 8–9.
35. Maurice Nau and Nemours Telhomme, *Code domanial* (Port-au-Prince, 1930), 241–249. Hereinafter cited as *Code domanial.*
36. Ardouin, VII, 66–67.
37. Armand Thoby, *La question agraire en Haiti* (Port-au-Prince, 1888), 31–32.
38. *Code domanial,* 250.
39. *Ibid.,* 30.
40. *Ibid.,* 32–33, 253–254, 255.
41. Boston Public Library, *Haiti MSS,* 66–264 (1–7).
42. Thoby, 10.
43. Edict of the King, July 14, 1819, British Museum, *Clarkson MSS,* Add. 41266 f81.
44. American State Papers, Commerce and Navigation, 1789–1823 (2 vols.: Washington, D.C., 1832–1834), II, 115, 175, 429, 485–486.
45. M. R. Lepelletier de Sain-Remy, *Saint-Domingue* (2 vols.; Paris, 1846), I, 169.

Emancipation in Action
Workers and Wage Conflict in Jamaica 1838–1840

Swithin Wilmot

The first of August 1838 marked a new era in labour relations in the British West Indies. With the termination of the apprenticeship system, ex-slaves were fully free to bargain for wages and to establish their general working conditions [see *Jamaica Journal* 17:3]. Walter Rodney has shown how the ex-slaves in British Guiana mobilized for improved wages and working conditions which led to protracted strikes in 1842 and 1848. However, the planters successfully undermined the workers' struggles by importing indentured labour and weakened the bargaining power of the ex-slaves in British Guiana.[1] This article looks at labour relations in Jamaica during the first decade of this fundamentally new interaction between planters and the new class of free workers. It will be demonstrated that the workers had very clear notions of their rights and determinedly protected them against various planter strategies to maintain a command over labour. Moreover, the article underlines the extent to which the new class of free workers had positions on issues such as immigration and free trade which affected their living standards.

Initial Wage Bargaining

The months after August 1838 were very unsettled ones throughout Jamaica. Deep suspicions and misunderstandings characterized the relationship between employers and workers. The former held their meetings and attempted to iron out a common approach to dealing with their ex-slaves, while the latter made it known that they were willing to labour after 1 August, once they were offered 'equitable' and 'just' terms. Generally, the workers were asking for a minimum of 1s 6d per day, the same rate which obtained during the apprenticeship when they had worked on the estates in their free time. There were workers who insisted that the daily rate ought to be twice that, but such demands were not as widespread as the planters complained. The planters too had varying wage offers. The

most common was 7 1/2d per day plus two days labour in lieu of rent for the continued occupation of the cottages and provision grounds belonging to the estates.[2]

Festivities dominated the first week of full freedom and the bargaining over wages began in full earnest after that time. In the initial stages both groups tenaciously adhered to their positions. The liberal newspapers, stipendiary magistrates, missionaries, and other known friends of the workers, tried to get them to moderate their demands and warned against 'avaricious requests'. For instance, the Rev. James Watson, Presbyterian missionary stated, and his appeal was published for others to read:

Do not arrest the progress of the cultivation of the country by refusing to labour for a fair rate of wages. If you demand more than is proper as a remuneration for your labour then the progress of cultivation must cease. Proprietors will withdraw their capital, and thus you will bring injury upon yourself, and the cause of liberty will be impeded. Far better to begin with a moderate rate at first, and as the country continues to improve under the state of things, masters will be enabled and encouraged to invest their capital and increasing prosperity will bring increasing wages . . .[3]

Such efforts failed to impress the workers who adhered to their initial demand of 1s 6d.[4]

Sir Lionel Smith, the governor, also intervened when it became abundantly clear that both employers and workers were unwilling to alter their original positions. He concentrated his efforts in the sugar areas near to his residence in Spanish Town. On 8 August 1838, he visited Bushy Park, one of the chief properties in the parish of St. Dorothy. There he met with the workers in that area and reminded them that he had no power to fix the rate of wages though he promised that he would do his best to encourage their employers to be 'liberal', provided that the workers adopted 'reasonable' positions. In conversation with the Bushy Park workers, Smith suggested that they agree to accept 1s per day and pay 2s per week as rent for the use of their houses and provision grounds. The spokesmen for the workers respectfully informed the governor that although they harboured no animosity towards their attorneys or their overseers, and held the greatest of respect for the governor himself, they would not work for less than 1s 6d.[5]

The workers' polite but resolute refusal so impressed the governor that he altered his proposals to resolve the stand off. With the support of stipendiary magistrates and missionaries, the governor formulated new terms to get the estates started. When he visited the parishes of Vere, Clarendon, Manchester, and St. Thomas-in-the-Vale, he successfully managed to convince the workers to resume once he assured them that their employers would pay them 1s per day and they would be permitted to occupy their houses and grounds rent free for three months.[6] Thus, by the middle of September, some amount of normalcy had returned to these areas due mainly to Smith's intervention.

In two other important sugar parishes, St. James and Trelawny, work resumed but only after the planters increased their offers. In St. James, the planters offered 7 1/2d for day labour. Though the workers were disappointed by such an offer especially when they had earned between 1s 6d and 2s during the apprenticeship, they offered to resume labour as early as 5 August, and to negotiate a final wage structure while they worked. The planters stubbornly refused this conciliatory proposal and prohibited any work until their terms were accepted. The workers stood firm and industry did not resume until George Gordon, an attorney with extensive interests in the parish, broke this deadlock by offering his workers terms similar to those which Smith had offered on the south side of the island. Gradually, the other attorneys offered Gordon's terms and by late September 1838 the estates were operating again.[7]

The behaviour of the Trelawny workers suggests that they were eager to resume labour on the estates after the festivities celebrating the advent of full freedom were over. All that was required was fair treatment and conciliatory action on the part of their employers. On 10 August 1838, Charles Mathew Farquharson, the attorney for Cambridge and Oxford estates, met with the stipendiary magistrate and workers and agreed on terms which were quickly adopted by other properties. The contract stipulated that able bodied workers would receive 1s per day and were expected to work four days per week out of crop and five days during. No rent was to be charged for the houses and grounds. The contract also included terms for skilled workers and for other categories of labourers. Moreover, the attorney agreed to provide free medical services for his workers and watchmen for

their provision grounds. As if to cement the agreement, the workers put on a 'sumptuous dinner' for the attorney and stipendiary magistrate in the evening of 10 August.[8]

On the 41 properties where employers adopted the 'Cambridge and Oxford terms', the ex-slaves quickly turned out for work while those properties that held out against these terms suffered from very irregular labour.[9] On Green Park for instance, out of the 404 resident agricultural labourers, only 35 were at work up to 15 October. The resident attorney had initially offered 7 1/2d per day. Later he increased his offer to 9d when his neighbours were offering 1s plus the other allowances mentioned in the terms above. In early October, the attorney belatedly offered these terms but still the labourers on his estate travelled elsewhere to work. He had antagonized his former apprentices by adhering to the old slave practice of shell blowing and sending drivers to the fields to supervise the work. Moreover, he refused to permit the workers to do task work which was already growing in popularity in the area. On Tiltson, similar recalcitrant behaviour on the part of the attorney drove away the resident labourers; only 26 had worked on that property since August.[10] Clearly, the workers in Trelawny where the provision grounds were not as fruitful as in other parts of Jamaica, were eager to come to terms with their employers.[11] However, their dignity was not for sale especially when other employers understood the need to handle their workers as free men.

Two other parishes stand out for very strained class relations during the first year of full freedom. These were St. Thomas-in-the-East and St. George. In both areas the workers resolutely resisted various strategies to coerce labour. In the former, the stipendiary magistrates managed to keep the peace and helped to smooth labour relations in time to take off the crop in 1839. However, in St. George, despite the efforts of the governor in 1838, relations deteriorated and violence erupted in 1839. In August and September 1838 the workers refused the planters' terms in St. Thomas-in-the-East. In the Morant Bay area the workers scorned offers of between 6d and 7 1/2d per day and insisted upon 1s 6d. When Morant's manager met the workers' demand, not only did the Morant people resume work in late August, but over 200 other workers offered their labour to cut canes.[12] The other properties gradually offered the terms which Smith had successfully proposed for the southern parishes and by early October more workers resumed.[13]

However, it was in the eastern section of the parish, the Plantain Garden River District, that the conflict between the planters and their former slaves was most pronounced. Up to the end of the apprenticeship, labourers had earned 1s 6d in their free time. Moreover, valuations for manumission purposes had used this figure. The workers were very aware that even when they received extra wages in the apprenticeship, their masters had provided housing, medical care and other allowances. The stipendiary magistrate in the area had warned workers that these 'indulgences of slavery' terminated on 1 August. Thus it was reasonable for the workers in the Plantain Garden River District to ask for at least 1s 6d per day. However, the planters offered 7 1/2d per day and combined this with three months notice to quit estate houses and provision grounds.[14] Clearly, at the same time that the employers were offering low wages, they were also threatening to deprive the workers of access to the grounds that could supplement these wages.

The labourers on Golden Grove led the way in opposing such terms. Interestingly, these workers enjoyed a higher degree of literacy than many others since the estate had had a chapel and a school room from the time of slavery.[15] Ten workers on the estate, led by Richard Edwards, who had been a slave for 27 years on Golden Grove, combined with other workers in the area and staged very successful strikes. The strikes ended in September 1838 when the planters dropped their rent claims and withdrew the notices to quit.[16] They also offered task work from which a very diligent labourer could earn up to 1s 9d per day.[17]

However, the women still refused to resume field work since they considered it incompatible with their new status. The planters led by the custos quickly revived the rent issue so as to penalize those who refused to labour on the estate but occupied estate houses and provision grounds.[18] The workers on Golden Grove, notably Richard Edwards, refused to meet the rent demands. Edwards travelled to Spanish Town and returned telling the other workers that the governor had told him not to pay rent. Of course, such a statement was a fabrication, but it strengthened the resolve of the workers to hold out against the rents demanded.[19] Furthermore, the literate workers had read accounts of stipendiary magistrates' decisions. These had forestalled ejectment proceedings against workers in St. Andrew who had refused to comply with iniquitous rents.[20] The impasse was resolved in January 1839 when the stipendiary magistrate in the area of Golden Grove convinced the workers that they had to pay rent.[21] The planters too adopted more reasonable rent practices so as to attract labour to take off the crop. The workers, though eager to make arrangements to secure their tenancies, steadfastly refused to enter into any contract with their employers unless the stipendiary magistrates were present.[22]

Class Conflicts

Once these contracts were agreed, estates operated smoothly throughout the parish of St. Thomas-in-the-East, but only after six months had passed since August 1838. Whenever the employers again arbitrarily altered the agreed terms of rent or wages, the workers promptly struck until the status quo was restored.[23] All the workers asked for was even-handed treatment. Nor did they necessarily have it all their own way. There were instances when the labourers tried to demand higher wages which violated the agreements. On Weybridge they tried this during the crop. However, the new owner, Charles Darling, who was also the governor's secretary, politely explained the property's financial state which did not allow for any increase. The workers understood and the issue was settled amicably. Indeed, Darling explained the ingredients of smooth labour relations in an otherwise unsettled area as 'civil treatment combined with cash wages regularly paid'.[24]

The first year of full freedom was marked by serious class conflict in St. George. Ridiculously low wages and oppressive rents intensified old antagonisms. The workers in this parish were particularly embittered and the stipendiary magistrates' efforts in August to mitigate the conflict failed.[25] When some of the more moderate workers tried to resume labour they were intimidated by the militants.[26] In the coffee areas of the parish the employers were forced to improve their offers when the berries began to ripen. The workers were offered 1s 6d per day with rent free accommodation, and in some cases, task work on even more favourable terms was proposed. Still, the workers refused. Such militancy alarmed even the usually moderate press. The *Morning Journal* criticized the workers especially since such terms had been gladly accepted by the labourers in other coffee areas such as Manchester and St. Andrew. The editorial commented:

It is not the refusal of a portion, or even half of the peasantry, but with one or two trifling exceptions, so trifling indeed as scarcely to be deserving of notice, the whole. All appear actuated by the same motive. It is not a struggle for high wages ... but one not to labour on any terms.[27]

Clearly, the workers of St. George had been deeply disturbed by their employers' oppressive tactics after 1 August 1838, and no attempt to repair the damage was about to restore labour in the parish.

It was against this background that Sir Lionel Smith had to intervene again to resolve a crisis in labour relations. Smith's address to the workers of St. George who had travelled over the mountains to meet with him at Dunsinane, in St. Andrew, on 6 September 1838, is instructive of the methods he had to use to get labourers to work for employers whose policies had precipitated serious class conflict and distrust. First, the governor appealed to the workers' gratitude and loyalty:

My friends, I am happy to see you. I wish you joy of your freedom. I have come up to this place to talk to you for your own good. A month and a week have now gone by and very little work has been done by you. This I regret very much. It is not in my power to satisfy you or to fix the rate of wages. You must make your bargain with your employers. . . . Perhaps your masters have made unfair proposals, and yourselves unjust demands. I would however recommend you to lose no time in coming to terms and commencing work or you will lose your characters, and give great offence to your good friends in England who have written and said many things in your favour. . . . I am sure no man feels more anxious about you than I do, and if you have any regard for me, or are willing to attend to my advice, the greatest compliment and obligation you could pay me would be to make your bargain at once with your employers and return to work. . . .[28]

Second, the governor appealed to the workers' material interest:

I am anxious to see you working hard, in order that you might get rich and independent. Some of the gentlemen have said that they will give you a macaronie [1s] a day, which is a dollar for four days labour, your giving a macaronie or the fifth day for house and ground. This will be a dollar a week clear. . . . Are you satisfied ? (Cries of yes and no). . . . If you consider that you have been offered too little, I can only inform you that in Manchester and several other parishes the people are working at a much lower rate. . . . On the subject of task work, I think that it would be more satisfactory. . . . I wish that you would think of this and come to any early arrangement with your employers. Believe me, I am consulting your best interests, idleness will bring you to poverty and misery. . . . By your refusal to work, you have been a loser of so much money which you should have earned. . . .[29]

Third, the governor followed this appeal to self-interest by a stern warning against any future strikes: 'If I hear of combination among you, I will punish the parties engaged in it'.[30] Finally, almost in despair, Smith pleaded with the gathering, 'I must leave you — Do for God's sake go to your masters, agree with them, and bargain to work.'[31] One can only speculate, but it would be hard to imagine that a colonial governor had had to use such imploring language elsewhere in order to get

workers to labour. Such was the determination of the St. George labourers.

Nonetheless, Smith's efforts were rewarded. The workers gradually resumed labour in the parish. By the middle of October 1838, more labourers were in the fields and the labour force was settling down on those properties where wages were paid punctually and employers were conciliatory.[32] However, rent remained a burning issue and was the cause of much misunderstanding and litigation in St. George. On some properties rent was levied on each occupant of a cottage while on others no rent was collected at all so that the labourers could be ejected as no tenancy would exist. Workers' requests for annual tenancy were turned down. Generally rent was manipulated in such a fashion that it was a penalty rather than a charge for the use of estate property. If the worker refused to pay increased rental, then the employer initiated legal action in the Courts of Common Pleas where the juries and not the stipendiary magistrates decided the issue.[33] Furthermore, the composition of these juries reflected old prejudices against free blacks. Whites of questionable character and notorious for their states of inebriation, were chosen over blacks known for their 'honesty, intelligence and respectability'.[34]

In July 1839, the workers on Spring Hill coffee plantation in St. George confronted by vexatious rents and denied justice in the courts, violently resisted parish constables who were levying on their goods for outstanding rent. Even when the stipendiary magistrates accompanied the constables on their second attempt, the workers, especially females, confronted them with missiles and 'violent language'. Indeed, the levy was only effected after the governor had dispatched military forces to support the civil authorities. Clearly awed by the presence of the military, the workers permitted the levy and the arrest of a female who had earlier wounded one of the parish constables.[35] Rent had also seriously affected labour relations in many of the other parishes of the island. However, remarkably, only the Spring Hill workers resorted to violence to settle disputes. Other workers resisted by moving to other properties where amicable arrangements were made or, as increasingly happened after 1839, they settled in free villages.[36]

The Decline of Sugar

Gradually, between 1839 and 1842 labour relations improved as the employers abandoned their coercive tactics in the face of determined opposition from the workers. Those connected with Jamaica who gave evidence before the select committee on West Indian colonies in 1842, stressed this improvement.[37] However, as willing as the workers were to offer their labour for fair wages, they were very vigilant in the protection of gains which they had won in the first year of full freedom. When sugar prices declined in 1841, some employers attempted wage reductions. This was done in an arbitrary manner in St. James, and the workers struck. They contended that the workers alone should not be called upon to bear any retrenchment necessitated by reduced prices. William Allen, a labourer on Virgin Valley, explained this position to over two thousand labourers at the Salters Hill Baptist Church:

De Busha dem all hab five to six harse; dem lib well nyam belly full; lib na good house; we lib no hut. . . . We pay half a dollar rent; den dem want to gib we shilling a day. Tell me now, how much lef fa you when week out? No half a dollar lef fe you? Den what fe buy fish? Den wha fe gib paason? . . . De Busha get ten shilling a day; dem want to rob we . . . Unoo will take one shilling a day; (Cries of no, no, no, no, from the audience) . . . Well den, tick out fe good pay and see if dem no blige and bound fee gee wha we ax a day.[38]

Other workers took a more militant position and demanded additional wages. The strikes were called off when the planters restored wages to the old levels.[39]

In St. Mary the attorneys used more conciliatory methods. Rather than summarily cutting the wages, they invited workers to a public meeting and tried to explain that the survival of sugar required reduced costs. The attorneys went even further. They agreed to lower rents by the same one-third that they proposed to reduce the wages. The headmen expressed agreement with this reduction and were expected to explain the proposals to the ordinary labourers. However, the field workers objected to the headmen negotiating for them and warned the employers that none of the headmen were empowered to make 'any promises' on their behalf. Robert Nelson, a spokesman for the workers, expressed the deep distrust of his class when he dismissed the proposals as a plan by the white people of taking them in'. The employers shelved their plan when strikes broke out on the properties which attempted to reduce wages.[40]

Opposition to Immigration

Confronted by the loss of control over labour and the effective bargaining by the ex-slaves, the employers in Jamaica increasingly turned to immigration after 1838.[41] However, the failure of the early schemes to import European and African labour strengthened the workers' position. Francis

Munroe, a carpenter, boasted to the Salters Hill workers meeting that 'All the great, lazy, big bellied fools send for Emigrants to do we harm, and now dat we find Emigrants cant harm we, it is we business to tick out for good wages whatever come'.[42] The Jamaican ex-slaves had rather unflattering views of the Indian immigrants and criticized the planters for importing labour when locals were willing to work, provided that they were treated properly and fairly. Ronald McArthur, a worker on Retrieve in the parish of Hanover, forcibly expressed this view at a workers' meeting summoned by Presbyterian ministers to protest the Sugar Duties Act:

The attorney bring Coolies to take their work and their bread. They make good house for Coolies, but anything good enough for we black nega. Now Coolie is the ruination of Jamaica. Coolie never can work with we; black people can work round about them; them is the most worthlessest set of people we ever saw; them can't work, and yet attorney give them fine house and a shilling a day for doing nothing; but when we black people do work them get plenty busing. Now dis is what ruin Jamaica. Send back the Coolies, them robbers that are brought to this country, and leave the country to us, and give us fair play and regular wages and Jamaica will stand good again . . .[43]

Phillip Dehaney, a labourer on Great Valley, echoed these sentiments and added a novel dimension. He claimed that the Indians were driving the younger workers from the estates:

The Coolies ruin Jamaica, the people often work for less than a shilling a day, and sometimes they no get paid for three and four weeks, and then when we go to get we wage them keep back half. Some time we work for four shillings a week them keep back two for rent. A worthless Coolie get him four and five shillings a week, a good strong man because him a labourer and have house on the estate only get two. This make young people are holding back them hands.[44]

Although McArthur and Dehaney were opposed to immigration, they were very clear about the importance to them of the survival of the estates. Both expressed strong sentiments against the free trade policies which endangered the Jamaican estates and the livelihood of labourers who were dependent on the estates. Dehaney boldly stated that 'Sugar is the best thing — we can't grow cotton, and ships no come from England for we yams and cocoas'.[45] But his message was clear:

Slavery in Cuba ruin the Jamaican proprietors, so Coolie in Jamaica ruin the Jamaican labourer; them both stand the same — put away Coolie, put away the slavery and gie we fair play, and you will see our young people hold up them heads, and Jamaica will turn around again. . . .[46]

These views were even more remarkable for they were expressed by workers in the parish of Hanover, one of the finest regions in the island for provision-growing.[47] This suggests that by 1847 some of the alternatives to labour on the estates had already become less attractive to ex-slaves. Benjamin Robertson, an ex-slave who made his living as a fisherman, complained that the failure of estates had affected his market. He and his family, who assisted him, had now to travel longer distances to seek markets for his catch.[48] This link between the estates and those who had left was also appreciated by Richard Nelster, a labourer who dismissed as 'foolish' the view that since 'there were no estates in Africa' no harm would come to the labourers if the estates in Jamaica were abandoned. He explained that 'if no money were made on the estate no one could live for if a carpenter sells a chair or a table, the man who buys it must get his money from the estate'.[49] These Jamaican labourers were as concerned as their employers about the future of the estates in Jamaica because of the free trade crisis.[50] Unfortunately for Jamaica the planter class failed to respond to the conciliatory sentiments expressed here. Instead, as credit dried up, wages were slashed by as much as 50% in some areas.[51] Planters agitated for stricter vagrancy legislation which 'would make a supply of labour attainable, upon more easy and convenient terms'.[52] Some misguided employers went even further. They openly stated that Jamaica would be better off under the 'American flag' and overseers boasted that such an event would restore their command over labour.[53]

These wild rumours of annexation to a slave republic, coupled with wage reductions, and in some cases, no payment of wages at all, revived class antagonisms to the extent that some militant workers were convinced that the 'White and Brown People were wanting to make them slaves again'.[54] Authorities in western Jamaica claimed that the militants were planning to stage violent strikes to coincide with the tenth anniversary of the termination of the apprenticeship. Panic and alarm spread throughout the western parishes as a repeat of the confrontation of 1831 seemed imminent. Fortunately, the governor acted quickly to defuse the situation by restraining the planters who wanted to mobilize the militia, and assured the workers that their freedom would be jealously guarded by the executive.[55]

Ten years after the era of free wage bargaining had begun in Jamaica, the executive had to intervene to forestall a class war. In this period the Jamaican workers had demonstrated that while they were willing to labour under reasonable and equitable conditions, they would resist any planter policies which failed to take account of their new status as free workers entitled to the fruits of their labour.

Notes

1. W. Rodney, **A History of the Guyanese Working People**, 1881–1905 (HEB: 1981) pp. 32–33.
2. C.O. 137/223, Smith to Glenelg, No. 140, 27 July 1838; **Morning Journal**, 8 August, 1 September 1838. (Wages and rents quoted in this paper are in Sterling).
3. **Falmouth Post**, 29 August 1838; **Morning Journal**, 4 and 21 August 1838.
4. **Morning Journal**, 3 and 4 September 1838.
5. **Morning Journal**, 20 August 1838.
6. **Morning Journal**, 5, 11, 19 and 24 September 1838.
7. C.O. 137/230, Smith to Glenelg, No. 189, 1 November 1830, enclosed Reports of Stipendiary Magistrate (S.M.) Finlayson and (S.M.) Carnaby. The George Gordon must not be confused with George William Gordon.
8. **Falmouth Post**, 15 August 1838.
9. **Falmouth Post**, 29 August 1838.
10. C.O. 137/230, Smith to Glenelg, No. 189, 1 November 1838, enclosed Reports of (S.M.) Lyon and (S.M.) Kelly.
11. P.P. 1842, XIII (479), Knibb's evidence before the Select Committee on West India Colonies, questions 6151, 6183–6191, Geddes' evidence question 6849.
12. **Morning Journal**, 1 September 1838.
13. C.O. 137/230, Smith to Glenelg, No. 189, 1 November 1838, enclosed Report of S.M. Ewart, 25 October 1838; **Morning Journal**, 1 September 1838.
14. C.O. 137/242, Smith to Glenelg, No. 41, 6 February 1839, enclosed Report of S.M. Chamberlaine, 31 January 1839.
15. Ibid.
16. C.O. 137/243, Smith to Normanby, No. 99, 11 May 1839, enclosure No. 1, McCornock to Darling, 8 May 1839.
17. C.O. 137/242, Smith to Glenelg, No. 41, 6 February 1839, enclosed Report of S.M. Chamberlaine, 31 January 1839.
18. Ibid.
19. C.O. 137/243, Smith to Normanby, No. 99, 11 May 1839, enclosure No. 1 McCornock to Darling, 8 May 1839.
20. Ibid.
21. Ibid.
22. C.O. 137/237, Smith to Glenelg, No. 53, 25 February 1839, enclosed Report of S.M. Ewart, 13 February 1839.
23. C.O. 137/242, Smith to Glenelg, No. 65, 23 March 1839, enclosed Report of S.M. Ewart, 6 March 1939; C.O. 137/243, Smith to Normanby, No. 103, 14 May 1839, enclosed Report of S.M. Ewart, 8 May 1839.
24. C.O. 137/243, Smith to Normanby, No. 100, 13 May 1839, enclosed letter of Darling to Smith, 13 May 1839.
25. C.O. 137/241, Smith to Glenelg, No. 8, 1 May 1839, enclosed letter of S.M. Fishbourne to R. Hill, 14 November 1838.
26. **Morning Journal**, 23 August 1838.
27. **Morning Journal**, 6 September 1838.
28. **Morning Journal**, 10 September 1838.
29. Ibid.
30. Ibid.
31. Ibid.
32. C.O. 137/230, Smith to Glenelg, No. 189, 1 November 1838, enclosed Report of S.M. Fishbourne, 10 October 1838.
33. C.O. 137/242, Smith to Glenelg, No. 74, 6 April 1839, enclosed Reports of S.M. Fishbourne and S.M. Hewitt, 20 March 1839.

34. C.O. 137/244, Smith to Normanby, No. 160, 16 August 1839, enclosed Report of S.M. Fishbourne, 7 August 1839.

35. C.O. 137/244, Smith to Normanby, No. 136, 17 July 1839, enclosed Report of S.M. Fishbourne, 15 July 1839.

36. C.O. 137/243, Smith to Normanby, No. 108, 27 May 1839, enclosed Report of Richard Hill, 23 May 1839.

37. P.P. 1842, XIII (479) Select Committee on West India Colonies, Knibb's evidence question 5994–5997; Geddes' evidence questions 6821, 6945; Barrett's evidence question 5443; McCornock's evidence questions 4798, 4802.

38. **Royal Gazette and Jamaica Standard**, 25 September 1841. Wages were reduced from 1/6d. to 1/- per day.

39. Ibid, 8 October 1841.

40. **Morning Journal**, 3, 6 and 28 January 1842.

41. Select Committee on West India Colonies, McCornock's evidence questions 4754–4755, 4844–4851; Geddes' evidence questions 6869 = 6874.

42. **Royal Gazette and Jamaica Standard**, 25 September 1841.

43. **Morning Journal**, 6 December 1847.

44. Ibid.

45. Ibid.

46. Ibid.

47. D.G. Hall, **Free Jamaica** (CUP 1969), p. 173.

48. **Morning Journal**, 6 December 1847.

49. Ibid.

50. Ibid.

51. **Morning Journal**, 13 September 1847, 6 December 1847.

52. **Falmouth Post**, 1 September 1848.

53. **Morning Journal**, 29 January, 28 March 1848; **Falmouth Post**, 27 June.

54. C.O. 137/299, Charles Grey to Earl Grey, No. 64, 7 July 1848, enclosure I.L.H. Evelyn to Pilgrim, 12 June 1848.

55. C.O. 137/299, Charles Grey to Earl Grey, No. 68, 22 July 1848.

The Flight from the Estates Reconsidered: The British West Indies, 1838–1842[3]

Douglas Hall

The purpose of this paper is to examine the reasons why after their emancipation many of the ex-slaves in the British Caribbean removed themselves from the estates and established households elsewhere. A related concern is the extent to which withdrawal of residence reflected an intention to withdraw their labour from the plantation economy. On these questions we have very little statement from the ex-slaves themselves, and it is necessary to rely on the information provided by others of whom the majority were estate-owners or managers whose views were very likely prejudiced by the effects of the withdrawals on their labour supply. The minutes of evidence given before the Select Committee of the House of Commons on the West Indian Colonies in 1842[1] provide a substantial body of such information and it is largely on that evidence that this enquiry is based. By 1842 the immediate reactions of both planters and ex-slaves to the emancipation had occurred, and although some measure of stability had been achieved in labour relations there was general complaint on the part of employers of the scarcity, the unreliability and the high price of estate labour. By 1842, also, the initial excitement in Britain over 'the great social experiment' of emancipation was on the wane, and there was a colder curiosity about the way in which the ex-slaves in the Caribbean were conducting themselves.

The Select Committee of 1842 was appointed to make particular enquiry into two matters: the general moral, religious and economic condition of the ex-slaves; and the need for immigrant labour to support the continuation of sugar production in certain colonies. Those planters who gave evidence were nearly all in complaint of loss of labour in terms of workers on the estates, and, even more so, of their loss of command over such labour as still, from time to time, was offered to them. They were likely to exaggerate the withdrawal of the ex-slaves and their labour from the estates, and they would be likely to emphasize their own explanations (such as the 'easy' winning of subsistence from a small plot of land in the lush and bountiful tropics)

of the 'pull' of labour away from their employment, rather than other factors (such as their own policies towards labour) that would have tended to 'push' the workers in search of better conditions of life.

The prevailing impressions conveyed in the general body of literature on the history of the post-emancipation period are: that the majority of ex-slaves wished to remove themselves from the estates on which they had suffered so much in the days of bondage; that the ex-slaves were, apparently with some reluctance, forced to leave the estates because of the harsh attitudes and demands of their masters, the ex-slaves owners; and, in either case, that their movements clearly depended on the availability of somewhere else to go.

In discussing 'The Rise of village Settlements in British Guiana' Rawle Farley expressed the view that:

The roots of the village settlements are to be found in the days of slavery. The forces which were fundamental to the establishment of these settlements were, for the most part, the same economic and social forces which had led to the end of slavery as such on August 1st, 1838.

The most decisive and continuous of these forces was the desire, on the part of the slave, for personal liberty and for land of his own. This desire was responsible for the persistent pressure of the slaves to destroy the system which deprived them of these rights.[2]

He went on to argue that 'the rise of the village settlements was symbolic of the continuation of the revolt against the plantation system by free labour, reinforced after 1838 by the advantages denied them under slavery.[3]

Later accounts of the movements of ex-slaves from the British Guianese estates have, with but slight modifications, followed Farley's explanation. Parry and Sherlock wrote that 'the establishment of free villages was not begun as a result of emancipation but with freedom it became possible for many people to do legally what a few had hitherto done illegally.'[4]

55

Mandle, in his book on population and economic change in Guyana since the emancipation, referred to the movement as 'the escape of the "inmates" from "the total institution", facilitated by the abundance of available land for settlement.[5] And, more recently, Alan Adamson has put much the same explanation, but with a slightly different emphasis.

In the generation prior to abolition the so-called coloured free of the colony began to play an increasingly important role in economic life: They became hucksters, butchers, skilled workers, overseers, managers, and even small-scale planters. But a free black man had never been known voluntarily to work with a shovel or to cut cane. These were the vocations of the slave. Thus, there were clear signs, well before emancipation, that free Negro labour would leave the estates.[6]

Accounts of the movement in Jamaica have, however, differed from Farley's 'escape' explanation. Hugh Paget, in 'The Free Village System in Jamaica', argued an almost opposite point of view:

This was the crux of the whole matter. As a general rule the people would have preferred to continue to live in their old villages on the estates and to cultivate their old provision grounds. If however, they were ejected or were subject to ejectment at notice so short that they were in danger of losing each crop that they had planted, and had, in addition, to pay high rents, they had perforce to leave the estates and make new homes for themselves where their tenure was sufficiently secure. . . Thus only could a man make a home for his family consistent with his self-respect; by that means alone could he obtain that measure of independence which could give him some bargaining power in the matter of wages.[7]

Parry and Sherlock, when discussing Jamaica, take Paget's view.[8] In another general history of the Caribbean, *The Making of the West Indies*, the authors (of whom I am one) tried a wider generalization about the whole British Caribbean based on Farley's theme:

Freedom of choice had at last come; the abiding question of whether or not labourers would remain on the sugar estates was to be answered. The answer was largely decided by the alternatives available; but it was clear what most ex-slaves wanted to do, if they had any real choice. Where there was an opportunity of living off the estates, they departed in large numbers.[9]

But, a year earlier, with specific reference to Jamaica, I had followed Paget's rather than Farley's view:

But this sudden demand [i.e. for high rents for houses and provision grounds] proved offensive to the labourers, who had never thought of these places as being anybody else's property, and they complained, often with very good reason, that the rents demanded were exorbitant, and that if they paid rent they were free men and should be allowed to work for whom they chose.

These disputes became general throughout the island; and . . . a stalemate was encouraged in which both estate labour and the cultivation of provision grounds suffered. The situation was broken by the exodus of labourers from the estates. In some cases they were ejected by estate owners who thought that by doing so they would divorce them from their provision grounds and force them into the market for estate labour . . . but, because of the availability of land and the ability of the ex-slaves to purchase it, the planters found it necessary to retreat from their aggressive policies, which had so obviously backfired.[10]

In an even earlier work, Gisela Eisner had put the two sorts of explanations together and sided with Paget's view. The exodus of the ex-slaves from, the Jamaica estates, she wrote:

is usually explained in terms of an association in the ex-slaves' mind between sugar-planting and slavery and the consequent literal interpretation of freedom. But this is hard to believe . . . [and] . . . had they been assured of attractive wages and conditions of employment there is no reason to suppose that they would not have remained on the estates.[11]

And so, in other accounts, both of the British Caribbean in general, and of individual colonies in particular,[12] historians have tended to follow Farley or Paget, and occasionally, to give less consideration to the 'push' factors, which influenced ex-slaves to leave the estates, and to emphasize more the extent to which 'pull' factors, such as the availability of land or alternative employment, attracted the ex-slaves away from estate labour.

The information provided in 1842 seems to make it very clear that movement of residence from the estates came as a consequence, not of burning recollections of brutalities suffered during slavery, but rather of the terms of the emancipation itself and the behaviour of estate-owners after 1834.

British Guiana was one of those colonies in which land was plentiful and labour was scarce. Wage-rates were high. Following a decline in the price of sugar in 1841 planters in Demerara and Essequibo issued, without reference to the Special Magistrates or to the Governor, certain Rules and Regulations for the employment of labour.[13] The general intention was to reduce the cost of labour by lowering wage-rates and eliminating other 'allowances' of free medical attention, housing and provision grounds, and to bind the ex-slaves to labour on the estates on which they resided. The reactions of the ex-slaves were to stop work and to raise complaint.

From Plantation Affiance the labourers addressed the local Stipendiary Magistrate, Captain J.A. Allen, on 3 January 1842.

It appears that within the pale of this week certain resolutions has passed, debiliting the wages of us labourers. We do now wishful of ascertaining the case from you in its minute order. Wheather we are bound by our Queen to act in accordance with these resolutions, or wheather we are to submit to what offer the managers choose to give. We leave it to you to give us your opinion on this most momentous subject. It is offered three bitts to one guilder per day for our labour per day. We are told we must pay for our provision ground, doctor fees, finding ourselves with all necessarys, etc. What will be remaining for us in case of sickness? We feel this case too hard upon us, and we hope that your worship will not consider that we have spoken hard, but it is a fraud that is wishful of placing on us, and unless other measures are adopted, we will be obliged to send to Her Most Gracious Majesty to justify us.[14]

There are several interesting points to be made about that message. First, it seems that as late as January 1842 the main body of the ex-slaves of Plantation Affiance were still resident and labouring there. Secondly, there is the explicit claim that they are being unfairly treated. Thirdly, their reaction to such treatment is not simply to go on strike and bargain for what they can get, but rather to appeal to higher authority to see that justice is done. Fourthly, their complaint takes no notice of the reduced financial circumstances of the planters as a consequence of falling prices for sugar, it is based entirely on what they conceive to be their rightful due as residents and labourers on the property.

These views are even more forcibly made in another message to Captain Allen from the workers on Plantation Walton Hall, dated 6 January 1842.

Sir! We free labourers of Plantation Walton Hall are already to work our liberty hours in putting hands and heart providing in we getting what is right. As to say for taking one guilder per day, we can not take it at all. Sir, you will be pleased to understand us to what we say (those few years since we got free), and so soon brought on a reducing price, which is now offered to we labourers. We certainly thinks it to be very hard. If you take it in consideration, when calling on us. We shall be proud to know from, if such laws came from the Queen, or any of Her Majesties Justice of Peace. During our slavery we was clothed, ration, and seported in all manner of respects. Now we are free men (free indeed), we are to work for nothing. Then we might actually say, we becomes slaves again. We will be glad to know from the

proprietors of the estates, if they are to take from us our rights all together. You will be please to understand very well. Satisfied we labourers with the former price we was getting. For we were also allowed a doctor in case of sickness. But now it is said we must pay house rent, and we is also made to understand that our negroe ground to be taken from us. Therefore we cannot work for a smaller price. You will be please to take the law in consideration in settling this matter.[15]

These were two of several similar messages addressed to the Stipendiary Magistrate.[16] There is nothing in them to support the view that on emancipation the ex-slaves, even in British Guiana where land was available for purchase, had rushed from the abhorrent scenes of slavery. Nor is there much evidence to support the view that those who had left the estates were determined to withdraw their labour as well as their households. In this the reports of the several Stipendiaries throughout the colony are almost totally in agreement.

In his half-yearly Report for the period ending 31 December 1841, in the Section dealing with 'Relations between the Peasantry and the Proprietors' the Stipendiary Magistrate in District (A) (Upper Division), in the County of Demerara, reported[17] that the ex-slaves were 'making a good deal of progress in establishing themselves as freeholders' but while

these changes cannot but have an effect upon the supply of labour, particularly at first, while the ground is preparing for cultivation and the houses building, I do not think however the consequences will be so injurious in this respect as is generally supposed, when the occupants are settled in these freeholds. The manager of Plantation Fellowship, the nearest estate to 'The Recess' [a newly formed hamlet] informed me that many of his labourers were supplied from it.

In the eleven other Reports sent in from Demerara, Essequibo and Berbice the comments were very much the same; but, as would be expected, the different magistrates in the different Districts made their particular emphases. In District (B) of Demerara it was said that many of the new freeholders 'generally continue in their former situations, and employ less effective labourers to do such work as may be required on their freeholds'. Even in District (C) on the outskirts of Georgetown where settlers had established 'a flourishing and populous suburb, called Albert's Town', many of the people continued to give labour on neighbouring estates, 'the majority [working] as porters, carters, &c.' In the more rural areas of District (C) it was reported that

During the last half year the labourers in this district have been allowed houses or cottages free from any rent;

within that time their progress in establishing themselves as freeholders has been very inconsiderable and no new hamlets or villages have arisen in this district; but those heretofore established have increased in population which has to a certain degree lessened the supply of labour for the [estates].

In District (D), also in Demerara, the provision of rent-free cottages seemed not to have affected the rapid growth of small freeholds; but here too the freeholders sought estate employment. In District (F) in Essequibo, the Stipendiary emphasized the withdrawal of labour from the estates as the ex-slaves settled in small villages; but even he predicted a return to estate labour 'when these plots are planted'. He was convinced that small cultivation could not enable the new freeholders 'to obtain those comforts which the negroe cannot now dispense with'. In District (L) in Berbice there was said to be 'mutual good feeling and confidence' between employers and employees; but 'the peasantry on estates are mere tenants at will; they continue anxious to become freeholders'. Perhaps the most appropriate summary came from District (K) in Berbice, where the Stipendiary Magistrate, Mr Charles Whinfield, reported

The relation between the peasantry and the proprietors is, as stated in my last report, a perfect independence on the part of the people of their employers, owing to the totally inadequate supply of labour to maintain the cultivation of the staples of the country. Notwithstanding this, there is a mutual good feeling and confidence daily gaining ground with both the employer and employed. The peasantry on estates are mere tenants at will; they continue anxious to become freeholders, a feeling which, in my opinion, cannot be too much encouraged.

Although the notions of a growing 'mutual good feeling and confidence' were to be shattered within the week by the attempt of planters in Demerara and Essequibo to inflict their stringent, and unlawful, Rules and Regulations, it is abundantly clear from the reports of late 1841 and from the reactions of the labourers to the Rules and Regulations, that in British Guiana memories of misery did not lead the ex-slaves to withdraw from estate labour. Their behaviour reflected far more positive reactions to current rates of wages, local market prices and the wish to preserve their newly acquired freedom.

Throughout the entire Caribbean the same was true. Many of those who removed their residences from the estates continued to give estate labour, though not regularly; and many of those who remained on the estates were not to be depended on to labour there five days a week. On these matters the evidence of planters before the Select Committee of 1842 is perfectly explicit.

One question put to nearly all those who appeared before the Committee referred to the population of ex-slaves who remained resident on the estates on which they had lived during slavery. The answers are instructive. Beyond a doubt they show that a considerable proportion of ex-slaves did remain in residence, that those who left did not entirely withdraw their labour and that those who remained did not always give it.

Thomas MacCornock, for thirty years resident on Golden Grove Estate in St. Thomas-in-the-East, and for several years Custos of the parish, was a prominent estate attorney in Jamaica. On Golden Grove there had been between 500 and 600 'apprentices' resident at the termination of the Apprenticeship Period in 1838. Of those, about 400 were still in residence in 1842. Of that 400, about 100 were 'agricultural labourers of both sexes'.[18]

Henry Lowndes, a proprietor, trustee, attorney and lessee connected with eight estates in St. Thomas-in-the-Vale, had lived 27 years in Jamaica. His ex-slaves all remained 'on the estates or in the neighbourhood'. Those who had left the estate still worked for him from time to time.[19]

Hinton Spalding, a medical practitioner in Kingston since 1815, had in 1835 given up his practice and devoted his full attention to his five coffee plantations: Hermitage, where he resided, in the parish of St. George's, Grove and Lancaster in the parish of Manchester, Platfield in St. Mary, and West Prospect lying adjacent to Hermitage, partly in St. George and partly in St. Andrew. The exchange between him and John Somerset Pakington, Chairman of the Select Committee, is full of interest.

PAKINGTON: 'Can you state to the Committee what is the difference, if any, in the number of labourers residing on your estates, between the latter years of slavery and the present period of freedom?'
SPALDING: 'At the Grove I have had a slight increase in the number of labourers, but that has not compensated for the want of continuous labour there. At Lancaster, in the same parish of Manchester, the numbers have greatly diminished. At Platfield they have increased in consequence of the circumstances I mentioned, that they returned from the locality where I had placed them, to their old locality of Platfield from which I had removed them; but the consequence is, that I had a great diminution in labourers at the Hermitage, and at West Prospect all the labourers have deserted the latter plantation and purchased or hired land in the neighbourhood or elsewhere.'
PAKINGTON: 'Are you able to state to the Committee with respect to the whole five, what is the ratio of reduction in number?'
SPALDING: 'I should say about half.'

PAKINGTON: 'In so speaking, are you speaking of the total numbers, or available labourers?'
SPALDING: 'The total numbers.'
PAKINGTON: 'What has become of the remainder, the half that have left you, where are they?'
SPALDING: 'They have gone to different districts where land was to be purchased.'
PAKINGTON: 'Are they still within reach of you?'
SPALDING: 'Some of them are, but some are not.'
PAKINGTON: 'Do you find that those who have purchased land, and settled on land within reach of you, give you their labour?'
SPALDING: 'They do when it suits their purpose.'[20]

Another Jamaican planter, Alexander Geddes, had lived in the island for 22 years up to May 1841. He was a property owner in St. Ann and claimed to have 'concerns embracing every description of cultivation', in the parishes of Clarendon, Vere, Manchester, St. Thomas-in-the-Vale, St. Mary, St. George's, Trelawny, Westmoreland and, of course, St. Ann. He had managed sugar estates, pens and coffee plantations. On his properties he estimated that since emancipation one-third of the ex-slaves had moved off to establish freeholds. Those living within reach occasionally gave him labour, but, he added, 'they do so as regularly as the labourers remaining upon the estate.'[21]

William Christie had lived in Jamaica for about fifteen years during the period 1816–36. He owned three sugar estates, one in St. Andrew and two in Hanover. The Hanover estates had lost more than half their ex-slaves, who had bought land 'all round the neighbourhood'.[22]

In British Guiana 'almost all' the ex-slaves remained resident on the estates of Henry Barkly in Berbice.[23] Mungo Campbell, co-proprietor of estates in Demerara, claimed that although he did not know the exact number there remained in residence on his estate 'a great number . . . who were formerly slaves thereon'.[24]

In Trinidad, on Harmony Hall and Paradise estates, of which Robert Henry Church was attorney, 'nearly all' the resident labourers in 1842 had formerly been slaves there, but the labour force was much diminished.[25]

George Estridge, estate attorney in St. Kitts for eleven years up to 1841, explained that on the estate on which he lived, Taylor's, 'we have as many labourers . . . as during the time of slavery, but the labour seems to melt away in freedom'.[26] In Antigua, on the estates of Nicholas Nugent, about two-thirds of the ex-slaves remained in residence.[27] In Barbados, of about 400 who had been slaves on the Carrington estates many had moved away, but most workers were resident and there were other residents who did not work there.[28] In the same island, William Sharpe said that most of his employees in 1842 had previously been his slaves and 'the only additional persons are those that have since come to join their nearest relatives; that is, husbands to join their wives, wives to their husbands, and children to their parents.[29]

And in St. Vincent, Hay McDowell Grant said that of 130 workers on his pay-list in 1842 about 100 had been his slaves.[30]

Withdrawals there were, everywhere, both of residence and of labour, but in the face of the array of evidence, and notwithstanding all sorts of variations of conditions in the different colonies and even different estates within a single colony, it is clearly not valid to claim that when emancipation came the ex-slaves rushed to remove themselves from the haunts of slavery. Indeed, not only did many remain where they were, but there is evidence that some, as at Platfield, had of their own choice 'returned . . . to their old locality'.

Ironically, the real reason for the post-emancipation movements away from the estates lay in the fact that the coming of freedom jeopardized the continuing enjoyment by the ex-slaves of the one real source of privacy and independence that they had enjoyed during their degrading enslavement.

It is well known that during slavery the slaves had been housed by their owners. In addition, they had been allowed the use of small areas around their dwellings, and where sub-marginal cane (or coffee or other staple) land was plentiful on the estate they had been allowed 'grounds' where in their spare time they might grow food provisions. In slavery these houseplots or gardens, and the provision grounds where they were available, were the only places in which the slaves were able to grow what they wished, unsupervised, and to enjoy with their households the fruits of their labours. Moreover, they were allowed to take the produce of these gardens and grounds to the weekly local markets and to keep for their own use any earnings by sales or exchanges of goods.[31] Set against the harsh, driven labour in the estate's fields from sunrise to sunset, sweating to produce the sugar which enriched his master only, the garden and provision ground enabled the slave, even if in a very circumscribed way, to be in some respects a man unto himself.

Immediately following emancipation planters sought to bind their 'apprentices' and, after 1838, their ex-slaves to continued labour on their estates in one of two ways; they either imposed high rents on houses and provision grounds, or they insisted that continued occupation would only be allowed if the occupants worked daily on the estate. The first was calculated to diminish the net earnings from sales of provisions in local markets, and so make the ex-slave more dependent on wages for

his livelihood. The second, more commonly practised where land off the estates was scarce and
dear, was intended to force the labourers to work
in order to continue having roofs over their heads.

The reactions of the ex-slaves were immediate
and, from our vantage point, predictable. To them,
obviously, emancipation should only mean a bet-
tering of their condition. Yet now in freedom they
were being charged for the continuing use of what
they had used without charge when they were
slaves. Or, alternatively, in order to continue in
rent-free enjoyment, they were being called upon
to surrender their newly acquired right to work
when, at what, and for whom they chose. Sometimes, it is true, their choice was limited, but even
then it was the freeman's right to do nothing rather
than do what was unpleasant or unprofitable.

These masters' policies seemed to the ex-slaves
to be a betrayal of the principles of emancipation.
The addresses to Stipendiary Magistrate Allen in
Demerara make the views of the ex-slaves very
clear. Nor are those two documents the only basis
for this assessment. In 1842 the following
exchange took place between Mr Grantley Berkeley, a member of the Select Committee, and Mr
Henry Barkly in evidence:

BERKELEY: 'In British Guiana have you known a
belief to exist among the negroes, that when they were
made free the Queen gave them their houses and land?'
BARKLY: 'I believe that was a very general belief at
first. I was told by negroes on Highbury estate, when I
went there, that it was all nonsense that the Queen made
them free without giving them a free house and land; and
they called upon me to carry out that proposition, by
giving up the houses and grounds. I attempted to explain
the system of tenancy, but I could not make them comprehend it in the least; they had no idea of paying anything at all. They have of course gained considerable
experience upon the subject since; and I do not think at
present there would be any obstacle to the introduction
of a system of tenancy, if an efficient law were passed.'[32]

It was, of course more than mere 'fancy'. For
the ex-slaves the circumstances were ironical in the
extreme. For generations they had occupied
houses, gardens and grounds free of rent; and even
more, according to their owners, they had seldom
been disturbed in their occupancy.[33] Had they been
freemen and not slaves they would long before
emancipation have acquired rights by undisturbed
occupation. Because they had been slaves, that is,
along with the houses, gardens and grounds they
had themselves formed part of the property of the
estate-owner, they had been able to establish no
such claim. Now that they were free they were to
lose that part of their livelihood which in their
view, had been the only real 'freedom' they had in

slavery; unless, of course, they surrendered their
new freedom to choose their employer and their
place of work.

By 1842, the withdrawals of residence from the
estates was well forward. So, too, was the withdrawal of labour; but not simply because ex-slaves
hated the estates, and not even because they disliked cane-field work so much that they would not
indulge in it. Obviously, there were many who with
the ending of compulsion would have withdrawn
from fields and factories — the old, the very
young, women who wished to give their time to
their own households, and others who preferred
village or 'urban' to estate employment, or town
life to country life. Our main concern is with those
who remained in agricultural and estate work.

As has been shown, those who moved their
households and set up on small freeholds did not
entirely withdraw their labour from the estates.
They did, however, show three very marked tendencies; they preferred job-work or task-work to
day's-work,[34] they exercised their judgement in
choosing their employers, and they did not offer
their services regularly. By 1842 day's-work, that
is labour from sunrise to sunset, was almost totally
given up even by those labourers who remained in
residence on the estates. It gave the labourers too
little time for their own affairs. Moreover, industrious labour earned more by the job or by the task.

In 1842, John Candler, who had spent the year
1840 travelling through Jamaica, put his observations very succinctly.

MR BENJAMIN HAWES: 'As to continuous labour, did
you hear complaints of the want of continuous labour?'
MR JOHN CANDLER: 'Very often.'
HAWES: 'Did you find that they were well founded?'
CANDLER: 'I think they were to some extent.'
HAWES: 'What was the cause of that?'
CANDLER: 'A natural love of independence on the part
of the negro, not wishing to be tied down to give so many
days' labour continuously and continually; wishing to be
at liberty to do anything else that he might want for himself.'
HAWES: 'Was there any variation in the complaints in
some districts, as compared with others?'
CANDLER: 'On some estates, as compared with others,
a great difference.'
HAWES: 'Did you arrive at any opinion as to the causes
of the difference in the complaints with reference to particular estates?'
CANDLER: 'Certainly.'
HAWES: 'What were the causes which appeared to produce that difference?'
CANDLER: 'I found that where the labourers were
wisely and fairly treated, there was generally very little
complaint on the part of the masters of the want of continuous labour.'
HAWES: 'Where you say fairly treated, do you mean by
paying fair wages?'

CANDLER: 'Not coercing labour by means of rent, paying an average rate of wages, and paying those wages duly.'[35]

Alexander Geddes emphasized the importance of the provision ground in the slave-household economy and claimed that was the prime source of post-emancipation labour shortage in Jamaica.

PAKINGTON: 'What in your opinion is the principal cause of the present difficulties of the Jamaica planter?'
GEDDES: 'I consider that the great source of his difficulties is not so much the want of population, as their having been habituated to depend for support during slavery upon the cultivation of ground provisions, to which they have now frequently recourse in place of cultivating the estates. They have been habituated to that system, and I consider it impossible in any way to stop them.'[36]

In other words, the ex-slave traditionally viewed his provision ground rather than the estate as his source of food and income.

However true this might have been in Jamaica it certainly could not have applied to the ex-slaves in the tight little 'sugar islands'. Nonetheless, the same sorts of complaints, if not the same sorts of explanations are to be found.

George Estridge seemed not to have much to complain of by way of labour shortage, and he admitted that the export of sugar from St. Kitts had not fallen off 'since the commencement of freedom'. Nonetheless, he bemoaned his loss of command over his labour force:

PAKINGTON: 'On the whole, your supply of labour is sufficient for your purposes of cultivation?'
ESTRIDGE: 'I should say there were labourers, but not labour enough.'[37]

George Carrington of Barbados (but an absentee proprietor who was a landowner in Britain) said that the labour obtainable from his resident labour had 'considerably diminished; because they go when they please, and come when they like and stay as long as they please. . . .'[38] But he was, apparently, a fair and just employer, for he had no great complaint about shortage of labour. He employed non-residents who augmented his resident workers.

John Candler's assessment was supported by others, in Jamaica and elsewhere. Joseph Allen, a Stipendiary Magistrate in British Guiana from August 1834 until April 1842, had no doubt whatsoever that where the ex-slaves were fairly treated and paid they evinced 'a full disposition' to give 'any reasonable labour'.[39] For Jamaica, an account given in 1842 by Captain Philip Browne provides

an excellent even if unusual illustration of Candler's remarks.

SIR CHARLES DOUGLAS: 'What [wages] did you offer them?'
PHILIP BROWNE: 'I asked them first what would satisfy them; they would not state any sum, but simply said, "We leave it to you, master, to give us what you think fair." I did not hesitate a moment, because I knew I had been paying 2s 11d currency for hired labour and I said I would give them 1s 6d sterling if they would work for me from sunrise till four o'clock in the afternoon. They thanked me, and in less than two days every man, woman and child upon the estate was at work.'
DOUGLAS: 'Were they all money payments which you made?'
BROWNE: 'All.'
DOUGLAS: 'What were the conditions as relates to the use of house and grounds, medical attendance, etc.?'
BROWNE: 'When I spoke to them I told them they were now as free as myself, and that they would have to find themselves in every article necessary for their sustenance, clothing, food, medical attendance, and even implements of husbandry; and I said to them, "As the property is not wholly my own, you must pay a certain rent for your houses and grounds; the condition I wish you to come to is this, if I give you 1s 6d sterling, you must pay me 2s a week for the use of your houses and grounds. A man with his family, and his children under 12 years of age, were to be included in that, but if they had sons and daughters grown up, who had separate houses or separate grounds, they must pay some small amount in addition to what their parents paid." They all agreed to that, and did pay it.'[40]

Beyond a doubt the 'rent question' was the one which most disturbed relations between employers and employees. The ex-slaves had soon learned that they would no longer have both unrestricted access to houses, gardens and grounds, and unrestricted freedom to choose their employers and employments. Where land was available for purchase they established freeholds and so, at the cost of leaving the estates and uprooting households, they escaped the limitations which their employers sought to place upon their freedom. Where land was not so readily available for purchase, they had, of necessity, to remain in residence on their estates, but they showed a great anxiety to purchase, and they pressed for the separation of rents and wages.

There were three clear practices. The least acceptable to the ex-slaves was that by which they occupied houses and gardens and grounds 'free of rent' on condition that they labour for the estate. An intermediary practice was to separate money payments — wages to the employee/tenant, and rents to the landowner/employer -but still with the requirement that the tenant (and usually his family household) must work for the landlord. This was hardly better than the first, but it did make a desirable distinction. The third, which by 1842 was being strongly recommended by the magistrates and had begun to be adopted by a few of the more far-sighted planters, was a complete separation of rents and wages. To reside on an estate the ex-slave would have to pay a rent for house, garden and grounds; but he would be completely free to find employment elsewhere. This, to which the ex-slaves most readily acceded, was already in 1842 the admitted practice of George Carrington in Barbados and Alexander Geddes in Jamaica.[41] Doubtless there were a few others. At any event, it was more and more recommended.

John Scoble, who had visited British Guiana in 1836 and 1838, remarked:

I found on inquiry of the negroes, that the tenure by which the negroes held their huts and provision grounds was not that by which they desired to hold them; they wished to rent their huts and provision grounds, and I suggested to the planters the propriety of at once coming to terms with the negroes, by allowing them to become renters, rather than to make the tenure by which they held their huts and provision grounds dependent on the amount of labour to be extracted from them.[42]

The magistrates of the Barbadian Assistant Court of Appeal, in April 1842, commenting on the reports of the Police Magistrates advised the Governor:

Although the plan of renting to the peasantry their cottages and grounds, whereby they became at liberty to dispose of their labour at the most profitable rate, is far from being generally adopted throughout the island, it is gratifying to note that the majority of the police magistrates advocate the latter view, and one writes, that the rent system is gaining ground in this parish (St. James), and beneficial effects have resulted on every property whereon it has been tried. In connection with this inquiry it is also important to add, that wheresoever the experiment of rent system has been tried, the supply of labour for the cultivation of the staple commodities of the island, has not been diminished. . . .[43]

In other colonies in the Windward Islands, St. Lucia, St. Vincent and Grenada, the better relationship between employers and employees was apparently beginning by a different means. From Colonel Graydon in St. Lucia to Sir Charles Grey, Governor at the end of April 1842: 'On some of these estates, however, a more cheering prospect has opened by a practice recently adopted between the planter and labourer of cultivating canes in halves, the latter furnishing labour to the planter in exchange for the use of land and machinery, and the profits being divided between them.'[44]

And before the Select Committee of 1842, Henry James Ross explained the working of 'the share or allotment system' on his estate in Grenada where he produced coffee and cocoa.[45]

When, however, Ralph Bernal, MP, an absentee proprietor of estates in Jamaica, suggested something of the kind to his attorney Mr McCook, the latter replied in April 1842:

The negroes of this country are too independent to wait for remuneration of their labour by any interest in the proceeds of the soil, and their minds are by no means yet settled down. So long as they have the waste lands to cultivate, they will only work for the estates when they please; and to adopt summary means to rout them out where they are squatting, and even located on the estate, would be dangerous.[46]

It was the McCooks of the post-emancipation period whose attitudes led to the exodus from the plantation.

John Scoble had visited Barbados, Trinidad and British Guiana. His views are corroborated by much of the other evidence given in 1842, and in the following passage the argument of this paper is nicely summarized.

MR BENJAMIN HAWES: 'What has generally been the conduct of the managers of estates towards the labourers, so far as you are acquainted with it from your own personal visit to the colony [British Guiana]?'
SCOBLE: 'I should say that the conduct generally, on the part of managers of estates towards the negroes, has not been conciliatory; on the contrary, they have brought with them into the state of freedom the habits and associations of slavery, and a degree of harshness has characterized their general conduct towards the negroes, both as to the manner in which they have conducted themselves towards them in the time of work and . . . out of the time of labour; they have treated them with great hauteur and distance, and exhibited much of pride and sometimes of violence towards them.'

[and then, later, on the same topic]

HAWES: 'What has been the result?'
SCOBLE: 'The result has been a great dissatisfaction on the part of the negroes. The consequence has been that they have turned out very reluctantly to work; that they have availed themselves of opportunities of changing their masters; and above all, they have thought it necessary to become purchasers of lots of land, and to render themselves by that means independent of that kind of conduct against which they have objected.'[47]

The movement of the ex-slaves from the estates in the immediate post-emancipation years was not a flight from the horrors of slavery. It was a protest against the inequities of early 'freedom'. It is possible that, had the ex-slaves been allowed to continue in free use of gardens, houses and grounds, and to choose their employers without reference to that accommodation, there would have been very little movement of agricultural labour at all from the communities apparently established on the estates during slavery.

If that conclusion be valid, certain other questions arise about the slave in the British Caribbean and his view of his own condition and of the estate on which he laboured. To say that the movement from the estates was not primarily motivated by desire to escape the scenes of slavery is not to say that the ex-slave remembered his servitude with any fondness. What seems to be of essential importance is whether the slave, as is described in Orlando Patterson's novel **Die the Long Day**,[48] clearly distinguished between his abject and miserable servitude on the **estate**, that is, in the service of his master, and his self-asserted independence in the privacy of his house and garden and the circle of his family. If he did, and there is some evidence of this in the reports of the slaves' attachment to their dwelling-places and to the burial plots of their relatives and their sense of belonging to the 'negro-house' community of the estate, then it is possible to argue a dichotomy of view: hatred of the estate, and love of home on the estate. If the slave did not so distinguish, his apparent reluctance to leave the estate as soon as he could would be very difficult to understand.

Notes

1. In quoting from this evidence I shall abbreviate by giving only the name of the person(s) giving evidence (where it is necessary to do so); the date, 1842; S.C. for Select Committee; and the number(s) of the Minute(s) of evidence quoted. For example, Campbell, 1842, S.C. 1914–20.
2. In **Caribbean Quarterly** Vol 3 No. 2, UWI Extra-Mural Department. Reprinted in Vol 10 No. 1.
3. Ibid.
4. **A Short History of the West Indies** (Macmillan, 1957), p. 195.
5. Jay R. Mandle, **The Plantation Economy, Population and Economic Change in Guyana, 1838–1860** (Temple University Press, Caribbean Edition, 1974), p. 22.
6. **Sugar Without Slaves. The Political Economy of British Guiana, 1838–1904** (Yale University Press, 1972) p. 34.
7. In **Caribbean Quarterly** Vol. 1 No. 4, UWI Extra-Mural Department. Reprinted in Vol. 10 No. 1.
8. Op. cit., p. 196.
9. F.R. Augier, S.C. Gordon, D.G. Hall, M. Reckord, **The Making of the West Indies** (Longman, 1976 edition), pp. 185–6.

10. Douglas Hall, **Free Jamaica, 1838–1865. An Economic History** (Yale University Press, 1959), p. 20. See also Don Robotham, 'Agrarian Relations in Jamaica' in **Essays on Power and Change in Jamaica** edited by Dr Carl Stone and Dr Aggrey Brown (Jamaica Publishing House, 1977), pp. 45–57. Robotham also takes Paget's argument and, I think, misrepresents mine quoted above.
11. **Jamaica, 1830–1930. A Study in Economic Growth** (Manchester University Press, 1961), p. 192.
12. See, for instance, William A. Green, **British Slave Emancipation. The Sugar Colonies and the Great Experiment, 1830–1865** (Clarendon Press, 1976), pp. 296–7 (following Paget), and Donald Wood, **Trinidad in Transition. The Years After Slavery** (Oxford University Press), p. 48 (following Farley).
13. Appendix III to the Report from the Select Committee on the West India Colonies, 1842.
14. Ibid.
15. Ibid. (One guilder was equal to about 1s.5d. sterling.)
16. But the others were not included in the correspondence sent by Captain Allen to the Governor.
17. This, and all other Reports from other Districts quoted below, are taken from Appendix III to the Report of the Select Committee.
18. MacCornock, 1842, S.C. 4551–4.
19. Lowndes, 1842, S.C. 4993–5.
20. 1842, S.C. 5648–54.
21. Geddes, 1842, S.C. 6645–8, 6764–7.
22. Christie, 1842, S.C. 7107–12, 7183–5.
23. Barkly, 1842, S.C. 2384.
24. Campbell, 1842, S.C. 2384.
25. Church, 1842, S.C. 2007–8.
26. Estridge, 1842, S.C. 3054.
27. Nugent, 1842, S.C. 2780–3.
28. Carrington, 1842, S.C. 1718, 1759–65.
29. Sharpe, 1842, S.C. 1519.
30. Grant, 1842, S.C. 83–5.
31. Sidney Mintz and Douglas Hall, 'The Origins of the Jamaican Internal Marketing System', in **Yale University Publications in Anthropology**, No. 57, 1960, pp. 3–26.
32. 1842, S.C. 2532.
33. 1842, S.C. 6974–5.
34. This is very clearly shown in the evidence given in 1842.
35. 1842, S.C. 7575–81.
36. 1842, S.C. 6845.
37. 1842, S.C. 3092–4, 3109.
38. Carrington, 1842, S.C. 1720.
39. Allen, 1842, S.C. 3698.
40. 1842, S.C. 6504–6.
41. Carrington, 1842, S.C. 1758–67; Geddes, 1842, S.C. 6652–74.
42. Scoble, 1842, S.C. 4250.
43. Appendix VI to the Report from the Select Committee on the West India Colonies, 1842.
44. Appendix IV to the Report from the Select Committee on the West India Colonies, 1842.
45. Ross, 1842, S.c. 7482–564.
46. Bernal, 1842, S.C. 6466.
47. 1842, S.C. 4272–4.
48. H. Orlando Patterson, **Die the Long Day** (Wm. Morrow, New York, 1972).

Metayage in the Sugar Industry of the British Windward Islands, 1838–1865

W. K. Marshall

Metayage[1] was an expedient adopted by many sugar planters in the British Windward Islands[2] during the economic depression of 1846–1855[3]. The coincidence of the commercial crisis of 1847–8, the loss of the protected market for sugar between 1846 and 1854 and a disastrous fall in sugar prices[4] in the same period produced an acute capital shortage in the islands and a great increase in the indebtedness of many estates. Proprietors, 'despondency' having 'quite taken possession' of all their energy, feared that they would have to abandon their estates.[5] Planters found it difficult and sometimes impossible to raise the necessary capital to pay the labourers who were already scarce and irregular in attendance but who nonetheless were vital to the existence of an estate-based sugar industry. At this juncture, many planters in St. Lucia, Tobago and Grenada resorted to metayage, that 'last resource of poverty'[6] which was already being exploited on a limited scale in St. Lucia and Tobago. They saw this system then, as planters in the Leeward Islands saw it then and later, as a 'desperate expedient' which would enable them to retain ownership of their estates and secure some profits from them during a period of depression.[7] They adopted a system which would allow them to pay wages in kind rather than in cash; the labourer, now in 'partnership'[8] rather than on wages, shared with the planter the risks, expenses and profits of sugar production. The labourer now supplied all the manual labour necessary for the cultivation, reaping and manufacture of the canes grown on a plot of land loaned to him by the planter: the planter supplied carts, stock and machinery for the manufacture of the sugar; and the sugar produced was shared between them.

This method of sugar production was never intended by the planters to be a system of land tenure or a permanent feature of industrial activity.[9] The planter had become, to some extent, a landlord, but he regarded this status as only temporary and, therefore, he refused either to regularize the new system or to examine its social and economic implications. The important point was that metayage could lead to a new system of land tenure and to vital and overdue structural reforms of the sugar industry. The fuller involvement of the labourers in the business of sugar production could lead to the establishment of large estate tenantries or to the creation of a class of cane farmers. Either of these innovations could have been exploited to secure a separation of cultivation of the cane from the manufacture of the sugar. At the same time, the enthusiastic participation of the negroes in the system certainly indicated the probable success of the reform. To achieve this reform would have involved a fundamental modification of the social attitudes of the planters. They would have had to realize that the appearance of a peasantry would neither affect seriously their positions of social and economic dominance, nor supply conclusive evidence of the negroes' supposed indolence and apathy.

Most of the planters could not make the necessary adjustment. The same attitudes of habituation which led them to refuse for a long time both to sell land to the negro labourers and to frame regulations to facilitate the disposal of Crown lands to labourers conditioned their reaction to metayage. Consequently, the significant implications of the metayage system never really engaged the attention of the planters. When they found that they could no longer maintain a successful opposition to the introduction or extension of the system they hoped to dispense with its unpalatable necessity as soon as the cycle of prosperity, repaired by imperial aid in the form of new protection for their sugar and pushed by immigration from Africa and Asia, inevitably turned their way again. But, fortunately, since they no longer controlled the situation as completely as they had done in the days of slavery, there was a limited opportunity for metayage to demonstrate its potential as an industrial reform and social solvent.

Metayage was a relic of French occupation of the islands, notably St. Lucia,[10] and it was used in that island on most of the early coffee and cotton estates.[11] In St. Lucia, metayage was extended to sugar cultivation around 1840 and its rapid and apparently successful extension in this industry ensured, with the help of official blessing, that it would be tried in the other islands experiencing similar problems of capital and labour shortage. The depression after 1846 provided the occasion for the extended trial of the system in the other islands. But it must be noted that there was more than a semblance of distinction between the economic positions of the different islands which was perhaps reflected in the several planters' use of the metayage system. All the islands were small[12] and the sugar industry in each groaned under the accumulated weight of encumbrance and indebtedness. But both Grenada and St. Vincent were more densely populated than St. Lucia and Tobago[13] and also possessed stronger economies as a result of the presence of a larger sugar industry and of elements of a less monocultural structure.[14] These factors might have given the planters some hope of acquiring and profitably exploiting immigrant labour. St. Lucia was roughly double the size of any of the other islands but its population was only about three-quarters the size of that of Grenada and St. Vincent. Tobago struggled with a very small population, constitutional crises, limited industrial activity and no money for immigration. In addition, its proximity to the more attractive area of investment in Trinidad further inhibited its chances of sustained capitalist economic development. These factors perhaps explain why metayage was used extensively in Tobago and St. Lucia, but only on a restricted scale in St. Vincent and Grenada.

In St. Vincent, metayage was hardly used on the sugar estates throughout the period. Between 1848 and 1850, a few St. Vincent planters did experiment with the system but they soon found, as stipendiary magistrate Polson reported, that it was 'certainly not an improvement'.[15] In the few instances that it was used many disputes developed between the planters and the labourers over interpretation of the metayage agreement; and in addition, the planters were reported to have persuaded the labourers, who presumably were pressing for the introduction of the system, that the sugar 'crop does not repay the grower the cost of cultivation'![16] However, the system continued to be used on the cotton estates of St. Vincent and perhaps also on the cotton provision estates of the Grenadines,[17] the dependency of St. Vincent. In December 1851, stipendiary magistrate Polson reported that one hundred and nine 'heads of families' were engaged in metayage cultivation on cotton estates in the Windward district of St. Vincent.[18]

In Grenada, the use of metayage in sugar production was limited by the attitude of many planters to the system. Stipendiary magistrate Hutcheson reported in June 1850 that five out of every seven planters had opposed the introduction of the system.[19] Hutcheson did not state the reason for this opposition, but presumably the planters were opposed to any innovation which seemed likely to lesson their profits and to weaken their control over the disposal of land and allocation of the negroes' labour. The depression in the sugar industry did force some of them to adopt the system between 1848[20] and 1850 but they hastened to abandoned or curtail its use in the mid-fifties when the promise of immigration and rising sugar prices[21] provided them with a palliative for their troubles. A 'majority' of the ninety-five estates used the system in 1850,[22] but by the late fifties it seemed as though it was the coffee and, particularly, the cocoa estates which provided a stimulus for the survival and extension of the system.[23] The new and expanding cocoa estates which enjoyed little if any of the small scale boom in the sugar industry needed the system and used it extensively. By 1854, nearly all of these estates were being cultivated exclusively on some sort of metayage system.[24] The result of this conversion and of peasant activity in cocoa cultivation was that the cocoa industry dethroned sugar by 1880.[25]

In St. Lucia and, particularly, in Tobago metayage cultivation became an important and more permanent part of the sugar industry. In St. Lucia, metayage enjoyed its first extended trial even before the depression, and was described in 1842 as 'an important and distinguished feature of agricultural process' in the island.[26] As early as December 1840, the proprietor of Beau Sejour estate had received so many applications for metayage contracts that he said that within two years he could cultivate his estate completely on the system.[27] In 1844, M. Beauce proprietor of Anse Canot estate, was encouraged to buy the neighbouring estate so that he could 'meet the demands of his labourers for more land to clear away and plant in canes' on the metayage system. Stipendiary magistrate de Brossard reported that the neighbouring planters were so impressed by this display that they were following Beauce's example.[28] By the end of the same year, all estates appeared to be using the system to some extent,[29] and by 1848, metayage was responsible for a quarter of the sugar cane cultivation.[30] Stipendiary magistrate Drysdale reported in 1848 that metayage labour had produced 8,768 cwts of one district's total sugar crop of 19,881 cwts.[31] This type of development, aided by the depression, continued until the mid-fifties when the improvement in the sugar market and the promise of immigration caused a general decline in the use of the system. By 1861, Administrator Breen was rejoicing at its disappearance: he reported that only one estate was still cultivated completely on the system and that 'the few estates' on which it was 'still found to linger' were 'among the least prosperous in the colony.'[32]

In Tobago, chronic financial distress which was compounded by a constitutional crisis in 1846–7[33] and a devastating hurricane in 1847[34] provided the ideal conditions for the most extensive use of metayage and for its permanence. The system was first introduced in 1843 and, according to H.I. Woodcock, was 'generally resorted to' in 1845 because 'such was the depression' that metayage seemed the only means of ensuring against abandonment of the estates lacking the 'means to pay in money for labour'.[35] During the economic depression extension of the system was very marked: in six months in 1852–3 the number of metayers in one district increased from 208 to 500.[36] This process continued throughout the fifties because, unlike the other islands, Tobago had little or no capital available to pay wages or finance immigration. Lieut.-Governor Drysdale reported in 1858 that 'there was scarcely an estate on which the share system had not been introduced to a greater or less extent, many of them, even some of the larger, being entirely worked by metayers'.[37] In 1862, he wrote that metayage still prevailed 'to a considerable extent' despite 'all its defects' because of the 'present low rate of wages'.[38] Drysdale estimated in 1858 that 'at least one-third' of the island's sugar crop for 1857 was the product of metayers' labour;[39] and by 1897 when metayage was disappearing in most of the islands the Royal Commission discovered that sugar cane cultivation in Tobago was carried on solely on the metayage system.[40]

From this survey it becomes clear that the planters' necessity was the main reason for the trail and extension of the system. Renee Augier proprietor of Mount Lizard estate in St. Lucia and one of the first planters to convert an estate metayage cultivation, spoke for many planters when he declared in 1842:

From the impossibility to which I find myself reduced and with the full knowledge I have of the country, I may say, from the impossibility to which we are all reduced, of continuing the cultivation of our land, I consider that there remains but this experiment in the art of cultivation to sustain our manufactories until more prosperous times may, with the blessing of Providence, arrive.[41]

Official opinion, both local and metropolitan, shared this conclusion. Col. Graydon, the Lieut.-Governor of St. Lucia, described metayage in 1841 as 'one of the surest foundations of the wealth and prosperity of the colony' provided it could be properly regulated.[42] The Colonial Secretary, Lord Stanley, was favourably impressed by this type of enthusiastic comment and report. He asked the Governor-in-Chief for full details of the system, and gave it his blessing because, as he said, the system 'appears to be well adapted to the present circumstances of the colonies, but which seems to have been proportionately much more generally introduced into St. Lucia than in any other colony from which reports have reached me.'[43] Planters in the other islands were thus encouraged to adopt the system, and after 1846–8 they did so because they could ill afford to spurn any measure of relief, no matter how temporary.

Continuing distress tended to change the character of the innovation. Since 'more prosperous times' obstinately refused to reappear, particularly after 1846–8, metayage became a more permanent feature of the sugar industry than the planters had intended it to be. Smaller profits, sometimes an inability to pay money wages and strikes for higher wages forced further extensions of metayage 'not from choice but from necessity'.[44] In Grenada in 1848 payment in money wages was generally suspended and replaced by metayage or by labour for rent.[45] Stipendiary magistrate Dowland reported from Tobago in 1849 that an extension of metayage had been stimulated by the embarrassment of the planters whom, he thought, calculated 'best for their own interest'.[46] In St. Lucia, the crisis situation also gave impetus to the extension of metayage and defeated any further attempts by the planters to 'swamp' it by offering the inducement of higher wages to the labourers.[47] A St. Lucian planter bluntly declared at this time: 'if we cannot get a good day's work at reduced wages, we must then work our estates on the Metairie system'.[48] H.H. Breen, the Administrator of St Lucia, summed up in his 1860 report the case for the stark necessity, which brought the system into operation on a large scale.

'So long as the price of sugar continued unsatisfactory', he wrote, 'the planters and labourers were drawn towards each other for mutual cooperation and assistance; each possessed what the other wanted; and a union of means and division of profits was natural result'.[49]

The planter-labourer relationship was secured by the metayage contracts or agreements. These contracts were the planters' instruments for securing the objectives of continued production through retention of the traditional labour force and economies in production costs' and largely because of these emphasis interpretation of the contracts was one of the most fruitful sources of dispute between planters and labourers. The contracts differed greatly from estate to estate, were made orally,[50] and usually extremely and deliberately vague in the definition of rights and responsibilities. Consequently, they furnished many opportunities for misunderstanding and even for fraud.

Generally, the planter supplied the land, usually one acre in size,[51] to be cultivated in canes by the labourer in 'a proper planter-like and regular manner'.[52] The labourer was entirely responsible for providing the labour used in clearing the land where necessary and in the cultivation of the canes. On some estates, particularly those in Tobago and Grenada,[53] the metayer was also responsible for the cutting of the canes and for the haulage to the planter's factory with the help of the planter's carts and stock. On these estates, he was also responsible for supplying the labour used in the manufacture of the sugar: he was to perform, said a printed contract in one of the Tobago districts, 'all the work usually done by the Mill Gang, Megass Carriers, and Firemen'. In addition, he had to assist in the potting of the sugar.[54] On some other estates, particularly those in St. Lucia, the labour costs of manufacture and sometimes the costs of cutting and haulage were equally shared by the planter and the metayer.[55] In return for this labour the metayer received half of the sugar produced from the canes grown on the plot of land. But if he had received a field of ratoons from the planter he only received one-third and, sometimes, one-fifth of the sugar. The metayer usually had to wait until all the sugar was sold before he realized his share of the proceeds; but some contracts left the metayer free to dispose of his sugar as he wished. In those cases he could either sell it to the planter who was obliged to pay the market price promptly and in cash, or he could ship it off to Britain on his own account.[56]

The planter was usually responsible for superintendence of the cultivation of the canes and the manufacture of the sugar and for the provision of stock, carts, and machinery for the manufacture of the sugar. Occasionally, he also supplied pen manure and the plant canes. In return for these services he received half of the sugar (or a larger share when he supplied a field of ratoons) and in most cases, all the molasses and rum. On some estates in Grenada and Tobago the rum was shared between planter and metayer, with the metayer receiving a gallon of rum for every barrel of his own sugar.[57] For contracts were clearly defined. In general, whether they were oral or written, they seemed to conform to the specimen of a contract, certified by the stipendiary magistrate, which was supplied in Colquhoun, a St. Lucien stipendiary magistrate. This contract was brief, vague and, though written, highly informal:

It is agreed between the undersigned AB Proprietor of ----- estate, on the one part, and CD labourer, of the other part, that the said CD shall cultivate in canes certain lands on ---- estate as shall be pointed out by the said AB more particularly; the canes when ripe to be cut, carried to, and manufactured into sugar at the work of ---- estate; the expense of such cutting, carriage, manufacture to be deducted from the gross proceeds of the sugar, after which deduction the remaining balance to be equally divided between the proprietor of ---- estate and the said CD whose signatures are affixed below.[58]

The one notable example of a clearly defined contract was that adopted on the Black Bay estate in St. Lucia during 1848. This written contract included exact provisions on the amount of stock to be included in the 'association' and how much stock should be replaced and divided, the number of weedings the canes should receive, the time and place for the division of the sugar, the allocation of provision grounds to metayers, the penalties on the metayers for breach of contract, and machinery for the dissolution and renewal of the contract.[59] This was clearly an exception; many stipendiary magistrates reported that there was no stated time limit to most contracts (though the customary contractual period was one year); and there was often doubt, uncertainty and dispute over the agreed provisions of the contract.

The deficiencies of the general type of contract were obvious. Such contracts guaranteed little to the metayer while they seemed to secure most of the planter's objectives. Such contracts, as stipendiary magistrate Dowland said, were 'one-sided' since the metayer was left 'very much open to the will and caprice of the landlord'.[60] These contracts had no provision for notice to quit, no machinery to secure compensation for the metayer if he was forced to surrender land with a crop on it, and no stipulation of the extent of the metayer's responsibility for damage to the planter's stock, carts and machinery. But, most important of all, these contracts offered no firm guarantee to the metayer of his rights of possession, security of tenure and a clear claim to a share of the crop. This last omission or imprecision was particularly important in the context of heavily encumbered West Indian property. Often, the proprietor who sanctioned a contract was merely in nominal possession and, consequently, had no power to enforce all its provisions; and lessees often had no authority to enter metayage contracts. Thus there was an urgent necessity to create machinery for the rational administration of the system and especially for the protection of the metayer against his planter-employer-landlord.

Metayers' complaints against the working of the system highlighted those deficiencies. Many metayers were dissatisfied with the arrangement for the manufacture of their canes and for the division of the sugar produced. Some felt that the planters never divided fairly and honestly either the expenses of manufacture or the sugar itself. They alleged — and were supported by at least one stipendiary magistrate[61] — that when the costs of manufacture were shared by planters and metayers the planter seldom rendered an honest account of these costs. They suspected that when the planter made money advances against the metayer's crop he proceeded to fiddle the accounts to ensure that the value of the metayer's share of sugar equalled the advances.[62] Many metayers objected to the retention of the molasses and rum by the planter; they thought that this represented an unfair loss of a share of their own produce since the planter could choose to make more molasses than sugar.[63] Many metayers also objected to the delay in fixing a time and place for the division of the sugar or its cash value. They did not relish the long wait while the sugar was sold on the British market; the delay fed their suspicions of the planter's honesty and scrupulousness. If they did have to wait, they often considered the return 'too remote, too small and unsatisfactory'.[64] They preferred an early division of the produce even if this did mean that the price they received for a local sale did not 'realize their expectations'.[65]

Far more serious was the metayers' grievance over the reaping and manufacture of their canes. Stipendiary magistrates in Tobago, St. Lucia and Grenada concurred in the opinion that many planters either from 'Motives of personal pique or petty revenge' seemed to have decided 'to postpone indefinitely the manufacture of canes brought to maturity at the cost of much toil and solicitude on the part of the poor labourer'.[66] The planter, perhaps naturally, gave priority in manufacture to the estate canes produced by wage labour. But this should not have meant, as it often did, that the metayer's canes were reaped so late that the sugar yield was reduced and the cane stools for a crop of ratoons damaged. Sometimes, indeed, the metayer's canes were not reaped at all.[67] A case in Grenada illustrated the nature and the extent of the loss which metayers could and did suffer. A metayer, Grand Frere, asked his landlord, Charles Renwick to reap his canes because rats were destroying them. The landlord delayed six months before he acceded to the request, but by that time the sucrose content of the canes had virtually disappeared. The metayer was forced to accept his loss because he could not afford to seek compensation through a civil action against the landlord.[68] As stipendiary magistrate Dowland said of a similar and more extreme incident in Tobago in 1850, 'such a spoil-

ation of property' led 'to heart-burning and distrust' and rendered the labourers 'unsettled and erratic'.[69]

These grievances pointed to the central weakness of the general type of contract — its failure to give the metayer real security both to a share of the crop he produced and to tenure of the land he cultivated. Apparently, the landlord could not be held guilty of breach of contract; he could terminate the agreement whenever he chose. He might be forced to give merely nominal verbal notice to quit — eight days 'to clear' his land as in the Black Bay contract — or he was not obliged to give notice at all. He could not be compelled to offer compensation, and some planters even felt, as Dowland reported, that if a labourer left employment on an estate then the estate's manager could confiscate the canes which the labourer might have been cultivating on a metayer contract.[70] The metayer could thus in summary fashion lose all the profit on his investment in a plant crop and in his succeeding crops of ratoons. This would indeed have been poor reward for these who had, as stipendiary magistrate de Brossard reported, 'cleared up uncultivated lands, felled forests and built houses, open canals, put up enclosures, and given themselves up to the culture of the sugar cane'.[71] In this situation, the metayer's only real protection lay in what Stanley had called 'the present circumstances of the colonists'. The landlord could be tempted to end the metayer's contract summarily by the fact that the metayer's labour had provided him with a field prepared for cultivation or in cultivation, but he would be restrained by a realization of the likely effect of his action. Such action, as stipendiary magistrate Johnston observed, would 'alienate his labourers' who would almost certainly desert the estate because of 'such unfair dealing'.[72]

The total situation could only be remedied by clear and precise rulings in the law courts and by legislation. The law courts of St. Lucia and Tobago managed to give definite status to the contract, but only the St. Lucia legislature succeeded in providing adequate guarantees for the metayers. But, in St. Lucia, some six years were spent in persuasion and correspondence before the ordinance was finally accepted by the legislature. Two factors probably accounted for the general hesitation or reluctance to clarify the legal position of the system and the contract. Firstly, most planters regarded metayage as a temporary expedient and therefore were not prepared to take any action that might render it permanent. Secondly, the legislatures were forced to be most circumspect in tampering with 'the rights of property'.[73] Most proprietors were absentee and many of those resident were in nominal possession. Therefore, it was difficult for the planter-legislators to act, even if they wanted to, on an issue which affected so closely the interest of their vital capitalist connections in Britain. But, in hesitating, they sacrificed the rights of labourers who had no spokesmen but the stipendiary magistrates.[74]

But the stipendiary magistrates themselves possessed little political influence and, worse, had no solid basis for the judicial authority they partially exercised over metayage agreements. From the inception of the system they had certified the few written contracts and had urged all metayers to seek written contracts with clear guarantees of their rights. They had attempted to mediate in disputes between planters and metayers and had tried without much success to treat these disputes and the general administration of the system as part of the functions of their magistracy. But they had soon recognized that this treatment was wholly inadequate. Metayer-planter disputes could not be regarded merely as labourer-planter disputes over which the stipendiary magistrates had been explicitly given jurisdiction. The metayer was not obviously a labourer, though he might still be a day labourer as well; he might be termed a tenant. The planter was not only an employer; he was, to some extent, a landlord. In such a new and complex situation the stipendiary magistrate's authority over metayage agreements could be challenged — and was successfully challenged in St. Lucia in 1843 and 1844. Therefore, the magistrates, from their vantage point of the third party most involved in the operation of the system, saw right from the start the necessity to create efficient machinery to administer the system. Perhaps they had a vested interest in securing such reform since the reform would most likely involve an extension of their own power and authority; but clearly too they were so conversant with the many deficiencies in the system and contracts that they were the persons best qualified to suggest and administer the remedy. Many of their reports listed a 'public law' on metayage to be administered by the stipendiary magistrates as one of the most urgent reforms. Drysdale called in 1844 for 'one uniform and well digested system founded on rules of justice and enforced by rules and restrictions calculated to sustain the interests of both proprietors and cultivators'.[75]

Many of the magistrates concentrated their attention and criticism on that weakest section of the system — the metayer's security of tenure and his unquestioned right to a full and fair share of the crop. Repair of this deficiency involved, they recognized, a definition of the status of the contract as well as the creation of machinery to administer the system. The question had to be asked and

answered: was the metayage agreement a lease of land or a contract for labour with payment in kind? If the metayer was a tenant it would be relatively easy to establish his rights to tenure and to a share of the crop; the civil courts could order compensation for the injured party. But if the metayer was merely a labourer he was always liable to lose the fruits of his industry, particularly on mortgaged and encumbered estates, unless some check was placed on the unscrupulous exercise of the planter's power. Needless to say, there was no doubt how the planters would have answered the question; they saw metayage as merely a device to retain labourers. But, on the other hand, the metayers, supported by the stipendiary magistrates, obviously saw themselves as tenants.

These problems were highlighted and partly solved in St. Lucia and Tobago by law court cases and judgements. In St. Lucia, the decisions in two cases in 1843 and 1844 caused great confusion because they upset customary practice; and this confusion was only dissipated by eventual legislative action which itself was perhaps precipitated to some extent by the decisions. In the first case, metayers on the Saphir estate petitioned against a court order which had allowed the proprietor of the estate to seize all the sugar produced by the estate in settlement of the proprietor's claims against the deeply indebted lessee of the estate. The metayers, with oral contracts, had been unaware of the lessee's indebtedness and they only discovered their error of omission when their sugar was seized along with the rest of the estate's sugar. The stipendiary magistrates and the Attorney General interceded on their behalf, but without success. The Chief Justice ruled that since he could find no evidence of a metayage contract (and in any case the lessee had no authority under his lease to use the metayage system) the metayers were entitled to one month's wages. Clearly, the Chief Justice was inclined to treat the metayers as labourers; the compensation he awarded was the maximum amount of wages labourers could claim under the Master/Servant Acts, if they held unwritten labour contracts on the estates.[76]

The Rabot estate case in 1844 was more important because it was the occasion of the expression of Attorney General Athill's opinion on the status of the metayage contract. Two metayers, possessing a written contract, certified by a stipendiary magistrate, had petitioned with the support of the stipendiary magistrate for a privileged claim on the occasion of the judicial sale of the heavily encumbered estate. Their petition was dismissed, but when the issue was referred to the Attorney General he dissented from the courts' decisions in both cases. He argued that the metayage contract was a lease of land, — a civil issue requiring civil remedies which did not bring it within the competence of the stipendiary magistrates. He wrote:

As this case, in my opinion, does not come within the classes of cases contemplated by the order in Council regulating the duties of Special Justices, and as their interference leads to erroneous impression and false hopes on the part of the population taking land for cultivation, especially where the lessor or proprietor is insolvent or embarrassed circumstances, I would respectfully suggest the propriety of cautioning the Special Justices against having executed ... before them any instruments not positively coming within the operation of the abovementioned Order in Council.[77]

This opinion had the weight of a definitive ruling because it had the support of the decisive official opinion, local as well as metropolitan. By the middle of 1844, Lord Stanley, the Colonial Secretary and the Governor-in-Chief, Sir Charles Edward Grey were both advising that the metayage contract was a farming lease.[78] 'The metayer' said Stanley, was 'in fact a tenant paying rent in kind', and it was evident that 'the nature of the cultivation requires a longer term. The longer the term, indeed the greater the interest in the land, and the approximation to ownership which it is so important to encourage'.[79] The lead was followed to some extent by the Tobago law courts. In 1853 and 1857, the Tobago Chief Justice ruled in the face of strong planter opposition that tenancy under the metayage contract existed from crop to crop, and could be terminated either by mutual consent or at the end of the crop if six months' notice had been given.[80]

Serious difficulties remained, however, as Athill's ruling had serious implications for the existence of metayage in St. Lucia. In the first place, though the contract was elevated to the status of a lease, the challenge to the stipendiary magistrates' authority had destroyed the only cheap and efficient machinery for the creation of the new contract in written form. Secondly, since it was the needy proprietors and lessees who required the expedient of metayage most urgently, the failure to create simultaneously the machinery to administer the system would paralyze the whole system and thus deprive these planters of a vital respite. Thirdly, there was little point in directing the metayers to seek redress for their grievances in the civil courts. Many labourers seemed to fear that they would lose their previous freedom if they became involved in litigation. Moreover, litigation was too expensive for the majority of them. A metayer could ill afford to lose a day's wages (if he was a day labourer as well) and pay the costs of travel and legal representation out of the £7 —

'the one or two barrels of sugar' — which might be at stake.[81]

Consequently, it was not surprising that a great deal of uncertainty and confusion was created among the metayers and stipendiary magistrates in St. Lucia after 1844. The judicial decision and Athill's ruling had gone far to upset customary procedure, to weaken what few guarantees of protection the metayers might have possessed, and to threaten the existence of the system. In such a situation, the negro labourers were both quick and apt to imagine the worst. A rumour, originating with a metayer who had been told by a stipendiary magistrate to seek redress for his injury in the civil courts, circulated strongly around St. Lucia during 1845: the British government had abolished metayage and the penalty for defiance of this order was a return to slavery.[82] It was obvious then that, in the absence of a clearly defined ordinance, the prospects for the continued existence of the system were not bright; stipendiary magistrate Johnson feared in 1845 that metayage might become 'a thing that was',[83] and Governor-in-Chief Sir William Colebrooke reported in 1850 that the continuing uncertain situation was not only a 'check to industry in the cultivation of the staples' but also created 'the possibility of Agrarian disturbance'.[84]

Fortunately for the existence of the system in St. Lucia, official opinion, both local and metropolitan, concurred in the suggestions for reform of the system made biannually by the stipendiary magistrates. This combination eventually wore down the planters' opposition to regularization of the system. By 1845, the British Colonial Secretary, Stanley, and the Governor-in-Chief, Grey had agreed on the type of legislation necessary in St. Lucia. The ordinance should contain provisions for written contracts which would be drawn up, certified and supervised by the stipendiary magistrates who would possess summary jurisdiction in cases of dispute involving a maximum of three acres of land or £20 in claims for compensation. Yet there was delay for another five years before the ordinance was passed by the Legislative Council. The reasons for this delay were the familiar ones: there was no anxiety on the part of the planters to protect the rights and existence of the metayers; but there was great solicitude for the guarantee of the rights of property. The deadlock was eventually broken, apparently by the promise of concessions and by the persuasiveness and energy of Henry Darling, the Lieutenant-Governor. Darling, unlike the governors in the islands with representative assemblies, was well placed to use his initiative. Crown Colony government, which existed in St. Lucia, did not erect the imposing and formal political and constitutional barriers against the acceptance of the

Executive's recommendations which often hampered administration in the islands under the Old Representative System. Darling probably did not understand fully the distinction between metayer and labourer, but with the impressive support of his superior in Barbados[86] he was intent on securing guarantees of the metayers' and labourers' rights through legislation. He sought their protection against the intervention of estates' creditors:

I am a strong advocate myself for making the labourer's remuneration, whether in kind or wages, a prior lien to all other claims of every description except the public taxes; but this doctrine finds little favour among those interested in the colonies, whether residents or absentees.[87]

In addition, some concessions to the planters interest had to be granted, and these were clearly written into the ordinance which was finally proclaimed in St. Lucia in April 1850.

Compromise was the chief characteristic of this ordinance for 'the better protection of lessees and of persons cultivating land in shares upon the Metairie System'.[88] The general administrative and judicial details of the system were settled by three essential provisions. Firstly, the metayage contract was given legal equality with a lease, which itself was given a nine year limit. Secondly, contracts had to be executed in writing in duplicate before the stipendiary magistrates of the particular districts who had to certify that they were voluntary and understood by both parties; and, in addition, the magistrates then had to send the contracts to the Registrar's office where they could be filed. All other contracts were declared void, but those who held informal contracts were guaranteed their shares and were entitled to recover losses through the courts. Thirdly, disputes would be settled in the local Courts of Requests, which could not adjudicate on questions of original title, nor award more than £8 in claims. Appeal from the courts was also guaranteed.

The more delicate question of the rights of proprietors and mortgagees, on the one hand, and those of metayers, on the other, was settled by a nice balance of guarantees. In the first place, before the contract was finalized, the stipendiary magistrates had to secure a certificate from the Registrar showing whether the land was encumbered or mortgaged. If it was encumbered, the magistrate had to serve notice within ten days on the mortgagee or his legal agent calling on him to reply within three months with his objection or assent to the intended contract. If there was no objection or no reply, the contract was executed. This served the dual purpose of informing the metayer of the

financial position of the estate, and at the same time, it gave the mortgagee the power to refuse the contract. Secondly, if some of the mortgagees refused the contract, the judge in the local High Court was given the authority to execute it so long as three-quarters of the mortgagees and encumbrancers in amount and number agreed to it; and such contracts would be limited to three years. This would prevent a minority of the mortgagees from wrecking the system or from securing for themselves a more privileged position in respect of claims on the estate. The balance of argument was against Earl Grey who feared that the court might decide to execute the contract even though it might be obvious 'that the assent of a majority of encumbrancers had been obtained under circumstances of hardship, possibly even fraud'.[89]

Thirdly and most important, all purchasers of land, in private and judicial sales, were obliged to respect all metayage contracts registered before the sale; and the Provost Marshal was directed to publish all contracts before judicial sales were finalized. This ensured not only that the metayer's security of tenure and right to a share of the crop were respected, but also that his priority of claims on the estate was established against succeeding mortgages and encumbrances. At the same time, the balance of guarantees was preserved by explicit regulations, in the case of judicial sales, to inform the new proprietors of the extent of their obligations.

This was a fair measure in the circumstances and, as such, was a triumph for its chief advocates — the stipendiary magistrates, Attorney General Athill and Lieutenant-Governor Darling. Their efforts fully merited Earl Grey's commendation of the Ordinance as 'well considered and framed with careful attention to detail'.[90] Perhaps these details were its slight weakness. The three months' moratorium on the new contracts involving encumbered property might have serious consequences in an agricultural community where the seasons never obeyed the exigencies of legislation. In addition, the stipendiary magistrates, their duties now multiplied, had to be particularly conscientious and vigilant if they were to afford the metayers the protection the law provided. But generally, there could be no serious complaint; the Attorney General could be excused his self-congratulation:

It is scarcely possible . . . that any injustice, surprise or inequitable interference with vested interests can arise, while the most obvious injustice in the existing laws of the island are swept away by the provisions of an Ordinance, upon which (I believe) more minds have been engaged, and to which more anxious attention has been directed than upon almost any recent subject of local legislation.[91]

Unfortunately, the planters in the other islands were not disposed towards following this lead even though the situation in those islands also required similar comprehensive action. This refusal to act was perhaps explained by two factors. Firstly, it was far more difficult in these islands with representative assemblies for official opinion, local and metropolitan, to win its way. Secondly, the planters in Tobago and Grenada had much less experience in the system than those in St. Lucia and, consequently, had been exposed to less pressure for reform of the system. To the former, metayage, because of its more recent introduction, seemed more obviously an expedient; and they could more fervently hope that the necessity for it would quickly disappear. In the meantime, they could and did resist action; and Tobago planters continued to resist even when it should have become clear in the late fifties and early sixties that metayage had come to Tobago to stay. In addition, there was the force of the general factor which applied to all the islands. The metayers, not the planters, suffered most keenly from the tardy definition of the status of the contract and from the delay and refusal to create machinery to administer and supervise the system. The planters were mainly concerned with exploiting the material advantages inherent in the temporary expedient they had adopted; they were not interested in creating conditions for its permanence.

The advantages of the system to the planters were clear. Generally, it helped to salvage the depressed estate-based sugar industry, for metayage usually succeeded in maintaining the extent of cane cultivation and the level of sugar production without increasing the already crippling liabilities of the estates. As a result, many estates, particularly those weighted down with debt and encumbrance, were saved from abandonment during and even after 'the period of great industrial distress'.[92] Three specific advantages could be noted. In the first place, the planter avoided some of the costs of production, and he achieved economies in the costs of superintendence of cultivation and protection of the growing crops. The planter, stipendiary magistrate Colquhoun reported, was exempted from 'all those heart-burning annoyances, from theft of canes and trespass of stock' which were 'such fertile sources of disputes between employers and labourers'.[93] Secondly, sugar production did not decline; indeed in some cases, it increased significantly, while in others relatively high profits were made. In 1846, Grenada, St. Lucia and Tobago exported 8,966 tons of sugar to the U.K.; in 1850 and 1852 these exports rose to 9,552 tons and 13,342 tons[94] respectively; in 1855 these exports fell to 8,613 tons. In St. Lucia and Tobago where

metayage was used most extensively the situation was similar. In St. Lucia there was a steady increase in sugar exports throughout the period, while in Tobago the level of sugar exports remained constant.[95]

An increase in production after metayage had been introduced, was noted on some of the St. Lucia estates. The Balembouche and Saphir estates produced ninety-five hogsheads of sugar by wage labour in 1840 but the managers of these estates forecast a crop of 350 hogsheads produced by metayage labour for 1842.[96] Lieutenant-Governor Darling's analysis of production costs on six of the St. Lucia estates during 1847 revealed that the only two which showed a profit in that year were operating on metayage — one partially, the other completely. These two estates returned profits of £84.5.11d and £482.5.9d respectively, while the other four estates incurred losses ranging from £337.17.2d to £845.15.0d. Stipendiary magistrate Drysdale, who supplied these details,[97] declared that a higher yield per acre and cheaper production costs achieved through the avoidance of certain costs were the reasons for the relative success of the estates operated on metayage.[98] Finally, metayage helped to maintain the dominance of the staple concept and of the sugar industry over the islands' economies. As stipendiary magistrate Colquhoun reported from St. Lucia, metayage encouraged the labourers to accept 'the paramount necessity of cane cultivation', and helped to attach many of them and their children to the soil.[99] Planter and labourer were linked, between all parties concerned in the cultivation of the same tracts of land'.[100] Such a situation, in its turn, might have helped to improve industrial relations by softening the mutual antagonisms of planters and labourers.

The economic advantages were perhaps most readily apparent on the smaller estates. Operations on these estates involved a limited area of land and small outlays of capital. What was required for continued and even successful operation was some stock and a serviceable mill, which the planter might be able to afford, and labour for cultivation and manufacture which the metayer could provide. Little, if any, loss of production might result from this 'union of means'. But on the larger estates this advantage was not so easily apparent. A decline in production could follow the adoption of metayage because on such estates more capital was required to run the estates and the factories, and because the fragmentation of the labour force implicit in metayage could inhibit the operations of those large units where, as S.M. Bennett said, 'all operations from one end of the year to the other, both on the field and in the sugar works, must be in intimate, orderly and well timed relation to each other'.[101] But this probable disadvantage could be discounted during the period of depression. Then metayage seemed the one barrier against complete ruin of many estates, large and small. The traditional props of the industry had been removed and only metayage seemed to ensure against immediate and total collapse. The system became important at this time to many planters in Tobago, St. Lucia and Grenada because it represented almost completely the possibilities of the continued cultivation of the sugar estates.

On the other hand, the planters did experience some disadvantages which strengthened their opposition of the extension and formalization of the system. The planters' principal grievances, related to their loss of control over the traditional labour force. To them, it seemed that this loss of control entailed a diminution in size of the labour force, a deterioration in the quality of cultivation, a reduction in the amount of sugar normally produced, and a loss of profits. In the first place, the planters contended that the metayers devoted so much time and energy to their provision grounds and to cultivation of the land held under metayage agreement that routine estate labour was neglected. It would have been surprising if this had not been the situation. Regular wage labour for the estates was scarce before the depression, and during the depression there was less money available either to pay wage labour at the new reduced rates[102] or to offer the inducement of higher wages which alone could have attracted a larger labour force. Obviously, this particular criticism ignored the *raison d'etre* of the metayage system.

Secondly, the planters accused many metayers of slovenly un-'planter-like' cane cultivation which resulted in reduced sugar yield. Lieutenant-Governor Drysdale of Tobago reported that in some instances the canes were left 'to struggle against weeds and weather, without the aid of the hoe or the benefit of manure of any kind', and that the land impoverished in this manner was 'soon abandoned for the repetition of a like exhausted and fruitless attempt elsewhere'.[103] From this type of example, the planters, like those in many countries,[104] concluded that the permanent use of metayage would constitute an unsurmountable obstacle to agricultural improvements. This criticism could be applied to those metayers (estate labourers as well as tradesmen and domestic servants)[105] who were so intent on improving their social status and material position that they either cultivated more land and at greater distances than they could manage comfortably, or used metayage 'as secondary to, and as an excuse for obtaining land for extending that of provisions'.[106] The criticism could also be applied to those metayers who were dissatisfied

with either the arrangement for, or effects on their profits of, cash advances from landlords. If the metayers received liberal advances, they made little or no profit on their crop, and this often led them to abandon the estates 'in discontent'.[107] If, on the other hand, they failed to receive either liberal advances from their landlords or extensive credit from the shopkeepers, some of them, as stipendiary magistrate Bennett reported, were prone 'to relax their exertions' and 'not to do justice either to themselves or to the property' on which they held metayage agreements.[108]

The incidence of these practices could, however, have been limited by frugality on the part of more planters, by a meaningful superintendence of cultivation by the planters, and by attempts to provide examples of efficient farming methods for their 'assistant small farmers'.[109] One of the outstanding successful planters on metayage in St. Lucia recognized early that if the system was to be successful the planter had to retain 'a strong right of immediate superintendence over the work in the field'. Under his metayage agreement the land was prepared and planted in canes before it was handed to the metayers who then did 'all the rest of the work' until the sugar was divided.[110] But, unfortunately, few planters seemed to recognize the necessity for this vigilance.

The third planter grievance referred to the effect of metayage on the operations of the sugar factories. The position of the factory was crucial in the sugar industry. It represented by far the greatest capital outlay of the planter; it was his most valuable fixed capital asset; it absorbed in regular improvements, repairs and replacement most of the little capital the planter could raise. It also determined to a large extent profit or loss on the crop. Consequently, a regular supply of labour was vital to it in order to ensure the prompt manufacture of all the estate's canes. But the introduction of metayage could place the operations of the factory in jeopardy. Most estates did not use metayage as an exclusive system and, consequently, there was nearly always a large amount of canes produced by wage labour which had to be manufactured into sugar. Labour for the manufacture of the metayers' canes was usually supplied by the metayers, but if these labourers left the factories as soon as their canes were manufactured the continued operation of the factory and the planters' profits could be imperilled. This was the planters' fear and grievance. Perhaps it was the presence of this fear which led some planters to postpone the manufacture of the metayers' canes; but, at the same time, there was little evidence to suggest that the metayers generally behaved in this fashion. Such incidents did occur on the Black Bay estate in 1842 and 1844 in St. Lucia,[111] but the incidents might have been explained away, as the stipendiary magistrates did, by a general tendency on the part of all labourers to take 'a few days' relaxation from their labour' at the end of 'all contracts or great operations'.[112] But, in any case, punitive action by the planters to ensure a regular labour supply for the factory could only crystallize more rapidly the very object of their fears.

The basis of the planters' reasonable grievances might have been removed if the planters themselves had been prepared to exploit the full potential of the system. Such exploitation could have involved a radical structural reform of the industry which in turn could have benefitted the whole industry and the economies of the islands. The system might have been modified in the direction of a cane farming system to produce additional economies in production. Capital being very short and labour scare it was in the planters' interest to think in terms of converting more, if not all, of their estates to metayage production. A class of metayer-tenants might have been established on estate land which would cultivate canes and sell them to the landlord-manufacturers. The conditions would thus have been created for a rationalization of sugar production through a division of labour and costs. The labourers would have welcomed the reform, and the planters' problems would have been minimized. The latter would now need to find capital and labour to service their factories, not to operate their complete estates.

Such a reform was frequently suggested by many of the local officials. For those stipendiary magistrates and lieutenant-governors, metayage was a desirable and superior method of cultivation to wage labour; de Brossard described it in 1842 as 'the safest and most profitable means by which the cultivation of the staple articles of our exports can be conducted'.[113] Dowland suggested in 1848 that all estates should convert completely to metayage in order to establish a separation of cultivation from manufacture.[114] Lieutenant-Governor Keate of Grenada saw the system in 1854 as 'an approach and distant resemblance to that farm tendency towards which it will lead, if judiciously directed; while if left to itself and to change, there is great fear that it will eventuate in a general subdivision of the whole property of the country, and an abandonment of all attempts at sugar making on a large scale'.[115] In 1858, Lieutenant Governor Drysdale lamented that under the metayage system 'the advantage which will naturally result for a proper division of labour is invariably set at naught.'[116] Governor-in-Chief Sir William Colebrooke reminded the planters through the lieutenant-governors that there was a greater possibility

of securing labourers 'by establishing an intermediate class of tenant employees' than by 'interference with the distribution of labour' through higher wages which 'unduly' raised the costs of production.[117]

This impressive advocacy had little effect on the planters. Few bothered to investigate the possibilities of the system. Too many of them were, as stipendiary magistrate Johnston said, either 'blind to their own interest' or 'considered it a species of unworthy apostasy to yield to anything bearing the character of an innovation'.[118] They regarded metayage as an expedient to retain labourers and to ease their financial difficulties; for them it was never intended as an instrument to create tenants and peasants who would continue to receive a share of the profits of sugar production which had been traditionally monopolized by the planters. Therefore, whenever their fortunes improved even slightly they hastened to dispense with the expedient. In St. Lucia metayage declined in the late fifties mainly because the planters were determined to exploit to the fullest all the advantages in immigration and rising sugar prices. In Tobago, the planters tried to abandon the system in the same period because as Drysdale said, they wanted to 'monopolize all the advantages resulting from the improved state of the country, and the encouraging aspect of the market for sugar'.[119] These Tobago planters were prepared to go further; they attempted to re-impose an export tax on sugar to raise money for immigration.[120] By this date, at least one-third of the island's sugar was being produced by metayage, and the imposition of the tax would have meant a levy on metayers' labour to provide themselves with competition in the labour market. It was highly unlikely that immigrants would have been allocated to metayers, and in any case, the planters would have seized the opportunity provided by the availability of immigrant labour to dispense with metayage.

The planters' distrust of and opposition to metayage were also clearly and perhaps, mainly determined by a realization of the likely and actual social consequences of the existence of the system. Metayage and, to a great extent, the development of the peasantry could be described as emancipation in action. In contrast to slavery, the metayage system as de Brossard observed 'opens up and establishes a competition to which everyone is invited'.[121] Such an invitation was not wasted on the ex-slaves. They, like the planters, were ready and willing to exploit metayage in their own interest. What they wanted above all else was an independent economic status freeing them from the routine of estate labour with its dependent status, low wages and associations with slavery. Therefore, 'their chief ambition' was to possess freehold land which they regarded as the high road to economic independence. But since a lack of capital and the refusal of many planters to sell surplus estate land often prevented the possession of land, metayage, as semi-independent cultivation, became one of the stepping stones towards the attainment of the main objective. Many negroes, therefore, used the expedient in conjunction with or as an alternative to small leaseholds and freeholds to secure for themselves large freeholds, some material comfort and higher social status.

Naturally then, labourer participation in metayage was enthusiastic. This support was one of the main reasons for the extension of the system in all the islands and for its permanence in Tobago. Drysdale reported from St. Lucia that the labourers were 'partial in the extreme' to metayage and that land was 'eagerly sought for' to continue and extend the system.[122] Stipendiary magistrate Child reported from Tobago that metayage was 'excellently suited to the ideas and habits of the labourers' and therefore 'much liked by the peasantry'.[123] Such participation ensured that the system could never be lightly abandoned. Two Grenada planters found themselves without labourers in 1852 when they tried to abandon metayage and revert to wage labour.[124] The Tobago planters discovered in 1857–8 that they had little power to act on their determination to abandon the system and monopolize all the profits from the improved sugar market. By then, as Drysdale pointed out, the system had become 'too deeply identified with the interests of the labourers', to be discarded.[125]

The labourers' 'interests' were both the substantial profits which could be realized from metayage and the respectability of small-farming which this semi–independent activity in the major staple crop conferred. The actual financial rewards, were, on the stipendiary magistrate's testimony, comparatively large and certainly larger than 'the mere pittance of plantation wages'[126] of 9d or one shilling per day. Drysdale reported from St. Lucia in 1845 that metayers in his district had cultivated 182 acres of canes and had produced more than 285 hogsheads of sugar for a share of £24.1.6d to each metayer.[127] In 1848, he reported that metayers in the same district had produced 657 hogshead of sugar from the 1847 crop and had received £3,507.4.0d as their share of the proceeds.[128] Pringle estimated that the Tobago metayer's share of sugar from one acre of cane land over a three year period would exceed three and a half hogsheads.[129] The size of this return was impressive when it is noted that the crops were produced in the metayers' spare time or in conjunction with other profitable activity. Since the first crop of canes on an acre of land did not, on Pringle's reckoning, consume more than eighty-three days' labour, the metayers were left relatively free to work on the estates if the estates required wage labourers and to tend their provision grounds which were also reputed to be fruitful sources of profit.[130] Pringle concluded that these combined profits 'would tend to speedily raise such a person from the rank of mere labourer, whether such an effect may be desirable or not'.[131] In addition, the metayers benefitted from the higher prices for sugar in the mid-fifties while at the same time the extension of the system, as occurred in Tobago, widened the area of distribution of the profits from the industry.

The presence of these advantages helped to reveal the potential in social terms of the system. In the first place, the apparent profits and the respectability of metayer activity attracted to sugar production many persons who had recently left it and some individuals who had always despised labour in the sugar industry. This accession of cultivators included the residents in the newly established villages and the creole lower middle class. The appearance of the latter was especially significant. This class included the poor whites and the coloureds, the 'respectable' individuals, 'people of higher class than mere labourer', and 'numerous small proprietors and tradesmen free from birth and who can look forward for a year or two'.[132] Earlier, these individuals had considered labour in sugar cane cultivation as 'degrading',[133] but now they sought metayage contracts and as stipendiary magistrate Bennett reported, 'generally do well'.[134] This development probably provided for a degree of social cohesion: as Johnston said, it might have helped to promote 'that good understanding which has always been so desirable but which has not been hitherto manifested by the old free and later emancipated class towards each other'.[135] At the same time, this accession of cultivators helped to explain why the area of cane cultivation was increasing while the supply of wage labourers was steadily declining.

The other important consequence was the stimulus metayage gave to the creation of a self-conscious 'useful middle class of yeomanry' which could enhance social stability and internal security.[136] Drysdale wrote from Tobago in 1858 that the metayers, being small farmers as well as smallholders, 'must naturally desire to maintain the laws made for the protection of their property and of the general peace and tranquility of the country, with the prosperity of which their individual interests have become identified'.[137] The stipendiary magistrates found great 'moral advancement' among those labourers who participated in the system.[138] The metayer, Drysdale and Dowland reported, felt himself 'above the ordinary class of less industrious labourers' and as a result of 'the trust and confidence' that had been placed in him, was 'impressed with a proper sense of his obligations and responsibilities' to those above as well as those below him in the social scale.[139]

Two examples of metayers' 'moral advancement' were provided by local officials. In 1843 labourers in Dennery, a St. Lucia district, established a Metayer Association — a small cooperative -to cultivate six acres of land to pay 'the cost of worship and the expense of an agricultural school for the children of that quarter'.[140] In 1858, the Inspector of Prisons in Tobago attributed the decrease in crime to the existence of metayage which, he said, was 'gradually elevating many of the peasantry to a higher social standing than they could otherwise have attained'.[141] Clearly, Sir William Colebrooke's recommendation of the establishment of an estate tenancy to tap this potential had been well founded. Some of the metayers were behaving in the way Colebrooke had hoped the new tenants would behave; they were helping to give 'stability to property' by sustaining the sugar industry, and they were trying to establish 'those relations which could conduce to the improvement of native society'.[142]

But this potential, like its industrial counterpart, received little recognition from the planters. This was not surprising. The planters were utterly opposed to any innovation which might loosen or shake their dominance of the socio-economic structure. Therefore, they saw metayage (and, particularly, the development of a peasantry) as a threat to their oligarchic positions since these developments represented significant modifications of the traditional social structure. Their attitude to metayage was well expressed by H.H. Breen, the St. Lucia historian. In 1844, Breen, then mayor of Castries, admitted that metayage was supported by the 'sinking planter' and the 'aspiring peasant', but he found its worst feature in

the direct tendency to give an undue and overstrained impetus to the growth and accumulation of wealth amongst the labouring population; to induce consequent habits of indolence; by lowering the condition of the landowners and elevating that of the labourers, to place both on a footing of quality; thereby to increase the number of small farmers and ultimately to divert a large amount of capital and industry from the more legitimate, because more lucrative, cultivation of the staple commodities.[143]

By 1861, Breen, now Administrator of St. Lucia, was even more destructive and partisan. He rejoiced at the partial disappearance of metayage from St. Lucia because the existence of the system was an indication of lack of resources, an encouragement to absenteeism, and because it had 'a tendency to disturb the social equilibrium by giving the illiterate classes a degree of weight and importance which should be the concomitants as well as the rewards of intelligence and education'.[144] This was the statement of rejection which the planters clearly endorsed by their reluctance to reform the contract and rationalize the system, and by their anxious attempt to abandon it whenever the circumstances seemed favourable to the resumption of traditional methods of production.

In spite of this rejection, however, there can be little doubt that the system was important to the Windward Islands both because of its actual achievement and because of its potential. It was partly successful as an expedient in the sugar industry and as a solvent inside the society. But it also contained a range of possibilities which were never fully explored and, therefore, never exploited. It remained a stop-gap while pointing to a new frontier. The exploitation of the potential of metayage together with active encouragement of the development of a peasantry would have rendered emancipation more of a reality to the ex-slaves. This was clearly recognized by Downland when he wrote his eloquent and optimistic tribute to metayage in 1849:

By this system the land will become as it were the natural inheritance of those who live and toil on it, and I doubt not that they will make it more fruitful by the sweetness of their own uncontrolled labour, — freedom will no longer be nominal, as the right of the landlord will become almost conventional, subsidiary and conditional.[145]

Unfortunately, no comprehensive scheme for small scale land settlement has yet been adopted in these islands to exploit fully the potential possessed by the land and its people.

Notes & References

The following abbreviations are used:

C.O.   Colonial Office Papers
P.P.   Parlimentary Papers
S.M.   Stipendiary Magistrate

1. The name of the system varied in the islands. It was called the shares system, the halves system, the half and half system and, most commonly metairie.
2. The British Windward Islands comprised at this time Tobago, Grenada, St. Vincent and St. Lucia. These islands shared a Governor-in-Chief who was stationed at Barbados. St. Lucia was a Crown Colony while the other islands possessed Representative Assemblies.
3. Cf. R.W. Beachey, The British West Indies Sugar Industry in the late nineteenty century (Oxford 1957) p. 114.

Metayage was used in all the islands by 1848; it was not, as Beachey writes, 'introduced from the French West Indies shortly after the mid-century'.

4. The price of British West Indian raw sugar, excluding duty, fell from 34s.5d. per cwt in 1846 to 23s.8d. in 1848, and to 21s.1d. in 1854. See Douglas Hall, *Free Jamaica, 1838–1865* (New Haven 1959), Appendix 2, p. 270.

5. This was the lament of Melcher Todd, one of the more efficient St. Lucia planters. The Governor-in-Chief, Col. Reid said in 1848; 'there will be found many other instances like Mr. Todd's where the Planter is cultivating his estate at a loss and cannot do otherwise' (C.O. 253/91 Reid to Earl Grey, 31 January 1848).

6. C.O. 260/72 Colebrooke to Earl Grey, 30 May 1850, Lieut.-Governor Campbell's comments on metayage.

7. C.Y. Shepherd, *Peasant Agriculture in the Leewards and Windwards* (I.C.T.A., Trinidad 1945), Report to the Colonial Office 58948–1, pp. 6–7.

8. C.O. 290/4 Tobago S.M. Reports, Child, Dec 1849.

9. Cf. Shephard, op. cit., p. 7.

10. C.O. 253/103 Colebrooke to Earl Grey, 13 July 1850, Solicitor General Mallet Paret's review of the legal position of the system.

11. C.O. 253/67 McGregor to Normanby, 26 June 1839. McLaurin's S.M. report for April 1839.

12. Tobago comprised 116 sq. miles, Grenada 120, St. Vincent 133 and St. Lucia 233 sq. miles.

13. The census returns for the period were:

	1844	1851	1861
Grenada	28,923	32,671	31,900
St. Vincent	27,248	30,128	31,755
St. Lucia	21,001	24,318	26,705
Tobago	13,208	14,378	15,410

14. Grenada exported sizeable crops of cocoa, cotton and spices; St. Vincent had thriving export crops in cotton and arrowroot.

15. C.O. 265/3 St. Vincent S.M. Reports, June 1849; Sutherland, Dec. 1848; McNicol, Dec. 1849; Polson, Dec. 1849, June 1850.

16. Ibid. Polson, June 1850.

17. C.O. 260/58 McGregor to Glenelg, 23 Feb. 1839, Polson's S.M. report.

18. C.O. 265/3 St. Vincent S.M. Reports, Dec. 1851. Metayage probably still survives in St. Vincent. See Shepherd, op. cit., p. 127.

19. C.O. 106/14 Grenada S.M. Reports, June 1850.

20. Thirty-seven estates used metayage in 1848. (P.P. 1849 XXXIV (1126) Colebrooke to Earl Grey, 15 March 1849, Lieut.-Governor Hamilton's 1848 Report on Grenada.

21. Sugar prices rose from 21s.1d. per cwt in 1854 to 26s.4d. in 1855 and to 35s.2d. in 1857. By 1860 they had fallen to 26s. 10d. and then they slumped to 22s.1d. by 1865 (Hall, op. cit., p. 270). During the same period conditions for the immigration of Indian labourers were relaxed by the British Government.

22. C.O. 106/14 Grenada S.M. Reports, Dec. 1850.

23. P.P. 1854–5 XXXVI Colebrooke to Newcastle, 16 May 1854, Report of the Agricultural Society's Treasurer enclosed in Lieut.-Gov. Keate's 1853 Report on Grenada. Between 1856 and 1865 Grenada received 2,408 Indian and African immigrants.

24. C.O. 101/107 Colebrooke to Newcastle, 20 March 1854, Keate's comments on metayage; P.P. 1857 X Hincks of Labouchere, 7 July 1856, Lieut.-Gov. Walker's Additional Report on Grenada, 1855.

25. W.A. Lewis, *The Evolution of the Peasantry in the B.W.I.* (1830, folio 656 Colonial Office library) pp. 15–17. There are few available details on the way the system operated in the cocoa industry, but metayage might well have been the origin of a practice of 'contracting' which Lewis described as in use on the cocoa estates after 1880.

26. C.O. 253/76 Grey to Stanley, 22 June 1842, de Brossard's comments on the system.

27. C.O. 253/73 McGregor to Russell, 20 January 1841, Johnston's S.M. Report.

28. C.O. 253/82 Grey to Stanley, 16 September 1844 de Brossard's S.M. Report.

29. C.O. 253/83 Grey to Stanley, 5 April 1845, S.M. Reports. In each of the five districts there were at least 200 acres being cultivated by metayers. de Brossard noted, however, that the estates of the sugar brokers — Cavan Bros. & Co. Marryat & Sons — used little metayage.

30. P.P. 1849 XXXIV (1126) Colebrooke to Earl Grey, 6 July 1849, Lieut.-Gov. Darling's 1848 Report on St. Lucia.

31. P.P. 1847–8 XLVI (749) Reid to Earl Grey, 3 May 1848, report on metayer sugar production.

32. P.P. 1862 XXXVI Hincks to Newcastle, 22 June 1861, Breen's 1860 Report on St. Lucia. Between 1856 and 1865 St. Lucia received 1,715 Indian and African Immigrants.

33. The crisis was precipitated by a dispute between the Assembly and the Chief Justice; and for two years no supplies were voted.

34. Seventeen lives were lost during the hurricane and damage to property was estimated at £84,853 (C.). 285/58 Reid to Earl Grey, 24 January 1848).

35. H.I. Woodcock, *A History of Tobago*, (Ayr 1867) pp. 189–190.

36. C.O. 290/4 S.M. Reports, Dec. 1852, June 1853.

37. P.P. 1859 XXI Hincks to Lytton, 24 June 1858, 1857 Report on Tobago.

38. P.P. 1863 XXXIX Walker to Newcastle, 30 June 1962, 1861 Report on Tobago.

39. P.P. 1859 XXI Hincks to Lytton, 24 June 1858, 1857 Report on Tobago.

40. Beachey, op. cit., p. 115 (note)

41. C.O. 253/76 Grey to Stanley, 22 June 1842, enclosed in de Brossard's comments on the system.

42. C.O. 253/76 Grey to Stanley, 20 May 1842, 1841 Report on St. Lucia.

43. C.O. 254/13 Stanley to Grey, 26 Jan. 1842. H.H. Breen, the St. Lucia historian, felt that it was this encouragement rather than any real awareness of the value of the system which caused it to attract attention in St. Lucia (St. Lucia: Historical, Statistical and Descriptive, London 1844, p. 300).

44. P.P. 1847 XLVI (1005) Reid to Earl Grey, 18 April 1848, Lieut.-Gov. Hamilton's 1847 Report on Grenada.

45. P.P. 1849 XXXIV (1126) Colebrooke to Earl Grey, 15 March 1849, Hamilton's 1848 Report on Grenada.

46. C.O. 290/4 Tobago S.M. Reports, Dec. 1849.

47. C.O. 253/76 Grey to Stanley, 16 May 1842, stipendiary magistrate Colquhoun's statement on the system.

48. P.P. 1847–8 XLVI (1005) Reid to Earl Grey, 3 May 1848, planter's letter enclosed in Lieut.-Gov. Darling's analysis of the costs of production on six estates.

49. P.P. 1862 XXXVI Hincks to Newcastle, 22 June 1861, 1860 Report on St. Lucia.

50. Stipendiary magistrate Harris of Grenada reported in 1849 that 62 out of the 654 contracts in the island were written (C.O. 101/101 Colebrooke to Earl Grey, 18 Oct. 1849). Some of the magistrates observed that some labourers seemed to fear that they might sell themselves back into slavery if they signed any document.

51. In St. Lucia, a carre, about 3 1/3 acres, was the usual area of land. Sometimes the area granted was as large as six acres.

52. C.O. 290/4 Tobago S.M. Reports, Dowland, Dec. 1849, a printed contract.
53. Ibid.; C.O. 106/13 Grenada S.M. Reports, Harris, Dec. 1848; Dec. 1849, S.M. Gurley's Plan and Deed of Agreement.
54. C.O. 290/4 Tobago S.M. Reports, Dowland, Dec. 1849.
55. C.O. 253/73 McGregor to Russell, 24 March 1841, Colquhoun's S.M. reported for January 1841; C.O. 258/16 St. Lucia S.M. Reports, Johnston, Dec. 1848, the Black Bay estate contract.
56. C.O. 253/76 Grey to Stanley, 22 June 1842, de Brossard's comments on the system. S.M. Drysdale reported a case from St. Lucia where two metayers in 1843 shipped their eight hogheads of sugar on their own account to the London firm of Marryat & Sons. (C.O. 253/79 Grey to Stanley, 11 Sept. 1843, S.M. reports.
57. C.O. 106/13 Grenada S.M. Reports, Frazer, June 1849; C.O. 106/14 Grenada S.M. Reports, Hutcheson, June 1851 and June 1853; Woodcock, op. cit., p. 190; C.O. 290/4 Tobago S.M. Reports, Child, Dec. 1853. In one contrct on the Rabot estate in St. Lucia the planter and metayer's shared the molasses equally (C.O. 253/82 Grey to Stanley, 16 Sept. 1844, the Rabot estate case).
58. C.O. 253/73 McGregor to Russell, 24 March 1841, Colquhoun's S.M. report for January 1841.
59. C.O. 258/16 St. Lucia S.M. Reports, Johnston, Dec. 1848.
60. C.O. 290/4 Tobago S.M. Reports, Dec. 1849.
61. C.O. 253/82 Grey to Stanley, 7 May 1844, Lafitte's S.M. report; C.O. 290/4 Tobago S.M. Reports, Dowland, June 1849.
62. C.O. 253/78 Grey to Stanley, 24 April 1843, Drysdale and Johnston's S.M. Reports.
63. C.O. 290/4 Tobago S.M. Reports, Dowland, June 1849.
64. Ibid. C.O. 106/13 Grenada S.M. Reports, Gurley and Frazer, Dec. 1849.
65. C.O. 101/101 Colebrooke to Earl Grey, 18 Oct. 1849, Hamilton's comments on metayage.
66. C.O. 253/82 Grey to Stanley, 16 Sept. 1844, Drysdale's S.M. Reports. C.O. 106/13 Grenada S.M. Reports, Frazer, Dec. 1849; C.O. 290/4 Tobago S.M. Reports, Dowland, Dec. 1849.
67. Ibid.
68. C.O. 106/13 Grenada S.M. Reports, Frazer, Dec. 1849.
69. C.O. 290/4 Tobago S.M. Reports, June 1850.
70. Ibid. June 1853.
71. C.O. 253/82 Grey to Stanley, 7 May 1844, de Brossard's S.M. Report.
72. C.O. 283/78 Grey to Stanley, 24 April 1843, S.M. Reports.
73. P.P. 1849 XXXIV (1126) Colebrooke to Earl Grey, 6 July 1849, Colebrooke's comment on the 1848 St. Lucia Report.
74. These were the paid officials who had been appointed to the West Indian Islands after the passage of the Emancipation Act. They administered the act and possessed jurisdiction in all disputes between ex-masters and ex-slaves. See W.L. Burn, Emancipation and Apprenticeship in the British West Indies, (London 1937).
75. C.O. 253/82 Grey to Stanley, 16 Sept. 1844, S.M. Reports, Cf. C.O. 290/4 Tobago S.M. Reports, Dowland June 1849, June 1853; C.O. 106/13 Grenada S.M. Reports, Gurley and Harris, Dec. 1849.
76. C.O. 253/82 Grey to Stanley, 7 May 1844, S.M. Reports, Chief Justice Reddie also argued that there was no evidence that the sugar belonged to the metayers and that there was strong presumptive evidence of collusion on the part of the lessee to defraud the proprietor.
77. C.O. 253/82 Grey to Stanley, 16 Sept. 1844, S.M. Reports.
78. C.O. 253/80 Grey to Stanley, 18 May 1844, Grey's comments on metayage.
79. C.O. 254/13 Stanley to Grey, 3 Aug. 1844.
80. P.P. 1859 XXI Hincks to Lytton, 24 July 1858, enclosures in Drysdale's 1857 Report on Tobago.
81. C.O. 253/82 Grey to Stanley, 16 Sept. 1844, Johnston's S.M. Report; C.O. 253/83 Grey to Stanley, 16 Sept. 1845, Johnston's S.M. Report. Harris S.M. in Grenada described civil action as a 'tedious and expensive process'.
82. C.O. 253/83 Grey to Stanley, 16 Sept. 1845, Johnston's S.M. Report.
83. Ibid.
84. C.O. 253/103 Colebrooke to Earl Grey, 13 July 1850, Colebrooke's despatch to Darling, 19 Nov. 1849.
85. C.O. 253/80 Grey to Stanley, 18 May 1844; C.O. 253/83 Grey to Stanley, 16 Sept. 1845; C.O. 254/13 Stanley to Grey, 8 Nov. 1845.
86. C.O. 253/98 Colebrooke to Earl Grey, 1 May 1849; C.O. 253/99 Colebrooke to Earl Grey, 7 Aug. 1849, 30 Aug. 1849.
87. P.P. 1849 XXXIV (1126) Colebrooke to Earl Grey, 6 July 1849; Darling's 1848 Report on St. Lucia.
88. C.O. 255/6 St. Lucia Ordinances, 1850/2.
89. C.O. 254/15 Earl Grey to Colebrooke, 18 Sept. 1850. Earl Grey was in doubt about whether the judge's authority was discretionary or directory.
90. Ibid.
91. C.O. 253/103 Colebrooke to Earl Grey, 13 July 1850, Athill's comments on the ordinance.
92. This was Drysdale's description of the depression period (P.P. 1863 XXXIX Walker to Newcastle, 30 June 1862, 1861 Report on Tobago).
93. C.O. 253/76 Colquhoun to Stanley, 2 April 1842.
94. This was the largest crop produced in the islands during the entire period.
95. Exports from Tobago and St. Lucia at five-yearly intervals were:

	Tobago	St. Lucia
1840	2577.4 tons	1883.3 tons
1845	3135.4 "	3562.5 "
1850	2214.8 "	2695.1 "
1855	1966.7 "	3297.6 "
1860	2574.1 "	3647 "
1865	2487.4 "	4973.5 "

96. C.O. 253/77 Colquhoun to Stanley, 5 April 1842, Supplementary report on Metairie.
97. P.P. 1847–8 XLVI (749) Reid to Earl Grey, 3 May 1848. Darling wrote that since the report was prepared by Drysdale it 'may therefore be implicitly relied upon as correct'. Drysdale was later promoted from stipendiary magistrate in St. Lucia to Lieut.-Governor of Tobago.
98. On the metayage estates the yield was 19 3/4 and 29 cwts per acre. On the others it ranged from 19½ to 25¼ cwts per acre. Costs of production were 13s.6d. and 10s. 0½d. per cwt on the metayage estates, while on the others it ranged from 16s.10d. to 22s. per cwt. Success on the metayage estates was also due to the personnel management of the resident proprietor and lessee.
99. C.O. 253/73 McGregor to Russell, 24 March 1841, Colquhoun's S.M. Report for February 1841.
100. C.O. 253/76 Grey to Stanley, 16 May 1842.
101. C.O. 253/78 Grey to Stanley, 24 April 1843, S.M. Reports. This opinion was shared by many stipendiary magistrates, especially by Dowland and Child of Tobago.
102. Between 1847 and 1849, wages, were reduced by about 2d. per day in all the islands and the prerequisite of free medical attention was withdrawn from all the labourers.

103. P.P. 1863 XXXIX Walker to Newcastle, 30 June 1862 Drysdale's 1861 Report on Tobago.
104. Cf. R. Schickle, 'Effect of Tenure Systems on Agricultural Efficiency', *Journal of Farm Economies, Vol. 23 No. 1 Feb. 1941*, p. 194.
105. It was to the tradesmen and domestic servants especially that Drysdale had applied his criticism.
106. C.O. 101/107 Colebrooke to Newcastle, 20 March 1854, Lieut.-Gov. Keate's comments on Metayage.
107. C.O. 253/78 Grey to Stanley, 24 April 1843, Johnston's S.M. Report.
108. Ibid., S.M. Reports.
109. Ibid., Drysdale's S.M. Report.
110. P.P. 1847–8 (749) XLVI Reid to Earl Grey, 3 May 1848, planter's letter enclosed in Darling's analysis of the costs of production on six St. Lucia estates. He was the planter who managed the two metayage estates.
111. C.O. 253/76 Grey to Stanley, 28 July 1842, de Brossard's S.M. Report; C.O. 253/82 Grey to Stanley, 16 September 1844, Drysdale's S.M. Report. Drysdale believed that the planters suspected such an intention rather than possessed evidence of the fact.
112. C.O. 253/78 Grey to Stanley, 4 Feb. 1843, de Brossard's additional comment in response to a Colonial Office enquiry.
113. C.O. 253/76 Grey to Stanley, 22 June 1842, de Brossard's comments on metayage.
114. C.O. 290/4 Tobago S.M. Reports, December 1848.
115. P.P. 1854–5 XXXVI Colebrooke to Newcastle, 16 May 1854, Keate's 1853 Report on Grenada.
116. P.P. 1859 XXI Hincks to Lytton, 24 July 1858, 1857 Report on Tobago.
117. C.O. 101/101 Colebrooke to Earl Grey, 18 Oct. 1849, Cf. C.O. 260/70 Colebrooke to Earl Grey, 2 July 1849.
118. C.O. 253/78 Grey to Stanley, 24 April 1843, S.M. Reports.
119. P.P. 1859 XXI Hincks to Lytton, 24 July 1858, the 1857 Report on Tobago.
120. Ibid.
121. C.O. 253/82 Grey to Stanley, 7 May 1844, S.M. Reports.
122. Ibid.
123. C.O. 290/4 Tobago S.M. Reports, Dec. 1853.
124. C.O. 106/14 Grenada S.M. Reports, Hutcheson, June 1852.
125. P.P. 1859 XXI Hincks to Lytton, 24 July 1858, 1857 Reports on Tobago.
126. Ibid.
127. C.O. 253/83 Grey to Stanley, 5 April 1845, S.M. Reports.
128. P.P. 1847–8 XLVI (749) Reid to Earl Grey, 3 May 1848, Drysdale's Report on the Metairie system.
129. C.O. 290/4 Tobago S.M. Reports, Dec. 1852.
130. Child, a Tobago stipendiary magistrate, estimated that an acre of yams could produce a profit of £30 (C.O. 290/4 Tobago S.M. Reports, June 1850).
131. C.O. 290/4 Tobago S.M. Reports, Dec. 1852.
132. C.O. 253/73 McGrgor to Russell, 24 March 1841, Colquhoun's S.M. Report for February 1841; C.O. 253/78 Grey to Stanley, 22 June 1842, Bennett's S.M. Report; C.O. 290/4 Tobago S.M. Reports, Child, June 1850.
133. Ibid.
134. C.O. 253/78 Grey to Stanley, 24 April 1843, S.M. Reports.
135. C.O. 253/79 Grey to Stanley, 11 Sept. 1843, S.M. Reports.
136. P.P. 1859 XXI Hincks to Lytton, 24 July 1858, Drysdale's 1857 Report on Tobago. Drysdale, like Lieut.-Gov. Eyre in St. Vincent, was mainly concerned about the effect on the public peace of the withdrawal of British troops in 1854.
137. Ibid.
138. C.O. 253/78 Grey to Stanley, 24 April 1843, Drysdale's S.M. Report. Cf. C.O. 290/4 Tobago S.M. Reports, Dowland, Dec. 1849.
139. Ibid.
140. C.O. 253/82 Grey to Stanley, 7 May 1844, de Brossard's S.M. Report.
141. P.P. 1860 XLVI Walker to Lytton, 28 June 1859, enclosed in Drysdale's 1858 Report on Tobago.
142. C.O. 101/101 Colebrooke to Earl Grey, 18 Oct. 1849.
143. Breen, op. cit., pp. 301–303.
144. P.P. 1862 XXXVI Hincks to Newcastle, 22 June 1861 Breen's 1860 Report on St. Lucia.
145. C.O. 290/4 Tobago S.M. Reports, Dec. 1849.

Labour Relations in Martinique and Guadeloupe, 1848–1870

Rosamunde Renard

The abolition of slavery in 1848 revolutionized labour relations in Martinique and Guadeloupe. A dependent and submissive labour force was transformed into one which was determined to take full advantage of its newly found independence from plantation labour. However, the plantocracy persisted in seeing the principal function of the blacks as one of supplying steady labour to the sugar plantations. The two opposing interests were bound to clash. In the French islands, however, a third element was added to this ongoing conflict. The planters were aided and abetted in their attitude by the metropolitan administration, particularly during the Second Empire. Methods of legal control, designed to keep the blacks on the plantations, were formulated. The impact of these labour laws on the lives of black women and men reached such startling proportions that it can be suggested that in the French West Indies, systematic attempts were made on a governmental level to create for black labour, as for immigrant labour, 'a new form of slavery'. The black workers devised their own means of countering these legal attempts to control them.

On the proclamation of abolition many blacks left the plantations. One ship captain, commenting on this, noted that:

I left Havre . . . for the destination of Pointe-a-Pitre. On my arrival in this harbour I found the colony in the saddest state of commercial affairs. The blacks (in very large part if not at all) no longer wanted to work or else were demanding salaries so enormous that they were rendering onerous the work of the most unfortunate proprietors.[1]

This mass flight from the plantations was particularly prevalent in the month just before and the two months after the abolition of slavery. In those months, sugar production, and production in general, came to a standstill. Captain Christiaem, arriving in Saint-Pierre on April 21 1848, reported that his cargo had been put in storage because buyers could not be found, even when the articles for sale

were offered at prices below normal. This situation he attributed to the refusal of blacks to work. Business, he continued, was paralyzed through a shortage of money.[2]

The planters, already dismayed at the very idea of abolition itself, reacted hysterically to this refusal on the part of the blacks to work on the plantations. They predicted the reversion of the colonies into a state of disorder and 'barbarism'. For instance, one planter wrote:

You will see . . . that work has fled us; that the barbarism of Africa will, as in San Dominigue, replace civilization and industry. . . .[3]

Another wrote imploring the Minister of Marine and the Colonies to:

. . . send immediate orders to the honourable Governor of this colony, to force the blacks to gather in the harvest which is being lost. It seems in all fairness that since the workers were so insubordinate and lazy during the last two months of slavery, they should be compelled, in their own interests of course, to bring in this harvest which is rotting underfoot with no profit to anybody. . . .[4]

In their attempts to become independent of the plantations after emancipation, the blacks utilized all means at their disposal. Some ex-slaves sought to cultivate cane on land that they had bought or rented and searched for factories where cane could be sold. Others approached Governor Gatine, for example, requesting grants of state land for clearing wood, only to meet with refusal. The cultivation of provision grounds increased tremendously as quite a few ex-slaves turned solely to this form of economic subsistence. In Guadeloupe, for instance, the number of market gardens rose from 1,128 in 1847 to 2,170 in 1849. By 1859, the number of market gardens in this colony was 3,567.[5]

The emancipation of the slaves gave rise to the growth of small proprietorships. The blacks used various means to acquire these properties. They squatted on any available land. They bought small lots; and reports also indicated that on occasions ex-slaves simply appropriated land abandoned by indigent planters. Some plantation owners also tended to give small quantities of land on and surrounding their plantations to their ex-slaves, in this way assuring themselves of a steady work force of sorts. Blacks paid for land acquired in this manner either by working on the plantations or by paying an annual sum of money towards the cost of the land. On the lands they grew ground provisions, raised cattle, chicken and other livestock, and sold their produce in the markets of the boroughs and towns. Small property farming was more prevalent in Guadeloupe than in Martinique between 1848 and 1870. The principal reason for this was that, according to Acheen, in Martinique the amount of cultivatable land which was not devoted to sugar production was smaller than in Guadeloupe.[6]

Blacks also tried to supplement their income by fishing, but this remained a periodical and not very dependable occupation. In addition, the newly freed migrated to the towns seeking the few jobs available, such as dockers and porters. This continuing desertion of the plantations by black workers was even more significant in Guadeloupe where the number of sugar workers immediately after emancipation was quoted at only 18,739.[7] One year previously, the figure had been twice as large. However, this mass desertion of the plantations was very brief and by 1849 the number of sugar workers in Guadeloupe had again increased to 26,755.[8] Nevertheless, although desertion had lessened, it did not terminate completely. By 1853 it was claimed that, since emancipation, more than one-fifth of the sugar workers in both colonies had abandoned plantation work altogether.[9]

Those ex-slaves who continued to do plantation work did not do so voluntarily in many instances. The ex-slaves incurred expenses unknown to the slave. Food, medical bills, clothing, rents — all wholly or partly supplied by the plantation before the plantocracy and the administration increased these expenses even more in the attempt to create an artificial need for money wages so that the blacks would be forced to work on the plantations. Subsistence farming alone, the blacks quickly realized, could not meet these expenses. In addition, few possibilities other than plantation work were, in fact, open to them. The colonies had no industries of any significance. Traditional alternatives in the countryside and the towns such as domestic work, washing, cart-driving, masonry, carpentry, road construction work and dock work, remained limited indeed, although they did increase after emancipation.

Moreover, those who decided to live off the produce of their lands met with fierce opposition from the planters and, later on, the administration.

Yet, the conditions of labour had radically changed. From the slave who could be exploited at will, the planter found himself confronted with the independent labourer who had the ability to choose not only his employer, but the type of contract she or he was prepared to adopt. There were, for instance, the *travailleurs cases*, rent-free tenants who exchanged several days of wage labour for the free use of a hut and provision ground. This type of worker increased in number after 1870 when the planter had a significant number of abandoned immigrant houses at his disposal. There was also the system of the *colons partiaires* or the metairie system by which the planter allocated an area of land to the worker who grew cane on it and who, at crop time, received a half to a third of the value of the cane before it was ground. This worker generally also had free use of a hut and provision grounds. There were also the wage labourers. Among this group could be found the *gens strangers*, workers not normally resident on the plantations but who came to work at crop time for wages.

The planter who was often heavily indebted and pressed for cash, tried at first to avoid paying money wages as much as possible. On the other hand, workers in both colonies preferred to be paid in cash. Both Governor Bruat of Martinique and Governor Gatine of Guadeloupe reported that after emancipation, it was cash, and not the metairie system, for instance, which produced results.[10]

Yet, the wage labourer did not necessarily predominate. While the plantations in certain communes of Martinique, like Robert, tended to favour the *colon partiarie*, in others like Francois, called by the Governor-General Bruat, Martinique's model commune, all three types of the work contracts (the rent-free tenants, the share cropper and the non-resident salaried worker) could be found on the same plantation. Still others, like Vauclin, tended to adopt wage payments.[11] By 1870, payment by wages had, at least in Martinique, gained the upperhand.[12] In both colonies task work was introduced. However, as late as 1890, task work, predominant in Martinique, was still not widespread in Guadeloupe.[13]

Yet the planters complained bitterly that even those plantation workers who did not return after the initial rush from the plantations showed a marked irregularity in their work habits. One report claimed that only half of the workers worked on plantations at any time, and that those who did so, worked no more than an average of five hours per day.[14] Another planter, who employed his labourers by the payment of daily wages, complained.

On my brother's plantation they had agreed by the day. Wages were agreed on in writing. The workers however broke the contracts. They would work only several hours during the day, and very badly, and would retire the next day, to return the day after, or later, or else they would cut the canes and leave them there instead of carrying them to the mills, thus putting the proprietor in the position of either losing the canes or being held to ransom for them. It was necessary to abandon this method of payment. . . .[15]

There were also some blacks who refused to work on the plantations, although they remained resident there and occupied their former slave dwellings. Such refusal to work by resident plantation blacks was widespread enough to warrant promulgation of a decree which condemned this practice and punished offenders by a fine.[16]

Thus, in the years following abolition, black workers resisted attempts by the planters to coerce them into furnishing steady and reliable employment. Reports indicated that this refusal on the part of the workers lay not only in the fact that they were enjoying their newly found liberty and searching for alternatives to plantation work, but was also based on the resistance to what they considered the unreasonable demand of the planters. In addition, the sugar planters refused to consider the workers' demands for better working conditions. In one commune, the field labourers went as far as to demand the right to choose their own managers, that is the post-slavery equivalent of drivers. The Mayor of Goyave in Guadeloupe reported to the Home Affairs Director that:

Jean Batisle Dupre, known as Couton, inhabitant of Goyave and a great friend of negroes, told Mr. Revert who repeated to me: — that the negroes would revolt if they were forced to work on certain plantations; that they would only vote for black and coloured managers; that the government should have known that in giving them liberty, they would no longer work the cane; that finally, if Mr. Revert proposed as manager of the plantation, the few workers who have remained would leave immediately.[17]

Blacks also made persistent appeals for free grants of land, appeals which were just as persistently refused. In the face of these setbacks, black workers displayed even less inclination to satisfy the planters' demands that they should be at the latter's disposal. Reporting on the 1848 revolt in Martinique which precipitated the abolition of slavery,[18] he noted that when he encouraged the blacks to work they replied that:

the land belonged to the good God, that it belonged to everybody, and that when they were given their portion, they would work. . . .
There was I for all my pains. And all of them left me much later on, saying, 'give us our part of the land and we will work.[19]

The majority of the claims made by the black focused, however, simply on demands for higher wages. As was customary, the planters responded by refusing to pay these and, on the contrary, attempted, through immigration, to force wages down even further.

Unfortunately, there is not much precise information on workers' wages. However, we do gain some important insights into wages from one local decree of 21 August 1848[20] which outlines the salaries on plantation Fonds, St. Jacques, Martinique, as the following:

Refiners, labourers, chief workmen,

first class unskilled daily	-	1 franc
Second class unskilled workers	-	0 franc 75c
Children aged 10–14	-	0 franc 35c

Article 2 stated that work would last five days each week for nine hours per day between sunset and sunrise while Article 3 noted that cultivators who fail to furnish the sum of work deemed necessary would receive the following sums:

First class workers	-	15	centimes per hour		
Second class workers	-	10	"	"	"
Third class workers	-	5	"	"	"

Neither does it seem that wages rose much during the nineteenth century. The Governor of Guadeloupe in a report noted that the Director of the Clugny factory had received the following anonymous letter. He cited the following phrase:

Since they ordained you to the post of Director, it seems that earth is no longer for you; understand this well that Grande-Terre is not Martinique where one only earns 70 centimes;[21]

As late as 1902, Jacques Adelaide remarks, wages were 80 centimes per day for *travailleurs cases*, while specialized agricultural workers i.e. labourers, cart-drivers and so on earned between 1 franc to 1 franc 50 centimes.[22]

Confronted then with a problem which plagued most West Indian colonies after emancipation — that of the workers' refusal to work regularly on the plantations on the employers' terms — the French West Indian planters, with the help of their administration, were able to retaliate with certain unique strategies.

The planters pressed for measures which would control the local labour force. Their demands were particularly rewarded during the period of the Second Empire when, under Napoleon III, the French government installed an elaborate series of labour laws designed to ensure that the blacks worked, in a steady manner, on the plantations. However, although many of these laws were actually formulated and elaborated during the Second Empire, the state was set for the promulgation of the labour laws before 1852, during the short term of government by the Second Republic.

During the preliminary months of the Second Republic's term of office, when liberal and socialist factions dominated the assembly in France, certain revolutionary transformations were introduced into the domain of labour relations. The colonial decision-makers during this very brief period were propelled, it seemed, by two distinct motivations that is, of assuring that the workers were not exploited while, simultaneously, guaranteeing that the employers were not overwhelmed by a general desertion of the fields.

In response to the primary motivation, that of assuring that the workers were not exploited, the system of *jurys cantonnaux* was voted on the same date as the law abolishing slavery, 27 April 1848 and was officially promulgated in Martinique, on 4 June 1848.[23] One *jury cantonnal* was instituted in the district of each Justice of the Peace, that is in each canton[24], and was presided over by the Justice of the Peace himself. Each jury was composed of six members, three chosen from among the proprietors and industrialists and three from among the workers. The Justice of the Peace publicly picked the members from the electoral lists of the canton, and a third of the jury's membership was renewable every three months. The *jurys cantonnaux* met once a week to vote on all disputes which arose between employers and managers on the one hand, and workers on the other. Article 8 decreed that any coalition of workers or employers which 'attempted to unjustly lower or raise salaries, to prevent work, ... will be ... punished by a fine of 20 to 3,000 francs'.[25] In conjunction with this law, the decree stating that the master, in a dispute between employer and worker, was believed on the basis of his word alone, was abolished. Likewise, work fetes, in which prizes to deserving workers were to be distributed, were established.

However, together with its desire to prevent worker exploitation, the Commission appointed to prepare for the abolition of slavery was also eager to assure that the abolition of slavery would not cause the economic ruin of the colonies, for it was the general sentiment of the colonial administration that:

The blacks will refuse to work because they have few needs to satisfy. They are never cold and only dress in light clothes, walk barefooted and do not drink wine. They prefer to live in bamboo huts and to eat ground provisions and fruits, rather than to work for a better existence. It is thus, consequently, necessary to create an artificial need, and this need will be the payment of a tax.[26]

In fact, this tax, already imposed before 1848 to counter the movement of freed blacks to the towns, served also as a means of restricting the displacement of the ex-slaves from the countryside to the boroughs and the towns. The law imposed a personal tax per head on every inhabitant of the colonies. The sum payable annually by the inhabitants of the boroughs was higher than that payable by the inhabitants of the countryside. In 1849, the personal tax jumped from 10 francs 50 centimes per year in Pointe-a-Pitre to 15 francs. The tax rose from 7 francs 50 centimes to 10 francs in Moule and from 7 francs 50 centimes to 12 francs in Basse-Terre. In all boroughs the personal tax was increased from 7 francs 50 centimes to 10 francs. Even in the country areas, the personal tax rose from 4 francs 50 centimes to 5 francs.[27]

The varied incidence of the personal tax was supposed to fulfill two functions. The first was to induce the workers to live in the countryside, and thus arrest any departure from the plantation centres. The second motive, as adequately outlined in the quotation above, was to force the blacks to work, to be able to pay the tax. In case of an inhabitant's inability to pay the tax, she or he was required to work for the state for the number of days necessary to meet its payment.

One decree in 1848 established that it was the duty of the 'proletariat' to contribute to the economic progress of its country. To do so, a certain amount of steady work supplied to the production of the country's principal export, was declared to be essential. The meaning was clear. The 'proletariat', that is the black workers of the countryside, was being told that it was its bounden duty to work on the plantations.

So as to counter any vagrancy, workhouses called *ateliers de discipline*[28] were created in 1848. Initially used in France as a means of providing labour for the unemployed, these workhouses quickly became, in the colonies, an integral part of the legal mechanism established to control the black workers. All persons who were declared 'beggars, unavowed people or vagabonds' were to be committed to workhouses. The inmates of the workhouses were supposed to work on the construction and upkeep of roads, embankments, drainage, the excavation and upkeep of canals and rivers as well as, finally, all other work which was demanded of them.[29]

The discipline and workload of these *ateliers de discipline* closely approximated those on the old slave plantations. The day began before sunrise when roll call was followed by prayer before work commenced. At 8:30 a.m. breakfast was taken. Work began again at 9:00 a.m., and continued to midday. At 2 p.m., the inmates were back at work and continued up to sunset. One hour after sunset, prayers were again held.[30] Apart then from the absence of the whip, there was little difference between the day of the workhouse inmate and that of the slave.

The timetable established for Sundays was especially revealing. On that day, the workers were taken to mass in the town or the nearest borough. Supervised by workhouse guards, they were supposed to march in twos and 'in perfect silence'. The services consisted mainly of exhortations by the priest that they fulfil their duty to the state by working ardently. At one o'clock, back in the workhouse, the workhouse steward then explained to the inmates, 'the laws, decrees, rulings and decisions concerning the rights of persons, the organization of liberty in the colonies, and the advantages accorded to work'. The steward then demonstrated to them 'by calculations and examples, the positive benefits that the cultivation of the land offers them'.[31]

The workhouses, therefore, were both supposed to supply labour to the colony and to serve as indoctrination centres to instill in the inmates that it was their duty and responsibility to work on the land, in other words, on the plantations.

Attempts were also made to curtail the cultivation of crops other than sugar and coffee, thus directly attacking ground provision cultivation. A 20 franc tax per hectare, on land producing crops other than sugar and coffee, was established. By so doing, it was hoped that the development of provision grounds would be arrested. Moreover, an additional tax of 6 francs per inhabitant was introduced for, so it was claimed, the upkeep of the roads. This tax, like the others, was obviously designed so that the blacks would have no other alternative than to work on the plantations, if they were to pay it and thus avoid the workhouse.

At this point, it would be useful to give some brief account of the nature of metropolitan government 1848–50 and trends therein. Government by Political Assimilation was operative between 1848 and 1851 under the Second Republic. During this period, government by Political Assimilation ran counter to the older, monarchist, white hegemonic rule which already, even before the presidential election of Louis Napoleon on 10 December 1848, had started to install itself.

Political Assimilation can be defined as a governmental system which granted to every male colonial inhabitant, regardless of colour, equal civil and political rights with their metropolitan counterparts in France. This definition remains however theoretical and insufficient because Political Assimilation also implied the economic assimilation (or more precisely expropriation) of the colonies by the metropolis and, even more subtly, their cultural assimilation. This threefold means of assimilation occurred gradually, the product of a slow bargaining process between the colonial and metropolitan politicians. Nether did Political Assimilation involve the entire colonial population between 1848 and 1851. Instead, it was confined to a white, coloured and later on black elite who were for the most part already culturally assimilated and convinced proponents of Political Assimilation. It is thus evident that some of the harsh labour laws already applicable during this period did not conflict with the nature of metropolitan government between 1848–1850. These countryside and other plantation blacks were not culturally assimilated and thus had to be persuaded by law to become assimilated.

The introduction of the domestic passport, known as the *passeport a l'interieur* became a principal means of worker control. Voted on 19 October 1850, when the Napoleonic administration already dominated the metropolitan assembly, this law required every person of either sex, of 16 years and over, living in the colonies, to have in his or her possession a domestic passport. This passport was essential for travel from commune to commune within the colonies themselves.

The communal police force had already been enlarged and re-organized in 1846 for tracking down beggars and vagrants. The communal militia, as it was called in Pointe Noire contained an infantry composed of two companies with 2 captains, 2 quarter-master sergeants, 16 Corporals, and 4 drummers. This communal militia could also form a calvary under the direction of a Marshall.[32] Communal militia or police also served for the legal apprehension of domestic passport offenders.[33]

As early as 1849, the second motivation — that of ensuring that the workers did not abandon the plantation fields — predominated in colonial policy. It is hardly possible to estimate the success of such liberal experiments as the *jurys cantonnaux*, since they functioned for such a brief space of time. Scattered reports suggest that the worker representatives in the *jurys cantonnaux* functioned with great moderation and discipline, and that, in the first few months at least, the workhouses were almost empty. Documents, however, do not provide enough proof to allow us to make this allegation with any certainty. Nevertheless, the fact that the second motive of colonial labour policy — that of ensuring that the blacks worked — was reinforced during the Second Empire, permits a more serious and detailed examination of this policy and its success.

In the Second Empire's famous decree of 15 February 1852, it introduced the pass system, which was distinct from the domestic passport. While the domestic passport was especially designed with the purpose of arresting inter-communal travel, the pass system attempted to force the blacks to adopt contractual labour. It was decreed under the pass system that 'every individual working for a salary or a daily wage, or every holder of a work contract of less than one year, should possess a pass'. It must be emphasized that although both systems were so worded as to imply that they concerned all individuals, they were geared principally to the blacks of working age. The pass system gave a very curious definition of what was considered a vagabond.

Vagabonds or unattached people are those who, not having some means of subsistence and exercising neither trade nor profession, are able to prove habitual work neither by their possession of a work contract valid for one year at least, nor by their possession of a pass.[34]

The blacks were forced into accepting a work contract for a year or more, possessing a pass, or being declared a vagabond.

The names of all persons possessing a pass were to be entered on the official register of the commune to which they belonged, along with their surname, first names, age, profession, date of birth, address and birth certificate.[35] On the pass itself was entered the surname, first names, nicknames, date of birth, domicile and profession of the bearer. In addition, a description of the bearer, the dependents and a registration number of the owner were noted. The pass was then signed by the mayor or by one of his assistants, and then by the bearer of the pass himself. If the bearer was unable to sign, this was stated on the pass.

The bearer of the pass was obliged to pay a cost of 1 franc 25 centimes for his or her pass. This pass was renewable each year, after 1 January 1854, at the cost of a one franc stamp, also payable by the bearer. Facility was available for those holding passes who wished to exchange them for domestic passports, on condition that they proved they possessed a work contract of at least one year.[36]

The freedom of movement of the pass-holders was even more restricted than that of the holders of domestic passports who possessed work contracts of one year or more. It was necessary for pass-holders who moved from one commune to another to declare themselves at the town hall within the first three days of their arrival and to enter their names on the official register of the

commune. Before they moved, the pass-holders had to obtain a clearance, entered on the pass, from the town hall. Consequently, within each colony, laws were designed with the purpose of virtually imprisoning the workers within the confines of their communes.

The pass was supposed to be perpetually in the possession of the bearer. On the demand of the police officer, (the communal militia previously referred to), the pass had to be furnished immediately, failing which the individual was arrested and taken before the mayor and the police commissioner.[37] One decree in 1854 specified that the monthly earnings and debts of each pass-holder, settled every Saturday morning according to the law, should be put on the pass on the first Saturday of every month. Every worker whose pass showed a statement of advances made to him by the planter, had to reimburse the planter, either in cash or by working the number of days required to repay the sums advanced, before she or he could obtain a clearance stamp on their pass.[38] The planters capitalized on this Article in particular, as a means of keeping the workers tied to the plantation.

The pass system was also specifically aimed at what was termed the 'vagabond'. It was further established that anyone found fraternizing with 'vagabonds' was punishable by the penalties pronounced against vagrancy. Thus, one was not only actively discouraged from being a 'vagabond' oneself, but one was penalized for frequenting with 'vagabonds'.[39]

Special laws were also implemented for those who through the nature of their jobs, found it impossible to know who their employer or employers would be in advance of assuming their jobs. It was possible for such persons to obtain the pass of a *journalier* or day-worker which she or he was obliged to present once every three months to the city hall, under the penalty of a 5 to 20 franc fine for not doing so.[40] The attestation of two *Conseillers Municipaux*, again members of the planter class or their close associates, or the police commissioner, was necessary to obtain a day-worker's pass. The day-workers had then to constitute themselves into trade-guilds. The mayor nominated three representatives in each trade-guild to assist him 'in the verification of the work of the day-workers of the trade-guild, to give their opinion on the number of day-workers necessary for the proper functioning of the diverse industries, and to establish the aptitude of those who demanded admission to the trade-guilds'.[41] Article 116 of the same decree obliged the porters, retailers, washerwomen and other day-workers to wear on work-days, a badge or medal which was delivered to them by the mayor, at their expense, and which indicated on it their profession, registration number in the trade-guild and the commune from which they came. Any day-worker who used the badge of another, or who loaned his badge to another, was punished by a fine of 61 to 100 francs and one to fifteen days imprisonment. This fine was also, of course, payable by days of work.

The attitudes governing the pass laws were explicit in so far as self-employed cultivators were concerned. Inspectors inspected the self-employed population on their own private properties and tried to ascertain whether the days of work furnished on their own land were sufficient to justify exemption from work for another. Every self-employed cultivator who did an insufficient number of work days on his own land, was obliged to make up the surplus by working for another, more often than not for a planter. All self-employed cultivators who, with no legitimate motive, did not cultivate their land, or neglected its upkeep on the days reserved for this by the mayor, were liable to a fine of 61 to 100 francs and to 1 to 15 days imprisonment, or to one of these penalties, according to the circumstances.[42] Article 3 of an 1854 decree stated that it was not enough to simply claim self-sufficiency. One had to establish it.[43]

If the pass system chose to limit and regulate the duties and movement of the workers, the local government, by a yearly registration or census, attempted to supervise and control the entire population, with particular reference of course to the native and immigrant workers.

After slavery, the ex-slaves use of different names to refer to the same person posed innumerable problems to the administration. The blacks, using inadvertently and voluntarily their nicknames and first names, changed their names at will and in this manner confused criminal proceedings and rendered extremely difficult any attempt to implement the type of control which the local administration was advocating. As Governor de Gueydon put it:

You see each day, in fact, individuals baptized under one name, married under another, taxed under a third and unknown under all these names. You see others thwarting the ends of justice by presenting themselves under different names.[44]

An increase in the numbers of the police force still did not solve this problem. Yet, the local government found this situation intolerable, preventing as it did the control of the workers, necessary if work on the sugar plantations was to continue smoothly. In an introduction to the law on registration, Governor de Gueydon summed up his opinions on the matter.

The large proprietors should not have to deal, beyond due measure, with the abandonment of their fields by the workers. Immigration will fill up space, but it is necessary that the deserters of the principal crop be convinced that they will find neither respite nor rest, if, by the production of useful commodities, that is export commodities, they do not meet the deficit which results from their own desertion of the principal crop. . . .[45]

Although de Gueydon's language was somewhat veiled, his arguments were explicit. The blacks had to work on the plantations, if only to fill the gap that their own desertion of the plantations had produced. One of the ways that the blacks escaped control over their labour power was through the adoption of a medley of names. It was necessary that they were shown, and forcibly, that the administration would give them 'no respite nor rest', as long as they refused to work on the sugar plantations. Therefore, registration, as one means of controlling the black workers, had to be established.

This census included an official register of the declarations of jobs, residences, changes of employers and departures from the commune for all individuals residing in the communes; an official survey of all properties, with or without buildings; an annual register for the enumeration of families, plantation gangs, servicemen and women, industries, properties and professions. Every person of sixteen years and over had to be registered. The head of the family, or the employer, was supposed to supply a list of all persons under his authority, or employed or housed by him, indicating their age, date of birth or approximate age, profession, registration number, pass or contract number or evidence of exemption from work by the mayor. The city-halls were in charge of the registration and the results were to be published each year before 31 December.[46]

Combined with the pass system, registration and other laws designed to control the native labour force, laws governing the domestic passport and the workhouses were also elaborated during the Second Empire. Yearly stamps (or as they were more correctly called, visas) given by the mayor for the native passports came to be preceded by the words 'subject to the pass' or 'not subject to the pass'. Everyone who did not possess a domestic passport was subject to a 5 to 100 francs fine.[47] Similarly, all those who were fined and could not afford to pay the fine, were transported to the workhouses where they were required to work out their fines at the rate of one franc per day. What was highly significant was that these sentences could also be carried out on the rural plantations of individual planters. In that case, the employer retained half of the worker's salary.[48]

The labour laws were, consequently, directed against two types of 'vagabonds', those who tried to escape plantation work completely and the irregular workers. Not even the stable plantation workers escaped this control although they were exempt from the pass and personal tax[49], they were by no means exempt from the domestic passport and registration.

These coercive labour laws were thus interlinked. The decree, for example, which demanded that tax collectors indicate payment or non-payment of the personal tax on the pass, tried simultaneously to ensure the payment of this tax. Similarly, the phrase, 'subject or not subject to the pass' which was compulsory on the domestic passport, ensured that all pass-holders were subject to even further supervision. The linking of one law to another ensured, in theory, the smooth functioning of the coercion apparatus.

It was for this reason that the so-called Gueydon decree passed in Martinique was so significant. This decree assembled all the labour laws into one cohesive and coherent code. Adelaide has emphasized the importance of the Gueydon decree.[50] However, few of the articles of this decree were in themselves original. The originality of the Gueydon decree lay in its codification of the labour laws and their forceful enactment during his term of government. Admiral de Gueydon, ardent supporter of the planter class, was able by his efficient and determined administration to ensure that the labour laws were carried out. To achieve this, he was blessed with no more significant apparatus than his predecessors but instead followed up the theory of the laws with practice. Through his efficient administration, his own personal and forceful style, he presided over the laws' implementation through the use of the communal militia who were unaccustomed to such forceful demands from the chief administrator. Gueydon's view on labour relations vis-à-vis the native workers was adequately illustrated in the quotation cited above when he urged that 'the deserters of the principal crop be convinced that they will find neither respite or rest if . . . they do not meet the deficit resulting from their own desertion of the principal crop . . .'[51] The planters rewarded him with their warm support. Souquet-Basiege, a nineteenth century member of the planter class, saw de Gueydon as the Governor responsible for setting the most forceful imprint on the exemplary government during the Second Empire in Martinique.

From 1852, Martinique entered into an epoch of material transformation which was almost uninterrupted. The population applied itself to improving its own well-being and, everywhere, a spirit of initiative, solicited by diverse enterprises, undertook the astonishing progress realized from that date. In the midst of it all, Admiral de Gueydon, remained the veritable creator of our present colony. . . .[52]

When, however, we look at the penalties imposed by these labour laws on the employers, in contrast to the penalties imposed on the employees, we are struck by a remarkable disparity. In the first place, relatively few laws concentrated on the obligations of the employers to their employees as compared to the superfluity of laws on the employees' obligations. Employers could not, for instance, refuse the entry visa without good cause.[53] They were supposed to keep a control book in which they entered the payments of wages to workers, worker debts, breaches by indentured servants, and advances made to workers. The penalty for failing to keep this law was a fine of between 5 and 20 francs.[54] In addition, employers who employed any individual without a pass, or with an irregular pass, were fined from 5 to 20 francs.[55]

When these penalties are compared to the 5 to 100 francs fine of an employee who did not have a pass, and who in addition earned a minuscule income compared to his employer's, the injustice of the labour laws becomes evident. This injustice

Penalties for breaches of reciprocal conventions between employers and employees, 1858[57]

Designation of Commune	No. of Disputes	Sentences Pronounced	
		Against Employee	Against Employer
Deshaies	3	3	–
Pointe-Noire	15	15	–
Bouillante	2	2	–
Habitants	23	23	–
Baillif	11	11	–
Saint-Claude	18	18	–
Gourbeyre	6	6	–
Trois-Rivieres	10	10	–
Capesterre	9	7	2
Goyave	5	5	–
Petit-Bourg	17	17	–
Baie-Mahault	23	23	–
Lamentin	15	15	–
Sainte-Rose	4	4	–
Point-a-Pitre	9	9	–
Gosier	6	6	–
Abymes	26	26	–
Morne a L'eau	5	5	–
Moule	16	16	–
Sainte-Anne	5	5	–
Saint-Francois	33	33	–
TOTAL	261	259	2

to the workers becomes even clearer when one considers the disputes between employers and workers which were taken before the courts. Fallope reported that in 1861 there were 365 penalties pronounced, only three against the employers.[56] The preceding chart, which lists the condemnations pronounced against the employers and employees in the different communes of Guadeloupe for the year 1858, highlights this discrimination practised against the workers.

In addition to these 'strong-arm' tactics employed by the administration, persuasive means were devised to encourage blacks to do steady work on the plantations. In both Guadeloupe and Martinique laws were formulated establishing a system of model workers. In Martinique, it was decided that each year, four gold medals, twenty-five first class silver medals, twenty-five second class silver medals and seventy awards of 20 francs each would be distributed to deserving workers. On one side, the medals held the likeness of the Prince-President, Napoleon, and on the other, the inscription of 'Reward for morality and zeal of work'.[58] Following is a list of only a few such individuals in Guadeloupe who were awarded prizes for being model workers. It allows us to appreciate some of the precise reasons for which the awards were granted.

Mayor's Presentation[59]	Motives	Attorney General's Proposal
Joseph L'AMOUR, 56 years, commissioner of plantation Doulogne	Devoted man, laborious upright, intelligent having always been and still is one of the workers of the plantation. He has always displayed sentiments of order and good conduct.	Pecuniary award of 50 francs
Marcelin, TOMBA, 36 years, cultivator plantation, Eloi Bain	Worthy of being cited and rewarded. Former plantation driver. Father of eight legitimate children. Honest and labourious. He brings up his large family to love order and work. Has never left his former master who is today very old, yet he continues, as formerly, to assist him with his work and his services. Strongly recommended by the mayor.	Pecuniary award of 50 francs
Fevriette BIRALD,	Of rare intrepidity at work. Cultivates the cane as a sharecropper. Has done, in 1851, one thousand barrels of sugar. Has brought back to the plantation six members of her family, who left in 1848. She employs them in the cultivation of her cane.	Second class silver medal
Philadelphe PLANTY,	Exemplary conduct, wise, invariably honest man. When liberty was proclaimed and the workers deserted the plantation, he proposed himself to work at the manufacture of the sugar. Has kept guard for more than fifteen days and nights to oversee the instigators of disorder.	Honourable mention
Rosillette LEMORNE,	This woman has not abandoned her unfortunate mistresses after 1848, and has contributed to helping and serving them without receiving any retribution.	Pecuniary award of 50 francs

The medals awarded from 1852 to August 1858 were given under the heading of 'The General State of Titulars of Medals'[60]

1852 and 53	51 medals
1855	34 "
1856	40 "
1857	18 "

A clear diminution could be noted.

Even schools were incorporated into this reward programme. Gold and bronze medals were distributed to the pupils of religious schools who distinguished themselves in agricultural work. In this way, it was hoped that the youth would be directed towards 'the honourable profession of agriculture'.[61] As still another means of enticing the population to this 'honourable profession', agricultural schools were established. In Martinique, an Arts and Crafts school was created in Fort-de-France with the special purpose of training plantation workshop leaders and good workers. It was the view of the Martiniquan *Conseil General* that in order for education to fulfil 'its moral and social aim', agricultural work had to be introduced into the educational system.[62]

Black men and women responded to these attempts to control them with acute hostility. The planters, together with the administration were attempting to replace the driving whip of slavery by the labour laws which allowed the workers little leeway for escape from plantation work. As Cochin remarked:

To the law which said: 'The worker is free', the decree added, 'work is compulsory'! One will agree that the newly freed found it difficult to grasp this nuance. Having escaped from constraints, they were defiant of all which resembled them.[63]

The system of awards proved unsuccessful. Governor Bertier of Martinique declared in 1867 that the system of medal distribution had turned out to be 'impotent', and that a bonus of encouragement offered to workers who fulfilled 250 days of work per year had produced no effect whatsoever.[64]

Various incidents resulted from the passing of these labour laws, and in particular the pass system. In Capesterre, Guadeloupe, one plantation gang reacted to attempts to implement the pass system by brandishing their cutlasses outside the town hall, and threatening to kill the mayor. Not one cultivator in this commune presented her/himself to the town hall to collect a pass. In the commune of Trois-Rivierre, members of another gang stated that they preferred to die rather than accept the passes and no passes were distributed in this commune. In Vieux–Fort also, workers refused to accept the passes while demonstrations took place in Moule and Anse-Bertrand. In the latter commune, workers unanimously refused to hand back the passes to the proprietors or managers.[65] The Governor of Guadeloupe summed up the attitude of the black population in the following manner:

The memory of slavery is still present in the mind of the masses. All which is new for this ignorant population, all that tends to restrain, I will not say their liberty of movement but only the abuse which has been made of that liberty up to now, awakens among the population a sentiment of defiance which causes a certain anxiety.[66]

In Martinique, the Governor reported in 1852 that the workers were very anxious about the new pass system and that the passes were being distributed very slowly indeed. In the two communes where the distribution of passes were the highest — Fort-de-France and Saint-Pierre — the number of passes distributed was only 257 and 5 to 600 respectively.[67]

In fact, so strong was black reaction against the passes that certain clauses had to be retracted by a decree of October 1852. In this way, Article 63 which took away from the worker the right to cancel her or his contract before the termination of the harvest, was replaced by a clause which allowed both parties to give only eight days notice. Article 64, which allowed the proprietor to take away from the worker the day reserved for the cultivation of his garden, was also withdrawn. So was Article 69, which allowed the proprietor to cut out the two and a half hours afternoon rest period if he felt it necessary.[68] The members of the Commission responsible for the elaboration of the labour laws, themselves facing charges of wishing to institute a new form of slavery, became divided over certain clauses of these laws.[69]

The hostility of the black workers to these labour laws was so intense that differences arose even between the planter class and the administration over them. The differences, however, did not focus on the fundamental principles of the labour laws, but on the too forceful implementation of some of them. In Guadeloupe, Garnier illustrated this disagreement with the example of a contractor, Mr. Belbeze, who said of his 42 employees:

I received word to dismiss all the workers without a pass. Now, out of 42 I would have dismissed 38. I employed them all. And averaging the work that is given them, they will earn (1) the wherewithal to pay the tax, (2) the wherewithal to live; (3) they can, moreover, obtain a pass, since it is refused to those who have not paid their taxes. If, on the contrary, I had dismissed them, they would be without work, without a means of existence, unable to pay the tax, and to obtain a pass. They would have been forced to become vagrants.[70]

The workhouses also came to be looked upon with some disfavour by the planters as they were seen as further contributing to the abandonment of the plantation fields.

In the long run, the blacks, and even those whites who continued to employ workers without a pass, were forced to comply. In Martinique, the Attorney-General sent a circular to the Attorneys, instructing them that the police force should, from 26 November 1852, begin to seek out actively all offenders against the labour laws. According to the Attorney-General:

Active searches should be scrupulously undertaken by the policemen and all the public authorities. These searches should be especially geared to, primarily, the town and borough populace, the proprietors and the workers of the principal plantations in order to repress the offenses committed not only by the domestics, workmen and cultivators . . . but also by the proprietors and the industrial heads.[71]

Prosecutions of the black populace for bodily attacks on policemen rose astronomically. To subdue the angry black population, the Governor of Martinique was constrained to order several police detachments to march through the more recalcitrant communes so as to impress on the population not only the undesirability of resorting to such acts as strikes,[72] but the superior military strength of the forces of 'law and order'. By 1853, the number of passes distributed in Martinique to the native black workers was calculated as follows:[73]

	Plantation Workers	Other Workers	Domestics
Men	13,454	5,264	1,160
Women	12,767	3,600	3,375

Compliance, however, did not mean acceptance. And the hazards of open and violent resistance gave way to what Adelaide termed 'passive resistance'[74] and what one report from Capesterre, Guadeloupe, called 'inertia'.[75] If they were forced to work, then by loitering on the job and generally refusing to accept contractual labour, the blacks managed to show their disagreement and to render the labour laws, to some extent, ineffectual. One report from Port-Louis, Guadeloupe, stated in 1858:

One still remarks among the cultivators, the same tendency to desert the regular gangs to go and establish themselves in the Grands Fonds of Moule, Morne-a-l'eau and Abymes on little portions of land that they buy, or

else as sharecroppers, in the communes where this mode of work exists.[76]

In Martinique, Governor de Lapelin reported in 1865:

The native workers do not generally enter into contracts on the rural properties. Most of them only want to acquire the means to make themselves independent so as to buy a portion of land where they can construct a house and consecrate themselves to the cultivation of provisions. Others, having already achieved this desire, or less worried about the future, will consent to hire their services by the day, but they show a marked repugnance to adopting long-term contracts. It is then, most often, by the help of financial advances, which force the cultivator, under the sanctions resulting from the local decrees on the policing of labour, to work, that the proprietors manage to attach some of them to their plantations.[77]

The labour laws provoked enormous problems in the society. They did not increase the native labour force. The number of native workers in Martinique dropped from 26,865 in 1848 to 23,840 in 1874.[78] The total population in Martinique around 1850 was estimated at 120,000.[79] While in 1876 Martinique's population was cited at 150,695.[80] Likewise, the number of native workers in Guadeloupe only rose from 25,755 in 1849 to 27,310 in 1874.[81] And these 1874 figures in both colonies were still significantly lower than the number of slave workers in 1847 for instance.

The active and passive resistance of the native workers ensured that the labour laws were thwarted at almost every turn, if, in fact, enforcement was every really practicable. They still managed to achieve some freedom from plantation work and adopted contractual labour only when forced.

If anything, the labour laws increased the blacks' repugnance towards work on the sugar plantations. In addition, it hardened the tendency of the younger black generation to desert plantation labour completely. One of the principal reasons for the inauguration of the agricultural school in Martinique in 1865 was to 'introduce the taste for agricultural work among the young generations who tend more and more to distance themselves' from this labour.[82] Needless to say, this attempt failed.

Nevertheless, the planters were loath to see the labour laws abolished for they were seen as a guarantee of a fairly stable, however inadequate, labour supply. We learn from Chester, a visitor to the French West Indies in 1869, that there were, in contrast to the British islands, no beggars on the French streets.[83] This was most likely a direct result of the labour laws. Despite proposals to reduce the personal tax in Martinique because of the misery it entailed to many 'honest cultivators and the families', most *Conseil General* members refused to support such a measure. They continued to look on the personal tax as the 'most assured guarantee of work and order'.[84]

Only in a negative light could the labour laws be deemed successful, for they did not encourage an increase in the numbers of native workers on the sugar plantations. They prevented, however, the plantation fields from being even more deserted than they would otherwise have been.

Notes

1. Archives Nationales, Section Outre-Mer (A.O.M.), Guadeloupe, C 4 D49, Ship Captain's Report, July 30.
2. A.O.M., Martinique C 56 D 463, Ship Captain's Report, July 30 1848.
3. A.O.M., Guadeloupe, C 4 D 49, Extract from a planter's letter, August 10, 1848.
4. A.O.M., Martinique, C 56 D 463, Extract from a planter's letter, June 14, 1848.
5. Josette Fallope, 'La Guadeloupe entre 1848 and 1900' (Universite de Paris, These pour le Doctorat de 3eme cycle 1972) p. 86.
6. Rene Acheen, 'Fondements Historiques' in **Encyclopedie Antillaise: Economies et Perspectives**, (Pointe-a-Pitre, Editions Des Ormeaux, 1973) p 186.
7. **Notices Statistiques**, 1848, pp. 33–35.
8. Ibid., 1849, pp. 33–35.
9. Fallope, 'La Guadeloupe', op. cit., p. 129.
10. A.O.M., Guadeloupe C 4 D 49, Governor to the Minister, August 10, 1848.
11. A.O.M., Martinique, C 11 D 109, Governor to the Minister, December 28, 1849.
12. B. David, 'La Population Martiniquaise au fil des ans, 1633–1902' (Memoires de la Societe d'Histoire de la Martinique, 1973) No. 3, p. 110.
13. **Annuaire de la Guadeloupe**, 1890, p. LVII.
14. A.O.M., Martinique, C 56 D 462, Extract of a letter by Delandre, businessman and proprietor, July 24, 1848.
15. Ibid.
16. **Bulletin Official de la Martinique**, 1848, No. 496.
17. A.O.M., Guadeloupe, C 7 D 71, Attorney-General to the Governor, December 12, 1848.
18. Before the arrival of the commissioners bearing the act of emancipation, the slaves had revolted in Saint-Pierre on May 22, 1848, causing the death of thirty whites. The Governor pronounced the emancipation Act on the same day.
19. A.O.M., Martinique, C 12 D 123, Colson 'Notes on certain episodes of the 1848 revolution in Martinique, able to elucidate several points of the colony's history in these ill-fated days', 1848.
20. **Bulletin Official de la Martinique**, August 1848, p. 721.
21. A.O.M., Guadeloupe, C 39 D 415, The Governor to the Minister, May 28, 1899.
22. Jacques Adelaide, 'Troubles Sociaux en Guadeloupe a la fin due X1Xe siecle et au debut due XX siecle (1895–1910)', Groupe Universitaire de Recherches Inter-Caraibes, No. 10, Mars 1971, G.U.R.I.C., Centre d'Enseignment Superieur Litteraire, Pointe-a-Pitre, p. 39.
23. **Bulletin Official de la Martinique**, June 4, 1848.
24. Between 1802 and 1848, administratively speaking, both Guadeloupe and Martinique were first divided into **arrondissements** or districts, further sub-divided into cantons, then finally sub-divided into communes. There were two

districts, four cantons and twenty-six communes in each colony.
25. **Bulletin Official de la Guadeloupe**, July 13, 1849.
26. J. De Crisenoy, **Etude sur la situation economique des Antilles Francaises**, (Bibliotheque Nationale, 1860) p. 48.
27. **Bulletin Official de la Guadeloupe**, July 13, 1849.
28. The word 'workhouse' is but a clumsy translation of the term **ateliers de discipline** which differed greatly from the old English workhouse. It is hoped that the implications of the **ateliers de discipline** will become clear from the explanations which follow.
29. **Bulletin Official de la Martinique**, 1848, Decree No. 449.
30. Ibid.
31. **Blletin Official de la Martinique**, 1848, Decree No. 449.
32. **Gazette Official de la Guadeloupe**, Nov. 20, 1848.
33. **Bulletin Official de la Martinique**, August 21, 1848. Unfortunately, the decree did not go into the details of this enlargement.
34. **Bulletin Official de la Martinique**, February 13, 1852.
35. **Bulletin Official de la Martinique**, October 9, 1852.
36. **Bulletin Official de la Martinique**, October 9, 1852.
37. Ibid.
38. **Bulletin Official de la Martinique**, October 9, 1852.
39. Ibid, February 13, 1852.
40. Ibid, May 16, 1854.
41. Ibid.
42. **Bulletin Official de la Guadeloupe**, December 2, 1857.
43. **Bulletin Official de la Martinique**, May 16, 1854.
44. **Bulletin Official de la Martinique**, January 9 and September 1, 1855.
45. Ibid, September 1, 1855.
46. **Bulletin Official de la Guadeloupe**, December 2, 1857.
47. **Bulletin Official de la Martinique**, September 10, 1855.
48. Ibid.
49. **Bulletin Official de la Guadeloupe**, December 2, 1857.
50. Jacques Adelaide, 'Les Origines du Mouvement Ouvrier a la Martinique de 1870 a la Greve de 1900' (Fort-de-France, CERAG, No. 26, 1972) p. 41.
51. See page 12.
52. G. Souquest-Basiege, **'Le Prejuge de Race aux Antilles Francaises'** (Martinique, Imprimerie du Propogateur, 1883) p. 135.
53. **Bulletin Official de la Martinique**, September 10, 1855.
54. **Bulletin Official de la Guadeloupe**, December 2, 1857.
55. **Bulletin Official de la Martinique**, February 13, 1852.
56. Fallope, op. cit., p. 108.
57. A.O.M., Guadeloupe C 108 D 757.
58. **Bulletin Official de la Martinique**, September 2, 1852.
59. Ibid.
60. **Gazette Official de la Guadeloupe**, October 26, 1858. In passing, it is interesting to note the high number of married men who figured among those awarded medals in proportion to the low number of married within the total black population.
61. **Bulletin Official de la Martinique**, 1852, Decree No. 380.
62. **Conseil General** Report, Martinique, November 10, 1863, 2nd sitting.
63. Augustin Cochin, 'Abolition de l'Esclavage' (Paris, Jacques LaCoffre ed., 1861) p. 227.
64. A.O.M., Martinique, C 12 D 117, Governor's annual report on the situation of the colony, 1867.
65. A.O.M., Guadeloupe, C 108 D 757, **conseil Prive**, deliverations, December 2, 1858, 6th sitting.
66. Ibid.
67. A.O.M. Martinique, C 79 D 652, Governor's annual report, 1852.
68. A.O.M., Guadeloupe C 108 D 757, 'Regime du Travail a la Guadeloupe' (no date given).

69. Ibid.
70. Alphonse Garnier, 'Journal Du Conseiller Garnier a la Martinique et a la Guadeloupe', presented and annotated by G. Debien, ed. (Fort-de-France, Societe d'Histoire de la Martinique, 1969) April 7, 1855.
71. A.O.M., Martinique, C 79 D 655, Attorney-General's Proclamation, Fort-de-France, November 23, 1852.
72. A.O.M., Martinique, C 79 D 652, Governor to the Minister, November 11, 1852.
73. A.O.M., Martinique, C 145 D 1229, Annual Report by Home Affairs Director, 1053.
74. Adelaide, 'Les Origines du mouvement ouvrier' op. cit., p. 42.
75. **La Gazette Officielle de la Guadeloupe**, October 18, 1858.
76. Ibid, November 11, 1858.
77. A.O.M., Martinique, C 12 D 117, Governor's annual report, 1865.
78. **Notices Statistiques**, 1849, pp. 33–36, A.O.M., Martinique, C 12 D 124, 1874 and A.O.M. Guadeloupe C 3 D 25, 1874.
79. **Les Cahiers du Centre d'Etude Regionales Antilles-Guyane**, 'La Population Martiniquaise et Ses Migrations' see Besnard Jean-Louis and Mariell Jean, p. 7.
80. A.O.M. Martinique, C 12 D 124.
81. See Footnote 78.
82. **Conseil General** Report, Martinique, November 10, 1862, 2nd sitting.
83. Grenville John Chester, 'Transatlantic Sketches in the West Indies, South America, Canada and the United States' (London, Smith, Elder and Co., 1869) p. 154.
84. **Conseil General** Report, Martinique, October 21, 1865, 11th sitting.

SECTION THREE
Peasants and Planters

Caribbean peasantries pre-dated the maturity of the sugar plantation economy. The abolition of slavery, however, provided the principal impetus for the growth of the Afro-Caribbean peasantry. The immigration of Indian indentured workers after emancipation also created the context for the rise of an Indo-Caribbean peasantry.

During slavery, according to Mintz, some land remained in the hands of the peasantry — freed black, coloured and white — or an enslaved proto-peasantry; but it was with emancipation that any significant shift occurred in traditional land-use and landownership pattern.

The rapid expansion of the peasantry in the post-slavery period, according to Marshall and Renard, came about despite the attempts of large-scale proprietors to deny ex-slaves and ex-indentured workers access to significant amounts of quality land. For example, though the planter-class had been defeated in Haiti, it was the conviction of Toussaint, and subsequent leaders, that the plantation system should remain the fundamental base of the economy. Only Pétion had consistently encouraged the rise of the peasantry.

Bolland indicted that much of the conflict which characterized the relations between planters and ex-slaves centred on land matters. The ability of ex-slaves to cement their freedom with the ownership of land was limited by several factors; the monopoly of 'land rights' by the politically dominant plantation sector; the reluctance of the planters to sell or rent land to the ex-slaves; the absence in some colonies of large tracts of Crown lands, and the ability of the planter state to prevent access to such lands. In many cases the accumulated wages of workers did not enable them to buy available high priced land. Above all, proprietors were intent on maintaining a landless proletariat rather than creating an independent peasantry. Where Crown lands existed, planters used their political power to place severe restrictions on their sale or occupation.

Ex-slaves partially overcame some of these obstacles by participating in a range of land use arrangements. Johnson shows for example, how they obtained land under an exploitative share-cropping system in the Bahamas. In places where the sugar sector experienced difficult times, planters were forced to sell or rent land, and missionaries oftentimes assisted ex-slaves with finances for land purchase, or themselves buying land for resale to ex-slaves. In Guyana, ex-slaves pooled their resources to facilitate group purchase and in Jamaica a peasantry formed on captured Crown lands. After 1865, however, the government of Jamaica also made more of this land available. In Barbados and Antigua, particularly after 1846, some ex-slaves did manage to obtain a small measure of freehold ownership with respect to tiny amounts of land, and functioned socio-economically as 'petty peasants'. The tenantry system in Barbados, noted Marshall, allowed ex-slaves access to if not ownership of, some land. But the insecurity of land use under this arrangement, like the share system Johnson describes for the Bahamas, meant that ex-slaves could hardly have perceived this form of access as an effective way of entrenching their socio-economic freedom. In both places they found it near impossible to insulate themselves from the coercive powers of the white ruling class.

The Origins of Reconstituted Peasantries

Sidney W. Mintz

The history of the Caribbean region begins in 1492, and its present character shows the effects of five centuries of complicated contact. This lengthy and complex past creates genuine analytic difficulties, when one seeks to classify the peasantries of the region in any orderly fashion. An attempt is made here to describe these peasantries as expressive of forms of resistance to European enterprise, as modes of escape or of contrary adaptation. But the origins of the peasantries have been diverse: some came into being only relatively recently; others flourished — and withered — at an earlier time. We lack anything like a complete account of the present distribution of peasant peoples in the islands, and even our criteria for defining a peasantry are open to serious question.

Nonetheless, there may be some utility in seeking to describe some of the main ways in which Caribbean peasantries came into being, if only to indicate what we know of the history of these groups. By and large, Caribbean peasantries have been 'interstitial' groupings, living on the margins of Western enterprise. But reflection on these 'interstices' tells us something about the direction and intent of imperial strategy in the islands, and allows us to discern more clearly how the peasantries responded to such strategy. If the emphasis seems to rest unduly on conflict, on resistance, this is because only rarely and briefly have European powers or even local governments viewed the peasantry as more than an 'obstacle' to development; and the reasons for this negativism, as well as the negativism itself, still persist.

It is certainly not our intent to describe the peasantries of each and every island and mainland Caribbean society as they are now constituted, nor even to examine the full list of historical processes by which such groups came into being. Rather, we shall describe a few major modes of peasantry formation, each of which enables us to perceive, from a somewhat different viewpoint, the challenge of European or state power, and the reaction of local people. Each such instance is substantially independent of the others, though commonly one mode of formation might lead eventually to the appearance of a different adaptation at a later time.

The Squatters

The first such adaptation is that which typified the early period of settlement in the Greater Antilles, in the period before Spain was seriously challenged by its North European rivals. The period begins soon after the Conquest, and continues until the rise of large-scale sugarcane plantations in Cuba and Puerto Rico and, to a much lesser extent in Spanish (that is, eastern) Hispaniola, near the start of the nineteenth century. In these large islands, held uninterruptedly by Spain until nearly the mid-nineteenth century in the case of Santo Domingo, and until 1899 in the cases of Cuba and Puerto Rico, peasantries of mixed cultural and physical origins seem to have come into being as a mode of escape from official power. The locus of settlement was invariably in the interior of the islands, and the settlers were often deserters, escaped slaves from other islands, freedmen of colour, and Europeans seeking to detach themselves from government surveillance and control. Such settlers were often squatters on Crown land, engaged in what was, technically, illegal settlement. Their crop repertories and horticultural techniques are little known, but appear to have included elements originating in Amerindian (Arawak), African, and European cultural heritages. They produced most of their own needs and sold little to outsiders — most such trade, in fact, seems to have been based on smuggling through illegal ports.

Fray Iñigo Abbad y Lasierra, whose *Historia Geográfica . . . de Puerto Rico* was published in 1782, gives us some idea of the life and manners of this curious peasantry (Fernández Méndez 1969). He is astonished, for instance, that they preferred their hammocks (*hamacas*), an item of Amerindian origin, to regular beds; that their meat consumption was low, and that they could be satisfied with a bit of rice and land crab; that they used heavily sweetened coffee to still their hunger pangs, that they loved cockfighting and dancing; and that they were not given to long hours of hard work in the fields. But it is clear that the people Abbad is describing represent a local adaptation to non-plantation life — that they are, in fact,

94

quite happy to be barefoot, to sleep in hammocks, and to limit their labour to their own notions of necessity.

As we have already seen, this was the group out of which the Puerto Rican sugar industry was to fashion a work force of almost 50,000 for the new plantations of the nineteenth century. In so doing, the sugar industry undercut badly the competitive position of its interior frontiersmen, and the highland areas of the island probably never fully recovered. Thus, this first category of peasants — the term is only barely applicable — consisted of people whose adaptation probably depended on the absence of a fully developed sugar industry; and the growth of the industry constituted a major element in its destruction. This is not to say, of course, that Puerto Rico's peasantry disappeared in the early nineteenth century, but rather that the balance was thereafter heavily weighted in favour of plantation enterprise.

The Early Yeomen

A second peasant category stems from the development of indentured labour systems in the islands of the Lesser Antilles, such as Barbados and Martinique, under the influence of British and French planters, in the mid-seventeenth century. Such indentured labourers received a grant of land when their term of labour ended, and it was common for them to settle down in the Lesser Antilles as a peasantry. This category approaches much more closely one part of the conventional definition of peasantries as landholders who produce much or most of their own consumption, while also producing items for sale; in most cases the former indentured servants of the Lesser Antilles produced tobacco, indigo, and other products for European markets. But the growth of the plantation system — a system which accounted in good measure for the original importation of indentured servants — was also to lead to the destruction of such peasantries. Not surprisingly, this process of destruction took on a clear racial character, since the original indentured servants were all Europeans, while those who supplanted them were African slaves. Merivale (1841: 75–76), referring to the British islands, states:

The early settlers who occupied in such numbers the soil of the Antilles, seem to have been chiefly small proprietors, who lived on the produce of their estates. When the cultivation of sugar was introduced about 1670, the free white population rapidly diminished, and continued to do so for a century afterwards. The whites in Barbadoes are said to have increased until they amounted about 1670 to 70,000; but these early calculations must be received with doubt; in 1724, there were only 18,000, there are now [1841] 16,000. Antigua contained 5,000 in the reign of Charles II, now only 2,500. The history of the other Windward Islands is precisely similar. Jamaica, from its extent of surface, and fitness for a variety of productions, did not present the same diminution; yet even there the number of whites remained stationary at about 8,000 from 1670 to 1720. This declining condition of the white populations, showing how unsuited these islands were to become, what their first occupiers imagined they would, the scenes of extensive colonization from Europe, chiefly proceeded from the monopoly of land, consequent on the cultivation of sugar. As mentioned in a former lecture, it was found that the small proprietor could not compete with the large one, in raising this staple product. Coffee, and still more sugar, requires a number of hands, and the simultaneous application of much labour at particular seasons. Thus this species of agriculture resembles in some respects a manufacture; and, as in manufactures, the large capitalists have great advantages . . . Hence all accounts of our West Indian colonies, in the first half of the last century, teem with complaints of the decay of small proprietors, and the consolidation of all classes of society into two, the wealthy planters and the slaves (Merivale 1841: 75–76).

The economic fundamentals which made the plantation more expeditious than the small farm as a medium of colonial development under mercantilism need not detain us. What matters is that the process was general in the New World area embraced by what Philip Curtin (1955: 4–7) has aptly called 'The South Atlantic System'. The slave plantation was, in general, an expansive agrosocial enterprise, land being regarded as the expendable factor in production. Improper land utilization led swiftly to exhaustion, whereupon new land, rather than improved agriculture, became the solution. Eric Williams quotes Merivale: 'It is more profitable to cultivate a fresh soil by the dear labour of slaves, than an exhausted one by the cheap labour of freemen'. And Williams continues: 'From Virginia and Maryland to Carolina, Georgia, Texas and the Middle West; from Barbados to Jamaica to Saint Dominigue and then to Cuba; the logic was inexorable and the same. It was a relay race; the first to start passed the baton, unwillingly we may be sure, to another and then limped sadly behind' (1944: 7).

The accompaniment of this relay race was the persistent and successive extirpation or degradation of yeoman cultivators. L.C. Gray (1941) has documented part of the process in the United States South. Merivale, as cited, did much to reveal the underlying dynamics of the process for the British West Indies. Ortiz, in his *Contrapunteo Cubano* (1940), and Guerra y Sánchez in his *Sugar and Society in the Caribbean* (1964) touch on the parallel theme for Cuba. Though much work remains to be done in order to clarify how yeomen and free squatters were driven out of other parts of the Caribbean by the plantation system, everything we know makes clear that this was not a racial but an economic matter, intimately connected with the plantation system, and the support it consistently received in the metropolis, whether in London, Paris, Madrid, or elsewhere.

However, since the plantation system depended so heavily on slavery, and since slavery fell most cruelly upon African peoples, an assumed relationship has been posited between slavery and race, which conceals a significant part of Caribbean historical reality. All that we know about the social history of the Caribbean plantation system convinces us that the planters were, in one important respect, quite without prejudice: they were willing to employ any kind of labour, and under any institutional arrangements, as long as the labour force was politically defenseless enough for the work to be done cheaply and under discipline. Hence it is a serious error of interpretation to posit any necessary relationship between slavery and race, ignoring all of those instances where non-Africans were enslaved, or otherwise coerced, by the plantation system. This is by no means to say that slavery in the Caribbean region was the same as slavery in other places and at other times; throughout Afro-America, the slavery institution assumed a highly distinctive character, probably never duplicated anywhere else. But just as Caribbean slaves were sometimes Indian, so Caribbean peasants have often been African; the key to the processes by which plantations and peasantries arose or declined is fundamentally economic and political, not racial.

The Proto-Peasantry

A third category of peasantry I have referred to elsewhere as a 'proto-peasantry' (Mintz 1961a), by which I meant simply that the subsequent adaptation to a peasant style of life was worked out by people while they were still enslaved. The full story of life on Caribbean plantations has by no means been written. But we may be sure of a number of general characteristics of Caribbean slave systems: the formal slave codes never represented, other than very superficially, the actual character of life in each society; each island society differed in certain important ways from every other, with regard to its treatment of the slave population; and in each and every system, the slaves were able to work out certain creative adaptations, in spite of the profoundly repressive conditions under which they were forced to live. 'There is something in human history like retribution,' wrote Karl Marx (1857), 'and it is a rule of historical retribution that

its instrument be forged not by the offended, but by the offender himself'. The chronicle of Caribbean proto-peasantries seems to confirm this ringing assertion.

Repeatedly, activities which the slaves were compelled to carry out in order to benefit the planters also enabled them to demonstrate their intelligence, resourcefulness, and creativity. Repeatedly, the planters were struck by the slaves' capacities to function very differently in new contexts — when producing their own foods or going to market, for instance — from the way they functioned under the whip. The planters, of course, explained the difference in terms of the slaves' contrariety; but the slaves — and occasional foreign visitors — knew better. Often these selfsame skills turned out to be basic in establishing the freedmen's independence from the plantation after emancipation; and Part III deals with just this development.

The proto-peasantry, then, are slaves who later became peasant freedmen, either through emancipation (as in the case of Jamaica) or revolution (as in the case of Haiti), and whose particular repertories of agricultural skills, craft techniques, crops, and all else represent important 'blendings' of traditional and new materials. Commonly, among such peasantries today, one finds both African religious elements and European religious elements; African crops and European, Asian, and Amerindian crops; African food-processing techniques and food-processing techniques from many other areas; and so on. Those of a proto-peasant past form the largest Caribbean peasant category, both numerically and in terms of historical origins. But this category has remained rather poorly defined, in contradistinction to other categories of rural agrarian people in the region.

The Runaway Peasantries

A fourth category shares much with the preceding categories but also differs in important ways and deserves separate treatment. These are the 'runaway peasantries', which were formed by escaping slavery rather than by submitting to it. Throughout the Caribbean region — in Mexico, Colombia, Puerto Rico, Cuba, Saint-Dominigue and Jamaica, as well as in Brazil and the Guianas — the creation of maroon communities in defiance of slavery and the plantation system was a common occurrence. Such communities must be separated, for some purposes, from individual escapees — who could attach themselves to the maroon communities only when they were accepted into the maroon bands — and from instances of resistance or rebellion in situ, in which slaves attacked their masters locally. The rationale of the maroon pattern was to create a new and free kind of community outside of, and in opposition to, the slave plantocracy and, where possible, to establish diplomatic relations with the plantocracy on the basis of some kind of reciprocal treaty. The best-known instances are probably those of Jamaica and Surinam (Dutch Guiana); but maroon communities elsewhere also established treaty accords with the slave society, as in Mexico (Davidson 1966) and Cuba (Pérez de la Riva 1952), and sometimes became runaway-slave hunters themselves as part of their compact.

Since the slave-owners and the metropolitan governments carried out frequent attempts to destroy the maroon settlements, their inhabitants often lived under the threat of war, and their economic integration with the outside world was correspondingly impaired. To the extent that they were compelled to maintain complete isolation, such settlements were not, typologically speaking, 'peasant communities'. But the history of such groups, in general, has been one of extermination or of transformation into peasantries. Thus, to take the Haitian case, we know that substantial maroon bands survived for generations in the borderlands of Spanish Santo Domingo. We do not know whether such bands had formal contact of any kind with the Haitian revolutionary movement after it became a movement of the slaves themselves; but we are inclined to assume that the maroon bands, like the revolutionaries, became settled peasantries after the Revolution. Debbasch, in his monograph on *marronage* (1961, 1962), has indicated what evidence we have that the maroon groups of pre-revolutionary Haiti maintained their previous contacts and amities after the Revolution; but it is likely that they became part of the Haitian peasantry in general in the post-revolutionary period. The relationships between proto-peasantries and maroon bands, though hardly known at all, could prove of immense significance for our understanding of slave resistance. For the moment, what we know is largely surmise.

These attempts to define certain historical trajectories in regard to peasant sub-cultures do not take the place of serious studies, either in the form of fieldwork or documentary research; in fact, fieldwork and research should test and refine (and, if necessary, discard) such formulations. Nor should a typological category as wide and as loose as that of 'the peasantry' disguise in any way the immense cultural variety that typifies peasant societies everywhere. Certain features of the Caribbean peasant adaptation originate in the general conditions — ecological, economic, political — under which the emergence of peasant groups occurred. We are able to trace the particular effects of these conditions in single cases, as is done in some of the following chapters. Thus, for instance, in both Haiti (French Saint-Domingue) and Jamaica, the slavery regime produced two highly variant responses among the slave population: escape and struggle on the one hand, accommodation and the learning of specific skills on the other. But the general sociological conditions under which the slaves had to respond to the immense pressures put upon them do not in any way explain the contemporary differences between, for example, Haitian and Jamaican peasants, nor even, necessarily, their contemporary similarities. The heavy commitment of the Jamaican peasantry to market-oriented production of pimento (allspice: *Pimenta officinalis* Lindl.) and bananas, when contrasted with that of the Haitian peasantry's production of coffee, implicates significant differences in seasonal activity, the use of family labour, attitudes toward the land, and much else, that are dependent on the nature of the crops themselves and on the marketing arrangements imposed from outside on the peasantry. Such differences cannot be 'explained' by reference to history as such, nor do they hinge on any shared characteristics of the peasantry, except in the most general sense. In other words, the delineation of a 'developmental path' along which the peasantry has evolved in any particular Caribbean case is little more than a highly abstract exercise, until the necessary historical and ethnological research to confirm or disprove such postulations is carried out.

Caribbean Peasantries as a Social Science Problem

The assertion that it is useful to study Caribbean peasantries as cases of resistance to the plantation regime is likewise open to attack — though a number of scholars (e.g., Marshall 1968) have begun to make very good use of this perspective. A core feature of the argument rests on the assumption that Caribbean populations, whether slaves, indentured labourers, or contract labourers, have consistently struggled to define themselves either within culturally distinctive *communities* or as members of family *lines* — that is, they have not *generally* responded to the plantation regimen in terms of their class identity but along other dimensions of social affiliation. A key to this assertion is the significance of land for Caribbean rural folk — a significance that far exceeds any obvious economic considerations. The slaves sought desperately to express their individuality through the acquisition of material wealth, and some of the following selections indicate the ways in which this might be done. Torn from societies that had not yet entered into the capitalist world, and thrust into settings that were profoundly capitalistic in character on the one hand, yet rooted in the need for unfree labour on the other, the slaves saw liquid capital not only as a means to secure freedom, but also as a means to attach their paternity — and hence, their identity as persons — to something even the masters would have to respect. In these terms, the creation of peasantries was simultaneously an act of westernization and an act of resistance.

Such responses were not limited to the formation of peasantries alone, however. All kinds of skills could be pressed into use to achieve the same results: craftsmanship, fishing, trade, veterinary science, hunting, and much else. In all such cases, the slaves — and at a later time, the contract labourers who succeeded them — sought to *become persons*, to define themselves, in terms of what they knew and could do. We have already seen how, on the Puerto Rican plantations, special skills were a source of prestige, wealth, and self-respect for black freedmen. This was even truer for the peasantries, and for all those who managed to escape the plantation regimen in order to define their lives outside its iron order.

This may very well be one of the most important ways in which a contrast may be drawn between the North American and the Caribbean instances. If one were asked to specify the single feature of the Caribbean past that might best account of the differences in circumstance facing the North American freedman and the freedmen of the Antilles, this — in the view of the present writer — would be the feature to explore. By what processes of disfranchisement, terror, and psychological pressure were the black freedmen of North America deprived of the means to define themselves *economically* as men? I would say that the answer to this question would explain, at least on some very general level, all of the derivative destructions of individuality, dignity, and self that white North America has sought — ultimately, in vain — to impose upon its black victims. Such an assertion

remains surmise, for the most part. But the endless controversies about 'culture deprivation', the supposedly non-existent black nuclear family, and much else that now typify the North American politico-intellectual scene, cannot be resolved only by revalidating the cultural norms of black Americans; it is essential to revert at some point to lower-order explanations of a more molar kind.

All of this takes us far from the task of formulating a typology of Caribbean peasantries. But it does suggest one way in which these peasantries must be evaluated historically: namely, by assessing the means used by the Caribbean masses to resist a system designed to destroy their identity as human beings.

References

Curtin, Philip, *Two Jamaicas: The role of ideas in a tropical colony* (Cambridge: Harvard University Press, 1955

Davidson, David M., 'Negro salve control and resistance in colonial Mexico 1519–1650', *Hispanic American Historical Review*, 46 (1966), 235–53

Debbasch, Yvan, 'Le Marronage: essai sur la desertion de l'esclave Antillais', *L'Annee Sociologique* (1961): 1–112; (1962)

Fernandez Mendez, Eugenio, *Cronicas de Puerto Rico* (Spain: Editorial Universidad de Puerto Rico, 1969)

Gray, Lewis C., *History of Agriculture in the Southern United States to 1860* (New York: P. Smith, 1941)

Guerra y Sanchez, Ramiro, *Sugar and society in the Caribbean* (New Haven: Yale University Press, 1964)

Marshall, Woodville K., 'Peasant development in the West Indies since 1838', *Social and Economic Studies*, 17 (1968): 252– 63

Marx, Karl, 'The Indian revolt', *New York Tribune*, Sept. 16 1857

Merrivale, Herman, *Lectures on colonization and colonies* (London: Longman, Orme, Brown, Green and Longmans, 1841)

Mintz, Sidney W., 'The question of Caribbean peasantries: a comment', *Caribbean Studies* 1 (1961a) 31–34

Ortiz, Fernando, *Contrapunto Cubano del tabaco y el azucar* (Havana: Jesus Montero, 1940)

Perez de la Riva, Francisco, *La habitacion rural en Cuba* (La Habana: Contribucion del Grupo Guama, Antropologia No. 26, 1952)

Williams, Eric, *Capitalism and Slavery* (Chapel Hill: The University of North Carolina Press, 1944)

Peasant Development in the West Indies Since 1838

Woodville K. Marshall

Modern West Indian history begins without peasantry, and [this] is of particular interest because in tracing it, we trace the birth and development of an entirely new class which has profoundly affected the foundations of West Indian society.[1]

Introduction

The West Indian peasant (in this paper 'West Indies' refers to the former British West Indies), because of the circumstances of his origin, cannot be fitted neatly into conventional definitions of the peasant. He has no long-established 'ties of tradition and sentiment' to the land which he controls. He cannot be seen as the 'rural dimension of old civilizations'.[2] The West Indian community is relatively young, and moreover no peasantry survived the establishment of the plantation and slave labour-based sugar industry during the seventeenth century. Whatever elements of a peasantry existed then — the yeoman farmers — quickly disappeared. The small settlers sought new opportunities in North America as the plantation swallowed their holdings; and the negroes who escaped the estates and established settlements in the bush and the mountains were always in danger of extermination by those who controlled the plantation.[3]

The only tenuous link that can be established between the present-day peasantry and the pre-1838 period is in the activity of the slaves as producers of most of their own food, and even of surpluses, on land granted them by their owners.[4] In this role the slaves were partly peasant cultivators or, as Mintz calls them, proto-peasants.[5] But of course they controlled neither the land nor their own time and labour.

Our peasantry then starts at emancipation in 1838. It comprises the ex-slaves who after 1838 started small farms 'on the peripheries of plantation areas',[6] wherever they could find land — on abandoned plantations and in the mountainous interiors of the various territories. 'They represented a reaction to the plantation economy, a negative reflex to enslavement, mass production, monocrop dependence, and metropolitan control.

Although these peasants often continued to work part-time on plantations for wages, to eke out their cash needs, their orientation was in fact antagonistic to the plantation rationale'.[7]

To summarize, then, the West Indian peasantry exhibits certain special characteristics. It is recent in origin; its growth — in numbers and in acreage controlled — was consistent during the first 50–60 years of its existence; it exists alongside and in conflict with the plantation; and it did not depend exclusively on cultivation of the soil for its income and subsistence. The early peasants, and many of the later ones as well, often combined the cultivation of their land with activities like fishing or shopkeeping and casual estate work. So, for the purposes of our discussion, we shall use the term 'peasant' to refer to all those variously called peasant farmers, small farmers and small cultivators. They are the individuals, who, as Lewis points out, devote 'the major part' of their time to cultivating land on their own account 'with the help of little or no outside labour'.[8] The size of holding which this requires varies with fertility of the soil and with the type of farm enterprise; but a minimum of 2 acres is probably what was (and is) required. Finally, these peasants are the founders and residents of the new village communities which sprouted near the estates and occasionally in the mountains immediately after emancipation.[9]

Available statistics do not allow us to estimate the size of the peasantry or the average size of its holdings with any precision. It is therefore probable that many of those we shall call peasants were those in possession of a 'house-spot' and a garden. These individuals are perhaps more accurately described as smallholders, but their desertion of the sugar estates and their participation in the development of the new village communities place them near, if not inside, the peasant sector.

The Growth of the Peasantry

Three states of growth can be identified. First, there is the *period of establishment* marked by the rapid acquisition of land holdings and by a continuous increase in the number of peasants. This stage lasted from 1838 to around 1850–60. Secondly, there is the *period of consolidation* during which there was continuing expansion of the number of peasants and, more important, a marked shift by the peasants to export crop production. This state lasted to about 1900. Thirdly, there is the *period of saturation* during which the peasantry did not expand and might even have been contracting. This is the period from 1900 to the present, when the peasantry reached the limits of possible expansion inside the plantation-dominated society and economy.

The period of establishment: A combination of factors explains the ex-slaves' desire to leave the estates at emancipation and to establish themselves as independent cultivators. Emancipation had widened the range of their expectations, and these, in many cases, could not be satisfied in plantation labour and residence. Moreover, the planters, over-anxious to safeguard their entire labour supply, attempted by various means to keep all the ex-slaves on the estates in relationships closely approximating to their earlier servile condition. In particular, they devised a system of tenancy which compelled the ex-slave to labour 'steadily and continuously' on the estates in return for secure residence in the house and ground which he had occupied as a slave.[10] Consequently, insecurity of tenure, as well as relatively low wages for plantation labour, sometimes high rents, and long contracts reinforced many ex-slaves' determination to seek new and better opportunities away from their estates. Some indulged in a measure of occupational differentiation; and there was a marked increase after emancipation in the number of artisans, porters, fishermen, seamstresses etc. But most of those in flight from the estate attempted to acquire land. The reason for this was obvious. Cultivation of the soil was the one skill the ex-slaves possessed; moreover, in many of the territories enough land seemed to be available to furnish the would-be cultivator with at least the elements of subsistence.

Opportunities for land acquisition did not exist to the same extent in all the territories. In Barbados, St. Kitts and Antigua — three of the older colonies — small size, a large population and a long established sugar industry left few, if any, opportunities for land acquisition. Consequently, it was difficult for a peasantry to emerge in these islands; those ex-slaves who wanted to 'better' themselves away from the estates had to think of emigration. On the other hand, Jamaica and the Windward Islands, Trinidad and British Guiana (now Guyana) offered opportunities for land acquisition. In Jamaica and the Windwards the sugar industry had left undeveloped much of the mountainous interior; in Trinidad and British Guiana a small population and a young sugar industry created many opportunities for land acquisition.[11] It must be noted, however, that in both of these latter territories, relatively high wages and, in British Guiana, the high cost of drainage might have moderated the desire for land acquisition. The point remains, however, that Jamaica, the Windwards, Trinidad and British Guiana provided the best opportunities for land acquisition by ex-slaves.

These opportunities were eagerly grasped, but they were not won without opposition. The ex-slaves' land hunger was enormous and evident. Observers said that the 'great and universal object' of the ex-slaves was the acquisition of land 'however limited in extent'.[12] One St. Vincent planter said as early as 1842 that the labourers were always 'on the look-out' for land on which they could settle and allow their wives 'to sit down' and 'take charge of the children'.[13] Throughout the period immediately after emancipation there is overwhelming evidence of a desire to acquire portions of the surplus land — estate land not in cultivation and Crown land.[14] But this desire brought the ex-slaves into direct conflict with the plantation. Planters feared the effect on the labour market and on the sugar industry of widespread independent land settlement. Consequently, they placed obstacles in the way of its development. The planter-dominated legislatures refused to initiate surveys of Crown land as a preliminary to smallholder settlement, and they adopted strict legislation against squatting on Crown land. The planters either refused to sell surplus and marginal estate land, or they charged high, even exorbitant, prices for small portions of it. Moreover, the legislatures instituted costly licenses for the sale of small quantities of manufactured sugar and coffee and for the production of charcoal and firewood. They also levied land taxes which discriminated against the owners of smallholdings.

Small-scale land acquisition became possible, however, because of the determination of the would-be peasants and because of the failure of the planters to maintain a united opposition. Some planters were anxious to win advantage in the labour market, and these sold land to the ex-slaves in the hope that this would secure them a portion of the ex-slaves' labour. In addition, many planters were chronically in debt and therefore welcomed the cash returns they could get from the disposal of small portions of their marginal land. This particular advantage was often exploited during and after the depression of 1847. But most important was the action of the ex-slaves. They practised thrift and industry, and, as a result, labouriously accumulated the purchase money for land. Some put their savings from wages and provision cultivation in the Friendly and Benefit Societies; some, as in British Guiana, started informal co-operatives and joint stock companies. Others, as in Jamaica, got the assistance of Baptist ministers in their attempts to bargain with landowners. Generally, they paid high prices for the land. Prices ranging from £20 per acre were common, and prices of £100, £150 and even £200 per acre were often reported.[15] The land itself was of variable quality — more often than not marginal land which was barely accessible, not surveyed and even uncleared. The lots, too, ranged in size from about ½ acre to 5 and sometimes 10 and 15 acres.[16]

So successful were the efforts of the ex-slaves that within four years of emancipation officials were reporting an 'almost daily' increase in the number of freeholders and an obvious extension of cultivation in territories like Jamaica, British Guiana, the Windwards and Trinidad. Eisner shows that Jamaica possessed 2,114 persons owning holdings under 40 acres in extent in 1838. By 1841, however, that number had reached 7,919, and by 1845 there were 19,397 persons with holdings under 10 acres in extent. She estimates that by 1842 nearly 200 free villages with a total extent of 100,000 acres had been established, and about £70,000 had been paid by the settlers for land.[17] Farley has described a similar pattern of development in British Guiana. By 1842 there were in Demerara and Berbice over 4,000 freehold properties with an extent of about 22,000 acres which had been purchased at a cost of about £70,000.[18]

This rapid development continued throughout the rest of this first period. The profits of provision cultivation provided more labourers with the means to desert the estates for the new villages and for independent small-scale cultivation. And the perennial difficulties of the planters afforded labourers many more opportunities to acquire land at lower costs. By 1852 in British Guiana there were more than 11,000 new freehold properties with an estimated value of £1 million.[19] By 1860 in Jamaica the number of holdings under 50 acres in extent had reached 50,000.[20] By 1861 the Windward Islands of St. Lucia, St. Vincent, Grenada and Tobago possessed more than 10,000 freeholders, while the number of residents of villages built since emancipation totalled about 20,000 in Grenada and St. Vincent.[21]

The period of consolidation: The rapid increase in the number of peasants continued during the second phase of development. In Jamaica, the only territory for which we have almost complete figures for the period, the number of small landholdings (i.e. those under 50 acres) increased spectacularly between 1860 and 1900 and up to 1930. Eisner's figures show that these holdings more than doubled between 1860 and 1902. The total figure for the later date was 133,169. Also important was the increase in the number of substantial peasants or small farmers. The number of holdings of between 5 and 49 acres increased from 13,189 in 1880 to 24,226 in 1902 and to 31,038 in 1930.[22] Moreover, as a share of the total population, the ratio of peasants rose from 11% in 1860 to 17.5% in 1890 and 18% in 1930.[23] Similar developments occurred in Grenada where the number of smallholders increased from about 3,600 in 1860 to more than 8,000 in 1911. By the latter date there were more than 2,000 proprietors of lots varying in size between 2½ and 10 acres.[24]

But the most important feature of this phase of development was the emergence of what Eisner calls a 'new peasantry'. The presence of this new group is partly indicted by the increase in the number of farms of more than 5 acres; but it is mainly indicated by a 'dramatic' change in the peasant's pattern of production. Eisner's national income estimates for Jamaica for 1850 and 1890 reveal a shift from mainly provision production to a mixed provision and export crop production by the peasants. The value of export crops (sugar, coffee, rum, pimento, ginger) in 1850 is estimated by Eisner at £1,089,300, of which 'small settlers' contributed £113,500 or just over 10%. In 1890 the value of cash crops (to which had been added logwood, bananas, oranges, coconuts, cocoa and lime juice) was estimated at £2,028,300; and the small settlers' share had risen to £798,800 or about 39%.[25] At the same time, the peasants had increased the value of ground provisions from £854,000 in 1850 to about £2,601,200 in 1890.[26] This meant that whereas in 1850, 83% of the peasant output consisted of ground provisions and only 11% of exports, in 1890 the share of ground provisions had dropped to 74% and that of exports had risen to 23%. It meant also a remarkable increase in the peasants' share was about half but by 1890 it had risen to about three-quarters.[27]

This change in the pattern of peasant production was also apparent in the Windward Islands. There, increased peasant activity after the 1850s in the production of arrowroot, cotton, spices, cocoa, citrus, bananas, logwood and sugar resulted in increased exports of most of those commodities. Indeed, arrowroot and cotton in St. Vincent and cocoa and spices in Grenada were regarded as peasant crops from the 1850s onwards, while sugar in Tobago was produced exclusively by peasants and sharecroppers by 1898 and was already in the process of disappearance as a major cash crop in that island as well as in Grenada.

The period of saturation: In general, the shortage of land for continued peasant expansion imposed a limit on this type of development. The characteristic of the most recent stage of peasant development is the failure of the peasantry to expand at its earlier pace. Moreover, there is increasing evidence that the peasantry income territories has been declining in numbers during the last 20 years. Table 1 provides some of the evidence for Jamaica.

The striking feature of these figures is the evidence they provide of the dramatic decline in the numbers of *smaller* holdings in the period 1930–61. So sharp was this decrease that the total number of these holdings in 1961 barely exceeded the number recorded for 1902. There is also clear evidence that the number of *larger* holdings increased throughout the entire period. These almost doubled in number in 1902–61 despite a sharp decrease in the period 1954–61.

This pattern was not uniform throughout the West Indies. Table 2 supplies some evidence of the size of the peasantry in the other islands and of its growth during the period 1946–61. In all the Windward Islands there has been a continuing and substantial increase especially in the number of smaller holdings. In Barbados and in all the Leewards there has been a decrease in the number of smaller holdings, and only a small increase in the number of larger holdings in Antigua and Montserrat. In Trinidad, there has been a slight increase in the number of smaller holdings, but a marked increase in the number of larger holdings.

This suggests that the peasants' shift to cash crop production has operated in conjunction with other factors to exhaust the opportunities for peasant landholding in the larger territories of Jamaica and Trinidad as well as in the longer-settled

islands of Barbados and the Leewards. These opportunities had always been limited in the latter islands where the plantation was well established and has remained dominant.[28] A relatively small peasantry did come into evidence in these islands, but the increasing pressure of numbers on the land as well as non-availability of land for expansion of peasant cash-crop production seems to have resulted in both the amalgamation of some of the smaller holdings into larger ones and a drift of peasants away from the land. Since there are few alternative means of employment available inside these islands, most of the ex-peasants must have emigrated.

In Trinidad and Jamaica a combination of other factors are involved. The expansion and consolidation of the plantation ever since emancipation has been one limiting factor. In addition, various types of non-agricultural economic activities during the last 40 years have competed with agriculture both for land and labour. For example, industries like bauxite and tourism in Jamaica and oil in Trinidad have not only attracted the peasant away from cultivation on his own account but have also imposed limitations on the growth of the peasantry by occupying land which was either peasant agricultural land or land which might have become available for peasant expansion. At the same time, the opening up and exploitation of migration opportunities, particularly after 1945, might well have made the peasantry more conscious of its neglected and depressed condition and more determined to improve it. It is suggested that these simultaneous pressures, added to the familiar ones of increasing population, shortage of fertile land for expansion, and demands for improved living standards, explain the 'crisis' of the peasantry in territories like Jamaica and Trinidad.

The situation has been somewhat different in the Windward Islands. In these islands the peasantry has continued its expansion. The reason for this is partly historical. Mainly because of late settlement, a sparse population and mountainous terrain, these islands have never possessed a plantation system which exercised full dominance over the economy and the landscape. As a result, the plantation system was (and is) less well equipped than in other islands to withstand long depression in the sugar industry (or in other staple production). This created perennial opportunities for peasant acquisition of land. Moreover, there has been no alternative economic development in these islands to compete with agriculture or to attract the peasant away from the land. The peasantry has thus been able to sustain a competition with the plantation for land and labour in conditions more favourable to it than in any other territory. This has ensured its continuous

Table 1. Peasant Holdings in Jamaica, 1902–1961

	Under 5 acres	1.5 acres	5–25 acres	25–100 acres
1902	108,943	—	24,226[a]	—
1930	153,406	—	31,038[a]	—
1954	138,761	95,851	53,237	5,572
1961	113,239	—	40,769	3,803

[a] Returns for holdings of 5–50 acres.
SOURCES: G. Eisner, op. cit.; Department of Statistics, *Survey of Agriculture 1961–2*; Federal Statistical Office, *Agricultural Statistics*, series 2, no. 1, 1960.

Table 2. Peasant Holdings in Selected West Indian Islands, 1946 and 1956–61[a]

| | 1–5 acres | | | |
	1946	1956–61	1946	1956–61
Trinidad and Tobago	18,120	19,200	11,563	14,400
Barbados	4,208	2,400[b]	454[c]	292[c]
Dominica	2,760	3,781	1,934	1,748
Grenada	4,991	6,773	1,361	1,615
St. Lucia	857[d]	4,887	1,976	2,361
St. Vincent	3,271	4,636	1,230	1,229
Antigua	2,926	2,800[b]	344[c]	476[c]
Montserrat	1,317	1,302	142	194
St. Kitts-Nevis-Anguilla	2,237	n.a.	351	n.a.

NOTES:

[a] The dates of the second set of data for the several islands are: Trinidad and Tobago 1957, Barbados 1961, Dominica 1956–9, Grenada 1956–9, Montserrat 1957, St. Lucia 1958, St. Vincent 1958.

[b] Estimates based on the returns of total number of holdings under 5 acres for the date 1956–61.

[c] Holdings of 5–100 acres.

[d] This low figure reflects incompleteness of the Census (see West Indian Census 1946, Part A, para. 43, p.51).

SOURCES: *West Indian Census 1946, Parts A and B; Agricultural Statistics,* Series 2, no. 1; *A Digest of West Indian Agricultural Statistics,* Dept. of Agriculture Economics and Farm Management, Un. of the West Indies, St. Augustine, 1965.

growth. These islands, then, are more nearly peasant communities than any of the other islands in the West Indies.[29]

The role of the peasantry

Peasant activity modified the character of the original pure plantation economy and society. The peasants were the innovators in the economic life of the community. Besides producing a great quantity and variety of subsistence food and livestock, they introduced new crops and/or re-introduced old ones. This diversified the basically monocultural pattern. Bananas, coffee, citrus, coconuts, cocoa and logwood in Jamaica; cocoa, arrowroot, spices, bananas and logwood in the Windward Islands: these were the main export crops introduced or re-introduced by the peasantry after the 1850s. All of these were subsequently adopted by the planters and became important elements in the export trade by the 1870s. Not all of these crops succeeded; peasant coffee in Jamaica, for example, was seldom of good quality. In addition, the success of the peasants in combating attacks of disease on crops like cocoa and bananas was always severely limited by their shortage of resources of capital and knowledge. However, this many-sided activity of the peasants represented not only 'a great new area of peasant advance',[30] but also served as a vehicle for expanding the production possibilities of the region. The plantation-staple economy was being mixed with elements of a peasant-subsistence

economy; and it seemed probable that a peasant economy could replace the plantation economy without any serious economic loss to the community. Peasants were producing cash crops as well as food which might have cancelled out the advantages of large-scale production for export markets by introducing important elements of self-sufficiency into the economy.[31]

The alternative foreshadowed by the presence and activity of the peasants had great social significance as well. The peasants initiated the conversion of these plantation territories into modern societies. In a variety of ways they attempted to build local self-generating communities. They founded villages and markets; they built churches and schools; they clamoured for extension of educational facilities, for improvement in communications and markets; they started the local co-operative movement.

Informal co-operatives made their appearance immediately after emancipation; groups of ex-slaves pooled their resources to buy land, to lay down drainage systems, to build churches and schools. Participation in more formal organizations came later. This could be seen in peasant activity in the Friendly and Benefit Societies, in the Jamaica Agricultural Society and particularly in the People's Co-operative Loan Bank of Jamaica.[32] These banks, first established in 1905, represented a considerable initiative in the area of self-help. They were located in peasant communities and were intended 'to encourage thrift and to provide the small farmer with loans on reasonable terms and at the lowest possible rates of interest'.[33] The importance of these banks in rendering vital financial assistance to the peasants, particularly in times of natural disaster, can be judged from the fact that by 1949, 119 branches of the bank with 72,700 members had been established, and the bank had made advances and loans of nearly £2 million.[34]

So the peasantry, because of the extent of its social investment and self-conscious community-building, was a persisting factor both for stability and change inside the West Indian community. As 'a nucleus of importance', which could constitute 'the stability of the country',[35] the peasants' presence and activity combined to soften the rigid divisions of race and class which were a feature of the plantation society.[36] At the same time, their increasing numbers and their economic importance made a cogent case for the adoption of broader-based institutions. In this respect peasant development was emancipation in action.

Government policy towards the peasantry

The potential of peasant development was never fully realized because government had tended, most of the time, to ignore the existence of the class. The peasants, as Eisner says, 'were left to themselves to experiment with different crops and techniques'.[37] This helps to explain why wasteful practices like 'firestick agriculture' (clearing virgin land with fire and then working it without rotation or artificial aids) still persist with their terrible consequences of soil exhaustion and soil erosion.[38] It also helps to explain the general backwardness in agricultural knowledge, the inadequate credit and marketing facilities and the shortage of fertile land for peasant expansion.

This neglect can be explained by the dominance of the estate-based sugar industry over influential opinion both at home and in the metropolis. Planters feared that peasant expansion would ruin the sugar industry by creating labour shortages. They convinced official opinion in England that both the prosperity and civilization of the West Indies were dependent on the survival of the estate-based industry. Metropolitan official opinion, though sometimes skeptical about the economic argument, seemed to accept (for no very good reason) the cultural argument. Both sides, therefore, co-operated for a long time in maintaining the traditional industry and in protecting the ex-slaves against 'a relapse into barbarism and the savage state'.[39] Both these ends could be served by ensuring that the ex-slaves continued to work for wages on the estates 'not uncertainly or capriciously, but steadily and continuously'.[40] Consequently, neither the Colo-

nial Office nor the local legislature exerted themselves at first to assist peasant development, which nonetheless thrived in spite of this official difference and, occasionally, open hostility.

Government attitude was modified only when discontent and restlessness among peasants and labourers combined with prolonged depression in the sugar industry during the 1890s and again in the 1930s to create a situation of crisis. The wisdom of the traditional policy was then questioned by those who had initiated it. The establishment of the Jamaica Agricultural Society and the appointment of a travelling agricultural instructor in the 1890s hinted at a new policy, and the Report of the Royal West India Commission in 1897 seemed to point in a new direction. The Commission recognized that the peasantry was 'a source of both economic and political strength'. Accordingly, it recommended land settlement and diversification of agriculture, 'no other reform affording so good a prospect for the permanent welfare in the future of the West Indies as the settlement of the labouring population on the land as small peasant proprietors'. The ironic point is that these sentiments had to be repeated by the Sugar Commission of 1929 and by the Moyne Commission in 1939.[41] Fundamental reform had been stillborn.

The 'agricultural revolution', proclaimed as official policy in Jamaica since 1902 and hinted at in these Reports, has still not occurred. New government policy has consisted principally of the provision of agricultural credit facilities and the institution of land settlement schemes. The first is a new departure, beginning in the 1940s,[42] and for that reason it is open to question whether it is not too little and has not come too late to ease the crisis among the peasantry. Land settlement schemes have a longer history. They were started in Jamaica in 1896, and have been used in most of the territories ever since. The schemes have not been pursued as consistent and coherent policy; rather they have been used as expedients whenever a general crisis seems to have threatened the existence of the community, as in the 1920s and again in the 1930s and 1940s. Consequently, little attention has been paid to the choice for settlers for the land or to the problem of the small farmer's deficiencies in knowledge, capital and organization. Moreover, much of the land distributed was not particularly fertile; half of the settlements in Jamaica between 1929 and 1949 possessed soil of the 'red dirt' variety which is notorious for its incapacity to retain water and plant nutrients.[43] Government has concerned itself only with distributing the smallholdings, but if land settlement is to solve reform rather than a palliative, government must commit far more resources to this type of project.[44] The amount of land distributed in many of the territories suggests that only the surface of the problem has been scratched. The peasants require access to a large quantity of 'fertile' land (i.e. estate land) in order to improve their living standards and also to increase their numbers. Land settlement, which in Trinidad between 1933 and 1948, for example, involved the disposal of 4,120 acres to 2,940 settlers, will neither halt the drift from the land nor encourage permanent settlement.[45]

A more determined assault on the problem is necessary if the position of the peasants is to be strengthened and if the potential of the peasantry is to be realized. This would seem to involve a reconsideration of the role of the plantation in this community and, ultimately, a basic re-arrangement of priorities in agrarian policy.

Notes

1. W.A. Lewis, *The Evolution of the Peasantry in the British West Indies*, Colonial Office Pamphlet 656, 1936. p.1
2. R. Redfield, *Peasant Society and Culture*, Chicago, 1956, pp. 27–9.
3. See V.T. Harlow, *Barbados, 1624–1685*, Oxford, 1926; H. Merivale, *Lectures on Colonies and Colonization*, London, 1841, pp. 75–6; S. Mintz, 'The Question of Caribbean Peasantries: A Comment', *Caribbean Studies*, vol. 1, no. 3, pp. 32–4.
4. See S. Mintz and D.G. Hall, 'The Origins of the Jamaican Internal Marketing Systems', in *Papers in Caribbean Anthropology*, New Haven, 1960.
5. Mintz, 'The Question of Caribbean Peasantries', op. cit., p.34.
6. S. Mintz, foreword to R. Guerra and Y. Sanchez, *Sugar and Society in the Caribbean*, New Haven, 1964, p. xx.
7. Ibid., pp. xx–xxi.
8. Lewis, op. cit., p.3. See, in particular, F.L. Engledow's Report on Agriculture, Fisheries, Forestry and Veterinary Matters (Supplement to *West India Royal Commission Report 1945*) Cmd. 6608, 1945, pp. 41–5.
9. See H. Paget and R. Farley, 'The Growth of Villages in Jamaica and British Guiana', *Caribbean Quarterly*, vol. 10, no. 1, pp. 38–61.
10. See W.G. Sewell, *The Ordeal of Free Labour in the British West Indies*, New York, 1861; W.K. Marshall, 'Social Economic Problems in the Windward Islands, 1838–1865' in Andic and Mathews (eds), *The Caribbean in Transition*, Rio Piedras, 1965, pp. 247–52.
11. In 1838 Barbados had as many slaves as British Guiana, and Antigua had more than Trinidad. The figures for Barbados and British Guiana were 82,807 and 84,915; for Antigua and Trinidad they were 29,537 and 22,359.
12. These were typical comments by stipendiary magistrates in the Windward Islands and in Jamaica.
13. H.M. Grant's evidence before the 1842 Select Committee on West India Colonies.
14. See Paget and Farley, op. cit., also R. Farley, 'The Rise of the Peasantry in British Guiana', *Social and Economic Studies*, vol. 2. no. 4, pp. 87–103; D.G. Hall, *Free Jamaica 1838–1865*, New Haven, 1959.
15. See Hall, op. cit., and Farley, op. cit.
16. See Lewis, op. cit., p. 7.
17. G. Eisner, *Jamaica 1830–1930*, Manchester, 1961, pp. 210–11.
18. Farley, 'The Rise of the Peasantry in British Guiana', op. cit., pp. 100–1.
19. Ibid., pp. 101–2. According to Farley, the recovery of the sugar industry in British Guiana led to a slump in peasant development after the 1850s.
20. Eisner, op. cit., p. 220.
21. Marshall, op. cit., p. 252.
22. Eisner, op. cit., p. 220.
23. Ibid., p. 221.
24. The *Grenada Handbook 1946*, p. 70.
25. Eisner, op. cit., pp. 53, 80.
26. Ibid., p. 9.
27. Ibid., pp. 221, 234. It fell to about 68% in 1930.
28. This is confirmed by statistics on the amount of farms with a size of more than 100 acres. In Barbados (1961) these farms occupied 81.7% of the total area; in Antigua (1961) 59.1%; in St. Kitts (1946) 78.8%; in Montserrat (1957) 68.4%. (See *A Digest of West Indian Agricultural Statistics*, p. 14.)
29. This is confirmed to some extent by statistics on the percentage distribution on the area occupied by farms of different sizes:

	Under 5 acres	5–100 acres	100 + acres
Dominica	12.7	32.0	55.3
Grenada	22.9	29.9	47.2
St. Lucia	14.9	37.5	47.6
St. Vincent	22.5	28.0	49.5
Jamaica	11.8	32.2	56.0
Trinidad and Tobago	12.5	40.1	47.4

Source: A Digest of West Indian Agricultural Statistics, p. 14.

30. Lewis, op. cit., p. 14.
31. Ibid., pp. 36–8.
32. See Eisner, op. cit., pp. 227–30.
33. R. Colon-Torres, 'Agricultural Credit in the Caribbean', *Caribbean Economic Review*, vol. IV, nos. 1 and 2, p. 95.
34. See 'Rural Welfare Organizations' and Credit Facilities for Small Farmers', in 'Land Tenure in the Caribbean', *Caribbean Economic Review*, vol. II, no. 2, pp. 90–2, 107–11. The actual figure was £1,793,658.13.7, of which £856,541.3.8 was still outstanding.
35. This opinion was expressed in 1850 by Drysdale, a stipendiary magistrate in St. Lucia.
36. Lewis, op. cit., p. 37.
37. Eisner, op. cit., p. 225.
38. See Mintz and Hall, 'The Origins of the Jamaican Internal Marketing System', op. cit., pp. 6–7; Eisner, op. cit., p. 225.
39. Merivale, op. cit., pp. 312–13; Earl Grey, *The Colonial Policy of Lord John Russell's Administration*, London, 1853, pp. 54ff.
40. This was the advice, contained in the Queen's Letter, which the Colonial Office offered to Jamaican petitioners for relief in 1965.
41. W.A. Lewis, 'Issues in Land Settlement Policy', *Caribbean Economic Review*, vol. 3, nos 1 and 2, pp. 58–9.
42. R. Colon-Torres, op. cit., pp. 85ff. See also 'Credit Facilities for Small FArmers' in 'Land Tenure in the Caribbean', *Caribbean Economic Review*, vol. II, no. 2, pp. 101–16.

43. P. Redwood, Statistical Survey of *Government Land Settlement in Jamaica*, BWI, 1929–1949, pp. 18–21. Only 4% of the settlement possessed soil of the best (alluvia) variety.

44. Lewis, 'Issues in Land Settlement Policy', op. cit., pp. 77ff. See also LeRoy Taylor's 'A Review of Land Policy in Jamaica', mimeo., 1965, ISER, Univ. of the West Indies, pp. 7ff.

45. Figures provided by Lewis for the period 1916–49 show that 5,300 acres were settled in the Leeward Islands; 14,400 acres in the Windward Islands; and 106,100 acres in Jamaica. In British Guiana 8,500 acres were settled between 1944 and 1949.

Systems of Domination After Slavery: The Control of Land and Labour in the British West Indies After 1838

O. Nigel Bolland
Colgate University

During our slavery we was clothed, ration, and seported in all manner of respects. Now we are free men (free indeed), we are to work for nothing. Then we might actually say, we become slaves again.[1]

Four years after their 'emancipation' in 1838, the former slaves of British Guiana protested against their conditions and their unfair treatment by the planters who sought to bind them to labour on the estates. When the planters introduced certain rules and regulations, which were intended to regulate the quality and quantity of work, and to reduce labour costs by lowering wages and abolishing customary allowances of free medical attention,housing, and provision grounds, the workers complained to the stipendiary magistrates and stopped work. Such conflicts between planters and former slaves were common in the British West Indies after 1838. The former sought to retain full control over what they still considered to be 'their' labour force at as low a cost as possible, while the latter sought to improve their quality of life by increasing their income, often through a combination of provision-ground cultivation and wage labour on the estates, and by organizing a more stable family and domestic life. Woodville Marshall recently summarized this situation:

Strikes, sometimes lasting as long as two or three weeks, occurred in most islands; many ex-slaves refused to surrender their provision grounds and some resisted violently; and nearly all of them objected to the wage rates. Eventually, a fragile industrial peace was created on the basis of a few concessions — small wage increases, a shorter working week for women and guarantees of right to growing crops in event of eviction.[2]

With few exceptions, however, most histories of the British West Indies view emancipation in a less critical light than did the former slaves themselves, and uncritically conceptualize the post–1838 colonies as 'free' societies in contrast to the slave societies that preceded them. A clear distinction is rarely made between emancipation as an event (sometimes understood as occurring in 1834 when slavery was abolished, but more sensibly understood to refer to the termination of the apprenticeship system in 1838), and emancipation as a human, social condition. It is too glibly assumed that the former produced the latter. William A. Green's recent study of emancipation in the British sugar colonies exemplifies this approach. It is a careful but conventional history that reflects Colonial Office attitudes and policies, rather than history from a Caribbean perspective.[3] For example, Green states, 'Finding a workable arrangement which permitted the survival of the plantation system without sacrificing the liberty of freedmen was clearly the most difficult and elusive problem of the free society'.[4] Green conceives the 'problem of the free society' as a problem of colonial administration whereas, for the colonized former slaves, the problem was that their liberty was not yet a reality. In other words, the problem should be defined not in terms of the survival of the plantations and the prosperity of the planters, but in terms of the survival and improved living standards of the former slaves. While the former masters sought

I am grateful to the Research Council of Colgate University for financing research in London in 1978, and to the officials of the Archives of Belize, the British Museum, and the Public Record Office, London, for their assistance over many years. I wish to thank the many people who have helped me formulate the ideas which appear in this paper, especially Arnold Sio who criticized an earlier version, and to absolve them from responsibility for its remaining shortcomings.

new forms of coercion, the former slaves sought new forms of freedom. The change in legal status changed the terms of, but did not abolish, their struggle: They were no longer defined as 'forced labour', but they were still defined as a 'labour force'. Whatever workable arrangement the colonial administrators were likely to devise would not resolve the real problems of most members of the society but would merely create a 'fragile industrial peace' between social formations whose interests were incompatible.

It would be inaccurate, of course, to suggest that all the colonies experienced the same situation after 1838, and erroneous to imply an evolutionary development in labour system, but it is essential to examine, critically and comparatively, the shift from slave to wage labour as a transition from one system of labour control to another, each system characterized by its own mode of struggle. The various attempts to control the former slaves as a labour force after 1838 met with differing degrees of success. The critical factor which determined whether or not ex-slaves would emerge as a 'reconstituted peasantry'[5] or would remain dependent upon estate labour is generally considered to be the availability of land. This factor is usually explained in terms of favourable or unfavourable man/land ratios or degrees of population density,[6] and it is this aspect of the society which is subsequently deemed crucial in determining the extent to which the masters were able to continue to control their former slaves. I intend to show that this explanation is simplistic and inadequate.

This essay has two goals. The first is to examine critically the prevailing explanation of the differing degrees of success with which masters controlled their former slaves in the British West Indies. The second purpose is to suggest the need to abandon the concept of the antinomy of slavery and freedom and to seek to promote the comparative study of transition from slave to wage labour, in terms of varieties of labour control, as an aspect of the transformation of systems of domination.

The study is in three parts. The first is a summary of the various attempts at labour control after 1838 in the British West Indies, and of the prevailing explanations of the differing degrees of success of these attempts. The second is an account of the interrelationship of the control of land and of labour in Belize (formerly British Honduras), a case which is neglected in all previous studies and which cannot be accounted for by their explanations. Finally, the third part suggests some general and theoretical implications of this study, including the suggestion that dialectical theory provides the most useful framework for examining systems of domination.

I.

Colonial societies are not autonomous social realities; they are subject to the fluctuating demands and interests of the metropolis. Even those people who appeared to have almost complete and untrammelled power in the British Caribbean colonies in the nineteenth century, namely, the planter class, were dependent in a number of ways — economically, militarily, psychologically — upon the mother country. These planters considered that slavery was necessary for their own economic survival and hence, they argued, for the continuing economic value of the West Indian colonies but, as the influence of the West Indian lobby declined in Westminster, the slave-owning planters were unable to halt the movement toward abolition. When 'An Act for the Abolition of Slavery throughout the British Colonies' was passed by the British Parliament in 1833, it changed the legal framework of certain social relations, especially labour relations, within the plantation societies of the British West Indies.

That Parliament took the planters' concerns seriously and decided to minimize the social impact of the abolition act is evident from the debates surrounding its formulation and from its final terms. In order to make the change gradual, and to ensure the continued dominance of the planters and dependence of the freed slaves, the act included two important elements which were very sympathetic and generous to the slave-owners. One element was compensation: The act empowered the treasury to raise twenty million pounds, to be paid to the slave-owners as compensation for their loss of property. The other element was the provision introducing the system called 'apprenticeship', under which all registered slaves over the age of six years were initially to become 'apprenticed labourers' who would be compelled to work without pay for forty-five hours each week for the same masters as they had prior to abolition. The original intention was to apprentice field workers for six years and others for four, but eventually all were freed in 1838. Apprenticeship afforded 'an interval intended to facilitate the creation of social and economic machinery that would perpetuate the established order'.[7]

There was widespread opposition to the apprenticeship system from the apprentices, who wanted complete freedom; many of them considered it a conspiracy on the part of local elites to keep freedom from them. In St. Kitts, martial law had to be declared and the militia was also needed in Montserrat; there was disorder in Essequibo, Guiana, and hundreds demonstrated in opposition to apprenticeship in Port-of-Spain,

Trinidad. In Antigua, the planters themselves rejected this apprenticeship system. They abolished slavery immediately in 1834, arguing that it was in their own interests to do so. In the other British colonies, however, the apprenticeship system, until its abolition on 1 August 1838, provided the planters with a temporary means of controlling their labour forces. The planters, feeling betrayed by their imperial parliament, then sought to devise new ways to control labour.

The masters, for so they still considered themselves, tried a variety of techniques of labour control after 1838 throughout the British West Indies. These included enactment of laws to restrict emigration and 'vagrancy', various forms of taxation to pressure people into wage labour, and the development of systems of police, magistrates, and prisons to punish those who broke the new labour laws. Several of these techniques had already been tried in Antigua, and planters elsewhere in the British colonies frequently sought to benefit from the Antiguan experience. For example, one technique was the use of contracts to ensure regular and obedient supplies of labour. The Antiguan legislature passed an act on 29 December 1834 to regulate and enforce labour contracts. Contracts were not required to be written but needed only to be made orally in the presence of two witnesses. If a labourer under contract absented himself from work, even with a reasonable excuse, he forfeited his wages for the lost time, and if absent without such an excuse for a half a day or less (a term sufficiently elastic to be used to enforce promptness), he forfeited the whole day's wages. If absent for two successive days, or for two whole days within any two week period, the labourer would be liable to a week's imprisonment with hard labour. Other offenses, such as drunkenness or the careless use of fire or the abuse of cattle, could be punished with up to three months' imprisonment with hard labour. The maximum punishment of the employer, however, for any violation of the contract, was a fine of five pounds. The British government was still sensitive to the view that the abolition of slavery should result in 'unrestricted' freedom, however, and the Antiguan act was disallowed, to be replaced in the following year by another only slightly less severe. The new act provided that verbal or implied contracts should be for a year, terminable only at a month's notice, and that the occupation of a tenement should be *prima facie* evidence of the existence of such a contract between the tenant and his landlord. Under this contract act, the Antiguan labourers worked nine hours a day, with one day free in a week or sometimes only one in every two weeks, for wages of nine pence a day. Not surprisingly, it has been concluded that 'the purely material condition of the Antiguan labourers showed little real advance over that of the days of slavery'.[8]

The Antiguan system introduced another mechanism of labour control which was adopted, with variations, by many planters elsewhere after 1838. This mechanism was the wage/rent system, which combined the roles of employer and landlord on the one hand and those of employee and tenant on the other. The ex-slaves, who during slavery had generally had access to personal provision grounds as well as to their family homes, often built by themselves, discovered that, as free men, they had a rental obligation for access to these traditionally gratuitous facilities. The employer/landlords were then able to reduce labour costs by charging rent, or by lowering wages in lieu of charging rent, and were also able to threaten their labourer/tenant with eviction if they did not work to the master's satisfaction on the estates. The former slaves frequently desired to continue to occupy the grounds and houses to which they had had customary rights of usage, supplementing a peasant livelihood with occasional cash earnings from casual estate labour.[9] The masters, however, needed regular and continuous labour, especially during crop time when cane was harvested and sugar produced, and asserted their legal property rights over the houses and grounds in order to extract this kind of labour from their former slaves. The conflicting interests of the two groups thus clashed in the wage/rent system: The planters, who continued to depend upon plentiful and regular supplies of cheap labour, which they were accustomed to controlling in a coercive manner, and their former slaves, who sought to avoid the persistent limitations imposed on them in estate work.

The application of the wage/rent system varied considerably from one colony to another. In Barbados, a house was often occupied rent free on the condition that the tenant work on his landlord's estate for five days a week. Those who worked less were fined, and the fine effectively constituted a rent. In order to prevent the tenants from paying rent with money earned by marketing provisions or labouring elsewhere, the planters deducted the rents from estate wages, thereby obliging the tenants to work for wages on the home estates, on pain of eviction. Until the mid–1840s in Barbados, rents and wages were generally associated with resident labourers being paid 10d daily, but after 1845 they became increasingly independent. There were wide variations in the rent charged. In Jamaica, the average was 2s a week, but it was sometimes as high as 6s.8d per household. In some cases in Jamaica, rent was charged '*per capita* against husband, wife and each of the children, as a *penal exaction*, to compel labour'.[10] However, in Trinidad and Guiana former slaves who worked on the estates continued to enjoy their houses and grounds rent free, and also had the customary allowances and relatively high wages. When considering rents as a percentage of wages, there was wide variation between colonies: In Tobago and Barbados rents were about 20% of wages, in St. Vincent they were 33%, in Grenada 35%, and in Jamaica as high as 48%.[11] There was also great variation in the planters' ability to collect rents: On Worthy Park estate in Jamaica, £342, more than 10% of the total wages, was deducted directly from the labourers' pay in 1839, but in the following year, when the total rent on houses and provision grounds was assessed at £2,827, attempts to collect it proved futile. 'Those from whom rents were collected proved even less willing to work, and those who did not work had no money to pay'.[12] In 1842, only £49.8s was collected for all rents on Worthy Park.

Above all, the wage/rent system varied considerably in its ability to promote continuous supplies of reliable labour. In some colonies, the planters maintained control over labour supplies, but in others the system became self-defeating; while the threat of eviction may coerce some tenants to work on the estate, implementation of the threat would throw labourers on the general market and alienate them still further from the landlord and would-be employer who had evicted them. Often, as in Jamaica, the coercive nature of the tenure arrangements was sufficient to cause the newly freed slaves to reject the system and flee the estates. Whether they fled or were evicted, the planters lost their labour force. By the mid–1840s, Jamaican planters had recognized the failure of the system and grudgingly abandoned it.

Why did the wage/rent system work in some colonies and not in others? Variations in the success of the system in securing labour supplies for the estates depended to a large extent on the availability of alternatives for the ex-slaves. Though some former slaves and field labourers became artisans and some became small traders,[13] the chief option was peasant farming on a small property to produce a variety of crops for family consumption and for sale. Thus the availability of land to provide former slaves with an alternative to estate labour in the form of peasant agriculture has been widely regarded as the critical element in the success or failure of the system. The availability of land is then evaluated as a function of the size of the territory, its state of development, and the population density. For example, the classic account of British slave emancipation distinguishes between the 'developed' and the 'undeveloped' colonies and finds that labour remained generally plentiful in the former and both scarce and hard to control in the latter.[14] A recent evaluation of the planters' success in coping with the labour shortage after emancipation states that the 'territorial heterogeneity' or 'territory diversity' of the colonies accounts for the variations.[15] Most recently, it has been stated that 'in the free West Indies, the supply as well as the quality of labour was mainly determined by two factors: population density and the availability of arable land. . . . Where the ratio of people to arable land was high — as in Barbados, St. Kitts, and Antigua — estate labour was comparatively plentiful. Where the ratio was low — as in Jamaica, Trinidad, and British Guiana — estate labour was scarce'.[16] Variations in labour relationships are viewed, in these explanations, as dependent upon the control of land, which is itself viewed as a product of geophysical factors and population densities. Thus, Green distinguishes between 'high density colonies', in which 'planters controlled virtually all arable land', and 'low and medium density colonies' where 'the propensity of the freedmen to pursue peasant agriculture on accessible fertile lands rendered it impossible for most planters . . . to command an abundant pool of reliable estate labourers'.[17]

These accounts of the labour situation and of the circumstances favouring the emergence of a peasantry in the British West Indies after 1838 arrange the various colonies on a continuum, extending from those small islands with high population densities where the planters controlled labour successfully, Antigua, St. Kitts and Barbados to the large colonies where land was plentiful and population densities were low, where the labourers left the estates in large numbers and created a substantial peasantry (Jamaica, Trinidad, and British Guiana). All the other British West Indian colonies (with the notable exception of Belize, which is not discussed in these accounts[18]) are viewed as falling somewhere in the middle of this continuum, exhibiting some retention as well as some loss of plantation labour (St. Vincent, Tobago, Grenada, Nevis, Montserrat, St. Lucia and Dominica).

In Barbados, St. Kitts, and Antigua, the monopolization of arable land by the planters restricted the growth of a peasantry and limited the independent cultivation of provisions to the function of supplementing wages earned from regular estate labour. Though provision agriculture was quite extensive on these islands, it was on such a small scale as to prelude an independent livelihood. In Barbados in 1844, about 30,000 persons, or 25% of the population, were employed in agriculture, chiefly as estate labourers. In St. Kitts in the same year, about 8,000 persons, or 30% of the population, constituted the plantation labour force; in

Antigua in 1847, as much as 40% of the population regularly provided labour on the estates.[19] The price of freehold land in these islands was the highest in the West Indies in the 1840s, ranging from £40 to £80 per acre in Antigua, and £60 to £200 in Barbados. A contemporary visitor commented: 'Of the large number of the labouring class who have purchased freeholds . . . the space of ground they have been provided has generally been so small and its quality so inferior (the poorer lands being sold to them) as not to suffice under culture for the support of themselves and family, being little, if any, more than they were allowed to have during slavery'.[20] Since neither the size nor the quality of these plots permitted production beyond the very limited levels used to supplement the family diet, estate labour for wages remained essential to survival for the former slaves.

At the other end of the scale are the colonies of Jamaica, Trinidad, and Guiana, where the loss of plantation labour and the growth of a peasantry were the greatest. As British colonial office records indicate, the planters in these colonies were continually hampered by the inadequate or irregular nature of the labour supply. Of Jamaica in 1842, for example, it was stated that 'the want of continuous labour is still very much felt on many estates as the labourers generally work *very irregularly*, without any regard to the wants or wishes of their employers'.[21] The exodus from the estates continued in Jamaica through the 1840s and 1850s. In 1861 it was reported that 'there are possibly forty thousand labourers in all who give transient work to the estates, but at one and the same time the number actually at work, or the number that can be commanded, does not average more than twenty thousand. These twenty thousand labourers, taking them *en masse*, do not work for estates more than one hundred and seventy days in the year, sometimes three and sometimes four days in the week'.[22] The 40,000 labourers who provided irregular and transient labour on the estates constituted only 9% of the total population. Of Trinidad it was said in December 1838 that 'there is not at present more than half the force willing to be employed on the sugar estates that was in operation previous to the first of August last',[23] and in 1848 planters could 'command' only 19% of the labour force they had available in 1838. In Guiana it was estimated in 1844 that only 30% of those who had been slaves a decade earlier had continued in plantation labour. Though about 36% of the total population in 1851 worked on plantations, less than half of these were ex-slaves, the majority consisting of recently imported Indian, African, and Portuguese indentured labourers.

Because so much land was available in these colonies, its price per acre was the lowest in the West Indies in the 1840s: from less than £1 to £50 in Guiana, between £4 and £20 in Jamaica, and from £1.10s to £13 in Trinidad. The great variation in price, especially in Guiana, reflected a wide range of quality and location, but the generally low prices, combined with relatively high wages and an initial rapid expansion in the internal market[24] enabled thousands of former slaves to purchase land and establish themselves as substantial peasant producers. In Jamaica the number of freeholds increased from about 2,000 in 1838 to 27,379 in 1845, and to about 50,000 in 1861. By the latter date, therefore, there were more peasant producers in Jamaica than there were people employed in casual estate labour. In Trinidad the number of proprietors, mostly smallholders, increased from about 2,000 in 1832 to over 7,000 in 1849, while only 3,116 labourers were said to work regularly on the plantations in 1851. In Guiana in 1842 some 15,000 former slaves had settled on 4,506 acres, 40,000 ex-slaves owned 17,000 acres in 9,797 freeholds in 1848, and by 1851 there were 11, 152 smallholdings and 46,368 people lived in villages which had been formed since emancipation.

It is an undeniable fact that planters were able to continue to control labour in Antigua, St. Kitts, and Barbados to a much greater extent than in Jamaica, Trinidad, and Guiana. The ascendant explanation of this fact identifies the availability of land as the crucial factor. Thus, it is argued, the planters' control of labour in Antigua, St. Kitts, and Barbados stemmed from their prior control of the land, made possible by a high population density, and, conversely, the former slaves' ability to establish themselves as an independent peasantry in Jamaica, Trinidad, and Guiana was the product of an abundance of available land, resulting from the low population density. Though this analysis of the relation between the control of land and of labour (which ultimately rests upon the factor of population density as the chief determinant of the degree of success of labour control strategies) appears to be satisfactory, it is not. The unusual case of Belize, a British settlement in Central America which was a colony in all but name, does not fit within the continuum provided, nor does the usual analysis, described above, of the relationship between control of land and labour in the British West Indies account for the facts in Belize. If, as is frequently the case, Belize is ignored or dismissed as an anomaly, we will continue to miss the issues and insights which its study can provide. After examining the situation in Belize, it will be clear that the availability of land, though important, is not the only factor, nor is it determined by population density. And the prevailing explanation for the differing degrees of success in controlling labour in the British West Indies after 1838 can then be seen to be partial and inadequate. The emphasis on, and the apparent success of, this explanation has resulted in the neglect of other factors affecting the systems of domination which emerged after slavery.

II.

Despite the fact that Belize was a very large and largely unoccupied territory, the masters were able to control both land and labour to a degree comparable to that in the small, densely populated islands. Their monopolistic control of land was certainly one way in which the masters were able to control labour, but their control of land requires an explanation. Excluding the islands of the barrier reef, Belize consists of about 8,600 square miles of land. In the 1830s the population did not rise above 4,000 persons, so that the density was very low — one person for every two square miles, approximately. According to the generally accepted ideas of the relationship between population density and the control of land and labour, and the influence of that relationship upon the emergence of a peasantry after emancipation, Belize should belong at one end of the continuum, along with Jamaica, Trinidad, and Guiana, but this is clearly not the case.

The history of the British settlement at Belize differs in many respects from that of the rest of the British West Indies.[25] Initially settled by buccaneers and pirates in the seventeenth century, Belize became an important source of logwood in the first half of the eighteenth century. The logwood cutters imported African slaves after 1720 and by the end of the eighteenth century the settlement's population consisted of almost three thousand persons, three quarters of them slaves, only a tenth of them white, the remainder being 'free people of colour'. When the logwood trade declined in the 1760s, it was replaced by the extraction of mahogany, in searching for which the settlers penetrated the interior and drove back the indigenous Maya.

The shift from logwood to mahogany extraction entailed an increase in the size of economic enterprises, because mahogany cutting required more land, more capital, and more slaves. As a result, ownership became increasingly concentrated, and the number of white settlers declined. By the beginning of the nineteenth century, a handful of settlers dominated the entire political economy of Belize, owning most of the land and people, controlling all of the trade, import and export, wholesale and retail, and also controlling the judicial,

legislative, and administrative organs of the settlement, called the Magistracy and the Public Meeting.

The British government had played little part in the emergence of this settlement, apart from providing military and naval assistance against periodic threats from both the Spanish and the slaves. By treaties of 1763, 1783, and 1786, Britain had acknowledged Spanish sovereignty, the British settlers having only limited usufructuary rights to natural produce. After the Spanish were defeated at the Battle of St. George's Cay in 1798 they made no further attempt to control the territory. As Spain declined and lost its Central American colonies early in the nineteenth century, Britain slowly assumed colonial authority over Belize. One important consequence of the early status of Belize was the absence of any agricultural development, cultivation being limited to the growing of slave provisions. Another consequence was the unusual system of land tenure,[26] whereby the principal settlers simply allocated land to themselves, claiming *de facto* freehold rights through their 'location laws'. When the Crown's representative, superintendent George Arthur, tried in 1817 to challenge the legitimacy of this system, he failed to restructure the pattern of landholding, though he did succeed in proclaiming all remaining unclaimed land as Crown land, to be distributed henceforth only by the superintendent.[27] This belated assertion of the Crown's authority regarding disposition of unclaimed land could affect only the remote areas of the south and west, much of which was mountainous or thickly forested and unsuitable for agriculture.

Though superintendent Francis Cockburn requested in 1831 that Arthur's recommendations regarding a more equitable distribution of land be implemented,[28] this was never achieved, and it was not until the 1850s that the system of land tenure was regularized. The Laws in Force Act of 1855 (18 Vict., c.22, cls. 2, 3) provided retroactive legitimacy to ownership of land that had been appropriated prior to 1817 under the old location laws, thereby confirming the extreme concentration of land established during the preceding century. When finally, after two centuries of settlement, the British government asserted its sovereignty in the mid-nineteenth century, declaring 'British Honduras' a colony in 1862, it chose not to disrupt the old structure of monopolistic land ownership. In fact, as a decline in the mahogany trade and in the power of the settler elite progressed after the middle of the nineteenth century, the concentration of land ownership and its alienation to metropolitan capital increased to the point where one British company, the Belize Estate and Produce Co., Ltd., owned about half of all the freehold land of the colony.

At the time of emancipation, therefore, a handful of large Belize landowners — many of whom were involved in partnerships between original settlers (who claimed the land under their own 'location laws') and London merchants (who provided capital and controlled the trade) — owned virtually all the land in the north and centre of the settlement, leaving the remaining remote and largely non-arable areas of the southwest in the hands of the Crown. The mahogany trade suffered from a trade cycle and at the time of emancipation was experiencing its biggest, but also its last, boom, exporting a peak of nearly fourteen million feet of mahogany in 1846. The mahogany lords were unable to reorganize their enterprises or to introduce new techniques to make their labourers more productive; in fact, the methods of felling and trucking mahogany trees hardly changed until mechanization was introduced in the twentieth century. Unlike many of the sugar planters in the West Indies, who were already experiencing prolonged depression and curtailment of production, resulting sometimes in bankruptcies and abandonment of estates, or who were able to operate with a smaller but more productive labour force by introducing new technology, the mahogany lords were eager to expand production using the old methods and thus needed to increase, or at least to maintain, the size of their labour force.

The supply of labour had always been the chief production problem for the mahogany lords in Belize. They acquired the land gratuitously in most cases, but labour was scarce and expensive because Belize was remote from major slave markets and because a great premium was placed on strength and fitness in the business of mahogany extraction. Early in the nineteenth century, the value of a recently imported African was stated to be between £120 and £160 Jamaican currency, but a 'seasoned' slave was worth £200 to £300.[29]

An estate of thirty-one slaves, four of whom were described as 'very old', realized £9,710 in 1820, an average of over £300 per slave.[30] When the value of slaves in the settlement was assessed in 1835, the estimate was £230,840, or an average of about £115 per slave, and the portion of the £20 million compensation fund that was set aside for the proprietors of Belize was £101,958.19s.7½d.[31] The per-slave rate of compensation in Belize, £53 6s 9½d, was higher than for any British sugar colony (British Guiana: £51.17s.1½d; Trinidad: £50.1s.1¼d; Barbados: £20.13s.8¼d; Jamaica: £19.5s.4 3/4d). Though the census figures of the 1830s are unreliable, they suggest that the number of slaves may have been decreasing (see Table 1),

Table 1. Population of Belize, by Colour and Status, 1829–39

	Whites		Free Coloured and Blacks		Slaves		Total
	N	%	N	%	N	%	N
1829	265	6.8	1,591	41.0	2,027	52.2	3,883
1832	223	5.9	1,788	47.1	1,783	47.0	3,794
					Apprentices		
1835	222	8.7	1,137	44.7	1,184	46.6	2,543
			Coloured		Black		
1839	163	5.5	809	27.5	1,974	67.0	2,946

Source: Census of Belize

and certainly the number of adult male slaves was viewed by the masters as inadequate.

According to the slave register of 1834 there were just under two thousand slaves in Belize, 62% of them male. At age forty years or more, however, men outnumbered women by ten to three, while under the age of forty they outnumbered women by only seven to six. This can be explained by the fact that during the years when slaves were imported, before the abolition of the trade in 1807, there was a premium on young men who could become mahogany cutters. The slave register list by occupation shows that 795 slaves were woodcutters, and over half of these were forty years old or more (see Table 2). Since the masters could command only a small and aging group of slaves in the 1830s, they sought other ways to augment the labour force, including the acquisition of 'liberated' slaves from illegal slavers and the coercion of members of the legally free population into wage labour.

In 1834 a Public Meeting decided that they needed 1,800 Africans captured from slaving ships; a petition was sent to the British Secretary of State in 1835 requesting that 825 of the Africans captured at Havana be sent to Belize, to be apprenticed for 'the Cutting of Mahogany' for a period of eight to sixteen years, 'or at the option of the Employer'.[32] Accordingly, 459 'liberated' Africans arrived in Belize[33] during 1836, but many died of cholera, 5 were drowned, and 2 committed suicide. After a year only 357 were alive, and only 229 of those were male.[34] The intent behind this importation of Africans, whose status was to be virtually that of slaves, was to increase the labour supply and also to make their present apprentices more tractable after emancipation:

The introduction of the successive Cargoes of Africans which have arrived in the Settlement, will tend to depreciate the services of the apprentices after August next,

Table 2. Slave Woodcutters, by Age, 1834

Age in years	0–9	10–19	20–29	30–39	40–49	50–59	60+	Total
	1	88	158	144	244	121	39	797

Source: Slave register, Archives of Belize, Belmopan.

and will render it the more necessary for the latter to conduct themselves with increased activity and attention, to enable them to obtain employment.[35]

However, this attempt to augment the labour force in the 1830s met with very limited success and it certainly did not fulfill the hopes or satisfy the needs of the masters.

The landowners had more success in coercing members of the legally free population into cutting mahogany as wage labourers. As early as 1790, a classification of settlers by property, occupation, and colour, indicated that about 30% of the free persons (whites and of 'mixed colour' with little or no property) were 'employed by Wood Cutters and others' as clerks and labourers.[36] Owing to the Spanish treaty restrictions on agriculture, the extreme concentration of land ownership, and a monopolistic control of trade, the mahogany exporters were able to keep 'the people poor and totally dependent upon them'.[37] Many of the free coloured were refugees from the Mosquite Shore who arrived in Belize in 1787 and were denied land by the magistrates, who were the principal land-owners. The superintendent complained that the refugees 'are entirely excluded from any means of gaining a Subsistence, unless they will become the Servants of these Legislators'.[38]

Since slaves continued to escape from the settlement into the interior or across the borders (especially after adjoining Spanish territories became independent and abolished slavery) and since after 1807 escapees could not be replaced by the slave trade, the masters sometimes improved their treatment of the slaves or granted manumission. The very high rate of manumission in Belize (573 manumissions between 1808 and 1830, or about one fifth of the slave population[39]) suggests that the masters preferred a free black labourer to a runaway slave. The landowner thus resorted to manumission while devising the means to control this increasing free population, which by 1838 was as numerous as the slaves.

The free people of colour always occupied an intermediate and ambiguous social position in Belize, as elsewhere in the Caribbean.[40] (The expression 'free people of colour' generally included the free coloured, who were of mixed race, and the free blacks, though distinctions were often made between these two sub-categories). Though legally free, they were denied many of the civil rights and social privileges accorded to whites and, although a few were quite wealthy slaveowners, the majority remained poor and economically dependent. A law passed in 1805 excluded 'free persons of colour' from possessing a logwood works unless such persons also possessed 'four able negro men slaves', and that at a time when the logwood trade was permanently depressed. Such economic restrictions, combined with exclusion from the judicial institutions and from commissions in the militia, and property and residence qualifications for the Public Meeting which were double those for whites, confined these people to an inferior social and economic position. When, under pressure from Britain, an act was passed to grant full civil rights to the free coloured in 1830, an attempt to extend this to free blacks was defeated.

In addition to the free coloured and black populations, the masters employed members of the Carib, or Garifuna, community which had established itself in the south, and also 'foreigners', that is, Spanish-speaking migrant or immigrant labourers. In 1833, the current superintendent pointed out that 'the Free Labourer and Slave work together, but tho' with the Gangs for months together, it would be impossible to discover the one from the other unless they were separately pointed out'.[41] A report from the same year stated: 'There are no gangs at present employed in cutting mahogany exclusively composed of Slaves, half of each gang being free labourers ... the freeman and slave labour together side by side, are subject to the same restraint and management in every respect, eat, drink, and sleep together ... It is however necessary to remark that the free labourers alluded to, are for the most part foreigners'.[42] In 1836, it was noted that between twelve and fifteen hundred 'foreigners and free Labourers are hired annually for the Mahogany Works, and they are by no means sufficient to answer the demand'.[43] The total work force in the mid–1830s was probably about 2,000 men, consisting of around 800 apprentices and 1,200 free labourers, half of the latter being coloured or black Creoles and Garifuna and the remainder being 'foreigners'.

Though it had been shown that the masters obtained a mixed labour force to cut mahogany in the 1830s, consisting of slaves or apprentices, free coloured and black labourers, 'liberated' African apprentices, Garifuna, and Spanish migrant labourers, it remains to be seen how the owners maintained control after emancipation in 1838. Though most of this population was still, in a general sense, dependent upon those few individuals and companies that dominated the economy of Belize, this circumstance does not indicate the specific means by which the labour force was controlled and disciplined. The monopolistic concentration of land ownership was clearly one way in which the mahogany lords had, since the eighteenth century, deprived the poor members of the free population of an independent livelihood and thereby made them dependent upon wage labour. This strategy continued to be effective after 1838. However, given the very low population density, it is necessary to explain how the concentration of land ownership was maintained. It will now be argued that the control of labour, through a combination of techniques and circumstances unique to Belize, was actually one of the ways by which the masters maintained their monopolistic ownership of land and thereby inhibited the development of a peasantry, such as occurred in other 'low density' colonies.

The employers used a system of labour laws and practices designed to keep their labourers under very firm control. At the heart of this system was a labour contract which worked with a combination of 'advance' and 'truck' systems to bind the labourer to his employer by keeping him in permanent debt. These practices, which originated in relation to the free labourers prior to emancipation, were certainly an effective mechanism of control long before they became incorporated into the laws of the settlement n 1846.

An attempt to regulate practices of hiring labourers having failed in 1830,[44] a committee was later established, on the superintendent's recommendation, to consider proposals for 'regulating the relative duties of Master and Servant'.[45] As emancipation neared, it was necessary to prepare a smooth transition in labour relations, and this led to an examination of existing practices of hiring labour. The report of the clerk of the court to the superintendent makes it clear that the contract system had existed prior to emancipation, and the clerk emphasized the inadequate legal protection for labourers which that system contained:

The employment of Household and all other servants, whether Journeymen or otherwise, within the Town of Belize, is regulated upon much the same principle as in England. The great bulk of the Lower Classes, however, and almost all the Charibs and Spaniards who resort to the Settlement, are employed in the Mahogany Works in the Interior, and with them it is the practice to enter into Contract by which they hire themselves generally for six or twelve months. This is usually done at the commencement or middle of the year, when the servant goes before a Magistrate, & volunteers a Contract for his services.

It is in the enforcement of these Contracts, however, that the great evil lies. There is no law on the subject further than what custom has sanctioned. That custom has been, that where the Servant has failed in his Contract, the Master has had the power to bring him up at once on Warrant, and have him summarily punished by Imprisonment and public Whipping. If however the breach of Contract lay with the Master, — if for example, the Master was deficient in the payments he had contracted to make to his servant, the Servant could only sue the Master as in the matter of a common debt.

To send the Servant into Court for the recovery of his wages amounts to an absolute denial of justice to him. People in his condition are not supposed to possess the means of their remaining for months at Belize to prosecute their suits for those very earnings which would enable them to reside there for a little. They only add to their embarrassment by being debarred from leaving the Town and entering into another contract.[46]

When, again under pressure from Britain, the settlers of Belize concurred in the superintendent's request to terminate the apprenticeship system on 1 August 1838, the Public Meeting hastily approved some regulations for resolving disputes over wages and other contractual matters between 'Masters and Servants'. Not only could the employer take his employee to court for 'absenting himself from his duty, or for unruly and disobedient conduct', but the employee could also take his employer to court before three magistrates empowered to fine the employer for 'unlawfully withholding any wages due to such complainant'. It was further stipulated 'that every servant or labourer shall be henceforth hired in writing', and the contract was to be registered at the office of the clerk of court, 'in order to remedy the great evil and inconvenience which has of late arisen to masters or employers by reason of labourers engaging themselves to several individuals at or nearly the same time to work for and during the same periods, and receiving considerable advances from each person on account of their wages'.[47]

That the law was primarily oriented toward controlling the labourers is indicated by the way it was applied shortly after emancipation. Though a general amnesty had released all prisoners from jail on 1 August, the jail had 103 prisoners only a few months later. Nine prisoners were listed as 'runaways', and twenty-four were guilty of insolence, disobedience, or breaking an agreement. A typical example of the severity of sentences appears in the case of Pedro Chabia, who was sentenced to 'six months' imprisonment with hard labour on the Public Works' for a 'breach of contract'.[48] When the labour laws were amended in the 1850s, the penalty imposed on a 'servant' who failed to fulfill a contract after receiving advances was reduced to three months of imprisonment with hard labour but, among other repressive measures, the amended law allowed the employer, or his agent, to apprehend a labourer without warrant and remove him forcibly to his designated place of work.[49] It is clear from these labour laws that the struggle between former masters and slaves was continuing, although in new forms.

Central to effective control of the labour force was the practice of paying wages in advances. The hiring period for mahogany work, which was a seasonal occupation, was generally during the Christmas holidays, when both employers and labourers congregated in the town of Belize. The advance system was ostensibly designed to permit the labourer to purchase his supplies prior to going to the forests for the season, an experience that had been compared to 'a long confinement on shipboard'.[50] The employers knew that the advances they gave were rarely used for purchasing supplies but were, instead, spent on 'keeping Christmas' in the festive fashion traditional in the settlement. This was often the only time the mahogany workers spent with their families, kin, and friends before the long, arduous, and isolated season in the mahogany camps, so they were motivated to spend lavishly on gifts and luxuries. The result was that the labourers then had to purchase their supplies on credit and at exorbitant prices from the employers' stores in the forests, a practice known as the 'truck' system. Frequently, labourers were paid a mixture of 'cash and kind', the goods being regularly inferior and overvalued. Sometimes labourers never saw any wages, as the company bookkeeper would simply reduce their debts by the amount of their earnings. Often, the balance of the wages a worker received in the forest was insufficient to meet his expenses, he ended the season in debt to his employer, and had to work off the debt in the following season. The effect of the combination of the advance and truck systems, therefore, was to bind the labourer to his employer by keeping him eternally in debt.

Voices were periodically raised against the advance and truck systems, but without effect. Some blamed the scheme upon the Yucatecan refugees who settled in Belize after the Guerra de las Castas began in 1847. Certainly the system was used on estates to the north of Belize, where Maya labourers were 'overwhelmed with debt [and were] regarded, in course of time, as a portion of the value of the various ranchos or Estates on which they live and work',[51] but the system had been used in Belize long before that. It was only with the depression in the mahogany trade in the second

half of the century that the employers, perceiving the supply of labour to be more than sufficient for their needs, let the system decline somewhat: 'Since the abandonment . . . of the mahogany works the Truck System has been in some measure given up . . . Employers are anxious to do away with the system altogether, and have made comparatively trifling advances this year'.[52] Nevertheless, a lengthy description of the colony's prevailing employment practices a dozen years later shows that the system persisted:

The first principle in this system . . . is the advance of three or more months' wages at the time of hiring. The labourer engages himself some time during the Christmas holidays for the ensuing year at say nine dollars per month. But he has just entered upon, or is in the height of, his few weeks' annual festivity, and he and the woman he lives with, and the children, if any, require money 'to keep Christmas'. He applies for, and is granted four months' advance of wages; probably taking three to begin with, and spending it out, returning for another month's advance. But by his agreement he is bound to take half of his wages in goods from his employer, who keeps in his store a stock of such goods as his hands require, and of a certainly inferior quality. First of all there is an undue advantage on the employer's side . . . the evil of his purchasing in the dearest market, instead of being allowed to take his money where he likes, is the lesser one only; the greater is that he receives these goods and the cash in the middle of a saturnalia of dissipation, and the consequences are the hard cash disappears like butter before the sun, finding its way into the tills of the rumsellers. The goods are next sold at one half what he is charged for them; that money, or the greater part of it also disappears, and another advance follows. The labourer has therefore to start his year's engagement three, four, or even five months in debt. On the works the same rule of half goods half cash is pursued, but he sees no more cash although he gets goods. The bookkeeper of the gang keeps his account, debiting so much for every day he is absent from work, even for sickness, and exacting fines rigorously, the contract being in every way a tight one for the labourer. It is hardly necessary to add that when his season's work is over he finds himself in debt when he comes down to Belize for his Christmas spree. At no time is he capable of understanding his accounts clearly, and the time chosen for settling his year's accounts is when he is enjoying a continuous carousel . . . the system is a most pernicious one in every way.[53]

The system was, of course, backed by the power of the police, courts, and prisons. A series of magistrates' reports in 1870 shows that a large proportion of their work consisted of enforcing the labour laws, called 'Masters and Servants' Acts, and this meant, almost entirely, disciplining the labourers. Thus the magistrate at Corozal decided 286 cases under the labour laws in 1869, all of them constituting discipline imposed upon labourers: there were 245 punished for 'absenting themselves from work without leave', 30 for 'insolence and disobedience', 6 for 'assaults on masters and bookkeepers', and 5 for 'entering into second contracts before the expiry of the period of former ones'.[54] In 1868 and 1869, there were 146 cases brought by masters against their servants at the police court in Belize. Only one of these cases was dismissed; a common punishment among the others was three months' imprisonment with hard labour. In the same period, ten cases were brought by servants against masters, only one of which resulted in punishment, namely, a two dollar fine.[55]

The high incidence of absenteeism, 'neglect of work', and disobedience shown in the magistrates' records is evidence of persistent dissatisfaction and discontent among the labourers and of continuing labour problems for the employers. Similarly, the severity of the sentences against labourers and the lack of cases resulting in punishment of employers demonstrate that the labour laws and the magistrates who enforced them were instruments of the employers for controlling and disciplining the labour force.

The consequence of this system of labour control was that the former slaves remained dependent upon and indebted to their masters. Belize was a small settlement with an undeveloped internal market (the Sunday markets having been abolished by the 9 July 1838 Public Meeting which agreed to end apprenticeship) so there was little incentive for the growth of any domestically oriented agriculture. In fact, the merchants of Belize, many of them also being big landowners, benefitted from the advance system and were opposed to the development of locally produced foods or of a self-sufficient peasantry. The great reliance upon imported food that characterized the period of slavery has remained a feature of Belize, much to the advantage of the commercial sector.

With regard to land, the mahogany lords were able to maintain their monopolistic control and to legalize their vast landholdings in the mid-nineteenth century. When freehold land was sold, it was sold by the small settlers to the large companies, thereby further concentrating landownership and excluding the former slaves. Crown land, originally granted free, was priced at £1 per acre in 1838 in order not 'to discourage labour for wages'.[56] and was chiefly in remote locations and of poor quality, therefore not an attractive or practical proposition for former slaves who may have wished to become independent peasant farmers. No Crown land was sold in the period up to 1855,[57] and by 1868 the total amount of Crown land sold since emancipation was said to be 'utterly insig-

nificant'.[58] Apart from some squatters on river banks, and the Garifuna and Maya subsistence cultivators in the south and north, respectively, there was virtually no peasantry in Belize in the mid-nineteenth century. On the contrary, the structure of landownership became increasingly concentrated and the majority of the population remained landless and wholly dependent upon the merchant and landowner elite.

The ability of this elite to continue to control the land must be explained, in part, by their effectiveness in continuing to control the labourers after emancipation. Unlike the former slaves of Jamaica, Trinidad, and Guiana, many of whom left the estates and became independent peasant producers, the majority of the former slaves in Belize continued to work for the masters in mahogany gangs. The indebtedness induced by the combination of advance and truck systems provided the means to maintain a submissive labour force, disciplined now through law enforcement by police, magistrates, and prisons. This system of domination, which trapped the labourers in a form of debt servitude, was unknown in the rest of the British West Indies but was successfully applied in Belize, despite the existence of a low population density and vast areas of unused land which would otherwise have favoured the development of an independent peasantry.

In 1888 a handbook on the colony criticized the predominant employment practices:

It is well known that a system has prevailed in the colony unchecked . . . of labourers being kept in debt by their employers for the purpose of securing a continuance of their labour, as such labourers consider themselves bound to serve until such debt is extinguished. Advantage has been taken . . . to keep them in debt by their supplying them with goods or drink for the purpose, and they thus become virtually enslaved for life.[59]

Half a century after the institution of slavery had been declared abolished, the labourers of Belize were far from being emancipated. Despite the change in legal status, the free labourer, like the slave, remained 'completely at the mercy of his employer' and 'virtually enslaved for life', as a result of this truly pernicious system of labour control.

III.

Examination of the Belize cases indicates the necessity to study the interrelationship of the control of land and the control of labour as two aspects of a system of domination which persisted long after slavery was declared illegal. At this point, we can examine two connected and more general issues which have been raised by this study, namely, the use of dialectical theory and the critique of the concept of the antinomy of slavery and freedom.

First, we should reconsider the theoretical framework within which systems of domination are examined. The fact that most historical writing lacks any explicit theoretical framework does not mean that it does not have an implicit one, which generally is based upon two assumptions concerning the nature of social action — that it is rational and that it is individualistic. In other words, this theoretical framework implies that, under certain given conditions, individuals will choose to act in certain predictable ways. This framework views labour control, and social action in general, as a series of relations between individuals, rather than as a social institution or as an aspect of a system of relationship which is already in operation.

Functionalism is most frequently invoked as the framework alternative to this 'rational individualism' because it appears to meet the problem of examining institutions as ongoing structures. However, though functionalism is not so reductionist, it avoids the question of the historical origins of social structures. When an institution is studied in terms of its function, that is, in terms of the part it plays in maintaining a systemic whole, the problem of examining the origins and the transformation of the institution remains.

Yet another framework exists in the comparative method which approaches problems of function and change by comparing specific factors and variables in a quasi-experimental manner. However, the fact that one can compare only those phenomena which have shared qualities produces the danger that the search for commonalities may be at the expense of drawing on the uniqueness of specific socio-historical situations. When factors are isolated from their contexts, in order that they may be compared, they lose their particular meaning. In this way, then, over reaching comparisons may lose sight of the real meaning of what is being compared, and the result is a historical theory and abstract generalizations. Of course, we must always make comparisons, but when the search for universals makes a 'methodology' out of the comparative method, then the tail is wagging the dog, and the quest for increasingly sophisticated techniques overwhelms the concern for understanding the meaning of specific historical structures.

In contrast to these approaches, dialectical theory is critical in that it identifies the conflicts that produce change in social structures and it emphasizes the importance of studying all factors as part of a historical 'totality' which the factors affect but from which they also derive their meaning. Dialectical theory consequently offers an important corrective to some of the possible extremes of the comparative method as well as an alternative theoretical framework to those of rational individualism and functionalism. These points may be illustrated by our present example, in which it may be seen that arbitrary abstraction of certain factors from the totality induces explanations that are deterministic, monocausal, and reductionist, and that dialectical theory provides a preferable framework.

While it is incontrovertible that the abolition of slavery in 1834 and of apprenticeship in 1838 changed the forms of domination that had prevailed in the British West Indies, it is necessary to distinguish between the ideological claims made for the new system and its reality. One of the illusions of the period is that, with the end of apprenticeship in 1838, labour power suddenly was freed as a commodity, but the fact is that labour power, like land, was not freed from the very real constraints of existing and persistent power structures. The uncritical acceptance of this illusion is compatible with the rational individualist approach which considers land and labour as two separate and distinct variables, abstracted from the socio-historical totality which gives them their real meaning. In this approach, the availability of land is determined by the degree of population density, and the latter is the factor that is taken to account for variations in the effectiveness of attempts to control labour. This conceptualization, which is characteristic of the explanations ordinarily advanced for the differing degrees of success with which masters controlled their former slaves after 1838, is doubly flawed. First, it fails to take into account the real continuity of structural constraints which remained undisturbed through the apparent change in systems in 1838 and, second, it arbitrarily separates and abstracts 'land' and 'labour' and makes their control dependent upon the supposedly objective factor of population density. Such a conceptualization constitutes a 'hollow abstraction'[60] which fails to take into account the dialectical interrelationships between land, labour, and population within a particular historic mode of production and, consequently, explanations based upon such a conceptualization are deterministic and monocausal. Further, by attempting to explain social relations in terms of a non-sociological variable, namely, population density, these explanations are also reductionist.[61] The density of population, while it is certainly a socially relevant factor, is not itself a social phenomenon; that is, it specifies nothing about social relationships, but only about the numerical distribution of people in space. Hence, all explanations which rely upon this factor to account for varieties of systems of labour control, or indeed of the division of labour or any other structure of social relations, are essentially reductionist.

In contrast to these theories, dialectical theory promotes examination of the interrelationship of social factors, including cultural and political, as well as of economic and demographic aspects, in the totality of a social system, which is conceived as an ongoing and changing structure of relationships. Moreover, generalizations concerning the interrelationship of such factors are valid only within the limits of the particular system to which they give rise, as Marx made clear with regard to the special 'law of population peculiar to the capitalist mode of production'.[62] When 'land' is considered in this framework, it is not as a geophysical determinant of social life, but as a factor which is itself socially produced and defined. It is in this sense, therefore, that the dialectics of 'historical materialism' are less materialistic, as well as less deterministic, than those theories that abstract land and population statistics from their socio-historical contexts.

As examined in the light of dialectical theory, it is clear that the control of land and the control of labour in Belize were but two aspects of an interrelated totality, of a changing but persistent structure of domination. The amount of arable land which is available is not determined simply by the size of the territory, nor by the population density. Moreover, while the quantity of potential arable land is affected by technology (including aspects such as land clearance and irrigation capacity as well as the types of crops and cultivating tools available), technology does not determine the quantity that is actually available, nor to whom it is made available. The availability of land is primarily determined by the power structure. In Belize, the unavailability of land to former slaves was the consequence of a policy to limit land ownership to a minority in order to make the majority more dependent. However, the ability of the landowners to enforce their monopolistic claims did itself depend on the degree to which they controlled the labourers. That the control of each aspect was a means for the further control of the other indicates the inadequacy of conceptualizing them as independent variables. The examination of the Belizean case suggests, therefore, that a dialectical analysis of the dynamics of domination in the rest of the British West Indies may also prove fruitful. We should examine the 'land factor', not as a geophysical fact determined by man/land ratios, as has been the tendency hitherto, but as a social aspect which is affected by such factors as available technology and, especially, the distribution of social power. At the same time, land influences the maintenance of that power structure by enabling those who control it to multiply their resources at others' expense.

The second point, implied in the previous statement, is that the study of the interrelatedness of the control of land and labour as key aspects of a structure of domination suggests the need for a more critical examination of the real meaning of the terms 'emancipation' and 'freedom' for the post-slavery period. These are ideological terms, the use of which promote and perpetuate illusions about the nature of an epoch whose real characteristics are those of systems of domination. M.I. Finley has persuasively argued that the 'simple slave-free antinomy' has been 'harmful as a tool of analysis'[63] and that it is necessary to distinguish among the kinds of servitude that exist between slavery and freedom, yet this antinomy persists in the historiography of nineteenth-century Caribbean societies. If historians are to be anything other than representatives of the Colonial Office and the planter class, self-confessed or otherwise, we should commence a critical re-evaluation of these concepts in relation to the changes which occurred in the mid-nineteenth century.

While not denying that the change in legal status of the majority of the population, and their subsequent attainment of some limited civil rights, constituted an important social event, it is nevertheless clear that the social condition of 'full emancipation' or entry into the 'realm of freedom' was not, and arguably has not yet been achieved. As has been seen in Belize, some nineteenth-century colonial administrators and apologists themselves recognized the likeness of the post–1838 system of labour control to slavery, as did the Guianese workers quoted at the beginning of this paper, and we should do no less. If we can emancipate ourselves from the slavery/freedom antinomy we may better examine and understand the continuities (as well as changes) in structures of social relationships, and in particular the continuities in the structure of power, in the nineteenth century.

The comparative study of systems of labour control could benefit from a classificatory scheme which would be capable of distinguishing among categories along a broad spectrum of 'unfreedoms', including slavery, serfdom, and debt peonage, as well as remunerated tribute labour, indentured labour, convict or captive labour, coerced wage labour, and so-called free wage labour. Finley has criticized the inadequate conceptualization of types of labour and has sought to distinguish sharply between, on the one hand, the various forms of compulsory labour and, on the other, hired labour, 'which implies the conceptual abstraction of a man's labour power from the man himself'.[64] Slavery, in which the *labourer* himself is the commodity, and free labour for wages, in which *labour power* is the commodity, are thus at the extreme poles of systems in which some people labour involuntarily for others. W. Kloosterboer has termed as 'compulsory' that labour in which 'the labourer cannot withdraw if he so wishes without being liable to punishment, and or for which he has been accepted without his willing consent to it'[65] However, such contract labour, performed under the threat of penal sanction, and wage labour which, despite the absence of direct external compulsion, is compelled as a means of survival, may both appear as involuntary in the minds of the labourers. Moreover, Arnold J. Bauer has recently emphasized that debt does not always mean bondage and that cash advances may be seen by some workers as an 'indirect wage increase' in the form of credit extended without interest.[66] Such credit, then, can indicate the weakness of the employer in a situation of labour shortage, while in the situation where the employers are powerful, such advances can tie the labourers to an enterprise against their wills. Any such classificatory scheme, therefore, must take account not only of the cultural definitions of such concepts as 'ownership', 'property', and 'work' in the legal system of the ruling class, but must also take account of the meaning of the labour system for the labourers.[67] While it is necessary to avoid undue abstraction of these concepts from their social context, which would result in comparison of unequals and overgeneralized ahistorical theorizing, there is clearly a need for a more systematic conceptualization of types of labour control, based on, an adequate theory of structures of domination.

If we abandon the simplistic slavery/freedom antinomy, productive comparisons of change in the forms of compulsory or coerced labour can be made, provided that these comparisons take into account the specifics of changing structures of domination and avoid attempts to create universalistic evolutionary sequences.[68] We may then usefully pose the question: How do we account for the fact that in some situations of labour shortage the workers are able to increase their benefits in terms of greater freedom and better remuneration, while in others the employers exercise ever more powerful coercion, in the form of violence or bondage? Or, similarly, why does an expanding economy sometimes result in the greater hegemony of the ruling class, while at other times it provides an opportunity for workers to win more concessions? These questions require a comparative analysis of historical specifics within a framework of dialectical theory.

In conclusion, the critique of domination in the British West Indies in the nineteenth century must analyze the interrelationship of land control and labour control. The system of labour control must be examined in a wide variety of aspects, including the wage/rent system, the advance and truck systems, contracts and taxation, sponsored and indentured immigration and restrictions on emigration, vagrancy laws, and the role and function of the magistrates, police, and prisons. In addition, the structure of the political system, with its restricted franchise and colonial administration, and the ideological role of ministers and missionaries in churches and schools should be examined. We need, also, to examine the race factor, to ascertain the degree to which the persistence of the powerlessness and rightlessness of the former slaves was related to their racial identity and the extent to which the dominant structure was sustained by racist ideology. All these aspects are dialectically interrelated with the responses of the labourers, which included a variety of techniques of withdrawal from and resistance to the coercive system, in the form of task-work gangs, strikes, absenteeism, noncooperation at work, and the creation of mutual aid societies, 'free villages', and independent peasantries, and even emigration.

To say that freedom or full emancipation was not attained after 1838 is not to deny that there were important changes. However, we must learn to examine and distinguish between forms of coercion which exist within systems in which labour is legally free, just as we need to distinguish between varieties of legal bondage. Frederick Cooper has drawn attention to 'how much richer and more precise studies of forms of agricultural labour that can be called "slave" have been, compared to forms of labour that can be called "free",' and has pointed to the 'great need to understand economic and social structures — of which direct coercion was only a part — that defined the options that ex-slaves had'.[69] Above all, what we need to accept is that domination persists even while the relations of domination change, and that the status of legally free people often may be depressed into various kinds of dependency and unfreedom. By rejecting the simple antinomy of slavery and freedom, we can view the nineteenth century as a period of transition from one system of domination to another, each involving different forms of labour control. This perspective encourages further comparative analysis of the transition from slave to wage labour systems in the Caribbean area, as well as in the United States, Brazil, and elsewhere.

Finally, to reject crudely deterministic theories and reductionist explanations is not to abandon all theory in favor of the descriptive study of historical particularities. I hope I have shown the contrary: that the application of dialectical theory provides a superior analytical base for comparative studies. An important part of such an analysis, which has been neglected hitherto, will be the examination of the labourers' resistance to the coercive system, as important in wage as in slave labour societies. As the negation of slavery made way for a new form of domination, so the new system also generates the social conditions which provide for its eventual dialectical transcendence.

Notes

1. Petition from workers on Plantation Walton Hall, British Guiana, to Captain J.A. Allen, stipendiary magistrate, 6 January 1842, in *Report from the Select Committee of the House of Commons on the West India Colonies, 1842,* Appendix III.
2. Woodville K. Marshall, 'Commentary', in 'Roots and Branches: Current Directions in Slave Studies', Michael Craton, ed. *Historical Reflections* 6:1 (1979), 247.
3. William A. Green, *British Slave Emancipation: The Sugar Colonies and the Great Experiment, 1830–1865* (Oxford, 1976). In this connection, see the critique of colonial historiography in Eric Williams, *British Historians and the West Indies* (London, 1966).
4. Green, *British Slave Emancipation,* 190.
5. See Sidney W. Mintz, 'The Question of Caribbean Peasantries: A Comment,' *Caribbean Studies,* 1:3 (1961), 31–34; *idem, Caribbean Transformations* (Chicago, 1974) 132–33.
6. Two recent studies concerned with areas outside the British West Indies which identify population density as a factor determining the availability of land to former slaves, are Poly Hill, 'From Slavery to Freedom: The Case of Farm-slavery in Nigeria Hausaland', *Comparative Studies in Society and History,* 18:3 (1976), 421; and Francisco Scarano, 'Slavery and Free Labor in the Puerto Rican Sugar Economy: 1815–1873', in *Comparative Perspective on Slavery in New World Plantation Societies,* Vera Rubin and Arthur Tuden, eds. (New York, 1977), 561. Whereas the former suggests that a low density meant land was available, the latter suggests that a high density limited access to land.
7. Green, *British Slave Emancipation,* 130.
8. Douglas Hall, *Five of the Leewards, 1834–1870* (Barbados, 1971), 28; see also William Law Mathieson, *British Slave Emancipation, 1838–1849* (London, 1932), ch. 1.
9. For an evaluation of the motives and interests of the ex-slaves, see Douglas Hall, The Flight from the Estates Reconsidered: The British West Indies, 1838–42', *Journal of Caribbean History,* nos. 10–11 (1978), 7–24. Hall concludes, 'The movement of the ex-slaves from the estates in the immediate post-emancipation years was not a flight from the horrors of slavery. It was a protest against the inequities of early ''freedom''.'
10. Joseph John Gurney, *Familiar Letters to Henry Clay of Kentucky Describing a Winter in the West Indies* (New York, 1840, 79.
11. W. Emanuel Riviere, 'Labour Shortage in the British West Indies after Emancipation', *Journal of Caribbean History,* no. 4 (1972) 7–8.
12. Michael Craton and James Walvin, *A Jamaican Plantation: The History of Worthy Park, 1670–1970* (London, 1970), 217.
13. See Riviere, 'Labour Shortage'.
14. Mathieson, *British Slave Emancipation.*
15. Riviere, 'Labour Shortage', 5.
16. Green, *British Slave Emancipation,* 192.
17. Ibid., 192, 194.
18. In some cases, Belize is deliberately excluded (Green, *British Slave Emancipation,* discusses only the sugar colonies), but Belize is generally neglected in histories of the British West Indies, perhaps because it is considered an anomaly.
19. Riviere, 'Labour Shortage', 12.
20. John Davy, *The West Indies, before and since Slave Emancipation* (London, 1854), 397.
21. T. McCornock, March 1842, encl. in Lord Elgin to Lord Stanley, 6 June, 1842, CO. 137/263, no. 6, Colonial Office Records, Public Record Office, London. (Hereafter cited as CO.)
22. W. G. Sewell, *The Ordeal of Free Labor in the British West Indies* (London, 1861), 265.
23. Sir George Hill to Lord Glenelg, 11 December 1838, CO. 295/122.
24. See Michael Moohr, 'The Economic Impact of Slave Emancipation in British Guiana, 1832–1852' Economic History Review 2nd Ser., 25:4 (1972) 588–607.
25. See O. Nigel Bolland, *The Formation of a Colonial Society: Belize from Conquest to Crown Colony* (Baltimore, 1977).
26. See O. Nigel Bolland and Assad Shoman, *Land in Belize, 1765–1871: The Origins of Land Tenure, Use, and Distribution in a Dependent Economy* (Kingston, 1977).
27. See encl. in 'Report of the Commssioners . . . 27 July 1820', George Arthur to Earl Bathurst, 13 September 1820, CO. 123/29.
28. Francis Cockburn to Lord Goderich, 10 April 1831, AB, R6, Archives of Belize, Belmopan. (Hereafter cited as AB).
29. Captain G. Henderson, *An Account of the British Settlement of Honduras. . . .* (London, 1809), 60.
30. 'Sales negros Est. of P.C. Wall', 29 August 1820, CO. 123/40.
31. 7 July 1835, CO. 318/117.
32. Francis Cockburn to Secretary of State, 21 January 1835, AB, R6.
33. J.G. Anderson to Lord Glenelg, 10 August and 20 December 1836, CO. 123/48.
34. William Gow to Alexander Macdonald, 1 March 1838, CO. 123/53.
35. Ibid. 1 February 1838, CO. 123/53.
36. CO. 123/9. See also O. Nigel Bolland. 'The Social Structure and Social Relations of the Settlement in the Bay of Honduras (Belize) in the 18th Century', *Journal of Caribbean History,* no. 6 (1973), 40.
37. Letter from Edward Despard, 11 January 1788, CO. 123/6.
38. Edward Despard to Lord Sydney, 24 August 1787, CO. 123/5.
39. Returns by George Westby, 15 December 1823, CO. 123/34, and 31 December 1838, CO. 123/37; and Francis Cockburn to Lord Goderich, 25 April 1831, CO 123/42.
40. See David Cohen and Jack Greene, eds., *Neither Slave nor Free* (Baltimore, 1972); and Jerome Handler, *The Unappropriated People* (Baltimore, 1974).
41. Francis Cockburn to Lord Stanley, 29 October 1833, AB, R6.
42. Memorial to Francis Cockburn, from minutes of Public Meeting, 26 October 1833, CO. 123/44.
43. J.G. Anderson to Secretary of State, 28 April 1836, AB, R6.

44. Minutes of Public Meeting, 1 March 1830, CO. 123/41.
45. Ibid. 6 November 1837, CO. 123/50.
46. James Walker to Alexander Macdonald, 12 February 1838, CO. 123/52.
47. Minutes of Public Meeting, 9 July 1838, encl. in Alexander Macdonald to Lord Glenelg, 28 August 1838, CO. 123/53.
48. Alexander Macdonald's report, 8 April 1839, CO. 123/55.
49. 'An Act to amend the Law relating to Contracts for Hire and Service', 18 Vict., c.12, *Laws of the Settlement of British Honduras* (1857).
50. Henderson, Account of British Settlement, 75.
51. Edwin Adolphus to James Longden, 15 January 1870, AB, R105.
52. Francis Cockburn to James Longden, 24 February 1870, AB, R106.
53. Archibald Robertson Gibbs, *British Honduras: An Historial and Descriptive Account of the Colony from Its Settlement, 1670* (London, 1883), 176–78.
54. Edwin Adolphus to James Longden, 15 January 1870, AB, R105.
55. Francis Cockburn to James Longden, 24 February 1870, AB, R106.
56. Lord Normanby to Alexander Macdonald, 22 April 1839, AB, R15.
57. William Stevenson to Sir Henry Barkly, 30 July 1855, AB, R48.
58. James Longden to Sir John Grant, 6 March 1868, AB, R98.
59. Lindsay W. Bristowe and Philip B. Wright, *The Handbook of British Honduras for 1888–89* (London, 1888), 199.
60. Friedrich Engels to Conrad Schmidt, 27 October 1890, in *The Marx–Engels Reader*, Robert C. Tucker, ed. (New York, 1972), 647.
61. To explain variations in the systems of labour control in terms of the determining factor of population density is actually Durkheimian. In 1903 Durkheim defined what he called 'the material substratum of society'. 'What is it', he wrote, 'which forms the main substance of society, if it is not social space plus the population which occupies this space? . . . a society is of greater or lesser density'. See Anthony Giddens, ed., *Emile Durkheim: Selected Writings* (Cambridge, 1972), 83. It is this concept of 'material density' which underlies Durkheim's explanation of the development of the division of labour and hence, also, his conception of the historical development of societies.
62. Karl Marx, *Capital*, 1, in *The Marx–Engels Reader*, 2d ed., Robert C. Tucker, ed. (New York, 1978), 422–23.
63. M.I. Finley, 'Between Slavery and Freedom', *Comparative Studies in Society and History*, 6:3 (1964), 236.
64. M.I. Finley, *Ancient Slavery and Modern Ideology* (New York, 1980), 68–69.
65. W. Kloosterboer, *Involuntary Labour since the Abolition of Slavery* (Leiden, 1960), 2.
66. Arnold J. Bauer, 'Rural Workers in Spanish America: Problems of Peonage and Oppression', *Hispanic American Historical Review*, 59:1 (1979), 36–48.
67. Further, the interests of those who control the labour should also be considered, in order to distinguish, for example, between labour for the public good and labour for private profit. The duration of the labour control system is another variable, ranging from a temporary duty, which may be accepted in unusual and extreme conditions such as wartime, through long contracts or lifetime bondage, to slavery as an inherited status.
68. For the series of changes that took place in systems of labour control in sixteenth- and seventeenth-century Mexico, see Silvio Zavala, *New Viewpoints on the Spanish Colonization of America* (Philadelphia, 1943), 93–103, and Charles Gibson, *The Aztecs under Spanish Rule: A History of the Indians of the Valley of Mexico, 1519–1810* (Stanford, 1964), 220–56.
69. Frederick Cooper, 'Commentary', in Craton, 'Roots and Branches', 82.

Bibliography

Adamson, Alan. *Sugar without Slaves: The Political Economy of British Guiana, 1838–1904*. New Haven, 1972.
Bauer, Arnold J. 'Rural Workers in Spanish America: Problems of Peonage and Oppression'. *Hispanic American Historial Review*, 59:1 (1979), 34–63.
Bigelow, John. *Jamaica in 1850*, New York, 1851.
Bolland, O. Nigel. 'The Social Structure and Social Relations of the Settlement in the Bay of Honduras (Belize) in the 18th Century', *Journal of Caribbean History*, no. 6 (1973), 1–42.
———, *The Formation of a Colonial Society, Belize, from Conquest to Crown Colony*. Baltimore, 1977.
Bolland, O. Nigel, and Shoman, Assad. *Land in Belize, 1765–1871: The Origins of Land Tenure, Use, and Distribution in a Dependent Economy*. Kingston, 1977.
Bristowe, Lindsay W., and Wright, Philip B. *The Handbook of British Honduras for 1888–89*. London, 1888.
Burn, W.L. *Emancipation and Apprenticeship in the British West Indies*. London, 1937.
Cohen, David, and Greene, Jack. eds. *Neither Slave Nor Free*. Baltimore, 1972.
Craton, Michael, and Walvin, James. *A Jamaican Plantation: The History of Worthy Park, 1670–1970*. London, 1970.
Craton, Michael, ed. 'Roots and Branches: Current Directions in Slave Studies', *Historical Reflections*, 6:1 (1979).
Curtin, Philip D. *Two Jamaicas: The Role of Ideas in a Tropical Colony, 1830–1865*. Cambridge, Massachusetts, 1955.
Dalton, Henry G. *The History of British Guiana*. 2 vols. London, 1855.
Davy, John. *The West Indies before and since Slave Emancipation*. London, 1854.
Eisner, Gisela. *Jamaica, 1830–1930*. Manchester, England, 1961.
Finley, M.I. 'Between Slavery and Freedom', *Comparative Studies in Society and History*, 6:3 (1964), 233–49.
Frucht, Richard, 'From Slavery to Unfreedom in the Plantation Society of St. Kitts, W.I.', in *Comparative Perspectives on Slavery in New World Plantation Societies*, Vera Rubin and Arthur Tuden, eds. New York, 1977.
Gibbs, Archibald Robertson. *British Honduras: An Historical and Descriptive Account of the Colony from Its Settlement, 1670*. London, 1883.
Gibson, Charles. *The Aztecs under Spanish Rule: A History of the Indians of the Valley of Mexico, 1519–1810*. Stanford, 1964.
Giddens, Anthony, ed. *Emile Durkheim: Selected Writings*. Cambridge, 1972.
Green, William A. *British Slave Emancipation: The Sugar Colonies and the Great Experiment, 1830–1865*. Oxford, 1976.
Gurney, Joseph John. *Familiar Letters to Henry Clay of Kentucky Describing a Winter in the West Indies*. New York, 1840.
Hall, Douglas. *Free Jamaica, 1838–1865: An Economic History*. New Haven, 1959.
———, *Five of the Leewards, 1834–1870*. Barbados, 1971.
———, 'The Flight from the Estates Reconsidered: The British West Indies, 1838–42', *Journal of Caribbean History*, nos. 10– 11 (1978), 7–24.
Handler, Jerome. *The Unappropriated People*. Baltimore, 1974.

Henderson, Captain G. *An Account of the British Settlement in Honduras.* . . . London, 1809.

Hilly, Polly. 'From Slavery to Freedom: The Case of Farm-Slavery in Nigeria Hausaland', *Comparative Studies in Society and History,* 18:3 (1976), 395–426.

Hovey, Sylvester. *Letters from the West Indies.* New York, 1838.

Kloosterboer, W. *Involuntary Labour since the Abolition of Slavery.* Leiden, 1960.

Knox, A.J.G. 'Opportunities and Oppositions: The Rise of Jamaica's Black Peasantry and the Nature of the Planter Resistance', *Canadian Review of Sociology and Antropology,* 14:4 (1977), 381–95.

Madden, R.R. *A Twelvemonth's Residence in the West Indies during the Transition from Slavery to Apprenticeship.* London, 1835.

Marshall, Woodville K. 'Notes on Peasant Development in the West Indies since 1838', *Social and Economic Studies.* 17:3 (1968), 252–63.

———. 'The Termination of the Apprenticeship in Barbados and the Windward Islands: An Essay in Colonial Administration and Politics', *Journal of Caribbean History,* no. 2 (1971), 1–45.

Martin, Robert Montgomery. *History of the Colonies of the British Empire in the West Indies.* London, 1843.

Mathieson, William Law. *British Slave Emancipation, 1838–1849.* London, 1932.

Mintz, Sidney W. 'The Question of Caribbean Peasantries: A Comment', *Caribbean Studies.* 1:3 (1961), 31–34.

———. *Caribbean Transformations.* Chicago, 1974.

Moohr, Michael. 'The Economic Impact of Slave Emancipation in British Guiana, 1832–1852', *Economic History Review,* 2d ser., 25:4 (1972), 588–607.

Riviere, W. Emanuel. 'Labour Shortage in the British West Indies after Emancipation', *Journal of Caribbean History,* no. 4 (1972), 1–30.

Rubin, Vera, and Tuden, Arthur, eds. *Comparative Perspectives on Slavery in New World Plantation Society.* New York, 1977.

Scarano, Francisco. 'Slavery and Free Labor in the Puerto Rican Sugar Economy: 1815–1873', in *Comparative Perpsectives on Slavery in New World Plantation Societies.* Vera Ruben and Arthur Tenden, eds. New York, 1977.

Sewell, W.G. *The Ordeal of Free Labor in the British West Indies.* London, 1861.

Stanley, Edward Henry. *Claims and Resources of the West India Colonies.* London, 1850.

Thome, James A., and Kimball, J. Horace. *Emancipation in the West Indies.* New York, 1838.

Tucker, Robert C., ed. *The Marx–Engels Reader.* New York, 1972.

Waddell, Hope Masteron. *Twenty-nine Years in the West Indies and Central Africa.* London, 1863.

Williams, Eric. *British Historians and the West Indies.* London, 1966.

———. *From Columbus to Castro.* London, 1970.

Wood, Donald. *Trinidad in Transition: The Years after Slavery.* London, 1968.

Zavala, Silvio. *New Viewpoints on Spanish Colonization of America.* Philadelphia, 1943.

The Share System in the Bahamas in the Nineteenth and Early Twentieth Centuries

Howard Johnson

Introduction

The existence of metayage in the sugar industry of the British Windward Islands in the post-emancipation years has been well documented.[1] The system of sharecropping was not,however, confined to those sugar colonies. In the 'marginal' non-plantation colony of the Bahamas the share system had been introduced as early as 1836 and was by the mid-1880s a significant feature of the rural economy of those islands.[2] As one contemporary observer remarked in 1886: '[the share] system prevails to a very large extent throughout the Bahamas especially at the pine-apple growing islands'.[3] The existence of a sharecropping system has, up to this point, escaped the notice of those few historians of the post-emancipation years in the Bahamas.[4] This is understandable for the references to the share system in the Bahamas are scattered, unlike the British Windward Islands where the metayage system was frequently the subject of official scrutiny and reports. This chapter examines the origins of the share system and its operation in the period up to the early years of the twentieth century.

Before examining in greater detail the circumstances which led to the adoption of the share system in the Bahamas it is necessary to describe the economic structure of the colony in the years before the abolition of slavery. The influx of loyalist refugees in the colony after 1783 had resulted in the establishment of a plantation system based on the production of cotton.[5] By 1800, however, the cotton plantation economy in the Bahamas had collapsed. In 1834 cotton was a crop of only minor importance. As Governor Balfour reported in that year, 'cotton which was formerly cultivated with great success . . . is now little more than a nominal article of Export'.[6]

Without a plantation staple many of the estates in the Out Islands practised a diversified agriculture, raised livestock, and supplied the Nassau market with a wide range of foodstuffs.[7] In 1834, for example, the island of Eleuthera sent 'Corn, Pease, Potatoes and Yams also Plantains and Bananas' to Nassau.[8] Although an export trade in pineapples had developed with the United States by 1832, pineapple production was confined to a few islands where the soil was considered suitable. As Governor Carmichael Smyth noted in that year:

The real truth is that these islands with the exception of salt do not offer any real encouragement for the employment of capital. Pine-apples to a very large extent have lately been cultivated; but they only answer in particular situations, and in a particular soil.[9]

By 1834 very few of the colony's exports were produced 'by the land, or the labour of the inhabitants'.[10] The main props of the colonial economy were salt production and wrecking. As Balfour stated in February of that year:

Our principal means may be put down as proceeding from the three chief sources, Salt, Wrecks and the money which is directly drawn by the Troops and Civil Servants from England.[11]

The emergence of the share system in the Bahamas after emancipation was directly related to the fact that there was no major agricultural export staple to replace cotton. The decline of cotton production had resulted in the migration of planters from the Out Islands to the United States and to other West Indian colonies as well as to Nassau where they often became merchants.[12] This was a trend which continued after the abolition of slavery. In 1836, for example, Special Justice Thomas Winder, after a visit to Southern Eleuthera, was able to report that since 1835 'the whole of the proprietors have either deserted their Estates or died'.[13] One result of these developments was that the owners of large estates on the Out Islands were usually absentee proprietors.

Without a profitable export staple most proprietors lacked operating capital. During apprenticeship this 'utter want of capital'[14] was reflected in the failure of some employers to properly maintain their apprentices. In a visit to Exuma, early in 1835, two Special Justices had listened to the complaints of apprentices whose employers had not supplied them with the food and clothing to which they are entitled by law. The Justices reported:

Upon enquiry we found that many of the Employers were unable to give their Apprentices the proper Supplies from *real Poverty* some of them stating that a Mr. Farrington at Nassau held Mortgages on their Estates, which so hampered them, that without his assistance, they really could not supply their Apprentices.[15]

In the years after emancipation the proprietors, because of a shortage of capital, could not offer steady employment to the ex-slaves for money wages. C.R. Nesbitt, the Lieutenant-Governor of the colony in 1842, noted that a large proportion of the colony's land was owned by private proprietors who cultivated only a negligible portion of it and offered 'no continuous employment on it for money wages'.[16] In 1847 H.E. Cartwright, a stipendiary magistrate in the Out Islands, commented even more perceptively on 'the proprietors of lands not having means or knowledge of an available staple article to employ labor'.[17]

It was in this context of absentee proprietorship and capital shortage that the share system was adopted in the years after the end of slavery. In fact there is evidence which indicates that one landlord had settled ex-slaves on his estate on this system as early as 1836.[18] The adoption of the share system may be explained by the fact that the labour requirements of absentee proprietors were met without the payment of a regular wage bill or supervision costs. Landlords hoped that land which was cultivated by tenants would retain its value. It was also anticipated that ex-slaves would work more productively as tenants on the share arrangement since they had a 'direct interest in the produce of their industry and in the protection of the property entrusted to them'.[19] Finally, proprietors expected that the share system would provide them with an income without risking scarce capital. As the editor of the *Bahama Argus* remarked in an editorial on sharecropping in 1835: 'what a revenue, without risk, might the judicious landholder thus derive!'[20]

It is possible in these early years to discern the outlines of the share system as it later developed. The editorial in the *Bahama Argus* (to which we have referred) provides us with an insight into those considerations which might have determined the division of crop yields between tenant and landlord. It suggested:

granting them [the sharecroppers] leases on a rent payable in cotton, or other produce, not exceeding one third

of the crop, allowing a third for the farmer's expenses and improvements, and another third for his subsistence.[21]

It is also clear that proprietors expected to benefit from the labour of the family unit on their estates. As the editorial pointed out in a discussion about the possibility of producing pineapples on the share system: 'the work would be performed by him [the tenant], with his family, at little cost'.[22]

In the Bahamas farming on shares was, in effect, an application to agriculture of a system which had previously been used in fishing and wrecking during slavery and persisted into freedom. It had been a common practice for slaves, especially in Nassau, to find employment for themselves and then pay their owners a fixed sum.[23] Many of these slaves engaged in fishing or wrecking and were paid 'in shares'. According to Governor Carmichael Smyth, writing in March 1830:

The greater part of the slave population here are seafaring People. The crews in the wrecking vessels are in a great measure composed of slaves — These people are paid in shares, and they almost invariably work out their freedom.[24]

This was a practice to which the Collector of Customs also called attention in 1832:

slaves often hire themselves from their owners, and join in trips with other slaves or with free people 'on shares'.[25]

In the post-emancipation years absentee proprietors recruited a labour force for their estates mainly by the share system and labour tenancy. The willingness of the labouring population to work on shares may be explained by the fact that this system made land available in a context where few ex-slaves were able to purchase land. There was in the Bahamas (as elsewhere in the British West Indies) an enthusiasm for landownership among the freedmen. In 1840 Governor Francis Cockburn had remarked on 'the prevailing inclination amongst the lower Classes to possess Lands at all risks and hazards'.[26] However, official policy on the devolution of Crown lands served to thwart the ex-slaves' ambitions to own land. As early as 1836 Lord Glenelg, the Secretary of State for the Colonies, had ordered, in a circular despatch to the Governors of the West Indian colonies, that Crown lands should no longer be sold for less than £1 per acre. According to Philip Curtin:

This document accepted the view of both [Edward Gibbon] Wakefield and the West Indians that too much land was dangerous to the production of staples.[27]

It is clear that the main idea which informed both metropolitan and colonial policy on Crown lands was to create a rural proletariat by limiting land-ownership. These ideas were expressed, in the case of the Bahamas, by John J. Burnside, the Surveyor-General, in a letter to Governor Cockburn in July 1838 in which he suggested changes in the regulations governing the sale of Crown lands. He recommended that individuals applying for Crown lands should purchase an allotment valued at a minimum of seventy-five dollars. He pointed out that:

by fixing the minimum extent to purchase at $75 it will bring into the market only those persons whose industrious habits have enabled them to lay up the requisite sum and which may be fairly considered as giving them a right to claim the privileges of being freeholders, and it may stimulate others to work as hired labourers until they have acquired the requisite sum to enable them to the like privileges.[28]

The effect of the regulations on the sale of Crown lands in the immediate post-emancipation years was to severely restrict the ownership of land by the ex-slaves. This was clear to C.R. Nesbitt who remarked in 1842:

The above classes of persons [ex-slaves and liberated Africans] continue desirous of possessing land but their limited pecuniary means do not admit of their purchasing the same under the present regulations.[29]

In this situation the ex-slaves turned to squatting, labour tenency and to the share system.

Despite the obstacles to landownership there were ex-slaves who purchased land. In Eleuthera, for example, liberated apprentices bought Crown land at the settlement of Pitman's Cove in 1835, for an average price of £5 sterling, to engage in the profitable business of producing pineapples for export. It was then estimated that an acre of land planted in pineapples could yield an income of £100 to £150 sterling after expenses.[30] Most of the land suitable for pineapple cultivation in Eleuthera was, however, the property of private proprietors who often owned tracts of several hundred acres.[31] As a result, ex-slaves who were unable to purchase land were often prepared to work on shares. Evidence for this development is provided by an advertisement for the sale of a pineapple plantation at Pitman's Cove which appeared in *The Observer* in August 1838:

The plantation consists of two distinct Tracts, joining each other, and the whole, with the exception of a small Turtle Pond, of the very best Pine Apple land . . . Several

persons have applied to the Subscriber, offering to work on shares.[32]

The arrangement by which the tenant cultivated the land assigned to him on the share system was relatively uncomplicated. Landlords supplied the land and received in turn from their tenants, who provided the labour, a share of the crop yield. In the early years after emancipation the division of the crop varied with soil conditions. An official report for the year 1847 described the 'conditions of tenancy on the estates' throughout the Bahamas in this way:

On some Estates if New Land one half, if old one third of the produce; and on others from two to three days labor are given for the privilege of cultivating the land.[33]

There is evidence which indicates that those tenants who cultivated crops such as Indian corn, guinea corn, and ground provisions often divided only the corn crops with the landlord and kept the rest of the crops for their own subsistence. As Sir Henry Blake observed in 1887:

the cultivators considered that the corn crops only ought to be considered as shareable with the owner, all ground provisions being the property of the cultivator.[34]

Tenants who worked on the share system (as well as on the system of labour tenancy) had a measure of security of tenure on the land they cultivated. By 1847 it had already been established by custom that tenants could not be ejected without reasonable notice and without an opportunity to reap the crops which they had planted. Writing in 1847 H.E. Cartwright observed:

By custom it has become a rule to give six months [sic] notice to the tenant to quit possession, and where the tenant pays rent in kind or gives two days [sic] labour per week in lieu, he is entitled to remain until he has reaped all the growing crops planted by permission of the Landlord.[35]

In the early years of the operation of the share system there was little to complicate the basic share contract to which we have referred. The landlord provided the land but contributed little else to the production process. Few landlords attempted to exercise supervisory functions or to control decisions on production methods. In fact, as we have argued, one of the main advantages of the share system for the absentee proprietor was that he incurred no supervision costs. As we shall see, this situation changed in the case of pineapple production in the latter part of the nineteenth century.

Most of the sharecropping agreements through-out the nineteenth century seem to have been ver-bal and informal. As early as 1847 the main fea-tures of these tenancy arrangements were firmly established by custom. There is evidence, however, that on the estates owned by the heirs of Charles Farquharson on Watling's Island written contracts (which were signed in the presence of a Justice of Peace) were used in 1865. Contrary to the general practice there was also on these estates an attempt to supervise the tenants who worked on the share system.

The share system was not introduced on these estates in Watling's Island until 1865. In the imme-diate post-emancipation period there had been a general reluctance among the ex-slaves on that island to work on shares. A description of eco-nomic conditions in the Bahamas between 1837 and 1840 noted of Watling's Island:

Almost abandoned by the Landed Proprietors being una-ble to cultivate their lands by hired labour and the work-ing class not being willing to work on shares; the old plantations are converted into grazing farms — sends a small supply to the Nassau market.[36]

Until the early 1860s the estates on the island con-centrated on the raising of stock for the Nassau market but by 1864 this had ceased to be the case. As Governor Rawson noted in his report on the Blue Book for that year: 'Cattle for slaughtering are imported from Cuba and Florida'.[37] It was per-haps in the light of these developments that the emphasis on the Farquharson estates shifted to agricultural production on the share system.

In the written contracts which have survived from 1865 the rights and obligations of the tenants on the Farquharson estates were explicitly stated. In the contract which was signed by the tenants who worked on the William J. Hall and John Har-rison tracts of land, for example, the owners made it clear that one-third of all the products of the land should be delivered to their resident manager. The crops specified in this contract were corn, sugar cane, plantains, yams, cassava, potatoes, beans, peas, pumpkins, melons and groundnuts. This agreement also mentioned the tenants' responsi-bility for keeping the land in good condition and emphasized the manager's supervisory functions:

the persons or tenants aforesaid . . . promise to be honest faithful and careful of the interests of the owners of said lands by not destroying the Standing woods by fire or abandoning the fields to weed before the same is worn out, and generally to obey all lawful orders of the afore-said Jacob Deveaux Senior[,] Manager as regards the portions of the said tracts to be farmed and cultivated.[38]

These provisions were clearly intended to discour-age the use of the 'slash and burn' agricultural techniques commonly employed by Bahamian cul-tivators of that period.[39] Any person who failed to comply with the terms of the contract had to pay two pounds sterling to the other party. This agree-ment could be renewed after a period of one year 'by mutual consent of both parties'.[40]

The detailed nature of the contracts signed by tenants on the Farquharson estates in 1865 is also demonstrated by the fact that even the number of pigs which could be kept on the estates was spec-ified. An addendum to one of these agreements read:

Every Tenant, working on Farquharson lands are [sic] hereby allowed the privilege of keeping free of Rent, or charge one Breeding Sow and the Barrow increase from the same, any person wishing to keep a larger number of Hogs must deliver one pig from each Litter for the own-ers of the land in lieu of Rent.[41]

Separate agreements were signed by those per-sons who performed the duties of manager on the estates. The manager's main function was to mon-itor the performance of the tenants. The contract signed by Jacob Deveaux, Senior, for example, mentioned that he had been employed 'for the pur-pose of directing and controlling the tenants'. For the performance of his duties Deveaux was allowed to keep one-fourth of the crops which he collected from the tenants and 'the use for culti-vation free of all Shares or Rent Three Acres or twelve tasks' of the land which he managed.[42]

During the latter part of the nineteenth century landlords who rented 'pineapple lands' on the share system began to take a more direct interest in the production process. By the mid–1880s they extended credit to the share-tenants and supplied them with pineapple slips, manure and fertilizer. The cost of these inputs was the first deduction from the proceeds of the sale of the tenant's crop which was marketed by the landlord. With this increased financial involvement landlords came to exercise a greater measure of supervision over the agricultural activities of their tenants. Thus Sir Henry Blake observed of pineapple production on the share system in the Bahamas in 1886: 'Here the initial expense of purchase of slips, and plant-ing, have necessitated the use of capital and with it, of supervision'.[43] The provision by landlords of these inputs was reflected in the share of the crop yields which they received. In the late nineteenth century it was usual for landlords who rented pine-apple land on the share system to receive one-half rather than one-third of the net proceeds.[44]

These developments followed on a heightened interest in pineapple production after 1865 when the economic boom based on blockade-running during the American Civil War had come to an end. Governor Rawson in 1866 admitted that blockade-running had not 'increased the commercial relations of the Colony with any other country'. It had, however, he suggested, focused the attention of the colony's merchant class on the commercial possibilities of local resources:

It has turned the attention of the Mercantile Community to the means of developing existing resources, and of opening up new employments for the population of the Out Islands, and fresh sources of profitable industry and commerce for all portions of the Colony.[45]

The 'existing resources' to which Rawson referred were pineapples and sponges.

The interest in the development of the pineapple industry by the merchant class in 1865 coincided with a sharply increased demand for tropical commodities by the industrialized countries of the North Atlantic. W. Arthur Lewis has noted that the rapid rise in tropical exports after 1870 reflected, in part, 'the growth of demand resulting from the increase in the national incomes of the leading industrial states'.[46] In the Bahamas (as in other parts of the tropical world) the expansion of the markets for certain foodstuffs led to increased production. In the case of pineapples the stimulus to production came from a demand for canned as well as fresh fruit. As the administrator of the colony noted in 1881:

The cultivation of pineapples has had an impulse given to it by the enormous demand for canned preserved pineapples, operations of which are on an extensive scale in New Providence.[47]

It was with the hope of profiting from this demand that landlords advanced loans,pineapple slips, manure and fertilizer in order to increase productivity and output.

The demand for pineapples was also reflected in the increased purchases of land by Bahamian merchants in order to extend its production. This trend was already discernible in 1869. Sir James Walker, governor of the colony, pointed out in his report on the Blue Book for that year:

Notwithstanding the discouraging return of the present year and the general precarious character of the pine cultivation, large tracts of land have been lately purchased with the view of extending it.[48]

One result of this trend was the concentration of the ownership of 'pineapple lands' in the hands of a few individuals. Thus Charles Mooney of the

Baltimore Geographical Society remarked, in 1905, after a visit to the Bahamas:

Although there are pineapple soils on all the islands, and particularly the larger ones, yet the industry is centred on Eleuthera and Cat Islands. On these the value of the lands has increased greatly, and they have now come into the possession of a comparatively few wealthy men. The fields are owned either individually or in partnership.[49]

Despite the growth and prosperity of the pineapple industry in the late nineteenth century the share system remained the dominant form of labour organization. Although pineapple production was sufficiently profitable to make a system of wage labour feasible, the share system continued to have important advantages for merchant-landlords who were intent on maximizing profits. First, it was a means of minimizing costs by restricting the outlay of working capital. Second, the landlord benefitted from the additional labour of his tenant's family. In fact the tenant's family constituted 'a cheap labour reserve'.[50]

The rapid extension of the pineapple industry in response to the export stimulus created an increased demand for a stable labour force, which would provide steady supplies of this commodity. Initially, merchants experienced difficulty in attracting such a labour force for most persons in the Out Islands eked out a relatively independent existence by engaging in subsistence farming and sea-going activities.[51] As we have argued elsewhere, however, merchants recruited and retained this labour force by the operation of a credit system whose effect was to bind labourers to regular employment by the creation of a debt relationship.[52] This method of recruiting labourers (used by merchants in both the pineapple and sponging industries) was remarked on by Governor Henry Blake in 1884:

The owner — generally a shopkeeper — requires labour for his shop or on his land. The sponger or 'farmer' is contented, indolent, and not disposed to work beyond his immediate necessities. To secure labour some inducement must be held out that will at the same time bind the labourer to his work, and that inducement is the opening of an account by advancing food and clothing, to be repaid out of the proceeds of the share in the new voyage or crop.[53]

Most cultivators who produced pineapples on the share system in this period relied on their merchant-landlords for credit in the eighteen months which elapsed between the planting and the reaping of a crop of pineapples. The evidence indicates that these tenants came increasingly to depend on the advances of cash and provisions from their landlords because they concentrated on the production of pineapples to the exclusion of subsistence crops. These developments and their consequences were noted by the Resident Justice of the island of San Salvador in his report for 1885:

Although the export [of pineapples] is large, there is no visible benefit among the majority of the small proprietors and the labouring classes who, here, as on some of the other Out Islands neglect other and necessary agricultural pursuits. The consequence is that ground produce is very scarce, and should any unforeseen circumstances arise to retard the growth of pineapple crops in the field, the usual method of bartering of the fruit of the coming season will have to be entirely adopted, this in some cases has been already done.[54]

The terms on which the merchant-landlord provided credit virtually guaranteed that at the end of the season the cultivator would be in debt to him. The loans were repaid from the tenant's share of the sale of the crop which the merchant-landlord marketed. The prices for provisions supplied and the interest on cash advanced were so highly inflated that the cultivator's income (after deductions for credit) was usually inadequate for the maintenance of himself and his family over the next crop cycle. As Governor Blake observed in 1884:

Be the year good or bad the closing of the account rarely leaves any but the smallest margin in favour of the debtor. There is therefore hardly any circulation of money in the Out Islands.[55]

Without cash reserves the cultivator resorted to the landlord for consumption loans. In this context the credit system was a mechanism by which the landlord strengthened his hold over a labour force and appropriated surplus in the form of the high rates charged on advances.

This system of credit (and debt) was a source of dissatisfaction to the share tenants in the pineapple industry. They complained that this credit relationship provided their landlords with an opportunity to cheat them. As Governor Haynes-Smith noted in 1896: 'The cultivator alleges the owner cheats him in the price he charges for the truck and in the statement of his accounts'.[56] Some tenants retaliated to his exploitation by selling illicitly a portion of the pineapple crop in order to obtain cash.[57]

In the twentieth century two factors converged to undermine the importance of the share system. The first of these was the growth of opportunities for lucrative wage employment in the southern United States and in New Providence. In Florida, for example, the expansion of agricultural production in the late nineteenth and early twentieth centuries attracted Bahamian labourers in large numbers. The economic prosperity in New Providence in the 1920s based on bootlegging, tourism and the land and construction booms also resulted in the depopulation of the Out Islands. The second of these factors was the decline of the colony's pineapple industry in the early decades of the twentieth century and with it a decrease in the demand for labour by the merchant-landlords. Exports of pineapple in 1892 were valued at £56,000 but in 1927 were worth only £7.[58] Although the share system has not disappeared, it has ceased to be an important form of land tenure in the Bahamas.

The share system emerged in the Bahamas after the abolition of slavery to supply the labour requirements of absentee proprietors most of whom had no capital to operate a wage system. This system was retained throughout the nineteenth century mainly because it involved lower costs than wage labour. Unlike metayage in the British Windward Islands, the share system in the Bahamas did not result in the elevation of the ex-slaves and their descendants on the social and economic scale, nor did it provide a stimulus to the development of an independent freehold peasantry.[59] In fact it was the share system which kept the estates of the absentee landlords intact and financially viable by lowering labour costs. In the Bahamas, under the share system, tenants remained basically 'permanent hired hands' whose main resource was their labour.[60] Operated in conjunction with a system of advances, the share system became for the landlords an effective mechanism for surplus appropriation and the retention of a reliable and impoverished labour force.

Notes

1. W.K. Marshall, 'Metayage in the Sugar Industry of the British Windward Islands, 1838–1865', *Jamaican Historical Review 5* (1965), pp. 28–55.

2. For a useful typology of the colonial economies of the British West Indies in the pre-emancipation era see B.W. Higman, *Slave Populations of the British Caribbean 1807–1834* (Baltimore, 1984), pp. 66–7.

3. Letter by Jas. C. Smith, 'The Industrial Progress of the Bahamas during the Period since 1865 to 1884', *Nassau Guardian*, 29 Sept. 1886. In the Bahamas the share system was also referred to as the metayer or the metairie system.

4. Michael Craton, *A History of the Bahamas* (rev. edn., London, 1968); Paul Albury, *The Story of the Bahamas* (London, 1975). The term 'sharecropping' is here used as defined by Ralph Shlomowitz: 'a labor arrangement by which individual family units, in payment for their labor on a separate parcel of land, receive a share of the output produced on that parcel of land', Ralph Shlomowitz, 'The Origins of Southern Sharecropping', *Agricultural History 53* (1979), p. 557, note 2.

5. Gail Saunders, *Bahamian Loyalists and their Slaves* (London, 1983), p. 36.

6. Balfour to Stanley, no. 78, 19 Feb. 1834, CO 23/91.

7. Higman, p. 65; Michael Craton, 'Hobbesian or Pangloss-ian? The Two Extremes of Slave Conditions in the British Caribbean, 1783 to 1834', *William and Mary Quarterly* (1978) p. 352.
8. Minutes of evidence taken before Commissioners of Crown Lands and Woods on 6 Aug. 1835 reprinted in *Bahama Argus,* 22 Aug. 1835.
9. Carmichael Smyth to Goderich, no. 178, 17 Sept. 1832, CO 23/86.
10. Balfour to Stanley, no. 78, 19 Feb. 1834, CO 23/91.
11. Ibid.
12. Michael Craton, 'We shall not be Moved: Pompey's Slave Revolt in Exuma Island, Bahamas, 1830', *New West Indian Guide 57* (1983), p. 21; Sir Henry Blake to the Earl of Derby, no. 108, 12 Aug. 1884, CO 23/224. Blake was governor of the colony between 1884 and 1886.
13. Report of Special Justice Thomas Winder, 6 July 1837. Enclosure in Joseph Hunter to Glenelg, no. 51, 12 Aug. 1837, CO 23/99.
14. Balfour to Spring Rice, no. 39, 15 Jan. 1835, CO 23/93.
15. Report of Special Justices, D. McLean and H. Munro, 23 April 1835. Enclosure in Colebrooke to Glenelg, no. 28, 27 Aug. 1835, CO 23/94.
16. C.R. Nesbitt to Stanley, no. 18, 12 July 1842, CO 23/113.
17. Enclosure in Nesbitt to Grey, no. 36, 7 Sept. 1847, CO 23/126.
18. Report of Special Justice Thomas Winder, 6 July 1837. Enclosure in Joseph Hunter to Glenelg, no. 51, 12 Aug. 1837, CO 23/99.
19. Ibid.
20. *Bahama Argus,* 24 June 1835.
21. Ibid.
22. Ibid.
23. Carmichael Smyth to Goderich, no. 163, 2 Aug. 1832, CO 23/87.
24. Carmichael Smyth to Sir George Murray, no. 30, 8 March 1830, CO 23/82.
25. Quoted in Higman, p. 84.
26. Francis Cockburn to Lord John Russell, no. 20, 6 April 1840, CO 23/107.
27. Philip Curtin, *Two Jamaicas* (paperback edn., New York, 1970), p. 137.
28. Burnside to Cockburn, 11 July 1838. Enclosure in Cockburn to Glenelg, no. 101, 5 Sept. 1838, CO 23/103.
29. C.R. Nesbitt to Stanley, no. 18, 12 July 1842.
30. Colebrooke to Glenelg, no. 79, 8 Aug. 1835, CO 23/94.
31. Minutes of evidence taken before Commissioners of Crown Lands and Woods on 6 Aug. 1835 reprinted in *Bahama Argus,* 22 Aug. 1835.
32. Extract from *The Observer,* 18 Aug. 1838. Enclosure in Cockburn to Glenelg, no. 101, 5 Sept. 1838, CO 23/103.
33. 'Statistical Summary for the half year ending 30th June 1847'; Table C. Enclosure in Nesbitt to Grey, no. 36, 7 Sept. 1848, CO 23/126.
34. Blake to Sir Henry Holland, no. 34, 15 March 1887, CO 23/229.
35. 'Statistical Summary for the half year ending 30th June 1847'; Table C. Enclosure in Nesbitt to Grey, no. 36, 7 Sept. 1848.
36. Records of the United Society for the Propagation of the Gospel. Records Relating to the Bahamas 1726–1858, Microfilm Reel 3. Table and Comments. Statistical Account from 1837 to 1840.
37. Rawson to Edward Cardwell, no. 33, 20 Jan. 1866, CO 23/183.
38. See duplicate of agreement made between Alexander Forsyth and tenants on William J. Hall and John Harrison tracts, 18 Aug. 1865. O'Brien Family Collection (BPRO).
39. For a description of the 'slash and burn' technique as practiced in the Bahamas see Blake to Derby, no. 108, 12 Aug. 1884, CO 23/224.
40. See duplicate of agreement between Alexander Forsyth and tenants, 18 Aug. 1865. O'Brien Family Collection.
41. See duplicate of agreement between Alexander Forsyth and tenants on the lands of the Estate of the late Charles Farquharson, 29 Aug. 1865. O'Brien Family Collection.
42. See original of agreement between Alexander Forsyth and Jacob Deveaux, Senior, 14 Aug. 1865. O'Brien Family Collection. My thanks to David Wood of the BPRO who brought these references to my attention.
43. Blake to Earl Granville, no. 32, 20 March 1886, CO 23/228.
44. W.F. Haynes-Smith to Joseph Chamberlain, no. 76, 7 July 1896, CO 23/244.
45. Report on Blue Book for 1865. Enclosure in Rawson to the Earl of Carnarvon, no. 142, 1 Sept. 1866, CO 23/185.
46. W. Arthur Lewis, 'The Export Stimulus' in W. Arthur Lewis (ed.), *Tropical Development 1880–1913* (London, 1970), p. 14.
47. E.B.A. Taylor to the Earl of Kimberley, no. 100, 29 July 1881, CO 23/221.
48. Walker to the Earl of Kimberley, no. 489, 30 Nov. 1870, CO 23/202.
49. Charles N. Mooney, 'Soils of the Bahama Islands' in G.B. Shattuck (ed.), *The Bahamas Islands* (New York, 1905), p. 175. For an example of the concentration of landowner-ship see advertisement 'Valuable Pineapple Land for Sale', *Nassau Guardian,* Feb. 1899.
50. Verena Stolcke and Michael M. Hall, 'The Introduction of Free Labour on Sao Paulo Coffee Plantations' in T.J. Byres (ed.), *Sharecropping and Sharecroppers* (London, 1983), p. 174. See also Stanley J. Stein, *Vassouras* (paperback edn., New York, 1976), p. 272.
51. For a discussion of the economic activities of the Out-Island population see Howard Johnson, ''A Modified Form of Slavery'': The Credit and Truck Systems in the Bahamas in the Nineteenth and Early Twentieth Centuries'. For a brief discussion of the expansion of the pine-apple industry in the late 19th century see Craton, *A History of the Bahamas,* pp. 247–8.
52. Ibid.
53. Blake to Derby, no. 108, 12 Aug. 1884, CO 23/224.
54. Report on San Salvador for 1885 in Appendix to *Votes of the House of Assembly* (23 Feb.–26 May 1886), p. 29.
55. Blake to Derby, no. 108, 12 Aug. 1884, CO 23/224. For an excellent discussion of indebtedness as a feature of the sharecropping relationship see Adrienne Cooper, 'Share-croppers and Landlords in Bengal, 1930–50: The Depend-ency Web and its Implications' in T.J. Byres (ed.), *Share-cropping and Sharecroppers,* pp. 240–3. See also Jay R. Mandle, *The Roots of Black Poverty* (Durham, 1978), pp. 48–50.
56. Haynes-Smith to Joseph Chamberlain, no. 76, 7 July 1896.
57. See Johnson, 'A Modified Form of Slavery'.
58. Memorandum by the Colonial Secretary, 'Agriculture in the Bahamas' (Nassau, 1938), p. 34.
59. See discussion in W.K. Marshall, pp. 50–5.
60. The phrase is Edward E. Malefakis'. Quoted in T.J. Byres, 'Historical Perspectives on Sharecropping' in Byres (ed.), *Sharecropping and Sharecroppers,* pp. 22–3.

SECTION FOUR
Immigrants and Indentured Labourers

Immigration has been a central feature of Caribbean society ever since the genocidal assault upon the indigenous population by colonizing Europeans in the sixteenth century, and the development of large-scale plantation production in the seventeenth and eighteenth centuries. While there has been interest in the voluntary movement of settlers to the region, the systematic analysis of various types of bonded or coerced labour continues to be the dominant area of scholarly investigation. For the slavery period, attentions focused on the transatlantic trade in enslaved Africans; for the post-slavery period scholars shifted their attention to the study of the fundamental causes which extended the relationship between the capitalistic plantation economies and contract labour from Asia, Africa and Europe.

In their essays, Laurence and Renard show that Caribbean planters, faced with a reduction in their labour force after emancipation, devised several labour recruiting strategies designed to increase both the supply and social control of workers. They suggest that planters, not satisfied with the effects of their extemporaneous means of controlling labour, convinced imperial governments that ex-slaves were opposed to advancing productivity and that immigration of workers was a major answer to the economic problems caused by emancipation. The call for immigrant labourers became particularly strident in the British and French West Indies. Once the view was accepted in Europe that immigration was the grand panacea, various schemes were instituted. This was so despite the clear opposition of anti-slavery groups and the Afro-Caribbean labouring class.

As Turner and Moore also show, five major sources of immigrant labour were tapped: Europe, the Portuguese Atlantic Islands, Africa, North America and Asia. Asian immigration — undertaken in French, Spanish, British and Dutch colonies — became the most numerically significant, with over 500,000 workers from the Indian sub-continent coming to the region between 1838 and 1917. The majority of immigrants went to Guyana and Trinidad; but Cuba, Suriname, Martinique, Guadeloupe and Jamaica imported significant numbers. Cuba, as Turner indicates, was a major destination for Chinese workers, who played a significant role in the reconfiguration of the labour market there before and during the period of the abolition of slavery.

Most immigrant labourers were employed as contract workers. Proprietors argued that only long contracts could compensate for the expense of importing and maintaining servants. Consequently, renewable one-year contracts soon developed into five-year contracts, with repatriation, in the case of Indians, being available only after another five-years' continuous residence in the region.

These essays also examine the socio-cultural consequence of immigration upon Caribbean plantation societies, and explain how the interaction between creole formations and Asian tradition ushered in another major stage in the cultural development of the region.

Chinese Contract Labour in Cuba, 1847–1874

Mary Turner

Cuba was the last of the Caribbean islands to undergo a 'sugar revolution'. Until the end of the 18th century it had a sparse population of 200,000 people, some 20% of whom were slaves, engaged in ranching and tobacco farming. Then, increased imports of slaves were allowed, sugar cultivation developed and by 1828 Cuba was producing more sugar than all the British West Indian islands put together.[1]

Slave labour was the basis of the sugar industry but, after 1820, when the slave trade was officially abolished, the slaves were all imported illegally. The Cuban planters, consequently, were threatened with a labour problem, a threat which became acute in the 1840s.

This article discusses the efforts they made to solve this problem and in particular their use of Chinese contract labour and its role in the development of the economy.

The 1820 treaty was at first completely ignored. Since slaves were needed both to expand sugar production and as replacements the slave traders flourished; expeditions were fitted out in Havana and arrivals and departures were advertised in the local press.[2] The demand for slaves was such and the connivance of the Spanish authorities in the island so complete (the Captain Generals were said to be paid for every slave landed in the island) that the slaves rescued from slavery by the British navy and landed in Havana were simply used to supplement the illegal slave trade. In 1835, however, the British put an end to this abuse and a new treaty with Spain drove the slave traders to take refuge in Portuguese and American flags. Pressure from the British continued; in 1840 a well-known abolitionist, David Turnbull, was appointed as British consul in Havana and in 1845 Spain made a new abolition law which exposed to punishment not only ships' personnel, pilots, captains and sailors, but also the ships' owners, the cargo owners and the traders; they were to be exiled more than 50 leagues from home and fined 1–100,000 pesos. The law caused a 'drumbeat of alarm' in Cuba; where were the labourers to come from? Some proprietors in panic began to sell their property.[3]

Their panic was, perhaps, premature. The Spanish government was essentially concerned to continue ownership of a prosperous plantation colony. Stripped of all other American possessions, Cuban revenues were an essential element in the Spanish budget and served as one sure guarantee for foreign loans.[4] Cuba provided a protected market for Spanish products especially flour, oil, wine and textiles; stimulated shipbuilding and created the capital which, invested in Catalonia, helped to boost the Spanish economy into an industrial phase. For the planters, however, and for Cuban society in general, the problem was more complex. By 1845 it was clear that, though the slave trade was profitable in itself and slave labour the cheapest available the slaves themselves posed a threat to security. So far as the Spanish government was concerned, as long as slave rebellions were small enough and infrequent enough to be contained by the military, the slave trade remained a viable institution. Individual Cubans, who stood at the very least to lose substantially by any rebellion and worse, risked being murdered, were forced to take a more progressive political position and ask: Was the continuation of the slave trade necessary? This question, which had long been discussed by Cuban intellectuals, who connected free trade, and a free wage economy with the achievement of a free Cuba, was forced on the whole ruling class by a sequence of slave rebellions which took place between 1841 and 1843. In the summer of 1841 there were a number of risings on the sugar estates and coffee plantations and in the autumn, slaves building a mansion in Havana for the largest slave owner in the country rebelled. The rebels were crushed and a new slave code instituted a pass system for slaves leaving their own plantation and substantial reward for informers. But in March 1843, in the heart of the sugar lands near Matánzas, rebellion broke out again; several plantations were involved and this outbreak was obviously better planned than the others. Further rebellions followed in November near Cárdenas.[5] All were easily contained, but they were followed in January 1844 by a government attack on the free black and coloured population. On the strength of a supposed conspiracy, revealed under torture, 4,000 people, mostly free persons, were arrested and many flogged into confessions: 78 were condemned to death, 400 to exile, 1,292 to prison and arrests of 'suspects' continued into the following year.[6] This conspiracy of La Escalera gave the government a chance to eliminate leading members of the rising coloured middle class, potential trouble makers, but at the same time, it demonstrated the frailty of the social order. The nightmare fate of St. Dominigue loomed over the future.

The result was that for the first time in Cuban history, the slave owners themselves petitioned for the abolition of the slave trade. In the jurisdiction of Matánzas, for example, the scene of the March 1843 rebellion, a petition signed by 93 planters called the trade 'a stain on our civilization, a horrible abyss in which all our hopes for future well being and security are buried, a hydra that frightens those capitalists who would come and settle on our soil.'[7]

The Captain General, Leopoldo O'Donnell, checked the circulation of a similar petition near Havana; but such opposition among the Cuban land owners could not be ignored. The new law of 1845 was passed in Spain with a view to placating the planters of the 'ever faithful' isle as well as the British government.

The planters, however, soon recovered from the fears induced by the slave rebellions. The market prospects for sugar seemed very good; Britain passed the Equalization of Sugar Duties Act, European and North American sugar consumption was increasing. Cuba seemed ideally suited to supply the market and, it was hoped, destroyed the prospects of the beet sugar producers if only sugar production could be increased.

The planters considered their problem within the framework created by the slave system. Increased production meant an increased labour force and the norm of labour costs was provided by the cost of slave labour. Salaried workers could be found within Cuba for planation work; by 1862 no less than 41, 661 whites, most of them peasants, were employed in the 'zafra', the sugar harvest.[8] But salaried workers were 'expensive'. Freemen had ample opportunity in Cuba to make a living outside the estates. Havana itself, which was the most important port in the Caribbean, the centre for an opulent ruling class, and with facilities that led tourists to make comparisons with Paris, provided a myriad of opportunities for employment. In the countryside, land was plentiful and the peasants played an important role supplying food both for Havana and the plantations since the practice of allowing the slaves provision grounds, 'conucos', was not uniform in Cuba.

Estimates of the earning power of free labourers vary. Free labourers in the country might earn as much as 20 pesos a month in the 1840s, rising to 40 pesos a month in the 1860s. In the town, wages might run to 40–50 pesos a month in the same period.[9] The Cuban historian, Fraginals, suggests 15–20 pesos a month.[10] According to Humboldt, slaves were hired at a daily rate of 10 cents per 100 pesos value of the slave in the 1820s; a 600 pesos slave earned 60 cents a day, 3.60 pesos in a six day week, just less than 15 pesos a month.[11] This probably represented the lowest wage bracket and a free labourer could aspire to 20 pesos. This meant that a years' hired labour cost 240 pesos. Slaves, however, could be maintained for 100 pesos, and with a buying price of 600 pesos spread over a 10 year working life, their labour was much cheaper.

Labour supply and labour costs were closely related to labour discipline. The slaves were valuable partly because they were at the command of the planter. Free labour, on the other hand, could only be either bought at competitive prices, or coerced by the existence of surplus labour. The planters did not want to increase their costs and Cuba had a frontier economy. How were the planters to command regular work from free labourers? Further than this, how were free labourers to be incorporated as part of the permanent plantation work force without further disturbing the slaves themselves? What the Cuban slave owners needed was a system of tied labour which approximated to the 'apprenticeship' system imposed on slaves in the British West India colonies after emancipation, a system with guaranteed hours of labour and recourse to corporal punishment.

To palliate the labour problem the planters made tentative experiments in dividing sugar growing from sugar manufacturing; they also became involved in railway building to cut costs in time and labour transporting cane to the mill and sugar to the ports. They made important innovations in the process of sugar manufacture.

Steam engines, introduced during the 1820s eliminated the use of oxen and of the slaves to tend the oxen. Mills with iron rollers were also imported from England and the United States in the 1820s which could be fed by a 'dumb turner', again cutting down the numbers needed to feed cane to the mill. In the 1830s vacuum pans, which boiled the liquid sugar at a low temperature and could be heated by the same force that drove the steam engine, cut down again on the numbers needed for stoking and on the numbers needed to get fuel to the mill. Early in the 1840s new 'sugar machines' coordinating all the manufacturing processes and requiring the supervision of only one person, began to be introduced and ten years later the 'centrifugal' machines, which turned the cane juice into sugar in one quick process, made their appearance.[12]

The sugar machines represented high capital investment and had been installed on only 55 estates out of 1,365 in 1860. But they represented not only reduced dependence on labourers, but increased productivity. The estates with the sugar machines, 4% of the total in 1860, produced 20% of the sugar.

To a degree the labour problem was aggravated by the development of sugar technology. The mechanized mill needed fewer workers, but they needed to be trained. Assistants to the 'sugar masters' and the engineers, salaried Americans or Europeans paid 1,200 or 1,500 pesos for work in the zafra,[13] would normally expect to be paid on the same scale, and since such training could only improve their bargaining power among the mill owners they would not be reliable. The use of slaves was also problematical; they were accustomed only to handle the machete and brutalized into an apparent incapacity to learn anything.

It was in the light of these factors that the Cubans debated the labour problem and, with the sanction of the Crown, conducted experiments in recruiting free labourers. Aldama, one of the most substantial planters defined the Cubans' position when he told a friend, 'Today there exists a great number of landowners who are bent on bringing in labourers and we must bring them from somewhere, even if it be from Siberia.'[14]

The experiments were conducted both by individuals and by the Junta de Fomento, the Council for Economic Development, a body approved by the Crown which represented planter and merchant interests. The first contract labourers were whites from Spain and the Canary islands. The contracts had certain features in common; the wages were lower than the wage rates current in the island; the immigrants were expected to pay for their passages out of their earnings, and, most important, they were subjected to disciplinary methods appropriate to labourers intended to work within a slave system. One large contingent of Canary Islanders were recruited by a Havana-Catalan firm to work with the Irish on the Havana-Guines railway line. They were paid 9 pesos a month (50% current wage rates) for as long as the work continued; they were to pay back the cost of their passage and some other expenses for medical care, etc.; and they were to be kept under a military régime. Absenteeism became desertion punishable by imprisonment and, in aggravated cases, by the firing squad. Galicians, imported to work at 6 pesos a month for five years, were also kept under coercion. In the latter case one of the first groups mutinied and

broke out of the barracks where they were being acclimatized. Efforts were made to capture them without success and the company which financed the scheme went bankrupt.[15]

White contract labour was clearly difficult to discipline, the workers knew the language and arrived with certain expectations; they proved, also comparatively difficult to recruit. In these circumstances the Junda de Fomento made a new move and in 1846 sanctioned the import of Chinese contract labour. The Junta continued to experiment with other sources of supply; some two thousand Indians from Yucatan, for instance, were imported in the following decade,[16] but the Chinese, together with the illegally imported slaves became the mainstay of the Cuban sugar economy from 1853 to 1874.

The offer to recruit Chinese labour was made by Zulueta & Co., one of the numerous enterprises associated with Julián Zulueta. Zulueta was a Spanish-born slave trader, merchant and multiple plantation owner; this 'prince of slave owners' and 'acknowledged political boss' of Cuba[17] was in many respects representative of the great planters, the prospective millionaires, the 'sacarocracia', which included the Aldamas, the Poeys, the Diagos and the Torriente families. These were the sugar tycoons who bought the new machinery, invested in railway building, maintained an interest in the slave trade and, like Zulueta, developed an interest in the trade in Chinese labour.

Zulueta, experienced slave trader that he was, grasped the crucial problems of supply, cost and discipline and saw China as supplying the solution. China had been forced to open its ports to foreign traders by the Treaty of Nanking in 1842 which followed the opium wars. English, French and American consulates were established there by 1844. The weakness of the Chinese government and the poverty of the peasants suggested that China might serve as well as Africa had done as a supplier of labour. Zulueta, like the British West Indian planters who applied for permission to import Chinese labourers in 1846, saw a rich opening. The Chinese would clearly be cheaper to contract than the Spaniards; they could be contracted for longer periods and at the same time subjected to plantation discipline in exactly the same way as the slaves.

The first 600 Chinese labourers were landed in the summer of 1847 and promised to fulfill all these requirements. They were contracted to work at 4 pesos a month for 8 years. They were to work at the order of their 'patrono', the contract holder, at any kind of work, for 12 hours a day in the country, or more in domestic service, for 4 pesos a month, 2 changes of clothing a year and food; 12 pesos were paid in advance (an incitement to indebted peasants) to be deducted from wages in Cuba. With a fine touch of legality the labourers subscribed to the following declaration:

I am in conformity with the stipulated wage although I know quite well that the wage earned by other free labourers and slaves in the isle of Cuba to be much higher because I consider the difference to be compensated for by the other advantages which the master will give me and those which appear in the contract.)[18]

Discipline was to be enforced in the terms of official regulations which subjected the Chinese to the same discipline as the slaves. The regulations of 1849 permitted 12 lashes for disobedience, 18 lashes for persistent disobedience the stocks and shackles for recalcitrance. Runaways were given bouts of this punishment for two, four or six months according to the frequency of the offence.[19]

To 'buy a chino' on these terms was clearly economical: a years' labour for 48 pesos plus maintenance and the cost of the contract. Since the Chinese cost no more than the slaves to maintain and the contracts rarely cost more than 340 pesos (the first cargo was an unusual bargain at 158 pesos) eight years labour could be bought for 720 pesos. This compared favourably with the cost of a slave bought for 600 pesos. The planters had achieved their ideal and found a wage slave substitute for chattels slaves.

It is scarcely surprising that the planters found the Chinese, on the whole, satisfactory; they had achieved a form of the apprenticeship system. When the Junta de Fomento circularized 'patronos' to enquire whether it would be 'convenient' to increase the number of Chinese, their answers were positive. Some emphasized their utility; Francisco Diago testified on behalf of his friends and family that the Chinese gave 'complete satisfaction in the tasks we are accustomed to give our slave population.' Some emphasized costs:

Because we cannot import slaves, we must have contracts which will assure us of getting back the expenses of the journey and the greatest equity in daily pay and I believe that the contracts of the Chinese meet both these demands and this is the best thing we could possible achieve.[20]

Some planters gave the problem of discipline priority even over questions of costs; Feijóo Sotomayor summarized their viewpoint,

We need them to work with the slaves and for this the only people of any use are the sons of a country which is governed by the stick, and this quality is very evident in the Chinese.

Sotomayor might have added that rule by the stick was not the planters only means of discipline. The Chinese were insulated initially by a language barrier, and permanently marked as a distinct racial minority; they were ideal material for policies of divide and rule. It is interesting that the British planters, recruiting for a free economy encouraged Chinese emigration on the ground they were 'a sort of ambidextrous people who can turn their hand to anything.' The Junta concluded Chinese immigration was 'not only convenient, but indispensable and invited special attention from the Junta and from the government.'[21] The trade was re-opened in 1853, partly in response to an epidemic of small pox and cholera, and continued, with only one break in 1860 until 1871; the last cargoes of contract labour arriving in the island in 1874.

Chinese immigration, as the Cuban historian Juan Pérez de la Riva points out, is the best documented immigration in Cuban history, including the European and West Indian immigration into the island in the twentieth century. The numbers derive from the Customs registers which omit only a few dozen Filipinos, who arrived before 1847 and the few thousand Chinese 'Californians' who went to the island via New Orleans, or Mexico in the 1860s. At the same time the trade was a legal, profit-making enterprise and its promoters advertised their profits and refuted the calumnies of English critics.[22]

Some 124, 813 Chinese labourers were imported between 1848 and 1874; the numbers fluctuated from year to year the extreme variants being 344 in 1862 to 14,263 in 1867. (See Table 1). In the years of regular trade, 1853–74 the average was roughly 6,000 p.a. The majority imported were men between the ages of 20 and 39; hardly any women were imported.[23] Most of the Chinese during their contract labour and after, worked in the country; the proportions for contracted labourers were 75% rural to 25% urban and of the rural labourers 45% were concentrated in the Matanzas-Cárdenas-Colon triangle of large-scale sugar plantations.[24]

What was the contribution of this labour force to the Cuban economy? The trade was important in two ways: it was profitable in itself and at the same time it facilitated the continued development of the sugar industry.

The first 'monzones', the Cuban term for cargoes of Chinese contract labour, organized by Zulueta and Co. were contracted for through Spanish merchants in Manila who had contacts with English merchants, and notably with Messrs. Tait and Co. of Amoy and Messrs. Syme, Muir and Co. of Canton.[25] These firms had already taken charge of Chinese immigration to the British West

Table 1. Chinese Arriving in La Havana

Year	Left China		Died on Voyage			Sold in Havana	
	Quantity	%	Quantity	%A	%B	Quantity	%A
1848	612	0.4	41	0.3	6.7	571	0.5
1853	5,150	3.6	843	5.1	16.3	4,307	3.8
1854	1,750	1.2	39	0.3	2.2	1,711	1.5
1855	3,130	2.2	145	0.9	4.6	2,985	2.6
1856	6,152	4.4	1,084	6.5	19.3	4,968	4.4
1857	10,168	7.1	1,575	9.5	15.5	8,547	7.5
1858	16,414	11.6	3,019	18.2	18.4	13,385	11.8
1859	8,549	6.1	1,345	8.1	15.7	7,204	6.4
1860	7,204	5.1	1,011	6.1	14.03	6,193	5.5
1861	7,252	5.1	279	1.7	3.8	6,973	6.1
1862	356	0.2	12	0.1	3.3	344	0.3
1863	1,045	0.8	93	0.6	8.8	952	0.8
1864	2,664	1.9	511	3.1	19.1	2,153	1.9
1865	6,794	4.8	94	2.4	5.7	6,400	5.7
1866	13,368	9.5	977	5.9	7.3	12,391	10.4
1867	15,616	11.1	1,353	8.4	8.6	14,263	0.3
1868	8,100	5.7	732	4.4	9.03	7,368	6.3
1869	6,720	4.7	1,060	6.4	15.7	5,660	5.0
1870	1,312	0.9	85	0.5	6.4	1,227	1.1
1871	1,577	1.1	89	0.5	5.6	1,448	1.3
1872	8,915	6.4	755	4.6	8.4	8,160	7.2
1873	5,856	4.2	(763)	4.6	13.02	5,093*	4.5
1874	2,863	2.0	(373)	2.3	13.02	2,490	2.2
TOTAL	141,391	100.0	16,576	100.0	—	124,813	100.0

Note: %A Refers to total 1847–74
%B Refers to total for each year
*The figures for this year and the following have been completed with those published by the Boletín de Colonización for May, 1874 and include all the 'monzón' of 1873, which was the last one organized.
SOURCE: Pérez de la Riva, *Demografía de los Culíes Chinos en Buca (1853–74), Revista de la Biblioteca Nacional*, año 57, núm. 4, 1966, p.

Indies.[26] The subsequent development of the trade seems to have remained largely in Cuban hands and the profits accrued to Cuban capitalists. In this the Chinese contract trade contrasted with the slave trade which, although it involved important Cuban interests, was dominated by the Americans. The Havana trade, 'could not be called a Cuban trade at all: it was financed by American capital carried in American ships, manned by American seamen and protected by the American flag.'[27] When the Chinese trade was re-opened, however, in 1843 it provided, like the slave trade, ample opportunity for speculators large and small and the conduct of the trade in China, as in Africa, was a prolonged scandal.

In China all the agents used kidnappers to recruit for them. The Cuban agent in Amoy, a disappointed Colombian politico with literary ambitions, was known as the 'Man-stealer'. Mr. Syme of the British firm Syme, Muir and Co. was indiscreet enough to try and rescue one of his agents from a Chinese court, an action which prompted a consular investigation of the British commercial community in Amoy.[28]

Although the Chinese government issued warnings against 'pig-stealers', it is clear that kidnapping and intimidation were common and torture not unknown. The Cuban investors and prospective buyers were only concerned that their agents should have enough expertise to avoid shipping the old and the sick.

The ships employed in the trade were 500–1,000 tons and were on the whole larger than the ships in the slave trade, but the journey was much longer, 110–115 days via Cape of Good Hope.[29] They were prepared like the slave ships with gratings over the holds to allow only one person on deck at a time: small cannon, ready loaded, guarded the mouth of the hatches and the steam ships had neat contrivances for letting steam into the hold in case of real trouble. As Pérez de la Riva comments only the chains were missing.[30] Water shortages, disease and mutinies characterized the voyages. The death rates recorded for each year in the customs figures, varied between 19.3% and 2.2%; less than 10% was considered 'reasonable', though between 1853 and 1860 the average was 15%. The sailors called them death voyages.[31] High death rates was bad business, but the profit margin was high enough to absorb the risk.

Some of the great planters maximized profit by organizing a vertical monopoly; Domingo Aldama, for example, had his own agent and maintained his own barracoons in Macao and Havana and absorbed his own recruits. Other planters formed a company, organized along these lines, the *Empresa de Colonización o Colonizadora,* which also had its own agent and barracoons in Manila and Havana.[32] In 1861 the *Empresa* was encouraged to increase its assets: a yellow fever epidemic in 1858–59, plus the emancipation of the slaves in the United States and its repercussions on the slave trade, promised opportunities for expansion and the *Empresa* merged with *La Compañía de Seguros y Créditos* and formed *La Alianza y Cía.* It has been suggested that the merger marks a transition from a trade financed by the slave traders to a trade financed by the plantation owners, a move made in response to rising prices for contract labour.[33] Slave trading capital and plantation owners' capital seem to have been involved in the trade from the outset: and the dual function Zulueta and Aldama, for example, dictated this should be the case. The creation of *La Alianza,* however, marks the emergence of the substantial plantation owners as a class from independence on merchant creditors to plantation capitalists in their own right. The first generation to graduate to this position, Pérez de la Riva, suggests, were either Spaniards (like Zulueta) or Hispanicized.[34] In 1871 a new firm inspired by Zulueta was founded, *La Compañía de Hacendados,* whose title reflected this shift. This company had a working capital of 1 mil. pesos and was evidently interested, in true Zulueta style, to exploit to the full the last months of the legal trade. The trade was abolished in 1871, but imports were allowed until 1874. In the closing years of the traffic, imports were 8,160, 5,093 and 2,490. (See Table 1). The Chinese imported by *La Compañía de Hacendados* were swept through the Suez Canal by steamship.[35]

What was the net gain of these enterprises? Given the continuing need for labourers in Cuba and the guaranteed sale of the contracts made in China, a basic consideration was the price of the original contract. In the first years this cost a mere 15 pesos and the contract was sold in Havana for 125 pesos: prices, however, increased to 150 pesos in China to 300–400 pesos in Havana. Expenses included agents fees and commission: bounties of 3–5 pesos paid to the ships captain for each healthy labourer: insurance for the cargo and the cost of the barracoons. To finance an expedition required 50,000 pesos, but only half was needed in cash. Capital could be borrowed at 8–12% interest and

the returns were made on a mere six months investment. Taking all these expenses into account there was a clear probability of profits in the 100–150% region on each 'monzón'.[36]

The ships, however, were usually engaged in a triangular trade; they carried to China arms, ironware and textiles from Europe and left Cuba for the United States and Europe with sugar and molasses. The profits, as Pérez de la Riva says, were 'succulent': not as succulent as in the slave trade, where profits were estimated in the 200–300% range,[37] but they were legal and it was on the basis of the gains that the Cubans were able to buy the clippers and steamers that completed the vertical organization of the trade as well as promote the development of their plantations.[38]

The contribution of the Chinese to the Cuban sugar economy can only be assessed in relation to other sources of labour and the fact that the slave trade was illegal during this period means that, until detailed local research has been completed in Cuba, the comparison must be based on reasonable estimates, rather than proper statistics. Estimates compiled from British Parliamentary Papers suggest an annual average import of about 12,000 slaves in the period 1835–64.[39] Some estimates are lower than this: for example, 10,000 annually for the period 1830–50.[40] P.D. Curtin's estimates made by comparing figures from different sources and relating them to a projected death rate suggests a sharp reduction in average annual imports in the period 1841–50 from an average of roughly 12,000, 1827–40 to roughly 5,000 increasing again, 1851–64, to about 12,000 a year. Pérez de la Riva argues that after 1853 the Chinese trade exceeded the slave trade, if not year by year, yet in toto.[41] Curtin's figures, however, suggest a total slave import 1851–65 of 184,500 slaves as compared with a total Chinese import of 124, 242 between 1853 and 1874. (Tables 1 and 2).

The pattern of illegal slave imports seems to have been influenced primarily by the demands of the planters which fluctuated in relation to the slave death rate. The epidemics of 1833–34, 1852–53 and 1858–89 multiplied demands for slaves as well as, in the later period, for Chinese labourers and the demand for slaves is witnessed by the higher than normal numbers of slave ships captured off the island.[42] Fluctuations were also created by the degree of complicity Cuba's Captains' General gave the trade; Federico Roncali, Count of Alcoy, Captain-General 1848–52 was very popular with the slave merchants and slave buyers who gave him 50,000 pesos when he left so he could promote their interests in Madrid.[43]

Whatever the relationship between the slave trade and the coolie trade it is clear that, by the

Table 2. Nineteenth-Century Cuba: Accepted Estimates of Slave
Imports Subdivided Assording to Census Dates

Period	No Imported	Annual Average	Source of data	Implied annual rate of net natural decrease (%)
1801–7	46,000	6,570	Aimes	—
1808–16	57,800	6,420	Aimes	—
1817–26	103,500	10,350	Aimes	0.7
1827–40	176,500	12,610	Saco, based on ann. average est. for 1835–39	0.5
1941–47	33,800	4,830	F.O. estimate 1848, adjusted for Cuban imports only	—
1848	2,000	2,000	Aimes	—
1849–50	11,800	5,900	F.O. estimate 1865	—
1851–60	123,300	12,330	F.O. estimate 1865	—
1861–64	49,500	12,380	F.O. estimate 1965	3.0 (1841–60)
1865	12,000	—	Sheer guesswork	
Total	616,200	9,480		
Total (1805–65)	750,200			

SOURCE: P.D. Curtin, *The Atlantic Slave Trade*, p. 40.

1860s, the Cuban planters depended increasingly on Chinese and other sources of free labour. Lincoln's accession to power in the United States, a new effective treaty for the suppression of the slave trade with Great Britain, and the exemplary hanging of a Yankee slave trading captain, deprived the traders of the sanction of the American flag and the trade was abruptly closed off.[44] According to Lloyd's estimates the total number of slaves exported to Cuba and the Spanish colonies dwindled from 23,964 in 1861 to a mere 6,807 in 1864.[45] Chinese imports on the other hand zoomed upward: 6,400 in 1865, 12,391 in 1867 and 14,263 in 1968. The use of white creoles in the 'zafra' of the 1860s underlined this dependence. By 1862 there was 1 Chinese contract labourer for every 10 slaves; the census of 1862 indicated 377,143 slaves, the Chinese under contract numbered at that date 34,429,[46] Though the census figures for slave population are not accurate, since newly arrived slaves were not registered, the figure gives a rough idea of the importance of the Chinese. By 1877, bearing the same limitation in mind, the Chinese were 17.5 to every 100 slaves.[47]

Chinese labour was used in tobacco growing and coffee growing and every variety of urban work; about 45%, however, were in the Colón-Matanzas-Cárdenas triangle. They were used as cane cutters and as factory workers. The Chinese proved the ideal solution for work in the mechanized mills: capable of training, and cheap. On *La Flor de Cuba,* owned by the Arrietas, which produced the

second largest quantity of sugar in the zafra of 1860, 1,360 hogsheads, there were 170 mills. *El Alava,* propriety of Zulueta, third in the 1860 'zafra', there were 130. Production at *El Progreso* was in the hands of a French technician with 40 Chinese assistants. The same pattern obtained at *La Pomina,* property of the Diagos, at Juan Poey's *Las Canas* and at *Santa Susana,* property of the Spanish Crown.[48]

Between 1840 and 1860 the sugar market, as the planters had anticipated increased; but prices fell by half. To develop with the market the Cubans had to produce more sugar. This they succeeded in doing 392,000 tons in 1855, 620,000 in 1865, 718,000 in 1875.[49] Their success was due in part to their ability to increase their labour force and hold down labour costs.

The overall effect of Chinese contract labour in the development of the Cuban economy, however, was to prolong the life of the slave system. The Chinese were conformable to plantation slavery, and enabled the planters to deal with the crisis of the 1840s, within this framework and in terms of labour supply.

The Ten Year War for Cuban independence 1868–78, however, changed conditions. Spain conducted a notably vicious and brutal war, the Vietnam of the decade. To counter worldwide criticism and secure international support Spain was forced, in 1870, to make legal provision for the abolition of slavery and the following year abolished contract labour. Slavery and contract labour came to

Table 3. Chinese Imports to Cuba: 1947–73[1] Statement of the
Number of Chinese Coolies imported into Cuba yearly since 1847

| | Vessels | | Chinese | | |
Year	Number	Tonnage	Shipped	Died at Sea	Landed
1847	2	979	612	42	571
1853	15	8,349	5,150	843	4,307
1854	4	2,375	1,750	39	1,711
1855	6	6,544	3,130	145	2,985
1856	15	10,677	6,152	1,182	2,970
1857	28	18,940	10,101	1,554	8,547
1858	33	32,842	16,441	3,027	13,384
1859	16	13,828	8,539	1,332	7,207
1860	17	15,104	7,227	1,008	6,219
1861	16	15,919	7,212	290	6,922
1862	1	759	400	56	355
1863	3	2,077	1,045	94	951
1864	7	5,513	2,664	532	2,132
1865	20	12,769	6,810	407	6,043
1866	43	24,187	14,169	1,126	13,043
1867	42	26,449	15,661	1,247	14,414
1868	21	15,265	8,400	732	7,668
1869	19	13,692	7,340	1,475	5,864
1870	3	3,200	1,312	63	1,249
1871	5	5,825	1,827	178	1,649
1872	20	12,886	8,194	766	8,148
1873	6	4,786	3,330	209	3,121
TOTAL	342	249,065	138,156	16,346	121,810

[1]Estimates by the British Consulate-General
SOURCE: H. Thomas, *History of Cuba,* London, 1971, p. 1541.

an end together; the last cargoes of Chinese arrived in 1874 and the same year a Chinese delegation visited Cuba, at the instigation of the British, to ensure the 1871 suspension of the trade remained in effect. The last contracts expired in 1883 and in 1886 slavery ended.

No section of the Cuban ruling class proved eager to relinquish slavery: neither the great planters of the sugar belt who supported Spain,nor the small planters of Oriente who rebelled. The rebel leader, Céspedes, freed his own slaves, but declared for 'gradual, indemnified emancipation' and won more support than his policy deserved from slaves and Chinese alike.

In the 1880s the Cuban faced a new crisis in world market conditions. Competition with beet sugar pressed hard: beet sugar interests developed even in Spain. Sugar prices, already in decline, dropped between 1883–84 by one third: from 19/- to 13/3d a ton on the London market and the price did not recover before the first World War. Deprived of slaves and contract labour the Cubans met the demand for cheaper sugar by re-organizing production. Economies of scale, technology, and numbers of labourers led to the development of the 'centrales', sugar factories, fed by railways, linking plantations employing seasonal labour: solutions all considered in the 1840s, but postponed, partly

as a result of the 'enterprise' of Zulueta, Aldama and company in finding Chinese contract workers to supplement the African slaves.

Notes

1. Franklin W. Knight, *Slave Society in Cuba* (Madison: University of Wisconsin, 1971), p. 28.
2. Arthur F. Corwin, *Spain and the Abolition of Slavery in Cuba, 1817–1886* (Austin: Unversity of Texas Press, 1970), p. 62.
3. Ibid., pp. 84, 86.
4. H. Thomas, *Cuba or the Pursuit of Freedom* (London: Eyre and Spottiswoode, 1971), p. 196.
5. Philip S. Foner, *A History of Cuba and its Relations with the United States 1492–1495* Vol. I (New York: International Publishing Co., 1962), pp. 205, 211–13; Corwin, *Spain and the Abolition of Slavery in Cuba,* p. 81.
6. Foner, *History of Cuba,* pp. 214–15.
7. Durvon C. Corbitt, Immigration in Cuba, *Hispanic American Historical Review 22,* (May 1942): 300.
8. Corwin, *Spain and the Abolition of Slavery in Cuba,* p. 136.
9. These estimates are made by Denise Helly, Chinese Contract Labourers in Cuba. Unpublished Ms.
10. Moreno M. Fraginals, *El Ingenio* (La Habana: Comisión Nationalal Cubana de la UNESCO, 1964), p. 147.
11. A. von Humboldt, *The Island of Cuba* (New York: Derby and Jackson, 1856), p. 212.
12. Thomas, *A History of Cuba,* pp. 116–18.
13. Ibid., p. 115.
14. Fraginals, *El Ingenio,* p. 154.

15. Ibid., pp. 149, 159; Corbitt, Immigration to Cuba, p. 302.
16. Corbitt, Immigration to Cuba, p. 302.
17. Thomas, *A History of Cuba,* p. 262; Knight, *Slave Society,* p. 134.
18. J.J. Pastrana, *Los Chinos en las luchas por la liberación cubana, 1847–1930* (La Habana: Instituto de la Historia, 1963), p. 29.
19. Ibid., p. 39.
20. Ibid., p. 36.
21. S. Basdeo, East Indian Immigration to the British West Indies, 1838–1860, p. 28. M.A. Thesis University of Calgary; Pastrana, Los Chinos en las luchas, pp. 35, 36, 37.
22. Juan Pérez de la Riva, Demografía de los culíes Chinos en Cuba, 1853–74, *Revista de la Biblioteca Nacional José Martí* 57, no. 4 (1966): 3, 4.
23. Ibid., pp. 7, 11; 1861 — 57 women; 1872 — 32 women; 1877 — 81 women.
24. Ibid., pp. 21, 26.
25. Juan Pérez de la Riva, Aspectos Económicos del Tráfico de culíes chinos a Cuba, 1853–74, *Universidad de la Habana,* no. 73 (mayo-junio, 1965): 97.
26. Basdeo, East Indian Immigration, p. 29.
27. C. Loyd, *The Navy and the Slave Trade* (London: Frank Cass & Co. Ltd., 1968), p. 163.
28. Basdeo, East Indian Immigration, p. 30.
29. Juan Pérez de la Riva, Documentos para la historia de las gentes sin historia: El viaje a Cuba de los culíes chinos, *Revista de la Biblioteca Nacional José Martí* 6, nos. 3–4, p. 47.
30. Ibid., pp. 47–48.
31. Ibid., pp. 49, 50.
32. Pérez de la Riva, Aspectos económicos del tráfico de culíes chinos a Cuba 1853–74, pp. 99, 101.
33. Ibid., p. 97.
34. Ibid., p. 97.
35. Ibid., pp. 99–101.
36. Ibid., pp. 105–106.
37. Fraginals, *El Ingenio,* p. 143.
38. Pérez de la Riva, El viaje a Cuba de los culíes chinos, p. 51.
39. Lloyd, *The Navy and The Slave Trade,* p. 276. This estimate is accepted by Thomas, *Cuba,* p. 169 and Knight, *Slave Society,* p. 53.
40. Corwin, *Spain and the Abolition,* p. 54.
41. Philip D. Curtin, *The Atlantic Slave Trade: A Census* (Madison: University of Wisconsin Press, 1969), p. 42; Pérez de la Riva, Demografía de los Culíes Chinos en Cuba, p. 20.
42. Knight, *Slave Society,* pp. 54–55.
43. Corwin, *Spain and the Abolition,* p. 104.
44. Knight, *Slave Society,* pp. 56–57; Lloyd, *The Navy and the Slave Trade,* pp. 174–75.
45. Lloyd, *The Navy and the Slave Trade,* p. 276.
46. Pérez de la Riva, Demografía de los Culíes Chinos en Cuba, p. 30.
47. Ibid., p. 30.
48. Fraginals, *El Ingenio,* pp. 155, 167: Thomas, *Cuba,* pp. 137–38.
49. Thomas, *Cuba,* pp. 1561–62.

The Evolution of Long-Term Labour Contracts in Trinidad and British Guiana 1834–1863

K.O. Laurence

The question of indenting immigrants to labour for a term of years in the West Indies dates from the very start of the post-emancipation immigration movement. When this began in 1834 with the arrival in Trinidad of the first group of liberated Africans from Cuba the London West India interest, on behalf of the local planters, demanded that regulations be issued for what they called the 'efficient control' of these new labourers. Secretary of State Spring Rice agreed, with the greatest reluctance, on the grounds that they were destitute and uncivilized and so would need careful supervision.[1] An ordinance of March 19, 1835, authorized the apprenticing of liberated Africans on their arrival in Trinidad for periods not exceeding three years, the employers being bound to provide food, lodging and medical attention in addition to money wages in order to ensure that the immigrants would be well treated as well as that they would perform a 'reasonable amount of work'.[2] This departure from the literal interpretation of freedom for negroes was perhaps easier to defend in the era of the Apprenticeship System and lasted until the end of Apprenticeship in 1838.[3]

A new Secretary of State, Lord Glenelg, regarded the welfare of those liberated Africans as the paramount principle to be observed in dealing with them, and so guarded it most solicitously. In July 1835 he disallowed a set of rules governing their allocation among the different estates because they provided for distribution by lottery, 'as if they were so much property come up for division'. Fearing lest any rigid system of distribution might lead to that great Colonial Office bogey, a new and disguised slave trade, Glenelg directed that they should be distributed entirely at the Governor's discretion.[4] Subsequently he rejected a Guianese demand for the extension of the period of apprenticeship to five years as not in the Africans' own best interests. A similar system was authorized in British Guiana in March 1836.[5] This determination to guard the welfare of the apprenticed immigrant, as such welfare was understood in London, remained in later years a fundamental principle

behind the attitude of the Colonial Office to labour contracts.

For free immigrants who could not be classed as uncivilized there were at first no special contract regulations. The Portuguese who arrived during 1834 and 1835 were imported on contracts for three or five years the enforcement of which at law was, in the absence of special provisions, highly problematical, especially in British Guiana.[6] As immigrants arrived in increasing numbers, however, the Court of Policy in British Guiana demanded that regulations be issued for 'enforcing the duties and securing the rights' of immigrants in general,[7] and eventually the Masters and Servants Ordinance, no. 74 of 22 June 1836, empowered Justices of the Peace to enforce on both parties performance of contracts for up to seven years which were concluded before a Justice.[8] Lord Glenelg however required that the contracts should be limited to three years (one year if concluded outside the Colony) and that immigrants from Africa should be specifically excluded — again the standing fear of a revived and disguised slave trade. Thus amended, the Ordinance was confirmed by Order in Council on 1 March 1837[9] with the result that a few months later a special Order had to be passed to enable John Gladstone to offer to Indian immigrants contracts for five rather than three years.[10]

Now that contracts for labour could be enforced in British Guiana, the number of articled servants imported into that Colony, especially from neighbouring British and Dutch colonies, suddenly began to increase. Trinidad seems to have had fewer problems over facilities for enforcing contracts, and there too the inflow of immigrants was soon noticeable.[11]

Private speculators soon began engaging labourers in the smaller islands on contracts which they then sold at a profit to employers in British Guiana and Trinidad. Lord Glenelg thought that this practice might lead the inexperienced ex-slaves into signing unfavourable contracts and that they should be protected from this danger;[12] and so in

141

July 1838 came a celebrated Order in Council requiring all contracts to be concluded in the Colony in which they were to be performed.[13] There quickly followed the yet more famous Order in Council of 7 September 1838, 'the handmaiden of Emancipation' as it had been called,[14] limiting all contracts to a single year. These Orders together subsequently became the corner stone of the British government's labour policies in the West Indies. That government regarded it as a vital principle that immigrants must have complete freedom to choose their employers after their arrival;[15] and the reluctance of successive Secretaries of State to depart from this and permit contracts to be concluded abroad, despite constant pressure from the West Indians, became a major obstacle to large scale immigration. The prohibition of overseas contracts strongly deterred the planters from importing labour privately since immigrants were under no obligation to work for those planters who had paid for their importation. Hence any significant immigration would have to be financed from public funds. The West Indians argued that the prohibition of overseas contracts infringed the negro's right to dispose of his labour as he pleased, and involved a great injustice in depriving him of an opportunity to seek higher wages overseas, while preventing only 'an imaginary evil'.[16] But the Imperial government, supported by a public opinion which was violently opposed to any measures which might conceivably be represented as coercion of negro labour, did not change its attitude until several years later.

Between 1841 and 1843 however, successive exceptions were made to this blanket prohibition of overseas contracts. First, in 1841, European immigrants were exempted after it had proved impossible to attract skilled artisans unless they were allowed to enter contracts before leaving Europe; and in January 1843 Lord Stanley decided to permit overseas contracts with coloured immigrants from North America.[17] Then in July 1843, when Chinese immigration was being canvassed, it was generally agreed that Chinese would not emigrate without firm contracts any more than would Europeans. The Colonial Office however still viewed all proposals for overseas contracts with acute suspicion, perhaps the more so because of the exceptions which it had felt obliged to make, and only the Under-Secretary, G.W. Hope, supported the West Indian demand for overseas contracts with Chinese. Stanley's decision was symptomatic: 'I am not prepared so hastily to sanction so important an alteration'.[18] Hope however continued to plead the West Indian case; he supported contracts with Chinese for five years, the minimum they were thought likely to accept, provided the immigrant was allowed the option of terminating his engagement at the end of each half-year in case current wages should rise above the contractual rate. Such a scheme was finally approved in September 1843.[19] Another breach had been made in the rigid contract policy adopted in 1838, in the face of its restrictive effect on immigration as a whole.

These exceptions were allowed on the ground that European, coloured Americans, and Chinese from British Colonies in the East appeared sufficiently intelligent and civilized to judge the merits of a contract for themselves, and sufficiently competent generally to decide what was for their best advantage. They therefore had no need of special protection from the imperial government.[20] Prospective immigrants generally, and negroes especially, were still deemed not to be thus competent, and so to need protection from overseas contracts. Although forced to abandon the position taken up in 1838, therefore, the Colonial Office's theory on contracts remained unchanged; it was their conception of who was and who was not competent to decide on his best advantage which was changing. All contracts had to be attested by a special magistrate, whose duty was to ensure that no deception was practiced in persuading emigrants to sign them.[21]

At the same time the renewed importation of liberated Africans provided yet another exception to the general law concerning contracts. When the regular importation of liberated Africans from Sierra Leone and St. Helena began in 1842, Governor Macleod of Trinidad argued that,unlike the free emigrants who had experienced some sort of civilization at Sierra Leone, these people were 'perfectly uncivilized' barbarians who should be placed under moderate restraint, both for their own protection and to ensure that they did in fact work. Their case was similar to that of the liberated Africans brought from Cuba in 1834–5, and Macleod suggested a similar form of engagement.[22] In July 1842 compulsory indentures for one year providing fair wages, house, garden, and medical attention were sanctioned for liberated Africans despite protests from the Anti-Slavery Society.[23] In effect, here were one year overseas contracts for liberated Africans.

The rigidly prohibitionist attitude once relaxed, the imperial government gradually developed a more practical approach to the contract question, and in 1844 it agreed that Trinidad might import Madeirans on two-year contracts, as a means of ensuring that such immigrants should not in future work in the canefields, where experience had shown that their health was likely to suffer severely.[24] Where immigrants were imported under contract, however, the imperial government refused to allow bounties to be paid from public funds under the system which had been established in 1838. The importer had therefore to choose between importing labour on contract at his own expense and importing it under the system of bounties but without contracts.[25] It was on this principle that the first Indian immigrants to arrive under government sponsorship, in 1845–6, were left free to wander idle about the countryside when they chose, with disastrous consequences to their health leading to a very high rate of mortality.[26]

In 1846 prospects that the new Indian immigration would attain very large proportions led the West Indian planters and Colonial governments to press for a new contract law.[27] The Anti-Slavery Society objected to attempts to revise this 'in favour of the Masters',[28] but Mr. Gladstone, the new Secretary of State, acknowledged that changes were needed. He now sanctioned overseas contracts for three years, but specifically excluded Indians and Africans, who were still thought too ignorant and backward to be left to make their own arrangements. In effect, the new three-year contracts therefore applied only to Madeirans, North Americans, and Creoles from the smaller islands, who seemed well able to look after themselves. Contract immigrants were allowed the option of being paid at current rather than the contractual rates. Gladstone agreed that the 1838 prohibition had tended to produce 'some artificial scarcity of labour' and a fall in production, which it was the government's duty to remedy if possible; but he believed that the West Indians were over-estimating the probable results of three-year contracts.[29]

Convinced that contracts which attempted to bind free labourers after they became dissatisfied with a particular job would never succeed, Gladstone announced that if these new contracts proved difficult to enforce he would consider that a ground for abandoning three-year contracts. His view that if a workman declined to honour his contract there must be some inherent defect in its terms sprang from Gladstone's rooted belief in the superiority of 'indefinite hiring' over any system of contracts, and a blind conviction that immigrants on contracts must become discontented when they discovered that native labourers would not work on contracts.[30] In fact no immigrants had had any opportunity to work on long contracts since John Gladstone's Indians had returned to India in 1843, and Mr. Gladstone's picture of widespread dissatisfaction among immigrants on contract was wholly imaginary in 1846. Three-year contracts with Madeirans and Creoles were sanctioned not because Gladstone thought they would do any good whatever, but because, having admitted that these immigrants could look after themselves, he could find no valid grounds for objecting. And he accepted the West Indian opinion of three year engagements 'as requisite for the satisfaction of the immigrant, or at least as tending to encourage his immigration more than the system of bounty, by giving him an assurance of employment for a certain and considerable period'.[31] This experiment with voluntary three-year contracts was however intended essentially to reimburse employers for the cost of importing immigrants, and contracts were still not allowed where public funds were employed. The West India Committee demanded that such contracts should be 'rendered effectual in practice' by special contracts laws; but Gladstone refused to allow this and the Committee accepted a substantial concession from the Colonial Office without thanks.[32] New Ordinances were accordingly passed in British Guiana in November 1846 and in Trinidad in April 1847.[33]

The Order in Council of 17 September 1838 was thus largely repealed. The West Indian planters had always thought its restrictions 'wholly indefensible', and argued that 'the most perfect freedom of intercourse should prevail . . . . throughout the British dominions and that no restraint upon either employers or labourers, in seeking employment or service, ought to be permitted.[34] But Gladstone still refused to allow overseas contracts in African immigration, arguing that they had produced no evidence that to do so would attract more emigrants. But this could only be a matter of conjecture; the West India Committee replied that they could not pretend to know how many Africans would enter such contracts, 'because they have never been permitted to make the attempt'.[35] Gladstone's attitude was conditioned by the old fear lest improper pressure should be used to induce ignorant Africans, or Indians, to sign unfavorable contracts. He never defeated the Committee's contention that this should scarcely occur where the contracts were concluded before a properly vigilant government official, and that the Africans could be adequately protected by regulations less restrictive than a complete prohibition of overseas contracts. But where abuses seemed likely to arise he distrusted the planters, and he was seeking the easiest way out; granted the risk of abuses, it was naturally easier to rely on a complete prohibition than to devise an adequate code of lesser regulations.

With the increase in immigration following the Sugar Duties Act, and the advent of Lord Grey to the Colonial Office in 1846, the Imperial attitude towards compelling immigrants to work began to change. When the illness, mortality, and general wretchedness of the Indian immigrants during

1846 made imperative the enactment of regulations to control their movements, Grey in October 1846 forwarded to the West Indies the 'Heads of an Ordinance for Promoting Immigration', embodying his proposals.[36] He concluded that some change in the existing system, as well as 'more effectual regulations for securing the continuous labour of immigrants brought to the colony at the public expense', was urgently required, a substantial departure from the negative policy of his predecessors.[37] He insisted that these must be based on normal incentives to labour, rather than on compelling immigrants to give the labour for which they had contracted by accepting a free passage. Experience had proved, thought Grey, that labour could be extracted from the unwilling only by 'extreme compulsion', which could not of course be allowed. He suggested that for Indian and African immigrants voluntary one-year contracts would suffice if immigrants not under contract were required to pay a monthly tax on pain of imprisonment. In order to quality for a return passage Indian immigrants would have to serve five years of such 'Industrial Residence'. The Colony paid their passages for a special purpose; if they ignored that purpose they might fairly be asked to repay their passages in instalments. A stamp duty on contracts would help to raise money for immigration purposes from the employers themselves. But Grey still stood by 'indefinite hiring' while recognizing its untoward consequences in practice, although sanctioning yearly contracts for Indians, he remained 'persuaded that these contracts would be found to work much better, if either party, in case of being dissatisfied, had it in his power to annul them' under certain conditions.[38]

In February 1847 Trinidad passed an Ordinance based on Grey's proposals, though the planters disliked the contract duty. The monthly tax was fixed at 5/-, the contract duty at 40/-. The penalty provided for inexcusable absence from work was 2d. per day.[39] Not until February 1848 did British Guiana finally follow suit and then she attempted to legalize contracts for three years instead of one for all immigrants, pleading that this would make the planters take greater care of their immigrants.[40]

As might have been expected, Grey disapproved of a general system of three-year contracts. Nevertheless, he was prepared to allow them provided they were made strictly voluntary.[41] It will be noted that a radical change of outlook had occurred in the Colonial Office since Gladstone in 1846 had refused to allow any contracts with immigrants imported from public funds. A less doctrinaire approach now permitted the compulsory allocation on one-year indentures of precisely such immigrants. The Court of Policy, already spoiling for a

fight with the imperial government, maintained that experience had shown that contracts for at least three years were 'absolutely essential to the well-being of all immigrants introduced as agricultural labourers', and would have prevented much of the mortality among the East Indians since 1845.[42] It would not agree that three-year contracts should be purely voluntary. The employers were reluctant to incur expenditure in locating immigrants unless assured of a reasonable contract; while three-year contracts were temporarily in force in 1848 and 1849 pending the final decision from London the incidence of sickness fell considerably and it does seem that employers took greater care of their immigrants.[43] Without three-year contracts the elected members preferred 'not to have immigrants at all', and the question soon involved the stoppage of the supplies and consequent suspension of all immigration to British Guiana in 1848–49. A final settlement remained in abeyance until 1850.[44]

Meanwhile Trinidad's 1847 Ordinance had proved abortive, through failure to collect the monthly tax. With many planters unable to pay wages or indenture fees as a result of the severe depression affecting the colony in 1847–8, the Indians were able to claim that although willing to enter contracts they could not find employment; others found their wages up to three or four months in arrears.[45] The penalties for breach of contract proved generally unenforceable; locating offenders in a sparsely peopled, largely forested, countryside was excessively difficult, and the planters consequently avoided employing Indians at a cost of £2 in contract duty. Lord Harris argued cogently in favour of compulsorily indenturing all immigrants for three years. 'They must be treated like children, and wayward ones too', he said of the Indians. It was extremely difficult to make them fear the law, and 'the only independence which they would desire is idleness, according to their different tastes in the enjoyment of it'.[46] Events had shown that Grey's 1846 principle of placing the immigrants in a position where normal incentives to labour would operate was extremely difficult to apply. Harris suggested that strict contract regulations should be applied, not by their employers but by government officials. Trinidad too, while less adamant than British Guiana, now wanted three-year contracts.[47]

During 1848, in the face of deteriorating economic circumstances West Indian opinion hardened in favour of long contracts. 'All in the least interested in property' supported them, eventually contracts for five years were legalized in Trinidad under Ordinance No. 3 of 1849. Supporting this, Harris hoped that English popular prejudices against long contracts had been 'overruled at length by better information'. He pointed out that although several thousand immigrants had been introduced at great cost since 1838, 'the intention has been frustrated in consequence of there not being sufficient restraint imposed on the immigrant'. Too many immigrants had simply deserted the estates for whose benefit they had been imported. Vagrancy must be stopped if the immigration system was to bear any real fruit. Contracts must be better enforced, and should preferably be for five years.[48] Lord Harris continued, 'I believe that it would prove not only more beneficial to the proprietors than the system hitherto adopted, but also to the immigrants, inasmuch as it would tend to give them regular habits, attach them to certain localities, and give them the opportunity of becoming intelligent and industrious men'.[49]

Although a new Permanent Under-Secretary, Herman Merivale, was doubtful about 'the application of the principle of free labour to immigrants from savage countries', the imperial government could not yet stomach compulsory contracts for so long as five years. Lord Grey however was anxious to conciliate West Indian opinion as far as possible, and believed that the opposition of the British public to any form of restriction on West Indian labourers was declining.[50] Grey acknowledged the difficulty of reconciling 'freedom of labour with such personal restraint as may be indispensable to secure, not merely the industry, but the health and the very life of certain classes of immigrants'. Certainly a strict discipline must be maintained. 'But if . . . we are really in the dilemma of having to sacrifice either the principle of free labour . . . or . . . the utility and even the lives of those particular classes of immigrants', then their introduction must cease; under the proposed law 'the condition of the immigrants would be neither more or less than slavery in a mitigated form and for a limited period', the only incentive to work being 'dread of punishment'.[51]

Trinidad's Ordinance No. 3/1849 which called forth this criticism proposed that immigrants under contract should not leave their estates without a pass and that absence from work should be punished by imprisonment, and that the only remuneration for the first year should be food and clothing. Grey thought it provided no proper incentive to hard work for the immigrants' own profit. Finally, Grey believed that if the government permitted a law based openly on the coercive principle, Parliament would certainly step in and prevent it. Demanding that the 1849 Ordinance be amended, and urging Trinidad to try the system of annual contracts and monthly taxes once more, Grey pointed out that in 1847 its failure had been due to special circumstances. In Mauritius it had

worked well, stopping vagrancy and ensuring regular labour. He would permit 'a strict police discipline and rigorous regulations, such as shall induce a strong compulsion of circumstances, so long only as . . . the labourer is made from the first to understand that he has an interest in being industrious, and that while he cannot escape a certain amount of toil, he will reap the advantage of working cheerfully and well'. 'They should be at liberty to choose their employer, and yet be compelled to work, and should be able to change their employers, although forbidden to wander', Grey and Harris now agreed that strict labour regulations were necessary, but differed on the relative definitions of 'stringent regulations' and 'slavery'.[52]

Indian immigration having now ceased, a long argument developed over the question of three-year contracts for liberated Africans.[53] Free negroes imported from Sierra Leone were subject to voluntary three-year contracts, to repay the colony for importing them. But in June 1849 Henry Taylor pointed out that liberated Africans were now transported at Imperial expense,[54] and Grey restricted their indentures to one year on the ground that there had been financial outlay for the colonies to recover. The Imperial Government, as the Africans' mentor, maintained that longer indentures were not strictly necessary in their own interests.[55] It was a confusing situation. The Parliamentary Secretary, Benjamin Hawes, could see no valid distinction between newly liberated and other Africans, and accepted the West Indian contention that in order to break a raw African to the ways of civilized society a three-year contract was not too long. 'Admitting contracts at all' he said, 'the operation and administration of the law will sufficiently protect the African from oppression or ill-usage'.[56] Some definite and uniform ruling was now urgently needed since contracts of different lengths in the different colonies and for different groups of immigrants could only lead to discontent. In July 1849 therefore Grey confirmed that contracts with liberated Africans must not exceed one year, while strictly voluntary three-year contracts might be allowed with African immigrants imported at the colonies' expense. In no case were compulsory contracts to exceed one year.[57] This decision was adhered to despite strong pressure from the West India Committee for straightforward three-year contracts with all immigrants.[58]

Grey remained convinced that long contracts would do nothing to encourage industrious labour but would rather exacerbate the relations existing between employers and labourers. He believed that a disturbance in May 1849 on Plantation Zorg in British Guiana, where a body of indentured Africans had struck work, had demonstrated that indentures exceeding one year were not in the best interests of the liberated Africans themselves.[59] That fracas was apparently due essentially to a misunderstanding, but Grey regarded it as 'a natural consequence of the relations established between labourers and employers by indentures on contracts for long terms'.[60] He accorded a disproportionate importance to this episode, and an instance of ill-treatment in Jamaica, referring to 'serious disturbances' caused by long contracts.[61] It was this belief, plus a feeling that they would certainly fail, which led Grey to oppose a general system of compulsory three-year contracts for all immigrants. His conditional consent as regards one class of immigrants had been due purely to a desire to avoid thwarting the planters' wishes if possible. His consistent advocacy of short, easily terminable contracts for labour was fundamentally due to the fact that such was the system familiar to Europeans; he constantly called up in his support 'the experience of this and of every country in which industry flourished', rather than the particular conditions of the West Indies.[62]

Governor Barkly of British Guiana had a strong point when he asserted that if Grey could only see the immigrants as they were he 'would hesitate to judge them by the light which experience throws upon the motives and conduct of English labourers in relation to their employers'. The Colonial Office tendency to judge the West Indies by English standards and apply English customs to them did not make for a real understanding of their problems.[63]

Pressed by the West India committee to reconsider his decision and allow three-year contracts generally, Grey merely reiterated that 'such a system would partake too much of the character of compulsory labour'.[64] When the stipendiary magistrates of British Guiana reported that the attempt of three-year contracts had worked excellently, he remarked that such a conclusion was 'at variance with a consideration of the motives which generally govern men's conduct in the relation of employer and labourer'. From such a standpoint, he not unnaturally concluded that where the immigrants had indeed worked well under these contracts they had done so under compulsion, and regarded the sparsity of complaints against the employers as 'in fact the most decisive proof of how little the immigrant is a free agent'.[65] The argument continued, Governor Barkly stressing the difficulties of indenturing different groups of immigrants for different periods, and claiming that 'immigration without contracts would require to be almost infinite in extent to produce any permanent effect upon the supply of labour'.[66] But Grey still believed that 'such long engagements must . . . deaden the operation of all those motives by which

men are usually stimulated to strenuous industry'. He did not understand that contract labourers received precisely the same wages as free labourers resident on the estates, and concluded that a contract must in some way lessen the labourer's ability to earn. Grey however was justified in claiming that there was no apparent reason why one-year contracts, backed up by a monthly tax on immigrants not under contracts, and properly enforced, should not prove entirely satisfactory. In the West Indies this system had never had a fair trial.[67]

Although indignant at the disallowance of their 1849 Ordinance, the Trinidad Legislative Council acquiesced with a surprisingly good grace. While pressing for a reconsideration, and urging Grey at least to approve restricting immigrants to their locations, even if on short contracts only, they expressed willingness to modify the Ordinance but pointed out that the frequent disallowance of local laws caused much confusion and inconvenience.[68] Lord Grey however now approved a modification proposed by Henry Taylor, requiring liberated Africans to follow their one-year indenture by working on contract for a second year for any employer they might choose. Harris deemed liberated Africans 'savages in the completest sense of the term'; for their own sakes close supervision was necessary.[69] But it is not easy to evaluate how long an indenture was strictly necessary before they could safely be left to themselves; and however much the planters' general advocacy of long contracts may have been motivated simply by a desire to obtain more labour, and to make the expensive immigration system 'pay', where liberated Africans were concerned the Colonial authorities were genuinely anxious about the need to keep a close rein on such 'savages'.

On the basis of what Grey would concede, Trinidad produced new Immigration Ordinances in 1850. These provided that liberated Africans should serve two years and retained the five-year Industrial Residence, redeemable at £3 per annum, as the qualification for a return passage to India; the alternative to yearly contracts was a monthly tax of 5/- on pain of 14 days imprisonment. The penalty for unauthorized absence from work was 6d. per day and immigrants found more than 2 miles from their contractual estate without a pass, except at weekends, could be apprehended without a warrant. Elaborate regulations were provided to enable the authorities to keep track of each immigrant.[70] This Ordinance was in some respects rigorous, but Taylor commented: 'Having admitted that long terms of engagement shall be enforced . . . it becomes indispensable to fall back upon a principle of rigor'.[71]

This Ordinance served Trinidad reasonably well for the next four years. Lord Harris was so glad to have a settled immigration law after three years of confusion and uncertainty that he resolved to suggest no further alternations.[72] In September 1852 imprisonment for 14 days was substituted for a fine which had proved 'quite inoperative' for preventing breach of contract and desertion.[73]

The Guianese were less ready to accept Imperial dictation over their labour laws. In practice native and immigrant labourers received the same wages, had the same opportunities to earn, contract or no contract. Governor Sir Henry Barkly could not therefore appreciate Grey's persistent objection to three-year contracts, the main effect of which would be to ensure regular labour and prevent frequent changes of employers.[74] All influential Guianese, planters or not, seemed convinced that three-year contracts were necessary to ensure the civilization of liberated Africans, and that with two year indentures only such immigration 'will eventually prove a curse instead of a blessing, and put the colony to enormous expense'.[75]

At this point Grey capitulated so far as to sanction compulsory three-year contracts for free immigrants. In July 1850 he agreed that free African immigrants might be indentured for three years on arrival in British Guiana; though he did not believe many would be obtained on such terms, they were the only ones on which Guiana would pay for free Africans.[76] In August 1850 therefore the long-condemned 1848 Immigration Ordinance was at length replaced by four new ones, Nos. 20–23/1850. Their basis was again a monthly tax, $1.50 for Indians, $2.00 for Africans, and a series of contracts for one to three years, to make up a five-year Industrial Residence for Indians, three years for Africans and Portuguese. For liberated Africans the Trinidad law was adopted, providing for a two-year indenture. Contract duty was fixed at $2.00 for the first year and thereafter $4.00 per annum. Provisions for enforcing the law were similar to Trinidad's except that the fine for unauthorized absence was 24¢ per day.[77]

The 1850 Immigration Ordinance quickly led to protests from the anti-slavery society, who again argued that the planters were trying to reduce the immigrants to 'a state of modified slavery', and opposed the monthly tax.[78] But these measures had been sanctioned by Grey after a very lengthy and searching discussion, and their objections were not taken seriously.[79] Grey agreed with the East India Company that in British Guiana the penalties for absence from work were unfairly high.[80] The 1850 Ordinances were therefore replaced by Ordinances nos. 20–22 of 14 October 1851, reducing these penalties: Indians were to pay 4¢ a day, other

immigrants to forfeit two days wages or spend two days in gaol. Otherwise the 1850 law remained unchanged, except that all immigrants were explicitly given the right to redeem their contracts for cash at the end of each year. Still the cost of introducing immigrants on overseas contracts to work for a specified employer could not be paid from public funds, but it was now provided that if such contracts were prematurely terminated a proportion of any bounty might be paid to the disappointed employer.[81]

Immigrants however continued capriciously to desert their estates; and the colonies proposed still longer indentures, preferably five years, as a probable solution.[82] The arrival of Sir John Pakington at the Colonial Office in 1852 was the signal for a renewed agitation supported by the Governors of Trinidad, British Guiana, and also Jamaica, in favour of indenturing liberated Africans for three years, so consistently opposed by Lord Grey. It was an old West Indian tactic to present previously unsuccessful demands to a new Secretary of State, hoping for a change of policy, and Pakington was well-known for his sympathy towards the planters. He at once asked the Emigration Commissioners for a full report on the contract law, and the position of liberated Africans was carefully reconsidered.[83] The Commissioners concluded that indentures did help to prepare the liberated Africans for life in a free society. 'During the first years of residence, they do in fact acquire some habits of industry and order and a decided understanding of the nature of a bargain and the value of money'. But the Emigration Commissioners did not accept the contention that one-year contracts had worked badly. Though finding no positive need for three-year contracts, they could see no good reason for disallowing them 'beyond that which lies against any gratuitous change in a system which is proceeding satisfactorily' — a salient departure from the previous Imperial attitudes that contracts were objectionable hindrances to a free labour system, to be permitted only in face of proven necessity. They now accepted that in 1848–49 three-year contracts had worked well in British Guiana, as indeed they had done in Mauritius, and accepted *prima facie* the old West Indian view that longer indentures would enhance the Africans' chances of 'moral and educational training'.

Ever careful, the Commissioners proposed that if three-year contracts were sanctioned the system of government supervision should be tightened as a safeguard against any form of coercion or exploitation. Henry Taylor as usual opposed longer contracts, expressing the too prevalent official view that 'when there is so much doubt as to what is best to be done, it is generally best to do nothing'.

Another Assistant Under-Secretary, T.F. Elliott, agreed with the Commissioners, adding that three-year contracts were allowed with all other immigrants and 'Uniformity is very desirable when there is no cogent reason to the contrary'.[84] Pakington, favourable from the first to three-year indentures for liberated Africans, now authorized them, and recommended closer government supervision.[85]

When British Guiana introduced compulsory three-year indentures for liberated Africans under Ordinance No. 3 of February 1853, she took the opportunity to require Indian immigrants to enter contracts for five rather than three years, providing an option of terminating them after three years. Pakington had now been succeeded by the less sympathetic Newcastle, who thought five years much too long and that all three-year contracts even with liberated Africans, should be strictly voluntary. The attempt to apply to Indians five-year contracts which could be terminated after three years but only on terms 'so onerous and vague as to be negatory', was regarded by Newcastle as a 'hasty subversion of existing arrangements', and immediately vetoed. With some justice he observed that 'the Court of Policy cannot possibly have been unaware that the duration of contracts was a subject which successive Secretaries of State had considered with a care approaching to jealousy; that the extension of these contracts even to three years had been conceded gradually and with hesitation by Mr. Gladstone, Lord Grey and Sir John Pakington; and that the further extension to five years was very liable, if not most likely, to be disapproved'. Changes in the contract law, he thought, should not be introduced without prior agreement with the Imperial government.[86] But further changes were now inevitable. It had again proved impossible to collect the monthly tax, and difficult to prevent desertion; some alternative means of enforcing 'Industrial Residence' was required. It was difficult to see any alternative save requiring the immigrants to serve the whole period of 'Industrial Residence' under contract. Newcastle however still refused to allow contracts for five years; he maintained that the existing three-year contracts were quite enough to compensate the planter for the initial cost of the immigrant, who must thereafter be free to choose his own employer. He therefore proposed making Indian immigrants follow their initial three-year engagement with two further one-year contracts with any employer of their choice, which could be commuted at $12 per annum. This would ensure five years fair labour if the contracts were enforced. This proposal differed from the disallowed Guianese law merely in the option reserved to the

immigrant of choosing his contractual employer with complete freedom after three years.[87] When the term of Industrial Residence for Indians was extended to ten years in 1853, it was eventually agreed that they should spend their five years on annual contracts, in order to provide some security that they would work during the second half of their term.[88]

This new system was finally introduced in both British Guiana and Trinidad in 1854,[89] as Governor Wodehouse of British Guiana remarked, the changes in the Imperial attitude to contracts over the years 'render it clear that it is no longer considered fair towards the colonist, or even beneficial to the immigrants, to leave the latter so absolute an exercise of their own discretion in respect to employment as was for some time after the commencement of immigration perseveringly advocated'. The government was now prepared to allow almost unlimited indentures for free immigrants, so long as after three years the immigrants were allowed to choose their own employers at annual intervals. In fact, Madeirans were required until 1856 to serve only one year on contracts, since they were cheaper and needed no external stimulus to work hard. Africans, liberated or otherwise, were to be indentured for three years. Chinese were now placed on the same footing as Indians.[90] Overseas contracts with Indians and Africans to work for a specific employer on arrival were still prohibited. In 1856 British Guiana, and in 1857 Trinidad, brought all immigrants imported under government auspices, except Africans, under the Indian system involving five years on contract.[91]

By 1857 Imperial objections to a straight five-year contract for all immigrants, with no power to change employers but with the option of redeeming the last two years for cash, had disappeared, and only the disinclination yet again to alter a law the frequent changes in which were a too common cause of confusion prevented the immediate adoption of such a system. When next the Immigration Law was amended such contracts seemed certain to be accepted,[92] and the renewed Chinese immigration in 1859 was based on them.[93]

The contract system of 1854 worked much more smoothly than any earlier law. Few complaints were heard from either side, and cases of breach of contract seem to have been fewer. Admittedly the employers were very reluctant to alienate their labourers by prosecution at law, but greater harmony in the labour relations of both colonies was clearly evident.[94] Sir Clinton Murdoch, Chairman of the Emigration Commission, subsequently defended the indenture system as absolutely essential to the interests of both employers and immigrants; this view can scarcely be gainsaid for the

1840s and 1850s at least, although the precise length of the contract could always be a subject for conflicting views. Without indentures the Indians had proved to suffer severely from the illness consequent on wandering, and the planters would have refused to bear the cost of importing them. Immigration without indentures could have been maintained only on a small scale and from sources reasonably close at hand like Madeira and the smaller islands. The West Indian authorities all asserted that 'the indenture system is not and cannot be worked oppressively'; labour was so valuable at this time that employers generally dared not antagonize their labourers too much, it was claimed.[95] Replying to anti-slavery protests against the whole system the Emigration Commissioners thought that in the last resort it must be judged by its effect on the immigrants, and not according to abstract principles of liberty, so prominent in official minds in the earliest days. 'As a general rule it appears to us that persons competent to take care of themselves should be allowed to make what contracts they please not being contrary to public policy, and that incompetent persons should only be so far restricted as to prevent them from making contracts manifestly hurtful to themselves'.[96] This represents a greater change from the views even of the reasonably sympathetic Grey, who thought that contracts with liberated Africans should be allowed only in so far as they were positively to their advantage; while the Imperial concept of who was and who was not 'competent' had changed remarkably since the restrictive days of 1840.

In 1862 came the long sought opportunity to introduce simple five-year contracts for Indians. Newcastle explained that 'experience has satisfied me that with proper government superintendence the welfare of the coolie can be sufficiently secured without the safeguard of that artificial form of contract'.[97] But in this respect West Indian conditions had not changed; Newcastle was applying the principle put forward by the Emigration Commissioners in 1859, in strong contrast to his attitude in 1853. The new contracts were much simpler to operate, and in 1864 were applied to the Chinese also.[98] In October 1863 Sir Clinton Murdoch approved five-year indentures for liberated Africans, on condition that they were afterwards settled on the land.[99] The logical conclusion of the repeated extension of the period of indenture had at last been achieved, though few liberated Africans subsequently arrived.

At all stages of its development, the contract system included provisions for the Governor to cancel contracts at his discretion where immigrants were ill-treated, and withdraw all indentured immigrants from the estate concerned. The Imperial govern-ment always regarded this power as a *sine qua non*, though it was seldom, if ever, used. In British Guiana the Governor could exercise it only where an employer was actually convicted of ill-treatment, but in Trinidad he was empowered to cancel contracts entirely at will.[100] That these powers remained dormant in the hands of many conscientious Governors is evidence that the employers generally were careful not to permit cases of blatant ill-treatment which would justify this extreme penalty, such as occurred more than once in Grenada, however hard on their labourers, and otherwise negligent, some of them may have been.

This history of the contract law is one of an Imperial Government constantly withstanding the demands of the planters but gradually giving ground before their pressure, a changing public opinion in Britain, and its own changing attitudes towards indentured labour; until a complete veto on overseas of compulsory contracts was by slow degrees converted into a system of simple contracts for five years, maintained as the indispensable condition of a free passage. But in all circumstances the Imperial Government was concerned first to protect the interests of the immigrants, to which the planters' demands for more effective labour were always subordinated. No change was ever permitted until the Secretary of State was convinced that the immigrants would not suffer materially; and the slow development of the system was largely due to exalted official concepts of the principle of free labour, and the apprehension about effect of a contract upon the immigrant, which had to be modified gradually by long experience.

Notes & References

The following abbreviations are used:

C.O.   Colonial Office Records, Public Record Office, London.

P.P.   Parliamentary Papers

C.L. & E.C.   Colonial Land and Emigration Commissioners.

1. C.O. 296/11: Spring Rice to Hill, 2 Nov. 1834, no. 26.
2. C.O. 295/106: Hill to Aberdeen, 26 March 1835, no. 12.
3. P.P. 1840. XXXIV. 367–8: Glenelg to West India Governors, Circulars, 15 May, 31 Aug. 1838.
4. C.O. 296/12: Glenelg to Hill, 15 July 1835, no. 22; C.O. 111/144: Glenelg to Smyth, 29 June 1836, no. 124.
5. C.O. 111/114: Smyth to Glenelg, 10 March 1836, no. 123.
6. C.O. 295/103: Hill to Spring Rice, 3 Nov., no. 29; C.O. 111/137: Smyth to Aberdeen, 25 May 1835, no. 40.
7. C.O. 111/114: Smith to Glenelg, 10 Feb. 1836, no. 117.
8. P.P. 1837–8 LII.3: Smyth to Glenelg, 27 June 1836, no. 179.
9. P.P. 1837–8, LII.11, 14: Glenelg to Smyth, 31 October 1836, no. 163; 1 March 1837, no. 194.
10. I.M. Cumpston, Indians Overseas in British Territories, pp. 17–18.

11. C.O. 111/150: Smyth to Glenelg 7, 23 Oct. 1837, nos. 383, 389; P.P. 1837–8. LII.12: Smyth to Glenelg, 22 Dec. 1836, no. 264.
12. P.P. 1839, XXXV.150: Glenelg to West India Governors, Circular, 30 July 1838.
13. P.P. 1837–38. LII 171–2: Order in Council, 30 July 1838.
14. Cumpston, op. cit., p. 8.
15. P.P. 1839 XXXV.445, 751: Glenelg to Light, 19 Dec. 1838, no.86; Hill to Glenelg, 11 Dec. 1838, no. 120; P.P. 1841. LII.463; C.L. & E.C. to Stephen, 29 July, 1840.
16. C.O. 295/127: Glasgow West India Association to Normanby, various dates, Feb.-May, 1839; C.O. 295/128: Trinidad Merchants of Bristol to Normanby, various dates, April-May, 1839.
17. P.P. 1846. XXVII.177: Lyttleton to West India Committee, 28 March 1846.
18. C.O. 318/160: West India Committee to Stanley, 24 July 1843; 9 August 1843 and minutes.
19. C.O. 318/160: Minutes, Hope to Stanley, 26 August 1843; Minute by Stanley, 28 August 1843.
20. P.P. 1844. XXXV.557: Hope to West India Committee, 4 Sept. 1843.
21. P.P. 1844. XXXV.571: Enclosure in C.L. & E.C. to Stephen, 14 Oct. 1843.
22. C.O. 295/136: MacLeod to Stanley, 15 Feb. 1842, no. 39.
23. C.O. 296/16: Stanley to Macleod, 30 April 1842, no. 59; C.O. 295/138: Anti-Slavery Society to Stanley, 5 October 1842; C.O. 295/136: Actg. Govr. Fuller to Stanley, 8 July 1842, no. 68 and minutes.
24. C.O. 295/145: C.L. & E.C. to Stephen, 28 Aug. 1844.
25. P.P. 1844. XXXV.560–1: West India Committee to Stanley, 13 Sept. 1843; Stephen to West India Committee, 3 October 1843.
26. Cumpston op. cit., pp. 118–121; P.P. 1847–8 XXIII, pt. III 277, 246, 249; Harris to Grey, 21 Feb. 1848, no. 21; Light to Grey, 11 Jan. 1848, no. 10; Dr. Bonyun's Report on Hospitals and Immigrations, 6 Jan. 1848.
27. C.O. 318/169: West India Committee to Gladstone, 7 Feb. 1846.
28. C.O. 295/148: Anti-Slavery Society to Gladstone (10 Feb. 1846); C.O. 295/148: Anti-Slavery Society to Stanley, 17 Mar. 1845.
29. P.P. 1846. XXVII.176–80: Lyttleton to West India Committee, 28 March 1846; West India Committee to Gladstone, 9 April 1846.
30. Ibid., also C.O. 318/169: West India Committee to Gladstone, 7 Feb. 1846, and minutes.
31. C.O. 318/169: Minutes by Gladstone on West India Immigration, 25 Feb. 1846.
32. P.P. 1846. XXVII.177–80: West India Committee to Gladstone, 9 April 1846.
33. P.O. 1847. XXXIX.188–93, 251–2: Enclosures in Light to Grey, 4 Dec. 1846, no. 249; Harris to Grey, 6 May 1847, no. 40 and enclosure.
34. C.O. 318/169: West India Committee to Gladstone, 26 May 1846.
35. C.O. 318/169: West India Committee to Gladstone, 29 June 1846.
36. P.P. 1847. XXXIX.123: Grey to West India Governors, Circular, 23 Oct. 1846.
37. P.P. 1847. XXXIX.266–69: Grey to Sir W.W. Gomm (Mauritius), 29 Sept. 1846, no. 38; C.O. 318/166: Minute by Grey, 15 Oct. 1846.
38. Ibid.
39. P.P. 1847. XXXIX.237, 253: Harris to Grey, 18 Feb., 12 June 1846, nos. 17, 52.
40. P.P. 1847–8. XLV.215–16: Light to Grey, 5 March 1848, no. 39.
41. P.P. 1847–8. XLVI.433: Grey to Light, 23 May 1848, no. 338.
42. P.P. 1847–8. XLVI.609: Report of Committee of Court of Policy, May 1848.
43. P.P. 1851. XXXIX.90: Barkly to Grey, 18 April 1850, no. 63.
44. P.P. 1847–8. XLVI.555–6: Actg. Govr. Walker to Grey, 18 July 1848. Private.
45. P.P. 1847–8. XLIV.585: Harris to Grey, 4 Dec. 1847, no. 100; C.O. 295/162: Harris to Grey, 20 June 1848, no. 72.
46. P.P. 1847–8. XXIII, Pt. III.277–8: Harris to Grey, 21 Feb. 1848, no. 21.
47. P.P. 1847–8. XXIII, Pt. V.62: Draft Report of Chairman of Select Committee, 1848.
48. P.P. 1850. XL.497–9: Harris to Grey, 6 Feb. 1849, no. 21.
49. Ibid.
50. C.O. 295/166: Harris to Grey, 6 Feb. 1849, no. 21, minutes.
51. P.P. 1850. XL.524: Grey to Harris, 28 April 1849, no. 327.
52. P.P. 1850. XL.524, 529: Grey to Harris, 28 April, 15 Dec. 1849, nos. 327, 376.
53. P.P. 1850. XL.447–8: C.L. & E.C. to Merivale, 23 March 1849.
54. C.O. 318/181: Minute by Taylor, 11 June 1849, bound with correspondence for April 1849.
55. C.O. 318/182: C.L. & E.C. to Merivale, 12 July 1849; Minute by Grey, 17 July 1849.
56. C.O. 318/182: Minute, Hawes to Grey, (24) July 1849: Jamaica: Immigration.
57. C.O. 318/182: Minute by Grey, 25 July 1849; P.P. 1850. XL.449, 491: Grey to Barkly, 31 July, 15 Dec. 1849, nos. 80, 128.
58. P.P. 1850. XL.661, 664: West India Committee to Grey, 25 July 1849; Merivale to West India Committee, 14 Aug. 1849.
59. C.O. 318/183: West India Committee to Grey, 25 July 1849, minute by Grey.
60. P.P. 1850. XL.459, 487: Barkly to Grey, 4 May 1849, no. 72; Grey to Barkly, 16 June 1849, no. 61.
61. P.P. 1850. XL.449: Grey to Barkly, 31 July 1849, no. 80.
62. P.P. 1850. XL.488,489: Grey to Barkly, 21 Sept., 15 Dec. 1849, nos. 96, 128.
63. P.P. 1850. XL.485: Barkly to Grey, 1 Feb. 1850, no. 20.
64. P.P. 1850. XL.666, 668: West India Committee to Grey, 23 Nov. 1849; Hawes to West India Committee, 20 Dec. 1849.
65. P.P. 1850. XL.489: Grey to Barkly, 15 Dec. 1849, no. 128.
66. P.P. 1850. XL.473, 486: Barkly to Grey, 30 Oct. 1849, no. 156; 1 Feb. 1850, no. 20.
67. P.P. 1850. XL.489: Grey to Barkly, 15 Dec. 1849, no. 128.
68. P.P. 1850. XL.508–14: Harris to Grey, 5 Sept. 1849, no. 68, and enclosure.
69. P.P. 1852–3. LXVII.441: Harris to Grey, 23 Nov. 1850, no. 91.
70. P.P. 1850. XL.677–80: Trinidad Ordinance no. 5/1850 'for the encouragement of Immigration and the promotion of the Industry of Immigrants'.
71. C.O. 295/170: Harris to Grey, 20 April 1850, no. 31, minute by Taylor.
72. P.P. 1852–3. LXVII.441: Harris to Grey, 23 Nov. 1850, no. 91.
73. P.P. 1852–3. LXVII.541: Harris to Pakington, 24 Sept. 1852, no. 60.
74. P.P. 1850. XL.485: Barkly to Grey, 1 Feb. 1850, no. 20.
75. P.P. 1851. XXXIX.86: Barkly to Grey, 18 April 1850, no. 62.
76. P.P. 1851. XXXIX.405: Grey to Barkly, 16 July 1850, no. 212.

77. P.P. 1851. XXXIX.169–72, 559–77: Barkly to Grey, 11 Sept. 1850, no. 130; British Guiana Ordinances Nos. 20–23/1850.

78. P.P. 1851. XXXIX.396, 437: Anti-Slavery Society to Grey, 22 March, 4 Oct. 1850.

79. P.P. 1852–3. LXVII.467, 477: Harris to Grey, 7 Jan., 10 Feb. 1851, nos. 2, 17.

80. P.P. 1851. XXXIX.453: Grey to Barkly, 16 Jan. 1851, no. 290.

81. P.P. 1852–3. LXVII.696–712: British Guiana Ordinances, Nos. 20–22/1851.

82. P.P. 1852–3. LXVII.527: Report of Trinidad's Superintendent of Immigrants, H. Mitchell, 1 April 1852.

83. C.O. 318/196: C.L. & E.C. to Merivale, 22 July 1852, and minute by Pakington, 26 July 1852.

84. C.O. 318/197: C.L. & E.C. to Merivale, 11 Aug. 1852, and minutes.

85. C.O. 318/197: Pakington to West India Governors, Circular, 16 Aug. 1852.

86. P.P. 1852–3. LXVIII.657–9: Newcastle to Barkly, 14 May 1853, no. 48.

87. P.P. 1859–i. XVI.31–4: Newcastle to Actg. Govr. Walker, 16 Jan. 1854, no. 175.

88. P.P. 1859–i. XVI.116: Labouchere to Wodehouse, 27 March 1856, no. 50.

89. P.P. 1859–i. XVI.448, 488: British Guiana Ordinance No. 7/1854; Trinidad Ordinance No. 24/1854.

90. P.P. 1859–i. XVI.190: Wodehouse to Newcastle, 7 June 1854, no. 21.

91. P.P. 1859–i. XVI.230, 144: Wodehouse to Labouchere, 6 Sept. 1856, no. 117; Labouchere to Wodehouse, 17 Dec. 1856, no. 196; P.P. 1859–ii. XX.307, 377: Keate to Labouchere, 6 Aug. 1857, no. 74; Labouchere to Keate, 9 Nov. 1857, no. 97.

92. P.P. 1859–ii. XX.380: C.L. & E.C. to Merivale, 25 Sept. 1857.

93. P.P. 1859–ii. XX.509: British Guiana Ordinance No. 17/1858.

94. P.P. 1860. XLIV.42: Annual Report of Trinidad's Agent General for Immigration for 1858.

95. P.P. 1859–ii. XX.501: Minute by Murdoch on Indian Immigration to the West Indies, 18 Feb. 1859.

96. C.O. 318/224: C.L. & E.C. to Merivale, 21 Jan. 1859.

97. C.O. 318/236: Newcastle to Hincks, 14 Aug. 1862, no. 477; Newcastle to West India Governors, Circular, 13 Aug. 1862.

98. C.O. 318/243: C.L. & E.C. to Rogers, 21 March 1864.

99. C.O. 318/241: C.L. & E.C. to Rogers, 27 Oct. 1863.

100. C.O. 318/224: C.L. & E.C. to Merivale, 28 March 1859; P.P. 1859–i. XVI.84: Sir Grey to Wodehouse, 13 Sept. 1854, no. 33.

The Social Impact of Portuguese Immigration Into British Guiana After Emancipation

Brian L. Moore

Perhaps the singularly most outstanding feature characterizing societies in plantation America is the overwhelming dominance of the plantation on the society and economy as a whole. Wherever the plantation emerged as the supreme socio-economic institution, civilization arose in which European-derived racial and cultural phenomena enjoyed supreme social and political dominance, while the staple crop of the plantation dominated the economy. These salient features were most evident in the South of the United States, the North-East of Brazil and throughout the Caribbean. The history of British Guiana, both during and after slavery, proved no exception to this trend; and the Portuguese immigration into that colony after emancipation was but one manifestation of the extent to which the white-dominated plantation civilization in the colony dictated the development of the society even after the vast majority of the population — the slaves — were freed.

Portuguese immigration into British Guiana during the nineteenth century formed but a trickle in relation to migration movements to the New World in that period. Even in relation to other immigrants into British Guiana itself, it was comparatively small. Between 1835 and 1850, only 17,098 Portuguese from Madeira went to the colony; while between 1851 and 1881, when the last group arrived, only 13,535 Madeirans and 164 persons from the Azores emigrated to Guiana.[1] Yet, on account of their racial affinity to the dominant white classes, they enjoyed a social importance out of proportion to their numerical position. It is the thesis of this paper that race was the overriding determinant of the social status of the Portuguese immigrants in British Guiana during the nineteenth century; and that this criterion was dictated by the need to preserve and bolster the social supremacy of the small dominant white minority of that plantation civilization in the face of the new challenge occasioned by the emancipation of the slaves.

The act of final emancipation in 1838 ushered into West Indian and Guianese society a new era of social and labour relations. Emancipation meant that for the first time in the history of the plantation society, black and white were rendered equal before the law. The ex-slaves were free to dispose of their labour as they wished. This freedom was most feared by the white classes of society. Not only might the blacks, who formed the large majority of the population, withdraw their labour altogether from the plantations and opt for an 'independent' and 'lawless' life of 'barbarism' in the densely forested interior of the colony; but by extension the plantation economy and, with it, the white civilization in the colony would decay. It was even feared that the freed blacks might run wild and attack the whites and the plantations before decamping to the 'bush'.[2]

Consequently, the objectives behind the desire to introduce Portuguese immigrants were two-fold: to create a white middle class; and to secure a regular and reliable supply of cheap labour to supplement the existing local resources of ex-slave labour to set an example of industry to the blacks.[3] The rationale underlying the first aspect was to augment the total white population in order to bolster the numerical strength of the white sector of society, and thereby to offset any social advancement likely to be made by the ex-slaves from their newly gained status of freedom. The Portuguese labouring population would create an industrious buffer group between the dominant whites and the ex-slaves who could be depended upon to buttress the perpetuation of white supremacy in the colony in the interest of race. Simultaneously, the second aspect would be fulfilled if a sufficient number of Portuguese could be procured to fill the void occasioned by a withdrawal of the ex-slaves from plantation labour, thereby maintaining the continuance of the primacy of the plantation in the economy and setting an example of industry to the blacks who were considered inherently lazy and indolent.

These motives were clearly expressed by government officials. In 1846, Governor Light asserted that 'it is of immense importance to the future prospects of the Colony that a large industrious body of whites should be established ...'[4] Similarly,

Governor Wodehouse noted that the Portuguese were the only immigrants who 'could ... be advantageously treated ... in as much as they possess habits of industry, coupled with other qualities calculated to render them peaceful and valuable citizens when set free from all artificial control.' Portuguese immigration was justified on the grounds that the preservation of the European interests in the colony was the antidote to a reversion into barbarism by the blacks.[5] The Colonial Office was in full agreement with these views, it being argued that in the absence of European employers the blacks would indeed revert to barbarism.[6]

Portuguese immigration was consequently encouraged in the interests of white racial supremacy and the preservation of white civilization in the colony. Although they were imported at public expense they were treated as a privileged group of immigrants in contrast to other (non-white) immigrant groups, namely the Africans, Indians, and later the Chinese. For instance, during the years 1845–1846 when there was agitation in favour of long contracts for Indian and African immigrants introduced at public expense (the bounty system), the planting interests ignored the fact that the Madeirans imported on bounty were then entirely free of any such obligation.[7] When placed under obligation of engaging in contract or paying a monthly tax to offset the cost of their introduction, they chose the latter course,[8] being advised by their countrymen on shore that the authorities were indisposed to levy the tax under the existing machinery.[9]

Subsequent efforts to ensure that the Portuguese complied with their contractual obligations were half-hearted and ineffective.[10] The one serious attempt to ensure that they entered contracts for three years without the option of commutation, Ordinance No. 25 of 1856, resulted in the cessation of the flow of Portuguese immigrants to the colony during the following season. The immediate upshot was that the planter class, in the interest of race, chose to consider the Portuguese a special category of immigrants and decided to continue to finance this immigration at public expense though exempting the Portuguese from such obligations as other (non-white) immigrants were subjected to.[11] Even when financial necessity forced a return to a contractual obligation of two years in 1859, the option to commute the service by payment of a given sum was reinstituted.[12] In effect, therefore, the Portuguese obligation to labour for a given period on the plantations was waived, or at least treated leniently, in contrast to other immigrants who were also introduced at public expense. For the post-emancipation social situation dictated that white racial interest should take priority in order to preserve the existence of white social supremacy in the colony. In this respect, even the demand for cheap labour by the plantations took second place.

The search for white labour in British Guiana began soon after the abolition of slavery in 1834, even before the ex-slaves were freed from the obligation to labour on the plantations by the final act of emancipation in 1838. Small groups of white immigrants were introduced from Madeira, Germany, England, Ireland, Scotland, and Malta between 1835 and 1838. But it was not until 1841 that a system of publicly financed immigration from the Portuguese Atlantic Islands was inaugurated.[13] In that year bounty payments were made on 4,312 Madeiran immigrants.[14] The mortality rate among these Portuguese was enormous. Between February and November 1841, some 282 died[15] (a rate of 98.025 per thousand per annum). As a result, this bounty-supported immigration was stopped in May 1842.[16] Such Portuguese immigrants who arrived during the stoppage paid their own passage money.[17] However, the mortality rate among those who had survived the rigours of the period of acclimatization seemed no worse than that for other race groups resident in the colony. For instance, only 78 deaths were recorded in twelve months ending in July 1846, while the mortality rate was just 2.45% for the first half of 1846.[18] Consequently, the Colonial Office was soon induced to consent to a resumption of large-scale bounty immigration from Madeira (September 1846).[19]

The renewed immigration proved no better than before. In the latter half of 1846, the death rate rose to 12%.[20] Throughout the period from 1841 to 1847, it was estimated that about 40% of the Portuguese immigrants died not long after arrival. In 1847, 5853 were resident on the plantations, but only 2,116 were scattered throughout the colony. This left 7,730 out of 15,099 who had arrived since 1835 unaccounted for or dead. In Georgetown alone, 1,062 deaths had been recorded among the Portuguese.[21] This high mortality continued into the early 1850s. For instance, in 1851, the death rate per thousand was 50.3; in 1852, 90.9;[22] and in 1853, 79.9.[23] But as fewer Portuguese arrived after 1850 and those who were already present became fully seasoned and acclimatized, the mortality rate decreased.

The excessively high mortality among the Portuguese immigrants was attributed to a number of factors. The first set of immigrants (1841–1842) arrived at a time when a yellow fever epidemic was raging in the colony. Many deaths, however, were attributed to their alleged uncleanliness; their premature and extreme exertion in the sunshine; to parsimony which prevented them from using sufficient diet; and to their alleged aversion to medical treatment.[24] They were said to be over-anxious to obtain money, thus generally overworking themselves and earning in a few cases as much as $1.50 (6s.3d. sterling) per day.[25] But the mortality was also due to their location on many of the rivers, creeks and islands which were reputed to be less salubrious than the coastlands; to the fact that many of them arrived with their constitutions shattered by disease from starvation and famine in their homeland; and finally to the almost total deficiency of hospital accommodation and judicious hygiene treatment.[26] Moreover, the apartments generally allotted to them on arrival were unhealthy, and very little attention was paid to the contiguous drainage and to the ventilation of the houses — quite apart from the fact that medical attention was poor.[27]

Notwithstanding the health problem, Portuguese immigration was encouraged mainly for social reasons, in order to augment the white population. The Portuguese not only presented a numerical bolster to the white sector, but they were facilitated to constitute an effective middle or buffer group between the dominant white minority (mainly British) and the subordinate black majority. Their numerical contribution was vividly reflected in the population statistics. In 1851, the dominant whites numbered only 3,630 out of a total population of 127,635 (2.8%); but the Portuguese added another 7,928 (6%) to the white plantation. By 1891, the Portuguese contribution was no less important. For the dominant whites numbered just 4,558, while the total population had increased to 278,328 — the white element constituting 1.6%. But the 12,166 Portuguese (4.3%) made a significant difference.[28]

In a society where agricultural labour was regarded as socially degrading because of its association with slavery, the Portuguese could not fulfil their middle-class status by remaining as plantation labourers. For this reason, therefore, it was important that they should be able to establish an economic base by which they could underpin their designated middle-class role. It is in this context that their accession to a position of monopoly over the retail trade of the colony achieves its crucial significance.

The facilitation of the Portuguese to a position of dominance over the retail trade was ideal in a number of respects. First of all, it was a new field of economic enterprise in the colony in which the dominant white classes evinced little interest. As such there was unlikely to be any competition or clash of interest between the British and Portuguese elements in this sphere of activity. Secondly, the ready market for retailing created by the desires

of the freed slaves to acquire essentials and luxuries provided the trade with lucrative potential sufficient to augment the socio-economic status of any group which should dominate it. Thirdly, if the Portuguese were channelled into that field, although they could become potentially wealthy rivals to the dominant classes, their 'middleman' role would be emphasized by their dependence on the dominant white commercial interests which controlled the wholesale import trade. Thus although they could be facilitated to rise above the general socio-economic level of the black labouring population, their subordinate or second-class social status in relation to the British element was to be clearly defined in the local society. The latter indeed regarded them as no better than lower-class Irish peasant folk,[29] having in fact originated from humble backgrounds and being for the most part illiterate even in the Portuguese language.

The Portuguese establishment of a stranglehold over the retail trade in the colony was conditioned by four main factors. First, the relaxed attitude of the planters in enforcing the contractual obligations of the Portuguese as opposed to other immigrants enabled the former to leave plantation labour very soon after arrival or not to enter it at all. It has already been shown that whereas the planters were eager to pin down the Indian, and later the Chinese, immigrants to plantation labour by means of the system of indentureship under legal contracts, their efforts to do likewise where the Portuguese were concerned were at best lukewarm and half-hearted; and that indeed by 1856 they were prepared to waive all obligations of the Portuguese to indenture themselves although their introduction to the colony continued to be financed out of the public revenues. This meant that the Portuguese were able to enter the retail trade long before any other group of immigrants could attempt to do so, and moreover, just at the time when that field of enterprise was being developed as a result of the new market created by the ex-slaves.

Secondly, the familiarity of the Portuguese with the operations, and financing methods and institutions of a capitalist money economy gave them a clear advantage over their Creole rivals who were just emerging from a slave system which had had no scope for the development of such business skills and enterprise. During slavery, the internal trade was small and insignificant, being geared principally to the supply of food and clothing in large quantities to the plantations at high prices.[30] Such retail trade as there was, consisted of servants employed by their masters in the selling of cakes and other small articles.[31] As late as 1841, there were no retail shops outside of Water Street (in

Georgetown), except those of druggists and chemists, who sometimes added the sale of dry provisions. Liquors, groceries, provisions, and dry goods could generally only be obtained in Water Street.[32] The Creoles were consequently rather inequipped in terms of know-how to compete effectively even in an open situation in which the Portuguese were not given artificial preferences. Thus, the latter were more cognizant of the long-term advantages which would accrue if they were prepared to forego immediate profits by selling at low rates[33] in order to out compete and undersell their rivals.[34]

However, it was not simply their know-how which rendered the Portuguese more willing to sell cheaply in the face of Creole competition, but the artificial assistance extended to them by the white merchants. The latter advanced credit to many Portuguese whereas the Creoles were either given no credit at all, or else given on very stringent terms.[35] This meant that the Portuguese could in fact readily undersell their rivals who had to pay cash for their supplies from the wholesale merchants. By so doing, the Portuguese retailers increased the circulation of money in the colony, generated more profits among their wholesale suppliers, and could clear off their initial debts rapidly and soon conduct their business transactions entirely in ready cash,[36] as opposed even to those Creoles who were granted some form of credit but at high rates of interest. This was the main basis on which the Portuguese could establish their retailing enterprises and thereafter generate their own growth.

Fourthly, the system of government taxation played a vital role in the Portuguese domination of the retail trade. Huckstering licences, which had been instituted since the days of slavery, were lowered from fifteen to ten dollars in 1843,[37] thereby facilitating the Portuguese enterprise by virtue of the fact that funds which would otherwise have been used to purchase goods could, in the event of such goods being procured on credit, be channelled towards the purchase of these licences. Thus although the licences were lowered they still remained high enough to hinder Creole participation as the latter had no credit facilities. Similarly, shop licences which stood at twenty dollars in 1850[38] operated against Creoles[39] for the same reasons. The Portuguese themselves recognized the hindrances to Creole competition occasioned by this licensing system, and during the Civil List dispute of 1848–1849 when no taxes were voted, they actually petitioned the government for the reimposition of these licences.[40]

Any system of licensing of the retail trade was bound to militate against Creole involvement and in favour of those immigrants who could escape the contractual obligations of plantation labour. Immigrants to the colony came with the prime objective of accumulating enough savings in the shortest possible time in order to return home in relative comfort.[41] As mainly single individuals, they could hoard their earnings and invest in the retail trade. The Creoles, on the other hand, with wives and families to maintain, could not save to the extent of the immigrants.[42] In addition, as 'birds of passage' with a transient outlook, the Portuguese's main concern was to extract as much wealth as possible from the colony in a relatively short period of time. The retail trade as a service industry, fitted their extractive or profit orientation far more than investment in the soil as farmers. On the other hand, the Creoles knew no other home than the colony, and having just been released from servitude, their primary orientation was towards investment in the land and to establish a permanent stake in a country where they had toiled so unremittently for generations. Having expended all their savings on the purchase of land and property after emancipation, there was little left to buy licences and goods for sale. If an open retail trade were to be fostered, that enterprise should have been free from taxation, the deficit in revenue being made up by taxes on plantation supplies and produce, which were exempt from taxation.

With such advantages, natural and artificial, the Portuguese were soon able to close the inefficient and expensive forms of the old internal trade,[43] and to out-compete the Creoles. By March 1842, there were 139 new shops in Georgetown, 42 of which were owned by Portuguese, and others partly so.[44] Likewise, in the rural areas, Portuguese could be seen in many districts, along the roads, in the villages, and up the rivers, literally bringing goods to every door.[45] Shops which were found unprofitable to operate by Creoles were rented or purchased by Portuguese whose activity at once seemed to attract customers.[46] In 1843 alone, one shop in Essequibo realized a net profit of £1,000, essentially through sales to the black labouring classes.[47] In June 1843, 91 Portuguese left for Madeira with large sums of money to invest there.[48] The retail trade rapidly became a Portuguese stronghold,[49] and by 1844 they were effectively driving the Creoles hucksters out of the market.[50]

By the 1850s, the Portuguese had established firm control over the retail trade, and later even began to oust the English merchants in Water Street.[51] Indeed, by 1856, they were thought to occupy nearly as high a position as any European, and many were probably in a more secure and substantial financial position than most Europeans.[52] Portuguese shops could be found at almost every corner in Georgetown.[53] The vast majority of shops and stores, drug stores and butcher shops were Portuguese owned; and so were the vast majority of hucksters both in the city and the rural districts.[54] Similarly, they predominated in other licensed occupations — owning the best carts and cheapest cabs and carriages for hire, and fitting up their boats as shops which plied up and down the rivers, calling at every hamlet.[55] In some cases, one individual owned or had a share in three or four shops in the city and perhaps more in the countryside.[56]

The virtual monopoly of the Portuguese in the retail trade meant that by the 1860s their position was so unchallengeable that they could fix the prices of goods unilaterally either for profit or to keep out competitors. *The Creole* newspaper asserted that they had established a sort of private Exchange where they met and fixed the prices and uniform quantities of goods to be sold. This system operated both in town and country, being further facilitated by the ownership of more than one shop by some.[57] So strong were they that in 1867 they even dared to combine to deal with any wholesale merchant who refused to give them three months' credit instead of six weeks'.[58]

From the 1850s onwards, therefore, the Portuguese monopoly of the retail trade was more or less complete. This provided that firm economic base which was necessary to underpin their social role as buffers between white and black. In short, their middleman economic role corresponded to their middle class social role. Their socio-economic elevation above the broad mass of the labouring population, both native and immigrant, was a *fait accompli* by the mid–1850s. But although some Portuguese became so rich as to present a challenge to the social exclusivism of the dominant white classes, they were still as a group dependent on the white (British) wholesale importers for the bulk of their supplies, as well as being clearly differentiated from the ruling whites culturally and in national allegiance. For as late as 1890, the generality of Portuguese resident in the colony had not been naturalized as British subjects, but remained subjects of the Portuguese Crown;[59] and as aliens they continued to be excluded from the representation in the legislative institutions of the colony,[60] even though they could vote when qualified for members of those institutions, had free ingress and egress to and from the colony, could move freely within it,[61] could serve on juries, own landed property and devise it, and could own British ships.[62]

However, their control and conduct of the very retail trade which underlined their middle class status in the society attracted to them as a class the animosity of the labouring classes, particularly the Creole element. Portuguese retailing practices caused considerable hardship on the labouring

classes. Their virtual monopoly position enabled them to mark up the prices of goods, which together with the government duties rendered the cost of living exorbitantly high. The bitt or eight cents (four pence sterling) was used most extensively in measuring the value of articles. For instance, in 1862, one bitt was the price of one pint of rice, one pound of flour (two pints), one pound of salt fish, one pound of biscuits, and half a pound of pork.[63] Many retailers refused to sell anything in quantities smaller than half a bitt (two pence) and many articles in no less than a bitt's worth.[64] Consequently, the half-bitt tended to be the smallest coin in circulation, the next being the bitt. The smallest increase in prices was thus never less than four cents (two pence).[65] This meant that the copper cent was only a denomination of account and not practically a coin,[66] perhaps because it had no intrinsic value of its own. In short, the ordinary labourer was deprived of the use of copper coinage; and some retailers further refused to sell certain articles unless the purchaser chose to buy others with them.[67]

Quite apart from this, the mark-up on prices of essentials were exorbitant. For instance, in 1862, yellow rice which cost three cents per pound wholesale (inclusive of duty of a quarter cent) was sold for eight cents (one bitt) per pint of about fourteen ounces. Likewise, the prices of salt fish and flour were five cents per pound wholesale and eight cents retail; while pork was ten and a half cents and sixteen cents per pound respectively. The profit of the retailer was, therefore, 60% on these latter articles, and as high as 166% on rice.[68]

Notwithstanding such great profits, some Portuguese retailers exacerbated ill-feelings towards them as a group by blatantly fraudulent practices. 'There is hardly a district where the inhabitants get full measure and eight for their money.'. Dishonest trading took interesting forms. By the use of lead in the scale customers got short weights.[69] False weights were also used. In a few cases, the two-ounce weight was noted to be as light as half an ounce. Naturally, the labouring classes were most affected, being purchasers of small amounts of goods: 'for scarcely a cases is brought before the Stipendiary Magistrates in which the smaller weights are not proved to be more unjust than the larger'.[70] Retailers also used false-bottom measures for selling rice and other goods. In one case, this enabled the rogue to cheat customers of about one-fifth of their due on every transaction.[71] Such malpractices continued unabated despite many convictions in court. In one swoop on the West Bank of Demerara in March 1875, for instance, 28 Portuguese shopkeepers were fined between ten and twenty dollars for such practices.[72] Of course, these retailers probably made far in excess of such fines in their 'dealings'.

It is not surprising that in a society in which white aliens were facilitated to occupy a privileged socio-economic status in preference to the large majority of the black and coloured labouring classes, and to exploit the latter on a day to day basis, they (the Portuguese) should have aroused the animosity of the Creoles which on occasion burst forth into open hostilities. To the Creoles, the Portuguese were of alien status, different in race and colour, language, religion and customs. They were like 'oil in water; among us, but not of us'.[73] Having originally been introduced to do the sort of work which the Creoles regarded as degrading they were considered inferior — white trash.[74] They were viewed as enemies more than as rivals, despised and taunted with the appellation of 'white nigger'.[75]

More important, however, the Creoles were aware that the whites favoured the Portuguese. The whites persistently asserted that 'the Negro lacks the industry, the energy, the tact, the self denial, and the perseverance of the European';[76] that 'there is no reason to believe that any of these envious natives would have been in any better circumstances than they are at this day, had no Portuguese ever been introduced'.[77] The Creoles developed a complex of oppression with respect to the Portuguese. 'The Portuguese have come to take over our country'; 'the Portuguese take away all our money'; 'we poor Creoles have no chance'; 'the Governor favours the Portuguese'[78] — such statements were frequently mouthed by the Creoles in expression of their dissatisfaction over the favours accorded to the Portuguese. So disgruntled had they become by the 1850s that some openly began to agitate for 'Black Power' in the colony — ' "Black Ministers, Black shopkeepers, Black Merchants, Black planters," in fact everything Black.'[79]

As a result of such deep-seated racial prejudices on all sides, the ill-feeling generated between these two groups from their first encounters never died out, but slumbered, waiting for opportunities to break out in open violence;[80] and, indeed, anti-Portuguese riots occurred thrice in forty years: 1848 in Berbice, 1856 in Demerara and Essequibo; and 1889 in Georgetown. It is significant that on each occasion the immediate pretext was created by the inefficient and partial conduct of affairs by the white ruling classes, which seemed favourable towards the Portuguese.

In 1848, after two and a half months of a general colony-wide strike against an attempt by the planters to impose a 25% wage reduction, the Creole labourers were forced to return to plantation labour and accept the reduced wages. The Portuguese immigrants had contributed to the failure of the strike in two respects. Those Portuguese who were still working on the plantations broke the strike by refusing to join the Creoles. Simultaneously, the retailers refused to allow credit to the strikers who were earning no wages and maintained prices at a high level. This, combined with the financial crisis of 1847–1849 caused the Creoles considerable hardships. A squeeze on credit led the Creoles, who had saved money in bank notes, to rush to the banks in Georgetown to convert their notes into specie which the banks refused to do. They were thus forced to sell their notes to Portuguese shopkeepers during the strike at 20% below par, only to find a few weeks after that the governor had restored confidence in the banking system by depositing $50,000 in the banks. This combination of factors raised Creole anger to a boiling point as they evidently considered themselves to be victims of the Portuguese retailers who had not been unwilling to exploit the severe economic plight of the Creoles at a time of distress. Indeed, that the 1848 riots should have been confined to St. Clement's parish in Berbice[81] is a rather surprising feature.

The 1856 riots were more commonly attributed to the work of the so-called instigator, John Sayers Orr, alias 'The Angel Gabriel'. He was a coloured man and a skilful orator, albeit with firm anti-Catholic sentiments. His persuasive and skilful oratory had left civil disorders in his wake in Glasgow and Greenock in Britain, and in Boston in the United States. On his return home in December 1855, he took to the streets of Georgetown in a campaign against the Catholics who were mainly Portuguese. These street-corner meetings were largely attended by the black and coloured townsfolk and on Sundays he held his meetings in the front of the Stabroek Market in Georgetown.[82]

Orr skillfully blended his anti-Papism with an assault on the Portuguese retailers whose introduction, he pointed out, had been financed by the Creoles through taxation and who were enriched by exploiting those very Creoles. He stressed that the Portuguese were aliens and should be repatriated to Madeira.[83] Orr's views were technically sound from an economic point of view, especially since the Portuguese were simply extracting wealth from the colony and contributing very little to the development of the economy by means of any permanent investment for production. As such he presented a threat to Portuguese interests which resulted in a threat on his life on February 9th when a group of Portuguese led by an Irish Catholic agitator, John Taggart, gathered to assault him physically.[84]

Orr had presented the Creole population with the first semblance of effective political leadership since emancipation which was evidently interpreted not simply as a confrontation with the Portuguese, but as a potential threat to the white social and political supremacy in the colony, especially in view of Orr's proven ability to mobilize the Creole labouring population. It was thus in the interest of the ruling class to snuff out this potential threat at the earliest moment. Hence, it only required a protest from the Catholic bishop to induce Governor Wodehouse to issue a Proclamation on Friday 15th, forbidding public assemblages, and to arrest Orr for having on the 10th ostensibly incited a crowd by displaying a life preserver and dagger[85] which he understandably needed after the threat on his life the day before.

The predetermination of the ruling whites to remove Orr from the public arena was vividly revealed at his indictment on Monday 18th, when no allusion was made by the Crown Prosecutor to the unlawful threat on his life by the Portuguese. This the Creoles regarded as highly partial administration of justice. Some irritation had already been caused by the Proclamation which had been correctly viewed by the Creoles as an infringement of the right of meeting to prevent their politicization in their best interest. Similarly, it was felt that if Orr had indeed exceeded the law on the 10th, he should have been arrested and dealt with before the Proclamation of the 15th.[86]

The final straw, however, came when bail for Orr was set at £500, plus two sureties at £250 each. When Orr's mother and a respectable black man, both with property, offered themselves as sureties, they were turned down on peculiar legal grounds and Orr was gaoled.[87] The Creoles responded by attacking Portuguese property in Georgetown, and the disorders spread into the countryside of Demerara, into Essequibo and to the West Coast of Berbice.[88] Even those Creoles who defended the Portuguese and their property from the rioters sympathized with the latter, hoping that the violence would occasion the exodus of the Portuguese from the colony.[89] In these riots, the Portuguese lost property to the extent of $267,204.[90]

Similar partial mismanagement of justice occasioned the riots of 1889 in Georgetown. On 3 November 1888, Manoel Gonsalves cold-bloodedly shot and killed his coloured paramour, Julia Chase, for alleged infidelity and was sentenced to death by the Chief Justice.[91] This trial had aroused keen interest among all sections of society since only one Portuguese had been executed for murder in previous years.[92] It was essentially a test case, it being commonly believed that Portuguese would not be hanged since they were white. Indeed established precedent in murder cases involving black and white seemed to suggest that black life was not valued in law.[93] As if to prove the validity of this notion, Gonsalves' sentence was commuted on a petition for mercy to the Governor by the Jury.[94]

This commutation revived Creole hatred for the Portuguese in all its pristine bitterness. From the day Gonsalves had killed Chase, the common cry was that the Portuguese would not be hanged -the Governor would let him off; and as Portuguese could kill black people without being hanged, other steps would have to be taken to protect the blacks.[95] The Creoles stated that 'a Portuguese can buy his life, while the black man and the coolie [Indian immigrant] are hanged'; for there was reason to believe that Gonsalves' reprieve had been bought.[96] A Portuguese newspaper, published in Lisbon and circulated in the colony, had printed two supposed telegrams from the Portuguese King to the British Queen and a reply on the subject. And the Portuguese went about boasting that 'Our King will not allow any of his subjects to be hanged'.[97]

It only required a spark to set off a conflagration; and this was provided on 19 March 1889 in the Stabroek Market when a black boy took a penny loaf from a Portuguese stall instead of a cent loaf for which he had paid, and was beaten into a state of unconsciousness by the Portuguese attendant. It was alleged that the Clerk of Market ordered the release of the attendant saying: 'Loose the Portuguese and throw the damn nigger on the street'. This was said to have infuriated the black crowd which had gathered and the news circulated that the unconscious boy had in fact been killed. What thus seemed like another incident of a Portuguese taking the life of a black served as the immediate pretext for the 1889 riots in Georgetown.[98] In these riots the Portuguese lost property to the extent of $39,459.[99]

The peculiar 'middleman' status held by the Portuguese in the racially segmented society of post-emancipation British Guiana rendered them the most vulnerable section of the population. Caught 'betwixt the earthy grovelling of the more uncultured races and the heavenly exaltation of the other Europeans',[100] they were differentiated from the latter by their Lusitanian culture and language, and despised by the former on account of their race, social elevation, and economic status and wealth. Moreover, they remained in a sense marginal to the entire host society by the retention of their Portuguese citizenship and by their disinclination to identify themselves as permanent residents of the colony.

Their introduction, which was originally occasioned partially by the economic demands of the plantation to alleviate the labour problem created by the emancipation of the slaves, assumed an increasingly social character to meet the demands of the white dominated plantation civilization in the colony. It was white racial considerations which pointed to the need to augment the white population in the colony to offset the social effects of the freedom of the blacks. It was the concept of race which determined that the Portuguese should be facilitated to occupy a middle class or buffer social status between the dominant whites and the subordinate blacks. It was the pull effect of racial affinity which motivated the dominant whites to favour the Portuguese accession to a position of monopoly in the retail trade in order to underline the social middle role which it was desired that they should play. For white racial supremacy was considered essential for the preservation of the plantation economy and white civilization in the colony, and even for the maintenance of the colony connection itself. The Portuguese contributed to this not so much as plantation labourers, but as a vital numerical buttress to the white population and by their effective closure of a lucrative alternative economic enterprise to the black labouring classes, whom it was reckoned would be forced to remain dependent on the plantations and so under the complete surveillance and control of the dominant whites.

Portuguese immigration was thus a most conservative feature in the social objectives of the ruling classes after emancipation. It was designed to foster and bolster white social supremacy and to nullify some of the social effects likely to accrue to the freed slaves in the post-slavery situation. Hence, it tended to facilitate the effective subjugation of the black majority and help to reduce them to a state of social degradation and persistent economic poverty. Equally important, however, was the fact that as a buffer group in society, the Portuguese had to bear the brunt of anti-white animosity generated among the Creoles. Their middle role, determined as it was by race, thus fulfilled two main functions: first, to erect a physical human barrier to protect the dominant whites from the mass of the black population — which emphasized the importance of their numerical position; and secondly, to foreclose to the Creoles the most lucrative economic alternative, thereby preventing any effective challenge by the latter to the social supremacy of the dominant white minority, while effectively reducing the Creoles to chronic socio-economic degradation. In both cases, it was the interests of the plantation civilization which dictated the social role of the Portuguese immigrant community in the segmented society of post-emancipation British Guiana.

Notes

The following abbreviations are used:

C.O.	Great Britain, Colonial Office Papers
Encl.	Enclosure
L.M.S.	London Missionary Society. Papers relative to (Bce) Berbice, and (Dem) Demerara
M.M.S.	[Wesleyan] Methodist Missionary Society
Ord. No.	Ordinance Number . . .
S.J./B.G.	Society of Jesus (English Province). Papers relative to British Guiana
S.M.	Stipendiary Magistrate
P.P.	Great Britain, Parliamentary Papers

Dates are recorded thus: Day/Month/Year.

1. P.P. 1873. L.1: Returns of Immigrants; C.O. 116: Blue Books of Statistics.
2. M.F. Milliroux, *Demerara: The Transition from Slavery to Liberty* (Paris, 1843; Translated edition London, 1877), p. 18.
3. K.O. Laurence, *Immigration into the West Indies in the 19th Century* (Barbados, 1971), pp. 9–10.
4. C.O. 111/235: No. 180, Light to Grey, 3/9/1846.
5. C.O. 111/316: No. 69, Wodehouse to Labouchere, 6/6/1857.
6. C.O. 318/215: No. 7294, Rogers to Merivale, 8/8/1857.
7. K.O. Laurence, 'The Establishment of the Portuguese Community in British Guiana', *Jamaica Historical Review* 5, No. 2 (1965): 65.
8. P.P. 1851. XXXIX.1 No. 75/26, Barkly to Grey, 11/3/1851; C.O. 318/190: No. 4251, Emigration Commissioners to Merivale, 19/5/1851.
9. C.O. 111/291: No. 146, Barkly to Pakington, 22/9/1852.
10. C.O. 111/324: No. 63, Wodehouse to Lytton, 18/5/1859, Encl. (See Ordinance No. 13 of 1853 by which one year contracts were instituted).
11. C.O. 111/316: No. 69, *supra cit.*. A sum of $35,000 was voted for encouraging Portuguese immigration in 1857.
12. C.O. 111/324: No. 63, *supra cit.*.
13. A. Adamson, *Sugar Without Slaves: The Political Economy of British Guiana, 1838–1904* (New Haven, 1972), pp. 43–44.
14. P.P. 1847. XXXIX.15: Returns of Free Immigrants to British Guiana.
15. C.O. 111/183: No. 157, Light to Stanley, 22/11/1841, Encl. 4.
16. Adamson, *loc. cit.* (note 13).
17. C.O. 111/379: 1870 Commission of Inquiry into the Treatment of Immigrants in British Guiana, Section 4.
18. P.P. 1847. XXXIX.115: No. 9/158, Light to Gladstone, 3/8/1848, Encl..
19. K.O. Laurence, *op. cit.* (note 7).
20. Ibid..
21. P.P. 1847–48. XXIII. Pt. III.1: No. 3/20, Light to Grey, 11/1/1848.
22. C.O. 111/294: No. 69, Barkly to Newcastle, 22/4/1853, Encl.
23. C.O. 111/301: No. 41, Wodehouse to Grey, 21/7/1854, Encl.
24. P.P. 1847. XXXIX.115: No. 9/158, *supra cit.*.
25. C.O. 111/244: No. 150, Light to Grey, 16/7/1847, Encl.
26. C.O. 111/250: No. 10, Light to Grey, 11/1/1848, Encl.
27. C.O. 111/275: No. 147, Barkly to Grey, 16/10/1850, Encl.
28. C.O. 116: Blue Books of Statistics-Censuses, 1851–1891.
29. P.P. 1847–48. XXIII. Pt. I.395: No. 5/150, Light to Grey, 16/7/1847.

30. K.O. Laurence, *op. cit.* (note 7), pp. 54–55.
31. C.O. 111/227: No. 70, Light to Stanley, 7/4/1845. Encl.
32. C.O. 111/222: Separate, Light to Stanley, 8/4/1845.
33. C.O. 111/208: No. 31, Light to Stanley, 10/2/1844, Encl., Report of Stipendiary Magistrate J. Macleod.
34. C.O. 111/224: No. 174, Light to Stanley, 2/8/1845, Encl., (S.M.) Britain.
35. *Royal Gazette,* 30/10/1843.
36. C.O. 111/212: No. 183, Light to Stanley, 28/8/1844, Encl., (S.M.) Carbery.
37. C.O. 111/227: No. 173, Barkly to Grey, 31/12/1850.
38. Ibid.
39. *Colonist,* III (373), 26/2/1851: Governor Barkly's speech in the Court of Policy.
40. C.O. 111/227: No. 173, *supra cit..*
41. R. Schomburgk, *Travels in British Guiana, 1840–44* (Translated by W.E. Roth; Georgetown, 1922), p. 25.
42. *Creole,* 1 (2), 29/11/1856.
43. *Royal Gazette,* XLVIII (7375), 19/5/1853.
44. C.O. 111/190: No. 97, Light to Stanley, 31/5/1842.
45. C.O. 111/222: Separate, *supra cit..*
46. C.O. 111/224: No. 174, Light to Stanley, 2/8/1845, Encl., Report of E. Carbery (S.M.).
47. C.O. 111/212: No. 183, Light to Stanley, 28/8/1844, Encl., (S.M.) Carbery.
48. C.O. 111/201: No. 83, Light to Stanley, 10/6/1843.
49. C.O. 111/227: No. 1/248, Light to Stanley, 30/11/1844.
50. C.O. 111/208: No. 31, Light to Stanley, 10/2/1844, Encl., (S.M.) Macleod.
51. S.J./B.G. 12: Sherlock to Barrow, 25/5/1858.
52. L.M.S. 8a/2 (Dem): Rattray to Tidman, 25/2/1856.
53. A. Trollope, *The West Indies and the Spanish Main* (London, 1859), p. 189.
54. C.O. 115: Official Gazettes — half-yearly lists of licenses.
55. J. Jones, Mission of British Guiana, *Letters and Notices* (Society of Jesus), vol. 1, 1862.
56. *Creole,* V. (333), 12/5/1860.
57. *Creole,* 12/5/1860; 16/4/1862.
58. *Colonist,* V (829), New Series, 19/6/1867.
59. C.O. 111/455: No. 4, Gormanston to Knutsford, 3/1/1890.
60. C.O. 113/8: Ord. No. 1 of 1891.
61. C.O. 111/226: No. 243, Light to Stanley, 28/11/1845.
62. *Creole,* II (74), 25/11/1857.
63. C.O. 111/334: No. 50, Hincks to Newcastle, 5/5/1862.
64. A. Adamson, 'Monoculture and Village Decay in British Guiana', *Journal of Social History,* 3, No. 4 (1970): 395.
65. L.M.S. 8/2 (Bce): Foreman to Tidman, 24/9/1858.
66. C.O. 111/334: Minute of H. Taylor, 6/5/1862 [appended to No. 50].
67. A. Adamson, 'Monoculture', *op. cit.* (note 64).
68. C.O. 111/334: No. 50, *supra cit.; Colonist,* 2/4/1862.
69. *Daily Chronicle,* 4147, New Series, 27/2/1889.
70. *Royal Gazette,* LXX (18066), New Series, 27/3/1875.
71. *Coloniest,* 25/8/1875; *Daily Chronicle,* 21/3/1885.
72. *Royal Gazette,* 27/3/1875; *Colonist,* 2/3/1975.
73. L.M.S. 8a/2 (Dem): Scott to Tidman, 19/5/1856.
74. B. Premium, *Eight Years in British Guiana* (London, 1850), pp. 191–92.
75. H. Bronkhurst, *The Colony of British Guiana and Its Labouring Inhabitants* (London, 1883).
76. M.M.S./W. iv/5: No. 363, Hudson to General Secretaries, 24/2/1856.
77. L.M.S. 8a/2 (Dem): Rattray to Tidman, 25/2/1856.
78. L.M.S. 8a/2 (Dem): Wallbridge to Tidman, 23/2/1856.
79. M.M.S./W. iv/5: No. 363, *supra cit..*
80. H. Kirke, *Twenty-five Years in British Guiana* (London, 1898), p. 202.
81. C.O. 111/252: No. 60, Light to Grey, 4/4/1848. and Encl..
82. P.P. 1856. XLIV.9: No. 1/16, Wodehouse to Labouchere, 24/2/1856; L.M.S. 8a/2 (Dem): Wallbridge to Tidman, 23/2/1856.
83. P.P. 1856. XLIV.9: No. 5/57, Wodehouse to Labouchere, 9/5/1846, Encl. 3.
84. L.M.S. 8a/2 (Dem): Wallbridge, *supra cit..*
85. P.P. 1856. XLIV.9: No. 1/16, *supra cit..*
86. L.M.S. 8a/2 (Dem): Wallbridge, *supra cit..*
87. Ibid.
88. C.O. 111/310: No. 16, Wodehouse to Labouchere, 24/2/1866; *Royal Gazette,* 21/2/1856; 23/2/1856.
89. L.M.S. 8a/2 (Dem): Scott to Tidman, 19/5/1856.
90. C.O. 111/312: No. 115, Wodehouse to Labouchere, 6/9/1856, sub. encl.
91. *Argosy,* 2/2/1889; *Daily Chronicle,* 31/1/1889.
92. C.O. 111/451: Confidential, Bruce to Knutsford, 1/3/1889.
93. C.O. 111/451: No. 66, Bruce to Knutsford, 9/2/1889.
94. Ibid.: Encl. A in No. 66.
95. *Argosy,* 17 (443), 23/3/1889.
96. C.O. 111/451: No. 109, Gormanston to Knutsford, 29/3/1889; *Echo,* 23/3/1889; *Argosy,* 23/3/1889.
97. C.O. 111/451: Confidential, Gormanston to Knutsford, 29/3/1889; *Echo,* 23/3/1889; *Argosy,* 23/3/1889.
98. *Argosy,* 23/3/1889; C.O. 111/451: No. 111, Gormanston to Knutsford, 30/3/1889; *Daily Chronicle,* 20/3/1889; *Echo,* 23/3/1889.
99. C.O. 111/453: No. 296, Gormanston to Knutsford, 16/8/1889, Encl.
100. J. Heatley, *A Visit to the West Indies* (London, 1891), p. 42.

Immigration and Indentureship in the French West Indies, 1848–1870

Rosamunde Renard

Between 1852 and 1859, approximately 6,126 African immigrants were introduced into Guadeloupe, and 10,658 into Martinique. By 1884, when Indian immigration was abolished, about 41,828 Indians had been introduced into Guadeloupe, and 25,509 into Martinique. Operating under the auspices of the British government, the French planters' demand for Indian immigrants, even more than that of the planters in the British West Indies, was never satisfied. Yet, immigration played an essential role in the recovery of the sugar industry after 1852, although it could not alone have prevented the collapse of this industry in 1882. For the Indians, however, plantation life was rigorous, especially during the Second Empire when, in accordance with this regime's general policy of the necessity of labour for the principal export industry, planter abuses of the immigrants and the immigration laws were left almost entirely unchecked.

Among the first immigrant workers introduced in Guadeloupe were those brought from the British West Indies. Approximately one hundred and fifty immigrant workers from the British islands, eighty of whom were of Madeiran stock, and the rest black, arrived in this colony on 10 November 1848.[1] Black immigrant workers originating from the British West Indies were estimated in November of the same year, as representing two thirds of the four hundred immigrants in the island — in other words, about two hundred and sixty-six individuals.[2]

This immigration attempt was, however, a miserable failure. Governor Fiéron suggested, somewhat uncertainly, that it would be necessary to place some restrictions on the importation of these labourers, although he did not state his reasons for arriving at this conclusion. Fiéron was, however, unwilling to take this step immediately. As far as the Controleur Colonial was concerned, there could be no equivocation on the matter. The British West Indian immigrants were:

Bad subjects for the most part, who with inveterate habits of laziness, not being able to provide for their existence in the neighbouring islands, profited from the occasion which was presented to them to go and carry elsewhere their wretchedness and vices.[3]

The Controleur was fearful that these immigrants would prove bad examples to the native labourers.[4] No documents indicate that Martinique had received any of these immigrants.

European immigration was the next to be attempted. Following on a ministerial dispatch on European immigration to the colonies, the Governor-General of Martinique allocated a fund of 100,000 francs 'to facilitate European immigration to the colonies'.[5] The government was prepared to support European immigration to the sum of 250 francs per adult and 150 francs per child.

The first reports from Guadeloupe about this immigration were promising. The Governor noted:

The intelligent and active work of these newcomers has been a happy example for the cultivators of several neighbouring plantations, not wishing to remain behind in what the foreigners could do . . . .[6]

Yet, shortly after, it was generally acknowledged in both colonies that this immigration had also failed miserably. In Guadeloupe, Governor Fiéron denounced the Europeans as 'weakly, overworked, and beaten up'.[7] He noted that they succumbed easily to various diseases and stated that the planters did not consider them suitable workers for cane production. One year later, Governor Aubry-Bailleul commented on the difficulties that these workers faced, noting that there had been many deaths among them, through a drought which had been followed by a shortage in food supply. These workers, he stated, were 'eagerly soliciting their repatriation'.[8]

Likewise, in Martinique, Governor-General Bruat claimed that 300 Madeirans and 190 to 200 Europeans from France had been imported. Apparently, all the Madeirans, sick, covered with sores, and begging on the streets, had abandoned work after a few months. Bruat, however, did not refer to the death rate among these immigrants, although he did point out that it was necessary to treat and repatriate the sick ones. Of European immigration he said:

European immigration to which all the planters were so enthusiastically attached after emancipation, now encounters only doubt and apprehension . . . .[9]

Yet, the planters reckoned, these initial immigration attempts had two positive results — bringing the native workers back to the plantations and driving the wages down. Although these particular efforts had failed, it was unanimously agreed that the policy of immigration, for these two reasons alone, should be encouraged. For, 'the renewal of the same means, whatever the origins, will lead to the same precious result'.[10]

There was, in fact, no initial rush on the part of the planters in either colony for Indian immigration. On the contrary, they evinced extreme caution, having just recently outlayed expenditure on disastrous immigration escapades at a point when they could least afford it. In Martinique, only a few large proprietors (Assier, Pécoul, Clerc and Hervé) undertook to receive a shipload, recruited under governmental supervision, of 350 Indians.[11] Attempts by these planters to get other proprietors to support the operational costs were only met by 'evasive responses, without any direct engagements'.[12]

It must be stressed that in their recruitment of immigrants on Indian soil the French were operating in an area which was dominated by the British. Up to 1861, the commercial houses of Pondichery and after 1856, the Emigration Society of this town were the suppliers of the different French agents. This was not a situation conducive to pleasing the French who complained that priority was always given to the British recruiters, that they always got an inferior quality of immigrants and, moreover, that their demand was always by far greater than the supply. The Immigration Commission of Guadeloupe reported that the General Maritime Company had on 26 October 1854 and 13 January 1855 concluded a contract with the colonies of Martinique and Guadeloupe for the introduction of 10,000 Indian immigrants in the former colony and 5,000 in the latter. By 1 January 1859, the date of termination of the contract only about half of the immigrants had been delivered.[13] On 4 March 1858 there was a demand for 10,332 Indian immigrants in Guadeloupe and only 1,411 were received that year.[14] Similarly, in Martinique, there was a demand for 7,570 Indian immigrants on 26 February 1857. That year only 1,534 Indians were imported into the island.[15] Nor did passing time

improve the ratio of supply to demand. In 1863 Governor Frébault of Guadeloupe pointed out the difficulty of recruiting Indians, noting that only a third of the immigrants asked for, had been received that year.[16]

From Singaravélou, we learn that between 1854 and 1873 the two main ports of recruitment in India for Guadeloupe and Martinique were Pondichery and Karikal, after which Calcutta was included. Before the 1861 Franco/English convention, the area of the recruiting agents was wider than in the subsequent period going beyond the present state of Madras to cover part of the present Central Provinces, Bihar and Hyderabad. The recruiting agents recruited wherever they could find immigrants. The 1861 convention however limited the terrain of the recruiters to the districts of Salem, Arcot du Sud, the provinces of Madourai and Tinnevely, and the districts of Tritchinopoly and Tanjore. The areas of recruitment were of course subject to variations as, for example, in the year 1867 when famine in the Bengal region veered recruitment to this area.[17]

French agents charged with the actual transportation of the Indian immigrants to Guadeloupe and Martinique changed. Auguste Blanc, who had been charged with recruiting for these colonies at the price of 250 francs per adult immigrant, was replaced by le Campion and Théroulde, by the General Maritime Company, by the General Transatlantic Company and by the House of Peultvé, Petit-Didier and Co. The terms of the contracts with the different agents did not vary considerably although there were significant minor changes as, for example, in Louis Blanc's contract, the insistence of a one-sixth woman contingent among the immigrants (article one) as compared to a one-eight minimum contingent by the General Maritime Company.

Immense problems surround the identification of the precise areas of origin of the Indian immigrants introduced into Martinique and Guadeloupe. Suffice it to note here that Singaravélou asserted that for Guadeloupe, the immigrants took their origin from the South-East of Tamoul country and the centre of the Indo-gangetic plain.[18] This conclusion was based on inadequate evidence and there is a definite need for more research in this area.[19] More adequately documented was the background of the Indians in terms of their professions and their castes. The majority of the immigrants in both colonies hailed from the agricultural profession.

They belonged to varying socio-professional milieus, but agricultural workers from 'inferior castes' were the most numerous.[20]

The Second Empire heavily subsidized immigration costs. Indian immigration was seen as one vital part of the desired recovery of the French West Indian economy. The preamble to an 1852 decree, establishing a contract between Louis Blanc and the French government, set out government's policy clearly:

Considering that it is the government's duty to encourage all seriously conceived efforts, which aim to augment the agricultural population and to ameliorate the conditions of work in the colonies, the fortunate results obtained from the introduction of Asiatic workers in the island of Réunion render desirable recruitment to the American colonies . . .[21]

Without government subsidies and aid, it is unlikely that Indian immigration would have got underway. The wealthier planters would have secured all the benefits of this system, as they did during the initial years of Indian immigration. This problem was particularly serious in Guadeloupe where the financial position of the planters was much more precarious.

The planters were aided by the creation of an immigration fund. This body was funded through the combination of an immigration tax of 30 francs per year payable by each planter, together with an initial annual subvention of 200,000 francs by the metropolitan government.[22] The fund was also used to pay the various immigration agents for example. The main function of the fund, however, was to defray the introduction and repatriation cost of the immigrants. In 1859, the Conseil Général of Martinique reported that the colony had benefitted from nearly 2,600,000 francs in subsidies furnished by the state.[23]

The alleviation of the introductory costs per immigrant was tackled in a series of laws which established a system of a down payment by the planter to be complemented by contributions from the immigration fund. The planter later followed up the down payment with two or three interest-free annuities. The cost of the different immigrants varied slightly from decree to decree, but the Chinese were the most expensive immigrants, the Africans second and the Indians the least expensive.[24]

The immigration fund also aided planters desirous of undertaking immigration on a private basis. Article six of a May 1857 decree accorded a sum not exceeding 200 francs per immigrant to any proprietor or 'undertaker' who decided at his own expense and risk, to import foreign workers into the colony.[25] Private immigration, however, never became important in either colony.

The Indian immigrants seemed to have little hesitancy about complaining against planters who did not stick to the contracts agreed upon. An Immigration Commissioner in Guadeloupe reported in 1857 that:

The Indian, more intelligent than the African, knows to claim from his *engagiste* the fulfillment of his contract for all his dues. He proves himself sometimes excessively exigent and does not stop at lies to give weight to his recriminations.[26]

We will not attempt to discuss here whether the higher incidence of complaints on the part of the Indians, as opposed to the Africans, was indicative of the Indians' higher intelligence. Suffice it to note that the Indians did not fail to manifest their discontent when they had any cause to feel that the planters had failed to fulfill the contracts or had abused their privileges.

Most of the Indians' complaints centred on the insufficiency and low quality of food, excessive work and bad treatment by the planters. Before making an official complaint to the immigration agent, they often engineered a strike. In fact, strike action seemed to be quite prevalent among this group while the documents do not allow us to estimate the number of complaints and strike actions orchestrated by the Indian immigrants, if one lists the number of these culled from documents from Guadeloupe between 1856 and 1860 (and these by no means represent the real number since some may have been overlooked, and one would imagine that some of the smaller complaints might not even have been mentioned in the immigrant agents' reports) one can get some idea of the type, if not the frequency, of these complaints.

Complaints were equally prevalent in Martinique. One report noted the desertion of a plantation in Saint-Esprit, proprietor one Déring, by fifteen Indians, recently arrived in the colony, to bear complaint. The report stated that the fifteen Indians were 'perfectly informed about their rights'.[28] In 1856, the Immigration Commissioner in Martinique noted that Indian immigrants imported from Trinidad were fomenting discord among the Indian immigrant population and encouraging the bearing of complaints to the syndics.[29] In 1857 a refusal to work by forty Indians on Plantation Sempré in Lamentin was reported and the Commissioner remarked in March 1859 that numerous complaints had been received of Indians who had deserted the plantations in all the communes of the islands to bear complaint to the capital.[30]

Yet, the possibility of these complaints being, first, even taken into account by the immigration agents and secondly, resulting in any condemnation of the planter, was very small indeed. The Indians came to understand that, in the majority of

Indian Complaints Revolts in Guadeloupe[27]

Year	Plantation	Commune	Type of Complaint	Nos. who Complain	Reason
1856	Bouvier	Baillif	refusal to work	5	Delay in food distribution
1857	Hurel	Moule	" " "	—	overwork
1857	Grand Rivière	Capesterre	" " "	—	food
1857	Lignière	Basse-Terre	" " "	—	food
1857	Bois-Debout	Capesterre	" " "	32	food
1857	Moulin à l'eau	"	beats mestry	—	planter's blows to Indian leaving marks.
1857	Beauvallon	"	—	—	food
1858	—	"	complaints to Pointe-à-Pitre	12	insufficient food. Overwork
1858	Navarre (owner)	"	complaints to Marine	—	food
1859	de Pombiray (owner)	—	"	—	—
1859	Claret	—	complaints to commissioner	—	—
1860	Reizet	—	—	—	food

cases, except when a sympathetic Attorney General happened to be in office (and this occurred only once during the entire period of this study and not during the Second Empire), complaints against the planters were not only a waste of their time, but resulted more often than not in their own harassment. They thus resorted to other means of manifesting their dissatisfaction. The case of Arrandissing and Ragounath gave adequate illustration of how, complaints ignored, the Indians were forced to other expressions of struggle. The Governor who reported this case totally disavowed the claims of these two Indians but did give some detail about the case.

Arrandissing and Ragounath were arrested as deserters and put in the depot in Basse-Terre, one of the two depots existing especially for housing deserters, the other being in Pointe-à-Pitre. They formally refused to return to their employers. Arrandissing, in the course of the trial, declared that he had tried to lodge several complaints against his employer, none of which was listened to. The two Indians also refused to do any work during their stay in the depot and, the Governor reported, responded to the steward and the inspector who were sent for, with insults and threats. Arrandissing and Ragounath were put into a cell, on a diet of flour and water. The day after, Arrandissing set fire to the floor of his cell. The two were

sentenced to five years imprisonment with hard labour.[31]

This practice of incendiarism among the Indian immigrants, convinced of the futility of complaints, began to rise especially after 1860. The Indians were merely following a pattern already set by the black field workers. But whereas the black workers then tended to use arson against a private enemy of their own race and class, the Indians used fire as a means of reprisal against the planters.

In 1861, four Indians who had formerly lodged several complaints against their engagistes — complaints which had come to nothing — burned the bagasse hut, a piece of cane land, and then tried to burn the purifying plant.[32] Out of twenty accused brought before the court, Governor Desmazes reported in 1868, there were 15 Indians, 13 of whom were accused of incendiarism. The reason given by the thirteen for their action as that they had been subjected to bad treatment by their engagistes.[33] In 1869, the Attorney General in Guadeloupe reported that out of 31 accusations for arson, 8 of the charged were creoles and 23 Indians. All of the fires set by the blacks were set for reasons of private vengeance among themselves. With the accused Indians, there was only one incident of private vengeance. The rest were directed against the planters for delay in the payment of salaries, insufficient food and especially for bad treatment.

When one asked them, he noted, why they did not complain to the syndics they all replied that 'The syndics do not listen to you. They are more the friends of the masters than ours . . . .'.[34]

With the Indians, magistrate Corré noted, there seemed to have been one special reason for their crimes — resentment against the planter for insufficient food, no medical care, unpaid wages and so on. This resentment accounted, he continued, for 34 out of every 100 crimes among the Indians. At times, to avoid bitter recriminations by their own particular planter against whom they held a grudge, the Indians set fire to neighbouring plantations. They then delivered themselves willingly up to justice, often remarking that imprisonment in French Guiana was a better alternative to their miserable lot in Guadeloupe or Martinique.[35]

Yet, as widespread as it was, arson never became as prevalent among the Indian immigrants as desertion for example. One principal reason for this was that the planters, frightened at this turn of events, began to impose very stiff penalties on incendiaries. Despite this, incendiarism remained, after 1860, quite significant. Following is a list of only those Indians incendiaries who reached the high courts and were actually condemned.

Guadeloupe[36]

Year	Condemned for Incendiarism
1865	16
1866	20
1867	11
1868	35
1869	28
1870	15
1871	20

Among the Indian immigrants, desertion, defined as an unauthorized absence from the plantation, was, for the most part, a temporary affair which rarely went beyond eight days. After this short period, the Indians, one Commissioner remarked, were caught by an efficient police force.[37] This type of temporary desertion, however, remained frequent. In the first three months of 1862, the Home Affairs Director reported, there had been 37 desertions in Martinique.[38] A valuable and more detailed report, as late as 1884, permits us not only to estimate the number of desertions in Martinique at the end of that year, but, more precisely, the number of desertions per canton.[39]

Evidently, the economic depression in that colony in 1884 must have served to increase the rate of desertion among the Indian immigrants. Nevertheless, even in the period of economic recovery between 1852 and 1870, the work and general liv-

ing conditions of the Indians remained such that they were encouraged to desert the plantations.

Before 1870 and even after this date, this type of temporary desertion did not unduly preoccupy the planters. But they were far more worried about the Indians' escape to the neighbouring islands of Dominica, Antigua, and Saint Lucia. One immigration agent in Guadeloupe reported connivance on the part of the British planters of Antigua whom he said paid an old fisherman from the commune of Anse-Bertrand 60 gourdes per immigrant. This information, he noted, resulted from a letter addressed by the Secretary of the Governor of Antigua to Mr. Bouvier of Port-Louis, the employer of a certain number of deserting immigrants.[41] Another Guadeloupean immigration agent reported, in 1862, the escape of nine Indians to Dominica. All the Indians, he said, carried with them relatively large sums of money that they had obtained by economizing and borrowing from their friends. There was still, he pointed out, a group of 'hirers' who were working in the Baie-Mahault, Abymes and Petit-Bourg regions and inciting the Indians to escape. He believed that the immigrants were taken in fishermen canoes and that they left from the Gosier, Goyave zone.[42]

In Martinique, apparently, such escapes were fewer. One immigration agent, while reporting the escape of two Indians, gave the impression that this was a rare occurrence. He went on to say that:

One need have no fear of the organized desertion of Indian immigrants for these people are not sailors, and to leave the country it is always necessary for them to have foreign help and an organized police could easily arrest such attempts if they happened to become frequent.[43]

In both colonies, the planters seemed to be less concerned at the number of Indian immigrants who actually escaped to the neighbouring British islands, and more at the fact that it was 'setting a bad example' and, that if allowed to go unhindered, it could grow to far wider proportions. Moreover, they were extremely wary of the encouragement given to the Indians by the British West Indian planters. Two planters, Roussel and Cardonet, went to Dominica to search for their immigrants who, even when found, refused to return with them. Neither did their new British West Indian **engagistes** demand that these immigrants return with Cardonet and Roussel.[44]

So serious a view did the French West Indian planters take of this practice of foreign escape that the French Minister of Foreign Affairs wrote a complaint to Her Britannic Majesty. Lord Russel apparently replied to the effect that his government

Indian Deserters in Martinique at the End of 1884[40]

Canton	No. of Plantations Involved	No. of Plantations Involved	No. of Indentured Servants	Deserters on Dec. 31, 1884
Basse-Pointe	29	1,222	94	7
Saint-Pierre	35	966	119	12
Saint-Esprit	32	403	81	20
Trinité	38	949	306	32
Lamentin	25	392	65	16
Diamant	7	158	30	18
Marin	5	56	0	0
Fort-de-France	9	50	9	18
TOTAL	180	4,196	704	13

would take measures to prevent the renewal of such occurrences, but up till then, the immigration agent stated, whatever measures Lord Russel had taken remained without effect.[45]

The Indians remained a population in transit. The majority of them viewed their stay in the colonies as temporary and, as a result, made little effort to integrate themselves into a society with which they felt they had little in common. They were in the colonies not only to escape the miseries and hardships of their own native land, but to save money with which they could return and, possibly, build a better material life for themselves and their families. This factor was, thus, a determinant of their attitudes and behaviour within the colonial society. Although, with passing time, many Indian immigrants decided to make the two islands their home, this decision was certainly not common between 1853 and 1870, and even after. This transience was much more pronounced for the Indian immigrants in Martinique than for those in Guadeloupe, as the following table shows:

Indians Repatriated Between 1853 and 1900[46]

	Total No. of Indians Introduced	Repatriated	% of repatriated of the total pop. introduced
Guadeloupe	41,828	8,902	21.2%
Martinique	25,509	11,951	46%

No definite explanations can be offered here for the higher repatriation figures in Martinique. Certainly, it seemed to have little to do with the fact that the Indian immigrants in that island suffered from greater physical and material hardships than their counterparts in Guadeloupe. The mortality rate of the Indian immigrants in Martinique remained well below that of Guadeloupe for the entire period of Indian immigration. It is evident however, that the greater facilities for repatriation which were offered in Martinique, which even encouraged the Indians to repatriate, was partly responsible for the higher rate of repatriation. Yet, was it also partly because the Indians, with smaller numbers in Martinique, felt their isolation more acutely and, consequently, had less urge to stay in this colony? This question is, pure conjecture, and can by no means be substantiated.

Notes

A.O.M. = Archivo d'outre-mer

1. A.O.M., Guadeloupe C 15 D 155, Governor to the Minister, November 10, 1848.
2. A.O.M., Guadeloupe, C 15 D 155, Deliberations of the *Conseil Privé*, November 13, 1848.
3. A.O.M., Guadeloupe, C 4 D 49, *Controleur Colonial* to Governor, 1848 (precise date indistinguishable).
4. *Ibid.*
5. *Bulletin officiel de la Guadeloupe*, 1849, No. 240.
6. A.O.M., Guadeloupe C 15 D 155, Governor to the Minister, November 10, 1848.
7. A.O.M., Guadeloupe C 4 D 47, Governor to the Minister, December 27, 1850.
8. A.O.M., Guadeloupe C 15 D 155, Governor to the Minister, July 28, 1851.
9. A.O.M., Martinique C 11 D 109, Memoirs of Governor-General Bruat, 1851.
10. A.O.M., Guadeloupe C 15 D 155, Report of the *Conseil Privé*, August 20, 1851.

11. *Conseil Général* Report, Martinique, November 14, 1858.
12. *Ibid.*
13. A.O.M., Guadeloupe C 187 D 1138, Report of the Immigration Commissioner, 1859.
14. *La Gazette Officielle de la Guadeloupe*, March 4, 1858.
15. A.O.M., Martinique C 130 D 1170, Governor's Annual Report to the Minister, 1857.
16. *Le Commercial*, November 23, 1864.
17. See Singaravélou, *Les Indiens de la Guadeloupe*, (Paris, Imprimerie Deniaud, 1975) Chapter on 'Les Origines des travailleurs recrutés en Inde'.
18. See Singaravélou, *Les Indiens de la Guadeloupe*, p. 24.
19. This Singaravélou concluded after scanning 9,251 immigrants embarked from the port of Calcutta during the 1875–76 season, of which only a seventh was actually bound for Guadeloupe. In addition, he used statistics culled by Wood on the origins of 6,384 Indians bound from Calcutta to Trinidad and those of Smith establishing the origin of 9,393 workers in British Guiana to establish the origin of Indian workers bound for Guadeloupe. See Singaravélou, pp. 23 and 24.
20. *Ibid*, p. 36.
21. *Bulletin officiel de la Martinique*, March 27, 1852.
22. *Conseil Général* Report, November 10, 1854 and October 27, 1855.
23. *Conseil Général* Report, December 1, 1859.
24. One decree fixed the price per adult immigrant Indian at 350 francs 55 centimes, of which 318 francs 05 centimes were destined for the company introducing the immigrants and 12 francs 50 for the indentured servant. For the non adult Indian immigrant (boys between 10 and 16 years and girls between 10 and 14 years), the sum of 185 francs of which 172 francs 50 centimes was for the company and 12 francs 50 for the indentured servant. Chinese immigration cost 659 francs 60 centimes per adult and 436 francs 50 per non-adult. The price of African labour was 4   5 francs per adult, 291 francs per non-adult and 48 francs 50 per child. There was a fixed down payment and the rest of the cost was payable in two or three interest free annuities. See *La Gazette Officielle de la Guadeloupe*, March 15, 1859. For definitions of adults (men between 16–36 years and women between 14–30 years), non-adults and children, see A.O.M., Guadeloupe C 187 D 1138, 'Project de révision du Traité du 13 Janvier 1858', Pointe-à-Pitre, February 27, 1858.

25. *Bulletin officiel de la Martinique*, 1858, No. 121.
26. A.O.M., Guadeloupe C 180 D 1116, Immigration Commissioner to the Home Affairs Director, September 10, 1857.
27. A.O.M., Guadeloupe C 180 D 1116 and C 56 D 399. These figures were culled from different documents, sometimes with insufficient information, thus, the blank spaces, represented by a dash.
28. A.O.M., Martinique C 130 D 1170, Commissioner to Home Affairs Director 1856 (date not distinguishable).
29. A.O.M., Martinique C 130 D 1170, Immigration Commissioner to Home Affairs Director, May 11, 1856.
30. *Ibid*, Commissioner to Home Affairs Director, March 10, 1859.
31. A.O.M., Guadeloupe C 56 D 398, Governor to the Minister, August 8, 1883.
32. A.O.M., Guadeloupe C 180 D 1116, Commissioner to Home Affairs Director, November 8, 1861.
33. A.O.M., Guadeloupe C 188 D 1144, Extract of Governor's letter, October 1, 1868.
34. A.O.M., Guadeloupe C 188 D 1144, Attorney General to the Governor, June 10, 1869.
35. Armand Corré, *Crime en pays créole*, (Paris: G. Masson, (ed.) and Lyon A. Storck (ed.), 1859) 2 vols A-G., pp. 138 and 140.
36. A.O.M., Guadeloupe, C 56 D 276, Report *Conseil Général*, November 11, 1878.
37. *Ibid*, C 180 D 1116, Commissioner to the Home Affairs Director, May 4, 1859.
38. A.O.M., Martinique C 130 D 1170, Home Affairs Director's Annual Report, 1860.
39. *Ibid*, C 32 D 276, Home Affairs Director's Annual Report, 1884.
40. A.O.M., Martinique C 32 D 276, 1884.
41. A.O.M., Guadeloupe C 56 D 399, Commission to Home Affairs Director, December 20, 1859.
42. *Ibid*, November 6, 1862.
43. A.O.M., Martinique C 130 D 1170, Commission to Home Affairs Director, October 13, 1858.
44. A.O.M., Guadeloupe, C 188 D 1144, Commissioner to the Home Affairs Director, December 9, 1862.
45. *Ibid*.
46. Figures calculated from lists given by Singaravélou, p. 50 and David, p. 120.

SECTION FIVE
Government, Political Control, and Popular Revolt

With the collapse of slave systems in all places, except Haiti, former slave owners were able to retain control of the state in order to maintain their interest at the expense of the emancipated. They sought, above all, as Augier and Belle show, to prevent the emergence of popular democratizing methods and systems of political organization and praxis. The established order, however, was aggressively challenged politically by blacks and coloureds. The majority of them, however, lacked the vote, and their interests were not well represented in the legislature.

Attempts to weaken the grip of the ruling elite were unremitting. In Trinidad and Guyana authoritarian Crown Colony Government offered limited latitude for 'in house' constitutional politics, and in Barbados, institutional political life remained the preserve of the plantocracy. The French islands continued to be administered as overseas departments of France, and the Spanish islands increasingly came under the economic and political influence of the United States and their local agencies.

Craton examines some of the most well-known instances of popular protest and unrest in the post-slavery period British West Indies — the 1856, 1865, and 1876 revolts in Guiana, Jamaica and Barbados respectively. Protest was not confined to the Afro-Caribbean people; Haraksingh shows that indentured and ex-indentured workers were equally outraged by the repressive terms of their labour in the region and consistently registered their disaffection. He outlines the characteristic features of Indo-Caribbean resistance throughout the period of immigration and indentureship and rejects the stereotype of the docile Indian workers.

These essays, then, when linked to those analyses of the revolts against slavery, and the early twentieth century labour and independence movements, demonstrate that protest has been an enduring feature of the Caribbean peoples as they struggled to free themselves from oppressive regimes.

Before and After 1865

Roy Augier

A bare list of the events which followed the riots at Morant Bay provokes no argument. But whether these events are, or are not, the consequences of that affray, is a matter of debate. We offer the remarks which follow as a contribution to this debate.

If we interpret the events at Stony Gut and at the Court House in Morant Bay correctly as a statement, uttered in blood, about the unjust relations between men who belonged to different economic classes and also to different ethnic groups, then the direct effects of the riots must be sought in the subsequent attitudes of social groups towards one another. That is we have to answer such questions as, to what extent did the riots change the attitudes of blacks, browns and whites towards one another? Did such changes take place in St. Thomas alone, or over the whole island, or nowhere? Did the riots change the conception each ethnic group had of itself? Did it stiffen the spine of the one and make the other more accommodating? How did it affect the relations between planter and labourer? Did it alter the balance of political power between economic classes?

We cannot give satisfactory answers to most of these questions for three reasons. Firstly, we are limited in what we write here by the kind of historical documents we have used. The information we possess does not allow us to discuss the direct consequences of the riots on social attitudes. But we do have enough information to discuss the effect of the riots on politics.

Secondly, to answer questions of the kind which we have instanced, it is not enough to know what social attitudes were after the riots; it is also necessary to know with some precision what they were before that social disturbance. And this we do not know.

Thirdly, two events intervened between the riots and some of their possible consequences. The intrusion into the society of an alien military force which found no riot to suppress but remained to terrorize a part of that society. And following closely, the imposition of political authority from outside.

So although it is possible to sketch answers to some questions, such as the attitudes of employers to labourers, or the attitudes of ethnic groups to one another for the years before and after 1865, and although we know in general what the society was like before 1865, and what it was like afterwards, it remains difficult to assess the direct consequences of the riots on relationships within the society, because the British interposed themselves in ways which were bound to influence the relations of social groups one to another.

If this is so, it is not the riots which make 1865 a watershed in Jamaican history, but the abdication in that year of political authority by the Jamaicans who possessed it. Later, we shall discuss the relationship between the riots and the passing of responsibility for the society over to foreigners. Now we wish to notice that both the riots and the events which followed them were the working out of tendencies already existing in the society. Since the society survived the riots without alteration of its social and economic structures, the history of Jamaica after 1865 may be read as a record of the extent to which these tendencies were assisted or frustrated by crown colony government.

Notice first that crown colony government strengthened a relationship which already existed. This change in the intensity of the relationship between the society in Jamaica and the government of Great Britain had this effect, among others: it made the society as a whole more dependent, less responsible, less self-directing than it had been. But the society in Jamaica had always been a colonial society. That is to say it had always been dependent on a metropolitan society and its government.

To say that the society had always been dependent, is not to say that early in the life of the society, the white settlers wished it so. They appreciated the advantages, particularly the economic advantages, of independence; but they also understood its hazards. Nor, we may be allowed to guess, did the slaves wish it so. Rebellious slaves surely appreciated that the dependent status of the society was a disadvantage to them.

It was a relationship imposed by superior power, and one to which the white settlers accommodated themselves. Within the bounds set by this power, white property-holders made their lives and fortunes. Foreigners were kept at sea and slaves on the estates. The white community was dependent on the imperial power for its trade and its protection. This was the basis of the accommodation: the white community had an exclusive market for its produce and was protected from slaves and foreigners.

The accommodation of inferior to superior power was made palatable by a concession which the white community had risked much to achieve. In matters which concerned exclusively the ordering of their society, they were allowed to be their own masters. In general this meant that taxes were not imposed on them by the English Crown in order to pay its servants in the colony. The white settlers taxed themselves and so would keep the arrogance of the King's servants within some bounds by withholding public money from them. It meant also that they were left to police the slaves and repress the free black and brown inhabitants without English interference. Finally it meant that they could tax themselves for the few services such as roads, forts, harbours and public buildings which they required in common.

As if to make up for the realization that the important decisions governing the life of their society were taken outside of it, the white community vehemently defended the political jurisdiction they had gained, and even sought to encroach upon what the Crown had marked out for itself.

Fighting with governors, complaining to the Crown and Parliament about the condition of trade and repressing the lower orders is not high politics; but it left its mark on the society. It gave the community a political style which survived at least to the nineteen-thirties. Long after emancipation it was the chief substance of our politics. And it gave to succeeding generations the rhetoric of liberty which has in modern times been put to more substantial use. The seriousness with which the whites conducted their limited politics gave them a cohesion which justifies us in describing them as a community. It was of course the politics of a minority, male, white, propertied and Anglican.

For most of the eighteenth century this accommodation was, on balance, to the advantage of the white community. Gradually it became less so. But by then both the sugar economy based on an exclusive market and the social structure erected to support that economy, the slave society, had become to the white community the natural order of the universe. What had begun as a convenience had become a necessity. Sugar and slavery bound them to Great Britain.

But even in Great Britain the natural order changes. In that country critics of the old imperial economy and critics of the slave society that went with it, became sufficiently powerful to abolish both.

Emancipation did not shock the white community into a posture of independence. To adopt such a stance they would have had to embrace the doctrine of social equality of all men. What they chose to do, once they had stopped their trans-Atlantic debate with Great Britain about its invasion of their constitutional rights, was to use their political power to make of emancipation a mere word, without economic and social reality.

They were tempted to play this game because although emancipation had conferred civil rights on all ex-slaves, political rights accrued only to those who possessed property to the value required by the laws then in force. By the eighteen-forties their game had been stopped. But unfortunately for the society it had not been stopped by the ex-slaves swarming over the field. It had been whistled off by Great Britain in its role as referee. The white community had been stopped, the black community had been protected, by the British government using its imperial authority to declare null and void any colonial law which offended it.

The imperial power to review colonial legislation had in the past been used to regulate the relations between the two societies, Jamaica and England; now after emancipation it was being used to regulate the relations between two groups within the Jamaican society, ex-slaves and ex-masters. In the earlier period the superior power of England had been exercised to maintain an economic relationship between Jamaica and herself according to the principles of political economy then in vogue. Now British power was being used to establish social relations between ex-slaves and ex-masters according to such humanitarian principles as survived political expediency.

But although British power was now informed by different principles and used for different ends, its exercise served to reinforce the state of dependence of the society. Emancipation brought the blacks into a relationship with the British government which was analogous to the one which the whites had long had.

The society then was comprised of two communities living cheek by jowl; one white, rich and small in number; the other black, poor and numerous; dependent each in its way on an outside power for protection against the other. The whites were protected against the physical force derived from numbers and the blacks protected against the physical force derived from wealth and political power. This arrangement was on balance to the disadvantage of the black poor.

It is difficult for an outside power to protect the poor effectively, while the rich are allowed to exercise political power over them. Moreover, the presence of the alien power denies the poor their one advantage. For if they resort to force, it is unlikely that they will do so in the full strength of their numbers; and in the circumstances, inadequately armed, they can be speedily curbed. It needed more concern for the society, greater moral stamina than the British power was able to summon, to protect the poor effectively from the rich.

The machine of British imperial administration could, and for the most part after emancipation, did prevent the white community from using the law to fasten the blacks to the plantation; but that machine was ill-designed to promote the interest of the black community in more positive ways. Why did not the black community exert itself to correct this imbalance in the society?

We noticed earlier white accommodation to English superior power and its effect on that community and the whole society. Now we notice black accommodation to local white superior power. To discuss those who accommodated is not to deny the existence, or the importance, of the rebellious, the suicide and the saboteur. It is only to discuss the majority: and it is also to discuss less than extreme attitudes. We do not wish to make Uncle-Toms of the majority of the slaves, but wish to notice the existence of patters of behaviour, simulated at first, but later becoming ingrained, becoming authentic elements in the personality.

The blacks lived in a society which was composed of a congeries of petty domains, the plantations and pens. But these were not merely forms of economic organization, not merely farms and mills for producing sugar. They were also to some extent isolated, self sufficient social and cultural systems. Within their confines the authority of the master was hardly trammelled by law. Beyond its gates all depended on the whim of the master and on the whim of those appointed to authority by his grace. The kick and the caress were equally arbitrary. This was the system of authority that a slave lived with, frequently imitated, and transmitted to his children.

It was on the plantation too that the slave was de-tribalized and slowly made into a creole. Into this creole culture his children were born. Later in the history of the society, if they lived on a plantation which permitted missionaries to instruct and baptize slaves, they could become Christians. But of necessity Christian instruction concentrated on redemption, love, obedience. It was the price missionaries paid for being allowed beyond the gates of the plantation.

It was not merely that the predominant values transmitted by the plantation to the slave reinforced the subordination to power inherent in his status. Men can and do reject some of the values of a social system not organized for their benefit. But, more important: conduct appropriate to a free society is a social habit, an art which can only be learned in a society which is engaged in the never ending process of helping all its members make themselves free men. There was hardly opportunity for black or white to learn so to conduct themselves before emancipation.

It is therefore no surprise that the black population did not seek power through political means to redress the imbalance in the society. It is more surprising that they did not attempt to do so by force. Riots there were; but when one considers the bitterness engendered during the period of apprenticeship, and the economic deprivation and injustice suffered afterwards, surprisingly few riots occurred. Explanations which refer to the geography of the island and to habits learnt during slavery do not seem adequate. Taken by themselves they are not. But add to them the freedom to starve, guaranteed by the British government after the apprenticeship period, and we may have a clue to the absence of widespread violence and agitation. The blacks did not seek to change the political system because so many of them could ignore it. And of those who could not ignore it? Did they cling to some belief that the Missus Queen would protect them from the worst?

Emancipation was carried by votes, instead of being seized after bloodshed. The British thus had an opportunity to try to arrange its terms in ways which would have set the two communities to learning to live as free men from the date of the establishment of a legally free society. This opportunity was neglected. The society was reconstituted by the will of the British. But for the work to be solidly founded, it needed close and sympathetic supervision. That the British could have done, though they were not fit to do more than that. They were themselves only just beginning to learn how to run a free society. Their disgust with slavery had allowed the ground to be cleared. But although they appropriated the office of supervisor of the society in 1833, it was some time before they worked out what functions they were willing to perform.

The British policy of intervention in the domestic affairs of the society had been adopted reluctantly. It was the only way to end slavery peacefully. The policy was justified on the assumption that the slave masters would never themselves dismantle the slave society. But after the Act of Emancipation had been passed, the British government acted as if that assumption had been wrong. It seemed to believe that the masters would govern the society and manage their estates in harmony with the principles of the Act. Instead of co-operating, the masters sabotaged the Act again and again. They thus goaded the British government into accepting the argument that the only way to give substance to the Act of Emancipation was for it to take complete charge of the affairs of the society.

But the half-hearted effort made in 1839 to suspend the Jamaican Constitution for five years was carried in the House of Commons by so small a majority that the government regarded it as a defeat. So within five years of emancipation the British government's resolve to function as the supervisor of the new society had been weakened by those Englishmen who had a sentiment for liberty as an abstraction. They were unwilling to disturb the political privileges and the property rights of their kith and kin in Jamaica.

The British government now adopted the policy which would determine the way it exercised the role of supervisor between 1840 and 1865. The basis of the new policy was the conciliation of the white community. The old policy had been founded on mistrust of the masters. The hostility of the House of Assembly to the British government had been one result. The second was more grave than the first. For the old policy had served to exacerbate the painful social relations of slavery. To prolong that policy was to delay the beginning of new social and economic relations. It would be better for the blacks, better for the whole society, to change the policy. So argued the British administrators who recommended the new policy to the British government.

The attempt to make the white community accept responsibility for the whole society by force had failed. The attempt to assume full control of the affairs of the society had been abandoned. The attempt would now be made to persuade the white community of the wisdom of themselves conducting responsible politics.

The old policy assumed the absence of goodwill in the white community. The new policy assumed the absence of self-interest in the black community. This policy professed to have at heart the interest of all parties. In fact it suited the interest of two only, the white community and the British government. The essence of the new policy was that it put away a big stick which was never to be used anyway. To that extent it was more honest than the old policy. But it was equally ineffective. It put away a stick, but dangled no carrots. The British government should have done in 1839 what it eventually did in 1944: enfranchised the whole population. Instead the British government coaxed the whites into lowering the voting qualifications they did, but only enough to enfranchise a minority.

It is true to say of the black that he was then unfit; but in all the senses in which this judgement is true and relevant, it is also true of the white. In both cases their disabilities were due to their being the creatures of a slave society. Therein lies whatever justification there was for allowing the British government a role in the affairs of the society. An effective role would have for a time, put both communities at an equal political disadvantage. The policy of conciliation buttressed the existing advantages of the white community and encouraged the blacks to be dependent on Missus Queen. We may judge the success of that policy both by the Appeal of the Poor People of St. Ann and by the reply to it, the Queen's Advice.

Some of the elected members did turn their energies to the constructive politics of establishing a free society. But they had to work within the old parliamentary system of the House of Assembly which had been perfected for opposing policies of the Executive. It was relatively easy for those who preferred to live in the past to use this machinery to wreck or frustrate efforts to grapple with the present. The result of such politics, the persistent neglect of the welfare of the society as a whole, was the riots which erupted in the middle years of the nineteenth century.

There is another reason why British intervention in the society did not take a more positive form. It was due to the eclipse of the humanitarians by the accountants, as a major force in British parliamentary politics. British colonial policy after 1830, so far as it was concerned with the protection of indigenous peoples against settlers in South Africa and New Zealand, and of ex-slaves in the West Indies, meant spending money on the soldiers and the administrators necessary for its execution. Between 1834 and 1845 the Negro Education Grant largely supported primary schools in the West Indies. But the accountants in the Imperial Parliament persistently questioned the philosophy behind these activities until the Colonial Office and the Treasury understood that it would be very difficult to get the House of Commons to vote the money necessary to sustain that policy. When in 1841 he signalled the approaching end of the Negro Education Grant, Lord John Russell justified the decision on the grounds that the Negroes were much better able to pay for the education of their children than could English labourers.

In equity the British government should have helped to pay for the building of a free society. Since it was unwilling to do so, it should have used its office of supervisor of the society to ensure an equitable incidence of taxation; that is to make those who benefitted most from the economic structure of the society contribute significantly to the public coffers.

The British government let the poor carry the public services for nearly a hundred years. Before 1865 it was content to lecture the House of Assembly. After 1865, although Governors reported on the tax structure from time to time, the Colonial Office did not go beyond the hand-wringing of the impotent. The British government reserved its largest gestures for propping up the plantation economy. When the policy of free trade had severely damaged that economy the government guaranteed in 1848 the interest on a large loan which the planters could use to import labourers to work on the sugar estates. Again when the inept financial management of the Assembly had made Jamaica practically bankrupt, the British government in 1854 guaranteed a loan of half a million pounds sterling to restore the country's public credit.

If one assumes that two communities, such as those in Jamaica after emancipation, whose lives and history are extensively intertwined, are better integrated, and if one also assumes that societies are the better for being self-governing and democratic, the years between 1838 and 1865 were largely wasted.

The British presence frustrated both processes. The whites did not accept political responsibility for the whole society and catered to their own interests. They resented the British for emancipating the slaves and for changing British commercial policy from imperial protection to free trade. They resented the blacks for refusing to work on the plantation at all, or for working there only when it suited them.

The services, notably education and health which the society needed after emancipation, were scarcely provided for out of local funds. The administration of justice particularly in the courts of petty sessions, was dominated by the white community and the property owners. Injustice flourished.

The blacks were for the most part excluded from the political system, and of those who qualified by virtue of property, many stayed outside. The black community also opted out of the plantation economy wherever possible. This process meant a search for land to buy or squat on, and the beginnings of the drift to the towns. Immediately after emancipation those who lived in the free villages shared a communal existence, even though it was one made rudimentary by poverty, and paternal by close missionary supervision. But progressively, the rejection of the life of an estate casual laborer meant living in isolation. And after about 1845 there was a falling away of that interest in church membership and school attendance which had marked the early years of emancipation. Some of the people had begun to opt out of the cultural system as well.

In the five years before the riots at Morant Bay the society was marked by a certain restlessness. The religious revival had involved its devotees in a long march around the island. Their provision grounds untilled, they poured out their energies, physical and emotional, in repeated acts of devotion. Their unrestrained fervour indicated how sick the society was. The American civil war had brought to all an economic depression, worsened by a succession of floods and droughts on provision grounds. To some it also brought the fear of invasion.

A section of the white community began to advocate the abolition of the representative constitution in its present state. The meetings held after Dr. Underhill's letter to the Secretary of State became public, criticized the House of Assembly for wasting taxes and demanded not its abolition but its reform. In 1859 there was prolonged rioting in Sav–la–Mar and in Falmouth. The rioters in both instances were tried with results which on the evidence seem equitable.

We may learn from these riots and from the Assembly's debates on the future of the constitution what dangers threatened the society. We can also see how they might have been averted. If one part of the society had not been able to look for help overseas, if it had no choice but to find its own solutions within the society, it would probably have responded, even at so late an hour, by providing political remedies. Indeed had a more balanced judgement presided over the Jamaican administration in 1865, would Ramsey and Hobbs and the Maroons have been let loose over seven hundred square miles of eastern Jamaica? As it was Eyre had his bad judgement reinforced by those who themselves sought the solution for the ills of the society overseas. Eyre unleashed an alien force at Morant Bay and two months later opened the door to alien political authority. Who remembers the Falmouth rioters? Who would have remembered the Morant Bay rioters? We remember them because as Eyre himself wrote, 'The retribution has been so prompt and so terrible that it is never likely to be forgotten'. Since so many were innocent the act of October 1865 was not retribution, it was murder. Ought we not to remember Morant Bay in greater measure for the many who suffered, rather than exaggerate the achievement of the few who rioted?

We wrote earlier that although the evidence with which we are familiar did not allow us to say in what ways social attitudes and social relations changed as a direct consequence of the riots, it did allow us to discuss whether the political changes after 1865 were directly due to the riots.

It may be said in support of the argument that the loss of the old constitution was a direct consequence of the riots that one of the accounts usually given of this event is that 'the English took it away'. And when it is so stated, it is implied that the English took the constitution away because the Morant Bay riots showed them that the society was unable to govern itself, that it was not fit for self-government.

About the British government's policy it need only be said that although the Colonial Office would have liked the constitution changed or abolished, the policy of waiting for Jamaicans to change their own constitution had been accepted by the Secretary of State in July 1865 as the only feasible policy. The constitution could not be touched in any way by the Minister simply acting in the name of the Crown, and exercising the Royal Prerogative. It could only be changed by the Imperial Parliament; and after the experience of 1839 no British government would lightly have gone to the House of Commons with a bill for suspending the Jamaican Constitution.

The decision not to use the Imperial Parliament meant that change could only come from the Jamaican Parliament itself. But even so the British government adopted the policy of keeping quiet and waiting hopefully for the deed to be done, because it feared that to give public encouragement to those who wished for change would cause such widespread resentment in the society that it would make it doubly difficult to get a majority for change in the House of Assembly.

Another explanation given for the change of constitution is that the white members of the House of Assembly panicked after the riots, fearing that they were about to be massacred by the blacks, and accepted Eyre's invitation 'to immolate the constitution on the altar of patriotism'. This explanation has the merit of looking for the reason for change in the local society, but it does not fit the information we have of the final session of the House of Assembly. It is true that the Assembly passed very quickly all the repressive laws which Eyre had prepared for them. But not the bill to change the constitution. That the members took of their leisure, trading concessions among themselves, and producing a hodge-podge of a law which changed

the constitution but left political power in the hands of the white community.

The constitution was not changed by the British; it was changed by Jamaicans. They changed it after the riots, but not because of the riots. They did not intend to change representative government for crown colony government, they were tricked into this by Eyre.

We have already elaborated on the first two assertions, we now turn to the others. Was the constitution changed by the House of Assembly because of the riots? Notice first that the desire to change the constitution existed before the riots; also that this desire was felt and expressed by a variety of groups. The question then is why was the constitution not changed before? Is it because a majority did not exist in the Assembly for change before the riots, but was produced by the riots?

A majority existed for the abolition of the existing constitution, or as it was sometimes said, for the reform of the constitution but for how long before 1865 it is difficult to say. What did not exist was a majority for a constitution to replace the old one. For crown colony government there was hardly a vote. The 1865 Session of the Assembly ended without a majority for any definite form of government. It was Eyre's triumph that he got the second amending act through a much depleted House of Assembly. Before we elaborate on Eyre's role let us look at the attitudes expressed before Eyre took a hand.

We have to guess in the absence of precise information, but we guess that the largest group was the one moved by the desire to put the representative constitution out of reach of the black population. They argued that now was the time. The numbers of negroes qualified to vote had grown, was growing and would soon be such as to allow them to control the legislature by electing black members. There were other motives for changing the constitution; some thought that for its institutions to work well they had to be staffed by a greater number of able men than the island could supply. Others thought that as a device for making the old constitution more efficient the Executive Committee had failed; it had been the cause of faction and of party and it had been the source of corruption. Their remedy was to give the executive offices to Englishmen appointed by the Secretary of State. At the Underhill meetings yet another group expressed its opinions. The black propertied tax payers criticized the Assembly for waste and they warned it that if it persisted in its old habits it would be abolished.

Before 1865 the abolitionists were unable to agree on what was to replace the old constitution. This was not simply a division between those who wished to let the British have a bigger role in politics and administration and those who did not. It was also due to factions among the whites. The division was crudely between those who had, however timidly, worked for an integrated society, and those who were against them for this act of collaboration. Such men, angry both against the British and the blacks, wished to hoist the constitution above the reach of propertied negroes, abolish the Executive Committee and keep the British out of Jamaican politics.

What did the riots do to these attitudes? So far as one can tell, nothing. What it did do was to provide the abolitionists with a broker, or to use the metaphor of a contemporary, a midwife. It is of course possible to combine the explanation which adduces panic with the broker-midwife description of Eyre's role, though the description does modify the notion that the constitution was surrendered in a moment of intense panic out of fear of the blacks. But it is best for us to treat the two matters, the attitudes of the members of the Assembly and the role of Eyre in changing the constitution separately.

The attitude pre–1865 of those who wished to keep the blacks outside of politics was not to surrender power to Great Britain, but to raise the property qualification both for membership of the House of Assembly and for voting. The attitudes of those who thought the society could not produce forty-seven members of the House and seventeen members of the Legislative Council was manifest in their proposals to consolidate both houses into a single chamber legislature. There were a few voices raised before 1865 for 'strong government', by which was meant government by Englishmen. We do not know the evidence which shows panic because panic would have meant a wholesale conversion of the first two groups to the position of the third, government by Englishmen. This obviously did not happen.

What happened was that the various groups none of which before or after the riots was large enough to get its own way, were kept talking long enough to produce a law, the first act amending the constitution. This was the product of horsetrading; it was untidy, contained tidbits for everybody, and was certainly not what any of the parties wanted, least of all Eyre. Did the riots put the various groups in a mood for horsetrading which would have been absent without the riots? Almost certainly, but they would not have continued talking but for Eyre.

The riots gave Eyre the opportunity to propose a change of constitution which without them he would not have been able to do. That is, in the interval between the riots and the meeting of the legislature Eyre felt able to prepare a draft bill and introduce it to the House through the Executive Committee. An act which in normal times would have been difficult, since Westmoreland for instance, would not have introduced such a bill. Even so, Eyre understood from the start that although what he wished was crown colony government, if he drafted such a bill it would never pass the Assembly. So he drafted a bill to establish a single chamber, with half its members elected and half nominated, and the Crown in control through the casting vote of the governor. But even this bill the Assembly mauled according to its own prejudices and interests.

Whatever it was that kept them talking, the magnet, the force that held them together was spent by the time the deed was done. Badly mauled as was the first amending act, particularly where it sought to give control to the Crown, Eyre urged the Colonial Office to accept it rather than send it back to the floor of the House, for then it was sure to be entirely lost.

If this was the mood of the Assembly why was Eyre able to get the second act passed? Briefly he took advantage of two things; one was that the House had thinned towards the end of the session as the country members went home for Christmas. Secondly he made brilliant use of the general disagreement over what sort of constitution should replace the old. He had told the Secretary of State that there were almost as many opinions on that as there were members. Yet even in the reduced House Eyre could not have got a positive bill written. He was able to let each group feel that if they merely repealed the first amending act and left it to the Crown to enact a new constitution, they would get the constitution they wished for. Hence the consternation with which the crown colony government constitution was greeted in 1866.

Eyre was able to insert himself a second time into the legislative machine through his use of a despatch which the Colonial Secretary had written before he received the first amending act. This despatch he sent to the House in an abbreviated version, suppressing those passages which did not support his plans.

He explained to the House that since it passed the first amending act, a despatch had arrived from the Colonial Office which laid down the conditions on which the British government would accept responsibility for Jamaica, that is protect whites against blacks. He had informed them of these conditions by excerpts from the despatch because it was confidential, and so they could not see it all. In the process he made the Colonial Secretary say clearly, what in his despatch, could at most, be only doubtfully inferred. That is, he made it look as if the first amending act was certain to be rejected.

This was enough to tempt those dissatisfied, for whatever reason with the first act. Here was the opportunity to get the form of constitution they preferred.

Eyre did not realize that what was clever politics was illegal. The English Attorney General informed the Secretary of State that the second amending act was *ultra vires*. The Assembly could amend the constitution but it could not abolish it and leave to the Crown the making of a new constitution. It matters here that the Secretary of State had decided before the riots that he would accept changes in the West Indian constitutions. The task of his staff was now only to find a way around the Attorney General's opinion. The only answer was an act of the Imperial Parliament. The Colonial Office staff was not sure that they could depend on the House of Commons. But the choice was between the Commons and the Assembly. The Assembly was certain to reject a third amending act. The Colonial Office chose to use the House of Commons. There, the act to give the Crown authority to make a constitution for Jamaica passed quickly enough. Thus was the old constitution abolished.

We now discuss some of the consequences of crown colony government. What benefits did the society gain from passing political authority over to the British? And what price did it pay for the benefits? We may draw up a crude balance sheet by assessing how the British used the political authority they had acquired in 1866. They had claimed that their presence in the society was justified because only they would be able to do three things, all of which the society badly needed. First they would tidy the public service and administration and make them more efficient; secondly they would provide impartial government between conflicting classes; thirdly they would look after the interests of the blacks, protect them from the whites and from themselves. These statements of principles to guide the administrators who would make, in each case, their own political programme. The British said from time to time that crown colony government was temporary; that it worked towards its own death; that as soon as the society had learnt the arts of responsible politics, it would again govern itself.

The constitution of 1866 gave the British political authority in an autocratic form. The governor was sure of his majority and the society was represented only by his nominees. The Order-in-Council of 1884 set some limits to the extent that any governor could play the autocrat, by permitting the elected members when acting in concert to veto his bills and resolutions. But it did not modify the essentially autocratic character of the crown colony constitution. For the next sixty years this was the constitution of Jamaica.

We begin our assessment of the use the British made of their political authority in Jamaica by distinguishing between the constitution as written and politics as practised by the functionaries of the crown colony constitution. The theory of the constitution asserted autocracy. The practice of politics assumed an oligarchy.

The autocratic power was not in general use. It was conceived for a form of opposition which died with the old constitution. The Colonial Office likened the governor's permanent majority to a phalanx. If any group was unreasonable enough to block the road to progress, the governor had the powers with which to scatter them. But after 1865 the mercantile and planter classes had no need for such crude tactics. And so the autocratic power which originally was to have been the instrument for transforming the society, became merely the instrument for asserting the imperial interest, even when that was as crassly conceived as it was in the 'Florence' case; and later still the autocratic power was used principally to protect the salaries of civil servants from the attacks of the elected members. On such occasions it appeared only after the governor had uttered the formula 'of paramount importance to the public interest'.

To say that crown colony government was in practice an oligarchy, is to gloss over the differences in style and in substance which distinguished the administrations of different governors. But, with one exception, it is not to distort significantly. Grant was the exception. He was the only autocrat. He had the will, and he had the advantage of inaugurating the new constitution. The export economy was buoyant, and it was too soon after Morant Bay for the old politicians to engage in unrestrained protests. Towards the end of his regime, they did protest over his failure to consult them, but their voices were still muted. After he had retired, they attacked his policies in earnest, particularly the Rio Cobre irrigation works.

Grant's practice may have been true to the letter of the constitution, it was not true to the spirit in which the Colonial Office expected crown colony government to work. Sir Henry Taylor was against governor-autocrats on practical grounds. He feared that they would inflame the local populations and bring down crown colony government in a very short time. The nominated unofficial members of the Legislative Councils, were not for him mere window-dressing. He justified their nomination on two grounds. First they embodied the principle of no taxation without representation. As the owners of the largest properties, agricultural and commercial, Taylor presumed them the mainstay of the revenue, and so the most appropriate local voices. He was wrong; but the despatches on the incidence of taxation did not perceptibly shake his belief in this argument. Secondly he wished for an opposition to the governor, and through the protests of that opposition, for local criticism of schemes sent up by governors for his approval.

Yet Taylor did not expect the governors to become the creatures of the local oligarchies. He expected career officials to resist the influence of the larger commercial and agricultural interests. It was asking too much of them. By choosing the unofficial members to represent interests in the Council, by expecting them to be consulted, Taylor created within the system itself the opportunities for the large property holders to influence the decisions of the crown colony administrators. When one also takes into account that these men, for the most part, could be expected to share the general opinions which the local oligarchies had about the society, it is not surprising that crown colony government failed to live up to the large claims Taylor made on its behalf in 1865.

It was easier to establish a relatively efficient administration than to be both an impartial administrator and the protector of the blacks. It was impossible to prepare a people for responsible government and democratic politics by surrounding foreign administrators with propertied men, elected on a restricted franchise, and able to exercise a veto on expenditure. That was the way to teach sterile and irresponsible politics.

There is no doubt about the accomplishments of crown colony government. It came as close as was humanly possible to fulfilling the first of the three claims made on its behalf. Grant established the administrative apparatus of a modern state. Old departments were made more efficient, new ones were created. Rational procedures for the administration of the country's finances were introduced; detailed estimates of revenue were prepared, debts funded, taxes collected. New courts were established to dispense justice to the poor. Abandoned land was declared forfeited to the Crown, and squatters were given titles. The public system of elementary education was started. So too was the public medical service. Roads and bridges were built.

This list tells us that in seven years Grant did most of the things which the society needed since 1838, but had not done for itself. It is perhaps an exaggeration to say that emancipation created the state. But it may serve to emphasize the limited nature of public responsibilities before emancipation. The sessions of the House of Assembly during the period of slavery were the occasions when the slave-masters met to treat with the King and to set-

tle a few matters of mutual concern. Whatever else was needed each master provided within his own domain. At emancipation one function was formally taken from him; that of judging and punishing the labourers on his estate. The Act of Emancipation specifically enjoined him to his other functions. He was to continue to provide the apprentices with the traditional services. He successfully flouted the act. He found ways to judge and to punish, and to withdraw the services he had provided.

The British at first paid for justice and education. In neither case was the service adequate, but that it was provided at all was a great boon to the newly emancipated population. When the British stopped paying, the masters, still in control of the public purse, left the services to volunteers; education to the churches and justice to themselves. The cholera epidemics forced them to spend large sums of money, but when it was over Jamaica was still without a public health service. So up to 1865 the state had barely acknowledged its responsibility to provide services for the whole society.

The British government lectured the Assembly on its duties to the society. The Assembly invariably replied that the economy ruined by emancipation and free trade could not afford public services. Is it then to the lack of means rather than to the absence of will that we must look for an explanation? The state of the economy may well have explained wide disparities in the public expenditure for services, between one year and the next. But what has to be explained is not uneven expenditure from year to year, for it was not the case, but the pittance spent on some things and the large sums spent on others, between 1838 and 1865. Compare for instance the total sum spent on education to that spent on immigration.

The explanation lies in the belief of the planters that widespread education was against their interest since it would quickly reduce the numbers of those willing to labour on estates. Moreover, they were convinced that the state had one responsibility above all others. And that was to keep the sugar estates in existence. The priority thus accorded sugar over welfare services was justified by equating the private interests of estate owners with the public interests of the state. Sugar was the revenue and the revenue was sugar. No sugar, no revenue, no public services.

It is to Grant's credit that he challenged the assumptions which made this reasoning plausible. The failure of his successors in office and of their superiors in the Colonial Office to construct alternative bases for economic development was in great measure due to their acceptance of this reasoning as correct. The most important economic event of the last century, the export trade in bananas owed nothing to crown colony government. But the country was fortunate that the trade was so firmly established by the eighteen-nineties when sugar prices steeply declined.

However inadequate we judge the explanation that the Assembly gave for its neglect of the interests of the whole society before 1865, there is a connection between the export economy and the public welfare services. Where so much of the revenue came from import duties, the revenues were affected by the decline in imports which followed whenever the value of exports was reduced. When world market conditions for sugar and other products deteriorated, it was bananas and other fruit which prevented a disastrous decline in the revenue.

Eisner calculates that public expenditures between the end of the eighteen-sixties and the beginning of the nineteen-thirties rose seven-fold on health, eight-fold on public works and twenty-four times on education. It may also be appropriate to notice that from Eisner's calculations it does not seem that the expenditure on education or on health was ever steadily above 10% of the expenditure during the crown colony period up to 1930.

We have acknowledged what was done; we must now estimate its worth to the society. First we consider the machinery of administration; the claim that the system would be rationalized and made more efficient was fulfilled, but without wishing to deny what was accomplished, its limits are suggested by two comments. The efficiency of crown colony government, particularly during its first period when it shone by comparison with the inefficiency of representative government, need not overawe us. It was the inability of the Colonial Office to tell exactly where the finances of Jamaica stood in 1882 which led to the appointment of the Royal Commission of that year. Secondly, efficiency was attained by concentrating all power of making decisions in the hands of the Colonial Secretary.

So the price paid for the advance in administration, was centralization and paternalism. Almost certainly any reforming government would have centralized administration in the capital; but one which had its roots in the country would not have perpetuated the ascendancy of the Colonial Secretary and the Colonial Secretariat. As a device to bring order out of near chaos, the institution may have been necessary in the years after 1866 but if the functionaries of crown colony government had taken seriously their professed intention of working towards its death, authority would have been dispersed, at least after 1884.

Equally damaging to the society was the practice of appointing foreigners as heads of departments long after there had been time to train natives for these posts. In most cases it was simply alleged that natives with the qualities required were not available but for some posts, such as that of Chief Justice and that of Attorney General, it was argued that natives were not desirable in the interest of justice.

In general we may conclude that the price paid for administrative efficiency was high. In 1865 the high posts in the administration were no longer the preserve of white natives and during most of crown colony government such posts were reserved for white foreigners. Paternalism and the social importance of a white skin were still characteristic of the society in 1865 although these values were by then no longer sacrosanct. By restoring whiteness as a necessary quality for jobs at the top of the administration, crown colony government reinforced the racial prejudices inherent in the society.

Secondly, we consider the services provided through the administrative machinery. For most of the period the British adhered to the principle that a crown colony could have all the services its revenues could afford. Within these limits it was left to individual governors to divide the cake. The society benefitted from the public services in at least three ways; Jamaica became a more orderly and law abiding, a more healthy and less isolated society after 1865.

The administration of justice during crown colony government restored the confidence of the poor in the court as a place where they might expect a fair trial in a dispute between unequal contenders. They preferred to use the District Courts presided over by foreigners rather than go before the native justices in courts of petty sessions. However the weaknesses of crown colony government are apparent; there was not enough trained justices, those in offices were overworked and with the consequent delay in hearing cases and increased cost of seeking justice. Moreover there was no sustained examination of the substance of the law administered, nor of the extent of the punishment inflicted on the guilty. From time to time administrators in the Colonial Office had good intentions, but here as elsewhere these remained on paper. For instance against its better judgement the Colonial Office sanctioned flogging as part of the punishment for praedial larceny in response to local demand.

The building of roads and bridges gradually connected isolated communities. For a long time even the coastal towns had depended on communication by sea; the network of roads not only made it easier for some small settlers to market their crops, it also made possible the growth of that feeling of oneness which later served as the basis for nationalism. If less was done to open up the country than was possible, it was because peasant agriculture remained the unattended step-child of crown colony government, land settlements notwithstanding.

The impetus for much that was attempted came from the report of the Royal Commission of 1897. In urging the British government to establish a department of Economic Botany in the West Indies, they commented that 'the cultivator of one product is often quite ignorant of the best means of cultivating any other, and does not know whether his soil and climate might be better adapted for something else. These remarks have special reference to the small cultivators, but they are not wholly inapplicable to persons interested in the larger estates'. The Imperial Department of Agriculture was established and the local department of agriculture was enlarged, but the money spent on the crops of the small cultivator, the time and energy spent on his problems, were as nothing compared to what was lavished on estate agriculture.

Thirdly, we consider how far crown colony government achieved the other aims it set itself. The claim that it would provide impartial government and protect the interests of the poor and ignorant, can be stated as a promise to bring the society into equilibrium. Then when the contending classes were in equipoise crown colony government would come to an end. During the time when the poor were being developed and the rich restrained, the whole society would have learned the style of responsible politics appropriate to a free society.

The British failed to live up to claims made in a moment of hubris. British civil servants temporarily stationed in a foreign society, were supposed, without check, to adequately protect the interests of the poor and ignorant. They did not. This was not because they did not care, but because they should not have been expected to care so much. They were not subjected to pressure on behalf of the poor while the nominated and elected unofficial members effectively lobbied in their own interest. When the early vision had faded, the major concern of crown colony government became to avoid another riot. By rioting in 1938 the poor and ignorant wrote their own epitaph on the system. It did not bring two unequal social groups into equilibrium; it reinforced the dominance of the power of wealth and frustrated the thrust of the power of numbers.

Although the British failed in large measure to be impartial administrators and to protect the interest of the poor and to teach the society responsible politics, even here they achieved a measure of success. What the gain was to the society is difficult to assess, but bits of evidence suggest that some of the poor were persuaded of their impartiality between contending classes.

One bit of evidence comes from a memorandum submitted to the 1882 Royal Commission by a group who claimed to speak on behalf of the 'hundreds of the negro inhabitants of Kingston and its neighbourhood'. They said among other things that they were 'fully conscious that without the protection of the government our fellow colonists would not permit us to enjoy the breath we breathe'. The document is redolent of the belief that their enemy was the white and brown propertied class who controlled the island since slavery. The relevant question is how widespread were these opinions among the black population? The literary sources known to us do not say.

So we now only suggest that the opinions expressed in the document to the 1882 Royal Commission seem to make sense of the campaign and the results of the 1944 election. The party which made the immediate goal bread rather than independence, and which made the enemy the propertied class rather than the British, may have owed its victory in part to an appeal which was in harmony with the beliefs of a large portion of the electorate. The electorate may have been mistaken in identifying the party led by the professional men with the propertied class, but if so it was a natural mistake for them to make in the circumstances of the island's history. The slogan 'self-government is slavery', whatever it may have meant to those who used it, echoes the voice of 1883, 'without the protection of the government our fellow colonists would not permit us to enjoy the breath we breathe'. And it may well be that those to whom it was addressed took it to mean more than those who used it ever intended.

So at the end of 1944 the upward thrust of the power of numbers which had been stopped at the end of 1865, reasserted itself. It would please us to add that the thrust now took a form which showed the benefits that had accrued to the poor from eighty years of crown colony government. But of that there is no sign. They voted, as they might well have voted in 1866, in their own interest. How much had they learnt of democratic politics and of responsible government in the interval? One test is that they voted into power a party to whom the forms and nuances of parliamentary democracy were alien. The apprenticeship in responsible government may well have started for the society in 1838 or 1866 or 1884. It only began in 1945.

The Abortive Revolution of 1876 in Barbados

George Belle

The political events of 1876 represent a critical juncture in the political history of Barbados. The 1876 political crisis was the most serious the society had experienced since the 1816 slave rebellion and the adjustment problems of the emancipation years of the 1830s. Indeed it is reasonable to argue that the 1876 political crisis was the most serious in the history of Barbados. For these reasons alone 1876 presents itself as a nodal juncture in the political development of the island. In addition, the 1876 crisis facilitates the analysis of three features critical to the politics of development of Barbados and to an understanding of that politics: oligarchy, democracy, and revolution.

By 1876 slavery had been abolished for some forty years. Changes, of course, had occurred since the 1830s, but the basic political order, social structure and socio-economic conditions of the early post-emancipation period remained intact. The island was still ruled and economically controlled by a rigid oligarchy; no extension of the franchise had taken place since 1842, and the planter class with some exceptions still elected the planter class to the House of Assembly. With a population of some 162,042 persons in 1876, only some 1,664 were recorded as registered electors by the Blue Book.[1]

The vote could be exercised by those who (i) had freehold possession of an estate valued annually at not less than £12.16s.6d. sterling for life or in right of marriage or as a dower of wife; or if himself or his wife had a life interest in the rents and profits of lands of a similar annual value; (ii) were lessees or assignees of land or of tenements paying rent of not less than £64.2s.0d. sterling and the term of the lease was in its original creation not less than five years; (iii) occupied any house, warehouse, store, counting house, shop, or other building in a town, parochially rated at not less than £32.1s.0d. sterling rent per annum or (iv) paid parochial taxes for two years of at least £3.4s.1d. sterling.[2]

So in 1876, 1,664 voters elected twenty-four members from twelve constituencies to the House of Assembly for one year. New elections were held annually with very much the same results. This elected Assembly was the lower house of planter government; the upper house consisted of the Legislative Council made up of nominated members, usually highly influential and experienced planters. Colonial authority of course stood above these local institutions, the governor representing the imperial government. The executive of the government consisted of the governor and the Legislative Council who combined to form the Executive Council. The colonial secretary, the attorney general and the officer commanding Her Majesty's troops also sat in the Legislative and Executive Councils. The Legislative and Executive Councils were made up of eight and nine persons respectively at the beginning of 1876.

Of the 162,042 persons in the island's population of 1876, some 16,560 were white and 145,482 black and coloured.[3] There were, according to the 1876 Blue Book of Statistics, 44,133 Barbadians engaged in agriculture; 1,863 of these were proprietors and employers, while the labourers were made up of 18,947 males and 22,323 females. Persons employed in manufacture were listed as 8,347 in number. Engineers, artificers and mechanics (partly employed on estates) numbered 6,848 and there were also some 1,499 artisans. Some 4,889 persons were engaged in commerce. Merchants and their clerks made up 1,078, shopkeepers

Registered Electors in 1876		
Constituency	Population	Electors
St. Michael	27,000	215
Bridgetown	21,000 +	398
Christ Church	18,000	102
St. Philip	17,000	221
St. George	14,000	125
St. John	10,000	65
St. Thomas	10,000–	115
St. James	9,000–	97
St. Lucy	9,000–	107
St. Andrew	7,000 +	38
St. Peter	7,000 +	69
St. Joseph	6,000–	94

SOURCE: Blue Book 1876, K1, *Political Franchise*

numbered 817, and hucksters, hawkers and ped-
dlars numbered 2,994.[4]

The class relations of these people remained
very much as in the post-emancipation period, only
now the black and coloured middle class would
have expanded and their political outlook had
become generally more conservative. The social
and economic conditions of the labouring classes
remained most unsatisfactory by any criterion.
Moreover, the sugar economy of the island on
which most of these depended was suffering from
the competition of European beet sugar. Beet sugar
competition had been an increasing grievance to
West Indian cane sugar producers since 1864 when
the sugar conference had granted bounties to beet
sugar exports. The ill-effects of this were, as far as
possible, passed on as a further burden to the
masses by the local producers.[5] Bruce Hamilton
commenting on this states:

. . . In times of stress . . . the labourers were the principal
sufferers. Hennessey reports in May 1876 the dismissal
of labourers, the reduction of wages and the demand of
more work for the same wages . . . Combinations to raise
wages remained, apparently, illegal. . . . Although it was
claimed that the working classes paid no taxes except
indirectly as consumers, and that there were infinitesi-
mal, as the import duties on food were so low, £24,330
was levied on imported foodstuffs of the sort used by the
poor in 1873. Hennessey quoted Hincks in 1858 and the
West Indian newspaper in 1874 as calling attention to
how taxes on provisions used by labourers had been
largely substituted for taxes on land . . .[6]

Moreover, the Masters and Servants Act, or the
notorious Contract Act, remained to exacerbate
matters. Hamilton says of it: 'This law of a type
common in the West Indies in the years following
emancipation, but which survived for Barbados far
longer than anywhere else, yielded in its operation
abuses so gross as to be almost incredible to a modern reader studying the institutions of a supposedly
free community'.[7]

The cost of consumption goods and the wages
worked for by the labouring class[8] additionally
give some indication of the material burden on that
class. Praedial labourers worked for eight pence a
day or, if working per ton or job, an able bodied
labourer could earn from 10d. to 1s.8d. within ordinary working hours. Domestic servants who were
hired by the month had wages varying from 8s.4d.
to £1.17s.6d. A tradesman would earn 2s.6d. per
day and masons and carpenters 2s. to 2s.6d. per
day. It must of course be remembered that there
was no job security for any of these workers and
work could be very irregular. The sugar crop for
instance lasted six months and the employment of

many of the labouring class depended on crop
work.

The 1876 Blue Book of Statistics[9] gave the following prices as average for articles of use for consumption: wheaten flour, £1.13.4d. per barrel of
196 lb; wheaten bread, 3d. per lb; horned cattle,
£15 per head; horses, £40 per head; sheep,
£1.13s.4d. per head; goats, £1.5s. per head; milk,
1s.4d. per gallon; fresh butter, 1s. per lb; salt butter,
1s.8d. per lb; cheese, 1s.6d. per lb; beef, 10d. per
lb; mutton, 1s. per lb; pork, 6d. per lb; rice, 3d. per
lb; coffee, 10d per lb; tea, 3s.4d. per lb; refined
sugar, 7d. per lb; salt, ½d. per lb; wine, per dozen
£1.13s.4d.; brandy, 16s.8d. per gallon; beer,
10s.6d. per dozen; tobacco, 2s.6d. per lb.

Not surprisingly, emigration remained a convenient method of relief for the labouring class; all 613
emigrants in 1876 for instance, were from the class
of agricultural labourers.[10] Despite hostility and
hindrances from the planter class and the effect of
poverty and disease on the labouring class emigration continued.[11]

It was the attempt to implement Colonial Office
policy relative to this social condition in Barbados
that acted as a catalyst to the social upheaval of
1876. The local instrument delegated by the Colonial Office to implement its policy was John Pope
Hennessey, who was appointed governor of Barbados at the end of 1875. The policy was to implement direct rule by the imperial government, a policy otherwise known to us as crown colony
government. The Colonial Office had in fact been
concerned to introduce this policy in the Caribbean
since the abolition of slavery but the strong and
successful resistance to it by the Jamaican Assembly in 1839 had forced it to wait until persuasion
could induce it, or opportune circumstances facilitate it. The 1865 rebellion in Jamaica moved the
Jamaican Assembly to surrender to crown colony
government in the interest of security;[12] in Barbados in late 1875 Hennessey had been sent out to
be a strong persuader.

Hamilton summarized the attitude of administrators in the Colonial Office in 1876 which led
them to believe their strategy might then be successfully followed. He argued that, first, they
believed that the local legislature was not only
hopelessly incompetent, but also unwilling to perform its duties. Second, they thought that the
errors of the legislature might be expected to produce such chaos as to lead eventually to its abolition and to the setting up of crown colony government. Third, they knew that in the last resort
the home government was in a position to insist
on this or some such lesser reform as the securing
of the initiation of money rates to the Executive.
Fourth, they were however unwilling to override

The Emigration of Four Years

	M	F	Total	% Males
1873				
(9¼ months)	1886	790	2676	70
1874	885	310	1165	73
1875	483	199	682	72
1876	400	213	613	65

SOURCE: *Blue Book 1876*

or interfere with the Barbados constitution as an act of power, and wished to bring about confederation, their own solution for the problem, by methods of persuasion. Fifth, they hoped to effect this persuasion by demonstrating that the confederation would result in greater economy. Sixth, when, after the Leeward Islands were federated, the expected result of economy was not achieved, they realized that this line of persuasion was unlikely to succeed. Seventh, they believed, however, that there was a substantial body of Barbadian public opinion either favourable to confederation or reform or at least capable of being won around.[13]

The form crown colony government was to take in Barbados was to be first through implementation of a confederation with the Windward Islands, with Barbados as the central unit. The policy had quickly run into vehement opposition from the Barbadian oligarchy, and Governors Rawson and Freling, the predecessors of Hennessey, had been blocked in their attempts to introduce it. Consequently Hennessey's task on his arrival seemed to be to approach the problem cautiously, but with determination, and if possible subtlety. His introduction of the notorious 'Six Points' soon after his arrival, by which time he had carefully cultivated a popularity with most sectors of the Barbadian society, seemed to be the following of this line. After his first weeks in office Hennessey was being referred to in glowing terms as 'a first rate man',[14] and 'the right man in the right place'.[15] His appointment was suggested as the return to a policy by the Colonial Office of appointing outstanding men as governors and not the mediocre.[16] Going further, *The Agricultural Reporter* pronounced: '. . . the Governor . . . continued to win the golden opinions by the sagacity and discrimination of his political principles . . . by the happy combination of the *fortiter* and *sauviter* which he displays; in the promptitude of his measures for the correction of abuses; by his liberal patronage of Literature; by the hospitality of his sumptuous entertainments . . . by the unostentatious display of his acts of private generosity'.[17]

Hennessey's 'Six Points' quickly changed all this, at least for the planter and middle class col-

oured interests. They saw in these proposals, as undoubtedly was the case, an attempt by the governor to quietly reintroduce the policy of confederation and crown colony government. The 'Six Points' declared:

(1) That the Auditor of Barbados should be appointed Auditor-General of the Windward Islands, his salary and clerical staff being increased, with the additional expenses resulting to fall entirely on the other islands.
(2) That the power of transporting prisoners from Barbados to the other islands and of receiving prisoners from the other islands in Barbados should be secured to the Governor-in-Chief.
(3) That the new lunatic asylum in Barbados should be open for reception of lunatics from the other islands.
(4) That a similar arrangement should be made about a common lazaretto.
(5) That there should be a Chief Justice of the Windward Islands, and a remodelling of the judicial system, based on the necessity of centralizing it in Barbados.
(6) That there should be a Police Force of the Windward Islands . . .[18]

The immediate and deep hostility to these proposals by the Barbadian press must quite quickly have indicated to Hennessey that neither subtlety nor persuasion would succeed with the sensitive upper classes of Barbados. The *Times* was not to be taken in: 'We need hardly reiterate how profound a sensation has been created throughout the entire community by the publication of this startling and revolutionary document . . . Mr. Rawson's perverse stolidity was the result of compact political stupidity. Mr. Sanford Freling was simply an empty-headed military tyrant but Mr. Hennessey is evidently an astute, wily politician . . . His predecessors were neither of them capable of committing an injury to our constitution, of any conceivable magnitude. But Mr. Hennessey having first fairly ensconced himself in popular estimation craftily endeavours to pervert that very popularity into an instrument for inflicting evils upon us of a most irreparable character . . .'[19] The planter newspaper, *The Agricultural Reporter*, fully agreed with the organ of the coloured middle class, as indeed did the more liberal *West Indian*.[20]

Governor Hennessey's response to the hostility of the Barbadian upper classes was to make a show of power. He informed both houses of the legislature that by the Letters Patent of his appointment as governor of Barbados and the Windward Islands he had been invested with powers out of the ordinary. 'Our sovereign has been graciously pleased on this occasion to entrust me with powers, usually given no doubt to Her Majesty's Representatives in other parts of the British Empire but not conferred for many years past on the governor of the Windward Islands'. He further announced a radical change. His intention was to remove from the Legislative Council its executive capacity; instead, a separate Executive Council was to be set up in which the governor would sit along with the public officers directly responsible to the Crown. Governor Hennessey further took the opportunity to make a scathing attack on the social conditions under which the mass of the people had to live. He referred to the comment made to him by the heads of the Anglican, Wesleyan and Moravian Churches that: 'In all our experiences, we have never seen a community in which there existed such intense and apparently hopeless poverty as in this'.[21]

The reaction from the planter interests to this challenge to their local power by imperial authority was a deepening of their hostility for Hennessey and his policy. Hennessey reported to the Colonial Office, that they were evidently disappointed and angry at losing some of their executive functions and that most of the influential members of the Legislative Council were now determined to join and throw their full weight behind the opposition. In Hennessey's opinion, some of the members 'seemed to regard executive powers as a part of their birthright'.[22]

The firm stand taken by the governor and the deepening opposition and hostility to his policies by the plantocracy ushered in the first significant aspect of the politics of 1876. The ruling class was split by a contradiction not easily resolved. There was clearly no way that the character and class outlook of the local plantocracy was going to come to terms with a Colonial Office policy which meant the loss of their political authority; just as significantly, Governor Hennessey, the local representative of the imperial interest, did not seem inclined to compromise. A politician himself, his strategy was to campaign publicly against his antagonists, making full use of his position and powers as local representative of imperial power and authority in order to carry through Colonial Office policy. This was the first setting for the revolutionary condition that was to be created in Barbados in 1876.

The development of the political division in the ruling class in Barbados in 1876 can be examined. Governor Hennessey in March 1876 was able to report to the Colonial Office that persons in the island opposed to confederation and crown colony government had started to organize politically in the interest of that opposition. A 'provisional committee' had been set up by the newly launched Barbados Defence Association, a political organiza-

tion which stated that its object was 'the preservation of their "constitution", the protection of their interests, and the maintenance of order, and a good understanding between the different classes of the population'. Hennessey listed the following as members of the provisional committee. S.H. Collymore, D.C. DaCosta, B. Inniss, J. Innis, T. Gill, J.A. Lynch, Doctor Pilgrim, Thomas H. Sealy (the honorary secretary of the Defence Association and son of Sir John Sealy of the Legislative Council), J.H. Shannon, J. Smith, J. Spencer, and S. Yearwood.[23]

Likewise, the planter press proceeded to identify to the public the confederation party, (if somewhat more abusively), charged to be led by the governor and some of his closest official advisers. *The Agricultural Reporter* listed the names of persons known or suspected of confederation tendencies. First listed was Bishop Mitchinson, Lord Bishop of Barbados, then Sir T. Graham Briggs, a member of the Legislative Council. The others were C. Kemp Sturgeon, 'late of the Pearl gang St. Kitts', Benjamin D. Sandiford, H.R. Semper, a member of the Legislative Council and Attorney General, T.J. Davis described as a 'Quack Doctor'; John Clements, Inspector General of Police; J.R. Douglas, described as a 'late coachman and insolvent debtor'; R.A.P. Bibby, described as a 'Briefless Barrister'; T. Kerr, a judge of the Assistant Court of Appeal; J.T. Dottin, described as a 'Bankrupt Merchant'; W.D. Griffith, Auditor General; F.B. Griffith, Inspector of Inland Revenue; S. Cowes Ellcock, described as a 'Constable and Village Lawyer'; E.R. Stuart, Assistant Master of Harrison College, described as a 'protege of the Bishop'; B.C. Howell, ex-member of the Assembly; W.T. Armstrong, Inland Revenue Officer; David Morris, coal miner; Charles A. Carew, described as a 'Rum Seller in expectancy of a berth in the excise department'; D. Stroud, described as 'a gentleman particularly fond of paying debts'; 'Cudjoe' Lovell, a 'Constable recently wounded in the mouth for praising Pope Hennessey'; James S. Loyd, 'late mission student of Codrington College Mission house, rusticated, alias expelled for abusing a Reverend Gentleman, at present orderly to Briggs and Hennessey'. J.W.B., 'a half crazy old tailor, excluded from the Public Library by Mrs. Bayne for scribbling on the margin of the books'; Young, 'sheep-stealer, Confederate Agent for St. Joseph', Providence Holder, 'late of the Penal Gang, Confederate Agent for St. George'.[24]

The anti-confederation camp carried their campaign to the public through public meetings, some public demonstrations and continuously used the established press, which was practically unanimously behind them, for wide propagation of their political point of view.[25] A report of the inspector general of police to the governor towards the end of March indicates that public meetings by the anti-confederationists were being taken to all parts of the island, even though the head of the police suggests it was either not reaching or appealing too much to the mass of the coloured and black working class. The report informed the governor that five public meetings had taken place; one at the Promenade Gardens in Bridgetown, one at Black Rock in St. Michael, another at Codrington Hill, one in St. Philip and one other in Christ Church. Although the Defence Association had also held meetings at which only members were admitted the head of police did not think that the people attending the public meetings totalled together more than 5,000. The principal speakers at those meetings were identified as Mr. Shannon, a Mr. King, an undertaker, a Mr. Pitt, a linen draper, Mr. Brewster, a Clerk at DaCosta and Co., Mr. Thomas Gill, a former speaker of the Assembly and proprietor of Kent Estate and Mr. Joseph Connell, proprietor of Oughterson's Estate. Several members of the House of Assembly attended these meetings but had not addressed the people. In the opinion of the inspector general of police the agitation for confederation in the towns was conducted amongst the merchants and their clerks and porters, and in the country, amongst the planters.

The report also indicated the way the case against confederation was presented at the public meetings. Individuals identified as supporters of confederation were denounced and confederation was described as 'damnation not salvation' which would bring with it 'starvation', 'increased taxation' and 'oppression'.[26] *The West Indian Newspaper* also contributed to this point, when reporting the anti-confederation public meeting held at Rosemong Black Rock. It noted that the following topics were listed for discussion.

(i) What is Confederation and what has it done for the people of the Leeward Islands?
(ii) Is it safe for the people of this island to be guided by the statements which are being made by the advocates of Confederation respecting the benefits which will accrue to Barbados in the event of our consenting to be federated with the Windward Islands?
(iii) Is the present form of government in Barbados with an efficient and liberal Executive at its head equal to the wants and calculated to advance the interests of the masses'.[27]

The pro-confederationists, organized with equal determination. They were, however, unable to use the established press and in fact had to launch their own newspaper organ, *The Barbados People and Windward Islands Gazette*.[28] This campaign had less of the public demonstration about it and was more organized to direct an intense agitation at the grassroot level, by grassroot agents.[29]

The West Indian was by mid-April indicating the state to which the agitation carried on by the opposing parties had brought the society. It placed the blame at Hennessey's door, asserting that in pursuit of his policies he had managed to create an agitation in the public mind, and a state of things unparalleled since the passing of the Emancipation Act forty years before.[30] In fact, *The West Indian*, in another strong editorial of 13 April, argued that a state had now been reached in the agitation where 'class stands arrayed against class', where bands of men were roving the country 'committing outrages' and 'exciting the minds of the labourers'. The paper had, indeed, already reported a number of violent incidents which included shootings and mob violence;[31] and there had been a major incident of mob violence and shooting at an anti-confederation meeting at Mount Prospect in St. Peter during the previous month.[32] In the editorial of the 13 April, however, it took care to note the non-intervention of the police in this increasingly violent agitation.

It was not surprising therefore that the editorial further pointed out that it had now become necessary for people to carry revolvers to protect their person and that it was no longer safe to travel in some places day or night. The editorial raised the question. 'How are they to be resisted except by force?' Violence was now clearly being placed on the agenda as a part of the political struggle between two factions of political authority in Barbados.

Two further aspects of the agitation emerged from the editorial, which suggests why this conflict in the ruling class had become so intense. The editorial alleged that the agents of confederation had been engaging in 'Communistic raving' to the mass of the people, telling them that when confederation was established there would be 'a division of the land amongst the black population. The blacks are to take the place of the whites and those who ride now will have to walk and their horses and carriages turned over to their former servants. Everything is to be held in common, the land, houses, stock, the very wives and daughters of the proprietors . . .'[33]

The two significant points which arise from such a picture of the pro-confederation agitation is that the case could now be made by plantocracy, even if opportunistically, that confederation was not now only a struggle which would cut back their monopoly of local power but that the confederation agitation, as put to the masses, would end in a revolution destructive to plantocracy as a class or at least an insurrection which would severely damage them materially. Evidence emerging later will indicate that agitation carried on among the people did seem to suggest to them that confederation meant revolution. In the context of our present discussion which seeks to recognize the depth of the division between the contending factions of the Barbadian ruling circles, this indicates that just as the planters had by April 1876 been ready to carry and use weapons to protect their person against the confederationists and were prepared to use violence in this cause,[34] so also the confederationists had decided to agitate the masses to, if not revolution, then at least to insurrection, if necessary or desirable, or at least create such chaos in the society as would lead to surrender by the local Assembly to crown colony government as happened in Jamaica in 1865. In respect then to the two centres of political rule in Barbados, both in this sense had reached such heights of antagonism to each other, that they had come to the position that violence against one another was a natural extension of their political agitation, if their particular political objective was to be attained or, in the case of plantocracy, maintained. It seems evident to us that factions of the ruling circle of Barbados were convinced that they could not continue to rule in the old way and this had brought serious and deep division between the rulers of Barbados to the point of a crisis of government.

The presence of a governmental crisis of the ruling class was quickly appreciated by the underclass; but the response by the two sections of the underclasses to that crisis was diametrically different. The growing petit bourgeois black and coloured section objectively defended the oligarchy by naively perceiving oligarchy as embryonic democracy. Consequently they opposed confederation, crown colony government and Pope Hennessey; and finally they joined forces with the plantocracy to attack the mass action of the labouring class.

The labouring class, on the other hand, knew and understood oligarchy to be despotism. They knew and understood through their own experiences as had Prescod and his early band of strugglers that direct imperial rule, when compared to planter despotism, was a benign despotism although naturally hypocritical. They knew that planter oligarchy and democracy were to each other as are the like poles of a magnet. They repel each other. The labouring class' response to the crisis of 1876 was mass insurrection.

The spread and intensity of the 1876 insurrection can be gathered from numerous contemporary 1876 sources.[35] It affected every part of the island; its duration was longer and its threat to the state agencies of law and order far greater than even the 1937 rebellion; and the physical possibility of overturning and removing the ruling order in Barbados far more likely. It was the nearest post-slavery Barbados has ever come to revolution.

The editorials of *The Agricultural Reporter, The West Indian* and *The Times*, despite their clear hostility to the masses, are useful in their description of the insurrection. The military report contained in the Command Papers on the disturbances, on the other hand, provides a military point of view, which indicates a more precise judgement of the threat to the security forces of the state and the intensity of the insurrection as seen by the military.

The most intense period of the insurrection lasted for just under two weeks, with most of the incidents taking place between 18–26 April 1876. One of the first important features to emerge is that the disturbances were not spontaneous; organization, planning and coordination are quite apparent in the way in which the rebels went about their business. Mobs of people, sometimes in their thousands, were assembled by the blowing of bugles or conch shells. Then, escorted frequently by bearers of red flags, they proceeded to raid and terrorize the estates, raiding the potato fields and slaughtering the livestock. This was, however, done after the reading of a document authorizing them to do this in the name of Pope Hennessey and confederation. Where confronted by the police they were prepared to attack them, throwing stones and using cane bills, cutlasses and sticks as weapons. In fact, some policemen were captured by the rebels, ridiculed and threatened with death, and attempts were made to rescue from detention comrades who had been arrested.[36] It would appear, however, that during the first three days of the rebellion, there was little intervention by the police with both the inspector general of police and the governor making the case that there was not much cause for alarm, despite the besieging of Government House by persons of property, demanding to see the governor because of the threat to themselves and their property. In fact the governor was only prepared to entertain a deputation from the merchants of Bridgetown and a few members of the Legislature.[37] Colonel Sargeant, the commander of the troops, also reported that he had twice gone to Governor Hennessey informing him that various people had come to him asking for military assistance, and this was some ten days before the troops were eventually allowed to intervene.[38]

The intensity of the rebellion clearly increased by 21 April, by which time the rebels were no longer content to stick to raiding fields of provisions, but were moving on the personal property of the estate owners and the threat to the lives of the plantocracy was becoming most real.[39] It was only at that point that Governor Hennessey allowed the military to intervene.[40] A section of the report of one of the military commandeers, Major Blythe, gives a picture of the growing intensity of the insurrection at that point in time. Major Blythe reported:

Being informed that the rioters had gone in the direction of Applewhaite, Mr. James Hickson's estate, . . . we followed them and I may say arrived not a moment too soon as the visitors had gutted the house and threatened the lives of the inmates; . . . on our approach we noticed a number of people dispersing in various directions some of them carrying what I now conclude was plunder, but a large portion (perhaps two or three hundred) were loitering about, most of them appeared to be armed with bill hooks and long cane knives, . . . In the avenue leading to the house we found a man apparently dead, shot through the right lung; . . . On getting to the house we found large stones strewn all around in the verandah which had evidently been used as missiles for breaking in the doors. All glass smashed, doors, windows, sashes, and venetians hacked and broken as if by hatchets or bill hooks, in this way an entrance appeared to have been made.

The house was completely gutted of all portable articles and the heavier furniture destroyed; for instance the piano smashed, chandelier pulled from the ceiling and broken to pieces, also marble tables shattered in pieces and locked-up places for the reception of papers and money burst open and in fact the lower part of the house a complete wreck, as would doubtless have been the case with the upper part where the family had retired to, and the mob had just gained access to when the report reached them of our approach which caused them to decamp. Another rioter was lying dead, shot through the forehead in the rear of the house — the man's name was Smith Baird whom the mob recognized as their 'Colonel', or second in command, the man 'Green' (previously mentioned as being shot through the right lung) being their or 'general' as they called him, . . . On going upstairs where Mr. Hinckson's family had gone for safety, we found them in a deplorable condition caused by the threats that were used by the rioters as to murdering him and carrying off his wife. Mr. Hinckson had given the man, Green, all the money in the house about 200 dollars in the hopes of appeasing them, which expedient failed, on the estates (six) policemen were stationed when the mob arrived; we only saw three . . .[41]

Also with respect to the intensity of the rebellion it is important to note that the military quite quickly appreciated that they were over-extended. For even though the attacks on the estates were often serious only in very special cases were troops sent out to them. Colonel Sargeant instead saw the necessity of making secure St. Ann's Fort, where the magazine was based and most of the plantocracy and white families had to take up residence within the fort or in ships in Carlisle Bay. This was the position up to 26 April at least.[42]

Colonel Sargeant in his report to the Secretary of State for War summed up his appreciation of the situation in Barbados at the height of the insurrection as follows:

. . . There can be no doubt that since the commencement of those riots, a great amount of wanton destruction of property of planters and others has been perpetuated throughout the country and the marauders and rioters from the 21st instance and during the 21st, 22nd, and 23rd instance have committed the most extensive and wanton, indeed, the expression is not too strong to say brutal destruction of cattle, poultry and other farm yard stock, sufficient in itself to create the greatest and most intense alarm in the minds of landed proprietors evidenced in what these scoundrels would do if not deterred to a certain extent by the knowledge that there were European troops at hand. There can be no doubt whatever that after the experience gained by the present transaction that Barbados can never be left without the presence of European troops. I am fully convinced that if we had not sufficient force to stem the spirit of riot and disorder openly and unreservedly shown by the evil disposed on this occasion, that the white population and I have no doubt, would have met with consequences of the most grave and painful character.

Situated as we are at present as regards our military position the prospect of the immediate arrival of H.M.S. 'Angus' from Jamaica and 180 of the 2nd West Indian Regiment, and 150 troops from Demerara, I have not the least apprehension but that we shall be prepared to meet any emergency that may arise. Colonel Cox telegraphs that in the event of 180 men from Jamaica not being required they are to go on to Honduras without landing but I think under all the circumstances they had better be landed and do so accordingly; the Detachment from Demerara I would also keep here for a short time and until the country is in a settled state . . . The presence of these two detachments here besides restoring confidence, will also enable me to relieve the extreme pressure of duty necessarily imposed on the troops already here during the events of the last few days.

During these three days 21st, 22nd, 23rd instant a large number of families, hundreds of ladies and children flocked in from the surrounding country and neighbourhood for protection leaving their estates and residence with nothing but the clothes they had on them or a few articles of value, money etc. St. Ann's was crowded with ladies and children as was also the pavilion at the General's residence, Queen's House, and it is only within the last few days that these families have returned to their homes . . .[43]

Statistical information provided by *The West Indian* newspaper on some of the material damage done during the disturbances, and the statistics on persons killed and wounded provided by the inspector general of police, establish that 9 estates in St. Joseph suffered damage to crops, livestock, furniture and equipment amounting to $2,181. At Waterford Plantation in St. Michael a gang of four to five hundred men, women and children was reported by *The West Indian* as doing damage to the tune of $1,206. The damage at 3 St. Andrew estates was $224 and to poultry, hogs, potato fields and sundry other goods and property totalled $150.17. At Salters, St. George, 9 acres of ripe and 3 acres of unripe potatoes were stolen. At the Valley, 9 acres of potatoes were stolen and at New Market 1 acre.[44]

Seven rioters were killed or died of wounds during the riots from 18 to 21 April 1876. On 21 April, Robert E. Sendhourse, aged 35, of St. Joseph was bayoneted in the left breast and died on the spot. The wound was inflicted by a police officer reputedly in self defence. On 22 April, London S. Bird, 33, of St. George was shot dead at Applewhaite. He was reported as killed during the riots by a policeman, or some unknown person. On 21 April, Charles Cummins, 24, of St. John suffered a gun shot wound in the right thigh and died on 22 April. His leg was amputated and he was reputedly shot by police at the Halton riot. Joseph Went, 17, of St. George suffered the same fate; he died on 10 May. On 22 April, Joseph Braithwaite, 30, of St. Philip, was wounded in the right leg, and died on 12 May. He was shot by a soldier of the 35th regiment on the direction of Mr. J. Hinckson, J.P. Henry Green, 27, of St. George sustained a gunshot wound in the right lung and died on the 29 April. He was reportedly shot by Mr. Hinckson of Applewhaite on 22 April. On the same day, Murray Clarke, 20, of St. Joseph suffered a gun shot wound in the left groin. He was found dead on Richard Olton's land on 26 April.

Thirteen rioters were wounded on 21 April, most of them at Halton, St. Philip. Rebecca Daniel, 19, of St. Philip was shot through the abdomen. John Bagley, 26, was shot in the right thigh and had his leg amputated. Isaac Ward, 23, of St. Philip, was shot in the left leg. Hubert L. Sealy, 10, of St. John, was shot in the instep. Rebecca Alleyne, 21, of St. John was shot in the left arm and her arm was amputated. William Hill, 26, of St. George, was shot in the thigh. Joseph Hoyte, 30, of St. John, was shot in the leg. Mary Belle, 33, of St. John, was shot in the feet. Mary Taylor, 46, of St. Philip, was wounded by a bayonet. Margaret Shepherd, St. Philip, 28, received a bayonet wound of the hand. R.W. Critchlow, 15, St. Joseph, was shot in the right arm and knee. Critchlow was not shot at the Halton riot, but allegedly by a police officer at Hackleton's Cliff.

Twelve rioters were wounded on 22 April. Mary Forde of St. Michael was bayoneted in the thigh at the Bush Hall riot by a policeman under the orders of Corporal Jones. Edward Payne, 42, of St. Michael, was shot in the bowel at the Staple Grove riot by Mr. Haynes. Henry Jones, 23, of Christ Church was shot in the back at Fairy Valley by the manager of the estate, Mr. Griffith. John, alias Hardy Clarke, 45, of St. Joseph was shot in the right arm during the Crab Hole riot by a police officer. George Thomas, 34, of St. George was shot in the back. John Codrington, 25, of St. Thomas was shot in the right thumb, and his thumb was amputated. John S. Holder, 40, of St. Michael was shot in the face. Mary Blackman, 38, of St. George was shot in the left arm by Mr. Whitehall, manager of Rowans; and her son was also shot. Alexander Small, 19, of St. George was wounded in the head by a stone. James Griffith, 19, of St. Michael was shot in the breast; and William Blackman, 12, of St. George suffered a fractured skull.

Eight policemen were wounded. On 18 April at Byde Mill, Sergeant Taylor, 36, of St. Philip received stone wounds of the head, arms and feet; Constable William Harrison, 28, of St. Philip had his chin cut open by a stone; and Constable Mapp, 30, of St. Philip, Constable Griffiths, 43, of St. George and Acting Corporal Ashby, 39, of St. George all received head wounds from stones. On 21 April, Colonel Clements, inspector general of police, 48, of St. Michael was wounded during a riot and had a branch of the left temporal artery cut, supposedly by a stone. He also suffered blows to the body. On the same day Constable Forde, 32, of St. Michael had his cheek cut open by a cane bill during a riot; and on 22 April Sergeant H. Lyder, 40, of St. Andrews suffered a head wound from a stone during a riot at Crab Hole, St. Joseph.[45]

The details on wounds suffered and the areas of the island from which persons wounded or killed came indicate graphically the widespread nature of the riots. More important, the nature of the wounds, particularly bayonet wounds, indicates the hand-to-hand character of the combat and therefore provides an indication of the intensity of the revolt. As would be expected, advantage in arms was with the police and military. Most policemen wounded had been struck by stones, although there is the one case in which a cane bill had been applied to the face of one constable. There is one other important advantage in having the list of wounded and killed available. More often than not we see in the accounts of riots merely the mass side of insurrection, masses and not persons[46], but the data here tell us clearly that a 12 year old boy of St. George was involved in the rebellion and suffered a fractured skull. We also know the names of the many amputees who carried the marks of 1876 to the end of their days. We know further that the 12 year old boy's mother, Mary Blackman, was shot by an estate manager and that she was 38 years old.

The non-spontaneous, organized and planned character of the mass disturbances of 1876 already provide an indication of the political consciousness of the masses at that time. The sequence of the disturbances, particularly the change in character after 21 April, suggests even more about this political character. What the first stage of the disturbances might have suggested — a passive body of people being acted upon by agitators and used for opportunist political ends — is denied by the events after 21 April which indicated a political awareness and independence on the part of the masses that most certainly Hennessey and the confederationist camp had made little or no calculation for.

What has been ascertained so far with respect to the pro-confederation agitation, particularly as described by the planters press, was that the agitation was conducted either by wily opportunists, as they described Hennessey, who did not see the full consequences of their actions, or by malicious agents too ignorant to perceive or care about the implications of their agitation. It was the latter, the agents who took the campaign to the grass roots, who were substantially accused of imbuing the confederation campaign with revolutionary rhetoric. The planter class apparently perceived that involvement of the masses in the pro-confederation campaign was either opportunistic, hypocritical or the result of ignorance of the masses.[47] There seems to be little point in denying this planter perception. But the pro-confederationists' and the anti-confederationists' perception of the masses' role in the politics of that time was misplaced. In the case of the confederationists, they saw the masses as there to be used, since in the confederationists' view the overall imperial plan for the colony was wise and would benefit all classes; so that to use the masses for the achievement of such an end was in fact in this view a service to the masses. For the anti-confederationists, on the other hand, the masses were an ignorant, simple, people who could easily be deluded by malicious and naive agitators.

In our view, one voice of the masses, apparently recorded in letter form and found by accident, might start to give an indication of how the labouring masses of Barbados in fact perceived the politics of 1876:

To his Excellency,

My deer Sir we has made up in our mines from seeing the white people is so much against Confedoraction which is for our good to raise up a rebellion on the eveinin afater ester against them so you but stand pun we side with the sogers but I here Mr. Spenser say at Sumervil that if a rebelion was to cum for Confederaction you would be in a set a truble and you cant make the sogers do as you likes. let us no by Mr. Davis that time as if it is tru it will bring you in truble we shant do it but you no when the white people ses the firs — they gets very friton it will do good on that nite as the people will be in a good temper so tel us if the sogers will fite for us; sum of the peple in St. Johns has promis to goin as you servent.[48]

John Jackman
St. Philips

This letter in the best of 'Bajan' sums up in a most singular way the politics of the masses in 1876. To a very great extent it put in writing what the masses did in practice during the course of the 1876 insurrection. It shows, further, as their practice also suggested, that they did not see themselves as being used and indeed did not allow themselves to be used in 1876; but with remarkable astuteness, the grassroot leaders of the masses were in fact using the political crisis in the ruling class for their own ends. Their perception in other words was that while the cat is away, the mice will play.

It seems to us that the labouring class in Barbados perceived that the ruling class in Barbados was in crisis over the confederation issue and that the governor in his effort to implement Colonial Office policy needed to have mass support, or create chaos in order to counter planter resistance. They moreover agreed and knew that Colonial Office policy had always been professedly declared to be less hurtful to their interests than planter policy. When the agitation took place they became conscious of how serious and deep was the division in the ruling class and when the confederationist party agitators linked confederation with the amelioration of their social condition and suggested a programme to overcome this situation through the removal of plantocracy and its economy, the masses knew that was their (i.e. the masses) natural political programme.

It is not surprising, then, that they co-operated with the confederation agitators and that, consequently, the uprising was so well foreplanned and organized. But the appointment of their own leadership, giving individuals the ranks of 'general' and 'colonel', seems to suggest that they understood that at some point in the insurrection they had to lead themselves. Their initiative after 21 April seems to confirm this, and it is no accident that Hennessey's close collaborators in the confederation party and chief of police, Colonel

Clements, was on that date thrown from his horse, beaten with stones and sent packing back to Government House. It is no accident that Hennessey quickly realized that the Barbadian masses were no passive factor in the action, simply to be agitated and used, but that they represented the threat of an overthrow of his government and everything else with it. So that on 21 April Hennessey called his commander of troops, Colonel Sargeant, and turned out the military.[49] Because of the political consciousness of the Barbadian masses, because of their political action, Hennessey, their professed champion, had to counter their revolution.

Notes

1. Barbados Blue Book of Statistics, R.1. *Return of the Population;* in C.O. 33/86. and K.1 and K.2 *Political Franchise.* The last census was taken in 1871.
2. Ibid. K.1. The Blue Book gives the equivalent amounts in local currency as respectively £200, £100, £50 and £5.
3. Ibid. R.1.
4. Ibid. R.2.
5. Cf. Bruce Hamilton, *Barbados and the Confederation Question 1871–1885.* (Millbank, London: The Crown Agents, 1956).
6. Ibid. p. 3–4.
7. Ibid. p. 4.
8. The statistics for goods and wages are based on Barbados Blue Book 1876, Y1, Table of Average Rates of Wages for Labour. In C.O. 33/86.
9. Ibid. Y3, Table of Average Prices of Various Articles of Use or Consumption.
10. Ibid. From the Fourth Annual Report of the Superintendent of Emigration.
11. Ibid. Emigration Acts had been instituted to contain emigration after the end of the Apprenticeship system. Another Emigration Act was passed in 1873, which discriminated particularly against the agricultural labourers and artisans excluding them from benefits to facilitate emigration. Cholera had been a big killer particularly among the poorer classes in the preceding decades.
12. For a discussion on this question and on the implications and impact of Crown colony government. Cf. Roy Augier, 'Before and After 1865', *New World Quarterly,* 2(1966), pp. 33–40.
13. Bruce Hamilton, op. cit., pp. 26–27.
14. *The Agricultural Reporter,* Bridgetown, Barbados, editorial of 3 December 1875. This newspaper was one of the organs of the planter interests.
15. *The Agricultural Reporter,* editorial of 4 January 1876.
16. *The Agricultural Reporter,* editorial of 23 November 1875.
17. *The Agricultural Reporter,* editorial of Friday 31 December 1875.
18. C.O. 31/67, in Message of Governor Hennessey to the House of Assembly. Minutes of Proceedings of Legislative Council Session 1875–76, at Legislative Council.
19. Meeting of Tuesday, 18 January 1876.
20. *The Times,* (Bridgetown, Barbados), editorial of Tuesday, 25 January 1876.
21. C.O. 31/67 Appendix II, Document No. 3. of the Minutes of the House of Assembly meeting of Friday, 3 March 1876.
22. C.P. 13.39; Papers relating to the Disturbances in Barbados, presented to both Houses of Parliament by her Majesty 1876. No. 58, O. 107 of the C.P. Governor Hennes-
    sey to the Earl of Carnarvon, 4 March 1875. In Account and Papers (12), 1876, Vol. LIII.
23. C.P. 1539. Papers relating to Late Disturbances in Barbados. Accounts and Papers (12) 1876, Vol. LIII. No. 64, p. 122 Hennessey to Carnarvon, 11 March 1876.
24. *The Agricultural Reporter,* editorials of 4 April and 11 April 1876.
25. Cf. Editorials of *The Times* of 1 April 1876; *The West Indian,* editorial of Tuesday, 14 March 1876; *The Agricultural Reporter,* editorial of Friday, 31 March 1876.
26. C.P. 1539, No. 80, p. 143 of C.P., Enclosure 3, Hennessey to Carnarvon, Report on Anti-Confederation Meetings by the Inspector-General of Police.
27. *The West Indian,* Tuesday, 14 March 1876.
28. The newspaper was launched in late March 1876.
29. *The Times,* editorial of 26 April 1876. Also see 'Message of the House of Assembly to Queen Victoria, 11 July 1876 (C.O. 321/11).
30. *The West Indian,* editorial of 11 April 1876.
31. *The West Indian,* of Friday, 31 March. See also *The Times* of 8 April.
32. Accounts of the incidents at Mount Prospect on 28 March were recorded in all the established press at the end of March. See also Bruce Hamilton's account in *Barbados and the Confederation Question 1871–1885,* pp. 65–66.
33. C.O. 321/10 Chief Justice Packer to the Colonial Secretary. Enclosure 2, in Despatch No. 190, 19 August 1876, Hennessey to Carnarvon.
34. C.P. 1539, No. 88, p. 171. Indeed Governor Hennessey himself was threatened with assassination, and additional guards had to be placed at government house. (Despatch of Hennessey to Carnarvon, 30 March 1876 in Accounts and Papers (12) 1876, Vol. LIII.
35. See Message of the House of Assembly to Queen Victoria requesting Hennessey's recall in C.O. 321/11. See also *The Agricultural Reporter,* Tuesday, 25 April 1876. See also Hamilton op. cit., pp. 71–5.
36. See the Report of Major Blythe of the 35th Regiment, Commanding the Gun Hill detachment, to Colonial Tisdall, Commanding 35th Regiment, 29 April 1876. In papers relating to the disturbances C. 1559, No. 24, pp. 83–86. War Office to the Colonial Office, 20 May 1876. (Accounts and Papers (12) 1876, Vol. LIII).
37. See *The Agricultural Reporter,* editorial of 21 April 1876.
38. The Report of Colonel E.W. Sargeant to the Secretary of State for War, 26 April 1876. In C. 1559, papers relating to the disturbances, No. 24, pp. 86–88, War Office to the Colonial Office, 20 May 1876 (Accounts and Papers (12) 1876, Vol. LIII).
39. Ibid, as well as Major Blythe's report, pp. 83–86.
40. Ibid, Lt. Col. Sargeant's report, pp. 86–88.
41. Ibid, Major Blythe's report, pp. 83–86.
42. Ibid, Col. Sargeant's report, pp. 86–88.
43. Ibid.
44. In *The West Indian,* 12 May 1876.
45. Based on the report of Col. John Clements, Inspector-General of Police, 10 June 1876. Enclosed as Appendix Y., Document No. 7 in the Message of Governor Hennessey to the House of Assembly Meeting of Tuesday, 13 June 1876. Minutes of proceedings of the House of Assembly Session 1875–1876 in C.O. 31/67. Bruce Hamilton makes an interesting comment on these statistics of Clement's. Hamilton states that during the period of the 20–25th April: '. . . eight persons appear to have been killed and something over thirty wounded. The figures published by the Chamber of Commerce . . . are by including small injuries not requiring medical treatment brought up to a considerably higher total than the returns of Clements which based on admissions to the General Hospital is probably too low . . .' Hamilton, op. cit., p. 75. Despite

this, however, Clements statistics and details on injuries provide information which assists substantially in the further understanding of the character of the 1876 insurrection.

46. See G. Rude, *The Crowd in the French Revolution,* O.U.P. 1969, for a discussion of this issue.

47. See *The Agricultural Reporter,* editorials of 25 April and particularly the editorial of 12 May 1876. It would be useful to remember again, at this point, that a part of the Colonial Office strategy for introduction of Crown Colony government was the opportune use of a situation of chaos created by the ineptitude of the local assemblies which would lead to the local ruling class surrendering political power in the interests of security.

48. This letter was enclosed in a letter to the *Agricultural Reporter* of 14 April 1876, it was said by the writer of the letter of the Reporter that it was found in the parish of St. George.

49. See Col. Sargeant's report.

Continuity Not Change: The Incidence of Unrest Among Ex-Slaves in the British West Indies, 1838–1876

Michael Craton

The observation that ruling classes tend to sustain their hegemony by shifts that are merely superficial, and the contention that oppressed classes will always resist their oppression, are ideally tested by focusing attention on the plight and political behaviour of the ex-slaves of the British West Indian colonies in the period after slave emancipation, particularly between 1838 and 1876.[1]

At the imperial level, the adoption of 'liberal' social and economic policies gave British slaves their nominal freedom while allowing freer trade with areas outside the formal empire where profits were greater and chattel slavery continued for a further fifty years. At the colonial level, plantocracies continued to dominate. No colony with its own Assembly lost its power of self-legislation before 1866, and in all colonies — including Crown Colonies directly ruled from London — the ex-slaves were cleverly kept in their place. Education was minimal, the franchise restricted, and law and order maintained by a scarcely reformed and even more impersonal magistracy and police force, and by the translation from Britain to the colonies of allegedly liberal but in fact class-regulating masters and servants, vagrancy, police and poor laws.

Most ex-slaves aimed to be peasant proprietors, yet they were denied cheap land by the application of Wakefieldian principles, and kept from squatting by the increased efficiency of government surveyors and lawyers insisting on proper title. In colonies with little spare land they were forced to compete with each other for the limited wage employment available, but elsewhere the planters' 'labour problem' was solved by the importation of cheap and reliable 'coolie' labourers from India. As a result, British West Indian ex-slaves were less a free peasantry than a wage-slave proletariat, employed only when needed on their former owners' terms, and competing with each other and with new immigrants of different ethnicities.

A closer look than has previously been given shows that the ex-slaves were far more restless and resistant than has been suggested by imperialistic writers or those who considered that emancipation was an end in itself. Unrest in the earliest years of nominal freedom stemmed from problems of adjustment, from official opposition to a return to traditional ways, especially in religion, from tensions occasioned by questions of rents, wages and the availability of land, and from conflict with new immigrants, government surveyors and the police. These incidents multiplied and spread in times of economic slump such as the late 1840s, early 1860s and mid–1870s, or in times of natural disaster, such as drought, flood or cholera epidemic.

In Jamaica, for example, recent research has shown that there were dozens of riots hitherto unpublicized between 1838 and 1865; localized for the most part, but approaching islandwide revolts in 1848 and 1859.[2] This paper, though, concentrates on the three most serious outbreaks in the British West Indies as a whole; the 'Angel Gabriel' Riots in Guyana in 1856, the Morant Bay Rebellion in Jamaica in 1865, and the Federation Riots in Barbados in 1876. It argues that the fact that these happened in the same colonies in which the chief of the late slave rebellions occurred (Barbados in 1816, Guyana in 1823, and Jamaica in 1831–2) was not coincidental, pointing up the telling parallels between slave and ex-slave grievances, the tactics, aims and expectations of rebels and rioters, and the savage responses of the white colonial plantocrats.[3]

In Guyana by 1856 the slave revolt of 1823 was a long closed entry in official ledgers but still a potent folk memory, for attitudes, issues and conditions had not changed fundamentally. In August 1823 the slaves on the East Coast of Demerara had come out in their thousands to demand freedom, or at least far better conditions of labour and more time to work their own provision grounds, from which they supplemented their meagre diet and made some money at informal local markets. For the most part they were convinced that they had already been granted concessions by the imperial government which were being withheld by the oligarchy of planters and Georgetown merchants. Many of them recently Christianized, the slaves did not wilfully damage the estates and offered little violence to the whites, calculating that the imperial troops (some of them black) would not be used against them except in retribution. In fact, the rebels were dragooned by the regular troops, white militia and Amerindian auxiliaries at the behest of a governor who was himself a soldier-planter, and as many as 250 slaves lost their lives.[4]

With emancipation in 1838 the ex-slaves had moved to achieve their aspirations, but with very limited success. As many as could left the estates, some to settle in the colonial capital, Georgetown, but more to find land for themselves and form 'free villages'. Yet these ex-slaves villages were free only in the senses of being unregulated and neglected by the plantocratic regime, emancipation having chiefly freed the planters from their previous legal and moral responsibilities. In a country where the only fertile land was near the coast and rivers, and extensive drainage works were necessary, suitable land was scarce and expensive. Though they often co-operated to buy land, the ex-slaves were unable to grow export staples and were restricted even in marketing local produce. Increasing cash needs (exacerbated by a growing population) could only be met by continuing to work for wages on plantations on terms compatible with peasant proprietorship, at a time when increased mechanization and economies of scale meant that ordinary labour was ever more cruelly seasonal. Planters, however, complained that negro labour was spasmodic, unreliable and insufficient — arguments used to justify the importation of Madeiran, Chinese and Indian labourers from 1835 onwards.[5]

The cultural gap between whites and blacks remained as wide as the socio-economic. In Georgetown, considerable numbers of both races lived close together, with resulting tensions. Yet over the rest of the colony only two small categories of whites lived in permanent contact with the Afro-Guyanese, both of them acting in an intermediate role between ruling whites and peasant-proletarian blacks. The few non-conformist missionaries willingly accepted the function of bringing 'under a more efficient moral culture'[6] a people whom Governor Wodehouse referred to as being 'a good measure beyond the reach of the law, and who lead a life little less savage than that of the beasts of the fields'.[7] Such missionaries admired the religious fervour of the black congregations, but no more understood what Christianity meant to them in terms of solace and inspiration than had Rev. John Smith 'The Demerara Martyr' in 1823.[8]

The Madeiran Portuguese were in an even more uncomfortable position, being not only foreign and Catholic, but having been encouraged by the white merchants and planters to move from mere labouring into the local retail trade, at a time when credit was almost entirely denied to those of black complexion. 'The negro was envious', wrote the negrophobic local historian James Rodway in 1894, 'but not ashamed of his own laziness or want of thrift. Instead therefore of blaming himself for his poverty he ascribed it to cheating and overreaching on the part of his competitor, and unfortunately the Madeiran gave some slight cause for this'.[9] In a situation where blacks were very easily indebted to the retailers and the truck system was not unknown, some would place much less equivocal blame on the Portuguese, but a fairer assessment might see them as the unfortunate catspaws of, and scapegoats for, an extremely exploitative ruling class.

Guyana was ignited in February 1856 by an apocalyptic coloured preacher called John Sayers Orr, who had recently returned from a stormy itinerary of 'sixteen of the United States, the Canadas, Nova Scotia, New Brunswick, . . . Scotland, England and the Protestant part of Ireland'. A sort of proto-Paisley, who announced his meeting with a blast on a trumpet and was nicknamed 'The Angel Gabriel', he purveyed an inflammable mixture of Protestant zeal, populist radicalism, racism and appeals to patriotism, along the lines of the doggerel on one of his American posters:

Scorn be on those who rob us of our rights
Purgatory for Popery and the Pope
Freedom to man be he black or white
Rule Britannia![10]

In his native Georgetown Orr was at first received kindly by the Governor, but 'immediately after he commenced walking about the town and its vicinity, carrying a flag, wearing a badge, and blowing a horn occasionally at the corners of the streets, followed by small groups of the rabble of the place'.[11] His preaching at the market place on Sundays attracted huge crowds of town and country blacks, in Wodehouse's words, 'blending together skillfully and amazingly . . . political and religious subjects in a manner calculated to arouse the passions of the Black and Coloured Population against the Portuguese Immigrants'.[12] Rioting began on Saturday and Sunday, 16–17 February 1856, after Orr was summoned for unlawful assembly, and spread like wildfire throughout the colony once he was committed to prison on Monday, 18 February. 'In the afternoon the town may be said to have been in open insurrection, and the true character of the disturbances was at once revealed', wrote Wodehouse.

The Pope, the Bishop, the Nuns were clean forgotten — Nothing remained in the minds of the actors but the long subsisting hatred and jealousy of the Portuguese Immigrants from Madeira and the love of plunder, aggravated by the gross and brutal character of the female population, who have throughout the Colony taken a most active part in the Riots, and who are of course the most difficult to punish.[13]

Long before the forces of law and order could be fully mobilized the riots had spread throughout Demerara and into the nearer parts of Essequibo and Berbice, and within four days virtually every Portuguese shop had been ransacked and plundered with the few local policemen who tried to intervene being pelted with broken bottles and brickbats. It was reported that 'men, women and children all joined in, and in some parts of the country every Creole of the lower orders seems to have been one of the mob'.[14] So unexpected, sudden and general were the disturbances that the Governor at first presumed a deep conspiracy. The most likely conspirators, he suggested, were the members of a black mutual aid society wishing to invest their funds in a trading transaction, who, disappointed by the way in which previous efforts had failed because 'either the Members were defrauded by their own leaders, or the shops from mismanagement gradually dwindled away', had used the coming of Orr to foment a plot to destroy the opposition and promote 'the establishment of Creole Shops upon its ruins'. In this imaginative scenario the agents of the black syndicate went rapidly through the country districts, not waiting for the actual riots but sowing the seeds by showing fictitious orders from the government not to kill the Portuguese but to seize all their property and give it to the people.[15] Certainly such wish-fulfilling rumours of benevolent actions by the imperial government did circulate in 1856, as they had in 1823 and all the late slave rebellions, though their origins were never ascertained and none of the members of the mutual aid society were actually implicated in the riots. Wodehouse himself found it incredible that anyone would be so ignorant as to believe that the government supported the plunder of the Portuguese, though he could not 'quite assert that they altogether disbelieved a statement which harmonized so agreeably with their own inclinations'.[16] The more plausible alternative that the riots stemmed from a universal socio-economic malaise only gradually dawned on the Governor, and he never publicly drew the most obvious conclusion from the fact that it was mostly food which the mobs plundered from the Portuguese shops.[17]

Governor Wodehouse, whom even the Colonial Office called 'an energetic officer with no disinclination to the old planter system, and with many of his advisors no doubt attached to it',[18] quickly disabused the rioters of the notion that the government was on the people's side and acted as forthrightly as had Governor Murray, his predecessor in 1823. Martial law was not declared, probably because the garrison consisted almost entirely of the black troops of the Second West India Regiment. But the troops were rapidly deployed, reinforcements called for from Barbados and offers of assistance from warships stationed in the neighbouring Dutch and French colonies gratefully accepted. Hundreds of whites and 'respectable' coloureds were sworn in as special constables and the old militia regulations, in abeyance since 1839, reintroduced.[19]

Loss of life was minimal, but so many rioters were arrested that the jails overflowed and a special penal settlement was set up. At the trials, more than 100 'ringleaders' were sentenced by the plantocratic judges to terms of one to three years at hard labour, in addition to fines or floggings. John Sayers Orr, despite being the only prisoner defended by counsel, was sentenced to three years at hard labour, with sureties of £600 to keep the peace on his release.[20] Another 600 prisoners were treated in what Wodehouse regarded as an ingenious and magnaminous way but which nonetheless betrayed his plantocratic bias; they were given a conditional pardon, dependent on the satisfactory conclusion of contract labour on designated estates, at a rate of six months' work for each month's sentence. Such an unprecedented measure Wodehouse defended by declaring 'that a Negro requires to be under a necessity to do right. As long as that necessity exists, he not only obeys but appears to have no wish to avoid. Remove the necessity, and the spirit of licence comes into operation at once'. He went on to state his belief:

that the people of England are no longer under the delusion that these people can be controlled by precisely the same forms of law as prove sufficient in highly civilized communities; and that they no longer wish freedom from slavery to mean anything less than freedom from all legal control . . . The late events have shown beyond the possibility of doubt that the mass of the population are in no degree able to govern themselves than they were at the time of the Emancipation — some will say even less so.[21]

Subsequent actions by the Guyanese regime reflected Wodehouse's dire assessment, and were endorsed by the Colonial Office because they were cleverly consonant with contemporary trends towards socio-political efficiency and *laissez-faire* principles, particularly the belief that colonies should be as self-supporting financially as was possible. A flurry of ordinances passed by the Court of Policy reformed and extended the police force and system of local courts and tightened the code against petty offenders (including, incidentally, a ban on the use of 'horn or other instrument to call people together'). An ordinance against vagrancy virtually defined as 'idle and disorderly persons', 'rogues and vagabonds' or 'incorrigible rogues' any persons who chose not to work for the estates and were found far from their settlements without visible means of support, at the same time as masters and servants legislation put all the onus of observing labour contracts on the labourers.[22]

The most controversial legislation, though, involved the payment of compensation to the Portuguese. Claims for damages amounted to some £59,000, of which no less than £53,000, or 91%, was allowed by a local tribunal — not so much because of representations made by the Portuguese Government to the Foreign Secretary Lord Wodehoue (a relative of the Governor), as through the determination of the Guyanese regime to rescue and restore the retail system, and its superstructure of Georgetown merchants. The compensation, more than the entire annual budget for the colony, was to be paid over five years and financed ostensibly out of the general revenue, but in fact through a novel poll tax. A special registration ordinance was promulgated on the pretext of facilitating the payment of compensation claims in this and possible future cases, but with two other quite different purposes; to arrive at an accurate census of population and property for taxation purposes and to facilitate the control of the free villages.[23] These purposes were transparent to the persons upon whom the new taxation pressed most heavily, at a time of special economic hardship. It was opposed in England by the Anti-Slavery Society, which made a deputation to the Colonial Secretary, and condemned in a petition from the ordinary people of the colony carrying 18,000 signatures.[24] When Governor Wodehouse left Georgetown on vacation in August 1857, he was pelted with stones, cane stalks and offal at the dock, and when he finally left the colony in May 1861 without ceremony and at dead of night, it was suggested that it was 'to avoid a salute of dead cats and dogs'.[25]

In Jamaica, the great slave rebellion at Christmas 1831 and the Morant Bay Rebellion in October 1865 occurred at opposite ends of the island, but in both cases they were merely the conflagration of islandwide tinder. Besides, the combustible material remained unchanged in many respects between 1831 and 1865, despite emancipation in 1838.

By 1831 the creolized slaves of Jamaica had become intolerably frustrated, while at the same time seeing a glimmer of hope that by concerted action they might enforce improved conditions or even speed their own emancipation. Over the previous fifty years, slaves had come to regard the working of provision grounds as a customary right and had established an effective informal market network; yet the more recent decline of the plantation economy and the ending of the slave trade in 1808 had led many masters to extract more work, while expecting the slaves to be more self-supporting. Likewise, the spread of Christianity — originally through the agency of black preachers from America and only later through white missionaries from England — had given slaves opportunities for organization and self-expression, as well as a message with apocalyptic overtones; yet the slaves' sense of self-justification through religion was frustrated, or at least challenged, by plantocratic opposition, to the point of martyrdom. Meanwhile, liberal reform — economic, political and social — was gathering momentum in the metropolis, and the planters' reactions to the threats of free trade, political interference and enforced emancipation occurred in dangerous conjunction with the slaves' growing realization that they had allies, of a sort, in England.[26]

Certainly, the slaves' most implacable enemies were the local whites, but rumours circulated by the elite slaves among their humbler brethren exaggerated the case for external support, claiming, for example, that emancipation had already been granted by the King and withheld by the Assembly, and that Governor, military and missionaries alike would support them if they rose to assert their freedom. In fact, all whites, including missionaries, had a horror of social unrest, particularly when it involved 'uncivilized' blacks. They ignored the clear evidence that a majority of dissidents simply planned a stoppage of work without harming any persons or even damaging the estates, and concentrated their paranoid fears on that minority of realist slaves who knew that the regime would never surrender without a fight and consequently drilled black guerrilla 'regiments'.

The revolt centred on the Great River valley in western Jamaica, far from the centre of government and the colonial armed forces, in ideal peasant farming (and guerrilla) country — a traditional area of maroon resistance. It was also the part of Jamaica where the native Baptists had made their most, and most fervent, converts; indeed, so many of the participants in the rebellion were Baptist church members and so many of their leaders Baptist deacons, that it became popularly known as 'The Baptist War'. Over 200 estates were involved, on which lived some 60,000 slaves. For a week the rebels controlled a fifth of the island, and it was six weeks — after thousands of troops, militia and maroons were deployed, using terror tactics — before the last embers were extinguished. Though no more than a dozen whites were killed in all, about 200 slaves perished during the campaign and no less than 340 were executed after court martial or civil trial.

The Jamaican Assembly assessed damages as well over a million pounds, and the planters received compensation from the imperial government despite the fact that the largest item was the value of the 540 slaves 'lost' in the rebellion. In the wake of the suppression, white Anglican vigilantes torched nearly all the non-conformist chapels in western Jamaica, and it was this and the maltreatment of white missionaries, rather than the death of the 540 slaves, which convinced waverers in Britain of the need to enforce emancipation upon the West Indian slaveholders. The parliamentary select committee to consider the means to effect emancipation 'at the earliest period compatible with the safety of all Classes in the Colonies' was convened just one week after the execution of Sam Sharpe, the noble chief of the Jamaican rebels.[27] Pretty soon the debate centred entirely on the questions of how much compensation the slaveholders should receive for their emancipated property and the means by which the ex-slaves could be compelled to work for their former owners as 'free' wage labourers.

It was, indeed, the attempted enforcement of local adjustments by the plantocracy that provoked much of the tension in the first phase after emancipation. Even in the initial period of optimism, when land seemed plentiful and the prices of peasant produce remained satisfactory, localized disturbances occurred between employers and employed over the trimming of wages and attempts to tie the labourers by charging rents for houses and provision grounds, and between planters and missionaries over the establishment of church-related free villages. With the economic collapse of the later 1840s and in subsequent slumps brought on by drought, hurricane, epidemic or worldwide depression, tension heightened. By 1865 Jamaica enjoyed only a fraction of its former prosperity, but the decline of the richest of all British plantation colonies did not mean that the ex-slaves were left to enjoy the life of free, if impoverished, peasants; rather the reverse. Sporadic conflict occurred over the more efficient application of the laws governing labour contracts, vagrancy and petty offenses, through a magistracy that remained essentially plantocratic and a more officious police force, following a policy of stationing officers in parishes other than their own. Conflict also broke out with more obvious strangers; the new Africans, Indians and few poor whites cynically introduced by the legislature to provide a more reliable plantation labour force while driving down wages through labour competition.[28]

Meanwhile, land for peasant farming grew scarcer; not so much because of a rapid growth of population as the tightening of rules about formal title and the payment of a 'sufficient price' for Crown lands. The situation was particularly anomalous in the light of the steady decline of sugar plantations — so many of the decayed estates being bought up for conversion into inefficient cattle 'pens' by middle-class Jamaicans (coloured as well as white) that one writer has referred to the creation of a 'penocracy' to reinforce the traditional plantocracy.[29] Fights flared between government surveyors and peasant farmers and over the eviction of squatters, and the police were kept constantly busy over cases of praedial larceny, fence breaking, and the rustling and maiming of stock.

The Jamaican countrymen remained a deeply religious people, and the normally high level of observance was periodically raised by waves of frenzied revivalism, particularly during the 1850s and early 1860s. Yet even the people's preoccupation with revivalist religion heightened rather than lowered tensions. Missionaries deplored the way in which the revivalists reverted to spontaneous and unsupervised worship (much of it akin to traditional African 'myal'), and the local whites, as usual, treated what they could neither understand nor control with a mixture of contempt and fear, complaining at the same time that episodes of religious fanaticism kept labourers from the estates and even led to a shortage of peasant-grown ground provisions.[30]

Localized disturbances became general during the depressed mid–1860s, and erupted into a major revolt in St. Thomas-in-the-East in October 1865. A few months before, a Baptist missionary, Edward Underhill, had written a forceful letter to the Colonial Office calling attention to the desperate plight of the Jamaican blacks, particularly now that provisions were scarce because of drought and prices of imports high because of the American Civil War. At the same time, some peasants of St. Ann's parish sent a petition for relief to Queen Victoria herself. The Underhill letter was debated throughout Jamaica, but the only official response was the so-called Queen's Advice to the St. Ann's petitioners callously enjoining hard work and thrift as the only solutions to the hardships.[31]

The Queen's Advice was inspired by the recently-appointed Governor, an obstinate mediocrity and ardent Anglican named Edward Eyre who, on the basis of experience with Australian and New Zealand natives and Indian 'coolies' in Trinidad and St. Vincent, believed that West Indian blacks should be ruled with an iron rod.[32] Eyre's most formidable opponent in the Jamaican Assembly was George William Gordon, an upwardly mobile coloured planter, businessman and independent Baptist church leader, who made himself the people's champion in a personal quest for political status. The real rebel leader in 1865, though, was the equally remarkable Paul Bogle, one of Gordon's black deacons, a peasant smallholder of Stony Gut in St. Thomas, a parish backed by the traditional maroon fastness of the Blue Mountains, with many decayed estates owned by absentees and thousands of land-hungry former slaves and recently freed indentured African labourers.

Events accelerated after Gordon was sacked as a St. Thomas Vestryman and JP for criticizing the operation of justice and a lack of social services in the parish, blaming by implication the Anglican Rector and the Custos (who, rather absurdly, was a German baron, Von Ketelhodt). In August 1865, Gordon allegedly told an audience of St. Thomas blacks 'You have been ground down too long already . . . Prepare for your duty. Remember the destitution in the midst of your families, and your forlorn condition', and went to say of the Queen's Advice, 'it is a lie; it does not come from the Queen'.[33] Shortly afterwards, Governor Eyre refused even to see petitioners, including Bogle, who had walked the 45 miles from St. Thomas's into Spanish Town. Unknown to Gordon, oaths were taken and drilling began in Stony Gut, based on Deacon Bogle's chapel.[34]

On Saturday, 7 October, a market day, a band of Bogle's men rescued a black whom the police were trying to arrest for a breach of the peace at Morant Bay courthouse, a commotion that immediately preceded a case involving eviction for non-payment of rent (in which the plea was 'on the ground that the land was free, and the estate belonged to the Queen').[35] Three days later, police sent from Morant Bay to arrest Bogle were driven back the seven miles from Stony Gut. Von Ketelhodt called out the volunteers and sent to Spanish Town for troops, while at the same time Bogle and 19 others signed a letter to the Governor asking the 'due protection', which, if refused, would compel them 'to put our shoulders to the wheel, as we have been imposed upon for a period of 27 years with due observance to the laws of our Queen and country'.[36]

Before any response could come from Governor Eyre, on Wednesday, 11 October hundreds of crudely armed men marched, to the sound of drum, cow horn and conch shell, upon Morant Bay, where the hated Vestry was in session. Fired on by the volunteers, who killed seven in their only volley, Bogle's forces burned down the Courthouse, released 50 prisoners, looted the town and estate provision grounds, and in all killed 20 whites, including Custos Ketelhodt and several unpopular estate managers. Back at Stony Gut, Bogle held a prayer meeting, allegedly declaring, 'It is now time for us to help ourselves. War is at us; black-skin war is at hand'. Within three days, insurrection had spread from Monkland in the west to Elmwood in the north-east, a distance of 75 miles.[37]

Retribution, though, was swift and terrible. Martial law was immediately declared in the County of Surrey, the eastern third of the island. Two naval vessels were sent from Port Royal to Morant Bay and the troops at Kingston and Newcastle were force-marched through the mountains. The Moore Town maroons crossed the Blue Mountain ridge and fell on the rebels, and even the Hayfield maroons, whom Bogle thought were behind him, sided with the government. More than 430 men and women were shot down or put to death after trial — scarcely fewer than in 1832 — with 600 publicly flogged and more than 1,000 houses burned. Paul Bogle, caught by maroons in a cane-piece, was hanged from the burned-out Courthouse. George William Gordon, carried by ship from Kingston to Morant Bay so that he could be tried by court martial, was hanged within three days, on 23 October.[38]

In keeping with better established methods of parliamentary inquiry, a more realistic effort was made by the imperial government to arrive at the causes of the revolt and the details of its suppression than in 1832. Over a three-month period, a three-man commission took evidence from 730 witnesses in 60 separate sittings, including some in the actual locations of the revolt. Yet some of the difficulties and prejudices of the commissioners can be gauged from remarks at the beginning of their 1,200 page report:

As regards the negroes, it is enough to recall the fact that they are for the most part uneducated peasants, speaking in accents strange to the ear, often in a phraseology of their own, with vague conceptions of number and time, unaccustomed to definiteness or accuracy of speech, and, in many cases, still smarting under a sense of injuries sustained.[39]

In their conclusions, the commissioners found that the revolt was at least partly fuelled by racial animosity and constituted 'planned resistance to lawful authority'. Governor Eyre was praised for his 'skill, promptitude and vigour', and it was stated that though there was no evidence directly implicating Gordon, had there been in fact a long-plotted conspiracy he must have known of it. Yet the commissioners also ascertained that the rebels were 'for the most part what are called free settlers, occupying and cultivating small patches of land', whose 'great desire was to obtain, free from the payment of rent, what are called the ''back lands'', and added that 'disputes between employers and labourers, and questions relating to the occupation of land, which are decided in the first instance at Petty Sessions, are adjudicated upon by those whose interests and feelings are supposed to be hostile to the labourer and the occupier'. Particularly in St. Thomas-in-the-East the existing bench of magistrates was unfit to dispense justice in the cases that most commonly came before it, and Jamaica as a whole was in sore need of 'a good Master and Servant Act', arrived at and administered by an independent and impartial tribunal. In their most damning passage of all, the commissioners concluded that in the suppression of the revolt martial law had been kept on far longer than was necessary, that punishments by death were 'unnecessarily frequent', that the floggings were 'reckless' and sometimes 'barbarous', and that the burning of 1,000 houses was 'wanton and cruel.[40]

These findings provoked scandal among conservative imperialists and, as Bernard Semmel and Gertrude Himmelfarb have shown, the controversy that raged in England in the later 1860s over the conduct of Governor Eyre polarized attitudes and helped to crystallize imperial policy.[41] Yet even the 'liberal' position in the debate went no further than the principle 'that if British rule was to prevail (as prevail it should), it should be just'.[42] For the ordinary black Jamaicans the only obvious change was the self-dissolution of the Jamaican Assembly and the substitution of Crown colony government in 1866, but this was far from a benefit to them. The voluntary change was motivated by a fear, inspired by the career of George William Gordon, that popular radical elements might in due course take charge of an elective Assembly, and by the thought that the plantocracy might more easily sustain itself through Councils nominated by 'right-thinking' Governors. Events after 1866 proved the Jamaican ruling class largely correct. Though an extremely limited franchise was gradually reinstated after 1884, land policy, laws and magistracy were not substantially changed in the nineteenth century, and what V.S. Reid called Jamaica's 'New Day' — democratic self-government — did not dawn until 1957, 119 years after slave emancipation.[43]

An even more repressive scenario characterized Barbados, where the widespread revolts of 1816, 1876 and 1937 punctuated, at remarkably even intervals, a largely unchanging tale of plantocratic dominance. The revolt in 1816 that was to take its popular name from its chief slave leader, Bussa, came as an immense shock to the Barbadian whites, whose slaves had not even been detected in a plot for over 100 years. With the threat of invasion removed by the ending of the French wars, the whites were preoccupied by the effects of reduced economic protection on sugar prices, and almost up in arms about plans by the imperial government to impose a slave registration bill with or without the consent of the Barbadian Assembly — loosely talking in terms of revolution and secession much like the Americans in 1775. Over 95% of the Barbadian slaves were island-born, regarding themselves as much Barbadians as the whites. They grew much of their own food on their tiny plots and even made money selling surpluses, including ginger for export.[44]

Yet the Barbadian slaves were far from content, particularly in the southeast of the island, the area with the highest density of slaves, the driest soils, the harshest working conditions and a tradition of resistance that went back to marronage in the early seventeenth century. Groups of elite slaves in St. Philip parish, in conjunction with a few disgruntled free coloureds who had more slave than free kin, plotted at weekend dances. They believed, on the evidence of newspaper reports and loose talk overheard, that the imperial government was in favour of slave emancipation, and calculated that if they closed down the mills and drove the whites into Bridgetown, the plantocracy would be forced to come to terms. The majority convinced themselves that if they refrained from violence the Governor and imperial troops would be on their side; only a few believed that their only option was to follow the lead of the 'Mingo' slaves (that is, the Haitian rebels of 1791–1804).[45]

The revolt erupted on Easter Sunday, 14 April 1816, with the firing of trash houses as beacons. Within hours the rebels controlled a third of the island, over 100 estates. Bussa's followers seized the armoury of the St. Philip's militia and marched towards town under the captured standard, as if they were now the effective parochial militia.[46] Not a single white was killed at this stage and very few injured, though hundreds were at the slaves' mercy.

The regime, however, showed no mercy at all. Martial law was declared, and the army commander confidently sent forward the black regular troops with orders to shoot when necessary and unleashed the undisciplined white militia, who shot on sight and wantonly burned slave huts and grounds. Two whites died in all, but 50 slaves were shot in the fighting and another 70 summarily executed in the field. Later, a further 144 were executed (including three of the four free coloureds charged) and 132 deported. The bodies of dead rebels — sometimes just their heads — were displayed on their home estates, and security measures were tightened up in all respects. Yet an official local report published in 1818 insisted that the Barbadian slaves had no grounds for discontent, putting the blame firmly on meddling by the imperial government.[47]

Unequivocally, 1816 was a lasting victory for the Barbadian white oligarchy of planters and Bridgetown merchants. Alone of the older sugar colonies Barbados was able actually to increase production after slavery ended through the planter's complete monopoly of fertile land and control of the former slaves, who had virtually no chance of owning farmland and no alternatives to labour on the estates on the planters' terms.[48] The increase in production tapered off in the 1870s with declining world prices, and many planters and even merchants were threatened with bankruptcy. But their socio-economic dominance was not seriously eroded. The few middle-class coloureds and blacks with money were denied the chance of competing as sugar producers by a united front of white planters and their merchant bankers, and the minority of blacks who owned parcels of freehold land were denied the capital and favourable legislation necessary to cooperate and become more efficient producers even of non-sugar crops.[49]

The lot of the black majority, crowded into Bridgetown or tied to agricultural labour, was bleakest of all. Though the population increased by more than 50% between 1838 and 1876 despite serious cholera epidemics, emigration was positively discouraged,[50] at least until 1870. In a community which the whites — like those of the American South — claimed was uniquely civilized, eight out of ten blacks were technically illegitimate, a majority of the children of school age received no schooling whatever, there was no free medicine and no medical facilities at all outside Bridgetown, the poor law system brought practical relief only to poor whites, and the Bridgetown jail and workhouse were accurately described as dungeons. In 1876 the only efficient institutions were the Assembly, the Anglican church, the police force and the magistracy.[51]

The linchpin of the planters' dominance was the oppressive Masters and Servants Act of 1840.[52] By this, every agricultural labourer was required to be located on a plantation, his tenancy of a minute house and plot requiring him to work when called, five days of nine hours' work per week. If he failed to turn out, he was liable to the forfeit of a month's wages and/or 14 days in jail, with or without hard labour. If no work were offered, the labourer, the-

oretically, could go to court to sue for five days' wages, but was then liable to eviction at one month's notice. In fact labourers never went to court for wages due, and worked on the average far less than 45 hours a week while at the same time having to pay rent for houses and plots which, by another law, was deducted by owner/employer before wages were paid. Many planters also trimmed wage-bills by selling ground provisions to their labourers which the labourers could not grow for themselves.

The consequences were inexorable. At the best times wages were close to subsistence, and in times of depression or drought destitution was common and starvation not unknown. For example, in 1870 an inquest was held at Clifden in St. Philip on a labourer named Samuel Dottin, aged 55, who was found dead in his hut while his wife was away at The Crane scavenging sea urchins for food. It was testified that Dottin had been receiving 10 pence a day as a contract labourer, but that most weeks he worked only three days and some weeks not at all. Even the estate manager admitted that Dottin 'tottered as he walked', and the coroner decided that he had suffered 'from no disease but starvation'.[53]

Yet the Barbadian proletariat was not so long-suffering and complaint, or the whites so calm and confident, as the plantocracy pretended. At the day-to-day level, by far the most common cases that came before the local magistrates involved canefield arson and other forms of malicious damage, trespass and, especially in times of hardship, stealing of food. For example, in the month before the 1876 riots, no less than 152 persons were charged with food stealing, compared with a total of 75 charged with all other offences.[54] As to more serious and general manifestations of resistance, there had been riots in St. Philip in 1863 which Governor Walker confidentially attributed to insufficient wages,

although the planters are very angry with me when I say so. They aver that there has been little or no reduction of wages, but whatever it may have arisen from, whether from the inability of the planters to give the same quantity of work, or from the difficulty with which the labourer can, on account of the hardness of the soil, accomplish his ordinary task, or from the task having been increased, the labourer is undoubtedly not earning the same amount of money which he has been accustomed to do.[55]

A few years later, a disillusioned Anglican curate leaving for England wrote:

One predominating characteristic of the white people of Barbados is their abject fear of the Negroes. Whether, on the principle that 'conscience doth make cowards of us all,' this feeling be only the natural offspring of past tyranny and present scant or unwillingly rendered justice, or has any more solid foundation, I am unable to say.[56]

Governor Pope Hennessey, who quoted the anonymous curate in 1876, added that even in comparatively good years when food was cheap and the people apparently worked cheerfully, 'panics sometimes spring up among the white people that are quite inexplicable', quoting Colonel Clements, the Inspector General of Police, as saying that he hardly knew an easter over the previous 18 years (that is, the anniversary of Bussa's Revolt) 'to pass without some leading white people talking of an insurrection amongst the labourers'.[57]

Conditions were desperate by 1876, but what triggered an explosion, as in 1816, was not the whites' fears of the blacks so much as of imperial interference, coupled with the blacks' reaction to white paranoia and their own miserable servitude. In this case, the immediate issue was the imperial government's campaign to create a Windward Islands Federation including Barbados.[58] The Barbadian blacks saw no practical advantage in a federation, but instinctively felt that if the planters and merchants were so adamantly against it, it must be good, especially since it was strongly espoused by a Governor, John Pope Hennessey, who was clearly on the side of the ordinary blacks.[59] From his arrival in Barbados late in 1875 Hennessey went on personal missions of inquiry into local conditions, being accused by the planters of holding court for disgruntled blacks at his country retreat, what is now called Sam Lord's Castle, in St. Philip.[60] In speeches before the Council and Assembly the Governor not only promoted federation but condemned the levels of wages, the burden of taxation on ordinary people, the lack of social services and the appalling state of the Bridgetown jail. On one occasion his carriage was dragged by exultant black townsfolk from the legislative building back to Government House.[61]

As so often in the past, exaggerated rumours spread through the rural areas, to gain additional force when relayed to the master class. For example, the fervently plantocratic *Agricultural Reporter* claimed on 4 April 1876 that pro-federation agents:

have been going about the country with Federation petitions for people to sign, have invariably employed as their great argument, a promise to the labourers, not only of higher wages, but of 20 acres of land in some neighbouring el dorado, where they would become gentlefolks, and be elevated from the position of labourers to that of landed proprietors in their own right ... [and] have not scrupled to impose upon their illiterate dupes the lying impression that the land of estates in Barbados

is to be freely apportioned to them, that they are to drive in their carriages, and indulge in other luxuries. The consequence is that the labourers are already heard selecting the spots of land for which they have a preference, and otherwise manifesting the results of the evil influences which are thus brought to bear upon their impressionable and excitable natures.[62]

An even more authoritative statement was made in a document signed by all the Anglican clergy from the Bishop downwards, sent to the Governor on May 26 after the riots subsided:

there was a general impression made upon the minds of the labourers that the ground provisions of the planters and their live stock were given to the labourers by the consent of the Governor ... The belief is still very general that the land and other property of the white, coloured, and respectable black owners, is wrongfully held back from the blacks, to whom at the Governor's insistence it had been awarded by the Queen.[63]

However, it was anti- not pro-Federation agents who provoked the first bloodshed. On 28 March 1876, a group of white members of the Barbados Defence Association attempting to hold a meeting at Mount Prospect, St. Peter's, was stoned by the audience and in the resulting fracas a black labourer, Moses Boyce, was shot.[64] Far worse was to follow as the true issues came to the fore, beginning, significantly, on Byde Mill estate, at the junction of St. Philip's, St. John's and St. George's, on Easter Tuesday, 18 April 1876 — almost exactly the sixtieth anniversary of Bussa's Revolt.[65]

Labour conditions at Byde Mill, under a hated manager called Reece, were notorious even by general Barbadian standards. In 1870 there had been a case of a labourer's child dying of starvation, and earlier in 1876 a female labourer, Emily Howell, had been served with notice of eviction after ten years' residence for complaining of wages of sixpence for a full week's work. On Easter Sunday, most of the labourers had received from 2 to 8½ pence for the week, the estate's attorney later telling the Governor 'he supposed the wind had been slack and there had not been full work for them all', while calmly adding as justification that these were net wages, Reece having duly deducted all rents due.[66]

On Easter Tuesday the labourers went to Reece's house, told him they were starving and asked for potatoes. When he refused, a mob of several hundred ransacked the estate's provision grounds. They were led by two brothers called Dottin, said to be relatives of the man starved to death at Clifden in 1870, the one blowing a conch shell, the other carrying a red flag.[67] From Blyde Mill, semi-organized bands of labourers fanned out in all directions, to plunder provision grounds on 50 estates. Local constables and armed and mounted whites were defied with sticks and stones, but no lives were threatened and very few buildings damaged. At Welch's, for instance,

The cellars, pantrys, potato store, pigsties, rabbit hutches etc. had been completely rifled, and in some cases pulled down, but the mob seemed to have been under control of some leaders with a system of their own, for no glass had been damaged in the dwelling house proper, nor had it been entered, although there were marks of bill hooks on the doors and other woodwork.[68]

In this manner, it seems, the labourers intended mainly to bring attention to their miserable condition, making the points that they intended no destruction of the plantation system, wanting merely a living wage, along, perhaps, with more land of their own from which to feed themselves and their families.

Neither white nor black Barbadians expected that Governor Pope Hennessey would act forthrightly, but he surprised all by the degree to which he emulated earlier governors. He resisted demands by panicked whites who fled into Bridgetown that he declare martial law, issue guns to the police and permit the public flogging of prisoners, but he immediately mobilized the troops, formed a column of irregulars from the ships at anchor and authorized the JPs to swear in hundreds of special constables. These last, needless to say, were exclusively whites and avowed anti-federationists, and pursued the rioters with traditional venom. There were skirmishes at Halton, Applethwaite's and elsewhere, but within a week the riots had been suppressed, with eight blacks killed, at least 36 wounded, and 450 taken prisoner.[69]

When they were eventually brought to trial in October 1876, before a judge specially imported from Natal, the prisoners were treated with comparative magnanimity — only 47 being given further terms in jail.[70] But the Barbadian regime successfully used the Federation Riots as a pretext to retain and reinforce its socio-economic system, finally to defeat the Windward Islands Federation proposal and to pursue the vendetta against Governor Pope Hennessey. Alone with Bermuda and The Bahamas — the other two colonies in the region with sizeable white minorities — Barbados never lost its right of self-legislation, though in the 1870s the franchise was exercised by only 1,300 out of 162,000, and no more than one in 20 adults ever voted before 1945. The Colonial Secretary, Lord Carnarvon, made only a token effort to support Pope Henessey's actions, the Federation project was quietly shelved and the Governor himself

transferred to Hong Kong before the end of 1876.[71] In one of their last petitions calling for Pope Hennessey's removal, the arrogant whites of the Barbados Defence Association had almost the last word, consigning the black majority of Barbadian back into the apolitical limbo from which they were not to emerge for another 70 years:

our society [that is, the B.D.A.] consists of persons belonging to every class, colour, and condition in life, representing the owners of property in contra-distinction to those not possessed of any property . . . This class of people being possessed of no real property whatever, never had shown the slightest disposition to take any interest in political questions, politics having all along been confined to people possessed of property without regard to colour or class.[72]

Elsewhere, I have tried to show how all three of the chief late slave rebellions in the British West Indies not only followed traditional patterns of slave resistance but also foreshadowed the will of the slaves to become free peasants.[73] This paper attempts to show the degree to which the major outbreaks in the same three colonies in the 40 years after emancipation not only demonstrated the frustration of would-be free peasants forced to continue to toil for former owners, but also harked back to the mass outbursts of slave resistance, on the part of rebels and masters alike. Of course, there were differences between the colonies affected and changes over time, but these, it is felt, were outweighed by fundamental similarities and continuities. Over an even longer period, if there were any important changes at all they were regressive.

There were substantial differences between the colonies in respect of racial composition, population density and the intensity of plantation agriculture, yet these resulted in socio-economic differences that were quantitative rather than qualitative. Jamaica had proportionally less land suitable for efficient sugar production than either Barbados or the settled part of British Guiana, and Barbados had far less land available for peasant farming than either British Guiana or Jamaica — as well as having a proportion of white inhabitants some five times as high as either. Yet these differences were reflected, if at all, in the form and intensity of the planation system rather than in the relative strength and weakness of the planter and peasant classes.

Jamaica, it is true, steadily declined as a sugar producer, falling behind Barbados around 1860, while British Guiana went ahead of Barbados around 1850 and by 1875 produced twice as much as Barbados and three times as much as Jamaica.

By then, British Guiana obtained its 100,000 tons of sugar a year from only 70,000 acres of canes, processed through a mere 70 factories — nearly all steam powered — but needed 90,000 sugar workers. This system was almost as labour intensive as Jamaica's, which required 40,000 workers to produce 33,000 tons from 30,000 acres, with over 150 factories. Barbados' 50,000 tons a year, on the other hand, were produced by only 42,000 workers, but most inefficiently, from about 75,000 acres of canes through no less than 440 factories, only a fifth of them powered by steam.[74] Had labourers been willing or able to migrate from one major British West Indian sugar colony to another they could have found few differences, and certainly no improvements in respect of the balance of wages received, work required and social conditions.

Each of the colonies had a different constitution, and from time to time there were imperial moves for simplification and consolidation. Yet with an imperial government dedicated to the principles that colonies be efficiently self-sufficient and left as much as possible to their own devices, constitutional issues remained largely academic. British Guiana was a Crown Colony from the beginning and Jamaica became one in 1866, but both were almost as free of Colonial Office control and as plantocratic as Barbados, which remained self-legislating from beginning to end. Paradoxically, the meek endorsement of Governor Wodehouse's spate of 'liberal' ordinances by British Guiana's Court of Policy in 1856-7 and the Jamaican Assembly's 'surrender' of 1866, had much the same plantocratic purpose as the fervent opposition by the Barbados Defence Association to dictation from Westminster over the question of the Windward Islands Federation.

This pragmatic uniformity applied to the local administration of laws as well. Stipendiary Magistrates, intended to be impartial, were introduced into all colonies from the time of Apprenticeship (1834-38), but they were never numerous or independent enough and, as in Britain, unpaid JPs drawn from the propertied classes remained the backbone of the system of petty justice.[75] Backing this plantocratic magistracy were police forces which, in line with metropolitan reforms, were intended to be an impartial and efficient alternative to the traditional militias and military garrisons. Yet to the very degree that they impartially administered the law, the police were seen as the agents of a hated system. Moreover, financial stringencies continually hampered the ideal. Trained professional policemen were augmented in the country districts by untrained local constables who were not only unreliable in times of stress but actually heightened tensions by insensitive officiousness.[76]

In times of widespread riot, police forces had to be augmented by special constables drawn from the 'respectable' classes who were realistically seen by blacks as little different from the old racialist militias and, in extreme cases, by the regular armed forces, kept in reserve throughout the age of the *Pax Britannica* as in slavery days, as much against internal as external foes.

In each colony throughout the period the will of the planters effectively determined local policy and planters controlled the magistracy and forces of order, while the black majority of former slaves were kept tied to the plantation economy, depoliticized, denied education and other social services, yet disproportionately taxed. Though metropolitan interest in the British West Indies declined along with plantation profits, no-one, it seems, could conceive of an alternative to the plantation system, let alone encourage the West Indian blacks to determine their own socio-economic fate. Whatever help was given — such as the delay in the removal of protection, the passing of the Encumbered Estates Act or the authorization of 'coolie' immigration — was designed to shore up the plantation system, not improve the lot of the black majority.

As we have seen, there were special features of each of the three outbreaks of 1856–76 — especially from the metropolitan point of view. But each of these differences cloaked fundamental realities. In British Guiana the riots concentrated on the Portuguese shopkeepers, in Jamaica the disturbances were overshadowed by Governor Eyre's actions and the fate of George William Gordon, and in Barbados the ostensible issue was whether or not the island should become part of the Windward Islands Federation. But the real local issues were common; the way in which the blacks were denied land and forced to work on their masters' terms, competing with immigrants and each other with a local economy over which they had no control, subject to actual starvation when times were bad, and with no means of being heard save through violence or its threat.

Over the longer duration, significant major changes did occur but, like the switch from formal slavery to competitive wage labour, they were more apparent than real, or represented simply a deterioration of general conditions. The world economic order shifted so that old style sugar plantations within formal colonies became less profitable, but for the British West Indian labourer this simply meant working more for less in a system that became yearly more impersonally exploitative in the quest for economies of scale. The black population also grew steadily, pressing on the limited land available, increasing the competitive squeeze on wages, and crowding poor people into towns woefully unprepared to receive them.[77]

The planters themselves became ever more subject to outside economic forces, and merchants and bankers proportionately grew in power. Many whites, defeated, retreated to the metropolis, but at the island level, merchants and planters acted in unison in order to preserve the socio-economic system — refusing in Barbados, for example, to break up even bankrupt estates before the twentieth century.[78] Likewise, as the proportion of whites declined, the middle class was gradually reinforced by coloured or even black recruits, even in Barbados. Yet all this represented in a structural way was an extremely gradual shift away from the complex dialectic of race and class in slave society, to that simpler class structure in which Paul Bogle would spare even policemen who would join his cause but encourage the beating to death of the black man Price because 'he has a black skin but a white heart'.[79]

Some white commentators have argued for the occurrence of a gradual change in imperial sensibilities, humanizing relations between races and classes as a continuation of the noble cause that created the Anti-Slavery Society and sent out missionaries to the benighted blacks.[80] From slavery days too blacks themselves were predisposed to imagine a sharp disjunction between their immediate oppressors and benevolent 'others'. Slaves expected help from distant authorities — an owner who was an absentee, the Governor in the colonial capital, 'Saint Wilberforce', or 'Big Massa', the English King — while, with remarkable unanimity, slave rebels and later black rioters alike believed in rumours that granted concessions were being withheld by the local regime, and that they would receive at least tacit assistance from imperial authorities if they acted positively in their own interests.

These were the cruellest delusions of all. In the event, governors invariably aligned themselves with plantocracies in the cause of law and order, and the imperial authorities automatically endorsed the activities of local regimes in suppressing disorder. Even the most ardent philanthropists, seeing riots as evidence of setbacks in the 'civilizing' process to which they were dedicated, found it far easier to condemn barbarities committed in the maintenance of law and order than actually to condone civil unrest. Bloodshed may have been rather less in 1856 and 1876 than it might have been 50 years earlier, but the suppression of the Morant Bay Rebellion was quite as savage and cynical as that of the late slave rebellions, and missionaries were just as much concerned to dissociate themselves from the unrest in 1856–76 in 1816–32.

Theoretically, control by the Colonial Office over the colonies was facilitated by improved communications, particularly the extension of the submarine cable to the West Indies in the 1870s. Formal Royal Commissions certainly became more frequent, efficient and voluminous after 1847, and the volume of printed materials on colonial affairs available for circulation also increased hugely with the introduction of the Command Paper system in the 1860s.[81] Yet faster mailboats and the telegraph made it easier to control and frustrate governors than to curb colonial regimes — as Governor Pope Hennessey found in contrast to Governors Eyre and Wodehouse — while the outpouring of Command Papers was more an index of the vastly increased efficiency of British printing than of greater metropolitan interest, and the reports of the Royal Commissions remained little more than 'maps of oblivion'. In each of the major inquiries into the British West Indies at least one commissioner noted with amazement, if not shame, that nothing had been changed since the last report.[82]

Yet, from the present perspective, the most remarkable of all continuities was the steadfast behaviour of the black majority; to endure when they had to, to resist however and whenever they could. In the period 1856–76, as in slavery days, the plantocratic regimes, with at least the tacit support of the imperial government, were everywhere able to localize and stamp out unrest. It was not until a hundred years after emancipation that concurrent unrest occurred throughout the British West Indies and major changes became inevitable. Even then similarities prevailed. For example, the scrupulous historian of the Federation Riots, writing in 1959 (in a book actually published by the Colonial Office), noted with surprise the remarkable parallels between 1876 and the 1937 Barbados riots he had witnessed for himself, in respect of the aims and methods of the rioters and the forces of law and order alike.[83] Moreover, though the wave of unrest throughout the British West Indies between 1935 and 1938 shook the imperial fabric in a way that the outbursts of 1856, 1865 and 1876 had not, an increasing number of commentators now feel that even the sweeping changes that occurred after the catalytic delay of the Second World War were by no means as revolutionary as they were once thought to have been.[84]

Notes

1. This paper is a substantial extension of a section in the Epilogue of *Testing the Chains; Resistance to Slavery in the British West Indies* (Ithaca, Cornell University Press, 1982), pp. 323–30.
2. Lorna E. Simmonds, 'Riots and Disturbances in Jamaica, 1838–1865', unpublished M.A. dissertation, University of

Waterloo, 1982. See also Swithin Wilmot, 'Emancipation in Action: Workers and Wage Conflicts in Jamaica 1838–1848', paper presented at Sixteenth Annual Conference of Caribbean Historians, Barbados, 1984.

3. The Guyana, Jamaica and Barbados episodes, however, were simply the most outstanding and best documented examples. Comparable outbreaks occurred at least in Dominica (1844, 1884, 1893), St. Lucia (1849), Tortola (1853, 1885), Antigua (1856), St. Vincent (1862), and Tobago (1876). Parallels are doubtless awaiting rediscovery in almost every colony and even some of the above await detailed analysis. However, see the following fine articles: Russell E. Chace Jr., 'Protest in Post-Emancipation Dominica: The "Guerre Nègre" of 1844', paper presented at Fifteenth Conference of Caribbean Historians, Jamaica, 1983; 'Religion, Taxes, and Popular Protest in Tortola: The Road Town "Riots" of 1853', paper presented to the South-South Conference, Montreal, May 1984; Woodville Marshall, "Vox Populi": The St. Vincent Riots and Disturbances of 1862', in B.W. Higman (ed.) *Trade, Government and Society in Caribbean History: Essays Presented to Douglas Hall* (Kingston, Heinemann Caribbean, 1983), pp. 85–115; Bridget Brereton, 'Post-Emancipation Protest in the Caribbean: The "Belmana Riots" in Tobago, 1876', *Caribbean Quarterly*, V, 30, 1984, pp. 110–23. For the general question of the formation of Caribbean peasantries and peasant responses to post-emancipation conditions, see Sidney W. Mintz, 'Slavery and the Rise of Peasantries', and the subsequent Commentary by Woodville Marshall in Michael Craton (ed.), *Roots and Branches: Current Directions in Slave Studies* (Toronto, Pergamon Press, 1979), pp. 213–248; O. Nigel Bolland, 'Systems of Domination after Slavery: The Control of Land and Labor in the British West Indies after 1838', *Comparative Studies in Society and History*, 23, 4, October 1981, pp. 591–619; Russell E. Chace Jr., 'The Emergence and Development of an Estate-Based Peasantry in Dominica', unpublished ms., 1986.

4. Craton, *Testing the Chains*, Chapter 21. The fullest contemporary account was Joshua Bryant, *Account of an Insurrection of the Negro Slaves in the Colony of Demerara*, Georgetown, *Guiana Chronicle*, 1824. See also Edwin A. Wallbridge, *The Demerara Martyr, Memoirs of the Rev. John Smith, Missionary to Demerara* (London, 1848); James Rodway, *The History of British Guiana*, 3 vols., (Georgetown, 1891–4), II, pp. 75–81; Cecil Northcott, *Slavery's Martyr; John Smith of Demerara and the Emancipation Movement, 1817–1824* (London, Epworth Press, 1976).

5. For the post-emancipation condition of Guyana see Alan H. Adamson, *Sugar without Slaves; The Political Economy of British Guiana, 1838–1904* (New Haven, Yale University Press, 1972); Jay R. Mandle, *The Plantation Economy; Population and Economic Change in Guyana, 1838–1960* (Philadelphia, 1973); Walter Rodney, *A History of the Guyanese Working People, 1881–1905* (Baltimore, Johns Hopkins University Press, 1981).

6. The phrase is from a report by Rev. William Woodson, General Superintendent of Wesleyan Missions in British Guiana, dated 7 March 1856, enclosed in Governor Wodehouse to Colonial Secretary, 10 March 1856, Public Record Office, London, C.O. 111/310. Woodson, who referred to 'the large number of Vile and abandoned Women in these Riots and I regret to add of *wild, rude, and half savage children*', specifically advocated 'putting villagers more firmly under Government', and compulsory work for three days, 'whether on their own provision grounds or on the Estates', as well as three days' schooling for all 'wild children'.

7. Wodehouse to Colonial Secretary, 10 March 1856, *ibid.*

8. See the transcript of Smith's journal, 1817–1823, C.O. 111/46.

9. Rodway, *British Guiana*, III, p. 114.

10. C.O. 111/309. Orr's rhetoric still has power. In one memorable phrase he referred to the militiamen come to arrest him as 'Glazed hatted dogs of war'. *Ibid.*

11. Wodehouse to Colonial Secretary, 24 Feb. 1856; C.O. 111/309.

12. *Ibid.*

13. *Ibid.*

14. Wodehouse to Colonial Secretary, 10 March 1856; C.O. 111/309.

15. *Ibid.*

16. *Ibid.*

17. Wodehouse to Colonial Secretary, 25 March 1856; C.O. 111/309.

18. Annotation by Permanent Under Secretary H.M. Taylor following Wodehouse to Colonial Secretary, 24 Feb. 1856; C.O. 111/309.

19. *Ibid.*

20. Wodehouse to Colonial Secretary, 9 May 1856; C.O. 111/311.

21. Wodehouse to Colonial Secretary, 10 March 1858; C.O. 111/310.

22. Local Ordinances were initiated by the Governor in Council, endorsed by the Court of Policy and approved, or disapproved, in due course, by the Colonial Office. In practical terms they could therefore be even more arbitrary than Acts passed by Assemblies in self-legislating colonies. The key Ordinances here were Numbers 20 and 21 of 1856, enclosed in Wodehouse to Colonial Secretary, 24 Feb. 1856; C.O. 111/309.

23. Ordinances Numbers 28 and 29 of 1856; C.O. 111/312, 313.

24. Rodway, *British Guiana*, III, p. 130.

25. *Ibid.*, pp. 135–6. One of the most interesting coincidences between 1856 and 1923 was that John Sayers Orr and the ordinary black Guyanese were defended in the local press by Rev. Edmund Wallbridge, a Nonconformist missionary who had written the biography of Rev. John Smith, 'The Demerara Martyr', in 1848. For his pains, Wallbridge earned an outpouring of obloquy from the planters and praise from British Nonconformists to rival that accorded his hero 33 years before, and was forced to leave the colony. *Ibid.*

26. Craton, *Testing the Chains*, Chapter 22. The most detailed of the many contemporary accounts, from opposite sides, were Bernard Martin, Sr., *Jamaica, As it was, as it is, and as it may be* (London, 1835), and Rev. Henry Bleby, *The Death Struggles of Slavery* (London, 1853). For modern analyses see Mary Reckord, 'The Jamaican Slave Rebellion of 1831', *Past & Present*, 40, July 1968, pp. 108–125; Stiv Jakobsson, *Am I Not a Man and a Brother? British Missions and the Abolition of the Slave Trade and Slavery in West Africa and the West Indies, 1786–1838* (Uppsala, Gleerup, 1972); Philip Wright, *Knibb 'The Notorious,' Slaves' Missionary, 1803–1845* (London, Sidgwick and Jackson, 1973), pp. 56–133. Edward K. Braithwaite, *Wars of Respect* (Kingston, Savacou, 1979); Mary Turner, *Slaves and Missionaries: The Disintegration of Jamaica Slave Society 1787–1834* (Urbana, University of Illinois Press, 1982).

27. Committee appointed, 30 May 1832; evidence taken, 8 June — 11 Aug. 1832; report ordered to be printed, 11 Aug. 1832. Samuel Sharpe was hanged on 23 May 1832. The first Emancipation Act was passed on 31 July 1833.

28. For the condition of Jamaica between 1834 and 1865 see Philip D. Curtin, *Two Jamaicas: The Role of Ideas in a Tropical Colony* (Cambridge, Harvard University Press, 1955); Douglas G. Hall, *Free Jamaica, 1838–1865: An*

Economic History (New Haven, Yale University Press, 1959); Mavis C. Campbell, *The Dynamics of Change in a Slave Society: A Sociopolitical History of the Free Coloreds of Jamaica, 1800–1865* (Rutherford, Fairleigh Dickinson University Press, 1976); Gad J. Heuman, *Between Black and White: Race, Politics, and Free Coloreds in Jamaica, 1792–1865* (Westport, Greenwood, 1981).

29. Professor Douglas G. Hall at Association of Caribbean Historians Conference, Guadeloupe, 1981.
30. Monica Schuler, *Alas, Alas, Kongo: A Social History of Liberated African Immigration into Jamaica, 1841–1865* (Baltimore, Johns Hopkins University Press, 1980).
31. Edward Cardwell to Governor Eyre, 14 June 1865; C.O. 137/391.
32. For Governor Edward Eyre, see Sydney H. Olivier, *The Myth of Governor Eyre* (London, Hogarth Press, 1933); Geoffrey Dutton, *The Hero as Murderer: The Life of Edward John Eyre, Australian Explorer and Governor of Jamaica, 1815–1901* (London, Collins, 1967).
33. Poster by Gordon to people of St. Thomas-in-the-East, 11 Aug. 1865, quoted in *Report of the Jamaica Royal Commission, Part I, British Sessional Papers, Reports 1866, XXX*, pp. 489–531.
34. *Ibid.*
35. *Ibid.*
36. *Ibid.* The letter was delivered to Governor Eyre in Spanish Town on the morning of 11 Oct. 1865, when the revolt was already irreversibly under way.
37. *Ibid.* Geoffrey Dutton quotes a similar letter signed by Bogle and four others and allegedly found at Stony Gut: 'Blow your shells! Roule your drums! house to house; take out every man; march them down to Stony Gut; any that you find take them in the way; take them down with their arms; war is at my black skin, war is at hand . . . Every black man must turn out at once, for the oppression is too great'; Dutton, *Hero as Murderer*, p. 275.
38. *Ibid.*, p. 286.
39. *Report of the Jamaica Royal Commission (1866), Part I, B.S.P., Reports, 1866, XXX*, p. 490.
40. *Ibid.*, p. 529.
41. Bernard Semmel, *Jamaican Blood and Victorian Conscience* (Cambridge, Houghton Mifflin, 1962); Gertrude Himmelfarb, *On Liberty and Liberalism: The Case of John Stuart Mill* (New York, 1974).
42. Michael Craton, *Sinews of Empire: A Short History of British Slavery* (New York, Doubleday, 1974), p. 315, quoting Frederic Harrison: 'The precise issue we raise is this, that through our empire the British rule shall be the rule of law; that every British citizen, white, brown, or black in skin, shall be subject to definite, and not to indefinite powers. . .'.
43. Victor S. Reid, *New Day* (London, 1973 [1955]); Sydney H. Olivier, *Jamaica the Blessed Island* (London, Faber & Faber, 1936); Samuel J. Hurwitz and Edith Hurwitz, *Jamaica: A Historical Portrait* (London, 1971).
44. Craton, *Testing the Chains*, Chapter 20. The fullest contemporary account, though heavily biased was *The Report from a Select Committee of the House of Assembly appointed to inquire into the Origin, Causes, and Progress of the Late Insurrection* (Barbados, 1818). But see also, Sir Robert Schomburgk, *The History of Barbados* (London, Longman, 1847); Karl Watson, *The Civilised Island: Barbados, A Social History, 1750–1816* (Barbados, 1979); Hilary Beckles, *Black Rebellion in Barbados: The Struggle Against Slavery, 1627–1838* (Barbados, Carib Research and Publications Inc., 1987).
45. *Report from a Select Committee*, pp. 25–34.
46. *Ibid.*, pp. 28–29.
47. *Ibid.*, pp. 34–57; Governor Leith to Lord Bathurst, 21 Sept. 1816, C.O. 28/85; Spooner to Bathurst, 4 Feb. 1817, C.O. 28/86.

48. Claude Levy, *Emancipation, Sugar and Federalism: Barbados and the West Indies, 1833–1876* (Gainesville, University of Florida Press, 1980).
49. See, for example, the petition of black freeholders of Carrington's Village, St. Thomas parish, dated 7 Aug. 1876; C.O. 321/10, pp. 473 sqq. The petitioners, who claimed to have held land since 1838, chiefly blamed absentee proprietors and the financial depression in general for crippling 'the emergence of our skilled and industrious peasantry', but pointed out that the island's great increase in sugar production had been achieved by labourers drawn from their own class, who were yet paid wages 'no more than affords the necessaries of life notwithstanding that food and the articles in general consumption are, at this time, plentiful and cheap'. They stated that many of them would have emigrated but for their attachment to their land and the fact that conditions in other islands were even worse, and begged the Government to put up capital for small producers as had the Danish Government in St. Croix, where estates were 'not even paying expenses'.
50. The population at the time of Emancipation had been 101,000, of whom 82,000 had been slaves. In 1874 the total population was 162,000, of whom 66.4% were blacks, 24.4% coloureds and 10.2% whites. The 'agricultural population' totalled 42,000. There were said to be 27,000 'seamstresses, laundresses and domestics', 29,500 school children and 40,000 unemployed, the latter being 'nearly all children under the age of 15'. Of the 42,000 agricultural labourers, 36,500 were over 15 years of age, 16,000 males and 20,500 females. Levy, *Emancipation, Sugar and Federalism*, pp. 134, 80–83, 101, 135.
51. The essential evidence is to be found in the three relevant Command Papers, C. 1539 and C. 1559 of 1876, and C. 1679 and C. 1687 of 1877; B.S.P., Accounts & Papers 1876, LIII, and 1877, LXI.
52. This was succinctly described in Governor Pope Hennessey to Colonial Secretary, 3 May 1876 in C. 1559 of 1876, and memorably criticized by Samuel Jackson Prescod the black editor and Assemblyman in *The Liberal* newspaper of 25 Sept. 1858 — enclosed in Governor Hincks to Colonial Secretary, 25 Sept. 1858.
53. Pope Hennessey to Colonial Secretary, 16 May 1876, C.O. 321/9.
54. Pope Hennessey to Colonial Secretary, 11 July 1876, C.O. 321/10. Canefield arson had also steadily increased in recent years. In a speech in March 1876, the Governor quoted the following figures: 1873, 68 fires; 1874, 116; 1875, 141; *Barbados People*, 23 March 1876, enclosed in Pope Hennessey to Colonial Secretary, 28 March 1876, C.O. 321/9.
55. Despatch of 25 Jan. 1863, quoted by Pope Hennessey to Colonial Secretary, 1 May 1876, C. 1559.
56. Unpublished manuscript quoted by Pope Hennessey to Colonial Secretary, 8 May 1876, C.O. 321/9. The anonymous parson was probably a Rev. Chester.
57. *Ibid.* In the same despatch, Pope Hennesssey quoted Governor Rawson (1869–75) as saying that the Barbadian whites would rather have had no troops at all than to have the black West India Regiment in garrison, and the Rev. Chester to the effect that the whites believed that if all white troops were removed the West India Regiment soldiers would fraternize with the 'creole negroes' and a general massacre of whites ensue. This was 25 years after Emancipation.
58. Bruce Hamilton, *Barbados and the Confederation Question, 1871–1885* (London, Crown Agents for Overseas Governments and Administrations, 1956). But see also Levy, op. cit.
59. James Pope Hennessey, *Verandah: Some Episodes in the Crown Colonies, 1867–1889* (London, Allen & Unwin, 1964). Also Hamilton, Levy, op. cit.

60. Then called Long Bay Castle. Governor Pope Hennessey also spent some time at Blackman's in St. Joseph's parish. After a disorderly meeting on the Federation question in St. John's on 23 March 1876, the plantocratic Barbados *Times* claimed that the trouble had been caused by 'some liberated persons and some of the dwellers near Long Bay Castle in St. Philip', and noted that, 'by looking at the Map, we find St. John comes between the two last places where Mr. Hennessey has been residing, at Long Bay Castle and Blackman's'; *Times*, 25 March 1876, enclosed in Governor Hennessey to Colonial Office, 28 March 1876, C.O. 321/9.

61. This was after Pope Hennessey's outspoken speech to both houses of the legislature on 3 March 1876; Hamilton, *Confederation Question*, pp. 54–7.

62. Quoted in C. 1559 of 1876, p. 67.

63. Enclosed in Pope Hennessey to Colonial Secretary, 30 May 1876, *ibid.*, pp. 168–9. The Rev. T. Clarke was also quoted as having heard of a black countryman saying: 'De gubnor say de Queen gib de rest of Gubnor's money fou help we, but dey no gib we. He gwine gib we, and gib we land too'; Hamilton, *Confederation Question*, p. 64.

64. Fullest details enclosed in Pope Hennessey to Colonial Office, 7 April 1876. C.O. 321/9; Hamilton, *Confederation Question*, pp. 65–6.

65. Voluminous details in Pope Hennessey to Colonial Secretary, 16 May 1876, C.O. 321/9 and in C. 1539 and C. 1559 of 1876; Hamilton, *Confederation Question*, pp. 71–4.

66. Pope Hennessey to Colonial Secretary, 1, 14 May 1876, C. 1559.

67. Pope Hennessey to Colonial Secretary, 16 May 1876, C.O. 321/9; Hamilton, *Confederation Question*, p. 71.

68. Major Tatton Brown to C.C. Sargent, 28 April 1876, C. 1559.

69. C. 1559, pp. 190 sqq.

70. There was an excellent full account of the trials, including the humane summing up by Judge Lushington Phillips in the London *Times*, 15 Nov. 1876, a copy of which was interleaved in C.O. 321/11.

71. Hamilton, *Confederation Question*, pp. 93–5; Pope Hennessey, *Verandah*, pp. 180–2.

72. Barbados Defence Association to Colonial Secretary, 9 Aug. 1876, C. 1687.

73. Michael Craton, 'Proto-Peasant Revolts? The Late Slave Rebellions in the British West Indies, 1816–1832', *Past & Present*, 85, Nov. 1979, pp. 199–125; 'The Passion to Exist; Slave Rebellions in the British West Indies, 1650–1832', *Journal of Caribbean History*, 13 (Summer 1980), pp. 1–20; *Testing the Chains*, Chapters 19–22, pp. 239–321.

74. Noel Deer, *The History of Sugar*, 2 vols. (London: Chapman and Hall, 1949, 1950), II, pp. 194–203; Eric Williams, *From Columbus to Castro: The History of the Caribbean, 1492–1969* (London, Deutsch, 1970), pp. 39–40, 366–73; Levy, *Emancipation, Sugar and Federalism*, pp. 57, 93, 107.

75. W. L. Burn, *Emancipation and Apprenticeship in the British West Indies* (London, Cape, 1937); Woodville Marshall (ed.), *The Colthurst Journal, 1835–1845* (Barbados, Caribbean Universities Press, 1979).

76. In each of the major outbursts, whites reported cases where the local constables stood on the sidelines or actually sided with the rioters.

77. There is not yet the work needed to relate the West Indies to the process of modernization in general, along the lines of Immanuel Wallerstein's study of the whole world in an earlier period, *The Modern World-System: Capitalist Agriculture and the Origins of the European World-Economy in the Sixteenth Century* (New York and London, Academic Press, 1974), or Walter Rodney's *How Europe Underdeveloped Africa* (London, Bogle L'Overture Publications, 1972). Perhaps the closest so far is George Beckford, *Persistent Poverty: Underdevelopment in Plantation Economies of the Third World* (Oxford, Oxford University Press, 1972).

78. See, for example, Cecilia Karch, 'The Role of the Barbados Mutual Life Assurance Society during the International Sugar Crisis of the Late Nineteenth Century', paper presented at the Twelfth Annual Conference of Caribbean Historians; Trinidad 1980. For the slight relaxation that came in the early twentieth century, see Woodville Marshall et al., 'The Establishment of a Peasantry in Barbados, 1840–1920', paper presented at the Sixth Annual Conference of Caribbean Historians, Puerto Rico, 1974.

79. Report of Jamaica Royal Commission, B.S.P., *Reports, 1866, XXX*, p. 495.

80. This philanthropic/liberal stance, culminating in Reginald Coupland's *Wilberforce* (Oxford, Oxford University Press, 1923), W. L. Mathieson's *British Slave Emancipation, 1838–1849* (London, Longmans, 1932), and G.R. Mellor's *British Imperial Trusteeship, 1783–1850*, was notably pilloried by Eric Williams in *British Historians and the West Indies* (London, Deutsch, 1966). Echoes of the older 'imperialist' tradition linger in William A. Green, *British Slave Emancipation: The Sugar Colonies and the Great Experiment, 1830–1865* (Oxford, Oxford University Press, 1976), which sparked off a memorable exchange between Green and Nigel Bolland: *Comparative Studies in Society and History* 26, 1 (Jan. 1984).

81. The series prefixed simply 'C.' began in 1861. When it reached 10,000 in 1900 it was superseded by the 'Cd.' series. The 'Cmd.' series began in 1930, 'Cmnd.' in 1950.

82. *Report of the West Indies Royal Commission, 1898, C. 8655* (Norman Commission); *Report of the Hon. E.F.L. Wood M.P. on his visit to the West Indies and British Guiana, 1922, Cd. 1679; Report of the West Indies Sugar Commission, 1930, Cmd. 3517* (Olivier-Semple Report); *Report on Labour Conditions in the West Indies, 1939, Cmd. 6070* (Orde Browne Report); *Report of the West Indies Royal Commission, 1945, Cmd. 6607* (Moyne Commission). See also Margaret Olivier (ed.), *Sydney Olivier: Letters and Selected Writings* (London, Allen & Unwin, 1948), pp. 181–2.

83. Hamilton, *Confederation Question*, Appendix A. 141.

84. The original position was that of Eric Williams' *From Columbus to Castro*. The present view is that of the numerous West Indian critics of Williams. See, for example, Gordon Rohlehr, 'History as Absurdity', in Orde Coombs (ed.), *Massa Day Dead* (New York, Doubleday Anchor, 1974), pp. 69–108.

Control and Resistance Among Overseas Indian Workers: A Study of Labour on the Sugar Plantations of Trinidad 1875–1917

Kusha Haraksingh

The sugar plantations of the Caribbean have been the location of much of the history of the region, and especially in relation to the period of slavery, for a recurring theme in that history has been the ways in which the labour force was controlled and the means by which it sought to resist. Thus, a great deal of attention has been directed not only to the slave codes imposed by the different European nations with possessions in the area but also to their modification by local assemblies and councils, as well as to the actual practice of slavery itself. In terms of resistance, investigations have been undertaken on both passive and active manifestations, with the events in St. Dominique in the 1790s being regarded as something of a zenith.[1] However, following the emancipation of slaves in 1838 attention in the British colonies at any rate is switched to the emergent peasantry, which is seen as constituting the more progressive sector of the economy, contributing directly to indigenous development, as opposed to the plantations, which supposedly continue primarily to promote metropolitan economic growth. The historians now explore the hardships and obstacles faced by the upcoming peasants and, as though with emancipation the battle had been won, tend not to be too concerned with the trials of free labour on the plantations.[2]

Part of the reason for this shift in the focus of concern is the impression (unfortunately, now almost axiomatic) that emancipation was accompanied in the larger territories by a general exodus of freedmen from the plantations. This picture is based on a number of considerations, including the feeling that any freedman worth his salt, and with the opportunity, would naturally have left the estates on which he had suffered so much as a slave. In truth, however, historians have been more eager to follow the freedmen out of the estates than they themselves were to leave. In Trinidad, in particular, the evidence would seem to suggest that far from withdrawing from plantation labour, freed-

men (especially women, children and those males past their prime) were being systematically pushed out by planters, making way for contract workers from the smaller West Indian islands and, to a more limited extent, from the United States.[3] At the same time a vigorous campaign of planter propaganda about the extent of arable land in the island and the shortage of labour was laying the foundation for a more elaborate system of contractual arrangements to replace slavery. For the planters had never been reconciled to the loss of servile labour; schooled in that tradition, they were convinced to a man that a tractable and dependable labour force was absolutely indispensable. By 1845 they had successfully persuaded the imperial authorities to sanction a scheme of Indian indenture, and in May that year the first shipload of indentured immigrants from India arrived in Trinidad. By the time indentureship was abolished in 1917, owing largely to nationalist pressure in India, some 143,000 Indians had come to Trinidad. Fewer than one in four returned to their homeland, claiming the return passage to which they were entitled under the terms of their contract. The remainder exchanged their passage home for a grant of land and cash and continued, for the most part, to work on the estates. The steady influx of immigrants, averaging 2,328 per year for the last three decades of the nineteenth century,[4] enabled the planters to stick to their policy of displacing free black labour. By the mid–1870s, when the traffic in indentured Indians was well established and the rules governing the system firmly entrenched, Indians constituted 90% of the sugar estate labour force.[5]

The Indian workers can be divided into three distinct groups, each of which transcended barriers of age and sex. The first category comprised indentured workers (that is, those still under contract); these lived on the estates in barracks provided by their employers. The second group was composed of workers who had served out their contract but who still continued, with their employers' permission, to live in the barracks. The third category of workers had also completed their contracts; however, they lived not on the estates but in freehold or rented plots in surrounding villages. Each estate had its complement of indentured, free residential and free non-residential workers. Generally, over the period the proportion of free non-residential to the other two groups combined remained fairly stable, while there was a close inverse relationship between indentured and free residential labour.

The preference for Indians over Blacks (though not for all types of work) has sometimes been attributed to their supposed docility. But this general stereotyping is wide of the mark, as the frequent outbreaks of strikes, riots and violence at workplaces attest. The real explanation is that the system rendered the Indians controllable — to varying degrees, obviously, for it was easier to control those still under indenture than those who had completed their contracts. The aim of this paper is to explore the means by which that control was exercised and the difficulties encountered.

In defining the context of control, one has to view the labour force as being held 'captive' at several different but connected levels. First of all, where the indentureds were involved there was a legal framework; they were obliged to work or, in default, to face penal sanctions. Then, for all workers there was a spatial ambit; the planters, through their influence in the legislature, were able to champion and secure policies which confined the workers either to the estates themselves or to their vicinity in the countryside. The promotion of indebtedness among the workers kept them imprisoned in economic terms and, consequently, under compulsion to perform at their workplaces. The ablest among them were often co-opted to serve as 'drivers' or foremen in the managerial system; ostensibly, they were required to perform the functions of a go-between, but in reality they simply concentrated on executing the wishes of their masters.[6] Thus the workers were kept in check by their institutional leaders; the very agency which ought to have been the avenue for registering complaints and protest was subverted to other ends. In psychological terms, the prison walls were clearly discernible, for even the ordinary run of plantation life fostered a general feeling of helplessness; few, if any, of the workers could have believed that man was the master of his destiny. Added to all of this, recurrent and wasting diseases, malnutrition, poor housing conditions and the low standards of amenities, as well as a low life expectancy, which together should have induced an inclination to escape, served only to create an oppressive sense of inertia. Those who did try to escape often discovered that to slip one of the bonds was simply

to tighten those that remained. It was, in essence, a model of 'interlocking incarceration'. The avenue of escape was either total revolt — in which all the bonds would be removed at a stroke — or a slow, painful struggle for economic independence through hard work and an attempt to save, during which the labourer would actually be fulfilling the purposes of his employer. The very presentation of these alternatives was itself a measure of control.

The Mechanics of Control

Immigrant labour is generally easier to control than local labour, for it is less secure, less confident and, in instances of confrontation, finds itself facing the weight, if not the wrath, of other social groups. This is so even when the immigrant comes from a society which in overall cultural terms is not dissimilar to the host environment. The less pronounced the similarity, the more effective is the physical uprooting itself as a weapon in the arsenal of control. In the case of immigrant Indians in the Caribbean, the degree of similarity was minimal. The North Indian villages from which most of them came were quite literally on the other side of the globe. Profound distinctions in language, religion, social customs and world view separated the Indians from the Creole society into which they were being introduced. Nor could it be expected that the differences would be transcended with ease, for the Indians were possessors of an elaborate and sophisticated cultural baggage which historically had demonstrated, even under sustained attack, a most formidable resilience.

In one area, however, the Indians could discern a certain continuity: this was in the metropolitan presence. In India the countryside had been able to ward off some of the social and cultural effects of foreign rule but had been less successful in resisting its economic impact. The penetrative tentacles of the land revenue administration stretched deep into the villages, and generally the disruption wrought by imperial policies that promoted the growth of non-food crops and the weakening of village craft industries was too extensive to resist. The ordinary villager who knew of the ultimate power of the British government and its representatives in the countryside had developed, over generations of foreign control, a marked deference towards the *hukm* or government. In the case of the elite that deference was sometimes no more than a cultivated air, adopted to mask an elaborate ploy to retain in Indian hands the substance of control, but the villager's awe of the government was usually genuine. Growing rural population, increasing pressure on the land, recurring floods and famine, as well as, in the individual case, unfortunate personal circumstances induced many to listen to, and to believe, the suitably embellished tales of the *arkatias* or recruiters. Those most willing to listen and to be convinced were, in the nature of things, generally among the least of the enterprising and successful. Thus when in 1883 an Indian government official investigated a group of 1200 emigrants, he found that almost all of them were illiterate and that almost none had any experience outside the narrow limits of his village. Further, he discovered that one of the things which really united the group was their common experience of personal misfortune — they had lost their land, or antagonized a village big-wig, or had run foul of the authorities.[7] It was not so much that the system deliberately sought out the weak, though deliberate efforts were made to exclude some groups who were regarded as potential troublemakers, such as disbanded soldiers, members of the higher castes or second-time emigrants — but the entire operation, like a whirlpool in the ocean of life, had a way of turning up the flotsam and the jetsam, those most susceptible to pressure and those most unlikely to resist.

The intending emigrant's first brush with rootlessness would come before he left his native land, in the emigration depot while waiting to embark. Here he would encounter people whom ordinarily he would not have met — people from different regions, speaking unfamiliar dialects — and those whom he normally would have avoided, members of other religions and other castes. The strange world of the depot would follow him on board ship, where the regulation clothing and the identity disc would proclaim him and his fellows to be coolies, a designation which would confuse customary reference points and threaten established concepts of status and rank. Unsympathetic and sometimes cruel treatment at the hands of the ships's officers, as well as the physical discomfort of the long voyage, often marked by storms at sea or serious outbreaks of disease, would serve to heighten the sense of disorientation. And as one day slowly merged into the next some would begin to have an inkling of the recruiter's forked tongue and would come to realize that, in contrast to what they had been led to expect, Trinidad was not a short, simple journey away.

Those who were finally 'landed alive', as the ship's papers would describe them, had gone through a formidable experience; ahead lay another, not any less trying.[8] The daily routine of plantation life, long and arduous hours of physical work, punctuated by brief periods of rest in cramped and uncomfortable conditions, generated its own crippling yet steady momentum. Disease

hung heavily over the estates, and early death often removed those on the verge of acquiring, in traditional terms, a 'suitable' age to impart direction and guidance to their uprooted countrymen. There was little scope for diversion or recreation, and the overwhelming presence of males in the recruiter's bag meant that many were denied the solace and support of female companionship. Again, it was not that these conditions were deliberately engineered to sap will and initiative or to keep the workers responsive to authority, though one could justify the claim that plantation owners or managers did not go out of their way to make improvements. The truth was that neither the plantation nor the life which it dictated was in practice an easily malleable institution. The general sense of defeatism which most workers must have felt was matched only by the ponderousness with which the plantation, for so long accustomed to slavery, had responded to the changed circumstances of indentureship.

Indeed, throughout the indenture period the assumptions and premises of slavery continued to inform management attitudes. The need to keep the workers under the strictest control was never questioned. In this context an elaborate system of coercion was established, which included laws curtailing freedom of movement outside the estate. Thus the worker who was legally entitled to prefer complaints against his employers to the Protector of Immigrants, whose office was located in the capital, had first to obtain his employer's permission to leave the estate in order to make the complaint at all. In addition, of course, worker mobilization beyond individual estates was rendered almost impossible. In any case, the magistrates who were empowered to investigate charges of maltreatment or violations of contractual obligations generally shared the class interests of the plantocracy. Frequently, while making their rounds in the countryside, they would be entertained or even hosted for the night by a manager who had a case to answer in court the following morning. No wonder, then, that the regulations notwithstanding, the plantocracy hardly hesitated to impose upon the workers an array of punitive devices — floggings and beatings on some estates, arbitrary fines and court-sanctioned imprisonment, which had the effect of lengthening the time under indenture, for periods spent in jail were not discounted.[9] In addition, the planters devised a 'trust week', whereby one week's wage was withheld as a guarantee of satisfactory performance in the next. Those who were not cowed by these stratagems and were regarded as potential troublemakers were either co-opted into the system of control and made 'drivers' or leaders of work gangs or neutralized by the threat of banishment (or banishment itself) to estates where they had no contacts and were unknown. The dominant quality of the overall arrangements justified the label of a 'new system of slavery'; though the regulations were supposed to act as a bulwark against the return of the bad old days, the rules were seldom in line with reality.

The attitude of resignation which characterized the psychological profile of many of the workers could also be linked in several instances to provisions in the indenture contract which assured them of a return trip to India at the end of the stipulated term — by the 1870s five years of indentureship plus a further five years of 'industrial residence'. Without that guarantee it is doubtful whether many Indians would have been induced to leave their native land. Once in the colony, some took the view that they must act so as not to jeopardize or unduly delay their homeward passage. Thus they tolerated unexpected and unsuitable conditions, just as a man, coming to the end of a long prison term, might decide to risk nothing which would delay the day of freedom. The nearer one came to qualify for return, the more decisive was this consideration. Thus the most vulnerable workers were precisely those who had almost travelled the distance.

As a group the indentured Indians were institutionally subject to more controls than time-expired workers. Therefore the planters insisted on replenishing their stock of indentureds by securing new arrivals. These were often provided with rations at deliberately inflated cost and so commenced their working career in the colony saddled with debt. Of course, the planters could justify the provision of rations to their workers by reference to nutritional requirements and similar considerations, but what seemed on the surface a helpful gesture had sinister implications. The indebted worker was not only more vulnerable, in that he was under greater pressure to perform at the work place, but he also would find it difficult to accumulate the money which might enable him to buy out the final years of his contract. Thus in 1889 the workers actually implored the Protector to put an end to the practice of rationing.[10]

The right to redeem through purchase up to the last two years of the five-year term of indenture had been stipulated in the early ordinances. But the planters naturally wished to make the most of their indentureds. So they began to argue that redemption was not in the interest of the sugar industry, since it allowed the more experienced hands to withdraw their services. Nor was it in the interest of the Indians themselves, they claimed, for many workers were tempted to borrow money at exorbitant rates of interest in order to exercise that

option. The planters gained some ground with their argument, so that in 1876 redemption as a right was cancelled; thereafter, the employer's consent had to be obtained. At the same time the planters sought to induce time-expired Indians to re-indenture themselves for further periods of one year at a time. The carrot was a cash bounty. The heyday of this scheme was the 1880s, but by the mid–1890s the planters had little use for it.

In terms of control, a pivotal role was played by the driver. The person appointed to that position (and on the typical estate there would be a number of them, each in charge of a group of about twenty-five workers) was generally hand-picked by the planter or his overseer. Selection was based on criteria which were sometimes at variance with the qualities which Indians expected in their leaders. This could lead to trouble, as when a low-caste individual was appointed to head a gang of higher-caste workers. The driver, by virtue of his office, was separated from the ordinary workers, and the distinction was sealed by higher remuneration and by certain modest fringe benefits which he enjoyed. These the driver would do his best not to lose, and so he strived to secure the approbation of his masters. However, merit and worth were gauged merely in terms of his efficiency in driving the workers to execute their tasks. Towards that end some drivers surrounded themselves with henchmen who threatened and beat the workers and who were least restrained precisely on those estates where the managers were inclined to be the most exploitative. But, apart from physical assault, there were other ways in which the workers were rendered compliant. One such avenue was to pay the wages of the workers through their gang leader, who simply pocketed a share for himself. Another arose from the existing lines of communication: the workers knew that the driver had the manager's ear and could identify individuals as poor performers, in which case their pay might be withheld. But the most widely used method was the assignment of work. The driver could allocate easier jobs to favoured or tractable workers, who would then be able to complete more units of work, which would enhance their earnings.[11] For the impoverished indentureds financial reward was a prime mover; in ordinary circumstances they were inclined to calculate long and hard before engaging in any activity or behaviour which could result in a reduction in earnings.

The methods used to control free workers naturally required some additional ingenuity as compared with those employed in the case of indentureds. The efforts of the plantocracy in four main areas can be isolated. First, time-expired Indians were encouraged to continue to reside on the estates or to settle in neighbouring plots. Second, earning potential was cleverly manipulated, as in the case of contract workers. Third, seasonal unemployment and (as the population grew) general under-employment rendered the labourers only too ready to turn out when work was offered. Fourth, the maintenance of a stock of indentured workers served to undermine the bargaining position of free workers.

The planters correctly calculated that if the free workers were settled close to the estates, they would have little option but to earn their livelihood in the sugar industry. (As a matter of fact, those who stayed in the estate barracks would have no other choice.) But it was not a one-way street. The time-expired Indian who was already decided about returning to India and who therefore merely wished to complete his five years' industrial residence in order to claim his passage might deliberately elect to remain in the barracks and so avoid the expense of having to set himself up in a plot of his own. Those who were as yet undecided about returning could keep their options open by living on the estates. Some single males undoubtedly preferred the communal atmosphere of barrack life to a lonely village hut, while other workers chose to remain on the estates to be near relatives or friends who were still indentured. For a significant number the question of whether or not to remain on the estate was decided by the fact that they could not meet the expense of doing otherwise. In addition, force of habit, as well as uncertainty about the world outside the estates, must have played a part. But whatever may have been the reasons for their continuing to live on the estates, those who did so opened themselves to planter pressure. In the daily run of things the distinction between them and the indentureds was often obscured. Also, the threat of eviction hung over their heads and doubtless was used as a lever to enforce labour demands.

The free workers residing in villages surrounding the plantations had more independence than other categories of estate workers, but the planters could still remain reasonably certain, once alternatives were minimized, that they would work on the estates. It was for this reason that they themselves rented or sold portions of their lands to the workers and also used their influence to have adjacent Crown lands opened up for settlement. But the planters were not comfortable unless they could be assured that the workers were rendered tractable and would perform reliably. Their inherited experience of sugar cultivation led them to believe that there could be no other way of doing business. They could point to the limitations imposed by the climate, which restricted harvest to the first six months of the year, and to the need to be able to

take advantage of favourable weather conditions at short notice, to orchestrate activities and deploy the labour force to advantage, to keep as short as possible the time between cutting and crushing the canes, and quickly to harvest a field which was accidentally burnt.[12] All of this necessitated a certain degree of responsiveness on the part of the workers and planter strategy was to rig the situation so that this could be assured.

The technique they chose was based on a perception which they had also inherited and accepted: the more the workers earned, the less reliably they would work — or, to put it another way, the quicker their requirements were satisfied, the less would be their total output at the workplace. Hence, while stressing in reports and speeches cases of individual workers who had managed to accumulate comparatively tidy sums, the planters proceeded to manipulate the earning potential of the workers — not, indeed, to discourage the labourers altogether but simply to ensure that they would have to work more hours in order to maintain their overall earnings level.

Beginning in 1875 considerable efforts were made to reduce the wage rates of non-residential workers. By 1885 planter expectations were substantially fulfilled. They no longer needed to offer inducements for re-indentureship, and the bounty system was accordingly phased out. Not only that, but with the reduced rate of pay to non-residential workers they were still able that year to turn out the 'largest crop of sugar the island [had] ever produced' up to that time'.[13] However, the planters apparently continued to reduce wage rates still further; by 1896 non-resident free workers were readily accepting and seeking work 'at all times' at indentured rates; and debate on an amendment to the Immigration Ordinance in 1897 revealed that they were prepared to do overtime at even lower rates.[14] In explanation, one manager offered that the coolie was showing a 'greater love of money' than heretofore.[15] But the real reason lay elsewhere: not in an increased thirst for wealth, but in the constantly increasing pressure to work.

Lowering wages was one simple way of reducing the earnings of the workers; another method was to increase the size of tasks. This was a recurring planter strategy which the nature of the task system itself conveniently accommodated. For though there were guidelines, there could be no standard task, especially in the fields where ground conditions varied from place to place and from time to time. Even a short downpour could make a big difference in the work of digging trenches, for example. The general effect of larger tasks was to increase the ratio of time and effort to money earned. But another result was a reduction in the units of work offered, and that paved the way for a policy of under-employment.

Over the years, as the level of earnings fell, the normal cycle of family development led to a growing burden of dependency. One contributing factor was an increase in the proportion of females to males, stemming from both recruitment policy and local births. More children survived as infant mortality declined, and as more Indians settled in Trinidad, the age structure of the population whose livelihood was based on the sugar industry altered. The accustomed bulge around the years 15 to 30 (which was the age group favoured by the recruiters) showed a tendency to flatten out, as the age composition of the population assumed a more normal mix. The pattern of family development increased the general compulsion of the labourer to perform especially as he was under-employed, and also assured that estates had a corps of child labourers at their command.

Within this general context some workers were rendered more controllable than others by individual circumstances, such as indebtedness. This might arise from borrowing to meet the expense of initial settlement in the villages, or from events like the performance of life-cycle rites or other religious observances, or from expensive habits like alcoholism. But the most serious cause of indebtedness, then as now, was under-employment in the rainy season, which forced the worker to rely on the credit facilities of village shopkeepers (not unusually ex-drivers) through the period July to December. The heavier this reliance, the greater was the compulsion to work during the harvest season, which was exactly what the planter wanted.

Those in peculiar circumstances, whether a result of indebtedness or of some other contingency as well as the general population of free workers, had to reckon with the continuing presence of the indentureds. It was not only that the standards applicable to the coercive regimen of indentureship were transferred to free workers, or that over the years wage rates showed a tendency to move down from free rates to low contract rates;[16] more important, the presence of a group of workers who were legally bound to work undermined the bargaining power of free workers and reduced the pressure which a strike could exert on the planters. When the free workers contemplated withholding their services, they had to consider that the critical work might continue to be done by the indentureds. Thus there was in operation a process of 'expansive control', whereby the planters, in holding a part of the labour force 'captive', could use it to capture another part. They were well aware of the value of their contract workers in this regard, so that even though by 1900 there was a surfeit of labour, they continued to press for the retention of indentured immigration. Their arguments and the counter-claims of opposing groups dominate the literature on indentureship in Trinidad in the closing years of the system.

Resistance

Data on resistance among sugar workers of all categories are not easy to come by. In the case of indentureds the local authorities, conscious of the watchful eye of the India Office and anxious to prevent any questioning of the system, consistently tried to convey the impression that all was well. If there was trouble, it was because, as everybody knew, the workers were both indolent and grasping. As for the free workers, the records do not deal with them in any depth, for they were, strictly speaking, no longer the responsibility of the Protector of Immigrants. However, it is possible to identify behaviour patterns which fall within the scope of resistance, from those which might be classified as active on the one hand to those which may be deemed as passive on the other.

The Indians demonstrated the capacity, not unknown to disadvantaged groups, to draw from vicissitude elements of strength. In this connection the experience of the ocean passage stands out. Those who survived that trip discovered in themselves resources of fortitude which they perhaps never knew they possessed. Emigrants on the same ship also developed the enduring ties of *Jahaji bhai* or 'brotherhood of the boat'. This new bond was also an example of cultural versatility, for it transcended the ordinary divisions of caste and religion, thereby demonstrating that the Indians were prepared to devise new approaches for new circumstances.[17]

Cultural resilience and adaptation might indeed be regarded as the most outstanding, as well as the most persistent form of resistance among Indian workers. It permitted a definition of otherness which amounted to defiance, both in the insulation and consequent feelings of solidarity which that engendered, and in the divergent concepts of status and rank which were implied. Culture defined an area to which Indians, after defeats at the workplace, could retreat to heal and bind the wounds before sallying forth again. The self, derided and degraded, could be refreshed and injected with new esteem. For within the safety of the cultural boundaries the idea of caste allowed notions of status to be overturned, so that the white planter, for example, who had no caste, was accorded a place beyond the pale.

The culture of the Indians in Trinidad was to some extent a blend of various local practices and beliefs brought from India, but before long the Bhojpur tradition became dominant. This was derived from a cultural area in northeast India which was characterized in language by the Hindi dialect Bhojpuri and in relation by the great epics, the *Mahabharata* and the *Ramayana*. These two religious works, but especially the latter, provided the basis for folk songs and stories and defined ideals and values. Without promoting dogmatic attitudes, they nevertheless allowed Indians to feel that those who did not share their ideals were the poorer for having yet to discover what life was all about. The performance of life-cycle rites and ceremonies of a private kind set the seal on all of this. The public celebrations and festivals served to reinforce the point.

Public festivals could also become undisguised demonstrations against the established order. The most famous incident of this type occurred during the *muharram* of 1884, when grievances connected with the size of tasks as well as misgivings about new regulations concerning the conduct of the celebrations led Indians to defy the authorities. When the storm cleared thirteen Indians, mostly in their late twenties, had been killed by police bullets and several others maimed and wounded.[18]

The odds were heavily stacked against achieving much by open defiance, but that did not prevent Indians from trying and occasionally succeeding. Even on board ship, as during the voyage of the *Hesperides* in 1882, violence could break out. In the fields violence was never far below the surface, though it was usually directed against the driver rather than the planter. Such acts of violence were usually spontaneous and unco-ordinated but often managed to achieve the desired effect. In fact, the vulnerability of the drivers to a sudden assault in a deserted cane piece by an aggrieved worker wielding the tool of his trade — a cutlass — did force many drivers to moderate their demands on the workers.

As one would expect, the indentureship period was not a happy time for labour relations; there were too many areas in which conflict could develop. In a general sense, one could say that both indentureds and free workers were constantly engaged in a struggle to re-possess the definition of the task. Sometimes the struggle took the form of starting work late or of staying away altogether and pretending, in the case of indentureds, to be ill. At other times it took the form of an attack upon the plant — that is, burning the canes or mistreating the draught animals. It often developed into a local strike especially in the 1880s and 1890s, but it was not long before that expedient was abandoned in the face of pressure to earn in the case of free workers or police action in the case of indentureds.

The planters might describe burning the canes as the mischievous and wilful destruction of property but the Indians knew what they were about. It was one way of gaining some initiative in their dealings with the plantocracy. For one thing, there was little risk of being caught. The Indians developed simple but crude incendiary devices, such as a lighted candle set in a bundle of straw; by the time the straw was set alight and the wind was doing the rest, the workers would be far away. Burned canes had to be quickly reaped and crushed, and with time then on the side of the workers, they could attempt to hold out for better conditions.

For many of the Indians resistance had to be seen in terms of who would have the last laugh. They would be compliant and would work hard, which undoubtedly kept the planters happy, but at the same time they were trying to lay the basis for their eventual escape from plantation life. Towards that end they resurrected caste-affiliated skills — such as that of the jeweller or the potter — and engaged in their own private agricultural pursuits. A not inconsiderable number even became sugarcane farmers. They also rediscovered the economic usefulness of traditional institutions such as the *bhaiacharaya* or co-operative brotherhood, which proved especially helpful in the cultivation of rice, and the box money arrangement — a kind of pool to which all would contribute at stated times and from which each in turn would draw a lump sum. The longing for economic independence earned some Indians a reputation for being tight-fisted, and the sacrifices which they were prepared to make even tempted the planters to lower their inducements to them. The argument was that the Indians would be satisfied with less, but it missed the point that the whole idea was to create a situation in which more might be achieved.

Of course, not every Indian had the singlemindedness to pursue the strategy outlined above, and the resistance patterns into which some fell were less positive. Taking to drink was one response, and by the 1880s that had become a serious problem.[19] In the same light may be considered the attitude of resignation and long-suffering which some developed — resistance by turning off. Others went further and took their own lives. A small number took a less final and more positive gamble and absconded to neighbouring Venezuela. Again, individual circumstances — knowledge, elements of character, family connections and so on — would make one option more feasible than another and so determine how workers would respond.

The major consequences of the entire network of control and resistance, as far as the Indian population as a whole was concerned, can be traced to facilities which were provided for the development of schismatic tendencies. Thus, the dominance of the Bhojpur tradition resulted in a situation in which the Madrassis — workers who originated from South India, admittedly small in number — had some grounds for feeling awkward. And religious dominance in that tradition meant that Muslims, even though they might have come from North India, would find themselves at a little distance from the main body of Indians. So too would those who had begun to respond to the ministrations of the Presbyterian missionaries. In addition, groups like drivers and shopkeepers, who did have some community of interest with the workers, nevertheless stood somewhat apart. The contradictions which began to emerge, basically of religion and class, would assume great significance when constitutional politics entered the system and the Indians began to extend their presence beyond the confines of the plantations.

Notes

1. See C.L.R. James *The Black Jacobins: Toussaint L'Overture and the San Domingue Revolution* (New York, 1963).
2. Some of this literature is surveyed in J. R. Ward *Poverty and Progress in the Caribbean 1800–1960*, Macmillan, 1985. See also *Labour in the Caribbean From Emancipation to Independence*, M. Cross and G. Heuman eds., Macmillan, 1989.
3. I have argued this in 'Sugar Estates and Labour in Trinidad in 1838–1845', 11th Conference of Caribbean Historians, Curacao, 1979. See also, at the same Conference, D. Hall, 'Fort George Penn, Jamaica: Slaves, Tenants and Labourers, 1832–1843', and W. Marshall, 'The Ex-slaves as Wage Labourers on the Sugar Estates in the British Leeward Islands 1838–1846'. See also, D. Hall, 'The Flight from the Estates Reconsidered: The British West Indies 1838–42'. *Journal of Caribbean History*, 10, 11 (1978).
4. Compiled from reports of the Protector of Immigrants printed in *Council Papers* of the Trinidad Government.
5. See my article 'Labour, Technology and the Sugar Estates in Trinidad, 1879–1914'' in *Crisis and Change in the International Sugar Economy 1860–1914*, B. Albert and A. Graves (eds.) ISC Press, Edinburgh 1984, pp. 133–46.
6. See K. Haraksingh, 'Indian Leadership in the Indenture Period', *Caribbean Issues*, 2 (3), (December 1976).
7. For a profile of the emigrants, see H. Tinker, *A New System of Slavery: the Export of Indian Labour Overseas 1830–1920* (London, 1974).
8. See Tinker, op. cit., ch. 6.
9. For a fuller discussion of the application of the criminal law to the workplace, see D. V. Trotman, *Crime in Trinidad: Conflict and Control in a Plantation Society 1838–1900*, University of Tennessee Press 1986, pp. 183–212.
10. Protector of Immigrants' Report for 1889, *Council Paper* 29/1890.
11. For a fuller description of the role of drivers, see Haraksingh, 'Indian Leadership in the Indenture Period'.
12. See evidence of several planters to the West India *Royal Commission*, 1897, cd 8657.
13. Protector of Immigrant's Report for 1885, *Council Paper* 33/1886.
14. *Council Paper* 157/1898.
15. Cd 8657, p. 239.
16. Just how these circumstances might have dictated emerging social stratification is discussed in R. K. Jain 'Plantation Experience East and West: Overseas Indians in Malaysia and the Caribbean' in *One World One Institution: The Plantation*, S. Eakin and J. Tarner (eds.) Louisiana, 1989, pp. 165–214.
17. Argued in Haraksingh, 'Estates, Labour and Population in Trinidad 1870–1900', 10th ACH Conference 1978.
18. 'Correspondence Relating to the Coolie Disturbances in Trinidad 1884–5', cd 4366. For a fuller discussion of these events see K. Singh *Bloodstained Tombs: The Muharran Massacre 1884*, Macmillan 1988.
19. Protector of Immigrant's Report for 1881, *Council Paper* 35/1882.

SECTION SIX
Women and Gender

The sexual division of labour that shaped social and economic relations during slavery continued to have a significant impact upon civic society and economic life. Planation-based patriarchy sought to tighten its grip upon the female section of the labour force in an effort to reduce labour cost and maintain strong links with the working class family.

Women, of course, as Momsen stresses, were the most exploited sector of the slave community, and had resisted their enslavement in many ways, including the pursuit of functions within the economy that offered significant autonomy. After emancipation, according to Mintz, their tradition of resistance and struggle was consolidated, especially at the economic level; they could then be identified throughout the region as independent peasant producers and hucksters.

Momsen, Reddock, Mintz and Shepherd suggest the necessity of using gender as an instrument of Caribbean historical investigation by illustrating the richness of interpretation and the range of evidence to be derived from such an approach. Reddock and Shepherd document the experiences of Indian women within the labour market, while Mintz assesses the economic roles of black women as commercial agents. Trotman shows that as African and Indian women sought to remove the restrictive forces that contained their survival endeavours, many walked that narrow path between legitimate protest and criminal activity. Ultimately, they confronted the post-slavery world as the least emancipated social group. In seeking to examine their 'half-free' experience, the arguments found within this section also outline the institutional and ideological expression of the male-power centres, and indicate how it continued to shape socio-economic relations within the market economy.

Gender Roles in Caribbean Agricultural Labour

Janet Henshall Momsen

Boserup[1] in her pathfinding study of *The Role of Women in Economic Development* identified the British Commonwealth Caribbean as an anomalous region in terms of gender roles in agriculture. She suggested that since Jamaica, as distinct from Cuba, the Dominican Republic and Puerto Rico, had a relatively high proportion of women farmers it was more like Africa than Latin America according to her continental-scale regional classification. Boserup explains this anomaly in ethnic terms relating it to the preservation of African farming traditions among a population mainly descended from African slaves.[2] This hypothesis appears to contradict her basic materialist thesis in which gender roles in agriculture are seen as being principally determined by the system of production, primarily through the workings of the labour market and the level of technology, with cultural perceptions of gender roles considered to be irrelevant. This essay examines the Boserup hypothesis using evidence from both historical sources and contemporary fieldwork.

The development of the sugar plantations in the Caribbean during the seventeenth century created a demand for labour which was met by the importation of slaves from West Africa. By 1663 it was said that 'the very being of the plantations depended on the supply of Negroes'.[3] More male slaves than female were imported and planters alleged that they preferred male workers. They blamed the low rate of reproduction among the slave population on this sex-specific migration which resulted in a shortage of women.[4] However, contemporary statistics belie this explanation as they show that by 1800 the sex ratio was in balance in most of the region and with the cessation of the slave trade women soon came to outnumber men. By 1817 there were 116 female slaves to every 100 male slaves in Barbados and Montserrat, 114 per 100 in Antigua, 108 and 104 in St. Kitts and Nevis respectively while Jamaica and the Bahamas had a relatively balanced sex ratio.[5] This increasing predominance of women in the slave population, despite the plantation owners' declared preference for male slaves, occurred, according to Kiple[6] because women were physiologically better able to

withstand the stress of the Middle Passage and slave life although they were often even less well nourished than the men. There was a higher rate of male than female fetal mortality and infant mortality in the slave population.[7] Reproduction remained low not because of the sex ratio but rather because malnutrition and overwork depressed the fertility rate of the female slaves while the mortality rate remained high.[8] In addition, even when slave owners improved conditions for female slaves in an effort to raise the birthrate, social factors still inhibited an increase in the fertility rate.[9] The numerical dominance of women in the slave labour force had a marked effect on the gender division of labour. Yet the planters generally refused to recognize the existence of a high female sex ratio and Bush[10] feels that this may have been done in order to conceal from the abolitionists the degree to which women slaves were exploited.

It is clear that under the forced labour of slavery the gender division of labour amongst Caribbean slaves was decided not by slave memories of African traditions but by the European slaveowners and their perceptions and traditions. Planters were aware that women worked in agriculture in Africa and used this knowledge as justification for the utilization of female slaves as field labourers in the West Indies. In fact, women had very specific roles in African agriculture and rarely undertook the heavy work of land preparation which was expected of them in the West Indies. The use of women as field labourers appeared natural to the planters because it was also the pattern of farm labour in England. There is strong evidence that between 1690 and 1750 in England there was little difference in male and female participation in agricultural work. During that period gender roles were undifferentiated by employers.[11] This metropolitan pattern, which in England continued for a relatively short period, was transferred to the Caribbean colonies and became associated with the slave labour system.

Gender in the 'formal' plantation economy

Under slavery men and women were seen merely as labour units. Not until the slave trade had been brought to a halt did women's reproductive role assume as much importance as her productive role. 'The woman was expected to work just as hard, she was as indecently exposed and was punished just as severely. In the eyes of the master she was equal to the man as long as her strength was the same as his'.[12] Women had a narrower range of occupations than men. Apart from the midwife, doctoress or traditional healer, the chief house-keeper (often a concubine of the master), and to a lesser extent, washerwomen, cooks and domestics, the slave élite consisted almost entirely of men. Reddock sees this as 'the introduction of the sexual division of labour that had been instituted in Europe into one sector of slave society while not extending it into areas in which it was not econom-ically advantageous'.[13]

In agriculture the élite positions were held almost entirely by men. Consequently planters were increasingly forced to rely on women as field labourers. Craton[14] shows that as the overall pro-portion of women slaves on Worthy Park planta-tion 'rose from 46 to 60%, their numbers in the fields increased almost proportionately: from around 58% of the 'field' labour force in the 1790s, to over 65% throughout the 1830s'. As early as 1756 on Roaring River Estate in Jamaica, of the ninety-two female slaves, seventy were field work-ers, while of the eighty-four men only twenty-eight were labouring in the cane fields.[15] From the age of four years children were also expected to work in the fields and data from the Codrington estates in Barbados (Table 1) show that the gender divi-sions of labour of the parents were visited on the children. In 1781, 73% of the active slaves at Cod-rington were field labourers of which over half were women and young girls. Of the working child slaves 95% of the girls but only 80% of the boys were field hands.

Although fieldhands performed the hardest labour, their living conditions were far inferior to those of élite workers and, in consequence, they experienced a higher mortality rate and suffered more frequently from illness than the more privi-leged slaves, but, despite these hardships, women field labourers lived five years longer than men on average. Pregnancy did not guarantee a lighter workload nor a reduction in physical punishment until very late in the period of slavery. As Mathurin indicates 'Slavery, in many essentials made men and women roughly equal in the eyes of the master. Their jobs on the plantation were distributed not according to sex but according to age and health. In theory men were supposed to do the backbreak-ing tasks of the field and the factory; in fact as long as women were young and fit they were recruited into the same work force as men and shared more or less the same labour'.[16] The majority of women remained in the fields in harsh conditions and unlike the men, they had the dual burden of child-care and housework on top of their agricultural work. As Levy[17] points out in Barbados slave women in the fields 'toiled as strenuously as the men, carried baskets of manure weighing as much as seventy pounds, and when they returned to their cottages at night faced additional family duties'.

Gender in the 'informal' slave economy

The cost of feeding a large labour force persuaded the plantocracy to allow peasant-like activities to develop. Male and female slaves were granted plots of land on which to grow subsistence crops in their own time. Mintz has shown that as early as 1672 in Jamaica, slave women were involved in buying and selling the surplus production from their provision grounds on Sunday mornings in public markets.[18] This growth of marginal produc-tion and internal trade within the plantation slave economy with its concomitant gender division of labour occurred to varying degrees on other West Indian islands, including Montserrat, Tobago, St. Vincent, Dominica, Grenada, Barbados, and St. Kitts, as well as in Jamaica.[19]

Table 1. Occupations of slaves at Codrington, Barbados, 1781

Occupation	Number of Slaves				Percentage of Slaves			
	Men	Women	Boys	Girls	Men	Women	Boys	Girls
Field workers	37	52	34	39	22.8	32.1	21.2	24.1
Artisans and watchmen	17	0	1	0	94.4	0	5.6	0
Stockkeepers	10	5	7	1	43.5	21.7	30.4	4.4
Personnel workers	3	15	0	1	15.8	78.9	0	5.3
Non-workers	4	4	19	27	7.4	7.4	35.2	50.0

SOURCE: Adapted from Bennett, J.H. 1958. *Bondsmen and Bishops: Slavery and Apprenticeship on the Codrington Plantations of Barbados, 1710–1838.* Berkeley, University of California Press, p. 12.

Such was the importance of the Sunday market to the entire population that the stringent laws restricting the mobility of slaves were relaxed where marketing activities were concerned. The consequent unusual mobility of market women enabled them to facilitate communication between plantations. Thus they came to play an important role in organized slave resistance and in the development of a creole society. By 1800 there were more women than men in the Jamaican Maroon communities. Women in these maroon groups had special tasks during campaigns, such as helping to carry off spoils, but their main role was to grow food.

Post-emancipation gender divisions of labour

By the end of the eighteenth century in England regional variations in types of agriculture had produced different practices in the division of labour by gender.[20] In the new, capitalist agriculture of southeast England technological change had had the effect of squeezing women out of agriculture to a very large degree, with their role being reduced to work such as weeding and haymaking. Gradually women moved away from agriculture and rural areas into domestic service and later manufacturing in the urban areas. The increasing scale of production and commerce led to the separation of public and private spheres of work with the men in the public sphere and the women in the private sphere of the home. These developments have been identified with Victorian morality and new middle-class assumptions about the role of women. By the mid-nineteenth century such metropolitan attitudes

Table 2. Occupations of slaves in Kingston, St. Vincent, 1817

Occupation	Number of Slaves		Percentage of Slaves	
	Male	Female	Male	Female
Domestics	297	751	28.3	71.7
Skilled trades	249	32	88.6	11.4
Transport	187	0	100.0	0
Retailers	0	25	0	100.0
Other	179	98	64.6	35.4
None	178	227	44.0	56.0
Unknown	12	8	60.0	40.0
Totals	1102	1141	49.1	50.9

SOURCE: Adapted from Higman, B.W. 1984, 'Urban Slavery in the British Caribbean'. In E. Thomas — Hope (ed.) *Perspective on Caribbean Regional Identity*. Monograph No. 11, Centre for Latin American Studies, University of Liverpool, pp. 49–50.

had been transferred, with the usual time-lag, to the colonies and the planters found themselves torn between moral certitude and economic preference in their search for non-slave plantation labour.

With the ending of slave apprenticeship in the British West Indies colonies in 1838, many women ex-slaves sought the private sphere hitherto denied them and it was said that 'mothers of families have retired from the field, to the duties of the home'.[21] Even before 1838 many women came to dominate the movement to the towns but, as on the plantations, the range of jobs for women was much narrower than for men, with most women working as domestic servants or in retailing (Table 2). Inter-island migration, encouraged by regional differences in wage rates, was mainly undertaken by men, exacerbating the female sex ratio in the smaller islands and leaving many women as *de facto* heads of households. The mid-nineteenth century rapid rise in food prices forced many women back into the agricultural labour force in order to feed their children. Women's fluctuating participation rate in the agricultural work force during this period was reflected in the planters' ambivalent attitudes towards women workers, for 'while the planters criticized mothers for neglecting their offspring, they preferred to hire females, whom they considered more regular than males in their work habits'.[22]

Indentured labour from India was used to replace slaves in many Caribbean territories. Throughout the period of indenture the attitude to women immigrants from India varied with the problems of recruitment and with the perceptions of the role of women in both production and reproduction by the plantocracy and the Imperial power. As Reddock[23] indicates 'contradictions continued between the planters' short-term preference for adult male migration and their long-term need for a self-reproducing, cheap and stable labour force. Among the male Indian workers, their desire for docile, secluded and controllable women as befitted their aspirations for higher caste status, conflicted with the planters' need for women as labourers and the non-availability of women of the "right kind" for migration to the colonies'. Both Reddock[24] and Emmer[25] have shown for Trinidad and Surinam respectively that the women who left India to work in the Caribbean were more independent than most Indian women. Indenture was an escape route for many Brahmin widows and child-widows offering both the opportunity for re-marriage and for economic improvement. Only about one-third of the women who arrived from India were accompanied by husbands. These women did not easily accept the prevailing male orthodoxy of the British view of women as 'housewives' or the Indian insistence on the seclusion of women of high caste. Indenture gave Indian women an escape from poverty and a chance for emancipation but Emmer[26] demonstrates that most women married and retreated to the private sphere. In Surinam, in principle, workers of both sexes were given equal pay but in Trinidad women indentured workers were paid less per task than men, as were all women workers. Emmer[27] indicates that the average number of days worked per year by women in Surinam was a quarter to a third less than men, while Reddock[28] asserts that in Trinidad, despite pay differentials, some women managed to earn as much as men by working harder.

In general, indentured labourers of both sexes were treated as severely as slaves had been since many estate managers wished to exact the maximum returns from their investment in labour during the period of the contract.[29] There was little gender division of labour and women were expected to perform a wide range of tasks on the plantation. Harry[30] quotes a newspaper report based on interviews with three women who had been indentured in Trinidad in the late nineteenth century. According to their story:

In the cultivation you will find that the women dominated the group. They were out early in the fields performing hazardous duties like dropping lime and phosphate of ammonia, planting foods on the estates, that is vegetable crops and ground provisions, manuring, cutlassing, weeding, cutting canes, loading them on carts, and most of the time carrying the canes on their heads.[31]

In addition to this field work, women were responsible for childcare, housework and general family maintenance. Thus, under forced labour there was very little differentiation of agricultural activities based on either gender or ethnicity.

Gender roles under a free labour system

Since the ending of apprenticeship and indenture, gender roles in West Indian peasant agriculture have been largely determined by two factors: family structure, and, to a lesser extent, type of agriculture. Women have had to accept responsibility for the financial support of their children since emancipation because of both male migration and male economic marginality. In 1970 the Commonwealth Caribbean had 238,781 female-headed households constituting 35% of all households in the region.[32] The proportion of female-household heads displays both cultural and spatial variation, ranging from one-half amongst the highly migratory Afro-Caribbean population of St. Kitts-Nevis

to one-quarter in Trinidad and Tobago where the rural population is largely East Indian. That this pattern is of long standing is clear from Brodber's[33] study of the Jamaican free women in which she showed that second generation free women even when married, chose and could choose economic independence and autonomy.

Female members of Caribbean farm households may play three economic roles related to agriculture. They may be the decision maker or they may assist on their own family farm, providing subsistence for their household; they may market the surplus production of their own and other farm enterprises or they may join the rural proletariat and work as agricultural labourers on other small agricultural holdings or on plantations. These roles are not mutually exclusive and any one individual may move between the informal and the formal economy at different times of year or at various stages in her life cycle.

Women as peasant farmers

Peasantries in the Caribbean have grown up in the crevices of their societies, interdependent but in conflict with the capitalist plantation economy.[34] In this situation it was perhaps, inevitable that women, in their reproductive role, should play a major part in the peasant sector.

Census data on gender divisions of labour on small farms is not widely available and is subject to the usual caveats concerning the effect of enumerator's and interviewees attitudes on underreporting of women's economic activity rates in agriculture.[35] Although the data presented in Table 3 for the Eastern Caribbean comes from a wide range of sources and is somewhat spotty in its coverage it is adequate to identify certain trends related to type of agriculture, inter-island variation and changes over time.

Female farming is most common on subsistence holdings and less so on those farm enterprises oriented towards commercial cropping, as the figures for St. Lucia, Montserrat and Grenada in Table 3 show. In the large island of Trinidad there are several distinctive types of farming, and Harry[36] in her survey found that one-quarter of the rice and dairy farmers, 22% of the cocoa farmers, 18% of the vegetable farmers, 14% of the tobacco and 13% of the cane farmers were women. These differences are related to income, land ownership and type of farm work. Cane farmers had the highest levels of living and women provided the smallest amount of labour on these farms. Most cocoa farms were on freehold land and the women farmers in this group had generally inherited their land from their

Table 3. Sex of decision makers on farms of less than 10 acres in selected Eastern Caribbean territories

Island	Year of survey	Sample Size	Percentage farms with female decision makers
Barbados	1963	207	53.1
Barbados	1987	146	23.9
Barbuda	1971–73	234	28.2
Grenada	1969	256	20.7
Grenada*	1969	214	18.7
Martinique	1964	203	35.5
Martinique	1981	17,919	20.0
Montserrat	1972	527	44.2
Montserrat	1983	125	32.1
Montserrat*	1973	60	36.6
Montserrat*	1985	136	27.9
Nevis	1950	205	29.2
Nevis	1979	91	30.8
Nevis	1985	407	38.3
St. Lucia	1964	187	42.8
St. Lucia	1980–81	7,520	23.0
St. Lucia*	1971	47	17.0
St. Lucia*	1984	152	15.8
St. Vincent	1972	6,862	46.2
Trinidad	1979	80	28.8

*Sample drawn from commercial farmers only.
SOURCE: Field surveys for Barbados, Martinique (1964), Nevis (1979), Montserrat (1973) and St. Lucia (1964 and 1971). Data for St. Vincent and Montserrat (1972) comes from the 1972 Agricultural Census. Data for Grenada from John S. Brierley *Small Farming in Grenada W.I.*, Winnipeg, 1974; for Barbuda from Riva Berleant-Schiller, 'Production and division of labor in a West Indian Peasant community', *American Ethnologist*, 4, 1977, pp. 253–272; and for Trinidad from I.S. Harry, *Women in Agriculture in Trinidad*, unpublished MSc thesis, University of Calgary, 1980. St. Lucia 1980–81 and 1984 data supplied by Department of Agriculture, Castries. Montserrat (1983), Census of Agriculture, 1985 data supplied by Department of Agriculture, Plymouth. Nevis 1950 and 1985, Farmers on Land Settlements, data supplied by Department of Agriculture, Charlestown. Martinique, 1981, Recensement General de L'Agriculture, 1980–81, Martinique, SCEES, SRSA-DOM DDA Martinique, 1983.

spouse. Tobacco and vegetable farms were predominantly on rented land. Female labour inputs were relatively high in rice and dairy farming.

Examination of the structural characteristics of farm operated by women shows that these farms are generally smaller, have poorer quality land, are less accessible to markets and are less likely to include rented land than those operated by men. The structure and economic level of the female-headed household, which is commonly associated with these farms, gives rise to labour problems and to a dependence on the land for subsistence rather than for commercial production. Women appear to view the farm as an extension of their domestic responsibilities, concentrating on subsistence production of food crops and small stock rather than on the export crops and cattle preferred by men. Sometimes, where the land is jointly operated, women may see the land as a source of economic independence from the male partner and thus may specialize in the production of fruit, herbs and vegetables which they can sell on the local market. The overall picture of female-operated farms is that of marginality in terms of capital, land and labour resources, and largely reflects the economic insecurity of the matrifocal household. However, the dominant characteristics of these farms vary from island to island indicating intra-regional differences in the availability of human and physical resources.[37]

On the whole the proportion of small farms operated by women has declined over the last two decades as the economic base of most islands has widened and alternative opportunities in the labour market have become available (Table 3). Only in the small, impoverished island of Nevis, of those islands for which time-series data is accessible, has this defeminization of agriculture not occurred. Indeed, in Nevis it is not merely the case that women are maintaining their operation of the family farm but that women are also actively taking up vacant lots on government land settlements in order to grow food with which to feed their families.

Women in the agricultural labour force

In addition to their role as peasant farmers, women have continued to play an important role in the agricultural labour force, as they did in the days of slavery (Table 4). The decade following emancipation was marked by a rapid decline in the agricultural labour force, as the women and children among the ex-slaves moved into domestic occupations and education respectively and, where land was available, the men became peasant farmers. The economic difficulties of the mid-nineteenth century resulted in a slight increase in the rural proletariat but then followed a century of relative stability in the absolute numbers of agricultural workers in most parts of the Caribbean. The food shortages of the Second World War brought the agricultural work force to its highest level since slavery but this peak was followed by a rapid decline as alternative occupations became available to the proletariat.[38] Within this overall trend the participation rate of women fluctuated as women came to see themselves as a reserve labour force responding both to seasonal and to longer term shortages in agriculture.

In the late nineteenth century, as men left the poorer territories in search of economic opportunities overseas, the unskilled agriculture work force became once more predominantly female as it had been in the later stages of slavery. Brizan indicates a ratio of 132 female to 100 male agricultural workers in Grenada at this time.[39] Even in Guyana where labour shortages were less marked than on the smaller islands the proportion of women agricultural labourers rose from 31% in 1881 to 39% in 1891 and 41% in 1911.[40] In Jamaica, on the other hand, women dominated migration to the towns and so their participation rate in the agricultural labour force fell from 49.2% in 1891 to 19.9% in 1943.[41]

The postwar decline in the agricultural labour force was accompanied by a relative increase in the proportion of female workers, especially in the unpaid family worker category. These postwar changes support Boserup's theory that agriculture comes to depend increasingly on unpaid female family labour as the number of paid agricultural workers decreases. However, as the tourism and manufacturing sectors of the Caribbean economy expanded under the stimulus of investment by trans-national companies, agriculture became less important as an employer and women, especially the younger, better-educated ones, moved into these new growing sectors. By 1970 only about one-third of the workers in agriculture were women and the decline was most marked in Antigua where agriculture was very depressed (Table 5).

The most striking development in the West Indian labour force since 1970 has been the increased economic activity rate of women, and the service sector, in which women predominate, has superseded agriculture as the major employer in the region. Yet agricultural labouring remains the main source of income for poor, rural women and in addition, there is anecdotal evidence that high inflation during the 1970s has forced many women back into dependence on subsistence agriculture. Agricultural surveys in the Windward Islands during this period indicate a continuing and in some cases increasing participation rate for women (Table 5).

Le Franc[42] found that women in Grenada made up 50% of the unpaid family workers but had declined from 40 to 38% of the paid workers whereas in St. Vincent and St. Lucia their role had increased with women constituting 47% of the unpaid workers and 41% of the paid in St. Vincent and 34% of the unpaid and 35% of the paid work-

Table 4. Occupation of Farm Workers, Dennery Estate, St. Lucia, 1985

	Number of Workers		Percentage of Workers		
Occupation	Male	Female	Male	Female	Total
Labourers	109	111	49.5	50.5	100
Field supervisors	20	—	100.0	0	100
Tractor drivers	5	—	100.0	0	100
Totals	134	111	54.7	45.3	100

SOURCE: Agricultural Statistical Unit, St. Lucia, 1985.

Table 5. Percentage of women in the agricultural labour force of selected Caribbean territories, 1946 to 1980

Territory	1946	1961	1970	1980
Antigua	47.6	59.2	25.3	N/A
Barbados	48.8	52.5	38.3	36.0
Dominica	40.4	55.0	32.8	N/A
Grenada	48.9	48.9	40.4	38.0
St. Kitts-Nevis	44.0	44.4	33.8	N/A
St. Lucia	39.3	47.0	29.9	35.0
St. Vincent	46.9	49.9	31.8	41.0

SOURCE: West Indian Census, 1946, Vol. 1, (Kingston, Jamaica, 1950); Agricultural Census of the West Indies, 1961, Eastern Caribbean Territories, (Bridgetown, Barbados, 1968); 1970 Population Census of the Commonwealth Caribbean Vol. 4, Part 16, (Kingston, Jamaica, 1976). 1980/81 Population Census of the Commonwealth Caribbean; Barbados, Vol. 1. Statistical Service, Barbados. 1885 Le Franc, E.R. 1980. 'Grenada, St. Vincent and St. Lucia', in Small Farming in the Less Developed Countries of the Commonwealth Caribbean, Barbados. Caribbean Development Bank, 1–143.

ers in St. Lucia. In Barbados, although agriculture's share of employment almost halved between 1970 and 1980, the proportion of women workers fell only from 38% to 36%.[43] In Montserrat, on the other hand, the absolute number of male agricultural workers increased between 1970 and 1980, and the number of women workers decreased so that the female percentage of the agricultural labour force declined markedly from 33.4% to 22.6%, in response to male return migration and increased female employment opportunities in tourism and the textile industry.[44] It is clear that West Indian women today, in general, consider agriculture as an occupation of last resort to be followed only when there is no alternative way of feeding their families.

Gender divisions of labour time

The local context, household structure and stage in the domestic cycle are all important in determining the gender division of labour time in any particular area. However, there is considerable evidence that, in general, women have shorter resting hours, greater intensity and fragmentation of work and more frequent recourse to multiple simultaneous occupations than men.

Throughout the Caribbean women members of farm families work long hours. Knudson and Yates[45] in their survey of small-farming on St. Lucia, found that women worked five to six hours a day on the farm, three to four hours on housework, two to five hours on childcare depending on the age of the children, and occasionally spent time on marketing. It is scarcely surprising that 22% of the women in this survey felt that they had no leisure time at all. In terms of farm work, the relative time input of men and women varies with the economic status of the farmer, the type of farming, seasons, the importance of off-farm employment and the sex of the farm operator. Both Edwards[46] working in Jamaica and Macmillan[47] in Trinidad found that women's labour input on the farm differed according to the male partner's economic status: in poor families women performed all field tasks but as prosperity increased dependence on female and child family labour declined. Harry[48] in her Trinidad survey found very little difference in the mean hours worked on the farm by men and women, with men averaging 4.9 days per week and women 4.8. Both sexes worked seven hours a day in the busy season and three hours in the quiet season. However, women worked longer hours than men in rice and vegetable farming while men put in longer hours on cane and tobacco farms. Men who had off-farm jobs worked fewer hours on the farm than average and women who operated their

own farms worked five to seven days per week on the farm. In the Leeward Island of Nevis, on the other hand, there were distinct gender-based differences in the average hours worked and in the seasonal pattern of employment. On average, women worked the same number of days per week as in Trinidad, 4.8, but men put in 5.5 days. At the busiest time of the agricultural year women averaged 25 hours and men 35 hours per week, while in the quiet season women worked 18 hours compared to 27 hours for men.[49] Thus the weekly hours worked by women fell from 72% of male hours in the busy season to 66% in the quiet season suggesting that women form, to some degree, a reserve supply of labour for the farm to be drawn on at periods of peak demand.

Gender divisions of agricultural tasks

The allocation of tasks by gender has become gradually more marked. Under slavery both men and women carried out the full range of farming tasks in the field and divisions of labour were based more on age than on gender. This situation was still evident in Grenada in the 1930s when, as Brizan[50] comments, 'rural womenfolk were engaged in all agricultural activities pursued by men, in addition to their domestic chores'. Today gender differences largely conform with the pattern found by Murdock and Provost[51] in their cross-cultural sample of 185 societies. In general, as shown by field surveys in Nevis, Trinidad,[52] St. Vincent (Table 6), and St. Lucia (Table 7), women perform the less strenuous tasks such as planting, weeding, fertilizing, moulding up of soil around young plants and harvesting. Men undertake the preparation of the soil, the hoeing or ploughing, and the transporting of the crop from the field. Some of these tasks are

Table 6. Gender divisions of labour on small farms in St. Vincent

Type of job	Percentage distribution of labour			
	Male	Female	Joint	Not applicable
Preparation of soil	90	5	5	0
Planting	28	40	32	0
Hoeing	85	8	7	0
Weeding	8	50	35	7
Pest control	23	5	2	70
Fertilizing	43	35	22	0
Harvesting	22	13	65	0
Storage	2	3	2	93
Marketing	25	45	27	3
Keeping records	5	3	0	92
Care of livestock	23	10	59	8

SOURCE: Adapted from a sample survey of small farms in St. Vincent undertaken by Barbara Yates in 1981, Women and Development Unit, Barbados.

Table 7. Gender divisions of labour on small farms in St. Lucia

| Type of job | Percentage distribution of labour | | |
	Male	Female	Joint
Preparation of soil	83	3	14
Planting	76	4	20
Weeding	48	17	35
Pest control	75	15	10
Fertilizing	56	22	22
Harvesting	54	8	38
Storage	52	25	21
Marketing	48	37	25
Care of livestock	55	23	22

SOURCE: Adapted from Tables III–13 and III–15 in *The Economic Role of Women in Small Scale Agriculture in the Eastern Caribbean — St. Lucia,* by Barbara Knudson and Barbara Yates, Women and Development Unit, Barbados, 1981.

gender-neutral or interchangeable, especially harvesting and fertilizing. Pest control is least likely to be undertaken by women because they feel that the use of chemical sprays is dangerous to them, especially when they are pregnant or lactating. Women farmers without available assistance from male relatives will hire male agricultural labourers for this task alone. Weeding is the task most often seen as suitable for women only, especially on tobacco and vegetable farms, but weeding and pruning is considered a masculine task for crops such as cocoa and bananas.

The gender division of labour associated with livestock is often considered to relate to the size of the animal, with men caring for large animals and women for small stock.[53] In the West Indies these gender divisions appear to be more closely linked to specific tasks and to the level of commercialization of the particular animal. Yates' work in St. Vincent and St. Lucia revealed that the construction of sheds and fencing for stock, and the slaughter of animals are jobs done only by men. Women help with daily care of farm animals and with the milking and collection of eggs and are responsible for the marketing of these products. In Trinidad men care for the beef cattle and the equines while women do much of the work with the dairy cattle and look after all other animals.[54] In Nevis, where sheep and goats are of major economic importance, men are normally in charge of all the animals, except poultry, and do all the marketing of animal products.[55] It would appear that in both Trinidad and Nevis it is the level of commercialization of stock raising which determines gender roles, rather than the type of animal.

Rural women in the West Indies fulfill their roles within the constraints of household structure, occu-

pational multiplicity, time and space. The presence of older children reduces the demand for the mother's labour in the fields and possibly may determine how far the family is able to market its agricultural produce. Younger children keep the mother tied closely to her private sphere of the home but many women develop home-based income-earning opportunities such as baking, sewing or storekeeping. Women are responsible for the dooryard garden of vegetables and herbs and for the poultry and pigs which are kept close to the house and fed on household scraps. Women are least likely to work in the most distant fields which are usually kept in tree crops or crops unlikely to suffer from praedial larceny and requiring little attention. These fields may be left uncultivated on farms operated by women if adequate family labour is not available.[56]

Conclusion

Under slavery, roles in agriculture were differentiated according to strength rather than sex. Only in the last 50 years have agricultural wage rates reflected gender differences. Today most rural people feel that women's roles are changing, according to Yates' surveys in St. Vincent and St. Lucia. In Trinidad, Harry noted that the 'female coolie syndrome', with women working up to sixteen hours a day in the fields and the home from the age of 10, was disappearing with the improved educational attainment of young women and the new opportunities for non-farm female employment. Yet the traditional pattern of male-dominated gender relations is not changing[57] and as women expand their horizons and become more confident they find themselves unable to alter their domestic work patterns.[58] It is essential if West Indian peasant agriculture, which depends so heavily on women's work, is to become more efficient that the conflicts between women's productive and reproductive roles at the household level are reduced.

This examination of gender roles in the rural Caribbean has provided evidence that productive activities organized through the relations of reproduction, of kinship and of community, have existed under a range of economic systems, though often in hidden and invisible form and varying in time and space. These activities adjust, counter-balance or disintegrate under the effects of the decline or continuing structural absence of capitalist relations. It is hoped that this study has shown the necessity for settling technological and economic developments in their local and historical contexts and has refuted Boserup's reliance on the preservation of African cultural traditions as an explanation of the role of women in Caribbean agriculture.

Acknowledgements

Thanks are due to the Social Sciences and Humanities Council of Canada for funding the field work in 1979 and to the Nuffield Foundation for supporting the 1985 field work.

Notes

1. For a critique of Boserup's theoretical approach see L. Beneria and G. Sen. 1981, 'Accumulation, Reproduction and Women's Roles in Economic Development: Bo9serup Revisited'. *Signs*, Vol. 7, pp. 279–99.
2. See Boserup, 1970. op. cit. p. 63.
3. Eric Williams, *From Columbus to Castro*, p. 136.
4. Bryan Edwards, 1801, op. cit. Vol. II, pp. 106, 118.
5. For details of the slave sex ratio in the British Caribbean see Higman, 1976, pp. 67–69.
6. For an analysis of gender differences in slave physiology see Kiple, op. cit. p. 149.
7. *Ibid.*
8. Kiple, *op. cit.* pp. 110, 114.
9. See Morrissey, *op. cit.*
10. Bush, *op. cit.* suggests this interpretation after considering female resistance to slavery.
11. See Snell, 1980, for a discussion of female agricultural labour in England.
12. Orlando Patterson, 1967, p. 67.
13. See Rhoda Reddock in *Latin American Perspectives*, Vol. 12(1), p. 65.
14. See Craton, 1977, in *Searching for the Invisible Man*, p. 142.
15. See Sheridan, 1974, *Sugar and Slavery*, pp. 257–8.
16. See Lucille Mathurin, 1975, *The Rebel Woman*, p. 5.
17. See C. Levy, 1980, *Emancipation, sugar and federalism*, p. 10.
18. This situation is described in Mintz, 1964. Currency problems in eighteenth century Jamaica.
19. M.R. Edwards, 1980, provides an overview of the growth of higglering in the region.
20. See R.E. Pahl, 1984, for a review of changing gender divisions of labour in England.
21. H. Morsen, 1841, provides a contemporary description of post-emancipation changes.

22. See Levy, *op. cit.* p. 113.
23. See R. Reddock, 1985 in *Economic and Political Weekly*, p. 81.
24. R. Reddock, *Ibid.*
25. See R.C. Emmer, 1986.
26. *Ibid.*
27. See Emmer, *op. cit.* p. 257.
28. See R. Reddock, 1985 in *Economic and Political Weekly*.
29. See Lowenthal, 1972, *West Indian Societies*.
30. See Indra S. Harry, 1980 for a discussion of women's role in Trinidadian agriculture.
31. See the *Battlefront*, 1978, Vol. 2, 19 May, p. 7.
32. This is reported in Buvinic and Youssef, 1978, *op. cit.*
33. See E. Brodber, 1980, *op. cit.*
34. See S.W. Mintz, 1985, *op. cit.*, pp. 127–154.
35. Dixon-Mueller discusses these probles in *Women's work in Third World agriculture*.
36. See I.S. Harry, 1980.
37. A detailed description of female operated farms is given in Henshall 1981, *op. cit.*
38. For a survey of agricultural labour in the Eastern Caribbean see Momsen, 1969.
39. See George Brizan, 1985.
40. Reported in W. Rodney, 1981, *History of the Guyanese Working People*.
41. See Roberts, 1957, *op. cit.*
42. See E.R. Le Franc, 1980, *op. cit.*
43. *1980–81 Population Census of the Commonwealth Caribbean, Barbados*, 1985.
44. *1980–81 Population Census of the Commonwealth Caribbean, Montserrat*, 1984.
45. In their 1981 sample survey of St. Lucia, Knudson and Yates provide considerable detail on gender roles.
46. See David Edwards, 1961.
47. See A.A. Macmillan's, 1967 study of market gardening in Trinidad.
48. See Harry, 1980, *op. cit.*
49. See J.D. Henshall (Momsen), 1984.
50. This is mentioned in George Brizan, 1979.
51. See Murdoch and Prevost, 1973.
52. Henshall, 1984, compares gender roles in Nevis and Trinidad.
53. This is described in Murdoch and Prevost, 1973.
54. Harry, 1980 provides further details on women farmers in Trinidad.
55. See Henshall, 1984.
56. See Vasantha Chase's 1986 paper on farming systems.
57. Henry and Wilson, 1975, discuss female status in the Caribbean.
58. See John, Elwin, Charles and Clarendon's 1983 report on a project in Dominica.

Indian Women and Indentureship in Trinidad and Tobago 1845–1917: Freedom Denied

Rhoda Reddock

When Indian Indentureship to Trinidad began in 1845, what later became known as the 'Indian Women Problem' had already reared its head. The initial phase of migration to the Caribbean of Indians destined for indentured labour on the plantations began as early as 1838 when migrants to the then British Guiana were among the 6,000 men and 100 or so women who were shipped to Mauritius, Australia and British Guiana between 1834 and 1839.[1] The initial phase of indentured Indian emigration followed fast on the heels of the abolition of slavery. This was an attempt (and eventually a successful one) by the plantocracy to reduce labour costs as well as to re-establish some degree of labour control of the plantation.

The first prohibition of indentured Indian migration which took place in 1839 was fuelled by the activities of the re-organized Anti-Slavery Society against this 'new system of slavery'. One of their major objections had been the small numbers of women among the migrants during this initial phase. In November 1844 therefore when the government of India lifted its ban on indentured Indian emigration to the Caribbean, one of the conditions was that at least 12½ per cent of the emigrants be female.[2] The inclusion of quotas for women was mainly for public consumption.[3] On 30 May, 1845 when the *Fatel Rozack* brought the first 227 Indian immigrant labourers to Trinidad, 206 were men and 21 women.[4] In addition to the factors in the receiving countries which favoured migration, there were also developments in British India where:

To natural hazards and traditional fragmentation of family holdings to an excessive degree, were added changes in production following the training of British rule[5]

which encouraged migration.

In the eighteenth century, India had supplied cotton goods on a large scale to Europe, but now she was losing her position as a manufacturing country and had been transformed into a consumer of British goods. The textile industries were the first to collapse before competition; weavers and other workers were left without employment and had no alternative but to fall back on the land. The land, however, did not welcome them. According to J.C. Jha, British land policy in India had sought to create and perpetuate a class of large landowners to the detriment of the small peasant proprietors through, for example, the permanent settlement of Bengal in 1793.

This settlement destroyed the land tenure rights of small holders while increasing the powers of landlords or *zamindars* over the tenants or *ryots*.[6] This situation was further aggravated by the recurrent famines in north India during the 19th century which affected peasants and rural artisans whose conditions were worsened by the annexation of Oudh to the British Empire in 1856.[7]

Within India itself, one of the apparent effects of this combination of destructive colonial policy with natural hazards was the migration of those affected to the towns from surrounding areas. For these landless unemployed, facing the increasing competition for survival in the towns, emigration to the British colonies was one alternative.

The system of indentureship was organized though two Emigration Agents in Calcutta and Madras. They were responsible for the recruiting, safe-keeping and transportation of immigrants from India to the Colonies. In each recruiting territory there as an Agent-General of immigration later known as the Protector of the Immigrants to estates, looking after their well-being — health, food, working conditions — and the prosecution of estate owners who failed to provide adequately in any of these areas.

In spite of the experience of Caribbean slavery where women engaged in planation labour manifested a higher survival rate than their male counterparts,[8] the planters adopted the notion of women as unproductive and generated policies from this idea. The relations of production between planters and their female indentured labourers must, however, not be seen only in ideological terms but also as resulting from the planters' initial unwillingness to finance the cost of reproducing a second generation of workers in the Caribbean. This fact went a long way in creating the possibilities for Indian women's independence in the Caribbean.

Recruitment Policy and the Reproduction of the Labour Force

From its inception, Indian indentureship in Trinidad, as all receiving territories, was characterized by a numerical disparity between the sexes: far fewer women were recruited and a number of reasons could be used to explain this. In India, since the 19th century to the present, unlike in most other countries of the world, the ratio of women to men in the population is much lower. In 1911, the ratio of women to men in the United Provinces was 915 to 1,000[9] while in Punjab and Delhi, at this time, the ratio was only 817 women to every 1,000 men.[10] Recruiting therefore took place in a situation of an already existing unequal sex ratio.

Throughout the indentureship period, the approach towards the recruitment of women varied over time in relation to the desire of the plantocracy and the exigencies of the recruiting situation as mediated through the policies of the colonial authorities. Some of these have already been identified and include the relative necessity to reproduce the labour force locally, the need to stabilize the male labour force and the problems incurred in securing the 'right kind of woman',

During the early period therefore, as noted by Ramnarine,[11] while the planters were interested in immigration as a source of direct labour, women as a source of labour were seen as financial liabilities due to the financial risks of child-bearing and child-rearing. 'Thus, in the early period, little encouragement was given to family migration or for women to migrate. In addition, the supposed 'natural weakness' of women was assumed to be another discouraging factor and, in a search for 'able-bodied' labour, few women were recruited. During the initial phase therefore between 1845 and 1848 no legal restrictions on the proportion of males to females existed. At least two authors, Weller and Cumpston, stated that encouragement was given to men to bring their wives and families.[12] However, this could not have been very successful. In 1857, the ratio was set at one woman to three men (1:3) and in 1859 it was changed to one to two (1:2). In 1860, due to difficulties in recruiting the 'right type of women' this was reduced to one to four (1:4) by Act XLVI of 1860. According to Weller,[13] the Protector of the Emigrants in Calcutta had the discretionary power to alter this standard.

The main areas of recruitment were the markets, railway stations, bazaars and temples. The main towns in the north were 'nakas' between Delhi and Benares and included Allahabad, Fyzabad and Agra. Muttra (Mathura) was apparently a main area for the recruitment of women.[14] From time to time although statements were made against the recruitment of women from these areas because of their 'low moral character' similar reservations were never made about men recruited from these same areas. The emigration agents were at pains to explain to the planters and Colonial Office the difficulties of obtaining the 'better class of women' and pointed out that these, if recruited, would be totally unsuited to estate work.

Certain magistrates carried out thorough investigations of single women's backgrounds before they would allow them to migrate. This was usually done through the police and could take from one to three months.[15] The women's statements were not accepted. An obvious disqualification was, of course, the manifestation of pregnancy by single women during the waiting period. Known prostitutes or those who were described as 'coarse low caste females' were also disqualified. But in periods of great shortage these controls could not be maintained and this contradictory situation was never adequately resolved. In 1913, Mr. A. Maisden, the Trinidad Government Emigration Agent writing from Calcutta to the Under Secretary of State in the Colonial Office, had this to say:

. . . it is in the recruiting of women that more than half our difficulties in emigration consist, and which causes recruiters to get such a bad name, and fall into disfavour with magistrates. In one district where the recruitment of women had come to a full stop for several months a new Magistrate was appointed who refused to register any woman for the colonies unless the recruiter who presented the woman at the Court for registration gave some evidence that he had been to the woman's village and obtained the sanction of her husband for her to go abroad. The recruiter replied 'if I do this I shall get my throat cut as the husband will be sure to attribute the cause of the woman's leaving her home to my influence, no matter how little truth there may be in the allegation'.[16]

By the mid–19th century, much concern was being voiced over the 'kind of women' who were being recruited. Many of the alterations in the official recruitment ratios were made with this in mind. Throughout the period, contradictions continued between the planters' short-term preference for adult male migration and their long-term need for a self-reproducing, cheap and stable labour force. Among the male Indian workers, their desire for docile, secluded and controllable women as befitted their aspirations for higher caste status, conflicted with the planters' need for women as labourers and the non-availability of women of 'the right kind' for migration to the colonies. The effect of this latter contradiction was manifested in the increasing violence among Indian men over women and towards women in all recruiting territories during the latter half of the 19th century.[17] In July 1868, therefore, the proportion was again increased, this time to 1:2, but the Government of Bengal complained that this would lead to the recruitment of 'a low caste of women' mainly 'prostitutes'. The figure was altered once more by the Government of India to 1:3 but finally it was fixed by the Colonial Office at 2:5.[18]

This did not persist and, according to Weller, in 1878–79 the proportion was once again reduced to 1:4 on the plea that females migrating prior to 31 October that year had had a high mortality rate.[19] The recruiters used this opportunity to turn back family groups and individual women and to send single men. Contrary to common belief, the majority of Indian women came to the Caribbean not as wives or daughters, but as individual women. As late as 1915 the commissioners, McNeil and Lal, described the composition of women indentured labourers thus:

The women who came out consist as to one-third of married women who accompany their husbands, the remainder being mostly widows and women who have run away from their husbands or been put away by them. A small percentage are ordinary prostitutes. Of the women who emigrate otherwise than with their husbands and parents the great majority are not, as they are frequently represented to be shamelessly immoral. They are women who have got into trouble and apparently emigrate to escape from a life of promiscuous prostitution which seems to be the alternative to emigration ... What appears to be true as regards a substantial number is that they ran away from home alone or accompanied by some one by whom they were abandoned, that they drifted into one of the large recruiting centres and after a time, were picked up by the recruiter.[20]

Following on this observation, it is interesting to note the types of women who did migrate. Of the two-thirds who were not wives of migrating husbands, the majority as mentioned earlier were windows. In India then as now, in many cases the position of widows was particularly abhorrent. In particular, Brahmin widows and those of other twice-born castes who, in spite of certain possible escapes suffered the stigma of impurity, were forbidden to remarry and were forced to live miserable lives in the homes of their in-laws. In particular, the case of child widows was especially difficult and was an issue eventually taken up by the nationalist movement.[21] As a result of this,

Brahmin widows comprised a large proportion of those migrating.

The remaining number usually comprised women who had left their husbands or been deserted by them for whom prostitution or destitution was the only remaining alternative in India. A smaller number included unmarried women who were pregnant or already practising prostitutes seeking a new life. Thus, it can be seen that the decision to emigrate, in itself, was a sign of the independent character of these women and the decision to emigrate alone was a sign of their strength. According to David Dodd writing on British Guiana-

... many of the women who did come to the colony tended to be already more independent and self-seeking than those whose fathers, husbands and brothers decided that they should not go ... .[22]

This contrasts greatly with the commonly-held image of the docile, meek Indian woman arriving five steps behind her husband. Within India itself, the usefulness of this image for certain categories of women was recognized by the colonial authorities.

In 1882–83, Tinker noted that two reports were forwarded to the Indian government on this question. The first was by Sir Alfred Lyall, Lieutenant/General of the North Western provinces, and Major D. J. Pitcher.[23] They believed that:

A very large proportion of the women who now emigrate are persons who have been turned out of the home, or have lost their friends by famine or pestilence; some were Hindu girls who have been forced to become Muslims in some inter-communal quarrel; many were widows; therefore women might benefit more by emigration.[24]

The other report was written by G.A. Grierson, a scholar of ethnographic and linguistic studies. It was forwarded by the secretary of the Bengal government to the Indian government in March, 1883.[25]

'Grierson also saw emigration as a necessary outlet for women in trouble. He asserted that the best sort of female recruit was drawn from those abandoned and unfaithful wives who could make a fresh start by getting out of the home environment (the only alternative for them was prostitution). Many magistrates refused to register an absconding wife; but said Grierson, women have rights too, and if an alienated wife was determined to go, no officer has the right to stop her'.

According to Tinker, 'It was a radical suggestion within the conservatism of Indian society and Anglo-Indian officialdom'. These two reports, however, did have some effect and once more the ratio of two to five (2:5) was advanced. It is interesting to note that the social reality of life in India did not always conform to the ideology of 'conservatism' which was and is often propounded: women were 'deserted' or abandoned or had children outside of marriage. It is possible that the government of India saw this as an opportunity to rid itself of some of the aberrations.

Reports vary as to the actual nature of the recruitment process. It is possible that differences can be explained chronologically. But it is also possible that in any one period different methods were used, depending on the character of the recruiters. The main question usually discussed in relation to this is the extent to which people had come of their own free will and the extent to which they had been forced to come. If one attempted to use the two approaches mentioned above, it is possible to suggest that at all times both were used. Tinker points out that a clear correlation can be seen between increases in migration and years of economic difficulty. For example, he states:

Thus in 1860–61, there was famine in the North-Western Provinces and a high departure rate from Calcutta (17,899 in 1860 and 22,600 in 1861). The year 1865–66 produced famine in Orissa and Bihar and a high emigration (19,963) while from 1873–75 there was acute scarcity in Bihar, Oudah and the North-Western Provinces . . . [26]

While this general rule with regard to migration could largely be accepted, the recruitment of women presented special problems. After the initial period when no specific sex proportions were laid down, the effects in the colonies were such as to make the recruitment of women an issue throughout the period of immigration. The independence of character of the first female recruits left much to be desired as far as the planters and Indian men were concerned. To large extent both groups desired women who could facilitate a certain degree of 'stability' in estate life, who could accept a subordinate position and also work diligently in the fields. The following letter gives an example of this feeling:

Trinidad,
April 26, 1851.

No.40,
MY Lord,

I have the Honour to report the arrival of the "Eliza Stewart" with 173 Coolies on board.

The number is small, but the appearances and condition of the people are highly commended.

There is but a small proportion of women (eleven) which is to be regretted.

I am happy to say that a great number of Coolies who have completed their five years have declared themselves ready to accept the bounty.

If a cargo entirely of women could be sent over, I have little doubt that the greater number of the Coolies would remain here permanently.

I have the honour to be My Lord
Your Lordship's Most Obedient
Humble Servant
Harris

The Right Honourable
Earl Grey
(CO 295/173)

There was clearly a need for some women as a means of keeping experienced male workers in the country and as available labour themselves on the estates. Later in the century, the need for women became increasingly apparent, but the old contradiction of the 'kind of women' continued to rear its head. In 1891, the sex ratio for the entire Indian population in Trinidad was 637 women to 1,000 men.[27]

In 1893 therefore surgeon-major D.W.D. Comins recommended the reduction in the period of indentureship for women from five to two years as a means of encouraging the migration of women.[28] In making this recommendation, which was eventually accepted, Comins was pandering to the prevailing ideology within the Indian and Trinidad ruling classes, which accepted the definition of women as 'housewives' and of seclusion as a sign of high caste status. The hypocrisy of this ideology, however, and the way in which it was/is used to mask women's productive contribution to the society and economy were clear in his addendum to this recommendation. He assured the planters that, after the two-year indentureship period, he was certain that the husbands would not allow their wives to 'sit idle' if plentiful and good wages were available.[29] By the early 20th century, the recruitment of women became a much more serious issue as complaints were being made to the Government of India and increasing opposition was emerging against the 'slavery of Indian men and the prostitution of Indian women'. It is interesting to note the way in which the exploitation of women was characterized, not in terms of their work as labourers, but in terms of their morals. In other words, while the realization of men's life-potential was seen in terms of their labour work, for women who were also workers, it was seen in terms of the necessity to control their sexuality. In this period, therefore, in an effort to:

(i) ensure a self-reproducing labouring population in the face of the threats to end emigration;

(ii) supply an adequate number of women to stabilize the male population, and

(iii) to assuage complaints that women were placed beyond the control of their menfolk and leading an independent life, family migration was reluctantly supported.

In response to the demands for an increased number of women migrants, in the early 20th century new rates of commission were established which offered a much higher commission for women than for men. At the same time, however, attempts were made to place more stringent controls on the type of women recruited.

In 1915, for example, Mr. C. W. Doorly, emigration agent in Madras, informed the Under-Secretary of State for the Colonies of recent changes in rates of commission for recruitment. The new rates were:

Original Rates	Men	Women
1–10	35	45
11–20	45	60
21 and over	55	70
Alterations beginning		
October		
1–10	35	55
11–20	40	70
21 and over	45	80

He gave as reasons for these alterations the difficulties he was having in filling the required quota of women. He said,

the continued scramble for women does undoubtedly lead recruiters to take a certain number of persons who are not desirable emigrants. As an instance, I may mention by occasion of my last shipment to British Guiana. I was very short of women and yet in a week prior to the embarkation I had to reject nearly 20 women as undesirables.[30]

In 1916 and 1917, the period immediately preceding the abolition of the system of indentureship, great debate ensued within colonial circles in India on this question. In August 1916, W. M. Hailey, Chief Commissioner of Delhi, argued that 'if a high proportion is insisted on, the females will always tend to comprise a proportion of prostitutes and women who were seeking to escape their husbands or their families . . . '[31] This view was shared by many others who, after years of experience, distrusted the establishment of proportions as a means of dealing with their 'problem'. In December 1916, in a pamphlet 'Labour in Fiji', Mr. Andrews

advised that a bonus be given to men migrating to encourage 'the taking out of female children by married persons' rather than recruit a number of 'unattached women'. On this same issue, E.L. Hammond, Secretary to the Government of India, argued that married emigrants should be encouraged to take their families with them to the colonies; that greater facilities to be given to unmarried immigrants to find wives among the free population and married immigrants whose families had been left behind be given part of the costs of bringing them over.[32] In December that same year, Sir Wilmot G. Golvin, chief commissioner of Ajmer-Merwara, also rejected the fixing of sex proportions and instead recommended the giving of 'large bonuses in the case of Fiji and Trinidad for married couples taking out daughters of age between 10 and 14 bonuses of less amount in similar cases emigrating to Jamaica and British Guiana'.[33]

In 1917 the debate continues, but the emigration agent took on a more defensive posture. Mr. Doorly, emigration agent for Madras, argued that:

It must be borne in mind that genuine field labourers such as the planters require can be obtained only from the lowest castes i.e. from the non-moral class of the population. A more moral type is found higher in the social scale, but such women would be useless in the fields . . .

He continued:

In my view, the class of women recruited during the recent years is not an undesirable class for the men who accompany them and who are drawn from the same social stratum as themselves . . . .[34]

To prove that family migration was accepted out of the needs of planters, Doorly in another confidential letter noted that, while he had always favoured family recruitment, the Colonies always objected to receiving dependents. 'Now' however, he admitted, 'we must look to families for our chief source of supply and in order to get them we must take a fair number of old and broken down . . . . . dependents . . . . .'[35] Unfortunately, it was too late to have much effect on the existing system. Many of these recommendations were incorporated into new proposals made initially in 1917 for the replacement of the system of indentureship by one of assisted migration. By 1917, however, in response to the great public outcry in India, the system was abolished.

For a number of reasons, the majority of Indian women who came to the Caribbean were not the docile, subordinate wives which the traditional understanding of Caribbean history would have us believe. In spite of the many cases of kidnapping, enticement and false information, it is clear that a large proportion of women did make a conscious decision to seek a new life elsewhere.[36] Unfortunately, their intentions did not fit in with those of the planters or the Indian men in the Colonies and already at this recruitment stage attempts were made to control the situation.

Women's Labour in Plantation and Peasant Production

Much less consistent data exist on the exact nature and character of estate work than exist on recruiting. There is general agreement that it was hard and inhuman but exact details of changes over the entire period are hard to come by. Most of the data easily available are relevant to the latter period when changes had been made after various commissions had reported,and not for the earlier period. Most of the information on estate labour is derived from these reports —

1. Surgeon-Major D.W.Comins, Note on Emigration from India to Trinidad,1983.
2. Report on Emigration from India to the Crown Colonies and Protectorates (Part I) and Minutes on Evidence and Papers laid before the Committee (Part II), 1910. (The Sanderson Report).
3. James MacNeil and Chaimman Lal, Report to the Government of India on the Conditions of Indian Immigrants in the Four British Colonies and Surinam (Part I) Trinidad and British Guiana, 1915.

Unfortunately, many historians writing on indenture have ignored this fact and taken this information of the latter eighteen (18) years of indentureship to be relevant for the entire seventy-two period.

Plantation work in general meant work on sugar estates but it also included work on cocoa and coconut estates. As would be expected, tasks differed; on sugar estates, the degree of work varied with the season of the year. During the production season, work continued up to 15 hours a day and all indentured labourers — men, women and children — were involved. Most work was allocated according to 'tasks' — a kind of piecerate system — and the 1875 Ordinance specified five tasks a week to an immigrant. The main occupations on the estates as outlined by D. W. Comins for Woodbrook Estate[37] were:

Driver	35¢ per day
Carters	30–35¢
Watchmen	30¢
Weeding	25¢
Stock-keepers	25¢
Planting Cane	25¢ per 450 holes

Supplying	25¢ per day
Banking chiefly by contract and free Coolies	$6½ per acre
Forking, flat	40¢ for 6,000 to 7,000 ft.
Forking, burying trash	40¢ for 4,000 ft.
Forking, furrows	40¢
Manuring (pen)	10¢ per 100 holes
Manuring (Foreign), (small children)	10¢ to 15¢ per day
Cane cutters, chiefly free	25¢ for 20 to 55 rods
Cane carriers at mill	25¢ to 30¢ per day
Mill workers	25¢ to 30¢ per day
Fuel carriers	30¢ per day
Stokers	35¢ per day

While in general wages were low for all indentured labourers, for women it was even lower. Comins noted that 'women' boys and weakly men are given permanently some sum less than 25 cents per task because it has been decided that they are unable to do a full task . . . '[38] (my emphasis). McNeill and Lal found that women normally earned 'about a one-half to two-thirds the wages of male immigrants'.[39] Even in periods of high season when, for example, at Palmiste Estate in 1891, men got 50,60 and 70 cents for a task, all women received a flat rate of 25 cents a day on task-work.[40] In addition to the payment of low wages, Comins found on some estates the practice of carrying forward 'an ever accumulating debt' for rations supplied to women during pregnancy. This resulted in them earning no wages for months or years.[41]

Some writers found, however, that in spite of wage differentials, some women could earn a gross salary almost equal to that of the men by doing more tasks and/or working extra hours. For example, McNeill and Lal found that

The best woman workers earn almost as much as the average man . . . [42]

Unfortunately, the wage differentials in most instances served their traditional purpose of making the Indian woman dependent on men in spite of the fact that they were full-time workers. This practice, although universally in existence, was contrary to the terms of agreement made in India which stated that adults over 10 years should be paid as adults with no differentiation made for women, weakly men, boys or girls.[43]

The appendix to the Sanderson Report gives a breakdown of wages on various estates. Ross Shiels[44] noted that the statistics given in this report are often incomplete and inadequate, but are nevertheless used for an illustrative rather than an accurate analytical purpose, helpful in the absence of comparable data.[45]

Brechin Castle Estate 1st April, 1907 — 31st March, 1908

1. Average Wage per Day Actually Worked

Number of Immigrants		Average Actual Days Worked per Head	Total Wages Earned	Average Wage per Day per Head
Males	461	195.44	$22,830.44	25.33 cts
Females	181	94.02	3,512.85	20.64 cts

2. Average Wage Earned per Legal Working Day

Number of Immigrants		Average Actual Days Worked per Head	Total Wages Earned	Average Wage per Day per Head
Males	461	280	$22,830.44	17.68 cts
Females	181		3,512.85	6.93 cts

3. Average Wage Earned per Day at 365 Days per Annum

Number of Immigrants		Average Actual Days Worked per Head	Total Wages Earned	Average Wage per Day per Head
Males	461	365	$22,830.44	13.56 cts
Females	181		3,512.85	5.31 cts

A further factor differentiating female indentured labour, especially during the latter period, was the length of indenture. As the pressure to encourage large numbers of 'respectable' females to emigrate grew, a number of actions were taken to facilitate this. In the mid–1890s therefore the indentureship period for women was limited to three years.[46] While a few 'well-off' Indian men could afford to keep their wives at home, the large majority of women did continue to work on the estates. This change was used as a bait to encourage men to migrate with their wives, during this latter period when family migration was encouraged. In 1892 when Comins recommended the reduction of the indentureship period of women to two years, he assured the planters that he was certain that the husbands would not allow their wives to 'sit idle' if plentiful and good wages were available,[47] although he noted in his 'Diary' that the women are so well off that many of them do not work.'[48] Another source, however, states that in 1891 when the sex distribution for the entire Indian population was 637 females to 1,000 males, there were 14,131 female agricultural labourers to 26,771 male.[49] This view is also supported by Shiels who stated that not only did the majority of women continue working after the three-year period but they worked harder during the next two.[50]

During the late 19th century, the Trinidad sugar industry faced one of its perennial economic crisis.

Among the measures taken to control the falling rate of profit was the introduction of cane farming in conjunction with the reduction of wages. The system of cane farming, like most peasant proprietorship, was based on the existence of at least the basic nuclear family where the wife would work 'at home' in cane production and subsistence food production but could provide additional labour on estates when needed during harvest. Men on the other hand continued to work on the estates but could contribute to their private production during their spare time. This system served a number of purposes for the planter by providing a ready reservoir of cheap labour; providing an alternate source of sugar cane, thus removing dependence on wage-labour (in the light of numerous strikes during this period); and subsidizing wages by allowing workers to produce a certain proportion of their own food (Johnson, 1971).[51]

Between 1869 and 1879, therefore, 19,055 acres of Crown Land were given to Indian immigrants in lieu of return passage and between 1885 and 1900 a further 37,256 acres of Crown Land was sold to Indians.[52] This system allowed many men to fulfil their desire for a 'secluded' wife who did not labour for a wage on the estates. This withdrawal of women from plantations to peasant production also fitted in with the overall colonial policy of defining all women first as 'housewives' as this was the period when Indian men were being supported by the Colonial State in the reconstruction of their family system in the colonies. Thus, the yard-stick eventually used to determine whether suitable conditions existed on an estate was in terms of men's labour. The Sanderson Report said:

It is provided in the Ordinance (#70) that when by the returns of the Protector is that 30 per cent of the adult males indentured to any estate during the year earn a wage averaging less than 6d. per diem for the whole 365 days, it shall not be lawful for the Protector to entertain any application for fresh immigrants on behalf of that plantation . . . (my emphasis).[53]

In spite of a relatively sizable working female population on the estate their wages were of no consequence in determining conditions on the estate. This criterion was uncritically accepted by the Trinidad Workingmen's Association (TWA) in their fight against immigration.

With few exceptions, Indian women, like their African counterparts before them, came to the Caribbean as workers and not as dependents or, as the planters wished to portray them, 'for other purposes'. During the initial stages, the planters were unwilling to cover the costs of the local reproduction of their labour force which large numbers of female workers apparently implied. At later periods, however, the ideology of woman as 'unproductive labour' facilitated their exploitation as cheap labour at half the cost of male labour; through their availability as part-time labour during harvest and eventually as a means of reproducing the cheap labour force when indentured migration was abolished.

Social and Domestic Organization

As alluded to earlier, one of the main factors affecting the position of Indian women in Trinidad and Tobago was the low proportion of women in relation to men. That this was considered a major problem by the State, the Church and the men is apparent from the records. The following table gives an idea of the sex ratio between 1871 and 1911.

Sex Ratios (Male per 1,000 females) Among Estimated Net Immigrants to Trinidad, 1871–1911

Period	Sex Ratio	
	East Indian	Other
1871 – 1881	2,143	1,101
1881 – 1891	2,117	1,246
1891 – 1901	1,748	1,147
1901 – 1911	3,037	4

SOURCE: Jack Harewood: *The Population of* Trinidad and Tobago, *CIRCLED Series, 1975.*

The records, as would be expected, express the views of the dominant groups. Nowhere, except in quotations, is the voice of women heard.[54] Even the oppressed Indian men through their illustrious letter writer Mohammed Orfy were able to have their views made public. The way in which the women perceived their situation, therefore, has to be judged from their actions and analyzed without colonial and religious moralism. As to how women were perceived by these various institutions the following quotations give us some idea.

The Presbyterian Church

'There were no zenanas in Trinidad.[55] Our women immigrants are not recruited from the class that in India are shut up in zenanas. In Trinidad they find themselves of added importance through the small proportion of their sex. They have great freedom of intercourse and much evil example around them. Sad to say they often show themselves to be as degraded as they are ignorant. On the other hand many are beautiful and lovable, faithful to their husbands and devoted to their children. This however is by no means the rule'.[56]

'S.E.M. (Sarah Morton) — The loose notions and prevailing practices in respect of marriage here are quite shocking to the new-comer. I said to an East Indian woman whom I knew to be a widow of a Brahman, ''You have no relations in Trinidad, I believe''. ''No Madame'', she replied, ''only myself and two children; when the last (Immigrant) ship came in I took a papa. I will keep him so long as he treats me well. If he does not treat me will, I shall send him off at once; that's the right way is it not?'' This will be to some a new view on woman's rights.'[57]

The Colonial State

'The proportion of Indian females in the colony is so much smaller than that of males that it is impossible for every man to have a wife of his own even if he wished to have one. This evil is also increased by the fact that in some cases Indians, such as shopkeepers, landholders etcetera who are in comfortable circumstances have more than one wife and though they may be married to one, keep another as a concubine . . . '[58]

'Predisposition to immorality among women emigrants. The Government of India in paragraph 7 of its despatch observes that it is inevitable under existing conditions that among females immigrants there should be ''a large proportion of persons who are prostitutes, social outcasts or who have been unhappy in their domestic relations''. These persons besides being prone to immoral conduct themselves must by their example exercise a corrupting influence on the respectable woman who are compelled under present conditions to live in barracks with them . . . '[59]

The Men

'. . . another most disgraceful concern, which is most prevalent and a perforating plague, is the high percentage of immoral lives led by the female section of our community. They are enticed, seduced and frightened into becoming concubines, and paramours to satisfy the greed and lust of the male section of quite a different race to theirs.

. . . they have absolutely no knowledge whatever of the value of being in virginhood and become, most shameless and a perfect menace to the Indian gentry.'[60]

'Is it permissible for a male member of the Christian faith to keep a hindoo or muslim female as his paramour or concubine? Is this not an act of sacrilege and a disgraceful scandal according to the Christian faith to entice and encourage Indian females to lead immoral lives? It is a burning shame, and a grave cancer of a disgraceful and scandalous nature, which is predominantly amongst the females of India. This tends to prove most detrimental to the welfare in general to our community. Is it plausible that as those females desire to live as paramours with males of a different race to hers. Fathers nor husbands, nor brothers, who are their lawful protectors have power over them and are not in the least heard when such matters are brought before the authorities; all the consolation these lawful protectors derive are, so long as the girls are pleased, no one has power to interfere.'[61]

What is evident from these quotations is that many Indian women, probably for the first time in their lives, got an opportunity to exercise a degree of control over their social and sexual lives which they had never had before. As pointed out in an earlier section, the majority of women who did migrate were already independent women who were seeking a new life. These were hardly the type of women who would fall back into the oppressive life patterns from which they had fled. This situation in relation to the women differed greatly from the desires of the men. To them migration was an attempt at improving their economic and if possible their caste status. The practice known as 'sanskritization', common in other areas of high Hindu migration, was not absent here. Maria Mies in her book, *Indian Women and Patriarchy* shows clearly the increased restrictions on the social, sexual and economic freedom of women

the higher up the caste and/or economic ladder. In fact a restricted wife was/is a sign of high caste. That this was/is the position, at least of Mohammed Orfy (although apparently muslim), is clear by the use of the words 'Indian gentry' to describe the indentured or ex-indentured labourers in Trinidad and Tobago. These words obviously express an aspiration on their part to recreate themselves as an Indian gentry in Trinidad.

Many writers on this subject have chosen either to ignore the situation of Indian women in this period or to accept the judgments based on colonial and religious moralism. Tyran Ramnarine, for example writing on British Guiana, noted that 'This Ordinance (16 of 1894) apparently brought no improvement in the class of women recruited . . . ' (my emphasis), while J.A. Weller noted that the 'paucity of women created various sorts of immorality in the depot, on shipboard and in the colony.[62] These authors accepted uncritically these definitions of morality as well as the class prejudices of the colonial authorities. It is, however, in relation to the registration of non-Christian marriages that most of the discussion has taken place.

In discussing the question of marriages, one first has to come to terms with the phenomenon of 'depot marriages'. According to Tinker, in spite of the strict segregation of the sexes, relationships did develop between them. It is interesting that while still on the Indian sub-continent, people were willing to disregard caste, religion and custom, and get married. One can suggest that among the poorer agricultural classes/caste from which the majority of the immigrants were drawn, restrictions on marriages were less strict. Or the explanations could be seen on a more subjective level as Tinker:

The advantage to the man is obvious: he had someone to cook for him and to attend to him in a society where females were very scarce. But there was also advantage to the woman in securing a protector in a savage new environment, and in establishing some sort of recognized position in a social order, which held no place for an adult single woman.[63]

These marriages were, however, the exception rather than the rule, for Ramnarine notes that among the 4,000 adults who travelled to Guiana in 1892, 421 marriages took place on board ships.[64] These marriages, despite their legality, had no claim on stability after the arrival of the ships. Indian women apparently preferred to leave their 'depot husbands' for men who had lived longer on the colony and could offer them a better standard of living. So great was this problem that by 1882 the immigration authorities in Trinidad and Tobago were considering the possibility of registering these marriages 12 months after the immigrants' arrival in the country.

In relation to the legal registration of marriages which had taken place in the country other problems arose. These arose from the fact that the majority of Indians saw no necessity to register marriages at a government's registration office when an elaborate wedding ritual had already taken place. In India itself there was no need for registration. The discussion on this subject has occurred extensively.[65] Much of the discussion (not necessarily in these texts) has centred around the obvious failure of the Colonial government to automatically accept Hindu and Muslim marriages as being legally constituted. Most writers quite rightly condemned this as the means through which thousands of Indians were robbed of their land and other inheritances by being declared 'illegitimate' as well as being debarred from attending secondary schools. With the exception of Professor J. C. Jha, few have sought to explain why, in spite of the immeasurable economic and social loss incurred by this practice, the majority of the Indian population, up until the 1930s, refused the relatively easy solution of registering their marriages. The following may serve as an explanation.

In 1893, Sarah Morton noted a case where a father had sold his daughter nine times for money and goods and on each occasion had refused to deliver her.[66] Similar instances were noted by other authors. Tinker noted that this was common in all receiving countries. He states:

Because females remained in scarce supply the parents reversed the usual Indian custom of providing a dowry for their daughter when she became a bride and often instead demanded a bride-price . . . [67]

Among the labouring classes (and tribals) from among whom the majority of migrants came, bride-price and not dowry was the norm. In their new situation, however, girl children did gain an increased value to the shortage of women. Weller noted that 'female infant children were considered a valuable addition to a family and were reared with great care'.[68] This improvement in the 'marketability' of girl children by their fathers did not really represent an improvement in their position per se. Rather, child marriage from as early as ten years became the rule.

The advantage of this new situation, however, was that women could now, on their own accord, leave one husband for another or have parallel relationships with more that one man. Sarah Morton noted with dismay many such cases, including one where the mother left her child with its father when leaving to go to live with another man. Of course,

reports vary as to the degree to which women left one man for another or were enticed or seduced away from one man to another. Proponents of the former position viewed this action as immoral, while proponents of the latter viewed the woman as hapless, childlike victims of adult, worldly men. In either case, the independent intelligence or decision-making capacity of the woman was not considered. The independence of the Indian woman was seen therefore as a source of shame by the Indian man. In addition, the inability to have one woman upon whom he could exercise all the power and authority denied in a colonial situation only added fuel to the fire.

It was for this reason therefore that around 1880, according to Weller, 274 Indian men in the presence of the Presbyterian Reverends Morton, Grant and Christie petitioned the government for the right to prosecute an unfaithful spouse and her partner in guilt in the magistrates court, the complaint court or the supreme court with damages of £10, £25 or more or imprisonment. The wife was to be imprisoned if she did not return to her husband. In other words, the men sought less to punish the women than to possess and control them. These recommendations were accepted and promulgated as the Indian Immigrant Marriage and Divorce Ordinance, No.6 of 1861, which was later incorporated into the Immigration Ordinance of 1889.[69]

The law was one means through which the Indian men sought to re-establish control over their women in a situation which denied them any other source of power. In addition to this, another weapon more easily available to them was used. A weapon used by men internationally to maintain control over women — violence and in the specific case of the sugar plantation, the cutlass (machete). One Guyanese clergyman, Archdeacon Josa, sympathetically put it this way:

Is it any wonder then that the Hindu who, according to his own religion, is so far superior to the woman, when he finds that his wife has proved unfaithful takes his 'cutlass' and makes mincemeat of such a thing? He considers woman a mere chattel, we feel for the man. We could almost wish that capital punishment were abolished for such as he — until he learns to understand that woman is his equal — his helpmate — his wife.[70]

The murder of women was a phenomenon common to all areas of high Indian migration. Trinidad and Tobago was by no means at the head of the list. According to Donald Wood, between 1859 and 1863 twenty-seven (27) murders were committed by Indians and in each case it involved the wife or mistress of the murderer.[71] In British Guiana between 1885 and 1890, 40 murders of women occurred of which 33 were of wives killed by husbands or reputed husbands.[72] But not only did the men kill women; to a lesser extent they killed other men and/or committed suicide. To some extent, these actions had the effect of stereotyping Indian men but this violence had the much more lasting and important effect of placing Indian women once more firmly under the control of the men through the reconstruction, albeit in a different setting, of the Indian patriarchal family system.

That violence was necessary for such a reconstruction is apparent. The continuous letters of Mohammed Orfy to the Secretary of State for the Colonies, the Indian government and numerous other authorities bear testimony to this. In addition, the inclusion of clauses in the immigration ordinances prohibiting the 'harbouring of an immigrant's wife', and the continuous court cases resulting from breaches against this law, are all evidence of the struggle which ensued. The Indian woman did not 'naturally' give up her new found freedom as some writers would have us believe, but was forced to do so and kept in that position through similar means. This is not to deny, however, that the equalization in the proportion between the sexes over a period of time would have had the effect of changing the relationship between the sexes.

The dissolution of caste endogamy was another important effect of this situation. Although the majority of migrants came from the lower agricultural castes, it is know that members of higher castes including Brahmins and Kshatriyas (mainly Rajputs) also came.[73] Indeed, Donald Wood goes so far as to suggest that between 1845 and 1870 Brahmins comprised the second largest caste represented among the immigrants.[74] Wood notes that Brahmins falsified their castes in order to be allowed to migrate as they could be rejected by the officials as unsuitable labourers.[75] In addition it was known that a large number of the widows who migrated were from the higher castes where widow marriage was totally forbidden. On the whole, most of the five main factors governing Hindu marriage — endogamy, exogamy, prohibited kin, virgin marriage and hypergamy, Brahmin widows formed relationships with and/or married men of lower castes and the opposite occurred to a much greater degree. Comins noted in 1893 that:

Thousands of men have been for years past living with women who are not of the same caste with the result that their children would in India be looked on as outcasts; I refer here of course to the Hindu part of the population . . .[76]

Attempts to re-establish strict caste endogamy had much less success as it was obviously in the interests of only minority in the Hindu community.

Similarly, among Muslims (as among Hindus), the practice of polygamy was virtually impossible. Comins noted in 1890 that among the 282 marriages declared on arrival, there were six cases in which two women were entered as the wives of one man.[77] He did not state the religions involved. Polygamy is in theory permissible for all Hindus but, in practice, rare. In a situation such as existed in the migrant colonies, more often than not the opposite situation of consecutive relationships occurred.

Education

It was through the Church that the Christian community was able to establish its greatest influence over Indian women. This was through the Canadian Presbyterian Indian Education system. This mission began work in 1862 under Reverend John and Sarah Morton and they worked specifically among the Indians. The views of Sarah E. Morton on Indian womanhood have already been expressed in this paper; her efforts to change it call for an analysis of the Mission's education programme.

By 1890, Comins noted, there were 49 East Indian schools with 1,958 boys and 926 girls, with an average attendance of 1,876 pupils.[78] He also noted that while education of boys comprised industrial training and land cultivation, that for girls comprised 'Needlework and cutting-out underclothing . . . '[79] This finding did not diverge greatly from the stated aims of Mission Education as outlined by John Morton, which was' . . . to teach the largest number of the three R's, a knowledge of the way of life and duty, and to the girls sewing'.[80] Comins found that very few children of indentured labourers attended school. One can only suggest that they were too busy working on the estates. On visiting Tunapuna Presbyterian School on 11 June 1981, he found 12 Indian girls present and was informed by the mistress, Miss Blackadder, that the girls were 'merely sent here to be taken care of to save their mothers trouble, and not for any educational advantages they might receive'.[81]

Post-primary education of girls usually meant an extension of housewife-oriented training. In 1890 a 'Home for Christian girls' was opened with the express purpose of developing girls who 'would naturally be qualified above all others to be wives of our helpers' (my emphasis) or Biblewomen for the Church.[82]

This imposition of Western European middle-class housewife ideology taught in all 'Indian schools', when combined with a strengthened Indian patriarchal family system re-established partly through violence, served to create the prototype of the submissive, subordinate, docile Indian housewife who many would have us believe followed her husband from India. On the contrary, the women of the agricultural castes were not then or now housewives. The prerogative of a zenana or secluded housewife was not that of the majority of Indian men who migrated during the indentureship period. But it was their aspiration and in this they were supported by the Colonial Church and State.

Abolition

The position of women in the colonies was one of the main 'whipping horses' of the Indian nationalists against migration. It reflected the colonials' acceptance of Victorian ideology on immorality and 'women's place'. As noted before, the campaign was seen as one against 'the slavery of men and the prostitution of women'. The reports on the 'immorality' of women in the colonies were seen as inflicting a blot on the image of India which should be removed. Because of this emphasis on women, the campaign made much use of women's organizations associated with the nationalist movement. Meetings held throughout India, mainly among middle and upper-class 'ladies', passed resolutions calling for the abolition of this system. Telegrams of protest were received from the superintendent of the Widows Home in Cawnpore; the Ladies Branch of the Home Rule League and from public meetings of 'ladies ' of Ahmedabad, Godhra, Surat and Amraoti, dated January-February, 1917.[83] Fiji appeared to be the focal point of discussion, but it is possible that 'Fiji' became a generic concept for all colonial territories of migration. At a public meeting of women of Ahmedabad, the women resolved to approach the wife of the Governor-General of India, Lady Chelmsford, to intercede with her husband on this matter. In this the governor's wife was appealed to as a woman who could identify with conditions of women overseas. The resolution read in part as follows:

. . . the system of indentured labour under which Indian women are taken to Fiji compels them to lead a bad and immoral life and subjects them to indignities and outrages. Children born in such immoral conditions are brought up in degradation. This shocking state of things requires that the system of indentured labour should be stopped immediately. We humbly beseech Her Excellency to hear this cry of defenseless women and children of India and to champion their causes. We are confident that as a woman and a mother, Her Excellency will appreciate the deep feelings of Indian women on this subject, and we pray that Her Excellency may be graciously pleased to lay before His Excellency the Viceroy this supplication of women and children of India . . .[84]

So great was public agitation in India that even the proposal for the system of assisted emigration had to be shelved. In the latter years, attempts were made to address these complaints, such as the implementations of the law giving the governor the discretionary power to transfer estate employees (presumably Europeans) found guilty of 'immorality with an East Indian woman'. This and other actions aimed at protecting the 'chastity of Indian women' by the Government however came too late for the abolitionists and virtually all migration of laborers from India was abolished in 1917.

Notes

1. I. M. Cumpston, *Indians Overseas in British Territories*, Oxford Historical Series, Oxford University Press, London, 1953, p. 21.
2. J. C. Jha, 'Indian Indentured Migration 1835–1917', n.d. (mimeographed).
3. See Cumpston, 1953.
4. M., Kirpalani, Rameshwar Sinanan, S. M. & L. J. Seukeran, *Indian Centenary Review: One Hundred Years of Progress 1845–1945*, Trinidad, B.W.I. Guardian Commercial Printery for Centenary Review Committee, 1945.
5. See Cumpston, 1953.
6. See Jha.
7. See Jha.
8. Rhoda Reddock, 'Women and Slavery in the Caribbean: A Feminist Perspective' in *Latin American Perspectives*, Issue 44 Vol. 12, No. 1, 1985.
9. E.A.H. Blunt, *The Caste System of Northern India: With Special References to the United Provinces of Agra and Oudh*, S. Chand & Co. New Delhi, 1969, p. 67.
10. C.O. 571/5:11985.
11. Tyran Ramnarine, 'Indian Women and the Struggle to Create Stable Marital Relations on the Sugar Estates of Guiana During the Period of Indenture, 1839–1917', Paper presented at the 12th Conference of Caribbean Historians, University of the West Indies, St. Augustine, 1980.
12. Judith A. Weller, *The East Indian Indenture in Trinidad*, Institute of Caribbean Studies, University of Puerto Rico, Caribbean Monograph Series, No. 4, 1968.
13. Ibid., p. 4.
14. High, Tinker, *A New System of Slavery: The Export of Indian Labour Overseas 1830–1920*, published for the Institute of Race Relations by Oxford University Press, 1974, p. 123.
15. Ibid., p. 131.
16. C.O. 571/1 No. 33014, 1913, p. 8.
17. Arthur & Juanita Niehoff, *East Indians in the West Indies*, Milwaukee, Public Museum Publications in Anthropology No. 6. Milwaukee, Wisconsin, 1960., David Dodd, 'The Wellsprings of Violence: Some Historical Notes on East Indian Criminality in Guyana', in Caribbean Issues, Vol. II No. 3 December 1976, and Ramnarine.
18. Bridget Brereton, 'The Experience of Indentureship 1845–1917' in Calcutta to Caroni, John La Guerre (ed.), Longmans Caribbean 1974, p. 75; Weller, p. 4.
19. See Weller.
20. Sir Henry Cotton, 'Indian Indentured Labour in our Colonies' in the Indian Emigrant, July, 1915, p. 372.
21. Maria Mies, *Women and Patriarchy*, Concept Publishing Company, 1980, p. 49.
22. See Dodd, p. 9.
23. See Tinker, pp. 266–7.

24. Ibid.
25. Ibid.
26. Ibid., p. 119.
27. H. H. Clarke, 'Introductory Note to the Census of East Indian Population'. Government of Trinidad and Tobago, 1891, Appendix in Comins A note on Immigration from India to Trinidad, Bengal Secretariat Press, Calcutta, 1892.
28. See Comins Diary 1893, p. 49.
29. Ibid., p. 49.
30. C.O. 571/3, 54685, p. 3.
31. C.O. 571/5, 27270.
32. Ibid.
33. Ibid.
34. C.O. 571/5, 27680.
35. C.O. 571/5, 27681.
36. See Tinker, p. 124.
37. Surgeon-Major D.W.D. Comins Diary, 1893, p.3.
38. Comins Diary.
39. James Mac Neill, & Chaimman Lal, Report to the Government of India on the Conditions of Indian Immigrants in Four British Colonies and Surinam. Part I: Trinidad and British Guyana, London, 1915, H.M.S.O. Cmd. 7744.
40. Comins Diary, p. 36.
41. Comins Diary, p. 15.
42. See Mac Neill and Lal, pp. 20–21.
43. Comins Diary, 1893, p. 9.
44. Ross Sheils, 'Indentured Immigration into Trinidad 1891–1916' unpublished thesis, University of Oxford, 1969.
45. Sanderson et al, Report on Emigration from India to the Crown Colonies and Protectorates (Part II) and Minutes of Evidence and Papers laid before the Committee (Part II) Cmd. 5192, 5193, 5194, 1910, pp. 139–40.
46. Tikasingh, Gerad, 'The Establishment of Indians in Trinidad, 1870–1900', unpublished Ph.D. thesis, Department of History, University of the West Indies, St. Augustine, 1973, p. 112.
47. See Comins Diary 1893, p. 49.
48. Ibid., p. 4.
49. See Clarke.
50. See Shiels, p. 162.
51. Howard Johnson, 'Immigration and the Sugar Industry in Trinidad during the last quarter of the 19th Century' in Journal of Caribbean History, Vol. 5, 1971.
52. See Brereton, 1979, pp. 179–181.
53. See Sanderson et al, p. 66.
54. Interviews with ex-indenture labourers have been carried out by Peggy Ramesar.
55. Zenanas — 'part of house for the seclusion of women of high caste families in India and Iran, Pocket Oxford Dictionary, 1982, 1054.
56. Sarah E. Morton, *John Morton of Trinidad*, Westminster Company, Toronto, 1916, p. 185.
57. Ibid., p. 342.
58. Note by the Protector of Immigrants to Surgeon-Major D.W.D. Comins, 1893, pp. 30–31.
59. A note on the System of Assisted Emigrants to the Colonies, 1916, CO 571/5: 27270.
60. Mohammed Orfy on behalf of destitute Indian men of Trinidad, CO 571/4 W.I. 22518 (1916).
61. Petition of Indentured Labourers in Trinidad, 1916.
62. See Weller, 1968, p. 3.
63. See Tinker, 1974, p. 140.
64. See Ramnarine, 1980, pp. 3–4.
65. See Jha, J.C. 'The Background of the Legislation of Non-Christian Marriage in Trinidad & Tobago'. Paper presented in the conference on East Indians in the Caribbean: A Symposium on Contemporary Economic and Political Issues, University of the West Indies, St. Augustine 1975: Marianne Ramesar, Indian Immigration into Trinidad, 1897–1917, unpublished Master's Thesis, Department of History, University of the West Indies, Mona, 1973 and also Weller, 1968.
66. See Morton, p. 342.
67. Tinker, p. 203.
68. See Weller, pp. 71–72.
69. Ibid., p. 69.
70. See Dodd, pp. 11.
71. Donald Wood, *Trinidad in Transition: The Years after Slavery*, Oxford University Press, 1968, p. 154.
72. See Ramnarine, p. 2.
73. See Weller, 1968, Appendix: Table 7.
74. See Wood, p. 143.
75. Ibid.
76. Comins Diary, p. 31.
77. Ibid., p. 30.
78. Ibid., p. 33.
79. Ibid., p. 35.
80. Morton 1916, p. 225.
81. Comins Diary, p. 15.
82. Morton, p. 347.
83. CO 571/5, 27270.
84. Ibid.

Black Women, Economic Roles and Cultural Traditions

Sidney Mintz

In Jamaica and Haiti (Saint Domingue), the leading slave colonies of the Antilles, slaves were early enabled (or compelled) to produce much of their own subsistence on the peripheral lands of the plantations; and in both colonies, the slaves soon became purveyors of their surplus products in local marketplaces (for Jamaica, see Mintz and Hall 1960; for Haiti, see Mintz 1964). During the slavery periods in these two societies, however, there is no evidence that women predominated in marketing — in fact, the evidence suggests that men, or whole families, engaged in local market trade, while still enslaved. But in both of these societies, the end of slavery (by revolution in one case, and by emancipation in the other) led to an emergence of a class of predominantly female traders.

I hypothesize that freedom signified an opportunity for many male ex-slaves to acquire land in sufficient quantity so that they could devote themselves full-time to agricultural production. In other words, female domination of the marketplace trade may have been correlated in these cases with a new division of labour made possible by increased access to land. Such an hypothesis, however, does not 'explain' the presence of female traders, any more than 'Arab influence' can be used to 'explain' their absence. Even where males are taken up with agricultural production, it does not follow automatically that women will become traders. Boserup writes: 'Thus, in Southeast Asia we seem to have a basically "female pattern" but, owing perhaps to Arab and Chinese influence, there is Malaysia to Western Indonesia. Within this belt, only one-tenth of the traders are women, as against one-half outside this belt' (Boserup 1970:91). 'Arab and Chinese influence' or no, in this subregion male domination of agriculture does not lead inevitably to female domination of trade. Boserup reasons that 'those regions are usually the regions which are characterized by female farming traditions' (*ibid*). This may be the case in West Africa — it is difficult to generalize — but it is emphatically not the case in the Afro-Caribbean, where trade by females seems better correlated with *male*-dominated agriculture.[1]

Thus, if one wishes to seek to analyze the trading patterns of Afro-Caribbean females by contrasts within and outside the region, it becomes clear that 'values' as such are an inadequate explanation of these patterns, even while they undoubtedly played a part in the emergence of contemporary norms for the sexual division of labour. From the cultural perspective, we are dealing with situations in which the society at large — or, at least, substantial segments of it — acknowledges an equal economic status for women in local, culturally-prescribed terms. Métraux (1951:147) tells us that some Haitian farmers are left at such a loss by their marketer wives' absence that they 'fast stoically for two or three days' until their spouses return from market. In general, our own findings, partly supported by the work of others (e.g., Métraux 1951:120–126, 146–147), indicate that Haitian men are not prepared to insist that their wives forsake *any* trading activity at all, merely in order to fulfill their domestic obligations. For Africa, Le Cour Grandmaison and Hill both describe women whose commercial activities are far more successful than those of their husbands, and quite independent of them; Le Cour Grandmaison offers one instance of a highly successful *dakaroise* who employs her husband on salary (1969:150). Marshall, writing of the Yoruba of Awe, Nigeria, gives lively instances of trade relationships between husband and wife that are in no way confused with (nor substituted for) the non-commercial aspects of the relationship (Marshall 1964:187–188).

In all of these instances, in fact, we are dealing with societies concerning which, for our purposes, it probably makes more sense to think of the rights of individuals, in terms of age, sex, kinship to the category of the rights of men or women. The Haitian *habitant* who fasts while his wife is at market (or who cooks his own food) plainly does not perceive this situation as one in which his status as an adult, husband, father, male, or otherwise is at stake. To put it differently, cultural prescriptions

238

do not permit the male individual to interpret his temporary inconvenience as a status deprivation; women are *supposed* to market, and men to fend for themselves meanwhile. Similarly, the husband employed by the *dakaroise* Awa G. presumably does not perceive her economic success as his failure, at least not in terms of male-female differences. Such examples may be easily multiplied; we draw a final case from the commentary of an American visitor, 'J.B.,' to the Republic of Haiti in 1854. The writer was invited to the baptism of a house owned by one of the leading women merchants of Port-au-Prince, and he has described the relationship between the hostess, called 'Elsiné', and her consort, 'Emilien', in a revealing fashion:

Elsiné — I name her first because she was the head of the house — was a wide-awake, intelligent, amiable and well-conditioned black woman, about forty years of age; Emilien, her faithful consort, was not near as intelligent, nor quite as fat, nor quite as tall, nor quite as dignified as Elsiné . . . His whole heart was evidently in the gaiety of the occasion, and his whole dependence for his enjoyment of it, seemed to repose upon the administrative talents of his better half. Their relations to each other and to the public, though not peculiar here, need a brief explanation, to be intelligible to American readers. She is the capitalist of the concern, owns all the property, and does all the business. He has no more to do with the direction of affairs, in or out of the house, than if he were her child. She is worth from fifteen to twenty thousand dollars, all of which she has made as a dealer in provisions.

Elsiné began her commercial career in the market without any money; by gradual accumulations she got some capital ahead, and now buys from the commission merchants in large quantities, and sells on credit to retail dealers — mostly to girls whom she has trained, and upon whose business she keeps a careful eye. Her monthly purchases, I understand, average about $8,000 a month, and though neither she nor her husband can read or write a line, she has an unlimited credit — that is, any merchant in Port au Prince would be glad to trust her all they could induce her to buy . . . Besides this house, she owns all the other houses on the block, and is building all the time. When I was informed of all these evidences of female enterprise and success, I very naturally inquired what might be her husband's function, and why he was such a silent partner in the connubial firm. The reply which I received revealed to me a glimpse of one of the 'peculiar institutions' of the country. Elsiné and her companion-at-arms are not married, but in conformity with the practice of the country, sanctioned by law, they are *placéed.*, as it is termed. This is a temporary marriage, determinable at the will of the parties, and the offspring from which, inherit as heirs-at-law. I mention the usage now, to explain what appear to me a strange inversion of the ordinary relations of husband and wife. They have been *placéed.* a long time, but have never married, because she thought Emilien made a much better lover than husband; in other words, she

did not think him competent to manage her business, and she did not care, therefore, to place herself or her property irretrievably in his power. Emilien appeared perfectly conscious of his inferiority, and as contented with the narrow sphere of connubial duty assigned him, as a prince-consort to the mightiest Queen in Christendon (J.B. 1854).[2]

We cite this lengthy passage, in part because it reveals nearly as much about the cultural values of the observer as it does about those of the observed. That the male should have no say in the economic affairs of the female is perceived by this Westerner as 'a strange inversion of the ordinary relations of husband and wife'; the male is depicted as 'conscious of his inferiority', and yet proud and contented. But it should be perfectly apparent that the male's 'inferiority' in this instance is, at worst, far less demonstrable than that of most females in Western society who, in their 'ordinary' family relations, may neither participate in their husbands' businesses nor engage in their own. That 'J.B.' should read as 'a strange inversion' what is, in fact, a much more equal relationship than that typical of his own society is not surprising, given the dominant tone of male-female relationships in the West.

These various cases point up some special valuation of female economic roles and particularly an acknowledgement right of the female to economic *independence* are of special interest because they implicate no corresponding loss of status for the male. They reveal that Western conceptions of male 'integrity', 'dignity', 'pride', and 'worth' are much more deeply imbedded in notions of male economic dominance than may be generally widely recognized. They also suggest that the supplantation of such non-Western values by Western values may, in some cases, eventuate in a regressive social direction for women — or, at any rate, for some women.

The point here is, first of all, whether a given society regards a substantial and publicly recognized economic contribution by the female spouse as 'normal', 'natural', desirable, and appropriate; and secondly, whether the rewards of that economic contribution to some other member of her group, as an individual or as an executor of group wealth. Both of these points plainly have to do with local conceptions of the kinship group, especially with its internal organization of statuses and roles, and the accompanying values. The particular composition of such kinship groups must be analyzed according to our understanding of their *internal* allocations of authority, resources, and prerogatives, especially the charter of rights and duties as applying to men and women. A very brief comparison of two Caribbean cases, the first Hispano-

Caribbean and the second Afro-Caribbean, may help me to enumerate certain differences.

The first case is that in Puerto Rico, the data based on the research of Eric Wolf (1956) in a peasant community in the interior. The field work was completed thirty years ago*, and the details cannot be generalized in any sense to Puerto Rican rural society at large; yet the case provides a striking contrast to the non-Hispanic Caribbean. Wolf notes that the keystone of peasant productivity is the low cost of labour within the family. The economic tasks of the family are carried out by family members; the family is an indivisible unit, economically, and there are no payments of cash among family members for work done. If a dependent child is paid for work done outside the family, the money must go to his father. The father, as family head, disposes of all of the family resources; in fact, he is in a position to sell the labour of his dependent children, or to dispose of their labour within the traditional labour exchanges of the peasant community. Among the peasants of whom Wolf writes, he discusses with special care that subgroup consisting of smallholders who cultivate ten *cuerdas* (approximately 4 hectares) or less. Such small-scale peasants cultivate tobacco and coffee for sale, as well as many subsistence crops, but hardly anything to be sold locally. In other words, these peasants produce one or two cash crops for sale to the world market, and much of their own food, but do not participate significantly in any system of local sale of commodities. They depend above all upon family labour; more and more, local out migration has made it difficult to employ others, at the same time that many of them must seek wage payments elsewhere themselves, in order to supplement their own limited productivity. Family labour is hence heavily engaged in production on the limited land available, with the father as executive. On one *cuerda* (ca. 4/10 hectares) of tobacco land, Wolf determined that a male might invest as much as thirty-nine days of labour; yet at the same time his wife might invest between forty-eight to fifty-four days of labour. In other words, the family commitment of effort, as managed by the father-husband, varies for each family member, and the quantity of work of the wife-member is fixed by her spouse according to his estimate of what is required.

In this milieu, the economic rights and privileges of the wife-mother are intimately tied to the status and role of the husband-father as head of the family enterprise. We take account of a situation in which there is what we would call one single structure of

risk, and one center only of authority. The wife must prepare all of her husband's meals, even though they do not eat together. When they go elsewhere together, the wife follows behind her husband. Of course the wife may not attend festivals or dances by herself, or other than in the company of her husband. Wolf's description is precise: 'Her status is tied to that of her husband. Her standing is judged according to the possessions which he owns and the treatment he accords her ... A woman does not acquire any rights to assert herself directly in her own behalf until she is beyond the child-bearing period' (1956:223). It may be worth adding to this decription that the husband has the right to insist that his wife *bathe him* weekly, and that she wash his feet daily! To which one may say that the differences between this situation and that typical of peasant Haiti are absolutely staggering.

In the Haiti situation, the husband-father's control of family labour is much less sweeping, at least today. The fundamental expression of this difference lies in the woman's wholly recognized entitlement to independent trading activity. 'African usage', writes Herskovits (1973:258), 'has here been reinforced by the historical fact of Haitian political instability. The fact that the proceeds from trading belong to the woman who does the trading, and that in consequence women are encountered who, though married, command independent means and exercise full control over their resources, is a carry-over of African tradition and, as in Africa, this gives women a position in the economic world quite foreign to conventional European practice'. While we may ponder with some doubt Herskovits' description of 'reinforced' African usage, the fact is that a sexual division of labour that acknowledges and validates women's independent roles in commerce typifies Haitian peasant life, and comparable expressions of female economic independence occur even in urban bourgeois segments of the Haitian population.

Peasant wives and *placées* can and do carry out agricultural tasks; a very complete list of tasks by sexes is provided by Métraux (1951:89–91), and women are not by definition exempted from most agricultural labour, even hoeing. But, in fact, the husband's claims on his wife's or *placée's* labour are powerfully qualified by her own enterprises, and most Haitian peasant women vastly prefer trade to agricultural work. We lack adequate detail on the divisions of authority along sexual lines among Haitian peasants. Simpson (1942:662) claims that 'the husband's caprices have the force of law in the peasant family. His wife or *placée*

*Thanks go to Melle François Morin and to Jacqueline W. Mintz for helpful criticisms of an earlier draft of this paper.

must give him unquestioning obedience'. Our own impressions are radically different, particularly insofar as the sphere of economic activity is concerned. It is of some interest, then, that Simpson goes on to say: 'However, because of the knowledge which she has gained in her trading contacts with the villages and towns, the woman is more practical than the man, and she acts as the treasurer of the family' (*ibid.*) — hardly convincing evidence of the crushing authority of the male. 'A peasant will often say he has no money in the house', adds Simpson, 'when the truth is that he does not wish to do business without his wife or *placée*'. These and similar comments suggest that the male-female division of authority is much more complex among Haitian peasants than among Puerto Rican peasants — or, at least, that male authority is substantially more qualified in the case of peasant Haiti.

The cultural origins of the majority of Haitian rural folk are in large measure African, as we have already suggested, while those of the majority of Puerto Ricans are predominantly Hispanic. Of course elements from many other traditions enter into the contemporary cultures of both groups: Amerindian in the case of Puerto Rico, for instance (and to some degree in the case of Haiti as well), African in the case of Puerto Rico (though to a much lesser degree than in Haiti). It needs to be recalled that the western third of Santo Domingo (French Saint Dominigue) only became a French colony in 1697, and received its strongest impulse to growth in the ensuing century, during which time perhaps 850,000 African slaves were imported (Curtin 1969:79), while the European population remained relatively small.

The Revolution, beginning 1791, eliminated the bulk of non-Africans, and the subsequent century of virtual isolation facilitated the consolidation of a culture that was in good measure African in origin. In Puerto Rico, on the other hand, though African slaves were present almost from the moment of Spanish domination, the numbers of slaves always remained very small relative to the population of European freemen (many of whom were part Indian in origin). Moreover, Puerto Rico remained Spanish from the Conquest until the North American occupation in 1899; during almost exactly four hundred years of continuous Spanish rule, it acquired a cultural character that might fairly be described as much more European (Hispanic) than anything else. Thus one could perhaps argue that, with regard to the economic role of women, at least, such differences find their origins in a difference between the values of West African and Southern European cultures, without taking account of immediate economic, ecological and other factors. This is, indeed, the way Herskovits has appeared to argue, for instance, in the quotation cited earlier, and as Boserup has argued in discussing 'Arab' and 'Chinese' influences upon the sexual division of labour. In our opinion, such a view does not explain enough. Within Puerto Rico itself, for instance, data on rural proletarian groups (cf. Mintz 1953, 1956) reveal sharp contrasts with the Puerto Rican peasant materials collected by Wolf, and these contrasts do not lend themselves to explanation in terms of different ancestral values. Rather, they seem to suggest that specific local conditions have had their differentiating effects upon traditional patterns of behaviour.

In other words, it seems to us necessary to distinguish between those characteristics of a particular situation that express the acceptable limits of variability of behaviour at one point in time, and the values, beliefs and attitudes of the local population — an ideological assemblage, so to speak, ultimately attributable to forces in the past. The Puerto Rican peasant woman who dutifully washes the feet of her husband does not do so *because* he completely controls the labour resources and wealth of the family — rather, the economic domination of the husband furnishes the context within which this custom is permitted to survive. Again, the Haitian peasant husband does not make his own dinner *because* his wife is the independent head of her own enterprise — rather, that economic independence furnishes the context within which he finds it expectable and acceptable to be required to do so.

Thus there is not, in my view, some single simple formula according to which one can resolve the problem of the association of a particular value or item of behaviour with a particular society or social group. Generally speaking, we are still unable confidently to assign a precise estimate of importance to specific contemporary economic conditions, on the one hand, or to specific historical traditions, on the other, in attempting to 'explain' the presence or absence of some mode of behaviour. Instead, we are required to state as fully as we can the conditions imposed by ecological, economic and other factors, within which family structures, models of intra-familial authority, and notions of status and role, of obligations and rights, of values, take on their characteristic forms. In each specific instance a set of values and attitudes is expressed in behaviour, but particular conditions may serve to facilitate that expression, or to hamper or modify it. We have only a vague idea of the ways older values maintain themselves in the face of new pressures, when change does (or does not) occur.[3]

Hence, we are left with the important problem of determining as best we can why Haitian rural women enjoy so wide a field of economic man-oeuver while their Puerto Rican sisters are corre-spondingly deprived of all significant access to economic independence. Though various eco-nomic factors undoubtedly played a crucial role in the evolution of Haitian marketing, and probably in determining its absence in Puerto Rico, I remain unconvinced that these factors fully account for the pre-eminence of women in Haitian commerce. At the same time, I suspect any *direct* reference to West Africa for the explanation of the Haitian case, not only because the slaves were drawn from many different African societies and because slavery itself intervened between the African past and the post-revolutionary present, but also because we lack evidence that women played a paramount role in Haitian marketing during the period of slavery itself.

Cultural traditions do not merely reassert them-selves unmodified after long intervals; and one may reasonably doubt whether any Haitian free-men in 1804 carried about in their heads an ideal image of women as marketers. Herskovits (1937) and others (Leyburn 1941) have suggested that women emerged as marketers after the Haitian rev-olution because the periodic warring and forced conscription typical of Haitian life after 1804 made rural men wary of towns, so that women perforce became the intermediaries. Yet women also became the intermediaries in Jamaica after eman-cipation (1838), when internal peace was undis-turbed. Ottenberg, writing of the Nigerian Afikpo Ibo, tells us that *men* are the principal marketers in that society precisely because of the previous absence of internal peace! Neither the Jamaican nor the Ibo case, in other words, can be wholly explained by this argument. In both Haiti and Jamaica, however, it was only after the end of slav-ery that rural males were able to acquire their own land, as I have already indicated, and this doubtless had something to do with the emerging pattern of female marketing. This assertion, however, fails to 'explain' the pattern; as we have seen, there are of course many places in the modern world where men have land but women do *not* market, Puerto Rico being only one of them.

Can one go any further than this in attempting to clarify the Haitian case? I believe so, but only by invoking a general principle for which there is no specific evidence as yet in the case of Haiti. The real question, perhaps is not that of the tasks men and women may do, but the psychological signif-icance of this division, in terms of the comparative status of members of the other sex. As I have sought to explain, it is not so much a matter of what men or women can do — but rather of what they do do without endangering the social status of their opposite numbers. Haitian peasant males are plainly not diminished, but elevated, by their wives' economic success. In contrast, it seems quite likely that Puerto Rican peasant males are diminished by an *independent* economic activity on the part of their wives — the question of success or failure cannot even rise to the surface. What, then, in the history of Haitian (and Jamaican) peas-ant life might explain the thorough-going accep-tance of independent economic roles for women, other than simply the acquisition of more land by the men, and the harking back to a 'tradition' sep-arated from the aftermath of slavery by a century or more of radically different life conditions?

I think that the answer is of a culture-historical order — that is, that one may explain the present by reference to some aspect of the past — but not in terms of culturally defined male-female differ-ences as such. The emergence of women as mar-keters in Jamaica and Haiti presumably did not rep-resent a radical change in the relative statuses of men and women, though the success of women as marketers may eventually have contributed to a rel-ative improvement of feminine status. I find it dif-ficult not to suppose that the ease with which Jamaican and Haitian market women were able to dominate trading activities was related to their spouses' views of themselves (according to local conceptions of masculine status), and not only to their views of their wives. In the Afro-Caribbean as in West Africa, the social manipulation of those values enabling women to function in independent economic fashion apparently represented no prob-lem to the effective functioning of traditional kin-ship groups or sex-based status attributions. And while it may be argued that, in the West African case, this was possible because of far-flung kinship networks limiting the primary family to a very minor role, such an argument (if it had any merit at all) certainly would not make sense for the Afro-Caribbean. The central question, we believe, con-tinues to be not whether the kin group can function when women's economic activities have grown as important as men's — the answer is, of course, 'yes' — but whether men can accept women's independent participation in a different risk struc-ture without feeling threatened *as men*. Obviously, there is expressed in this view the now familiar association between female submission to male economic domination on the one hand, and the view of women as property on the other. Such an association should be of more than passing interest when we reflect that, in Haitian and Jamaican soci-eties, slaves of both sexes were viewed as property by their masters, and won the right to independent economic activity as slaves only because such activity was ultimately profitable to the masters, as well as to the slaves themselves. We are very far from understanding the 'personalities' of Haitian and Jamaican slave men and women on the eve of freedom. Yet it would not surprise us to discover that regard for *individual* prerogatives in these groups was at least as strong as that for the prerogatives of males as against females — given the fact that slavery itself had not always made it possible for male slaves to assert 'paterfamilias' domination over female slaves.

Hence, I am seeking to suggest that it may have been partly in the experience of slavery itself that Jamaican and Haitian males found the capacity to tolerate female autonomy, while Jamaican and Haitian females were finding the capacity to exercise that autonomy — eventually in ways remarkably consistent with those of their West African sisters. Such a view is not intended to slight the force of the African past in the lives of Caribbean peoples of African origin, but it does raise a question about assertions of uninterrupted continuities with that past, surviving unchanged through slavery, as if cultural traditions were not responsible even to radically changed life conditions. My suggestion does not, of course, explain whey marketing by women develops in some societies and not in others; nor does it assign differential weight to the variables that probably affect such emergence. From a historical point of view, it might be useful to amass whatever commentary is available for these two societies, on relations between male and female slaves, and for the free rural peoples of these societies thereafter. We are quite unable at present to specify any steps by which female marketing gradually became the rule in these societies, or to relate such steps to prevailing attitudes about male and female roles. Thus the case continues to rest largely on surmise and assumption, rather than on hard data, either ethnographic or historical.

To sum up, the various West African patterns of sexual division of labour were probably profoundly modified under slavery in the Caribbean region. However, in situations where slaves were compelled or permitted to grow their own subsistence, as in Jamaica and Saint-Domingue, slave family groups of some kind apparently engaged in this practice, and slave family units also participated in the marketing of agricultural surpluses. While some of the related tasks may indeed have been restricted to one or the other sex, our descriptions indicate that men and women both cultivated and marketed. After freedom, however, female-dominated marketing rapidly developed in these Afro-Caribbean societies, in marked contrast to the Hispanic Caribbean (Puerto Rico, Cuba and Santo Domingo). The emergence of such female-dominated marketing was probably related, on the one hand, to the acquisition of larger amounts of agricultural land by the freemen, requiring their fuller commitment to agricultural labour.

But acquisition of more land by males could not be expected to result in female domination of trade, if such domination were to run counter to male values and male prestige notions in the society in question. In other words, we hypothesize that independent economic activity by females in these societies was not only concordant with new agricultural conditions, but also not discordant with existing male-female relationships. Posed this way, our 'explanation' becomes no less 'historical' on the one hand, and no less 'functional' on the other. Nor do we discount the possible significance of cultural continuities with the African past, though our view of such continuities may share little with older conceptions of this kind. The massing of historical data on male and female attitudes among slaves (and, later, freemen) in these societies of the sort recounted by 'J.B', could conceivably allow us to sharpen our assertions or to set them aside if they do not, in fact, explain adequately.

In the absence of more information, it may appear that we leave off not far from where we began. And yet this exercise may not be entirely in vain. The fact is that West African and Afro-Caribbean societies have been able, in some contexts to achieve sexual equality still quite unheard of in Western societies, for all of their vaunting of individual freedom. The independence and authority exercised by a West African or Haitian market woman in regard to her uses of her own capital, or in regard to the economic influence of her husband, has few parallels in the Western world, where individual prerogatives are commonly seen as flowing from individual *male* wealth, embedded in a nuclear family organization. With histories radically different from those of the Caribbean and West Africa, Europe and America have busily exported doctrines of equality rooted in their own past — their own primary-family, monogamous, male-property past. Meanwhile, West Africa and the Afro-Caribbean, influenced so profoundly and for so long by European power and domination, have demonstrated a version of equality in some population sectors that European societies, with their quite basic view of *women as property*, neither understand nor accept.

The day may yet come when the contribution of black women to the perpetuation of their respective societies will be recognized; it is still far off. Further off still, perhaps, is the recognition that African and Afro-American societies have contributed a good deal more to a vision of individual equality transcending sexual chauvinism than has the West itself.

Notes

1. I have dealt with this matter at somewhat greater length in Mintz and Price, 1976.
2. The writer is grateful to Prof. Joseph Boromé for calling his attention to this unusual report.
3. It would be useful to compare the development of marketing institutions and the roles of men and women in these institutions throughout Afro-America. Such an exercise might help us to assess somewhat more precisely the importance of antecedent values in affecting the ways new institutions develop, in this case. Among the factors that would enter into this comparison would be: African traditions of female marketing; African traditions of economic autonomy for spouses; the role of slavery in levelling and homogenizing the sexual division of labour; the allocation of marketing roles, if any, under slavery; the Spanish pattern of male dominance in economic life as in all else; the role of internal strife in affecting the sexual division of labour; and, finally, ideal role-models for slave men and women in each society. Needless to add, a complete picture of these factors will probably never be possible; but assembling the relevant data might prove useful and revealing, nonetheless.

References

Boserup, E. *Women's Role in Economic Development.* London: Geo. Allen and Unwin, 1970.

Curtin, Philip. *The Atlantic Slave Trade.* Madison: University of Wisconsin Press, 1969.

Herskovits, M.J. 'Preface' to Bohannan, P. and G. Dalton (eds.), *Markets in Africa.* Evanston: Northwestern University Press, 1962 pp. vii–xvi.

Hill, P. 'Hidden Trade in Hausaland'. *Man,* (1969) 4:392–409.

J.B. 'Notes of a Tour in Haiti'. *The Evening Post,* Vol. LIII (Friday, 19 May 1854), p. 1.

Le Cour Grandmaison C. 'Activités économiques des femmes dakaroises'. *Africa,* XXXIX: (1969) 138–52.

Leyburn, James A. *The Haitian People.* New Haven: Yale University Press, 1941.

Marshall, G.A. 'Women Trade and the Yoruba Family'. Ph.D. Dissertation, Columbia University, 1964.

Métraux, A. *Making a Living in the Marbial Valley (Haiti).* UNESCO Occasional Papers in Education 10. Paris, 1951.

Mintz, Sidney W. 'The Folk-Urban Continuum, and the Rural Proletarian Community'. *American Journal of Sociology* 59 (1953) 2:136–143.

———. 'The Employment of Capital by Haitian Market Women' in Firth, R. and Yamey, B. (eds.), *Capital, Saving and Credit in Peasant Society.* Chicago: Aldine Publishing Co., 1964, pp. 256.86.

Mintz, S.W. and D. Hall 'The Origins of the Jamaican Internal Marketing Pattern'. *Yale University Publications in Anthropology,* 57, 1960.

Ottenberg, Phoebe. 'The Changing Economic Position of Women among the Afikpo Ibo'. in Bascom, W., and M. Herskovits (eds.), *Continuity and Change in African Cultures.* Chicago: University of Chicago Press, 1959.

Simpson, George E. 'Sexual and Familial Institutions in Haiti'. *American Anthropologist* 44 (1942) 4:655–674.

Wolf, Eric R. 'San José: Subcultures of a Traditional Coffee Municipality'. in Stewart, J.H., et al., *The People of Puerto Rico.* Urbana: University of Illinois Press, 1956, pp. 171 – 264.

Emancipation Through Servitude: Aspects of the Condition of Indian Women in Jamaica, 1845–1945

Verene Shepherd

Introduction

One of the more interesting analytical issues relating to the history of Indian women in the Caribbean to be raised in recent years is that surrounding their aims in contracting for indentured servitude, and the degree to which such objectives were realized. Among those involved in this are Reddock and Emmer. Reddock has argued that the majority of female Indian immigrants to Trinidad were not those considered 'suitable' by the planters — that is, obedient daughters and docile wives, 'arriving five steps behind their husbands',[1] who would fulfil their designated role as housewives. Rather, they were single, independent women whose intentions were to remain in the host society on the expiration of their contracts and seek to improve their socio-economic position.[2]

Emmer has posited even more definitely that, for the Indian women who emigrated to Suriname — particularly the single ones — emigration represent a vehicle of female emancipation.[3] This was despite the fact that they had to serve out a period of contract under harsh conditions of servitude. However, according to him,'more women than men used the system of contract labour as it operated in the Caribbean in order to increase their social status and . . . emancipate themselves from an illiberal, inhibiting and very hierarchial social system in India'.[4] Thus emigration was undertaken not only in order to attain better material conditions but to create a social and cultural environment with fewer social barriers than existed at home.[5] Indentured servitude, then, was arguably the price female emigrants paid for eventual 'freedom' and an improved lifestyle.

Though female emigrants to Jamaica left no known statements of their intentions, and while it is impossible to ascertain quantitatively the proportion which emigrated voluntarily and that which may have been coerced,[6] there is no reason to believe that the objectives of the majority differed markedly from those of women who went to Trinidad and Suriname.

In the first place, a principal 'pull' factor in all migration schemes is the promise/hope of betterment at the point of destination. Second, as was the case in Trinidad, the majority of women emigrating to Jamaica from India were single. Even some of those categorized as 'married' were unaccompanied by spouses, though a few had their children with them. Third, those recruited failed to fit planter preference for wives to keep male emigrants 'happy'.[7] Fourth, the majority settled in Jamaica at the expiration of their contracts.[8]

This paper will, however, show that, far from providing Indian women in Jamaica with an opportunity to improve their economic condition, indentured servitude served to tie them to plantation labour and an economically depressed life. This condition continued well into the mid-twentieth century, and affected urban women as much as those who remained as rural settlers.

Immigration and indentureship

Between 1845 and 1916 approximately 37,000 East Indians were imported to Jamaica to provide a nucleus of continuous labourers on Jamaican properties (estates, plantations and pens) after emancipation.[9] From its very inception, Indian immigration was characterized by a numerical disparity between the sexes. A preliminary analysis of close to 7,000 emigrants' passes in the Jamaican Archives reveals that women generally comprised less than one-third of each shipment of immigrants. Of the 812 on the SS *Indus* of 1905, only 217, or 25.7%, were women.[10] In the first few years of the scheme, the male-female ratio was even more disproportionate. Of the 261 Indians imported on the *Blundell* in 1845, 200 were men, 28 (or 10.7%)

were women with children completing the shipment.[11] Even after the British government imposed a ratio of 40 women for every 100 men on each ship,[12] the difficulties experienced in recruiting women left the situation relatively unaltered.

Once in the island, Indian women were distributed to proprietors who had contracted their services. They were located primarily on rural properties. Only a few were indentured to estates in the Liguanea Plain. In 1871, for example, only 83 women were noted in the latter area.[13] Most of the women who made up the female indentured population were single. Of those who arrived on the *Indus* in 1905, for example, only 29% were married and accompanied by spouses, while 71% had emigrated as single/unattached workers. A similar trend was observed among those who had come by the *Indus* in 1906. On that shipment, 38 of the 114 women were married and 76 were single.[14]

Initially, female immigrants, like their male counterparts, were indentured for one year, with the requirement to renew their contracts at the end of each year. Three-year contracts were introduced in 1850 and five-year contracts in 1862.[15] After 1893 an unsuccessful attempt seems to have been made to reduce contracts for female workers to three years. The suggestion to do so had been made by Surgeon Major Comins. He felt that it might have had the effect of inducing more married women or women of 'a respectable class' to emigrate.[16] Some planters objected on the grounds that 'a woman who is not occupied otherwise than in cooking her husband's food is more likely to get into mischief'.[17] Other planters were, however, prepared to let women work for three years 'provided that . . . absence from work does not merely mean exposure to temptation and the possibility of serious trouble'.[18] Indian men seemed not to have been too keen on the proposed three-year indentureship. One reason seems to have been that their economic status as indentured servants did not allow them to be able to support a wife 'in relative ease'. Married men reportedly (and secretly) asked planters to send their wives out to work.

The wages paid to indentured servants varied. In the 1840s, Indian women's wages were fixed at 9d. per day.[19] When task work was introduced in preference to day labour, it became theoretically possible for female emigrants to improve their earnings by increasing the number of tasks done per day. Nevertheless, very little change occurred in women's wages. Very often, women on some plantations even earned less than the stipulated rate. Lal and McNeil's report contains statistics on comparative wage rates which serve to illustrate this point. These statistics show that wages earned by women per working day ranged between 4¾d. and 9½d.,

though the upper level was rarely attained. On the 36 St. Mary estates visited by the two officials, for example, only two paid between 9d. and 9½d. per day or per task (which coincided with a day's work) to female immigrants. These wage rates of female workers represented roughly one-half to two-thirds of those earned by men on the same estates.[20]

In reality, however, as the annual expenditure for female workers was said to have been higher than that for males, their economic status was even lower than their rates of pay would at first suggest. At a conservative estimate based on rough statistics supplied by the two officials, it would seem that the annual expenditure for male workers was 57% of annual earnings, while for females it was 76%.[21] Although women may have tried to increase the number of tasks in an attempt to improve their earnings, they were still at a disadvantage compared to male workers who were given the more remunerative tasks — thought to be too strenuous for 'fragile females'. On banana estates these included forking, trenching, ploughing, lining, circling and cutting. Some men could earn from 7s.6d. to 10s. per week[22] doing some of these tasks — wages which were hardly ever earned by Indian plantation women.

Ex-indentured female workers in rural Jamaica

On the expiration of their period of indentureship, Indian women were theoretically free to move out of the low status agricultural labour on the plantations into more remunerative areas. They were not free to leave the island until after ten years' continuous residence — either to return to India or to seek jobs in Cuba and Central America, as thousands of Jamaicans were doing from the 1880s.

In reality, however, illiteracy and lack of access to land kept them tied to rural plantations as wage labourers. In 1891 when the female Indian population numbered 4,467, 58.36% were agricultural labourers.[23] A further 399, or 9.2%, were general labourers, 151 were shopkeepers and 113 were doing household domestic duties. There were 1,063 females categorized as 'persons and children of no occupation'. Only a comparatively small percentage of Indian women were in the professional, commercial and industrial sectors. There was, for example, only one female Indian teacher.[24] When one considers the general absence of schooling among East Indians in Jamaica — particularly among the girls — the occupational pattern becomes more understandable; for there was a close correlation between the educational standard of the wage-earning population and the industry to which they were attached. Of 2,145 school-age Indian children (1,082 boys and 1,083 girls), only 110 girls and 126 boys were attending school in 1891.[25] A combination of socio-economic factors militated against a more significant school attendance, and by 1943, 48.6% of the Indian population was still illiterate, compared to 28.1% blacks, 13.8% coloureds, 3.2% whites, 13.9% Chinese, and 5.6% Syrians.[26]

All the censuses up to 1943 indicate a similar trend in the occupations of rural Indian women in Jamaica. In 1911, for example, out of a total of 7,452 Indian females in the island, 3,734 were engaged in agriculture, the majority as estate labourers;[27] and in 1921, 3,828 Indian women were in agriculture, most being employed on banana and sugar estates in rural parishes.[28] By 1943, 76% of the women engaged as wage earners were East Indian women. More especially, of those women engaged as agricultural labour, 56% were Indian women compared to 28% blacks, 13% coloureds, 1% Chinese and 1% Syrian.[29] By contrast, whereas 56% of Syrian women and 49% of Chinese women were engaged in the retail trade, only 12% of Indian women were similarly occupied.[30]

The high proportion of female ex-indentured workers in agriculture as wage earners combined with the low wages they were paid militated against any upward social mobility and led J.D. Tyson to comment on their special plight in the 1930s.

The 1930s were terrible years for Jamaica. The worldwide economic depression, the cessation of emigration as an outlet for those seeking higher wages, the return of migrants to swell the already growing mass of unemployed labourers, the recession in the banana and sugar industries, and the general oppression of the rural and urban poor had culminated in widespread labour unrest in 1938.[31] In 1939, the Moyne Commission was sent to investigate the causes of the riots which had occurred. Tyson was sent to investigate and report to the Commission on the condition of Indian workers. Tyson found that a scarcity of work existed among women on the banana, coconut and sugar estates. Many women went for weeks without a single day's work at a time when close to 60% of Indian women depended on the estates for employment. Of the Indians in general, Tyson observed that:

the complaint of short work for Indians — all the time on the banana estates and out of 'crop' season on the sugar estates — was general wherever I went. Indians on banana and coconut plantations were thus living in a state bordering on destitution. Those who got 2–3 days' work per week and made thereby from 3s. to 5s. were considered fortunate.[32]

As Indian women were hardly ever among those getting this 2–3 days' work per week, their plight was understandably grim. Tyson also gave the reason for this situation. While admitting that Indians suffered along with the rest of the labouring population of the island from the general wave of unemployment, he said that to this had been added, in the case of the Indians, 'a growing competition in fields hitherto regarded as his own from West Indian labour returning from Cuba and elsewhere, with some training and experience in estate work'.[33] To compound the situation, it was alleged that headmen on the estates, who were generally black, tended to 'favour their own people in the distribution of piece work, especially where there is not enough to go around'.[34] He added:

unemployment is general in the island but Indian labour has been especially hard hit by limitation of production in the two crops in which this labour is principally utilized — sugar (owing to the quota) and bananas for which, owing to the prevalence of various banana diseases, coconuts have been substituted.[35]

The substitution of coconut for banana cultivation, however, not only reduced the demand for labour but also had the effect of depriving the labourers of the use they had hitherto enjoyed of estate land for their own cultivation. Indian labour so displaced was not 'fluid' and was therefore unable to seek an outlet in the industrial fields.

The condition of female Indian plantation workers had not improved by the early 1940s, as is indicated by the population census of 1943. In that year, the total Indian population in Jamaica was 21,393, consisting of 10,924 males and 10,469 (or 48.9%) females. This Indian population was 2.1% of the island population, making them the largest minority group. Indian women residing in Kingston and Port Royal comprised 7.7% of the population in those parishes, with 13.8% in St. Andrew. Though 76% of Indian women depended on wage labour, only 1,168, or 45.56%, were employed in December 1942. The majority of these (658) earned less than 6s. per week; 302 earned between 6s. and 10s. per week; 141 earned between 10s. and £1; 48 earned £1 — £2; 15 earned between £2 and £3; and 3 earned between £3 and £4. No East Indian woman earned over £4 a week.[36]

Compared to other immigrant minority groups, East Indian women were the worst off economically. Whereas 658 Indian women earned under 6s. a week, only 28 Chinese women, 9 white women and one Syrian woman earned in this category.

While no Indian woman earned over £4 a week, all other races had women earning in this category, with one coloured woman and one woman from the British Isles earning over £20 a week.[37] It is significant to note that 45.9% of women who earned under 6s. a week and 31.1% who earned between 6s. and 10s. a week were illiterate or barely literate.

The occupational breakdown of rural Indian women was significant. Of 2,418 Indian women employed, 1,535 were agricultural labourers. Those who were not plantation workers were mainly seamstresses, milliners, messengers and domestic servants.[38]

Ex-plantation women in the urban sector of the plantation economy

From the 1850s, time-expired Indians began to move to the urban core of the plantation economy in their search for greater opportunities for capital accumulation and upward social mobility. Women comprised a significant proportion of this rural-urban migration. Along with ex-indentured women who had formerly been indentured on estates in the Liguanea Plain, the urban Indian female population by 1881 numbered 200.[39] The harsh economic and social conditions in the 1930s, particularly in the banana parishes of St. Mary and Portland, caused an increase in the trek of Indian women to Kingston and St. Andrew, so that by 1943 there were 2,297 Indian females in these parishes. This represented 52% of the 4,418 Indians in Kingston and St. Andrew.[40]

Indians were in the minority in Kingston and St. Andrew, however. In 1943, they comprised only 2.6% of the total East Indian population in the island. By contrast, 32.9% of Chinese women lived in Kingston and Port Royal, with 17.8% living in St. Andrew.[41]

Indian women in Kingston were largely single women. The population census of 1943 revealed that 1,539 single Indian women lived in Kingston and St. Andrew, 835 were legally married, 270 lived in common-law relationship and 173 were widowed and thus supporting themselves.[42] To do so, they engaged in a variety of occupations, including the growing and selling of flowers, market gardening and the service industries.

By the 1890s it was generally accepted in Kingston that the growing and sale of flowers was an East Indian specialty. An Afro-Jamaican in Kingston reported in the 1890s that 'the Coolie agriculturalists supply all the flowers and decorations, for this is their specialty and they certainly make excellent gardeners'.[43]

A large number of Indian women also were in the service industries in the urban centres. These included professional, public and personal services. The census does not allow for a parish by parish analysis of the number of Indian women in these service industries; but one can safely assume that the majority were in domestic service, which employed the highest number of women (mainly black, coloured and Indian) in Kingston and St. Andrew in the 1940s. This, however, was a low-paying job. On the all-island level, 50.7% of women who earned below 6s. a week were employed in personal service.[44] Only a few Indian women were engaged in service industries other than the personal service industry. A few were messengers and occasional labourers.

One of the most important income-generating activities of Indian women in Kingston was market-gardening and the peddling of the products from their gardens from house to house or to the Chinese shops. The East Indian National Union observed in 1940 that 'East Indians are well-known for their traditional contact with the land. Nearly all the vegetables sold in the Corporate Area are grown by East Indians'.[45] In 1931, however, this activity was severely curtailed by the Kingston and St. Andrew Corporation (KSAC) Law, Section 136. By this law:

any person who shall expose or exhibit for sale in the urban or sub-urban district of the Corporate Area any fresh . . . vegetables, ground provisions or fruit elsewhere than in a public market or in a shop licensed . . . for the sale of such articles shall forfeit a sum of ten pounds for every day in which he shall so offend.[46]

Four Indian women were, in fact, charged under this KSAC law in 1941, despite the fact that they claimed to have been selling their goods to a Chinese shop. According to one of the women, Beatrice Setal:

this morning about 6.30 o'clock myself and three other East Indian women were supplying greens and vegetables to Chinese [sic] in a Chinese shop at 115 Barry Street . . . Constable Hewett who is an employee of the KSAC came to the door and said, 'Hai, unnu don't run', and took our names. He then told us to go to the Sutton Street Police Station.[47]

They further claimed to have been the victims of racial discrimination as 'there was a black woman also selling fowls also banned by the above-mentioned law, in the Chinese . . . shop, but they let her go and prosecuted us'.[48]

Indian women were also affected by the programme of general metering of water by the Water Commission in the Corporate Area which began in the late 1930s. Their inability to pay the subsequent increase in rentals for market garden plots caused hundreds of them to be thrown out of employment. Wilfred Thompson of the East Indian National Union, in his evidence before the Moyne Commission of 1938, claimed that 'the water meter system of the vegetable crops has come in and that has choked out their means of earning a livelihood'.[49]

East Indian women were, therefore, beset by many problems in their efforts to improve their economic status in the plantation economy.

Conclusion

The plantation experience was an oppressive one for the majority of Indian women in Jamaica. The low wages paid to female indentured servants caused the majority to be unable to break the ties with the plantation system even after the abolition of indentured servitude in 1921. Thus the majority remained plantation labourers up to the 1940s. This was unlike other immigrant women, who, either because of higher educational standards or an early break with the plantation system, functioned primarily in the industrial, professional and commercial fields.

The plight of Indian women in Jamaica became even more acute in the late 1930s as a result of the effects of the worldwide economic depression. Thousands of Indian women were jobless and the inability of Parochial Boards to respond to all the appeals for poor relief rendered them destitute. An indication of the level of this destitution was the hundreds of letters of appeal which the Protector of Immigrants had to contend with from the 1920s.[50]

Despite the beliefs — or hopes — of the Indian population of Jamaica, who, long after the indentureship ended, continued to take their problems to the Protector of Immigrants, the latter was powerless to alleviate their plight. Like the rest of the poor people of the island, therefore, Indian women, and men, had to find their own solutions to their prevailing socio-economic plight.

Notes

1. R. Reddock, 'Indian Women and Indentureship in Trinidad and Tobago, 1845–1917: Freedom denied', Third Conference on East Indians in the Caribbean, Trinidad, 1984, p. 13.
2. Ibid.
3. P. Emmer, 'The Great Escape: the migration of female indentured servants from British India to Suriname, 1873–1916', in D. Richardson (ed.), *Abolition and Its Aftermath: The Historical Context, 1970–1916*, 1985, p. 248.
4. Ibid.
5. Ibid.
6. Efforts so far made to provide even partial answers to these questions through the techniques of oral history have not been successful.
7. See V. Shepherd, 'The Emigration of East Indian Women to Jamaica and their Experiences in the Plantation Society', Social History Workshop, University of the West Indies (UWI), Mona, Jamaica, 8–9 November, 1985.
8. V. Shepherd, 'Transients to Citiznes', *Jamaica Journal*, 18, August-October 1985, pp. 17–25.
9. For an elaboration of the reasons Jamaican proprietors opted for Indian immigrants and the details of the scheme, see H.S. Sohal, 'The East Indian Indentureship System in Jamaica, 1845–1917', PhD, University of Waterloo, Canada, 1979; and V. Shepherd, 'Separation vs Integration: the experiences of the Indian group in the Creole Society of Jamaica, 1879–1945', M. Phil, UWI, Jamaica, 1985.
10. Central Government File (hereafter CGF) 1B/9/34, Protector of Immigrants' Papers, Jamaica Archives.
11. Ibid., 1B/9/3, Papers of the *Blundell*, 1845.
12. K.O. Laurence, *Immigration into the West Indies in the Nineteenth Century*, Barbados, 1971, p. 46.
13. *Jamaica Census*, 1871, p. 20.
14. CGF 1B/9/35B.
15. Laurence, op. cit., p. 24.
16. Reported in C. Lal and J. McNeil, *Report on Emigration from India*, HMSO London, 1915, p. 313.
17. Ibid.
18. Ibid.
19. CGF 1B/9/3, Papers of the *Blundell*.
20. Lal and McNeil, op. cit., pp. 223–5 and 228–9.
21. Ibid., p. 320.
22. CGF 1B/9/128B.
23. *Jamaica Census*, 1891, Abstract M, p. 68.
24. Ibid.
25. Ibid.
26. *Jamaica Census*, 1941, p. lii. See also V.A. Shepherd, 'The Education of East Indian Children in Jamaica, 1879–1950', Postgraduate Seminar Paper, UWI, Mona, December 1983.
27. *Jamaica Census*, 1911, pp. 80–1.
28. *Jamaica Census*, 1921, p. 119.
29. *Jamaica Census*, 1943, p. liii.
30. Ibid.
31. See K.Post, *Arise Ye Starvelings: the Jamaican Labour Rebellion of 1938 and its Aftermath*, 1978.
32. J.D. Tyson, *Report on the Condition of Indians*, n.p., 1939, p. 6.
33. Ibid., p. 33.
34. Ibid.
35. Ibid.
36. *Jamaican Census*, 1943, Table 125, pp. 220–1.
37. Ibid.
38. Ibid., Table 93, p. 181.
39. *Jamaica Census*, 1881, p. 358.
40. *Jamaica Census*, 1943, pp. 96 and 113.
41. Ibid., p.l. See also V.A. Shepherd, 'From Rural Plantations to Urban Slums', *Immigrants and Minorities*, vol. 5, 1986, pp. 130–43, and 'Depression in the "Tin Roof" Towns', in D. Dabydeen and B. Samaroo (eds.), *India in the Caribbean*, 1987, pp. 173–88.
42. *Jamaica Census*, 1943, p. 96.
43. Livingstone Collection, MS 59, Scrap Book 1, National Library of Jamaica.
44. *Jamaica Census*, 1943, p. lxxvi.
45. CGF 1B/9/111/8, Secretary of the East Indian National Union to Allan O. Ritchie, Protector of Immigrants, 28 July 1940.

46. CGF 1B/9/111/31, Laws Affecting East Indians in Jamaica.
47. Ibid. Evidence of Beatrice Setal, 6 May 1941.
48. Ibid.
49. *Daily Gleaner,* 2 December 1938.
50. See CGF 1B/9/166, Protector of Immigrants' Outward Letter Book, and CGF 1B/9/154, File 9, Poor Relief 1940–6.

Women and Crime in Late Nineteenth Century Trinidad

David V. Trotman

This paper examines the patterns of crime and criminality among women in late 19th century Trinidad. Its focus is on the last three decades of the nineteenth century which could be rightly called the golden age of the *jamettes* or 'loose women' in Trinidad's social history. Although females constituted less than half of the total population, they managed to exasperate the ruling classes and had a stamp on the socio-cultural patterns of the emerging creole cultural complex. Their behaviour caused consternation among the moral arbiters of the time — established clergy, police and judges as well as those citizens who considered themselves representatives of the respectable classes. The essay concentrates on those women who found themselves before the courts or in the prisons and who consequently were labelled criminals. The behaviour of this small segment of the female population became the basis for the castigation of all urban working-class women, especially those of African descent.[1]

The Female Population

The nineteenth century was a period of rapid demographic growth in Trinidad. The population, which at the time of full emancipation in 1838 was approximately 30,000, reached 84,438 thirty years later. It continued to increase rapidly and the decennial censuses from 1871 to 1901 showed a steady rise from 109,638 to 255,148 people. These increases did not come from natural reproduction but rather from immigration, as the sugar interests promoted the movement of labour from nearby West Indian colonies, Africa, China, Portugal and India in an attempt to redress the land-labour imbalance on the plantation frontier. Like the slave trade, the nineteenth century indentured labour migration was male-biased and youthful. The movement of these predominantly West and East Indian immigrants essentially into rural Trinidad coincided with an internal migration of Trinidad creoles into urban areas.

The female population increased as part of the general pattern of growth, although at a much slower rate. While the overall population advanced by 132% between 1871 and 1901, the female segment increased by only 72%, from 49,233 to 119,328. The smaller ratio of female to male immigrants accounts for this slower growth rate. But although overall the female increases were smaller, the urban female population grew at a rate equal to the general pattern. The emergence of this urban based female population was crucial to the development of the *jamette* culture of the nineteenth century.

Females dominated the urban centres in 1839. Port-of-Spain had 6,781 females to only 4,912 males and by 1861 the number of females had risen to 10,436 as compared to only 8,544 males. In 1881, when females constituted only 45% of the general population, they amounted to more than 50% of the Port-of-Spain population, and ten years later San Fernando, Arima and St. Joseph all had a surplus female population as well. Moreover, creoles dominated this urban female population, in contrast to the rural area where male immigrants predominated. Females were 46% of the overall population in 1891, but they were only 50% of the East Indian and 46% of the British West Indian population. Among the creole group, however, the female component was over 50%. In 1891, 60% of Port-of-Spain's female population gave their place of birth as Trinidad and 31% said they were from another West Indian colony.

The female population, like the general population and its immigrant segments, tended to be young. Between 1871 and 1891 the age group twenty- to forty-year-olds formed roughly 40% of the general population; and if we include age twenty, then at least three-quarters of the population were below age forty. The urban pattern was similar. In 1881 20% of Port-of-Spain females were under twenty and in 1891 23% were between the ages of ten and twenty, with 35% between the ages of twenty and forty. The majority of these young women were reported to be unmarried — a general condition — since 75% of the Port-of-Spain population in 1881 were also listed as unmarried. This figure refers only to those considered legally married, of course, for the census does not recognize other cohabitation arrangements then common among the lower classes. Given the predominance of young women, however, one may assume that most women lived alone, were involved in lesbian relationships, or had relationships with men whom they shared with other women.

Female concentration in the urban areas was part of a general movement of labour away from the rural areas as women, like men, sought a greater degree of flexibility and independence which they could only find away from the plantations. Although women continued to be significant in plantation labour, these were mostly East Indians and British West Indian immigrants. Non-plantation occupations which could be considered gender specific or traditionally associated with women increased in the nineteenth century and tended to be dominated by Trinidadian women of African descent.

The 1881 census listed 5,838 domestics (an increase from 3,780 in 1871), 4,545 laundresses and washers, 7,855 seamstresses and 2,865 shop-keepers/hucksters (an increase from 1,884 in 1871). Port-of-Spain alone had 3,094 or 53% of the domestics; 3,138 or 40% of the seamstresses; 1,086 or 38% of the hucksters; and an overwhelming number who listed their occupation as washers.

Employment as store-clerks was considered to be a high status occupation and tended to be dominated by females of the coloured lower middle class. Shop-clerks, like all other female workers, were poorly paid, however, and seamstresses earned the lowest wages for the longest period of daily labour. Many of those who mentioned such occupations to census takers were probably expressing vocational preferences rather than actual occupations, for urban women had few job choices. Some rural re-migration occurred during the reaping season, but women had to develop a variety of urban survival strategies, especially during the economic crisis of the late nineteenth century. More often than not, the price women paid for independence from the plantation was economic marginality in the city.

In summary, the female population of nineteenth century Trinidad tended to be predominantly creole but with a significant non-Trinidadian rural component; young and unmarried; urban; and marginally employed. Crime statistics acquire meaning only against this peculiar demographic, residential and occupational background, for women became victims of their socio-economic situation, and in the ensuing struggle to overcome their disadvantages, they emerged as statistics in the prison and court records.

Women as Victims

Nineteenth century Trinidadian women, urban and rural alike, were vulnerable to three particular types of crime: uxoricide, common assault, and rape.

A clear reflection of demographic pressures, sexual imbalance, and other social and cultural changes wrought by immigration, as well as the brutalizing effects of a harsh labour system, uxoricide was most prevalent among the East Indian community. Between 1872 and 1880, 27% of all Trinidad's murders were committed by East Indian immigrants; East Indians accounted for 60% of the murders between 1881 and 1889, and 70% between 1890 and 1898. The majority of these homicides were murders of women who were either wives, concubines or fiancées. All of the victims of the twenty-two East Indian murderers from 1872 to 1880 were wives; 60% of Indian murder victims between 1881 and 1889 were women, of whom 88% were wives; and 70% of those murdered in the 1890s were women, of whom 58% were wives.

East Indian uxoricide stemmed from the sexual imbalance of the East Indian population. The entire population showed a male bias, but it was most acute within the East Indian community. The plantocracy was slow to recognize the importance of imported females in a labour-short society, and this, combined with the reluctance of single Indian females to emigrate, made the Trinidad East Indian community a male-dominated one. Between 1871 and 1891, Trinidad received 49,855 East Indians, of whom 70% were males. Approximately 25,037 East Indians arrived in the following decade: 85%, or 21,220, were listed as adults, that is, above the age of fifteen; 11% were children, and the remaining 4%, infants; 70% of the adults and 57% of the children were males.

Because planters preferred males above age thirty-five, the immigrant male population tended to be young, single, and in the prime of their lives. The scarcity of women increased the competition for female spouses. Although men used the services of Afro-Trinidadian prostitutes and had other sexual liaisons with creoles, they were generally reluctant either to marry or set up illicit long-term relationships with non-East Indian women. The available women therefore became valuable and the source of numerous jealousies and quarrels that ended in violent conflict. Married men guarded their wives as if they were prized pieces of property.[2]

Marital infidelity with employers — proprietors, managers and overseers — tempted many East Indians, for numerous advantages accompanied such liaisons, and non-compliance caused problems. Plantation officials could make or break any immigrant. They could affect immigrants' quality of life by the way they regulated rations and work loads. They could influence the justice system, convincing magistrates that immigrants had contravened some clause of the Immigration Ordinance for which imprisonment was the punishment. When employers behaved like feudal lords or old slave masters and imposed a sexual *droît de seigneur* over female employees, they frequently precipitated violence by concerned Indian men. Such a situation underlay the 1873 indictment and manslaughter conviction of Louis Thomas, an East Indian, for the murder of his wife Romain. The deceased Romain 'had for sometime left her husband and formed a connection with Nivet, the manager of an estate adjoining that on which Louis Thomas lived'. Managers' and overseers' relationships with East Indian women were so common that the Chief Justice attacked the practice in a letter to the Agent-General of Immigration precisely because it could lead to the women's murder.[3]

Despite the inequality of the relationship and the difficulty of resisting, East Indian women received little understanding, and most authorities merely echoed the popular denigration. Justice placed the blame on 'the very loose character of the majority of coolie women, and the temptations to which men in the position of managers and overseers are subjected'.[4] It was a classic case of blaming the victims. The benefits of liaisons with employers tended to be illusory, temporary and dangerous. Women were frequently sexually used and then abandoned, sometimes with offspring. Single women faced ostracism from an unsympathetic community or death from a jealous rejected East Indian suitor, and married women often died at the hands of a cuckolded husband.

Unfortunately for these East Indian women, they were part of a male-biased culture where perceived slights to male pride had to be avenged. In a misguided manner, but dictated by East Indian tradition, the wife paid with her life for daring to cause the East Indian male to lose face and suffer dishonour among his community and peers. It did not matter if some of these women merely sought to ease the conditions of their husbands' lives by alliances with employers, managers or overseers. Transgressions brought death.

The situation in the new East Indian society forming in Trinidad undermined many traditional Indian values, particularly those surrounding male-female relationships. Males, pressured by sexual hunger in a female-scarce situation, abandoned traditional respect for marital ties and seduced wives away from their spouses. That marriages performed according to Indian religious rites were not recognized by Trinidadian law only aggravated the problem.

The ability of women to sign individual indenture contracts and to become independent breadwinners undermined traditional Indian female dependence. Rations, wages, land and money awarded in lieu of return passages further encouraged female independence. Realizing that their scarcity increased their value, some single female immigrants exploited the situation, challenged traditional ideas of female subservience, and changed lovers frequently. For many death at the hands of rejected lovers ensued. The murder of Rookmania in 1872 is a good example. She rejected Darsan in order to live with an East Indian overseer. The fact that Rookmania chose to live with her new lover on the estate where her previous lover resided probably hastened her demise, for three weeks later the rejected lower killed her.[5]

Some calculating parents exploited the female-scarce situation. The tradition of arranged marriages, where females of tender age were betrothed to a male suitor on the payment of a dowry, lent itself to ready exploitation. Parents of daughters manoeuvered between multiple suitors, manipulating them and exacting large dowries or tribute in the form of services. That, too, was a dangerous game that sometimes ended in death. In October 1878, for example, an East Indian immigrant, killed the ten-year-old Chetapeah and her mother Palowa. The homicide took place during a dispute over the return of a $400 dowry or the giving of Chetapeah in marriage as Palowa had promised.[6]

Afro-Trinidadian creoles shared with East Indians the belief that men had indisputable rights over the bodies and lives of women, and men used corporal punishment to enforce domestic law and order. It was taken for granted that men were entitled to punish women for real or imagined transgressions against their domestic sovereignty or to avenge real or imagined slights against their ego.

The phenomenon of battered women was a public matter, since the spatial arrangements of the plantation range or the urban barrack yard made privacy virtually impossible. Although onlookers sometimes became participants and took sides in the dispute, generally little intervention occurred. The idea prevailed that 'a little blows' indicated love; and the folly of interfering in 'husband and wife business' was well known.

Many domestic disputes were settled out of court so that there is no reliable statistical information about them.[7] Although on the spur of the moment women might report incidents to the police or lodge complaints in court, once passion cooled they usually failed to pursue their cases. Legal spouses were less prone to report disputes and to prosecute. Unless the violence did extensive physical damage, women tended to consider abuse part of the price of marital respectability. Women in common-law unions, the predominant form of marriage, pursued the matter of abuse according to their interpretation of the purpose of the chastisement. They might report the matter initially in order to save face; and if they considered the beating a notice of the termination of the relationship, they might proceed with the case. If the beating was interpreted merely as the exercise of conjugal rights, however, then convention ruled, and the matter never reached the courts. Since many wives, married or common law, were either unemployed or marginally employed, they often preferred to suffer brutalization in silence rather than face a life of poverty without the financial support of some man.

Rape was the classic example of the oppression of women in the society. Given the understandable reluctance of women to report it, the number of reported rape cases is noteworthy. Between 1870 and 1899 two hundred and six such cases were tried before the superior courts. In the two five-year periods, 1870–1874 and 1875–1879, seventeen rape cases were tried; this number increased to twenty-six in the following five-year period. The number of rape cases continued to increase, peaking at fifty-six in 1885–1889 and decreasing to fifty and forty, respectively, in the two succeeding periods.

The number of rape reports was small by any standard, and should not be taken as an index of the actual incidence of rape. The decrease in the number of court cases after 1889 is also no evidence of real decrease in the number of rapes; rather, it is more probable that fewer cases were being reported and tried. Curiously enough, the decrease in court cases coincided with the decrease in the conviction rate of rape. The acquittal rate for rape increased between 1870 and 1899. During that thirty-year period, 59% of the 206 cases before the courts ended in conviction, 27% of the accused being acquitted, and 14% of the cases falling through, or being returned *nolle prosequi*. In the period 1871–1877 only twenty cases were tried, but 65% ended in convictions and 35% in acquittals. Between 1893 and 1899 this situation changed, however; seventy-seven cases were tried of which only 46% ended in conviction, 30% in

acquittals, 24% of the cases were aborted before the completion of prosecution.

The reasons for the decline are unclear, but a number of possible explanations come to mind. It is quite possible that some miscarriage of justice occurred in the earlier part of the century when judges may have been more disposed to believe the rape accusations of women against men of colour. After all, judges and juries were well aware of the scarcity of women in the immigrant population, and therefore might have found it plausible that some would resort to rape to satisfy sexual needs. In the minds of many whites, rape by an accused African or Indian man was quite believable given prevalent racist beliefs that darker peoples suffered from uncontrollable passions. It is also possible that, in the interim, legal defence improved in quality thus increasing the acquittal rate. There is also little doubt that some acquittals and aborted cases resulted from bribery of juries, witnesses, and sometimes even plaintiffs.[8]

Racist and sexist traditions of the society had their impact on the legal system and discouraged more women from bringing rape cases before the courts and completing prosecution. The stereotyping and characterization of non-European women as people of loose character and questionable morals constituted a major problem in proving rape, and became a favourite defence in the courts. The idea that all non-European women were inveterate liars, sexually promiscuous, and devoid of any 'womanly sense of shame' dominated the nineteenth century thought. A working-class complainant in a rape case had to fight against these racist and sexist stereotypes.

The argument of one defence attorney in an 1869 rape case typified the defence used in rape trials. He claimed that the plaintiff had previously had sexual intercourse with the accused as well as others, and suggested the possibility of consent. Citing British precedents, he argued that the more promiscuous the woman, the more stringent the evidence required to establish absence of consent. In the absence of convincing evidence, he claimed, consent might reasonably be presumed. This line of defence prompted a response which surely constituted one of the few glorious moments in nineteenth century jurisprudence in Trinidad, when the Chief Justice retorted that even the greatest strumpet had a right to assert an assumed chastity against a trespasser to her will.[9]

A low age of consent provided an exploitable line of defence for those accused of the rape of girls. Ordinance 1 of 1889 lowered the age of consent from sixteen to thirteen years. One of the reasons advanced for this reduction was that under the Immigrant Marriage and Divorce Ordinance of

1881, the large East Indian population was at liberty to marry at the age of thirteen, although the age of consent for the general population was sixteen. The proponents of reduction claimed that this created a number of legal problems. The non-official members of the Legislative Council, who represented the interests of the plantocrats, also argued that 'girls developed more rapidly in tropical climates and sooner attained the age of puberty'.

This justification disguised the real reason for the age reduction. The plantocrats, always concerned about their labour supply, understood that a lower age of consent would increase the number of people who could legally sign labour contracts or seek employment, and would therefore expand the labour pool. Two years later, when Ordinance 20 sought to fix age sixteen as the age of consent for all purposes, the planting interest unanimously expressed its dissent and walked out of the chamber to prevent the bill's passage. They refused to accept the observations of some magistrates and the police that a higher age of consent was valuable in policing brothels and checking the growth of prostitution among female juveniles. As a result, official members, representing the Governor and Colonial Office, were forced to compromise, and the plantocrats accepted fourteen as the age of consent.[10] The interests of the plantocracy therefore triumphed and served to perpetuate a situation that facilitated the exploitation of women, propelling them into the courts and prisons.

Women as Criminals

Prison records reveal that while female prisoners existed in nineteenth century Trinidad, the numbers were small in comparison with the number of male prisoners and the general female population. That refers only to statistics for prison committals, however. Other sources, such as newspaper, suggest that a greater number of women were brought before the courts. However, most women were probably fined rather than imprisoned. In the closing years of the nineteenth century judges tended to favour fines over prison terms, except in the case of indentured immigrants, but statistics fail to differentiate between the sexes in such cases. One can only guess at the reasons for the smaller female prison population. Some magistrates may have felt that prison was the wrong environment for women, and would impose prison terms only where imprisonment was mandatory. Many women may have been in a better position than men to pay fines and avoid imprisonment.[11]

Total prison committals increased by 64% in the last three decades of the century, from 20,935 in 1872 to 30,459 in 1899. Female prison committals increased by 57% over the same period, from 2,850 to 4,485. Some of the increases are explained by the large number of people lodged in prison for non-penal purposes. These included people awaiting trial who were either refused, or unable to post bail; witnesses in protective custody; individuals detained because the police feared they would not otherwise appear for trial; and debtors, who were not considered criminals.

While all committals for penal imprisonment increased by 32% in the 1870s and 1890s, the female component increased by 46%, from 2,506 to 3,665. Even with a decrease in the number of debtors, committals of unconvicted detainees rose to as much as 20% of the prison population. Prison detentions, excluding debtors, grew by 128%, from 2,939 in the 1870s to 6,729 in the 1890s, with the female component increasing by almost 200%, from 271 to 811. At the same time female debtors, like debtors in general, declined from forty-six to fifteen. During the 1870s and 1890s, the female contingent of the prison population never exceeded 15% of total committals, 18% of penal imprisonments, or 12% of non-penal committals.

The female prisoners were also as youthful as the general population. The sample years 1895 and 1899 show that more than 70% of female prisoners were between sixteen and thirty years of age, with 23% between sixteen and twenty and 50% between twenty-one and thirty. Statistics for the seventies and eighties fail to differentiate between the sexes, but there is no reason to believe that the situation was any different. Female juvenile offenders (under age sixteen) constituted roughly 30% of all juvenile committals between 1872 and 1899. Convicted women could be found in the older age groups as well, and women between forty and sixty years of age accounted for roughly 8% of female prisoners; a number of female prisoners over sixty years of age could also be found.

Female prisoners' occupational status also reflected that of the general population. Labourers dominated, but since the records do not differentiate between the sexes, they cannot provide a precise picture of the number of the females in each occupational category. For those categories generally associated with women, however, such as domestic service, huckstering, sewing and washing, the picture is clearer. Out of 1,144 convicted female prisoners between 1873 and 1875, 802 or 70% were from these four categories, with washing and domestic service as the chief occupations. No major change occurred by the end of the century. In the 1890s 4,060 females were committed to penal servitude, 2,987, or 74% of whom listed themselves in the same four categories. There was a ten point increase in domestics and a fourteen point decrease in seamstresses.

The whole judicial system, including prisons, served more as an irritant to women than as a mechanism for dispensing justice, imposing punishment or providing rehabilitation. A high rate of recidivism existed throughout the nineteenth century as lower class people were repeatedly imprisoned for short periods with neither harsh penal conditions or social stigma attached to their short sojourns. Between 1885 and 1889, 37% of 2,742 females were first-time prisoners, another 37% were incarcerated for four or more times. A combination of unchanging socio-economic conditions accounted for the original criminal activity and brevity of most sentences. Most sentences were for three months or less. In the 1880s, 95% of 4,940 female committals were for three months or less, with 4% sentenced to terms longer than three months but shorter than a year. Only 1%, or eighteen committals, were for five years and over.

Recidivism and short terms were clearly related to the kinds of crimes women committed. Since prison records, like court records, did not always distinguish between the sexes, the female crime profile is unclear. Criminal activity among women, no less than among men, reflected their particular socio-economic status in a colonial plantation economy. Women participated in all kinds of illegal activities, but were more prominent in gender-specific crimes such as prostitution.

There is no doubt that women committed crimes against property and offences against labour and social economy ordinances. They, like their male counterparts, were affected adversely by changing economic conditions, especially the sugar crisis of the late nineteenth century, and it seems reasonable to include women in that period's characteristic pattern of petty theft and larceny. They were victims of a complex of legislation regulating plantation and non-plantation labourers of both sexes. Indentured East Indian women could not escape the numerous pitfalls of the Indentured Immigration Ordinances, and British West Indian immigrants and Trinidadian women who sought to escape the plantations found themselves trapped in the web of the Masters and Servants Ordinance and numerous other ordinances regulating marketing and other economic activities in urban areas. In short, women were victimized by the laws as a mechanism of labour and economic control.[12]

No record exists of the execution of women for murder or their imprisonment for life during the late nineteenth century, although females were convicted for terms of five years and more. Fourteen of these long-term committals occurred during the 1880s and one during the 1890s. Since long-term imprisonment was reserved for serious crimes against property and person, these sentences might have been for serious crimes such as manslaughter. With the exception of uxoricide the majority of assaults during the nineteenth century tended to be impulsive outbursts, rather than premeditated attacks. Although often resulting in bodily harm, they were rarely fatal, and they were frequently committed by women.

The brutality of slavery and its perpetuation in the conditions of post-emancipation colonial plantation society encouraged violence in women as well as men. The slave era had women who responded to the violence of slavery with as much violence as physique and their social position allowed. This pattern did not disappear in the post-emancipation period: during the first generation after slavery, from 1838 to 1869, women could be found in the forefront of the affrays and riots that so typified that era of transition. They were highly visible participants in the violence of the late nineteenth century and a shocked elite commented frequently on their behaviour.

Women played active as well as supportive roles in all the violent activities in Trinidadian society. The police reported that it was women who encouraged men to riot during a massive demonstration marking the departure of Chief Justice Gorrie, a hero of the lower classes. In an 1849 riot prompted in part by an attempt to shave the heads of female prisoners women took the same leadership role.[13] In both cases women taunted men for their lack of aggression. Women were the *chantwells* who sang fighting songs to intoxicate male stickfighters as they prepared to do battle on Carnival and other days. The singing of East Indian women served a similar function for the *gatka-wallahs*, the East Indian stickfighters, as they re-created the battle of Kerbala at the annual Hosein celebrations.

Among the many bands or gangs that existed in Port-of-Spain were a number of female ones.[14] Clementia Mills was one of twenty women charged with causing an affray in the public streets of Port-of-Spain in June 1864 and 'being unlawfully assembled and arrayed in warlike manner'. Clementia, armed with a horsewhip, led a band of women, the 'Mourcelines', against another group called the 'Don't care dams', whose leader carried a flag. Both groups carried stones in their aprons, and were armed with knives and razors. With their frocks tucked up, they fought each other in a battle which spread from George Street to an open field on the banks of the Dry River.[15]

Annie Coals, Myrtle the Turtle, Alice Sugar, Alice's younger sister, Piti Belle Lily, and Boadicea were some of the more notorious fighting women of the time. Their exploits earned them places in those archives of the oppressed, the calypso. Boadicea fought Alice Sugar for over an hour for the right to the sexual favours of a well-known stickfighter called Cutaway Rimbeau. The fight became grist for the calypsonian's ready mill. In an ironical twist, Boadicea subsequently whipped Rimbeau with his own stave for having dared to offer his sexual services to the defeated Alice's sister, Piti Belle Lily.[16] The scarcity of males prompted violence in the urban community and often led unemployed or marginally employed women to use force to secure and retain male companionship.

The elite complained continually about the number of prostitutes in Trinidad and cited them as further evidence of female immorality. The Chief of Police, L.M. Fraser, in particular, seemed to have his eyes constantly on the prostitutes, for he commented regularly on their increasing numbers. He observed, in 1877, 'that each succeeding year shows a rapid spread of prostitution, and no one can pass through the streets of our Towns without having ample evidence of the utter degradation of our lower class females'.[17] Four years later, he was appalled at the increase in 'the number of female children who take to habits of prostitution at an age so early that the fact might almost be deemed impossible'.[18] In 1884 he was shocked at 'the steady increase in the number of girls of very tender ages who unblushingly enroll themselves amongst the recognized and registered prostitutes'.[19] He was concerned, moreover, with the financial support these women gave to men, making men disinclined to seek regular employment and more prone to criminal activities. How much of this was fact and how much was the police chief's conjecture, however, is difficult to ascertain.

The fact is that the uneven sexual composition of plantation society tended to make prostitution almost inevitable. During the slave period, the existence of a large number of enslaved women at the disposal of a minority of ruling class males may have restricted the opportunity for women to sell themselves on the street. But slaves were available for hire as prostitutes, and mulatto women operated both as prostitutes and brothel owners. Prostitutes began by servicing urban men who had no authority over slave women. One visitor claimed that a Mrs. Perry ran 'The British Coffee House', the best brothel in Port-of-Spain and most of Port-of-Spain's taverns were in fact brothels. Their clientele included soldiers of the militia and numerous sailors who regularly visited the port. In 1869, Charles Kingsley hinted at the existence of prostitution in Port-of-Spain, linking it to the town's role as a port, 'aggravated by the superabundant

animal vigour and the perfect independence of the younger women'.[20] The existence of a large male market thus prompted the emergence of a group of women who were willing to satisfy male needs outside of the confines of marriage, and for a price.

The development of prostitution can be linked also with economic distress in the 1880s. As we have seen, Port-of-Spain developed a surplus female population in the immediate post-emancipation period as women deserted the plantations and flocked to urban areas. This drift continued throughout the nineteenth century. Marginal employment opportunities — sewing, laundering, and domestic service — decreased, however, as the supply of women increased. As a result, some women may have been forced into prostitution in order to survive. During periods of relative prosperity, other women may have made prostitution a more deliberate career choice, since prostitutes' earnings may have surpassed the wages of the menial jobs to which women were restricted.

Court and prison statistics are not particularly useful guides to the extent of prostitution. The offence is not listed separately under convictions, and we have to depend on imprisonment figures alone. Prostitution was, however, a 'victimless' crime, and had no complainants unless a transaction ended in a brawl over payment and services. In many instances, however, policemen did pose as prospective clients to entrap prostitutes. As prostitution was a highly charged moral issue, statistics on arrests, convictions and committals reflected the prevailing elite moral climate, more than they did the actual number of prostitutes. In many cases police raids netted women who, although charged with prostitution, or labelled as prostitutes by the press, were merely friends and neighbours of prostitutes. Committal statistics indicate that the number of women imprisoned for prostitution decreased steadily after 1880. But if Police Chief Fraser's constantly articulated fears and the number of letters to the press complaining about prostitution reflected actual conditions, then many more prostitution cases should be concealed under 'miscellaneous' cases and convictions.

An 1874 list provides some indication of the age and nationality of known common prostitutes. It includes ninety Port-of-Spain women and thirty-eight San Fernando women between the ages of seventeen and thirty-eight. Another group of fifty-three San Fernando prostitutes includes two girls of about 11 years whose identity as prostitutes is debatable. They may have been arrested with their parents or older friends. Prostitution at such a young age must have been unusual, since the presence of two children among the older prostitutes created a public sensation. Creoles dominated the

1874 list; sixty of the ninety listed for Port-of-Spain were from Trinidad, eighteen from Barbados, and ten from other West Indian islands, and one 25–year-old Calcutta woman. Thirty-one of the thirty-eight San Fernando women gave Trinidad as their place of birth; one 28–year-old woman was born in Madras, India, and a 26–year-old was born in Venezuela. Unless most of these women claimed Trinidad as their birth place to avoid deportation, this 1874 profile of prostitutes contradicts the commonly held opinion that criminals and prostitutes were immigrants. The list does not represent all prostitutes in Port-of-Spain and San Fernando, however, only 'the most notorious and flagrant cases' registered according to the Contagious Diseases Ordinances.[21]

The Contagious Diseases Ordinance was one of the weapons in the campaign against prostitution. It was modelled on British legislation to combat the spread of venereal diseases in towns with garrisons of unmarried soldiers and sailors. This legislation was introduced to Trinidad as Ordinance 18 of 1869, suspended for three years but reactivated in 1875 and remained in operation until 1887. The Act required women accused of common prostitution to register and to be periodically examined for venereal disease and, if diseased, to be incarcerated in a certified hospital ward.[22]

In the hands of the police the ordinance became a tool to harass not only prostitutes, but all lower-class women. The term 'common prostitute' was so vague that it left the interpretation to the discretion of the police. Women were expected to submit voluntarily to a medical examination. If they refused they were taken before a magistrate and had to prove that they were virtuous. Evidence of sexual activity, regardless of the circumstances, was often all that was needed to establish guilt. As a result, many innocent women were forced to register as common prostitutes and were subjected to periodic examinations. Some women who were thus harassed either left town or changed their addresses, for when the Act was reactivated in 1875 the police could not locate many of the original registrants.[23]

Unscrupulous policemen abused their powers and exacted sexual favours from women. For instance, women who refused the advances of Sergeant Holder, a Barbadian, often found themselves arrested and forced to register as common prostitutes. Magistrate Mayne of the Port-of-Spain court accepted Holder's word on any case connected with the ordinance and 'out of twenty cases decided by Mayne against unfortunate women, victims of this man's rapacity and lust, nineteen were decided on Holder's unsupported evidence'. Finally, a petition made by Elizabeth Walcott was

investigated and Holder was found guilty and dismissed from the force. He returned to Barbados but irreparable damage had been done already to the lives of innocent women whose only crime was that they were poor and non-white.[24]

Those who failed to petition against the unfair working of the ordinance did not necessarily accept their fate, however, for there were other ways to protest. Residents of Upper Charlotte Street and St. Ann's Road, a new upper-class suburb, witnessed 'scandalous scenes of obscenity and scandal occasioned on Wednesday mornings by the band of prostitutes who go up in a body to the Hospital, in compliance with the provisions of the Contagious Diseases Ordinance'.[25] Without political power, unorganized and mostly illiterate, they used the only tools available to them, shouting and screaming their way to their weekly examination, flagrantly demonstrating their resentment in ways that attracted attention to them as a group. Ironically, such behaviour only reinforced the negative stereotypes that 'decent' society already applied to them.

Charges of indecent behaviour, riotous and disorderly conduct, and obscene and profane language were the most frequent charges made against working-class women. Many of these charges reflect the cultural gap between the elite and working class. The charge of obscene language resulted from the elite's attempt to impose the English language on a multi-ethnic society, and reflected the different values attached to language by the elite and lower classes. The problem was exacerbated by an aggressive West Indian immigrant police force which rarely understood the popular patois of the lower classes. Charges of indecent behaviour and disorderly conduct were used to restrict those types of working-class behaviour which seemed directly opposed to the ideals of an elite influenced by Victorian ethics. Lower-class behaviour seemed to emphasize noise, turmoil and lack of sobriety, while the elite code emphasized sobriety, decorum and respectability. The behaviour of lower class women in particular represented everything that was antithetical to ruling-class notions of respectability.

Women were the chief victims of cultural conflict in such areas as religion, language and behaviour, since they tended to be more involved than men in those activities which attracted the attention of the ruling classes and brought them into immediate contact with the law. Urban working-class women as representatives of the emerging creole culture were the prime casualties of a cultural struggle which had as its aim the imposition of a cultural hegemony supportive of perpetuation of plantation interests in post-emancipation

Trinidad.[26] Women were perceived as perpetuators of a code of ethics and a pattern of behaviour antagonistic to the plantation order. They were isolated, labelled criminal, and continually harassed by the law. They formed a small but significant portion of those continually before the courts or in the prisons.

Abbreviations

CO   Colonial Office Series, Public Record Office, Kew
PP   Parliamentary Papers, Great Britain, House of Commons
TCP   Trinidad Council Papers

Notes

1. On the history of Trinidad in the nineteenth century see Bridget Brereton, *Race Relations in Colonial Trinidad 1870–1900* (London: Cambridge University Press, 1979); Donald Wood, *Trinidad in Transition* (London: Oxford University Press, 1968); and Eric Williams, *History of the People of Trinidad and Tobago* (Port-of-Spain: P.N.M. Publishing Co., 1962).
2. Keate to Cardwell, No. 79, 21st May, 1864, and enclosures, CO 295/227.
3. Longden to Kimberley, No. 161, 21st August, 1873, CO 295/269.
4. Longden to Kimberley, No. 161, 21st August, 1873, CO 295/269.
5. Longden to Kimberley, No. 74, 6th April, 1872, CO 295/269.
6. No. 88 and enclosures, CO 295/313.
7. The offence 'assaulting female or child' was not distinguished from' assault and battery' in the statistics prior to 1901. In the decade 1901–1910, 275 persons (256 males and 19 females) were imprisoned for 'assaulting female or child'.
8. For example, see rape cases reported in *Port-of-Spain Gazette,* 19th October, 1892.
9. Gordon to Granville, No. 59, 8th May, 1869, and enclosure, CO 295/247.
10. Robinson to Knutsford, No. 127, 11th April, 1889, CO 295/322; No. 312, 8th October, 1890, CO 295/330; and No. 311, 27th November, 1891, CO 295/334.
11. See TCP 30/1883, p. 3.
12. For crimes against property see David V. Trotman, 'Crime and the Plantation Society: Trinidad 1838–1900', Ph.D. dissertation, The Johns Hopkins University, 1980, pp. 132–173; and on law and labour see David V. Trotman, 'The law and labour control in nineteenth century Trinidad', in *Latin America and the Caribbean: Geopolitics, Development and Culture* (Ottawa: CALACS, 1984).
13. Harris to Grey, No. 1, January 1850, CO 295/170.
14. These bands were not purposeless groupings given only to senseless violence, as the Chief of Police and others described them, but were sororities that served as friendship and support networks in the sometimes strange and alienating urban situation. See also Brereton, *Race Relations,* pp. 166–9.
15. *The Trinidad Chronicle,* 23rd December, 1864.
16. Andrew Pearse, 'Mitto Sampson on Calypso Legends of the Nineteenth Century', *Caribbean Quarterly,* 4 (1956): 250–262.
17. TCP 45/1878, Report of the Inspector of Prisons 1877, p. 2.
18. TCP 53/1882, Report of the Inspector of Prisons, 1881, p. 3.
19. No. 107, Enclosure from the Inspector of Prisons, 1884, CO 295/306.
20. V.S. Naipaul, *The Loss of El Dorado: A History* (New York: A.A. Knopf, 1970), p. 162; Charles Kingsley, *At Last: A Christmas in the West Indies* (London: Macmillan and Co., 1889), p. 72.
21. TCP 17/1875.
22. TCP 17/1875; PP 1887, LVII, pp. 675–87; Robinson to Knutsford, NO. 26, 21st January, 1891, CO 295/332.
23. TCP 17/1875.
24. *Port-of-Spain Gazette,* 10th December, 1881, and *Trinidad Palladium,* 19th November, 1881.
25. *Port-of-Spain Gazette,* 5th November, 1881.
26. For a more extensive discussion of the struggle for cultural hegemony see Trotman, 'Crime and the Plantation Society', pp. 294–361; see also Brereton, *Race Relations,* pp. 193–212.

SECTION SEVEN
Social Policy and Class Formation

Post slavery societies were characterized by the movement towards the assumption of responsibility by central government for social policies designed to enhance the public good. During slavery, there were attempts by government to address certain social issues by means of the financing of public policy, but such efforts were restricted by the identification of the plantation, and urban vestries, as the proper fora for implementation. Emancipation, therefore, resulted in a considerable shift of responsibility for issues such as the health and education of the labouring poor to the central government.

Public policies designed to improve the conditions of former slaves, however, according to Laurence and Campbell, did not meet with enthusiasm within English Caribbean governments which were still dominated by former slave owners, and who persisted with the ideological perspectives that the poor were by and large undeserving of public welfare. As a result, as Campbell shows, measures designed to improve educational facilities for the disenfranchised met with considerable opposition but as Bacchus points out, the colonial authorities wanted to ensure that the transition from slavery to a 'free labour market' was achieved without any major disruptions, and saw that the 'right type' of education was important for this to happen. Thus despite the negative attitude toward education held by a substantial number of planters and the depressed economic condition of the region, there was a growing recognition by the legislators and other sections of the population that popular education had come to stay. Its expanded provision, indeed, was deemed vital for social stability in the colonies. Thus the spirit of social reform was an important feature of the nineteenth century Caribbean world. But according to Bacchus and Laurence, the will to finance social measures from public revenues remained weak. These financial difficulties led to the strengthening of the denominational system of education and the increase in the numbers of private schools.

The educational opportunities available to the black population in most places, did expand considerably after the abolition of slavery. Facilities, however, remained insufficient with respect to popular demand and the ideals projected by radical thinkers and social reformers. One immediate consequence of such opportunities, notes Brereton, was the increase in literacy, and the emergence of a professional elite within the black community. The implications for class formation were very significant. For the very first time in Caribbean history, Brereton shows, social mobility for non-whites was seen as an option based upon merit in addition to white patronage. Blacks became teachers, lawyers, politicians, writers and medical practitioners, professions hitherto monopolized by whites and a few of their coloured offspring. In some places social mobility was also based upon economic accumulation within the business community.

It was not difficult, then, to speak of social progress for a section of the emancipated community, which for the first time was clearly divided by internal class considerations. These essays examine the background to public policy formulation, the difficulties of implementation, as well as their impact upon social structure and class formation.

Social and Economic Obstacles to the Development of Popular Education in Post-Emancipation Jamaica 1834–1865

C. Campbell

Slavery and the formal education of the slaves were considered incompatible by the slave owners in Jamaica. The abolition of slavery, although not complete in 1834, provided the first opportunity for a mass provision of day schools for negro children on the island. The main impetus to develop such a programme came from England — from the swell of British philanthropy, Protestant missionary zeal, and from a conscience-aroused government.

Between 1835–45 an annual subsidy of £30,000, reduced gradually after 1841, was made available to the Mico Charity and the missionary societies by the British government.[1] Each year the missionary societies — the Scottish Missionary Society, the Moravian Missionary Society, the Church Missionary Society, the Society of the Propagation of the Gospel in Foreign Parts, the London Missionary Society, the Baptist Missionary Society, the Wesleyan Missionary Society[2] and the non-denominational Mico Charity[3] — submitted development plans for popular education in the West Indies. The agreement was for the British government to meet two-thirds of the cost of erecting new schoolhouses, and a moiety of the salaries of some teachers.[4] The missionary societies were to find the remainder of the cost from whatever sources they could command. Most of the funds of the missionary school promoters in Jamaica emanated from religious and philanthropic groups in England, and from religious supporters in the colony. The government of Jamaica gave the missionaries little or no funds for education between 1834–44, and after 1845, as before this date, it offered most of its meagre aid to the schools of the Church of England.

The achievement in the field of popular education in the post-emancipation years was more remarkable for the expansion of facilities for schooling than for any growth in the quality of education. In any education system it is easier to increase the number of school places than to raise the standard of education. This was particularly the case in Jamaica, because many of the facilities

essential for popular education were being developed for the first time. The availability of a British subsidy to competing missionaries and clergymen of the Church of England, whose schools were not required to meet any established standard of attainment, resulted in a fairly rapid multiplication of small denominational day schools for the masses. The denominations, apart from the Mico Charity, were the only agencies owning schoolhouses and conducting popular schools in Jamaica; schools were therefore a vital means of recruiting church members[5] and it was felt to be more important to have as many schools as could be afforded, than to have good, but fewer, schools. Anglican clergymen, as well as dissenting missionaries, consistently subordinated schools to churches, children to adults, and teachers to ministers of the gospel. Perhaps the most fundamental obstacle to quality was that those who planned and controlled popular day schools had too limited a view of the social purpose of these schools, and for this reason could not see the wisdom of investing heavily in them. Negro parents also contributed to the low standards of the schools by not sending their children regularly to classes.[6] Irregular attendance was usual not only because parents were uneducated and unaccustomed to the idea of schooling, but also because some of them recognized the educational shortcomings of the schools.

Every assessment of the work of the schools by inspectors not in the employ of the churches amounted to a strong indictment of the quality of teaching and the methods of learning. The exception to this was the Latrobe Report, written by Peter Latrobe, the British government inspector of schools who visited Jamaica in 1837. After only four years of popular education, Latrobe felt it unwise to be sharply critical of the schools. At any rate he tended to accept the outlook of the clerical school promoters. As he saw it, 'in the present state of education in Jamaica every class of schools must be considered a blessing as long as they tend to impress moral and religious principles upon the minds of the coloured population'.[7]

In 1846, Jasper Cargill, the first inspector of schools in the service of the government of Jamaica, severely criticized the attainment of children, even in religious knowledge[8], the major subject on the curriculum of the schools. Worse yet, Mr. Savage, another government inspector, could write of the schools he had examined in 1864:

it happens, that after a child has spent 5 or 6 of the best years of his life dabbling with bare words and dry abstract figures, he has to enter the business of life with scarcely a single practical principle or intelligent thought, derived from his schooling, to enable him successfully to cope with its difficulties, and attain if only to a plain but decent standing in society. His education for all useful purposes to him has been a complete failure, and he like thousands before him, sinks into the condition of the illiterate and uneducated.[9]

When Savage made this comment he had just returned from a tour of 289 schools in the island. Of these he rated 154 in the fourth or last class, 110 in the third class, 17 in the second class, and 8 in the first class. Some of the first class schools, Savage confessed, had been assigned to that class by courtesy.[10]

Though quality lagged behind quantity in the development of popular education, provision was never made for even a majority of the children of school age. The school statistics of the period are not accurate, partly because of the brief existence of some of the schools and also because of the failure of teachers to keep proper records of pupils. In 1834 there were only 7 day schools for popular education.[11] Three years later this number leaped to 183 schools,[12] and in 1846 Jasper Cargill counted 178 schools with an average daily attendance of 9,530 children.[13] At this time Cargill was able to estimate from the last census that there were 75,558 children between the ages of 5–14. In 1864, Savage calculated from the 1861 census that there was a total of 110,538 children between the ages of 5–15. The total number of popular schools in 1864 was about 490, and there were 18,850 children in average daily attendance.[14]

Growth of schools between 1834–64

Year	No. of schools	Average daily attendance	No. of children 5–14 years
1834	7	—	—
1837	183	—	—
1846	178	9,530	75,558
1864	490	18,850	110,538 (between 5–15 yrs)

The fundamental obstacles to qualitative and quantitative development of education in post-emancipation Jamaica were social and economic. Like the mass of the English people,[15] the negro ex-slaves never evolved genuine schools of their own. The native Baptists, the most authentically indigenous religious body in Jamaica,[16] failed to build any schools. Schools were provided for the negroes from above, by their social superiors, who were almost always Englishmen or white creoles in the island. For this reason, and also because provision of day schools for the masses in England had a headstart of scarcely thirty years,[17] a programme of popular education in Jamaica had no chance of being un-English. The denominations, Anglican and dissenters, which undertook to build schoolhouses and conduct schools for the masses in Jamaica were the same agency which had pioneered popular education in England.[18] They did not feel the necessity to think out an original philosophy of education for Jamaica because they already had one for the English masses which was applicable, so it was thought, to the Jamaican masses.

Despite the early phase of the industrial revolution, and the Reform Bill of 1832, the prevailing notion in the 1830s of how English society should be organized was still largely medieval. The primary duty of the lower classes was to work, to be contented with their lot and to respect their social superiors. The existing popular culture of the English masses was completely set aside as 'idle and trivial',[19] and useful skills of reading, writing and arithmetic, together with simple craft work and a tremendous amount of moral and religious instruction, with a strong emphasis on the virtue of obedience to social superiors, were the staple of the schools. There was another kind of education available in England: this was of course the classical humanist education of the grammar schools and universities. But this was for gentlemen.

The British government as well as the missionary societies conceived of a programme of popular education in Jamaica as the path to moral reformation rather than as a lever of upward social mobility. By giving missionaries and Anglican clergymen a free hand in conducting schools, the British government signified its acceptance of the clerical conception of the purpose of popular education. Of the more influential members of the Colonial Office staff immediately after emancipation, Lord Glenelg, James Stephen and Sir George Grey shared the evangelican sentiments of the missionary societies. To these men, to the British government, and to the missionary societies, moral reformation for the negro ex-slaves was more important than secular knowledge, and social stability more vital than social change.

The government of Jamaica in the post-emancipation years was typical of what has been called the 'old representative system'.[20] The central government consisted of a Governor, an elected House of Assembly and a nominated Legislative Council which also acted as a Privy Council.[21] In theory the direction of colonial government was the business of the Governor, but in practice the initiative and power of government had long passed to the House of Assembly. The hold which the Assembly had upon the island was strengthened, at the level of the 22 parishes, by vestries which possessed large taxative and administrative powers over parochial affairs.[22] The working of the Assembly and vestries did not remain unaffected by emancipation. But these vital political institutions remained substantially in the hands of the white planting and mercantile interests which had stubbornly resisted the emancipation of the slaves.

Emancipation, of course, was a blow to the labour supply of the sugar plantations. And these plantations, in the view of those who ruled Jamaica, were the irreplaceable life blood of the island. The plantations in Jamaica were always voracious consumers of unskilled labour; and after 1834, as before emancipation, the planters and their attorneys were anxious to ensure an adequate supply of labour.

From at least two points of view, day schools were viewed as a threat to the plantations. There was still a role for the 'little gang'[23] on the plantations; and during the apprenticeship[24] the most consistent attitude of the planting interest towards the 'free children',[25] was that they should be incorporated into the apprenticeship and forced to work like the apprentices.[26] What was more frightening to the planters, however, was the prospect that the next generation of negroes, undisciplined by the rigour of plantation slavery, might have their alleged distaste for agriculture sharpened by exposure to literacy. Since the curriculum of the denominated day schools was literary and not agricultural, there were widespread fears on the part of the white upper classes that book learning would stimulate the negro's ambition for white collar jobs[27] and upward social mobility. As a rule the stronger the interest of the upper classes in the persistence of the plantation system, the greater the likelihood that they would disapprove of the development of any kind of education which might present lower class children with alternatives to plantation work. It was easier for the British government and the missionaries, who were less committed to the plantation system, to accept upward social mobility of some negroes, even if

their schools were not designed principally to produce this result.

The ruling class in Jamaica could not prevent schools and chapels from springing into existence. Missionaries and clergymen had money from the British government, and from their denominational supporters abroad and within the island. The British government stood ready, in the name of religious liberty, to protect the missionaries from oppressive legislation by the Jamaica Assembly; in fact the back of open, hostile resistance to the work of missionaries had already been broken in the years immediately before emancipation.[28] The question which faced the ruling class was whether they should attempt to influence or control the day school movement, or stand aside and allow it to run its course. What happened was that the ruling class, in the hope of turning the teaching of the schools to the service of the plantations, attempted to influence the school movement by calling for agricultural education and by allotting most of the government grants to the church it trusted most: the Church of England. But the ruling class refused to pay for any efficient system of popular educating, whoever controlled it or whatever was its purpose.

With the exception of a few Baptist missionaries,[29] the clerical school promoters in Jamaica, as well as the British government and the ruling class in the colony, had limited views of the social purpose of educating negroes. It followed that they were not prepared to spend substantial sums of money on schools for the ex-slaves. Missionaries and clergymen spent more money on their churches than on their schools. When in tight financial corners, they tended to cut back on their schools rather than on their churches. The financial partnership between clerical school promoters and the British government was never on solid ground: by 1838 the missionary societies were the first side of the partnership to weaken[30] and the scheme collapsed in 1841 when the British government, after only six years,[31] disavowed any long-term responsibility for education in the West Indies.

In 1841 the British government decided to reduce its grants gradually and to cease subsidizing education in 1845.[32] The British government had paid the slave owners £20 million as compensation, and the ex-slaves had been allotted less than £300,000 for education over a ten-year period.

Popular education in both England and the West Indies needed greater attention from the British government, for the sad fact was that between 1834–41 the British government spent approximately the same amount of money on popular education in England as it did in the West Indies.[33] It would be an obvious over-simplification to maintain that in the 1840s the British government cut off the subsidy for West Indian education in order to increase the grants for popular education in England. It was true that the Secretary of State for the colonies, Lord John Russell, who agreed to end the subsidy for West Indian education, was an ardent and successful advocate[34] of increased government expenditure on, and direction of, popular education in England. If Russell had not cut the subsidy, however, some other colonial secretary would have done it.[35] The tide of imperial policy was turning against the West Indies in the 1840s. The abandonment of the subsidy for education formed a part of new and larger measures of imperial Government to further its own interest at the expense of the colonies. Less tariff protection was to be given to West Indian sugar in the interest of cheaper sugar for the consumer in England.[36] The British government was under pressure to reduce its expenditure in the colonies, and to concentrate on the social and economic needs of the English people in England.[37] From the middle of the 1840s the people in the West Indies would have to pay for their own development, and not only in the field of education. There were to be no gifts from the British government; only perhaps loans with interest.

Education for the masses was believed by the British government to be an important part of the transition from slavery to freedom. But it never sought to force the Jamaica Assembly into supporting a program of popular education. Money for education was not included in the negotiations for the abolition of slavery; the veto of power of the British government was not used[38] to influence legislation in favour of popular education. It was not on the issue of education that the British government came into conflict with the Jamaica Assembly, but about such other matters as prisons, conditions of work for the ex-slaves, and constitutional reforms.[39] Compared with these issues, education was in the back-water of metropolitan-colonial relationships.

If Jamaica was a crown colony in which the governor had both the responsibility and the power to rule, some governors, for instance, Sligo[40] and the Earl of Elgin[41] would have given a higher priority to popular education than did the Jamaica Assembly. Sir Henry Taylor, an official of the Colonial Office who advocated crown colony government in Jamaica, used the slender record of the Jamaica Assembly in education as part of the evidence of its failure to govern progressively.[42] Yet if we are to judge from the crown colonies of Trinidad and St. Lucia in the post-emancipation period, crown colony government of itself did not guarantee a high priority to education. What would be done depended on the interest and on the vision of the

governor of the crown colony, and on the possibility of satisfying the major groups interested in the matter. On the whole, the British government did not press education projects upon the colonies, whatever the nature of their constitutions. The burden or the challenge of initiating legislation on education was always in the hands of the local authorities.

In terms of financial support for education, the record of the ruling class over the years 1834–65 got slightly better, not worse. This response was due partly to the passage of time which made everybody more accustomed to the idea of schools for the masses; partly to new forces and movements in Jamaica which made it impossible to govern the island like a slave colony. The political enfranchisement of coloured men[43] led immediately to the establishment of a small party of non-white members of the Assembly. These coloured politicians were more sympathetic to the black masses than the old white planting and mercantile oligarchy.

The geographical bounds of the society expanded as thousands of negro ex-slaves moved off the coastal plantations and established themselves as peasant farmers, or at best occasional plantation workers, living on the island hills. The dissenting missionaries followed the ex-slaves into the interior of the islands in greater numbers than the Anglican clergy, and in furious denominational rivalry brought into existence chapels and schools, which the ruling class feared might produce serious social change unless subordinated to the social and economic purpose of the plantations.

A new society was in the making, and it demanded new and subtle strategies to maintain the plantation system and white political control of the island. There was a limit to the amount of coercive legislation by which the Assembly could hope to hold employers and employees in an unequal partnership to produce sugar. More money would have to be spent to rule the new Jamaica. The ex-slaves, whether on the plantations or in their provision grounds, would have to be reached and made to understand that emancipation did not mean freedom from work in general, and plantation work in particular.

Between 1834–44 the Jamaica Assembly voted little or no money for schools but it invested heavily in staffing and erecting Church of England places of worship in all the parishes of the island.[44] The argument that appropriate religious instruction could make the negroes better sugar workers, more submissive, more moral, had gained wide currency in philanthropic circles[45] in England in the years before emancipation. But as long as slaves could be coerced by the time-tried method of the whip and treadmill, the majority of the ruling class in Jamaica felt no need to believe this argument or to try the experiment. They insisted rather that religious instruction would encourage the idea of liberty.[46]

Emancipation was imposed upon the slave owners, and religious instruction of the ex-slaves then became less objectionable to the ruling class. This did not mean that they no longer believed that it had a potential to further the breakdown of the plantation system: they planned to minimize the risk while extracting whatever potential religion possessed to induce social subordination. Not all the clerical school promotors and preachers, however, could be trusted with such a delicate assignment. Clergymen of the Church of England best suited the purpose, because they were all white men, who were often related to local white planters, attorneys and merchants, and they were amenable to government control and the ecclesiastical discipline of the Bishop of Jamaica, with salaries of clergymen and money for church buildings coming mostly from public revenues.

To a lesser extent the conservative dissenters, i.e. the Moravians, some of the Methodists and a few of the Presbyterians, could be aided with smaller grants for the same reason as the Church of England. But the less conservative Independents,[47] and the radical Baptists, native and European, had to be contained by Church of England competition, and prevented from capturing the religious and political allegiance of the black masses.

The vestries also put their trust in the Church of England, and for the same reasons as the Assembly. But as far as education was concerned, the alliance between vestries and the established church proved more fruitful, because the vestries, unlike the Assembly, had a tradition of providing for schools, and they felt morally bound to support the institutions of the Church of England which were organized on a parochial base. The vestry and the local Anglican chapel were the foci of white upper class parochial loyalties and this narrow allegiance, before 1834 and long afterwards, made the provision of formal education a matter for the vestries rather than the Assembly.

The superior role of local government in education can be seen clearly from the history of the endowed[48] schools and parochial schools. In the 18th century, and even in the early 19th century,[49] a number of wealthy plantation owners had bequeathed money to endow schools for poor white boys and girls of their parish. Legislation by the Jamaica Assembly implementing[50] these bequests usually gave the parish in which the benefactor resided control of the management of the endowed schools. For this reason, and also because the pupils of these schools were usually restricted to parishioners, the endowed schools became in effect parochial institutions. Vestries in the early 19th century also accepted some responsibility for parochial poor relief[51] and a few parochial schools for children of poor white and free coloured parentage developed.[52] Such parochial schools as institutions ranked with the parochial poor house. But they fortified the parochial sense of accountability for schooling of the poor in the parish.

After emancipation, the Bishop of Jamaica turned first to the vestries, not to the Assembly, for funds to support a programme of 'national schools'.[53] He succeeded in getting some vestries to assist him with land for school sites, money towards building and usually a commitment to meet a part of the teachers' salaries.[54] It was only insofar as the Bishop made such agreements with vestries that there was any integration between the use of the British subsidy for education and any organ of government in Jamaica. The Bishop's strategy was to use the promise of money from the vestries to assure the society for the propagation of the gospel that the Anglican church could find the money to back the British subsidy; and in turn he dangled before the vestries the prospect of getting assistance from the society and the British government. The result was that up to 1845 at least, more money for popular education came from the vestries than from the Assembly, although all vestries, like the Assembly, invested more heavily in churches and clergymen of the Church of England than in their schools and their teachers.

It was unfortunate that the vestries should have taken the lead in financing education from public revenues, for they were poorly positioned to deal with the task of developing education in a religiously divided society. Each vestry did not look beyond the boundaries of the parish, and within the parish it tended to assist only the Church of England's schools. The dissenters who had set the pace in popular education could not find any satisfaction in vestry control over the development of education in the colony. Their best hope for assistance lay in the Assembly.

The Assembly was affected earlier than the vestries by new political forces which complicated the white settlers' problems of governing the colony. The freedom of the slaves had been followed by the political enfranchisement of men of colour who outnumbered the whites in the island. By 1835 the coloured men had made a tiny dent in the amount of white planting and mercantile monopoly of the Assembly. Messrs. Osborn and Jordon, the first coloured assemblymen in the history of the island, took their seats[55] in 1835. This trend towards coloured men winning seats in the Assembly became established in the post-emancipation period. A growing number of coloured men, together with a few Jewish merchants, formed the legislative arm of the so-called 'Town Party'.[56] These men often had a wider and more generous conception of Jamaica's needs than the older planter-mercantile oligarchy.

The full effect of the Town Party, and particularly the coloured core of the party, upon the political life of the island have not yet been unravelled. It seems safe to assume that the participation of coloured men in politics tempered the political performance of the white ruling class; and in the field of popular education the coloured politicians and the Town Party stood from 1834 to 1865 for increased government grants, and increased government supervision. Governor Sligo saw this in 1836, for he informed the British government in a private despatch[57] that the best hope for popular education in the Assembly lay with the Town Party. Osborn, Jordon and Richard Hill, all coloured assemblymen in the 1830s, showed an interest in education. But the energies of the Town Party until 1838 went into the defence of the apprenticeship policy of the British government and Governors Sligo and Sir Lionel Smith. In the 1840s and 1850s, however, Osborn, Jordon and Hill[58] and another coloured politician, the wealthy George William Gordon[59] of Morant Bay fame, were among the leaders of the town Party's efforts to get increased government subsidy for popular education.

These efforts failed, for the Town Party and the coloured politicians lacked political power for most of the period.[60] If they had had it securely they would have increased the government subsidy for education, but not on a scale adequate to give every child, or even the majority of children, a school place. The increases which they supported were pitiably small in absolute terms: in 1844 Osborn and Jordon voted[61] for £2,000 instead of £1,000, and in 1855 Jordon[62] fought for £6,000 instead of £3,000. It was not the age of the welfare state in England, and colonial ideas on social legislation were never ahead of the mother country. At any rate the coloured politicians, always prone to ambivalent social behaviour and attitudes, were not free from the white bias that was built into Jamaica society by centuries of white power and superior influence and black slavery and humiliation. Because of their racial affinity to the black masses, because some of them were not sugar planters blind to social and economic alternatives, because they were largely dependent on the votes

of the non-white electorate, the coloured politicians had a more liberal view of the existing needs and the future role of the ex-slaves in Jamaica. But their programme was primarily political,[63] and they probably would not have supported a campaign for equal access to equal schools for all classes. The move towards creation of a society in which a government would make educational opportunity available to all irrespective of race and class, would have to await the democratization of the politics of the island.

Notes

1. For correspondence on the British subsidy, or, as it was called, the Negro Education Grant, see C.O. 318/122, 318/126, 318/130–1, 318/138–9, 318/145, 318/152, 318/156, 318/163. P.R.O.
2. The following abbreviations are used: B.M.S., Baptist Missionary Society; L.M.S., London Missionary Society; M.M.S., Moravian Missionary Society; W.M.S., Wesleyan Missionary Society; S.P.G., Society for Propagation of the Gospel.
3. Founded in July 1835 as a non-denominational trust for education of Negroes in the West Indies. For early history of the Lady Mico bequest see report of trustees of Mico Charity, 1838. C.O. 318/138.
4. Grey to secretaries of missionary societies, 18 March 1835. C.O. 318/122.
5. Minutes of annual meeting of Jamaica District, 17 January 1839. S/M 1838–41. Methodist School Records, Archives of Jamaica.
6. Latrobe. 1837. *Negro Education in Jamaica*, p. 12. Also report of Jasper Cargill for 1846, p. 11, appendix II. Votes of the House of Assembly, 11 December 1846.
7. Latrobe, *Negro Education in Jamaica*, p.14.
8. Report of Jasper Cargill, pp. 8–9.
9. Report of Inspector Savage, appendix 46. Votes of House of Assembly, November 1864 — April 1865.
10. *Ibid.*
11. Sligo to Glenelg, 19 January 1835. Enclosures: returns of schools. C.O. 137/197.
12. Latrobe, *Negro Education in Jamaica*, pp. 72–3. Recapitulation and appendix to Schedule B.
13. Report of Jasper Cargill, p. 27.
14. Report of Inspector Savage.
15. Clarke, Fred. 1940. *Education and Social Change — an English interpretation*, London, p. 40.
16. Black, Clinton. 1958. *History of Jamaica*, London, p. 109.
17. Curtis, S.J. 1948. *History of Education in Great Britain*, London, pp. 206–23.
18. *Ibid.*
19. Clarke. *Education and Social Change — an English interpretation*, p. 30.
20. Wrong, Hume. 1923. *Government of the West Indies*, Oxford, pp. 36–45.
21. Hall, Douglas. 1959. *Free Jamaica, 1838–1865: An Economic History*, New Haven.
22. *Ibid.*, p. 6.
23. *Ibid.*, p. 45. Sometimes the gang of young children was augmented by old people.
24. The apprenticeship was the period (1834–40) which the slaves had to sere before full emancipation. It came to an end in 1838 instead of 1840.
25. The 'free children' were those of six years and under on 1 August 1834. The Abolition Act exempted them from forced labour.

26. Sligo to Glenelg, 19 February 1836. Enclosures: letters from the custodes. C.O. 137/209.
27. *Six Essays on the Best Mode of Establishing and Conducting Industrial Schools adopted to the wants and circumstances of an Agricultural Population* London (1845). See in particular the winning essay of Mr. Lyndon Evelyn of Savanna-La-Mar.
28. Curtin, Philip. 1955. *Two Jamaicas: The Role of Ideas in a Tropical Colony, 1830–1865,* Cambridge, Mass., pp. 87–9.
29. James Phillippo, a Baptist missionary, proposed a university college open to all races. But it was not to be supported by government funds. See Phillippo, J.M. 1843. *Jamaica: Its Past and Present State,* London.
30. Beecham of W.M.S. to Grey, 12 May 1837 and 7 June 1838. C.O. 318/139.
31. Vernon Smith to secretaries of missionary societies, 18 March 1841. C.O. 318/152.
32. *Ibid.*
33. Curtis, *History of Education in Great Britain,* pp. 223–37.
34. Walpole, S. 1889. *The Life of Lord John Russell, vol. I, p. 229.*
35. There was general agreement in the Colonial Office in 1841 that the subsidy should be terminated. James Stephen, using the Baptists as an example, speculated that education could prosper without the subsidy. C.O. 318/152, 424.
36. Augier, F.R. *et al.* 1960. *The Making of the West Indies,* London, p. 193.
37. *Ibid.*
38. The British Government did this successfully in Dominica. See Colebroke to Lord John Russell, 18 July 1840. C.O. 71/93. Also Russell to Macphael, 20 February 1841. C.O. 71/94.
39. Black. *History of Jamaica,* p. 184.
40. Sligo claimed that one of his reasons for dissolving the Assembly on 6 February 1836 was its failure to do anything for the education of the apprentices. See Sligo to Glenelg, 5 February 1836. Enclosure: speech to the Assembly. C.O. 137/209.
41. Elgin to Stanley (confidential) 3 August 1845. C.O. 137/284. Elgin's policy in education was to teach agriculture as a science.
42. Barkly to the Duke of Newcastle, 21 February 1854. Analysis of returns of stipendiary magistrates by Taylor. C.O. 137/322.
43. Black. *History of Jamaica,* p. 157.
44. Votes of House of Assembly, 1 March 1838. Session December 1837 — March 1838. Also Votes of House of Assembly, 7 April 1840. Session October 1839 — April 1840.
45. Porteus, Bishop of London. 1808. *An Appeal to Governors, Legislatures and Proprietors of plantations in the British West Indies,* London, pp. 22–5.
46. Curtin. *Two Jamaicas: The Role of Ideas in a Tropical Colony, 1830–1865,* pp. 87–9. The Jamaica slave revolt of 1831–2 was attributed by planters to the teaching of dissenting missionaries.
47. The Independents were the missionaries sent out by the L.M.S.
48. In the post-emancipation period there were nine endowed schools: Beckford's (St. Catherine); Walton (St. Ann); Mannings (Westmoreland); Rusea's (Hanover); St. James Free School (St. James); Smith's (St. Catherine); Titchfield (Portland); Vere (Vere); Wolmers (Kingston). There ought to have been one called Munro and Dickenson School, but the trustees stole a large part of the endowment. See Votes of House of Assembly, appendix 6. First Report of Charity Commissioners. Elgin to Stanley, 21 November 1844. C.O. 137/280.
49. The money to found Smith's (St. Catherine) was left in 1830. First Report of Charity Commissioners.
50. *Ibid.*
51. Duncker, Sheila. 1960. *The Free Coloured and the fight for Civil Rights in Jamaica, 1800–1834.* Unpublished MA thesis for London University, pp. 132–8.
52. *Ibid.*
53. The Title which the Church of England assumed for its schools.
54. Bishop of Jamaica to Secretary of S.P.G., 1 June 1836. Also Rev. G.D. Hill to secretary of S.P.G., 22 March 1838. Also table showing grants of moieties of salaries from local sources. Jamaica, 1838. S.P.G. Archives, London.
55. Votes of House of Assembly, 10 November 1835. *St. Jago de La Vega Gazette,* 7–14 November 1835.
56. Hall. *Free Jamaica,* pp. 7–8. Abrahams, Peter. 1957. *Jamaica, An Island Mosaic,* London, p. 89.
57. Sligo to Glenelg (private), 31 December 1835. C.O. 137/205.
58. *Falmouth Post,* 14 December 1849, editorial. *Falmouth Post,* 11 January 1850, editorial. *Falmouth Post,* 28 and 31 October 1856. Also Votes of House of Assembly, November-December 1856, appendix 15. Proposals of Richard Hill.
59. *Falmouth Post,* 18 November 1856. Gordon combined his concern for education with his non-conformist religious zeal by proposing at a public meeting in Kingston a tax upon alcoholic beverages to underwrite a higher government subsidy for popular education.
60. Abrahams. *Jamaica, An Island Mosiac,* p. 107. He claims that the Town Party won a majority in the Assembly at the 1864 elections.
61. Votes of House of Assembly, 17 December 1844. Session October-December 1844.
62. *Falmouth Post,* 6 November 1855. Speech of Jordon in presenting the Education Bill.
63. Hall. *Free Jamaica,* p. 8.

The Development of Medical Services In British Guiana and Trinidad 1841–1873

K.O. Laurence

One of the earliest problems with which the governments of British Guiana and Trinidad had to cope when they first accepted responsibility for introducing immigrants into their respective territories after emancipation was that of providing medical attention for the sick. Public hospitals existed in both Georgetown and Port-of-Spain, but there was no public health service in the country districts, where medical attention of any sort was difficult, sometimes impossible to find. Yet the accepted official view was that since government was encouraging immigrants to come, under contract, from places as far afield as India and later China, government had a duty to see that when these immigrants fell ill they were able to make contact with a qualified medical practitioner, and to get his advice without having to consider its cost. Experience soon proved that it was useless to rely on the employers to provide such medical attention in the belief that it was to their advantage to see that their labourers maintained good health. Despite government exhortations to the employers, which were supported by the colonial press,[1] and advice to the immigrants to take work only on estates which provided adequate medical attention for the sick, Lord Harris reported in 1846 that many Trinidad planters provided only 'the cheapest and worst medical advice if any at all'.[2] The Coolie Magistrate described the arrangements as 'utterly inadequate'.[3] Conditions in British Guiana were no different. If the governments of the two colonies were going to take seriously their supposed obligation to ensure that medical attention should be available to all contract immigrants, they had only two alternatives: they could undertake to provide medical attention themselves, through some form of public health service, or they could pass legislation to compel the employers to provide it. The idea of a system of public district hospitals to which sick immigrants could easily be admitted found much favour both with the Colonial Secretary, Lord Grey, and with the Governor of British Guiana, Sir Henry Light. It was frequently mooted in the years 1847 to 1850, but always it was

deemed too expensive for the then impoverished colonial governments; when revised in 1866 it was similarly brushed aside. Thus both colonies were reduced to using compulsion on the employers.

It was British Guiana who led the way in establishing an effective medical system for immigrants. She had of course the more serious problem, since her immigrant population was much larger than Trinidad's and the rate of sickness among her Portuguese immigrants was far higher than anything in Trinidad's experience. The Georgetown hospital was chronically overcrowded: since immigration had attained large proportions in 1841 it had often had to pack 300 or 400 patients, most of them Portuguese or East Indians, into accommodation designed for 200.[4] Therefore in March 1847 the Court of Policy passed an Ordinance 'to provide medical attendance and medicine for immigrant labourers', which obliged employers of immigrants to maintain a hospital on each estate and employ a doctor to visit it every 48 hours. Sick immigrants could be compelled to enter the hospital though Lord Grey warned the stipendiary magistrate to watch carefully for any abuse of this power.[5]

It was many months before every estate had its hospital. In January 1848 the system was 'as yet incomplete';[6] only 98 out of 220 estates had hospitals in operation, 24 more being under construction, and the government's medical advisor report that in practice three medical visits each week were not always sufficient.[7] When the Hospital Ordinance was amended in 1848 nothing was done to increase the frequency of the doctor's visits, but the allocation of new immigrants to estates without hospitals was forbidden.[8] When the planters began to grumble about the expense of the system Lord Grey replied that he was willing to agree that a compulsory contribution towards its cost should be introduced with regard to immigrants who had been in the colony for more than two years; but in view of the strong opposition which this would inevitably have aroused among the immigrants, who commonly preferred to go without medical advice rather than pay for it, it was never adopted.[9] However the enormous incidence of sickness and mortality among immigrants in the past few years had made such an impression on the employers in general that most of them seemed ready to make at least some effort to comply with the law.[10]

Subsequently the system of estate hospitals in British Guiana worked fairly well for several years. Most of the planters and managers gave their full co-operation. But of course the large number of vagrant immigrants who were not regularly employed on any particular estate were beyond its scope, and while in practice negro labourers were usually allowed to make use of the hospital of an estate for which they worked regularly, this was entirely by courtesy of the employers. Their legal obligation applied only to immigrants working under contract. Among the various estate hospitals, too, there was no common standard, and the arrangements for inspections were defective.[11] In 1853 it was reported that in many cases the visits of the estate doctors were so hurried that they frequently left without seeing any sick immigrants who might have remained in their own homes.[12] Information concerning the health of the immigrants is haphazard, and only partially reliable;[13] among Indian immigrants mortality was usually heavy during the first 18 months after their arrival, before they became 'acclimatized';[14] but otherwise the general average was reasonably low during the 1840s. Official estimates of 3.6% per annum[15] were probably too low, but there is no doubt that but for the system of estate hospitals introduced in 1847 the rate would have been much higher than it was. In 1859 a new Hospitals Ordinance was passed, laying down that each hospital was to have a nurse and a certain minimum standard of equipment; a Medical Inspector of Estates' Hospitals was appointed to visit each hospital every six months; each hospital was to keep a register, and provision was made for serious cases to be moved to the public hospital in Georgetown. Still only immigrants were legally entitled to treatment — it was considered unfair to impose on the employers the medical charge of the general population. And while in practice most estates hospitals remained open to all estate workers, the inhabitants of the negro villages who worked elsewhere found that medical attention was still largely beyond their reach.[16] But many estates spent large sums of bringing their hospitals up to the standard now required.[17] And by 1864 the system, within its limitations, was working tolerably well.[18]

In Trinidad however not only was there no regular system of estates' hospitals, but some remote estates were beyond the normal reach of doctors. Lord Grey in 1850 had given instructions that no immigrant labour should be allocated to such estates, but these do not appear to have been strictly observed.[19] In 1862 investigations revealed that there were occasions when an employer, with his eye on his pocket would wait until the last possible moment, by which time the immigrant had become seriously ill, before sending him to the public hospital — moreover immigrants frequently resisted entering hospital. Vagrant immigrants often became very distressed for lack of medical attention, and the Agent General for Immigration believed that during the wet season half the immigrants on an estate might well be ill at any one time.[20] The medical arrangements in Trinidad, under which each estate was supposed to engage a doctor to pay regular visits either once or twice a week, were clearly inadequate: in 1850 doctors were to be found only in the towns of Port-of-Spain, San Fernando, Couva and St. Joseph, since elsewhere the general indifference to medical advice made it difficult for them to earn a living;[21] by 1862 this situation had improved very little.[22] To provide more doctors would have involved the creation of government medical posts, which no one yet envisaged; but it was clear that a great improvement could be effected by establishing a system of estate hospitals on the Guianese model. Even this however would have meant heavy expenditure, if not to the government at least to the employers; so the government contented itself with appealing to the employers to honour their obligations.[23]

This brought little change until in 1865 Trinidad at last passed an Ordinance which provided for the erection of estate hospitals; though in order to save the planters' pockets this was not made compulsory, as it had been from the first in British Guiana. Only now were powers taken to compel sick immigrants to enter even a public hospital, though the need for them had been obvious for years.[24] In the following year, 1866, Trinidad at last began to approach really seriously the medical care of her immigrant population, and attempted to emulate the Guianese system. The able Agent General for Immigration, Henry Mitchell, now insisted that provision of estate hospitals should be made compulsory, and the requisite Hospitals Ordinance was passed. The Agent General's efforts to improve the service were supported, and sometimes improved on, by Sir Arthur Gordon, one of the few able men to govern Trinidad during the nineteenth century, and one who made the welfare of the immigrants his special concern. Now that the employers had proved unwilling to erect estate hospitals voluntarily under the 1865 law, the Council proved quite willing to sanction compulsion. In 1865 they had attempted to make employers pay for the treatment of their immigrant labourers at one of the two public hospitals with a view to encouraging them to provide estate hospitals; but in practice this had combined with a general apathy, difficulties of transport and the employer's reluctance to spare their labourers, to delay in sending immigrants to the public hospitals until they became seriously ill.[25]

But even now Trinidad's medical regulations with regard to sick immigrants remained much less detailed than British Guiana's, whose enforcement machinery was much more elaborate. Trinidad relied on a system of inspection, and the Governor's power to remove immigrants from estates which failed to comply with the law, and her Ordinance depended for maximum effect upon the co-operation of the planters. In British Guiana wide range of penalties was provided for neglect in the hospitals. In Trinidad only two medical visits were required each week as against three in British Guiana, and even so it seemed very likely that for sheer lack of doctors many estates would receive only one, in future as in the past. Nevertheless, immediately after the new Ordinance was passed six employers ordered the construction of hospitals on over 30 estates, a good augury; by the beginning of 1867, 92 of the 155 estates in Trinidad had their own hospitals, 50 more were under construction, and the remaining 13 had chosen to cease employing indentured labour rather than erect hospitals. Planters employing large numbers of indentured immigrants soon realized the advantages of the new scheme, though some of the smaller employers naturally complained of the expense involved in building and equipping hospitals.[26]

A year later Henry Mitchell stated that most of the estate hospitals in Trinidad were well built, though not all were well appointed. Of 104 which had been inspected, only four had less than two wards, and although 14 had no cleaning utensils, 10 neither kitchens nor sanitary conveniences, and a few no drains, all but one were well sited and well ventilated.[27] They proved extremely valuable and the planters spent much money ungrudgingly on them.[28] In January 1868, a new set of regulations for the management of estate hospitals was issued, calculated to remedy the deficiencies which had been noted.[29] Trinidad's medical facilities for immigrants were now roughly comparable to those in British Guiana.

Immigrant mortality in British Guiana was always higher than in any other West Indian colony — it was in general the most unhealthy of them all — but following the reorganization of the hospital system the mortality rate was said to have fallen from 10% in 1861 to 4.4% in 1866.[30] Prob-ably the proportionate fall which these figures illustrate is not much exaggerated, and the 1866 rate was considered satisfactory at the time. It is beyond dispute that the immigrant mortality rate fell sharply in the 1860s and that the provision of better medical attention was the most important factor in this development. The Commission of Inquiry which investigated the immigration system in British Guiana in 1870 concluded that the hospital system was perhaps the brightest star on the Guianese immigrant's horizon.[31] In 1859, on his very first tour of inspection, Dr. Shier, Medical Inspector of Estates' Hospitals, found the buildings in much better condition than might have been expected, though ill-ventilated and very short of trained nurses. In November 1859 minimum hospital standards were laid down, requiring at least ten beds, plus five more for every hundred immigrants on the estate, and separate wards for the two sexes. Buildings of all sorts were used as hospitals, but by 1870 'the old ill-adopted buildings' were being superseded by hospitals built for the purpose. Particularly good hospitals were found on De Kinderen and Hampton Court estates. Though the Commissioners in 1870 found several bad hospitals and all sorts of minor defects in the service, 'yet the system taken as a whole must be considered a credit to the colony'. Most of the bad hospitals were found on estates which were either insolvent, on lease or up for sale.[32]

Many hospitals had rather less than their prescribed complement of beds, and the space allowed for each was often less than the required 100 square feet. There had been many instances of hospitals with more patients than beds; in November 1867 Shier found 79 patients in 43 beds Versailles. In other respects estate hospitals were often inadequately equipped. But the government had not been entirely apathetic; in extreme cases new allocations of immigrants had been withheld pending improvement of the hospital. Some estates, like Providence, had proved most recalcitrant in this matter; those in financial difficulties, like Good Hope, Annandale, and Belle Plaine, had been prone to economize on the hospital, and the Medical Inspector had sometimes acquiesced. The Commissioners thought that estates which could not afford to maintain an adequate hospital should be relieved of their immigrants. The law requiring all hospitals to have baths was 'utterly neglected', notably on Hope and Experiment and De Kinderen estates, and even where they were provided it was evident that they were almost never used. Only Enmore had a bathroom efficiently supplied with water.[33]

Many estates had also departed from the hospital diet as laid down by law, usually by issuing short rations, and though the Medical Inspector had discovered 20 cases of this abuse over a period of three years, he had never done more than issue empty threats of prosecution. The hospitals needed to keep more exact records, and to employ better qualified nurses; of the 118 'head nurses' in 1870, 25 held no qualification whatever. The doctors' obligations to visit each estate every 48 hours was very generally honoured, the required frequency often being exceeded, but certain serious cases of neglect had been allowed to pass unnoticed, and one had been put right only after two years' delay and four letters from the government. Most doctors regarded themselves as responsible only for visiting and not, as the law had clearly intended, for the general condition of the hospitals they visited. Allegations against the doctors in general of neglect, and gross servility to the managers of the estates who employed them, were unfounded, but the hospital system, for all its merits, was clearly capable of greatly improved efficiency, and to this end the Commissioners recommended that in future the doctors should be paid by and responsible to the government.[34]

Such a system had already been introduced in Trinidad, where under the 1870 Immigration Ordinance government medical officers had been appointed to take over the care of sick immigrants, with a view to achieving a more efficient and more easily controlled service. The existing fifteen estate doctors became government officers, paid from funds appropriated to immigration, (which came largely from taxes paid specifically by planters) in proportion to the size and number of the estate hospitals under their charge. The doctors were paid £30 to £50 per annum in respect of each hospital, a rate which usually amounted to between 12 and 15% less than their previous earnings; but they were free to make up this difference by private practice among the proprietors and managerial staff of the estates, and their families, who had previously been covered by the general estate arrangements. The island was divided into fifteen districts, based on groups of the local authority areas (wards), with one doctor to each. These District Medical Officers also acted as Sanitary Inspectors.[35] By making the doctors responsible to the government rather than to the very employers against whose interest they might need to act in attending to the immigrant labourers, the new arrangements placed the doctors for the first time in a position effectively to enforce their instructions.[36]

In British Guiana the proposals of the Commission of Inquiry for reform of the medical service were considered at great length. The government was anxious to retain the goodwill of the doctors

and as there were twenty-three of them in British Guiana who earned through the estate hospitals incomes ranging from £1,018 for a practice spread over ten estates to £104 from a single estate, their attitudes differed. In July 1871 Governor Scott submitted a plan for a government medical service which would serve not only the indentured immigrants but the whole population, based on a series of medical districts drawn with regard to area rather than the incidence of estates, as had been done in Trinidad. Scott proposed to create twenty-five medical districts; three which contained only scattered villages would be placed in the care of dispensers at salaries of £300 a year, the others would have medical officers who were to be paid £800 each, and three *locos tenentes* were to be employed at £350 a year. To finance this scheme Scott proposed to pay about £4,135 from the government's revenue and to raise the balance through a capitation tax of 7s.3½d. a year on indentured immigrants, to be paid by the employers.[37]

These proposals were opposed by some estate mangers who thought they represented undue interference by the government in private concerns, by others who employed so many immigrants that their payment in respect of the capitation tax was likely to exceed the salary paid to the doctor under the old system, and by many doctors who seemed likely to suffer a reduced income. On the other hand some estates which employed few immigrants were likely to pay less for medical attention in future. The argument dragged on for many months, but Scott's proposals were eventually implemented in 1873.[38]

Thus by 1873 both British Guiana and Trinidad had a system of District Medical Officers whose prime responsibility was to take charge of the estate hospital which had been established to meet the problem of sickness among immigrants, but whose services were also available to the general population. Previously, especially in Trinidad, remote estates had found it very difficult to secure a doctor's services; now each district had its own doctor, and no estate was beyond the reasonable reach of one. The government had now accepted full responsibility for maintaining the rudiments of a medical service, and abandoned its earlier policy of trying to compel private employers to undertake this task. Experience proved that this would not suffice. Clearly this development was the direct result of the decision to spend large sums of government-sponsored immigration. After emancipation neither the imperial nor the colonial governments took any interest in the health of the former slaves. As it was no longer to the obvious economic advantage of the individual planter to provide medical attention for his labourers, and they in their turn could seldom afford it and frequently spurned it even when they could, there was little inducement to doctors to practice in the rural areas. Were it not for the arrival of the indentured immigrants this position might well have endured for much longer than it did. As it was, the imperial government felt that it could not in good conscience encourage people to migrate to colonies where their expectation of life would not be at least reasonable; since events proved that the rate of sickness among newly-arrived immigrants was always very high and sometimes politically intolerable, it followed that some form of skilled medical attention had to be provided if the immigration was to continue. Hence after 1847 the imperial government, and following it the colonial governments, always paid close attention to the provision of a reasonable medical service for sick immigrants. It was no part of their original intention to create a service for the benefit of the settled population, which in any case was usually regarded as enjoying 'good health', barring occasional outbreaks of epidemic disease; it seemed no part of their business to give such assistance to people who were not regarded as the direct responsibility of the government. But it followed naturally that one section of the population came to derive great benefit form a service created essentially for another.

Footnotes & References

1. The Port-of-Spain Gazette printed many items arguing that the planters would serve their own interests by strict attention to the health of the immigrants, e.g. 15 May 1846.
2. Colonial Office Records (C.O.) 295/152: Harris to Grey, 6 Oct. 1846, private.
3. Colonial Office Records (C.O. 295/156: Fagan to Harris, 15 Jan. 1847, enc. in Harris to Grey, 20 Jan. 1847, private.
4. Parliamentary Papers (P.P.) 1847. XXXIX. 206: Speech by Light on opening the Combined Court, 23 March 1847. P.P. 1847. XXXIX. 317–18: British Guiana Hospital Statistics, 1838–46.
5. P.P. 1847. XXXIX. 208, 211: Light to Grey, 29 March 1847, no. 58, & enc. Grey to Light, 22 June 1847, no. 187.
6. P.P. 1847–8 XXIII–iii 246: Light to Grey, 11 Jan. 1848, no. 10.
7. P.P. 1847–8 XXIII–iii. 250: Dr. Bonyun's Report on Hospitals and Immigrants, 6 Jan. 1848.
8. P.P. 1847–8 XLV. 243–6: British Guiana Ordinance No. 4/1848.
9. P.P. 1847–8 XXLV. 216–17: Light to Grey, 5 March 1848, no. 39. P.P. 1847–8. XLVI. 434–5: Grey to Light, 23 May 1848, no. 338.
10. P.P. 1847–8 XLVI. 556: Actg. Govr. Walker to Grey, 18 July 1848, private.
11. C.O. 111/324: Wodehouse to Newcastle, 22 Sept. 1859, no. 93.

12. C.O. 318/202: Caird to Colonial land and Emigration Commissioners (C.L. & E.C.), 18 March 1853, enc. in C.L. & E.C. to Merivale, 21 March 1853.
13. P.P. 1859–ii XX. 499–502. Memo by Murdoch on Indian Immigration, 18 Feb. 1859, C.O. 319/–25. Murdoch to C. Cox, 7 Sept. 1859, bound after C.L. & E.C. to Merivale, 25 Aug. 1859.
14. C.O. 318/202: Caird to C.L. & E.C., 18 March 1853, enc. in C.L.& E.C. to Merivale, 21 March 1853.
15. P.P. 1859–ii. XX. 499–502: Memo by Murdoch on Indian Immigration, 10 Feb. 1859.
16. C.O. 111/324: Wodehouse to Newcastle, 22 Sept. 1859, no. 93. C.O. 318/226: C.L. & E.C. to Merivale, 3 Nov. 1859.
17. C.O. 111/332: Actg. Govr. Walker to Newcastle, 19 Nov. 1861, no. 83 C.O. 318/235: C.L. & E.C. to Rogers, 5 Feb. 1862.
18. P.P. 1865 XXXVII. 34: Hincks to Cardwell, 6 Sept. 1864, no. 146.
19. P.P. 1852–3 LXVII. 564: Grey to Harris, 30 Oct. 1850, no. 455.
20. C.O. 295/216: Keate to Newcastle, 4 June 1862, no. 112: Newcastle to Keate, 8 Aug. 1862, no. 499 C.O. 295/219: Keate to Newcastle, 16 Sept. 1862, no. 166 & enclosure. C.O. 295/241: West India Committee to Murdoch, 7 Dec. 1863, enc. in C.L. & E.C. to Rogers, 10 Dec. 1863. P.P. 1865. XXXVII. 28–9. Enclosure in Keate to Cardwell, 4 June 1864, no. 84.
21. P.P. 1852–3. LXVII. 439: Harris to Grey, 23 Nov. 1850, no. 91.
22. In 1856 about 100 Indian immigrants on remote estates were still clearly beyond the reach of regular medical attention. P.P. 1859–i. XVI. 350: Annual Report of Agent General of Immigration for 1855.
23. C.O. 295/219: Agent General Mitchell to Colonial Secretary Cuyler, enc. in Keate to Newcastle, 16 Sept. 1862, no. 166.
24. C.O. 295/230: Manners Sutton to Cardwell, 8 March 1865, no. 32 & encs; 23 March 1865, no. 42.
25. C.O. 295/235: Actg. Govr. Rushworth to Cardwell, 20 July 1966, no. 94.
26. C.O. 295/235: Actg. Govr. Rushworth to Cardwell, 20, 23 July 1866, nos. 84, 91. Vide also J.K. Chapman, The Career of Arthur Hamilton Gordon, unpublished Ph.D. thesis, University of London, 1954, p. 224.
27. C.O. 295/240: Gordon to Buckingham, 20 Sept. 1867, no. 121.
28. C.O. 318/250: C.L. & E.C. to Rogers, 26 Nov. 1867. P.P. 1867–8. XLVIII. 43: Gordon to Buckingham, 8 Nov. 1867, no. 144.
29. C.O. 295/243: Gordon to Buckingham, 10 Jan. 1868, no. 10.
30. C.O. 295/250, 252: C.L. & E.C. to Rogers, 22 Jan. 1867, 13 June 1868.
31. P.P. 1871 XX 624: Report of Commissioners of Enquiry into Immigration in British Guiana, 1870.
32. Ibid. 625.
33. P.P. 1871. XX. 626–30: Report of Commissioners of Enquiry into Immigration in British Guiana, 1870.
34. P.P. 1871. XX. 636–60: Report of Commissioners of Enquiry into Immigration in British Guiana, 1870, passim.
35. C.O. 295/251: Gordon to Grenville, 24 June 1870, no. 94. C.O. 295/255: Longden to Kimberly, 19 Jan. 1871, no. 6.
36. Chapman, op. cit., p. 225. C.O. 318/261: C.L. & E.C. to Rogers, 2 March 1871, minute by Kimberley. 'A very well conceived reform'.
37. P.P. 1872. XLIII. 22–6: Scott to Kimberley, 25 July 1871, no. 115.
38. P.P. 1872. XLIII. 28–9: C.L. & E.C. to Herbert, 27 Sept. 1871.

The Development of an Identity: The Black Middle Class of Trinidad in the Later Nineteenth Century

Bridget Brereton

After the emancipation of the slaves in 1838, a black and coloured middle class developed slowly in Trinidad, as in the British West Indies as a whole. Its origin lay in the 'free persons of colour' and the 'free blacks' of slave society, and after 1838 this nucleus was expanded as ex-slaves and their descendants, liberated Africans, and coloured and black immigrants from the Eastern Caribbean rose to middle class status.[1] Middle class status, in Victorian Trinidad, seemed to depend on two essential criteria: an occupation which involved no manual labour, and command of European, or British, culture, especially the ability to speak and write correct English. These two criteria were more crucial than either material prosperity or lightness of skin colour. Many members of this class in 19th century Trinidad were comparatively penniless, and some were black. A fairly prosperous but uneducated smallholder would not belong to the middle class; an elementary schoolteacher on a miserable salary would.

Members of the coloured and black middle class, then, were distinguished from the black masses by their education, their familiarity with European literary culture, and their 'white-collar' jobs. They were distinguished from the dominant whites by their African descent. They were, generally speaking, excluded from the white elite, who dominated the political as well as the economic and social life of the colony. They were not a part of the ruling class, but their literacy and their intellectual skills, which they valued highly, clearly marked them off from the black and East Indian masses.

Forming as they did an intermediate group, their position in post-emancipation society was certain to be difficult. Historians have generally concluded that the coloured and black middle class, in the generations after 1838, aspired to move in 'white' social circles, to adopt 'white' values, and to be accepted by the dominant group. As a result, members of this group, it is said, downgraded or rejected totally their African heritage, their slave past, and their race. Donald Wood writes 'the col-

oured people — and the few educated Negroes — continued after 1838 to look towards the whites as they had done during slavery days; rarely were there any expressions of pride in their African heritage'.[2] Selwyn Ryan, writing of the period 1838 to 1919, thinks that 'generally, the aim of the coloured strata was to penetrate as far as possible into white society. They disparaged their ancestral past and strove to eliminate or conceal all evidence of their negroid origin. They accepted and internalized all the myths about black inferiority, and imitated with exaggerated fidelity the cultural patterns of the Europeans'. This class was characterized by 'its deculturation, its lack of pride in its negritude, in Africa, in any aspects of the slave past'.[3]

It is in part the purpose of this paper to suggest that these judgements need to be modified, at least with reference to the black middle class of later 19th century Trinidad. While many members of this class no doubt tried to reject the racial heritage, a significant number of educated Afro-Trinidadians expressed pride in their race and advocated race consciousness. Inevitably, their developing racial consciousness was shaped by the society they lived in and by the place in that society assigned to them by the dominant classes. For this reason, the paper will indicate briefly the social and economic characteristics of this non-white middle class in the later nineteenth century, its occupations, its economic life, and its education. It will then discuss the nature of racism in Trinidad during this period, both institutional and ideological, which thwarted the mobility of the educated blacks, and forced them to confront the problem of identity. Finally, we shall consider how middle class blacks reacted to this racism. They showed their resentment by protesting in the local press, and elsewhere; they reacted in terms of political action; and they began to develop an ideology which countered the prevailing white racism. It is the thesis of this paper that an awareness of race — a black identity — began to emerge among educated black and coloured Trinidadians in the last half of the nineteenth century.

The nucleus of the black middle class was the 'free people of colour' and the 'free blacks' of pre-emancipation society. And it is significant that Trinidad had a headstart over most other Caribbean societies, in that the 'free coloured' group was exceptionally large in proportion to the whites and the slaves.[4] Emancipation in 1838 destroyed the legal basis of the free coloureds' distinctive position. Nevertheless, the families of French free coloured origin continued after 1838 to form a distinct and self-contained sector within the developing non-white middle class. Like the white French Creoles of Trinidad, they cherished the past. There was the same nostalgic feeling for birth and breeding, for aristocratic traditions, the same tendency to intermarriage. They were often highly educated and refined, planters, merchants, and professionals. Catholic, French-speaking, strongly conscious of their worth and their breeding, this group, though small in numbers, formed a kind of aristocracy within the black middle class.

The second and larger group within the black middle class was made up of blacks and mulattoes who were not descended from wealthy coloured planters and who had achieved their status mainly through their own efforts and through education. They might be descended from Creole ex-slaves, African immigrants blacks from the other islands, or Venezuelan immigrants of Spanish-Black Amerindian descent. For the Trinidad ex-slaves, emancipation, by removing the legal basis of their servitude, opened up the possibility of upward mobility. What is clear is that numbers of ex-slaves and their children became petty traders and artisans after 1838.[5] Few of them could have been prosperous, but they were better off than the estate labourers, they were more mobile, and they were more ambitious for their children, especially for their education. They formed a kind of 'respectable', ambitious, potentially mobile working class, and their children might well achieve the climb to middle class status.

Another significant result of the ex-slaves' entry into petty trade and skilled work was that they settled in towns, for these were activities which were carried on mainly in Port of Spain and the other towns and larger villages. By 1870 at least one quarter of Trinidad's total population was urban, an exceptionally high ratio for a 19th century tropical colony. It was naturally in Port of Spain and the towns that schools and other social and religious amenities were most available. The pronounced urban orientation of many of the more ambitious and mobile ex-slaves and their children was an important factor in the emergence of a black middle class after 1838.

Most of the 'self-made' black or coloured men who won middle class status through their own efforts were professionals, teachers or civil servants in this period. Relatively few middle class blacks owned plantations, unless they had inherited estates from their families, because of the difficulty of access to capital with which to buy land. Nor did the large sugar or cocoa plantations offer employment to educated non-whites. The same problem of access to capital prevented most middle class blacks from owning substantial businesses. The island's commercial establishments were almost exclusively owned by whites in this period, and even the 'clerks' or store assistants employed in these firms tended to be young white Creoles or Britons, though certainly many black and coloured clerks were also employed. Large scale commerce was effectively closed to Afro-Trinidadians, but a few of them owned and operated small businesses: a bookshop, pharmacies, printing establishments and newspapers. On the whole, the established plantation and commercial sector, dominated by a few white families, offered few opportunities to educated and socially mobile non-whites.

In many ways, primary schoolteachers were the nucleus of the coloured and black middle class. Teaching was one of the few 'respectable' white collar jobs available to young men from humble backgrounds, who had no chance of a university education and so could not enter the more favoured professions of law and medicine. The schoolteacher, moreover, was a prestigious figure, especially in the small rural towns and villages, where he/she became the natural leader and advisor of the whole community. A significant number of the emerging black middle class were teachers themselves, or the sons and daughters of teachers.

For the more fortunate members of this class who had access to a university, often through winning an Island Scholarship, the professions of law and medicine offered prestige, social position, and a good income. Coloured and black lawyers formed an important and articulate element in the black middle class.[6] Medicine was also a favoured profession. Several Island Scholars chose this profession,[7] and it was also possible to qualify in the United States after working through a university.[8]

Most middle class blacks, then, were employed in white-collar jobs; the majority were involved in neither agriculture nor in commerce. They were teachers, minor civil servants, journalists and editors, druggists, printers, doctors, lawyers and clerks. Education was the key to all these occupations, the crucial factor in black mobility in the two post-emancipation generations.

These generations availed themselves of a system of public elementary education, established in

1851 and modified in 1870, which provided for both government run and denominational, state-aided primary schools in the towns and in rural areas. Though this system was deficient in many important respects,[9] it provided an elementary education of sorts for most, though by no means all, of Trinidad's black children by the end of the century.[10] Secondary education, however, was largely the preserve of the upper class, for the two boys' secondary schools[11] charged fees high enough to exclude all but the most prosperous, who were mostly white, since colour lines coincided so neatly with income levels. The only chance for working class and even lower middle class boys to attend either of the colleges was through the free college places offered each year to boys from the government and assisted primary schools.

These free places, combined with the Island Scholarships for boys from the two colleges to British universities, represented the main chance for upward monility open to the coloured and black working or lower middle classes. The very able, or the very lucky, could hope to win free places to the colleges, and secondary education made possible careers in teaching or the civil service. The luckiest of all, a mere handful, might win an Island Scholarship and proceed to Britain to study for a profession. Education was, in fact, a crucial factor — almost certainly the crucial factor — in the development of a black middle class in post-emancipation Trinidad.[12]

Nineteenth century Trinidad, the society from which this class emerged, was one in which Europeans and white Creoles dominated economic, social, and political life. And it was a society pervaded with racism. This racism, of course, had its roots in the complicated network of European relationships with Africans since the fifteenth century saw a hardening of racist attitudes on the part of the educated British public, directed especially against Africans.

Africans had their champions after the 1830s, but the defence was weakening. Humanitarianism, for so long a dominant influence on British official circles, was becoming less sure of itself; and many overt defenses of the African gave way to cultural or racial prejudice on almost every point short of the minimum claim of spiritual equality.[13] Around the mid-century, pseudo-scientific racism was emerging in British scholarly thought, a body of ideas which 'proved' that the dark-skinned races, especially Africans, were inherently and biologically inferior to Europeans. Such ideas were to be enormously influential in the second half of the century.[14]

Victorian comments about Africans were often outspokenly derogatory, and by this time the black-est Africans were considered the grossest and the most primitive. The 'Jamaica Revolt' of 1865 crystallized many Victorian views on race; it strengthened the tendency to see all blacks as inherently inferior to Europeans, and the conviction that without firm control by whites, West Indian blacks would revert to the savagery of their ancestors. The revolt appeared to be a conclusive example of the innate savagery of black people. After 1865, Exeter Hall philanthropy was unfashionable with the educated British public. British humanitarianism was a spent force. The general climate of opinion in Britain in the second half of the century was hostile to black people, pessimistic about the success of emancipation, and favourable to despotic rule over the coloured races in the Empire.[15]

Many European and American visitors to the British Caribbean expressed this contempt for the race. Three well-known British writers, Trollope, Kingsley, and Froude, wrote books on the West Indies which echoed the strident negrophobia of Thomas Carlyle earlier in the century.[16] Kingsley, for instance, concluded that 'the Negro may have the corpus sanum without the mens sana' and thought it necessary to point out to his readers that the "Negro" was, after all, human.[17] W. A. Paton, an American traveller, was sure that if Europeans withdrew entirely from the West Indies, the blacks would relapse into 'hordes of mild-mannered, indolent semi-savages.' West Indian blacks were 'indolent, physically and mentally ignorant beyond belief, unambitious, superstitious, in fact, brutish.'[18] And the stereotypes revealed by these and other authors were probably held by most local whites in the period.

One incident in 1870, which became a *cause celebre*, illustrates the prevailing view of the African race. An English medical officer, Bakewell, became involved in a conflict with a doctor of French free coloured origin, Espinet. He had been criticized by the latter on a medical issue, and had replied in a letter in which he reproached Espinet with 'ingratitude .... towards an Englishman, who, for many years, paid his share of the interest of your redemption money from slavery.' The letter was published, and in the sequel Bakewell was tarred and feathered by unknown black assailants. He was obliged to resign, but remained convinced that he was in the right; he wrote to the Secretary of State that he had been 'grossly misrepresented by a man my inferior in education, social position, and race.'[19] Few British officials were quite as tactless as Bakewell, but no doubt many would have agreed with him privately.

Institutional discrimination against non-whites was a feature of the society. Because so many educated blacks were employed in the civil service, including teaching, discrimination in the service was a burning grievance. In this period, it was the unofficial policy of the Colonial Office that non-whites were rarely to be appointed to senior posts. For instance, Governor H. T. Irving wrote of J. O'Brien that he was 'a coloured man, and it is often difficult to find appointments for men of his class'; but 'the fact that he is annually chosen as Secretary of the Race meeting shows the sort of consideration with which he is held by the community generally'. In other words, he was acceptable to the whites.[20] In 1894 there was a notable scandal. An English department head, Ralph Monier-Williams, wrote to the Governor asking him to appoint to a vacant clerkship 'a person with as little coloured blood as possible and if practicable with no coloured blood at all, as these have given considerable trouble in the department within the last two years.' This letter became public knowledge before it reached the Governor.[21]

These racist conceptions also affected political life, as it was, in Victorian Trinidad. The British authorities, and local upper class whites too, profoundly mistrusted all coloured or black politicians. In Trinidad this attitude has its origins in the very early years of the British regime, when the free coloureds were suspected of cherishing Republican and Jacobin notions. Indeed, the fact that this class heavily outnumbered whites was probably the crucial factor in the denial of representative institutions to Trinidad in 1810.[22] The attitude persisted long after the Napoleonic era. In 1849 a riot in Port of Spain over a new rule that petty debtors in the Royal Gaol should have their heads shaved was blamed by the Governor on 'French coloured' troublemakers. He claimed that a 'revolutionary spirit' was being fostered by communications with French islands, and that the ultimate purpose was to get rid of the whites. The Port of Spain Gazette fancifully described the coloured immigrant from Martinique 'exciting our population with stories of shooting and roasting the *sacrés colon* of the islands he came from, and *endoctrinairing* our loyal Creoles with the outrageous notions imbibed by himself, at second hand, of equality and republicanism.'[23] Here mistrust of coloured agitators and dislike of the French, both characteristic of 19th century British colonial authorities, neatly coincided.

As late as 1903, the Commission of Enquiry investigating the riots of that year reported that 'for some years a group of persons has existed in Port of Spain whose main conception of public spirit and independence is to vilify the Government and indulge in personalities regarding the individuals who compose it. Conspicuous among this group are certain coloured lawyers, some of whom have studied in England, coloured tradesmen, and some less reputable persons.'[24]

Such was the network of racist assumptions which educated black and coloured Trinidadians were forced to confront. It is clear that they resented the prevailing European view of their race, and this resentment was often expressed in letters and editorials in the Trinidad press. The Port of Spain Gazette replied to an item in a London paper critical of West Indies blacks:

With regard to the intellectual capacities of the black race in the W.I . . . . It is on the authority of Bishop Rawle and other competent judges admitted to be quite on a par with the capacity of the whites either in Europe or America . . . the black man is as susceptible of religious impressions as the white man, as capable of labour, as docile, and equally qualified for social and political life . . . we are no longer to be reproached with being either black or illiterate.[25]

Another paper observed that many Europeans arriving in the West Indies believed that the 'natives' were savages and cannibals.[26]

The evidence is clear that educated blacks in Trinidad resented the arrogance of the Europeans and local whites, and their exclusion from upper class society. One editor thought that most Europeans coming to Trinidad imbibed colour prejudices through indoctrination soon after their arrival. It was 'adventurers' from Britain, carrying on a 'whispering campaign' against blacks, who poisoned race relations.[27] Educated blacks had a strong sense of their moral and intellectual worthiness to move in the 'best' circles. They thought society was divided between 'those who justly deem themselves entitled to a social position in the island consistent with their means and general behaviour and those who believe that they have a prescriptive right to dictate who shall, or shall not, be received into the ranks of the colonial aristocracy.'[28] A correspondent in 1858 complained that whites only treated educated mulattoes as equals during business discussions; otherwise they were coldly aloof.[29]

A correspondent to the Telegraph in 1872 wrote that no amount of wealth or education enabled a man to enjoy social prestige, if he lacked 'the correct tinge.'[30] Planters of wealth, merit, and good character were 'tabooed,' being without the 'colonial passport . . . more potent than education, habits, principles, behaviour, wealth, talent, or even genius itself.' People outside the West Indies had no idea of the actual position of the "educated man" of the incorrect tinge.' It was especially galling when coloured men of 'good' family were subjected to discrimination. For instance, the manager of a San Fernando hotel told a coloured man, 'whose ancestors held a fair name in the history of Trinidad,' that 'a negro had no right to sit at the same table as a white man.' The reporter of this incident commented that even during slavery, coloured men 'of a certain standing' were freely admitted to all public places 'within the scope of their social position.'[31]

The social dilemma of the middle class black was summed up in the obituary of a wealthy coloured merchant:

Rich, educated, strictly moral, yet he felt he had no place in society because of those social distinctions with which the country is cursed. And he was not without that manly pride that enabled him to be satisfied with a very small number of chosen companions rather than to court those whom he felt to be his inferiors morally and intellectually, and whose only claim to consideration consisted . . . in the purity of their Caucasian blood . . . He felt keenly the disabilities under which certain races, notably that to which he himself belonged, were subjected.[32]

At times, members of this class would protest against what they considered unfair treatment by local whites. In 1879 a public meeting was organized to draw up an address of condolence to the Queen on the death of a daughter, and the speakers were all white. A letter from 'Several Coloured People' objected: 'Surely (the coloured people's) importance, advancement and loyalty are sufficiently conspicuous to entitle them to have their feelings expressed on the occasion by someone who is one of their unmistakable representatives.' This letter suggests that educated blacks had a strong sense of being a distinct sector in the society, and an important part of the whole community.[33]

Educated blacks also criticized the churches for discrimination against their race. Samuel Proctor, a black headmaster, put his case against the Anglican church forcibly. Arguing against church services to mark the Jubilee of Emancipation, he wrote 'We are indebted to the church for less than nothing so far as freedom is concerned. The church has always snubbed us.' He refused to attend the thanksgiving services because 'no man who has seen slavery and how the negro was treated by the church could do so. The church taught that freedom never was ordained for the negro . . . I look upon the thanksgiving service as a farce. Certainly the way the church treated the negro, she may well blush, if blush she can, for shame.'[34] Proctor was clearly no uncritical admirer of the Christian churches in the Caribbean. The Catholic priests were often attacked by educated blacks for their hostility to mass education.

Numerous editorials complained of discrimination against black civil servants. Not only was Trinidad flooded with Colonial Office nominees, stated the Telegraph, but even the lesser posts to which Creoles were appointed were 'snapped up as the almost exclusive right of one race in the community at the expense of all others.' This confirmed the rumor that a Secretary of State had privately instructed West Indian governors 'that on no account whatever was the "subject race" to be employed in any office . . .of trust or responsibility.'[35]

When the Monier-Williams's letter became public, a petition from the 'coloured inhabitants' was sent to the Secretary of State, demanding his dismissal, and claiming that his letter was a wanton insult to the coloured population, especially those in the service. Feelings ran high. One letter hinted that Monier-Williams would be tarred and feathered; posters were put up in the city asking 'What shall we do with Monier-Williams?,' and a detective was assigned to protect him. The Governor, presumably deliberately, appointed a man of unmixed African descent to the clerkship in question, and this was interpreted as a 'lesson,' though the Secretary of State refused to dismiss Monier-Williams.[36]

The educated coloured and black middle class, then, resented the prevailing European notions about the African race; they resented too their exclusion from white society and the discrimination they suffered in social life and especially in the public service, where so many of them were employed. While these reactions may be seen as merely a defence of their class interests, at least they indicate that educated blacks did not meekly accept the inferior position to which they were assigned by local and European whites. And their indignation at discrimination in the public service and elsewhere was an important factor in their participation in political life in 19th century Trinidad, especially in movements to reform the Crown Colony constitution. For British colonialism, by providing a public education system, however limited, made possible the emergence of an educated black middle class which would become increasingly politicized and in the end would turn against Crown Colony government. Educated blacks kept closely in touch with metropolitan political developments, and whatever their ambivalence towards the ruling whites, they had 'natural' claims to be the political leaders of the non-white community. In the 19th century their participation in political life, limited in the years after 1838, broadened as the century progressed and as this class gained in numbers and in self-confidence.

Politically minded blacks in 19th century Trinidad participated in the various movements for constitutional reform partly, no doubt, because they hoped that they would benefit from the introduction of semi-representative government by being elected to the Legislative Council. They were also active in the elected borough councils, which were one of the few fora open to non-white politicians. One of the most prominent members of the class in the 19th century was M. M. Philip. As a young barrister Philip's views were mildly radical. He took part in the Catholic protest against the government in the 1850s and 1860s, and in the Reform movement of the 1850s. In 1867 he was elected mayor of Port of Spain, the first non-white to hold the office; he served for three terms.[37] He was appointed an acting Unofficial member of the Legislative Council, in 1869, and in the same year Solicitor General, the post he retained until his death in 1888.

Once he was appointed Solicitor-General, his position in the government prevented him from participating in local politics, and he was, of course, obliged to support the politics of the regime. For this reason radical blacks felt he had 'betrayed' his people. The Liberal Reform, ten years after his death, commented that Philip had had opportunities to put himself at the head of his fellow countrymen in a campaign against the oligarchy under which they suffered, but instead' he had supported the government in some of its most shameful acts.[38] A Grenada paper thought that Philip, though the 'first and ablest coloured West Indian orator,' was 'deficient in all the noble moral qualities which make a man a ruler of men'; he had left nothing by which 'members of his race could be guided to some higher and more masterful goal.'[39]

Lawyers seemed to provide the natural political leaders of the non-white middle class, because of their university education, their training, and the prestige they have enjoyed in the whole community. Henry Alcazar, called to the Bar in 1882, was perhaps the most prominent of this group in the later 19th century. He was Mayor of Port of Spain several times (1892–4) and (1896–8) and was appointed an Unofficial in 1894. He was the most prominent leader of the Reform Movement in the 1890s. Alcazar was coloured, but two black lawyers became prominent in local politics at the end of the century. These were Emmanuel Lazare and C.P. David. Lazare was of unmixed African descent, born in 1864, the son of black immigrant from Guadeloupe. He was educated in Port of Spain and qualified locally as a solicitor in 1895. He held a commission as Lieutenant in the Trinidad Field Artillery Volunteers (perhaps the first black to do so), and in this capacity he represented Trinidad at the 1897 Jubilee celebrations in London, being presented to the Queen and receiving the Royal message to the Colony.[40] He was a leader of the agitation which led to the Water Riots of 1903 and was one of those prosecuted and acquitted for instigating the riot. The local support for Lazare and the other agitators is indicated by the fact that the jury acquitted them on all the charges after deliberating for a mere fifteen minutes.[41] Lazare continued to be active in agitation for reform and was an Unofficial Member of the Legislative Council from 1920 to 1924.[42]

David, also a black, won an Island Scholarship in 1885 and proceeded to study law, being called to the Bar in 1889. In the 1890s he was Secretary to the Reform Committee. He was appointed the first black Unofficial in 1904, in order to placate black opinion after the 1903 riots.[43] The careers of Lazare and David mark the emergence of black men in Trinidad politics, around the turn of the century, and they also indicate that political dissent was becoming more radical at this time.

It is clear that educated blacks participated in political activities in 19th century Trinidad, much to the annoyance of the authorities. They could also express their political views through the press, for there were always one or two newspapers owned by Afro-Trinidadians and representing the outlook of the educated blacks. William Herbert was one of the more prominent coloured newspaper proprietors and editors. In turn he owned and edited the *Trinidad Press*, the *Trinidad Colonist*, and the *Telegraph*.

Born in Barbados, he lived in Trinidad from 1857 until his early death in 1873. His views were liberal, even radical, and his editorials against the government incurred the anger of several governors. Governor Arthur Gordon even thought that he might have attempted to assist the U.S. in annexing the colony, 'for the sake of notoriety . . . But he is too well known, and too personally despised, to be able to form a party, and is moreover a Barbadian, and as such an object of antipathy to the Creoles of Trinidad.[44] This may have been Gordon's opinion, but the educated black community regarded Herbert as their champion. In 1871 he received a letter signed by over 300 'coloured gentlemen' thanking him for refuting in his paper the criticisms levelled at Afro-Trinidadian by Charles Kingsley.[45] *New Era* called him 'the chief educator of public opinion in Trinidad and a great upholder of the oppressed race against the powerful few'.[45]

New Era (1869–90) was owned and edited by Joseph Lewis, who was coloured. It was the self-acknowledged spokesman of the coloured sector[47] and it consistently upheld the interests of that sector. The most consistently liberal paper in the later 19th century, however, was the *San Fernando Gazette*, owned and edited by Samuel Carter, a black man from Tobago. Carter defined its political stand in 1894. It stood for constitutional reform; the ending of state-aided immigration; free and compulsory primary education; the opening of the Crown Lands on a credit system; cheap administration of justice; reform of taxation to relieve the masses and to reach the absentee landowners; and the ending of special bounties to private industries (that is, sugar).[48] This was a coherent and sensible political programme for the time. Carter thought that the press was the only guarantee of popular interests in Trinidad: 'a Crown Colony is a despotism tempered by the press . . . In Trinidad more than in any of the other colonies has the existence of the independent press been an absolute necessity; in none has it done more good'.[49]

It is clear that members of the educated black community took part in political life, especially in the later 19th century, and held definite political views. They were among the strongest supporters of the movement for constitutional reform and they attacked many aspects of the Crown Colony regime. They also expressed a sense of racial pride and identity. The evidence for the existence of this racial pride among the coloured and black middle class is impressive, and it makes it impossible to state that this group made a whole-hearted effort to downgrade its black heritage. Many Afro-Trinidadians in the later 19th century defended their race against its enemies in the Caribbean and in Europe; they 'vindicated' the race, in the tradition of (for instance) J. T. Holly of the U.S. and Haiti, or Edward Blyden of Liberia.[50]

One of these 'champions of the race' was William Herbert. The address presented to him for refuting Kingsley's slanders against Afro-Trinidadians in 1871 declared that 'it raises our pride that you should identify yourself with your and our race, which, without advantages and with few opportunities, has placed itself nevertheless on an equality with the favoured class . . . You have ever been the true sympathizer of our race. You have in this as in other instances proved yourself their friend and defender'.

Herbert replied on this occasion that while he had always striven to secure real equality for blacks, he had 'wanted moral support'. He urged Afro-Trinidadians to 'work out your moral, social and political salvation for yourselves . . . strive by every legal and constitutional means to secure your rights, and cherish . . . those among you who give evidence of ability and the desire to be true to their race . . . . Let me warn you against your want of

cohesion, the absence of concerted action among you . . . (May these words) be instrumental in helping to elevate that race — my mother's race — that I love so well'.[51] In the same way, Carter of the *San Fernando Gazette* was praised for his consistent defence of the interests of the race. W. G. Donovan, editor of the liberal *Grenada People*, and himself a black man, told Carter 'there is no more vigorous champion of the Race in these Islands than you . . . none more uncompromising in its advocacy and defence of the Negro Race'; his people were grateful for his services.[52]

Numerous letters and editorials in the press spoke of pride in the race and in the African heritage. One editorial is interesting for its praise of African civilization. The editor argued that it was the slave trade which had led to the 'modern degradation' of Africa; there was a noble future in store for the 'pure' African race, if only they proved themselves worthy of their great pre-European past, by education and self-respect. For despite the obstacles the African race had risen everywhere and could not be kept down; the race would triumph over everything.[53] A letter insisted that blacks 'of light and leading' had a special obligation to lead the struggle against oppression. The success of the race depended on their grit and self-reliance in the fight against powerful antagonists.[54] E. Maresse-Smith, a coloured lawyer, was involved in establishing a branch of the African Methodist Episcopal Church. Explaining his involvement, he wrote that his standpoint was 'that of a person who, having African blood flowing in his veins, and not being . . . ashamed of the land of his mother, looks with pride and satisfaction upon any success achieved by those who, in common with him, are descendants of Africans'.[55]

Racial pride and identity were expressed in celebrations of the anniversary of Emancipation,which was regularly observed up to about 1870. In 1868, for instance, various meetings were held in Port of Spain and San Fernando to observe the anniversary. One speaker, Julien Maisonneuve, reminded his listeners that August first should always be remembered by anyone with even 'one drop of African blood'. Blacks should show themselves to be worthy of freedom and should show the world that differences of colour had no effect on the mind.[56] J. J. Thomas, the black author, consistently advocated celebrating the first of August, and he criticized 'the guilty reticence with which, year after year, we sneak through the 24 hours of the first of August, which should have been the great commemorative day'.[57]

An excellent example of race pride among middle class blacks is the celebration of the Jubilee of Emancipation in 1888. The event was surrounded by a great deal of controversy in Trinidad, and the whole incident reflects the society's ideas about slavery and race relations. From the start, influential men, white and coloured, warned against any 'fuss'. For this could only remind people of slavery and so perpetuate the unfortunate divisions of the past. But a group of young 'radical' blacks, led by Maresse-Smith, promoted a more conspicuous celebration; Maresse-Smith explained that he thought it the plain duty of all blacks to remember slavery and to celebrate its end. He disassociated himself from mulattoes who tried to sever all ties with their black ancestors and relatives 'Let us then not be ashamed of our race, and understand for good that the servitude of our ancestors was a misfortune for them for which we need not blush . . . Let us throw aside once and for all that weakness which causes us to be so cruel the one to the other, and so ridiculous to the world at large'.[58] Another correspondent agreed. Blacks should rejoice that they were free and progressive. The shame of slavery belonged not to the Africans, but to those who carried it out. Slavery was merely the abuse of superior power.[59]

A group of more conservative coloured men, and a few whites, alarmed at Maresse-Smith's 'radicalism', and at the prospect of divisions of class and colour, set up a rival banquet for the night of August first. The speeches at their banquet were bland and non-committal; it was patronized by the Governor, and Maresse-Smith derisively called it 'the official affair'. His group stressed in their speeches racial pride, the horrors of slavery, and the intellectual and moral progress of blacks since 1838.[60]

The whole affair illustrates the ambivalent feelings of educated blacks about slavery and the race. The older and more conservative mulattoes, the 'respectable coloured portion of the community', thought it was dangerous to revive 'dormant' prejudices and grievances. It would set class against class and race against race. Better to play down the Jubilee; at the most, attend church services of thanksgiving. The younger radicals, both mulattoes and blacks, wanted to glorify the race and revive memories of past wrongs. They thought it was important to bring into the open the existence of race feeling and discrimination, in order to destroy it.

The San Fernando Gazette thought that the celebrations of the Jubilee in Trinidad testified that blacks had not lost all racial self-respect. 'It demonstrated that there was yet a spark of manly independence in the downtrodden race, and that with the advance of education . . . they may yet reach that crowning point of civilization which is marked

by an absence of that servile shame which acknowledges no race, no country, no ambition'.[61]

One correspondent, ironically calling himself 'Old Quashie' thought that Trinidad had many who stood up boldly for the 'despised sons of Ethiopia'. Many of Trinidad's most successful men descended from 'the poor, degraded, and despised slave women . . . sold in bondage to the fathers of our more favoured brethren'. He hoped that 'none of the genuine sons of Africa will be ashamed to own a common maternity'.[62] There were many calls for unity among blacks. One such exhorted 'unless unity be our motto, matters will go from bad to worse. Let us be set aside — a general separation of the two classes of society — White and Coloured . . . and let us support our class. No wolves in sheep clothing; all who have African blood in his veins cleave to his countrymen and leave all new blood alone'.[63]

One of the most prominent champions of the race in 19th century Trinidad was certainly J. J. Thomas, the self-educated black philologist and writer, author of Creole Grammar and Froudacity.[64] Thomas was acutely aware that the values of black inferiority had to some extent been internalized by Afro-West Indians. In a newspaper correspondence on the failure to celebrate Emancipation Day, Thomas wrote that blacks as well as whites were guilty of race prejudice. In the Caribbean 'colour prejudice is a ladder with almost numberless rounds. It is a system of social aggression and retaliation'. Everyone, of whatever shade, was in some way 'the ministers as well as the victims of this pernicious idolatry'. This 'preoccupation of the skin' was 'a fearful incubus on our social existence'.[65]

In a plea repeated throughout his writings, Thomas urged Africans of all shades to unite, for union was strength; they would never be respected when they were 'too frivolous to maintain their own identity and too spiritless to make it respected'. Instead of 'longing . . . after the fleshpots of our white fellow citizens', they should be preparing for the task of creating their own united society. Above all, educated and enlightened blacks had special duties and obligations to the race.[66] Elsewhere he wrote decisively 'no sympathy should be wasted on the negro sufferer from mortification at not being able to change his skin. The Ethiopian of whatever shade of colour who is not satisfied with being such was never intended to be more than a mere living figure'.[67]

Like Edward Blyden, Thomas was a 'vindicator' of his race. His book Froudacity was devoted to refuting the slanders cast by J. A. Froude against West Indian blacks. Through his successes — his book Creole Grammar was well reviewed and he was elected a member of the Philological Society of London — he 'proved' the black people's intellectual equality with the European, and his career was an important factor in the slow growth of self-confidence in the educated black community of Trinidad. Thomas is especially interesting for his concept of 'Afro-America' and his recognition of the links binding Africans in the New World with those in Africa. His thinking on this may have been influenced by Blyden, his contemporary, whose work laid the foundation for Pan-Africanism, African Nationalism, and Negritude.[68] Many of Blyden's ideas are found in Thomas. Like Blyden, Thomas thought that New World blacks were inextricably bound to Africa. Like him, Thomas was fiercely race conscious, and despised blacks who tried to ape whites. Thomas agreed with Blyden that European directed education was disastrous for blacks. And with Blyden, he appealed for race pride and for unity among all Africans.

Throughout *Froudacity* Thomas showed his concern for the progress of blacks in the non-British Caribbean and in the U.S. He grasped with absolute clarity the need to go back to the roots, to Africa and its history, culture and genius, in order to create a future for the 'extra-African' black people.[69] He insisted that it was time for New World blacks to occupy themselves with matters of importance to the Race. There were individually brilliant blacks. But there had to be 'some potential agency to collect and adjust them into the vast engine necessary for executing the true purpose of the civilized African Race'. In other words, unity of action was essential to carry out the upliftment of the race. 'Already, especially since the late Emancipation Jubilee, are signs manifest of a desire for intercommunion and intercourse among the more distinguished of our people. With intercourse and unity of purpose will be secured the means to carry out the obvious duties which are sure to devolve upon us. . .'[70]

No doubt Thomas was proud of his mastery of European literary culture, and especially of the difficult field of philology. He and his friends were gratified when his books were favourably received in the British press and when he himself was 'lionized' in London literary circles. It would probably be true to say that he accepted European culture as the highest form of civilization. But Thomas was acutely aware of his African heritage. He was intensely concerned for his fellow blacks, in Trinidad, in the Caribbean, in the world. He followed the progress of the race in Sierra Leone, Liberia, the U.S., Haiti, and Brazil. He showed little of the excessive loyalty towards the Mother Country typical of educated 19th century colonials. He was as informed as was then possible about Africa. He

perceived the unity of Afro-America. Above all, he was dedicated to the 'upliftment' of the race; through mastery of European culture and technology, educated and privileged blacks would raise up their fellows in the New World and in Africa. 'What is it', he asks rhetorically 'in the nature of things that will oust the African race from the right to participate, in times to come, in the high destinies that have been assigned in times past to so many races that have not been in any way superior to us in the qualities, physical, moral, and intellectual, that mark out a race for prominence among other races?'[71]

There were, it is clear, very many black and coloured Trinidadians in the later nineteenth century who expressed pride in their racial heritage. This development culminated in the establishment in 1901 of the Pan-African Association in Trinidad. H. Sylvester Williams, the founder of the Association in London, was himself a lawyer from Trinidad, and he visited the island in 1901. He was enthusiastically received, and branches were formed in Port of Spain, San Fernando, Princes Town, Arouca, and Chaguanas, as well as in smaller, rural settlements.[72] Among Williams' prominent colleagues in Trinidad were Lazare and Maresse-Smith, and the Pan-African Association found its supporters mainly from the black middle class whose views and attitudes we have attempted to describe.

After 1901, of course, the black middle class became increasingly involved in the development of what may be described as black nationalism. The First World War, the invasion of Ethiopia, the work of Marcus Garvey, all stimulated the growth of race consciousness. All this lay in the future. But perhaps we may draw two conclusions from this analysis of the developing ideology of the black middle class in the later nineteenth century. One is that this class did not wholeheartedly reject its racial heritage, its negritude, as historians have often stated. The other is that those who argue that the contemporary Black Power movement in the West Indies is wholly imported, that it lacks any indigenous roots, must take into account the pleas for black solidarity, the expressions of race price, which were made in Trinidad in this period. By the beginning of this century, the search for a black self-image, an identity, was well under way.

Notes

1. It is essential to define our terms. By 'coloured' I mean a person of mixed African and European descent, probably light-complexioned; 'mulatto' is used in the same sense; 'black' refers to someone of exclusively or predominantly African descent who is dark-skinned.

2. D. Wood, *Trinidad in Transition* (Oxford 1968), pp. 302–3.

3. S. Ryan, *Race and Nationalism in Trinidad and Tobago* (Toronto 1972), p. 20.

4. One estimate, for 1838, gives 3,993 whites, 12,000 free coloureds and blacks, and 20,656 apprentices (ex-slaves). Wood, p. 44.

5. Cf. W. Sewell, *Ordeal of Free Labour in the British West Indies,* (New York 1860), pp. 113–14.

6. Among the prominent Black lawyers in the second-half of the century were Alexander Fitzjames, M. M. Philip, E. Maresse-Smith, Vincent Brown, C. P. David, E. Lazare, H. A. Alcazar.

7. Eg. Stephen Laurence, who qualified from Edinburgh in 1888.

8. Eg. Eusebio Valerio, who wrote his autobiography, *Seiges and Fortunes of a Trinidadian* (Trinidad 1919); F. E. Brass and H. M. Lermont: see A. Burkett, *Trinidad a Jewel of the West* (London 1914), p. 38 and 30.

9. See The Keenan Report of 1869 for an indictment of the system; most of it is printed in S. Gordon, *Reports and Repercussions in West Indian Education 1835–1933* (London 1968), pp. 67–97.

10. *Trinidad Royal Gazette,* 25 December 1889.

11. The two colleges were: St. Mary's, established 1863, Catholic, state aided from 1870; Queen's Collegiate School, government run and secular, founded 1859 and renamed Queen's Royal College in 1870. After 1870 pupils from both competed for scholarships to British universities.

12. Lloyd Best has expressed this well: 'Black People's investment was in education, our business was the school. The tycoons of industry in this country have been the Primary Headteachers — the men who held that precious ladder which let our fathers out the hatch — first through the College Exhibition — and finally the Island Scholarship supreme'. TAPIA, May 7, 1972.

13. P. D. Curtin, *The Image of Africa* (London 1965), p. 385.

14. *Ibid.,* pp. 363–387.

15. See C. Bolt, *Victorian Attitudes to Race* (London 1971), pp. 76–107 and pp. 131–8.

16. A. Trollope, *The West Indies and the Spanish Main* (N.Y. 1860), p. 225. C. Kingsley, *At Last* (London 1889). J. A. Froude, *The English in the West Indies* (New York 1888).

17. Kingsley, p. 26.

18. W. A. Paton, *Down the Islands* (London 1887), p. 211, 214.

19. Wood p. 252 and L. O. Innis, *Trinidad and Trinidadians* (P.O.S. 1910), pp. 87–8.

20. H. Johnson, *Crown Colony Government in T'dad 1870–1897.* (unpub. D. Phil. Thesis, U. of Oxford, 1969), p. 86.

21. For this affair, see *Observer* June 15 to 24, 1894; *Herald* June 26, 1894; *Public Opinion* Aug. 15 and Oct. 5, 1894.

22. See J. Millette, *The Genesis of Crown Colony Government* (P.O.S. 1970), pp. 260–66. See also I. M. Cumpston, 'Radicalism in Trinidad and C. O. Reaction 1855–6' in B.I.H.R. Vol. 36, 1963, pp. 153–4.

23. *Port of Spain Gazette* (P.O.S.G.) Oct. 5, 1849; cited in Wood p. 176.

24. Report of the Commission of Enquiry into the Recent Disturbances at Port of Spain. (T'dad 1903). Cited in E. Williams, *History of the People of Trinidad and Tobago* (London 1964), p. 184.

25. P.O.S.G. April 16, 1875.

26. *New Era (N.E.)* April 18, 1870.

27. *Palladium* Nov. 12, 1881.

28. *Ibid.,* Aug. 3, 1878.

29. *Trinidad Sentinel* 29 April, 1858.

30. *Telegraph (Tel.)* Dec. 4, 1872: Letter from 'Democrites'.

31. *N.E.* June 10, 1872; Our San Fernando Correspondent.

32. *Tel.* May 22, 1872: Obit. of Etienne Gouffe.

33. *Fair Play* 23 January, 1879: Letter from 'Several Coloured People'.

34. *Truth* July 28, 1888; *P.O.S.G.* Aug. 8, 1888: Letters from Proctor.

35. *Tel.* April 3, 1872. Cf. also *San Fernando Gazette (S.F.G.)* July 20, 1887; *N.E.* Aug. 4, 1873.

36. See footnote 21.

37. See C. L. R. James, 'M. M. Philip, an Impression' in *The Beacon* Sept. 1931, pp. 16–23.

38. *Reform,* March 5, 1898.

39. *S.F.G.* Feb. 28, 1894: extract from the *Grenada People,* Feb., 1, 1894.

40. H.M. enquired if he spoke any English; he replied, with restraint, 'We all speak English in Trinidad, Ma'am'.

41. Moloney to Lyttelton, 16 Nov. 1903 and 19 Dec. 1903 (Tel.) C.O. 884/7. I am grateful to Dr. Brinsley Samaroo for these references.

42. Burkett, pp. 95–6. See also K. O. Laurence, 'The Trinidad Water Riots of 1903' in *Caribbean Quarterly,* Vol. 15, No. 4, 1969, p. 19, Note 11.

43. See B. Samaroo, 'The Emergence of the Black Man in Trinidad Politics — C.P. David' in *Journal of Caribbean History',* Vol. 3, 1971.

44. Gordon to Granville, Secret, 24 May, 1869. C.O. 295/247.

45. *P.O.S.G.,* Sept. 16, 1871: Correspondence published.

46. *N.E.* June 2, 1873.

47. Cf. *N.E.* Nov. 6, 1871.

48. *S.F.G.* Jan. 4, 1894.

49. *S.F.G.* April 14, 1894.

50. J. T. Holly, *A Vindication of the Capacity of the Negro race . . .* (1857) and E. W. Blyden, *A Vindication of the Negro Race* (1857).

51. *P.O.S.G.* Sept. 16, 1871.

52. *S.F.G.* April 28, 1894: Letter from W. G. Donovan.

53. *Palladium* July 9, 1881.

54. *Public Opinion* Feb. 19, 1892: Letter from 'Philo Negro'.

55. *S.F.G.* April 4, 1885: Letter from E. Maresse-Smith.

56. *S.F.G.* Aug. 8, 1868.

57. *Tel.* Oct. 2, 1872: Letter from J. J. Thomas.

58. *Truth* June 16, 1888: Letter from Maresse-Smith.

59. *Ibid.,* July 21, 1888: Letter from 'Titus Africanus'.

60. *Ibid.,* June to Aug., 1888. *N.E.* June 3, 29; July 20, Aug. 3, 1888. *P.O.S.G.* June 27; Aug. 4, 1888. Maresse-Smith was prominent in the Pan-African Association in 1901 and in the Water Riots of 1903.

61. *S.F.G.* Jan. 5, 1889.

62. *N.E.* Dec. 29, 1873: Letter from 'Old Quashie'.

63. *N.E.* Feb. 28, 1876: Letter from 'Sphink'.

64. For his life, see D. Wood, 'Biographical Note' in J. J. Thomas, *Froudacity* (New Beacon Edn., London 1969).

65. *N.E.* 31 Aug. and 14 Sept., 1874: Letters from Thomas.

66. *Ibid.*

67. *Froudacity,* p. 68.

68. See H. Lynch, *Edward Wilmot Blyden Pan-Negro Patriot 1832–1912* (London 1967), p. 248 and chapter four *passim.*

69. *Froudacity,* pp. 179–81.

70. *Ibid.,* p. 193.

71. *Ibid.,* pp. 180–81.

72. See B. Samaroo, *Constitutional and PoliticaL Development of Trinidad 1898–1925.* (Unpub. PH.D. thesis, University of London, 1969), pp. 68–71.

The Black Middle Class in Nineteenth Century Jamaica

Patrick Bryan

Between the mass of rural labourers and small-scale cultivators on the one hand, and the white and coloured elite who dominated ownership of the island's major resource — land — there was an evolving strata which constituted part of the island's middle class. This middle class has been described by R.T. Smith as two-tiered, drawing a distinction between a middle class of traders and a middle class of professionals some black, some brown.[1] Occupational status and the possession of European cultural attributes were important variables in definitions of class but the status associated with an occupation could, in the Jamaican milieu, be modified by race and colour divisions. It is always difficult to draw rigid lines of division between classes given that there is an almost infinite gradation associated with material well-being, place and type of residence, cultural attainments, and occupation. At the same time, it is not only that occupation determines class but that class determines occupation. The extent to which heterogeneity can exist within classes and yet permit the application of the homogenizing term 'class', is partly a question of philosophical outlook, and partly a question of how much weight we attach to the differences which people, within an objectively defined class, perceive between themselves. The factor of race was an important division within this middle class; there is also a significant division in occupation, income, and probably in education as well. The traders of Jamaica also constituted a diverse element in Jamaican economic and social life. Among the traders themselves there were substantial ethnic divisions, as well. The use of the term 'class', therefore, corresponds more with the need to find a convenient term to define a large group of people spread between the minorities and the masses, than with the accurate or scientific description of a group which shared common interests, aspirations, or a common consciousness.

The respectable peasantry

In rural Jamaica there was a layer of wealthy peasants and farmers who were generally termed 'respectable'. A respectable farmer was not, in the Jamaican context, the same thing as a 'gentleman farmer' who would have the term 'esquire' attached to his name. The respectable farmer was often of limited educational attainment, sometimes entirely illiterate, but his status was based on land-ownership and on his ability to employ labour. A rural farmer who attracted some attention and admiration was Mr. Hibbert of Clarendon, who had acquired 150 acres of land. Hibbert was described by the *Daily Gleaner* as an 'enterprising black man from the superior of his class to be found in the colony'. He produced coffee, owned a mill, a pulping house, tanks and barbecues, a machine for preparing arrowroot and cassava starch. He had 15,000 hills of yams valued at £400. He had, we are told, no problem with labour, or with praedial larcenists and worked along with his employees with his pick and hoe. His income was estimated to be about £1,000 per year.[2]

Another prosperous black agriculturist and pen-keeper was J.M. Gordon, who sat on the St. Catherine Parochial Board.[3] Over a three year period, Gordon had been able to purchase approximately £2,000 worth of cattle from Mr. George Sturridge, a large penkeeper near Mandeville. Gordon, described by his lawyer Mr. Vendryes as a black man who had 'lifted himself to his position through integrity, industry, and ability', became a member of the Parochial Board of St. Catherine in 1889. He received some dubious public attention in 1889 because of a charge made against him of theft of a steer. Gordon in the magistrate's court, insisted that he had been framed by men in league against him, and who desired to ruin him and hated him 'because I possess a certain amount of influence and respect among my people which they wish to destroy for their political ends ... who affect to despise me because of my success, who think it an injudicious and dangerous thing for a man of my class at all to succeed and to possess property, and who hate me because I prefer to stand by the respected custos of my parish, in his desire to keep things straight, and to discountenance robbery and dishonesty'.

Gordon was committed to stand trial in any case, but the jury unanimously agreed to release him 'amidst the deafening and prolonged cheering from the large number of spectators assembled in and outside the courtroom'. It was also established, by way of poetic justice that his accuser, Henriques, had been in the habit of selling his employer's stock for a commission of 33⅓% in exchange for selling below market value. But it was so tragically clear that had Gordon not had strong character references the case may have gone differently. Gordon's own statement illustrated the vulnerability of this segment of the middle class because of race.

The evidence points to an evolving layer of black society whose lifestyle differed from the mass of rural labourers and tenants. One of the major comments made on this group came from Sir Anthony Musgrave in 1880.[4] In his lecture to the Royal Colonial Institute Musgrave reproduced comments made on the standard of housing of this class. From Manchester, Rev. Panton described those who 'in material prosperity there is a large class now in the country whose means warrant their social elevation. But they are below the mark in education and taste'. Rev. Panton, one of the closest associates of Enos Nuttall, and a man much venerated in South Manchester, declared:

We want a good middle class of black population. To a certain extent we have this in Manchester — men who will appreciate education, morality, social rules, among themselves, and the ordinary customs of civilized life. Such men would see the necessity for taxation, and not grudge their quota.[5]

Rev. Webb, reporting from Stewart Town in Trelawny, referred to the improvement in the construction of cottages 'in the Gibraltar District where people are small settlers and growers of coffee'. In Watt Town, he reported, no less than 'fifteen houses had been built in the previous ten years, and others were being constructed on an improved scale, neat, commodious, peasant-family cottages. Webb described the cottages as having a solid base wall, 25 ft by 15 ft: 7–8 ft high. There were normally two rooms below, the sons occupied one as a sleeping room, and one was used as a lock-up for coffee or ground provisions for market. Upstairs, there were two sleeping rooms, one for parents, the other for the daughters. There was a hall, with a few pieces of mahogany furniture . . . Upon a corner table there were cups, saucers, and mugs all of the latest and most approved designs, more for show and ornament than use. There was another hall for dining and general family chit-chat. There was a front portico. Comparable descriptions of homes among well-to-do small settlers in Westmoreland, North Manchester, and St. Elizabeth confirm the existence of a middle group of black farmers whose daily life differed fundamentally from that of the rural workers and tenant farmers and small peasantry.[6]

This middle group of black farmers would no doubt have been among those 3,766 'Africans' mentioned in a tabulation of voters made in 1886. In that later year, of 7,443 qualified and registered voters 51% or 3,766 were listed as 'African', 35% or 2,578 as of mixed race, 13% or 1,001 Europeans or Europeans born in Jamaica, and 1% or 98 East Indians. The franchise was not particularly liberal. For a householder to quality to vote he had to occupy a floored and roofed dwelling, and pay a tax on a horse and nine acres of cultivated land. In the 1890s the franchise was limited by the imposition of a literacy qualification, while the economic hardships in the twilight years of the nineteenth century contributed to the removal of several people from the voters list as a consequence of inability to pay taxes.

One source for the emergence of the middle group of farmers was the migrants returning from Panama, though it is probably true that several Panama migrants had been farmers before leaving for Panama 'with God as their compass' (as one migrant so ably and picturesquely explained the migration). For the thousands who did not succeed financially or even survive the experience of emigration, there were a few, who having returned to the island became small settlers and shopkeepers. Newton speculated that 'in Jamaica and the Windward Islands, the recipients were probably also the main purchasers of the several hundred acres of crown lands which the governments of these islands sold during the first two decades of the twentieth century'.[7] A report of an officially appointed commission in 1888 suggested, however, that even before the government made crown lands available, returned migrants were purchasing land and establishing shops.[8] Several of the emigrants to Panama had been artisans in Jamaica. In 1886 they were able to earn, as tradesmen in Panama, between $2 and $2.75 per day if they reported directly to the Compagnie Universelle, or between $4 and $5 per day, if they were employed to contracting firms. Dr. Gayeard, who had been despatched by Governor Norman in 1887 to report on conditions in the Canal Zone, reported that tradesmen on the line (masons and carpenters) earned $3 to $4 per day. They were also supplementing their income by their small farm tenements, 'raising corn, bananas and fowls'.[9]

The rural middle class farmer sometimes had common interests with larger farmers, especially in relation to labour supplies. In 1890 small proprietors of Canoe Valley in Clarendon petitioned the Governor on the labour question. This particular group of proprietors shared some of the most reactionary views of the elite on the educational system which, they claimed, spoiled labour.

Dependent on the soil for our livelihood, we cannot express too strongly our disappointment at the present system of education. Most young men and women leave school, despise the soil, and regard agriculture as beneath them, and so strongly has this sentiment influenced the less informed that we find it difficult to obtain labour in our District even for high wages.[10]

Clearly, however, there was a distinction between education of one's own children, and the education of other people's children. For example, some small proprietors, also from Clarendon, complained that the education of their children was being hampered by the need to utilize their labour for conveying water for household use.[11]

Clarendon farmers grouped themselves into the Clarendon Agricultural Association, of which the President was George Douet. The association pleaded for 'practical training in agriculture, assistance to hardworking cultivators; some means to provide agricultural implements and machinery so as to economize labour'. The petition called for industrial schools, co-operative associations on the central factory principle, amendment of the Immigration Law, in respect of payment for immigrants so as to 'put it within the reach of a large number of those who want labour to avail themselves of East Indians, protection to certain of our exports from unscrupulous dealers'.[12]

The response to petitions such as the above was really the formation of the Jamaica Agricultural Society, which, founded in 1895, was to be the foremost organization colony-wide of small settlers. But the Jamaica Agricultural Society (JAS) was not a small farmers association in the sense that the initiative for its establishment came from the farmers themselves. It was organized by the colonial leadership, and its leadership remained in the hands of the country's elite. In the year of its formation the JAS had just over 150 members who paid 4s. for membership. The Board of the Society consisted of fourteen persons chosen from the Legislative Council, fourteen nominated by the Governor, and another fourteen elected by the membership. The Governor was president. There were to be four vice-presidents elected by members from among the Board. The Governor appointed the secretary and treasurer. The objec-

tive of the JAS according to Governor Blake was to improve the small stock of the people by importing breeds of pigs, goats and fowls. 'By this means I hope to confer immediate benefits upon small proprietors and cultivators to *win their confidence* and support in the general movement which must of course be slow'.[13] The Hon. John Pringle, of banana fame, and one of Blake's Privy Councillors was one of the vice-presidents of the society. A Board of Agriculture would serve as the executive body of the JAS.

The structure of the JAS was designed to ensure that agricultural policy would remain distinctly the business of the colonial bureaucracy and the Legislative Council. While providing a voice for black farmers it was intended to provide a platform whereby small-farmer production could more easily be influenced by the agricultural policies of the colonial state. Thus the JAS was expected to help redirect the energies of small farmers into export production. Small farmers were to be exposed to the use of more modern implements of agriculture, to be lectured on methods of cultivation, to be provided with practical demonstrations in the methods of planting and pruning crops such as cacao, kola and coffee. The architect of the organization, Governor Sir Henry Blake, made it clear that his optimism was much modified by the supposed inferiority of the black population:

What the ultimate result will be I cannot say. A black population not very intelligent and saturated with suspicion of any attempt to interfere with their crude and wasteful system is not easily influenced.[14]

The JAS was an organization of black farmers, by the colonial administration for the advancement of small-scale agriculture, under the paternal guidance of the Governor and the Legislative Council. In this respect it differed fundamentally from the Jamaica Union of Teachers, a professional organization of teachers, established by black teachers, for the welfare of education and teachers in general.

The Teachers

The middle-farming sector of the Afro-Jamaican population was always keen to provide education for their children. For this sector of the population the elementary school was the most probable avenue for learning basic literacy and numeracy.

The system of elementary education was aimed at the lower class of ex-slaves, but it found its principal support among the more prosperous small and medium-sized farmers engaged in the production of 'minor', that is to say non-plantation crops. Its existence also led to the creation of a lower middle class of primary school teachers who became a reservoir of black leaders. Whatever its shortcomings, elementary school teaching was almost the only means by which poor blacks could escape manual labour . . . However, in the rural communities where church and school were most effective, particularly among the middle farmers who could make enough money to maintain a respectable style of life, the schoolteachers were the local elite.[15]

Many teachers had been born to farming families, and in the absence of pensions until definitely the end of the nineteenth century, retirement often dictated a return to the soil. Indeed, many teachers left the schoolroom for the farm long before retirement, or became shopkeepers. One such example was Mr. Josiah Smickle who, after nineteen years, left teaching and devoted his time to his shop and to his grazing property in one parish and cultivation in another. He had about 160 acres of land in all. Smickle became a member of the Parochial Board, and of the Legislative Council.[16] Rev. C.A. Wilson also observed the tendency of teachers to abandon the classroom for more gainful occupation in farming.[17]

We should be careful not to exaggerate the importance of elementary education as a factor in social mobility, insofar as elementary education in itself was unable to provide that. Basic numeracy and literacy, while of themselves important, cannot offer a general preparation for a lifetime occupation. The majority of children left school and were abandoned as far as educational institutions were concerned for the rest of their lives unless deviant behaviour brought them under the umbrella of reformatories, which ironically did more to prepare children for occupations as masons, carpenters, tailors and other artisan-based occupations. An elementary education, however, did provide an opening for further education, especially for those who excelled and were able to move on to training colleges, and in a few cases to study overseas.

The black rural middle class, among whom we include the teachers, were not yet a stable social group, moving as they did from teaching, to the religious ministry, to farming, or combining these occupations. However, teachers were among the first of the professional groups in the island to establish associations designed to further the interests of the profession and of individuals within it. Beginning in about 1883, a series of parish associations of teachers were set up under Church of England auspices.[18] The strongest and most vibrant of these teachers' associations was the North Manchester Teachers' Association operating out of Mount Olivet.

The main function of these early associations was to improve the 'intellectual culture' of teachers. Some meetings conducted essay readings, lectures (called 'orations'), written and oral discussion. They also purchased books and periodicals for members. These organizations were strictly for Church of England teachers. Archbishop Nuttall explained this apparent exclusiveness:

While embracing some points of general interest, they are to a great extent such as only church teachers can benefit by. We are trying in various ways to train our teachers and catechists and improve their status. But much of this work is done on Church of England lines, so require these separate associations. But our teachers are at liberty to join general associations, and where these exist and work well it will be a benefit to our men to belong to both. You will therefore understand that we have not formed our teachers' associations in a spirit of exclusiveness but simply for the purpose of doing some needed work in our own way.[19]

So, then, the Anglican associations were being set up in 1883 to improve schoolmasters and catechists, and to elevate their status. The Westmoreland and Mountain Teachers' Association typically declared their objectives to be the 'promotion of the interests of teachers, and the advancement of their profession, the increase of efficiency of their work and a general furtherance of the course of elementary education. The Inspector of Schools, Mr. Thomas Capper, associated the work of the associations with the improved training of teachers and higher standards in schools, and particularly the efforts of teachers towards 'self-culture'.[20]

Parallel to the teachers associations which catered primarily for the professional development of teachers was a somewhat more subdued movement in the 1880s which began to agitate for the improved material welfare of teachers. The improvement of salaries was related, firstly, to the degree to which the government of the island was prepared to invest funds in education. It was related, secondly, to the more subjective factor of race. The late-nineteenth century witnessed an increased desire on the part of the Churches to encourage greater participation of government in education, in accordance with the experience of England, and in response to the reality that the Churches were experiencing financial difficulties in maintaining current establishments, at a time when the demand for more schools in the countryside was increasing. As far as the racial factor is concerned, most of the elementary school teachers were black and coloured, and they were probably correct when they argued that low pay and poor housing conditions emerged out of the low esteem in which blacks were held in the society.[21] Teachers clearly regarded themselves as an upwardly mobile section of the black population and were coming to demand incomes commensurate with their 'middle class' status. Current salaries, they argued, did not allow them to lead lives of dignity.

The Association of Schoolmasters established in 1884, at the instigation of Mr. Matthew Joseph, was concerned with the economic interests of teachers as well as with the competence of teachers. On behalf of the Association, Mr. Joseph sent a long memorandum to the Colonial Office. It is not clear how long the Association lasted, but of interest are the issues raised in the memorandum of Mr. Joseph.[22] His long memorandum can be summarized as follows:

Firstly, with all due respect to the wonderful work which the Churches had done, it was time for the Government to take a more active interest in education.

Secondly, the educational system was not providing facilities whereby the 'peasantry could be thoroughly civilized and enlightened'. The consequence was that the great majority of the black and coloured people who formed three-fourths of the population of this country are in a state of deplorable ignorance.

Thirdly, a proper system of education was particularly important in an island such as Jamaica 'inhabited by different races of people, with but little sympathy among them, such a state of gross ignorance is baneful to its peace and prosperity'.

Fourthly, there should be compulsory education, which would be the 'greatest boon' to the country since emancipation.

Fifthly, it was not true that such a system of universal education would lead to discontent among Negroes as 'put forth by strangers and others who have no real interest in the welfare and prosperity of our country and in the progress of its people. Rather, it would increase the loyalty of the people to the Crown'. 'Your memorialists who are all black men and coloured men and are natives of different parts of the Island, are the best judges in this matter; and we assert, that should the system of education which we are now advocating be introduced here, for the civilization and enlightenment of our people it will greatly add to their love for our Most Gracious Queen and their loyalty to her throne'.

Turning to the question of conditions of work, the memorandum pointed out that teachers were often driven to migrate to Panama, or to join the Constabulary, or to become time keepers and 'bosses' at the Canal. Others became schoolmasters 'among the people of their own race in the southern USA'. Addressing itself specifically to salaries, the memorandum expressed the view that 'the great majority of trained schoolmasters are of the view that their pay is small because they are black men. The saying 'Any pay will do for a Negro being a proverb in this Country'. On the question of profes-

sionalism the memorandum noted that there was 'a false economy by which these incompetent men are employed at starving salaries, to pretend to educate the peasantry of this country . . . waste of public money and an act of injustice to the people themselves'. The memorandum also called for a pension scheme and a widows and orphan fund on the basis of monthly deductions from salary.

The memorandum is instructive because it views education as the road to 'civilisation' of the peasantry; it associated race as a factor in the slow mobility of blacks; it emphasizes the need for a professional and properly trained corps of teachers. It advocates a widows and orphan fund, and hints at the movement outside the profession, of migration and change of profession. The Association viewed itself as a spokesman for the rural constituency, and makes a political point: education would reinforce rather than weaken loyalty to the Crown.

It is probably this trend among teachers which the Jamaica Union of Teachers (JUT) continued from its formation in 1894 — the idea of teaching as a profession of respectable black people; the dedication to the civilization of blacks by blacks within an unreformed status quo. The JUT, as an organization of black schoolmasters (and schoolmistresses), spoke in the same tones of education of the peasantry, and threw their support behind Legislative Council candidates who advocated educational causes.

In his history of the JUT, one of its founders, W.F. Bailey, emphasizes this professional outlook.[23] In 1891 guest speakers had been invited from the United States to speak to teachers 'to widen the outlook of those who were destined to mould or mar the lives of as many tender ones'. According to Bailey 'with aspirations kindled and outlook widened, teachers as a class soon found that the environment which surrounded elementary education in Jmaiaca did not lend itslf to progress'. The thinking behind the formation of the JUT was partly that since the government, the general public and the planter class cared little for mass education, this particular class of blacks had to take the initiative. Education had to be undertaken as a responsibility by teachers themselves grouped in a countrywide professional asociation.

The JUT was modelled on the National Union of Teachers in Britain. It was to act as an advisory body to teachers who were moving to districts which were not known to them: it was designed to co-ordinate all the various local associations of school teachers throughout the island in order to facilitiate the expression of the opinions of teachers. The JUT also committed itself to founding a Provident Benevolent Annuity Fund in connection with the Union, for the benefit of the scholastic profession.[24] Eventually a Teachers' Mutual Aid Society was formed.[25]

Black teachers and spokesmen, such as J.H. Reid, an ardent advocate of black racial unity, viewed the JUT as one of the columns of such unity. Even more he saw racial unity as cutting across class and occupational lines. In his response to the dock workers strike in 1895 he expressed the view that the formation of the JUT and the wharf strike were indicators of growing ethnic unity:

Is the sentiment of race affinity so completely disrupted in the Negro race as to render it powerless in bringing about a coherence of its members? Objects of ostracism by other races, why should each stand aloof from the other, when numbers so greatly preponderate in their favour? United we stand divided we fall.

Reid was going beyond the idea that black teachers were responsible for the 'civilisation' of rural black workers, to the more revolutionary idea of a cross-class black alliance.[26]

While the religious bodies never ceased to show creative interest in the growth of educational facilities in the country, the JUT was associated with an expansion of secular education at the end of the nineteenth century — a factor which was of some concern to the Church which feared the growth of agnosticism and even atheism if there were not a strong religious input in the schools of a non-denominational nature. The JUT was, at the same time, an important organization of black Jamaican professionals, many of them highly educated not by means of local institutions but through the acquisition of libraries. They would have constituted part of what was called the 'coloured aristocracy' of the country. Their intellectual rather than their possession of wealth made them 'respectable'.

The priesthood was another important middle strata profession for coloured and black men. The path to the priesthood was often via the road of teaching, and in fact, the two professions were at some points inseparable. The Minister of the Gospel enjoyed considerable prestige in rural Jamaican society, partly because of the old tradition of close association between preacher and labourer, the former often acting as surrogate for the interests of the latter; partly because the Church and/or the school was often the social centre of life in rural Jamaica. The origins of the black minister of religion also rested in the rural smallholding class. In 1881 the census listed 261 ministers of religion and in 1891 it recorded 329 fairly evenly spread throughout rural Jamaica. In comparison there were approximately 1,000 schoolmasters in the country between 1881 and 1891, not including governesses, music teachers and dancing tutors of which there were a few dozens.

Such prestige which the black minister of religion or catechist enjoyed among his flock was modified by his race. Coloured clergymen were given, as a matter of course, the less prominent cures. The fact that, inevitably, the majority of Jamaican congregations were black led some churchmen to conclude that there was no discrimination in Churches. The 'Little Kirk' in 1896 committed the blunder which revealed the truth. A Presbyterian clergyman (black) Rev. Dingwall was refused burial at the Little Kirk. Dingwall had served at the Little Kirk and was a member of that congregation. It is true that Rev. Dingwall had died in the mental asylum, but that hardly seemed grounds for disqualifying the uncomplaining corpse of Rev. Dingwall from burial in Holy ground. Rev. T.M. Geddes of Coke Chapel (Methodist) came to the rescue of the deceased minister.[27] Dingwall, it should be noted here, made forthright remarks (in print) on sexual license in Jamaica and had associated loose sexual behaviour with white society. His had also been an extremely forceful Africa consciousness.[28] Little Kirk tried to punish his soul by not burying the body.

Rev. P.F. Schoburgh, a local Baptist minister, was discriminated against on board Captain Walker's ship. He had been refused a clean cabin on board though there were clean ones available. The remark of the Captain was: 'And what do you expect, better?' The *Jamaica Advocate* described Rev. Schoburgh as 'one of the foremost black men in the Colony, in education, character, social standing'.

A denial of his rights not only wakes but startles, us all. If he is treated with indignity, what must be the lot of the many unfortunates of his race who travel on these boats?[29]

These two experiences demonstrate that social prestige as measured by cultural attainments was no barrier to discrimination on the grounds of race.

The artisans

An important social group in the country, whose members constituted a substantial number of blacks outside the agricultural sector were the artisans. It is essential to observe, however, that while there were men who dedicated themselves entirely to the trades, there were others who supplemented the tilling of the soil with work in one of the trades.

The artisan group proved mobile in two respects: first they were among the Jamaicans who migrated most; secondly, it was the segment which perhaps experienced most downward social mobility. What may appear puzzling in late-nineteenth century Jamaica is that there were regular expressions of regret at the absence of skilled artisans, while the reality was that poor opportunities at home encouraged an outward movement of artisans. The fact is that declining opportunities for artisans in rural Jamaica, particulary in the sugar industry, drove many artisans overseas. Secondly, the competition faced by artisans from cheap imported goods reduced opportunities for some categories of artisans.

In 1870, for example, the West End Foundry in Kingston, had employed an average of 120 mechanics, including apprentices, in addition to outdoor hands. Approximately £80 per week were paid in wages. In the decade of the 1870s the West End Foundry drew from the parish of Vere alone, for foundary and estate work, some £1,500 to £2,000 per annum. By the 1890s these contracts were not being renewed, and in 1897 the future apeared dim.

We got work only to the value of £26 from Vere in 1895 compared with £1,500 to £2,000 per year in 1870–80. In 1869 contracts were worth only £80. The staff had therefore been reduced significantly, from 120 in the 1870s to 38 in 1897; that is eight good mechanics and 30 lads (not apprentices).

The decline in sugar was the main cause of the problem, but the banana industry 'has not given us one pound of work in ten years'.[30]

The possession of artisan skills was no longer viewed with the respect once enjoyed. As Mr. Lazarus noted:

The intelligent and respectable lads, as a rule, do not take readily to mecahnical trades, nor are their families inclined to place them out. Their first object is to put them to the Civil Service examination, and if they should fail, they then make an attempt to put them to a trade; the lad is so spoilt and so above himself, that he becomes overbearing and has to be dismissed, for such an example would become a curse to any establishment.[31]

This statement confirms the view that browns and whites saw the civil service as the target of their aspirations. But their aspirations for civil service positions must have become associated with the decline in the standard of living of artisans and therefore with the view that artisans' work of any kind was beneath their social status. From the conduct of 'respectable lads' who were recruited, it was clear that foundry work was moving towards an occupation dominated by blacks — a movement comparable to that in the domestic service.[32]

The decline in demand for their services in the sugar industry combined with foreign competition to make the occupations of artisans hazardous during this period. W. Clarke Murray who had intimate knowledge of the artisan strata, having himself been a carpenter at Port Royal before his distinguished occupation as an educator in the island began, noted that the 'importation of entire buildings and parts of them, and also of dress lumber of every description, as well as ready-made clothing, boots, etc. have reduced the earnings of this class considerably, so that comparatively few of the youths see any prospect for making a living by trades, and do not seek instruction in them'.[33]

In 1898, two members of the Legislative Council (Mr. Leyden, representative for St. Elizabeth, and Dr. Johnson of St. Ann) presented petitions from artisans and tradesmen showing that their 'several trades were being ruined by the large importation of ready-made goods, and were consequently on the verge of starvation and could not find the means to pay their taxes and dues'.[34]

Earnings from the trades had, in the past, provided the cash for investments in land or in shopkeeping. The Custos of Westmoreland decribed the fall in status and fall in income as follows:

[Artisans] used to occupy a much more respectable position than the ordinary labourer, and had accumulated some means which as a rule, they put into the savings bank or with which they purchased a mule and cart, or built a good house and bought a few acres of land and cultivated it, who are now worse off. This class of people who derived all their progress at the time from the sugar estates in my neighbourhood now scarcely exists at all.[35]

Looking at artisan occupations over the period 1871–91 there was, according to census returns, a decline in the number of blacksmiths from 1,432 in 1871 to 1,377 in 1881, and to 1,185 in 1891, or a 17% decline between 1871 and 1891. The figures for coopers who were probably most affected by the decline of the sguar industry are not as clear. According to the 1871 census there were 2,089 coopers and 92 carpenters. In 1891 there were 8,982 carpenters and 1,487 coopers. In 1881 carpenters and coopers were linked; there were then 10,701 carpenters and coopers. It is not improbable that coopers took up carpentry. Shoemaking remained stable: 1,710 in 1871; 1,830 in 1881; 1,765 in 1891. There was a decline of hatmakers from 487 in 1871 to 412 in 1881, and 370 in 1891; a 24% decline in 20 years.[36]

But there were definite increases in the number of bricklayers and masons, from 1,058 to 2,527, and 2,502 for the period 1871–91. There was an increase in the number of tailors (1,939 and 2,422) and in the number of painters — from 152 in 1871 to 300 in 1881 and to 426 in 1891. The suggestion is that artisans and tradesmen associated with the construction industry still found their occupations among the most viable, though Clarke Murray had observed that pre-fabricated buildings were being imported. There is good reason to believe that the carpenter, bricklayer and mason were fully occupied in the late-nineteenth century in the construction of housing. The number of dwellings with shingle, metal or concrete roof and flooring increased from 44,027 in 1891 to 91,183 in 1911, while the number of dwellings with thatch roof and flooring increased from 35,683 in 1891 to 47,637 in 1911. In 1891 the number of dwellings with metal roofs was only 994. In 1911 there were 18,315.[37] It is true, however, that these figures must be treated with caution since there was no census in 1901 and there must have been much more feverish building after the earthquake of 1907.

In spite of foreign competition, milliners and seamstresses increased in number from 14,565 to 18,966 in 1891. These figures do not, however, say anything about the quality of life of milliners and seamstresses, and the large numbers found in this category are probably a more significant comment on the limited occupational opportunities for women than on the economic viability of such occupations.

The Blue Book indicates that in 1888–9 tradesmen earned between 2s.6d. and 6s. per day. Painters earned between 1d. to 1s.5d per superficial yard, per coat.[38]

Many tradesmen were probably of dubious skill. Young men were in the habit of setting themselves up in business as soon as they had 'picked up the merest smattering of their business, carpenters who cannot drive a nail, bricklayers who cannot lay a brick, set up for themselves as skilled labourers without the slightest qualification'.[39] The royal Commission of 1879 complained that these youths had been 'spoiled' for agriculture, but were no good for anything else. The skepticism concerning the skills of many of the young tradesmen continued to be vibrant in the late-nineteenth century:

Notwithstanding we have some good, hardworking, intelligent tradesmen, who are doing well and have brought up their families decently, who own their own houses; we have against these, a large number of incompetent, insolent, ignorant, lazy and worthless lot of grown-up tradesmen, who are really in the way of good men.[40]

The point is, though, that many of them continued to receive jobs because 'they were encouraged by gentlemen who give out work to be done, because they think it is cheap, and when a little experience teaches them that they have been deceived, they abuse the whole rank and file of tradesmen and call them worthless'.[41]

The system of apprenticeship had evidently broken down. Mothers apparently often expected their sons to receive an income as apprentices.[42] Masters found it difficult to maintain discipline among apprentices, so they claimed, because the boys continued to 'live in their parents' yards and spending their leisure time away from restraint, are not sufficiently separated from the demoralizing associations, and do not readily submit to the control of their employers'.[43] One cabinetmaker had been taken to court for strapping an apprentice, a sure indication of the conditions under which apprentices learned their trade.

Artisan's work, where it was closely linked to the sugar industry, witnessed a decline in the demand for skills: where there was demand particularly in the building industry, the artisan situation was not as precarious. There was decline in the prestige of the mechanical trades as they fell increasingly into the hands of black juveniles, and as 'lads' of higher 'social standing' agitated for employment in the more prestigious civil service.

The artisans did not confine themselves to employment in the trades. They often invested in land, partly because of the security arising out of investment in real estate, but more importantly for the income which good farm land could bring. In some respects, the artisans of the countryside were part of the small farmer complex. They cultivated their own land, but also engaged in carpentry, shingle splitting, sawing wood. In response to the reduction of opportunities in the sugar industry in Hanover one mason reported that he had converted full time to farming his twenty aces of land (three acres in coffee, and the rest in pasture and provision).[44] Another carpenter divided his time between carpentry and cultivating eleven acres of his own land.[45] Of course, opportunities for artisans arose from the construction of railroads and from the programme of bridge building during the 1890s.

The artisans were regarded as leading a precarious existence. One response was to seek opportunities overseas, thereby depriving the colony of experienced artisans. In this context, there was serious discussions on 'free trade' versus 'protectionism'. There were some Jamaicans who regarded free trade as an 'economic law', there were others who advocated a tariff to protect local industries.[46] Spokesmen such as W. Clarke Murray, despite his sympathy for the class of artisans, thought it would be unwise to offer protection to the possible disadvantage of other groups in terms of increased costs:

A goodly number whom I represent would seek a protective duty on such imported articles, but I would myself hesitate in recommending such a course lest in seeking to advantage a class, though large, a much larger number be made to suffer additional payments for necessary articles and work. . . .[47]

In any event Jamaica was not in the most favourable position to utilize the policy of protective tariffs. The colony's leverage was much reduced by the pressures placed on it by British and American trading policies — most favoured nation clauses on the one hand, and reciprocity conventions on the other. The US market absorbed, up to the end of the nineteenth century, considerable quantities of Jamaican sugar, and was in addition a favourable market for bananas, citrus, and cacao. Jamaica's small market also favoured British manufactured goods. There was little prospect that artisans would win legislative sanctions of the type which would make their goods competitive with cheaper manufactured imports or processed goods such as dressed lumber and pre-fabricated buildings. Meanwhile the increase in imports of clothing, footwear, and furniture supports the view that local production was faced with increased competition.[48]

There was not only a wide range of skills within the artisan layer, but differing levels of competence. The ambivalent attitudes of artisans is demonstrated by the fact that their 'attitudes and living standards had as much in common with lower middle class attitudes and living standards as with the attitudes of the unskilled'.[49] In Jamaica, some artisans supported industrial education for the sake of greater technical efficiency and a sense of professionalism. Others were hesitant to support educational policies which would have the effect of swelling the number of artisans.

Faced with severe competition from imports, the lower middle and middle class artisans were forced to support the Government's restrained approach to technical training in order to protect their small share of the local market. Those of the higher classes who were in favour of more vigorous action based their preference more on the supposed effectiveness of technical training in developing desirable attitudes to work than on marketable skills that could be gained.[50]

The artisans were not a united group, yet they were to establish one of the first occupational unions in the colony. One of the major divisions between the artisans rested on the existence of those who desired to maintain some degree of professionalism within the crafts and those, who

poorly trained, set themselves up as skilled labourers, and, so it was argued, brought all tradesmen into disrepute. At the lower level of artisanry the line between the skilled worker and the hustler could only have been a thin one, merging at the bottom with the vagabonds, vagrants, and, in Kingston, 'the dangerous classes'. At the upper level the artisan groups were a part of the emergent middle class. In 1897 one of the island's most well-known artisans showed strong support for technical education, which he thought should be given at least the same importance as elementary education. Once that was done, Mr. Lazarus argued, the 'disabilities from which the mechanical arts and crafts suffered, would be removed'.[51]

It is not that the upper levels of the artisan class were preoccupied with 'credentialism' or with the control of a market for their expertise, but definitely with the collective social status of respectable artisans.[52] Occupational role can become 'an integral part of a person's self-image', and it was with this self-image that the upper level of the artisan group was concerned.

It is in this spirit that we understand the formation of the Artisans' Union in 1899, an organization determined on a collective level to defend the rights of the profession, and to discourage the intrusion into the profession of untrained artisans who discredited the profession, in their view at least. It was not a labour union organization directed towards extracting concessions from capital, but an association of professionals to protect the integrity of the occupation by leaving membership open only to those who could prove their relevant skills.

When the Artisans' Union met in mid-December 1899, it is significant that the *Daily Gleaner* referred to the 'weekly general meeting of the Carpenters, Bricklayers and Painters Union' -the artisans of the construction industry.[53] The meeting of 11 December 1899, 'deprecated the system by which contracts were awarded', and recommended that the building public be cautioned against the 'instability of the lumber market and also the rule of thumb methods adopted by certain untrained and incapable builders and contractors in making valuation for building work, resulting in the detriment of the working man, sub-contractors and merchants'. At its meeting on 20 December 1899, the Union called for the establishment of a Technical School Workshop in connection with the Union for 'training of hand and eye of both women and boys, so that "botchers" may learn to have ambition'.[54]

Yet, despite its concern with professional integrity, the Union was to make strong comments on various social issues which did not affect artisans only. The Union, for example, protested against poor wages and 'in many instances labour minus wages'. It sent circulars to the Parochial Boards seeking information 'as to the rate of wages etc. for artisans and labourers. . .' It addressed itself to the unhappy state of affairs at the St. Catherine District Prison, and 'deprecated' the action of the St. Ann, St. James, and Manchester Parochial Boards in withholding information asked for in connection with social conditions of the people whom they represented. 'This union is entirely indignant at this treatment in trying to trample under their feet the intelligence of the Artisans' Union'. The Union also called for the abolition of taxes which now 'oppress labour and hamper production'. Taxes should be placed on land instead. Workmen should be given the opportunity to be 'producers of wealth for the social advancement of the community'.[55]

The strength/weakness of the Union was partly demonstrated by the resolution that 'Rule 55 be suspended to enable delinquent members to become financial'. The tendency of the Union to express itself in strong language prompted the *Daily Gleaner* to plead with the Union to 'bear and forbear; grievous words stir up anger'.[56]

Professional women

Dr. Robert Love, editor of the *Jamaica Advocate,* spoke strongly in favour of women's education, without which the negro race as a whole could not rise. In April 1895 the redoubtable editor spoke of the 'culture of our women' as the 'key to the whole problem'.

We have concentrated on the elevation of our men — clergymen, lawyers, etc. — but not on our daughters. The race must rise by families not by individuals. Men are still despised in spite of their achievements. The race rises as its women rise. They are the true standard of its elevation. We are trying to produce cultured men without asking ourselves where they are to find cultured wives. We forget that cultured families constitute a cultured race and that a cultured race is an equal race. The elevation of women to equality with [their] white counterparts is the Condition *Sine Qua Non* of the elevation of the Negro race.[57]

Returning to the same theme later that year the *Advocate* declared:

Every pound spent to educate the black boy tends to elevate a class only, but every pound spent to educate a black girl, tends to elevate the whole race. Fathers and mothers, bear these facts in mind, and send as many of your black daughters to England as you can. Some tell you that your girls can be just as well educated here. Ask them, why then do they send theirs to England.[58]

By the end of the nineteenth century efforts to educate girls had begun to reap their reward. There was clearly a decline in illiteracy among women. The number of women signing the marriage register with a 'mark' declined even more rapidly than men.[59]

It is not clear why employment requiring skills in shorthand, typing and telegraph operation is dominated by women, but such posts were filled in Jamaica by women rather than by men. In the 1890s Miss Maud M. Barrowes, principal of Wolmer's Girls School, added to the usual curriculum of French, English, Latin and German, a commercial syllabus which included shorthand, typing, book-keeping and French and English business correspondence. Miss Barrowes, so claims one grateful beneficiary, 'might be said to have put Jamaican girls on the map'.[60]

The health services also provided more occupation for women. The census gives only 20 nurses for the whole island in 1881, and 129 for the whole island in 1891, including three men.

Through the Deaconess programme the Anglican Church sought to develop a corps of nurses, though, as Nuttall indicated, the preference was for coloured women:

As regards nursing even more had been accomplished. In this work one real difficulty to contend with has been the prejudice against it on the part of many, especially among the coloured people to whom we chiefly look for volunteers, but who have not been in the habit of considering the vocation of nurse a very honourable one.[61]

Black Jamaican women took up the profession of nursing, which became open to them because coloured women did not think it prestigious enough, and because of increased educational facilities for women. In 1904 the Jamaican Nurse Union was established, with the encouragement of the Anglican Church, and its objectives were to facilitate communication between nurses and medical men as well as patients who required their

Table 1. Comparison of literacy between men and women as indicated by the marriage register

Year	Men	Women	Mean
1883–4	49.6	68.8	59.2
1886–7	46.8	64.8	55.8
1889–90	47.6	64.9	56.3
1892–3	45.3	60.0	52.6
1895–6	41.5	55.5	48.6
1899–1900	41.1	51.6	—

services.[62] For those who, in their dedication to the cult of 'true womanhood', preferred women to be 'Queen of the Home' the nursing profession could be explained as an extension of the nurturant role played by women at home.

There was a concerted effort to encourage women to take up the teaching profession. In 1883 ministers of religion came together to draft a memorandum to the acting Governor advocating the establishment of a training college for women. As the clergymen saw it, the young women were to come from a 'grade in life higher than that of most of the students who enter training colleges . . . they would be persons of a higher social culture and of more general intelligence'. The ministers also thought that women were more efficient teachers than men. Their claim rested on British and United States authorities who claimed that females had a 'greater natural aptitude for teaching children and bearing with their ignorance and restlessness'.[63] Female teachers were also expected to exercise a healthy moral influence on their charges.

In view of the social condition of the people, the moral influence of well-trained female teachers upon scholars of their own sex would be of incalculable value.

Finally, the memorialists argued that such a programme 'would have a beneficial effect on the community by opening careers of such honorable employment to young women'.

There was one other pressing consideration, and that was the lack of moral restraint on the part of male teachers with respect to their older female pupils; though the Inspector of Schools admitted that 'under temptation, more or less severe, the moral stamina of several teachers has given way'.

The most painful feature of the matter is that fact that in several instances the change of teacher has been rendered necessary under Government Regulation respecting the maintenance of moral character . . . Among them, I regret to say, are some whom I have heretofore had occasion to commend highly for efficient work in the schoolroom.[64]

The Inspector commented on the 33% turnover of teachers for that particular year, a turnover closely associated with the larger problem of sexual immorality. The introduction of more women in the classroom would stabilize staff, offer an ideal role model for girls, introduce gentler forms of discipline, and provide honourable work for women.

Women played an active role in the Jamaica Union of Teachers and from that platform tackled, in a particular manner, issues relating to women. Firstly, they asked for equal salaries; secondly, they protested against restrictions imposed on the professional mobility of women. Impediments to mobility arose precisely because of the policy of the Churches to employ men who could serve as catechists, according to the assumptions of the time.

Women were also employed as telegraph clerks. In 1889 they earned 10s. per week, and apparently were expected to pay rent, provide their own furniture, and to present a 'respectable appearance'.

I think myself that when the Government can stoop to insult a class of respectable females who carry on the work of a responsible and paying institution, by paying them six–pence per day, allowing only for the first hour one shilling for working after official hours, it is time the matter was taken up by the new representatives of the country and set right.[65]

Artisans, teachers, nurses, constables, and prosperous small farmers represented a diffuse group of occupations standing between the minorities and the masses. They constituted the 'respectable' blacks of colonial society and probably represented a fair number of people who emigrated to seek superior opportunities elsewhere, for the obvious reason that their material circumstances could not support their 'respectability'. It was sometimes noted that many of the emigrants came from the 'middle walks of life' in Jamaica.

Out of this group has emerged the professional strata of black Jamaicans, whose 'respectability' and status rested upon education and professional attainments, rather than upon ownership of the means of production. Within this group can be identified the black intelligentsia which for a long time had been in formation.

Notes

1. R.T. Smith, 'Race and Class in the Post-Emancipation Caribbean', in Robert Ross (ed.) *Racism and Colonialism: Essays on Ideology and Social Structure,* Leiden: Martinus Nijhoff 1982, p. 108.
2. Daily Gleaner (hereafter DG), 28 March 1886.
3. DG, 6 September 1889.
4. Sir Anthony Musgrave, *Jamaica: Now and Fifteen Years Since* (Proceedings of the Royal Colonial Institute, 1879–80, vol. 41).
5. *Ibid.* p. 14.
6. *Ibid.* p. 13.
7. Velma Newton, *The Silver Men, West Indian Labour Migration to Panama 1850–1914,* Kingston: ISER 1984, p. 106.
8. *Jamaica Gazette* (JG), Vol. XI, 1888. Report of Committee on Immigration, p. 686. The Committee consisted of Messrs. Neale Porter, Michael Solomon, W. Bancroft Espeut, Charles Mosse.
9. CO, 137/532, 1887. Norman (no. 364), 25 October 1887. Enclosure Dr. Gayleard's report on conditions in Panama.
10. CO 137/541, Vol. 1, 1890. Blake (No. 47), 1890. Enclosing petition of Clarendon farmers.

11. CO, 137/542, 1890. Blake (No. 59), 10 February 1890 reporting on tour of the island and enclosing petition of farmers.
12. *JG* Vol. 17, No. 39, 22 March 1894. Address to Blake by Clarendon Agricultural Association.
13. Jamaica Archives, 1B/5/18, Vol. 50. Blake (No. 234), 3 July 1895, 'Jamaica Agricultural Society'.
14. *Ibid.* Blake (No. 326).
15. R.T. Smith, *Race and Class,* p. 109.
16. West India Royal Commission (WIRC), 1897. Evidence of Mr. Thomas Smickle, 5 April 1897, p. 325/333.
17. Rev. C.A. Wilson, *Men with Backbone and other pleas for progress* (Kingston, 1913), p. 8.
18. Manuscript (MST) 209, *Bishop's Letter Book,* Vol. 7, 14 July 1883. Nuttall to Mr. Asbourne.
19. *Ibid.* Nuttall to Mr. Asbourne, 14 July 1883.
20. Jamaica Minutes of the Legislative Council (JCM), 1887 Appendix XVIII. Annual Report of Inspector of Schools to 30 September 1886.
21. *DG,* 9 March 1885, 'A Son of Africa' to Editor.
22. CO 137/514, 1884. Memorandum signed by Mr. Matthew Josephs 'for and on behalf of the Meeting of the General Association of Schoolmasters in the Island of Jamaica'.
23. W.F. Bailey, *History of the Jamaica Union of Teachers,* Kingston: Gleaner Co. Ltd. 1937.
24. *Ibid.* p. 12.
25. C.A. Wilson, *Men of Vision,* (Kingston 1929), p. 86.
26. *Jamaica Advocate* (JA) 22 June 1895. J.H. Reid, 'Negro Isolation'.
27. *JA* 27 June 1896, 'The Little Kirk and the Rev. Robert Dingwall'.
28. Rev. R. Dingwall, 'Outlook for Jamaica and her People' in Rev. R. Gordon, et al, *Jamaica's Jubilee,* (London, 1888), especially pp. 119–128.
29. *JA* 21 September 1895.
30. WIRC, 1897. Written testimony of Charles P. Lazarus (West End Foundry, Kingston, Jamaica) for the information of the West Indian Royal Commission. pp. 405/413 to 406/414.
31. *Ibid.* 406/414.
32. B.W. Higman, 'Domestic Service in Jamaica since 1750', in B.W. Higman, *Trade, Government and Society in Caribbean History, 1700–1920,* Kingston: Heinemann Educational Books, 1983, p. 126.
33. WIRC, 1897. W. Clarke Murray D.D., Vice-President, Wesleyan Conference, to the secretary of Her Majesty's Commission, pp. 388/396 to 389/397.
34. Jamaica, *Legislative Council Proceedings,* 4 May and 11 May 1898.
35. WIRC, 1897. Evidence of Hon. W. Ewen, Custos of Westmoreland, p. 337/345.
36. See Jamaica Censuses of 1871, 1881, 1891.
37. Census, 1911. Housing, p. 5.
38. Blue Book, Island of Jamaica (JBB), 1889.
39. Report of Royal Commission upon the Condition of the Juvenile Population of Jamaica (RCJ), 1879, p. 16.
40. WIRC, 1897. Testimony of Charles P. Lazarus.
41. *Ibid.*
42. RCJ, 1879. Evidence of Mr. Alexander Berry.
43. *Ibid.*
44. WIRC, 1897. Evidence of Andrew Little, p. 330.
45. *Ibid.* Evidence of James Cox, p. 340/348.
46. DG, 27 March 1886, and 'O.P.Q.' to Editor, DG, 22 March 1886 and 4 April 1886.
47. WIRC, 1897. Evidence of W. Clarke Murray.
48. Trevor Turner, 'Social Objectives in the Educational Thought of Jamaicans 1870–1920', Ph.D. University of Toronto, 1975, p. 124.
49. E.H. Hunt, *British Labour History 1814–1914,* New Jersey: Humanities Press, 1981, p. 39.
50. Trevor Turner, *Social Objectives,* p. 401.
51. WIRC, 1897. Testimony of Charles Lazarus.
52. Keith McDonald, 'Professional Formation: the Case of Scottish Accountants', in *British Journal of Sociology,* Vol. 35, 1984, pp. 174–5.
53. DG, 13 December 1899, 'Artisan Union'.
54. DG, 20 December 1899, 'Artisan Union'.
55. *Ibid.*
56. DG, 21 December 1899.
57. JA, 6 April 1895, 'The Condition *Sine Qua Non* of the Complete Elevation of the Negro Race'.
58. JA, 14 September 1895, 'Truths to be Remembered'.
59. Jamaica Department Reports (JDR), 1895–6, 'Proportionate Numbers of Bridegrooms and Brides who signed by Mark, per 1,000 Persons Married'.
60. Jamaica Memories (JM) Essay of Mrs. Enid Pilgrim (née Carrington).
61. National Library of Jamaica (NLJ) MST 209a, Vol. 29, *Bishop's Letter Book,* Nuttall to Jamaica Church Ladies' Association in England, 9 August 1892.
62. F. Cundall, *Jamaica in 1912,* (Kingston, 1912), p. 62.
63. JG, 18 October 1883. Memorial from Ministers of Religion to Major-General Gamble (Acting Governor).
64. JCM 1887. Appendix XVIII, Report of George Hicks, Inspector of Schools.
65. DG, 11 March 1889, 'Fair Play', to Editor.

Consensus and Conflict Over the Provision of Elementary Education

M.K. Bacchus

The Provision of Elementary Education

While the provision of elementary education obviously depended on both supply and demand factors, the forces that influenced the former were far more crucial in determining the rate at which this level of education expanded in the region. This was largely because the masses, who were anxious for their children to receive an education, did not have the economic resources to meet its full cost on their own, or the political power to ensure that the state took on the entire responsibility of paying for it. The amount of resources that the state made available to meet the cost of education therefore became a key element in the expansion or improvement of this level of education. Hence, the support of groups which controlled or had some influence over the spending powers of the government was crucial.

There were a number of key groups with differential amounts of power who were able to influence the amount of government funds provided for elementary education in the West Indies which in turn determined its rate of expansion. Among the more important of these were the imperial authorities and their local representatives, i.e., the colonial governors, the planters, the missionaries, and the local legislators.

Obviously the attitude of the members of such groups to the education of the masses influenced the support which they were willing to provide in order to obtain government financial assistance for it. This in turn depended largely on their perceptions of the role which they saw such education could play in serving their own vested interests.

The major effort at formally educating the ex-slaves began after the abolition of slavery in 1834 and the termination of the 'apprenticeship' period in 1838. The British government made a grant for Negro Education in 1834 and also allowed the Mico Trust funds to be used for this purpose. This provided additional impetus to the missionary societies and other voluntary agencies to increase their contribution to education. The result was a substantial expansion of elementary education in the region in the years immediately following emancipation. As a result, by the time the Negro Education Grant was terminated in 1845, day primary schools were available in all these colonies and 'the idea of popular education was established for good in the West Indies.'[1]

But with the withdrawal of imperial funds and the declining financial support which the denominational bodies were able to secure from their parent organizations, the question which arose was whether and to what extent the local legislatures would step in to help bridge the financial gap. This was of some concern because most West Indian legislative assemblies had not offered any tangible help when the British government earlier sought their assistance in providing education for the ex-slaves. In addition, the colonies were facing severe economic difficulties due to the decline in the sugar industry and their treasuries were at times almost empty.

The support of the planters for the education of the masses became absolutely necessary because under the representative system of government, the final responsibility for allocating public funds still rested with the members of the local legislatures whose members formed part of, or were closely associated with the plantocracy. A major challenge, therefore, which faced those who were providing education in the region, was to win the support of the planters, and *ipso facto* the legislators, in assuming a larger share of responsibility for financing elementary education.

An important step in this direction was the attempt to define, or redefine, the role of education in such a way that its objectives would become more acceptable to the ruling groups. Therefore, it was suggested that the ex-slaves had to be taught to accommodate themselves to their new reality and to become aware of the need to adjust their occupational aspirations and behaviours accordingly. In commenting on the kind of education which was considered necessary for the black population, the editor of the *Colonist* suggested that:

it should be directed at motivating the Africans to work and respect authority ... [it] should *teach the Negroes not to disregard the diversities of rank and the corruption of life imposed [on them) for wise purpose.* They should be brought practically to love honesty, sobriety, reverence to authority and a *Christian respect for all whom Providence has placed in a superior condition [emphasis added].*[2]

Attention was also drawn to the fact that this type of education was supported by William Wilberforce, one of the foremost champions of abolition, who did not want the ex-slaves to aspire 'beyond their station in life.' In his *Practical Views of Christianity*, he suggested that, as far as the lower classes in general were concerned, 'their more lowly path has been allotted to them by the hand of God,' and that it was 'their obligation faithfully to discharge their duties' in their given station in life and 'contentedly to bear its inconveniences.'[3] These views were seen as applicable to the children of the ex-slaves as they were to the working class in England, and were likely to win the approval of the local legislatures in financing popular education.

A number of key groups in these societies became increasingly supportive of the expansion of primary education, especially in view of the goals which were being proposed for it. As a result of their efforts, pressures were increasingly brought to bear on the West Indian legislatures to raise their level of financial contribution to education and to play a more active role in its general administration and regulation. But while such efforts were commendable, they also represented an attempt by those who had greatly benefitted from the inhumane exploitation of the enslaved Africans to salve publicly their uneasy consciences by supporting the issue of their children's education.

Nevertheless, a point of view that many of the supporters of popular education espoused was that parents should be expected to make a greater contribution to the cost of their children's education and this was to be done by increasing school fees, encouraging local communities to raise additional funds and persuading parents to pay their children's fees punctually.

Moral Support by the Imperial Government

Despite the termination of its Negro Education Grant the British government maintained an interest in the long-term economic rehabilitation of the region. This was seen as partly dependent on the education of the masses, even though the imperial authorities did not have a consistent educational policy for the region and took 'direct action (only) ... in exceptional cases'.[4] The Colonial authorities wanted to ensure that the transition from slavery to a 'free labour market' was achieved without any major disruption, and saw that the 'right' type of education was important for this to happen. It was one reason why, around 1847 the Colonial Secretary again expressed the view that the agricultural and commercial prosperity, as well as the moral and spiritual well-being of West Indian communities, depended on the education of their population. He also suggested that the parents should not be allowed to refuse to send their children to school, even if this meant introducing compulsory school attendance in the region.

The British government's positive attitude to the education of the blacks was partly reflected in the crucial influence exerted by number of colonial governors in the development of education in these colonies. Many of them played an important role in trying to convince the local ruling groups, particularly the members of the legislatures, of the need for popular education and under the Crown Colony system some of them even led the way in proposing new educational policies and programmes.

The Support Provided by Various West Indian Governors

Many West Indian governors expressed strong support for popular education and recognized that the agencies providing such education faced great difficulties, in view of the limited support that they received from the various governments. They therefore tried to help correct this situation. For example, when Reid became Governor of Barbados, he was appalled at what he considered to be the 'low character' of the schools and, despite the economic difficulties which the colony then faced, called upon the legislators not to reduce the already limited amount of the education grant which they were providing. Instead, he suggested that they should increase the education vote, especially since some of the rural areas were not yet provided with schools, and urged that more efforts be made to improve the quality of instruction offered in the primary schools. His eventual hope was that popular pressure for education would be stimulated to a point where it would compel the Legislature to make publicly-aided schools free to the masses.

Colebrooke, who succeeded Reid, also put forward the case for more government assistance to education, suggesting that parochial schools be placed on a better financial footing to make them less dependent on voluntary support. He refused to accept the argument that government expenditure on education could not be increased because of the current economic position of the island, which, in 1848, was spending 34% of its budget on the police, 7.2% on jails and only 2.5% on education. Instead, he felt that a substantial reduction could be effected in the current expenditure on the repressive state apparatus (RSA) — the police, the courts, the prisons — without 'impairing' public security. Such a step would release additional funds for schools. This, in turn, would contribute to the educational and moral advancement of the people. His views probably had some effect on the members of the Barbadian legislature because, by 1852, there was a slight change in the structure of government expenditures with 3.8% of the total budget earmarked for education compared to 2.8% in 1848.

In Jamaica, Governor Grey also recognized that the failure of the legislature to provide funds for education during 1848/49, due to depressed economic conditions, was creating many problems for the voluntary agencies which operated schools on the island. He therefore called upon the members of the Legislative Assembly to recognize the value of education for the masses and urged that 'above all,' they should try to 'educate the people.' As a result, this item of expenditure was re-introduced into the budget in the following year.

Many governors went beyond simply requesting more state aid for education, with some even putting up their own proposals for educational reform in the different colonies. For example, when Grey was governor of Barbados, he developed an outline of a new educational policy for that island in which he proposed that, (i) a basic education should be provided, free of charge, for all children between 4 and 7 years of age, and that the curriculum should place a heavy emphasis on the inculcation of moral and religious values. (ii) that 'higher' elementary education, for which a fee was to be charged, should be made available to those between 7 and 10 years of age. This education was to be entirely secular, though the pupils were to be given religious instruction without charge on week-ends.

The Governor felt that because of the social benefits expected to accrue from the lower primary education, it was a worthwhile investment for the state. The proposed emphasis on the 'moral' development was considered important for the social stability of these colonies since it would help working class blacks to accept their 'ordained place' within the existing social order. The private returns from the second level of primary education was

considered to be high enough to induce parents to contribute to its cost.

Governor Reid was also concerned about the issue of equity of access to education and expressed the hope that the current admission policy that allowed some schools to exclude students because of their colour would soon come to an end. In its place, he urged that educational opportunities should be open to all children on the basis of their abilities — on the 'qualities of their mind' as he put it. In addition, he advanced the argument, later put forward by the advocates of the human capital theory, that, because education was important to increase economic productivity, a basic course of instruction should be made available to all members of the society.

The state should therefore play a more active role in producing 'an intelligent and educated' labour force. The Governor pleaded with the legislators that, 'whilst we strive to encourage religion and morality, let us strive to increase the general stock of intelligence (i.e. 'level of education') throughout the whole body of the community.'[5] Governor Grey of Jamaica made a similar point about the economic benefits of popular education when he suggested that there were important 'spin off benefits that would accrue from an educated work force because it was likely to attract more European capital and machinery and this could put the island on the first step toward becoming a 'happy and prosperous colony.'

Reid also drew attention to the importance of 'continuing education' because, as he pointed out, the education provided in schools for the young simply 'lays the foundation' which was necessary to enable all men to continue their self-education after they have entered the business of life.' As a result, he suggested that facilities such as a public library and a museum should be provided, so that those who had been to school could continue to educate themselves by their own efforts.[6] His proposals met with some success and the first public library in Barbados was established in 1848.

Governor Barkly of British Guiana expressed his regret at the 'little progress' that had 'hitherto been made in the education of the labouring classes,' especially since he too considered that 'the prosperity of all classes in the Colony' was 'entirely dependent' on the efforts which were made 'in the cause of education.'[8] In his desire to ensure that the government take a more active role in education, he established a Board of Education which was requested to prepare a 'plan of public instruction' that was suited to the requirements of the colony. In addition, he proposed that both the central and the local government authorities work together in their efforts to meet the future cost of education. The Governor also tried to get more financial support from the legislature to improve the amount and quality of elementary education offered, again using the economic argument that education was necessary to produce the steady and industrious work force that was a pre-requisite for improved agricultural production.

In his efforts to increase the spread of education in Grenada, the Lieutenant Governor tried to dissuade the legislature from making grants to schools conditional upon the levy of school fees because, as he argued, this was likely to reduce overall school attendance. Instead, he put forward the case for a general education tax or levy which would create less financial hardship on the poorer sections of the society seeking to educate their children. In 1853 he too recommended the creation of a Board of Education which was established by the Education Act of 1857/58. To secure the cooperation of all sections of the society both Protestants and Catholics were to be represented on this Board. The Act even provided for the establishment of a Model School, a Normal School for the training of teachers and a Grammar School. In that year also, all schools became eligible for government grants, partly due to Governor Keate's influence. With the arrival of Governor Sendall in 1886, education was again placed on the 'front burner.' He considered the financial allocation to education to be inadequate — a view which had been earlier expressed by the 1882 Royal Commission enquiring into public expenditure in the colony and made some attempts to improve the situation. In 1889 he called for the establishment of government-owned and operated schools, though the colony was to continue its financial support for the existing denominational schools.

Noting that during the year 1848, 'the education of the working classes has . . . greatly fallen off . . . owing to the (limited) financial resources of the government and the people,' the Administrator of Montserrat urged the legislature to provide some financial assistance to schools, adding that,

A grant from you, however small, voted with the view of retrieving lost ground and making further progress, (in education) would be of unspeakable use by affording a praiseworthy example, and showing every member of the community that you participate and sympathize with the universal yearning of the wise and good for the extension (of education) to those who so much need it, of a blessing so essential to the advance and amelioration of the human race . . . . A small grant from you would resemble the widow's mite; it would be like a flower in the desert, the more beautiful, the more grateful, the more acceptable, from our knowledge of the poverty of the soil which has produced it.[8]

Despite the fact that the legislators were still reluctant to provide funds for education, the Administrator did not fail to continue requesting them to make some provision for the maintenance of the schools. He even suggested that it was the first duty of every 'civilized community' to foster and encourage education. Eventually some success was achieved in 1868, when the legislature voted its first grant of £50 for schools.

The Governor of St Lucia tried to impress on the Legislature the view that education was 'a subject, the importance of which it is impossible to overrate, as upon its spread and encouragement will mainly depend the social, moral and physical well-being of a people'[9] In the Bahamas the Governor also tried to convince the members of the local legislative assembly that 'the demand for education is the most sacred of any that can be made on the public purse, and that any sacrifice should be made (for it) rather than that the laudable disposition of the rising generation for the acquirement of knowledge should be discouraged.'[11] The Administrator of Dominica expressed his hopes that education would continue to expand on that island. He saw it as being 'essential to the future well being of the colony' because it would ensure an ultimate improvement in the 'moral and intellectual culture' of the labouring classes.[11] However, in 1852, he pointed out that after four years of urging the House of Assembly for an 'augmentation' of the grant for education, the programmes continued to be 'sadly hampered' due to lack of funds.

The importance of education in helping to establish social stability was particularly stressed by individuals like Governor Barkly of British Guiana, who expressed the view that without a sound education it would be impossible to answer for the 'peace and safety' of the society. Governor Grey of Jamaica had emphasized the contribution which education could make to the moral and cultural development of the population. He advanced the argument that without the mental and moral culture which religious education provided, the population was likely to become discontented and restless and dissatisfied with the existing institutions of the society.

Other colonial administrators shared similar sentiments which became common throughout the region after the Morant Bay Rebellion of Jamaica in 1865. This incident was seen as a rude reminder to the Jamaican government and the elite groups in the other West Indian colonies, that there was a need to provide a 'proper' education for the masses if political stability in the region was to be maintained. Therefore, when Jamaica was reduced to a Crown Colony in 1867, the Governor, Sir John Peter Grant, began to give greater priority to education than his predecessor, partly because he was in a stronger constitutional position to do so. Under him, the education system was re-organized, elementary education placed on a more systematic basis and higher per capita grants paid for students as they moved up from one grade to another.

In Bermuda, the Governor noted that the Legislative Assembly was in 'a state of too general and deplorable apathy' on the subject of education. He argued that if there was no improvement in the education of the youths born around the 1850s, there was 'every reason to fear' that they will 'relapse into a semi-barbarous condition before the end of the century.' To him, the governing elites and the proprietors of large estates stood at a critical point in the history of the colony. They were 'between the progress of civilization and a steady improvement' of the population on one hand. and, 'unhappily, on the other,' there was the 'serious risk' of increasing 'ignorance, idleness and prejudice,' if they failed to adopt the right policies.[12] He suggested that it was only through an effective educational programme for the masses that they could succeed in guiding the development of the society along the 'proper' path.

Both Governors McLeod and Harris were also strong advocates of the view that government should assume greater responsibility for providing education for the masses. They argued that in Trinidad there was a great need to bring about a greater degree of social cohesion among the culturally diverse elements of the population. Since the colony was only more recently ceded to Britain from France, most of its inhabitants were still considered by the British authorities to be 'foreign.' Therefore, it was necessary to make a special effort to develop in the children in schools an allegiance to the British Crown and a sense of loyalty to the new Imperial authority. Another concern was the fact that most of the population did not speak the language of their new colonizers. As McLeod noted, 'two-thirds of the natives still speak exclusively either Spanish or French'- a situation that was regarded as unacceptable, since it was considered 'absolutely necessary that people living under British rule and claiming the benefit of British subjects should be able to read the laws by which they are governed.'[13] In addition, schools were to transmit a knowledge of English to all their students as part of an effort to develop in them a strong psychological attachment to the mother country.

McLeod saw that the only way that this could be achieved was through a vigorous policy of Anglicization and both governors therefore proposed that the state should assume a more direct responsibility for education. They recommended an end to the denominational system of schooling and making use of education to foster social cohesion and national integration in the society. The state should also have a role in deciding, or at least in directly influencing the curriculum that was being offered in schools, so that some of these concerns could be taken into account in the instructional programmes that were being offered.

When Lord Harris became governor he also observed that education in Trinidad had been neglected and that those attending school were receiving a poor quality of instruction. He reiterated the need for greater social cohesion among the population, pointing out that although 'liberty has been given to a heterogeneous mass' and 'a race has been freed, a society has not (yet) been formed.'[14] Another factor contributing to the social divisiveness among the local population was its religious composition and the inequality of the educational facilities available to children of these different denominational groups. He was convinced, therefore, of the need for common schools not only to help increase the amount of understanding and tolerance among the population but also to ensure a greater degree of equality of educational opportunity among them. This, he felt, could only be brought about if the state played a more active role in the provision of education. However, the dilemma which he faced and to which he drew attention was the 'scanty means of instruction' which were available in the colony. He recognized the need for more financial resources to extend educational facilities to all groups and was not convinced by the argument that the government could not afford to provide those additional funds. In fact, he felt that the subject was not given enough priority in the colony's budget.

To overcome some of these problems, Harris directed his efforts at developing a state operated system of secular education with fairly equal access to all sections of the society. He also wanted to ensure that there was an improvement in the quantity and the quality of education offered in the primary schools. To help achieve the latter goal, and to offer an 'encouragement' to the poorer classes to educate their children, he instituted a system of annual public examinations for the Governor's Prizes. These awards varied in value from $50 to $3.[15]

Many of Harris's ideas were ahead of their time and he initially made little progress with them. He had to modify some of them partly because of the prevailing poor economic conditions, and partly because of Catholic opposition to the secularization of education. These modifications involved the abandonment of a number of his crucial educational principles, one of which was to provide opportunities for intellectually capable students to move right up the educational ladder, irrespective of their social origins. Although he was of an aristocratic background and accepted the view that people had certain positions in life to occupy and 'given' duties to perform, he nevertheless believed in providing opportunities for upward social mobility among the 'lower orders' through education.

By 1851 Harris was successful in having a new Education Ordinance passed, which provided for the establishment of a decentralized system of education, offered through a system of 'Ward' schools and the provision of teacher training facilities. He also helped the legislature to develop a greater appreciation for the value of education. By the time his term of office ended in 1854, the government was much more heavily involved in providing elementary education than a decade before.

There were other West Indian governors, public officials and policy makers who tried to convince the local legislatures of the need to become more actively involved in the provision of education for the masses. The account given above provides only a sample of the individuals and the kind of arguments they were advancing in support of public education. It also suggests that, overall, the Colonial Office and its local representatives were willing to exert pressure on the local legislatures to make more government funds available for primary education. Some individuals even began to advocate the introduction of compulsory education throughout the region.

Pressures from Increasing Support for Popular Education

In addition to the positive attitudes to education shared by most West Indian Governors, there was also growing support for popular education among other influential groups in these societies. Many Church officials were concerned about the rising incidence of 'unruly behaviour' and delinquency among the young. In 1850 the Presbyterian Synod of Jamaica put forward a plan for a comprehensive State system of education to be administered by local boards. This was considered a means of checking 'the downward progress of society.'

The historian, Schomburgk, had also advanced the argument which was put forward by others such as Governor Colebrook, that, since moral and religious education would result in an improvement of 'the human mind,' the provision of education for a larger section of the population should eventually result in a diminution in crime and a concurrent reduction in public expenditure on the

physical control mechanisms of the State. This would, therefore, compensate for the additional expenses incurred by education. Around the late 1840s Maxwell, too, had urged that the responsibility for education should be taken over by the State, and that 'the advantages of an elementary education should be extended to every creed and colour without money and without price.'[17]

In Barbados, the proposal by Governor Grey for two levels of elementary education — one free, with a strong religious focus, and the other secular but paid for by the parents — was supported by various individuals who advocated that education should be provided on a universal rather than a parochial basis, and should be under public, not sectarian control. The Barbadian newspaper considered the government expenditure on education as highly inadequate. While it recognized that the existing state of the economy was partly responsible for this, it pointed out that when the first education grant of £750 was made by the legislature in 1846, the colony could have afforded a much larger sum. It also drew attention to the fact that, while the total government grant for popular education during that year was only £750, the island's upper class willingly diverted £1000 per annum from the Codrington estate to educate twelve of their children in England. One Dr. Bascom also argued that the local legislature had a special duty to help shoulder the responsibility for the education of the masses, since there was 'no question of greater importance' which could 'occupy its attention'. Rev. Richard Rawle, the Principal of Codrington College, pointed out that education was necessary in 'preventing mischief and promoting good' in the society. He, too, advanced the view that money spent on schools and teachers would eventually result in substantial savings on expenditure on the police.

Resistance to Increasing the Supply of Elementary Education

But while such support for popular education had an influence on the various West Indian legislatures, the planters were not always convinced about the need for extending educational facilities to the masses. This was partly because many of them did not want the colonial governments to extend their financial commitment to any item that might become a regular part of the recurrent budget. They de-emphasized the social returns to education, many of them subscribing to the views of the Trinidadian legislator, P.N. Aumaitre, who argued that the common man had no right to look to government to help raise himself to a more elevated sphere of life, which was what education was likely to do. This was one of the main reasons why the bills which sought to tax the propertied class to provide funds for education, such as the one put forward in the Jamaican legislature by Lyons in 1854, and the Compulsory Education bill which was part of a House Tax bill proposed in 1856, never found enough support to be made law.

Possibly even more important was the fact that many planters still believed that education was not only alienating the 'labouring classes' from their 'ordained' role as agricultural labourers, but was likely to make them a threat to the stability of these societies. In St. Kitts, there was 'a large and influential portion of the proprietary' class, who, in the late 1850s, continued to suggest that 'the worst labourers in their employment, the most deceitful, unruly, disrespectful, and impatient of direction and control were invariably those who had been to school.'[17] Therefore, some of the planters continued to oppose the extension of education to the masses, with the claim that it only made the newly emancipated averse to estate work and gave them 'strange' ideas of their social status.

In 1857 the Inspector of Schools for Grenada continued to draw attention to the lack of support for popular education from the elite on that island and observed that,

It is to be lamented that the efforts to educate the lower classes should be regarded by some persons here with a certain degree of jealousy and coldness. As likely to impair their usefulness as labourers, they cannot and will not believe that the more general education becomes, the less likely it is to have the effects they anticipate. They judge from the fact of the few who have acquired a little knowledge, having thereby raised themselves above the level of their more ignorant companions.[18]

Up to the late 1860s, the demand for popular education was opposed by many members of the local 'upper class,' who continued to regard it as a 'positive evil' calculated to induce the educated portion of the poor classes to regard their fellow labourers as beneath them and to withdraw themselves from the class to which they property belonged'.[19] As late as 1876 the Inspector of Schools for Antigua also observed that, 'even in the present day there are too many people to be found who regard an education given to the peasantry as serving only to unfit them for the labours which fall to their lot'.[20] In the same year the Education Commission for Barbados made similar observations noting that some local planters and estate managers still had misgivings about popular education, fearing that to teach the agricultural labourers' children was to unfit them for such duties which 'must necessarily' be their 'lot in life'.

Finally, members of the elite blamed the slow educational progress in the region not on the reluctance of the legislatures to provide additional funds for schools but on the attitudes of the blacks themselves. It was even suggested that instead of depending on more financial support from the state they ought to make a greater contribution to the education of their own children, eventually meeting the full cost of their schooling. Others expressed the view that any increase in the provision of education should only take place gradually, since, as the Administrator of the British Virgin Islands contended, the local population was not yet fully appreciative of its value. However, he saw that this would eventually come about as education became more available to them arguing that,

an appreciation of the value of education sufficient to induce the Negro to make a sacrifice of his means, for the education of his children, cannot be expected from the present generation of the emancipated classes in these colonies; it must be the *gradual result* of full experience by the people themselves of *the practical benefits arising from the acquisition of knowledge* it must be the result of a better educated state of the mass of the population, and this must be a work of time,[21] (emphasis added)

Support by Some Local Legislators for Elementary Education

With the conflicting pressures resulting from increasing support for popular education and opposition to it by some members of the plantocracy some legislators were caught in a dilemma. For example, around 1858 the Governor of Barbados, while deploring the inadequate provision that the colony was making for education, noted that many influential members of the community were 'unimpressed by this failing'. Nevertheless, they began to show a gradually increasing appreciation of the value of education.

Schomburgk, writing about Barbados during the mid 1840s, reported that, by then, 'a more liberal system (of education had) . . . spread over the Colonies; it . . . (was) no longer the wish of the great proprietors of the land to keep the labouring classes in the darkness of ignorance.'[22] The Mitchinson Commission also observed in 1876 that many planters were 'farsighted enough to recognize the superior value of labourers who had been under teaching and discipline to the entirely untaught child.'[23]

West Indian legislators, therefore, though sometimes with great reluctance, began to contribute a greater amount of financial support to the various missionary societies to help them continue their educational activities. In 1851 the Crown Colony government in Trinidad itself assumed the major responsibility for directly funding elementary education. The financial commitments made to the voluntary agencies were often on an annual or even on an 'ad hoc' basis, and the sums voted could be, and on many occasions were, reduced or withdrawn without much prior notice. Sometimes when new schools were built there were insufficient funds to meet their regular operating costs, even after the economy of the region had improved. But, despite the financial problems faced by these colonies, their expenditure on the state control mechanisms remained substantially higher than their allocations to education.

(a) *The Barbadian Legislature*: The attitude of the Barbadian Assembly to the provision of popular education was said to have been influenced by the 1846 Circular of the Education Department of Upper Canada, which stipulated that every member of a society must contribute to the support of its public institutions and that every child has a right to education 'which will fit him for the duties of a useful citizen of the country.' Further, he was 'not to be deprived of such education on account of the inability of the parents or guardians to provide it.'[24] Therefore, the local legislators made an initial grant of £750 for education in 1846 and doubled this amount four years later. In addition, most of them indicated some support for Governor Reid's proposal for a comprehensive system of education which was based on the assumption that 'instruction to all classes of the community ... would confer benefits eminently advantageous, both in the moral and economic point of view.'[25] But, they suggested that the time to implement such proposals was inopportune because of the prevailing economic circumstances. In fact, the government was then considering a reduction in the salaries of public officers and while this did not take place, the wages of agricultural workers on the sugar estates was cut by 20% to 30%. In such circumstances, it was felt that the colony could not afford the additional costs that would have been incurred if Governor's Reid's proposals were fully implemented.

Nevertheless, the 'legislature appointed a Joint Committee on Education in 1850 to examine the 'best mode' of promoting 'the more extensive and general education' of the people. Its recommendations, which were approved by both Houses of the Legislature, resulted in an Education Act that provided for an increase in the range of educational activities which were to receive government assistance. This included the establishment of 'dame' or infant schools in the rural districts, an extension of primary education for the masses, the development of secondary education for children of the middle class and the provision of scholarships for tertiary level education. Financial assistance was also provided to schools operated not only by the Anglicans but also by other denominational bodies such as the Wesleyans. The grant for education steadily improved, reaching £3,000 by the late 1850s and £9,000 by 1875. The Mitchinson Report of 1876 even attempted to widen the scope of the involvement of the government of Barbados in education by stressing the importance of nursery schools and this issue came under consideration again in the 1890s.

Despite the economic hardship which it faced, the government of Barbados was said to have been spending more per capita on education than the British government by 1850 — 5s.2d per head as opposed to 1s.6d per head in Britain, where most of the education costs were then being met by voluntary agencies. The establishment of a Barbadian Education Committee, comprising members of the 'two legislative houses', was recommended so that the government could exercise some control over the ways in which public funds voted for education were spent. Also proposed was the appointment of an Inspector of Schools to monitor the quality of education offered in schools and to evaluate pupil performance.

These recommendations were approved by the legislature and a part-time Inspector was appointed, which meant that the government had some mechanism in place through which it would could be kept informed about the activities of schools. The 1850 Education Act was the first real step toward some legislative control of public education and could be seen as a recognition by the legislature of the need to have education provided for all sections of the population. The policies established by the Barbadian legislature not only laid the foundation of the island's educational system but, in some ways, also served as a model for the educational services that were provided later by most other West Indian colonies.

The Education Committee, however, continued to place the main responsibility for the instructional programme of schools on the missionary societies and other voluntary agencies, arguing that the business of government was simply to stimulate, encourage and strengthen the educational work of these bodies, not to be totally responsible for it. Such involvement by the various denominational groups in the provision of education was considered particularly important since the island was unable to afford a 'free and extensive system' of general education. Finally, the view that the government should be financially supportive of, rather than be fully responsible for education, represented an improvement in the attitude of some members of the legislature who, in 1837, had argued that it was the responsibility of the Imperial Government rather than the colonial legislatures to provide funds for the religious and moral education of the West Indian masses.

By 1857, when there was a slight improvement in the finances of the island, the Education Committee requested more liberal support for education and in the following year there was a positive response to this request. Public funds were made available for Infant Schools and a full-time Inspector of Schools was appointed. By then the Barbadian government was providing financial assistance for education from the infant to the tertiary level. Therefore, while in 1849 only about 2.4% of the island's total budget was spent on education compared to 33.7% on the police, by 1856 the former figure had increased to 4.4%, while the latter had declined to 21.3%. By the 1860s, when about 50% of the population 4–15 years of age was enrolled in schools, the Inspector observed that there was no locality on the island which was 'not within a reasonable distance from a school.' He added, probably with some exaggeration, that education on the island was 'progressing at a pace equal to that of any other country' including the metropole.[26] In 1878 another Education Act resulted in the establishment of a new Board of Education, comprised mainly of members of the legislative assemblies. This resulted in a substantial increase in government expenditure on elementary education.

(b) *The Jamaican Legislature*: The Jamaican Legislature started to make an allocation for elementary education by the end of 1843. By 1845 it had appointed its first Board of Education to take over the responsibility of making grants to schools, though it initially had no system of inspection in place to ensure that the funds provided were properly spent. In 1849, an Education Act to establish a Board of Education on a more permanent basis was introduced. The legislature soon began to increase its educational grants and liberalize its funding policy to provide financial support for schools operated not only by the Anglicans but by other denominational bodies as well. Therefore, from 1844 onwards, the education vote rose substantially and by 1847/48 the island was spending about 3.5% of its total budget on education.

However, as the economic position of the island declined, the education vote not only fluctuated annually but was often reduced or even terminated quite abruptly. In 1852 the allocations for operating the Normal School of Industry and for paying the salary of the Inspector of Schools were deleted from the budget and the financial situation was so tight in the following year that the Jamaican government made no grant whatsoever to its Board of Education. However, by 1855 the situation had improved with the government providing an education grant to £6,000 p.a.

One measure that was proposed to ensure a reliable source of financial support for education was the imposition of an education tax on houses. While this bill failed to win the approval of the majority of members of the legislature, the Governor nevertheless was able to secure a 50% increase in the education vote, even though the amount provided remained at this level for the next nine years. Between 1864/65 and 1867/68, 'a remarkable impulse' was given to elementary education, when government grants rose by 18% over the three year period, and subsequently there was a relatively large increase again of about 50%.

As a result, the quality of education improved, and the number of schools that were classified as 'first' and 'second' class schools increased which meant that they were able to receive higher grants. The government introduced a system of 'opening grants' in order to encourage and aid 'trustworthy' managers or teachers to establish new schools in the more remote areas. In addition, funds were provided for the increased number of schoolmasters who were annually becoming available, and who were to help establish these additional schools.

In 1885 an Education Commission for Jamaica recommended an improvement in the conditions of employment for teachers by providing them with suitable residences and a superannuation allowance. It was also proposed that compulsory education for children between 7 and 13 years be introduced, that school fees be abolished, and that a Central Board of Education and local education boards be established. As a result of these proposals education was made free in 1893 and a house tax introduced to help recover some of the funds lost through the abolition of school fees. A new Board of Education was also formed. One outcome of these developments was the steady increase in the annual budget for education in Jamaica. Figure 1 shows the increasing amounts allocated to education between 1862 and 1881 and Figure 2. the rising per capita expenditure on students on the island between 1868 and 1896.

(c) *The Government of Trinidad*: The Crown Colony status of Trinidad generally gave the governor a greater amount of authority and responsibility for initiating legislation. In 1845 the colony provided a subsidy of £1,418 for elementary education. The legislature also supported Harris's new Education

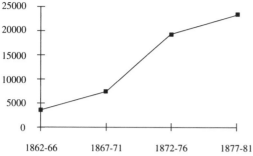

Figure 1. Graph showing the increase in the amount spent on education in Jamaica between 1862 and 1881 in pounds (£).

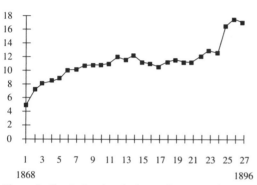

Figure 2. Graph showing the increasing per capita expenditure on elementary education for Jamaica from 1868 to 1896 in shillings.

Ordinance of 1851 which embodied the establishment of a Board of Education and a system of 'ward' schools. Thus, with the approval of the Colonial Office, a state system of education was in place, making the Government of the island almost fully responsible for financing its elementary schools.

The administrators of the wards — 'wardens' — were responsible for establishing schools wherever they were most needed and many of them immediately set upon this task. The costs of erecting such schools, of providing suitable accommodation for teachers and of paying teachers' salaries were to be defrayed from the funds made available by the wards with the assistance of the central government. The 1851 Education Act also approved the appointment of an Inspector of Schools and provided funds for the establishment of a teachers' training institution. But, despite these new provisions, the central government expenditure on education was still about 1.2% of its total budget in 1869, compared to the 15.8% allocated to its state control mechanisms — a figure which had fallen from 18.6% the previous year. As a result, at no time were all the wards able to provide enough facilities for educating the total eligible population.

By the late 1860s, as a result of Catholic opposition to the state funded secular schools, Governor Gordon made a request to the Colonial Office for someone to review the educational situation on the island and Patrick Keenan, the young Chief Inspector of the Board of National Education in Ireland, was appointed to undertake this task in 1869. His recommendation for a dual system of education with State-aided Church and Government Ward schools was accepted and introduced after 1870. This new provision resulted in a substantial increase in enrollments in the denominational schools. The 1888 Education Ordinance provided for even greater government involvement in education since it allowed the Board of Education to exercise complete control over most of the instructional activities of its elementary schools. It also made available 'liberal' grants for school houses and teachers' residences along with a new and somewhat more generous formula for the remuneration of schoolmasters. In addition, the government was to meet three.quarters of the expenses incurred by the denominational schools which had to accept all children, irrespective of their religious affiliation.

(d) *The Legislatures of Other West Indian Colonies*: In British Guiana, where the legislature allocated only 1% of its annual budget to education in 1846, many children in rural areas continued to have difficulties in securing access to schools. The number of institutions was simply insufficient to meet the growing popular demand for education. The Combined Court had withdrawn all salary payments for teachers in the late 1840s, which resulted in a substantial drop in school enrollment and the situation was made worse by the uncertainty as to whether the grant for education would be resumed. Around the late 1840s consideration was given to the establishment of an educational fund. the money for which was to be raised by the vestry of each parish through an assessment on every house. The sums collected were to help all schools which were operated by licensed teachers, irrespective of their denominational affiliation. However, this proposal, like others of its kind in the West Indies, did not find enough support among the legislators to be made into law.

In 1850 a Board of Education was established in British Guiana by the Governor at the request of the Combined Court and the first Inspector of Schools for the colony, George Dennis, appointed in 1851. Dennis tried to secure increased government support for education, arguing, like others of his time, that money laid out for the 'encouragement of virtue' and the 'removal of ignorance' was a far more profitable investment than that expended on the repression and punishment of crime. Partly as a result of such arguments, the legislature gradually became more supportive of education for the masses. A local Commission was appointed to examine the state of education in the colony and it too drew attention to the serious problems arising from the lack of national cohesion among the 'variety of races' in the colony. This was particularly marked with the arrival of a large number of Asian immigrants who were described as being immersed in the 'grossest paganism.'

On account of the ethnic diversity of the population, it was considered necessary to encourage the children of all groups to attend the same schools. To achieve this goal the Commission recommended the introduction of a secular system of education — a recommendation which received the support of the Combined Court. However, this measure was strongly opposed by the various denominational bodies and was eventually overturned by the Colonial Office. Therefore, church control of schools continued and educational opportunities for the population were extended along denominational lines. This explains why so little was done locally during this period for the education of East Indian children.

The economic situation continued to pose a problem for the legislators. While they provided financial assistance for the schools, this support failed to keep pace with increasing enrollments. For example, between 1880 and 1896 the average attendance in elementary schools rose by about nearly 50%, while the grant provided by the legislature was only increased by about 7% at current prices. As a result the number of pupils who were presented for annual examination rose while the expenditure per student examined fell. This can be seen in Figure 3.

The Government of Grenada not only reversed its 1842 decision to withhold funding from schools but also increased its grant to help with the costs which the denominational bodies bore on their own, when no State assistance was being provided. At the time, there were schools operating in the capital city of St. George's and at least one in each parish, to which the legislature granted aid. However, after 1845 the sum voted for education remained virtually fixed for a number of years and it was used to support only Anglican (£230) and Methodist (£117) schools, despite the fact that the majority of the population on the island was Catholic. In 1846 this policy was changed and government grants to education were extended to the Roman Catholic schools. In 1848, there was a marginal increase in the education vote, which rose from £347 to £390, and then to £500 by 1851. The island was also spending only a relatively small percentage of its budget on education — 2.3% in 1845 — compared to 25% on its repressive state apparatus. However this situation gradually changed and by 1852, these percentages were respectively 5% for education, compared to the 1845 figure at 2.3%, and 15.9% for the RSA, compared to the earlier figure of 25%.

Despite the financial difficulties which the various religious bodies faced, the Catholics continued to establish new schools on the island. This resulted in even greater pressure on the legislature to improve its funding for education. Consequently, in 1855 the government allocation for education was increased to almost double the 1851 figure, at current prices. In 1862 the legislature again decided to discontinue its education vote and financial hardships were once more imposed on the schools. Tremendous financial pressure was also placed on those church bodies which had decided not only to continue operating their existing schools, but even to establish new ones. The result was an increasing demand for a return of the education subsidy which occurred in the late 1860s.

In 1882 the Grenadian legislature, following the steps taken by Trinidad, enacted a new Education Ordinance which

(1) made grants-in-aid available to assist schools that reached certain standards in terms of their enrollment and academic results.
(2) provided for the establishment of schools in areas where no assisted schools existed.
(3) doubled the education vote between 1881 and 1882.
(4) allowed funds to be voted for the appointment of an Inspector of Schools.
(5) permitted the Roman Catholics to have a 50% representation on the Board of Education.

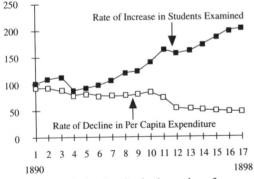

Figure 3. Graph showing the rise in number of students examined in the primary schools of British Guiana between 1880 and 1896 and the declining per capita expenditure per pupil examined.

The governments of most member states which formed the Leeward Islands had accepted the importance of education for the masses. In 1846, for example, the St. Kitts legislature made a liberal three year grant for the purpose of 'promoting the education of the industrial classes.' Yet, in 1849 the grant of £600 p.a. was withdrawn, and for some years after, no further subsidy to education was provided. In 1856 a new Act came into force which raised funds for education by means of a tax on provision grounds. In the 1860s there was again an improvement in the island's supply of school accommodation, after the government began to provide one-third of the cost of building 'proper school houses' and made education grants available on the basis on school enrollment.

While Nevis had schools which were 'creditably constructed,' the number of children admitted to them had to be limited, due to lack of financial support from the legislature. Up to the end of the 1850s, the government had not yet made any funds available for education, despite the obvious desire by the population to have schooling available for their children. The levy of an educational tax had been proposed, but no successful action was taken on the issue. The legislature did, however, make an annual grant of £50 to education, which was increased to £150 in 1866 and continued to rise after this date. In the neighbouring island of Anguilla, it was noted that money was not circulating in 1847, which meant that the government was unable to provide funds for the support of schools.

The continuing apathy of the Montserrat legislature toward the issue of education was a matter of constant complaint by the Administrator. The island's poverty, he asserted was no excuse for the legislature's neglect of this need, especially considering 'how small the grant was necessary to effect a vast amount of good and what large sums are constantly voted for objects comparatively trivial. They feel it is the duty of the people to provide education for their own families.'[27] It was, therefore, not until 1868 that the government made its first grant to assist the various bodies operating schools on the island. Although the initial sum was small, it represented almost 1% of the total government budget. The authorities, however, required a certain minimum attendance before schools could qualify for aid.

The Dominican Legislature also initially made little financial contribution to the operation of schools, though during the 1850s, its involvement in the provision of popular education substantially increased. For example, in 1849 it passed an Act which raised its grants for schools from £300 to £800. In Antigua, although overseas aid to the various missionary bodies involved in educational activities was declining, the colonial legislature nevertheless refused to make up the growing financial shortfall needed to operate the primary schools. As a result, many of them were forced to close and the total dissolution of the school system on the island was seen as a possibility. However, in 1857 the government began to provide additional funds for education.

In St. Vincent, there was a general reluctance on the part of the legislature to vote money for education after the withdrawal of the Negro Education Grant. A proposal was put forward for a small rate or tax to be levied to support the 'common school' and, with some reluctance, the legislature began to make a contribution to the operational cost of the island's schools. But it was so indifferent to this activity that not only was there a substantial reduction in school grants between 1854 and 1855, but in the latter year the legislators allowed the Education Act to expire, without introducing a new one. This led the Lieutenant Governor to enter an urgent plea to 'the honourable House' to make 'the largest provision possible . . . for ensuring the systematic and permanent establishment of schools.'[28] While funding was restored, yet in 1856, the education grant was again drastically reduced from £903 to £152. However, by the end of the decade the situation began to improve and the education vote eventually reached £1,000 p.a.. In addition, many schools were re-established and put on a better footing and a regional Inspector of Schools appointed.

In 1845 the government of St. Lucia made its first grant of £450 for education and raised it to £500 the following year. At the time the only public schools on the island were those operated by the Mico Trust. In 1848 the government established a Board of Education and Agriculture whose major responsibilities were to apportion government grants to existing schools and to extend educational facilities to districts where schools did not yet exist. In 1852, the government began to open its own schools and was also providing financial assistance for the denominational schools. Incidentally, two Infant Schools received a grant of £1000 in 1851 from the Society of Friends, which occasionally provided some limited financial assistance to schools in the region. By the 1860s, government support for education was provided by fines levied in the inferior courts, hawkers' and boat licences, an export duty on coffee, cocoa, charcoal, firewood, logwood, hides, and farine manioc, plus an annual grant of £500 from general revenue.

Because of the absence of schools in the more remote rural areas in the Leeward Islands the inspector of Schools recommended that the grant for a school not be withdrawn when it was the only one in a district, even if the school did not have the minimum enrollment, or if the students failed to attain the prescribed levels of academic performance. According to the Inspector, the closure of such schools would mean that 'the little flickering light of these schools will be extinguished and the children living in that neighbourhood will be left to grow up in utter darkness and ignorance,'[29] To some extent this advice was heeded, when funds were available.

For a number of years after the withdrawal of the Negro Education Grant, the legislature of the British Virgin Islands also provided no aid for education and schools had to continue depending on church or other private sources for support. The government later began to provide an occasional subsidy for education, but by 1853 there was still no regular annual government grant available to schools. The situation began to improve some years later, when the legislature granted aid to the Anglican schools. The hope was expressed that such assistance would be extended to other bodies, when 'the state of the public finances' permitted it. In the early 1860s an Education Grant Ordinance was introduced to provide funds for education from the annual budget. But a problem which the island faced was the emigration to St Thomas of a number of youngsters who having received an education locally were going over to this neighbouring island to fill clerical positions. This led the Administrator to observe that he did not think that it was fair for the colony 'to educate lads here at public expense so as to fit them for clerks at St. Thomas; if they desire this, they must educate themselves at their own expense.'[30] This point of view continued to affect the attitude of the local legislature to the provision of additional funds for education and partly, as a result, government grants to education were often subject to considerable fluctuations.

Overall, while the total expenditures incurred jointly by the Leeward Islands (Antigua, St. Kitts/ Nevis, Montserrat, the British Virgin Islands, and Dominica) during the two decades between 1869 and 1889 increased by 21.5%, the portion of the budget spent on education had risen by 36.3%. During the latter year, education was taking 3.73% of the budget, instead of the 3.32% which it did in 1869. While one has to be careful about interpreting data on educational expenditure because of their variability from one year to another, one can observe certain trends which are indicated by the following graphs. Figures 4, 5, 6 and 7 give an idea of what was happening to overall expenditures, in relation to expenditures on education, in the Windward and the Leeward Islands between 1867 and 1881 — years for which fairly reliable comparative

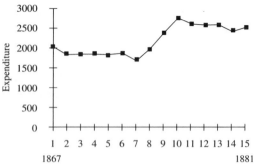

Figure 4. Increase in educational expenditure in three windward islands (St. Lucia, St. Vincent, and Grenada combined) between 1867 and 1881 in pounds (£).

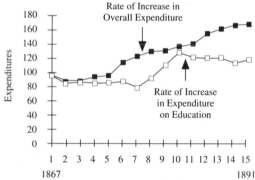

Figure 5. Rate of increase in total government expenditure as compared with increases in educational expenditures alone in three windward islands (St. Lucia, St. Vincent, and Grenada combined) between 1867 and 1881.

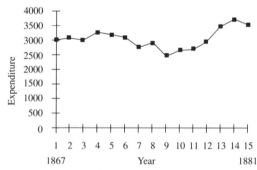

Figure 6. Increases in expenditure in the leeward islands (Antigua, St. Kitts, Nevis, Montserrat, Br. Virgin Islands, and Dominica combined) between 1867 and 1881 in pounds (£).

data was obtainable. Over the next decade and a half, between 1882 and 1896, expenditures on education by these West Indian colonies together, increased quite rapidly, rising from £95,000 to £180,000 — an increase of about 90% at current prices.

The graphs below indicate that educational expenditures for the two regions kept up fairly well, both in absolute terms (though at current prices) and in comparison to total government expenditures. However, an interesting picture emerges if the data for individual islands in these regions are examined separately as is done in Figures 7,8,9 and 10.

One can see from the graphs that, over these years, such islands as Grenada and St. Kitts, which were making higher grants to education at the beginning of this period, gradually reduced the percentages of their budget spent on education. On the other hand, the islands which originally made smaller contributions gradually improved their position. These islands included St. Vincent, St. Lucia, Dominica, Montserrat, Nevis and even Antigua. The marked variability in allocations to education in the British Virgin Islands (BVI) reflected the even greater fluctuations in the economic conditions in this colony.

During the latter half of the 1860s the government of the Turks and Caicos Islands began to provide financial assistance for education, increasing its funding between 1868 and 1869 by slightly over 50%. By then, the colony was spending about 7.2% of its limited government budget on education. Here too, while the actual figure was quite small, the percentage of the budget allocated to education was the highest in the region. Commenting on this point, the Governor observed in 1866 that, 'for the size of the colony and the number of children under tuition' the vote which the colony allocated to education was quite 'liberal' and would 'stand a favourable comparison with that in other portions of Her Majesty's dominions.'[31] However, after the colony began to face a tighter economic squeeze, the legislature abolished the public schools with the 1872 Act, and reduced its £700 p.a. education grant to £200 p.a.. This amount was then given as a subsidy to those teachers who continued to operate schools. By 1873 the government had further reduced this allocation to under £105.

In 1850, the government of British Honduras voted £100 for education which meant that up to the mid-1850s, about one-sixth of the pupils were attending schools that were unsupported by the legislature, even though the inadequacy of financial resources was recognized as one of the major obstacles to improving the local education system. However, in 1850 an Act was passed to provide educational assistance 'for the benefit of every denomination of Christians' and to establish a Board of Education. By 1856 the legislature made funds available for the Board to grant £30 p.a. for every school with no less than 50 children, to provide books and stationery for each school, and to

erect 'new and spacious' central schools. The Board was also charged with the responsibility of supervising these schools and providing improved salaries for teachers, in order to facilitate the engagement of 'superior trained' and 'certificated persons.' It also made financial assistance available for the 'proper' supervision of schools by competent head masters.

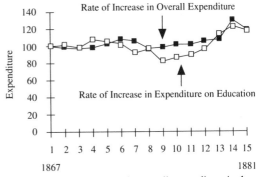

Figure 7. Rate of increase in overall expenditure in the leeward islands (Antigua, Nevis, Br. Virgin Islands and Dominica combined) as compared with rate of increase in expenditure on education between 1867 and 1881.

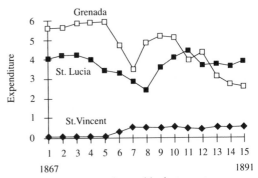

Figure 8. Percentage of annual budget spent on education in St. Lucia, St. Vincent, and Grenada between 1867 and 1881.

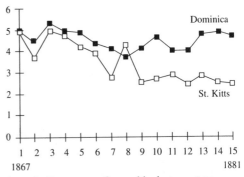

Figure 9. Percentage of annual budget spent on education in Dominica and St. Kitts between 1867 and 1881.

While the Legislature recognized the fact that there remained an unbalanced distribution in educational expenditures between town and country in favour of the former, it could do little to overcome the problem, partly because of the difficulty in finding qualified teachers for the rural areas. However, due to the financial situation which it faced, the government gradually let the responsibility for providing education shift almost entirely to the religious bodies. In the 1890s, it closed its one remaining school because it was too expensive to operate and finally decided that the money might be more wisely spent to assist religious agencies in their educational efforts. As the Governor stated at the time, 'the religious bodies are now to be recognized as the popular educators'.[32]

In 1845, the government of the Bahamas was allocating about 5.5% of its recurrent budget to education. Large though this percentage was, it was inadequate to meet the demand for schools in the 'Out Islands', especially in such areas as March Harbour, Abaco, Governor's Harbour, Grand Bahama, Deadman's Cay and Long Island. The reluctance of the legislators to provide additional funding for schools was again seen in 1851, when the education vote was exceeded and the Governor sought an increase in the allocation to cover the deficit. His request was not only turned down but legislators argued that there needed to be an overall reduction in the amount voted for education. Other efforts at reducing expenditure in the Bahamas and other islands with a scattered population was to consolidate existing school facilities, including the expenditure on education, and one of the steps taken was the closure of schools with limited enrolment. However, in 1860 the Legislative Assembly approved the continuation of grants for the 'education of our poorer classes'.

In 1873 the allocation for education in this colony was again reduced, by almost one half, thereby adversely affecting the level of enrollment and the level of remuneration received by teachers. By the mid 1870s the legislature discontinued its funding of schools in the more remote areas which often resulted in the closure of these schools. It was suggested that the steps taken by the legislature to reduce educational expenditure was partly a reflection of the fact that, up to the 1870s, there were still influential individuals in these island — most of whom were white — who continued to regard an education given to the masses — most of whom were black — as serving only to unfit them 'for a life of steady labour such as falls to the lot of a similar class in other countries.'[33] funds In Bermuda, an Act was passed in the late 1840s with the objective of promoting 'general education' in the colony. The aim was to assist and encourage edu-

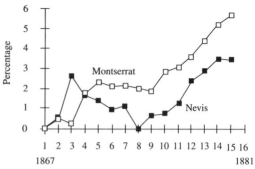

Figure 10. Percentage of annual budget spent on education in Montserrat and Nevis between 1867 and 1881.

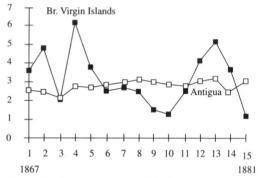

Figure 11. Percentage of annual budget spent on education in the British Virgin Islands and Antigua between 1867 & 1881.

cation along 'whatever lines' those who established schools might choose, while the government was to assume the responsibility for 'impartial' but 'vigilant' inspection. As a result, an initial sum of £300 was provided as aid to schools in 1847. The amount was then increased to £600 for two years and an Inspector of Schools appointed in 1858. However this grant fell to £400. Between 1868 and 1869, the colony experienced a drop of 13% in total government revenues which resulted in a substantial further reduction of the grant provided for education. The per capita expenditure on pupils declined by just under a half of what it had been previously, detrimentally affecting school enrollment and attendance, teachers' salaries and the overall quality of education. These various cost cutting measures particularly affected the education of the black population toward whom it was noted that the Bermudian legislature displayed 'deplorable apathy.'

In 1874 another Ordinance was passed by the Bermudian legislature which approved the payment of grants to private institutions, thereby resulting in the establishment of additional primary schools. This payment was subject to the schools maintaining certain standards which were to be verified by inspection. As a result, the education grant rose to £700 in 1876 and then to £1,200 by 1879 when a new Education Act was passed by the legislature. This Act levied a school tax of 6s. per quarter on all parents with children 6– 13 years of age, except those whose children were attending private schools. This made more funds available for education with the result being that school attendance doubled in two years. But, the nature of the provision was such that schools remained racially segregated and it was the children of whites who were said to have benefitted most from these funds.

All schools in the colony, even aided ones, therefore became regarded as private schools and were conducted 'how and where' the 'master or mistress pleases.' This enabled the predominantly white legislature to free itself from the responsibility of preventing racial segregation in schools, including those receiving government funds. However, the schools were still subject to inspection as a condition of receiving aid.

While a substantial increase in the education grant resulted this proved to be beneficial mainly to the 'poor whites' by compelling them 'to extend the blessings of education to their children, instead of allowing them to grow up in ignorance and barbarism.'[34] The benefits to the black population were much more limited.

Summary and Conclusions

An important factor in the 'supply' of educational facilities for the masses was the support for popular education provided by various influential groups, both within and outside these societies. In response to mounting pressure, the legislators became more involved, though often reluctantly, in increasing their votes for popular education. However, as a percentage of the total annual budgets of these colonies', the financial support which they provided was still modest, and in some cases subject to marked annual variations and even decline. In Jamaica, the data indicate that during the latter part of this period, the total education vote and the per student allocation for education rose steadily while for British Guiana the situation, was one of decline.

The British government continued to give 'moral' support to efforts at providing education for the black masses, even after it had terminated its Negro Education Grant in 1845. The Colonial Governors also played an important role in securing the financial support of the local legislature, as did a number of other groups, such as the missionaries, and the journalists. However, some

planters were sill not enamoured with the idea of extending educational facilities to all the children of the labouring classes. Many of them were not yet convinced that the provision of education for all, was a sound policy. It had been a common assumption only a few years earlier that education would produce discontent among the labouring population, and would result in social and economic unrest. Therefore, it was difficult for the planters to develop a sudden positive attitude toward education for the black population. They also suggested that those who had received some education tended to look down on their 'fellow labourers' as being beneath them in status. In addition, they were more likely to seek jobs away from the sugar estates which would allow them to enjoy a status superior to those without any schooling who were still working on the plantations.

However, despite such opposition, some West Indian legislatures began to make a growing commitment to the provision of popular education for the region by making financial support available for it and taking on an increasing responsibility for its administration and its monitoring. But, especially in the smaller colonies, the efforts were not always consistent and in many cases the local legislatures repeatedly withdrew their support for schools, thus placing a heavy burden on the various denominational bodies which were operating schools in the region.

There were many other constraints on the expansion of elementary education, including the reduction of funds that became available to the local missionary societies from overseas. Another was the difficult economic position which these colonies were experiencing, especially after 1845. With the fluctuating and declining prices of sugar, legislators were usually unwilling for the state to make any long-term financial commitment to fund education, on account of the difficulties they might face in meeting future payments, given the unpredictability of the amount of revenues that would be collected from one year to another. So that even though various West Indian governments were gradually making additional financial provision for primary education, as yet there was no consistent picture of an increasing commitment by the local legislatures to provide funds for it on a permanent basis. Commenting on this point, the Governor of Grenada observed that, in the provision of funds for education, the island's legislature was guided by 'no clear principle,' usually producing uncertainty for those who were involved in operating schools in these colonies. This had adverse effects on the amount and quality of elementary education which the missionary societies and other groups could provide.

However, despite the negative attitude toward education held by a substantial number of planters and the depressed economic condition of the region, there was a growing recognition by the legislators and other sectors of the population that popular education had come to stay. Further, its expanded provision was necessary for social stability in these colonies and possibly, even for their economic growth. The challenge therefore was to increase efficiency and effectiveness of the education being provided so that its social and economic returns would continue to justify the increasing expenditures required to expand the service and improve its quality. In this context, much controversy developed over the nature of the instructional programme which the schools should offer. These financial difficulties however, led to the gradual abandonment of the idea that the total cost of elementary education for all should be borne entirely by government. It also resulted in the strengthening of the denominational system of education and the provision of more private schools in most of these colonies.

Notes

1. Shirley Gordon, *A Century of West Indian Education: A Source Book* (London: Longmans, 1963),43.
2. Vere T. A. Daly, *A Short History of the Guyanese People* (Georgetown, Guyana: The Daily Chronicle Ltd., 1966),264.
3. Nicholas Hans, *Yearbook of Education*, 1938 (London: Evans Bros. Ltd.,1938),779.
4. F. A. J. Johnston, 'Education in Jamaica and Trinidad in the Generation After Emancipation' (Ph.D. diss., Univ. of Oxford 1971), p.266.
5. Gordon 43.
6. Gordon 43.
7. CO 111/259, John McSwiney, Report of The Inspector of Schools for British Guiana, 'The State of Public Schools in the Colony', 20 October 1848 (London: PRO, 1848).
8. Report of the Government of Montserrat, British Parliamentary Papers, Vol. XLVI, 1847–48 (London: Government of Great Britain),135.
9. Report of the Government of St. Lucia, British Parliamentary Papers, Vol. LXII, 1852–53 London: Government of Great Britain).
10. Report of the Government of the Bahamas, British Parliamentary Papers, Vol. XXXIV,1851 (London: Government of Great Britain, 1851),41.
11. Report of the Government of Dominica, British Parliamentary Papers, Vol. LXII, 1852–53 (London: Government of Great Britain),107.
12. Report of the Government of Bermuda, British Parliamentary Papers, Vol. XXXIV, 1851 (London: Government of Great Britain),28.
13. CO 295/134, MCLeod to Secretary of State for the Colonies, 13 October 1841 (London: PRO).
14. Governor Harris to Earl Grey, 19 June 1848, no. 71 (London: PRO).
15. *Royal Gazette* [Trinidad],8 October 1851.
16. James Maxwell, *Remarks on the Present State of Jamaica* (London: Smith Elder and Co., 1848), 36.
17. Report of the Government of St. Kitts, British Parliamentary Papers, Vol. X, 1857 (London: Government of Great Britain), 195.
18. Report of the Government of Grenada, British Parliamentary Papers, Vol. XL, 185758 (London: Government of Great Britain),46.
19. George Brizan, Grenada, *Island of Conflict, From Amerindians to People's Revolution 1498–1979* (London: Zed Books Ltd., 1984),157.
20. Report of the Government of Antigua, British Parliamentary Papers, Vol LI, 1876 London: Government of Great Britain),100.
21. Report of the Government of the British Virgin Islands, British Parliamentary Papers, Vol. XXXVII, 1847 (London: Government of Great Britain),56.
22. Sir Robert Schomburgk, *The History of Barbados* London: Longmans,1848), 108.
23. Report of the Commission on Education in Barbados (The Mitchinson Report), 1875–76 (Bridgetown, Barbados: Barclay and Fraser, Printers to the Legislature, 1876),6.
24. Schomborgk 109.
25. CO 31/56, Governor Reid's Address to the Legislature, 29 December 1847
26. Report of the Government of Barbados, British Parliamentary Papers, Vol. XXXVI, 1862 (London: Government of Great Britain), 45.
27. Report of the Government of Montserrat, British Parliamentary Papers, Vol XXXIX, 1846 (London: Government of Great Britain),109.
28. Report of the Government of St. Vincent British Parliamentary Papers, Vol XLII, 1856 (London: Government of Great Britain),90.
29. Report of the Inspector General of Schools in the Leeward Islands, British Parliamentary Papers, Vol. XLIV, 1882 (London: Government of Great Britain), 188.
30. Report of the Government of the British Virgin Islands, British Parliamentary Papers, Vol XXXVII, 1865 (London: Government of Great Britain),93.
31. Report of the Government of Turks and Caicos Islands, British Parliamentary Papers, Vol XLIX, 1866 (London: Government of Great Britain),68.
32. Report of the Government of British Honduras, British Parliamentary Papers, Vol. LV 1892 (London: Government of Great Britain),9.
33. Report of the Government of the Bahamas, British Parliamentary Papers, Vol LI, 1876 (London: Government of Great Britain),80.
34. Report of the Government of Bermuda, British Parliamentary Papers, Vol LXIV, 1881 (London: Government of Great Britain), 143.

SECTION EIGHT
The Sugar Industry: Crisis and Adjustments

Until the mid-twentieth century, Caribbean economic dependence upon the sugar industry was extreme. Sugar was king, and even when the evidence was clear at the end of the eighteenth century that the crown was in danger in the British colonies, there were no obvious contenders.

The decline in sugar production in various British colonies after emancipation resulted from a combination of causes; absentee ownership, negligent administration, lack of investment capital and labour shortages — all of which preceded the 1846 Free Trade legislation. These were problems identified by the planters from the beginning of the nineteenth century, particularly after the 1807 abolition of the slave trade. During the 1820s there was widespread rationalization of production, prompted largely by the realization that the easy control of the labour supply (after 1807) was a thing of the past. The Abolition Act of 1833, Curtin argues here, merely aggravated problems in the economy which were already evident, such as falling production, falling price of sugar, rising cost of production and falling profitability.

The principal complaint after 1838, according to Curtin, was rising cost of production which eventually more than the Free Trade development, undermined West Indian prosperity in the mid-nineteenth century. In spite of technological innovation, and rising productivity, the cost of sugar production continued to rise after 1846. In Jamaica, the planters attributed this to high wage levels which consumed all efforts made to cut cost at the point of production.

The 1842 Select Committee on the West Indies identified several issues, apart from the movement towards the full equalization of sugar duties, that were hampering sugar producers competitiveness. It stressed that capital shortage was having an adverse effect on production and productivity, and was likely to be the central problem in subsequent decades.

Lobdell explains the difficulties faced by West Indian planters in raising investment capital before and after the 1846 Act. In terms of the international movement of capital, the West Indian colonies were isolated. British trade and investments were flowing beyond the confines of the old colonial structures. The newly independent republics of Latin America emerged as both markets for British manufactures and as tempting markets for capital. In the 1830s and 1840s British capital flowed into Latin America for railway construction, expanding wheat farms and mining. These were the leading destinies of surplus British capital — the West Indies were generally abandoned by finance capitalists.

Fraginals and Williams show that only the Spanish colonies were able to attract vast sums of American capital for the technological modernization of the sugar sector. The Spanish colonies, emerging after a long period of economic stagnation, were able to dominate the other Caribbean islands within a very short time indeed. The Cuban economy, according to Fraginals, assisted by American capital and corporate management experienced a Sugar Revolution in the middle part of the nineteenth century. After 1846, Cuban sugar began to arrive on the London market at a rapid rate. By 1850, the English West Indians, probably with the exception of the Trinidadians and Guianese, were underpriced. In these older sugar colonies productivity levels were low and the cost of production rapidly rising. Cuban, and other foreign sugar, had no real competition in a free trade market.

The British Sugar Duties and West Indian Prosperity

Philip Curtin

The Sugar Act of 1846 stands in the same relation to the end of the old colonial system as does the repeal of the corn laws to the end of protection for British agriculture. Both measures were passed by the same session of Parliament and both were symbolic of the victory of free trade. The acts of 1846 were crucial because the struggle in Parliament and in public opinion was fought on these issues and not on the piecemeal reduction of other duties. Nor is their importance diminished by the fact that the Peel government was already moving toward free trade — nor by the fact that the wholesale removal of protective duties was not completed at once. In the public mind, the controversy over free trade was centered on specific commodities — corn and sugar.

With corn, the free traders themselves raised the issue and made it paramount in their campaign for repeal. But in the case of sugar it was the protectionists and the West India interest that chose the ground on which to make their stand. For several years after 1846 they worked intensively against the Sugar Act, principally trying to show that the prosperity of the West Indian colonies was being destroyed by free trade. The chief literary product of this campaign was Disraeli's *Lord George Bentinck,* and the chief legislative effort was made in the Sugar and Coffee Committee of 1848. In the end the campaign failed. The Sugar Act of 1848 succeeded only in postponing the final date of free trade in sugar. The import duties on British and foreign sugar were equalized in 1854 instead of 1851; but this was small satisfaction to the sugar planters, and the Act of 1846 was still the crucial turning point.

Perhaps a more lasting effect of the campaign has been that, while the repeal of the corn laws has gone down in history as a 'good thing', the Sugar Act of 1846 has generally had a bad press. In discussing the results of the act, historians have given a number of answers, varying from a clear statement that the West Indians were 'ruined' by free trade — a position on which the West Indians themselves were unanimous — through a series of modifications stressing other causes of West Indian decline. Many have simply shied away from the tangled question of West Indian decline, and, in spite of excellent analysis of the problem by some writers, we are no closer to a generally accepted answer than we were a hundred years ago.[1]

In searching for the results of the Sugar Act of 1846, the important point is this: the removal of protection could not, by itself, be the cause of West Indian decline. All it could do in the long run was to make other causes operative by removing a cushion against change, and in the nineteenth century there were three major changes detrimental to the interests of the West Indian planter. These were the reasons the planters wanted protection. The first was technological innovation. At the beginning of the century the West Indian industry was established on the basis of the small-scale 'estate', using animals for transportation and often for power, boiling the cane juice in open 'coppers'. Improved techniques and new machinery were introduced gradually throughout the century — central factories, vacuum and centrifugal processes in refining, steam power and tramways. But these changes came first to new areas of sugar production, and this development called for a complete renovation of the West Indian sugar industry if it were to continue to compete in a world market. A second challenge was presented by the emancipation of the slaves throughout the British Empire during the 1830s. In this case the problem was one of social readjustment and reorganization of labour system on a free basis. Finally, the development of beet sugar, which became increasingly important from the 1870s onward, introduced a new source of competition for all cane sugar producers.

From one point of view, therefore, the answer to West Indian decline is not to be found in the Sugar Act of 1846, but beyond this measure in other factors that made West Indian planters high-cost producers in the first place. And essentially it rests, as we shall see, in the way that each individual colony sought to meet the challenge of emancipation and technological backwardness. Before this problem can be approached, however, it is necessary to examine the intermediate buffer presented by the British sugar duties. Certainly some

314

of the West Indian colonies were in economic difficulties in the middle decades of the nineteenth century, and certainly all of them looked to tariff protection as a way out of their troubles; and the argument for protection rested on the assumption that tariff schedules like those in force before 1846 would have continued to protect them in the future. As a first step in clearing the way for deeper investigation, therefore, it is necessary to look again at the kind of protection that was being extended, to measure whether this protection, if continued, would really have isolated the West Indian planter from the competition he feared.

One aspect of the problem lies in the structure of British sugar duties in the early nineteenth century. Several different interests were being protected. There was a prohibitive duty on all refined sugar, protecting the British refiners from all competition, whether colonial or foreign.[2] As a result, the production of the British colonies was almost entirely an unrefined sugar known as 'muscovado', or, in the tariff schedules, 'not equal to white clayed'. The rate on muscovado, therefore, is of key importance. But before 1825 there were three different rates, according to the origin of the sugar. The lowest was for sugar from the British West Indies. A higher rate applied to sugar from the rest of the British Empire, and a very high duty was paid by foreign sugar. Foreign sugar, however, could be imported for refining, since a drawback was paid when it was re-exported to the Continent.

This structure of the sugar duties passed through two periods of important change. First, just before and during the social revolution of emancipation, Mauritius in 1825 and the East Indies in 1835 were given the same rate as the West Indies. At the time, this change was not a serious threat, but it broke the monopoly of the West Indians against the rest of the empire, and this fact later became very important. From 1836 to 1844 there were only minor general changes, the rates being set at 24s. per cwt. for the West Indian group, 32s. for the rest of the empire, and 63s. for foreign muscovado. The second major shift began in 1844 and continued through 1854, when colonial sugar was deprived of protection in the British market. The key act, however, was that of 1846. First, in 1844, foreign sugar not grown by slave labour was admitted at only 10s., more than the West Indian rate, then in the following year all rates were lowered. In 1846 the differential was further reduced to 7s. immediately — for all foreign muscovado, whether slave-grown or not — and then lowered each year until it disappeared. After 1854 there was a single rate on muscovado for revenue only, and it too was abolished in 1874, when all sugar entered free.[3]

It is possible to see the general results of these changes by comparing the annual average British imports from various sources and the average price of muscovado during three decades: 1821–1830, before either emancipation or competition from the rest of the empire had an effect on West Indian plantations; 1836–1845, the period of stable duties; and 1853–1862, the period following the shift to free trade. (Tables I and II).

In the decade 1821–1830 the British West Indies had a practical monopoly in the British market, but it made little difference in the price of sugar. West Indian output supplied the entire British market and some of the re-exports, which were sold on the Continent at the world price. This outlet had the effect of keeping the price of British sugar close to the world price, in spite of protection. During the period 1821–1830 the average premium for West Indian muscovado over Havana Yellow, a comparable foreign sugar, was only 6d. Thus the planters profited little from protection and, indeed, they may have suffered from the high rate of duty, which reduced the demand for sugar in Great Britain itself.[4]

In the decade 1836–1845 the average premium for British muscovado jumped to 12s.4d. (before duty) on the London sugar market, showing that the tariffs were finally influencing price. This change was caused by decreased production in the British colonies, which, in turn, was caused by slave emancipation. Since West Indian sugar production no longer exceeded the British demand, it did not have to be sold abroad. With less British colonial sugar entering the world market, the world price had less influence on the price of West Indian muscovado. The re-export trade was still carried on, but now largely with foreign sugar that could not be sold for consumption in Great Britain on account of the high duty. (Tables I and II).

Although these changes helped the West Indians to recover in higher prices a part of what they lost in lower production, it also brought new British colonial producers into the field. Higher prices combined with the tariff changes of 1825 and 1835 to bring about an increase of almost 300% in imports from the empire other than the West Indies, and this new production took over 28% of the British market. Clearly, a significant breach in the old dike of protection for the West indies had been made long before 1846. (Table 1).

In the decade 1853–1862 — with equal duties for sugar from all areas — the full effect of foreign competition came into play. But the duties were not only equal, they were also lower. The result was an amazing increase in the size of the British market, brought about by the lowered price. The greatest share of this larger market was satisfied, as would be expected, by sugar of foreign origin; but non-West Indian empire sugar continued to hold approximately its former share of the market, and imports from the West Indies, though a smaller part of the total, increased slightly. (Table 1). As a whole, however, the West Indian planters were not able to maintain the level of real gross return from the sale of the sugar crop in London. (Table 3). They could not meet the new conditions demanding higher output at lower prices. The Sugar Act aggravated these difficulties in the short run, but new production in other parts of the empire continued to increase after 1853, even in the face of foreign competition. In the longer run this increased empire production would have had much the same effect as foreign sugar, and the pre–1846 tariff structure had provided no protection.

It is clear, however, why the West Indian planters complained of their ruin and blamed the Sugar Act of 1846. What they saw was a sharp and permanent drop in the price of their product. (Table 2). And behind the drop in money price was a further drop in the real price of sugar. Like Alice, they had to run in order to stay in the same place. Comparing the annual averages for 1839–1846 with those of 1857–1866, a 45% increase in production

Table 1. Annual average imports of unrefined sugar into the United Kingdom.

| | Total | Consumed | Product of | | |
| | Million | in | | Rest of | Foreign |
Year	Cwts.	Britain	B.W.I.	Empire	Countries
1821–1830	4.37	82.3	88.0	7.8	4.2
1836–1845	4.83	82.9	57.8	28.1	14.1
1853–1862	8.71	92.1	37.4	24.8	37.8

Percentage change in volume of annual average imports

| | | | From | |
| | | | Rest of | Foreign |
	Total	B.W.I.	Empire	Countries
1821–1830 to 1836–1845	+ 10.31	− 27.5	+ 297.4	+ 374.0
1836–1845 to 1853–1862	+ 80.45	+ 16.7	+ 59.4	+ 384.2

SOURCES: PP, 1856, lv. (209), pp. 2–3; PP, 1863, lxvii (272), p.3.

Table 2. Annual average prices of B.W.I. Muscovado sugar and Havana yellow sugar in London, before duty (per hundredweight)

| | B.W.I. Muscovado | | Havana Yellow | | Difference | |
Years	(1)		(2)		(1) − (2)	
	s.	d.	s.	d.	s.	d.
1821–1830	31	10	31	4	+	6
1836–1845	37	5	25	1	+ 12	4
1853–1862	26	9	28	1	− 1	4

SOURCES: PP, 1856, lv (209), pp. 2–3.

Table 3. Annual average sugar production and gross income from sugar in British West Indies

| | Production | | Money Value in London | Real Value in London | |
| | | Percentage | | 1866–67 | Percentage |
Period	Tons	Change	£ Millions	£ Millions	Change
1824–1833	204,699	—	69.4	74.6	—
1839–1846	131,177	− 35.9	55.0	59.2	− 20.7
1857–1886	190,690	+ 45.4	55.7	55.8	− 5.7

SOURCES: Deerr, *History of Sugar*, II, 377; PP, 1856, lv (209), pp. 2–3; PP, 1863, lxvii (272), p. 3; PP, 1878–79, xiii (321), p. 402; A. Sauerbeck, 'On the Prices of Commodities and Precious Metals', *Journal of the Royal Statistical Society*, XLIX (London, 1886), 592, 648.

brought them a 6% loss in gross real value received for their sugar. (Table 3).

But, were they ruined? The answer, of course, depends on the costs of production, and reliable information is not available. A good deal of light is thrown on this question, however, by the changes in the quantity of sugar produced by different West Indian colonies. (Table 4). In comparison with changes in the world production between 1839–1846, the West Indian colonies fall into four different groups. Barbados alone increased sugar production at a rate greater than the world rate of increase for all sugars. In the second group, Demerara, Trinidad, and St. Kitts still led the world rate of increase for cane sugar. The sugar industry of Antigua and St. Vincent, however, was hardly holding its own, and that of Grenada and Jamaica was clearly in full decline.

These figures also go far in explaining why the 'ruin' of the West Indian sugar industry is often blamed on the Sugar Act of 1846. Jamaica had been the largest and most valuable of the West Indian colonies, while Trinidad and Demerara were relatively recent acquisitions. When many Englishmen of the period spoke of the West Indies, they were actually thinking of Jamaica. But in 1857–1866, the annual average sugar production of Jamaica amounted to only 14% of the West Indian total.[5] The ruin of the West Indian sugar industry was principally the ruin of Jamaica, the Leewards, and the Windwards. Other colonies were forced to operate in new, perhaps less favourable conditions; but, to maintain that the industry in these colonies was ruined, one would have to assume that the sugar planter was a species of philanthropist, willing not only to produce at a loss

for twenty years but actually to increase production by more than half.

Since the sugar duties and their equalization affected all the West Indian colonies alike, the problem becomes one of explaining the failure of some islands while others succeeded. It is shifted to the internal economic development of Jamaica and her neighbouring islands. This part of the problem is beyond the immediate scope of the present examination, but it is still worth while to point out some of the factors that must eventually be taken into account.

One that attracted most attention from the nineteenth-century Jamaicans was the supposed disequilibrium between the supply of labour and the amount of land in the island. While the quantity of unused land was not the only determinant of the wage rate, it was generally true that wages were lower in colonies where land was scarce and higher where land was plentiful. In 1848 the daily rate for field labour in Barbados and Antigua was only about 7d. In Dominica, St. Vincent, and Nevis it was 10d.; in St. Kitts 12d.; in Jamaica and St. Lucia 15d.; in British Guiana 20d.; and in Trinidad 25d.[6] There is, however, an alternative explanation of these wage differences. With the exception of Barbados, the low-wage colonies tended also to be colonies where the sugar industry was not doing well — where, consequently, the demand for labour was slack. The low wages in Barbados could be explained by the lack of alternative employment and an employers' combination to keep them low. The actual causes of wage differences can only be determined by further research, and this research will have to take account of the price levels. Real wages may have been very different from money wages. In Jamaica, for example, prices in the nineteenth century were generally 30 to 50% higher than those prevailing in England.

Another factor affecting the labour question was the importation of indentured labourers from India. Trinidad and British Guiana imported labourers in large numbers during the mid-century period. Jamaica made some attempts but was generally unsuccessful. Barbados made no use of induced immigration. Where induced immigration was practiced on a large scale, it surely had an influence on the fortunes of the sugar industry, but that influence cannot be determined *a priori*. Induced immigration might act as a subsidy for sugar planters at the expense of other taxpayers. It might simply have been an investment, paid for ultimately by the planters out of future income. Or it might have been, as it seems to have been in Jamaica, more expensive than local labour, but an expense that was borne for the sake of stricter control over the labour force.

Table 4. Changes in sugar production by type of area between 1839–1846 and 1857–1866

Kind of sugar and area of production	Percentage change in annual average production
World total beet sugar	+ 793.00
Barbados cane sugar	+ 132.00
World total — all sugar	+ 98.2
Demerara cane sugar	+ 92.5
Trinidad cane sugar	+ 77.1
St. Kitts cane sugar	+ 59.5
WORLD TOTAL CANE SUGAR	+ 56.4
Total British West Indies and Guiana cane sugar	+ 45.4
Antigua cane sugar	+ 12.2
St. Vincent cane sugar	+ 8.1
Grenada cane sugar	− 7.2
Jamaica cane sugar	− 24.7

SOURCES: Deerr, *History of Sugar* (2 vols.; London, 1949–50), II, 377, 490.

Still another factor to be taken into account is the distribution of cane juice between the three chief sugar products — rum, muscovado sugar, and molasses. Jamaica, for example, was not quite so badly off as sugar production figures alone indicate. About 30% of the total value of cane products exported was in the form of rum, rather than sugar. Trinidad, on the other hand, exported 90% of the value of its cane products in sugar, the rest being divided between rum and molasses. The other major sugar colonies fell somewhere between these two extremes, measured in the annual average declared value of colonial exports over the period 1859–1863.[7] Furthermore, Jamaica at this time was producing 5.5 puncheons of rum for each hogshead of sugar, as against only 3.7 puncheons during the period 1831–1835.[8]

Whichever of these factors will appear, after further research, to be the most important, the Sugar Act of 1846 can be ignored as an important cause of the decline of West Indian sugar. At its worst, the Sugar Act was a short-run difficulty, although it did show suddenly and dramatically that world conditions had changed. It did not, however, 'ruin' the sugar industry of the West Indies as a whole, because the industry of the West Indies as a whole was not ruined — only that of certain islands. Furthermore, the pre–1846 tariffs had only protected the West Indian planters from foreign competition, not from the competition of the rest of the empire and certainly not the failing islands from the competition of the more successful ones. To the extent that Jamaica's difficulties came from technological backwardness, continued protection might have been even more disastrous than a sudden shift to free trade, since it would have put off still further the eventual necessity of making a painful adjustment.

These considerations, of course, apply only to the competition of cane sugar and only to the period up to about 1870. In the last three decades of the century, all West Indian planters, and, indeed, all cane sugar producers, suffered increasing competition from beet sugar. Here the precedent of free trade in sugar, set by the Sugar Act of 1846, played a part in the economic difficulties of the period, but otherwise the beet sugar problem was a new one, only just appearing on the horizon in the 1850s and 1860s. This problem was not successfully solved in the 1880s and 1890s, but one should not — as some historians have done — place the blame on the policy-makers of the 1840s. In the same sense, it is hardly fair to read backwards from the economic policy of the twentieth century in prescribing for the nineteenth. Perhaps the sugar industry, even in Jamaica, could have been revived and protected by a careful system of price control, quotas, and government credit on easy terms. This was not a possibility in 1846. It was a question of no protection vs. the same kind of protection that had been extended in the past.

Notes

1. Compare A.P. Newton, *A Hundred Years of the British Empire* (London, 1940), p. 295; P. Knaplund, *The British Empire, 1815–1939* (New York: Harper and Brothers, 1941), pp. 244–45; C.E. Carrington, *The British Overseas* (Cambridge, 1950), p. 514; R.L. Schuyler, *The Fall of the Old Colonial System* (New York: Oxford University Press, 1945), pp. 155–56; W.P. Morell, *British Colonial Policy in the Age of Peel and Russell* (Oxford, 1930), pp. 265–69; W.L. Mathieson, *The Sugar Colonies and Governor Eyre 1849–1866* (London, 1936), p. v; C.W. Guillebaud, 'The Crown Colonies, 1845–1870', *Cambridge History of the British Empire* (Cambridge, 1940), II, 730–31; N. Deerr, *The History of Sugar* (2 vols.: London, 1949–50), II, 446; W.L. Burn, *British West Indies* (London, 1951), pp. 126–31.
2. British imports of refined sugar were negligible early in the century and rose to only 3.6 per cent of the total imports during the decade 1853–1862.
3. Parliamentary Papers (hereafter to as PP), 1898, lxxxv [C. 8706], p. 218.
4. The current West Indian duty of 27s. to 30s. per cwt represents an ad valorem rate of 87 to 97 per cent. Furthermore, the elasticity of the demand for sugar was very high. Per capita consumption in Great Britain doubled in response to a 44 per cent drop in the price of sugar between 1845 and 1854. — Deerr, *History of Sugar*, II, 430, 532; Guillebaud, in *Cambridge British Empire*, II, 706.
5. Deerr, *History of Sugar*, II, 377.
6. PP, 1849, xxxvii (280), p. 165.
7. PP, 1872, lxiii [C. 616], pp. 72–79.
8. PP, 1867–68, xlviii [C. 3995], p. 9.

Patterns of Investment and Sources of Credit in the British West Indian Sugar Industry, 1838–1897

Richard A. Lobdell

This essay was awarded the Newcomen prize for essays in Material History at McGill University in 1971

In this essay we attempt to describe the pattern of investment and identify the sources of credit in the British West Indian sugar industry between 1838 and 1897. During those years sugar planters faced three separate crises: Emancipation in 1838, Free Trade in 1846, and bountied beet sugar competition in 1884. In order to examine the response of the sugar industry to each of those crises, it is convenient to divide this study into three time periods. The first deals with the period 1838–45; the second examines the years 1846–83; and the last considers the period 1884–97. Within each of those sections, we attempt to discuss (1) the pressures on the industry to undertake technological improvements, (2) the pattern of capital investment as a result of those pressures, and (3) the major sources of credit which enabled that investment to proceed. In a concluding section we offer a brief summary of our findings and reflect upon the consequences of the industry's attempts to reduce production costs over the period.

The Post-Emancipation Crisis, 1838–45

The British West Indian sugar industry had been in recession for several years prior to the Emancipation Act of 1834. Responding to wartime demand in the British markets, West Indian planters had expanded production throughout the first decade of the 19th century, and in the process new and only marginally productive land had been brought under sugar cultivation in an effort to capture the profits of a distant war. With the peace of 1815, however, sugar prices plummeted, profits disappeared, and planters were faced with the difficult task of reorganizing production. As prices continued to fall, many marginal estates ceased production altogether as sugar cultivation retreated to more suitable lands.

Understandably, the Act of 1834 tended to complicate this rationalization of the sugar industry. Although emancipation was not immediate, few planters held much hope for the future prosperity of the sugar industry. Feeding on each other's wildest fears and recalling the generally unfortunate experiment called apprenticeship, most British West Indian planters gloomily awaited the collapse of the economy with the coming of full emancipation in 1838.

In the light of such forebodings, it is not surprising to discover that plantation accounts tend to show increasing costs of production following the Act of 1834. But as can be seen in Table I, most planters argued that during apprenticeship, production costs were only slightly higher, and in some cases even lower, than under the last few years of slavery. Predictably, the most spectacular increases in costs uniformly belong to the period immediately following 1838.

Table 1. Estimated annual average cost of producing a hundred-weight of sugar (exclusive of capital charges)

Colony	Slavery	Apprenticeship	Freedom
Jamaica[1]	10s 5½d	9s 2¼d	29s 2d
Trinidad[1]	9s 5d	8s 3d	32s 6½d
Tobago[1]	8s 5½d	11s 2d	27s 10d
St. Vincent[2]	7s 3½d	7s 1d	19s 7d
Grenada[2]	9s 5d	9s 8d	24s 3d
St. Kitts[3]	4s 5d	6s 7d	21s 10d
Antigua[4]	7s 8d	7s 6d	19s 7d

SOURCES AND EXPLANATIONS:
[1]Slavery – 1832–4; Apprenticeship — 1836–8; Freedom – 1838–40. (*The Sugar Question,* vol. 2, p. 62)
[2]Slavery – 1831–3; Apprenticeship — 1834–8; Freedom – 1838–40. (*The Sugar Question,* vol. 2, p. 62)
[3]Slavery – 1828–34; Apprenticeship — 1834–8; Freedom – 1842–6. (*The Sugar Question,* vol. 2, pp. 19–20)
[4]Slavery – 1829–33; Apprenticeship — 1834–6; Freedom – 1837–46. (*The Sugar Question,* vol. 2, pp. 10,14–15)

319

The accuracy of the data in Table I may be questioned. Since this evidence was presented to a committee of the British House of Commons with the hope of winning aid for the sugar industry, it was obviously in the planters' interest to show clearly 'the high cost of freedom'. Even if planter honesty and good faith are assumed, it is doubtful whether the costing of production was very sophisticated on most estates.[1] Nonetheless, although these estimates may be somewhat inaccurate, there is little reason to suppose that overall costs of production did not rise as labour was transformed from a slave to a wage basis. Antigua was probably not exceptional when its leading planters claimed that in 1848 somewhere between one-half and two-thirds of total production costs arose from wages.[2]

It is interesting to note that not all planters were convinced that labour was the chief cause of increasing production costs in the mid–1840s. According to one authority, the increased costs of sugar production in St. Kitts were mainly the result of mismanagement arising from absentee ownership of estates.[3] A planter in Trinidad believed that the principal cost of production was not high wage rates, but instead arose from 'waste, loss, destruction and damage' in field and factory operations.[4] In both men's view the situation could not be expected to improve until fresh capital, new management practices, and improved prices were forthcoming.

By 1840, therefore, most British West Indian planters were convinced that costs of production were rising as a result of emancipation and that some remedial action was urgently required if the sugar industry were to survive. Thus, when it began hearings in 1842, the Select Committee on the West India Colonies encountered a variety of proposals designed to check the declining fortunes of sugar. Without question the most frequently heard complaint dealt with the 'labour problem' and possible solutions to it. Mr. Burnley, whose particular interests were in Trinidad, echoed the opinion of many when he declared that if only labourers could be induced to work regularly, then profits could still be made in spite of the high wage rates.[5]

The Committee of 1842 also considered the usefulness of capital investment in reducing overall costs of production. Of course, certain improvements in field operations had been made long before emancipation. In Grenada, for example, ploughs had been employed since 1815, although they were not extensively used until after 1838.[6] This wider use of field implements after emancipation seems to have been common in most of the West Indian colonies. Hence, in Barbados it appears that more extensive use of artificial fertil-

izers and better drainage systems were undertaken mainly after 1838.[7] Similarly, cultivation machinery is said to have become widespread in Trinidad by the mid–1840s,[8] and certain estates had clearly improved production through the use of ploughs and harrows in Jamaica after 1838, but capital needed to finance further improvements was very scarce.[9]

It was in British Guiana that cultivation techniques were most advanced before 1845. Although extensive use of ploughs was limited by the layout of estates and soil conditions, British Guiana could easily boast the best cultivation and transportation systems in all the British West Indies. Steam engines, cane carriers, and megass carriers were widely employed in the transportation of estate products, while new techniques of fertilization and irrigation were known and used before 1845.[10] Indeed, the only obstacle to even greater employment of machinery in field operations (e.g. relaying of fields to facilitate steam ploughs) was the acute shortage of finance capital.[11]

Capital investment was not limited to field operations during the period 1838–45. Indeed, it is not unlikely that most new capital was invested in factory equipment during those years. One obvious innovation was the introduction of steam-powered mills for the crushing of cane. Although they were expensive, a number of estates installed these new mills in order to reduce overall production costs. In St. Kitts, for example, only one steam engine was to be found in 1833, but by 1847 some twenty-three were employed on the island.[12] Likewise in British Guiana a good number of steam mills were employed during the period 1838–45, though some planters seemed unwilling to risk capital in sugar's dubious future.[13] Barbadian planters ordered over £14,000 worth of factory equipment from one manufacturer alone in the two years ending in 1846.[14] Steam mills were widely employed in Trinidad in 1842. In fact, Mr. Burnley reported that while others might speak of a capital shortage, he was of the opinion that in Trinidad there was much more capital in relation to labour than prudence dictated.[15]

Nonetheless, steam mills remained the exception on most of the less prosperous sugar estates before 1845. In Antigua, for example, only six or seven steam mills were employed on more than 125 estates in 1842.[16] Virtually all sugar mills in Grenada were turned by water power in that same year,[17] and even in the previous most prosperous colony of Jamaica, investment in factory equipment was concentrated on a few estates, most notably at Worthy Park in St. Catherine.[18]

These attempts to reduce the costs of sugar production were not dramatically successful before

1845. Planters generally found it difficult to econ-omize on labour as it became virtually impossible to make substantial reduction in wage rates. On those estates where new factory and field machin-ery were introduced, the costs of transition, as well as inadequate accounting systems usually put an intolerable strain on finances. On the surface at least, costs of production continued to rise in spite of planters' efforts to rationalize production before 1845. And yet, there is some evidence that capital investment made during this period was useful in reducing costs of production in later years. Mr. Greene of St. Kitts, for example, reported that the previous introduction of machinery on certain local estates had led to a marked fall in production costs by 1848.[19] In 1850 Lord Stanley argued that Bar-badian planters who had made capital improve-ments before 1846 were in a stronger financial position than their less adventurous neighbours.[20] Even the ultra-cautious Guianese planter Henry Barkly admitted that some neighbouring estates' cost of production had been reduced through the employment of new machinery during this period.[21] In short, those estates which made sub-stantial capital investment in field and factory improvements before 1845 were generally in the best position to withstand subsequent crises.

A British West Indian planter interested in con-tinuing the operation of his estate, or in making capital investments in the hope of future profits, might acquire financial support from a number of sources after 1838. He might try to continue pre-vious credit arrangements with his agent in Britain. Under this system a planter acquired on credit from a British merchant the supplies necessary for the operation of his estate. The subsequent crop would automatically be consigned to the same merchant who would arrange its sale on the British market. Once the crop had been sold, deductions were made for supplies shipped to the estate on credit, commissions were subtracted, and the balance credited (or debited) to the estate's account. At the end of the Napoleonic Wars, however, many con-signee creditors began to despair of such arrange-ments as the indebtedness of planters grew with declining sugar prices. Consequently, advances were limited to the barest necessities and following emancipation only the financially strongest plan-tations could safely rely on this traditional source of credit for investment funds.

A second possible source of investment funds was the £17 million voted by Parliament in 1834 as partial compensation to British West Indian planters for emancipation of slaves. Had this money been used for rational investment, the pro-ductivity of sugar estates would have undoubtedly improved. Although a few planters did invest their

compensation payments in sugar estates[22], the greatest share of the compensation money seems to have been used to reduce indebtedness previ-ously contracted. Insofar as these debt payments increased credit worthiness, they may be consid-ered to have established a potential source of credit for future capital investment. But as suggested above, many consignee merchants had grown sus-picious of West Indian plantations and viewed the compensation money as a last chance to make good an increasingly worthless planter indebtedness.[23]

Thirdly, planters might have financed capital improvements from savings accumulated during periods of past prosperity. Unfortunately, only estates free of debt in 1838 and in possession of sizeable savings could consider such an undertak-ing. Although not unheard of, this alternative was not a very real one for the vast majority of plant-ers.[24]

Finally, sugar planters might turn to the newly established local banking system for help in financing estate operations. Of the local banks, by far the largest was the Colonial Bank of the West Indies which was granted a Royal Charter in May 1836. By the mid–1840s branches had been estab-lished in most of the British West Indies, as well as in Cuba and North America. Under its Charter, the Colonial Bank was empowered to carry on the normal operations of a commercial bank, includ-ing dealing in bills of exchange, accepting depos-its, and advancing money on commercial paper and government securities. However, the bank was expressly forbidden 'to lend or advance money on the security of lands, houses, or tene-ments, or upon ships or to deal in general wares or merchandise of any nature or kind whatso-ever'.[25] Consequently, the bank was legally for-bidden to undertake substantial loans to sugar estates. It might advance money to meet some working expenses of the estates if owners were willing to sign a personal guarantee of liability. But long term capital improvements were quite impossible for the bank to finance. Hence, although it prospered throughout the 19th cen-tury, the Colonial Bank had little beneficial effect on investment in the British West Indian sugar industry. Indeed, through its excessively high dis-counting rates, the Colonial Bank may have seri-ously hindered the industry's development.[26]

Other local banks followed the practice of the influential Colonial Bank and refused to lend money on the security of sugar estates. By the mid 1840s there was only one rival to the Colonial Bank in British Guiana. Established sometime in 1836, the Bank of British Guiana was granted a Charter very similar to that of the Colonial Bank.[27] There is no evidence that this smaller bank lent money to finance capital investment in sugar during the years preceding 1846.

Jamaican local banks appear to have adopted the same policy towards estate financing as did their counterparts in British Guiana. For example, an institution known as the Jamaica Planters' Bank was formed in 1839, but was never given a charter. There is no evidence that it undertook estate financing, but instead seemed particularly interested in financing commercial activities. It is not surprising, therefore, that the Planters' Bank fell victim to the British financial crisis of 1848 and was forced to close its doors in Jamaica.[28]

A final example of the kind of banking institutions which existed during these years is the Bank of Jamaica which was founded in 1837 and closed in 1865. Like the Planters' Bank, the Bank of Jamaica was refused a formal charter. But unlike other local banks, the Bank of Jamaica's Deed of Settlement hints at a more liberal policy towards advances and credit. According to the Deed, the Bank was allowed to

give credit or make advances to any person or persons whomsoever, to such amount, at such rate of interest, and upon such terms, as the Directors may think fit, and such credit may be given, and advances made, with or without security, at the discretion of the Directors. . .[29]

Whether in fact the Bank of Jamaica did pursue such a liberal credit policy is not known. From the lack of planter comment and enthusiasm, however, it is probably safe to assume that the Bank of Jamaica did little to finance capital investment in that island's sugar industry.

In summary, those British West Indian planters interested in capital improvement before 1846 had either to rely upon their own meagre savings or upon consignee credit which was becoming increasingly restricted. Undoubtedly, many planters and merchants had lost confidence in the future of sugar in the West Indies. The steady decline of sugar prices, the mounting indebtedness of estates as profits diminished, and the alluring prospects for investment elsewhere[30] all acted to divert capital away from the British West Indies between 1838 and 1845.

The Free Trade Crisis, 1846–83

Before 1825 British West Indian planters enjoyed a near monopoly in the British muscovado market. British import tariffs were such that the lowest rates applied to West Indian muscovado, slightly higher rates were levied on muscovado coming from elsewhere in the empire, and prohibitively high duties were placed on the muscovado of foreign planters. Beginning in 1825, however, slight alterations in the structure of the sugar tariff were introduced. In that year muscovado produced in Mauritius was allowed to enter the British market at the same tariff rates as West Indian muscovado. Ten years later muscovado made in the East Indian colonies was similarly admitted.[31]

Between 1836 and 1844 the British sugar duties were altered almost annually, though for most of the period the 'B.W.I. group'[32] muscovado paid 24s. per cwt in duties, as against 32s. for other empire producers, and a staggering 63s. duty on foreign muscovado. In 1844 all foreign muscovado not grown by slave labour was admitted to the British market at the rate of 34s. duty, and a year later rates were reduced on all categories of imported sugar.[33] Thus, even before the Act of 1846, alert British West Indian planters must have seen their preferential market slowly disappearing.

The Sugar Duty Act of 1846 announced the intention of the British government to reduce preferential duties so that by 1854, a single rate would apply to sugar of a given quality, regardless of its origin. The Act further prescribed that eventually all sugar would be admitted free of any duty. Consequently, beginning in 1846 British West Indian muscovado entered the British market with only a seven shilling tariff advantage over all foreign-made muscovado. And, as the Act had promised, all muscovado was admitted to the British market at a single rate beginning in 1854.

It is important to note, however, that even after 1854 different quality sugar was taxed differently when imported into the United Kingdom. The British government, anxious to protect its home sugar refining industry, introduced a tariff that progressively increased duties as the quality of imported sugar rose. Hence, the highest duties were paid by refined sugar and successively lower duties were charged on partially refined and muscovado sugar.[34]

This arrangement clearly favoured West Indian planters who had always concentrated on the production of muscovado. Even the vacuum pan yellow crystals made in British Guiana was allowed to enter at relatively favourable rates after 1854. Having installed a good deal of modern machinery after 1840, foreign competitors (e.g., Cuba, Brazil, Mauritius) produced relatively refined sugar, which almost always entered the British market at higher rates of duty. The duties were so favourable to muscovado that some West Indian producers, especially those in British Guiana where modern equipment had recently been employed, found it profitable to spoil refined sugar and export it as muscovado.[35]

This peculiar advantage disappeared only after 1874 when all sugar was admitted to British markets free of any duties. Some West Indian estates were abandoned as a result while others sought more satisfactory markets for their produce. Hoping to encourage a domestic sugar refining industry, the Americans restructured their sugar duties in 1872 and it became advantageous for West Indian planters to sell muscovado in the American rather than the British market. Between 1879 and 1883 exports of West Indian sugar to the United Kingdom fell by 25%, whereas by the early 1880s nearly half (47%) of all British West Indian sugar exports went to the American market.[36] Nonetheless, planters fully recognized that the American market was inherently unstable since muscovado prices were entirely dependent upon the whim of Congress which set the tariff in a generally unpredictable manner.

Between 1846 and 1883, therefore, British West Indian planters were faced with declining prices in the British market and great uncertainty in the American market. Although total British West Indian sugar exports had more than doubled over the period, on the whole it was difficult to maintain total revenues as prices continued to sag.[37] The only obvious way to earn even modest profits was to reduce overall production costs.

As most planters saw the situation after 1846, there were three possible ways by which sugar production costs might be significantly reduced. First of all, a new source of cheap and efficient labour would greatly lower production costs. After a good deal of experimentation, East Indian indentured immigrants were brought to the British West Indies and were found to be suitable estate workers. Considerable sums of money, both private and public in origin, were required for such immigration which may be considered an investment of sorts in the industry.

A second strategy used by planters to reduce costs of production between 1846 and 1883 involved the mechanization and rationalization of field and factory operations. Immediately following the Act of 1846, significant capital investment seems to have fallen off in the West Indian sugar industry, though it did not completely disappear. Between 1803 and 1851, for example, the firm of Boulton and Watt sent to the British West Indies at least 129 sugar mill steam engines, some of which must surely have been ordered and installed after 1846.[38] Furthermore, one witness before the Committee of 1848 claimed that '2,500 agricultural implements have been sent out to the West Indies during the last few years'.[39] Nonetheless, it is difficult to find much direct evidence of massive capital investment in sugar during the first few years following the Act of 846.

By 1850 the immediate shock and panic had begun to subside and West Indian estates which were still in operation increasingly turned to newer techniques of production. In spite of hardships in Barbados, for example, most estates were running profitably in the years after 1850, primarily as a result of 'investment of fresh capital in improved machinery, drainage, and expensive concentrated fertilizers'.[40] Indeed, between 1865 and 1883 a mild prosperity seems to have visited the West Indian sugar industry. With the momentary prosperity came renewed interest in investment. To be sure, some of the smaller islands seemed to prosper without undertaking capital improvements, but those same colonies were virtually ruined when the last remnants of preference in the British market disappeared in 1874.

It was in the large, relatively 'new' colonies of Trinidad and British Guiana that capital investment was most impressive during the period 1846–83. The Colonial Company in Trinidad made substantial investments in all kinds of new equipment. Vacuum pans, centrifugals, steam powered crushing mills, better techniques of cultivation, and a modern central factory were the main elements of the new investment in Trinidad. Similarly, in British Guiana large sums were invested in the sugar industry between 1846 and 1883. Especially in the latter years of that period, sugar machinery imports often averaged over £100,000 annually.[41] Vacuum pans, centrifugals, improved steam mills, better irrigation schemes, hybrid cane, and improved transportation represented the major areas of capital investment in British Guiana over those years.[42] Indeed, the capital stock of the industry was so improved by 1883 that estates in British Guiana were justly noted for their 'utility, economy, and latest manufacturing appliances'.[43]

The third method planters saw for reducing costs between 1846 and 1883 lay in the amalgamation of small estates into larger, well-managed, commercial enterprises. Such consolidations allowed for more efficient use of existing factory equipment, available labour supplies, and marketing facilities. In addition, as more acreage was absorbed by the consolidated estate, costs could be lowered by carefully concentrating cultivation on the most productive lands. Finally, and perhaps most importantly, these consolidated estates usually enjoyed the availability of sufficient credit necessary to undertake other cost-saving innovations.

Small inefficient muscovado-producing estates were often consolidated through direct purchase. In Trinidad these small estates usually found it financially impossible to modernize operations by investing in expensive machinery.[44] Consequently, many turned to cocoa or coconut production where soil and climate permitted. Still others were simply sold to buyers who wished to continue sugar production. Mainly through direct purchases, the joint stock company known as the Colonial Company had by 1871 managed to expand its Trinidadian holdings to such a degree that a central factory was considered economical.[45] Other companies and even some individuals in Trinidad followed this tactic in consolidating sugar estates during these years. By 1884 estate consolidation had proceeded so far that a hugh proportion of Trinidadian sugar was being grown, manufactured, shipped and marketed by a mere handful of companies.[46]

As in Trinidad, estates in British Guiana were systematically consolidated during the period 1846–83. Thus, the 404 estates producing sugar in 1838 had by 1870 been consolidated into 135 units of production, of which the greatest part was owned by non-resident companies. The Colonial Company, Messrs. Daniels of Bristol, and a few other British merchant houses controlled 'nearly all the largest, finest, and best cultivated estates'[47] in that colony by 1883.

The amalgamation of estates in St. Lucia proceeded in a slightly different manner. The multiple crises following 1815 had driven many muscovado estates into bankruptcy. In order to facilitate the liquidation of these debts, a local law was passed which allowed for the seizure and sale of immovable property. As might have been expected, these sales tended to concentrate land ownership into fewer hands.[48] Consolidation had proceeded so far by 1871 that the next logical step in the rationalization of production, the construction of a central factory, was undertaken. However, the central factory was unable to reduce substantially the costs of production before 1883, as it suffered from mismanagement and poor organization of cane deliveries.[49]

In the other areas of the British West Indies, systematic amalgamation of small estates was hindered by the legal peculiarities of indebtedness. The law did not make it easy to bring about the forced sale of insolvent estates. No strict priority of encumbrances was generally recognized, and that difficulty aside it became almost impossible after 1846 to find buyers willing to assume the estate's outstanding liabilities. Hence, it was often in the interest of insolvent proprietors to abandon production altogether and default on their debts.

In order to expedite the sale and legal transfer of land held by insolvent owners, the West India Encumbered Estates Act was approved by the British Parliament in 1854. By passing an appropriate local ordinance, any West Indian colony[50] could make use of the encumbered estates courts whose duties were to order the sale of land hopelessly in debt. In addition to courts in the various colonies, the Act provided for a central court in London in order to ensure equal protection to all litigants. The courts were most active between 1857 and 1883, although they were not formally abolished until 1895.

Estates processed under the courts were generally sold in London. Only rarely were such estates purchased by individual planters. Instead, the vast majority came into the hands of various British merchant houses. In St. Vincent, for example, the thirty estates sold by the courts were mostly bought by Porter & Sons or by Cavan Bros., who also held plantations in British Guiana, Trinidad, and Barbados. Similarly, court-processed estates in Montserrat, Antigua, and St. Kitts were usually purchased by the estate's former consignee merchant. By 1883 most of the land in these smaller colonies was controlled by non-resident proprietors.[51]

The courts were most active in disposing of insolvent estates in Jamaica. In that colony some 148 estates were sold by the courts, including some of the largest and best known plantations. Many of these estates were taken out of sugar production, but some were cultivated while muscovado continued to enjoy an advantage in the British market. However, only a limited amount of new machinery was introduced on these estates which often tended to concentrate on rum production.[52] As elsewhere, the sale of encumbered estates tended to concentrate ownership in the hands of non-resident merchants.

In summary, the consolidation of estates after 1846 tended to concentrate plantation ownership in the hand of British merchant houses specializing in sugar. The non-resident nature of these companies, which possessed considerable non-estate assets, gave them a credit worthiness which the smaller estates could not hope to rival. The extensive use of such credit and the more thorough organization of existing assets enabled these new enterprises to dominate the industry by 1883.

Moreover, the consolidation of sugar estates demonstrates a change in attitude towards plantation production. In former times a surprising number of estates had been operated by a curious combination of sentiments and family pride. With the crises of the first half of the 19th century, however, it was increasingly apparent that a more commercial approach to estate production was required.

Finally, consolidation of estates generally led to lower costs of production during the years 1846–65. The new credit worthiness of the amalgamated estates made possible the introduction of machinery and other improved techniques of production. It must be noted, however, that production costs were not significantly reduced during the years 1865–83.[53] Nonetheless, the consolidation of estates across the whole period 1846–83 laid the foundation for remarkable savings in cost after 1884.

Apart from consolidation under non-resident merchant ownership, other credit sources were available for the financing of capital investment between 1846 and 1883. In spite of a general hesitancy to do so, a few consignee merchants seemed willing to continue the advances on which planters had always relied. This traditional system of credit seems to have been particularly important in Barbados. Unlike neighbouring colonies, Barbados exhibited no tendency towards estate consolidation. Even as late as 1897 only 14 of 440 sugar estates were owned by public companies.[54] By virtue of their excellent quality muscovado and relatively low costs of production, Barbadian planters were usually able to earn modest profits, which in turn allowed them to finance their operations in the traditional manner. To planters in other West Indian colonies, however, merchants showed great reluctance to advance credit.

Secondly, planters might try to finance day to day operations through credit secured from the local banking system. Unfortunately, the Colonial Bank still refused to loan money on the security of land and so it was of little assistance in financing major capital investment. Nevertheless, the Colonial Bank could usually be relied upon to provide working capital in the form of personal loans to well-known and highly respected planters. Other local banks were of no more help in the financing of major investment. Moreover, many of these smaller banks closed their doors before 1884. In short, local banks might grant small loans to cover working expenses, but they would not provide the financing required for significant capital investment during the years 1846–83.

Finally, planters in a few colonies were able to take advantage of indirect financial aid offered by local governments. During these years many colonial governments employed skilled engineers to advise planters on improved manufacturing techniques, thus indirectly encouraging capital investment. In addition, many local governments had established, at least on paper, a Department of Agriculture which gave advice and some assistance to planters interested in improving production techniques. The St. Lucian government undertook an even bolder course of financial assistance to the sugar industry by granting some £40,000 for the construction of a central sugar factory in the 1870s.[55] The governments of Trinidad and British Guiana expended considerable sums of public money on the importation of indentured immigrants which may be considered a form of assistance extended to the industry. On balance, however, it would be difficult to argue that substantial government credit was available to planters interested in capital investment during the period 1846–83.

The Beet Sugar Crisis, 1884–97

Taking advantage of rapid technological developments, European beet sugar producers were able to reduce costs and increase output substantially during the second half of the 19th century. Better crop yields, more efficient manufacturing, and more systematic marketing placed beet sugar in a position to threaten cane sugar by 1870 when nearly one-third of total world sugar output was beet in origin. Only ten years later, beet producers were turning out 50% of the world's sugar.[56]

Although total world sugar production increased by 44% between 1870 and 1880, sugar prices in Britain remained reasonably steady at or near 20s. per cwt. Beginning in 1884, however, European beet sugar was 'dumped' in massive quantities on the British market. Protected by a disguised export bounty and enjoying the absence of a British tariff, beet sugar soon swamped the British market. Prices began to fall so precipitously that by the end of 1884 sugar was selling at 13s.3d. per cwt; by 1897 prices had fallen below 10s.[57]

The reaction of British West Indian planters to the threat of bountied beet sugar was immediate and frantic. Countless petitions, innumerable pamphlets, and seemingly endless interviews with government officials proved futile during the twelve years following 1884. Wedded to the principles of free trade and cognizant of the political advantages of inexpensive sugar for home consumption, the British government remained serenely indifferent to colonial complaints. Only after another round of bounty increases in 1897 was the British government prevailed upon to send a Royal Commission to their West Indian colonies.

Most planters of the time did not require a Royal Commission to point out the difficulties confronting their industry. By 1870 hardly anyone seriously believed that West Indian sugar would ever again be protected in the British market. Consequently, more and more West Indian muscovado found its way into the more attractive American market, especially after the revision of the American tariff in 1872. By the end of the century more than 65% of all British West Indian sugar was being exported to the U.S. markets.[58]

Furthermore, few planters needed a Royal Commission to explain that profits were determined as much by costs of production as by final product prices. As it became increasingly obvious that British prices were not likely to improve and that the American tariff was subject to the uncertainties of partisan politics, West Indian planters took more interest in reducing their overall costs of production.

In 1884 the least expensive British West Indian sugar cost 16s. per cwt to produce.[59] After that year, however, those sugar estates which were still in operation managed to reduce costs of production dramatically. The Royal Commission of 1897 found Guianese producers making sugar for about 9s. per cwt;[60] two years later costs were said to have been lowered to 8s.[61] Similar reductions were found in the principal sugar producing colonies by 1897, as can be seen in Table 2.

These relatively low production costs were the result of several important improvements. Firstly, significant economies had been realized in field operations between 1883 and 1897. In British Guiana, for example, cultivation costs involved in making one hundredweight of sugar had fallen from 6s.4d. in 1883–4 to 4s.3d. in 1896–7.[62] The Royal Commission believed that improved species of cane was the single greatest cause of such falling cultivation costs. Reductions in the wage rates had also been important, though by 1897 it was difficult to imagine that additional savings of this type could be expected. More widespread use of modern cultivation implements, more thorough application of artificial fertilizers, and better irrigation schemes also made significant contributions to lower cultivation costs.[63]

Secondly, improved factory operations helped reduce overall production costs after 1884. In British Guiana, for example, factory costs associated with the making of a hundredweight of sugar were calculated to be 9s.9d. in 1883–4, but had fallen to 4s.9d. by 1896–7.[64] This remarkable decline in factory costs must be laid to the heavy investment which proceeded even after the crisis of 1884. Hence, the value of sugar machinery

imported into that colony during the period 1879–97 has been estimated at between £1.4 million and £2.2 million.[65] In 1890 alone some £130,000 worth of sugar factory equipment was imported into British Guiana.[66]

In similar fashion capital investment played a large role in reducing production costs in Trinidad after 1884. By 1897 some £2.5 million had been invested in the sugar industry, of which at last 75% represented machinery of the most modern nature.[67] After 1885 these improved factories began to produce an increasing proportion of Trinidadian sugar exports. In 1891, for example, about 43% of sugar export earnings was vacuum pan produced; by 1896 that figure had increased to 53%.[68] Indeed, capital investment in Trinidadian factory equipment was so extensive that the Royal Commission could find little to recommend by way of improvement.

On the other hand, capital investment in sugar industries of other British West Indian colonies virtually ceased after 1884. In the technologically backward islands of Grenada, Dominica, Montserrat, and St. Vincent sugar production had all but disappeared by 1897. Certainly after the crisis of 1884 no major improvements were undertaken in sugar, though a few merchant companies with land in these colonies turned production to limes, cocoa, and sea island cotton.[69] Even the more prosperous islands of St. Kitts and Barbados saw little capital investment in sugar after 1884, though relatively cheap labour held production costs within manageable limits.[70] After 1884 even Jamaica ceased to be a major exporter of sugar, choosing instead to concentrate on the production of rum, bananas, and citrus. To be sure, a few extraordinary Jamaican plantations still profited from sugar production,[71] but methods of production were primitive and sugar investment negligible.[72]

Finally, production costs were reduced after 1884 through various economies resulting from consolidation of estate lands. Although interest in consolidation waned in some of the smaller islands after 1884, amalgamation of estates continued in Trinidad and British Guiana. We have already seen that such consolidation helped to reduce costs of production by co-ordinating various estate activities in the years between 1846 and 1883. Similar economies were realized after 1884 as amalgamated properties became better organized and new techniques of production were steadily introduced. In Trinidad, for example, the central factory built by the Colonial Company in the 1870s had reduced production costs by more than 50% between 1884 and 1894.[73]

The availability of credit to finance capital improvements was a major difficulty for most

Table 2. Estimated least costly production of sugar, by colony (exclusive of capital charges)

Colony	Cost per cwt, 1897
Barbados	8s. 7½d.
Trinidad	8s. 10½d.
Jamaica	7s. 4d.
St. Kitts	9s. 5½d.
British Guiana	9s. 0d.

SOURCE: Royal Commission of 1897, *Report,* Appendix A.

planters after 1884. The traditional sources of credit, the consignee merchants, had been almost unapproachable before 1884 and the events of that year offered little inducement to merchants to provide estates with additional capital. Increasingly, planters had to look elsewhere for the credit needed to finance their operations. The reluctance of consignee merchants to extend credit did not close the sugar industry to inflows of foreign capital. As noted earlier, by the mid–1880s most of the best estates had come under the control of a few British-based merchant houses. Relying on their own creditors in London, these enterprises were able[74] to secure the credit necessary to undertake modernization, and after 1884, if not before that date, this type of credit was the most important available to the British West Indian sugar industry.

A second source of credit for the industry lay in the availability of local investment funds. Some local capitalists were apparently willing to loan funds at 8% interest when the liability was secured by a mortgage on a large estate; smaller, less secure estates were often required to pay 40% interest for similar local financing.[75] Perhaps even more important, however, local capital available for such loans at any rate of interest was strictly limited. Giving evidence to the Royal Commission of 1897, the mayor of Port of Spain and other prominent Trinidadians bemoaned the lack of local credit for small independent planters.[76] Similar complaints were heard by the Commissioners in all of the colonies visited. Although it cannot be completely disregarded, local credit did not seem to play a very important role in the financing of sugar investment during this period.

The increasingly sophisticated banking system of the West Indies might have provided a third source of credit for the sugar industry after 1884. Unfortunately, although the banks continued to prosper, they provided little financing of investment in sugar. In most colonies the Colonial Bank held a monopoly on banking transactions, but the bank was still bound by its original charter which explicitly prohibited the extending of credit on the security of land. Even the personal credit that had proved so useful during the years 1846–83 had been severely restricted after 1885 as prices continued to fall and confidence waned.[77] Only in British Guiana was there to be found a bank willing to underwrite estate operations after 1884. But the Bank of British Guiana was too small, overambitious, and over-extended to remain solvent for long. By 1897 it had been forced to seek government help in meeting its commitments and its role as a financier of sugar had all but ended.[78] In short, the banking system after 1884 could no longer aid planters with even the most temporary advances.

That the banks, as they were then constituted, might have financed major capital investment was completely beyond question.

Finally, financial assistance to the sugar industry was occasionally made available by various colonial governments after 1884. The colony most active in the public support of sugar was Barbados, a colony which had little access to corporate financing so important to Trinidad and British Guiana. When credit became tighter and more expensive following the events of 1884, the Barbados government approved the Agricultural Aids Act of 1887, which allowed planters to borrow money on the security of their growing crop. The Act was so enthusiastically received that by 1896 some 138 estates comprising over 30,000 acres (about one-third of total plantation acreage) had borrowed more than £100,000 under the scheme. It is important to note that these funds were not governmental in origin; rather, they were loans made by private individuals whose confidence had been bolstered by the obvious interest of the government in the sugar industry. Unfortunately, the poor harvests of the 1890s placed many of these advances in danger of default.[79]

Government aid in other West Indian colonies was less significant. St. Lucia continued some public support for the central factory, but nothing on the scale of the 1870s. Most colonies had agricultural officers who advised planters on new techniques of sugar production and increasingly urged diversification into the production of bananas, cocoa, and limes. Large governmental expenditures were involved in the indentured immigrant programmes in Trinidad, British Guiana, and a few other colonies after 1884. Nonetheless, except for the policies of the Barbadian and St. Lucian governments, it is difficult to find much direct assistance given by governments to the sugar industry between 1884 and 1897.

Summary and Conclusions

Confronted with declining sugar prices during the last two-thirds of the 19th century, British West Indian planters desperately sought to reduce production costs. As we have seen, a number of possible economies presented themselves to the enterprising planter. Attempts to reduce wage rates and fevered efforts to secure an adequate and predictable supply of labour were the initial responses of most planters to rising unit costs of production. Although wage rate reductions proved difficult, the use of indentured immigrants did reduce labour costs of production in some colonies.

Most thoughtful planters were convinced that overall production costs could be lowered if field and factory operations were made more efficient. Consequently, newer milling machinery, more efficient use of factory equipment, and less costly transportation systems were employed after 1840. Improved species of cane, more enlightened use of fertilizers, widespread use of irrigation, and the introduction of new cultivation implements also contributed to lower production costs.

More importantly, overall production costs were reduced through the consolidation of small inefficient estates into larger units of production. Such amalgamation allowed for the more complete employment of factory equipment, more thorough organization of planting and cultivation, and more profitable marketing of final products.

We have seen that these strategies for reducing costs were most successfully undertaken in British Guiana and Trinidad during the period 1838–97. Of those colonies which undertook the importation of indentured immigrants, Trinidad and British Guiana probably benefitted most. Heavy investment in modern factory equipment and improved cultivation tools was widespread in both colonies. Perhaps because they were less encumbered, possessed more fertile soil, and were generally more suited to large-scale production, estates in Trinidad and British Guiana were steadily amalgamated so that by 1897 the sugar industry in those colonies was controlled by a mere handful of foreign based merchant companies. Although these strategies were attempted in the other islands, the newer colonies of Trinidad and British Guiana had by the end of the century succeeded in dominating the West Indian sugar industry. More convincing proof of the efficacy of these strategies would be hard to imagine.

During these years planters searched frantically for the massive credit with which to finance capital investment. As we have seen, the traditional system of consignee credit, savings from past profits, small loans from local banks, and occasional governmental assistance were all useful (though highly restricted) sources of capital. The most important sources of finance capital were the British merchant companies which came to dominate the West Indian sugar industry after 1880. Relying on credit secured by non-estate assets, these merchant firms alone possessed the capital necessary for significant investment in the newer techniques of production.

The rise of these large, foreign based, vertically integrated companies is the single most important development in the West Indian sugar industry during the last two-thirds of the 19th century. Indeed, the emergence and success of these companies mark the beginning of a fundamental change in the institutional organization of the West

Indian economies. Dispassionately shifting production and investment from estate to estate and colony to colony, these new enterprises were no longer bound by the tradition, nostalgia, and status considerations which had proved so important to earlier planters. With consummate skill and almost ruthless efficiency, these firms combined their ability to command massive outside credit with their talent for vertical integration. The ultimate result was the transformation of family based plantations into modern, impersonal, industrial enterprises. Indeed, their vertical integration, ability to command credit, reliance upon advanced technology, and foreign ownership may qualify these sugar companies of the late 19th century as the first modern multi-national corporations in the Caribbean.

Notes

1. D.G. Hall, 'Incalculability as a Feature of Sugar Production During the Eighteenth Century', *Social and Economic Studies*, Sept. 1961.
2. *The Sugar Question: Being a Digest of the Evidence Taken Before the Committee on Sugar and Coffee Plantations* (London: H.M.S.O., 1848), vol. 2, pp. 12, 14.
3. Evidence of Mr. Pickwood in *The Sugar Question*, vol. 2, p. 21.
4. Evidence of Mr. Burnley in *Report of the Select Committee on the West India Colonies* (London: H.M.S.O., 1843), pp. 91–2. Hereinafter referred to as Report (Committee of 1842).
5. Ibid., pp. 92ff.
6. Evidence of Mr. Barkly, Report (Committee of 1842), p. 205.
7. Earl of Derby, *Further Facts Connected with the West Indies* (London, 1851), pp. 28, 41.
8. Evidence of Mr. Bushe, Report (Committee of 1842), pp. 287–8.
9. Evidence of Mr. MacCornock, Report (Committee of 1842), p. 359. N.B. Alexander Geddes disagreed, believing that little machinery had been introduced in Jamaica and was of no value to those estates where it had been employed. See his evidence, ibid, p. 477.
10. Evidence of Mr. Campbell, Report (Committee of 1842), pp. 152ff.
11. Evidence of Mr. Barkly, ibid., pp. 187–8.
12. Evidence of Mr. Greene in the *Report of the Select Committee on Sugar and Coffee Planting* (8 Reports, London, 1848), *Third Report*, p. 138.
13. Evidence of Mr. Barkly, *The Sugar Question*, vol. 2, p. 86.
14. Evidence of Mr. Moody, ibid., p. 121.
15. Evidence of Mr. Burnley, Report (Committee of 1842), p. 76.
16. Evidence of Mr. Nugent, ibid., p. 227.
17. Evidence of Mr. Barkly, ibid, p. 205.
18. Evidence of Mr. Price, *Second Report* (Committee of 1848), pp. 62–70.
19. Evidence of Mr. Greene, *Third Report* (Committee of 1848), p. 138.
20. Earl of Derby, pp. 27–8, 41.
21. Evidence of Mr. Barkly, *The Sugar Question*, vol. 2, p. 82. See also the evidence of Dr. Rankin, ibid., pp. 74–6.
22. Evidence of Mr. Barkly, Report (Committee of 1842), p. 188.

23. That most consignees viewed suspiciously the future of sugar in the B.W.I. during these years is beyond dispute. The evidence collected by the Committees of 1842 and 1848 is full of such suspicions. See, for example, the evidence of Mr. Innes in *The Sugar Question*, vol. 2, p. 53, and that of Mr. Hankey in the *Third Report* (Committee of 1848), p. 26.

24. Although the evidence is not conclusive, Mr. Barkly seems to have been one of those who did so (Report (Committee of 1842), pp. 187–8). On the other hand, Mr. Tollemache's estates in Antigua were debt free and reasonably profitable, but he flatly refused to invest in new equipment (*Third Report* (Committee of 1848), p. 247).

25. As quoted in R.M. Martin, *History of the Colonies of the British Empire* (6 vols., London, 1843), vol. 4, pp. 20, 21. See also, Barclays Bank, *A Banking Centenary: Barclays Bank, 1836–1936.* (Plymouth, England, 1938).

26. R.W. Beachey, *The British West Indian Sugar Industry in the Late Nineteenth Century* (London, 1957), p. 159. J.W. Root, *The British West Indies and the Sugar Industry* (Liverpool, 1899), pp. 12–14.

27. Martin, p. 134.

28. D.G. Hall, *Free Jamaica, 1838–1865* (New Haven, 1959), pp. 122–4.

29. Bank of Jamaica, *Deed of Settlement of the Bank of Jamaica* (Kingston, 1837), p. 15.

30. Evidence of Mr. Barkly, *The Sugar Question,* vol. 2, p. 85. When one planter was asked by the 1848 Committee why investment was lacking in the B.W.I. sugar industry after emancipation, he replied: '[Investors] preferred India and Mauritus. . .' (Evidence of Mr. Higgins, *Fourth Report,* p. 101).

31. Noel Deerr, *History of Sugar* (London, 1949), vol. 2, pp. 430, 422–3.

32. Meaning muscovado originating in the British West Indies, Mauritius, and the East India colonies.

33. P. Curtin, 'Sugar Duties and West Indian Prosperity', *Journal of Economic History* (Spring 1954), pp. 159–61.

34. Deerr, vol, 2, p. 442.

35. Beachey, pp. 45–8.

36. Calculated from Beachey, p. 57.

37. Deerr, vol. I, pp. 194–203; Curtin, pp. 160–1.

38. N. Deerr and A. Brooks, 'The Early Use of Steam Power in the Sugar Cane Industry', *Transactions of the Newcomen Society,* Vol. XXI, (1940–41).

39. Evidence of Mr. Miles, *Fifth Report* (Committee of 1848), p. 260.

40. Earl of Derby, p. 41.

41. *Report and Evidence of the West Indian Royal Commission of 1897,* Appendix A, pp. 84–5.

42. A railway was begun in British Guiana in the early 1840s and substantial sums of money (£100,000) were invested by local planters. However, after 1846 English capitalists refused to pay in their subscribed funds as their confidence in the colony's future declined. See, *The Sugar Question,* vol. 2, p. 66.

43. Beachey, p. 120.

44. One authority in 1848 placed the cost of installing a modern factory capable of producing a modest output of 500 hogsheads of sugar at £8,000. (*The Sugar Question,* vol. 2, pp. 120–1).

45. Beachey, pp. 84–5.

46. Beachey, pp. 42, 84, 122, 127.

47. Beachey, pp. 118–21.

48. Royal Commission of 1897, Report, Appendix A, pp. 116–17.

49. Beachey, pp. 84–5.

50. With the exception of St. Lucia, Barbados, Trinidad, and British Guiana, all the West Indian colonies eventually passed such an ordinance.

51. Beachey, pp. 8, 36–8.

52. See both Beachey, pp. 6–9, 36, and Eisner, pp. 196–7. Both these authors suggest that during these years there was some absolute reduction of the industry's capital stock as some sugar factories were dismantled and sold to Cuban planters.

53. Beachey, p. 53.

54. Beachey, pp. 125–6.

55. Report (Royal Commission, 1897), p. 45.

56. Deerr, vol. 2, p. 490.

57. Deerr, vol, 2, p. 505.

58. About £2 per ton more revenue could be earned in the American market during most of the last thirty years of the 19th century. See Beachey, pp. 128, 129.

59. Report (Royal Commission, 1897), Appendix A, p. 84.

60. Ibid.

61. Root, p. 50.

62. Report (Royal Commission, 1897), Appendix A, p. 84.

63. Report (Royal Commission, 1897), p. 14.

64. Report (Royal Commission, 1897), Appendix A, p. 84.

65. Ibid., pp. 84–5; Root, pp. 16, 24.

66. Beachey, p. 176.

67. Report (Royal Commission, 1897), Appendix A, p. 100.

68. Calculated from data found ibid. In St. Lucia the central factory and other modern factories had all but eliminated muscovado by 1897.

69. Report (Royal Commission, 1897), Appendix A, pp. 110, 120, 122–3, 127.

70. In Barbados between 1886 and 1895 nearly £70,000 was spent annually on artificial fertilizers. Strictly speaking this may not qualify as capital investment, but it clearly shows a willingness to adopt technology suited to the Barbadian circumstance. See, Report (Royal Commission, 1897), Appendix A, p. 97.

71. For example, Mesopotamia estate averaged some £2,000 profit annually between 1874 and 1891 and other estates in the parishes of Westmoreland, Hanover, and Trelawny seem to have been equally prosperous. See, Beachey, p. 159.

72. Report (Royal Commission, 1897), Appendix A, p. 137.

73. In St. Lucia similar reductions in costs were claimed for these years as the central factory began efficient operation. See, Beachey, p. 86.

74. Though they were not always willing to do so. In St. Kitts, for example, foreign owners whose credit was excellent refused to undertake necessary investment after 1895. See, Report (Royal Commission, 1897), p. 57.

75. Report (Royal Commission, 1897), Appendix C, p. 282.

76. Report (Royal Commission, 1897), Appendix C, pp. 237, 241, 276, 282. See also, Root, pp. 16–17; Eisner, p. 196.

77. Report (Royal Commission, 1897), Appendix C, pp. 44–5.

78. The government's commitment to the Bank of British Guiana stood at £145,000 in 1897. See the letter from Gov. Hemming dated 26 April 1897, found in Report (Royal Commission, 1897), Appendix C, pp. 148–9.

79. Report (Royal Commission, 1897), p. 30, and Appendix C, pp. 151–3, 157; Beachey, p. 34.

Plantations in the Caribbean: Cuba, Puerto Rico, and the Dominican Republic in the Late Nineteenth Century

Manuel Moreno Fraginals

Historical phenomena, obviously, have never been static; but there are certain periods in which transformations occur slowly, and others in which the rate of change is such that in a few short years everything seems different. An example of this may be found in the industrial history of the Caribbean.

During the eighteenth century and the first half of the nineteenth, the patterns of sugar production and commerce changed very little, and what changes occurred were either geographical (shifts in production from one island to another) or determined by the partial adoption of certain technologies. On the other hand, starting about 1860 and within not more than thirty years, the centuries-old structure of the sugar industry was shattered, to be replaced by completely new forms of production and commerce and even by a new form of the final product itself, a sugar produced to different standards and shipped in different packaging. It is no exaggeration to say that as regards sugar in the Caribbean, in the nineties everything was completely different from what existed in the sixties.

It is almost impossible to list the successive developments in the sugar world from the 1860s on, and even more so to establish causal relationships among these developments in order to follow them like a chain reaction. These changes equally affected sugar producers, merchants, and consumers; they modified human and labour relations and altered age-old habits of consumption. This great transformation was at once the cause and the consequence of other economic, social, and political factors and was at the same time connected by innumerable links to other world events such as the crisis of the Spanish colonialism, the emergence of the United States as a world power, the rapid developments in science and technology, the universal increase in population, and the new systems of communications.

Changes in the Sugar Industry

Technical Changes

An overview of the process allows us to point out that, in the first place, from a technical point of view, Caribbean sugar-producing methods changed completely in the last thirty years of the nineteenth century. A series of radical innovations sprung up at every stage of the sugar-making process, causing the old manual machines (run by untrained workers) to be junked and replaced by highly sophisticated machinery that required skilled operators and efficient technical supervision.

The installing of this new machinery required an extremely large economic investment and the scrapping of the existing production lines and even of most of the buildings constructed under the previous system. Consequently, the new enterprise cannot be considered an old mill that had been modernized (as was the case with the introduction of the first steam engines into the sugar mills); rather, the old sugar mill was demolished, and in its place — or elsewhere — new buildings were erected to house new machinery run by new types of workers. The only holdovers of the old sugar mill complex were, in general, certain structures for social use, the communications infrastructure, and the cane fields, which in any case supplied only a part of the new production centre's needs: obviously, to be profitable, the new industrial plant had to process much greater quantities of cane than the old sugar mill.

This was the case when the new industrial plantation (the central or centralized factory, as it came to be known at the end of the nineteenth century) was set up in the zone previously occupied by one or more ingenios, the old sugar mills. One other solution, also quite typical, was for the organizers of the new central to seek out fertile new low-priced lands.

This change is both quantitative and qualitative. From the point of view of quantity, the old central differed from the old ingenios both in grinding capacity and a higher rate of extraction of sugar from the cane that it ground. For example, the so-called modern mechanized sugar mills of 1860 ground, on an average, the cane from 30 to 35 *caballerías* of land (roughly 400 to 500 hectares or about 1,000 to 1,250 acres); the central of 1890 could handle the production of 100 to 120 *caballerías* and those that could grind the cane from up to 150 or 200 *caballerías* were not uncommon. But production increased at an even greater rate than milling capacity because the new factories could extract almost twice the amount of sugar from the same amount of cane as the old mill.

This increase in production capacity accelerated the process of consolidation. In 1860 there were 1,318 sugar mills in Cuba producing some 515,000 metric tons of sugar; by 1895 the number had decreased to 250 while production was up to almost 1 million tons. In Puerto Rico, where a similar process began somewhat later, there were 550 mills in 1870 producing about 100,000 tons, the highest figure achieved there in the nineteenth century; by 1910, fifteen centrales were producing 233,000 tons.

This consolidation affected landowning practices from a legal standpoint and brought about the emergence of the sugar latifundia in Cuba and Puerto Rico; socially, the consolidation process undermined the old class of slaveowning planters, who were replaced to a great extent by a new type of industrial entrepreneur. In Cuba, by 1895 only 17% of the owners of centrales came from the old plantation-owning families.

This industrial revolution in the sugar industry also made it necessary to transform labour relations over the next thirty years, having finally triggered the crisis of the slave system on which the old *ingenio* had been based. But the industrial revolution of the Caribbean was not accompanied by a complementary agricultural revolution. On the contrary, the agricultural side of the sugar industry (planting, cultivation, and harvesting) retained its traditional backwardness, which had originated in slaveowning cultural patterns, though under a new political climate, for by 1873 (in Puerto Rico) and 1881 (in Cuba) slavery had been abolished.

Thus a technological gap arose between the industrial sector and its agricultural base. In contrast to the modernity of the central, the agricultural sector retained its obsolete ways: within a few years the law of diminishing returns (which applies where, as in this case, no efforts were made to improve crop yields by modern methods of cultivation) made its appearance, marked by the trend toward smaller cane yields.

The first response to this situation, aggravated by other social and legal factors, was to create an administrative separation between the manufacture of sugar (the industrial sector) and the supply of raw material, cane (the agricultural sector). The relationship between these two sectors was to be a permanent source of conflict from the end of the nineteenth century. The old creole sugar oligarchy, the sugarocracy of Cuba and Puerto Rico, was for the most part forced out of the manufacturing side of the industry, but in many cases stayed on as owners of cane plantations.

As a result of the industrialization process, the productivity of the industrial worker in the central rose steeply; but the productivity of the agricultural worker, especially that of the cane cutter, remained the same, for, as mentioned, the methods of cultivation and harvesting had not evolved. In order to take advantage of the enormous capacities of the new industrial installations, the *zafras*, or cane harvests, became bigger and bigger but were carried out in shorter periods, generally starting in January and ending in April.

This, in turn, created two problems of far-reaching magnitude: one with labour, the other with the amortization and the optimal utilization of the expensive industrial equipment. With respect to labour, the amount of cane required by the modern industry made it necessary to employ hundreds of agricultural workers (cane cutters) simultaneously in Cuba, Puerto Rico, and Santo Domingo for a period of three to four months of the employment during four months of the year, which for the majority of the labourers meant seasonal unemployment for eight months of the year. This situation had not occurred previously because with unskilled slave labour (which in any case had to be supported all year round), rudimentary manufacturing equipment, small daily millings, and long harvest seasons, there was almost always work for all hands. But the modern plantation required, for its optimal running, the existence of an army of unemployed workers, ideally located off the *ingenio* grounds but subjected to economic pressure that forced them to sell their services cheaply and with a minimum of social benefits, as cane cutters. These workers made up a migratory mass, and their migration could be either internal (from one part of the country to another) or external (from one country to another). A mixture of both kinds became the normal pattern.

The other problem created by the installation of modern industrial equipment was the need to find additional sources of income, not necessarily connected with the sugar industry, that would help to amortize the enormous economic investment. Certain double-purpose equipment (railways, power plants, foundries, etc.), as well as some specific services, became 'independent' enterprises, with autonomous economic existence. Thus in typical centrales the cane-hauling railway also offered passenger services; the power plant provided electricity for the centrales facilities as well as for the nearby settlements that would pay for it; the foundry made items ranging from park benches to manhole covers for the municipality — and all at high prices because the central enjoyed a monopoly of these services in its region, besides decisive economic and political influence. The typical Cuban central of the nineties controlled the general store where labourers bought, the hotels, house, and barracks, either permanent or temporary, the barbershop, the butcher, the drugstore, and sometimes even the gaming house and the brothel.

Partly for its own financial benefit and partly for increased control on all the surrounding region, the centrales issued their own coinage, in the form of tokens, as legal tender. By this system of private coinage, Cuba, Puerto Rico, and the Dominican Republic reproduced, under conditions of colonialism and underdevelopment, one of the most typical aspects of the English Industrial Revolution. There were two ways in which the sugar token was employed. One was for the central to pay its workers in tokens. These tokens were legal tender in all the shops and facilities around the mill and could be redeemed there, though at a discount (often this was the result of a 'secret' agreement between the management of the mill and the owner or manager of the store), which was the equivalent of a wage reduction. The other system was for the central to pay wages monthly in official currency; but since workers had to pay for their daily needs from their first day on the job, the storeowner would advance them small loans in tokens that could be spent only in his store or in the establishments of other members of the group. The storeowner would notify the management of the central of the advances made to each worker, and the totals would be automatically docked from his wages at the end of the month. In cases of illness or layoff, the mill would immediately notify the shopowners to withhold credit. Payrolls for Cuban and Puerto Rican mills show that at the end of the month many workers received only 10% of their wages in cash, the balance having been advanced.

In 1892, the Santa Lucía sugar mill in Gibara, Cuba, ran as subsidiaries five general stores, seven grocery stores, one shoe shop, one distillery, three barbershops, one drugstore, nine bars, one school, one confectioner's, two eating houses, three blacksmiths, three bakers, three clothing stores, two tailor shops, and one leather goods or saddlery. All of these accepted payment in the nickel tokens issued by the central. And what made this case even more unusual was that the official paper currency issued by the Bank of Spain was not accepted by these establishments; it had to be exchanged for Santa Lucía company tokens — at more than 10% off face value.

Within this group of transformations, there was one further and extremely important change that has been little noticed: the end product, the sugar produced by the new-style industry, was as different from the previous product as the central was different from the old slave-run *ingenio*. Indeed, it is enough to glance at any market report of the 1860s, in any market or colonial products to see that they do not give the prices for *sugar* (in the singular) but for *sugars* (in the plural). The Colleges of Brokers of Havana and Puerto Rico (up to the sixties, the Havana market played a key role in fixing world sugar prices) daily quoted prices for fourteen different types of sugar. And the Dutch Standard (Tipo Holandes in Spanish-speaking countries), which was accepted worldwide as the most suitable set of standards for trading in sugar, listed twenty-one different grades, based on colour, where grade 1 was practically muscovado and 21 was powdered white sugar.

This plethora of kinds of sugar was the logical consequence of sugars being manufactured with primitive equipment, set up in different ways in hundreds of small factories throughout the Caribbean: mills in which the quality of sugar depended on natural factors (the degree of ripeness of the cane), on the purity of the cane juice obtained by manual operations, on the intensity of the fire that heated the boilers (a fire led by slaves who might throw more wood or less wood on), and, in the final event, on the skill of a maestro (generally illiterate) who was guided only by his senses (smell, taste, touch, hearing), by his long experience, and by orally transmitted tradition.

On the other hand, the industrial processes of the sugar mills of the nineties were standard, supervised by technically trained professionals, who were aided by internationally recognized analytical methods carried out on modern laboratory equipment. Thanks to these controls, by the end of the century all the Caribbean mills were producing centrifugal sugar Pol 95 degrees. In the first few years of this century a sugar purity of Pol 95 degrees became the standard.

The different types of sugar produced in the pre-industrial stage required at least three types of packing: the box, the hogshead, and the bag. This last was little-used in the sixties (only 4% of total New York market sales), but by 1890 the situation had changed completely, with more than 95% of U.S. sugar imports in bags. By the beginning of the twentieth century the box and the *bocoy* (the hogshead) were virtually museum pieces.

One type of sugar, one type of packing: these factors influenced the transformation of the sugar trade. The Pol 95 degrees sugar of the new industrial period, as we have seen, was a standardized product, whose source (cane or beet) or region of origin(Cuba, Puerto Rico, Java, Australia, Mauritius, Brazil, or whatever place in the sugar-producing world) was impossible to determine. It was also a long-lasting product, that packed in bags could be stacked and stored cheaply. In contrast, the muscovadoes of the sixties differed widely in quality and spoiled easily; the hogsheads in which they were shipped could be stacked only three high without those on the bottom bursting. There were other essential differences: the hogshead was expensive, the bag was cheap; the hogshead was heavy (10 to 14% of the weight of the sugar it contained), the bag light (less than 1%); the hogshead was hard to handle and raised shipping costs enormously, the bag was easy to handle.

Commercial Changes

All these factors brought about a new commercial practice that had hitherto been little observed: the storing of large surpluses from successive sugar crops. As the new-type centrifugal sugar came more and more to be packed in bags, it became feasible to store it indefinitely. This was the beginning of a new dimension of the problem of initial stocks as a factor affecting sugar prices. Sugar traders had always taken the initial stocks into account in fixing their prices, so it was not a new phenomenon: what changed was its magnitude. Before 1860, stocks on hand rarely were as much as 10% of the estimated annual consumption; by the nineties it was common for them to run over 50% of estimated consumption, and the trend was constantly upward. The bigger the stocks sugar importers had in their warehouses, the more pressure they could bring to bear on the producers to lower their prices.

All these new conditions (uniform product, packing in bags, worldwide standards, large on-hand stocks) inevitably led to what can be called the revolution of the sugar trade. This commercial revolution was in part the result of the factors already detailed, but it was also caused by other features of the world's economy in the last third of the century. There were several significant dates in the sixties and seventies. For example, historians point to 1871 as the year in which the tonnage carried by sailing ships, subject to the whims of the winds, was first surpassed by that shipped in streamers — fast, punctual, and with low freight

rates. A steamer could carry five times the cargo that a sailing ship of the same displacement could. In addition, the opening of the Suez Canal had eliminated sailing ships from the regular Europe-Far East runs. In general, freight rates between American and Europe fell, on the average, 25% between 1860 and 1880, while those between Europe and the eastern sugar colonies (India, Java, Mauritius, Philippines) fell 63%. As a result, sugar could finally breach the wall that high freight rates had built around the colonies, thereby limiting their development. At the same time, sugar from Hawaii began to reach California.

So far, these new factors affected those countries that produced cane sugar. But simultaneously the last decades of the century saw a tremendous boom in beet sugar. In 1860 the 352,000 tons of beet sugar produced made up 20% of total world sugar production. By 1890, however, beet sugar production was up to 3.7 million tons, for a total of 59% of the world's production. From being a net importer of sugar, Europe became an exporter. And logically what had resulted was not by any means 'fair competition': an immensely intricate protectionist system, complemented by every sort of subsidy and direct aid, brought beet sugar prices below any possible competition and drove Cuban, Puerto rican, and Dominican sugar off the European markets.

The three Spanish-speaking countries (of which two were still Spanish colonies) had only one customer left for their sugar, the United States. Java and Mauritius benefitted, to a certain degree, from English protectionism as did Reunion (formerly Bourbon Island) from French policy. Cuba and Puerto Rico (and the Philippines), on the other hand, never had a protected market: of all the colonial countries of Europe, Spain had the lowest sugar consumption per capita, and, besides, its poor commercial and maritime development did not allow it to become a re-exporter of its colonies' raw materials. Santo Domingo's sugar was also in the hands of its almost exclusive customer, the United States.

By 1890 the commercial sugar world had required the same characteristics it was to keep until 1960. On one hand were the beet sugar-producing countries, highly developed and defended by protectionist barriers. On the other were the colonial countries that produced cane sugar (except Cuba, Puerto Rico, and the Philippines) with the protected markets offered by their respective mother countries (Hawaii, at this time a colony, must be included in this group). The difference between total European sugar consumption and the supply of local beet sugar plus the cane sugar from protected colonies made up the prize that Cuba,

Puerto Rico, Santo Domingo, and Brazil, principally, competed for. This minimal breach in the protectionist barrier — irregular, unstable, and residual — was to receive, in the twentieth century, the imposing name of *free market*.

As may be seen, then, at the end of the nineteenth century the European market for sugar imports was characterized by its lack of elasticity: only to a very limited degree (the 'free' or residual market) can we speak of free competition or of the interplay of supply and demand. The foregoing, obviously, refers to the European market. At that time the other great importer was the United States, which possessed characteristics of a free market in that its local producers, benefitting from protectionism, supplied a minimal percentage of the country's needs. Cuba was its principal supplier: in the 1860s Cuban sugar exports to the United States covered more than 60% of that country's consumption and the share was a rising one. The balance was supplied mainly by Puerto Rico and Brazil and to a lesser degree by Santo Domingo.

This overall picture shows a key fact: the European beet sugar producers were industrial powers (independently of sugar), countries with solid economies, a high degree of culture, and extraordinary political development. They thus met all the conditions necessary for being able to establish effective protectionist policies and, further, to set up a system of subsidies, the Sugar Bounties, that permitted beet sugar to compete all the more advantageously with cane sugar. For example, French and German raws drove sugar from Cuba, Puerto Rico, Santo Domingo, and Brazil off the British domestic market. In the eighties French refined sugar was selling in London at 15% under its cost of production.

Cuba, Puerto Rico, and Santo Domingo were colonial countries (even though Santo Domingo had become an independent country in the second half of the century, from an economic point of view it must be considered a colony), poor, tied to a single major crop and a single major export to a single major market, and completely lacked the means of economic self-defense. Nor did they have the remotest chance of forming a producers' pool to safeguard the prices of their raw materials. It was not until far into the twentieth century that the developing sugar-producing countries were able to bring about the holding of the first international sugar conference, which would set forth their points of view.

Since the cane sugar-producing countries were virtually defenseless, the sugar trade was rapidly dominated by the great international trade interests that drove out even the local traders: these became simple intermediaries of the great international firms. There was a corresponding shift in the location of the price-setting markets: in 1884 the FOB Hamburg price played a more decisive part in commercial decisions than the FOB Havana quotations. Another important development, moreover, marked the coming of a new age to the sugar trade.

Until the sixties sugar price were fixed in the market. But until that time the concept of the *market* was a strictly physical one: it referred to the geographical, urban region where warehouses were located and where the traders carried out their operations. In London it was Mincing Lane; in New York, lower Wall Street; in Le Havre, the great square where the Exchange Building stands today; in Havana, the dock area near the College of Brokers, where the principal trading firms — Drake and Brothers, Sama and Company, Ajuria and Brothers, and others — were located. What was meant by market prices were the highs and lows of the day's most important sales, that is, the maximum and minimum spot prices paid for sugar for immediate (fast or prompt) delivery. Payment for purchases was generally made on delivery (although it was also customary to ship sugar on consignment to European or U.S. markets to be sold through agents there, again for immediate delivery).

In this world of commerce, physical and tangible, the parameters to be fixed were equally objective and concrete, requiring the trader's personal attention in the solution of specific problems rather than the theoretical analysis of market conditions and trends. The trader's calculations were done with elementary arithmetic — thus the figure of the rich but illiterate sugar merchant. Just as the old slave-operated sugar factories were swept away by the modern industry, this type of trading (and consequently this type of trader) would be replaced by new firms, using new methods, in the last thirty years of the nineteenth century. There was a simple physical reality: the old trading organizations could no longer cope with the multiple factors that went into the making of a sugar sales agreement, or dealing with futures, on the exchanges of New York, Paris, London, or Hamburg.

In brief, then, the modern sugar industry of the late nineteenth century — an intricate economic complex with an enormous volume of production that had to meet international standards of quality — came into being in a world that since the sixties was being constantly shaken by new developments; the rise of monopolistic world capitalism, the ever-increasing speed of transport, and the radical techniques of handling information.

The application of mathematics to business (especially sampling surveys, the concept of indexes, the improvement of economic statistics); modern data processing (the declining classification system, other coding and retrieval systems,punched cards); new methods of transmitting information (the telegraph, telegraphic codes, the telephone, the Atlantic cable, the stock ticker); the concept of marketing; new methods for evaluating the efficacy of management and for manipulating public opinion; the use of sociological and anthropological studies to help the incipient international trusts achieve economic domination — all of this can be found in the large-scale sugar speculation of the last years of the nineteenth century. In that sense, the sugar trade led the field in international trade.

For example, the German firm of F.O. Licht, founded in 1861, was the first firm of sugar brokers to use successfully, and on a large scale, sampling to predict world sugar production. Licht's figures, published in the famous 'Monthly Report of Sugar' from 1868 on, were a fundamental tool of the big sugar speculators. C. Czarnikow Ltd., of London, did similar work to Licht but concentrated on the Caribbean. In 1897 this firm opened in New York a branch office that was to play a decisive role in the sugar trade of Cuba, Puerto Rico, and Santo Domingo: merging with the New York-based Cuban broker Manuel Rionda in 1909 as the Czarnikow-Rionda Company, within a few years it had so dominated the market that it could act as sole broker for the Cuban crops of the war years (1914–18) and for some 80% of both Puerto Rico and Dominican crops of the same period.

These and similar firms functioned simultaneously as market researchers, trade publishers, and brokers and acted as agents for certain powerful sugar interests, although this last was done more or less discretely: for example, Willet and Hallem (later Willet and Gray Inc.) acted for the American Sugar Refining Company, at one time one of the world's largest trusts.

In the last thirty years of the nineteenth century, the world sugar market fell into the hands of a small group of refiners and bankers, who used the most up-to-date big business methods to control the producers of raw sugar and eliminate the old traders. In this struggle the key strategy was to create a price-fixing mechanism that while appearing to observe the rules of supply and demand, would allow them to take over the market. The commodity exchanges played a fundamental role, opening a new era in the trade of colonial products. For the West Indies, especially Cuba, Puerto Rico, and Santo Domingo, the London Sugar Exchange and the New York Produce Exchange (which later became the famous New York Coffee and Sugar Exchange) were especially significant.

These exchanges, in theory at least, were of ancient origin; some scholars claimed that they were the direct descendants of the medieval bourses. But whatever the kinship, the similarity was only skin-deep. Commodity exchanges, before this commercial revolution, had been organizations made up jointly of buyers and sellers, a kind of organized market where the forces of supply and demand would meet to carry out commercial transaction. But the new exchanges were marked by an essential difference: here the products were not sold directly; the transactions carried out were exclusively speculative. Briefly stated, the commodity operations consisted of signing sales contracts in which one party undertook to supply a certain amount of sugar on a certain date: that is, a sale was made at the prices of the day for future delivery. When the date of delivery arrived, no sugar was delivered. The price of the sugar involved was calculated on the basis of the prices in effect on the delivery date, and the difference between the two prices was paid by one party to the other, in cash, less a commission paid to the exchange for its services. As there were many such operations daily, the exchange provided the means for setting the transaction: that is, it acted as a clearing house. Only in less than 1% of the deals did any sugar actually change hands. Thus the exchange did not replace the real market in which the actual sugar was bought and sold: it simply dominated it, imposing prices and terms. It is clear why in the nineties London's authoritative *Economist* described the London Sugar Exchange as 'Monte Carlo in Mincing Lane'.

As stated, however, the exchanges were not only places where one could gamble in commodity prices but also the brain children of economically dominant groups, whose purpose was to consolidate and broaden their control of the market. Appearing before a U.S. Senate hearing that was investigating a great sugar antitrust scandal, Theodore Havemeyer, president of the American Sugar Refining Company, stated that he used the stock exchange to bribe government officials and the commodities exchange to impose the prices that he wanted on the raw sugars of Cuba, Santo Domingo, and Puerto Rico.

As may be expected, in the last decade of the nineteenth century there was little regulation of the activities of the commodity exchanges. This allowed the carrying out, daily, of operations that could not even be attempted on today's exchanges. It must be remembered that data gathering and handling were new phenomena at the time and that there were no regulations affecting relations between different exchanges; it was possible to take advantage of the five-hour time difference between England and the East Coast to learn London's closing prices before the New York Exchange opened (thanks to the international telegraph, which was also poorly regulated and, furthermore, controlled by a group of speculators) and use this information advantageously. In general, in the United States (practically the only market for Cuban, Puerto Rican, and Dominican sugar at the time) sales of sugar futures lacked any regulatory legislation until the incredible speculating of 1920–21 led to the controversial Futures Trading Act of August 24, 1921, which was declared unconstitutional shortly afterward, though passed again, with minor changes, on September 21, 1922.

An interesting commentary on the changes at this time may be found in the following, first published in 1888: 'In the good old days merchandise seldom arrived to a loss, except in time of severe panic: dealers, when they speculated at all, had visible evidence of the goods in warehouses and docks, and prudence, foresight and intelligence reaped their reward. The introduction of steamships changed all this, and the telegraph completed the revolution. . . .'[1]

Cuba and Puerto Rico: Growth of Production

Throughout the nineteenth century Cuba's sugar production increased steadily, year by year, until 1875, when the slave plantations, which for some time had been showing clear signs of crisis, started on the path to their definite disintegration. Plotted on a graph, the fortunes of the sugar industry would show marked fluctuations, especially for the 1876–89 period, reflecting the transition from the old *ingenio* to the modern central. By the nineties, however, Cuba had regained its scepter as the world's largest sugar producer, with five successive crops of over or just under a million tons, only to fall into the great slump brought about by the War of Independence and the subsequent U.S. occupation of the island.

Puerto Rico, on the contrary, maintained its upward economic trend only until the fifties, when the series of ups and downs started that bore witness to the instability of its slave-based production. In 1873 (before Cuba, notwithstanding the fact that both islands were Spanish colonies) slavery was abolished in Puerto Rico. This occurred during a period marked by large harvests; but abolition in Puerto Rico was not accompanied by a general process of modernization, and production fell sharply in the nineties.

Diverse factors contributed to the dissimilar development of these two colonies of the same mother country and therefore with the same form of government, countries with similar climate and in the same geographical region. In the first place, historically they had different pasts. From the sixteenth to the eighteenth centuries and into the first two decades of the nineteenth, Cuba was a centre of defense of the Spanish Empire, a main maritime base (for both the navy and the merchant fleets), and an important productive region. Due to these factors, there developed on the island an oligarchy that came to wield almost unique political power and from the start accumulated large sums of capital derived from the service sector (trade, shipbuilding for the Spanish state, building of forts, etc.). This capital was subsequently invested in agro-industrial resources: tobacco, coffee, and sugar. The Cubans took advantage of the favourable conditions of foreign trade, which had been upset by the 1791 revolution in Haiti (until then the largest sugar producer in the world), emerging in the first third of the nineteenth century as the possessor of an important sugar complex that by 1829 was outproducing all the British West Indies together.

During the long process of formation of the Cuban oligarchy, its accumulated wealth and political experience also led to a cultural development of the highest order. In addition, it was able to impose, uniquely, its own terms on the home government; for example, the right to trade freely and directly with any foreign port and in ships of any nationality was a privilege won by the native oligarchy in 1792 (though officially recognized only from 1818 on).

Unlike the French or English West Indian colonies, in Cuba the sugar mills were the result of native investments, and with very few exceptions they were never the property of absentee owners. These owners, on the contrary, lived in Cuba and as a general rule at the beginning of the sugar harvest would move into their *ingenios* to watch over and manage their interests directly. Like modern entrepreneurs, they kept up to date regarding world technological developments and quite rapidly incorporated into the Cuban sugar complex those items of equipment and technical advances that could improve the capacity or the profitability of the industry.

As early as 1796 these native businessmen carried out the first experiments in adapting the steam engine to the cane mill; in 1837 they inaugurated the world's first railway devoted to hauling sugar and molasses from the mills to the ports (and the first railway of any kind in Latin America); in 1842 they started using vacuum evaporation for obtaining sugar; in 1844 (the same year as in the United States) they put up the first telegraph wires; in 1849 they installed sugar centrifuges. Cuba, a colonial possession, out-paced all the other Latin American countries in technological developments during the nineteenth century. Under the influence of legislative privileges and a dynamic class of entrepreneurs, and helped by extraordinarily favourable natural conditions (highly fertile lands, ideal weather conditions, large forestry resources, etc.), Cuba understandably was the world's largest sugar producer from 1829 to 1883. (Puerto Rico, which did not share these characteristics, was a much smaller producer).

With the arrival of the sixties, however, both Cuban and Puerto Rican plantations began to show the first symptoms of a crisis. Put briefly, the crisis was a structural one, provoked by the steadily decreasing profitability of slave-based labour and by the difficulties resulting from the adoption of the new technologies.

Thus there came into being a state of permanent instability in which the principal problem faced by the producers — and therefore by officialdom — was to find a viable solution to the transition from slavery to wage-earning labour. The objective of the producers was to obtain from Spain a law of abolition that would include indemnification to allow them to recoup the capital that they had invested in slaves for reinvesting in modern equipment. They also hoped for related legislation that would provide a cheap and constant supply of free labourers (by *free* meaning semi-enslaved, obliged to work 12 hours a day for starvation wages and then laid off at the end of the harvest). In Cuba in 1863 over 95% of all sugar properties were mortgaged. Economic studies of the period showed that the 300 million pesos invested in the sugar industry bore 200 million pesos in mortgages. That is to say, two-thirds of the sugar industry was in the hands of merchants who in Cuba and Puerto Rico carried out the functions of bankers.

In the sixties this critical situation on the two islands abruptly entered a stage wherein a series of external events acted favourably, not by solving the inherent structural difficulties (for the slave plantation had exhausted all possibilities of internal reform) but by extending the system's lease on life. The U.S. Civil War and the Franco-Prussian War for years created their classical effect of upsetting market conditions, bringing about increased demand and very high prices. In Cuba, the Ten Years' War (1868–78), the first gigantic struggle for independence, also heightened the panic in the sugar trade and extended favourable market conditions. There were almost ten years of good harvests and high prices (even though most of these, in Cuba, occurred during the Ten Years' War), which allowed the Cuban sugar producers to pay

off a great part of their mortgages, and their Puerto Rican counterparts to begin the mechanization of their sugar mills, which in general lagged behind Cuba in this respect. But this period was an exception to the trend, and once it had passed, the crisis made itself felt stronger than ever.

In Puerto Rico the process of disintegration of the old-style sugar plantations was extremely rapid. In 1870 there were 550 mills with a total production of 96,000 tons; by 1880 there were 325, producing 50,000 tons. Due to the existing backwardness, the crisis in production was matched by a crisis in quality, and many U.S. importers refused to buy the Puerto rico raw sugars that were rejected by refiners. But there was a more significant reason for the island's crisis: the basic problem was that Puerto Rico lacked the necessary physical and economic infrastructure on which to base its industrialization. Without investment capital or an adequate railway system, without concerted action by the producers, without what might be called the vision of sugar, the few efforts made were individual and for the most part limited to the purchase of machines (which were not always logically installed) and to the building of a few centrales that until the end of the century alternated between good and bad years, and generally with heavy

debts. To cite but one example, Central San Vicente, in Vega Baja, founded by Leonardo Igaravidez, Marquis of Cabo Caribe, by 1873 had taken over the larger surrounding plantations to ensure a supply of cane for his mill and was using the services of as many as several hundred cane cutters. But by 1879 his debts were over a million pesos (one pesos = one dollar), an incredible amount for the time. In 1880, besides the San Vicente, there were four other centrales: the Luisa, San Francisco, Coloso, and Canovanas. All through the nineteenth century, from the economic point of view, their histories were the same.

Another key point that limited the development of Puerto Rico's sugar industry was the failure to find a successful means of transition from slavery to free labour. It is generally said that slavery was abolished in Puerto Rico in 1873, but this is true only in the legal sense. In fact, the institution of slavery had for a long time been in a state of collapse, and by the seventies the island lacked a labour force that could be subjected to the conditions that the plantation owners considered necessary. Unlike Cuba, in Puerto Rico there was no significant influx of migrant labour: only small numbers of coolies came in from Cuba; efforts to set up a system of migrant workers from Spain (colourfully known at the time as *golondrinos* — swallows) met with no success; and the experiment of importing labourers from the British West Indies ended with a handful of groups that settled on off-shore Vieques and on the sugar mills of Ponce, Humacao, Loiza, and Carolina.

The Cuban case was different. The great sugar boom took place in regions that had easy access to ports that by mid-century were already served by an excellent rail network. In general, this railway system, originally designed to carry hogsheads and boxes of sugar, turned out to be exceptionally useful for carrying cane from the fields to the mills. As far as the labour force was concerned, 1847 saw the beginning of an impressive immigration of coolies that probably reached as high as 150,000 by the end of the century. Another source of labour for Cuba's sugar mills had an unusual origin. The Spanish regular army being needed at home for the Carlist Wars, garrisons in Cuba were manned chiefly by *quintos*, or conscripts from Spain. A series of Cuban regulations — which were considered thoroughly illegal in Spain — gave the draftee the choice of serving out his full term as a soldier or of signing on as a hand in a sugar mill. The Ten Years' War being fought in Cuba at the time, many *quintos* not unnaturally became cane cutters. And in the eighties the owners of the new centrales were able to set up an efficient flow of migrant workers, who would arrive in Cuba at the beginning of January and leave at the end of April, from the Canary Islands and from the Spanish provinces of Galicia and Asturias, where there were extremely low standards of living, overpopulation, and high rates of unemployment.

Large sums of capital being available, many Spanish merchants and some families belonging to the old *criollo* (Cuban-born) oligarchy invested in centrales, especially from the eighties. From an economic point of view, Cuba's bloody Ten Years' War for independence turned out to be profitable for the modernized sugar industry. The war, which was fought mainly at the eastern end of the island, destroyed over a hundred old sugar mills, all of which were technologically backward and unproductive. The western part of the country where the new 'giant' mills were located, and which produced 80% of Cuban sugar, did not suffer the ravages of the war.

Moreover, the *Banco Colonial* and the *Banco Español de la Isla de Cuba,* both controlled by the big Spanish merchants and some members of the Cuban oligarchy, had been charged with the financing of the war by the Spanish government, and this turned out to be an enormously profitable deal. Cuban-Spanish shipping and railway companies handled the transportation of military supplies. With a military colonial administration and under the psychological state-of-war pressures, legitimate business and shady deals of all types

were made, and illicit enrichment became the norm. It is evident that at the end of the war these groups would have the necessary liquid capital to invest in the great 'new' (i.e., radically modernized) sugar industry.

There were still other factors. With a sugar-oriented background and political experience, united by long-time common interests, the Cuban producers were well aware of the needs of the times and began to create a group of institutions to steer the new industry. In this way came into being the *Asociación de Hacendados de la Isla de Cuba* (Association of Mill Owners of the Island of Cuba) in 1879 for the purpose of coordinating the action of the principal brains (and capital) in the sugar world. From its beginnings, the association guided the activities of the producers, promoted projects for bringing in migrant workers, set up agricultural and industrial training schools, sponsored research, set up direct communications with the sugar exchanges in New York and London, published a widely read magazine, and formed a powerful lobby to defend the industry's interests. During this period arose many similar but local associations of *colonos* or cane planters.

Slavery was abolished in Cuba in 1881 (eight years later than in Puerto Rico). The concept of the abolition of slavery may suggest to many the picture of a mass of people, chattels subjected to their masters' every whim who suddenly, at a given point in time, find themselves free and in full possession of civil rights and responsibilities. Had this really been so, the abolition of slavery would have brought the total collapse of the sugar industry, for as late as 1877 (the last year for which reliable statistics on Cuban slavery are available) more than 70% of sugar production was based on slave labour. That this did not occur was due to the simple fact that the Law of Abolition was merely the *de jure* recognition of a situation characterized by the *de facto* disintegration of the slave system.

As a matter of fact, as early as the 1860s, and much more so in the seventies, the term *slavery* covered a wide range of means of exploiting labour. To begin with, there was the 'pure' slave, physically forced to work on the sugar mill. Next to him was the hired slave. These slaves were subject to totally different conditions from the first type: physical punishments were banned, and they received part of the money paid for their hire. There was the *jornalero* or wage earner, a variant of the preceding, the slave who personally signed on at a sugar mill for a certain figure and who periodically handed part of his wages to his nominal owner as payment for the status of a semi-freedman with the right to sell his services freely. There was the salaried slave (a very common feature of the time), whose wages were generally 50 to 70% of those of a freedman. Many slaves of all types enjoyed usufruct of small plots of land where they grew produce and raised animals, selling part of the *ingenio*. With them worked free blacks and whites, Chinese and contract labourers from the Yucatán (virtual slaves themselves), and, at times, convicts whom the state provided to the mills and who were paid a small wage. This anomalous situation in the labour supply acted as a break on capitalistic industrial development: the Law of Abolition was a means to the end of rationalizing the confused labour system efficiently.

Thus, the essence of the changes brought about in Cuban sugar production from the eighties were much more economic and social than technical. This does not mean that there were no significant improvements in equipment and processes; there were. But the complete renovation of the process of production was not a mere question of installing modern industrial equipment (which had begun in numerous Cuban sugar mills since the middle of the century); it also implied a renovation on the social, institutional level that could simply not be carried out by slaveowners. The more reactionary among these retained and exploited their slaves as long as they could: clinging to a past that was doomed to disappear, they held on to their slaves because they considered them part of their investment. Perhaps, for them, there was no alternative.

One other key point refers to the process of consolidation in Cuba. Industrialization, as we have seen, led to the early disappearance of the less efficient units. In Matanzas, Cuba's most important sugar region, there were 517 mills in 1877, producing some 350,000 tons; in 1895 the number of mills wa down to 99, but production was almost doubled, at 600,000 tons.

During these last years of the nineteenth century, however, the concentration of production in fewer but larger mills did not find a counterpart in land ownership. Possibly the liens and other obligations of land ownership (especially the unredeemable and indivisible type of *censo* or living pledge) conspired against all efforts to bring about a consolidation of lands that would complement industrial concentration. This led to a broad discrepancy between agriculture and industry and in part explains the backwardness of cane planting in a period of industrial and technological advance.

From the point of view of direct ownership, either of land or of mills, there are a few signs of the presence of U.S. capital in the Cuban sugar industry of the nineteenth century. There were, of course, individual American millowners, just as there were French, Canadians, and Germans. The figures of the U.S. forces, which occupied the island in 1898, show that at the time 93.5% of the sugar mills belonged to Cuban and Spanish capital, and only the remaining 6.5% belonged to foreigners, including U.S. citizens. Moreover, many of the mills then listed as American really belonged to native Cubans and Spaniards who had only recently acquired U.S. citizenship.

The preceding, in the main, has referred to the behaviour of those internal factors that shaped the development of the Cuban sugar industry during the last decades of the nineteenth century. But external factors also played a decisive role in the process. Thus, the statement about the lack of a U.S. presence in the sugar period refers exclusively to an internal situation. But from the point of view of international trade, the United States had long exercised hegemony. By the 1870s the Golden Age of Competition had disappeared from that country, at least where sugar was concerned: there existed an oligopolistic structure that, though legally established in 1887, had in fact come into being a decade before. The Sugar Act of 1871 was the first legislative tool of neocolonial domination forged in the United States, under pressure of the East Coast refiners, for the specific purpose of economically dominating Cuba, Puerto Rico, and Santo Domingo. By the eighties all three islands were selling virtually all their sugar to the United states, dealing with one sole firm in the market; their sugar was shipped in U.S. vessels; the sugar prices were fixed by the New York Produce Exchange; island planters and millowners got their market prices and production estimates from Willet and Gray, in news items reported by Associated Press and carried by Western Union. Without direct investment in lands or mills, the economic annexation of the three islands was underway: physical annexation by forcible means would come a few years later.

Cuban sugar development suffered an abrupt interruption. On February 24, 1895, in the middle of the harvest season, a new war of independence broke out, one that unlike the Ten Years' War was fought over the entire island. The magnitude of the war may be gathered from a few figures: Spain moved 400,000 soldiers, the largest army ever to cross the Atlantic until the days of World War II. This signified one Spanish soldier for each three inhabitants of the island. During the War of Independence (1895–98) thousands of hectares of cane fields were repeatedly set afire (cane is an easy crop to burn). An indeterminate number of sugar mills were also destroyed. Unfortunately, quantitative documentation is lacking that would allow an exact appreciation of war damages inflicted on the sugar industry. From the point of view of production, the last five years of the century are presented in Table 1.1. Using these figures as their basis, traditional

Table 1. Cuban Sugar
Production

1895–99	(unit: metric tons)
1895	983,265
1896	286,229
1897	271,505
1898	259,331
1899[a]	322,337

SOURCE: Manuel Moreno
Fraginals, *El ingenio* (Havana:
Editorial de Ciencas Sociales,
1978). 3:38.
[a]First year of peace.

Cuban historiography, influenced by the interests of the sugar magnates, created the myth of the total destruction of the sugar industry during the war. As no censuses of sugar plantations were taken during the period, the theory of total ruin still prevails among modern historians.

But painstaking qualitative studies, which analyzed thousands of dispersed sources, would seem to prove that although an enormous drop was evident in cane production (the result of repeated burnings), the industrial sector, on the contrary, received mush less damage. Of the fifty largest centrales to grind in 1895, only seven were destroyed during the war, four received some damage, and thirty-nine remained standing, ready to start a new grinding season. It is probably that the effective overall loss suffered by the industry was 20 to 25% of installed producing capacity, as a maximum. To start up the industry anew required an extensive programme of cane planting at a time when the traditional farm labourers had been widely dispersed (the war had completely changed the pattern of settlements in many areas). This explains the drop in production in the war and the immediate postwar years and why, within three years after the war, sugar production reached almost a million tons, which was about the total installed capacity in 1895.

Notes

This paper draws on work that will be published in more detail and with full documentation elsewhere. The translation was done by Arturo Ross.

1. 'The London Produce Clearing House', *Financial News* (London), as reprinted in *The Sugar Cane* (Manchester), July 2, 1888, pp. 350ff.

American Capitalism and the Caribbean Economy

Eric Williams

A new and more bitter revolution for independence began in Cuba in 1895. Spain was unable to restore order, the non-combatant population was caught between the depredations on both sides, and American commerce and interests suffered heavily. The United States urged Spain to terminate the revolt, but the revolutionaries refused to be satisfied with anything short of independence. The continuing disorders led the United States government to send the battleship *Maine* to Havana in January, 1898. It exploded shortly after with the loss of two officers and 258 men. The United States, blaming a submarine mine or some external cause demanded reparation and presented a virtual ultimatum to Spain on March 29, 1898 calling for an immediate armistice. The Spanish government, blaming an internal explosion, refused. On April 11, 1898, President McKinley, unimpressed by a joint note of the European Great Powers urging further negotiations with Spain, approached the Congress, which passed a joint resolution reading as follows:

First. That the people of the Island of Cuba are, and of right out to be, free and independent.
Second. That it is the duty of the United States to demand, and the government of the Unites States does hereby demand, that the government of Spain at once relinquish its authority and government in the Island of Cuba and withdraw its land and naval forces from Cuba and Cuban waters.
Third. That the President of the United states be, and he hereby is, directed and empowered to use the entire land and naval forces in the United States, and to call into the actual service of the United States the militia of the several states, to such extent as may be necessary to carry these resolutions into effect.
Fourth. That the United States hereby disclaims any disposition or intention to exercise sovereignty, jurisdiction or control over said Island except for the pacification thereof, and asserts its determination, when that is accomplished, to leave the government and control of the Island to its people.

After three months of war Spain sued for peace, preferring annexation of Cuba by the United States in order to guarantee Spanish life and property and Cuba's external debts to Spain. The United States

refused, and the Treaty of Paris, signed on December 10, 1898, provided for the relinquishment of Spanish sovereignty over Cuba, as well as Puerto Rico which was annexed outright by the United States. Thus ended the Papal Donation of 1493 and Spanish power was removed from the Caribbean.

The military government established by the United States concentrated on the relief of the starving population, the disarmament of the Cuban revolutionaries and loyalists, the control of yellow fever, and the promulgation of an electoral law as the basis of the election of a convention to frame a constitution. The convention, summoned in 1900, resisted American claims which were clearly and precisely set out in a proviso attached to the Military Appropriation Bill on March 2, 1901, which has come to be known as the Platt Amendment. The Platt Amendment, which was to govern American relations with Cuba down to the advent of Fidel Castro, read as follows:

I. That the government of Cuba shall never enter into any treaty or other compact with any foreign power or powers which will impair or tend to impair the independence of Cuba, nor in any manner authorize or permit any foreign power or powers to obtain by colonization or for military or naval purposes or otherwise lodgement in or control over any portion of said island.
II. That said government shall not assume or contract any public debt, to pay the interest upon which, and to make reasonable sinking fund provision for the ultimate discharge of which, the ordinary revenues of the island, after defraying the current expenses of government, shall be inadequate.
III. That the government of Cuba consents that the United States may exercise the right to intervene for the preservation of Cuban independence, the maintenance of a government adequate for the protection of life, property, and individual liberty, and for discharging the obligations with respect to Cuba imposed by the Treaty of Paris on the United States, now to be assumed and undertaken by the government of Cuba.
IV. That all acts of the United States in Cuba during its miliary occupancy thereof are ratified and validated and all lawful rights acquired thereunder shall be maintained and protected.
V. That the government of Cuba will execute, and, as far as necessary, extend, the plans already devised, or

other plans to be mutually agreed upon, for the sanitation of the cities of the island, to the end that a recurrence of epidemic and infectious diseases may be prevented thereby assuring protection to the people and commerce of Cuba, as well as the commerce of the Southern ports of the United States and the people residing therein.

VI. That the Isle of Pines shall be omitted from the proposed constitutional boundaries of Cuba, the title thereto being left to future adjustment by treaty.

VII. That to enable the United States to maintain the independence of Cuba, and to protect the people thereof, as well as for its own defence, the government of Cuba will sell or lease to the United States land necessary for coaling or naval stations at certain specified points, to be agreed upon with the President of the United States.

VIII. That by way of further assurance the government of Cuba will embody the foregoing provisions in a permanent treaty with the United States.

The convention was disinclined to accept the Platt Amendment, taking the view that such demands would deprive the government of Cuba of all real independence and would pave the way for constant American interference in its internal affairs. The United States made it clear that it would not withdraw from Cuba until the Platt Amendment was accepted, and so the convention backed down. The permanent treaty was signed on May 22, 1903. The United States received in 1903 bases at Guantanamo and Bahia Honda, agreeing to pay an annual rent of $2,000; in 1912 the United States surrendered its right at Bahia Honda in return for an enlarged area at Guantanamo, agreeing to raise the annual rent to $5,000. Ultimately in 1925 the United States abandoned all claims to the Isle of Pines which remained under Cuban jurisdiction. The American government intervened in 1906 when law and order in Cuba totally broke down, and an American Provisional government, under Taft, and later Magoon, was installed from 1906 to 1909.

All this was in accordance with the new interpretation of the Monroe Doctrine enunciated by Theodore Roosevelt. In its classic form, the Roosevelt Corollary, as it has come to be known, was thus stated by Roosevelt in 1904:

Chronic wrongdoing, or an impotence which results in a general loosening of the ties of civilized society, may in America, as elsewhere, ultimately require intervention by some civilized nation, and in the Western Hemisphere the adherence of the United States to the Monroe Doctrine may force the United States, however reluctantly, in flagrant cases of such wrongdoing or impotence, to the exercise of an international police power.

The international policeman carried a big stick. His was the duty, as President Taft wrote to Secretary Knox in 1909, 'to have the right to knock their heads together until they should maintain peace between them'. As stated frankly by Roosevelt himself in 1908 with reference to Venezuela, America had to 'show these Dagoes that they will have to behave decently'. So Roosevelt just 'took' the Panama Canal while Congress and the South Americans debated the issue. As Roosevelt himself wrote to Cecil Spring-Rice of the British Foreign Office in 1904:

It was a good thing for Egypt and the Sudan, and for the world, when England took Egypt and the Sudan. It is a good thing for India that England should control it. And so it is a good thing, a very good thing, for Cuba and for Panama and for the world that the United states has acted as it has actually done during the last six years. The people of the United States and the people of the Isthmus and the rest of mankind will all be the better because we dig the Panama Canal and keep order in its neighbourhood. And the politicians and revolutionists at Bogota are entitled to precisely the amount of sympathy we extend to other inefficient bandits.

The Caribbean itself was to become America's closed sea, the American Mediterranean. As Assistant Secretary of State Loomis stated in 1904:

. . . no picture of our future is complete which does not contemplate and comprehend the United States as the dominant power in the Caribbean Sea.

The need to control the approaches to the Panama Canal did the rest. The new policy was adumbrated by President Taft in his Annual Message to Congress in 1912, as follows:

The diplomacy of the present administration has sought to respond to the modern idea of commercial intercourse. This policy has been characterized as substituting dollars for bullets.

The United States was faced with new large British investments in Cuba which from 1909 to 1913 totalled $60 million (French and German about $17 million) as against $35 million from the United States, and with German interests in Haiti and the Dominican Republic related to naval bases and coaling stations. President Wilson was obsessed with his determination 'to teach the South American Republics to elect good men' and Secretary of State Bryan with the opportunities in the Dominican Republic for jobs for 'good deserving Democrats'. The stage was set for American intervention in the Dominican Republic and Haiti.

On February 8, 1907, there was signed at Santo Domingo a convention respecting assistance of the United States in the collection and application of the customs revenues of the Dominican Republic.

The pertinent sections of this convention read as follows:

I. That the President of the United States shall appoint a General Receiver of Dominican customs, who, with such Assistant Receivers and other employees of the Receivership as shall be appointed by the President of the United States in his discretion, shall collect all the customs duties accruing at the several customs houses of the Dominican Republic until the payment or retirement of any and all bonds issued by the Dominican government in accordance with the plan and under the limitations as to terms and amounts hereinbefore recited; and said General Receiver shall apply the sums so collected, as follows:

First, to paying the expenses of the receivership; second, to the payment of interest upon said bonds; third, to the payment of the annual sums provided for amortization of said bonds including interest upon all bonds in sinking fund; fourth, to the purchase and cancellation or retirement of said bonds as may be directed by the Dominican government; fifth, the remainder to be paid to the Dominican government. . . .

II. The Dominican government will provide by law for the payment of all customs duties to the General Receiver and his assistants, and will give to them all needful aid and assistance and full protection to the extent of its powers. The government of the United States will give to the General Receiver and his assistants such production as it may find to be requisite for the performance of their duties.

III. Until the Dominican Republic has paid the whole amount of the bonds of the debt its public debt shall not be increased except by previous agreement between the Dominican government and the United States. A like agreement shall be necessary to modify the import duties, it being an indispensable condition for the modification of such duties that the Dominican Executive demonstrate and that the President of the United States recognize that, on the basis of exportations and importations to the like amount and the like character during the two years preceding that in which it is desired to make such modification, the total net customs receipts would at such altered rate of duties have been for each of such two years in excess of the sum of $2,000,000 United States gold. . .

In 1915 the American government occupied the Dominican Republic for fear that the ordinary process of Dominican elections would produce a government not regarded with favour in the United States. The decree of the American Command stated:

All revenues accruing to the Dominican government, including revenues hitherto accrued and unpaid — whether from customs duties under the terms of the Treaty concluded on February 8, 1907, the Receivership established by which remains in effect, or from internal revenue — shall be paid to the Military government

herein established which will, in trust for the Republic of Santo Domingo, hold such revenue and will make all the proper legal disbursements therefrom necessary for the administration of the Dominican government, and for the purposes of the Occupation. . .

The Military government came to an end in 1924.

The Dominican pattern was followed in the case of Haiti with which a treaty was signed by the United States on September 6, 1915, respecting finances, economic development and tranquility. The Treaty set up a general receivership, associated with a Financial Adviser nominated by the President of the United states. Customs receipts were to be applied to the costs of the Receivership, the salaries and expenses of the Financial Adviser, the interest and sinking fund of the Haitian public debt, and to the maintenance of a constabulary. The Treaty continued:

Article VIII. The Republic of Haiti shall not increase its public debt except by previous agreement with the President of the United States, and shall not contract any debt or assume any financial obligation unless the ordinary revenues of the Republic available for that purpose, after defraying the expenses of the government, shall be adequate to pay the interest and provide a sinking fund for the final discharge of such debt.

Article IX. The Republic of Haiti will not, without a previous agreement with the President of the United States, modify the customs duties in a manner to reduce the revenues therefrom. . .

Article X. The Haitian government obligates itself, for the preservation of domestic peace, the security of individual rights and full observance of the provisions of this treaty, to create without delay an efficient constabulary, urban and rural, composed of native Haitians. This constabulary shall be organized and officered by Americans, appointed by the President of Haiti upon nomination by the President of the United States. . .

Article XI. The government of Haiti agrees not to surrender any of the territory of the Republic of Haiti by sale, lease, or otherwise, or jurisdiction over such territory, to any foreign government or power, nor to enter into any treaty or contract with any foreign power or powers that will impair or tend to impair the independence of Haiti.

The American officers of the Haitian constabulary were withdrawn by agreement on August 7, 1933, which provided for the Haitianisation of the constabulary, and the withdrawal of the American marines was to commence on October 1, 1934 and be completed within 30 days. A financial arrangement adjusting the financial guarantees stipulated in 1919 and 1922 limited the number of Americans employed by the Fiscal Representative to 18, and provided further:

Article XIII. Each year, by January 31 at the latest, the Fiscal Representative shall present a detailed estimate of receipts for the following fiscal year. Except by special agreement, the budget of the Republic shall not exceed the amount of probable ways and means which the Secretary of State for Finance and the Fiscal Representative shall have agreed upon. . .

Article XVII. Without the accord of the Fiscal Representative no new financial obligation will be assumed unless the ordinary revenues of the Republic, after defraying the expenses of the government, shall be adequate to assure the final discharge of such obligation. . .

Article XX. The government of Haiti agrees not to reduce the tariff nor to modify the taxes and internal revenues in such a way as to reduce the total amount thereof without the accord of the Fiscal Representative. . .

United States supremacy in the Caribbean was further underlined when, in 1917, the United States purchased the Virgin Islands from Denmark for the sum of $25 million, in order to get possession of the harbour of St Thomas.

World War II provided the setting for yet a further advance, this time in the British West Indies. In 1940 the United States received from Britain 99–year leases of naval bases in Trinidad, Guyana, Antigua, St. Lucia, Jamaica, the Bahamas — as well as in Newfoundland and in Bermuda. The difference was that no dollars were involved — only fifty over-age destroyers for Britain, with its back to the wall against submarines. How the deal appeared in United States eyes brought out in the opinion of Robert Jackson, the Attorney General, to President Roosevelt on August 27, 1940:

(b) In consideration it is proposed to transfer to Great Britain the title and possession of certain over-age ships and obsolescent military materials now the property of the United States and certain other small patrol boats which, though nearly completed, are already obsolescent. (c) Upon such transfer all obligation of the United States is discharged. The acquisition consists only of rights, which the United States may exercise or not at its option; and if exercised, may abandon without consent. The privilege of maintaining such bases is subject only to limitations necessary to reconcile United States use with the sovereignty retained by Great Britain. Our government assumes no responsibility for civil administration of any territory. It makes no promise to erect structures, or maintain forces at any point. It undertakes no defence of the possessions of any country. In short, it acquires optional bases which may be developed as Congress appropriates funds therefor, but the United States does not assume any continuing or future obligation, commitment, or alliance. . . The executive agreement obtains an opportunity to establish naval and air bases for the protection of our coastline but it imposes no obligation upon the Congress to appropriate money to improve the opportunity. . .

I am informed that the destroyers involved here are the survivors of a fleet of over 100 built at about the same time and under the same design. During the year 1930, 58 of these were decommissioned with a view toward scrapping and a corresponding number was recommissioned as replacements. Usable material and equipment from the 58 vessels removed from the service were transferred to the recommissioned vessels to recondition and modernize them, and other usable material and equipment were removed and the vessels stripped. They were then stricken from the Naval register, and 50 of them were sold as scrap for prices ranging from $5,260 to $6,800 per vessel, and the remaining 8 were used for such purposes as target vessels, experimental construction tests, and temporary barracks. The surviving destroyers now under consideration have been reconditioned and are in service, but all of them are over-age, most of them by several years.

Bryan Edwards, the historian of Jamaica at the end of the eighteenth century, had warned that 'the business of sugar planting is a sort of adventure in which the man that engages must engage deeply'. By the end of the nineteenth century the enterprise had become too big for the individual entrepreneur, and the West India Royal Commission of 1897 expressed the opinion that 'under any circumstances that can at present be foreseen, the days of very large or excessive profits from the sugar-cane industry appear to us to have passed away'. The tremendous outlay required for land, labour and machinery exceeded individual capacity, especially in the competition with the beet sugar industry. But the American corporation proved that it was more than ever possible to make the sugar cane industry pay. The age of mass production followed the emergence of American military power and political presence in the Caribbean, and, as Fernando Ortiz of Cuba writes, 'all becomes mass, shapeless, collective and anonymous: the company, the sugar and the syndicate; mass of capitalists, mass of products, mass of workers'.

The West India Royal Commission of 1897 had condemned latifundia and had suggested that experiments be made with the separation of cane production by small farmers and sugar manufacture in large central factories:

Where this system can be carried out, it offers many advantages, and in any of your Majesty's West Indian possessions where a tendency is shown to adopt it, and the production of sugar is likely to continue, we think the government concerned might fairly be expected to encourage it by providing means of communication between the cane-growing tracts and the central factories, and by offering every facility for the establishment of cane cultivation on suitable lands.

The Americans disagreed completely. The powerful Brookings Institution of Washington, in its comprehensive study entitled *Porto Rico and its Problems* in 1930 wrote:

From a strictly technical standpoint, sugar can be produced more efficiently and cheaply where both cane growing and sugar manufacturing are under a single administration. . . . The highest cane and sugar yields per acre, the best qualities of cane, and the maximum recovery of sugar per ton of cane, are found in countries where all operations from plowing the field to bagging the sugar are under one management.

The period between 1897 and 1930 saw the enormous concentration of latifundia in the Caribbean under the stimulus of American capital investment. The combined acreage of six plantations operated by the Cuban American Sugar Company totalled half a million acres; that of the nine plantations of the Cuban Atlantic Sugar Company 400,000. The Vertientes-Camaguey Company owned or leased over 800,000 acres; the Manati Sugar Company owned or controlled 237,000 acres of which 29,000 were in cane; the Punta Alegre Company on its three plantations owned 112,000 acres and leased 43,000 — 39,000 acres were in cane. Symbolic of the new age was the United Fruit Company. The backing for its control of 93,000 acres of cane land in Cuba was its various properties in the Caribbean, Central and South America, the Canary Islands, Europe and the United States, totalling at the beginning of 1941 over 3 million acres. Its sugar production in Cuba was part of a huge empire which controlled 65% of the world's supply of bananas, included a tourist hotel in Jamaica, embraced its own fleet of cargo and passenger vessels, and dominated 40% of the entire voting stock of the International Railways of Central America.

What was true of Cuba under American capital was also true of Puerto Rico. A law passed in 1900 immediately after the American occupation prohibiting corporations from acquiring plantations larger than 500 acres remained a dead letter for decades. Four large American corporations dominated the sugar industry which totalled 7,600 farms, 166 over 500 acres. These 166 farms comprised half a million acres or two-thirds of the total included in sugar-cane farms, but comprised 60% of the total cane acreage and produced 67% of the sugar in 1935. The four American companies held nearly one-quarter of all the cane land in the island and nearly one-half of all the land held in plantations. Central Aguirre owned nearly 25,000 acres and leased a further 18,000. The holdings of Eastern Sugar Associates totalled 51,000 acres, two-thirds of this owned outright. The Fajardo Sugar Company owned 30,000 acres and leased 20,000 — over 20,000 acres were planted to cane.

The Dominican Republic presented a similar pattern. Two American companies dominated — South Porto Rico Company and the West Indies Sugar Corporation. The former owned 150,000 acres of which half were in cane, and the latter 100,000 — apart from a further 123, 000 in Cuba.

The key to this American concentration of production was the railway. In 1899 there were less than 200 miles of railroads in Puerto Rico. By 1940 there were over 1,000. Nearly two-thirds of this mileage was owned outright by the sugar plantations and depended on sugar tonnage for 90% of its business. The public corporations were dependent only to a lesser extent on sugar. The most important independent system, the American Railroad Company, derived 85% of its freight revenues from sugar. Central Aguirre owned 17 miles of railway, Fajardo 27, South Porto Rico 50, Eastern Sugar Company 133.

Sugar was equally the life and soul of the Cuban railway system. In 1938–1939 the railways depended on sugar and its by-products for 80% of their tonnage and 60% of their freight revenues. The individual plantations were in addition well-equipped with their own private systems, and in some instances dominated the public corporations. Thus the Cuba Company owned all the stock of the Consolidated Railroads of Cuba, which extended from Santa Clara to Santiago and served the whole eastern part of the island. They ran through territory which was practically all sugar territory — half of Santa Clara province and the provinces of Camaguey and Oriente. In this region about 70% of Cuba's mills were located, producing 60% of the island's crop. The Cuban-American Company operated 570 miles of railway, Guantanamo Company owned 70 miles and in addition owned 80% of the stock of the Guantanamo Railroad Company. Manati Company owned 176 miles of its own railway and in addition operated the 44 miles of the Ferrocarril de Tunas. The Punta Alegre Corporation owned 228 miles of railway, the Vertientes-Camaguey Company 326.

In addition the American-style sugar plantation owned its own rolling stock on the railways; in many cases its own steamers; its own wharves and warehousing facilities. The scope of its operations can be gauged by the fact that the South Porto Rico Sugar Company found it possible and profitable to grind some of its Dominican cane in its Puerto Rican factories. The West Indies Sugar Corporation owned directly or through subsidiaries warehouses at the port of Santiago in Cuba having a capacity of approximately 100,000 bags of sugar. The same corporation owned the lighters which shipped its sugar from its Dominican factories to the port of San Pedro de Macoris. For the operation of its properties it owned a dairy herd and approximately 21,000 head of cattle. If the large plantation of Cantero's day in 1860 was a monster, the large plantation of 1942 was a colossus.

There were two casualties of this American mode of production. The first was the British West Indian sugar industry. Barbados was typical. The land in plantations totalled 52,000 acres out of a total of 66,000 arable acres. Barbados was therefore a plantation economy. But what sort of plantation was this to compete with the American juggernaut? Of the agricultural holdings, less than 300 were over 20 acres, over 200 were more than 100 acres, and only 9 were over 500 acres in size. British Guiana came closest in the British West Indies to the American pattern of concentration. But even there, the largest plantation, Diamond, was just over 7,000 acres. Three more were over 4,000 acres, while 17 barely had 1,000 acres.

The second casualty of the American system of production was the *colono* or small cane farmer. It is true that in Trinidad their numbers increased from 3,712 growing 17,500 tons of cane in 1896 to 20,000 growing 375,000 tons of cane (half the island's output) in 1928. But the situation was radically different in Puerto Rico. Nearly 75% of the sugar cane farms in Puerto Rico had less than 10 acres in cane; these farms represented merely 6% of the total acreage in cane. Farms with less than 25 acres in cane were 86% of all sugar farms, but only 12% of the cane area, while they produced 7½% of the total cane. The estimated yield per acre of these 25–acre farms was 20 tons in 1935, as compared with the average of 30 tons for the whole island. A study of 130 *colono* farms ranging from an average acreage in cane of less than 16 for small farms and less than 206 for large, revealed that the average was 30 tons per acre for all, 29 for small farms, 34 for those of middle size, and 30 for the larger farms. If the *colono* held his own in yield, he more than held his own in costs of production. The United States Tariff Commission, in a comparative study of 125 *colono* farms in Puerto Rico harvesting an area of 20,000 acres as against the large plantation, found that *colono* cane cost $4.79 per ton as against $5.60 pre ton for plantation cane.

But the *colono* could not withstand the American invasion. Between 1910 and 1935 in Puerto Rico the acreage of farms of 20–99 acres declined 11%, and of farms of 100 to 499 acres nearly 22%. As a Puerto Rican writer pleaded: 'the small *colono* is the romantic figure of individualism in an industry controlled by a handful of corporations or powerful partnerships. While farming to the sugar-cane corporation is merely a manufacturing business, it is a way of living for most *colonos*. The *colonos* constitute an element through whom

a better distribution of part of the large income produced by the sugar industry is obtained'.

The large planation was paralleled by the large factory. Centralization in the factory paralleled centralization in the field. Puerto Rican sugar production increased from 60,000 tons in 1898 to over a million in 1934 before the crop restriction programme. In 1898 there were 345 mills in the island, with an average daily capacity of 36 tons of cane each. In 1939 there were 41 modern mills, varying from Guanica with a capacity of 150,000 tons to Pellejas with a capacity of only 1,400; the average for the island was 28,000 tons in 1935. In 1898 each mill in the island ground the cane of only seven producers as compared with an average of 317 producers per mill in 1939. The four American sugar companies produced almost half of the total output in 1935.

American capital accelerated a similar centralization in the Dominican Republic. The West Indies Sugar Corporation and the South Porto Rico Company together owned six of the 14 mills in that island; the combined production of these six mills represented 75% of Dominican production in 1939–1940. The largest mill, Romana, owned by the South Porto Rico Sugar Company, produced 109,000 tons; Barahona, owned by the West Indies Sugar Corporation, 64,000.

But as centralization had proceeded furthest in Cuba during the slavery regime, so, stimulated by the flow of American capital, twentieth-century Cuba was well in advance of the other areas. The 2,000 factories in 1860 had been reduced to 158 in the 1930s; where the production was 447,000 tons in 1860, it was over five million in 1925 at the height of the sugar boom and 2,720,000 in 1939 under crop restriction. Production, centred in the western provinces of Havana and Matanzas under the Spaniards, shifted under the Americans to the eastern provinces of Camaguey and Oriente. Of the mills in the thirties, one-fourth were located in Oriente and one-seventh in Camaguey. The Oriente mills produced more than one-third of the total crop, Camaguey's nearly one-third. Together the two provinces produced more than the combined output of the other four provinces. Camaguey, with less than half the number of mills as Santa Clara province, surpassed Santa Clara's output by more than one-fifth.

Of the 158 mills in Cuba, fifty-eight or more than one-third were American-owned. These mills produced 55% of Cuban production. The average per America mill was 157,000 tons of sugar as compared with an average of 104,000 for the whole island; that is to say, the average of the American-owned mill was more than one-half greater than the island average. Even so, the picture of American domination is incomplete. Many American companies controlled more than one mill. Thus the Cuban Atlantic Company owned eight mills which together produced 195,000 tons; the Cuban American Company six mills which had a combined output of 138,000 tons. The mills of the West Indies Sugar Corporation produced 68,000 tons. Cantero's monsters of 1860 made a poor show in comparison with their modern counterparts. Thus Vertientes, with restricted output, produced 71,000 tons in 1939; Stewart 47,000; Moron 46,000; Jaronu 48,000; Delicias 54,000.

Here again the British West Indies could not keep up with the pace set by the Americans. Barbados and Jamaica seemed not to be living in the twentieth century. In 1939 Barbados produced 133,000 tons of sugar in 32 factories, an average of barely 4,000 tons per factory. Greater progress had been made elsewhere. St. Kitts had only one factory, to which all sugar producing areas were connected by a railway encircling the whole island; the normal capacity of the factory was 20,000 tons. Antigua had two factories — the larger produced 19,000 tons in 1929, the smaller 3,500. In 1928 there were 21 factories in British Guiana manufacturing what 64 had done thirty years before. The Trinidad average per factory was 12,800 tons; Trinidad had the largest factory in the British West Indies, the Usine Ste. Madeleine, with a capacity of 41,000 tons in 1939.

Sugar cultivation and manufacture on the scale indicated as a result of American penetration obviously called for a colossal investment of capital which only the United States could afford. The United States Tariff Commission estimated American investment in Cuba in the thirties at $666 million, in the Dominican Republic at $41 million, in Haiti at $10 million. Of these figures sugar represented more than one-third of the Cuban investment, though the money-value declined from $544 million in 1929 to $240 million in 1936. Ninety (90%) of the American investment in the Dominican Republic was in sugar, over 50% in Haiti. Another estimate put at $30 million the American investment in the sugar industry of Puerto Rico.

The individual American corporation represented a large investment. The Cuban American Sugar Company had a capitalization of over a million shares in common and preferred stock and total assets of $36 million, of which more than half was in land, buildings, railroad, equipment. The West Indies Sugar Corporation with its interests in Cuba and the Dominican Republic, had a capitalization of close to a million shares and total assets of nearly $30 million, of which over 60% was in land, buildings, equipment. The Punta Alegre Company, with assets of $19½ million, had over

75% in plants, railroads, land. The Cuban Atlantic Company had assets of $9 3/4 million; the Manati Sugar Company $8½ million; the Guantanamo Sugar Company nearly $6 million. Behind the United Fruit company's sugar operations stood total company assets of $186 million.

The Puerto Rican situation was similar. Central Aguirre Associates, with a capitalization of over $3½ million in common stock, had total assets of $19½ million, of which half was in plants and properties. The Eastern Sugar Company, with 250,000 shares in common and preferred stock, had total assets of over $13 million, with over 67% in lands and equipment. The Fajardo Sugar Company had a capitalization of over $6 million and abets of $14½ million, of which nearly half was in plant and properties. The South Porto Rico Company had nearly 750,000 shares of common stock plus $5 million of preferred stock; its total assets amounted to nearly $30 million, of which nearly half represented real property, plant and equipment.

Comparable data for the British West Indies are scarce, but we have sufficient to show that large scale investment was again involved. Where in 1897 the capital invested in the Trinidad sugar industry was estimated at $12 million, an estimate in 1935 put the investment in the British Guiana sugar industry at $26 million on an average of the six–year period 1929 to 1934, and after allowing for depreciation.

Contrary to what the West India Royal Commission had opined in 1897, this large investment yielded large profits. Of Puerto Rico Esteban Bird has written:

From 1920 to 1935 Central Aguirre, South Porto Rico, and Fajardo Sugar Company have paid cash dividends of practically $50,000,000 and slightly over $10,500,000 in stock dividends or total dividends paid of around $60,500,000. The surplus earnings of the three sugar mills for the same period amount to slightly over $20,500,000. Altogether, therefore, these three companies alone have paid dividends and have accumulated a surplus amounting to over $80,000,000. The average combined annual returns on capital since 1922 has been 19%. During 1928 the average return was as high as 31% but the average return in four years out of the thirteen years period has been over 25% and these companies, on various occasions, have declared stock dividends of 100% and more.

The Diffies, in their study, *Porto Rico, A Broken Pledge,* stated that the three largest sugar companies paid dividends ranging from 4 to 115% over a period of 20 years. Diffie's figures were challenged by Gayer, Homan and James in their study of the Puerto Rican sugar industry in 1938, who charged him with an inadequate interpretation of stock adjustments. Their own figures speak eloquently enough. Total earnings of the four American companies from 1923 to 1935 averaged 12% upon investors' equity. Deducting the taxes and profits on the Dominican cane of the south Porto Rico Company, the earnings accruing to investors on strictly Puerto Rican operations exceeded 10%. Central Aguirre earned over 12% after income tax deductions; South Porto Rico 11%; Fajardo 7%. In the bonanza year when according to the Diffies, South Porto Rico paid 115% and Fajardo 110%, actual cash dividends were 15% and 40% on par value of stock. It would seem that even with these reduced estimates investors had nothing to squawk about.

Detailed figures published annually in Farr's *Manual of Sugar Companies* confirm this view. From 1919 to 1920 Central Aguirre paid dividends ranging from 5% to 60%. In 1920, on the $20 par value stock, 70% was paid, 37½% in 1921, 30% from 1922 to 1928. In addition an extra cash dividend of 25% was declared in 1923, and 5% in 1927 and 1928, plus an extra stock dividend of 20% in 1925. Dividends from 1929 to 1941 were 7½%, plus extra stock dividend of 5% in 1928 and cash of 5% in 1936 and 1937.

For the six years 1908 to 1913 Fajardo paid average dividends of 7% with 10% in 1908 and 1910. From 1916 to 1921 the dividend increased to 10%, with extra cash dividends of 10% in 1916 and 30% in 1920 and a stock dividend of 70% in the latter year. From 1921 to 1923 the dividend was 5%, from 1923 to 1929 10%. None was paid thereafter until 1935, when 5% was paid. On the new $20 par value stock 7½% was paid in 1936, 20% in 1937 and 1938, 10% in 1939. Between 1923 and 1925 extra cash dividends were paid in addition on the old $100 par value common stock.

The Cuban picture admittedly was different, but after 1938, as a result of the depression and the United States tariff which favoured American capital in the sugar industry of Puerto Rico, the Philippines, Hawaii and the mainland, rather than American capital in Cuba and the Dominican Republic. But the Cuban American Sugar Company paid preferred dividends, except for two years, from 1905 to 1929, averaging 7% from 1915 to 1929; after 1929 payments were irregular. The Cuban Atlantic Sugar Company paid a dividend of 15% in 1937 and 10% in 1940. Vertientes-Camaguey Company paid 4% in 1940 and 1941; the West Indies Sugar Corporation 5% on preferred stock in 1941 and none on common.

These figures tell a sad tale when compared with the dividends of the Amsterdam Trading Company on its sugar, rubber, coffee and other tropical plantations in Java — 1924, 40%; 1925, 30%; 1926–1929, 16 ; 1930, 15%; 1931–1933, 5%; 1934, 4%; 1935, 8%; 1936, 16 ; 1937, 25%; 1938, 17%. They are higher, however, than the average annual profit of slightly over 2% estimated by a British Guiana Commission in 1936 and than the average of 6% reported for the British West Indies. But it must be remembered that the United States Tariff Commission in 1919 had estimated that only 43.3% of the production in Puerto Rico, 48.6% in Hawaii, little or more in Louisiana, and 56.8% in the beet sugar industry would have survived free trade.

The large aggregation of land, buildings, railroads and equipment represented by an American sugar corporation in the twentieth century called for a corresponding concentration of labour. What Cantero would have written had he seen the plantations of the thirties one can only conjecture. Of all the workers in Cuba engaged in sugar production, American corporations controlled nearly 60%. The average number of workers per mill in the whole island was 3,200; for American mills it was 5,150. The average per American mill in Camaguey province was 6,880. The Vertientes and Estrella plantations employed 10,000 workers each; Delicias, Manati and Preston 10,500 each. The plantations owned by the Cuban Atlantic Company employed an average of 5,570 workers; the Cuban American Company an average of 5,800; the Punta Alegre Company 5,250.

But the nineteenth century still survived. The gigantic expansion of the Cuban sugar industry after the wars of independence, coupled with the loss of manpower in those wars and the cessation of the negro slave trade, required the importation of labour. This was true also, though on a much smaller scale, of the Dominican Republic. Both countries turned to the Caribbean islands, those like Haiti and Jamaica, and lesser British areas like St. Kitts and St. Vincent, where the labour supply was over abundant. This importation was called 'swallow' immigration in Cuba; the majority of the workers would come only for the sugar season, after which they would return home. Not all of them, however: Cuba and the Dominican Republic found themselves threatened with a swarm of black alien labourers, on a lower cultural and economic level than the native Cuban or Dominican, white, coloured or black.

Between 1913 and 1924 Cuba received 217,000 labourers from Haiti, Jamaica and Puerto Rico; in the single year 1920, as many as 63,000 from Haiti and Jamaica. In 1931 there were 80,000 Haitians resident in Cuba. The Cuban working class demanded the repatriation of the immigrants, which the planters were less unwilling to concede in the depression. Thirty thousand Haitians were repatriated in 1936 and 1937. The average annual exodus from Jamaica, largely to Cuba, was 10,000 for the half-century before 1935; in the five years ending in 1935 approximately 31,000 were repatriated at the expense of the British government. The Dominican Republic resorted to speedier and more drastic methods; a wholesale slaughter of Haitians took place in 1937, straining relations between the two governments to breaking point. But despite the massacre and subsequent repatriation, there were still 60,000 Haitians resident in the Dominican Republic in 1937, and that government resorted to the familiar Latin American practice and insisted that in all employment a certain percentage — fixed at 70% — must be Dominican.

Latifundia, gigantic mill, extensive railroads, large labour force, colossal investment — all added up to monoculture. Sugar was as much king in the first fifty years of the twentieth century as it had ever been in Caribbean history. It was American capital that enthroned sugar in Cuba. From 1902 to 1939 sugar constituted more than 80% of the island's total exports. Less than half in 1902, the proportion was more than nine-tenths in the boom year 1920. There was a corresponding decline in the contribution of the tobacco industry to the economy. Tobacco, the field *par excellence* of small white farmers, represented 40% of Cuba's exports in 1902, only 10% in 1939. For the whole period 1902–1939 the average proportion of tobacco in the total exports was less than 14%.

Under American rule after 1898 sugar regularly constituted more than 50% of the exports of Puerto Rico; in 1939–1940 it represented over 40% of total exports. Coffee had been the staple of Spanish Puerto Rico. American Puerto Rico actually imported coffee. Coffee declined from nearly 5% of total exports in 1920 to less than half of 1% in 1939. During the same period tobacco exports declined from 20% of the total to slightly more than 5%.

Sugar was the largest single employer, employing about 20% of all workers reporting a gainful occupation. Almost half of all the agricultural labourers over ten years of age worked in some aspect of the sugar industry. This was more than twice the number employed by the next largest industry, coffee, three times the number employed in tobacco, and more than the workers employed in the coffee, tobacco, fruit, dairy and stock-raising industries combined. Whereas 100 acres in sugar provided employment for 46 persons, the same acreage in other crops provided employment for only 31 persons. The acreage in sugar in Puerto Rico increased more than fourfold between 1899 and 1935. In 1899 sugar represented less than 20% of the cultivated land, about 40% in 1940. The

value of sugar farms was about 67% of all the farms in the island. From 1926 to 1935 the value of the sugar crop was on the average over five times larger than the tobacco crop and nearly eight times larger than the value of the coffee crop. The value of the sugar cane crop was never below three times as large as the value of the tobacco or the coffee crop during these ten years, while in some years it was 32 times the value of the coffee crop and 45 times the value of the tobacco crop.

For the decade 1929–1938 sugar constituted nearly 67% of the exports of the Dominican Republic. Between 1903 and 1939 the output increased nearly ten times. Under the stimulus of American capital, sugar exports in Haiti increased from an average of 3% of total exports for the decade 1916–1926 to 14% in 1938 and nearly 20% in 1939.

Small as the sugar industry was in the British and French islands, it occupied an equally dominant position in the economy. In the British West Indies 33% of the population of St. Kitts and Antigua was directly employed by the sugar industry, 20% of the population of Barbados, 17% of British Guiana's, 12% of St. Lucia's, 10% of Trinidad's. With the ancillary occupations which have their whole origin in some phase of the sugar industry and its needs, and the families dependent on these sugar workers for support, the Olivier Sugar Commission of 1928 estimated that the extent to which the population of the British West Indies would be affected by the abandonment of sugar was as follows: the entire population of St. Kitts and Antigua, 67% of the population of Barbados, 50% of British Guiana's, 33% of Trinidad's, 25% of St. Lucia's, 10% of Jamaica's. 80% of the cultivated area in Antigua was planted to cane, 50% in Barbados, 67% in St. Kitts, 33% in British Guiana, 20% in Jamaica, 10% in Trinidad, 67% in Martinique, 50% in Guadeloupe, which depended on sugar and by-products for 60% of its exports.

Little change had taken place between the West India Royal Commission of 1897 and the Olivier Sugar Commission of 1928. Sugar and by-products constituted 97% of total Barbadian exports in 1896 and 95% in 1928. The percentage in Antigua was 94½% in 1896 and 97% in 1928; in St. Kitts-Nevis 96½% in 1896 and 86% in 1928 when Nevis had practically abandoned sugar. In Jamaica it remained the same, 18%. But the percentage declined in these two years in British Guiana from 70½% to 60½%; in St. Lucia from 74 to 45; in Trinidad, where oil had been discovered, from 57 to 20; in St. Vincent from 42 to 9.

The 1897 West India Royal Commission had called for agricultural diversification as a matter of the highest policy and the greatest urgency. The

Commission recognized that 'the representatives of the sugar industry in the West Indies have had special means of influencing the governments of the different colonies, and of putting pressure on the Home Government to secure attention to their views and wishes. Their interests have been to a very great extent limited to the sugar industry, and they have seldom turned their attention to any other cultivation except when the sugar industry ceased to be profitable'. The Commission continued: 'No reform affords so good a prospect for the permanent welfare in the future of the West Indies as the settlement of the labouring population on the land as small peasant proprietors'. The 1928 Commission explained the failure to take action on this recommendation: if the sugar planters 'encouraged action which in their belief, must tend to diminish their labour supply, they would be cutting away the branch upon which they sit'.

By 1928, therefore, precisely nothing had been accomplished. When the largest plantation in British Guiana was once asked about the possibility of land settlement of farmers on some of its lands, the manager wrote in reply:

We have about 1,000 acres of land uncultivated which will eventually be suitable for growing canes ... We cannot afford to part with any of this land. In fact, we are getting near the end of our tether as regards expansion. The estate is not prepared to lease any portion of these lands to cane-farmers or settlers.

Even in overcrowded Barbados in 1928 there was much land which was eminently suitable for growing fruit and vegetables, and no doubt these would have been grown 'had it not been deemed to be in the interests of sugar cane cultivation to abstain from encouraging such cultivation'. The Olivier Commission drew attention to the contrast between the prosperity of those colonies in which a peasantry existed and the degradation and squalor of those in which the lower classes were labourers on the sugar plantations.

The 1897 Commission had warned that 'so long as they remain dependent upon sugar their position can never be sound or secure ... Where sugar can be completely, or very largely, replaced by other industries, the colonies in question will be in a much sounder position, both politically and economically, when they have ceased to depend wholly, or to a very great extent, upon the continued prosperity of a single industry'. For this reason the Olivier Commission of 1928 refused to recommend the revival of the sugar industry in those places where it had died a natural or artificial death. Elsewhere the situation remained as described by Esteban Bird for Puerto Rico in 1935: 'sugar is everything and everything is sugar; it is the goddess that reigns over practically one-third of the private wealth'. What two students of the situation in Puerto Rico have said was applicable to the whole area: 'A significant change in the economy of the Island through the introduction and commercialization of new crops is very doubtful under present physical, economic and political conditions'.

SECTION NINE
The Labour Movement: Decolonization and Democracy

Emerging between the reformed post-slavery nineteenth century colonial world and the emergence of the 'modern' mid-twentieth century dispensation, was the movement of organized labour. It is now generally understood that the rise of popular democracy has its origins within the political process that emerged from workers' increasingly militant call for the political franchise; by the 1930s, the movement of organized labour had gained, in some places, revolutionary potential.

Associated with the demand for political self-representation was the call for the eradication of colonial relationships in the Caribbean. The democratic movement and the anti-colonial struggles, then, were closely integrated and located essentially within a broad-based ideological populism. It is possible, therefore to suggest that the beginning of the twentieth century constituted a critical watershed in the history of Caribbean self-expression.

The essays in this section indicate some specific circumstances that characterized that transformation of consciousness and political action. Rodney identified the origins of modern working class political radicalism within the circumstances surrounding the Ruimveldt Revolt of 1906. For him, the organizational methods, ideological articulations and collectivist consciousness of workers suggest that they had broken with the past and had reached a stage of development where their relationship with the owners of the means of production resembled those found within modern capitalism.

Perhaps the greatest mass movement among workers in several countries was built by Marcus Garvey during the 1920s and 1930s. Garveyism came to symbolize the hopes and aspirations of black people who, since their nineteenth century emancipation, had remained disenfranchised. Martin's essay outlines the spread of Garveyite organizations across the Caribbean, and focuses specifically upon the impact of his movement upon the struggle for Black Nationhood in Jamaica, the land of his birth.

By the 1930s, the Caribbean was in revolutionary turmoil, as workers and middle class radicals sought to redress many historical imbalances. In the English speaking region, as well as in the Spanish and Dutch speaking areas, workers resorted to militant methods of achieving their democratic goals. Richard Hart presents a detailed chronological survey and interpretation of the spread of workers' rebellions during the 1930s. Arthur Lewis describes the social background of the working classes and the rise of the labour movement in the various territories, outlines the objectives of the movement, analyses the degree of success of the uprising in these territories, and traces the impact of the decade of militancy upon workers' political consciousness and colonial political structures.

The Ruimveldt Riots: Demerara, British Guiana, 1905

Walter Rodney

were some who ran one way.
were some who ran another way.
were some who did not run at all.
were some who will not run again.
And I was with them all,
when the sun and streets exploded,
and a city of clerks
turned a city of men!

— Martin Carter

The Event and Its Causes

Riots and disturbances punctuate the history of the British West Indies. Most were minor phenomena with little significance beyond the small circle of lives touched by a brief explosion of social violence.[1] But there were times when the disaffection was more wide-ranging and the scale of violence larger; and when the level of consciousness and organization of the participants carried these elements forward into a moment of challenge to colonial authority. In different degrees, these characteristics were present in the riots of November-December 1905 in the county of Demerara.

The 1905 riots are often referred to as the 'Ruimveldt Riots', because several workers from Plantation Ruimveldt were among the first to lose their lives in the violence. But other sugar estates on the East and West Banks of the Demerara were significantly involved, while Georgetown remained — throughout — the hub of activity. Being close to the city, Plantation Ruimveldt was understandably first to respond to the agitation in Georgetown. Thereafter, social unrest became evident on other East Bank estates, and then on the estates of the left or West Bank which were in constant contact with Georgetown and with East Bank plantations like Ruimveldt and Diamond. In most instances, the estate strikes started and remained within the precincts of the factories. Sugar boilers, porters, stokers, and other building hands were the workers involved. When the unrest spread, it moved logically to creole cane-cutters who were friends, relatives and neighbours of the factory hands in the villages. But it was the Georgetown stevedores who provided the spark of rebellion when they decided to take a stand on the question of the wage rate, which had stagnated for nearly three decades.

Each shipping firm in the city of Georgetown retained a nucleus of permanent stevedores, but most of their needs were met by the hiring of casual 'outside' labourers who received two guilders, or 64 cents, on completion of a day's work of ten and one-half hours. One of the major complaints of these labourers was that they were paid pro rata on the basis of the daily wage when work ran out before the day was finished. Stevedores contended that they were willing to work the full day of ten and one-half hours and should receive a full day's wage when available tasks were completed. Alternatively, if they were to be paid for part of a day, the hourly remuneration should be far higher than the prevailing six cents per hour. A second sore point among the waterfront workers was that 'boys' earned 48 cents per day (16 cents less than grown men), but adults were often categorized as 'boys'. In the final analysis, workers were convinced that wages had remained at a low level for far too long. On Sunday, 26 November, the new Colonial Company offered a special rate of 16 cents an hour to have labourers complete the loading of a steamer. This was a practical demonstration of the value of their labour, and it precipitated strike action to back demands that wages be raised to that level.

352

The dramatic moments of the 1905 riots were on 30 November and 1 December. However, a diary of the entire event would span the period from 28 November to 6 December. It was on Tuesday, 28 November, that a strike was called on the wharf of Sandbach, the 'boys' refusing to take less than sixteen cents an hour. There was no disorder. Workers who came off the job got together in groups and discussed the matter quietly. On the following day, Wednesday, 29 November, the number of strikers increased considerably. All of the shipping firms were affected, and the strikers were vociferous and demonstrative. From early in the day, a large group of about three hundred young stevedores marched under a banner that read, '16 cents an hour or no work'.[2] They moved from place to place and persuaded others to withdraw their labour all along the waterfront. Other strikers congregated in groups of fifty to sixty at various points in the business district. Meanwhile, porters employed by Ruimveldt estate (East Bank Demerara) began a strike at midday. The scene was set for an alliance between urban workers and sugar estate workers — an alliance which was a distinguishing feature of the 1905 riots.

On Thursday, 30 November, masses of people took to the streets in Georgetown. Those who were on strike set out to persuade others of their fellow workers to likewise cease labour. Sometimes force was required. That Thursday morning, domestics were dragged out of private houses, while workers at the Railway Goods Wharf were threatened and pushed off the job site. By afternoon, crowds roamed the business centre, and some looting took place at pawnbrokers' and jewelers'. Most businessmen hastened to close their premises, but the scale of intimidation and larceny was very restricted, and, interestingly enough, there were no cases of arson.

The police response, when it came, was not to criminal acts but to what they interpreted as social rebellion. The inspector of police claimed that a large crowd of some fifteen hundred persons in front of Bookers' Wharf had stated an intention to prevent anyone working. There was no indication that they were bent on looting or damaging property. The strike was joined that evening by bakers who left their jobs because of a pay dispute and staged a march down Carmichael Street. The colonial state had but one answer to this escalation of industrial action: to declare parts of the city 'proclaimed areas' and read the Riot Act.[3] The Riot Act was read around 6:00 P.M. that Thursday at four different points of the city of Georgetown. The crowds dispersed, but instead of going home, people gathered that night in animated groups in Bourda, Alberttown, Wortmanville, and Albouystown.

'Fore-day morning' on 1 December found the Ruimveldt factory grinding. It began to consume coals, cane, and human labour from 4:00 A.M. However, work came to a stop by 5:00 A.M., and after 'dayclean', cane-cutters joined the factory hands to confront the manager, who not only rejected their wage demands, but sent for the police, alleging that he was assaulted and that the workers were rioting. At 7:55 A.M., the police and a detachment of artillery were in position at the Ruimveldt bridge, over which the East Bank workers were about to cross to link up with Georgetown and La Penitence workers who were assembled on the other side. The Riot Act was read, and the police opened fire when the crowd failed to disperse. Four workers were seriously injured. Their bleeding bodies were taken first to Government House and then to the Colonial (Public) Hospital. Word of the Ruimveldt shooting flashed through the city of Georgetown, which was already in a state of tension. According to one report, 'three-fourths of the population of Georgetown seemed to have gone stark staring mad'.[4] In spite of the Riot Act, thousands converged on the streets in the western part of the city from the Parade Ground to the Public Buildings. A hostile crowd invaded the Public Buildings, forcing His Excellency the governor to take refuge behind locked doors in the Court of Policy hall. They rushed up and down the galleries and stairs of the Public Buildings looking for the inspector-general of police, who was rumoured to have threatened to shoot down more people. One man was killed by police fire in the vicinity of the Public Buildings. As the police regained control of the western section of the city, the crowds were forced east of Camp Street, where they vented their anger on individual members of the ruling class who crossed their paths. The dead and the dying in the Colonial Hospital attracted many rioters to that part of the city. Along the length of Thomas Street, the police patrols were showered with stones and other missiles. They responded with rifle fire; and before the day was done, the toll rose to seven dead and seventeen critically wounded.

Predictably, the newspapers labelled Friday, 1 December 1905, 'Black Friday'. On the next morning, the population of Georgetown was extremely bitter but more cautious, moving in groups of no more than a dozen or so. Strikers repeated the exercise of invading the Railway Goods Wharf to dissuade labourers there from working. They also continued attacks on persons closely identified with the system of exploitation. The women in particular were said to have resorted to stone throwing, and a band of women attacked the police station in Hadfield Street that Saturday at midday, scattering the prepared meal which was being carried in. But several were arrested; and increased police and vigilante activity caused street manifestations to disintegrate into knots of a mere four or five persons. It was outside of Georgetown that the disturbances grew in scope and intensity after the shooting on 'Black Friday'. The sugar estate areas of the East Bank Demerara were all affected. In the wake of the Ruimveldt shootings, the deputy manager of Houston had been stoned, while the carts of Plantations Farm and Diamond were robbed of their groceries. The porters of Diamond demanded on Saturday, 2 December, an increase from thirty-six cents per day to forty-eight cents per day, while sugar curers asked for fifty-six cents instead of the forty cents per day that they were then receiving. A mixed force of twenty-seven police and special constables was sent to deal with these wage demands at Plantation Diamond.

Sunday was of course a day of rest for most workers. This did not apply to the tram conductors who chose Sunday, 3 December, to strike for more pay. A tram conductor who had been employed for less than a year earned five cents an hour, while those with one year's service or more received six cents an hour. The following Friday morning, estate workers again had an opportunity to demonstrate their grievances and their militancy. The porters and girls at Peter's Hall struck for higher wages, which meant that every estate on the East Bank Demerara had been affected by the industrial unrest. At the same time, factory workers on the West Bank Demerara decided to seize the chance to press their wage claims. The first group of workers to make this decision visited Plantation Nismes and called out the workers. Schoonord, Wales, and Versailles followed in quick succession. For the first time in decades, managers were forced to sit down by their own employees. At Schoonord and Versailles, the managers were prepared to negotiate, but the colonial state was not. The forces of repression had been immeasurably strengthened by the arrival of two Admiralty vessels. H.M.S. *Diamond* was a fast third-class cruiser of 3,000 tons, with a crew of 300. It had been commissioned one year earlier, and it was dispatched from Barbados. The British also sent H.M.S. *Sappho,* an older second-class cruiser of 3,400 tons, which arrived from Trinidad with its crew of 272 men plus a contingent from another cruiser then in Port of Spain. The bluejackets from the *Diamond* and the *Sappho* were used to arrest the so-called ringleaders of the strikes on the West Bank Demerara.

If the strikes were to grow to epidemic proportions as the governor feared, then they would next have affected the east and west coasts of Demerara. The governor was advised by police security that bands of men came from as far as Plantation Hope on the west coast and the island of Wakenaam on the east, trying to stir up strikes and rioting among the Afro-Guyanese labouring population. If this was true, then nothing came of their agitation.[5]

An alarm was soon raised by a disturbance in the hinterland among gold miners at Peter's mine in the Puruni river district. About 225 labourers employed by this American-owned quartz mine struck work on 12 December. Payment for labourers working underground then ranged between sixty-four cents and $1.20 per day, and the men were proposing $1.50 a day. When this was rejected, the men demanded to be paid off, and the company accepted this with respect to 67 of them. The official reaction at Bartica and in Georgetown was that the miners' dispute was an indication of 'strike contagion'. However, once more selective arrests and victimization put an end to all manifestations.

By Tuesday, 5 December, the streets of Georgetown were back to normal, but the wharves continued to be at practically a standstill, particularly with regard to the employment of 'outside' labour. The withholding of labour persisted on a few estates. Nevertheless, the end was in sight; and on Wednesday the sixth, the governor reported that all was normal in Georgetown and in the rural areas, with the exception of the West Bank factories where a few stokers had not yet returned to their jobs.

The collapse of the waterfront strike in Georgetown was dictated by sheer want, since the workers had no means of surviving without employment. Obviously, there were no strike relief funds; and in place of such a mechanism, a group of workers found themselves scrambling for a few coins and cigarettes thrown down by the mayor. It seems as though he intended to be charitable, but the result was thoroughly degrading. In any event, a handout like the mayor's was far from adequate. When workers surrendered to necessity and broke the strike, they did so with a sullenness born of the conviction that their demands were just, and that justice for workers was unobtainable.

The events of 1905 must be placed in the context of the sustained and unrelenting pressure brought to bear on the living standards of the working people ever since the depression of 1884, and more so since the acute depression of 1894–96. In the late 1880s, wages recovered briefly from their low rate in the period 1886–87. There had been no major upheaval in the city of Georgetown since 1889. Nevertheless, it should be recalled that in 1895 the colonial authorities were particularly concerned that urban workers and unemployed might resort to violence. Ten years later, wages were lower and unemployment was greater than ever. The recommendations of the Royal Commission of 1896–97 had had no impact on people's lives, and when the populace took to the streets in November-December 1905, it was in a desperate effort to deal with the endemic ills of low wages and high unemployment.

Most of the year 1905 passed by without social protest of an unusual kind. There were several small work stoppages and strikes occurring mainly on the sugar estates; but it does not appear that the authorities considered that the situation was building to a climax or that there was the possibility that 'things were getting out of hand'. What should be borne in mind was that the distress of the working people was at the time being publicly aired. Throughout the month of November 1905, a Mortality Commission was sitting in Georgetown and taking public evidence. Witnesses referred to a range of social and environmental factors which were responsible for high mortality, and especially for high infant mortality, in the countryside and in Georgetown. Sanitation and sewage disposal in Georgetown were frighteningly poor. The pit latrines or cesspits were cleared from time to time by a piece of equipment referred to as an 'odorless excavator', a name which proved to be a masterly euphemism. Quite apart from the asphyxiating smell, there was a direct threat to health because the contents of the latrines floated in the flooded yards in the rainy seasons. It was the poorer classes who had to wallow in that filth and to crowd into the many-roomed tenement houses in which tuberculosis was on the increase. They could do no better. Lengthy correspondence in the *Chronicle* back in February 1902 had clearly indicated that overcrowding of families into single rooms was inevitable, given that even a single room consumed in rent at least 25% of the three or four dollars which a poor man might earn in a week. The mortality commissioners eventually concluded as follows: 'We are of the opinion that the excessive mortality in the colony occurs chiefly among the poorer classes of the community ... and the high rate among the poorer classes is in part due to the absence of adequate measures of sanitation; overcrowding in rooms, in ranges of tenement rooms and in tenement houses... It is also due to poverty'.[6]

The mortality commissioners were drawn from the ruling class. In a circular manner, they attributed the distress of the poor to poverty. The poverty was explained in large part as due to ignorance and laziness. In other words, poverty was the fault of the poor. Such social analysis was not unusual at the time; however, the enquiry did illustrate the hard facts of social existence for the large number of persons who were to participate in the riots of 1905.

Some of the authorities were certainly aware that deplorable conditions in many parts of Georgetown (whoever was at fault), were the breeding ground for potential violence. Henry Kirke, an experienced magistrate and sheriff of Demerara, had commented on the subject a few years previously. 'Let anyone walk through the yards which lead out of lower Regent Street, Lombard Street and Leopold Street in Georgetown, and let him ask himself how he could expect respectable law-abiding citizens to be raised therein'.[7] Kirke was concerned with narrow, antisocial violence, but the conditions that he perceived and that were noted by the Mortality Commission were such as would encourage much more sweeping violence.

When the rains fell, Georgetown residents waded among floating feces; when casual labourers obtained two days' work per week, the entire earnings could barely cover the rent and keep away the bailiff's cart; when mothers gave birth, they stood a 30% chance of burying that child before the first year was up, given an infant mortality rate of 298 per thousand. Besides, the Mortality Commission had been sitting for nearly one month before the outbreak of the riots. The witnesses were not telling the poor anything that the poor did not know, but they were placing before the authorities common experiences that were otherwise hidden; and the poor were reminded of the intolerable nature of that which they tolerated from day to day. One witness referred to the houses of the poor as 'dog-houses'; another expressed his amazement at the capacity of labourers to do hard manual labour from 6:00 A.M. until noon, fortified merely by a cup of 'sugar-water' and a few biscuits.

Apart from sharing their living environment, many rioters had a special nexus with the stevedores. The casual or 'outside' labourer was poised uncertainly between unemployment and employment. Every day, large numbers of 'outside' labourers would assembly near the wharf gates and try to catch the eye of the wharfinger. The majority received work only for a few days a week and were permanently underemployed. Young men out of work were recruits for the 'centipedes' street gangs; they also spent a lot of time playing 'Cheefa', a Chinese gambling game which was comparable to the 'numbers' game of U.S. cities. Up until 1905, the government offered no solution beyond arresting 'centipedes' and 'Cheefa' gamblers. One correspondent in the press indicated his awareness that the colonial authorities were not exercising any social responsibility. He stated: 'I have often wondered at the supineness of the government in permitting so many men to go on existing without any visible means of livelihood'.[8]

With hindsight, it is easy to see that the unemployment, poor wages, atrocious living conditions, and the consequent riots of 1905 should all be placed within the context of the protracted crisis since 1884. But, in addition, it is of overriding importance to note that Georgetown workers themselves made a conscious connection between their current misery and the refusal of the system to provide amelioration over the previous three decades.

Among the stevedores, the demand for higher wages was accompanied by a clear exposition that the shipping companies owed workers back pay — meaning, as they themselves explained, that they had been underpaid for many years. The employers did not deny that wages had stood still. On the contrary, they used the stagnation of the wage rate as a justification for concluding that the remuneration was perfectly acceptable. The merchants put forward as a defense that 'as far back as 30 years ago, when sugar was fetching a higher price, the same wages were paid as are paid now when sugar is fetching a lower price'.[9] One of the most recalcitrant employers was the firm of J.H. de Jonge, auctioneers, importers, and sugar brokers. In 1897, a spokesman for this firm had admitted to the Royal Commission that urban wages were down by 15% while rents held at the same level. But de Jonge and most shipping employers failed to take account of the high cost of living and the decreased purchasing power of wages in 1905.

Planters likewise chose to emphasize that thirty years earlier they paid the same wage when sugar fetched a higher price. They completely ignored the fact that workers never shared in the profits realized through price rises or through negotiated markets in the U.S.A. and Canada, although that surplus realization was made possible by tariff concessions that raised the cost of living for the working class consumers in British Guiana. Indeed, the two years preceding the riots were years during which the cane sugar industry was emerging out of its slump. The international Brussels Agreement had at last limited European beet sugar subsidies, and the Guianese product was establishing itself in the Canadian market. Yet there was resistance to sharing any of these profits with the workers. An equally telling illustration of planter recalcitrance is that, in responding to wage demands from factory hands, planters made no mention of reduced production costs and enhanced labour productivity in the factories resulting from technological change and the ploughing back of earlier profits into factory renovation.

Planters seemed not to recognize that productivity and the cost of living were crucial variables which should have altered the rate of wages; and it was left to the workers to take up a stance that was much closer to modern concepts of industrial relations in the capitalist world itself. Stevedores, for example, correctly noted that changes in technology and work routines intensified the rate of exploitation of dock labour. At one time, they took four or five days to load a ship with sugar. By 1905, they were loading ships of the same capacity in one and a half to two days; and because they were paid by the day with no consideration given to output, they actually suffered de facto wage reductions. On the wharves and on the sugar estates, the working class vanguard demonstrated that it had achieved a sound grasp of the historical process of labour exploitation and that it knew the situation of colonial and oppressed races to be especially backward. One inspector of police assumed the role of mediator on behalf of business interests and sought to calm the crowd at the Parade Ground. He was rebuffed by a worker who stepped forward and got straight to the point. 'If you please to kindly go back and say for we that when white man work for 30 years if they don't get their money raise? We work for 30 years for the same money and now we want a raise; we want more money.....Is that 30 years cheap work sweeten them white man, that make so they think it hard to pay a price now?'[10]

Reports on the 1905 riots indicate a level of worker self-awareness that could only have been a leap consequent upon a long period of slow development. The stevedores of 1905 represented the highest expression of worker consciousness derived from the struggle both on and off the plantations. The clash between themselves and their employers was one between the working class and the sugar capitalists in a different guise. Most of the outward-bound cargo which the stevedores loaded was sugar. Most of the shipping firms were closely associated with the major joint-stock sugar companies such as Booker Brothers, Sandbach Parker, and H.K. Davson. Dockworkers were at a sensitive point of articulation of the colonial import-export economy. The significance of this sensitive location for the rebelliousness of dockworkers is to be seen from their history throughout the colonial world. Through contacts with seamen and through the popular press, Guianese waterfront workers would also have been aware of the struggle of dockworkers in metropolitan countries. Back in 1890, when there was an 'epidemic of strikes' in Georgetown, they were led by stevedores, and they followed on the heels of the great London dock strike of the previous year. This process of class education through glimpses of international experience must have continued in the years that came after. The stevedores and the clerks of the shipping firms were among the first to hear, read, and discuss news from the outside world. In 1905, they would have had a great deal to excite their imagination. The local newspapers carried not only the evidence before the Mortality Commission at home, but also lengthy accounts of the 1905 Revolution in Czarist Russia.

Ashton Chase's *History of Trade Unionism in Guyana* lays emphasis on the organizational weakness of the Guianese working class in 1905. He attributes this weakness to the semi-feudal conditions prevailing in the sugar industry, to the lack of modern large-scale industry, and to the attendant under-development of proletarian consciousness.[11] The untested assumption is that organization would not have lagged far behind subjective development; but the evidence suggests precisely this. What is beyond dispute is that Guianese workers in 1905 lacked any organization equal to the conduct of uncompromising struggle. The embryonic working class organizations of the late 1880s had not survived. The People's Association had called for the formation of a trade union, but this had not materialized. The result is that grievances burst to the fore spontaneously in November 1905, and there were no structures to plan or guide the worker movement either at the place of work or in the streets. At best, ad hoc committees of workers sought audience with employers and with the colonial authorities. Alternatively, middle-class spokesmen presented themselves as negotiators.

Neither in Georgetown nor in Ruimveldt nor in West Demerara was there any leadership with anything approaching a plan to advance the interests of the working class as a whole. On 28 November, stevedores at Sandbach Parker had acted on the spur of the moment and used their practical judgement in deciding to detain a steamer which needed to be loaded to catch the tide.* During the days that followed, spontaneity was all the more evident in working-class actions. There was certainly no plan to stage violent rebellion. The corollary to this was that state agencies were largely responsible for forcing the wage protests in the direction of mass violence. As observed on the sugar estates, the edgy authoritarian response to immigrant protests often precipitated tragedy. In like manner, the destruction of life, limb, and property in December 1905 came out of the operation of the coercive state apparatus.

Whenever they were presented with an opportunity, sugar and waterfront workers ably advanced their wage demands. They went first to their employers, but the colonial state acted with remarkable speed in interposing itself between capital and labour and in taking up the defense of the employers. Georgetown stevedores wanted to negotiate directly with the principal import-export firms such as Sandbach Parker, the La Penitence Company of Curtis Campbell, Thom & Cameron, Booker Brothers, T. Garnett, Wieting & Richter, and the New Colonial Company. However, the governor issued his proclamations on 30 November, which was only the second day of the effective waterfront strike. A few members of the Chamber of Commerce were prepared to compromise, but the hard-liners easily won out because the shelter of the state coercive apparatus made stubborn refusal a practical proposition. That the governor should come out in defense of 'law and order' was not surprising. But it was somewhat surprising that he never hid behind the formula of the colonial power being the evenhanded dispenser of justice, but instead, openly declared that his function was primarily to defend the capitalist class. Speaking to crowds at the Public Buildings on the morning of Friday, 1 December, Governor Hodgson admonished that 'if you break the law in connection with your grievance, as Governor of the colony and as the person who has to protect the lives and interests — more particularly the mercantile interests — of the colony, it is my duty to see that no one breaks the law'.[12] Besides, the governor's proclamation on the previous day had set the stage for the Ruimveldt tragedy, which must be in large part attributed to the refusal of the police to allow an industrial dispute to remain precisely that. The crowd continually told Major de Rinzy that their purpose was peaceful and that they only wanted to speak to the manager to resolve the wage question. 'We ent rowing', they said, 'We only come for seek for price, and we cannot go. We ent come to you [de Rinzy]; we come to the manager'.[13] Major de Rinzy himself testified that the cane-cutters said, 'We have not come to fight, we have come for higher wages'. In spite of this, Major de Rinzy appointed himself a planting attorney, one of his orders being that the artillerymen should go into the logies and bring the labourers out to work.

After Ruimveldt, official policy deliberately excluded the possibility of any wage negotiations. Governor Hodgson's strategy was to meet each labour claim with the maximum show of force, to arrest all who could be identified as ringleaders, and to pressure the planters to take the line of a blanket denial of wage increases. The governor

---

*Because of a silt bar at the Demerara estuary, ships leaving the port of Georgetown had to await the moment when (twice daily) the tides were at their highest.

distinguished himself by taking command over the planter representatives in the colony. He decided what was good for capital and the colonial state in the face of popular challenge, and he whipped into compliance those managers and planting attorneys who seemed weak or vacillating. This pattern emerged clearly on the West Bank Demerara on the fourth and fifth of December. The governor personally visited Nismes, Wales, Schoonord, and Versailles — accompanied by troops of H.M.S. *Diamond* and H.M.S. *Sappho*. Some managers were prepared to make concessions. At Schoonord and Versailles, the managers had agreed to new wage rates in their deliberations with workers. But Hodgson forced them to renege on such promises. He claimed that to concede wage increases would be to encourage the spread of wage demands; he criticized the manager of Versailles for panicking; and he implied that the manager of Schoonord was concerned only with getting his ripe cane cut. The governor told them plainly that they should follow his advice or he would withdraw the armed forces from their estates and leave them to the mercy of the 'rioters'. Endorsed in the final analysis by the entire planter class, Hodgson used coercive instruments against the workers in the belief that this was the only way to stop wage claims from spreading to estates in other parts of the country, and to discourage the vast majority of field workers from taking militant steps. The introduction of troops was also intended to be intimidatory. One Guianese in the streets suggested to a British soldier that there was no need for the latter's presence,

informing him tersely and eloquently: 'The people are doing nothing. It is the government who are rioting and shooting down the people'.[14]

Notes

1. See e.g., Frank Cundall, *Political and Social Disturbances in the West Indies: A Brief Account and Bibliography* (Kingston, 1906).
2. The *Chronicle*, 30 November 1905. The *Chronicle* gave comprehensive coverage to these events and subsequently published a compilation entitled *The Riots of 1905: Details of the Outbreak, Its Causes and the Measures Taken for Its Suppression; Inquest on the Victims and Punishment of the Rioters* (Georgetown, 1906). (To be cited subsequently as *The Riots of 1905*).
3. For the Proclamation, see Minutes of the Court of Policy, 28 December 1905.
4. The *Chronicle*, 2 December 1905.
5. C.O. 111/547, GD 364, 28 December 1905. This dispatch, along with all other telegrams and letters on the Riots, was presented to Parliament as *Correspondence Relating to Disturbances in British Guiana*. This document is available in the Guyana National Archives and in the Public Record Office, London, C.O. 884, vol. 9, West Indies no. 151 (1906).
6. Minutes of the Combined Court, Special Session 1906, 'Report on General Mortality and Infant Mortality'.
7. Henry Kirke, *Twenty-five Years in British Guiana* (London, 1898), p. 308.
8. The *Chronicle*, 21 January 1902.
9. Ibid., 30 November 1905.
10. *The Riots of 1905*, p. 6.
11. Ashton Chase, *A History of Trade Unionism in Guyana, 1900–1961* (Georgetown, 1964), p. 27.
12. *Correspondence Relating to Disturbances*, p. 14.
13. The *Chronicle*, 5 December 1905.
14. Ibid., 6 December 1905.

Marcus Garvey, the Caribbean, and the Struggle for Black Jamaican Nationhood*

Tony Martin

There have been several movements to federate the British West Indian Islands, but owing to parochial feelings nothing definite has been achieved. Ere long this change is sure to come about because the people of these islands are all one. They live under the same conditions, are of the same race and mind and have the same feelings and sentiments regarding the things of the world.

— *Marcus Garvey 1913*

The Honourable Marcus Mosiah Garvey (1887–1940) is undoubtedly one of the most important figures in West Indian history. At a time when African peoples all over the world were colonized, disfranchised and subjugated, he provided hope and helped sow the seeds for nationalist struggles in Africa, Afro-America, the West Indies and elsewhere. His Universal Negro Improvement Association (UNIA), founded in Jamaica in 1914 and re-established in the United States around 1917, in the process became the largest Pan-African movement in history. By the mid–1920s it boasted approximately 1,120 branches in over 40 countries.

Within the West Indies, Garvey's UNIA stands out as one of the few Pan-Caribbean political movements in our history, and probably the most successful. For there were UNIA branches in Cuba, Trinidad, Jamaica, the then British Guiana, the Dominican Republic, Barbados, the then British Honduras, the Bahamas, Antigua, Bermuda, Dominica, Suriname, Grenada, Haiti, Nevis, Puerto Rico, St. Kitts, St. Lucia, St. Thomas, and St. Vincent. This was therefore a genuine Pan-Caribbean mass movement, cutting across political and linguistic barriers. Cuba had more branches (52) than any other territory in the West Indies, and indeed more than any country other than the United States. Trinidad had at least 30 branches. Jamaica had 11, British Guiana 7 and the Dominican Republic 5.

In addition to the large number of branches in the West Indies proper, West Indian emigrant workers made up a very large percentage of UNIA members in such Latin American countries as Panama, Costa Rica, Honduras, Colombia, Guatemala and Nicaragua. Many West Indians also joined the movement in other countries, especially in such United States cities as New York, Boston, and Miami, which were major destinations for West Indian emigrants.

The rapid spread of Garvey's movement may be attributed to several factors. For one thing, the World War I period was a time of worldwide radicalism. African peoples were also at their most desperate point in history and so needed vigorous leadership. Garvey himself was a tireless and exceedingly able organizer, in addition to being an exceptional orator and a strongly charismatic figure. His ideological position also appealed to masses of people. He urged Black people to be self-reliant, to put their racial interest first in a world which universally oppressed them, and to strive to build a strong nation in Africa, strong enough to compel world respect and lend support to African people everywhere.

The UNIA's impact on West Indian affairs was almost immediate. Garvey's agents traversed the area establishing branches and spreading the word of nationalism and anti-colonialism. Some were deported from, and/or refused permission to land in certain territories. The UNIA weekly newspaper, the *Negro World* was widely distributed in the area practically from its inception late in 1918. Several of the British colonial governors responded by banning it, illegally in 1919, and from 1920 on by means of hastily introduced Seditious Publications Ordinances. Despite these measures the paper found its way in, sometimes through the mail, sometimes smuggled in by seamen. Copies intercepted by the authorities were burned.

---

*Originally published in 1978 as 'Marcus Garvey and the West Indies'

By 1919 the UNIA in the West Indies was firmly entrenched enough to figure prominently in the labour riots and racial unrest that swept the area. The British colonialists blamed the *Negro World* for the upsurge of race consciousness which formed a backdrop to the disturbances. In Trinidad, many of the leaders of the Trinidad Workingmen's Association, the major organization involved in the stevedores' strike of December 1919, were also members of the UNIA. It was reported that Garvey's editorials were read aloud at their meetings. In British Honduras, S.A. Haynes, one of the major figures involved in the riots, was a Garveyite. He later became a high-ranking UNIA official in the United States.

After 1919 the UNIA maintained its links with the budding West Indian labour movement. A. Bain Alves of Jamaica, members of Hubert Critchlow's British Guiana Labour Union and D. Hamilton Jackson, leader of the St. Croix Labour Union, were among those who established contact with the UNIA in the 1920s. Indeed, Basil Brenthol Blackman, former secretary-treasurer of the Caribbean Congress of Labour, once said that most of the working class leaders coming to power in the 1930s in the West Indies had been influenced by involvement at some level in Garvey's UNIA. Garvey himself founded a Jamaican Workers and Labourers Association after his deportation from the United States in 1927.

Garvey's impact generally on progressive elements in the West Indies, both within and without the labour movement, can be said to have been substantial. Grenada's T.A. Marryshow wrote favourably of him in his *West Indian* newspaper; in Trinidad the *Argos* and the *Labour Leader* (organ of the Trinidad Workingmen's Association) regularly supported him; in Barbados Clennel W. Wickham endorsed Garveyism in the pages of the *Barbados Weekly Herald*.

By the 1920s the UNIA had become, in several greater Caribbean territories, the virtual representatives of the black population. At a time when most black people in the area were denied the right to vote, and in an age mostly predating mass political parties, the UNIA often performed the function of quasi-political party as well as mutual aid organization. It was a major, sometimes the major, organized group looking after the interests of the mass of black people. In 1923 the British government seriously considered recognizing the Cuban UNIA as the body representing the British West Indian population in that island. To this day in Costa Rica the UNIA enjoys a position of importance among the black section of that country.

And when mass-based party politics did come to the West Indies, Garvey and the UNIA were again in the vanguard. For Garvey's Peoples Political Party, formed in Jamaica in 1929, was a pioneer in its class, at least for the British West Indies. A West Indian federation with dominion status was among its aims.

Garvey, in his travels in the West Indies, fared little better than his lieutenants, being occasionally barred from some areas. At various times he was refused permission to land in Bermuda, Cuba, the Canal Zone and Trinidad. Yet on other occasions he was received by such persons as the governor of Oriente province in Cuba, the president of Costa Rica and the governor of British Honduras. His most extensive trip to the British Caribbean came in 1937, three years before his death. On that occasion he was prevented by the British authorities from holding open air meetings in Trinidad. Nor was he permitted to refer to the labour struggles which had erupted there. Indeed, were it not for the personal intervention of Captain A.A. Cipriani, he may not have been allowed to land at all.

By 1927 Garvey was, of course, no stranger to Jamaican politics. Through workers' struggles, through his participation in the National Club, and through his leadership of the UNIA in Jamaica from 1914, he had amassed a wealth of experience prior to emigrating to the United States in 1916. And during his almost twelve years in the U.S. he maintained contact with Jamaica. In 1921 he suggested that Jamaican workers should unionize and elect their own representatives to the legislative council.[1] In 1923 the Kingston UNIA formed The Jamaica Political Reform Club which, though under UNIA auspices, was open to anyone wishing to take an active part in Jamaican politics. Fifty-four people were reported to have enrolled at its first meeting.[2]

The fear of a Garvey return to Jamaica had plagued some British colonialists, both in Jamaica and in London, for several years. In 1921, shortly after Garvey, on a visit home, had experienced difficulty in obtaining re-entry into the United States, a British Colonial Office official wrote, 'Garvey is a very dangerous man ... Unfortunately he is a native of Jamaica and from that Colony we could not deport him'.[3] In 1926, with Garvey's deportation from the United States seemingly imminent, the governor of Jamaica made an unsuccessful attempt to have London intercede with the U.S. officials against sending Garvey home.[4] Garvey sought to allay the fears of the colonialists on his return home by promptly disavowing any intention of seeking election to the legislative council.[5] He soon changed his mind though, and Governor R.E. Stubbs moved quickly to try and head him off. In February 1928, 'after a long talk with Garvey', he set forth his position in a despatch to the Colonial

Office. He compared Garvey with Sun Yat Sen of China. His observations are a singular mixture of sound insight and a colonialist mentality. He wrote:

[Garvey] reminds me curiously of San Yat Sen. There is the same devotion to an idea — possibly spurious but, if so, wonderfully well counterfeited -: in Sun's case the unification and independence of China; in Garvey's the improvement of the status of the black races. They both have the same magnetic power over men, even quite intelligent men, and in each case there is the same childish vanity, incessant talk of 'my organization', 'my party', my ideals' etc. In both cases I got the same impression that while the man was genuinely zealous for the cause, he would rather see it fail under himself than succeed under anyone else. In both cases this vanity had led the man into absurdities: Garvey as Emperor of Africa; Sun as President of the Southern Republic. The main difference is that Sun was honest in money matters; . . . .

Stubbs thought that Garvey himself was not a particularly harmful character but his 'followers, being mostly men by no means so well educated as himself or so skilled in the meaning of words', might misinterpret his pronouncements as a call to violence. The governor at this point was undoubtedly confused by Garvey's ability to uncompromisingly champion the cause of the disfranchised Jamaican masses while simultaneously employing the rhetoric of loyalty to the British empire. In any event he proposed amending existing laws specifically to remove any possibility of Garvey being elected to the legislative council. Under his proposals ex-convicts would be debarred from voting (and therefore, under existing legislation, from running for office) regardless of whether the sentence had been served or not. Alternatively, such persons would be ineligible to hold public office for ten years, regardless of where the imprisonment had taken place. (Garvey, of course, had been jailed in the United States on a trumped up charge of mail fraud). Such legislation was deemed necessary because Garvey on the legislative council would be 'bound to take up the position that the negro is being kept out of his rights and a series of speeches to that effect will pre-dispose the lower classes to violent action if, as must be expected, there comes a bad year for crops and they feel the pinch of hard times'.[6] By this time there were ample precedents in the Indies and Africa for laws passed by British administrations specifically to deal with Garvey and Garvey-inspired activities. Among them were Seditious Publications ordinances passed in several West Indian territories in the early 1920s and laws such as the 1924 Undesirable Persons (Prevention of Immigration) Ordi-

nance introduced into Sierra Lerone to forestall Garvey's projected African tour.[7]

On this occasion, however, the Colonial Office officials were uniformly against the idea of special legislation. They agreed that such a stratagem would be tactically unwise and from their arguments it would appear that they were not entirely aware of the existing precedents. One official argued: 'There is no precedent for a disqualification such as that proposed . . . it would be regarded as being 'The Marcus Garvey (disqualification from election) Law' . . . It is extraordinary that a man of Sir R. Stubb's intelligence should not see this'.[8] Another official, E.R. Darnley, argued that 'Legislation ad hoc and obviously if not ostensibly in personam' would be an unpalatable admission of fear on the part of the British administration. He alluded to Garvey in terms unusually favourable for one in his position and reminiscent of Stubb's own observations. Clearly Garvey was able to win the respect of at least some colonialist functionaries, even as they plotted to crush him. Darnley wrote,

I cannot follow the Governor in his indiscriminate condemnation of convicts. The list of them includes Jesus Christ, Bradlaugh, Parnall and innumerable others who will be remembered when Sir Edward Stubbs is forgotten, although, no doubt, they were highly inconvenient to the Government of the day. Imprisonment is the common penalty of the more drastic political and social reformers and other innovators, but if it were not for such innovators we should never have excelled the monkey.

Marcus Garvey specially excluded from the council and provided with a marketable grievance might well be more dangerous than Marcus Garvey on the Council, and if the electors of Jamaica emulated those of the United Kingdom in the case of John Wilkes, the Colonial Government would find itself involved in difficulties mainly attributable to its own unwisdom.

Darnley's condemnation of the Jamaican governor was a little too strong for the Secretary of State at the Colonial Office and he was forced to clarify his statement. 'I am sorry that the Secretary of State should have believed that I meant to show contempt of Sir Edward Stubbs', he explained, 'I have always reckoned him in the first rank of West Indian Governors. My remark was merely intended to indicate that he is not a conspicuous historical character like Parnell or Bradlaugh'.[9]

The Colonial Office eventually turned down Stubb's request, but with regrets. 'I am sorry not to be more helpful', wrote whoever drafted the official reply. 'I wish I could, as I know well what a d_____d nuisance Garvey will be if he gets into the Council'.[10] Yet the local ruling class did not give up the struggle. One year later Garvey reported an attempt, obviously aimed at him, by the legislative council to deprive of citizenship anyone who had ever applied for citizenship elsewhere, even if such foreign citizenship had not actually been obtained. Garvey commented, 'Some people really think that they own the world and that by owning the world they may sell it to their friends'.[11] As late as October 1929, shortly before Garvey's first electoral contest, local newspapers were spreading the rumour that he could not be elected due to his conviction in the United States.[12]

In April 1928 Garvey left Jamaica on a seven month trip which took him to Europe, Canada, (where he was arrested), Bermuda (where he was not allowed to land) and the Bahamas. By this time the prevailing view at the Colonial Office seems to have been one of resignation to an inevitable Garvey victory at the next general elections.[13] But events were to show, again, that the local ruling class and its British allies on the spot were much less inclined to prematurely concede defeat.

Shortly after his return home Garvey announced the formation of a Peoples Political Party. Dismissing as nonsense the frequently expressed opinion that party politics could not work in Jamaica, he argued that the government and its non-elected minions acted like a de facto party in the legislative council, so it was time for elected members to organize in a similar fashion.[14]

Simultaneous with his active entry into Jamaican politics, Garvey advanced three major demands. The first was for black majority rule. On this point his *Blackman* newspaper editorialized:

It is an Axiom that other things being equal
THE MAJORITY MUST RULE
and we shall see that other things are equal.[15]

The second demand flowed from the first and consisted of no less than a call for political independence for Jamaica. The expression used, 'dominion status', was simply the terminology then utilized within the British empire to denote the de facto independence soon to be granted to the 'white' colonies of Canada, Australia, New Zealand and South Africa. It implied, for the white 'dominions', (and for most of the Black and brown British colonies which became independent many years later) a continued ceremonial allegiance to the British crown. Garvey had no problems with this. Hence his expressions of loyalty to the colonial thrust. Besides, it was good tactics. And this anti-colonialism went back at least two decades to his days in the National Club. In 1913, before the formation of the Universal Negro Improvement Association, he was already railing against 'the red-tapists, who pull the strings of colonial conservatism from Downing Street, with a reckless disregard of the interests and wishes of the people'.[16]

The difference between Garvey's pro-empire statements and his anti-colonial actions were well illustrated during the Empire Day celebrations in 1929. He greeted the occasion with a lot of God Save the King rhetoric, which did not prevent him from sharply attacking Governor Stubbs, who, during the Empire Day celebrations at the Ward theatre, had interrupted the speech of a Black Rev. J.T. Hudson. Stubbs ordered Hudson to shut up when he mildly criticized the British empire. Garvey reprinted the whole speech in the *Blackman*.[17] This paper, begun as a daily on March 30, 1929, greatly facilitated Garvey's entry into Jamaican politics.

Garvey's third basic demand was for a West Indian federation, a logical step for one who had long advocated the unity of African peoples and the linking of Third World struggles. In May 1929 the *Blackman* editorialized: 'Federation of the West Indies with Dominion status is the consummation of Negro aspiration in this Archipelago'.[18]

These three basic demands reflected the tendency to long-range planning that had characterized Garvey's North American period. The first phase of this West Indian plan would involve a PPP foothold in the Jamaican legislative council. Phase two would call for the democratization of the political system and majority rule, leading to phase three, dominion status for Jamaica. Phase four would see an independent Jamaica launching an initiative throughout the islands to stimulate their own drives towards majority rule and incorporation within the West Indian federation. This West Indian plan was similar to that which Garvey had earlier intended to put into effect in Africa, using Liberia as a base. It is similar to the Pan-African plan that Kwame Nkrumah, an admirer of Garvey, used with partial success operating out of Ghana nearly three decades later. Garvey's West Indian federation would reach out to embrace the non-English speaking islands. In the UNIA, which had branches throughout the Caribbean area (English, French, Spanish and Dutch speaking), Garvey had a ready made vehicle to push for federation, and he intended to use it for this purpose when the time was ripe.[19]

The PPP received its first opportunity to engage in electoral activity several months before the 1930 general election, its major target. In April 1929 the Rev. Dr. F.G. Veitch, described by the *Blackman* as a PPP candidate, won a legislative council bye-election for the Hanover seat by forty-six votes. His opponent campaigned under the slogan of saving Hanover from Garveyism.[20] A mere two months later the PPP won its second victory, this time at a bye-election for the Kingston and St. Andrew Corporation council's No. 2 Urban Ward. The PPP's John Coleman Beecher led with 238 votes, followed by a Mr. Sheerwood, 107, Cyril B. Wilks, 87, T.A. Gayle, 37, and A. Bain Alves, 37.[21] Beecher's association with Garvey dated back to the National Club, and he, like Garvey, had been influenced by the pioneer black nationalist, Dr. J. Robert Love. He had run for election before but had been badly beaten at the polls.[22] Following his victory Garvey had cause to score his perennial adversaries at the *Gleaner* for commenting that 'Voters of the Class Higher Up Kept Away from the Polling Stations'.[23]

Fresh from these two victories, the Garvey machine rolled on, two months later, to the spectacular Sixth International Convention of the Negro People of the World, held in Kingston throughout the month of August. Of Garvey's status as a world leader there could by this time have been no doubt. However, this convention could not help but bring it home, in a most pertinent way, to all and sundry. Twenty-five thousand people representing 'nearly every Negro organization on earth' were said to have participated in the five mile long parade marking the opening of the convention. Ninety thousand were estimated to have lined the parade route. [24] With this kind of momentum going, and with the general elections less than half a year away, Garvey now loomed as a massive threat to the stability of British colonialism on the island. The British administration therefore reacted swiftly and ruthlessly. In the United States the courts had been a major device for harassing, and finally jailing and deporting Garvey. There he had been arrested and/or harassed for one thing or another during practically all of his international conventions.[25] The British colonialists now set out to emulate their North American co-thinkers, and within six months Garvey would be fined twice and imprisoned once for contempt, sentenced to six months for seditious libel (this conviction was overturned on appeal) and the courts would wrongfully sell the Kingston Liberty Hall.

As a preliminary to judicial harassment the authorities mounted a show of force. At the beginning of the convention extra police were placed in readiness with an extra ten rounds of ammunition each. They were augmented by British troops, the Argyle and Sutherland Highlanders, armed for the occasion with machine guns.[26] The convention had barely begun before the chief justice, Sir Fiennes Barrett Lenard, threatened to jail Garvey forthwith for contempt if he did not produce the books of his organization within half an hour.[27] This was in the case of G.O. Marke vs UNIA where Marke, a former UNIA depute potentate, was suing to satisfy a judgement against the UNIA awarded in New York. Despite the fact that the books of the local UNIA were not technically in Garvey's possession he was summarily fined 25 pounds for contempt. The fine was paid by delegates to the convention.[28] The case itself dragged on for the whole of the convention month. To coincide with the end of the convention the chief justice ordered the Kingston Liberty Hall sold. Many foreign convention delegates were present when it was auctioned for 1,005 pounds.[29] This action was eventually overturned by the supreme court but it was over two years before the UNIA regained its Liberty Hall.[30]

Less than a week after the confiscation of Liberty Hall, the *Blackman* announced that the first PPP meeting for the upcoming general election (now less than five months away) would be held shortly. 'It is to arouse the peasant to the consciousness of his power', the paper editorialized, 'that the Peoples Political Party has come into being'.[31] The meeting took place on September 9, 1929 at Cross Roads in St. Andrews parish, and Garvey delivered a major speech. He recalled his days in the National Club, when 'Men like the late Mr. S.A.G. Cox, Alexander Dixon, Mr. H.A.L. Simpson, Mr. DeLeon and myself fought . . . to break down the power of the plantocracy, and we succeeded, but another class took control of the Council . . .' He announced that the PPP would soon be holding a national convention at Edelweis Park (his headquarters) to let the people nominate fourteen candidates to contest the elections. The convention would also formulate a platform which would have to be endorsed by all fourteen candidates. In the meantime, he presented an interim fourteen point platform which he hoped would be endorsed at the convention. Much of the speech was taken up with presentation of the fourteen points together with his explanations of each point. The points and his explanations can be summarized as follows:

1. A 'larger modicum of self-government for Jamaica'. This could be either through direct Jamaican representation in Parliament at London (as in the French colonies) or dominion status.
2. Protection of native labour.
3. Minimum wage legislation.
4. 'The expansion and improvement of . . . urban areas, without the encumbrances or restraint of private proprietorship'. This was aimed at big landowners who held idle lands adjacent to towns.
5. Land reform. The bulk of the land, he said, was owned by one percent of the population.

He would tax huge landowners and force them to make unused land available to small holders. His uncle, a sharecropper, had been chased off his land on a trumped up charge before harvesting his crops. This kind of thing was still happening. He planned to change all that.

6. The United Fruit Company and other large corporations would be forced to contribute (e.g. hospitals, universities, docks) to the areas where they were extracting their billions.

7. The 'promotion of Native industries', to end unemployment and its reluctant emigration, leading to suffering in such places as Cuba.

8. A university and polytechnic with night courses.

9. 'A National Theatre in Jamaica, where we can encourage Negro arts'.

10. The impeachment of judges who abuse their authority.

11. Legal aid.

12. A law against procuring votes by duress, especially where this involved an abuse of the employer/employee relationship.

13. Granting Montego Bay and Port Antonio 'the Corporate rights of Cities'.

14. Upgrading the Kingston Race Course into a National Park'.[32]

The next step on Garvey's well-organized campaign was to be a ten day tour of all of the country's fourteen parishes. He would take his programme directly to the people and lay the groundwork for the national convention which would select candidates and endorse a platform. Before these plans could be put into effect, however, the colonialists struck again. Just over a month after being fined for contempt, and less than two weeks after the loss of Liberty Hall, Garvey was summoned to court to face new contempt charges. This was on the very first day of his country wide tour. This time the judges claimed to be peeved over 'scurrilous abuse of the Court' and remarks capable of 'inciting disaffection in the minds of the King's Subjects', arising out of Garvey's explanation of point 10 on his draft manifesto.[33] The judges were armed with affidavits by police inspector John Courtenay Knollys and reporter Oscar Joseph Durant, both present at the PPP's first election meeting.[34] Garvey's alleged contempt was contained in the following remarks:

A law to impeach and imprison such judges who enter into agreements and arrangements with lawyers and other persons of influence to deprive other subjects in the realm of their rights in such Courts of Law over which they may preside; forcing the innocent parties to incur the additional costs of appeals and other legal expenses which would not have been but for the injustice occasioned by the illicit arrangements of such judges with their friends.

Now, this is an evil that Jamaica has suffered from for a long time, and we have not been able to tackle it. The time has come now for us to bring changes, and if we cannot settle it in Jamaica, we are going to settle it in England. We are not going to have judges here who can meet their friends and others in their club houses and connive and conspire to take away an innocent man's property or his rights simply because they want to satisfy their friends . . . There is no man who is above the law, and if a judge breaks the law he can be dealt with as any other man who violates the law.

. . . the rich man sits beside the judge and the poor man cannot get his rights.[35]

At the contempt trial the supreme court asked for and received a written apology from Garvey, even though he insisted that his statement was not aimed specifically at this court. The three judge panel, with one dissenting, then imposed a sentence of three months in jail and a hundred pound fine, and admonished him for being a 'hot headed and foolish man'. The dissenting judge favoured a heavier fine and no jail.[36] The wrath of the judges was so great that they transgressed one of the rules of colonial etiquette and fined Garvey's white lawyer, Lewis Ashenheim, 300 pounds on two charges of contempt. He was ordered to pay the costs of a third charge. His offence had been to caution against meddling with UNIA property.[37] Representatives of the legal profession approached the chief justice at the exclusive white club where he was wont to hang out, in a vain attempt to stay his action against Ashenheim. He threatened to cite the delegation for contempt too.[38]

Garvey's trial and imprisonment took care of three and a half of the four and a half months remaining to the election campaign. The fine meant a further depletion of campaign funds. But these types of trials and tribulations were nothing new to Garvey, who had been subjected to all manner of harassments and who had been jailed twice during his stay in the United States, not to mention jailed (it is thought) in Costa Rica, arrested in Canada and barred from entering several areas. Once again he manifested that indomitable spirit that had kept him steadfast on his program of racial emancipation through all vicissitudes. On the same day that he was sentenced to jail for contempt, he announced that he would run for the vacant seat in the No. 3 urban ward of the Kingston and St. Andrew Corporation council. The campaign would be handled by the PPP's Councillor John Coleman Beecher.[39] He would thus be running for both municipal and national office at the same time, and from jail.

A few days after entering jail Garvey was officially nominated for the KSAC seat at a PPP conclave attended by 5,000.[40] A month later he was elected. *Blackman* headlines summed up the situation thus: 'Marcus Garvey, Negro Leader, Now Prisoner, Is Elected To Represent No. 3 Urban Ward In Corporation Council — An Event Without Precedent In The Political History of The World!'. The voting was Garvey, 321 votes and F.W. Bailey, 102 votes.[41]

Almost two months still remained before Garvey's release from jail, however. And as the day drew near, the exact date of his release became a matter for new maneuvering on the part of the British administration. No matter was too small to escape attention if it involved the possibility of harassing Garvey. An unsigned secret memo from the governor's residence to the Colonial Office tells his story:

[Garvey] was due to come out of prison on the 24th December but we learnt that his release on Christmas Eve would mean that he would be hailed as a 'Black Messiah' and a monster procession from the goal at Spanish Town to Kingston a distance of 12 miles, with bands and all the rest of it, was being organized. That, of course, would not have done at all, so with a secrecy which was highly applauded throughout the Island, Mr. Garvey was released about three or four days before the proper time. He was shown the door of the prison at a moment's notice and found his own way back to Kingston. I think he came back in a Police car which we sent out to assist him![42]

Upon his release Garvey took his oath of office on the KSAC council and was able to attend a few meetings before the powers that be (this time with the local ruling class taking the initiative) struck again. His seat was declared vacant since he had missed three consecutive meetings while in jail, and this though his application from jail for leave of absence had been refused. The council was dominated by the class that Garvey opposed and, buttressed by the opinion of their counsel, Norman Washington Manley, they had their way.[43] At this point the legislative council elections were less than three weeks away.

Simultaneous with these problems on the KSAC council, Garvey was trying his best to pick up the pieces of his election campaign. Within days of his release he resumed his tour of the parishes, cut short by the judges three months earlier. He also opened election headquarters at 107 Water Lane.[44] Then came a revised twenty-six point manifesto, consisting of the earlier fourteen points plus an additional twelve. The new points can be summarized as follows:

1. Workmen's compensation.

2. At least sixty per cent of local labour to be employed on 'all industrial, agricultural and commercial activities. . . .'.
3. An eight-hour working day.
4. Free secondary and night school education in each parish.
5. A public library in each parish.
6. The appointment of official court stenographers.
7. A government loan of at least three million pounds to develop Crown lands and thereby create 'employment for our surplus unemployed population, and to find employment for stranded Jamaicans abroad;' also to purchase ships to facilitate the marketing of local produce.
8. The expansion of electrification 'to such growing and prospering centres as are necessary'.
9. Prison reform.
10. Health outreach programmes for rural areas.
11. Decent low priced housing for the peasantry.
12. An end to profiteering 'by heartless land sharks' 'in urban and suburban areas to the detriment of expansion of healthy home life for citizens of moderate means'.

Garvey's manifesto was progressive by any standard. At least twelve of the twenty-six planks spoke directly to the immediate needs of workers and peasants. Another eight planks spoke to areas of broad social concern (free education, libraries, etc.), designed to raise the educational and cultural levels of the broad mass of Jamaicans. The oppressed classes obviously stood to benefit most from these. At least four planks directly sought to curb the power of multi-national corporations, landowners and the local capitalist class. In addition most of the twenty-six provisions could only succeed at their expense. The provisions for self-government and the impeachment of judges were of course direct challenges to British colonialism.

The crowd which was on hand to hear Garvey present his twenty-six points cheered repeatedly. Cheering was reportedly loud and long for the planks dealing with the minimum wage, eight-hour day, free secondary education, legal aid, an end to procuring votes by duress, the government loan to increase employment, the National Park for Kingston, cheap housing for the peasantry, and a move against the land sharks. Cheering was 'almost deafening' for the planks calling for workmen's compensation and a minimum of 60% local labour in all areas of employment.[45]

The coincidence of class and colour in Jamaica became a focal point of Garvey's campaign, since his main opponent for the St. Andrew seat which he contested was both white and mayor of Kingston up to two weeks before the election, making him an important member of the class that had harassed Garvey, both in and out of the KSAC council. In his campaign speeches Garvey therefore harped on the principle of race first, as a means of countering the historic injustices heaped upon black people by the white race. 'When you look at [Seymour's] face and lanky, overbearing personality', Garvey declared, 'you see there the brutal slave master. . .'. He could not understand why, in 1930, 'such men have the audacity to come to you and ask you — you the sons of the slaves whom they treated like brutes . . . to allow them . . . to exploit you'. The question of white rulers over black people naturally struck at the heart of Garvey's demand for black majority rule. He noted that 'The Legislative council for several terms past [was] made up chiefly of men of Seymour's race. . .'[46] The Council, during the term before the one that has just come to an end, was made up of men purely of his race'. The task facing voters was clear: 'There must not be one white man on the elected side of the House in January. We have white men on the official and nominated side. But the side which the people elects must be represented by themselves'.[47]

A few days before the election Garvey came up with a slate of twelve candidates whom he supported. Among them, perhaps surprisingly, was a Mr. R. Ehrenstein, a white man contesting the St. Thomas seat. This was not the first time that Garvey supported a white person he considered a renegade from his own race.[48]

To add to his imprisonment, the loss of his KSAC council seat, and all his other myriad problems during the campaign, Garvey also had to deal with sundry other election malpractices engineered by his opponents. He complained that people were telling taxpayers in Mavis Bank and Guava Ridge in St. Andrew that taxes were going up because of him. At a mass meeting a few days before the election he protested that Herbert George DeLisser, editor of the *Gleaner*, and D.T. Wint, a black political opponent, were suggesting that he now had black Jamaicans in a state of disorder similar to the 1865 Morant Bay uprising. For some days prior to the elections rumours were circulating that Garvey had been arrested and jailed again.[49] And to crown this incredibly relentless campaign of pressure, the judges struck again in the last days of the campaign, this time charging him with seditious libel.[50]

The elections were held on January 29, 1930, and Garvey lost. The results in St. Andrew were Seymour — 1,677, Garvey — 915 and Dillon (Black) — 269.[51] One of the governor's aides wrote, in a secret memo:

Garvey lives in the parish of St. Andrew a select residential area, where is also King's House, and he appeared as a candidate for the parish against a very well-known landowner, the sitting member who had recently been Mayor of Kingston . . . Garvey's people . . . were responsible for rowdyism and attempts to break up meetings. But the result was that all the decent people in St. Andrew rallied to the support of the sitting member — many bedridden old ladies going down to record their votes for him — and Garvey was very heavily defeated.[52]

Garvey's initial response to the loss was to angrily blame the voters for having sold themselves for a mess of pottage. He could not afford to spend on rum and transportation to the polls like the other candidates, he said. He had based his campaign solely on his programme.[53] There were factors militating against Garvey, however, which were beyond his control. A *Blackman* editorial addressed itself to these:

In Jamaica there is no universal suffrage. The bulk of the population is Negroes, with a very small proportion of them enjoying the franchise. According to the last census, there are 900,000 people in the island, of which 700,000 are Negroes. We will be very near correct in saying that of the 900,000 population only about 112,000 are registered . . . The supporters of the Universal Negro Improvement Association, we are told, are the voteless unit, and that being so, a paltry eighty or ninety thousand Negroes voting at a general election (although they did not all vote for the successful candidates), is no evidence whatsoever that [Garveyism] is on the wane.[54]

As for Garvey himself, his disappointment at his election reverse did not last very long. He bounced back with his accustomed resiliency and was soon explaining that this was only a retreat, not a defeat. The PPP had fared better, despite everything than the British Labour Party on its first election bid. And his paper noted, correctly, that reform is, in general, in advance of its time '. . . yet, such movements eventually succeed. Not today, not tomorrow, perhaps, but eventually. And the leaders of such movements are acclaimed, their country prospers and their names go down in succeeding generations'.[55]

In this post-election period Garvey also defended two of the major charges brought against him by the Jamaican ruling class. The first was the charge of racism. On this the *Blackman* editorialized: 'It is unfortunate that in this country the proletariat or common people belong to a group that is ethnologically described as Negroes, and when one stands up for their economical, social or industrial advancement, the cry goes up that racial antagonism and colour prejudice are being disseminated among the people.'[56] The other charge was that his manifesto was socialistic. On this Garvey retorted: 'The United Fruit Company makes millions of dollars every year through the banana industry. Why could not your government do the same? You would say that would be socialistic. Is it not social-istic for the government to run the Railway?' He continued, 'If the government can plant bananas on the Prison Farm and sell to the United Fruit Company, the government can plant bananas on a larger scale throughout the country and thus find employment for the people of the country'.[57] Gov-ernor Stubbs thought Garvey's proposals to be so 'grotesque' that they 'could not bear even looking into, still less encouraging'.[58]

Such election post mortems did not have Garv-ey's undivided attention, however, for the seditous libel case, initiated before the election was tried shortly thereafter from February 12 to 21, 1930. The judges based their case on a *Blackman* editor-ial entitled 'The Vagabonds Again', which took the KSAC council to task for refusing to hear a lawyer whom the burgesses of Garvey's No. 3 ward had retained, at their own expense, to fight the council's determination to unseat Garvey. The editorial further suggested that the council, a 'group of vagabonds', was campaigning for Mayor Seymour, and that as a result of their actions con-fidence in government was being 'sorely tried'.[59]

Charged along with Garvey were the PPP's John Coleman Beecher, business editor of the *Black-man*, and Theophilus Augustus Aikman, literary editor of the paper and national secretary of the PPP. (Garvey's official position in the PPP was chairman). The presiding judge was A.K. Agar, Kingston resident magistrate. He refused the defendants a jury trial.[60] Although the editorial had actually been written by Aikman, Garvey received the longest sentence. Indeed so carried away was the judge by his hatred for Garvey that he sen-tenced him to six months' hard labour. He had to be reminded by the crown solicitor that hard labour could not legally be imposed for such an offense. Aikman was sentenced to three months and Bee-cher, who had nothing to do with editorial matters, was acquitted. Garvey and Aikman appealed suc-cessfully.

Garvey wrote both Governor Stubbs and Phillip Snowdon, the British chancellor of the exchequer with whom he had corresponded while in England, setting forth his objections to these libel proceed-ings and other harassments. His imprisonment for contempt, he wrote, was a 'political dodge'. He had learned in advance of the chief justice's intention to convict him from the chief justice's chauffeur, a UNIA member. (The chief justice, according to Garvey, ordered the chauffeur to stop attending UNIA meetings). As for the libel case, Garvey argued that the judge used the courtroom to direct propaganda against UNIA members. The whole thing he saw as a 'conspiracy' to prevent him from representing 'the interest of the poor working and

labouring classes and give them a voice that may probably help them to improve and better their conditions'.[61]

The libel charge was designed to do several things — first it was a 'dirty trick' timed to do maximum harm to Garvey's campaign for the leg-islative council; second, it was part of the general campaign to tie up as much of Garvey's time and money as possible in court cases; third, if success-fully prosecuted it would have put Garvey behind bars again for six months; and fourthly, if Garvey went to jail he would once more have lost his seat on the KSAC council.

On the same day that the libel case began the *Blackman* announced that Garvey had decided to enter the bye-election for his former KSAC council seat. The two other candidates, Cyril B. Wilks and E.A. Walters, therefore withdrew and Garvey was returned unopposed.[62] This was a mere two weeks after the legislative council elections. The swearing in ceremony took place a few days after the end of the trial and was marked by anti-Garvey filibuster-ing and much general harassment. Garvey was warned that he was not qualified to sit on the coun-cil and much was made of the libel conviction.[63] He nevertheless could not be stopped this time, so in September 1930 the colonialists dissolved the whole council for a year using as a pretext an investigation into corruption on the part of some other councillors. Garvey and the PPP held protest meetings and the *Blackman*, none daunted by the recent libel proceedings, decided that the time for self-government had come, since the forcible dis-solution of the council was 'a most despotic act'.[64]

Garvey was re-elected to be a reconstituted council in 1931 while away in Europe and served until late 1934 when he declined to seek further re-election due to his impending relocation to Eng-land.[65] During this period he welcomed the for-mation of the Kingston Civic Voters League,[66] gave some qualified support to former members of the British West Indies Regiment who were demanding the vote,[67] and continued to make favourable utterances on the subject of socialism.[68]

Garvey's last few years in England (where he died in 1940) coincided with the workers' struggles in Jamaica which ushered into existence the Peo-ples National Party (PNP) and the Jamaican Labour Party (JLP), the two parties that have dom-inated Jamaican political life ever since. The strikes and riots met with his approval, as did the appointment of a British royal commission into the matter. He disapproved, however, of the appoint-ment of his old adversary, Sir Reginald E. Stubbs, as chairman, while welcoming the inclusion of the Labour Party's Sir Walter Citrine.[69] Eight years earlier, during Stubbs' administration, Garvey had called for a royal commission to investigate his persecution.[70] He submitted a memorandum to the 1938 commission.[71]

With Norman Washington Manley, who later emerged as head of the PNP, Garvey had had some unusual contact. For Manley, a prominent lawyer during the life of Garvey's PPP, became something of a fixture in legal proceedings against Garvey and the UNIA. In 1929 he appeared for the applicants in the case of *Bourne vs. UNIA*.[72] When Garvey was unseated by the KSAC council in 1930 it was partly on the opinion of Manley, who was retained by the council in that matter.[73] Later that year Manley represented the plaintiff, Mrs. Barnes Haylett, in a libel suit against Garvey and the *Blackman*. She was warded thirty pounds on a claim for a thousand pounds. Garvey defended himself.[74] Yet Garvey approvingly called him 'our popular barrister' and 'a first rate man' when Manley became a king's council in 1932.[75] Garvey's Edelweis Park headquarters in 1939 became PNP headquarters.[76] In August 1941 a PNP meeting chaired by N.N. Nethersole stood in silence for a few minutes as a mark of respect for the fallen hero.[77] In 1938 Garvey welcomed the entry of the JLP's Alexander Bustamante into politics.[78]

As in the case of his activities in North America Garvey's political struggles in Jamaica were both a failure and a success. He can be said to have failed in so far as he was thwarted in his bid to consolidate his party and move towards black majority rule, self-government and West Indian federation. But this is to take a very narrow view. He successfully demonstrated that political parties could work in Jamaica and in the process indoctrinated and politicized the workers and peasants on a scale probably more massive than they had experienced before. The hundreds and thousands who followed Garvey and attended his meetings were well-represented among the rioters and strikers of the late 1930s. In a way the leaders who emerged from these later struggles were more fortunate than Garvey. For one thing, they could build on foundations already laid by him. And people like Bustamante and Manley were able to reap the benefits of widespread and violent challenges to British colonialism. Garvey often cautioned his followers, at least in public, to be 'constitutional', but there is no telling what may have happened if he had been fortunate enough to walk into a ready made situation of mass unrest, such as was the case in 1938. The fact that the post-Garvey violence was Pan-Caribbean in nature and came at a time when British imperialism was about to be severely weakened as a result of World War II, are also objective advantages that Garvey could certainly have used.

S.J. Garrick, a JLP organizer, was correct when he observed in 1941 that 'if there wasn't a UNIA there could be no PNP or JLP. . .'[79]

Notes

1. *Daily Gleaner*, June 2, 1921, p. 6, quoted in Adolph Edwards, *Marcus Garvey* (London: New Beacon, 1967), p. 15.
2. *Negro World*, September 1, 1923, p. 4.
3. Minute, July 28, 1921, CO 318/364, Colonial Office records Public Record Office, London. On Garvey's 1921 efforts to re-enter the U.S. see Martin, *Race First*, pp. 184–187.
4. Destroyed file, March 31, 1926, register of correspondence for the West Indies, 1926, OAG/8674, Colonial Office records; ibid., destroyed file May 6, 1926, FO/8674.
5. Lenford Sylvester Nembhard, *Trials and Triumphs of Marcus Garvey* (Kingston: The Gleaner Co., Ltd., 1940), pp. 116–117.
6. Governor R. E. Stubbs to [Sir S.] Wilson, Colonial Office, February 24, 1928, CO 318/391/56634.
7. Martin, *Race First*, pp. 94–96, 115.
8. Minute by R. R. Sedgwick[?]. March 12, 1928, CO 318/391/56634. Of course he could have been correct if he meant that despite general precedents of special laws against Garvey, there was no precedent for the specific facts of this case, namely denying a person the right to run for office. Se also, ibid., minutes by S. H.[E?], March 15, 1928, J. S. R., March 15, 1928, and G. G. March 16, 1928.
9. Minutes by E. R. Darnley, March 13, 30, 1928, CO 318/391/56634.
10. Draft of reply from Colonial Office to Sir R. E. Stubbs, March 27, 1928, ibid.
11. *Blackman*, April 18, 1929, p. 7. Garvey had taken out his first citizenship papers in the United States.
12. *Blackman*, October 14, 1929, p. 7, quoting the *Jamaican Mail* of October 8 and the *Gleaner* of October 9, 1929.
13. Draft of Colonial Office to Lord Snowdon, June 14, 1928, CO 318/391/56634.
14. *Blackman*, April 12, 1929, p. 3.
15. Ibid., April 16, 1929, p. 2.
16. Marcus Garvey, 'The British West Indies in the Mirror of Truth', *Africa Times* and *Orient Review*, October 1913, p. 159.
17. *Blackman*, May 28, 1929, p. 2, May 28, 1929, p. 1.
18. Ibid., May 2, 1929, p. 2. See also ibid., May 16, 1929, p. 2, *New Jamaican*, September 9, 1932, pp. 1, 5.
19. Amy Jacques Garvey, *Garvey and Garveyism* (Kingston: A. J. Garvey, 1963), p. 204; Nembhard, *Trials and Triumphs*, p. 92. For Garvey's Liberian plan see Martin, *Race First*, pp. 122–137; for a list of UNIA branches in the West Indies (and the world) see ibid., pp. 15, 16, 359–73.
20. *Blackman*, April 25, 1929, p. 1, April 26, 1929, p. 7.
21. Ibid., June 27, 1929, p. 1.
22. Ibid., June 4, 1929, pp. 1, 7, November 6, 1929, p. 2.
23. Ibid., June 28, 1929, p. 1. He called the *Gleaner* 'the unofficial Government of Jamaica' — ibid., July 8, 1929, p. 1.
24. *Negro World*, August 10, 1929, p. 1; *Blackman*, August 2, 1929, p. 1.
25. Martin, *Race First*, p. 187.
26. *Blackman*, August 5, 1929, p. 1.
27. Ibid., p. 4.
28. Ibid., August 8, 1929, p. 1, August 13, 1929, p. 5. For more on this case see Garvey, *Garvey and Garveyism*, pp. 193–94.

29. *Blackman*, September 4, 1929, p. 7.
30. Ibid., August 30, 1930, p. 2; December 13, 1930, p. 5; October 24, 1931, p. 8.
31. Ibid., September 7, 1929, p. 4.
32. Garvey, *Garvey and Garveyism*, p. 196, lists the fourteen points. The embellishments can be found in *Blackman*, September 11, 1929, p. 7, September 12, 1929, pp. 1, 7.
33. *Blackman*, September 13, 1929, p. 1.
34. Ibid., September 14, 1929, p. 3.
35. Ibid., September 12, 1929, p. 7.
36. Ibid., September 26, 1929, p. 7, September 27, 1929, p. 1. The judges were Chief Justice Sir Fiennes Barrett Lennard, Mr. Justice C. E. Law, and Mr. Justice Adrian Clark, dissenting.
37. Ibid., October 1, 1929, p. 1, September 14, 1929, p. 4.
38. Interview with Mrs. Amy Jacques Garvey, Kingston, March 6, 1972.
39. *Blackman*, September 27, 1929, p. 1.
40. Ibid., October 1, 1929.
41. Ibid., October 31, 1929, p. 1.
42. Secret unsigned memo from King's House, Kingston, June 30, 1930, CO 318/399/76634. See also *Blackman*, December 20, 1929, p. 1.
43. *Blackman*, December 31, 1929, p. 1, January 6, 1930, pp. 1, 7, January 14, 1930, pp. 1, 7, January 13, 1930, pp. 1, 2; Garvey to Rt. Hon. Phillip Snowdon, Chancellor of the Exchequer, February 27, 1930, CO 318/399/76634.
44. *Blackman*, December 20, 1929, p. 1, December 24, 1929, p. 7.
45. Ibid., January 2, 1930, p. 8. The twenty-six points are at ibid., p. 2. They are reproduced in Amy Jacques Garvey, 'Political Activities of Marcus Garvey in Jamaica', op. cit.
46. *Blackman*, January 8, 1930, p. 1.
47. Ibid., December 28, 1929, p. 14.
48. Ibid., January 25, 1930, p. 1, January 23, 1930, p. 1. Ehrenstein's platform was similar to Garvey's and his manifesto appeared several times in the *Blackman*. It is not clear whether all twelve persons on Garvey's slate were actually PPP members. For other examples of Garvey's occasional support of renegade whites see Martin, *Race First*, pp. 31, 233.
49. *Blackman*, September 10, 1929, p. 1; ibid., January 25, 1930, p. 13, Garvey to Sir Reginald E. Stubbs, February 7, 1930, CO 318/399/76634; *Blackman*, January 28, 1930, p. 1.
50. Garvey to Rt. Hon. Phillip Snowdon, February 27, 1930, CO 318/399/76634.
51. *Blackman*, January 31, 1930, p. 1.
52. Unsigned secret memo from King's House, Kingston, June 30, 1930, CO 318/399/76634.
53. *Blackman*, February 1, 1930, p 1.
54. Ibid., February 4, 1920, p. 2.
55. Ibid., February 15, 1930, p. 12, February 2, 1930, p. 2.
56. Ibid., February 12, 1920, p. 2.
57. Ibid., March 29, 1930, p. 13.
58. Unsigned secret memo from King's House, Kingston, June 30, 1930, CO 318/399/76634. According to the memo, Garvey 'saw Sir Edward Stubbs two or three months ago' to put forward his proposals.
59. *Blackman*, January 14, 1930, p. 2.
60. Ibid., February 13, 1930, p. 1.
61. Garvey to H. E. Sir Reginald Edward Stubbs, governor of Jamaica, February 21, February 22, 1930, CO 318/399/

76634; ibid, Garvey to Rt. Hon. Phillip Snowdon, Chancellor of the Exchequer, February 27, 1930. In this correspondence Garvey expressed a desire to appeal the libel case all the way to the privy council, if necessary. Somebody at the Colonial Office commented (on the libel case) that though Garvey was 'a danger to good order' he should not be subjected to such blatant persecution — minute, June 30, 1930, CO 318/399/76634.
62. *Blackman*, February 12, 1930, p. 1.
63. Ibid., February 24, 1930, p. 1, February 26, 1930, p. 7.
64. Ibid., August 30, 1930, p. 4, September 13, 1930, p. 1, September 27, 1930, p. 1, September 27, 1930, p. 1, November 29, 1930, p. 4.
65. *Ethiopian World*, May 26, 1934. According to this report Garvey would not be contesting the November elections because he would be departing for England where he planned to become a Labour Party member of parliament for West Kensington.
66. *New Jamaican*, January 16, 1933, p. 1. The League was formed by a Mr. Vivian Durham and others.
67. Ibid., January 13, 1933, p. 1.
68. Ibid., October 12, 1932, p. 1, November 1, 1932, p. 2, November 23, 1932, p. 2. Included here are statements by Garvey as well as editorials in his newspaper. For a discussion of the complete relationship between Garvey, communists and communism, and working class struggles in Jamaica and elsewhere, see Martin, *Race First*, pp. 221–272.
69. *Black Man* (magazine, not to be confused with the *Blackman* newspaper), III, 10 July 1938, pp. 5–7, III, 11 November 1938, p. 19.
70. Garvey to Rt. Hon. Phillip Snowdon, February 27, 1930, CO 318/399/76634. Garvey thanked the Colonial Office for acceding to his request, but they expressed puzzlement since no royal commission was being contemplated at that time — *Blackman*, August 23, 1930, p. 1; Garvey to Secretary of State, Colonial Office, via the Officer Administering the Government, Jamaica, September 4, 1930, CO 318/399/76634; ibid., Secretary of State, Lord Passfield to OAG, Jamaica, September 18, 1930. In January 1930 Garvey and nine others had presented a petition 'On behalf of the Labourers of Jamaica' to a visiting West Indian Sugar Commission, led by Lord Oliver — *Blackman*, January 11, 1930, p. 2.
71. Garvey, Memorandum to West India Royal Commission, September 24, 1938, CO 950/44. The memorandum traced the history of Black West Indians after emancipation — the importation of foreign labour to depress wages, the consequent migrations to Panama, Cuba, etc. in search of work, the usurpation of commercial activity by Chinese, Syrians, etc. It also dealt with the race/class question in the islands and the persecution of popular black leaders.
72. *Blackman*, October 25, 1929, p. 1. Manley was instructed here by J. H. Cargill. Mr. N. N. Ashenheim appeared for the respondents.
73. Ibid., January 14, 1930, pp. 1 and 7.
74. Ibid., November 1, 1930, p. 10.
75. *New Jamaican*, September 19, 1932, p. 5.
76. R. N. Murray, ed., *J. J. Mills — His Own Account of His Life and Times* (Kingston: Collins and Sangster, 1969), pp. 110–111.
77. *National Negro Voice*, August 23, 1941, p. 8.
78. *Black Man*, July 1938, p. 6.
79. *National Negro Voice*, August 30, 1941, p. 5.

The Labour Rebellions of the 1930s

Richard Hart

What appeared on the surface was a picture of general working class subservience and docility. Surveying the scene, colonial officials, representatives of the big foreign owned enterprises and the local employers and upper middle classes generally felt confident and secure. Those who interpreted the situation differently, like the visiting professor W.M. Macmillan, whose book *Warning from the West Indies*[1] was first published in Britain in February 1936, were dismissed as alarmists or troublemakers. Sullen resentment and dissatisfaction were, nevertheless, swelling among the working people and the unemployed in all the British colonies of the Caribbean area. By the middle years of the decade the situation was like a cauldron of liquid coming to the boil, with isolated early warnings here and there disturbing the apparently placid surface.

The earliest warnings came from Trinidad where there was a small demonstration of unemployed workers in Port of Spain in 1933. In the following year came a larger demonstration of some 400–500 unemployed workers which led to the appointment by the legislature of a committee of enquiry.[2] Earlier that same year there had been spontaneous strikes and demonstrations of short duration on several Trinidad sugar plantations. Other early warnings came in 1935, from Guyana where there were strikes and disturbances on several sugar plantations,[3] and from Jamaica where there were strikes of port workers in several out-port towns and among banana loaders on Kingston wharves.[4]

From 1935 onwards a wave of militant working-class protest began to swell across the Caribbean area, as major social upheavals occurred in one British colony after another. The first of these explosions took place on the island of St. Kitts, an island entirely devoted to the production of sugar. Though an organization called the Workers' League had been formed there in 1932, it was still legally impossible for it to act as a trade union. The social upheaval which occurred three years later was spontaneous and unorganized.

The trouble began on 28 January 1935 when cane cutters refused to permit the reaping of the new crop to start at Shadwell plantation, on the outskirts of the capital Basseterre. The employers had offered work at 8 pence (16 cents) per ton, the rate which cane cutters had been forced to accept under protest in the previous year. This the workers now refused to agree to and the news of their refusal spread quickly to the adjoining plantations. Workers at the island's sugar factory also came out on strike, demanding a wage increase. Their wages had actually been reduced by one penny in the shilling in 1930 and subsequently by a further penny.

Workers on other plantations also refused to start the crop. At Lodge estate the owner-manager threatened the workers with a gun but when, instead of submitting or running away as expected, they disarmed him and broke the gun in two, they found that it was not loaded. This fact appears to have saved him from being harmed. At Estbridge estate, however, a party of armed police succeeded in arresting some of the strikers.

A new spirit of determination now spread throughout the length and breadth of the island as groups of workers went from plantation to plantation calling for a general strike. On Tuesday, 29 January, the workers everywhere were in a militant mood. Processions of workers were moving around the island on foot and no work was allowed to start. That afternoon, at Buckley's plantation, two to three hundred strikers, carrying sticks, entered the estate yard. Armed with guns, the manager and the overseer ordered the workers to leave but they were in no mood for retreat. Stones were thrown and the manager, either before or after the stone throwing fired into the crowd injuring three or four workers.

An armed party of police arrived under a former British army major, but the workers refused to obey his order to disperse and instead, demanded that the manager be arrested. At about 6:00 p.m. a contingent from the local military force arrived, by which time the crowd had increased to four to five hundred. The Riot Act was read and when this had no effect the armed men fired into the crowd. John Allen and James Archibald, both labourers, and Josephs Samuel, a factory watchman, were killed and eight others were wounded. According to the official report, fifty-five shots were fired. The report alleged that stones had been thrown at the armed forces.

Next day a British warship arrived and marines were landed. For several weeks thereafter unarmed workers were terrorized and intimidated by the police and soldiers. Thirty-nine workers were arrested and sentences of imprisonment ranging from two to five years were imposed on six of them.[5] Thus was the militant upsurge contained for the time being. But the fact that the workers on such a small island, so vulnerable to economic pressures from their employers, should have dared to offer a militant challenge to the plantocracy and the colonial government, was of tremendous significance. A new spirit or working class determination was now in evidence.

The events in St. Kitts signalled the start of the third upsurge of working class protest and organizational activity in the British colonies of the Caribbean area. Later that same year there was an eruption in St. Vincent, though the spark which ignited the social conflagration there was not primarily a strike. The riot that occurred in St. Vincent represented a protest against rising retail prices, including prices of articles of popular consumption, occasioned by the imposition of increased customs duties. These had been introduced in a situation of static and extremely low wages, threatening a further reduction in an already desperately low standard of living.

St. Vincent shared a colonial governor with the other Windward Islands. In October the Governor arrived to attend a meeting of the Legislative Council which at that time consisted of a majority of colonial officials and persons nominated by the Governor who represented the principal business and financial interests, and a minority of members elected on a franchise restricted by property and income qualifications to about 10% of the adult population. On 15 October the Governor, in a move designed to increase government revenues at the expense of the ordinary consumers, introduced his new taxation proposals. It was also proposed to maintain the high local tariff on sugar which had previously been imposed to assist the sugar producers at the consumers' expense. The legislature was scheduled to meet again on 21 October to approve the Governor's proposals and, during the intervening week, there was mounting popular opposition as more and more people realized that there would be an appreciable increase in the cost of living.

On the morning of 21 October, an angry crowd of workers gathered in the capital, Kingstown, at the chemist's shop of George McIntosh, a popular member of the Town Council. They wanted him to present their grievances to the Governor.[6] It is doubtful whether there was any clear consensus as to what their demands should be, withdrawal of the proposed tax increases and sugar tariff or increased wages to meet the increased cost of living or perhaps both. But McIntosh is alleged to have stressed that to avoid oppression the people had to fight for their rights.[7] He wrote an urgent letter to the Governor, seeking an interview on the people's behalf, which he then took to the building where the Legislative Council was in session. At about mid-day, while McIntosh was seated in the public gallery of the Council awaiting a response from the Governor to whom his letter had been handed, a large crowd armed with sticks, stones, cutlasses and other implements, assembled in front of the building.

McIntosh emerged from the building to say that the Governor had replied that he would be willing to receive a delegation later that afternoon at 5:00 p.m. This immediately aroused suspicions that the Governor was only buying time and intended to leave the island before that hour. The demonstration became increasingly militant and some workers forced their way into the building.[8] Among the remarks shouted the following were heard: 'We can't stand any more duties on food or clothing'; 'We have no work . . .'; 'We are hungry'; 'Something will happen in this town today if we are not satisfied'. Such was the alarm created that the Governor adjourned the session of the legislature.[9]

As the Governor and other officials emerged from the chamber and the former tried to restore calm, several incidents occurred. The Attorney General, who had drafted the taxation measures, was cuffed by a man who claimed that he had kicked him. The Governor was pushed and struck and is alleged to have received several cuts. Some of the Court House windows were smashed and the motor cars of several officials were destroyed or damaged. A crowd broke into the prison and released the ten prisoners there. The business premises of F.A. Corea, a member of the Legislative Council who was also the island's largest merchant and plantation owner, were ransacked.

The tables were turned when a large force of armed policemen arrived and the Governor personally took command of their operations. The Riot Act was read and the crowd at Corea's store was fired on. One person was killed and several others injured. Meanwhile the riot had spread beyond the city to Georgetown, twenty-one miles to the south, and Chateaubelair the same distance to the north. All telephone wires were cut and several bridges were destroyed. Armed police and 'volunteers' were posted to guard the cable and wireless station and the electricity plant.

At midnight on 21 October a British warship arrived. Military personnel known as 'Volunteers' were also brought in from other islands. On 22 October a state of emergency was proclaimed. Though the uprising was suppressed in the capital by the end of the first day, disorders in the rural areas continued for the next two days. Many plantation workers were involved. The police met particularly strong resistance at Byera's Hill, Campden Park and Stubbs. In these areas demands were made for land, for better wages and for better living conditions. Such was the level of unrest that the state of emergency was maintained for three weeks.[10]

In Kingstown the working-class leader who had emerged from the spontaneous uprising to play the principal agitational role in the demonstrations was Sheriff Lewis, previously known as Pablo but later nick-named 'Selassie' because of his advocacy of the cause of Ethiopia at the time of the Italian invasion of that country. Also mentioned as playing a leading role was a woman named Bertha Mutt, nick-named 'Mother Selassie'.[11] But the lime-light soon shifted to McIntosh who, despite his attempts to encourage 'law and order', was arrested on a charge of treason felony on 23 November. The weakness of the charge against McIntosh was revealed in the case presented against him at the preliminary examination before a stipendiary magistrate which lasted for five days. The magistrate, in dismissing the case, commented that all except one of the many witnesses called by the prosecution had given evidence which established the absence of guilt of the accused.[12] The effect of the prosecution was that McIntosh emerged as unchallengeably the most popular leader of the working class.

At the end of 1935 there was a strike of coal loaders in the neighbouring island of St. Lucia. With recent events in St. Kitts and St. Vincent very much in mind the Governor mobilized the local military force and called upon the British government for reinforcements. A warship was quickly on the scene and marines patrolled the streets of Castries while for several nights the ship's searchlights played upon the city. The show of force was extended also to the rural areas. Faced with this massive intimidation the workers returned to work to await the report of an official commission of inquiry set up to consider their demands. The commission, however, felt sufficiently secure to reject the workers' claim for increased pay.[13]

These events in the Leeward and Windward islands were followed by a social upheaval in the island of Barbados. Clement Payne, who could be described as the person responsible for the disturbance which occurred there in 1937, had been born

to Barbadian parents resident at the time of his birth in Trinidad. His parents had returned to their native land when their son was only four years old and it is doubtful whether he had ever become aware that he had not been born in Barbados. In later years he himself had migrated to Trinidad where his political awareness was no doubt aroused. He later claimed to have been an associate of Uriah Butler, the charismatic Grenadian who in the 1930s had been an active member of the Trinidad Workingmen's Association and had, along with others, broken with Cipriani in 1936.

In March 1937, at the age of 33, Payne returned to Barbados. To the immigration officer on duty he declared that he had been born in Barbados. Shortly after his arrival he began holding street meetings, announcing his intention of forming a trade union. On 1 May 1937 he distributed the first ever May Day celebration leaflets in Barbados. Arrangements he had made to rent a hall for meetings were frustrated when the proprietor discovered his purpose, but his public meetings at Golden Square in Bridgetown began to attract large working-class audiences. Others who joined Payne in his efforts to arouse support for launching a trade union were Fitz Archibald Chase, Olrick Grant, Mortimer Skeete, Israel Lovell and Darnley Alleyne.

Alarmed at the agitational effect of Payne's speeches, the Governor decided to act. The first move was to prosecute him for making a false declaration as to his place of birth. But although Payne's father testified that he had been brought back to Barbados at the age of four and might not have known where he was born, he was fined £10 with the alternative of three months imprisonment at hard labour. The fine of £10 was far beyond Payne's own ability to pay. He appealed and was granted bail. On the next day he led a march to Government House, demanding to see the Governor. The crowd refused to disperse when ordered to do so by the police. Payne was then arrested and taken into custody along with several others. He was refused a renewal of bail pending the hearing of his appeal three days later and, whilst in custody, was served with a deportation order.

Payne's supporters took up a collection to fight his legal battles and if necessary pay the fine. He had been unrepresented at the original hearing, having been unable to find the fee requested by Grantley Adams, the lawyer he had hoped would represent him. But by the time of the appeal enough money had been raised to secure Adams' services. Some 5000 of Payne's supporters assembled outside the Court.

Payne's appeal, heard by the Court on 26 July, was successful. It could not be seriously contended by the prosecution that his declaration of birth in Barbados had been made in the knowledge that it was false or with an intent to deceive. But he was not released from custody. Instead the Governor had the police smuggle him on to a ship bound for Trinidad and deported him in pursuance of the deportation order. In Trinidad the police were waiting for him and he was arrested for having forbidden literature in his possession.[14]

When it became known in Bridgetown that Payne had been deported, there was an angry popular reaction. On the night of 27 July a large crowd assembled in the Lower Green and Golden Square which was addressed by Payne's closest associates. Next morning there was widespread rioting and disorder in the city. *The History of the Barbados Workers' Union* records: 'Shop windows were smashed, cars were pushed into the sea, passers-by were attacked; police patrols, caught unarmed and unawares, fled beneath a hail of bottles and stones. . . During the next two days the ''trouble'' spread to the rural parishes where a few lawless souls stoned cars on the highways while the bolder spirits among the hungry poor took advantage of the general fear and confusion to break into shops and to raid the sweet potato fields in isolated incidents of spontaneous opportunism. Shops remained closed, work came to a standstill in town and country alike. . .'[15]

Three weeks before these disturbances a strike at the Central Foundry had begun and the workers were still out on strike at the time of Payne's deportation. On 28 July the lightermen, whose importance can only be appreciated when it is remembered that no deep water piers had yet been constructed in Barbados, went on strike. They resumed work on 4 August when their demands were met. Other sporadic strikes and threats of strikes occurred in numerous work places. The government however acted ruthlessly to suppress the widespread unrest and to intimidate the workers. Firearms were used on several occasions, the final toll being 14 dead, 47 injured and more than 500 arrested.

Payne's closest associates received sentences of imprisonment on charges of inciting to riot. Grant and Skeete were each sentenced to ten years imprisonment, Lovell and Alleyne to 5 years. The atmosphere was well illustrated by the sentencing of Chase to nine months imprisonment. The words he was alleged to have uttered on 27 July, for which he was arrested and charged for inciting to riot, were: 'tonight will be a funny day!'[16]

On Payne's behalf Grantley Adams challenged, unsuccessfully, the validity of the deportation order. His request that Payne be allowed to return to give evidence on the question of his domicile was adamantly rejected by the Governor. Rejected also was Payne's request in the following year to be allowed to return to give evidence to the West Indies Royal Commission.[17] But having so valiantly assisted in excavating the foundations for a trade union movement in Barbados and denied the opportunity to assist in laying them, his services were not entirely lost to the Caribbean workers' cause. In Trinidad he became a founding member and organizer for the Federated Workers' Trade Union, which he served for several years. He was also a member of the radical political group known as the Negro Welfare and Cultural Association. On 7 April 1947, he collapsed while addressing a meeting and died shortly afterwards.

The situation to which Payne had returned in Trinidad in July 1937 was tense. A strike in the oil fields in June, when the police attempted to arrest Uriah Butler, the strike leader, had developed into widespread rioting with loss of life and destruction of property. In the following year a working-class uprising in Jamaica escalated far beyond sporadic rioting into an all-island general strike.[18] Widespread strikes and demonstrations followed in Guyana in 1938 and 1939. Out of the womb of these events, affecting the entire English-speaking Caribbean area, the modern labour and trade union movements were born.

The Law and the Trade Unions

Prior to 1918 trade unions were illegal in all the British colonies of the Caribbean area. There was the English common law proscription against activity in restraint of trade, from which trade unions had been exempted by statute in Britain in 1871 but not in the colonies. There were, in addition, local statutes in force which made participation in such combinations a criminal offence. Law 15 of 1839 in Jamaica is a good example. The preamble to that statute stated:

. . . all combinations for fixing the wages of labour and for regulating and controlling the mode of carrying on manufacture, trade or business, or the cultivation of any plantation . . . are injurious to trade and commerce, dangerous to the tranquility of the country and especially prejudicial to the interest of all who are concerned in them. . .[19]

Legislation of this kind, initially designed to prevent the slaves emancipated in the 1830s from combining as free men to obtain better wages, was still in force.

So far as the writer is aware, no prosecutions were instituted against the organizers of the unions of skilled workers formed in Jamaica during the first stage or wave of working-class activity. It is worth considering why this should have been so. Certainly the Gleaner Company, the largest printer affected by the 1908 strike, was aware of the legal position. The fact that the printers' union was illegal would not have escaped the notice of the astute lawyer, Lewis Ashenheim, who was a Director of the company. Nevertheless, the reason given by the managing director for refusing to recognize the union was that it was affiliated to the American, rather than the British, trade union movement.[20] He did not resort to the argument that it was illegal. The explanation may be that, at that early period, the employers were confident that they could easily defeat this attempt of their employees to organize, and saw nothing to be gained by drawing attention to the fact that what was lawful for white workers in England was unlawful for black workers in the colonies.

The workers, however, appear to have been aware of their vulnerable legal position. On their behalf, in 1909, S.A.G. (Sandy) Cox, a progressive elected member of the Jamaican legislature, asked the governor to introduce trade union legislation along the lines of legislation existing in Britain. The governor referred the request to the Colonial Office, where it was placed before the Secretary of State with the following revealing memorandum from a senior civil servant:

this movement is apparently being engineered by the 'American Federation of Labour' and if it is successful, will mean that any unions formed in Jamaica will be controlled by the American organization, thus leading to a further development of the Americanization of Jamaica, which we are trying to hinder in other directions. Setting aside any questions of its merits as a matter between employer and employed, I think it is on this ground a dangerous movement which we should not help forward if we can avoid it.[21]

This cunning civil servant then went on to point out that if Mr. Cox were reminded that he could raise the matter himself in the legislature, the proposal would be killed there if he did so. The author of the memorandum was relying on the reactionary composition of the legislature, to a majority of whose members, as he explained, the proposal would 'probably be objectionable ... on other grounds'. The Secretary of State accepted this advice. It is interesting to note that the Governor of Jamaica at the time, with whose unprotesting co-operation this proposal for trade union legislation was killed, was Sydney Olivier, the well known Fabian socialist!

When the second wave of militant working-class activity broke upon the English-speaking Caribbean area, trade union activity was still illegal.

There were no local equivalents of the legal recognition conceded by statute to trade unions in Britain in 1871. But the second wave was far more widespread and militant than the first had been and before long the British government decided that the time had come to make concessions. On 25 October 1919 a trade union law was enacted in Jamaica. The legislation did not confer upon the unions and workers engaged in industrial disputes immunity from liability for tort or breach of contract. Nor did it legalize peaceful picketing. But it was, at least, a gesture that trade unionism would be tolerated. In June 1921 similar legislation was enacted in Guyana.

In Trinidad, unlike Jamaica and Guyana, there was no corresponding legislation of trade union activity. Indeed, the policy of the government there moved towards repression rather than token liberalization. The Habitual Idlers Ordinance of 1918, designed to discourage indentured labourers whose terms had expired from leaving the plantations, provided that any male, who could not prove that he had worked for four hours per day during the preceding three days, could be sent to a government labour camp or be contracted out by the government to private employers. The Strikes and Lockouts Ordinance, the first statute enacted in 1920 after the display of working-class militancy in November and December of the previous year, was a temporary measure which prohibited strikes and provided for arbitration to settle disputes between employers and employees. When this ordinance expired in June 1920 it was replaced by the Industrial Court Ordinance (No. 26 of 1920) designed to achieve the same purpose on a more permanent basis.

A particularly repressive statute was the Seditious Acts and Publications Ordinance (No. 10 of 1920) which, in addition to banning a number of publications, created the criminal offence of 'disaffection' against the King, the government of Trinidad and Tobago or any other British possession and the colony's Executive and Legislative Councils. Offenders could be sentenced to imprisonment for up to two years and/or fined up to £1000.[22]

A point which requires further elucidation is the reason why the government of Trinidad and Tobago failed to follow the example of Jamaica and Guyana in introducing trade union enabling legislation at this time, and set off so persistently in exactly the opposite direction. Is this divergence to be understood entirely in terms of the personal inclinations of the respective governors and the tendency of the Colonial Office to trust the man on the spot? Or could the development of the commercial production of oil in Trinidad and the fact that in 1910 Winston Churchill, First Lord of the Admiralty, had begun to convert the ships of the British Navy from coal to oil burning,[23] have had something to do with it? Further research into the official correspondence of the period may yet provide the answer.

One of the planks of the Trinidad Workingmen's Association in the 1925 election in Trinidad and Tobago had been a demand for legislation making trade unions lawful. As has been mentioned, the TWA's leader, Captain Cipriani, had discouraged the organization from fulfilling its trade union functions precisely because these were illegal. But although the TWA, even on the restricted franchise, had won three of the five elected seats in Trinidad, the Colonial Office could still not be persuaded to instruct the colonial governor to introduce trade union enabling legislation until 1932. Even then, the legislation followed the Jamaican Trade Union law of 1919 in failing to authorize peaceful picketing. Cipriani appealed on this point to the Secretary of State for the colonies, but the decision was against variation of the legislation.

Meanwhile, a trade union Bill had, on T.A. Marryshow's insistence, been introduced in the Grenada legislative Council in 1933. Learning of Cipriani's appeal to the Secretary of State, Marryshow secured a decision to delay final passage of the Bill until information could be obtained as to the decision on the Trinidad and Tobago legislation. When this had been received the Grenada Law was enacted in the same form, without the legislation of picketing.[24] Not until after the third wave of social upheavals had swept across the region in the late 1930s did trade unions become lawful in all parts of the English-speaking Caribbean.

Notes

1. W.M. Macmillan, *Warning from the West Indies,* (London, 1936, 2nd edit. Penguin Books, London, 1938).
2. Govt. of Trinidad & Tobago Council Paper no. 109 of 1934.
3. Ashton Chase, *A History of Trade Unionism in Guyana 1900–1961,* (Georgetown: New Guyana Co., 1964), p. 79.
4. Richard Lobdell, 'Jamaican Labour 1838–1938', (unpub.) Univ. of Wisconsin, 1968, p. 45.
5. Joseph N. France, 'Working Class Struggles of a Half Century', unpub. manuscript consisting in part of selected contemporary weekly articles in the *Union Messenger.* The writer is indebted to J.E. (Fidel) O'Flaharty for making this manuscript available.
6. Verbatim report of the Magistrate's examination of George McIntosh, a *Port of Spain Gazette* publication, n.d. Trinidad.
7. Ralph Gonsalves, 'The role of Labour in the Political Process of St. Vincent (1935–1970)', Univ. of the W.I. Kingston, 24 Oct. 1935.
10. *Ibid.* pp. 23–28, citing: *The Times,* 24 Oct; *The Investigator,* 29 Oct., 2 & 7 Nov., 1935; and an interview with an eye-witness.
11. *Ibid.,* pp. 26–77 and citing K. John & O. Peters, '1935 Revisited' in *Flambeau,* No. 8, (Kingston Study Group, Kingston, Sept 1967).
12. *Port of Spain Gazette* report of examination.
13. W. Arthur Lewis, *Labour in the West Indies,* (Fabian Society, London, 1939; new ed. (S. Craig, ed.); New Beacon Books, London & Port of Spain, 1977), pp. 21–22.
14. Francis Mark, *The History of the Barbados Workers Union,* (Bridgetown, B'dos Workers' Union, n.d.) pp. 1–5.
15. *Ibid.,* pp. 5–6.
16. *Ibid.* p. 7.
17. *Ibid.* p. 8.
18. For a detailed account of the labour rebellion in Jamaica in 1938 see R. Hart, *Rise and Organize: the Birth of the Workers' and National Movements in Jamaica 1936–39,* (London, Karia Press, 1987).
19. R. Gonsalves, 'The Trade Union Movement in Jamaica' in C. Stone and A. Brown (eds.), *Essays in Power and Change in Jamaica,* (Kingston, Jamaica Publishing House, 1977), p. 91.
20. Interviews with A.J. McGlashan.
21. P.R.O., CO 137/674 — memo initialled G.G. The writer is indebted to Richard Lobdell for identifying the author of this memo as G. Grindle, senior adviser and later private secretary to the Permanent Under Secretary for the Colonies.
22. Wendy Charles, *Early Labour Organization in Trinidad,* pp. 10–12, and *The Colonial Context of the Riots,* (St. Augustine, Trinidad, Univ. of the W.I., Dept. of Sociology, 1978), pp. 10–12.
23. NACLA, 'Oil in the Caribbean: Focus on Trinidad', *Latin America and Empire Report,* Part 2, (San Fernando, Oilfield Workers' Trade Union, 1976).
24. P.R.O., CO 104/52 — Grenada Leg. Co. Minutes, 15 Nov. and 29 Dec., 1933.

The 1930s Social Revolution

Arthur Lewis

Before the Emancipation the slaves rebelled frequently, and throughout the last hundred years there have been isolated strikes, riots, political organizations, and even trade unions. But not until recent years has there been anything that could be called a movement.

We propose to take the year 1935 as our starting point because it is the first year of the more recent series of upheavals. Early in that year there was a general strike of agricultural labourers in St. Kitts, out of which serious trouble developed. It was followed, in February, by a strike in the oilfields of Trinidad and subsequent hunger march, and later in the year by strikes in British Guiana, a serious disturbance in St. Vincent and a coal strike in St. Lucia.

After all this activity 1936 was a fairly quiet year, but there was widespread trouble in 1937. The strikes in Trinidad in June were followed almost immediately by an upheaval in Barbados and by strikes in British Guiana, St. Lucia and Jamaica. This series of protests first brought West Indian conditions to the eye of the British public.

But it was the general strike in Jamaica in the following year, immediately succeeded by further strikes in British Guiana, which really roused the public mind. By that time at least 46 persons had been killed in the course of suppressing these upheavals, 429 injured, and thousands arrested and prosecuted.

What accounts for this sudden burst of activity? Undoubtedly each occasion has had its own special features acting as the immediate spur to activity. But underlying it all have been certain factors common to all the islands.

In the first place it is generally agreed that the specially bad conditions which have ruled in recent years are a major predisposing factor. The prices of the principal West Indian exports were on the average almost halved between 1928 and 1933, and workers were forced to submit to drastic wage cuts, increased taxation, and unemployment.

A second factor has been the steady drift of unemployed workers from the plantations to the towns, where their numbers have been reinforced by labourers repatriated from Cuba and San Domingo. Long unemployment without any dole has made these workers very bitter and militant, and they have sometimes used periods of emergancy for looting and demonstrations. The official reports are usually content to describe such people as 'hooligans', but more often than not they are genuinely unemployed workers who have drifted into the towns and have no means of support.

Again, a number of factors have combined to increase the political consciousness of the workers. Foremost is the Italian conquest of Abyssinia. West Indians felt that in that issue the British Government betrayed a nation because it was black, and this has tended to destroy their faith in white government, and to make them more willing to take their fate in their own hands. News of sit-down strikes in France and America was also followed with the greatest interest.

Had there existed constitutional machinery for the redress of grievances, there might well have been no upheavals. But government and employers have always been hostile to collective bargaining, and the political constitution is deliberately framed to exclude the workers from any control over the legislature. Consequently the general strike and the riot have been the worker's only weapons for calling attention to his conditions.

In the following pages we shall trace these upheavals island by island, paying particular attention to the trade union and political organizations to which they have given birth.

St. Kitts

This island, which experienced the first of the recent series of explosions, is a tiny member of the Leeward group with a population of less than 20,000. It consists almost wholly of plantations owned by Europeans; there are hardly any peasants; and the general atmosphere is most reactionary. In the twenties and early thirties there was a fairly militant *Representative Government Association* led by some members of the middle classes, but this was mainly concerned with political questions. There have also been a number of working class societies, of which the *Workers' League* and the *Universal Benevolent Association* are the most notable, but they have not had a large membership.

Social conditions in this colony are so much worse than elsewhere that in 1929 a West indian Commission made them the subject of a special report, but no action was taken on this.

In the year 1935 the beginning of the sugar cane reaping season was set for 28 January, and throughout the preceding weeks labourers were discussing between themselves the necessity for wage increases. Some workers felt that no increase could be expected at the ruling price of sugar, while others thought that an increase was justifiable. However, when the 28th arrived it turned out that the employers did not intend to grant any increase.

The Governor states in his official report that the strike movement was started by some of the unemployed labourers in the capital. A group of these started to march round the island persuading the workers on the plantations to strike for an increase of wages. Their numbers grew steadily; the news flashed round the island, and by next morning there was practically a general strike.

Trouble arose when a crowd invaded an estate to demand higher wages from its proprietor. He fired upon them, wounding three. The crowd determined to beat him up, and when the police arrived they were unable to disperse the people until they had opened fire, killing three and wounding eight. With this the spirit of the strikers was broken. The police arrested large numbers, a warship arrived, and in a few days everyone was back at work — except the many who were consigned to prison on various charges and others whom the employers refused to take back. Wages were not increased.

This sporadic upheaval left hardly any permanent mark. It was not led by any organization, and with its collapse the workers were left merely with the discouragement of failure.

St. Vincent

Not so in St. Vincent, which exploded later in the year. With the death in the early thirties of the *Representative Government Association*, political conditions in this island of 50,000 had long been fairly quiet, until the October events came to ginger them up.

What precisely happened is still uncertain, as the government imposed a strict censorship on the press, and no official report was ever published. It appears however that the trouble was due to the decision of the government to increase the customs duties. The public was strongly opposed to this measure, and on 21 October while it was being debated in the Legislative Council a crowd demanded to see the Governor and present a petition. The Governor would not yield, and the crowd appears to have got somewhat out of hand, breaking some of the windows of the Chamber. Some of the unemployed started looting, and in the course of the subsequent disturbances 3 were killed and 26 injured. The Governor declared a state of emergency, instituted a strict censorship of the press, and summoned a warship; and in a few days all was quiet. Then began a series of prosecutions culminating in a trial for treason so ridiculous that at the preliminary hearing the magistrate threw out the case without calling on the defence.

The reaction of the general public throughout the West Indies, even as far as Jamaica, was amazement and deep resentment against the repressive measures adopted. In St. Vincent it resulted in the formation of a *Workingman's Association* with a radical programme, in the forefront of which stand land settlement and constitutional reform.

In three short years the Association has become the focus of radical opinion in St. Vincent, and a body of great political influence. It is not registered as a trade union, but represents the workers in all negotiations. It has also attracted wide middle class support, and its candidates were enthusiastically returned at the last general election. It is one of the new organizations which is changing the orientation of West Indian politics.

St. Lucia

Some 60,000 people live in St. Lucia, and although the principal occupation is wage labour on plantations, there is also an important trade in supplying ships with coal. This trade was at its best in pre-war days, providing employment for large numbers in the neighbourhood of Port Castries, and contributing largely to the colony's revenues, but it has now largely declined owing to the increasing use of oil.

Politically St. Lucia is one of the quietest islands, its *Representative Government Association* having died some years ago. There have been working class societies from time to time, but they have never taken root. The most militant workers have been those engaged in coaling ships, and there is a long record of sporadic strikes among them in the last fifty years.

One such strike occurred at the end of 1935. It was quite free from violence, but the Governor, with the events of St. Vincent on his mind, decided on a demonstration. He mobilized the Volunteer force, summoned a warship, had marines patrolling the streets, and at night played the ship's searchlights upon the town, dazzling the inhabitants and disturbing their sleep. Well accustomed to coal strikes, the peaceful inhabitants of Castries deeply resented this show of force.

On the Governor setting up a committee to investigate the coal trade, the strikers returned to work, and in due course the committee reported, on the basis of evidence taken *in camera* from the firms concerned, that no wage increase was possible. There was much dissatisfaction but the matter rested there.

In August 1937 the agricultural labourers on the sugar plantations struck for higher wages. This most unusual action followed close upon the news of strikes in Trinidad, Barbados, Jamaica and British Guiana, and was largely inspired by it. Again there was no violence, but again the Government was moved to demonstrations of force, this time being severely criticized by its own nominees in the Legislature for what they regarded as the waste of public funds entailed by unnecessary mobilization. A committee was set up to investigate agricultural wages, and it recommended slight increases subsequently embodied in a minimum wage order.

No new organization emerged in the succeeding months, but the evidence given before the committee and news of movements elsewhere created a profound impression, especially upon the minds of the younger members of the middle classes. The outcome of all this has been the formation in January 1939 of the first St. Lucian trade union, which proposed to function as a general union of agricultural and urban workers. It is as yet too early to say anything about its progress.

Barbados

This is a tiny island with a population of over 1,000 per square mile depending for its existence on plantations almost entirely in European hands. Its government is one of the most reactionary in the West Indies, and though in recent years a number of middle class leaders have appeared, until 1937 they had made little impression on either the government or the masses.

In March 1937 one Clement Payne arrived in Barbados. He was a friend of Uriah Butler, the man who was later to lead the oilfield workers' strike, and came from Trinidad to urge upon the working classes of Barbados the virtues of organization. He held a number of meetings and got so good a hearing that the government looked around for some means of suppressing him.

They found it in the formalities associated with his entry into the colony. Payne was the son of Barbadian parents and had grown up in Barbados,

but had been born while his mother was in Trinidad. On entering the colony, however, he had stated that he was born in Barbados, and the police charged him before a magistrate with wilfully making a false statement as to his place of birth. This happened just after the distrubances in Trinidad, and the Barbados masses, already excited by the news from the sister colony, realized at once its purport. Huge crowds followed him to and from the trial, and when on 22 July he was convicted and fined £10, he appealed and announced his intention of leading a procession to the Governor's residence to protest against the conviction. The police refused to let him see the Governor and as he persisted he and a number of his followers were arrested and an order issued immediately for his deportation to Trinidad.

On 26 July the Court of Appeal quashed his conviction on the ground that having been brought to Barbados very young he might not have known that he was born in Trinidad. Efforts by counsel to have the deportation order rescinded were, however, unsuccessful, and the same day he was deported.

His supporters were furious at this treatment. A large crowd assembled on the wharf where Payne was expected to embark, but the police secretly sent him off from another point. To quote the official report,

'when they learnt that Payne was already on board the steamer and that the possibility of preventing his deportation was gone, the passions of the crowd, which had been excited by the events of the day, became uncontrollable. A cornet sounded the assembly and the crowd marched to meetings in the Lower Green and Golden Square where they were again harangued. The mob then spread through the city in bands smashing motor cars and electric street lamps. When the police tried to stop these outrages the mob rained showers of stones and bottles upon them in a fray in which Sergeant Elias had two fingers fractured and three other police constables received injuries. The police, who were armed only with batons, succeeded with the greatest difficulty in restoring some sort of order; but it is noteworthy that in the face of the considerable disorder and damage to property they were unable to make a single arrest.'

Next morning large crowds again collected and once more began an orgy of smashing shop windows and cars. The disturbances spread quickly. Groups of unemployed commandeered cars and buses and spread the 'news,' and soon the country people were busily engaged in looting the shops and raiding potato fields. To quote again,

'The lawless acts committed in the country were more purposive than those committed in Bridgetown; and it would appear that hunger or the fear of hunger coupled with the news of the disturbances in Bridgetown were the chief causes of the outbreaks in the country districts.'

In attempting to restore order the police were forced to fire, killing 14 and wounding 47. Over 400 arrests were made, and many persons imprisoned for sedition, including a young man who was given ten years for a speech which 'tended to raise discontent or disaffection amongst His Majesty's subjects or to promote feelings of ill-will and hostility between different classes of such subjects' by urging workers to organize in trade unions.

These disturbances suddenly opened the eyes of Barbadians of all classes to the existence of poverty in their midst, an impression confirmed by the official Commission who attributed the trouble mainly to unemployment and poverty, and almost for the first time in Barbadian history directed attention to the conditions of the masses. Government, pushed by the Colonial Office, immediately began plans for old age pensions and legislation governing workmen's compensation, trade unions and minimum wage machinery.

Out of the succeeding middle and working class ferment the *Barbados Progressive League* was born in August 1938. Its main purpose is on the one hand to organize trade unions and on the other to run candidates for election in an attempt to force the government to provide adequate social services, to assist emigration, and to promote land settlement. Led by a prominent lawyer it has attracted widespread middle class sympathy, and is encouraged by the workers' response to hope that it will soon be able to sponsor trade unions for agricultural labourers, shop and clerical assistants, and waterfront workers; but it is handicapped by the continuous fear of victimization which keeps away many who would otherwise support it. The views of the League are expressed through the *Barbados Observer*, a radical paper of many years standing.

British Guiana

This colony, of which only a coastal strip has so far been developed, consists of a large portion of South America. Nearly half of its population are East Indians brought over as indentured labourers to work on plantations, and their descendants. There is also some Negro agricultural labour, but the bulk of the Negro element is to be found in the towns, in transport, or in the relatively small mining industry, extracting gold, diamonds and aluminium.

In 1919 the *British Guiana Labour Union* was formed, and its membership rose rapidly to 12,000. But with the general decline of economic activity which followed the slump of 1920 the union declined. It never ceased to exist, however, and its Secretary, Mr. Hubert Critchlow, is still active in preaching the virtues of organization, though with most success among the urban workers.

Until 1932 the East Indian agricultural workers had their interests supervised by an offical 'Protector of Immigrants' whose duty it was to enforce the elaborate legislation governing the employment of indentured labourers. This post was, however, abolished in 1932, and though the legislation remains, its enforcement is not very rigorous. Conditions on the plantations have always been very bad, since it has been regarded as axiomatic that the 'coolie' worker has the minimum of needs. Consequently there is a long record of strikes, dating from the nineteenth century.

In September 1935 a further serious outburst of strikes occurred. There was no violence, and the main demand was for increased wages in view of the record crop. The Labour Union was associated with the strikes, though it cannot be said to have organized them. The strikes were spontaneous, widespread and determined, and lasted off and on throughout September and October. A subsequent Commission of Enquiry stressed the need for setting up machinery through which the workers might represent their grievances to their employers.

Towards the end of 1936 the *Manpower and Citizens' Association* was formed, and it was registered as a trade union in September 1937. It has had remarkable success, especially in organizing the agricultural workers. East Indian agricultural labourers have proved easier to organize than Negro workers. They have a greater sense of national solidarity, being bound together by their own languages, religions and social customs. The principal leaders of the union are themselves East Indian, and there has been some fear that this may become a cause of friction with Negroes. This, however, is strongly denied by the leaders. They point out that the union is open to all, irrespective of race, and that all their propaganda is on class rather than racial lines. They point out, too, that there are a fair number of Negroes in the union, and that many of them occupy important administrative posts, especially in the country branches where the standard of literacy amongst the East Indians is not very high.

Within two years the Association attained a membership of 10,000, and though it has attracted the bitter hostility of the employers, the government has been forced to recognize it as the body with which to negotiate in case of dispute.

Since September 1935 there has been a series of further strikes on the plantations. None of these has been called by the union, which exercises all its influence in favour of collective bargaining. Thus in June 1938 when serious and widespread strikes occurred in one county, the union advised the workers to return to the plantations, and succeeded by negotiation in securing wage increases for them.[1]

The Association publishes the only labour paper in the colony, the *Guiana Review*, which campaigns for constitutional reform, an eight-hour day, a minimum wage, and reform of the trade union and workmen's compensation laws, the former to allow peaceful picketing, and the latter to include agricultural workers. At present it seems likely to capture the bulk of the agricultural workers.

Apart from this Association, there are several other small unions in the colony. Workers engaged in the mining industries (bauxite, diamonds and gold) are organized in the *B.G. Miners' Association.* There are also two general unions, the *B.G. Labour Union,* already mentioned, and the *B.G. Workers' League.* Waterfront workers are catered for by the *Seamen's Union,* and Government workers by the *Transport Worker's Union* (railway and inland waterways), the *Post Office Workers' Union,* the *Subordinate government Workers' Union,* and smaller unions such the *Medical Subordinates' Union,* the *Hospital Attendants' Union* and the *Government Messengers' Union.* Most of these unions are represented on the *British Guiana Trade Union Assembly,* a coordinating body consisting of members of the Executive Committees of the several unions, which meets fairly often. Thus since July 1938 the transport and postal workers have been negotiating with the government, and when in December the negotiations appeared to be breaking down, the *Trade Union Assembly* arranged for a general strike of all government employees in its constituent unions. The strike was, however, averted, and the negotiations are still in progress.

The British Guiana Unions are represented on the *B.G. and West India Labour Congress,* a body coordinating labour activities in all the colonies, of which more will be said later.

Trinidad

Trinidad is the only West Indian colony whose exports are not predominantly agricultural. An important extractive and refining oil industry has developed steadily in the southern part of the island since 1908, and today oil accounts for 60% of the value of the island's exports. Nevertheless the number of workers in the industry is relatively small, sugar and cocoa between them employing seven times as many people as oil. From the labour point of view, therefore, Trinidad must be regarded

with the other colonies as being predominantly agricultural. A small peasantry has emerged, but the large plantation with its dependence on large supplies of cheap landless labour continues to be the basis of the system.

Working class activity in this colony has a long history. The *Trinidad Workingmen's Association* was formed in the early nineties of the last century, and its radical programme attracted much attention. It declined, however, after the serious disturbances of 1903 (the 'Water Riots') when the police seized the opportunity of prosecuting some of its most prominent members, and it was not revived until 1919.

Under the leadership of Captain Cipriani, a European born in Trnidad, who had learnt in the war the worth of the 'barefooted West Indian' the Association grew steadily throughout the twenties, and was able in the early thirties to claim a membership of 120,000, out of a total population of 450,000. It never functioned as a union, but devoted its attention to legislative reforms. As an opposition party much of its work consisted in useful amendments to bills proposed by the government; but it also consistently agitated for proper trade union legislation, factory legislation, social insurance schemes, minimum wage legislation, land settlement, constitutional reform, etc., and was responsible for forcing the government to introduce workmen's compensation. Of the 26 members of the Legislative Council only seven are elected, but for years the Association has been well represented among the seven. It has also controlled the City Council of Port-of-Spain for many years, and used its power to improve the working conditions of municipal employees, to initiate slum clearance and other improvements which make Port-of-Spain one of the finest cities in the Caribbean area, and to acquire the tramway system for municipal ownership, after a long legal battle. The Association is affiliated to the British Labour Party, and fraternal delegations have been exchanged. When in 1932 the Government passed trade union legislation which did not permit peaceful picketing or protect against actions in tort the Assocation decided on the advice of the TUC not to register as a union, and changed its name to *The Trinidad Labour Party.*

The weakness of the party was that it had no trade union basis. In 1929 the *Trinidad and Tobago Trade Union Centre* was formed as a rival organization, and by 1930 had some 2,000 members, mainly engaged in transport. But it was in the south, among the oilfield workers, that the party's influence declined most rapidly, the workers there being prepared for more radical action than the party was capable of leading. The short oilfield strike of February 1935 and succeeding hunger march to Port-of-Spain were engineered by Uriah Butler, a man whom the party had expelled, and when in 1937 workers all over the island were coming out on strike the party was so out of touch that it could neither lead nor restrain.

The events of June 1937, destined to be a landmark in the history of Trinidad, started in the oilfields, and it is perhaps as well to start with a short description of the industry. Most of the twenty-two companies engaged in it are quite small, and in 1936 five companies produced 88% of the total output. The industry is pretty well organized as a monopoly, wages being fixed by the 'Petroleum Association' to which all the principal companies belong.

While some of the smaller companies are not faring very well, the major ones are prospering exceedingly. Profits of four of them in the year 1936–37 amounted to £1,540,000 on a total capitalization (including all reserves and premiums) of £6,770,000. As the profits of these four companies were more than three times the total sum paid in wages by the whole industry (£473,000) it is not surprising that one company was able to declare a dividend of 30% and another a dividend of 45%. It has been argued for many years that the income tax is too light at 2/6 in the pound, but so powerful are the oil interests and so closely have they the ear of the government, that no attempt has been made to increase taxation. It is often said that the real rulers of Trinidad are not the Governor or his Legislative Council, but the representatives of the oil industry.

The specific grievances which led to the strike of June 1937 were first the rise in the cost of living, officially estimated at 17%, and secondly the 'Red Book', a system for identifying the workers which they felt was being used to facilitate victimization.

To focus these grievances came Uriah Butler, already mentioned as organizer of a strike and hunger march in 1935. He formed in August 1936 the *British Empire Workers and Citizens Home Rule Party*. Butler was not a man of great education, and not always wise in his choice of language, but he impressed the Governor with his sincerity, and though practically unknown elsewhere in the island, had a sizeable following on the oilfields.

The strike was no sudden storm. Negotiations had been pending for some time, and according to the official report the police had expected it on 7 June, almost a fortnight before it actually occurred. On 19 June every single worker on the oilfields laid down his tools, and it is a measure of the general unrest and dissatisfaction in the colony that the oil workers were soon followed by agricultural workers, and even by some of the workers in Port-of-Spain.

This strike might have remained a peaceful industrial dispute like its predecessors but for an unfortunate incident which turned it into a riot. The turning point occurred when the police attempted to arrest Butler while he was addressing a meeting on the first evening of the strike. The crowd succeeded in routing the police, and thus gave the signal for a general uprising. Responsible opinion in Trinidad had urged that there would have been no uprising if the police had had the sense to wait until Butler had finished his meeting before attempting to arrest him, but tact has never characterized the attitude of West Indian officialdom towards labour leaders.

The Governor summoned the navy from Bermuda, and with its help the disturbances were quelled, but not until 14 had been killed, 59 wounded, and hundreds arrested. The government appointed a committee to mediate, and by 5 July most of the workers had returned to work. Subsequent history is best described under five heads (1) the oil industry; (2) the sugar industry; (3) urban unions: (4) the Labour Party; and (5) the general situation.

The Oil Industry

On the appointment of the Mediation Committee and the return of the strikers to work events moved fairly quickly. On 10 July the employers announced that the pay of the lowest workers would be increased to a minimum of nine cents per hour (three shillings a day). They also invited the workers to elect delegates for further negotiations. A meeting was held on 14 July at which the employers offered various concessions, notably an all round increase of one penny per hour, a pension scheme, one week's holiday with pay, and the replacement of the Red Book by a different system of identification. The offer was rejected by the delegates as inadequate.

On Sunday, 25 July, the *Oilworkers' Trade Union* was formed, and proceeded immediately to formulate its demands, the most important being an all round increase of threepence per hour and two weeks' holiday with pay. Almost immediately the Governor announced that the Secretary of State for the Colonies had appointed a Commission to investigate the entire situation in Trinidad. Negotiations were therefore suspended pending the arrival of the Commission, which was expected to act as a sort of mediator, and in the meantime the companies' increase of one penny per hour was accepted provisionally, and the Red Book suspended.

The Union set about the task of increasing the membership and has been so successful that it has now over 8,000 members in an industry employing 9,000, and fairly substantial cash reserves. Its power in the oilfields is unquestionable.

When the Commission presented its Report in February 1938 it was found that it had dodged the wage issue. The union therefore immediately recommenced negotiations, on the basis of the demands put before the Petroleum Association in July. At first the Association refused to discuss the issue at all, but through the intervention of the Government's Industrial Adviser, and in face of the serious threat of strike action, it finally agreed to negotiations, and eventually to arbitration. Accordingly a special arbitration tribunal of five members sailed from England for Trinidad in November, two members being appointed by each side, with an independent chairman appointed by the government. The tribunal took evidence throughout December, and after brilliant performances by both the union and the employers, failed to agree. The award was therefore made by the Chairman, using his special powers, and resulted in a victory for the union, which was granted 50% of its demands, i.e., an extra penny per hour beyond the penny already granted in July 1937, instead of the extra twopence which it was claiming. Both sides have agreed to respect this finding for a year.

The Sugar Industry

The leaders of the oilworkers' union also devoted their attention to organizing the workers in the sugar industry, the south being also the most important sugar area. The *All-Trinidad Sugar Estates and Factory Workers' Union* was founded soon after the oilworkers' union, and started a membership campaign. It was more successful in recruiting sugar factory workers than field workers, though it had a fair following among the latter, especially in the south.

In January 1938 the union formulated its demands, notably an all-round increase of ten cents per day for field workers, and an increase for factory workers of 20% for those earning less than 4/- a day and 15% for those earning more. The companies, through their union, the Sugar Manufacturers' Association, rejected these demands, but owing to the intervention of the Industrial Adviser and the threat of strike action a conference was arranged for 31 March 1938. This conference resulted in a deadlock, and was adjourned to consider the possibility of arbitration by the government.

But the members of the union's strongest branch, the employees of the largest company, were determined on a test of strength, and forced the leaders to declare a strike. The Union's leaders have been bitterly criticized for calling this strike, but reply that though they realized its inadvisability they could not but associate themselves with it in view of the determination of their strongest branch. The strike was a complete failure. Practically all factory workers went on strike and a considerable proportion of field workers. But the strike was broken by the 'cane farmers'. In Trinidad nearly half the total output of cane is grown by small peasants who own land or rent it from the sugar companies and sell them the cane to grind; these are called 'cane farmers'. When the strike broke out the companies cleverly used such labour as they could get to grind their own canes, leaving the cane farmers' canes to rot. These in turn proceeded to break the strike. Some offered their labour to the factories, while others called upon the union pointing out the hardships they were suffering and demanding that the strike should be called off. Thereupon the workers started returning to work by the end of the first week, and eventually the union fixed 16 April for the termination of the strike.

The consequences of failure were terrible for the union. Hundreds of workers were victimized, and this served only to frighten other workers away from the union. The employers took the line that the strike was a breach of faith in view of pending negotiations, and adopted an attitude tantamount to refusing to recognize the union. It will take much patient work before the union is able once more to gather enough strength to force the reopening of negotiations. A source of strength is its close association with the oilworkers' union, enabling it to bask in the reflected glory of the latter's successes.

Urban Unions

The events of June 1937 produced a great ferment in Port-of-Spain, especially under the leadership of the *Negro Welfare and Cultural Association*. With its more or less marxist philosophy and purely working class leadership this body was probably the most radical in the island. It had existed for many years, issuing leaflets, organizing street meetings and demonstrations, etc., and it seized on the general ferment left by the disturbances to organize new unions. Its project for a domestic servants' union fizzled out after a number of meetings which struck terror into the hearts of Trinidad's housewives, but it met with permanent success in organizing a *Seamen and Waterfront Workers' Union* and a *Public Works Workers' Union*. The former, after a successful strike in July 1937, was recognized by the seafront employers early in 1938; it includes about 30% of the eligible workers. The latter has a membership of 800 amongst employees of the Public Works Department, and has also succeeded in gaining wage concessions.

The leaders of the oilworkers and sugar unions have also founded a *Transport and General Workers' Union,* and a *Federated Workers' Union.* The latter operates mainly among railway and constructional workers; registered in September 1937 it entered into negotiations in January 1938 for shorter railway hours. Other unions are the *Amalgamated Building and Woodworkers' Union,* established in 1936 for building workers, and the *Printers' Industrial Union.*

In 1933 the Trinidad Labour Party founded the *Clerks' Union,* a section for shop assistants and clerical workers, which attained a membership of 500 but, in accordance with the general policy of the party, never registered as a trade union. Since 1937, however, a rival association, the *Trinidad and Tobago Union of Shop Assistants and Clerks* has been formed, with the intention of registering as a union, and seems likely to supplant the former organization.

Another branch of the Labour Party which must be mentioned here is the *Shipwrights' Union,* also unregistered, which is particularly notable in that it has started a cooperative section offering to build and repair boats for the public.

The Labour Party

All this trade union activity, proceeding independently of the Labour Party, has tended to cut the ground from under its feet, especially as the TUC has now written reversing its earlier opinion, and commending the formation and registration of unions.

There has been a remarkable decline in the influence and activity of the party, and a tendency to forget its long record of service. It is still, however, very strong in Port-of-Spain, where it continues to control the City Council.

The General Situation

Some friction arose in the early days of the new movement through the difference in outlook between the various sections. The leaders of the south are essentially trade unionists; they are not wholly in sympathy with the leaders of the *Negro Welfare Association,* and are themselves regarded with suspicion by the leaders of the Labour Party, who are not quite reconciled to the rise of powerful new organizations outside their control. Fortu-

nately the early mutual suspicion is disappearing, especially as cooperation in the *B.G. and West India Labour Congress* (of which more later) is proving that there is little essential difference of opinion. Three labour papers are now published regularly in Trinidad, the *Socialist* by the Labour Party, the *Pilot* by the *Seamen and Waterfront Workers' Union,* representing in general the views of the *Negro Welfare and Cultural Association,* and the *People,* an independent paper, giving full publicity to union activities.

Conditions are now fairly quiet. All the unions are busily engaged in increasing and consolidating their membership, and it is conceivable that the success of the oilworkers' union should lead to an increased demand for arbitration proceedings.

Jamaica

Jamaica, with its population of 1,150,000 is the largest of the islands. It is also from the agricultural point of view the most fortunate; for whereas the other islands depend upon sugar, cocoa, coconuts, citrus or cotton, products whose prices have all been very low, the prosperity of Jamaica is bound up with the banana. In 1937 bananas accounted for 55% of the value of domestic exports while sugar accounted for 18%. Recently banana diseases have been making serious inroads, but the relatively high prices secured have saved the colony from the fate of most of the others. But though as a whole the colony has been able to withstand the effects of the decline in the price of sugar, those large areas dependent on sugar production have suffered severe depression and unemployment.

Jamaica is fortunate in possessing a relatively large peasant population, estimated variously at between 100,000 and 150,000 holdings. Their conditions are doubtless deplorable; they have not enough land — most holdings are of less than two acres; they have suffered from banana diseases; and the decline of the sugar industry has diminished the demand for their food products. But the existence of such a large peasantry has prevented unemployment and starvation from being as great as it might otherwise have been.

For the last few years there has been growing unrest associated with the decline of the sugar industry and distress amongst the peasantry. Adding to it has been the repatriation of labourers from Cuba, who have tended to remain in the towns, and with minds widened by travel, to be quicker to protest against bad conditions. Kingston has been particularly sensitive to the general unrest, and a Parliamentary reply by the Secretary of State for the Colonies on 9th February 1938, indicates something of this:

'There was also a demonstration by unemployed and ex-servicemen at Kingston in Jamaica in August 1937, when it became necessary for the police to disperse the crowd with batons. A number of small strikes also occurred during the year in various parts of the Colony, but as I stated in reply to a question on 1 December, agreement was reached between the employers and the labourers, and increased wages have now been given in the case of the banana labourers who were those principally concerned. There was no disorder.'

Until 1938 trade unionism in Jamaica made little progress, though various attempts were being made to organize labour. A survey in June 1938 revealed that there were then in existence twelve unions, mainly very small organizations on a craft basis. Only two were of any significant size, the *Jamaica Workers' and Tradesmen's Union* and the *Jamaica United Clerks' Association.* The former claimed to have a membership of 5,000 and was organized so as to embrace every class of labour, but the majority of its members were agricultural labourers and waterfront workers. The *United Clerks' Association* catered for shop assistants and was very strong in Kingston.

Alexander Bustamante, who has recently sprung into prominence, was formerly a member of the *Jamaica Workers' and Tradesmen's Union,* but left it in 1937 and in the early months of 1938 conducted a strenuous campaign of meetings throughout the island, and especially in Kingston. Associated with him is William Grant, who had previously been a labour leader on his own. Both men have remarkable speaking powers and have stirred the imagination and won the loyalty of the working classes throughout the island.

In 1938 matters came to a head. One can do no better than quote the official Report:

'On 5 January this year a strike, which may be regarded as the forerunner of the recent disturbances, occurred on the sugar estate of '*Serge Island*' in the parish of St. Thomas. This necessitated the despatch of reserves of police from Kingston and a number of arrests. It was settled by wage concessions.

On 29 March the Governor announced in the Legislative Council that he had decided to appoint a commission to enquire into and report upon the rates of wages and conditions of employment of field and day labour in receipt of not more than thirty shillings a week, and the first sitting of this Commission was held in Kingston on 11 April. As a result of representations made by members of the Commission, the Governor gave instructions for acceleration of the programme of the Public Works Department in order to relieve unemployment.

A serious disturbance occurred on 2 May 1938 at Frome in Westmoreland, where a strike, principally affecting labourers constructing a new factory for Messrs Tate and Lyle (the West Indies Sugar Co.) resulted in a clash between strikers and police, four of the former being killed and nine wounded. This disturbance necessitated the despatch of the greater part of the Kingston police reserve, a part of which was still absent when the disorders under review occurred.

Between 11 and 20 May, a series of small strikes by wharf labourers occurred in Kingston, but these were quickly settled; there was no general demand then for higher wages, the stoppages being due to a variety of causes. During the same period, however, a series of meetings was held in and around Kingston at which speeches of an inflammatory nature were delivered, and workers of all classes were urged to unite together so as to be in a position to enforce their demands for higher wages. The principal speakers at these meetings were Alexander Bustamante and William Grant.

On 16 May a contractor engaged by the Kingston and St. Andrew Corporation on road construction in the Trench Pen area of St. Andrew attempted to engage labour, but the workers refused to work for him alleging that he cheated them when it came to payment of their wages. Nevertheless, he succeeded in engaging 45 men to begin work the following day. The next morning, however, a large crowd arrived at Trench Pen armed with sticks, pieces of iron, etc., and prevented any work being done. The police arrived on the scene and prevented any violence. In the result the contractor was induced to surrender his contract and the Corporation carried out the work by direct labour. This incident was not without its effect upon the labouring population of Kingston and St. Andrew.'

This then was the chain of events which led up to the explosion of May and June. As we shall see the trouble began with a general strike on the waterfront on the 21st, followed by a general strike of street cleaners on the 23rd, and immediately by an upheaval which spread rapidly throughout the island.

'On Saturday 21 May there was a general strike on the waterfront for higher wages, but a few ships were loaded and unloaded with labour procured from elsewhere; this strike continued without disorder or violence that day and the next. Crowds and strikers loitered on the waterfront until midnight on Sunday and then dispersed peacefully.

On Monday the street cleaners employed by the Kingston and St. Andrew Corporation failed to go to work with the consequence that dust bins filled with refuse remained unemptied in the streets.

From an early hour mobs began to collect and parade the streets of Kingston. They rapidly became mischievous. Dust bins were overturned and their contents scattered on the streets; some Chinese shops and bakeries were attacked and goods and money stolen. . .

Between the hours of 6 a.m. and 8 a.m. the police were able to control the situation by despatching parties of 10 to 20 men to different points where disorder was reported. They succeeded in dispersing mobs without the use of force and without incurring the hostility of the crowd.

However, as time passed the mobs were much increased by men and women who might have gone to work if left to themselves, but who were either intimidated from doing so by the mob or were unable to withstand the attraction of having a day out. They continued to parade the streets and began to threaten shopkeepers with violence unless they closed their shops and released their assistants; as a result all shops in the centre of the city had to close.

Disorder then became general and the police were insufficient in numbers to control the situation. Persons of all classes going to business were set upon, public property was destroyed, streets blocked and tramcars attacked.'

Thereafter disorder ruled for several days, despite the use of soldiers, the navy, and special constables. Moreover it spread rapidly throughout the island, and for the next fortnight soldiers and police were having to be rushed from one part of the island to another to suppress uprisings. It was clear that the unrest was not confined to Kingston; the whole island was seething with discontent. In the course of restoring order 8 persons were killed, 171 wounded, and over 700 arrested and prosecuted.

By about 10 June the island had more or less settled down to normal conditions. There were, however, further flare-ups during the rest of the year, which continued into 1939.

The events of May and June threw two men principally into relief, Bustamante and Norman Manley, KC, Jamaica's leading barrister. Arrested on 24 May, Bustamante became the hero of Jamaican labour, and after his release on the 28th devoted his energies to restoring order. Manley had not previously been associated with labour, but on the outbreak of the disturbances he came forward and put himself unreservedly at the disposal of the working classes, offering to negotiate on their behalf with government and the employers. He quickly won the confidence of the masses, and his negotiations played no small part in the settlement of outstanding grievances. In the past few months Bustamante has concentrated on organizing trade unions, while Manley has devoted himself to political organization. After some initial friction, both men now work in close association.

The *Bustamante Trade Unions,* as they are called, date from July 1938, and already claim a membership of 50,000. The organization takes the form of one general union with a central executive and seven divisions. The divisions are Transport, General Workers, Maritime Workers (including seamen and dockers), Municipal Workers (including workers employed by Government or municipal bodies on road or other constructional work), Factory Workers, Artisans of every description, and Commercial Clerks (including clerical workers but not shop assistants). It is expected that a new division will soon be formed for Hotel Employees. Bustamante is President of the whole organization, and it is believed that the constitution reserves wide powers to him, including the right of declaring strikes. The Central Executive consists of the President, the General Secretary of the whole organization, and the Vice-Presidents, who are the heads of the seven divisions.

The division of General Workers has the largest membership and includes agricultural labour. The most completely organized division is that of the Maritime Workers, which must include well over 90% of the dock workers and seamen in the colony.

As is to be expected of a movement in its infancy, the unions are faced with difficult problems of organization and discipline. Unauthorized strikes occur frequently, and in many cases the union heads are placed in a position of great difficulty because the strike may be about some very trivial matter or about some issue on which the leaders find themselves unable to support the men's contentions. This has thrown a great strain on the time and energies of officers, who have more than enough to do at present in trying to cope with the job of organization. At the moment hardly anyone but Bustamante himself has any influence over the workers, and as we have seen his constitutional powers are very wide. As with Trinidad, however, where there was exactly the same sort of situation in the months immediately following the disturbances of June 1937, the passage of time, education in trade unionism, and experience, will bring home to the workers the need for union discipline and the true nature of trade union functions.

In September 1938 Manley launched the *People's National Party* at a meeting at which Sir Stafford Cripps was present. The party has had an enthusiastic reception, and proposes to affiliate with the trade unions. Its programme is labour — land settlement, adult suffrage, social legislation, etc. The past few months have been spent in enrolling thousands of new members all over the island

and there is no doubt that its formation has profoundly altered the structure of Jamaican politics.[2]

Summary

It is now possible to ask what has emerged from these years of working class upheaval, with their tale of strike and riot, death and victimization. Two things: the rise of trade unions, and the entry of the working classes into West Indian politics.

Trade Unionism

As we have seen, new unions have sprung up in the bigger colonies for all the principal types of labour, while in the smaller colonies there are either new unions, or other organizations which though not registered as unions, perform the same sort of function. The sections which have proved easiest to organize have been oilfield workers, and people engaged on the waterfront, in inland transport, on public works, and in shops. In most areas their unions have already secured important wage concessions. Agricultural workers, however, have proved exceedingly difficult to organize, and it is only in British Guiana, where special circumstances prevail, that there can be said to be a flourishing agricultural union.

The legal obstacles to the growth of trade unionism have frequently been pointed out. The unions have not the right of peaceful picketing or protection against actions in tort, two rights conferred in Great Britain by the Act of 1906. The government of Trinidad has also on more than one occasion exercised its right of withholding registration from unions of which it disapproves. But it is not so much legal obstacles which have restrained the growth of trade unionism as the attitude of the government and employers. The Secretary of State for the Colonies has announced his desire to foster the growth of trade unionism and collective bargaining, and has appointed Labour Advisers in each colony to assist in bringing unions and employers together. But the colonial administrations have not yet rid themselves of the notion that trade unionism is treasonable. Union leaders are in some places continuously shadowed by the police, and the mildest utterance may provoke a prosecution for sedition. The Government of Trinidad has frequently exercised its right of prohibiting street processions in order to prevent labour demonstrations from taking place. Again, trade unionists are often prohibited from travelling from one colony to another on temporary fraternal visits. This is not the sort of atmosphere in which the object to which the Secretary of State has committed himself is likely to be achieved.

As for the employers, in general they detest the unions and their leaders. They withhold recognition as long as possible, and only the threat of strike action is able to wring concessions from them. The Labour Advisers are supposed to be of assistance in this connection, but whether because of their own lack of interest, or the obstinacy of the employers, the general rule is that they are never successful unless the union is already sufficiently powerful to be able to threaten the employers with strike action. The employers' principal weapon in fighting the unions is victimization, and they use it mercilessly. In a small community where everybody knows what everybody else is doing and saying, it is easy for employers to keep each other informed of the names of 'troublesome' workers. Many discharged workers have found themselves not only unable to get work with any other employer, but also forced to give up at short notice the house or land which they may have been renting. It is this easy victimization which is the main obstacle to the growth of the unions.

In view of all this it is surprising that the unions have met with such response from the workers. Indeed in many of the newer unions the leaders are faced with the problem that their members, with a bitter sense of generations of injustice, are over-militant, and anxious to strike on the flimsiest pretext. In the absence of trade union traditions it is a slow and difficult task to inculcate the subtleties of trade union strategy, and it will take some time before the workers have grasped the nature of trade union functions and methods, and grown to accept trade union discipline. That is why some leaders are tending to discourage strike action at present, and devoting themselves to consolidating and instructing their membership. In the task of education they are helped by the labour press which has been started in the larger colonies, by issuing pamphlets, and by regular meetings. There is also a great demand for literature on trade unionism, and any person or organization in Great Britain who desired to help the movement would probably serve it best by sending out such literature, and by endowing club rooms where libraries may be kept and where workers may gather after work for social intercourse and for educational meetings.

As for the leaders, it must be admitted that one or two are irresponsible extremists brought into prominence by their genius for agitation in a period of unrest and upheaval. But such men are a tiny minority. Indeed one interesting feature of the last few years has been the way in which the agitator who led a major upheaval has given way after the upheaval to sober responsible men who set themselves the task of building up trade unions. The vast majority of the new leaders are extraordinarily capable and intelligent; a few are lawyers or other members of the educated middle classes, but most of them are just workers with a genius for organization and a capacity for sacrifice. They are very conscious of their responsibility, and though the difficulties in their path are many, they are confident of eventual success.

Politics

Important as have been the results on the trade union front, on the political front nothing short of a revolution has occurred. It is not merely that the British government has been forced to appoint a strong Royal Commission specifically to investigate social conditions. Nor is it even the fact that governments have already been forced to adopt all sorts of measures to meet the grievances of the workers — land settlement, fixing minimum wages, expenditure on public works and slum clearance, old age pensions, enactment of workmen's compensation, etc. This is indeed a revolution, for hitherto West Indian governments have not regarded measures of this sort as of primary importance. But even more important than all this is the fact that the working classes have become organized politically, and that their interests have been forced into the foreground.

To understand the full significance of this revolution, we must take a glance at the history of West Indian politics. While some of the educated coloured elements sought to identify themselves with the ruling oligarchy others rebelled and sought through political action to secure for the Negro a higher status in society. This has always been true of West Indian politics; even before the emancipation of slavery the free coloured people were in constant conflict with the plantocracy, and throughout the nineteenth centry that conflict continued. It came to a head after the Great War with the formation of *Representative Government Associations* throughout the Lesser Antilles. These associations were narrowly middle class in their aims; they wished particularly to see more middle class representation on the legislative councils, and to increase the number of posts in the civil service to which educated Negroes might be appointed. Mass support was easily obtainable for such liberal ends, the urban workers willingly associating themselves in meetings, demonstrations and petitions with the demand for constitutional reform and racial equality in the civil service. But there was hardly anything in the programmes of these associations of direct working class interest, only the associations of Trinidad and Grenada (significantly called *Workingmen's Associations*) including in

their programmes such things as slum clearance and workmen's compensation.

Agitation for constitutional reform was intense just after the war, and as a result the Colonial Office sent Major Wood (now Lord Halifax) to visit the colonies in 1921. His recommendations were followed by constitutional changes in Trinidad, the Windward Islands and Dominica in 1924, providing for the election of a minority of middle class members to the Legislative Councils on a very restricted franchise. This was a victory for the movement, but it was felt that the numbers to be elected were far too small, and agitation continued. At the same time the Associations became convinced that the colonies could not achieve much if they acted separately, and federation sprang to the forefront of their programmes.

The further agitation led the Colonial Office to appoint in 1932 a commission to consider the possibility of closer union between Trinidad and the Windward and Leeward Islands. So soon as the announcement was made representatives from these colonies and one from Barbados met in conference at Dominica in November 1932.

The main task which the Dominica conference set itself was the elaboration of a West Indian constitution, on the two major foundations of federation and full elective control. All went well until the question of the franchise was raised, the representative of Trinidad leading the demand for adult suffrage. On this there was no agreement, and eventually the conference adopted a compromise solution permitting each colony within the federation to settle its own franchise qualifications. It was clear that many of the leaders of West Indian politics were unsympathetic to the aspirations of the working classes.

The real significance of the revolution of 1935–38 is that such narrow political thought has faded into insignificance. The major issues discussed today no longer revolve round the aspirations of the middle classes, but are set by working class demands. Federation and elective control are still in the forefront, but they are now desired in the interest of the masses, and side by side with them are new issues — industrial legislation, slum clearance, social services, land settlement, extension of the franchise and others — which were seldom discussed before. Initiative has passed into the hands of trade union leaders and new working class bodies like the *Progressive League* of Barbados, the *Workingmen's Association* of St. Vincent, and the *People's National Party* of Jamaica. These also have much middle class support, and many have strong middle class leadership, but their programmes are much wider than their predecessors.

Focusing all this new spirit is the *British Guiana and West India Labour Congress*, newly established as a clearing house for labour opinion. Its inaugural meeting was held in British Guiana in June 1938, and was attended by delegates of trade unions and labour organizations from British Guiana, Dutch Guiana, Trinidad, Barbados and Jamaica. The first meeting merely set up machinery and expressed solidarity, but on the announcement of the appointment of a Royal Commission a second meeting was summoned for November 1938 in Trinidad, and delegates invited from labour organizations in every colony.

It is a far cry from the Dominica conference of 1932 to the Trinidad congress of 1938. As will be seen from the report quoted in the Appendix, federation and full elective control figured prominently in the resolutions, but even more attention was devoted to the demands for adult suffrage, dismemberment of plantations and creation of a cooperative peasant community, nationalization of the sugar factories and public utilities, provision of old age pensions, health and unemployment insurance, and reformed industrial legislation. This was essentially a Labour Congress. It is mainly on the development of this united labour movement that future progress in the West Indies depends.

What Can Be Done

We have described the social background of the working classes and the rise of the new labour movement. We propose now to discuss the objects of the movement, and to analyze the possible methods of attaining them.

The general aims of the movement are to raise the economic and cultural standards of the masses, and to secure for them conditions of freedom and equality. The attempt to raise the standard of living itself has two sides. First the total income of the West Indies must be considerably increased, and in the second place it must be more equitably distributed. It would be a mistake to ignore either of these two aspects. A considerable increase in the price of sugar, followed by increased wages, would not satisfy the movement's demands for redistribution and equality; and yet without a considerable increase in total income the standard of living would still be very low even if everybody's income were equal. Let us therefore begin by asking what can be done to raise the total income of these colonies.

Economic Policy

Undoubtedly the major problem here is the low price of West Indian exports, and it is for this rea-

son that West Indians ask for special treatment in British markets, and particularly for an increased preference on sugar. They ask too for assistance by way of loans at low rates of interest and free grants of money to make a radical attack on poverty — to open up new areas and finance land settlement schemes, to improve housing conditions, to build new schools, and finance the proper training to teachers, and to build and equip hospitals and clinics, to drain swamps and supply drugs for a concerted attack on malaria, yaws, venereal diseases, children's diseases, and other ailments of the people. Undoubtedly many of these things can be done in the next hundred years relying solely on local taxation and the capital market, but if any fairly rapid progress is to be made — and conditions are so bad that it is essential to adopt drastic measures — it can only be done with British help.

What claim have West Indians to demand such sacrifices from the British people? Briefly this. It is the British who by their action in past centuries are responsible for the presence in these islands of the majority of their inhabitants, whose ancestors as slaves contributed millions to the wealth of Great Britain, a debt which the British have yet to repay. Moreover, if the islands were under French or American control they would come within the ambit of highly protective systems which make the prosperity of Guadeloupe or Puerto Rico put to shame the poverty of the British possessions. If it were possible for the inhabitants to migrate, distress would not be so acute, but restrictions on migration prevent this solution. Either Britain must help, or the people must remain very poor.

Yet, essential as it is that increased preferential treatment and grants and loans from the imperial treasury should be accorded if we are to see in the near future any noticeable improvement in West Indian conditions, no one proposes that these islands should live permanently on the charity of Great Britain. It is therefore necessary to discuss what measures can be taken in order to secure that in the long run they may be able to stand permanently and prosperously on their own feet.

First, what can be done permanently to improve the conditions under which the world's sugar is marketed? West Indian producers have always claimed that in the absence of foreign tariffs and quota restrictions discriminating against them, they would be able to hold their own in the world market, and this view was supported by the Sugar Commission of 1930. Not only do foreigners shut out their sugar, but even Britain by means of a subsidy produces as much sugar as all the islands put together. Recently an international sugar agreement has been signed in the hope of raising prices by restricting output, but it seems unlikely that the islands will gain as much from any slight increase in prices which it may bring about as they are certain to lose from restriction of output. More might be gained from an attempt to renew the Brussels Convention.

Secondly some attempt should be made to reopen the American market by a trade agreement. The United States' share of West Indian exports fell from 26% in 1930 to 7% in 1933 as a result of American restrictions, and is still very low. Great things had been expected from the recent Anglo-American trade agreement, but hopes were frustrated, and there is now a demand for a trade agreement to be negotiated directly. The United States is the natural outlet for West Indian exports, and it is vital that it should be open.

Finally, new sources of revenue must be found to replace the existing staples. It is possible that with care and encouragement fruit growing may become an important industry; also a greater cultivation of foodstuffs and greater attention to the home market would doubtless be profitable, and this is bound up with the question of land settlement discussed later. But despite this it is difficult to feel much confidence in the future of agriculture, and it seems necessary for the islands to seek other means of livelihood. The tourist trade offers some prospects, but seems unlikely ever to become a principal source of revenue. The policy which seems to offer most hope of permanent success is for these islands to follow in the footsteps of other agricultural countries in industrialization. There is scope for factories for refining sugar, making chocolate, utilizing copra, making dairy products, etc. Such enterprises would need to be subsidized at the start while local labour was trained and the local market won, but after the initial period should be able to stand on their own legs. No other policy seems to offer such permanent prospects as the development of local industries.

Redistribution

Now we can turn to the other aspect of the problem, redistribution of income to secure to the masses an adequate share of what they produce. There are four main weapons which can be used for this purpose: (1) collective bargaining and minimum wage machinery; (2) industrial legislation; (3) taxation; and (4) redistribution of property.

Collective bargaining and minimum wage machinery

These can be discussed together since their economic effects are more or less the same. The struggle for higher wages is the method of redistribution which appeals most strongly to the worker since it is the weapon he can most effectively use by direct action. But unfortunately it is probably the least efficient method of redistributing income, since it is so liable to have effects different from those which are intended. Much of the wage increases secured by one group of workers often falls not on the employers but on other groups of workers. This is because in general (we shall say something about the exceptions in a moment) the employer combines labour with other factors in whatever proportion is cheapest at existing prices. If then wages rise, he will react in one of several ways. He may use less labour per acre, and more capital, discharging some of his workers who will either become unemployed or be forced into less paid occupations, reducing wages there still further — one group of workers will have gained at the expense of another. Or he may raise the price of his product, if it is one being sold in the local market; and if it is bought mainly by other workers, it is they who will suffer. A special illustration of this is the way in which wage increases granted to municipal and government employees are passed on in the form of increased taxation, which may well fall on other workers. Or again the employer may react by reducing the price offered to some other grade of worker. For instance an increase in the wage of dock labourers may simply reduce the price the peasant gets for his bananas, just as an increase in the wage of workers in sugar factories may mean unemployment and lower wages for field workers, or lower prices offered to peasants for their cane. An increase of wages gained by one group so often falls upon another group that it has to be regarded as one of the least efficient methods of trying to redistribute income. And unfortunately the result is the same even if all workers are highly organized; an all-round increase in wages may simply be followed by an all-round increase in prices (as recently in France) or an all-round increase in unemployment.

The exception to this arises in three cases. First an increase in wages may stimulate employers to be more efficient; this is not likely to be of much importance in the West Indies where years of low prices have already taxed employers to the utmost. Secondly, by enabling workers to eat better and to live in better conditions it may so increase their productivity as to pay for itself; this point is likely to be of some importance in these colonies where malnutrition is responsible for a low productive efficiency. And thirdly, in so far as employers are combined monopolistically to keep wages low, an increase will not affect prices or the volume of employment; this point also may be of some importance. In so far as the last two conditions apply, the attempt to increase wages by collective bargaining and the issue of minimum wage orders will be entirely to the benefit of the workers, without one group of workers being driven to exploit another.

Discouraging as this picture is, it is no condemnation of trade unionism, for trade unions do not exist solely for wage fixing purposes. The union is the worker's solicitor, representing him in negotiations with his employer, and increasing his status and dignity; it is also his insurance company, protecting him against illness, accident and unemployment; and it is his political machine, through which he may hope to improve his conditions by legislative action. If its successes may sometimes be gained at the expense of other workers, this is merely an argument for close inter-union cooperation to prevent actions which may be mutually harmful.

Industrial legislation

Here again much of the cost of industrial legislation falls not on the employers but on the workers themselves. Shorter hours, workmen's compensation, better working conditions, restrictions on child labour, social insurances — all these things either cause employers to raise prices, or reduce the wages they are able to pay, or the volume of employment they are able to offer. But to point out that the cost in large measure falls on the worker, and not, as he may be tempted to think, on the employer, is not to say that such legislation is undesirable; on the contrary, it is well worth having, and paying for. And the part of the cost which falls on the worker can be reduced by appropriate taxation and subsidy.

Taxation

High direct taxation offers the best method of redistributing income, since we can be more or less certain where its burden will fall. It has, of course, its limitations. If it is too high, it will reduce the savings of the rich, and this in the long run will reduce the standard of living of the workers if it results in the community consuming its capital; or again if it is too high it will discourage foreigners from investing capital in the islands, and this can only help to keep the workers poor. This is a consideration of great importance, since the future development of the colonies will mainly depend on their power to attract capital from abroad. Yet direct taxation is at present so low, that it should be possible to increase it considerably with hardly any of these unfavourable effects.

At present the bulk of the revenue is raised by indirect taxation, expecially import duties, which fall most heavily on the poor. It should be a major aim of the labour movement to reverse this position, using the proceeds of high land taxes, income taxes and death duties to provide adequate social services, especially health, education, and social insurances.

Redistribution of property

The present distribution of land is the last legacy of West Indian slavery. In those grim days all the cultivated area was concentrated in the hands of a small white slave-owning aristocracy, and despite the rise in the past century of a not inconsiderable number of smallholders, the position remains more or less the same today. The consequences of this land monopoly are far-reaching. In the first place, the planters, few in number and bound together by social and racial ties, are able to and do combine to fix wages at the level which suits them best. Secondly, the distribution of income, and in particular the right to the rent of land, is most inequitable, the poverty of the masses contrasting sharply with the luxury of the landed aristocracy. Thirdly the shadow of the plantation carries with it the touch of serfdom, depriving the labourer of that sense of dignity and independence which would be his in a society in which property was more widely diffused, and this is a factor most important in debasing mentally and spiritually the West Indian labourer. Finally such a concentration of property gives to the planters in the political field a power which they have always used to advance their own interests. All independent authorities are agreed on this, and two Royal Commissions (1897 and 1930) have said:

'No reform affords so good a prospect for the permanent welfare in the future of the West Indies as the settlement of the labouring population on the land as small peasant proprietors, and in many places this is the only means by which the population can in future be supported.'

Granted the social advantages of such a measure, it is pertinent to consider how far it is economically advisable. Three considerations are relevant here. First it appears to be generally agreed that the greater cultivation of food and rearing of cattle which would result would not merely increase the national dividend but also reduce the effect of cyclical fluctuations. Secondly, the relative efficiency of peasant and plantation production is a subject much debated. To establish a prosperous peasantry it is necessary not merely to provide land, but also to provide instruction through schools, societies, and peasant advisers, to establish peasant banks or cooperative credit societies, and to provide for cooperative processing and marketing of the product. Given these essential institutions, there seems no reason why the West Indian peasant should not learn to utilize the land as capably as the planter. With the exception of the sugar-cane, most of their products are eminently suited to peasant production; and even in the case of cane smallholders in Trinidad already contribute almost half the output, despite the absence on any adequate scale of the institutions essential to peasant success. Finally the ratio of land to labour is highly relevant in determining how far a peasant policy can be pushed. In a community like Barbados, where severe over-population demands intensive cultivation of every inch of soil, definite limits are set to peasant agriculture, such as do not exist in British Guiana with its abundant spaces. In all these colonies it is necessary in addition to dismembering the estates to open up new areas which for want of roads are now uncultivated, in order to make available new land for peasant settlement. It is very desirable too, that roads and drains should be provided to open up the vast lands of British Guiana and British Honduras as outlets for surplus island populations; these are projects which have long been discussed and are now a vital necessity.

Political Questions

The labour movement is committed to this programme of redistribution, but there are many difficulties in its path. A major obstacle is the present constitutional structure.

The theory underlying these constitutions is that all power is vested in the Governor who through his control of the Executive Council (to which he appoints all the members) and of the Legislature (to which — except in Barbados — he appoints the majority) is able to put through, with the consent of the Colonial Office, any policy which appeals to him. When this type of constitution was extended to Jamaica and other islands after the emancipation of the slaves, these powers were given with deliberate instructions to use them to protect an inarticulate Negro proletariat against a vengeful white plantocracy. But it is a sad commentary on the failure of the system that the people who are most in its favour are those whom it was supposed to attack, while it is detested by those whom it was supposed to protect. Such has been the antagonism of government to proletarian needs, and so close its connections with vested interests, whose representatives are generally the only people chosen by the Governors for nomination to their councils, that the impression is now widespread among the people that the Governors and officials are little more than the tools of a white oligarchy of planters, merchants and bankers, in whose society they spend most of their time, and whose will it is that really governs the islands; indeed, that the policy of the government is the policy of the local club decided on, perhaps, over a round of golf or a whisky and soda.

It is difficult to explain in any other terms the indifference or hostility of governments to measures advanced by the people's representatives for improving the conditions of the masses, and even to the recommendations of Royal Commissions. Take for instance land settlement. This has been advocated by Royal Commissions for forty years and it is difficult to escape the conclusion that the only reason why it has made comparatively so little headway, is that given by the Commission of 1896:

'The settlement of the labourer on the land has not, as a rule, been viewed with favour in the past by persons interested in sugar estates. What suited them best was a large supply of labourers entirely dependent upon being able to find work on estates and consequently subject to their control and willing to work at low rates of wages.

It is manifest (as the Sugar Commission added in 1930) that where the economy of a community depends practically entirely, as that of Barbados, St. Kitts and Antigua still does, upon a single industry carried on by the employment of wage labourers on estates, the public policy of the class most influential in guiding the government must almost inevitably incline to this economic view. If they encouraged action which, in their belief, must tend to diminish their labour supply, they would be cutting away the branch upon which they sit'.

Vested interests, in close alliance with government, have held unchallenged sway in these islands for three hundred years, opposing not merely land settlement, but any measure which in raising the standards of the masses would react unfavourably (from their point of view) on the level of wages. They have so whittled down workmen's compensation ordinances, that they exclude the bulk of the workers, and have steadily opposed other industrial legislation. Proposals for cooperative marketing of fruit met with steady resistance for many years, and when a cooperative association did come into existence in Jamaica, a trading combine used its political and economic influence to wreck it. They are careful through the use of indirect taxation to keep the burden of taxation mainly on the masses, and they refuse to tax themselves sufficiently to provide decent educational, medical and other social services. Their power has lasted long, but its end is in sight.

The labour movement knows that measures of the kind which it proposes can only be enacted if there is strong mass pressure on the Legislature. That is why constitutional reform is in the foreground of its programme. Unconstitutional mass pressure in recent months has already forced through many measures, and unless constitutional methods are provided, it is likely that the masses will have to continue to resort to unconstitutional means of securing their ends as the only measures open to them. The alternative before the British Government is to provide in these islands the constitutional machinery which will make unnecessary a resort to violence.

It is fashionable in modern Europe to speak contemptuously of the vote. It is indeed no panacea, nor is it an easy instrument to handle. Yet is is the best method yet evolved for securing the freedom of the ordinary man and enabling him to protect and advance his interests. West Indian constitutions reserve the vote to the few, and permit only men of substance to set up for election. Until the franchise is extended as widely as possible, the income and property qualifications for membership of the legislature removed, the number of nominated members reduced, and the elected members given a real control over the policy of the government, it is unlikely that there will be any substantial improvement in the standard of living, and useless to dismiss the inevitable disturbances as 'political agitation.' Constitutional reform which will enable it to get into power, is the first aim of the labour movement.

One other important political issue is that of Federation. The demand for it is based on two sets of reasons; first West Indian national aspirations, which are a powerful force in its favour; and secondly economy. The latter argument has been accepted by most official reports since 1897, and has long been obvious to the people themselves. Everyone knows the benefits which have been derived from establishing one expert agricultural service for all the islands — such as no single one could by itself afford — and it has long been accepted that education, health, police, the judiciary, and in fact most of the services could be administered much better and at a smaller aggregate cost if expert central departments were established in place of the present independent services. Indeed tentative beginnings have been made with education in the Windward and Leeward Islands, and plans for many other services have long been drawn up.

What has stood in the way of federation is not the sea; that is no obstacle in these days of aeroplanes and wireless telephone. The real stumbling block has been the opposition of small local potentates, fearful that their voices, all-powerful in a small island, will be unheard in a large federation. Nevertheless it is essential in the general interest to ignore these small magnates and to proceed with the federation of Trinidad, Barbados, the Windward and Leeward Islands and British Guiana in the immediate future, leaving Jamaica perhaps until a later date when better communications have been established.

The labour movement is on the march. It has already behind it a history of great achievement in a short space of time. It will make of the West Indies of the future a country where the common man may lead a cultured life in freedom and prosperity.

Notes

1. On 2 March 1939 the employers' association signed an agreement with the union recognizing it for purposes of collective bargaining, giving it the right to negotiate in any case of dispute, and to hold meetings on the plantations.
2. Since the above paragraphs were written, there have been important developments. Friction between the Bustamante unions and the older *Jamaica Workers' and Tradesmen's Union* led Mr. Bustamante early in February 1939 to declare a general strike. This action was very unpopular; the Governor declared a state of emergency; and after much high feeling the strike was eventually called off.
   As a result of the general situation produced by Mr. Bustamante's action, Mr. Manley, after consultation with him and with the Governor, announced the formation on 22 February of a small 'Industrial Advisory Council' to advise the trade union movement. Its members are prominent in the People's National Party, and are mainly of professional and middle class status.
   The Council's first action was to take steps to heal differences between conflicting unions. On 25 February the *Jamaica Trades Union Council* was formed, and it has been successful in bringing the principal unions together. Its first meeting was attended by representative of the Bustamante unions, the *Workers' and Tradesmen's Union*, the *Montego Bay Clerks' Assocation*, the *Builders' and Allied Trades' Union*, and the *Jamaica United Clerks' Association*. A constitution was adopted giving the TUC important advisory powers.
   It is expected that the Council will soon urge that the constitutions of the Bustamante unions should be revised so as to make them more democratic, in view of continuous complaints of the autocratic position of the President.

SECTION TEN
Economic Diversification and Transformation

The political and constitutional break with the past that resulted from many of the struggles for nationhood and democracy in the years before the Second World War, created the context for a corresponding 'economic revolution.' In reality, this meant a departure from traditional mercantile ideas and system that had locked Caribbean economies into a division of labour whereby they specialized in the mass production of agricultural goods for export to their corresponding metropolitan centers.

Caribbean economic history prior to 1945 has been essentially that of plantation agriculture, and the commercial and financial network that maintained it. However, the argument in favour of industrialization as the way to achieve self sustained growth gained credibility at policy levels of government. This development signalled a rejection of the British colonial mercantile principle that 'not even a nail was to be manufactured in the colonies.'

In Puerto Rico especially, government wasted no time in putting in place legislative provisions for the encouragement of industrialization. Broad based manufacturing, tourism, and agro-industries were encouraged to replace sugar production at the centre of economic activity. Industries with a labour intense bias and an import substitution potential were encouraged to give life to the policy of open capital invitation. This policy became known as industrialization by invitation, or the Puerto Rican Model. Here, Dietz provides an assessment of what transpired in Puerto Rico during the period of so-called 'Operation Bootstrap', while Brewster and Thomas otherwise outline how, and with what effects, this approach to economic growth took root in the English speaking West Indies. Levitt and Best outline the characteristic historical features of the Caribbean economy, and show how attempts to introduce industrialization models contradict many of the persistent structural and ideological features of the economy. These characteristic features, they suggest, constitute inhibitions to economic efficiency. In addition, their deep seated historical nature indicates that balanced economic transformation would be rendered problematic in the long term. Inertia, then, was the logical result, which in turn unleashed frustration and negative attitudes within the economic environment to the detriment of entrepreneurial development. Goslinga examines the impact of oil refining upon the Netherland Antilles, and suggests that many of the socio-political problems remain in spite of unprecedented levels of economic accumulation.

Industrialization of the West Indies: The Manufacturing Sector In The Total Economy

Havelock Brewster and Clyde Thomas

During the past two generations West Indian economic thinking, if not policy, has seen some fairly sharp turns. First, there was the general and official belief that the industrialization of the area was both economically impractical and, in many ways, undesirable. It was assumed that the West Indies was and should be essentially an agricultural community. The economic facts of the area as well as the relevant economic theories were considered to have firmly established this as an absolute truth. In some ways it was fortunate, though it was used as 'proof' in support of these static ideas, that in the early post-war years, there was the coincidence of a relatively low level of unemployment with a state of 'prosperity' in the traditional industry, sugar. These relatively favourable circumstances were themselves the outcome of forces quite unrelated to the rationale upon which West Indian primary specialization rested. There was at the time a relatively high death-rate and a much lower birth-rate than at present. In addition, there was the general shortage of sugar in the sterling area whilst the sugar industry had not yet taken its great strides in labour-saving technical innovation. The accelerated mechanization of the industry in the late 1950s was an attempt to reduce unit cost in anticipation of less favourable conditions. The fundamental problem in this respect was not that the wage rate was too high but that the labour input made the total wage cost disproportionately heavy. Moreover, there was official and social pressure in some areas, which coincided with the effects of technological innovation, to rationalize the labour force by increasing the average number of days worked by labourers in the industry in order that the average level of earnings might rise.

In the early 1950s there took place a definite swing to the idea that industrialization was the only answer to the area's economic problems which, because of changing economic circumstances, were now becoming apparent. The natural increase to the population was reaching unusual heights, even by international standards. This was caused partly by the decline in the death rate and a more

satisfactory ratio of sexes. Although these were also years of 'prosperity' for the sugar industry, the process of labour-saving innovation was gaining momentum. In addition, despite this 'prosperity', the income contribution of the sugar industry was scarcely able to keep pace with the increments to the population as exemplified by the position of Barbados and St. Kitts. Jamaica was fortunate to find bauxite, Antigua, tourism; Trinidad and Tobago expanded the petroleum industry. Guyana was, in a sense, saved by the phenomenal growth of the rice industry, as bauxite in that territory, in contrast to Jamaica, played, right up to the early 1960s, a passive role in its economic development. Moreover, it appeared in several places as if the limits of readily cultivable land had been virtually reached. Large-scale unemployment was now becoming, if it had not already become, an endemic feature of West Indian life. The swing then was an understandable and even a rational one, founded, as it was, on the real economic conditions of the region and on the necessity to find a substitute for what was appearing more and more vividly to be a dead-end.

This new kind of thinking was not very accurately reflected in governments' policy. There were at the time several limitations to governments' behaviour. The more important of these were the conception of government's role as inherited from and applied by various United Kingdom governments; the heavy force of traditional practice; the fact that agriculture was indeed the largest employer of labour and that both large-scale spatial and occupational mobility would create more problems than could readily be handled; the scarcity of capital resources, fuel, industrial knowledge and skills and entrepreneurial ability. Despite these limitations it became more or less clear that there was a tendency to discuss the problem as a choice between agricultural and industrial development, with the proponents of the more 'enlightened economics' not hesitating to take the latter opinion.

The 'new economics', founded on the practical realities of the West Indian situation, was ushered on the scene by a more general revolution in this direction and by the much heralded industrial transformation that was taking place in Puerto Rico. In the West Indies it took its more striking form in the very generous and competitive concessions which were being given as incentives to industrial development. About this time, Professor Arthur Lewis's publication, *The Industrialization of the British West Indies* appeared and attracted fairly wide attention. Unfortunately, the general and incorrect impression which seemed to have been conveyed by this publication and its title was that the proponents of the new economics held the correct view. In fact, however, Professor Lewis's standpoint was differently stated, as may be shown by his words: 'Those who speak as if the choice in the West Indies lay between agricultural development and industrial development have failed completely to understand the problem'.

The general argument of that publication may be stated in different ways. One is as follows: The productivity of agriculture should be increased because, at the present level, it can give only a meagre standard of living and provide a small and inadequate demand for the products of industry. This increase in agricultural productivity can take place only if the number of persons on the land is reduced because the limits of cultivable lands are practically reached and because no very substantial increase can be expected from land productivity. The way to make possible this reduction in the number of persons practising agriculture is to provide alternative jobs in manufacturing industry. Thus, there is a closely complementary relationship between industrial and agricultural development. It is apparent, too, that this argument does not suggest that industry is the only avenue through which the West Indies can solve its economic problems. However, it lends itself to such an interpretation in that industrialization is made a necessary requirement for West Indian economic growth and expanded employment opportunities.

Now, we have been somewhat chastened by the apparent inability of industry to cure the major economic ill, unemployment. In a practical sense, the most disillusioning experience has been that of Puerto Rico which, lying in the midst of the region, is as much the showpiece of industrialization as of unemployment and the mal-distribution of wealth and income. Indeed, a similar statement may be made with respect to Latin American development in general. In principle too we have begun to question whether the capital resources as well as the level of internal and possible external demand required for the absorption in industry of the unemployed and of the increments to the labour force can, within the foreseeable future, be attained.

These doubts are rooted not only in the sheer physical size of the task, for the region now has about 280,000 persons in open unemployment alone, whilst the population of working age is being added to at the rate of 40,000 a year. It is also rooted in the operation of the economic system and in the nature of technology and of technical innovations. All this has now led to an increased willingness to think that the role of agriculture needs to be reviewed. In one sense, this takes the form precisely of the complementary relationship which Professor Lewis stressed in the early 1950s.

However, in another sense, it is different from Professor Lewis's view of that period which he himself seems to have recognized implicitly in his article 'Jamaica's Economic Problems' published in September 1964. The difference has several aspects. Firstly, the level of unemployment has become much greater than it was at the turn of the 1940s. In general, the rate and the absolute size of open unemployment have increased by at least 100%. This is itself partly caused by persons emigrating from the rural areas, voluntarily or by force of circumstances, partly by labour displacement in the sugar industry and partly by the structure of demand and the inability of these technologically dual economies to adjust to the factor proportions of the region. Not only have the technical coefficients of the 'modern sector' been totally incapable of adjusting to a labour surplus situation but the changing relationship of labour-costs to non-labour costs, in the absence of corrective measures, has permitted and provided an economic rationale for the reverse process of saving in the unit labour cost of production. Thus, the West Indies has been left with the paradoxical situation of 'saving', not of the relatively scarce resource but of the apparently relatively abundant resource.[1] At present therefore, it is highly impractical, though it probably was not so twenty years ago, to speak of industry absorbing labour at such a rate as to make possible a sufficient reduction of workers in agriculture in order that the productivity of that sector might be improved. The facts of the present situation are that even the most optimistic prospects for industry cannot ensure the absorption of the present unemployment, let alone the natural increments to the labour force, plus the disguised unemployed, plus the release from low-productivity agriculture.

Secondly, features are appearing in agriculture which permitted a somewhat less pessimistic interpretation of its ability to provide a moderate standard of living for the present agricultural labour force and probably for some addition to this. For example, there are some possibilities for both a more extensive and intensive cultivation, particularly in the larger territories. A variety of crops,

such as rice, bananas, root crops and other vegetables, tree crops like citrus and coffee, to name a
few, appear to be quite far from exhausting the
possibilities of land productivity increases. It has
been suggested that the yield of rice per acre in
Guyana can be increased from the present 1,230
lbs. per acre to somewhere between 2,220 and
4,440 lbs. per acre, based on the experience of the
United States, Italy, Australia, Japan and Indonesia. So also, it is possible, based on the experience
of similar areas in the Caribbean and South America, that the yield of banana cultivation could rise
from 2.5 to 8.0 tons an acre. Indeed, practically the
whole range of agriculture, with the exception of
sugar, falls into this category. Besides, new commodities and the quickly rising demand for existing
ones such as livestock, dairy products and vegetables will make it possible for the earnings per
capita of agricultural workers to rise. In addition,
opportunities do exist for large-scale co-operation
and for a reorganization of the pattern of land distribution with respect to idle land as well as with
respect to land in use. Lastly, there are the purely
administrative devices, such as those at the disposal of agricultural marketing corporations, for
influencing the returns to agriculture. These are
only some of the things which lead us to review
the role of agriculture in relation to what industry
can be expected to do. No longer now is it possible
to discard the likelihood of fairly good returns from
the ownership and cultivation of relatively small
areas of land.

In this study we shall look at the possibilities of
industrialization from the viewpoint of regional
import substitution. This is not intended to imply
that an export trade in industrial goods is either
impossible or undesirable. The feasibility of the
latter involves additional dimensions and forms
more conveniently a separate area of enquiry. The
more substantive reasons, however, for treating
import substitution in isolation are that it presents
immediate and assessable opportunities which
avoid the more difficult problems of finding export
markets and maintaining at once a high degree of
competitiveness with respect to quality and cost of
production.

At once it is important to form some idea of the
income and employment equivalent of the present
volume of imports. This sort of perspective, even
though it is a rather static one, is necessary in order
to set some rough limits to the prospects of industry
when this is judged against the background of the
total economic scene. At present, total West Indian
imports of manufactures (based on Sections 4 to 9
of the S.I.T.C.) from non-regional sources amount
to about $800m. Certainly all of this cannot be
replaced by domestic production but let us assume,

for present purposes, that it can. If we allow about
30% for the import-content of such production and
20% as the foreign distributors' margin, these
being empirically supportable estimates, it means
that something like $400m. can immediately be
added to the region's real gross domestic product,
as a maximum. This is equivalent to about 13% of
the present West Indian GDP, that is, to about two
years' growth. If, in turn, this addition to the
region's product should grow at the same rate at
which importation of these products was rising,
that is at 9% a year, then, other things not changing, it would add about 1.1% to the 'normal'
annual rate of growth (that is, the rate of growth in
the absence of such import replacement).

The employment equivalent of the present level
of imports can be approximated by dividing the
potential addition to domestic product by the
potential per capita value of such manufacturing
industry. In Trinidad-Tobago, at present, the per
capita value of manufacturing is about $2,500 but,
with the range of industry suggested by our import
replacement assumption, it would certainly be considerably higher than that figure. An estimate of
$5,000 is suggested by the experience of such rel-
atively small-scale and small-production countries
as Eire and New Zealand which, nevertheless, have
virtually the whole range of manufacturing industry which the West Indies might contemplate establishing. On this basis, immediate complete import
replacement of manufactured goods would create
directly employment for some 80,000 persons, as
a maximum, and for an additional 5,000 or so a
year thereafter.[2]

These estimates of income and employment,
whilst they give what might be regarded as the
maximum direct contribution of immediate total
import-replacement of manufactured goods, are
themselves, of course, very approximately
derived and can easily give rise to many fastidious
queries. For example, the creation of income
through import substitution will also be dependent on the prices at which the new commodities
can be produced and the price elasticities of
demand for such commodities. If the prices of
domestic production are higher than import
prices, as may well be the case, there may be a
tendency for the quantity bought to fall unless this
is offset by the purchases of the newly employed
and the indirect additions to the income of the old
industries. In an extreme case, where for example
the price elasticity of demand is very high, there
may be a fall in the aggregate demand for import-
substitute commodities.

In addition, the indirect contribution to income
and employment, working through the linkage and
multiplier effects, have not been estimated, though

they can certainly be expected to be quite substantial. With an overall combined marginal propensity to save and to import of 0.5 to 0.6, a realistic total West Indian coefficient, the indirect contribution may well be fully equal to the direct contribution. Indeed, it is becoming increasingly apparent that more attention needs to be paid to the indirect creation of employment, particularly in the 'Service' sectors.[3] A good example of this is offered by the recent experience of Jamaica and Trinidad and Tobago. In Jamaica, between 1957 and 1962, about 7,000 additional jobs were created in the manufacturing sector (excluding sugar) and, whilst employment in sugar and other agriculture declined, the number employed in distribution and other services increased by some 5,000.[4] In Trinidad and Tobago employment in manufacturing is recorded as having increased, between 1957 and 1963, by about 6,000. At the same time employment in agriculture and mining declined, but employment in services increased by 14,000 and by another 17,000 in commerce and communications.

Nonetheless, it would be reasonable on the basis of these orders of magnitude, despite their static limitations, to draw a conclusion that a large-scale regional import substitution programme for manufactures, if this were to prove feasible, has such an important contribution to make that it entirely warrants closer examination. At the same time, it is apparent that the direct and indirect impact of import substitution of manufactured goods may not be able to provide a complete answer to the West Indian problem of large-scale unemployment, though, together with the contribution of other sectors, it probably can give, in time, a satisfactory answer to the problem of low income.

Recent Industrial Development

Industrial development in the region has been confined almost exclusively to Jamaica and Trinidad and Tobago. Since the early 1950s substantial additions have been made to the manufacturing activity of those countries, both in quantity and in range. This was, indeed, a general occurrence in the underdeveloped world. In both Jamaica and Trinidad and Tobago the manufacturing sector (excluding sugar and alcohol) almost trebled its real output between 1950 and the early 1960s. Since, however, they, like other developing countries, were beginning from very low levels of industrialization (excluding sugar and alcoholic beverages) this rate of increase may convey an impression which is not warranted by the absolute volume of production. For example, in 1963 Jamaican production of manufactures (excluding sugar and alcoholic beverages) was valued at only

$119m. ($74 per capita) or 10% of its gross domestic product. In 1951, its value was $33m., that is 8.3% of the gross product. In Trinidad and Tobago, in 1962, the corresponding figure was $106m. ($132 per capita) or 10% also of its gross domestic product. In 1951, its industrial production was valued at $24m., that is 7.8% of the gross product. The relatively low level of West Indian industrialization is partly revealed through the low volume of intermediate transactions between the manufacturing sector and other sectors. The data which are available for the Trinidadian economy for 1962 are illustrative of this point. They are given in Table 3.1.

In general, the low coefficients of inter-sectorial transactions betray the relatively 'untransformed' nature of West Indian development, despite the substantial increases in income which have taken place over the past fifteen years. It is hardly surprising that this should be so, for industrial development in the Caribbean has depended little on indigenous material. The harnessing of this material has itself been blocked by the fact that it is bound up with questions of the scale of output. Thus, backward and forward linkages have been minimal for the most part.

This pattern of development leads to some severe disadvantages. Firstly, it inhibits indigenous technological research. For example, despite its obvious importance, West Indian science has more or less neglected these areas of organic chemistry which are most critical to the region. Secondly, the value-added of industrial production is proportionately smaller than in mature economies. The total employment created per unit of final output is correspondingly smaller and thereby partially explains the poor labour-absorptive capacity of Caribbean economies which appear to be industrializing at a fast rate. Thirdly, the significance of scale economies is obscured. The reason for this lies in the fact that the really substantial savings are made through the dimensional economies of the processes of manufacturing basic and intermediate materials rather than in fabricating end-products. Almost any large industrial sector can be chosen at random to illustrate this point, for example, paper, glass, iron and steel, rubber, plastics, automobiles. Even with respect to the fabrication of end-products, the most important economies are not gained since 'long runs' cannot be secured where a relatively small total demand is itself disaggregated into a large number of specifications.

Thus, the establishment of the so-called 'screwdriver' industries in Jamaica, Trinidad and Tobago and Puerto Rico (for example, automobiles, radio, television, aluminium, steel, rubber and plastic manufactures) strengthens rather than weakens,

Table 3.1. Cost coefficients of input structures, Trinidad-Tobago, 1962

Intermediate Transaction	Alcoholic Beverages and Tobacco	Food Manufacturing	Other Manufacturing
Oil	.0048	.0139	.0324
Alcoholic beverages and Tobacco	—	—	—
Food Manufacturing	—	.0199	—
Other Manufacturing	.0724	.0787	.0214
Transportation	—	.0071	.0064
Distribution	.0139	.0259	.0566
Services	.0281	.0199	.0168
Construction	—	.0193	.0062
Public utilities	.0061	.0063	.0113
Sugar manufacturing	.0163	.0302	—
Sugar growing	—	—	—
Other agriculture	.0163	.1368	.0442
Banks and financial institutions	—	—	.0081
Total	.1578	.3581	.2035

SOURCE: A.A. Francis, 'A Note on Inter-Industry in the Economy of Trinidad and Tobago 1962', Research Papers, Central Statistics Office, Trinidad and Tobago.

the case for functional integration in the Caribbean. It appears that the foreign manufacturer loses none or only a small portion of the firm's overall savings whilst he achieves lower unit cost of a portion of his output in areas which are not heavily dependent on scale and external economies, for example, labour, transportation, customs duties, taxes. In this way, the scale of production loses its pivotal importance as a cost-reducing factor (though, of course, the volume of turnover is always an important factor from the viewpoint of the absolute size of profits).

All this means that foreign manufacturers may be fairly well disposed to establish fabricating or assembling industries in the larger Caribbean countries (Jamaica, Trinidad and Tobago, Puerto Rico). The readiness to do so is promoted by two additional features — the possibility of exporting to nearby countries and the possibility of being eliminated entirely from the market by more enterprising competing companies. (Consider in this connection, the establishment of the Esso Petroleum refinery and the Goodyear tyre factory in Jamaica) Caribbean countries have been inclined and, indeed, forced to seize these opportunities since they are each operating separately under the severe limitations of small size.

What therefore we ought to emphasize is that the scale and external economies argument does not rest simply on the widening of the market for particular commodities, but on the extension of the market in such a way as to make feasible the har-

nessing of indigenous and semi–indigenous primary and intermediate material. It is the latter rather than the former which seems to be the more critical factor in the economic rationalization of functional integration in manufacturing industry. It is apparent that not only does the magnitude of the economies differ, but the minimum scales required for fabricating end-products differ from the minimum scales required for producing basic materials. In this way, the economically disintegrated state of the region is leading to a type of industrialization which has, in the macro-economic sense, inherent defects, whilst it is used to promote the fallacious idea that the ultimate level of development of this kind can be made to coincide with the achievement of high income and full employment. It is ironical that, at this juncture, the process of industrialization should follow Professor Lewis's list of favourable industries.[6]

The Jamaican data we have examined with respect to the cost of production by scale of industrial activity for 1960 give preliminary support to some aspects of the argument above. We have related the cost/sales ratio for a number of industrial sectors to the scale of operation according to number of persons employed. A large establishment is one employing fifteen or more persons; a small establishment, less than fifteen persons. Costs include all costs of production except indirect taxes. This analysis is not put forward as a thorough investigation of the economies of scale. There were problems with respect to the criteria

Table 3.2. Cost/Sales ratios in Jamaican manufacturing industry
(1960) by scale of activity

Industry Group	Large[a]	Urban	Small[b]	Rural
Bread and baking products	.89	.79		.32
Food products	.95		.65	
Beverages	.54		.85	
Tobacco and tobacco products	.33	.51		.52
Textiles and made-up textiles	.87		.38	
Curios and straw goods	.81		.63	
Dressmaking	—	.53		.44
Tailoring	—	.38		.27
Footwear and shoe repairing	.93		.54	
Furniture	.83		.76	
Sawmilling and boxes, other wood products etc.	.93		.80	
Printing and publishing	.77		.72	
Chemicals	.82		.82	
Cement and cement products	.92		.94	
Metal products, metal furniture etc.	.81		.84	
Machinery products	.85		.97	
Construction	.83		.76	

[a] Employs more than 15 persons.
[b] Employs less than 15 persons.
SOURCE: Adapted from information in Industrial Activity, 1960,
Department of Statistics, Kingston, Jamaica.

for determining the scale of operation as well as with respect to the heterogeneity of product. Nonetheless, on the premise that a lower cost/sales ratio may be indicative for some economies, the data suggest that the small operator is not at all outcompeted by the larger operator. The outstanding exceptions to this are the beverage and tobacco products industries. However, the small operator appears to have an advantage in construction, food products, bakery products, straw goods, wood products.

No direct evidence on this question exists with respect to Puerto Rico industry. The evidence, however, is that a significant proportion of the plants deliberately promoted up to 1963 by the Economic Development Administration of that country which has free access to the U.S. market has not been really large-scale. This suggests indirectly, though subject to the same qualifications stated above, that the disadvantage of small size may not have been judged, given the type of industrial development, to be so crucially decisive. Indeed, it suggests implicitly the existence of those features which obstruct the establishment of the larger scale basic manufactures. Table 3.3 shows, for example, that 30% of the 748 plants promoted by EDA up to 1963 employed individually less than twenty persons. In lumber and

wood products three of four plants were in this category; in paper and allied products 57%; chemical and allied products 50%; and fabricated metal products 62%. This is all the more disturbing when one considers that Puerto Rican industrial policy has been based partially on comparative advantages with respect to the United States and that the most important source of this advantage lay in the labour-cost element.

In Tables 3.4 and 3.5 the course of industrial development, as measured by rising output in current dollars, is shown for Jamaica, 1959 to 1963, and for Trinidad and Tobago, 1957 to 1962. In the case of Jamaica, industrial output averaged an annual rate of increase of 6% and maintained a constant 10% share of the aggregate product. Industrial output increased *pari passu* with the overall rate of growth. In Trinidad and Tobago, on the other hand, the manufacturing sector increased its share from the 8% level of 1957 to 10% in 1962. This was the outcome of two occurrences. Firstly, there was the usually fast rate of growth of the manufacturing sector itself. This, during the years 1957 to 1962, averaged, as measured in current dollars, 18% a year. The second occurrence was the below-average rates of expansion of the agriculture and mining sectors. These grew at about 3% and a little more than 4% a year respectively.

Table 3.3. Plants promoted by the economic development administration, Puerto Rico up to 1963, according to size by number of persons employed

Industry Group	Number of Plants Established	Percentage of EDA Promoted Plants up to 1963 Employing less than 20 persons	Dominant Size of Activity by Persons Employed
Total	748	30%	a
Food and food products	41	27	b
Tobacco manufactures	13	0	d
Textile mill products	52	22	b,d
Apparel	224	16	c,d
Lumber and wood products	4	75	a
Furniture and fixtures	28	36	a,b
Paper and allied products	21	57	a
Printing and publishing	12	59	a
Chemicals and allied products	28	50	a
Petroleum refining and related industry	6	17	b
Rubber and miscellaneous plastic products	27	30	a,b
Leather and leather products	49	12	d
Stone, clay and glass products	34	42	a
Primary metal industries	9	11	c
Fabricated metal products	54	62	a
Non-electrical machinery	13	46	a,b
Electrical machinery	60	34	a
Transportation equipment	3	0	b
Professional, scientific and controlling instruments	15	34	a
Miscellaneous manufactures	55	46	a

a = 1 to 19 persons, b = 20 to 49 persons, c = 50 to 99 persons, d = 100 to 249 persons, e = 250 to 499 persons and f = 500 or more.
SOURCE: Adapted from *Annual Statistical Report of* EDA Manufacturing Plants, 1963–64, July 1965, San Juan, Puerto Rico.

Table 3.4. GDP of the manufacturing sector, Jamaica, 1959 to 1963

Industry Group	1959	1960	1961	1962	1963
Food (excl. sugar)	35.5	34.0	34.5	36.0	36.0
Alcoholic beverages (excl. rum)	8.9	7.4	8.2	7.5	8.3
Non-alcoholic beverages	3.8	3.7	3.7	3.9	4.0
Tobacco and tobacco products	7.5	6.7	6.8	8.7	14.6
Footwear	2.9	3.3	3.4	3.6	3.6
Textiles	9.3	8.8	10.6	11.7	12.9
Wood and wood products	3.6	3.9	4.1	3.3	4.1
Furniture and fixtures	9.4	7.0	7.2	4.8	6.5
Printing, publishing, advertising and other paper products	8.6	8.7	11.0	11.9	12.2
Leather and leather products	0.8	0.9	0.9	1.1	1.2
Chemicals and chemical products	9.1	6.6	10.4	12.1	10.4
Cement and clay products	9.1	9.9	10.4	9.8	9.8
Metal products	12.7	14.6	14.7	17.2	17.0
Miscellaneous manufactures	3.1	3.2	2.9	2.9	33.1
Total manufacturing	124.3	118.7	128.8	134.5	143.7
Total GDP at factor cost	977.1	1,033.4	1,074.0	1,095.5	1,122.1

Table 3.5. GDP of the manufacturing sector, Trinidad and Tobago, 1957 to 1962

Industry Group	1957	1958	1959	1960	1961	1962
Food manufacturing					19.5	
(excl. sugar)	12.5	15.0	17.1	16.0		22.0
Shoes and other footwear:					21.0	
tailoring and textiles	13.5	16.2	18.7	18.2		22.9
Other manufacturing	28.9	34.4	41.3	45.5	51.7	61.0
Total Manufacturing	54.9	65.6	77.1	79.7	92.2	105.9
Total GDP at factor cost	659.1	719.4	799.1	865.9	954.8	1,005.7

A supporting index of the growth of industrial activity, the amount of electricity consumed, is given in Table 3.6 for both countries. By this measure, the late 1950s and initial years of the 1960s were a period of quickened industrial activity. In both countries, during that time, the consumption of electricity more than doubled. When this is taken in conjunction with the much slower rate of labour input it suggests, in so far as there is a correlation between increases in electricity consumed and increases in the capital stock, a very rapid process of capital intensification.[7] Thus the increase of labour productivity in these economies, which has tended to be of the order of 6% a year as an average, overstates the increase in total productivity. This fact is of added importance since there are differential rates of accumulation and labour input into the various sectors, particularly as between industry, agriculture and mining. It is important, to bear this point in mind when interpreting economic development and transformation in the West Indies. It is also relevant to our discussion of recent developments to note that these facts point, in a general way, to a (further) movement at the margin of comparative advantage in the direction of commodities which use intensively the apparently 'scarce' factor, capital.

The increase in manufacturing production was also reflected in an increased inter-West Indian trade in manufactures. We saw there that the value of this trade doubled itself between 1957 and 1963, though still remaining at a relatively small absolute value. In fact, the programme of industrialization, though it was closely related to the idea of import substitution has involved also a significant expansion of exports, the greater portion of which went to the West Indies. Some indication of this is given for Jamaica in Table 3.7. It is a sign of some encouragement in that it is a partial indicator that protected development has not, so far, involved such a complete loss of competitive standing, as for example in the Latin American case, that export opportunities for manfuactures have been forfeited. The range of Latin American manufactures

is, of course, much wider than that of the West Indies. A more severe test for the latter comes after the stage of light and elementary manufactures, where there may still be some flexibility with respect to the size of capacity installation and utilization.

In very few industrial manufactures, surprisingly, has import replacement exceeded 50% of domestic consumption. Those that have done so are fertilizers and cement which have virtually reached 100%, glass bottles, nails and tacks, paper bags and paperboard products, envelopes and exercise books, boxes and crates, paint and furniture. It is evident, therefore, that, even with respect to existing manufactures, there are considerable opportunities for expanding production through import substitution. Naturally, these, if they were to be pursued, would sharply restrict the range of choice. For example, footwear and textiles may necessitate a more rigid protectionist policy. West Indian countries, in fact, practice a rather mild degree of infant industry protection when judged by the standards of Latin America where outright prohibition or extraordinary high tariffs are generally to be found.

In Appendices 3A and 3B an indication is given of the range of industries established mainly since the 1950s in Jamaica and in Trinidad and Tobago. One of the immediately astonishing things about the present situation is that several industries which were considered unfavourable in the 1930s and 1940s[8] have since been firmly established. The original list was founded on the minimization of the scarce factor inputs. When compared with industries in actual operation it poses a severe reminder to us of the dynamic nature of industrial processes and the marked divergence which can exist between social and private profitability. The present list includes fertilizers, grain milling, milk, margarine, cement, china, beer, cattle food, soap, paint, petroleum refining. At the same time, in striking contrast, many of those industries which were regarded as favourable have not really got off the ground — fish curing, hosiery, watches and

Table 3.6. Electricity Consumption in Jamaica and Trinidad

	Jamaica		Trinidad-Tobago	
	Million KWH Commercial Industrial	Index	Million KWH Industrial	Index
Year				
1957			68.4	100.0
1958	123.9	100.0	84.7	123.8
1959	148.6	119.9	91.6	133.9
1960	145.1	117.1	80.2	117.2
1961	177.6	143.3	152.5	222.9
1962	195.8	158.0	157.2	222.9
1963	224.0	180.8	167.6	245.0
1964	263.8	212.9		

SOURCES: Annual Economic Surveys, Jamaica Annual Statistical Digest, Trinidad-Tobago, 1963.

Table 3.7. Distribution of sales of selected Jamaican industries

	$000	
Commodity	Value of Local Sales, 1963	Value of Exports, 1963
Jelly crystals	192	230
Paints	3,220	688
Toilet preparations	1,189	251
Pharmaceutical	653	124
Paper products	2,520	211
Pens	37	14
Footwear	n.a	681
Ladies underwear	"	4,022
Men's and boys' outerwear	"	1,185
Cloth	"	1,846

clocks, umbrellas, brooms and brushes, sports goods, plastics, weaving, electric lamps, to name a few. Apart from the dynamics of resource requirements and supply, it is evident that this kind of 'irrational' industrialization, undertaken as it was by private enterprise, was less concerned with the overall or social maximization of returns to factor inputs than with the absolute size of profits from any particular line of activity. Simply stated, it was more a question of the size of divergence between sales and costs of a commodity, which was itself largely determined by the size of the demand for it and the potential for exercising monopoly power rather than one of overall minimization of the scarce factor inputs per unit of social product. This divergence between social and private profitability is most dramatically reflected in the low rate of absorption of manpower, the resource in general surplus.

Currently the uncertain beginnings of a new phase of industrialization in Jamaica and Trinidad and Tobago are to be seen in such developments as the establishment of steel and motor vehicle factories. Sooner or later, a broader range of heavy manufacturing activity, which might include glass, paper, synthetic fabrics and so on, undoubtedly will have to be considered. At the same time, the remaining West Indian territories are fully intending, in so far as it is feasible, to follow the pattern of Jamaica and Trinidad and Tobago. These developments, in themselves, give some prominence to an urgent consideration of the possibilities for regional collaboration. The easy stage of import substitution soon will be well past in Jamaica and Trinidad and Tobago and the scope which it offers in the smaller units is very limited. Already in Jamaica the growth of the manufacturing sector (excluding sugar and alcohol), from 1961 to 1964, failed to exceed, in current values, an annual average of 3%. And certainly in Trinidad and Tobago a sharp deceleration from the speed of 1957 to 1962 is, ordinarily, to be expected.

However, as we remarked previously, there is, evidently, no deficiency of demand for expanding production of existing manufactures. Although this is so, there is to be found, at the same time, idle production capacity. Some prominent examples are textiles, footwear, chemicals, insecticides, paper products, paints, buttons, and processed food products. Fortunately, the evidence which has been coming forward on the economies of large-scale production, together with external economies, suggests not only significant savings of unit capital and production costs but a way by which may be overcome, partially at least, the problem of very narrow choice, which is a feature to be expected in small autarkic economies. However, even with the extension of the market to cover the entire region, a considerable lessening of the differentiation of products must be anticipated. If this involves a loss to the community, or to some sections of it, there will be the compensatory gains of income and employment creation, foreign exchange savings, and, probably, some wholesome social consequences as well. There can be little doubt that the failure to replace a higher proportion of imports by domestic production is due, in part, to the very wide range of alternatives to which West Indian consumers have been accustomed. It is hardly surprising that import substitution of manufactures has gone furthest where the product is, more or less, of a homogeneous nature, for example, fertilizer, cement, beer, paper bags, and so on.

Finally, the locational aspect of industrial development has become of much greater importance to the general strategy of economic transformation. Already, we have noted the geographical polarization of such development in Jamaica and

Table 3.8. Percentage income shares of ordinal groups of households, rural and urban Jamaica, 1958

Ordinal Groups % of Households	All Jamaica	Rural	Urban (incl. Kingston Metropolitan Area)	Kingston Metropolitan
0 – 20	2.2	2.5	3.7	3.8
21 – 40	6.0	6.4	7.8	8.0
41 – 60	10.8	11.2	12.2	12.2
61 – 80	19.5	19.0	20.8	20.9
81 – 100	61.5	60.9	55.5	55.1
Further breakdown on top groups:				
81 – 90	18.0	17.4	16.1	16.7
91 – 95	13.3	13.9	12.9	13.1
96 – 100	30.2	29.6	26.5	25.3
Index of concentration	56	55	49	49

SOURCE: E. Ahiram 'Income Distribution in Jamaica', Social and Economic Studies, University of the West Indies, September, 1964.

Trinidad and Tobago. This, however, has its counterpart within those countries themselves and gives rise to the more serious problem of social and racial polarization. Indeed, this type of development is generally found in the Caribbean. In Table 3.8 we partially illustrate this point with information relating to revenue shares in rural and urban Jamaica, where the problem is probably more acute than in other West Indian territories. The data relate to 1858 but the indirect evidence does not suggest any improvement since that time. The table shows that the degree of inequality in the rural area is much higher than it is in the metropolitan area (an index of concentration of 55 compared with 49). It should be noted, at the same time, that the income share of the lower income groups is higher in the metropolitan area than in the rural districts. The bottom 60% of households in the metropolitan area received 33.7% of its income. The corresponding percentage for the rural districts was 30.1.

Additional information on the concentration of income is provided in Table 3.9 for Jamaica and Trinidad and Tobago in the form of an index of *per capita* labour force GDP for 1960. This index, although it relates to sectors of the economy, is suggestive of the degree of locational and social polarization since in the West Indies the areas outside the city engage almost exclusively in agriculture, though there are the enclaves of mining and holiday activity. In both countries the index number for agriculture is well below the average for all sectors. In Jamaica it is 35 and in Trinidad and Tobago 70 (All Sectors = 100).

The general movement of population from country to town is made attractive by the government's policy of locating industries almost exclusively in the metropolitan area. Although this policy has met

with much valid criticism its reversal cannot be seen as an answer to the fundamental problem. There are many additional factors, inherent in the operation of the economic system, which contribute to the present situation.

Firstly, there is a fairly large and recurrent imbalance between the annual total increase in employment and the annual increment to the labour force. In some territories like Jamaica and Guyana the gap seems to be equal to about 50% of the increment to the labour force. The effect of this is exacerbated by another imbalance which arises from the fact that the rural population increases at a faster rate than the city population. This differential, even under a less skewed industrial location policy, would tend to cause unbalanced population pressures between the various districts. These facts suggest both a pre-determined minimum rate of growth of total real output, given the increase in labour productivity, and appropriate differentials in the rates of growth of the districts if the social tensions engendered by these imbalances are to be remedied. Regrettably, West Indian planning has not yet made any direct attempts to come to grips with these aspects of development.

Secondly, a continuous worsening of the commodity terms of trade between country and town would tend to encourage the movement of persons out of the rural areas. This movement is hastened by increases in productivity in two ways. By leading to a fall in relative agricultural prices the income terms of trade itself may not improve and, at times, may even decline. Indeed, the idea of 'immiserizing growth' becomes less of a theoretical curiosity when applied to inter-regional than to international transactions. Further, some of the more important aspects of immiserizing growth are

Table 3.9. Index of per capita labour force GDP in Jamaica and Trinidad and Tobago, 1960

Industrial Sector	Jamaica	Trinidad-Tobago
All Sectors	100	100
Agriculture	35	70
Mining, refining	425	375
Manufacturing	102	100
Construction, public utilities	153	106
Transport, communication	209	74
Distribution, finance	182	147
Services and government	124	51

SOURCE: See Table 3.8.

to be found in growing unemployment and increasing inequality in the distribution of income which do not form part of the theoretical analysis of this concept.[9] Increases in productivity also hasten the movement of persons out of the rural areas by reducing the quantity of labour input per unit of output. This would always take place unless the rate of increase of real output was greater than the rate of increase of productivity plus the rate of increase of the labour force. Productivity increases can be very large in agriculture, though erratic over short periods. The sugar industry is an example of this. Also, as we remarked earlier, the natural rate of increase of the rural population is higher than that of the city population. Thus, it rarely occurs that the growth of real output in agriculture can be sufficiently high to absorb the required quantity of man-power. Moreover, with a higher rate of natural increase of population in the rural areas than in the city the rate of growth of rural unemployment will tend to be corresponding higher unless this can be offset by a proportionately faster rate of growth of real output and/or lower rate of increase of labour productivity in the country than in the town. This also rarely occurs. Hence the movement of persons out of the countryside becomes necessary. It is interesting to note, at the same time, that this analysis provides an unconventional economic rationalization of the farming community's apparent reluctance to improve productivity or greatly increase the volume of output.

The result of this situation is that the flow of persons to the city is transforming it more and more into a nucleus of stark poverty, conspicuous inequality and social tension. Thus, the socially polarized and disintegrated nature of the society poses an additional problem for the functional integration of the region. It will be recalled that we adopted a concept of integration which, by displacing the principle of *laissez faire,* made way for the inclusion of social values at the regional level. In this way, these values became an integral part of our conception of integration. The problem which is now posed is the conflict which may take place

between the application of this notion at the regional level and a state of disintegration at the national level. The regional authorities, whatever they may be, cannot, of course, intervene in the latter problem, but it should be understood that some corrective to the dichotomy which we have presented will need to be undertaken.

Notes

1. There is a sense in which one may need to question whether labour is the relatively abundant resource in the West Indies. The capital reservoir has never been limited to the national boundaries, unlike the situation in many developing countries. Thus, not only is the private valuation of labour greater than its social (accounting) valuation, for various reasons, but the price of capital is depressed by the existence of the larger international supply. Although this depression of the price of capital is beneficial from the viewpoint of the real cost of the individual operations, it evidently helps to promote a capital intensive type of development which otherwise might not take place, even if both factors were valued at their private (national) cost.

2. The gross output of Eire's manufacturing industries in 1963 was $2,500m., just about double their value of the West Indian consumption of manufactured goods. Our estimate of job creation is also well supported by the parallel situation of New Zealand at the end of the 1930s.

3. Walter Galenson 'Economic Development and the Sectoral Expansion of Employment' *International Labour Review,* June, 1963.

4. 'Employment and Earnings in Large Establishments 1957–62', Department of Statistics, Kingston, Jamaica. Large establishments are defined as establishments employing ten or more persons. The position, 1957 to 1962, seems to have been that no net employment was created, and possibly there was some decline.

5. Jack Harewood, 'A Comparison of Labour Force Data for Trinidad and Tobago, 1946–1964', Research Papers, Central Statistical Office, Trinidad and Tobago, December 1965. The increases in the 'Service' sectors do seem to be unusually large but it should be recalled, as a partial explanation, that during this period, Trinidad and Tobago's Gross Domestic Product, in current values, increased by some 60 percent and that employment in Government services was growing at a rapid rate. However, we are not entirely certain that there may not be some exaggeration in these figures.

6. Arthur Lewis, *The Industrialisation of the British West Indies,* Caribbean Organization, Puerto Rico.

7. It is difficult to bring forward more direct evidence since there are no firm estimates of the stock of capital at any point of time. Approximate estimates show the first derivative to be much higher than the rate of increase of labour input. The second derivative which may be more firmly calculated is also well in excess of the rate of increase of labour input. Indirect evidence through the consumption of electricity, whilst it has obvious drawbacks, is better able to cope with the problem of changes in the intensity of utilization of the stock of capital.

8. W.A. Lewis, *The Industrialisation of the British West Indies, op. cit; Industrial Development in the British Territories of the Caribbean,* Report to the Caribbean Commission, Volume II.

9. J. Bhagwati, 'International Trade and Economic Expansion', *American Economic Review,* December 1958.

Character of the Caribbean Economy

Kari Levitt and Lloyd Best

Introduction

The central concern of postwar economic theory and policy in the Caribbean has been how to get the economy to grow fast enough. It was anticipated that rapid growth would place the territories in a position to close the gap in real income per head between the region and the metropolitan countries of the North Atlantic, to create sufficient employment to absorb population increase and enough social and economic equality to ensure political stability. It was expected that the regional economy would ultimately be better placed to reduce if not eliminate its traditional dependence on metropolitan areas for investment, technology, skills and business enterprise, for sheltered export markets and for the overwhelming majority of imported supplies. Eventually, it was argued, the economies would attain 'self-sustaining growth' which would clear the market of all factors offering themselves for employment and yield a dynamic equilibrium between capacity and wants simultaneously created. These expectations were based on a crude mix of Ricardian [Lewis 9] and Keynesian economics, the former being revised to allow for technical progress in agriculture, and the latter for autonomous capital inflows to an 'open' economy.

The 'Ricardian' component of the synthesis postulated a typical under-developed economy which had two sectors. On the one hand, there was a backward, traditional, primary and largely agricultural sector. This dominated the economy. On the other, there was an embryonic, modern, comparatively advanced industrial sector. The problem of development was seen to be one of eliminating this 'dualistic economy' by creation of new capacity in the modern sector. By this means, not only was labour expected to be drawn out of the agricultural sector, but it was also expected that the growing urban industrial sector would generate new demands for food and raw materials. Thus the traditional sector, too, would enjoy more favourable supply and demand conditions for its own modernization through the introduction of technical progress.

It was believed that the 'Ricardian' model as outlined above might be unworkable for several reasons. First, there did not exist — in the typical under-developed country — it was diagnosed — an entrepreneurial class large enough to mobilize the surplus, undertake accumulation, promote innovation or introduce the backlog of technology known to be available from the 'developed' countries. Secondly, there was little or no surplus to be mobilized. Income was so low that domestic savings were calculated to be below the critical minimum required to make the 'take-off' possible. Thirdly, in this low level equilibrium trap the demand of the dominant traditional sector was not for industrial output but largely for the bare necessities, i.e., for its own agricultural produce. There was therefore little or no home market for industry, or at least, few markets big enough to utilize to the full the minimum economic capacity of industrial plants.

The 'Keynesian' component of the synthesis with its heavy emphasis on government spending provided the strategy. A solution to the difficulties was to be found in intervention by the public sector. In demolishing the unstated neo-classical assumption that full utilization of resources was an automatic process, the *General Theory* helped unwittingly to draw poor countries into doctrinal community with the North Atlantic. Poor countries had always known growth to be hedged in by formidable obstacles but now they could be persuaded that all were somehow in the same boat. The sense of community was strengthened by the fact that the initiative in the development of doctrine remained in the rich metropolitan countries which were, moreover, deeply involved in managing the dissolution of the empires which the maritime nations of Western Europe had established since the end of the 15th century. The problem of economic change even in the poor countries of the hinterland has been formulated in terms of North Atlantic experience; the theory which has informed strategy has been basically the Keynesian adaptation of his still largely Ricardian heritage. Foreign businessmen were to be encouraged to organize industrial production,

405

introduce techniques from the developed countries, employ comparatively cheap local labour and sell their products either in their own metropolitan markets or in third markets to which they had or could gain access.

Government inducements to foreign business would be in the form of tax concessions and in the provision of social overheads — the so-called infrastructure — education, roads, public utilities, etc. Since enough money for social overhead investment would not be forthcoming from traditional taxes, measures were to be taken to increase the effective tax rate by fiscal modernization, to broaden the tax–base by negotiating better terms for traditional exports, and to expand investible resources by securing grants and loans from the wealthier nations.

By this strategy it was expected that in the short-run, the typical under-developed economy could be transformed at a rate fast enough to yield socially acceptable improvements in the living standards of the population and yet without undue imbalances in the budget, the foreign payments or the commodity market, or without much difficulty in matching savings with investment and the supply with the demand for labour.

In the long-run, it was expected that local entrepreneurs would take over the promotional role of government and displace foreign business as the agents of industrialization. In the process local savings would rise, technology would become more selective and more independent, and local products would create tastes in wider international markets and so improve their selling prospects.

This strategy was clearly articulated by the Caribbean Commission. The best statement of the case is to be found in two celebrated essays by Professor Arthur Lewis, [10] entitled 'Industrial Development in the Caribbean' and published by the Commission. Economic policy along these lines has been pursued with greatest vigour by the government of Puerto Rico but also with considerable persistence by other governments, in particular those of Jamaica, Trinidad and Tobago, Surinam and Barbados and by the Cuban government between 1952 and 1957.

We believe that the failure of these industrialization programmes is to be laid at the door of a basic weakness in the theoretical approach to policy-making. The procedure of adopting a model drawn from the experience of countries which have their own internal mechanisms of growth, and then prescribing the missing components to be imported into the Caribbean proved an inadequate guide to action. The legacies of plantation economy and the new endowments of economies dominated by branch plant subsidiaries of multi-national corporations have set limits on the capacity of the economies to adjust in the manner anticipated. Thus, low wage levels did not induce investment in labour-intensive industry on a scale needed to reduce unemployment. Nor did the shift of the traditional export sector to new products and more capital-intensive techniques enhance its ability to do without metropolitan market shelter. Nor again, has the increase in domestic product produced a corresponding increase in local savings. Nor has the dependence on metropolitan entrepreneurship and finance diminished. In spite of heavy out-migration, unemployment increased, both in absolute and relative terms.[2]

As it came to be appreciated that the strategy of development adopted in the early postwar period was not bringing the expected results, the first response of theorists and policy makers was to advocate schemes of regional economic integration.[3] The problem of development was interpreted as one of pooling limited national savings, or combining skewed natural resources and of integrating small domestic markets in support of more extensive programmes of import-substitution. Deeper investigation into these possibilities and actual experiments with schemes of integration such as the Latin American Common Market and the West Indies Federation have, however, revealed that the problems of economic stagnation and economic fragmentation are closely related [Jefferson and Girvan 6, Best 1], and that they are a process actively promoted by certain types of national and international economic organization. At the centre of this process is the multinational corporation, extracting the old traditional agricultural staple and the more recent traditional mineral ones and supplying metropolitan corporate goods through a multitude of assembly-type branch plants.

The predominance of the metropolitan subsidiary and the branch plant in Caribbean economies reinforces fragmentation. Each territory tends to engage in terminal activities of resource extraction at the one end of the spectrum and distribution and final assembly of imports at the other. Linkages both within and between Caribbean economies remain feeble, and metropolitan domination persists.

The frustrations of the postwar development programmes in the Caribbean can only be understood in the light of the legacy which all the territories have inherited from their common plantation history. In spite of important differences, the regional economies are embedded in a well-defined set of institutions and structures and are characterized by a distinct pattern of economic behaviour. Our central hypothesis is that this plantation legacy represents an endowment of mechanisms of economic adjustment which deprive the region of internal dynamic.

Essentially, the Caribbean economy has undergone little structural change in the four hundred-odd years of its existence. By this we mean that the character of the economic process in the region seems not to have been significantly altered over the period. Neither the modifications which, through time, have been made to the original institutions, nor the new institutions which have from time to time been incorporated into the economy, have relieved its dependence on external development initiatives. The economy remains, as it has always been, passively responsive to metropolitan demand and metropolitan investment.

It has for some time been clear that fresh theoretical initiatives are called for. The criteria which have guided our efforts to construct a model which is realistic, relevant and useful derive from our judgement that policy in the region must be directed towards the achievement of structural transformation. We have thus considered it essential to identity the relationships which prevent the Caribbean economy from adjusting in the manner taken for granted in general equilibrium models.[4]

We have sought to study contemporary economic problems in the perspective of the past performance of Caribbean economy. To this end, employing the method of *histoire raisonée* we have constructed a series of models. As an interpretation of economic history, these models may be conceived of as successive stages in the evolution of plantation economy. We must emphasize, however, that our primary interest lies in isolating the institutional structures and constraints which the contemporary economy has inherited from the planation legacy. The historical stages which underlie the models are to be seen in the contemporary perspective of successive layers of inherited structures and mechanisms which condition the possibilities of transformation of the present economy. Our major argument is that the study of the character of the plantation sector and its relation both with the outside world and with the domestic economy provides the single most essential insight into the mechanisms of Caribbean economy.

Our attempt to identify the objectives of transformation and the strategy for achieving them must therefore begin with an analysis of the nature and functioning of plantation economy. In this article we present some of the results of our work in the form of a series of generalizations meant to apply to all variants of plantation economy. It emphasizes modes of factor allocation and deployment, employment creation and destruction; income generation, distribution and disposal; it specifies associated patterns of supply and demand and tendencies in technology and accumulation. Finally, it indicates the policy choices open to the plantation economy under conditions of expansion and contraction of the staple.

The emphasis is placed on the case where new staples are developed in the hinterland by metropolitan corporations. This corresponds to the experience of Jamaica, Trinidad, Guyana and Surinam.

The result is a reinforcing of traditional economic and social structures of dependency, a ratooning of the old plantation relationships, both external and internal. It follows that structural transformation requires, as a precondition, the dismantling of the corporate mercantile links between the hinterland and the metropole.

Caribbean Plantation Economy

Insofar as Caribbean economy is the creation of metropolitan enterprise from the start, current economic institutions in the region have been formed by the historic accretion of the hinterland operations of the metropolitan economy from the slave plantations to the modern multinational corporation. It follows that the appropriate definition of Caribbean economy must include all those areas in, around and near the Caribbean Sea which have, in the last 450 years come under the influence of the sugar plantation and its characteristic culture and mode of social and economic organization. This includes all the Caribbean islands, the Guyanas (English, French and Dutch), Venezuela, the North East of Brazil, parts of the coastal area of Ecuador and Colombia, pockets of Central America and sections of the Southern United States. This is substantially the area defined by Wagley [13] as Plantation America.

Obviously, there are great differences in the historical experience of these areas. It is not our intention at this time to outline, even in the roughest manner, the economic history of Plantation America. Rather, we wish to indicate some concepts and themes which may be of assistance in understanding the influence of the historic legacy of the area on its contemporary structure.

Types of Hinterlands

If one ignores preliminary and transient forms of European colonization such as trading posts, military garrisons, and their supporting settlements by European colonizers, one may classify New World hinterlands into three broad types: hinterlands of conquest, of settlement and of exploitation. Hinterlands of conquest correspond to the case of Spain and Andean America and New Spain.

Hinterlands of settlement correspond to the case of the North and Middle colonies of North America. Hinterlands of exploitation are most clearly exemplified by the Caribbean plantation economies.[5]

A hinterland of exploitation is a direct extension of the economy of the metropole. Its *raison d'etre* is to produce a staple required for metropolitan consumption and for entrepot trade to third countries. It thus forms part of the overseas empire of the metropole. In its purest form, the source of its entrepreneurship and of its finance, and indeed, the locus of key decisions are metropolitan. Whereas in colonies of conquest the metropole provides only military and administrative infrastructure, in colonies of exploitation it provides economic enterprise, organization and initial capital as well. It organizes the importation of slave or indentured labour to extract its staple.

Plantation Hinterlands

The Plantation Hinterland is essentially a geographical area of production passively incorporated into the Overseas Economy of a metropolitan system. Plantation hinterland is not therefore a unit to which considerations of economic welfare can uncritically be applied. The national economy must be distinguished from the domestic economy as it refers to economic activity organized by foreigners. The latter is a technical concept relating to productive activity with a defined geographic area. The former is the relevant unit for discussions of economic welfare.[6]

A plantation hinterland does not trade in the sense that is implied by the theory of international trade. It does not import in order to complement domestic supply. Nor does it actively seek to exploit the comparative advantage of its national economy. Its trade is therefore ancillary to the production of supplies required in the metropole. In this sense, it imports in order to export and its imports are 'intermediate' goods in the earlier stages of metropolitan production. The role of plantation economy is embedded in its institutions and structures. These are biased in favour of staples needed in the metropole. A staple is a commodity which is produced for export and contributes a large share of domestic output, exercising disproportionate influence on the level of domestic activity and on national economy policy.

Mainland vs. Island Plantation Hinterlands

Mainland plantation hinterlands differ significantly from those which are 'islands'. By the former term we do not refer merely to the geographic concept, but to the existence of large areas of cultivable land not engrossed by plantations. In the context of this discussion the plantations of northeast Brazil and those of the American South are mainland hinterlands. Here the residentiary sector produces a significantly large part of domestic requirements and the planters themselves are residents in the full sense of the term. It is not our intention to discuss the evolution of plantation economy in mainlands at this time. By way of contrast, 'islands' are areas where the bulk of cultivable land has been preempted for plantation production and where a residentiary sector is, to the extent that it exists, principally an adjunct of the plantation sector.[7]

Because size and the existence of spare land are relative concepts we may usefully introduce here the distinction between islands which are demographically *closed* and those which are *open*. The *closed* island hinterland is one in which all available land is engrossed by plantations and is fully under cultivation. This is the case of mature plantation hinterlands such as Barbados, St. Kitts and Antigua since the latter part of the 17th century. Here the ratio of population to cultivable land is typically high, and the situation is unfavourable to the development of a residentiary sector.

The *open* resource situation in island hinterland is one in which there exists plenty of unsettled virgin land suitable for planation cultivation. It corresponds to cases of territories which came into the plantation system in more recent times such as Trinidad and the Guyanas, Cuba, Puerto Rico and Santo Domingo. Here the ratio of population to land is lower, and the planters have an interest in preventing the population from engaging in residentiary agriculture. Thus, there tends to be a severe shortage of labour, and labour is imported on terms which ensure its availability for plantation work. The intermediate cases are *mixed ones,* best exemplified by the situation in Jamaica. Here plantations co-existed with peasant production of export staples and some production for the local market. It was a situation created by the breakdown of the plantation system at a stage when spare land still existed. The situation was more favourable to structural transformation and shared some of the characteristics of mainland situations. One should mention also, in this context, territories which never came under the influence of the full plantation system, and where local producers began early to be predominant. This is exemplified by some of the Windward Islands, particularly Grenada, St. Vincent and Dominica.

The Plantation as a 'total economic institution'

When labour is introduced into an 'open' resource situation the merchant-pirate ethos with a short view dictates the need to impose a 'total economic institution' so as to encompass the entire existence of the work force.[8] The plantation, which admits virtually no distinction between economic organization and society, and chattel slavery which deprives workers of any personal rights, including the right to own or cultivate land, together furnish the 'ideal' framework. Hence the term 'plantation economy' for the Caribbean type of hinterland of exploitation.

Save for supplies produced and consumed on own account, the plantation produces a single crop. Accordingly, the hinterland is composed of a single industrial sector fractured into plantations. Each plantation is a self-contained, self-sufficient total institution. Pure planation economy is modified by the existence of some nomadic native survivors, runaway slaves who escape to inaccessible lands, and small settlers from the metropole.

Pure plantation economy is an ideal type and no exact historic counterpart exists. Barbados, St. Kitts and Antigua became full fledged sugar economies in the 17th century. Trinidad and the Guyanas were comparative late-comers in the 19th century. Although Cuba and Puerto Rico had some sugar plantations from early in the 16th century, it was not until the 19th century in Cuba, and the 20th century in Puerto Rico, that they came to dominate economic life. Slavery in Haiti was abolished in the early 19th century. In Brazil, Puerto Rico and Cuba it was abolished comparatively late in the 19th century; in the British territories in the 1830s and in the French islands in the 1840s.

The Overall Mercantilist Framework

The relations between plantation hinterlands and the metropoles are defined by institutional rules of exclusivist trading arrangements. These serve to secure the transfer of a surplus to the metropole. In the period of explicit political colonial systems, these rules were ultimately enforced by the military and naval power of the metropole. In contemporary times these patterns have persisted. The ultimate sanction of military intervention is still present as witnessed by the recent experience of Santo Domingo and Cuba. While rivalries between metropolitan powers persist, their impact on Caribbean hinterlands has been significantly modified by new cartel-type arrangements between rival metropolitan corporations. These international corporations largely ignore the remnants of the old political structures in the region. Thus, Alcoa, for example, which is a U.S. based corporation, operates with equal facility in territories formerly British, as Jamaica, presently Dutch, as Surinam or nominally independent, as Santo Domingo. Military intervention is thus 'internationalized' with the top role being played by the top metropole in the area, the United States.

The overall rules of the game in plantation hinterland can usefully be classified under four headings:

Division of Labour: The first rule specifies the division of labour. The hinterland is confined to terminal activity: primary production at the one end of the spectrum, and distribution or assembly of consumer goods at the other end. This we have termed the *Muscovado Bias*. Processing facilities are strategically located in the metropole. From here the multinational corporations have integrated forward to final product markets with the aid of direct investment in the manufacturing and distribution of finished goods in scores of countries.

Carriage of Trade: The second rule relates to the carriage of trade. Here goods are almost entirely transported by metropolitan carriers and associated services are provided by metropolitan intermediaries. This is the *Navigation Provision*. The control of transportation and distribution systems is a principal weapon of oligopolistic competition of multinational corporations. The resulting absence of price-forming markets for raw materials ex-hinterland contributes to the large margins of incalculable costs.

Monetary System: The third rule defines the character of the hinterland monetary system. The banking system is dominated by metropolitan bank and non-bank financial intermediaries. Hinterland currency is effectively backed by metropolitan assets and freely convertible into metropolitan exchange at fixed parities. This is the *Metropolitan Exchange Standard*. Although central banks have been established and legislation controlling the operations of the banking system introduced, they cannot be said to have altered in any fundamental way the basic constraints under which the monetary system continues to function.

Imperial Preferences: Finally, hinterland trade is conducted within a framework of imperial preferences. Exports enter the metropole at lower tariffs than rival output, and are typically accorded larger quotas. In the extreme case, facilities in the metropole are specific to the processing and distribution of materials drawn from the hinterland. On the other hand, metropolitan consumer and capital goods are accorded preferential entry into the hinterland. Together these provisions are termed *Imperial Preference*. The terms of participation in the various metropolitan-based preferential systems continue to be a major pre-occupation of Caribbean economic policy.

The Structural Characteristics of Plantation Economy

At the risk of some repetition, it is useful to outline here the structural characteristics of a plantation economy. These can be described as follows:

In a plantation hinterland, the dominant unit of production is a subsidiary or affiliate of a metropolitan firm. Its purpose is to extract the staple. To this end, it is typically organized as a total institution in the fashion of a plantation. That is to say, in regard to the hinterland, it tends to be a self-contained unit. Its primary links are external and almost exclusively with the parent firm in the metropole. This self-contained character of the production unit results in specific patterns in the markets for commodities, labour, land and capital, and corresponding patterns of price and wage formation, capital accumulation and technical change.

In regard to the labour market, the plantation encompasses its own resident labour force. Labour needs to be appropriately trained, to be available at cheap wages and in adequate supply during high seasons. To this end, labour is imported and land is engrossed so that the labour force has little option but to sell its wage-services. Education and training are made specific to the production of the staple. Tasks requiring expertise of a kind which gives occupational flexibility are reserved for a temporary imported cadre, specially rewarded for maintaining its distance from the labour force which is in permanent residence.

In regard to the commodity structure of output, the typical unit of production concentrates its resources on the direct production of the staple. Since it is established when export prices are high, provisions and supplies tend to be imported. Under these conditions, the diversion of land and labour to the production of these intermediate goods is more expensive than importing. Thus land and labour are from the beginning highly specialized in the direct production of the staple. This skewed pattern of resource allocation persists when the industry matures, i.e. when a secular decline in the terms of trade sets in, and when consequently diversification becomes necessary.

It follows from this pattern of commodity production and supply that within the hinterland there are few backward linkages and limited forward linkages to further stages of processing. What is more, when capacity is established to supply goods and services ancillary to the extraction or elaboration of the staple, these activities tend to be undertaken within the total institution. Thus, on both counts, the spill-over or 'spread' effects on the local economy are relatively feeble.

Even when the provisioning of the labour force with consumer goods and services is undertaken domestically, and a significant line of final demand linkage within the hinterland economy is created, the impact is limited by a taste constraint. The initial pattern of supply forms preferences for imported provisions. Thus, even when the decline of an export staple releases resources it is difficult to switch them to the profitable production of residentiary output.

A further constraint on the expansion of the residentiary sector derives from the fact that the production and distribution of consumer goods and services needed for employers tend to be undertaken within the confines of the unit of enterprise. Domestic demand is therefore fragmented by firm, and it is only a residual which is freely directed towards the residentiary sector of the national economy. The extent of final demand linkage varies markedly between hinterlands which are 'islands' and those which are 'mainlands'. In the former case, the resource constraint is more severe due to the relative shortage of land. In the latter case, spare labour can more readily be switched to the production of consumer output in the dead seasons and in times of depression.

Income and Employment Dependence

A plantation hinterland is also characterized by a distinctive process of income and employment determination. The orientation of the economy towards the metropole implies that the level of activity is determined by the level of metropolitan domestic and re-export demand for the staple, and by the share of the market commanded by the particular hinterland. Aggregate metropolitan demand may or may not be expanding. Even if it does, it is inherent in the situation that demand for the staple output deriving from one particular source of supply cannot remain buoyant for any extended period of time. Lower cost suppliers inevitably enter the market, for two reasons. The first reason derives from the *extractive nature* of hinterland operations which eventually results in the depletion or deterioration of the natural resource. The second reason relates to the process of accumulation and technical change imposed on the economy by the pattern of income distribution. Both the allocation of investment and the differential incidence of technological progress favour the newer hinterlands in competition with the older.

The dependence on metropolitan entrepreneurship and capital in the dominant sector of the hinterland implies that almost all property incomes from this sector accrue in the metropole. So long as reserves of the resource are enough to sustain the competitive position of the hinterland there will be re-investment and new investment in the widening of extraction facilities. The hinterland economy expands while employment tends also to expand and the level of local income to rise. However, when maturation sets in, as reserves are depleted, the metropolitan investors have an option. Either they may deepen their investment so as to maintain or reduce unit costs or they may switch to altogether new terrain.

Typically, the latter alternative is the more profitable. For one thing, technological improvements may be more readily introduced in capacity which is being newly established. For another, the fact that processing facilities are located in the metropole place the firms in a flexible enough position to exploit this option without sacrificing the external economies associated with the stages of elaboration and marketing. The resulting expansion of world capacity erodes the competitive position of the more mature hinterlands. Profits decline and older hinterlands are forced to seek ways to adjust.

The Staple Cycle

Throughout the phases of plantation economy, from its beginning as slave plantations producing the sugar staple for the metropole to the present times, a staple cycle asserts itself.

The cycle can be divided into a *foundation period, a golden age,* and a period of *maturity and decline.* Maturity and decline tends to be a chronic condition, terminated by the total collapse of the system or the arrival of a new staple. In the long decline of the older plantation economies, we distinguish between an initial phase of *Gall and Wormwood* and a terminal one of the *Liquidation.* These phases have already been described by Lloyd Best [2]. Here we focus on the process of adjustment as it relates to the emergence of a national economy.

Adjustment and Obstacles to the Emergence of a National Economy

When maturation sets in the export sector tends now to grow at reduced rates or even to contract. The main consequence of this is a reduction in the demand for labour and a slowing down of the rate of growth of demand for local goods and services.

Institutionally, the encompassing character of the typical unit of production is now modified. The plantations find it expedient to shift the incidence of redundancy on to the population by at least a partial switch from fully-bound labour to a quasi-proletariat. Part of the labour force is therefore

moved out of residence on to plots from which they cannot derive a livelihood without engaging in supplementary plantation work. In an 'island' hinterland, where land is scarce, this adjustment requires the release or activation of land and other co-operant factors. In a 'mainland' hinterland the release of labour is enough. In either event there emerges a national economy which is complementary to the traditional export sector. The national economy, like the wage earning quasi-proletariat which forms part of it is an out-growth of the slave plantations.

This national economy is circumscribed by the conditions under which it is founded:

1. Its endowment of skills and crafts are limited by the previous specialization of the labour force in plantation work.
2. The amount of land which the plantations make available to the residentiary sector is limited. The planters must keep land in reserve and they must secure access to wage labour in the event of a temporary revival of the staple. Thus, land must be withheld from the newly created quasi-peasantry to ensure their incentive to offer wage labour services to the planters.
3. The dependence of this economy on wage rather than on local property incomes both limits the size of the national surplus and narrows investment opportunities.
4. The inherited structure of demand favours imported rather than residentiary produce.
5. Finally, the instruments of the state are highly specialized to the provision of law and order rather than to the promotion of economic transformation.

The overall effect is that the national propertied class is born in circumstances which restrict its capacity for innovation and self-assertion, and stunt its growth. The national economy emerges with a bias towards the production of output requiring traditional plantation skills and serving traditional markets. The new sectors either produce minor staples for export with the assistance of metropolitan distribution agencies or they produce services for residentiary consumption including distribution and other commercial services associated with importation.

Thus, contrary to the theories of development economies, the plantation hinterland does not evolve from subsistence production to small-scale, wage employing business serving a national market and from there to large-scale corporate enterprise. Rather, as we have seen, the sequence begins with total institutions producing export staples for the metropolitan market on a highly commercial basis. The residentiary sector and the national economy are creations of the plantation sector and local enterprise comes into existence with a distinct plantation heritage. Metropolitan enterprise in the traditional export sector remains paramount. The plantation remains the dominant and exemplary unit of production. A somewhat modified total institution remains the representative firm. It follows from this that plantation economy is in no sense an 'enclave' economy in which large-scale capitalist enterprise is superimposed on a pre-existing peasant economy.

The key to an understanding of plantation economy lies precisely in the fact that it is, from its inception, an extension of the metropolitan capitalist economy. The quasi-proletariat, the quasi-peasantry and the quasi-bourgeoisie are creatures of the plantation export sector. The residentiary peasant sector comes into being to the extent that the plantation system breaks down.

The pressure on the traditional export sector eventually forces the economy to adjust. The presence of metropolitan enterprise with a continuing interest in its investments governs the nature of the adjustment. In theory, there are two options. First, the techniques of producing the traditional staple may be rationalized to cut costs. Second, the continuing ties with the metropole admits an increased reliance on imperial preference. In practice the two options are complementary. A rationalization of the total institution and a complete transformation would involve expenditures on a scale which are denied by the earning capacity of the economy, and social upheaval of a kind which is likely to place intolerable strains on the polity. We have seen that metropolitan enterprise has the alternative of investing in other locations and that national enterprise is not well placed to undertake speedy transformation. It is in this context that imperial preference becomes attractive to both local and metropolitan property-interests. The effect of this convergence of needs is to create an enduring preoccupation with the maintenance of traditional mercantile ties and traditional relationships of dependence vis-á-vis the metropole.

In the short run, financial support from the metropole is likely to maintain or even increase the level of employment in the traditional export sector. Although it is likely to discourage increased productivity and depress wage-rates, it nevertheless retards the decline in the aggregate wage-bill. The effect is to sustain demand for the output of the new residentiary sector. However, the stimulus is never enough to assign the sector a leading role in the process of transformation.

The coalition favouring protection unites the interests of planters and merchants on the one hand and small producers in the residentiary sector as well as the wage earners in the traditional export sector on the other. The coincidence of short term interest assists in explaining the durability of the imperial hinterland-metropolis relationship.

However, the short run solution of imperial preference adopted by the entire domestic economy involves a sacrifice of the long run interests of the national economy. The real cost of postponing transformation is the potential gain of income, employment and internal dynamic which could have resulted had protection been abandoned. A severance of the metropolitan ties is a precondition of structural transformation. A genuine programme of import-displacement and output and market diversification cannot proceed until the preferential props are withdrawn.

The consolidation of vested interests in protective shelter provides a prop to an economy which is fundamentally inviable. Occasional windfalls brought by fortuitous changes in market conditions provide additional supports but the economy remains in a precarious balance. It can be rescued only if the discovery of new natural resources revives metropolitan investment on a major scale. In this event, there will be economic growth and development of a type which further strengthens the hinterland-metropole relationship.

In the absence of a new staple it is inherent in the situation that the already slender base is progressively eroded by a widening gap between unit costs and market prices set by more efficient hinterlands opened by new metropolitan investment. The outcome is a reduction in the value of any given level of preferences and an increase in the support necessary to maintain viability.

The level of preference needed to maintain the standard of living is further inflated if population is growing. The ratio of labour to land in the residentiary sector rises, leading to the fragmentation of holdings and to technological retrogression, to low productivity, labour intensive techniques in the embryonic industrial trades and to under-employment in the services. In these circumstances, the only resource of the economy is to export labour. It follows that the more restricted are the opportunities for migration, the greater is the pressure for a total transformation of the economic order as large-scale unemployment becomes endemic. At best, an uneasy equilibrium is achieved on the brink of social revolution. At worst, there is a total breakdown.

Breakdown of the Staple Economy: Two Basic Options

When the system breaks down its path forward becomes indeterminate. *The extent and type of transformation which follows depends in the first place on whether or not the traditional mercantile ties are severed.*

In an island hinterland which is by definition weak and inviable, the most likely possibility is metropolitan interventions to restore order. In this event there is no modification of the institutional base.

Alternatively, the country may break traditional metropolitan ties. Such a country may, however, be forced into a new quasi-metropolitan relationship even where ownership of the traditional export sector is fully localized.

Where no new metropolitan ties are formed, the economy ceases, by definition, to be a hinterland. Options still remain open. However, the country may or may not participate widely in international trade and it may or may not stagnate.

We may usefully distinguish four cases:

Old metropolitan ties are cut, but the traditional export sector is maintained intact. The country which breaks traditional metropolitan ties may be forced into a new quasi-metropolitan relationship in order to solve the problem of marketing the export staple — or in order to protect the country's continued existence as a politically independent entity. This is the case of contemporary Cuba.

Although all incomes of the export sector accrue to nationals (whether as individuals or through their government), although there is flexibility in the allocation of investments and in choice of techniques, the problem of export pricing and sustained access to external markets remains crucial. The new quasi-metropolitan bilateral relations could restrict the freedom which the economy enjoys on account of having localized ownership of the traditional sector. Allocation of land and labour continue to be biased towards the requirements of the export staple.

Old metropolitan ties are cut and the traditional export sector disintegrates. The traditional export sector is dismantled, ownership is localized and old metropolitan ties are cut. The economy is closed with respect to the metropole. Haiti provides an example of a country which won political independence from the metropole, ceased to be a hinterland and has existed in a state of chronic stagnation ever since.

Metropolitan ties are maintained or restored and a 'quasi-staple' is developed. In an island hinterland which leaves its institutional base unaltered but does not discover a new major staple when the old staple economy breaks down, the only resources available are location and cheap labour. If these resources can be employed to establish quasi-staples it remains in the interest of the metropole to keep the hinterland passively incorporated

in its overseas economy. The quasi-staple economy specializes in finishing touch assembly manufacturing, tourism, and the provision of labour to the metropole by emigration. The more extreme case of a quasi-staple economy is Puerto Rico. Barbados and Antigua can also be characterized as quasi-staple economies.

While the corporate links with the metropole tend to be more diffused in a quasi-staple economy than is the case in a true staple producer the quasi-staple economy tends to be an even more dependent one. Its manufacturing and tourist industries are totally geared to the metropole. They are in every sense an appendage of metropolitan demand. Internal linkages are extremely weak. Incentives and subsidies given to new industries are almost exclusively directed to aiding export activity. The sector is mobilized to service tourism and export manufactures. In such an economy local initiatives are severely limited and the wage bill of the sector is the main contribution to the national economy. Such economies are particularly open to metropolitan cultural penetration. Consumption expenditures have a very high import content and government expenditure tends to be heavily financed by metropolitan grants.

Metropolitan ties are maintained and reinforced by the entry of a new staple. In the event that the economy is salvaged by the discovery of a new major staple, a fresh cycle of expansion and production begins. Income grows and the economy is pressed into a perpetuation of its traditional role as a hinterland. The new staple sector enters a hinterland system whose plantation legacy imposes continuation of the old structures on the new activity. The terms on which bauxite entered the economies of Jamaica, Guyana and Surinam, and the petroleum industry has expanded in Trinidad have resulted in a 'ratooning' of the structures of plantation economy. In the remainder of this essay we explore this fourth case.

Contemporary Caribbean Plantation Economy

Specifically, when a new natural resource is discovered or an old one is revived, the national economy has neither the capital nor the entrepreneurship nor the international marketing experience to organize production. Indeed its effective resource endowment is continuously being redefined less in terms of local potentialities and indeed, almost exclusively in relation to metropolitan demand requirements and metropolitan technology.

The economy is pressed therefore into a perpetuation of its traditional role as a hinterland. The effect is a renewal of links with the metropole which continues to be the source of entrepreneurship and capital. The continued dependence has to be seen as a consequence of the biases of the initial institutional framework — particularly the *Muscovado Bias* towards terminal activity. The metropole derives cumulative benefits in the form of external economies and a self-perpetuating advantage in its bargaining position Thus the old mercantilism facilitates the birth of the new [Levitt 7].

The relationship between the metropole and the hinterland, between the unit of enterprise in the former and the unit of production in the latter, and between the new traditional export sector and the national economy remains essentially unaltered. However, the forms within which the relationships of dependence express themselves are modified. The rules which typically define the new metropole-hinterland relationship are not those of the old colonial political systems.

At the level of the general institutional framework, the persistence of the metropolitan-hinterland relationship tends to be effected through the terms of multilateral and bilateral governmental agreements and through the rules of international and regional agencies.

In theory, the hinterlands are free to adopt more independent monetary systems, to establish their own facilities for production elaboration and import-displacement, to engage in multinational trading beyond the frontiers of the metropolitan system, to pursue commercial policies which discriminate against metropolitan suppliers and to arrange their carriage in the cheapest bottoms. In practice, however, the rules of the international agencies and the agreements which are contracted between metropoles and hinterlands are not impartial. Because of the difference in productive structure, in technological and financial strength and in access to information, the effect is often a perpetuation, if not an exacerbation of the traditional relationship of dependence.

At the level of the unit of enterprise, the controlling firm in the metropole tends to be a tightly knit complex combining capital, entrepreneurship, and technology within a corporate entity. The dynamics of competition and concentration call forth oligopolistic forms of organization on an international scale in which control over final markets is tightly exercised by the competing multinational corporations. The control of the modern corporation over primary production is tighter than that of the old time merchants over the planter-producers. Their time horizons is longer and their allocation of investments between hinterlands forms part of an overall competitive strategy.

For this reason they place a very high premium on exclusive control of subsidiaries. They have largely internalized transactions relating to the 'purchase' and 'sale' of products between scores of subsidiaries and the parent companies. Similarly, 'borrowing', 'lending', 'repayment', 'remittance of profit' and 'transfer of capital' between subsidiaries and parent companies are transactions with no clearly determined counterpart on a market. The *incalculability* of the old merchant-planter transactions has asserted itself in an international economy in which corporate strategy requires the elimination or suppression of price determining markets in the service of creating and securing quasi-monopoly rents and transferring them to the metropole.

It follows from this that metropolitan corporate investment in the hinterland has become the predominant form of economic penetration. The typical unit of production of the new major staple in the hinterland tends to be on the frontiers of metropolitan technology. It is, to use the jargon, capital intensive, i.e. a large amount of equipment per person is employed. Moreover its hinterland operations tend to be large in relation to other sectors of the local economy. What is more, it forms an integral part of a unit of enterprise whose operations are typically larger than those of an entire island hinterland and are almost always larger than those of the local government.

Owing to the high degree of mechanization, the share of the new staple in Gross Domestic Product and National Income far exceeds its contribution to employment. Moreover, the small share of the wage bill in total cost renders its profit position more or less insensitive to increases in hinterland wage rates [Seers 11]. This places the workers in the traditional export sector in a strong bargaining position. Furthermore, the multinational character of the unit of enterprise induces the adoption of the labour standards of the metropole. Still further, the subsidiaries typically engage in a continual process of technological modernization which results in a high rate of increase in output per man. Save during bursts of expansion and new investment the sector is typically shedding labour. In the particular conditions of superior labour organization this further reinforces wage differentials within the domestic economy.

Owing to the small share of wage income in total costs and the large share of property income, the retained earnings and depreciation allowances of the dominant export sector constitute a substantial part of gross domestic savings. These savings, however, do not accrue to the national economy but to the metropolitan parent companies. The only purpose for which they are available to the hinterland is for rationalization or expansion of the subsidiaries from which they are derived. If the hinterland's domestic savings arising from its traditional export sector are not re-invested in this sector they are transferred to the metropoles for investment in affiliated operations in other countries. Where these countries are also engaged in extraction of the staple, one hinterland is in effect financing capital investment in competing hinterlands; in this case a hinterland country is forced to transfer its domestic savings to finance its competitor and maybe aid the corporation in phasing out. As for the savings out of distributed profits, these accrue almost exclusively in the metropole, where they finance metropolitan consumption and investment.

The only means for a national economy to share in the savings of the new sector is by the intervention of government to levy taxes or to secure partial ownership. However, effectiveness of government in securing local participation — by taxation or by partial ownership — is circumscribed by the pattern of evolution of the new staple.

Constraints on the Hinterland Government

In the foundation period of the new staple the government is under great pressure. It is expected to ensure that the economy be salvaged from the stagnation and unemployment which marks the end of the cycle associated with the previous staple. In practical terms, it has to decide upon the conditions of entry to be accorded to metropolitan enterprise seeking to exploit the local natural resource. In this bargaining situation, the governments are handicapped by the absence of information in respect of the potentiality of the resource. Moreover, it is inherent in the situation that governments have far less information than the companies concerning the economies of the new industry. They are therefore inclined to make more concessions than may be necessary to attract the prospective investors. One effect of this is that the metropolitan corporations are likely to gain control of extensive reserves of the natural resource — thus making it more difficult for rivals to enter at some later date. Another effect is that the initial tax rate is low and the effective yield is likely to be negative if we remember that the provision of infrastructure at public expense is a direct subsidy to the company. Actual tax yields are further reduced by inflated depreciation and investment allowances. The main contribution which the new staple makes to the national economy consists in the boost to wage employment and to the demand for local materials associated with a construction boom.

Once the facilities have been established, however, the position of the government becomes stronger because the metropolitan investors now have a stake in the hinterland. In this Golden Age of the new staple, the yield to the national economy can be increased in the wage rate, in the tax and royalty rate, in the export price and in the scale of output. There are, however, limitations on the extent to which the public sector can use its powers to augment national income and government revenue. The integrated character of the companies with their metropolitan controlled complexes permits flexibility in manipulating the declared export price, and in choosing the locations where output may be expanded.

Thus, ultimately, whatever the tax rate the government levies, the actual yield to the national economy is determined by the companies. In this context, a high tax rate implies a high yield only because in the Golden Age, it usually pays the company to maintain the viability of the hinterland economy. It is for this reason that the bargaining position of the hinterland government is at its strongest.

The government's interest is as much in the maximization of revenue yield as in the direct national income yield. The reason for this lies in the comparatively low employment generated in the traditional export sector. In the context of an island hinterland with limited land and limited residentiary transformation, the responsibility for providing employment devolves most heavily on the public sector. There thus tends to develop a conflict between government and organized labour in the export sector over the division of the national income and of foreign exchange earnings.

High wage rates in the export sector exert an upward pressure on wages in the government and residentiary sectors, thus inhibiting employment creation. Furthermore, the expenditure patterns associated with higher wage rates typically imply a rising propensity to import consumer goods. This depresses the level of effective demand directed towards residentiary suppliers.

It is for both these reasons, as well as the obvious one — that larger taxation revenues give the government more direct means of determining national priorities — that there is a conflict over the distribution of national income and foreign exchange between the public and the national private sectors.

The Persistence of Mercantilist Ties

When the parent-affiliate relationships of new enterprises in resource extraction and in manufacturing are superimposed upon the pattern of the old mercantilism, the barriers to the emergence of indigenous enterprise are reinforced. The techniques of production, the consumption patterns and wage structures imposed by internal economic initiative frustrate transformation, particularly when income is growing.

Historical evidence strongly suggests that indigenous initiative is the key to the internal dynamic of development. Dependence on imported enterprise builds into the economy an assured backwardness *vis-a-vis* countries whose entrepreneurial dynamic is indigenous. The fact that it is the policy of many corporations to staff operations in hinterlands with nationals of these countries in no way modifies technological dependence. Local people working in a technical or managerial capacity are salaried employees who internalize the values and codes of the institutions of which they are a part. Their status within these corporations and their ability to do their jobs well forces upon them a style of life which mirrors metropolitan consumption patterns, and a view of themselves as people capable only of implementing decisions taken by others.

In a society in which the high import content of consumption has been a structural characteristic inherited from the past, the encouragement of a metropolitan economic presence is particularly questionable as a development policy. The so-called 'demonstration effect' whereby people in poorer countries aspire to metropolitan consumption patterns is, in good measure, the result of the setting up of metropolitan production facilities abroad. The pattern of income distribution which results from this type of industrialization is highly favourable to imports, and unfavourable to the increase in national savings and employment.

High wages in sectors dominated by profitable new export industries exert a strong upward pressure on wages in other unionized sectors, including the public services. When higher incomes are accompanied by a high propensity to spend on imported goods, the ratio of income saved does not increase. Nor is local enterprise stimulated. This does not interfere with the expansion of the foreign-owned mineral export sectors. They do not depend for expansion on local savings.

In fact the major contribution which this foreign sector makes to national income is in the form of wages and salaries and government revenue. Profit accrues as distributed factor income to the shareholders of the parent corporations or as retained income to the corporation itself. An economy of subsidiaries and branch plants thus chokes off the development of local entrepreneurs. Although the total savings generated by the activities of the subsidiaries are considerable, access to these savings by local enterprise is severely limited.

The savings out of employment income, even when the latter is high, come mainly in the form of contributions to insurance and pension plans and are channelled through financial intermediaries whose placements do not, as a rule, provide for investments of risk capital in the hinterland.

The fractured and partial nature of the capital market of hinterland countries is not due to low levels of income, or a low rate of saving from domestic product. It is the result of mercantilist relations of production with metropolitan corporations, and a system of financial intermediaries which is similarly characterized by the free flow of funds between branches of metropolitan commercial banks and their head offices. Domestic savings may be high, but very little of these are free in the sense that they are easily transferable from the sector in which they are generated to another sector of the national economy. There is thus the appearance of an excessive shortage of capital [Levitt 8].

In spite of the existence of much surplus labour, a strong bias towards the adoption of capital-intensive techniques of production is introduced by organizational ties with the metropolis. This bias is self reinforcing in so far as it leads to high wage levels, and continuing substitution of capital for labour. Further, the ability of the public sector to provide jobs for the growing number of unemployed persons is constrained by the tendency for expenditures to exceed revenues. To attract investment, governments undertake heavy outlays on infrastructure, involving substantial recurrent costs on salaries and debt servicing. Fiscal capacity however expands more slowly and further, cannot be fully exploited because fiscal concessions are one of the main instruments of industrialization policy.

The possibility of developing new exports of manufactures is severely limited. Activities which are attracted to cheap labour are limited and even here wage differentials are eventually narrowed by trade union organization. The possibility of expanding industries servicing the domestic market into exporting activity is constrained by their high unit cost and their imitative character. Branch plant manufactures are products initially developed for metropolitan domestic markets. Experience indicates that hinterland manufactures are likely to win external markets in spite of rising costs if they offer something unique to the foreign purchaser. This points to the need for indigenous product innovation. Branch plant manufacture is inimical to such a development.

Finally, and most important, the extension of the degree of processing of natural resources of the region is constrained by the mercantilist organization of the agricultural and mineral sectors.

The point here is that it is an insufficient diagnosis simply to note that in the Caribbean the units of production have, for the most part, been externally owned. What has also to be taken into account is that these units have usually been minor and dependent partners in wider international systems of resource mobilization and allocation. The lines of interdependence run, not laterally between local firms, but vertically to the metropole. As a consequence, the territorial economy is really comprised of a number of unintegrated segments held together by the political system. Production and pricing and other decisions are made more with reference to international than national considerations.

The internal functioning of firms operating in the Caribbean needs therefore to be explored in detail as the basis for a fresh approach to development. It is now becoming evident that the policies of active government were formulated without much reference to institutional factors such as these. It is for that reason that the ensuing development programmes have reinforced traditional relations.

It was assumed that the promotion of manufacturing activity would necessarily activate the economy. But it has to be appreciated that this depends — especially in a small country — on whether or not it is manufacturing of the branch plant type. On that turns the chances that local people will in fact learn 'the tricks of the trade' — the techniques of industrial enterprise and foreign marketing, that greater flexibility will develop in the choice of techniques and in the use of resources, and that a climate of experimentation and innovation will prevail.

It is also important here to appreciate the significance of the terms on which industry has been invited. For the premise of the open economy and the open society has set restraints on the use of foreign exchange, monetary, fiscal, and other governmental controls and on the availability of professional and skilled manpower. The so called 'brain drain' is partly a result of the imitative society which results from the type of development policies by the countries of the Commonwealth Caribbean.

Thus 'active' government in one sphere has led governments to be largely passive in others. Certainly there is a case for tighter monetary controls and more steeply progressive income taxes. But the governments have to calculate the effects of such changes on the investment climate — and that in a world of stiff competition for investment.

The argument here can perhaps be turned round. Possibly the choice of a strategy involving branch-plant manufacturing in the terms of a permissive open economy came naturally to the Caribbean countries because the traditional sectors had already charted the way. But, however the argument is put, it is clear that active governments must now conceive their role as involving a greater direct concern with the institutional facts of segmentation and the excessive openness of the economy.

Problem of Transformation

The economy which breaks traditional metropolitan ties may, as we said before, be forced into a new quasi-metropolitan relationship.

The act of changing external metropolitan affiliation, however, assists internal transformation. Established patterns of taste and techniques of production are disrupted. The commercial interests which serviced the traditional pattern of exportation and importation are eliminated. The immediate effect is a stimulus to local entrepreneurship. Shortages must now be met by drawing on local resourcefulness. However, the quasi-metropolitan relationship is bound to place pressure on the economy to accept supplies and techniques from the metropole. In this context, it is important that, on account of having localized the dominant sector, the government has greater freedom to resist this pressure and has the means to encourage and assist local enterprise.

Where traditional metropolitan ties are maintained, transformation is more difficult. It requires, above all, that the conditions must be created under which national entrepreneurship can be drawn from the margins to which it has traditionally been confined by the plantation heritage and directed towards the task of economic reconstruction.

When the export sector is in an expansionary phase, and generating high levels of income and revenue, the government is financially strong enough to initiate the process of diversification. But in the context of the institutional framework which has been inherited from the past, these attempts are typically frustrated. The restraints are internal as well as external, political as much as economic and tend even to be ideological.

During the boom, political and social limitations express themselves principally in the inability to control organized labour, to select patterns of investment which appear to discriminate against particular racial, cultural or class interests, and to resist expenditures and employment projects tailored to the needs of political support.

Equally constraining are the limitations placed on monetary and commercial policy by the rules of the international agencies and the terms of bilateral and multilateral agreements. The heavy dependence on metropolitan markets, investments and technology is inconsistent with the manipulations of the instruments of economic control necessary to change the pattern of taste, wage and price formation. Specifically, when the export sector is generating a high rate of growth of national income and foreign exchange earnings, the 'rules of the game' do not favour measures to impose controls on the use of foreign exchange. When the balance of payments is not in obvious 'fundamental disequilibrium' import controls are not internationally respectable. Yet it is precisely during an export staple boom that the potential resources available for transformation are greatest.

At such a time control over imports could divert considerable foreign exchange resources from consumption to development requirements. This implies a change in the composition of imports. Prices of food rise, thus providing one of the conditions necessary to induce a larger supply of domestic agricultural output. The rise in the price of other consumer goods and indeed, the total unavailability of luxury and semi-luxury imports is a form of forced postponement of consumption,placing command over resources in the hands of the public sector to undertake essential expenditures. In an open economy, this is an alternative to control of money wages or higher taxation. As an instrument of development policy it has the advantage of being more selective and discriminatory in its impact.

Because, however, the governments are restricted in their ability to mobilize and re-allocate internal resources they are forced into the only course remaining open to them — external borrowing and concessions even when revenue is plentiful as in conditions of a booming export sector. Thus, development programmes aimed at the diversification of export and residentiary activity are typically based on traditional reliance on metropolitan capital and entrepreneurship.

In point of fact, the strategy of 'industrialization by invitation' does not bring transformation. Rather it reinforces the traditional institutions of plantation economy. The outcome is the emergence of a residentiary sector which engages in import-replacement, rather than import displacement. The importation of parts and components takes the place of the importation of finished articles. What is more, 'finishing touch' consumer goods industries catering for the domestic market create a new rigidity in the import bill in the form of political pressure from wage-earners employed in these assembly-type industries and from consumers who come to regard these products as necessities of life. A reduction in imports of intermediate components and parts creates redundancy and unemployment. Substitution of local inputs may temporarily affect the quality of the product. The combination of protection and income tax concession with product differentiation fragments the local market, which is in any event not very large. The outcome is that the economy is burdened with a manufacturing sector producing too many similar products at high unit cost. Manufacturing firms typically employ few workers, import a large part of their supplies, and contribute little or nothing to government revenues. Indeed, when the substantial public infrastructure expenditures are charged against these industries, their contribution to the public sector may be negative.

In effect the economy is still engaged in terminal activity. Internal linkages remain weak. Imports of final goods yielding customs revenue have been replaced by the duty-free import of semi-finished goods assembled by a relatively small labour force employed by firms which pay little or no income tax and receive large subsidies in the form of public services. The availability of 'cheap labour' typically fails to attract export industries. In part this is due to the increasing tendency of metropolitan manufacturing firms to establish subsidiary production facilities within the countries, or common market areas, to which they then export materials and components. In part it is due to the fact that the cost of labour in the Caribbean is not really low when compared with other much poorer countries.

In these conditions, the distribution of income resulting from the introduction of branch plants into the economy reinforces the traditional weakness of the local capital market. Funds which find their way into commercial banks by way of personal savings from higher local incomes are not, in general, made available to local entrepreneurs. Metropolitan commercial banks prefer to extend credit to the distribution sector, either directly or indirectly, by extending personal loans to finance consumer purchases of cars or other durables, which are either imported or locally assembled from imported components. In so far as bank credit is available to industry supplying the local market, there is a bias to lending to foreign firms or joint ventures between local and foreign partners.

Although the strategy of transformation by industrialization was originally derived from the belief that the shortage of land imposed a physical limit to the extension of local food production, import substitution in agriculture has been more, rather than less successful than in manufacturing. But here, also, the constraints are those imposed by the traditional structures: the patterns of land and other resource allocation, the taste for imported foods, the difficulties of access to finance, the high import content of animal feedstuffs and the structure of distribution channels, to mention only the most obvious.

The result is that the typical manufacturing establishment is a taker of highly specific technology, tied to imported tastes, imported intermediate and capital goods, and imported managerial personnel and organizational procedures. Not surprisingly the manufacturing sector has not developed the dynamic which the early theorists who formulated the programme of 'industrialization by invitation' believed it would acquire.

It is evident that the dynamic for transformation derives from pressures exerted on domestic suppliers of consumer and intermediate goods. This is the main mechanism by which are induced secondary rounds of employment and income in the domestic economy. The typical manufacturing enterprise in the Caribbean, however, relies on infrastructure established by the government, on inputs imported from metropolitan sources, on tastes formed by advertising agencies and on purchasing power created by the expenditures of the large corporations in the traditional export sector augmented by consumer credit extended by local banks and government expenditures motivated by the necessity to buy political support. While it is obvious that the residentiary sectors benefit from income growth, it appears that it is only when there is an acute shortage of imported goods — such as during unusual conditions of World War II — that new residentiary activity, including domestic agriculture is generated.

The failure of employment to increase as fast as the labour force, the consequent rising number of unemployment, and the persistent and severe income inequality, force the government to seek means to create additional sources of employment and income, even when export earnings are rising. When the export sector slows its growth, as inevitably it must, the entire burden of adjustment falls on the public sector. Having failed to effect transformation when conditions were more favourable, the government is forced to turn to increased external borrowing to meet its rapidly rising development expenditures.

To give to the economy the internal dynamic necessary to create new internal linkages, it is necessary to change the pattern of tastes, to develop residentiary industries with lower import content and larger local purchases, to increase the degree of local processing of agricultural and mineral resources, to reallocate land resources, to halt the brain drain, to restructure financial institutions to widen the channels of national saving and investment flows, and to break down the economic barriers between individual territories within the region.

In conditions of plantation economy, such structural transformation is not possible without breaking the traditional plantation patterns whereby Caribbean economy is incorporated into metropolitan economy. It is for this reason that the localization of economic decision-making lies at the heart of transformation. This appears to be the principal lesson of the study of the legacy of the plantation on the contemporary economy.

Notes

1. This essay summarizes some of the conclusions which derive from work on plantation economy started in 1965. The assistance of the Centre for Developing Area Studies of McGill University in the academic years 1966/68 is gratefully acknowledged. For a more detailed exposition of the concept of plantation economy see Best and Levitt [4].
2. For a brief critique see Best [3].
3. See especially Demas [5].
4. These disappear from view in the conventional aggregative Keynesian models of open economies. The complaint against such models is that they are empty of significance. They thus direct attention from important structural relations to trivial equilibrium conditions.
5. For a brief elaboration of this topology and some bibliographical references see Best [2]. See also Best and Levitt [4].
6. That distinction corresponds to the accepted conventions of national accounting which distinguishes between National Income and Domestic Product.
7. Although part of the South American continent, the coastal settlements here are akin to 'island' hinterlands.
8. The concept of 'total institutions' comes from E. Goffman, *Asylums*, New York, 1961 and was adapted to the sociology of the plantation by R.T. Smith [12].

References

[1] BEST, L., 'Size and Survival', *New World Quarterly*, Guyana Independence Issue, 1966.
[2] ———, 'A Model of Pure Plantation Economy', *Social and Economic Studies*, Vol. 17, No. 3, September 1968.
[3] ———, 'The Economy of the British Commonwealth Caribbean: An Overview' in *West Indies-Canada Economic Relations*, Jamaica: Institute of Social and Economic Research, University of the West Indies, 1967.
[4] ——— and Kari LEVITT, *Externally Propelled Growth and Industrialization*, Centre for Developing Area Studies, McGill University, 1969 (3 Vols.) mimeographed.
[5] DEMAS, W.G., *The Economic of Development in Small Countries with Special Reference to the Caribbean*, Montreal: McGill University Press, 1965.
[6] JEFFERSON, O. and N. GIRVAN, 'Corporate Versus Caribbean Economic Integration', *New World Quarterly*, Vol. 4, No. 2, 1968.
[7] LEVITT, Kari, 'The Old Mercantilism and the New', *Social and Economic Studies*, Vol. 19, No. 4, December 1970.
[8] ———, *Silent Surrender: The Multinational Corporation in Canada*, Toronto: Macmillan of Canada, 1970.
[9] ———, *Industrial Development in the Caribbean*, Caribbean Commission, Port of Spain, p. 151. Reprinted from *Caribbean Economic Review*.

[10] SEERS, Dudley, 'A Model of the Open Petroleum Economy', *Social and Economic Studies,* Vol. 13, No. 2, June 1964.

[11] SMITH, R.T., 'Social Stratification, Cultural Pluralism and Integration in West Indies Societies', in S. Lewis and T.G. Mathews (eds.)

[12] ———, *Caribbean Integration,* Rio Piedras, Puerto Rico, University of Puerto Rico, 1967.

[13] WAGLEY, Charles, 'Plantation America: A Cultural Sphere' in Vera Rubin (ed) *Caribbean Studies: A Symposium,* U.W.I., 1957.

Operation Bootstrap and Economic Change in Puerto Rico

J.L. Dietz

Introduction

Between 1942 and 1952, all the institutional innovations that were to transform Puerto Rico from a rural, predominately agrarian society to an urban, manufacturing-based one were put in place. From 1952 to the mid–1980s, there were no fundamental changes of direction in development policy, only variations on the theme of industrialization dependent on U.S. markets, inputs, technology, financing, and ownership. The standard of living, and certainly the lifestyle, of most Puerto Ricans was made dramatically different and easier as the island became little more than an extension of the U.S. economy. While it is not meaningless to refer to the Puerto Rican economy, its distinctiveness has become blurred as a result of its nearly full integration with the mainland market, banking system, manufacturing methods, and labour, environmental, and juridical regulations. Integrated but not assimilated; part of but not of the United States, U.S. citizens by law but Puerto Ricans first — these are the tensions and contradictions that permeate society at all levels.

This chapter examines the evolution of the island's industrialization strategy from the early 1950s to the mid 1980s. Efforts to bring U.S. firms to the island dominates the story, and the government and Fomento continued their interventionist role. However, the local government's function as collective capitalist, entrepreneur, and social planner directly involved in the development process had come to an end with the initiation of Operation Bootstrap and its reliance on external sources of capital and entrepreneurship, except in those areas such as public utilities, where government ownership is commonplace in most capitalists economies. Despite an outward semblance of planning and the existence of a planning board and planning laws, there actually has been a surprising lack of instrumental planning for the domestic economy.[1] Fomento has done planning, of course, but of the sort designed to get results that appealed to U.S. investors. Planning has revolved around the issue of what is necessary to attract external capital to the island rather than around the issue of Puerto Rico's needs. This did not happen because Fomento, Munoz, and the PPD wished to benefit U.S. companies at the expense of local capital or to subject the local economy to external control, but because they believed that Puerto Rico's needs would be met by attracting U.S. capital, which was required for rapid growth, generation of employment, and an improved standard of living. The two issues, in other words, collapsed into one for local policy makers. 'Fomento under Teodoro Moscoso has seen the interests of Puerto Rico as one.'[2]

There are good reasons for this conflation of what in reality are distinct questions. They lie not in any conspiracy assimilationist PPD leaders but in classical and neoclassical economic theory, which has postulated that self-interested behaviour in a competitive market not only leads to results that are socially desirable but even allows society to approach an optimum state of well-being marked by a harmony of individual interests. Market systems are held to convert private greed into public benefit, since only by satisfying the desires of buyers will sellers profit. Practically the entire corpus of orthodox economic theory is devoted to the verification and elucidation of this result in the light of complicating factors.

As impressive as these efforts may have been, they are to great extent unconnected with reality. The theory that the public good is best served by private greed requires that there be perfect competition (or, in a more recent refinement, 'contestable' markets), no uncompensated externalities, independent individual utility functions, an optimal distribution of wealth, and quite a number of other factors.[3] In any real economic situation, these conditions obviously cannot all be met.

Despite the striking gap between theory and reality, Operation Bootstrap from its beginning was based, at least implicitly, on the assumption that self-interested behaviour does lead to public benefit, and on the further assumption that economic growth benefits all classes and groups —

i.e., the 'trickle-down' theory that the benefits of a growing output gradually spread throughout the social hierarchy. These assumptions, even if not always clearly articulated or well understood, are what gave justification to Puerto Rico's industrialization via the market, based overwhelmingly on self-selection by U.S. firms. As a consequence, external capital's interests have continued to shape the characteristics of the Puerto Rican economy.

Economic Growth and Equitable Development

The orthodox models of development first put forward in the 1940s and early 1950s exerted an intellectual influence on the design and extensions of Operation Bootstrap. All of these models — whether their strategy was balanced growth, unbalanced growth, a labour surplus, or some other — suggested means by which underdeveloped countries could attempt to repeat the development that had taken place in the already developed countries by focusing on measures — fundamentally productive capital formation — to increase the rate of growth of GNP. Invariably, these recommendations called for an expansion of industrial production and a decrease in the importance of agriculture. Labour was to be transferred from traditional and backward agriculture to the modern industrial sector, since it was believed that it had been precisely this social and economic transformation that had been responsible for the success of the developed countries. One of the best-known and most influential descriptions of such a strategy was that of W. Arthur Lewis, though he emphasized the importance of agricultural transformation as well as industrial expansion.

The basic problem with these models and with their practical application in the nations that have tried to apply them was not that they did not increase the rate of economic growth and the level of GNP. Very often the results on these counts have been quite spectacular; Puerto Rico and Brazil are two especially good examples of rapid growth, but there are others as well. But what has increasingly come to be questioned is the relation between economic growth and development and the reliability of trick-down as the transmission mechanism. Development is now understood to be something broader than economic growth. Though it is obvious that GNP growth can make the goals of development easier to achieve by providing the base for improving the standard of living of the poorest in society, economic growth alone has been found to be neither necessary nor sufficient for development to take place, and in some cases

it actually appears to have been a hindrance to the process.[4]

Development economist Dudley Seers has suggested three criteria for determining whether development is taking place: (a) a decrease in the numbers of those in absolute poverty; (b) movement toward greater equality; and (c) a movement toward full employment for all who wish to work.[5] The World Bank has utilized a similar definition of development, known as 'the basic needs approach'.[6] Both of these approaches begin from the premise that, while the trickle-down theory of 'growth first, equity later' may succeed in achieving economic growth, it often fails to meet other criteria of development. The basic needs perspective effectively turns the orthodox models on their heads by proposing that equity be accorded equal priority with economic growth. This implies a continuing need for state intervention and planning to meet the basic needs of the vast majority of the world's population, one-quarter of whom, by the World Bank's count, are in absolute poverty.[7]

Orthodox economic models had recognized the necessity for government intervention to get the growth process started, but they assumed that the market system would then take over and lead to development without significant further direction by the state. In the equity-with-growth approach, by contrast, government intervention is held to be necessary not only to launch economic growth but also to ensure that output is continuously used in ways that result in the production and distribution of goods and services that contribute to development in Seers's or the 'basic needs' sense. This perspective eschews any simple faith in the automatic workings of markets, especially in an era of international oligopolies with extensive market power and price-fixing arrangements, and it assigns an important role to government actions.

The PPD programme in the early 1940s was very much a forerunner of an equity-with-growth development model and was, to that extent, ahead of its time. Both social justice and economic growth had been primary goals. But the contradiction of pursuing both these goals in a colonial, capitalist economy once the relative autonomy of the war years came to an end became ever more intense. Bowing to market pressures, Operation Bootstrap represented the renunciation of the equity-with-growth strategy and its replacement by a growth-first, orthodox model of economic growth.[8] The way in which this change affected Puerto Rico's economy and society is the theme of this chapter.

Varieties of Economic Growth

Rapid economic growth in the 1950s and 1960s became the hallmark of Operation Bootstrap, and policy makers from around the world were brought to the island (as part of official U.S. policy under Point Four of the Truman Doctrine) to see the miracle at work. Puerto Rico went from being the 'poorhouse of the Caribbean' to the 'showcase of democracy', demonstrating, it was claimed, the possibilities of cooperation among developed and underdeveloped countries to the benefit of both. As table 1 shows, economic growth did indeed take place during Operation Bootstrap. From 1950 to 1960, GNP more than doubled, the rate of annual growth averaging 8.3%. From 1960 to 1970, GNP growth was even more spectacular, at an average annual rate of 10.8% per year, thus nearly tripling over the decade. Per capita GNP increased from $342 in 1950 (it had been $154 in 1940) to $716 in 1960 and to $3,479 in 1980. In this last year, Puerto Rico's per capita income exceeded that of all the Latin American republics except Venezuela.[9]

Gross investment grew even more rapidly: 219% from 1950 to 1960 and another 295% from 1960 to 1970. The growth rate slowed down to 45.5% from 1970 to 1980, but that was on a much larger base. More important, gross investment as a proportion of GNP rose from 14.8% in 1950 to almost 31% in 1970 (it had been but 8% of GNP in 1940), though the proportion declined during the 1970s until in the early 1980s it was at a level very similar to that which had prevailed at the beginning of the industrialization programme.

Table 1 also shows the level of real GNP (i.e., GNP adjusted for price changes). It rose 5.3% per year from 1950 to 1960 and 7.0% from 1960 to 1970; but then slowed down to 3.5% per year from 1970 to 1980. In total, real GNP increased 134% between 1940 and 1960 and a further 177% by 1980. There was a downturn in real GNP after 1980, the result of recession in the United States, a decline in exports, and a slowdown in federal expenditures on the island (to be discussed later). This was followed by a slight recovery in 1984 which brought aggregate real GNP back up to the 1980 level.[10]

The rapid increase in investment contributed greatly not only to the growth of GNP (total insular income) but also to the growth of gross domestic product, or GDP (the total value of output produced within Puerto Rico, regardless of its recipient). Until 1960, GNP exceeded GDP, primarily because of the payment of wages to federal employees on the island. After 1960, however, as can be seen in table 1, GDP exceeded GNP. This difference, as Freyre points out, 'is important for a capital importing country such as Puerto Rico, because interest and dividend payments on external investment can be considered as a drainage from territorial production which does not accrue to residents of the country, although it is produced with the participation of domestic capital stock'[11] — and, it should be added, local labour.

In 1960, the difference between GNP and GDP, the 'GNP/GDP gap', was equal to about 1% of GNP; in 1970, the gap was equal to 7.4% of GNP; by 1980, it had grown to 30.8% of GNP, and it remained near or above that level in the 1980s

Table 1. Gross National Product, Gross Domestic Product, and Gross Fixed Investments, Selected Years, 1950 to 1984

	Gross National Producton			Gross Domestic Product (millions of dollars)	Gross Fixed Investment	
	Current Dollars (millions)	Per Capita	Real Dollars[a] (millions)		Total (millions of dollars)	As Percent of GNP
1950	754.5	342	878.7	723.9	111.4	14.8
1960	1,676.4	716	1,473.2	1,473.2	1,691.9	21.2
1970	4,687.5	1,729	2,901.4	5,034.7	1,401.6	29.9
1972	5,771.0	2,045	3,231.2	6,342.6	1,761.0	30.5
1974	6,817.8	2,366	3,434.6	7,710.0	1,695.6	24.9
1976	7,555.8	2,537	3,458.4	8,996.4	1,819.0	24.1
1977	8,173.8	2,683	3,623.5	9,929.9	1,540.1	18.8
1978	8,994.0	2,903	3,817.4	11,172.4	1,744.9	19.4
1980	11,073.8	3,479	4,076.7	14,480.0	2,039.0	18.4
1982	12,626.5	3,879	3,977.5	16,414.5	1,778.6	14.1
1983[b]	12,907.7	3,953	3,891.9	16,969.3	1,636.3	12.7
1984[b]	13,993.6	4,248	4,074.1	—	1,957.7	14.0

SOURCES: Junta de Planificación, *Informe económico,* al goberador 1980, p. A–1, table 1; ibid., 1982–83 2:A–1, table 1; Government Development Bank for Puerto Rico, *Special Economic Bulletin,* (Dec. 1984), p. 6, table 1, and p. 7, table 2.
NOTE: The Junta de Planificación has been revising its accounting procedures retrospectively and many of the recent figures differ from those that were reported earlier.
[a] In 1954 prices.
[b] Preliminary figures.

(table 1). This widening gap, which there will be occasion to comment on again, is a rough measure of the volume of profits, interests, and dividends flowing out of the economy to non-residents, primarily in the United States. (Actually, it understates the magnitude of this outflow, since it is net of the inflow of federal wages paid on the island). Table 2 thus shows unambiguously that an increasing share of production and income created in Puerto Rico has been appropriated by external investors and has been unavailable as income or for consumption or for local investment.

The gross fixed investment shown in table 1 needs to be discussed in more detail. It can be divided into two components: (a) construction, and (b) machinery and equipment. The latter category is clearly capital — the physical tools that are used in the production process in combination with labour and raw materials to produce final outputs. Construction is a more problematic category. Some construction, as for factories, is also capital, since it contributes to long-term economic growth. Other construction expenditures, such as for residential housing, have but a short-term impact on growth. It can be seen from table 3 that the machinery-and-equipment component of investment increased relative to total investment from 1950 to 1960, at the same time that gross investment was increasing, but that its share of total investment then began to fall. Since 1977, its share has increased, returning to its 1960 level, but total investment has not grown during that time, and indeed from 1980 to 1984, it declined in absolute terms. This suggests a potentially deleterious trend for the longer term.

Stages of Operation Bootstrap

The activities of Operation Bootstrap can be divided into two fairly distinct stages. During the first stage, which lasted from 1947 into the early

Table 2. The GNP/GDP Gap, Selected Years, 1950 to 1983

	GDP – GNP (millions of dollars)	Percentage of GNP
1950	−30.6	
1960	15.5	0.9
1970	347.2	7.4
1972	571.6	9.9
1974	892.2	13.1
1976	1,440.6	19.1
1977	1,756.1	21.5
1978	2,178.4	24.2
1980	3,406.2	30.8
1982	3,788.0	30.0
1983	4,061.6	31.5

SOURCE: Table 1.

1960s, most of the firms coming from the United States were labour-intensive enterprises with relatively low capital requirements. For example, in 1949, the production of textiles and clothing — a notoriously labour-intensive industry — accounted for 13.7% of all manufacturing firms; in 1954, the figure was 19.5%, and in 1967, it was 19.9%.[12] They were attracted to Puerto Rico not just by tax exemption, but also by the possibility of being able to pay wages substantially below mainland rates and by the absence of such risks as political instability that are often associated with foreign operations. There was also a 'push' factor: labour was in short supply in the United States.[13] Even though most managers and other officials believed that tax exemption was the key reason for moving to Puerto Rico, careful analysis has shown that low wages actually provided a larger subsidy than did the tax holiday provided by the Industrial Incentive Law. In fact, it has been estimated that if wages had been 25% higher, they would have erased any savings from tax exemption for those firms that relocated before 1953 and tended to have a high ratio of labour costs to total costs.[14] Thus, low wage levels were the key to their profitability. This circumstance has led one observer to refer to this stage as Operation Bootstrap's 'sweatshop' phase.[15]

Table 4 compares wages paid in Puerto Rico to those being paid on the mainland at the same time. In 1950, at the beginning of Operation Bootstrap, the average hourly wage in manufacturing in Puerto Rico was but 28% of the U.S. wage. By 1965, it had increased to nearly half the level in the United States, still a substantial savings from an employer's point of view but possibly a threat to the development program, if a narrowing differential tended to reduce the attractiveness of tax exemption.[16] Yet, as already noted, labour-intensive firms continued to arrive, so the higher relative wage was evidently not having the negative effect that had been feared.

It may be more significant then, that the absolute difference in wages between the island and the mainland has tended to increase since 1950, and particularly since the mid–1960s. It is this lower absolute wage level in Puerto Rico that has attracted and retained many labour-intensive producers, which is precisely the result one would expect if productivity levels were similar between the two, as they were. As long as labour-intensive firms could pay lower absolute wages in Puerto Rico than they had to pay in the United States for equivalent work, they continued to have an incentive to produce in Puerto Rico.

Despite the absolute wage gap relative to the United States, however, Puerto Rico has been losing its comparative advantage to other low-

Table 3. Components of Gross Investment, Selected Years, 1950 to 1984

	Construction		Machinery and Equipment	
	Total (millions of dollars)	Percent of Gross Investment	Total (millions of dollars)	Percentage of Gross Investment
1950	78.7	70.6	32.6	29.3
1960	227.0	64.0	127.9	36.0
1970	988.6	70.5	413.0	29.5
1972	1,285.3	73.0	475.8	27.0
1974	1,281.9	75.6	413.6	24.4
1976	1,295.3	71.2	523.7	28.8
1977	1,003.7	65.2	536.4	34.8
1978	1,133.7	65.0	611.2	35.0
1980	1,303.1	63.9	735.9	36.1
1982	1,236.4	69.5	542.1	31.5
1983	1,266.0	64.7	691.7	35.3

SOURCES: Same as table 1.

Table 4. Wages in Manufacturing, Puerto Rico and the United States, Five-Year Intervals from 1950 to 1975, 1977, and 1979

	Average Hourly Wage			Puerto Rico as Percent of U.S.	U.S. Minimum Wage
	Puerto Rico	United States	Difference		
1950	$0.42	$1.50	$1.08	28.0	$0.75
1955	0.56	1.91	1.38	29.3	1.00
1960	0.94	2.30	1.36	40.9	1.00
1965	1.26	2.64	1.38	47.7	1.25
1970	1.78	3.37	1.59	52.8	1.60
1975	2.59	4.40	1.81	58.9	2.10
1977	3.11	5.60	2.49	55.5	2.30
1979	3.58	6.54	2.96	54.7	2.90

SOURCES: U.S. Department of Commerce, *Economic Study* at Puerto Rico, 2 vols. (Washington D.C. 1979) 2:56, table 4; Puerto Rico Economic Development Administration, *Manufacturers Ready Reference File*, 1979, 'Labour' folder.

wage countries. In 1969, the island was the largest supplier of clothing to the U.S. market; by the mid–1970s, it had slipped to fourth place. Of course, there are factors other than rising relative and absolute wage levels that explain this decline -e.g., the opening of the U.S. market as the result of the various rounds of the General Agreement on Tariffs and Trade and the tendency of international corporations to spread their operations among many countries. In any case, the apparel industry has remained the largest single employer in manufacturing in Puerto Rico, with 23% of total manufacturing employment in 1978 and more than 30% in the early 1980s, a good indication that labour-intensive production remains very important in the local economic structure.[17]

But prices in Puerto Rico were higher than in the United States,[18] so an industrialization strategy based on low-wage labour demanded a great sacrifice of Puerto Rican workers. Fomento was aware of this contradiction.[19] Pressure also was applied by island labour unions to win higher wages, and they were joined by the U.S. unions that feared a

loss of jobs to the island. But, just as had been true in the 1930s, U.S. firms in Puerto Rico had nothing to gain from paying higher wages, since the bulk of their output was exported to the mainland, not sold to Puerto Rican consumers. One director of Fomento, José Madera, wrote:

The industries attracted here by means of that [early] strategy had a common profile: Firms that needed only a modest investment (labour intensive and of a relatively low technological know-how) which produced consumer goods for unstable markets; and, moreover, industries which did not need each other, nor link themselves into a chain of economic development.[20]

The last part of this describes another important characteristic of the industries that were attracted by Fomento in the early years of Operation Bootstrap: they had few linkages or connections with the rest of the local economy. The firms were 'export enclaves', largely unrelated to other firms or industries in the local economy, typically as subsidiaries of a vertically integrated company headquartered in the United States. The unit located in Puerto Rico served as an assembly or production plant that imported raw or semifinished materials and reexported the finished output back to the United States. Very few inputs to the production process other than labour originated on the island, and the benefits to the island were limited to, in most cases, the wages paid. There were thus very few indirect or spinoff effects on the local economic structure, and few 'satellite' firms emerged to service the enterprises. To the extent that the promoted firms were more or less integrated into supply and distribution networks in the United States, they failed to provide opportunities for supply or distribution firms to develop in Puerto Rico.

Revision of the Tax Incentive

Under the Industrial Incentive Act, full tax exemption was to end on June 30, 1959, to be followed by three years of partial exemption (1960, 75%; 1961, 50%; 1962, 25%) and then an end to the exemption altogether. As the termination approached, it became apparent that it would become increasingly difficult to convince new firms to initiate operations with these reduced tax exemptions.[21] When industrial promotion began, the idea had been to provide a few years for companies to adjust to a new location in the favourable circumstance of untaxed, above-normal profits, and then the firms were expected to become tax-paying enterprises just like any other. However, corporate decision makers in the United States and on the island perceived tax exemption quite differently.[22]

One study found that officers of 95% of a representative sample of forty-four firms believed tax exemption to be the key to their operations, and it was ranked an 'important advantage' more often than any other factor that might have influenced a location decision. Other factors, in declining order of importance, were wage rates, efficiency of machinery and equipment, and the attitude of the community. Interestingly, the factor that was next-to-last in importance was the availability of a labour force with suitable skills. The conclusion drawn from this study was that 'the new industrialists apparently do not consider tax exemption to be in the nature of a short-run subsidy'.[23] One business leader commenting on tax exemption in the early 1950s said bluntly, 'It should be extended, otherwise I won't be here'.[24]

Fomento and the Commonwealth government thus faced the first real dilemma of the development strategy. Having embarked upon a path of tax exemption designed to attract firms that might cre-

ate employment, generate high incomes, and encourage spinoff or satellite industries, they ended up attracting firms that were labour-intensive but that had few local linkages, firms that were therefore highly mobile and might liquidate their investments if their tax exemptions were terminated.[25] Confronted with such a possibility, the PPD-dominated legislature passed a new Industrial Incentive Act, which became effective in 1954. This law permitted a firm to receive exemption for a period of ten years after it began operations on the island, whenever that might be. This measure helped to make Puerto Rico continue to look attractive to potential investors and helped to overcome the decline in relocations which began in 1953–54, though a downturn in the U.S. economy at the time dampened investors' confidence irrespective of Puerto Rico's promotional efforts. With this action, however, the tax–exemption programme shifted from being a temporary measure, as originally conceived, to being a permanent feature of the development strategy. This act essentially marks the point in time when external capital and externally owned enterprises were institutionalized as the long-term base of development.

In 1963, another Industrial Incentive Act was passed to correct some of the imbalances that had appeared after the 1954 law. One adverse consequence had been the concentration of firms in the San Juan metropolitan area (including Carolina, Cataño, and Bayamón), where more services existed, the amenities of a large city were close at hand, and most government offices were located. Almost half the new firms, accounting for more than one-third of the employment, were in this area, and two-thirds of them were in the combined urban areas of San Juan, Caguas, Ponce, and Mayagüez. This contributed to an influx of population into the cities that greatly exceeded the employment generated by the new enterprises locating there, while at the same time severely straining public services, health facilities, and the school systems. These higher social costs, moreover, could not be paid for out of additional tax revenues from the exempted corporations, and hence the growing urban population was becoming increasingly burdensome. In an attempt to remedy this, the 1963 law provided for varying periods of tax exemption depending upon where the new enterprise was to be located. In 'underdeveloped industrial zones' (typically in the interior), full tax exemption was possible for up to seventeen years. Location in an area of intermediate development provided for twelve years of complete exemption, and those firms choosing to operate in areas of 'high industrial concentration', like the San Juan area, were to receive 'only' a ten-year full tax holiday.[26] This revision in the tax law has had very limited success in bringing about decentralization, however.[27]

The 1963 law also permitted a delay of up to two years in the initiation of the exemption period, on the premise that if there were losses at the beginning of operations due to start-up problems, tax exemption would be meaningless for those years. (This provision also permitted subsidiaries of U.S. companies to include their losses in Puerto Rico on a combined income statement with the parent corporation, thus reducing their U.S. tax liability, another attraction for enterprises with high initial costs). The length of the exemption period also could be doubled by taking 50%, rather than complete, exemption.[28]

The Second Stage

As early as the 1950s, but increasingly in the 1960s, an awareness grew within Fomento of the desirability of attracting capital-intensive firms requiring a semi-skilled and skilled labour force.[29] Such a re-orientation was believed necessary for a number of reasons. First, if wages were to increase in Puerto Rico — and this was both a goal for the sake of a higher standard of living and a need imposed by the high prices on the island — the importance of tax exemption for firms with high labour costs relative to total costs would be somewhat diminished, given the low wages that prevailed in Asia and in other countries in the Caribbean and Latin America. Capital-intensive firms, though, could afford to pay higher wages because, with their heavier use of capital, labour productivity was greater, and because, with labour costs a small share of total costs, increases in wages had less of an effect on profits. The attractiveness of tax exemption would thus be retained, even with increasing wage scales.

Second, it was believed that capital-intensive industries would be more resistant to the cyclical variations of the mainland economy, which tended to affect subsidiaries of U.S. firms on the island more than the parent corporation in the United States.[30]

The first capital-intensive projects were in the petrochemical sector. Caribe Nitrogen, Gulf Caribbean, and Commonwealth Oil Refining Company (CORCO) were in operation by 1956. Between 1952 and 1958, new firms in this industry invested $78.4 million in Puerto Rico, equal to 27% of total investment in manufacturing.[31] Attracting this industry seemed to make economic sense to Fomento officials; since all energy sources were externally supplied, the construction of oil refineries would permit the capturing of at least a portion of the value added in the production process, thus contributing to local job and income creation. In actuality, however, this effect was much weaker than had been expected. In 1979, not long before the complete cessation of its refining operations in 1982, CORCO employed but 1,450 workers.

A second reason why the creation of a petrochemical sector seemed advantageous was that Venezuelan crude oil could be refined for the U.S. market, which not only was using increasing amounts of petroleum but also was relying on even greater quantities of imported supplies. There were negative aspects to the building of the refineries, of course, primarily in terms of the costs of infrastructure and the levels of pollution and ecological damage expected — and these came to be the focus of much popular discontent — but there is no doubt that the petrochemical sector was a basic part of the second-stage strategy of Fomento and was indeed, for a time, conceived as something of a showcase.

Other capital-intensive firms were successfully promoted in the machinery, chemicals, and metal industries. Within the chemical sector, drug and pharmaceutical firms have grown especially rapidly. In 1982, chemical and related products accounted for 32.1% of the gross output of all industry, though they provided only 10.1% of employment in manufacturing, which is an indication of the capital-intensive nature of this industry. A further indication is that, in the same year, the chemical industry earned $1.9 billion in net income, equal to 35.3% of net manufacturing income, and of that amount, $1.6 billion, or 84%, was what can be called 'capitalist income' — that is, the return accruing to owners and creditors of these firms as profits, interest, and dividends. Only 16% of net income in the chemical industry was paid to employees as wages and salaries, and it is this limited share which was retained in the Puerto Rican economy, since the capitalist income share was predominately repatriated to recipients in the United States.

In capital-intensive industries as a whole, 75% of net income was paid to owners of capital, primarily external, and only 25% to workers. The workers' share of income in all capital-intensive industries was $947.3 million in 1982, compared to $897.2 million in all labour-intensive industries. That can hardly be regarded as incremental gain to the economy from capital-intensive promotion. In 1981, in fact, employees in labour-intensive production received total compensation that exceeded the returns to labour in capital-intensive industry.[32] Though it is true that workers were better paid, on the average, in the more capitalized firms, there were fewer of them. From 1947 to 1961, Fomento firms employed an average of 70 workers; in the late 1960s, employment per firm had declined to just 33.3 persons. In the San Juan area, Fomento firms were providing jobs to only one of every thirty-nine inhabitants in the mid–1960s, only 28.7% of the jobs promised by promoted firms had actually materialized, and among the highly touted petrochemical firms the percentage was even lower.[33]

There was, however, something else expected from these capital-intensive, so-called 'core' industries. Besides the jobs and incomes they might directly create, and the greater stability they were thought to bring, it was believed that (1) backward-linked spinoff effects would emerge as new firms were created to supply raw and semifinished materials, and that (2) especially in the petrochemical sector, forward linkages would develop as new firms were founded to purchase the outputs of the capital-intensive firms. What actually happened was quite different. The firms that located on the island were integrated into sourcing and distribution networks with other firms in the United States or other countries. They made no attempt to forge linkages with the island economy, nor were they motivated to do so by the government or its incentive package. As a result, they had only minor indirect employment effects. The new industrial sector thus resembled the export enclave of the ear-

lier promotions in textiles and apparel and was not even very different from the sugar industry of the pre–1940 period.

Nevertheless, firms promoted by Fomento have dominated the manufacturing sector. In 1978, there were 2,411 enterprises operating that had been promoted by Fomento.[34] Whereas in 1960, promoted firms had provided 54% of all manufacturing employment, this share rose to 78% in 1970 and to 92% in 1980. Fomento firms have paid slightly better wages than other firms. For example, in 1981, they paid an average of $4.55 an hour, compared to $4.11 in non-Fomento firms.[35] In 1970, Fomento firms accounted for 70% of all exports and 75% of manufacturing net income. By 1977, they were responsible for 83% of total exports, and in the early 1980s for more than 90% of net income in manufacturing.[36]

Some 84 pharmaceutical companies have been promoted, an increase from the 47 in 1972. For the pharmaceuticals, Puerto Rico has become an extremely profitable link in their worldwide operations. Besides the ability to test new products with fewer restrictions and to produce under less hampering conditions than in the United States, nearly 50% of their worldwide profits are earned on the island.

There also were 367 promoted firms in apparel, 177 in food processing, and 93 in petroleum and related products in the late 1970s.[37] In food

Table 5. Gross National Product by Sector, 1950, 1960, 1970, and 1980

Sector	1950 Value[a]	%	1960 Value[a]	%	1970 Value[a]	%	1980 Value[a]	%
Agriculture	132.1	17.5	164.0	9.8	160.9	3.4	393.9	3.6
Manufacturing	119.7	15.9	366.3	21.9	1,190.0	25.4	5,322.5	48.1
Constructing and mining	30.4	4.0	101.1	6.0	379.1	8.1	370.1	3.3
Transportation and other public utilities	61.2	8.1	155.8	9.3	439.3	9.4	1,234.8	11.2
Trade	144.3	19.1	319.1	19.0	898.3	19.2	2,277.3	20.6
Finance, insurance, and real estate	74.5	9.9	197.7	11.8	613.8	13.1	1,598.9	14.4
Services	44.7	5.9	140.9	8.4	512.2	10.9	1,316.1	11.9
Government	75.1	10.0	187.1	11.2	609.9	13.0	1,896.3	17.1
External[b]	30.6	4.1	−15.5	(0.9)	−347.2	(7.4)	−3,406.2	(30.8)
Total[c]	745.5		1,676.4		4,687.5		11,073.8	

SOURCES: Junda de Planificación, *Informe económico,* 1980, p. A–5, table 4; ibid., 1982–83 2:A–4, table 4.
[a] Millions of dollars.
[b] Difference between income received from external sources (primarily federal wages paid in Puerto Rico) and income created in Puerto Rico but paid to external recipients (primarily payments of profits, interest, and dividends to U.S. residents). When the figure is negative, outflows exceed inflows. The percent measures the excess of GDP over GNP (or, when positive, the excess of GNP over GDP).
[c] Total value includes a category of 'statistical discrepancy', not shown here, which may be positive or negative. Percentages are based on the total shown.

processing, the tuna industry is the most important one, having displaced sugar as the leading export in that sector in 1969. In 1981, three U.S. and two Japanese firms were operating seven tuna canneries in Mayagüez and Ponce, and the Puerto Rican tuna-canning industry was supplying 40% of U.S. consumption. In this industry, not only the canneries but also individually owned boats are eligible for tax exemption.[38]

Changes in the Economic Structure

Table 5 shows how the productive structure of the economy has evolved during Operation Bootstrap. The share of GNP originating in agriculture had been more than 17% in 1950, but by 1960 its share had declined to less than 10% and by 1970 to slightly more than 3%. The share due to trade has remained remarkably stable, but there has been growth in services and in finance, insurance, and real estate, as would be expected from the spread of market relations and the rise in incomes, making the provision of services, which are income-elastic, more feasible and speculation more profitable. Government's contribution to GNP also has grown; if transportation and other public utilities (electricity, telephone, water, and sewage) are added to the direct contribution of government, the state's contribution to income generation appears to be second only to that of manufacturing.

The growth in manufacturing output has been by far the greatest: more than 4,300% in absolute terms and more than tripling in relative importance.

A word of caution in interpreting manufacturing's contribution to GNP growth is in order, however. The next-to-last row of figures in table 5 shows a negative contribution to GNP since 1960 arising out of the payments of profits, interest, and dividends to non-residents in excess of the inflows of income to residents from outside the local economy, and is the amount by which GNP differs from GDP (shown in table 2). Because it is primarily through ownership in the manufacturing sector that such income is received by non-residents, the percentage contribution of manufacturing to GNP and local income creation is overstated in the percentages reported in table 5. However, if the payments of profits and dividends to non-residents are subtracted from the share attributed to manufacturing, a quite different picture emerges (see table 6). A substantial proportion of income from manufacturing — in the 1980s, well more than half of it — has been repatriated to the mainland. In 1980, though manufacturing apparently produced about 48% of total GNP, its net contribution was only about 18% — only slightly more than its contri-

bution for the preceding twenty years. In 1982, the net contribution of manufacturing to GNP actually decreased and was once again near its 1950 level. Conversely, an increasing proportion of manufacturing's gross income has been paid to external owners: from 12.4% in 1950 to 34.4% in 1970 and 62.2% in 1980 and then to an extraordinary 68.7% in 1982, when repatriated profits equaled $4.132 billion, an increase of 9.5% over the $3,773 billion paid in 1981. By comparison, external income on direct investment had been $14.8 million in 1950 and $75.3 million in 1960.[40]

Table 7 contains further evidence on the relatively small contribution of manufacturing to the island's economy. Manufacturing's share of total employment nearly doubled from 1940 to 1980 (rising from 10.9% to 19%), a rate of increase which is closer to the rate of growth of manufacturing's net contribution to GNP than to its gross contribution (table 6). The decline of agriculture, seen before in its shrinking contribution to GNP, is reflected also in the change in its share of employment, where it is now less than 5%. On the other hand, the expanding role of the government sector is seen in the fact that it is now the largest employer. However, the crisis of the late 1970s and early 1980s affected employment in all sectors; in 1982, total employment had fallen below the 1978 level, a decline that continued into 1983. These changes in employment will be commented on more extensively below, but it is clear from this and the preceding tables that there is now an economic structure that exhibits the characteristics of a modern social formation, in which the leading sectors in terms of income and employment are industry (even after adjustment from gross to net contribution), services, and government. This transformation from an agricultural economy was compressed into less than twenty-five years, from the late 1940s to 1970 — one of the more rapid industrial revolutions.

Sources of Financing for Investment

The growth of output and income since the 1940s has been partly the result of greater investment, and it is important to examine where the funds for such investment have come from. In general, a surplus of funds that is available for investment use can be generated either internally or externally. One premise upon which Operation Bootstrap was based was that the domestic surplus would be insufficient and external funds would therefore have to be mobilized to finance industrialization. Over time, as the economy grew and incomes rose, a locally generated surplus of funds was expected to become available.

Table 6. Total and Net Contribution to GNP from Manufacturing, 1950, 1960, 1970, 1980, and 1982

	1950	1960	1970	1980[a]	1982[a]
Total contribution of manufacturing to GNP[bc]	119.7	366.3	1,190.0	5,322.5	6,017.0
Profits and dividends paid to non-residents	14.8	75.3	408.3	3,308.2	4,131.5
(Percentage of manufacturing GNP paid to non-residents)	(12.4)	(20.6)	(34.4)	(62.2)	(68.7)
Net contribution to GNP[c]	104.9	291.0	781.2	2,014.3	1,885.5
(Percentage of net contribution to GNP)	(13.9)	(17.4)	(16.7)	(18.2)	(14.9)

SOURCES: Freyre, *External and Domestic Financing*, p. 164, table V–8; Junta de Planificación, *Informe económico*, 1980, p. 26 and p. A–6, table 5; ibid., 1982–83 2:VII–9 and 2:A–4, table 4; ibid., *Balanza de pagos*, p. 18.
[a] These figures do not reflect the changes in accounting procedures made by the Junta de Planificación.
[b] From table 5, except for 1982.
[c] Millions of dollars.

Table 7. Employment by Sector, Ten-Year Intervals from 1940 to 1980 and 1982

	1940		1950		1960		1970		1980		1982	
Sector	N	%	N	%	N	%	N	%	N	%	N	%
Agriculture	229	44.7	214	35.9	124	22.8	68	9.9	40	5.3	35	4.9
Manufacturing	56	10.9	55	9.2	81	14.9	132	19.2	143	19.0	134	18.6
Home needlework	45	8.8	51	8.6	10	1.8	[a]		[a]		[a]	
Construction	16	3.1	27	4.5	45	8.3	76	11.1	44	5.8	36	5.0
Trade	54	10.5	90	15.1	97	17.9	128	18.7	138	18.3	141	19.6
Finance, insurance, and real estate	2	0.4	3	0.5	6	1.1	13	1.9	21	2.8	21	2.9
Transportation	17	3.3	23	3.9	24	4.4	27	3.9	25	3.3	25	3.5
Communications	1	0.2	—	—	4	0.7	6	0.9	8	1.1	9	1.3
Other public utilities	2	0.4	5	0.8	8	1.5	12	1.7	14	1.8	14	1.9
Services	73	14.3	77	12.9	75	13.8	116	16.9	135	17.9	132	18.4
Public administration	13	2.5	45	7.6	62	11.4	106	15.5	184	24.4	171	23.8
Other	4	0.8	—	—	7	1.3	[a]		[a]		[a]	
Total	512	99.9	596	99.0	543	99.9	686	99.7	753	99.7	719	99.9

SOURCES: Junta de Planificación, *Informe económico*, 1980, p. A–27, table 24; ibid., 1982–83 2:A–25, table 24.
NOTE: N's are in thousands. Percentages are based on totals shown and do not always add up to 100 because of rounding errors and lack of exact figures for some categories in some years.
[a] Exact figures not available, but less than 2.

However, this has not happened. The bulk of investment funds have continued to come from the United States. There has been no visible trend toward greater local financing of investments; if anything, there has developed a greater dependence on external sources (see table 8). In 1947, more than half of all investment funds were derived from external sources, including the U.S. federal government, external investors, and foreign banks. The proportion was lower during the early 1950s, but then, with the shift toward capital-intensive promotion as the focus of Fomento's activities, the share of external funds to the total increased, until, in the 1970s, about three-quarters of investment funds were derived from external sources, primarily from the United States. In the key sector of manufacturing, approximately 90% of investment funds have come from mainland firms.[41]

The sources of an internal surplus for investment consist of depreciation reserves of business enterprises (that is, funds set aside to take account of wear and tear on machinery and other capital), savings by government (budget surpluses), savings by corporations (retaind earnings), and personal savings of individuals. Of these internal sources, depreciation reserves and government savings have been the most important, supplying 52.9% and 29.2%, respectively, of local investment funds between 1947 and 1972.[42] Retained earnings of

Table 8. Total and Imported Capital, Selected Years, 1947 to 1980

Year	Total Capital Funds[a] (millions of dollars)	Imported Capital[b] Amount (millions of dollars)	Imported Capital[b] Percentage of Total
1947	51.6	28.8	55.8
1950	124.1	43.7	43.3
1955	236.4	96.3	40.7
1960	413.7	227.5	55.0
1965	810.0	441.3	54.5
1970	1,639.4	1,007.3	61.4
1972	1,835.9	1,310.3	71.4
1974	1,856.0	1,346.1	72.5
1976	2,104.4	1,734.9	82.4
1978	2,308.1	1,891.5	82.0
1980	3,519.5	2,607.4	74.1

SOURCES: Curet Cuevas, *El desarrollo económico*, p. 282, table 85; Junta de Planificación, *Informe económico*, 1977, p. 159; ibid., 1980, p. 240.
[a] Total funds available in Puerto Rico (including both private and public sectors).
[b] Funds invested in Puerto Rico derived from non-Puerto Rican sources.

business have also made a contribution, but individual savings normally have been a drain on surplus creation, since — contrary to conventional economic wisdom — consumption expenditures have risen more rapidly than incomes (see table 9). Net savings have exceeded income in only two years since 1947 (in 1952 by $4.4 million and in 1954 by $1.8 million). In fact, in 1977, 1978, and 1983, total consumption actually exceeded GNP. Increased incomes, instead of leading to increased personal saving which could be used for investment, have led to dissaving and the growth in personal loans to cover current consumption expenses. Hence consumer debt rose from $237 million in 1963 to $3,276.4 million in 1983, diverting funds that could otherwise have been used for locally controlled productive investment.[43]

In an exhaustive technical study, Freyre compared the dependence on external financing in Puerto Rico with that of other nations. In modern times, only the Philippines have come close to Puerto Rico's degree of external dependence, having been about 80% dependent. Such other countries as Italy, Denmark, Peru, Mexico, Jamaica, and Israel have shown a much lower degree of external dependence. In now developed countries such as Sweden, Canada, and the United States, external financial dependence tended to decline as production and incomes increased and industrialization expanded, which is just the opposite of Puerto Rico's experience.[44]

A high degree of external dependence brings in its wake, as Maldonado has pointed out, 'such interacting problems as perpetual balance of payments deficits, over-consumption, loss of domestic control over the factors of production, and, eventually, loss of domestic control over the politico-economic structure of the economy'.[45] These impacts in Puerto Rico will be considered later in the chapter.

Aspects of External Ownership

To speak of 'foreign', rather than 'external' ownership and control in Puerto Rico would be somewhat of a misnomer. Since most investment funds have come from the United States and since Puerto Ricans are U.S. citizens, these funds are hardly foreign in the usual sense of the term, especially when it is added that some of them have certainly come from Puerto Ricans living on the mainland. It does not follow, however, that Puerto Rico is, for questions of capital flows, the same as any state in the United States and thus that any dichotomy between external and internal financing is meaningless. First, Puerto Rico does calculate a balance-of-payments account, just like any independent country and unlike any state. Second, and more important, Puerto Rico is not a state or even a territory of the United States. Its status is not a resolved matter, and the island could become a politically sovereign entity at some future time, which is surely not the case for any state. Third, unless the Federal Relations Act which now governs relations between the United States and Puerto Rico is substantially revised, the island will not be treated exactly like a state for purposes of federal financing, laws, programmes, and the like.[46] Not having full rights as U.S. citizens, the people and government of Puerto Rico must be concerned about the sources of their income and the stability of the base of their income-earning potential. Awareness of the fact of Puerto Rico's second-class status vis-á-vis the United States has become particularly acute as a result of the cuts in federal funding since 1981, which have been especially severe in their impact on the island.

Finally, and perhaps most important, the role of external financing is wrapped up with questions of power, influence, and control in the local economy. This, of course, goes back to an issue raised earlier: unless one assumes that a market system more or less automatically tends to function to the advantage of society in general, its impact is something to be investigated, probed, and evaluated, not to be taken for granted as positive or even neutral, particularly in an era of huge international corporations, many of which individually have incomes larger than Puerto Rico's. The importance of external financing is underscored by the realization that in 1978, Puerto Rico had 34.1% of all direct investment in Latin America, an amount equal to U.S. investment in Mexico and Brazil together, and that 42.4% of all profits from Latin America came from Puerto Rico.[47]

Two issues need to be separated in the ensuing discussion. One is the more or less objective measurement of the extent of external ownership and control in the local economy; the other is the judgmental question of the desirability and inevitability of externally funded investment. This section will deal with the first of these issues.

Table 10 presents data on several measures of the degree of external ownership in manufacturing

in 1963 and 1967. It is true that, in absolute numbers, there have always been many more locally owned than externally owned firms. It is notable, however, that the proportion of externally owned firms increased during this period by about 10%, the number of locally owned firms declining from 1,655 to 1,502. (Even earlier, from 1954 to 1958, the number had declined from 1,718 to 1,665).[48] But even that is a misleading measure, because locally owned firms tend to be much smaller than externally owned ones. In 1963, nearly three-quarters of locally owned manufacturing enterprises employed less than twenty people, while only one-quarter of externally owned manufacturing firms

Table 9. Disposable Personal Income, Total Consumption, and Personal Savings, Selected Years, 1940 to 1983 (millions of dollars)

	Disposable Personal Income	Total Consumption	Personal Savings[a]	Net Personal Savings[b]
1940	218.2	235.6	−17.4	—
1950	637.8	662.5	−24.7	−38.0
1952	814.9	796.0	18.9	4.4
1954	931.2	911.8	19.4	1.8
1955	976.5	964.4	12.1	−9.0
1960	1,333.5	1,397.6	−64.1	−106.4
1965	2,232.9	2,197.4	35.5	−165.4
1970	3,564.8	3,746.5	−181.7	−290.2
1972	4,475.8	4,742.4	−266.6	−432.8
1974	5,582.2	5,753.3	−171.1	−347.6
1976	7,264.5	7,485.7	−221.2	—
1977	7,769.6	8,291.6	−522.0	—
1978	8,553.7	9,139.8	−586.1	—
1980	10,332.9	10,976.0	−643.1	—
1982	11,969.1	12,414.0	−444.9	—
1983	12,009.0	13,011.2	−1,002.2	—

SOURCES: Junta de Planificación, *Informe económico,* 1980, p. 425 and p. A–1, table 1; ibid., 1982–83 2:A–1, table 1; Colón de Zalduondo, *Puerto Rican Economy,* p. 17, table 5.
[a] Disposable personal income less total consumption.
[b] Disposable personal income less total consumption, interest on consumer loans, and funds sent abroad.

Table 10. Indicators of External Ownership in Manufacturing, 1963 and 1967

	1963		1967	
Indicator	Total	Percent Due to External Ownership	Total	Percent Due to External Ownership
Number of firms	2,243	26.2	2,367	36.5
Number of employees	98,597	59.8	121,537	70.7
Wages paid (thousands)	$241,021	60.1	$371,847	70.5
Value added (thousands)	$620,815	61.4	$1,002,817	70.6
Total sales (thousands)	$1,480,379	59.5	$2,272,647	68.7
Sales in Puerto Rico (thousands)	$686,012	43.1	$1,025,983	51.0

SOURCES: Curet Cuevas, *El desarrollo económico,* p. 253, table 81. For details onlocally owned industries, see Colón de Zaluondo, *Puerto Rican Economy,* pp. 176–81, tables 3–5, and pp. 190–93, tables 7 and 8.

were that small, and these figures were virtually the same in 1967.[49] The effects of this can be seen in the other figures in table 10. In 1963, externally owned firms were responsible for about 60% of employment, wages, value added, and total sales in manufacturing; in 1967, each of those figures had increased to about 70%.[50] In some areas of manufacturing, external ownership has been even more marked. In the 'core' industries so vigorously promoted by Fomento in the second phase of Operation Bootstrap, external ownership (by equity) in 1973 ranged from a 'low' of 60% in petroleum products to 99.988% in drugs. For the entire group of core industries, which produced 57% of total manufacturing output by 1977, external ownership averaged 98.3%.[51]

Fomento's strategy of industrialization has thus clearly enlarged the role of external ownership in the manufacturing sector. External investment has not been a complement to local ownership and control, but a substitute for it, despite the fact that one goal of Operation Bootstrap was to create an environment propitious for the emergence of local capital linked to firms promoted by Fomento. The Puerto Rican capitalist class has assumed an auxiliary or even subordinate relationship to U.S. capital as small businessmen in banking, trade, insurance, and real estate.

Foreign companies also predominate in the financial field. Of fifteen mortgage companies in the late 1960s, fourteen were U.S. branch operations. Of the 225 insurance companies, 196 or 87.1% were externally owned (182 of them U.S.-owned), and they controlled 99.97% of all insurance assets at the end of 1966. In commercial banking, the two U.S. banks in operation in 1967 — First National City (now Citibank) and Chase Manhattan — controlled 33.4% of total banking assets.[52] By 1977, the share of assets held by these two banks is not as high as in manufacturing, the global reach of Citibank and Chase Manhattan gives them greater leverage than these figures alone might suggest. Each is larger than any domestic bank on the island, and because they are international banks, they can move funds and assets in and out of Puerto Rico quite easily. More than 81% of the deposits of international corporations in financial institutions in Puerto Rico were deposited in the branches of these two banks — some $1.3 billion of the more than $1.6 billion of deposits in the late 1970s.[54]

The total gross wealth in Puerto Rico in 1974 amounted to some $22 billion. That represents the value of all tangible, reproducible assets (i.e., excluding land) — housing, capital, inventories, consumer durable goods, public works, and external financial investments owned by Puerto Ricans.

Of that amount, $6.1 billion were owned by external investors, and another $6.2 billion were offset by external debt. Thus, the net worth held by island residents was $9.7 billion, or 44.1% of total gross wealth. The other 55.9% was the property of external owners, of which 27.7% was owned outright.[55] In 1928, the proportion of total wealth that was externally owned was 27.1%. The share of external ownership had more than doubled since that time period. The total wealth of the island has grown more than 3,000% (it had been only $650 million in 1928), but external ownership had increased even more rapidly, displacing local ownership to a substantial degree.

As was also true in 1928, a considerable proportion of the reproducible assets owned by Puerto Ricans in 1974 were not productive assets. Housing accounted or $5.1 billion of total wealth, and consumer durables (e.g., refrigerators and cars) for an additional $2.9 billion. On the other hand, external ownership has been concentrated in productive wealth like plant, machinery, equipment, buildings, and financial instruments. With the elimination of housing and consumer durables, total productive assets in 1974 were $14 billion, and the net holdings of island residents in such assets (i.e., after deducting external liabilities) was only $4.3 billion, or 30.7%.

Thus, since the late 1920s, and partly because of the growth strategy pursued by Operation Bootstrap, there has been a progressive increase in absolute and relative external ownership of the capital stock and especially of the productive wealth of Puerto Rico's economy, so that 70% of all productive wealth is now owned by external investors. There is no indication that anything has changed since 1974. By 1977, net direct foreign investment had risen to $9.1 billion, and in 1982 it stood at $16.7 billion.[56]

Notes

1. '. . . . no había ni nunca ha habido una planificación de la actividad económia' (there was not and there never has been any planning of economic activity): Curet Cuevas, *El desarrollo económico de Puerto Rico 1940–1972* (Hato Rey: Management Aid Centre, 1976), p. 204.

2. Baver Sherrie, 'Public Policies and the Private Sector: The Case of Industrial Incentives in Puerto Rico' (Paper presented at the Latin American Studies Association, Indiana, Oct. 1920), p. 10.

3. Graaf, J. de V., *Theoretical Welfare Economics* (Cambridge: Cam. Univ. Press, 1967), pp. 142–54.

4. See Wood, C.H., 'Infant Mortality Trends & Capitalist Development in Brazil', *Latin American Perspectives*, 4 (Fall 1977), pp. 56–76 which demonstrates a worsening of living conditions among the poorest sectors during Brazil's period of most rapid economic growth. The seminal work on growth and development is the economic study by Adelman Irma and Morris, C.T., *Economic Growth and*

Social Equity in Developing Countries, (Stanford, Calif.: Stanford University Press, 1973) which shows that at low levels of per capita income, growth of GNP has worsened income contribution in a large number of instances. Only beyond a certain threshold of income does income distribution improve. This proposition is known as Kuznet's inverted-U hypothesis. See also Chenery, Hollis, et al., *Redistribution with Growth*, (New York: Oxford Univ. Press, 1924).

5. Seers, Dudley, 'Meaning of Development', *International Development Review* 11 (Dec. 1969), pp. 2–6.
6. World Bank, *Poverty and Basic Needs*, (Washington, D.C. 1980) and Streeten, Paul, *First Things First*, (New York: Oxford Univ. Press, 1981).
7. McNamara, Robert S., *Address to the Board of Governors*, (Washington, D.C. World Bank, 1976), pp. 5–8. Meier, Gerald M., *Emerging From Poverty: The Economics that really matter* (New York: Oxford Univ. Press, 1984), provides a balanced assessment of all the various approaches to development and suggests why orthodox economics has been incapable of meeting the challenge of helping the world's poor.
8. Curet Cuevas, *El desarrollo económico*, p. 221.
9. World Bank, *World Development Report*, 1980 (New York: Oford Univ. Press, 1980), pp. 110–11, table 1. Venezuela's per capita GNP was $3,630. However, quite a few Caribbean countries had higher incomes than Puerto Rico.
10. Junta de Planificación, *Informe económico, 1982–83* 1: chap. 2. There is no discussion of inflation in this chapter, not because of its absence, but because it is simply a product of inflation in the U.S. The wage earners' price index (1967 = 100) was 168.7 in 1976 and 216.6 in 1980, compared to 170. and 246.8 for the consumers' price index in the U.S.: Vélez Ortiz Benito, 'Methodology and Problems in Computing and Comparing the Rates of Inflation in Puerto Rico and the U.S. Mainland', *Puerto Rico Business Review* 6 (Sept. 1981), pp. 9–13. Of course, oligopolistic sellers in Puerto Rico can affect local prices, but most important are the prices that prevail on the mainland. Prices are, or have been, controlled on rice, sugar, coffee, bacalao, bread, milk, gasoline, and other products: Santiago, Ana, *'El control de precios en Puerto Rico*, (Masters Thesis, Univ. of Puerto Rico, 1963), p. 31. In June 1953, the Administración, de Estabilización Económica was created to replace the Administración General de Suministros.
11. Freyre, Jorge F., *External and Domestic Financing in the Economic Development of Puerto Rico*, (Rio Piedras: Univ. of Puerto Rico Press, 1969), p. 55.
12. Merrill-Ramírez, Maria, 'Operation Bootstrap: A Critical Analysis of the Puerto Rican Development Program', (M.A. Univ. of Texas), 1979, p. 87, table 1.
13. Taylor, Milton C., *Industrial Tax Exemption in Puerto Rico*, (Madison: Univ. of Wisconsin Press, 1957), pp. 11, 120–21, 144.
14. *Ibid.*, pp. 115–17.
15. Merrill-Ramírez, 'Operation Bootstrap', p. 22.
16. Taylor, *Industrial Tax Exemption*, p. 13.
17. USDC, *Economic Study* 2:270, and Junta de Planificación, *Informe económico, 1982–83* 2:II–11.
18. Federal employees in Puerto Rico receive a supplemental cost-of-living allowance of 5 to 12.5 percent. Some have estimated the cost of living to be as much as 25 percent higher: USDC, *Economic Study* 2:689–90.
19. Puerto Rico: Administración de Fomento Económico (PRAFE), *El desarrollo económico de Puerto Rico durante los ultimos viente años*, (San Juan: Fomento, 1971), pp. 3–5.
20. Madera, Jose R., 'Strategy of Development', *Industrial Newsletter* (PREDA) 22 (1982).

21. Taylor, *Industrial Tax Exemption*, p. 22.
22. *Ibid.*, chap. 9.
23. *Ibid.*, p. 124, table 4; p. 126, table 5; and p. 130.
24. *Ibid.*, p. 130.
25. *Ibid.*, p. 50, notes two cases that indicate how loosely were the criteria for granting tax exemption. In one, a needlework 'factory', the one piece of equipment differentiating production from home needlework (which was ineligible for exemption) was a time clock. In the other, exemption was granted to a fishing boat on one occasion but denied on another.
26. Curet Cuevas, *El desarrollo económico*, pp. 133–35, table 52, and Colón de Zalduando, Baltazara, *The Growing Puerto Rican Economy*, (New York: Gordon, 1977), pp. 155–56.
27. For an analysis of the effects, see Woodward, Robert S., 'Intra-Island Industrial Incentives in Puerto Rico', *Review of Regional Studies* 4 (Spring 1974), pp. 50–61.
28. Baver, 'Public Policies', pp. 13–14; USDC, *Economic Study* 2:74, and Curet Cuevas, *El desarrollo económico*, pp. 216–17. The 1963 law was amended a number of times to permit varying partial exemption periods and to extend the period of exemption to thirty years for firms locating on the islands of Vieques and Culebra off Puerto Rico's east coast.
29. PRAFE, *El desarrollo económico*, pp. 3–5.
30. *Ibid.* See also Junta de Planificación, *Informe económico, 1980*, pp. 60–61, and Ruiz, Angel L., 'The Impact of Economic Recession on the Puerto Rican Economy: An Input-Output Approach, *Caribbean Studies* 16 (Oct. 1976 — Jany. 1977), pp. 125–48.
31. Freyre, *External and Domestic Financing*, p. 89.
32. Junta de Planificación, *Informe económico, 1982–83* 2:II–3, II–5.
33. Gutiérrez, Elias R., *Factor Proportions, Technology Transmissions and Unemployment in Puerto Rico*, (Rio Piedras: Editorial universitaria, 1977), pp. 13–14, and *San Juan Star*, March 29, 1978, p. 3.
34. The peak number of establishments was 2,782 in 1973: *Puerto Rico Business Review* 5 (November 1980): 8–10.
35. Government Development Bank (GDB), *Monthly Economic Indicators*, Nov 1984, p. 10, and Junta de Planificación, *Informe económico, 1982–83* 2:II–10.
36. PRAFE, *El desarrollo económico*, pp. 6, 11, and Junta de Planificación, *Informe económico, 1977*, p. 39.
37. PRAFE, *Puerto Rico Official Directory 1980*, 12th edn. (San Juan: Witcom, 1980), pp. 11–13, 15, 33, and *Claridad*, June 1–7, 1979.
38. *Puerto Rico Business Review* 7 (June 1982): 2–7.
39. The same conclusion, though without numerical estimates, was reached in USDC, *Economic Study* 2:24 ('the manufacturing sector is not producing as much income for Puerto Rico as might be expected of it in light of its performance in terms of output'). One might not find this result so surprising, or the size of the repatriated share of income created so astounding, when it is realized that there is very likely substantial transfer pricing and other accounting devices to shift value added from the U.S. parent corporation to subsidiaries in Puerto Rico, where profits are tax–free. With the regulations in force since 1976, permitting immediate profit repatriation with minimal taxes, this effect has likely been exaggerated, though there are apparently no studies that have attempted to determine the extent of transfer pricing. See the comment in Weisskoff, Richard and Wolff, Edward, 'Linkages and Leakages: Industrial Tracking in an Enclave Economy', *Economic Development and Cultural Change* 25 (July 1977), p. 619, n. 21.
40. Junta de Planificación, *Informe económico, 1982–83* 2:VII–9, and Freyre, *External and Domestic Financing*, p.

164, table V–8. Repatriated profits on direct investment was the largest category of external payments to capital, amounting to 84.1 percent of the total in 1982.

41. Curet Cuevas, *El desarrollo económico,* p. 282, table 85, and USDC, *Economic Study* 2:5.

42. Curet Cuevas, *El desarrollo económico,* p. 281. See also Freyre, *External and Domestic Financing,* chap. 4 and pp. 53–54, where Freyre calculates the 'degree of self-sufficiency' as the ratio of foreign capital imports to total capital formation. Table 1.8 shows that this ratio has tended to increase since the beginning of industrial promotion and hence that the degree of self-sufficiency has declined.

43. Junta de Planificación, *Informe económico, 1982–83* 2:X–11. For most years since 1947, the average propensity to consume (APC) has been close to 1; since 1970, it has exceeded 1 in every year except 1975. The marginal propensity to consume (MPC) has shown wide fluctuations, but in some years (most recently 1980), it too has exceeded 1, though its instability probably indicates that it is not too reliable an indicator. Freyre, *External and Domestic Financing,* analyzed this tendency and the weakness of personal savings. He concluded that over the period from 1947 to 1963 the average propensity to save was close to zero and that 'the relative constancy of personal average and marginal propensities to save during the period of reference is especially striking if we consider the extraordinary increase of personal disposable income of Puerto Rican families, which rose by $1,292.3 million or 240.7 percent during said period' (p. 120). See also Colón de Zalduando, *Puerto Rican Economy,* pp. 13–23, for a review of some of the literature on estimating MPC and APC in Puerto Rico and comparisons of different definitions of 'saving'.

44. Freyre, *External and Domestic Financing,* p. 152, table V–2, and Economic Commission for Latin America (ECLA), *Statistical Yearbook for Latin America* 1979 (New York: United Nations, 1981), p. 106, table 102.

45. Maldonado, Rita M., *The Role of the Financial Sector in the Economic Development of Puerto Rico* (Washington, D.C.: Federal Insurance Corp. 1970), p. 36. See also Wasow, Bernard, 'Saving and Dependence with Externally Financed Growth', *Review of Economics and Statistics* 61 (Feby. 1970), pp. 150–54 in which a formal model of differing measures of dependence is developed.

46. The importance of this issue has recently been analyzed in a report by the United States Comptroller General, *Puerto Rico's Political Future: A Divisive Issue of MaNy Dimensions,* Report to the Congress of the U.S. March 2, 1981.

47. Bonilla, Frank and Campos, Ricardo, 'A Wealth of Poor: Puerto Ricans in the New International Order', *Daedalus* 110 (Spring 1981), p. 140, table 2.

48. Colón de Zalduondo, *Puerto Rican Economy,* p. 159.

49. *Ibid.,* p. 164, and p. 167, table 1. In 1961, Fomento organized a Department of Puerto Rican Industries to promote local ownership.

50. The trends since 1967 cannot be determined precisely, because detailed data on local and external ownership are no longer reported. However, one knowledgeable economist has estimated that the external share on each of these indicators was at least 80 percent in 1972, and it has probably been no less than that in the 1980s; Curet Cuevas, *El desarrollo económico,* p. 255. In 1975, it was reported that in ten of the preceding eleven years 'the Puerto Rican private sector has actually reduced its ownership of Puerto Rico's capital stock over a period in which that capital stock has been rising rapidly': Committee to Study Puerto Rico's Finances (Tobin Committee), Report to the Governor, Dec. 11, 1975, p. 25.

51. USDC, *Economic Study* 2:6 and 2:37, table 12. The 1973 figures for external equity ownership in other industries were: petrochemicals, 99.98 percent; other chemicals, 98.3; petroleum refining, 94.6; primary metals, 89.1; fabricated metals, 99.5; machinery, 99.7; and electrical machinery, 98.9. Rates of return on direct investment in these industries are well above those in the U.S. because only about 20 percent of assets are held in physical capital; rates of returns of 15 to 20 percent on total capital (financial and physical) are thus equivalent to rates of return on direct investment in the range of 35 to 60 percent: Tobin Committee, Report, p. 44.

52. Maldonado, *Financial Sector,* pp. 78–79, and p. 92, table 5.1.

53. USDC, *Economic Study* 2:544, table 1. It is also noted (pp. 548–49) that the shift toward external banks (which after 1975 included Spanish interests as well as U.S. and Canadian interests) has increased. See Puerto Rico, Dept. of the Treasury (PRDT), *Economy and Finances, 1976,* (San Juan: General Services Administration, 1976, '77, '78).

54. USDC, *Economy Study* 2:561–62, and Marrero Velázquez, Wanda I., 'The Economic Development: Strategy and Unemployment in Puerto Rico', M.A., Univ. of Texas, 1981, pp. 44–45. See also North American Congress on Latin America, 'Puerto Rico to New York: The Profit Shuttle; NACLA's *Latin American and Empire Report* 10 (1976), pp. 11–13.

55. Tobin Committee, Report, p. 63, table X–1. See also Curet Cuevas, *El desarrollo económico,* p. 254, table 82, for a similar accounting for 1972. The calculation by the Tobin Committee of external equity as $6.1 billion may be low; for 1972, Curet Cuevas calculated it as $6.6 billion.

56. Junta de Planificación, 1977, p. 124 and *Ibid.,* 1982–93 2:IV–30.

The Industrialization of the Netherlands West Indies

Cornelis Ch. Goslinga

The Economy of the Netherlands Antilles was, in the 19th century and during the first two decades of the 20th, tottering from smuggling and contraband trade to agricultural and industrial experiments which had their ups and downs and except for a few years of good phosphate exports, never made the islands self-sufficient. Poverty, already rampant around the turn of the century, spread in ever wider circles, prosperity was the privilege of a small class of merchants and government officials, and the future looked black indeed. Except for phosphate there were no raw materials for sale, nor did the black populations have purchasing power. The straw hat industry alleviated the problem but could not eliminate it. But there was little chance of a break-through of the old economic structure with its emphasis on navigation and trade — licit and illicit — which meant a commitment to uncontrollable factors. It also meant a continuous dependency on subsidies from the Mother Country, which acted more as a stepmother than as a loving parent.

The coming of the oil industry ended this situation. The dependency on uncontrollable factors was replaced by another dependency, undoubtedly much more ominous; on the goodwill of dictators and the decisions made in Venezuela's capital so close to their territory and under the Dutch flag. Oil moved Curaçao and Aruba into an energy field in which both islands became hand-cuffed by their neighbour. It was not oil from their own barren soil, but was foreign oil — Venezuela oil. Conflicts with Venezuela, were no longer possible as Willemstad could no longer afford to antagonize Caracas. The USA through the Monroe Doctrine played a certain key-role in this relationship. The powerful Anglo-American republic established strong financial ties with the islands supplying machinery and parts for the refinery and at the same time became the most important client of the finished oil products.

With the Netherlands, the relationship was a traditional one. Even though the Hague showed little interest in the islands' fate because of the burden for the Dutch taxpayer, the white, and especially the Jewish part of the population was fervently Orangist. The House of Orange had protected its freedoms and privileges for several centuries. Other factors played a role in this relationship; Dutch experts visited the islands with regularity to give advice on specific issues; the governors, appointed by The Hague without any consultation with the local representative institutions, were not always capable men and could certainly not follow their judgments, in political resolving dilemmas. These were solved by cabinets and ministers in The Hague who were notoriously ignorant of the issues involved.

The oil industry brought employment, income and purchasing power. Everything connected with this industry thrived — the port, trade, public affairs — while all the activities which could not cater to the oil industry declined: agriculture, stock-breeding, craft, home industry were among those that suffered. The long-standing desire for financial autonomy, however, was realized and it was not long before the political relationship between the Mother Country and the colony had to come up for a thorough revision. The oil company was given a vote in the *Koloniale Raad*, the Chamber of Commerce, the Council of Administration. A new wind blew, there was renewal and adaptation of the infrastructure to the new prosperity; health care and education expanded, the bureaucracy grew, roads were laid out, and the port modernized. Curaçao and Aruba were the two islands which profited most by this change. Bonaire and the three Leeward Islands could not keep in step with this new trend, and stayed behind, maintaining their rural character for a long time.

In 1901 the *Koninklijke Nederlandsch Maatschappij tot Exploitatie van Petroleumbronnen in Nederlandsch Indië* — the Royal Dutch Company for the Exploitation of Petroleum Wells in the Netherlands East Indies — founded in 1890 — came under the leadership of Sir Henri Deterding, a Dutchman. In severe competition with the Standard Oil Company of New Jersey it merged, in

1907, with the British Shell. This merger proved to be extremely profitable.

Some British companies had already received concessions to drill for oil in and around the Lake of Maracaibo. The Royal Shell bought concessions given by President Gômez, which covered a large area in the southern part of the Maracaibo basin. To operate this, the Colon Development Company was founded in which the Royal Dutch-Shell obtained a 75% interest. Another major development came in 1915 when the Venezuelan Oil Concessions, a company founded in 1913 to operate the Aranguren concession covering the districts of Bolìvar and Maracaibo, became associated with the Royal Dutch-Shell group. At Mene Grande, the Caribbean Petroleum Company started drilling at the end of 1914.

Commercial production began in 1917 and with it came the first export of oil from Venezuela. Naturally, successful production soon brought American companies more actively into the picture. The Lago Petroleum Company and the Gulf Oil Company acquired concessions in the same Lake Maraciabo region. Deterding offered the Standard Oil Company (of New Jersey) which at that time had no Venezuelan production under its control, a share in the Colon Development Company but the offer was declined. This concession was soon producing 20,000 barrels daily. The Standard Oil Company remained without production in Venezuela until 1928, when it acquired a predominant interest in the Creole Syndicate, a company owning concessions in the Lake bed, which then changed its name to Creole Petroleum Corporation. In June 1932, the Standard Oil Company acquired control of the Lago and thus became the second largest oil-producing group in Venezuela.

At first Deterding had planned to have a refinery in Venezuela and trans-shipment facilities in Curaçao. Two tanks were built there, but then the Dutchman changed his mind. In May 1915 the decision was made to locate most of the oil processing facilities in the Dutch colony. President Goméz of Venezuela took no action to prevent this choice.

The decision to construct a refinery in Curaçao was justified on the basis of the stability of the colonial government, the availability of cheap labour and the safety and spaciousness of the port. While these were valid reasons there was more to the decision. It was the custom to refine oil close to the wells; the Royal Dutch-Shell now deviated from this custom. Its interest was, of course, to support the Gómez dictatorship whose fall could mean the end of the concessions. The company had to be careful not to ruin this delicate relationship with the dictator. That it diverged from the regular

course of things must be seen from the point of Deterding's Mexican relations. Deterding needed a refinery which would refine Venezuelan oil, but could also, potentially, refine Mexican oil from Tampico and other wells. A refinery which provided the option to refine Mexican oil could not possibly be built in Venezuela.

Together with the positive factors mentioned, some negative ones also had to be taken into consideration. In Curaçao there were no skilled labourers. This was not an insurmountable problem. The merger of the Shell with the *Koninklijke* produced two other companies of which one, the *Bataafsche Petroleum Maatschappij* (BPM) would take care of the drilling of wells, the refining of the oil and manning its installations with its own professionals. 'Unskilled labour can be found in any quantity' wrote its representative, sent to Curaçao to make the necessary preparations. There was, however, a more serious problem: the lack of good water. A sufficient water supply was absolutely necessary for a smooth production process. The government had granted the Maduro firm a water concession. But the BPM was unwilling to buy this water from an agent of its biggest competitor: the Standard Oil Company of New Jersey. This difficulty was temporarily solved by digging a number of wells which then provided 200 to 300 tons daily.

On instructions from The Hague the colonial government exempted from import duties all oil and oil products and all materials needed for the construction of plant, offices and houses for employees. A Captain P. Jansen sent in May 1915 as representative of the Royal Dutch Shell to the island, had as his first task to buy the necessary real estate. This started with the plantation Asiento on a peninsula in the Schottegat, bought for f 40.000. He then added the peninsula on which it was located for f 53.000. In July 1915 the first Curaçaoans were appointed to various positions and by November the Royal Dutch Shell already employed over 400 people. In January 1916 Governor Nuyens laid the foundation stone of the office and the lab, in the presence of officials of the government, the clergy, the consular corps and prominent inhabitants of the island. Had not the Governor, shortly before, told the *Koloniale Raad*, that it would be 'of the utmost importance for the colony if refineries were established'? All were convinced of the epoch-making importance of this event for the islands' economy. The Colonial Report of 1917 stated somewhat dryly: 'As a result of these circumstances the purchasing power of the population increased . . . [and] only a few needed to emigrate in search of work'.

Soon the BPM bought the small island of Negropont situated in the Schottegat with permission to connect it with a dam to the shore. It planned to build there the local headquarters of the refinery, but mighty Hendrick Colijn, then director of the BPM and soon an important figure in Dutch politics wanted 'the centre of our business on the peninsula'.

Still the BPM lacked the necessary quay space and Jansen tried to solve it by buying or getting long-lease rights on several plantations which bordered on an accessible waterway. In these efforts he was supported by The Hague, but it led to a confrontation with S.E.L. Maduro & Sons, who had the support of the island's white elite and the Governor.

Maduro owned the Juliana wharf with access to the St. Ann Bay and the Schotteat. The directors of the BPM approached the Governor, before any real estate property was bought, to pressure the firm into selling the wharf to the BPM, without which plans for the refinery would have to be shelved. A proposal for an exchange of wharfs with the CHM (*Curaçao Handel Maatschappy* or Curaçao Trading Company) was rejected. Deterding again approached the Minister of the Colonies to exercise pressure on Nuyens. But Nuyens would not do anything as the firm's rights to the water areas was undisputed. Deterding had to settle the affair directly with Maduro: 'We were forced to come to the conclusion that Mr. Maduro was a greater authority, and had more power in Curaçao than the governor there, and that therefore the government practically wished us to do what Mr. Maduro desired'.

When negotiations with the Maduro firm started, they did not go smoothly as the BPM was aware that Maduro was an agent of the West India Oil Company (WIOC), a daughter company of the Standard Oil. It was during these negotiations that the BPM began to buy real estate. Deterding had to accept his first defeat, as Maduro defended its position successfully against the mighty English-Dutch enterprise. In this controversy Maduro tried to offer the BPM the firm's services, to build a dry-dock, and a wharf. The colonial government decided in April, 1916, to give the BPM a long-lease contract of 75 years, expiring in 1992 on the water areas in dispute.

The refinery was built by an American contractor with American materials and mostly skilled American labourers. At the beginning of 1917 the construction had progressed so far, that the BPM could transfer its responsibilities to the newly founded daughter company the *Curaçaosche Petroleum Maatschappij* — Curaçao Shipping Company or CSM — which because of the war had to content itself with wooden lighters towed by small tug-boats. It was the Maduro firm that

solved this problem after the CPM was unable to get the necessary material. It chartered a ship to get the wood from the USA and built two 800 ton lighters which were towed forwards and backwards between Willemstad and Maracaibo. This was the humble beginnings of a CSM fleet that in 1917 carried 8.000 tons of raw oil from the Maracaibo fields to Curaçao. In 1922 Venezuela's export rose to 263,000 tons of raw oil — close to 78% of the total production — with 17,000 tons coming from other sources. By 1924 only Venezuelan raw oil was imported and in 1929 imports amounted to 7,624,000 tons, or 38% of Venezuela's total production. The CSM fleet — now no longer consisting of wooden lighters but iron tankers, the so-called *lakers* — grew proportionally.

In the first four or five years of its existence the CPM thus had to iron out problems related to the transportation of the oil. It required some time to build a trained labourers' corps and it is understandable that in those first years the Company resorted to foreigners who did not create the problems the young company had with the native blacks.

Those first years were not yet very profitable. Opened officially May 23, 1918, the refinery operated only from 5 till 20 December, then stopped, and started again in April 1920. This strange schedule was caused by the insufficient supply of crude oil, though it improved somewhat in the course of 1921. By then it became clear that the storage depots of oil fuel were insufficient. Not until 1923 was the CPM able to report that work was proceeding without interruption.

The wooden lighters were far from satisfactory, even though in 1918 a third one was added to the fleet. In 1922 the first two iron tankers arrived by which time the problem of sufficient supply had been solved. Curaçao received the lion's share of the Venezuelan crude oil production. But the CPM did not place any orders with the Curaçao wharfs, a policy that estranged it from the Maduro firm.

From its very beginning the Curaçao refinery delivered 85% fuel oil and 15% other oil products which it sold all over the Caribbean. This meant, of course, a threat to The Standard Oil Company which was also selling to the area, but nowhere was the competition as strong as in Curaçao itself. Before June 1918 the island bought only Standard oil products and Maduro made good profits. At the end of 1919 the CPM sold 72% of the gasoline and 63% of the kerosene to Standard's former clients. These numbers increased in 1923 to 98% and 96% respectively. Here was where the Maduro firm lost the battle.

After half a dozen frustrating years ending in 1922, the Royal Dutch Shell shifted its operations from Mexico to Venezuela. Before the end of 1920 almost all the oil pumped in Venezuela came from this company's wells. Soon more than 3/4th of this production was shipped to Curaçao, the remaining 1/4th to the national refinery of San Lorenzo. Thanks to Deterding's foresight the Royal Dutch Shell stayed far ahead of its competitors. By now, the installations in Curaçao were working at full capacity and to match this development, the construction of a brand-new refinery was planned. It was built at Asiento between 1924 and 1926, and later expanded. The third phase in this growing process was completed in 1930, when the Great Depression loomed.

As long as no profits were made — the first four years — there were no tax problems. But as the refinery of the Venezuelan oil approached the dividend earning state, a new look at the organization of the company was required. The solution was found in the replacement of the CPM by the CPIM, the *Curaçao Petroleum Industrie Maatschappij* or Curaçao Petroleum Industry Company, which would pay taxes only in Curaçao. Thus the CPIM was created in March 1925 with a capital of f 30.000.000, of which the BPM paid one third. The new company also took charge of the CSM whose initial capital of f 2.000.000 was increased to f 10.000.000. Between 1920 and 1932 the CSM's fleet had grown from 4 to 26 tankers.

The colonial reports of these years noted in detail the growth of the new industry. In 1925 the refinery could handle 6,500 tons of crude oil daily. The CSM, at that time operating with 6 tankers, transferred in 1925 1,893,000 tons to Curaçao. Six years later, when the Great Depression hit the industry, its tanker fleet with 72,000 tons had to be reduced slightly to 26 tankers and 67,000 tons. They imported from Venezuela 6,971,000.000 kg. of crude oil down from 8,545,000,000 kg. the previous year. At the end of 1931 the CPIM and the CSM had 271 and 247 white collar employees and a blue collar labour force of 3,335 and 652 respectively on their payroll. At that time the CPIM paid a monthly amount of f 6,928,000 in wages and salaries.

After a short recession, the growth pattern resumed its rapid course. Indeed, in this decade the growth of the refinery seemed to be without limits. It revolutionized the rather static Curaçao society. A new element permeated the somewhat rustic island community of settled relations and accepted values. The enclosure of the oil premises with a high fence — in 1928 — demonstrated visibly the end of a period in which tradition was highly valued and the beginning of a new era in which traditions were unable to stop the modernization of a society.

Indeed, as Liewen put it neatly: 'Shell's Curaçao plant was the beginning of a great industry in the Netherlands West Indies', though, probably, it had better be called the 'distortion of an economy, which became affected by a process of deformation. The fortunes of the islands and of the colonial government began to hang by a single thread, that of oil. The traditional exports like straw hats and divi-divi began to wither away. Phosphate could maintain itself, but compared to the refined oil exports its revenues were small. In 1918 Curaçao exported almost f 1.716.500 of traditional goods and f 180,500 of oil and oil products. By 1933 these exports were f 566,000 and f 42,372,000 respectively.

The economic consequences of the establishment of the oil industry permeated both islands, Curaçao and Aruba. Direct and indirect revenues from the oil accounted by 1924 for the balancing of the colonial budget and although the Great Depression halted expansion, by 1935 the peak of 1929 was again reached.

The extraordinary income generated from the oil industry enabled the colonial government to undertake public works programs, including the building of roads, extension of port facilities; it took over the water concession of the Maduro House, improved health and education standards and embarked on social legislation.

Because the local laborer, in the view of the CPM, was lazy and indifferent, the Company resorted to the hiring of blue collar workers from Aruba. When this source of labour was exhausted, Bonaire and St Eustatius, Surinamese labourers were also hired. In 1925 a group of men from the Netherlands arrived to strengthen the labour force. Around that time efforts were also made to get people from Jamaica and Haiti. From 1926 onwards large numbers of Venezuelans from Maracaibo and Coro arrived on six–month contracts. By the end of December 1929 the CPIM had an international labor force: Curaçao blue collar workers, Arubans, Bonairians, people from the Dutch Leeward Islands, Venezuelans, men from the British Antilles and other nationalities. The CSM, at the time, had 2365 workers on its payroll. A total of 11,000 people were directly working for the oil company.

Prosperity was not evenly spread. A dry spell, though not causing catastrophic consequences as in earlier days, still could play havoc among the poor rural population. But because prices increased constantly, the urban population with fixed salaries could suffer. There were increases in wages and cost-of-living allowances, but these came almost always too late and were most of the time small compensation for hardships already suffered. The merchants did well; they prospered and could modernize and enlarge their shops. Many people, especially the Dutch employees of the CPIM, had sufficient purchasing-power.

The short-sighted policy of the CPIM not to favour the local merchants but to set up its own shops, caused enormous bad-feeling. In 1926 it opened a grocery store in Negropont with lower priced foodstuffs. Not only in the retail trade but also in the wholesale trade the CPIM followed this same policy, introducing the English firm of John Henderson & Co. Ltd., Shipstore and Export Merchants. Though this firm's prices were hardly any lower than those of the Curaçao merchants, it could count on a monthly sale of its products to employees and labourers. It also received a monopoly in the provisioning of all CSM vessels and those of which the CSM was the agent. The comment of the R.C. daily paper the *Amigoe* undoubtedly voiced the popular feeling: 'We thought that our Curaçao merchants at least would be given a chance to compete in the deliveries . . . . it seems strange indeed, ... that a Dutch company in a Dutch colony prefers a foreign firm. . . .

This insensitive attitude of the CPIM resulted in a closer union of the Curaçao merchant class with the firm of S.E.L. Maduro & Sons taking the lead. In spite of this conflict Maduro profited tremendously from the presence of the oil. Its capital, in 1915 of 4.3 million guilders, increased in 1929 to over 12 million, its capital stock doubled from 2.2 million in 1922 to 4.4 million in 1929. Other firms also profited in spite of the CPIM policy.

This policy may have been inspired by the worldwide custom of the Royal Dutch Shell to man its refineries with an expatriate staff. In the case of Curaçao it was of Dutch origin resorting to local labour for the lower level workers. Mention has been made of the heterogeneous character of these lower levels. Especially after 1925, due to the departure of Arubans and Bonairians, there was an increase in foreign labour, not always to the benefit of the company.

While the refinery promoted a massive increase in shipping — in 1922 about 50% of the ships that dropped anchor in Willemstad were directly involved in the oil-industry and in 1929 this had grown to 80% — there were other fields of economic activity which the oil succeeded in eliminating almost completely. One of them was agriculture. The number of people involved in agriculture shrunk considerably while the population increased as is shown by the following table.

In Curacao, agriculture was only practiced for its extra earnings by those who were willing to work in their spare time. The Colonial Report of 1910 concluded that it was not the climate but oil killed agriculture.

A similar depressing picture can be given of other non-oil productivity whose exports all declined. In 1932 Curaçao no longer exported aloe, and divi-divi. Goat skins exports amounted to only f 8,000, f 11,000 in orange peels and f 2,000 in salt. The value of the phosphate exports, in 1930 still f 1.4 million, was cut in half two years later. The revenues from straw hats in that year came to f 144,000, the lowest registered in a long time.

The Curaçao banks were well prepared to absorb this upsurge of industrial activity. The guilder was solid and the *Curaçaosche Bank,* in charge of supervising the monetary system, saw its position strengthened as is proven by the fact that it could work out a gentleman's agreement with the other banks to quote one common rate for the Dutch guilder. When the *Hollandsche Bank Unie* — Holland Bank Union — in 1936 terminated this partnership, it became necessary to prohibit the export of gold and silver.

The new prosperity, which gave rise to the establishment of various local banks, was also responsible for the continued existence of the *Curaçaosche Bank,* though its stability in the first half of the twentieth century was threatened by a rapid succession of presidents. In the space of three decades — from 1910 to 1940 — this bank evolved from everybody's bank to a bankers' bank. As a circulation bank it issued banknotes which were covered by gold and silver in its vaults. Its currency system was based on gold. For this reason a member of its board even advocated a dissociation of the Curaçaoan guilder from the Dutch guilder, a view which, understandably, appealed to the *Koloniale Raad.*

During the years 1924 through 1927 subsidies from The Hague were not needed. Then followed a few years in which the colonial budget again worked in the red, but from 1932 on Curaçao became financially independent of the Mother Country.

Import duties allowed the same trend during the short depression, increasing through 1929 and then declining. But by 1932 the depression, for the Curaçao Islands at least, was over and a new period of prosperity was on its way.

The depression, short as it may have been, also had its impact on the labour force of the oil industry and of the islands. There was a decline of many enterprises, indirectly depending on the oil industry. Contractors were out of work, building activities ended and in turn labourers were dismissed. A small tile factory had to close its doors, an ice company declared itself bankrupt, an effort to get Heinekens Breweries interested in a Curaçao daughter company failed. At the end of 1930 the phosphate company had to lay off 100 men

Islands	1910		1920		1930	
	popul.	agric.	popul.	agric.	popul.	agric.
Curaçao	30,930	2,715	34,021	3,140	44,344	1.527
Aruba	9,049	1,314	8,934	222	13,450	345

because of declining sales, though in spite of this dark perspective it still could pay, in 1932, a 7.5% dividend. Electricity experienced in 1932 lower sales of 15% and many people who could not afford the high price, tried to live without it. In the very dry years from 1929 through 1931 much water was used for the distillation plant, while at government's expense private wells after being deepened, were opened to the public. After consultation with the CPIM and the shipping companies it was decided to import water two or three times a month. For a few very critical weeks the CPIM supplied the government with another daily ration of 100 tons. A new distillation plant was built. But when in 1931 abundant rains began to fall, the distillation of seawater — an expensive procedure — was stopped. For the CPIM the problem was not that urgent. Its distillation plants produced 500 tons daily. On top of this the company imported 527.000 tons of water for its own use in 1931. Three years later this increased to 721.000 tons.

While the water shortage in Willemstad was acute, it never reached a critical level. However, the situation in the outer districts became very serious. The government solved this by buying a truck which brought water to the rural population in iron barrels.

A curious consequence of this short lull in the island's industrialization process was a return to agriculture. Many native labourers who were dismissed returned to the land while the foreigners returned to their native countries. The colonial government granted small lots to the many unemployed to cultivate maize. The dry spell of 1930 caused a failure of this crop but in the latter part of 1931 the rains saved part of the harvest. However, the Curaçao black had during the short years of oil prosperity lost his touch with the land and his ability to cultivate it. His heart was not in it. A revival of the *kleine landbouw* by these *malaise landbouwers* — depression farmers — failed miserably and only the Chinese labourers clung stubbornly and successfully clung to the land.

The plantations suffered a similar fate. The salt plantations could not sell anything because of the low prices. The decline of this industry is vividly illustrated by the following export table which also gives information on the salt production of Bonaire and St. Martin.

Prices of plantation products declined. Many were offered for sale including those owned by the CPIM which did not produce any water. Brievengat estate originally bought for f 100,000, was sold for f 17,000 and Groot Piscadera which it had bought for f 145.000 sale in public auction started at f 14.000. Their returns were assessed at only 0.2% but headquarters in The Hague was adamantly against these sales as it regarded the possession of the plantations as strengthening their power in Curaçao.

Stock-breeding also declined. During the serious droughts of the years mentioned many cattle had died or were slaughtered because of the lack of food and water. A Union of Stock-breeders, founded in 1931 could count on government support which exempted its members from the excise duty on slaughter to make competition with imported meat easier. This measure was successful. In 1932 the local livestock provided 70% of all slaughtered goats and sheep. After a decline, in 1933, it rose to even 85% of the slaughtered sheep and goats.

It is difficult to assess whether the oil companies have been beneficial to the islands. On the positive side, Curaçao's and Aruba's budgets no longer worked in the red and financial autonomy became the prelude for political autonomy which followed in the post-war years. The *Staten* could only be pleased with this development. For so many years they had risked conflict after conflict with the Colonial Office and had repeatedly been rebuked. These conflicts with The Hague now seemed to become a thing of the past. Surely, with balanced budgets the Dutch supervision and meddling in the islands internal affairs should end. But the presence of a new and mighty industrial company created a number of questionable aspects, which came to the fore in those early years. John de Pool in his *Del Curaçao que se va* strikes a nostalgic note in depicting the many facets of the island's folklore that fell victim to the continuous industrialization and mechanization of the island's economy and its social life. Improvements in all aspects of life: higher wages, a higher living standard, better education, were accompanied by a tougher struggle for survival, with more pressures and by tensions unknown to the pre-oil society.

A community within a community. That can be said of the Royal Dutch Shell in Curaçao and the

	Curaçao		Bonaire		St. Martin	
	tons	value	tons	value	tons	value
1922	5.730	f. 78.914	6.397	f. 39.915	6.332	f. 43.128
1926	853	12.184	4.215	26.155	5.091	44.682
1930	100	3.000	1.560	10.952	3.160	27.109
1931	100	1.100	3.489	22.494	2.703	24.417

LAGO in Aruba. They were never part of the islands' societies. The benefits they doled out were financial benefits and that was all. There was no concern for the islands' problems, no participation in the islands' life, no interest in their culture. There was hardly any question of imaginative management, or of investment in local development. What interested the management in Curaçao and in The Hague/London was profit. The making of Curaçao's society into a capitalistic one was the result of this policy.

The oil-industry meant the death knell for other industries with the exception of phosphate. The white elite had to write off its role in society. The small farmer was lured away by the high wages. And the merchants? They could still act as a pressure group because of their representation in the *Koloniale Raad* and later in the *States of Curaçao*. They maintained in the Chamber of Commerce their prominent position, keeping it closed to outsiders and adapted smoothly into a closely-knit group to successfully defend its privileges and its status in society. After World War I this splendid isolation was threatened by many newcomers: Ashkenazics, *macamba* Dutchmen, Syrians, and others. However, World War II would end also this prominent position. The writing was already on the wall when Governor Wouters extended the franchise, modest as it may have been.

Thus, the industrialization of Curaçao meant a *Umwertung allerWerte* — a change in accepted values — a kind of social revolution. It affected first of all Curaçao and Aruban societies and to a lesser degree the societies of the other dependencies. In this social and economic upheaval Queen Wilhelmina's radio speech of December 7, 1942 became a watershed announcing a period of changed relations with the Mother Country. It included the promise of autonomy, so long desired by the *Koloniale Raad* and its successor the *Staten*.

SECTION ELEVEN
Political and Economic Integration

Integration schemes of various kinds have always typified Caribbean history. Native inhabitants in the pre-Columbian period went about the task of establishing political and economic systems under which the region was manipulated. In the sixteenth century, for example, the Kalinago people (Caribs) had established an integrated political and economic network through which they implemented survival strategies.

In the period of European colonization the tendency towards the governance of the region as one unit was enhanced with Spanish imperialist claim to exclusive right of administrative authority. The defeat of the Spanish claim opened up the region to a series of competing imperial orders. All efforts were designed and fashioned to integrate colonies for purposes of administrative efficiency. The French, Dutch and English, for example, saw their various colonies as a unitary system for mercantile operation, political management and jurisdiction. The European colonial experience, then, had two fundamental consequences in this regard; one, the integration of territories along imperial, and therefore linguistic and cultural lines; second, the geo-political fragmentation of what was originally a unified Amerindian world.

The post slavery period witnessed a number of constitutional changes with respect to the administrative unification of sections of the region, but it was during the middle of the twentieth century that far reaching measures were adopted to address the long standing ideal of Caribbean integration. Wallace addresses in her essay the circumstances governing the rise and demise of the British West Indies federation between 1958 and 1962. She poses a number of questions with respect to the relation between the federation's conceptual origins, and the transcending nature of nationalist [insular] politics and consciousness. Axline, in turn, picks up these themes at the economic level. He does not address the failure of political federation, but deals instead with the development of Caribbean economic integration; that is, the movement from political disintegration to economic common market and customs union. Lasserre and Mabileau deal with the francophone Caribbean experience. They explain why political processes in France, and the French West Indies, moved in favour of the fuller constitutional colonial integration of government, rather than independence and Caribbean nationhood. The 1946 constitutional development is fully addressed, and stands in stark contrast to political developments that had taken place in the English-speaking countries. The Puerto Rican experience, however, is to some extent comparable. Lewis outlines the circumstances under which Puerto Rico became a colony of the United States, and indicates that the process parallels the experience the region has experienced at the hands of the Europeans. He suggests that Puerto Rico remains essentially a nation still seeking its independence, but is torn ideologically between the perceived notions of an impoverished nationhood and a more opulent subjugation.

The French Antilles and Their Status as Overseas Departments

Guy Lasserre and Albert Mabileau

The law of 19 March 1946 conferred the status of overseas departments (*départements d'outre-mer,* known as DOM) on France's four 'old colonies' in the tropics, Guadeloupe, Martinique, French Guiana (Guyane), and La Réunion. It was at the request of the General Councils of the territories themselves that the Constituent Assembly, immediately after the second world war, unanimously voted for this measure of assimilation. From then on the inhabitants of these territories were no longer 'colonials' but as wholly French as those of the metropolitan departments. The colonial problem seemed to have been finally settled by this measure of integration, which crowned the process of decolonization begun in 1848 with the abolition of slavery in the French colonies and with the grant of suffrage to freed Negroes.

It is undeniable that assimilation gave rise to a remarkable economic impetus in the islands and to some improvement of the social conditions of the workers. Nevertheless, for a dozen years this policy of change to department status has been contested, sometimes with violence, and it is evident that it has not been able to settle all the economic and social problems of the former French colonies. This chapter will only discuss the French Antilles and will begin by considering their distinctiveness from France; we will then deal with the evolution of their political status before analyzing aspects and causes of the current malaise.

I. The Characteristics of the French Antilles

The French Antilles consist of Guadeloupe and Martinique, but although they belong to France and are currently closely integrated with her through their departmental status, it should not be overlooked that they are very different from France and have their own specific problems arising from a tropical geographical situation and from over three centuries of colonial history.

1. Overpopulation

Martinique and Guadeloupe, which are separated from each other by the British island of Dominica, belong to the Lesser Antilles. These are tiny islands: Martinique covers 425 and Guadeloupe 583 square miles. Martinique would fit into an area 20.5 miles square and Guadeloupe into one 24 square miles.

The cultivable land is greatly restricted by the mountainous nature of the country and also by the climate. Situated between 14° and 16° north latitude, the Antilles have a hot and humid climate, but the rainfall, which is too abundant on the high slopes of the volcanic massif, is inadequate in the lower regions which cannot break up the Atlantic clouds, and even more so on the leeward coastlines sheltered from the trade winds. Thus it is its diversity that best characterizes the geographical personality of the French Antilles: the rocky, sun-scorched hills of the Caravelle, south Martinique, the Ile des Saintes, and St Barthélemy, the monotous limestone plateau of Grande Terre, the evergreen equatorial forest of the Pitons du Carbet or the slopes of the Soufrière, the windswept and remote summits of the highest mountain ranges.

Human settlement has reinforced this natural diversity in the variety of physical types because of the heterogeneity of the population and the differences in land occupancy and cultivation.

The settlement of the French Antilles is intimately related to the development of tropical sugar plantations. The labour force of the great domains, known as *habitations*, was drawn from Africa and poured into the sugar islands by slave ships. The rapid disappearance of the original inhabitants, the Arawaks and Caribs, who were few in number, the installation of whites, who were rapidly outnumbered by black slaves, the interbreeding between white and blacks, all resulted from the plantation system.

The Antilleans still distinguish between various groups within the population: the 'Blancs-France', the 'Blancs-Pays', Syrians, Negroes, 'Indians', and half-castes or 'coloureds' in the strict sense of the word. Each of these groups is in turn subdivided on the basis of criteria which are not only anthropological but also sociological. The Negro lawyer or doctor does not belong to the same group as the plantation 'Nég' because he does not come from the same social class. The 'Blancs-France' are either birds of passage or recent settlers: officials, technicians, soldiers, etc. Another stratum of whites is that of the 'Blancs-Pays', called 'Békés' in Martinique. These are Creoles, i.e. local-born whites of families who have been in the Antilles for several generations. They all speak the Creole patois and have property in the islands. In Martinique they are in possession of most of the land. Within this group are the 'Petits-Blancs', whose situation in the social scale is a good deal lower. In Guadeloupe this white population of modest rank is mainly represented in the 'petites dépendances' (Désirade, St Barthélemy) and the region of Grands-Fonds in Grande Terre, where the 'Blancs-Matignon' or poor whites live.

The Syrians are to Guadeloupe what the Chinese are to La Réunion, but there are very few of them in Martinique. They specialize in trade. As for the Indians, they are the descendants of workers recruited in India after the abolition of slavery in 1848. They were mainly introduced during the thirty years from 1855 to 1885. Most of the population of the Antilles consists of Negroes and coloureds, but each island has a different skin tone. Martinique is more hybrid than Guadeloupe. The 'petites dépendances', which are too small and too dry to permit plantation agriculture, have a very light coloured population, especially St Barthélemy, where an almost pure white element constitutes nearly 90% of the population. The history of settlement is thus indissolubly bound up with the occupation and exploitation of the land.

The population of the Antilles has a very vigorous growth-rate and its rate of increase gives much cause for concern and makes the problem of unemployment more and more serious. In 1954 the two islands had a total population of 468,250 persons; at the 1961 census they had 573,918; in October 1967, 633,000; of these 320,000 live in Martinique and 313,000 in Guadeloupe. The population has doubled in some twenty-five years. Population density per square kilometre is very

high: 175 per sq. km. in Guadeloupe and 290 in Martinique. Density per hectare of cultivable land is five or six times higher in the island overseas departments than in metropolitan France.

The growth-rates of the population are extremely high: 2.4% in Martinique and 2.9% in Guadeloupe, as against 0.7% in metropolitan France. This results from the fact that crude birth-rates are very high while crude death-rates are rapidly falling thanks to an improvement in public health conditions and in living standards and the continuing rejuvenation of the population. Between the two wars the natural population increase was about 4,500 a year in the French Antilles: 2,000 in Guadeloupe and 2,500 in Martinique. At present it is 16,500 a year, 8,000 in Martinique and 8,500 in Guadeloupe. This has had two main consequences. The first is the youth of the population. While in metropolitan France only 33% of the population consists in persons under twenty years old, in 1966 the percentages were 52.6 in Martinique and 53.1 in Guadeloupe. It is the youth of this population which explains why death-rates are lower in the French Antilles than in metropolitan France.

The second result is the importance of dependants which adults of working age have to support. In France in 1961, 100 adults had to support 99 persons (64 young people and 35 elderly). In the Antilles the burden is much heavier and consists mainly of young people. In Martinique 100 adults were responsible for 144 persons (126 young and 18 old); in Guadeloupe they were responsible for 148 persons (131 young and 17 old). Every plan for social and economic development must first take into account these truly alarming demographic facts.

2. Economy and Employment

The economy of the French Antilles is characterized by intensive specialization in agricultural products and by the high share of services — over 60% — in the GDP, while the share of agriculture has greatly diminished as is shown in the following table:

GDP *by sector (per cent)*

Sector	Guadeloupe			Martinique		
	1961	1965	1968	1961	1965	1968
Primary (agric.)	33	25	15	28	22	12
Secondary (bldg, public works, industry)	11	14	15	14	16	17
Tertiary (trade, rents, services, educ. & health)	56	61	57	58	62	58
Administration			13			13
GDP	100	100	100	100	100	100

SOURCES: Comm. Centrale Des DOM, *V^e plan 1966–70, rapport général*, p. 82 & Inst. d'Émission des DOM (IEDOM), *Rapport d'activité; exercise 1969* (1970), p. 17.

The major part of the population is engaged in some or other branch of agricultural activity: in 1961 37% of the Martiniquans and 46% of the Guadeloupans, and in both islands 62% of the population was rural, as against 38% which was urban. It is impossible to realize the economic and social problems of the French Antilles if one does not see them in their true context; they are essentially part of that group of tropical countries in which the peasant economy is at subsistence level and is of prime importance in the overall picture. However, alongside of this are great sugar plantations established by Europeans; they have the lion's share of the land, and it is because of them that the sugar islands have had the reputation of being rich and prosperous. The marked decline in agriculture between 1965 and 1968 has been mainly due to four hurricanes, to high wages and production costs, and to urban migration, especially of young people. Both islands lack raw materials for industry and have to import fuel from Curaçao and Trinidad to produce electricity; they are basically agricultural in outlook, depending on overseas trade — overwhelming with metropolitan France — for exports and imports. They have preserved a colonial-type economy and their sugar-island background and lack of natural resources have been responsible for this. A striking feature of the economy is the size of the sector devoted to the production of food for domestic consumption, but even so foodstuffs swell the imports of consumer goods required by the highly salaried employees in the public sector; these employees, who constitute only 10% of the employed population, share about half the total of all salaries.[1]

The major agricultural products are sugar-cane and bananas in Guadeloupe, bananas, sugar-cane, and pineapples in Martinique. In the northern part of Martinique bananas have been particularly important because they can be grown on small holdings and need no mechanization, and because cane was associated with slavery and has the disadvantages of requiring processing in factories belonging to *Békés*. Thus bananas totalled some 60% of Martinique's exports, as against 30% for Guadeloupe, until the plantations were severely damaged by hurricanes. The crop was in any case vulnerable to fluctuations in demand and there was no prospect for any increase in production since France is the sole customer. Other outlets are closed because bananas are produced more cheaply elsewhere.[2]

Sugar is still the basis staple of the economy. On average it accounted for half the value of exports from the islands (in 1969 for 115 m. francs out of a total of 412 m.).[3] Again, except for some 30% of the total for Guadeloupe, France is overwhelmingly the main customer. For 1955–68 Guadeloupe produced some 195,000 tons and Martinique 85,000, but because of hurricane damage, production fell in November 1969 to 165,000 and 32,000 tons respectively, and the islands have not been able to fulfill the EEC quota allocated to them. Replanting and reorganization are being undertaken with French help, which includes the provision of mechanical equipment and the introduction of new methods of cutting the cane.[4]

The production of fresh and tinned pineapples has been a notable feature of the economy of Martinique, accounting for 10% of the total of exports; in 1968 three factories produced 18,000 tins. However, since the islands became subject to EEC regulations for fruit and vegetables, Martinique has suffered from a fall in demand for tinned pineapples; half of the French market is supplied by the Ivory Coast and the overseas territories.[5] Another export is rum (108 m. hl. in 1969). Attempts to cultivate coffee and cacao have been almost abandoned, but there has been a limited success in producing fresh vegetables for export in Martinique (2,000 tons in 1969).[6]

Industrial production remains slight, despite considerable investment during recent years. In Guadeloupe it accounted for only 4% of GDP in 1965 and 6% in 1968, the figures for Martinique being 5% and 6% respectively (excluding industries of agricultural origin such as sugar mills, distilleries, and pineapple-canning factories).[7] The colonial heritage, shortage of raw materials, and the very limited local market for industrial produce all account for this, but so too does departmental status. For this has imposed on the islands a high level of salaries and social costs which deter private investment. They are financed by the metropolitan government, but such aid is non-productive. The metropolitan share of public expenditure has been steadily mounting: in 1969 it amounted to 834 m. francs compared with 551 m. francs generated locally, representing an increase of 9% in Guadeloupe and of 13% in Martinique.[8] In the four years 1961–5 public expenditure more than doubled, and in 1969 had gone up by 12%. It is these incoming public funds which encourages the serious adverse balance of trade, whereas in 1964 Guadeloupe's exports slightly exceeded imports and those of Martinique balanced.

As for tourism, on which so many hopes were founded, its contribution is still small. While the number of tourists has increased from 9,000 in 1961 to c. 50,000 in 1969, this is a negligible figure compared with the whole Caribbean (c. 3 m. in 1969).[9]

It is thus not surprising that unemployment and underemployment are serious problems. In the course of the fourth Plan, which ran from 1961 to 1965, only 24,000 jobs were created. A distinct falling-off in numbers employed in agriculture reflects progress in mechanization and the disinclination of young people to work on the land; the new jobs were created in the services and public departments. The fifth Plan (1966–70) envisaged creating rather more than 12,000 new jobs in each island, whereas it was estimated that demand would be some 22,000 in Martinique and 25,000 in Guadeloupe.[10] For the duration of the sixth Plan it was established that a minimum of 30,000 jobs would be necessary for each island, but industry has only a few dozen vacancies a year. According to a census of the potentially active population conducted by INSEE, in Martinique there were only 85,000 jobs for 180,000 persons and in Guadeloupe the same number of jobs for 110,000 persons.[11] The situation is especially alarming among young people. The fall in employment figures reflects the entry into an already saturated market of the postwar population bulge. The situation is one which can only deteriorate, for no increase in the number of jobs can keep step with the current population expansion. The only remedy is emigration, almost all directed to metropolitan France, which since 1963 has been organized by a Bureau known as BUMIDOM. In 1969 some 2,500 persons from each island migrated to France; the figure envisaged by the fifth Plan was 3,000, and is currently about 8,000 per year. French Guiana, which is very under-populated and is now the site of the National Centre for Space Studies, might attract immigrants from Martinique and Guadelopue, but at present they would rather go to Paris than Cayenne.

Even this brief analysis of the economic and demographic organization of the French Antilles is sufficient to show how profoundly they differ from metropolitan France. Their problems spring from their geographical location, their historical past, over-population, and in part from their departmental status. The tertiary sector occupies the preponderant place in the economy, paid for by public funds transferred from France, which also finances the cost of administration. Indeed, most of the islands' activities — industry, trade, tourism, and cultural life — are run from France. For some this overlapping of interests is an argument in favour of departmental status, but for others, who are eager to change the present economic and social structure, it is a powerful argument against the present status since it makes their dependence on France so absolute. Hence the interest of the analysis of the development of the political status of the French Antilles which follows.

II. The Evolution of the Status of the Antilles

Since 1635 the 'Isles d'Amérique' have been French dependencies. During these three centuries relations between the Antilles and France have oscillated between two contradictory political formulas. Autonomy was the incessant demand of the local councils and the white people of consequence, who believed that this would enable them to assert a local particularism and put a brake on metropolitan tutelage. Assimilation was the principal objective of the metropolitan administration and of the Negroes, the one bowing to the traditional centralization of the French political and administrative system, the others seeking to be brought into line with the metropolitan power and an end to the economic and social domination of the whites. This contradiction has largely obscured the evolution of the status of the Antilles from the time of the colonial regime to the current modified departmental status.

1. The Old Colonies

Under the monarchy, the Antilles were ruled by a governor appointed by the king, with the help of a Council, consisting of white grandees who were nobles of French origin. The Council was the supreme power and often refused to bend to the royal will; its constant preoccupation to preserve the autonomy of the islands has combined with a determination to maintain the servitude of the coloured population. With the Revolution of 1789 the great issue became the abolition of slavery which, with the propagation of revolutionary ideas, dominated the political life of the Antilles and conditioned their status. Paris leaned to the side of autonomy in creating General Councils in 1827, finally proclaiming the abolition of slavery by the Schoelcher decree of 27 April 1848.

This was a decisive turning point. Not only was political equality bestowed on all the inhabitants of the islands, but a democratic regime was installed in France. The new colonial regime, settled until 1946 by a senate decree of 1854, was based on a democratic ideology and institutions. It had autonomist tendencies in spite of developing ever stronger ties with Paris.

The basic instrument of government remained the Governor. Directly representing the Minister for Colonies, he appeared to be the agent of the colonial power. His powers were indeed regal. He was aided by a consultative Privy Council consisting of the heads of the administrative services and men of consequence nominated by the metropolitan government. Nevertheless, the position of the Governor was an uneasy one. He could not permit himself to engage in open conflict with the local élites who disposed of the political fiefdoms solidly entrenched in the islands and certainly all-powerful in Paris. There was also the General Council. It was the representative of the colony and exercised the autonomy bestowed on it; its budgetary powers and control of customs duties made it powerful. It was the centre of local political life and its presence prevented the setting up of any system of direct administration. It was, however, far more preoccupied by political problems than by sound administration. The General Council upheld a tradition of independence *vis-à-vis* the metropolitan authorities.

Nevertheless the desire for self-government was never absolute. The term was associated with the old colonial regime, and the word 'colony' evoked memories of slavery. On the other hand the fiscal and financial autonomy of the islands, which was the most cogent indication of their autonomy, lost some of its charm when there was a crisis and a fall in prices; it would then have been preferable for the country's status not to have prevented the granting of metropolitan subsidies. Finally, for the new coloured élite France had a growing attraction: democracy, liberty, progress, lay across the sea with all the enchantment lent by distance. This is why the trend was reversed during the years preceding the second world war. This latter event broke the ties with France and simultaneously re-established government by whites; it further loaded the scales of opinion in favour of integration. The Fourth Republic was rapidly to institutionalize this development.

2. The Change to Departmental Status

The status of the Antilles was transformed in a new political context: the socialist and communist parties of the Antilles demanded assimilation, and the tripartite left-wing coalition government in Paris voted the law of 19 March 1946, which transformed the former colonies into departments and enshrined the assimilation formula with a view to abolishing distinctions from the metropolitan power and to associating the inhabitants in the running of their own affairs. Guadeloupe and Martinique became overseas departments. But French policy, above all in colonial affairs, was often content to state principles, leaving their application to the whim of circumstance, thereby destroying any continuity. As Marius Moutet, an expert in colonial

problems, said so cogently during the parliamentary debates on the 1946 law: 'Will the populations of these former colonies always be governed by Paris or will they govern themselves?' This is the problem: centralism or decentralization, subjection or autonomy'.[12] The application of the new status was to lean towards the first solution but at the same time to bring about its first partial setback.

The new departments are totally assimilated with France in the political organization of the Republic. The Antilles are represented in parliament. The 1946 constitution put the legislative regime of the overseas departments on the same basis as that of France. The normal administrative services are each dependent on the relevant minister. The unity in conception and treatment resulting from the sole jurisdiction of the Minister for Colonies disappeared. The files were dispersed in various ministerial branches, more anxious to preserve their respective authority than to solve problems, while the local administrative organs became increasingly separated from one another, giving up what individual powers they had in order for all decisions to be taken in Paris. The horizontal dispersion of local services paradoxically reinforced the process of metropolitan centralization.

The classic French departmental structures were swiftly installed. A decree of 1947 gave each departmental Prefect the same prerogatives as his metropolitan colleagues. Like the former Governor, he is in addition responsible for the external defence and internal security of the island; he also has discretionary powers over prices and can regulate imports and exports. This extension of prefectoral powers was justified by distance and the necessity for some genuine local authority. But one must not be deceived: this authority does not give the Prefect any real weight *vis-à-vis* the ministries and governments in Paris. In fact he keeps in step with the metropolitan Prefects because his temporary sojourn in the Antilles constitutes only one step — sometimes a perilous one — in his career. He is above all the agent of the Minister of the Interior in a department where the maintenance of order is far more difficult than elsewhere. His administrative functions thus take second place, and he has an essentially political role, which consists in ensuring the 'fidelity' of the island and he occasionally plays this role at the time of elections.

The General Council is the principal element for him to take into account. The metropolitan regime is strictly applied to this assembly; a decree of 1946 abolished the former financial autonomy of the councils. The General Council has thus completely lost any authoritative role in local politics, even its right to control the administrative services. The symbol of Antillean autonomy and decentralization, it has been the greatest loser from the policy of assimilation. It was hardly astonishing, therefore, that the establishment of the new administrative system met with systematic hostility from the Council, which claimed over and over again that 'it could no longer have confidence in M. le Préfet' and went on to support social demands which could only bring disorder, even though to do so often brought the risk of its own dissolution.

Nevertheless, assimilation stops short at the threshold of the social and economic structure, the domain in which differences with and opposition to Paris are most pronounced. In this respect the policy does not aim higher than an attempt to prop up the economy of the islands and to bring some sort of equilibrium to the social structure. The change-over to departmental status has favoured the installation of the great national economic services, which permit state intervention and the progressive development of planning and long-term economic policy. This was the moving spirit behind the creation in 1948 of the Fonds d'Investissement des Départements d'Outre-Mer (FIDOM), which is financed by the state budget. But it was difficult to get the new system going, and its first social measures, conceived within the framework of assimilation, soon clashed and came dangerously near disturbing the balance of island society. Social security was introduced in 1947, but no system of family allowances was put into operation; wages were related to those operating in France, but in practice they could be fixed by the Prefect. Since 1950 the financial aid of the state, which for the most part forgoes the resources of taxation, has subsidized the local bodies and embarked on an expenditure on equipment without parallel in the metropolitan system, an indication of the limits and inadequacies of departmental status.

In fact, contrary to the hopes of those who supported the principles and ideology on which it was founded, the conversion of the French Antilles into departments has not been successful. Departmental status is totally ineffective, not to say in some cases a restraining mechanism, for the economic and social development of the islands. Whenever under-development was the basic fact, departmental structures and procedures proved ineffective. This inadequacy was accentuated by the haphazard way in which the new status was applied. The revolution it implied has profoundly shaken the structures of administration but without really affecting traditional mentality and behaviour. Further, the political basis of power was eroded,[13] and this intensified with the progressive weakness of the metropolitan government. Prefect and General Council clash, because one lacks responsibility and has no freedom of action, while the other has lost its jurisdiction and takes advantage of this by attributing all the difficulties to the administration, while at the same time the illusory promises of assimilation increase its disappointment. The government sometimes yields and recalls the Prefect; at other times it dissolves the General Council. But in the end there is always a return to the traditional system of a Prefect who 'governs with his majority'. Gradually people began to realize once again that, according to the celebrated saying of a Martiniquan politician of the Third Republic, an Antillean is 'a Frenchman in a continent which is not French'. The contagion of decolonization was the final blow, with the outbreak of the Algerian rebellion in 1954, and the Defferre *loi-cadre* for Africa in 1956, with which the French Antilleans felt in sympathy. That was the moment when assimilation lost its psychological attraction. By then the new departmental structures had already come under fire.

3. Modified Departmental Status

M. Conombo, Secretary of State of the Interior, announced to the General Council on 16 November 1954:

It is the wish of the government that the situation [of the DOM] should be the object of careful study, from all points of view, to discover the rate and terms whereby they could best profit from democratic and republican institutions which have been tried and proved in France. What is in question is an additional stage in the process of assimilation and no kind of retrograde step.

There was therefore no change in either basic principle or general purpose; this was still the assimilation of the French Antilles to the mother country at some unspecified date in the future. But means, methods, and basic structures had to be more realistic; it was these which had to be 'modified' to meet the situation in the islands.

Modification has taken place at three different levels. The first is that of political and administrative co-ordination of the DOM. The government was to have one member specifically responsible for the DOM. The co-ordination of administrative activity has been ensured since 1958 by a secretary-general of the DOM, who is consulted on all measures applicable to them and who presides over an interministerial council for the co-ordination of the DOM. The mechanism is repeated at the local level, where since 1960 the Prefect has been the 'co-ordinator of activities' of all the service heads. It seems that this reorganization has made it possible to re-establish a unity of conception in the administration of the islands which was largely overturned by the 1946 status.

But it is above all on the level of administrative organization that the reform is best known, on the basis of the decree of 26 April 1960 which increased the powers of local authorities. Besides his new co-ordinating activities, the Prefect is in full charge of all the administration of the island: he is kept informed of all the plans and activities of public enterprises, whether state or semi-public; he appoints local officials and can propose their recall to France since the 1960 ordinance, an arrangement much criticized because it was used to penalize subversive opinions held by the autonomists and the communists. Some measure of decentralization was added to this notable effort towards devolution, which resulted in increasing the powers of the General Council. Henceforth this was to be the instrument for the 'adaptation' of the islands to their particular situation: it is consulted on every draft law or decree issued with this in view, and even has the right to propose any special measure which seems desirable for its own department. It participates in the same way in economic and social policy by its role in the running of FIDOM.

In fact the new measures basically relate to the economic and social position of the Antilles. A decree of 1960 defines the machinery of FIDOM, whose investments in the local sector are decided by the General Council and the Prefect. A law of 1960 established a plan to improve the equipment and economic expansion of the DOM. All these measures have the objective of putting in hand the economic and social development of the countries by successive steps, of which the first landmarks were the agrarian law (1961), equalization of family allowances (1963), the alignment of wages with those of France (1965).

Modified departmental status decidedly marks a new stage in the status of the Antilles, if not in principle then at least in political and social reality. Considered from the point of view of the traditional options, the 1960 status — as it is currently termed — indicates some return to the machinery of autonomy and self-government. But this evolution is far more in line with efforts at regionalization and territorial improvement undertaken at the same time in France. The Antilles are treated as a special 'social and economic region'. This is translated into practice by means of a certain amount of administrative reorganization. But in the political sphere the dogma of departmentalism persists: regionalization stops where politics begin. Perhaps this lack of harmony explains the political malaise experienced in the Antilles at present.

III. The Political Malaise

In spite of the new reforms there is an undeniable political malaise in the islands. The frequency of strikes and disturbances, the incidental recurrence of outbreaks of violence and their inevitable repression bear unfortunate witness to this: riots at Fort-de-France (1959); arrest and trial of students accused of conspiracy (1963); new riots at Fort-de-France (1965); and explosions of violence at Basse-Terre and Pointe-à-Pitre (1967). It is nevertheless true that violence and repression have always been part of the political climate of the Antilles, and their persistence has not irremediably cut the ties between them and France. The extraordinary calm of the islands during the events of May-June 1968 which exploded in France is clear proof of this. That is to say that one must appreciate the real measure of this malaise before one can determine its place in Antillean opinion and its effect on French politics.

1. Reasons for Malaise

The underlying reason is certainly to be found in the impact on the Antilles of the contact between an underdeveloped society and the organization and techniques of an industrialized society. A consumer society, itself questioned in France where, however, it fits in with the prevailing social psychology, has directly clashed with the very basis of an underdeveloped society — if one views the development of the Antilles in the light of the standards prevailing in France itself. This conflict between two types of society affects the political structures as well as the psychological reactions of the Antilleans.

The reforms which have taken place since the end of the last war have been relatively swift and far-reaching, but they do not seem to have had any profound effect on local politics. In fact, political structures function without having the slightest effect. In colonial times, the local powers had both authority and prestige, something they no longer command today — even if the personality of General de Gaulle offered the islands an illustration of the power of France. Nothing has replaced this former legitimacy, despite the efforts made to provide the local élites with new responsibilities: the 96% of the population who are non-white have a (formally) dominant position in island politics.[14] The traditional élites have lost the confidence of a population in full demographic development. The traditional political game has continued alongside the new structures. The beneficiaries of all kinds of privileges — privileges of race (whites and mulattos), economic privileges (the local bourgeoisie, civil servants) put the brake on development and encourage the inertia of the political and administrative élites. Things are kept in order by the maintenance of the traditional *status quo*, whilst the existing institutions seem to undergo some sort of surface change and local confidence fades dismally. Island politics have an innate futility which dooms every reform to failure; this has been responsible for the collapse of almost every plan for agrarian reform.

Despite all this, as has been seen, the economic and social development of the Antilles since the war has been considerable. The per capita income of the inhabitants of Guadeloupe and Martinique is three times that of their neighbours in the neighbouring British islands.[15] The new structures, which operate largely on metropolitan funds, have been much more successful in the economic field than in the political context. But it is also noteworthy that economic progress has not had the expected results. Bearing in mind that economic changes can only have long-term social effects, the social climate of the islands remains uncomfortably disturbed. Social inequalities are intensified by economic development. Certain sections of the working population, notably administrative civil servants and higher economic personnel, have a considerable advantage over their colleagues in France, while in contrast the average wage-earner lags far behind his French counterpart. This disparity is the more hotly resented in that it corresponds with racial differences: 78% of the white population dominates the economic life of the islands.[16] To this must be added chronic and seasonal unemployment which migration to France and the start of industrial development has not succeeded in alleviating[17] — it is not without significance that outbreaks of violence usually begin with strikes and social clashes. Social inequalities inevitably express themselves in terms of political disorders and these, of course, are useful ammunition for the left-wing parties. They constitute a source of political unrest and bring to the forefront the problem of social and economic development of the islands.

However, this malaise goes deeper and its roots lie in the psychological make-up of the Antillean character. The history and particular characteristics of island society produce contradictions which come to the surface in times of crisis or change. The contact between under-development and a consumer society thus causes psychological reactions which currently seem to be the basic reason for the existing malaise. One must at this point acknowledge the fact that local aspirations vary. Island society is simultaneously introvert and

extrovert.[18] Everyone's gaze is constantly directed towards France. People adopt the mentality of those on public assistance, and they are also sensitive about anything that might be interpreted as heralding a policy of abandonment by France. But at the same time the islands wish to assert their 'local personality' and manifest their desire to be responsible for their own affairs, which would confer on them the dignity and equality of Frenchmen. These divergent reflexes are more marked among the autonomous than among the traditional élite, whose sense of dignity is blunted by the privileges they enjoy. Another psychological factor is international opinion. The myth of decolonization exerts a pressure favouring the loosening of ties with the metropolitan powers: it has affected the Antilles despite the care of the authorities to control news media. But one should note that this aspiration is counterbalanced by the experience of neighbouring islands; the recent independence of other Caribbean islands and even of Cuba was felt to be an object lesson in Guadeloupe and Martinique where the standard of living is much higher.

There is, in conclusion, one more factor that needs to be mentioned: the complex influence of island nationalism, or particularism. This is not basically directed against France as a whole, but against the white élite in the islands; there is also more than a trace of rivalry between the two islands themselves. It is not the classic nationalism of underdeveloped counties, for in some curious way it manages to include a genuine feeling of being French. This *romantisme de la France* is an accumulation of various things — a long-established attachment of local culture to French civilization, the prestige of France itself, and, in recent years, also the personal prestige of General de Gaulle. All these contradictions crop up in the political malaise and explain different nuances in public opinion in the Antilles.

2. Public Opinion in the Antilles

Between 1946 and 1956 opposition to the principle of assimilation was rather vague and ill-defined. The Communist Party criticized certain aspects of the idea of departmental status but on the whole maintained the basic concept of assimilation. The Socialist Party too supported the existing policies, but suggested a more decentralized status: centralization and the power of the 'technocrats' in Paris had increased after the islands had become departments.

The year 1956 marked a turning point in Antillean consciousness of the problems inherent in the status of the DOM. The Defferre *loi-cadre* launched French black Africa on the road of decolonization; destabilization and the events in Hungary caused a crisis in the French Communist Party. The deputy mayor of Fort-de-France, Aimé Césaire, broke with the French Communist Party, took up a position against departmental status, created the *Parti Progressiste Martiniquais* (PPM), and opted for a federal type of solution. To avoid being overtaken on the left by the PPM, the local communists also broke off from the French Communist Party (March 1958). From then onwards the Communist Parties of Guadeloupe and Martinique severely criticized departmental status and claimed autonomy for the Antilles. They demanded the setting up of a territorial assembly endowed with legislative powers and of an executive responsible to this assembly. These various demands led all political parties without exception to condemn France's integrationist policy and to recommend that the government 'modify' the existing departmental status to fit the special requirements of the islands, and to increase the decision-making powers of the General Councils.

On 4 May 1958 the *Revue guadeloupéene* organized a symposium on assimilation, which made a deep impression. There were two opposing viewpoints: on the one hand the supporters of the policy of 'modified departmental status' and on the other those of 'self-government' in a federal framework, or of 'internal autonomy'. Most of the political parties (*Indépendants, Union Nationale Radicale*, Socialists) came out in favour of the first point of view; they had a majority in the General Council and represented the opinions of both the local élite and of the majority of the population. The second point of view was promoted by the PPM, the local Communist Parties, the *Parti Socialiste Unifié*, and 'left' groups (the Association of Antillean Students in France, Catholic students of the *Jeunesse Étudiante Chrétienne*, etc.). The words 'self-government' or 'autonomy' in any case did not have the same political content for all the militants, but all wished to maintain union with France and demanded a legislative and executive power which would ensure the running of Antillean affairs by the Antilleans themselves.

The measures taken in 1960 to devolve and decentralize the administration by giving local authorities and elected members a greater part in local affairs did not put an end to the arguments about the status of the overseas departments. The defenders of modified assimilation do not fail to criticize the defects of the system, but they felt that the integration of the French Antilles into the French Union will mobilize national solidarity and in time give Martinique and Guadeloupe an economic and social standard more closely related to that of the metropolitan departments. *Match,* published at Pointe-à-Pitre, is the organ of the defenders of modified departmental status.

L'Étincelle (in Guadeloupe) and *Justice* (in Martinique), organs of the Communist Party, and above all *Progrès social,* organ of the Guadeloupe autonomist intellectuals, on the other hand, wage war on assimilation. The advent of Castroism in Cuba, the FLN victory in Algeria, the local independence of the French African states, the fascination exercised by the Chinese revolution on the young communists are all factors which have hardened the attitudes of the Antillean separatists. The legal opposition of the political parties has thus been outstripped by violent revolutionary action, which is met by arrests and deportation. The latest of these violent episodes were the serious riots of 26 and 27 May 1967 at Pointe-à-Pitre, riots which followed two months after those of Basse-Terre! It is possible that this uncontrolled burst of violence developed spontaneously at the time of a building strike and was led by workless youths who had never become integrated into the work force; it might also have been organized by autonomist political groups, in particular by GONG (the *Groupe d'Organisation National de la Guadeloupe).* The government acted on this latter supposition in arresting a large number of intellectuals (teachers, journalists, doctors) accused of undermining state security. But the State Security Court of France on 1 March 1968 gave a lenient verdict in the so-called 'Guadeloupe Nationalist' trial: there were thirteen acquittals and six of the accused received suspended sentences. This trial gave the maximum publicity to the autonomist cause. The future will show whether this has constituted an important step on the road leading to a revision of departmental status.

3. Current French Policy

There are those who have doubted the very existence of any French policy towards the Antilles. The memory of governmental ultra-conservatism under the Fourth Republic, the distance between the islands and metropolitan France, the natural inclination of local government representatives to avoid disturbing the precarious political and social equilibrium, all these have led to the notion that the great plan was to leave things as they were, while ready to make a few hasty concessions whenever the situation looked threatened.[19] But General de Gaulle's declarations during his visits to the Antilles, the speeches of his ministers, and the official communiqués have not given this impression, although one must, of course, make a distinction between the broad lines of this policy and the problems inherent in its application in distant islands where the social context is very different from that of France.

French policy in the Antilles is based on the assumption that the islands are French and wish to be French, that France alone is competent to solve their problems. In 1964 came the final parting of the ways between the former African territories and the Antilles. The decolonization policy was right and natural in Africa, since these countries consisted of 'autonomous peoples forming large units'. In the Antilles things were quite different, with a mixture of African and European peoples within a framework of French civilization. In the Antilles 'departmental status seems to be the only solution to fit our times'. Within this framework, French policy basically relies on the social and economic development of the islands: 'practical decisions . . . must be taken for the development and social improvement of the people'. It is assumed that the political malaise will disappear with the raising of the standard of living and the bringing about of a new economic and social balance. Two additional points complete this policy. The first relates the Antilles to France's global policy: they are a 'French outpost in the American hemisphere';[20] this effectively defines their role vis-à-vis the influence of the United States and revolutionary initiatives or movements for regrouping in Central or South America. The second point is a warning to those who seek a solution in a new political status and in independence: since 1958 and the experience of Guinea, the attitude of the French government has been clear and unyielding: all French aid ceases with independence.

In conception, this policy at least has the merit of being clearly defined. But at the local level, these declarations of principle arouse response only in so far as they are applied in practice. The agency to implement this policy is naturally a new economic and social administration. The development agencies envisaged by modified departmental status have been set up; they are run by the traditional establishment, who have been endowed with new economic and social powers. However, the change of function which has fallen to the administration is not proceeding without difficulty. The same old conflicts remain between administration and policy, and the Prefect and his colleagues find it difficult to forget their political preoccupations to devote themselves to their new responsibilities. Nor are the administrators themselves always properly equipped for their new functions. A development policy can succeed only when shock tactics sweep away all obstacles. In this respect the conduct of the administrators is often inadequate; 'There are too many people in positions of responsibility, civil servants who are never brought to book for their mistakes'.[21] Some of the civil servants who were transferred from Africa after the independence of the former overseas territories have been quite unable to cope with the situation, and local officials seem inextricably involved in nepotism and the clannishness typical of island behaviour. Not even the emergence of a body of specialists — the economic secretariat of the DOM prefectures — has been sufficient to inject a fresh spirit and new methods into the traditional administration struggling to cope with a new policy.

But what really hinders the proper development of this new policy is the attitude of the local élites, who form a barrier against the infiltration of government policy into the island environment. Many social and economic improvements threaten their privileges, and naturally they prefer the maintenance of the *status quo*. The Europeans want to maintain their existing position (though there are exceptions to this, and notable efforts have been made in certain economic circles): the planters through their monopolies. The local bourgeoisie, except for a fringe won over to gradual social change, are happy with a situation which ensures their social superiority and some equality with the whites. The local politicians are imprisoned by their political reflexes and positions which that social change might threaten. The government's new policy cannot hope to be successful outside the purely material field without the full co-operation of the island élites.

The French Antilles have now held departmental status for over twenty years, and in the final assessment this may be judged as an original experiment which is almost, but not quite, a type of decolonization. But its outcome remains in doubt. This uncertainty arises partly from the lack of continuity, which is often the defect of French policy, and partly from the want of harmony between official principles and the implementation of a policy which demands empiricism at every point. French policy in the Antilles has not yet been taken to a successful conclusion. It would be dangerous to make departmental status a step on the road to independence. That would be catastrophic for the Antilles in a world in which poverty and underdevelopment prevails, nor would it correspond with the wishes of a population where rich and poor alike are attached to French culture[22] and whose reactions are always permeated by a *romantisme de la France*. But the *status quo* is just as dangerous, and some evolution is clearly indispensable. It is still an open question to what extent economic and social development will be able to free the French Antilles from the prospects of underdevelopment. Moreover, considerable changes in behaviour and attitudes both for France and for the islands are required. The plans for regional autonomy which were announced in Paris after the crisis of May 1968 might well provide a framework for future developments:[23] they could ease the centralizing process by which the islands are assimilated to metropolitan France and allow the population of the Antilles to take on constructive and realistic responsibilities within the administration of an individualized regional unit inside the French Community.

Notes

1. *Le Monde*, 6 Jan. 1970.
2. *Ibid.*, 6 Jan. 1970.
3. IEDOM, *Rapport . . . 1969*, p. 42.
4. Guadeloupe Préfecture, *La Guadeloupe économique*, Sept. 1967 (mimeo); *Le Monde*, 23–24 Nov. 1969.
5. *Le Monde*, 6 Jan. 1970.
6. IEDOM, *Rapport . . . 1969*, p. 32.
7. *Ibid.*, p. 33.
8. *Ibid.*, p. 74.
9. *Ibid.*, p. 36.
10. Comm. centrale des DOM, *V^e plan 1966–70*, p. 565.
11. *Le Monde*, 7 Jan. 1970.
12. Cf. Descamps de Bragelongne, 'Le problème du statut des départements d'outre-mer: Guadeloupe et Martinique', *R. jurid. et écon. du Sud-Ouest* (sér. jurid.), 1964, p. 78.
13. Cf. the opinion of M. Mireau in *Marchés tropicaux*, 29 Jan. 1949: 'The new regime could easily cause a weakening of authority. A Governor's authority, less representative of the government than a Prefect's but nevertheless symbolizing the power of France itself, enjoyed a traditional prestige which was very important. . . . Authority will lose its strength when scattered between these different departments'.
14. Cf. Arvin Murch, *The Policy of Assimilation in the French West Indian Departments Opposed to Independence* (1966). This thesis, submitted at Yale University, was discussed in *Outre-Mer français* (1968).
15. See Murch.
16. *Ibid.*
17. See above, pp. 87–8.
18. Cf. A. Mabileau, 'Gouvernement et administration dans les îles françaises d'outre-mer', *Outre-Mer français*, Numéro spéc. 'Colloque', p. 20–2.
19. Cf. Aimé Césaire's pronouncement to the National Assembly on 26 April 1962: 'The history of the Antilles over the past few years has been the history of minimal measures when it has not been eye-wash pure and simple'.
20. Text of an electoral poster for the UNR during elections for the Legislative Assembly (*Le Monde*, 24–25 Dec. 1967).
21. Cf. Report of a parliamentary mission from the Commission des Finances to the National Assembly, 1963.
22. Cf. the results of Murch's investigations into the status of the French Antilles.
23. Cf. the study of the Association for the Defence of the Interests of Guadeloupe, *Le Monde*, 11–12 Aug. 1968.

The Break-Up of the British West Indies Federation

Elizabeth Wallace

The Jamaican Referendum

Norman Manley's successful insistence on a deflated national government ultimately defeated his own ends by enabling Sir Alexander Busta- mante to argue forcibly that such an emasculated federation was a useless luxury which West Indi- ans could not afford. From mid-June to mid-Sep- tember 1961 the referendum campaign dominated all other issues in Jamaica. At a political meeting on 3 August Mr. Manley announced that the ref- erendum would be held on 19 September and that he himself would stand for the national House of Representatives at the next federal election.

During the previous three years the island had been a leading member of the Federation. Yet only in these last three months of meetings, speeches, and letters to the press had many Jamaicans their first serious opportunity to learn what federalism really meant. The widespread ignorance and inertia about fundamental facts of political life were a comment on the ruling People's National Party which, during its six years in office, had officially supported the Federation but failed to cultivate an informed public opinion on what it involved. This failure, mainly caused by anti-federal sentiment within the party, was a major reason for the even- tual defeat. From the outset Premier Manley fought an uphill struggle, almost single-handed, whereas Sir Alexander enjoyed active help from his prin- cipal colleagues: 'It is a fight against odds', wrote *The Gleaner's* political reporter, 'against apathy, against a determined opposition and against the natural insularity of Jamaicans, grown proud in their own concept of nationhood'.[1]

Mr. Manley's campaign received little aid from his political cohorts in Jamaica and none from the rest of the West Indies. It was, however, supported by the powerful National Workers' Union and by an unlikely recruit, Kenneth Hill, formerly Acting First Deputy Leader and Whip of the Federal Dem- ocratic Labour Party. Late in July Mr. Hill announced his resignation, both from the national parliament and the Jamaica Labour Party, because he believed Jamaicans had 'no honourable or prac- tical alternative' to remaining in the Federation and

that their character and reputation were at stake. He later rejoined the People's National Party. If the vote went against federation, he declared, 'no country would ever trust Jamaica, its government or its people, for generations to come'.[2]

Mr. Manley himself argued that a vote against federation would be a breach of faith deserving worldwide contempt. More than a year earlier he had publicly recognized that if Jamaica seceded, the national union would come to an end. On his return from the London Conference he contended that the 43% of the federal budget paid by Jamaica was less than 1% of the island's local budget, and that to 'go it alone' would cost more than twice as much as remaining in the Federation. His main financial argument was that most national expenses were for common services such as the university and the two federal ships, for which Jamaica would have to pay her share whether in the union or not.[3]

The Jamaica Labour Party attacked these figures as 'a masterpiece of deception', argued that fed- eration meant dominance of Jamaica by the small islands, and appealed to voters to save their beloved country from this peril. 'Who', Sir Alex- ander demanded, 'ever heard of federating pov- erty?' The rich, he maintained, were arguing for a federation for which the poor had to pay. On a slogan of 'Jamaica — Yes — Federation — No' his party conducted an effective and ultimately vic- torious campaign based on an appeal to class and insular divisions.[4]

Although the Jamaican legislature ratified the constitution designed at Lancaster House, thus defeating Sir Alexander's amendment demanding immediate independence for the island, its people eventually chose to leave the Federation. The ref- erendum result was 256,261 or 54.1% against remaining in the Federation, as opposed to 217,319 or 45.9% in favour. Of the 60.8% of registered voters sufficiently interested to cast their ballots, a majority of 8.2% or 49,000 supported secession. Thus less than 10% of those who voted in one of ten constituent territories destroyed The West Indies. Jamaica's capital city of Kingston voted four to one for federation, but the day was carried by country constituencies which outnumbered urban by thirty-five to ten.

In all probability few Jamaicans realized the full implications of their decision or seriously considered the economic and political problems of independent nationhood. The referendum aroused far less popular interest than the Jamaican general election of 1962, in which almost 73% of the electorate went to the polls. 'It is something to be deeply regretted', said the *West Indian Economist,* 'that the long and often weary negotiations, the detailed studies, the hard-won concessions, the reluctant sacrifices, and the volume of sheer hard, grinding work involved in building the Federation should be negated in one day by one vital popular vote'.[5]

The issue was decided, not on the merits or demerits of federalism, about which ordinary Jamaicans knew little, but by the prejudices of up-country peasant farmers who, like rural peoples elsewhere, were suspicious of the unfamiliar. Repelled by the chilly logic of an austere intellectual like Norman Manley and by his idealistic challenge to support a wide concept of West Indian nationhood, they were attracted by the superb and humourous demagoguery of his cousin. They responded to Sir Alexander's appeal to isolationism and self-interest, to his contention that Jamaica's choice was between independence and subservience, that the referendum involved a vote for or against the Manley government's whole record, that the issue was in reality between the rich and the poor, and that the new brown ruling class favoured an expensive federal system which would further impoverish their unfortunate black countrymen, who would have to support impecunious little islands in the Eastern Caribbean. Edward Seaga (later leader of the Jamaica Labour Party) voiced an often reiterated argument when he maintained that there was too much need and want in Jamaica to think of using its resources to help others.[6]

The People's National Party had come to the fore on slogans of freedom and independence for the island. This made it difficult for its members to attack the Jamaica Labour Party's appeal to insular nationalism. Many voters were fearful of increased taxation and saw a conflict between continuance in the Federation and the long-sought goals of Jamaican self-government and nationhood. The question was not put to them as a choice between two alternative routes to independence, of which one lay through West Indian unity. Support for the Federation was among the most unpopular planks in Mr. Manley's platform and opposition to it perhaps the only popular one in Sir Alexander's. For the People's National Party to appeal to the electorate on this single issue was a calamitous mistake.

Despite more than one public statement that he staked his political career on the outcome, Mr. Manley did not throw the whole weight of his party behind the campaign. When he first announced the referendum, he stressed that his government would loyally support whatever decision the electorate made. This stand, widely condemned outside Jamaica as a sacrifice of principle to expediency, added nothing to his stature and precipitated his political downfall. Had he chosen to call a general election, or to gamble his future on the plebiscite by indicating in advance that he would resign if federation were rejected, his great personal popularity might have turned the scale. Instead, however, he explained that the referendum was a national issue on which voting would be free.

A majority of his followers rightly believed that he would not consider failure in it sufficient reason to resign. Many accordingly either abstained or cast their ballots against federation, in the comforting conviction that defeat would not mean the fall of his government. Had all of his professed supporters voted in favour, he would have won the plebiscite. His campaign was not helped by Sir Grantley Adam's concurrent attack on the Lancaster House proposals.

Mr. Manley's political opponents did not allow these circumstances to go unregarded, but stressed his pre-referendum statement that he had pledged his political future to the Federation and would stand or fall by it. 'Well', remarked "Thomas Wright" of *The Daily Gleaner,* 'Federation has fallen and Mr. Manley has decided to stand rather than fall'.[7]

It has seldom been possible to restrict a plebiscite to a single issue, detached from party considerations. The device is particularly unsuitable for a country with cabinet government. Where, as in Jamaica, the majority of unsophisticated voters were ill-qualified to determine a complicated political question, the decision to hold a referendum was singularly ill-advised. As a commentator in Jamaica pointed out, it was a means of 'playing political dice with destiny'.[8] Many Jamaicans probably believed that they were voting against change and for the *status quo,* as have most electorates in most countries, notably Australia, when asked to make a decision by a plebiscite.

The Jamaica Labour Party treated the matter as a straight party fight and, in the absence of other clear policies, was doubtless fortunate in being presented with a highly emotional issue. Since Jamaicans, like most West Indian parties, were distinguished more by the personalities of their leaders than by political tenets, this lack of ideas was not surprising. Yet, as the *West Indian Economist* observed, people who shrink from discussing principles can scarcely believe strongly in federalism, which is designed to give effect to certain ideas.[9]

Mr. Manley attributed the result of the referendum mainly to Jamaica's intense spirit of nationalism, fostered by geographical and psychological remoteness from the other British Caribbean islands. The internal autonomy won in 1959 undoubtedly exaggerated its already lively local patriotism, Mr. Manley admitted his own deep disappointment at the outcome, which blocked what he considered the best and only safe road for Jamaica. To the rest of the British Caribbean he expressed his 'profound sorrow and regret'. Tens of thousands of West Indians, he said, 'will grieve at this defeat of all their hopes for the future and I share their sorrow'. At the moment of defeat Mr. Manley probably realized better than anyone else the disastrous nature of his decision to hold a plebiscite: a last desperate gamble, with the stakes not simply his own political future but that of his island and of the concept of a united West Indies. His bitter disappointment at the outcome was unquestionable.

Six years later, however, he was contesting with Sir Alexander Bustamante which of them deserved more credit for enabling Jamaica to leave the Federation although, as Mr. Manley frankly acknowledged, the referendum was a breach of the national constitution and of legislation by the British Parliament which brought the West Indies into being. 'I relied', he said candidly, 'on the fact that no one would have dared to attempt to apply force to Jamaica'.[10]

To Sir Alexander the result clearly indicated that Jamaica was determined not to be ruled by Barbados, Trinidad, or any other territory. He called on the Premier to resign, but Mr. Manley refused, on the curious ground that the referendum showed no clear lack of confidence in his administration, because a substantial number of his party followers had obviously voted for secession. Neither he nor his supporters, he argued, had been defeated on a party issue. He promised, however, to hold an election to decide which party should have the honour of leading Jamaica out of the Federation.[11] Within a week after the referendum he resigned as leader of the West Indies Federal Labour Party and severed his party's affiliation with it.

Aftermath of the Referendum

The unexpected result of the referendum naturally shocked the federal government and the other territories. It also provoked much critical comment from outside as well as within the British Caribbean. Sir Grantley Adams described Jamaica's decision as a tragedy, but denied that this must break up the federal union. He urged his countrymen to profit from past mistakes and start afresh. 'If we want to make it succeed', he declared, 'it can succeed and I am optimistic that the West Indies can become a stronger Federation'.[12]

Jamaica, wrote a Grenadian journalist, 'has sounded the death knell of the West Indian Federation'. The hard-pressed backwoods Jamaican, said a St. Lucian, 'poor, ragged, barefoot, . . . has spoken and utter confusion and chaos reigns among the leaders of the remaining islands'. In the Jamaica Labour Party, a *Gleaner* editorial commented, 'much of the cohesion and thrust which were thrown into the anti-Federal drive derived not only from Sir Alexander's consistent distrust of Federation, but also from the passion of some of his close and more dynamic colleagues to get to power quickly and to see, each outdoing the other, who shall succeed'.[13]

Jamaica's decision raised the immediate problem of whether the union could survive. As far back as 1912 a perceptive advocate of federation, Sir Algernon Aspinall, had remarked that 'the West Indies without Jamaica would be like Hamlet without the Prince of Denmark'. Before the referendum Sir Grantley had said that without Jamaica the Federation's future would be bleak. After it he called an emergency cabinet meeting but declined to comment on the outcome. The Governor General interrupted a holiday in Scotland to confer with the Secretary of State for the Colonies, while Sir Grantley led a delegation to London to discuss the crisis. These September meetings were private and the official communiqué issued at their conclusion was noncommittal, although it indicated that the federal government would continue for the time being to operate under the existing constitution.[14]

Mr. Manley for his part, immediately after the referendum, cabled the Secretary of State for the Colonies, requesting prompt discussion of Jamaica's secession and of a date for its independence. Before the federal ministers had departed from London, a Jamaican delegation arrived. Sir Grantley was much irritated when, without consulting him, the Colonial Office announced on 5 October 1961 that the British government accepted the result of the plebiscite as a firm indication of Jamaica's views and would introduce legislation providing for the island's withdrawal from the Federation and for its independence in 1962.

Mr. Manley told a press conference that he thought the question of Jamaica rejoining a West Indian federation unlikely to be revived during his lifetime. To any surviving common services, however, his island would be willing to contribute its share.[15] On his return from England to Jamaica he received a tumultuous reception from enthusiastic supporters shouting 'power'. An opposition motion calling on his government to resign was defeated. A Select Committee of the legislature, composed of representatives from both major parties, was promptly appointed to draft a new constitution for independence.

The Position of Trinidad and Tobago

When the rest of the West Indies recovered from the initial shock of the Jamaican referendum and began to examine the situation, there seemed some reason to suppose that the Federation was not necessarily doomed and might even be strengthened. An Eastern Caribbean union of the remaining territories, although only half the size of the original state, would form a more natural geographic entity. Many West Indians, especially in the Leewards and Windwards, hoped it might be possible to agree on a revised federal constitution giving greater power to the centre and less to the units. The feasibility of this view clearly hinged on the attitude of Trinidad and Tobago, whose 850,000 people would provide half the population and over half the wealth in such a truncated federation.

Its Premier had more than once declared that, if Jamaica withdrew, his territory would follow suit. A few days after the Jamaican referendum the annual convention of the People's National Movement adopted a resolution that there should be no discussion of the national crisis until an election had been held in Trinidad. Dr. Williams explained that he could not interfere with his island's domestic needs by talking about federation, because Trinidad and Tobago came first. As the national constitution made no provision for secession, he argued that Jamaica's withdrawal was illegal, the Federation had consequently ceased to exist, and all that was left was a caretaker government. One from ten left nothing, not nine.[16]

Despite his official silence Dr. Williams's views were indicated, not only by his jocular arithmetic, but by his public description of the Lancaster House agreements as a 'violation of every federal concept' and a 'total sell-out to Jamaica', at the expense of antagonizing Trinidad and Tobago. To his mind their implementation would make the West Indies 'the laughing stock of the entire world'. The Jamaican referendum had set back for a generation the whole Caribbean region. He had refrained from stating his opinions at the London Conference of June 1961 only because the Colonial Secretary had persuaded him to hold his hand.[17]

The fact that the Trinidad opposition, led and dominated by East Indians, continued after the referendum to urge adherence to the Federation probably increased Dr. Williams's antagonism to it. He reiterated his determination to reject Dr. Capildeo's demand that Trinidad's position on the matter should be a major election issue.

If Trinidadians supported the proposed new federal constitution, Dr. Williams warned, he himself would retire from public life rather than become a party to bastardizing the Federation. In his view Trinidad had participated long enough in this 'tomfoolery'.[18] Unlike Mr. Manley, he was genuinely prepared to stake his political future on the issue. The Jamaican press argued that these statements clearly confirmed the wisdom of Jamaica's secession, since Dr. Williams would in any event have refused to support the Lancaster House agreements.[19]

As the Premier of Trinidad declined to attend any conference called by the Prime Minister of the West Indies, it was impossible during the crucial last three months of 1961 for the federal government to initiate discussions with the leaders of the remaining territories. Moreover Trinidad's official silence was paralleled by that of the United Kingdom. Presumably in the belief that the first necessity was for West Indians to set their own house in order, it neither suggested further constitutional meetings nor conveyed the promised conference on additional economic assistance for the Leewards and Windwards. Indeed when the Secretary of State for the Colonies was asked in the British House of Commons on 19 December 1961 what steps were being taken to give more financial aid to the Caribbean, his reply was discouraging. He regretted that, owing to Britain's own economic problems and adverse balance of trade, he saw no present prospects of increasing the £5 million a year already given the West Indian territories through the Colonial Development and Welfare Fund, plus £2 million additional for grants-in-aid.

Under these gloomy circumstances Sir Grantley Adams threw himself wholeheartedly into a struggle which required all his native optimism. 'I feel in my bones', he declared shortly after his return from London, 'that the Federation of the West Indies will survive'. It would remain in existence, he emphasized, until the Parliament of the United Kingdom modified the British Caribbean Federation Act of 1956. Its future depended on whether enough people believed in West Indian nationhood to preserve it.[20]

His views were supported by Dr. Philip Sherlock, later Principal of the University of the West Indies, in a moving broadcast on the crushing blow dealt British Caribbean unity by Jamaica's decision. 'The work of fourteen years of discussion and negotiation', he said, 'has been brought to nothing in a day, the expenditure of many hundreds of thousands of pounds turned to waste, a solemn compact between governments and peoples broken, the forces of separatism and faction strengthened, our stature as a nation diminished, . . . by a decision springing out of a heritage of colonial parochialism'. In this desolate moment he asked whether the sense of West Indian nationhood was a deception, whether the peoples of the region were doomed to remain fragmented and set apart from each other, not by the sea, but by decisions of their own making. Himself a distinguished West Indian, Dr. Sherlock concluded that there was indeed a recognizable British Caribbean community, if only because the islanders shared a common heritage of history, language, and laws.[21]

These sentiments were echoed by the Governor General, Lord Hailes, who stressed that the need for unity was never greater and the reasons for federating no less cogent than fifteen years earlier. In a radio address he appealed to West Indians to fight the parochialism and selfishness which were the enemies of all progress.[22]

Attitude of the Eastern Caribbean

The small islands, for their part, refrained from embarrassing Dr. Williams before the Trinidadian election by asking him to state his intentions, although it was difficult for them to make plans without knowing the attitude of Trinidad and Tobago. They themselves were divided as to their future, about which various views were propounded. Opposition members in Antigua demanded that it also should withdraw from the Federation. The Chief Minister of Dominica, E.O. LeBlanc, showed more grasp of reality in arguing that the Leewards and Windwards should espouse a strong central government and reduced local legislatures and ministerial establishments.

These views were supported by John Compton and J.D. Bousquet of the ruling St. Lucia Labour Party. The former contended that ministerial systems were too expensive in the smaller territories where money could be used more advantageously to improve their economies. He advocated a revamped national constitution with power concentrated in a strong federal government. Although anxious to see the union survive, Mr. Bousquet called on all the small islands to redouble their efforts to achieve full internal self-government. Hunter François, president of the Opposition People's Progressive Party in St. Lucia, announced, however, that he would rather see the island remain a colony than 'be tied to Trinidad's apron strings as a pauper'.[23]

By November 1961 Principal Arthur (later Sir Arthur) Lewis of the University College of the West Indies, who had visited the Eastern Caribbean islands after the referendum as a special adviser to Sir Grantley, reported that Barbados and the Leewards and Windwards all wished to continue to be federated with each other and with Trinidad and Tobago. Should Trinidad, like Jamaica, opt for independence alone, the remaining eight territories wanted to remain federated under the leadership of Barbados. They unanimously rejected the idea of a unitary state. He found widespread agreement that Jamaica's secession had made possible a much stronger and more practicable union, and that the small islanders were united by the common sympathy essential for any successful federation but never felt by Jamaica for the Eastern Caribbean.

Most thoughtful West Indians in the area, he believed, considered that its fragmentation into independent countries whose people regarded each other as foreigners, would be a tragedy for which its authors would have to answer at the bar of history. He proposed an Eastern Caribbean Federation with a strong central government and a marked decrease in the administrative structures of the constituent islands, but acknowledged that the latter suggestion would be strongly resisted by certain Chief Ministers.[24]

Trinidad and Tobago Election, 1961

As Trinidad and Tobago election campaign progressed, Dr. Williams's attacks on the Federation multiplied. He was soon describing it as 'the biggest scandal in the West Indies', conceived for the purpose of intriguing against Trinidad. The region, in his view, would have been 'in a bigger mess' if Jamaica had decided to remain in a union so weak as to be worthless. There had already been one referendum too many, and he did not propose to have another in Trinidad. If, however, one were held, he was convinced that 90% of the electorate would vote 'to go it alone'. When Jamaica withdrew, 'everything mash up'.[25]

Trinidad's opposition Democratic Labour Party continued strongly to support the Federation and vainly to demand that its future be an issue in the election. Dr. Williams steadily continued to refuse this and even declined to allow the legislature to debate what stand the island should take. He promised, however, after the election, to hold a series of public meetings to educate the public on issues involved in Federation.[26]

If some Trinidadians were alarmed by his attitude, they found little comfort in the exhortations of his rival, Dr. Capildeo, to Democratic Labour Party supporters to arm themselves to break up meetings of the People's National Movement, march on Government House, and take over the country.[27] Dr. Williams reacted with a threat to deal with profiteers who helped finance the opposition. Ten days before the election the tense political situation in Trinidad exploded into violence, when gangs armed with stones and cutlasses smashed cars, chased political opponents through the streets, and broke into homes.

There, as in Jamaica, short-lived minor parties proliferated. The Trinidad East Indian Congress, standing for equal rights for Indians, appeared on the scene in August 1961. In the following month, Victor Bryan, a federal member of parliament, launched the United Labour Party, a working-class body dedicated to the ideals of Captain Cipriani. The left-wing West Indies Independence Party, chaired by Lennox Pierre, a solicitor, and founded in 1952 but quiescent since 1956, briefly re-emerged but did not contest the election. Uriah Butler, leader of the Home Rule Party, returned to the political scene, and the African National Congress appeared on it. In October the West Indian National Party for American Federation was formed by Jeeboda Ramtahal two days after he had conceived the brilliant notion of federal union between Trinidad and the United States.

In a series of articles in the *Sunday Guardian* Albert Gomes, maverick member of the federal opposition, conducted a lively one-man campaign to preserve the Federation. He attacked as completely undemocratic the Trinidadian ruling party's refusal to state its stand on the one really vital issue: the future of the Federation. He condemned its acquisition of the British West Indian Airlines as 'a potentially dangerous anomaly' involving operation by one island of a 'patently national amenity'. He criticized Dr. Williams's recent appointment of a High Commissioner to London as implying independence for Trinidad, although the electorate had not been consulted. Why, he asked, should the man who had long advocated a Caribbean union including the French and Dutch territories, wish to break up the existing British West Indian Federation, the logical precursor to wider regional co-operation? Further fragmentation, he argued, would be disastrous.[28]

In the Trinidadian election of 4 December 1961, the first held under its new constitution, Dr. Williams was supported by two powerful factors in the community: the National Trades Union Congress and the Roman Catholic Church. In a record poll of over 88% of the electorate his party won a resounding victory and increased its majority, securing twenty of the thirty seats in the House of Representatives and 57.7% of the popular vote, as opposed to ten seats and 40.8% of the popular vote won by Dr. Capildeo. The People's National Movement captured all four seats in Port-of-Spain, both seats in San Fernando, Trinidad's second major town, and the two seats in Tobago. Other parties failed to elect any members. This outcome owed much to Dr. Williams's own conspicuous ability and to the success of his Five Year Development Programme, his scheme for free secondary education, his policy of spreading wealth, his effective party organization, and — a novelty in Trinidad — his administration's honest and stable government.

The rival Democratic Labour Party suffered from internal dissension, lack of any specific programme apart from support for the Federation and dislike of the People's National Movement, as well as from the fact that it was almost exclusively based on a racial appeal to East Indians. It retained three seats in the Caroni sugar belt and others in southern constituencies, but failed to win any in the suburbs or in Port-of-Spain, where election forecasts had favoured Dr. Capildeo. At a party meeting to celebrate his victory Dr. Williams described the Federation as a 'disgraceful episode', wherein Britain and the United States had brought constant pressure to bear on Trinidad and Tobago to support a union which Jamaica then proceeded to smash and Barbados to repudiate.[29]

Barbados Election, 1961

On the same day as the Trinidadians, Barbadians also went to the polls, where only 60% of their electorate voted. In the twenty-four-member House of Assembly the representation of the Barbados Labour Party, long presided over by Sir Grantley Adams and in power for the past fifteen years, dropped from fifteen seats to five. The seventy-year-old Premier, Dr. H.G. Cummins, who had succeeded Sir Grantley, lost his seat, as did all but one of his ministerial colleagues.

An impressive victory of fourteen seats was won by the able Errol Barrow's Democratic Labour Party, which had originated in 1955 as a splinter group composed of Sir Grantley's erstwhile followers who had become dissatisfied with his personal domination. Mr. Barrow, however, gained only 36.3% of the votes, as opposed to 36.8% for the Barbados Labour Party. Four seats and 22% of the votes were secured by the Barbados National Party led by Ernest Mottley, perennial Mayor of Bridgetown, while the remaining seat went to an Independent. The defeat of the Barbados Labour Party doubtless sprang in part from its very long term of office and in part from the absence in Port-of-Spain of its leading personality, Sir Grantley. While his prestige had helped to hold his followers together, his sometimes autocratic stand had often created irritation.

Trinidad's Decision

The new Secretary of State for the Colonies, Reginald Maudling, who had succeeded Mr. Macleod in October, visited the West Indies from 13 to 28 January 1962. After a brief initial interview with him Dr. Williams refused to discuss the question of federation, on the ground that he could not commit Trinidad and Tobago until his party convention reached a decision. Less than twenty-four hours later the General Council of the People's National Movement approved a resolution to reject unequivocally participation in any Eastern Caribbean federation and to 'proceed forthwith to national independence'.[30] The unitary state of Trinidad and Tobago would, it said, nevertheless be willing to contemplate incorporating any territory in the area whose people so desired. All the small islands except Grenada viewed this tactlessly worded proposal as a calculated insult, designed to parade their poverty. They promptly reacted by announcing their desire for a new federation without Trinidad and Tobago.

The resolution was, however, accepted both by the party as a whole and by Dr. Williams's government. An alternative motion by Andrew Rose, Federal Minister of Communications and later High Commissioner for Trinidad and Tobago in Canada and in the United Kingdom, was withdrawn when it became clear that this had no chance of success. Mr. Rose had advocated participation by Trinidad in a strong and centralized Eastern Caribbean federation.

The extremely lengthy resolution of the General Council of the People's National Movement set forth a detailed catalogue of Trinidad's grievances against Jamaica, the Leewards and Windwards, the United Kingdom, and the United States. Prominent among these was the complaint that Britain had not indicated how much aid it would in future provide for the small islands, to compensate for 'centuries of maladministration and underdevelopment;. The Federation, according to the resolution, had wasted time and money, frustrated the basic interests of the Caribbean peoples, and encouraged 'foreign intrigues in West Indian affairs, on such issues as Chaguaramas and Venezuela, thereby aggravating the basic conflict between the Government of Trinidad and Tobago and the Federal Government'. Trinidad was willing to associate itself with all West Indian peoples in a Caribbean Economic Community, but would not participate in an East-ern Caribbean union involving it in major expenditures for the seven grant-aided islands which could not pay their own way. The Federation, the Premier told the House of Representatives, had 'died at Lancaster House and was buried in Jamaica in September 1961'.[31]

In all this it was hard to recognize the party which in 1956 had promised support for a 'strong and vibrant Federation', or the leader who in 1960 in *The Economics of Nationhood* had stressed the need for harmonious co-operation between national and unitary governments and described the Federation as an opportunity to help bridge the gap between the richer and poorer territories. Clearly Dr. Williams considered the Leewards and Windwards a financial burden too great for Trinidad to assume, without Jamaica, and Barbados a questionable asset. His bitterness against other West Indian leaders may also have affected his decision.

Since the federal issue had been purposely excluded from the election campaign, it was impossible to tell how far the people of Trinidad and Tobago supported their government's policy of secession, strongly attacked by the East Indian opposition and by various voluntary groups in the two islands. It was consequently difficult to see on what grounds Port-of-Spain's leading newspaper contended that Trinidadians unanimously desired to advance towards full autonomy without hesitation or discussion of alternative solutions such as participation in an Eastern Caribbean union.[32]

The bitterness occasioned in Trinidad by different views about secession was illustrated by a letter to the local press. 'We were told to vote for Federation', it said, 'and we did so willingly. But no one explained clearly to the masses what Federation is and the benefits to be derived from it. . . Now the cry is independence. What really is independence? The masses do not know . . . One of these bright brains who led us blindly into Federation is leading the people into independence without an explanation, and again without giving us a chance to choose. What are we heading for and what are we to expect? The majority do not know'.[33] The South Trinidad Chamber of Commerce protested against dissolution of the Federation without proper recourse to the people or their representatives and without any serious attempt by Dr. Williams's administration to preserve West Indian unity.[34]

His government's intention to withdraw from the Federation was announced five weeks after Trinidad's election and the promised public meetings on the issue were not held. Many letters in the local press expressed 'profound disappointment' at the stand of the General Council and executive of the People's National Movement, while columnists variously described the decision to secede as 'a crime against West Indian history', and as 'unrealistic, untimely, and self-centred.[35] West Indians abroad, including the London branch of the People's National Movement, were equally critical about Trinidad seeking independence alone. With similar forthrightness Jamaican students in Britain and Canada had condemned their island's referendum and called for a strenuous campaign to reverse it.[36]

An Eastern Caribbean Federation?

The Leewards and Windwards reacted to the Trinidad government's decision to seek unilateral independence by holding a conference which agreed to continue the Federation without Jamaica or Trinidad but, if possible, with Barbados. To an invitation to attend this meeting Dr. Williams vouchsafed no reply. All government leaders in the Eastern Caribbean territories, except Mr. Bird of Antigua and Mr. Barrow of Barbados, who declined to attend, met with Sir Grantley, Sir Arthur Lewis, and Mr. Maudling to discuss the matter.

At subsequent meetings, Mr. Maudling examined the future of the smaller islands with the Premier of Barbados and the Chief Ministers of the Leewards and Windwards. From these conversations they insisted on excluding Sir Grantley and any other representatives of the national government. Their attitude was partially explained by the fact that the new Chief Minister of Barbados, the thirty-nine year old lawyer and economist, Mr. Barrow, was Sir Grantley's chief political rival in the island. The political leaders of the remaining units, promptly dubbed the 'Little Eight', told the Colonial Secretary that they wanted to form a new federation, with a capital in Barbados, to become independent in January 1963.[37]

Continuance of gradually declining grants-in-aid from the United Kingdom they considered essential to the success of this enterprise. They recalled Britain's promise, at the 1961 Constitutional Conference, to discuss financial assistance to the Leewards and Windwards. The Premier of Barbados stated that his island did not support Dr. Williams's suggestion about establishing a Caribbean Community and, indeed, wished in future to have no economic dealings with Trinidad.

The Secretary of State for the Colonies, while at first unenthusiastic, eventually described the proposal for an Eastern Caribbean federation as 'a very promising and encouraging idea', and said that Britain realized the dangers of fragmentation in the West Indies. He warned, however, that any

new union would require careful consideration, especially as to its constitution, distribution of powers, and economic and financial viability, and should not have local administrations too expensive for its members to support.[38]

His caution was understandable. Alleged financial irregularities in four of the eight territories were then being investigated by the Colonial Office. Barbados's revenues from income tax were almost seven times those of St. Kitts, the next most prosperous Eastern Caribbean island. The imbalance in population and wealth among the different units, which caused many of the old Federation's problems, would obviously be repeated and accentuated in the new. Most small islands showed little concern to reduce the cost of insular administrations or to establish a strong centre. Although supporting a modified version of Sir Arthur Lewis's recommendations, most wanted a far weaker national government than he had advocated.

Moreover there were obviously important differences of opinion in the Eastern Caribbean. In Dominica E.B. Henry, leader of the opposition United People's Party, cabled Mr. Maudling protesting against the proposed new federation, because its peoples had no assurance that they would benefit from it. To seek independence before economic stability had been achieved struck him as ludicrous.

A St. Lucian member of parliament thought that, while a federation of the Little Eight would be ideal, it should be based in St. Lucia, although Barbados would naturally command 'great deference'. The People's Progressive Party, one of St. Lucia's two opposition groups, also objected to an Eastern Caribbean federation as economically unviable, since seven of the eight territories, unable to balance their budgets, were financially dependent on British taxpayers. It preferred to see the individual islands go their own way. What, it demanded, had the Leewards and Windwards to gain from a new union which would once more saddle them with 'a ludicrous circus of Governors, Chief Ministers, Senators, etc., requiring an initial $4 million to establish?

John Compton, however, leader of St. Lucia's National Labour Movement, like Eric Gairy, Chief Minister of Grenada, urged careful study of Trinidad's offer of unitary statehood and accused the federal government of intrigue and sabotage.[39] George Charles, Chief Minister of St. Lucia, while supporting a new union of the Eastern Caribbean islands, emphasized their strong spirit of nationalism and insisted that they would never become wards either of any federation or of Trinidad and Tobago.[40] An editorial in the island's leading paper, the *Voice of St. Lucia,* said that, while there had always been much to recommend a unitary state or strong federation of the British territories, recent events demonstrated that West Indians were not ready for either. The thinly veiled contempt of Dr. Williams's party for the small islands was scarcely ingratiating.[41]

The Times (London) in an able leading article argued that it would be less wise for the small islands to embark on a 'Lilliputian Federation', with all the costs of independence, than to consider joining the united state of Greater Trinidad.[42] *The Daily Gleaner*, conveniently ignoring Jamaica's conspicuous contribution to West Indian disruption, observed ungraciously: 'It may be that Mr. Maudling is hoping that Trinidad will pull Britain's chestnuts out of the fire. . . In any event, opportunism and cynicism are not the answers to the problems of the "Little Eight" '.[43] The *West Indian Economist* criticized the Secretary of State for encouraging the small islands to view federalism as a means of preserving the privileges and powers of local politicians, and argued strongly for unitary government under Barbados.[44]

Jamaican Independence Conference and 1962 Election

Within a week of the Colonial Secretary's return to London the Jamaican Independence Conference of 1–9 February 1962 opened in the same hall at Lancaster House where, eight months earlier, Mr. Manley and his colleagues had helped to fashion a revised constitution for the West Indies Federation. If the Jamaican Premier detected any irony in the situation, it was not apparent in his reference to his island's 'experimental trial marriage' with the other territories, whose peaceful termination, he said, set 'an example to the world of democracy in action'. Mr. Manley and his colleagues (equally divided between government and opposition representatives) preferred laying ghosts to resurrecting them.

It was not a politician, but a distinguished West Indian journalist, Theodore Sealy, editor of the Jamaican *Gleaner*, who recalled that the last time he had sat in that hall, 'we all thought we were making history; we were starting a new nation, the Federation of the West Indies. How wrong we were!'[45] An opposition representative with an odd sense of history, Donald Sangster (later Prime Minister of Jamaica), observed that Jamaica had started on the road to independence and merely 'paused on the way to help the Federation'.[46]

In his opening address to the conference the Secretary of State for the Colonies said many people had hoped that Jamaica would exhibit the political maturity it had shown at home on a wider federal stage, in conjunction with its Eastern Caribbean neighbours. Many regretted that the referendum had ended this possibility, but the British government felt bound to accept and implement the Jamaican electorate's decision. In an apposite reference to Donne's famous passage, he reminded the delegates that in the modern world no country could be 'an island entire of itself'.[47]

The conference eventually approved a new constitution for Jamaica drafted by a bipartisan Joint Select Committee of its legislature. The United Kingdom agreed that on 6 August 1962 the island should become independent: an event likely to be greeted, observed a British writer, with 'muffled cheers'.[48] It also undertook to support Jamaica's desire, on achieving independence, to be accepted as a member of the Commonwealth.

The Jamaican election of 10 April 1962 determined that the presiding genius at these celebrations would be the seventy-eight-year-old Sir Alexander Bustamante, who defeated his cousin by a margin of under 1% or less than three thousand votes. Mr. Manley campaigned under the slogan of 'The Man with the Plan', the opposition as 'The Party with a Programme', with Sir Alexander described as 'The Father of Freedom'. The People's National Party, appealing as the spokesman of the poor black majority, adopted Marcus Garvey's motto: 'Forward Ever, Backward Never'. The campaign was tempestuous. Riot squads of policemen were unable to prevent clashes at political meetings enlivened by stone-throwing and the use of pistols.

In a record poll of 71.6% of the electorate the Jamaica Labour Party, with 49.7% of the votes, won twenty-six seats in the House of Representatives, while the People's National Party, with 48.9% of the votes, won the remaining nineteen. Millard Johnson's People's Political Party contested sixteen seats and Independent candidates eight, but all failed to return any members. In the referendum less than 62% of the electorate had voted. Clearly far more Jamaicans were interested in insular politics than in the future of the Federation. In view of the referendum results, those of the election were not unexpected. A majority of the voters evidently preferred Sir Alexander's warm-hearted understanding of ordinary people to Mr. Manley's hard-headed, efficient, and somewhat academic approach to the country's problems.

Last Days of the Federation

Before leaving Port-of-Spain the Secretary of State for the Colonies had told Sir Grantley's cabinet that he intended to recommend dissolution of the Federation. On 6 February 1962 he explained the situation in the West Indies to the British House of Commons. The Jamaican electorate, Mr. Maudling pointed out, had indicated its desire to withdraw from the Federation, as had the government of Trinidad and Tobago, which had also decided not to join any Eastern Caribbean union. The Premier of Barbados and the Chief Ministers of the Leewards and Windwards, while favouring a new federal union among their territories, agreed that the present one should be dissolved. Under these circumstances the government of the United Kingdom regretfully concluded that it had no alternative but to arrange for dissolution of the existing Federation and to set up an interim organization, under a commissioner appointed by Britain, to administer certain common enterprises (such as the university and national shipping and meteorological services) until some permanent arrangements could be made.[49]

The West Indies Bill to dissolve the Federation on 31 May 1962 was introduced in the House of Lords on 1 March and passed the Commons on 2 April. It provided for secession by participating units and enabled the United Kingdom to establish a new federation or any other form of government for the British Caribbean territories except Jamaica and Trinidad.

This was not a bill, said Mr. Maudling, that any Secretary of State could propose with pleasure. Marking the end of an experiment on which many people had placed high hopes, it was necessitated by divisions of principles and personalities. The long series of West Indian constitutional conferences had been bedevilled by economic and financial considerations. The British government, as it had told Sir Grantley Adams, had no power to object to the decision of a self-governing country like Jamaica to hold a referendum or like Trinidad to withdraw.

When during the debate in the House of Lords Britain's Conservative government was criticized for allowing Jamaica to hold a referendum, a Labour peer, Lord Ogmore, dissented. What, he asked, could Her Majesty's government have done to prevent this? 'Can anyone imagine, even if we had any battalions to spare, which we have not, that we could contemplate British troops shooting down Jamaicans because they wanted a referendum and we objected to it?' Your Lordships must remember, added the Earl of Perth, 'that these are free adult peoples, and, in the last analysis, they must do what they choose'.[50]

The United Kingdom, Mr. Maudling believed, should proceed with caution on the proposed new union of the eight Eastern Caribbean islands, to be sure that this would be securely founded and finan-

cially viable, with an adequate central organization and reasonable machinery of government. Their total land area was smaller than that of Shropshire or Wiltshire and their combined population less than that of Herefordshire. Under these circumstances, eight chief ministers, cabinets, and legislatures seemed an unnecessarily substantial and expensive governmental structure.

The Labour opposition regretted the need for the bill but agreed that there was no alternative, although various members pointed out that until recently Britain had refused the right of secession to members of the Central African Federation. One Labour member, however, Denis Healey, who supported Mr. Maudling's tribute to Sir Grantley Adams, complained that, although there was no part of the Commonwealth to which it owed a greater obligation, the United Kingdom had given many people in the British Caribbean 'an impression of bored indifference to their opinion' by its conduct over the Commonwealth Immigrants Bill. Despite the fact that most of their forefathers had gone there as slaves or indentured labourers, West Indians had always been distinguished by exceptional loyalty and all considered themselves British. It was time, he argued, for the United Kingdom to begin thinking about the region as part of the whole Caribbean and Central America. In this area of major concern to the United States it was possible that Canada, rather than Britain, would eventually be the most influential member of the Commonwealth. Like other speakers he argued consideration of a joint Commonwealth contribution to the British West Indies.[51]

Representatives of the Little Eight, meeting at Barbados from 26 February to 3 March 1962, could not agree to ratify the memorandum on a new union which they had presented to the Secretary of State for the Colonies. They forwarded a resolution to him declaring that the 'Save the Federation' mission then in London had no authority to speak for the Eastern Caribbean and requesting a meeting of the Little Eight before dissolution of the existing Federation. Despite diverse views about their future, they announced that, while they wanted a new union, they wished no further part in the old one.

The last days of The West Indies were undignified. The Premier of Barbados and the Chief Ministers of the Leewards and Windwards refused, as had Dr. Williams, to discuss future plans with Sir Grantley and his cabinet. After the Jamaican referendum, the announcement that Trinidad also would withdraw, and the defeat of Sir Grantley's party in Barbados, many members from these three territories ceased to attend sessions of the federal legislature. Thus the Prime Minister and the rump of his parliament were more and more isolated and increasingly powerless to influence the course of events. They made, however, determined efforts to do what they could.

Sir Grantley announced his conviction that posterity would condemn Jamaica and Trinidad and history prove them wrong. Never before, he said, had there been unilateral repudiation of a federation whose constitution made no provision for secession.[52] During the last sessions of the national House of Representatives debate degenerated into an unedifying post mortem on apportioning blame for destroying the union. The decision of Jamaica and Trinidad to secede was bitterly attacked, as was the Colonial Office for permitting them to do so and failing to give more financial assistance or to consult adequately with the federal government. Certain members, however, acknowledged the part played by West Indians' 'fatal tendency to quarrel with each other' and to put their own interests before those of the nation.[53]

Outside the national parliament there was severe criticism of its members' decision to vote themselves, from dwindling federal funds, BWI $352,000 or some $18,000 apiece as disengagement compensation, although a pension for the Prime Minister was generally approved. The sharpest criticism was provoked by the belated inclusion of a token sum of $10 to compensate federal civil servants. The West Indies' parliament concluded its final sitting without making any further provision for its public officials. On 2 May 1962 it was notified by the Secretary of State for the Colonies that the United Kingdom had approved a compensation scheme based on recommendations of a working party composed of officials of the British Colonial Office and the federal and unit governments.

Debate on a motion by an Independent member of the West Indian parliament to oppose attempts to destroy the Federation ended with an unanimous vote of approval and a standing ovation for Sir Grantley. In a speech condemning Dr. Williams's constant attacks on the national government, the Prime Minister blamed the Federation's failure primarily on Colonial Office intrigues in West Indian affairs. The United Kingdom, he complained, had neither informed nor consulted his government about the timing of the bill to dissolve the Federation.[54] A bi-partisan delegation including members of both federal houses was appointed to request discussions with the British government.

The so-called 'Save the Federation' mission, led by Sir Grantley, spent five days in London before obtaining an audience with the Secretary of State for the Colonies on 13 March. By that time the bill

to dissolve the union had passed its second reading in the House of Lords. Mr. Maudling then informed the West Indian delegation that he would neither withdraw his promise to allow Jamaica to secede nor force Trinidad to hold a referendum before doing likewise. In a letter to him Sir Grantley described the dissolution bill as retrograde, arbitrary, and hurried.

From Sir Grantley's point of view, insult was added to injury by a British order-in-council of 14 March 1962, about which he first learned from the London newspapers. This empowered the Governor General of the West Indies to act against the advice of his ministers and to refuse assent to measures passed by its parliament. The reason for its passage was to block payments by the national government of compensation and repatriation expenses to ministers and members of parliament when the Federation was dissolved. While the United Kingdom agreed that there might be a case for grants to parliamentarians, it considered the sum voted excessive in view of the West Indies' slender remaining resources and its failure to propose any adequate compensation for federal civil servants. Among the last acts of the national cabinet was a protest against a decision by the Secretary of State for the Colonies that the federal Prime Minister, Speaker, and ministers would receive terminal payments equivalent to three months' salary but that no such compensation would be given senators or members of the House of Representatives.

On his return to Port-of-Spain Sir Grantley attacked this British order-in-council as 'shabby treatment', designed to strip his cabinet of power. The United Kingdom's actions, he added, although legal, were highly immoral. The British order-in-council also provoked a telegram of protest to the Secretary of State for the Colonies from the Premier of Barbados, no friend of Sir Grantley, who pointed out that for over three hundred years the United Kingdom had not legislated in this manner for his island.[55]

The last session of the federal parliament, from 9 to 11 April 1962, was largely devoted to recriminations by the one-third of its members who attended. The legislature reiterated its previous condemnation of the United Kingdom, the Governor General, Mr. Manley, and Dr. Williams. It passed a unanimous motion deploring the fact that successive Secretaries of State for the Colonies had made no effort to preserve the Federation. Reporting to parliament on his mission to London, the Prime Minister stated that he had never been so humiliated as by Mr. Maudling, who had for five days refused to see him and eventually talked with him for only fifteen minutes. In a farewell message on his final departure from Port-of-Spain Sir Grantley described the Federation's collapse as 'a shattering blow, . . .fatal to the idea of West Indian unity'. Yet he voiced hope that time would heal present wounds and that from the ashes of the old union one Caribbean nation would eventually arise.[56]

His eloquence could not conceal the triumph of what Mr. Manley at Montego Bay had called 'the vested interest of ambition in power'. In the acid words of a St. Lucian, 'the power-spree that was the first West Indian Federation' had ended.[57] At midnight on 31 May 1962 the Federation was formally dissolved. The national flag was lowered, while buglers sounded the last post. This concluded the aspirations and hard work of many able West Indians and successive British Colonial Secretaries.

Trinidad and Tobago Independence Conference

Three days earlier the Trinidad and Tobago Independence Conference had opened at Marlborough House in London.[58] The opposition Democratic Labour Party had bitterly attacked the decision by Dr. Williams's administration to withdraw from the Federation without holding an election on the issue and without serious consideration of joining a new Eastern Caribbean union. Hence it was understandable that Trinidad's proposed constitution, unlike Jamaica's, was not based on agreement between the island's two major parties. This could scarcely have been obtained, since Dr. Capildeo accused the Trinidadian government of autocracy and of drafting the new constitution prematurely, and had made a fruitless visit to London to lobby members of the British House of Commons in the interests of what he described as preserving democracy in Trinidad and Tobago.[59]

The draft independence constitution published on 20 February by Dr. Williams's government had been widely distributed. The general public and private organizations were both invited to submit written comments by 31 March, a deadline the government refused to extend. The proposed new constitution ironically aroused far less general interest than preparations for Trinidad's famous carnival. Yet within the brief period allowed, over one hundred and sixty submissions requested constitutional changes, especially as to guarantees for civil and political liberties, which many considered inadequate.

Among the groups submitting comments were the Civil Service Association, the Indian Association of Trinidad and Tobago, and the African

National Congress. Wherever a right or freedom was guaranteed, the Civil Service Association protested, it was nullified by qualifications. The Indian Association complained that the new constitution struck 'at the very root of the independence of the judiciary' and of individual liberties, while completely ignoring such important safeguards in the British constitution as an informed public opinion. The African National Congress contended that the proposed constitution established a legalized dictatorship and recommended that it be scrapped.[60]

From 25 to 27 April the Trinidadian government discussed numerous proposed changes at a conference of some two hundred people. Although the press was excluded and opposition members walked out of the meetings, Dr. Williams described them as a landmark and their conclusions as the closest approximation to national unity yet achieved. Certain amendments arising out of these consultations were accepted by his cabinet and examined by a twenty-one member Joint Select Committee of both houses of the legislature, which included members of the opposition. The Democratic Labour Party nevertheless complained that, after several days' deliberation, its essential differences with the government remained. A revised version of the draft constitution, approved on 11 May by a majority of sixteen to one on a straight party vote in the House of Representatives, formed the basis for discussion at the Trinidad and Tobago Independence Conference at Marlborough House. These meetings, from 28 May to 8 June 1962, convened in accordance with the Secretary of State's agreement that the territory should become independent as soon as possible, were attended by two officials delegations from Trinidad and Tobago, one from the ruling People's National Movement and the other from the Opposition Democratic Labour Party.

Voluntary organizations also sent unofficial teams of varying sizes which presented diverse proposals, ranging from protest against the way in which the constitution had been drafted to suggestions for partition, proportional representation, or incorporation of Trinidad and Tobago into the United Kingdom. Among these bodies were two Indian organizations, the Samatan Dharma Mahasabha and the Indian Association. East Indians, who then formed over one-third of the population, were particularly fearful about their position in an independent Trinidad ruled by a predominantly black government. Local journalists promptly recognized that Trinidad's reputation was unlikely to be enhanced by all these rival delegations. To one sunday *Guardian* commentator the spectacle suggested 'a degree of immaturity unsurpassed in the smallest or weakest West Indian island'.[61]

A threatened deadlock at the conference was finally resolved, largely owing to tactful compromises proposed by the Secretary of State for the Colonies. Careful entrenchment of safeguards on important issues met the opposition's major demands. The last session culminated in wide agreement among government, opposition, and independent observers. At the delegates' unanimous wish, the United Kingdom willingly undertook to support Trinidad and Tobago's application to become an autonomous member of the Commonwealth. While Trinidadians were relieved by the outcome of the conference, many regretted that the independence inaugurated on 31 August 1962 was for their islands alone, not for the whole British Caribbean.

Why Did the Federation Fail?

The rapid decline and fall of the West Indies Federation, reminiscent of the inexorability of a Greek tragedy, provoked much discussion about 'the Federation betrayed' or 'Who killed Cock Robin?' Why did the principal protagonists act as they did? Was the union, as Premier Barrow of Barbados maintained, an essentially 'unfederatable federation?' Could anything have been done to avoid the death of a state whose birth only four years earlier had been so enthusiastically acclaimed? These questions were widely asked throughout the West Indies, where in many quarters there was a marked tendency to shift responsibility for the débacle to other shoulders.

The favourite but not invariable scapegoat was the United Kingdom. Jamaicans also blamed Trinidad and the federal government. Trinidadians blamed Sir Grantley, Jamaica, and the Colonial Office. The small islands blamed all three, but especially the two largest territories. The federal government blamed Britain, Jamaica, and Trinidad. Before the Federation's collapse its opponents criticized the United Kingdom for encouraging union in the first place. When Jamaica and Trinidad opted for withdrawal, its supporters attacked Britain for allowing them to secede.

During the years between the Montego Bay Conference of 1947 and the break-up of the Federation in 1962 two myths gained wide currency in the Caribbean. Federalism, it was said, had been forced on reluctant West Indians by a negligent imperial power indecently eager, after lucrative centuries of slavery and subjection, to slough off unwanted because no longer profitable dependencies. It was also alleged that the United Kingdom improperly withheld independence from the Federation. There is little evidence to support either of these views.

All British parties realized that it was impracticable, in the mid-twentieth century, to compel colonies eager for autonomy to remain dependent and none desired to do so. As far back as 1828 Wellington had declared in the House of Lords: 'We have not the power of governing . . . colonies by force any more than we have the power of governing this country by force'.[62] A decade later Macaulay said of India that the result of exporting free political institutions would be elimination of the British.

The United Kingdom's reduced economic position after 1945 rendered it unable to defray the obligations of empire and to provide monetary assistance on the scale which the Caribbean islands considered their due. Without help most smaller territories could not balance their budgets. Few West Indians sympathized with Britain's financial difficulties, produced by its major role in the Second World War. Many found it simpler to accuse the United Kingdom both of attempting to 'divide and rule' and of urging them to unite. Yet at least since the last 1940s their political problems stemmed far more from themselves than from the Colonial Office.

Acute economic distress during the 1930s fostered the rise of Caribbean trade unions and political parties which demanded first self-government and then independence. British and West Indians alike originally believed that the only way in which the Caribbean territories could fulfill this aspiration was through some form of union. For this reason successive Labour and Conservative governments in the United Kingdom supported the federation long debated and many times approved by all West Indian legislatures. Delay in its establishment was occasioned solely by Britain's insistence that the peoples concerned must be sure that they wanted to unite and agreed on the form which union should take. In response to the colonies' urgent demands, federation was fostered, never forced, by the United Kingdom. Final decisions were wisely left to West Indians.

The *Report* of the Standing Closer Association Committee, as its Grenadian member, J.B. Renwick, pointed out, was prepared by West Indians. No outside source determined its decisions, which resulted from 'West Indian imagination or lack of imagination'.[63] Grantley Adams had told the Barbados legislature in 1948 that the British officials on this committee emphasized that it was for West Indians to determine the type of constitution they wanted; 'all we are going to do is . . . our utmost to help you to go along the path that you are choosing for yourselves'. Eight years later he declared that nothing had been 'pushed down the throat of the West Indies by the Colonial Office; they have emphasized that they have left it to the West Indies to create their own constitution'.[64]

Norman Manley said in the Jamaican House of Representatives in 1955 that it was not 'the British Government which is keeping the Federal Parliament in a lower status. It is the inability so far of the people of the territories to agree to accept a large measure of responsibility'. When asked in 1958 why the Federation was not independent, he answered: 'Perhaps the timidity of West Indians . . . The British Government is not withholding self-government from the people of the West Indies; we can have full self-government whenever we ask for it, and we West Indians alone will decide when to ask for it'.[65]

Three years later, at the opening session of the West Indies Constitutional Conference, Sir Grantley Adams also referred to the United Kingdom's readiness to grant independence as soon as the British Caribbean peoples could resolve their difficulties. 'It is one of the very good features of our post-war relationship with Britain', he said, 'that the popular will in the West Indies and the policy of the metropolitan power have been directed at an identical dénouement of the historical drama in which we have been involved for more than three hundred years'.[66]

The facts of the matter did not deter the Jamaican press from asserting, both before and after dissolution, that the 'ill-starred Federation was the creation of the Colonial Office'.[67] The above comments by Caribbean leaders provide ample evidence, however, that, whatever its shortcomings, the Federation was made in the West Indies by West Indians and could have achieved autonomy when it wished.

As Harold Macmillan frankly told the federal parliament in March 1961, no matter how intoxicating the prospect of self-rule, its attainment would not abolish the difficulties the islands faced, but simply placed the onus for their solution more squarely on themselves. However poor a territory, he said, independence should be linked with determination to achieve the greatest measure of financial autonomy feasible. This in itself would stimulate economic effort but required a change of outlook in a region with few natural resources and long accustomed to financial aid from Britain. Some responsible West Indians agreed with him. Mr. Bradshaw, the Federal Minister of Finance, pointedly reminded his countrymen that they could not call themselves independent but 'keep going cap in hand . . . begging for technical assistance and everything else'.[68] Nevertheless a firm offer by the United Kingdom of additional financial aid for a given period might have helped to woo the Jamaicans and Trinidadians who anticipated from

federation heavy financial liabilities and few economic advantages, and considered hopelessly inadequate the assistance given to the Caribbean by British grants-in-aid and the Colonial Development and Welfare Fund.

When the Federation's difficulties multiplied, it was impossible for the United Kingdom to force increasingly divided territories to work together. Yet in the critical period between the referendum and Mr. Maudling's visit, Britain might possibly have helped by promptly convening a conference to discuss plans with federal and insular governments and by promising greater long-term financial assistance. Ultimately, however, the United Kingdom could not decently bribe unwilling peoples to co-operate.

Most West Indians believed that the Colonial Office had led them to suppose in 1960 that sizeable additional funds for the small islands would be forthcoming. Dr. Williams considered this extremely important because greater economic development, especially in the Windwards, might have reduced unemployment and consequently pressures on Trinidad to admit immigrants from neighbouring islands. At the Lancaster House Conference in 1961, however, the British government insisted that the agenda should be confined to constitutional problems, although it agreed that later in the year another meeting should consider economic aid to the Leewards and Windwards. Because of disputes about the national constitution, these promised discussions were never held.

The veto for each unit on extending the federal government's financial and economic powers, secured at Mr. Manley's insistence, meant that Jamaica or any other one territory could prevent both customs union and central control over development. Dr. Williams bitterly resented the fact that Trinidad and Tobago was given no similar power to block immigration. His strong objection to allowing free entry to other West Indians increased his existing hostility to the Federation. This, coupled with his longstanding belief in a strong national government and conviction that, without Jamaica, Trinidad could not bear the major costs of union probably explained his refusal, between the referendum of 19 September and the Trinidad election of 4 December 1961, to indicate his attitude towards the Federation or to discuss plans for its future.

Two major British policy decisions in 1961–2 created much bitterness in the Caribbean. The first was the Commonwealth Immigrants' Act of 1962, which severely restricted entry to the United Kingdom. Confronted by the acute problem of trying to support too many people in too little space, West Indians believed that this measure was dictated by pure colour prejudice. Dr. Williams was especially critical, because he thought British limitations on immigrations likely to increase neighbouring islanders' demands for admission to Trinidad.

Many people in the United Kingdom sympathized with such West Indian views, even if they thought Dr. Williams illogical in attacking Britain for imposing restrictions he considered reasonable when imposed by Trinidad. 'More than anywhere else in the old colonial empire', wrote Sir Jock Campbell of Bookers (later Lord Campbell of Eskan) in a perceptive letter to *The Times*, 'the West Indies are what we made them. Consciences cannot be cleared by a judicious and tidy withdrawal from sovereignty. We brought the Negro slave and the indentured Indian to the West Indies, and it was we who started the West Indies on their present course. Already, to the great majority of West Indians, the Commonwealth Immigrants Act has seemed like a repudiation of the consequences of our own actions'.[69]

The other policy with no less serious implications for the British Caribbean was the United Kingdom's decision to seek admission to the European Common Market. The Treaty of Rome, signed in March 1954, took effect at the beginning of the next year. In August 1957 the Regional Economic Committee in Barbados appointed an economist to study the consequences for the area of the proposed free trade area within the European Economic Community. West Indians watched the subsequent negotiations with anxiety.

This matter was discussed at the Lancaster House Conference in June 1961, when the government of Trinidad and Tobago circulated a paper on European union. In the following month the Earl of Perth, Minister of State for Colonial Affairs, visited the British Caribbean and discussed with federal and territorial governments the implications for the region if the United Kingdom decided to apply for entry to the European Common Market. He promised that in this event Britain would consult closely at all stages with West Indian and other Commonwealth governments and do its best to safeguard their interests. After his departure the federal House of Representatives passed a unanimous motion that, failing adequate safeguards, Britain's entry would be detrimental to the West Indies and was accordingly opposed by its parliament, which requested representation at every stage of the negotiations.[70]

The islands' economies were then still predominantly agricultural, and their sugar, bananas, and citrus not competitive without traditional imperial preferences. Sales of bauxite and alumina, vitally important to Jamaica and British Guiana, might also be seriously affected if the United Kingdom joined the European Common Market, as almost half of Canada's aluminium and its by-products were exported to Britain and a sizeable additional fraction to Norway and Sweden, who might follow the United Kingdom into the Common Market.

British Guiana's Dutch neighbour, Surinam, a major rival producer of bauxite and alumina, already participated in the European Economic Community as part of the Tripartite Kingdom of the Netherlands. The French West Indies, because Departments of France, were also entitled to free entry for their products, as was oil from French wells in the Sahara. Other members of the European Common Market, including Italy and Greece, produced a variety of citrus fruits, as did North Africa and Israel, which might at some future date apply for membership. While sugar was partially protected by the International Sugar Agreement, similar provisions for citrus and bananas seemed unlikely.

The West Indies Federation, as a British dependency, qualified for the status of an associated overseas territory, and its products might be exported without duty to the European Economic Community, if reciprocal exemptions were extended to member countries, including the United Kingdom. It would, however, face competition from the associated territories of France, Italy, and Belgium, as well as from Surinam.

Although no colony, the West Indies Federation once granted associated overseas status, would lose this on achieving autonomy, approval of an application from an independent West Indies for membership in the European Common Market would involve gradual abolition of the customs duties from which the islands obtained an important portion of their revenue. Membership might also lead to political involvement in European affairs. If Britain joined the European Economic Community, West Indians were afraid that this would accentuate the Caribbean's existing problem of concentration on a few crops produced at high costs. Without special terms of entry for their primary products, they feared that they might face economic disaster.

It was not surprising that few people in the islands were concerned about the plight of a United Kingdom outside the European Common Market. Yet at the Commonwealth Prime Ministers' Conference of 1962 Dr. Williams said that Trinidad, almost all of whose trade was with Britain and Europe, favoured both associate status for itself and the United Kingdom's membership in the Common Market. 'A weak Britain,' he declared, 'is of no use to us at all'.[71] When early in 1963 the United Kingdom's negotiations for entry were vetoed by France, Mr. Manley expressed regret.[72]

Such views, however, were not widely held in the West Indies. Hence, during the last two years of the Federation Caribbean relations with Britain were seriously strained on several grounds.

Most West Indians never really looked on the Federation as their own government. To many it seemed as remote and sometimes almost as unpopular as the British Colonial Office. The difficulty of forming a united community from widely scattered islands separated by geography and history and confronted by acute economic problems, was recognized from the outset. Yet some realistic West Indians acknowledged that their divisions sprang less from the estranging sea than from an estrangement of minds.[73]

The federal government never overcame the suspicion of the unknown which lay at the root of the British Caribbean's passionate insularity. West Indians' lack of familiarity with each other fostered a climate of misunderstanding, contempt, and suspicion uncongenial to the tolerance and co-operation essential for any successful democracy and above all for effective federalism. Brotherhood in race proved a frail bond among peoples who commonly viewed even adjacent islanders more as rivals than neighbours. The specious façade of unity, already crumbling when the Federation was established in 1958, turned out to be criss-crossed by divisions. Inter-island feuds challenged the concept of West Indianism, while hypothetical goodwill give way to bickering.

Even the most patient and experienced statesmen have found federalism difficult. It was no fault of West Indians that they had little practice in operating their own governments. Jamaica, for example, attained universal suffrage only in 1944 and did not gain full responsible government until 1959, a year after the Federation was launched.

Yet, despite all these considerations, failure of local leadership was beyond dispute. During the lifetime of the Federation British Caribbean politicians were noted neither for patience nor for willingness to compromise. A distinguished West Indian, Sir Arthur Lewis, believed it was primarily this failure, rather than internal problems, that destroyed the national union.

Sir Grantley Adams, Mr. Norman Manley, and Dr. Eric Williams, the three major figures in the ruling federal party (although only the Prime Minister had a seat in the national parliament), were all cultivated men of unquestioned ability and integrity. Their calibre would have made them outstanding in any country. So would that of the Federation's galaxy of dedicated senior public servants. Nevertheless acute personal antagonisms among these political leaders steadily exacerbated already difficult circumstances. For the most part they concentrated more on differences than on common goals. On controversial issues they had usually adopted well-publicized positions before arriving at federal conferences, where there was consequently little room for manoeuvre or conciliation. West Indian national parties did not, as in most federations, exert a unifying influence, because they never rose above their origins as loose aggregates of local groupings.

'Our sins, such as they are', a member of the federal parliament wrote in 1961, 'are not of our territories, but of leaders, whose political ambitions, despite their protestations, are still rooted in insular rather than regional achievements. . . The reason why our Federation threatens to fall apart has nothing whatever to do with economic difficulties or physical distances but everything to do with the psychological malady with which West Indian leaders are afflicted. It is the personal power factor that has been threatening the Federation all along the way'.[74] The peoples of the British Caribbean deserved better from able West Indians who preferred ruling their little island kingdoms to fashioning a new state.

'Devoid of programme and consideration for the people', C.L.R. James, secretary of the West Indies Federal Labour Party, said of local politicians, 'they saw federation and met among themselves only to arrange what their governments would get and what they would lose. That is always an important part of any political discussion. But if you are discussing nothing else, then the result is always the violent quarrels, in fact the unseemly squabbles for that is what they were, by which these gentlemen broke up the Federation and disgraced the West Indian people'.[75]

The largest and most prosperous territories naturally proved fittest in the struggle, as the independence, in rapid succession, of Jamaica, Trinidad, Guyana and Barbados subsequently indicated. The economic interests of the more powerful islands triumphed over the ideal of West Indian unity. The Leewards and Windwards, divided among themselves as to their future, had long had their inferior position firmly emphasized by the other territories, as was illustrated by the well-known calypso: 'Small island, go back where you come from'. The two largest and wealthiest units took for granted their natural superiority to the smaller, poorer, and less constitutionally advanced. After the federal election of 1958 they found themselves paying the major costs of a national union less autonomous than Jamaica and with a cabinet dominated by the little islands to which they had long condescended.

Jamaica and Trinidad, accustomed to considering themselves the twin giants of the British Caribbean, found such a position from the outset galling and soon intolerable. The fact that their own governments were largely responsible for this situation made it the more humiliating. A federal state in which Jamaica and Trinidad were subordinate partners never had any chance of survival. As time went on, this became increasingly evident.

The Federation sprang primarily from anti-colonial sentiment and a wish for independence, rather than from a positive desire for unity. Its failure resulted from a variety of causes: inadequate finances, uneven economic and political development in the constituent units, the clashing personalities of its chief architects, and above all from a lack of any positive fellow-feeling among its scattered peoples.

'Nothing', declared Dr. Williams early in 1962, 'least of all a disintegrated Federation of the West Indies', must block the path of Trinidad and Tobago to nationhood.[76] 'It was not that we loved others less', said Donald Sangster of the Jamaica Independence Conference, 'but that we loved Jamaica more'.[77] Mr. Manley echoed his political rival's sentiments.

If the leaders of Trinidad and Jamaica were clearly governed more by insular than national considerations, their people's views were less patent. The Federation collapsed because of the decision of one-third of the electors in one of ten constituent territories. Citizens of Trinidad and Tobago were given no opportunity to indicate whether they wanted to withdraw from the Federation or, when their government announced its intention of doing so, whether they preferred independence alone or as the leading partner in an Eastern Caribbean federation. What they thought about these crucial questions no one knew.

Ordinary people in Trinidad and Jamaica, catapulted into independence through a variety of circumstances largely beyond their control, viewed the prospect with a mixture of elation, curiosity, indifference, and natural misgivings. It was obviously difficult for even the most fluent orator to state precisely what independence meant or ought to mean. The less sophisticated were apathetic or puzzled because federalism did not solve their major problems, commonly attributed by Caribbean leaders to the evils of colonialism rather than to their islands' scanty natural resources, small size, and high birth rates. To the ill-educated and underprivileged majority of West Indians a national state unable to provide much needed concrete benefits made little appeal.

The federal government lacked money, power, and prestige. It could neither cure nor conceal the continued unemployment, illiteracy, poor health, and bad housing under which its peoples laboured.

Nor could it be expected promptly to substitute wealth for poverty, although it might ultimately have stimulated trade and industry, encouraged improved methods of agriculture, and provided a more intelligent attack on regional problems. It was not surprising that such a union never succeeded in capturing the imagination or loyalty of citizens unable even to move freely from one part of the West Indies to another.

After the Federation was launched, the United Kingdom deferred to the islands' unanimous insistence on full self-government for each unit, with an attendant proliferation of cabinets and local pride. If this was a cardinal error, it was of the British Caribbean's own making. Effective federalism necessarily involves diminution of territorial powers. Such abortive West Indianism as existed was steadily eroded by rising demands for more local sovereignty. Under such conditions no federation could flourish.

Colonial aspects of the national constitution antagonized regional politicians hot for independence and resentful because the British Parliament retained power to legislate for all the units. Yet the United Kingdom could not reasonably be blamed because the Federation was not independent from the outset. At varying stages of constitutional development in 1958, most participating territories depended on aid from Britain, and in some local administration of finances left much to be desired. When the Canadian and Australian federations were formed, their provinces and states were also colonies, and decades elapsed before these older nations achieved full sovereignty.

Jamaica was partly responsible for the fact that the West Indies Federation never attained complete autonomy. The national parliament passed a motion in December 1959 requesting the British government to set an early date for full independence. Jamaica objected on the ground that the revised national constitution, then bitterly debated, should be settled first. With this view the Secretary of State for the Colonies agreed.[78]

It is easy to point to flaws in the federal constitution. All constitutions reflect, with varying degrees of accuracy, their citizens' temperaments and aspirations, strengths and weaknesses. They also reflect the geographic, historical, and economic circumstances which help to shape their people's outlook. West Indian history and traditions developed from isolationism, not co-operation. Whatever the formal provisions for amendment, constitutional inadequacies or mistakes, when recognized, can be changed when there is a will to do so. But to transform attitudes of mind, to put aside ancient animosities, to transcend familiar hurdles imposed by geography and long-established economic practices requires statesmanship of a very high order.

West Indians could have made their federal constitution work, whatever its shortcomings, had they been sufficiently eager for union and convinced that its assets outweighed its liabilities. In the British Caribbean such eagerness and convictions were conspicuously absent. This might perhaps have been altered by an early and intelligent attempt to develop among ordinary West Indians an informed public opinion on federalism and on the consequences of failure.

It can be argued that, for its own sake and that of the other territories, Jamaica should never have joined a union of far-away islands, many smaller than a Jamaican parish, about whose people it knew little and cared less. As Michael Manley observed in 1970, however central the idea of federation was in the rest of the Caribbean, 'it was always an afterthought in the dialogue of Jamaican politics'.[79]

Jamaica's secession gave Dr. Williams an opportunity to fashion an Eastern Caribbean union to his own specifications, with the obviously desirable strong central government he had consistently supported. His unwillingness to assume financial responsibility for economically inviable islands was understandable. Yet it was sad that, at a critical juncture, the cause of West Indian nationhood was rejected by the regional leader who best comprehended what federalism involved and who had long advocated Caribbean unity.

Administrative costs in the Leewards and Windwards, although high enough to discourage Jamaica and Trinidad from assuming them, were in fact relatively small. The most serious objection to the inflated trappings of insular cabinet governments, much prized as status symbols, was that by fostering the little islands' sense of importance and pseudo-statehood they made united action on anything extraordinarily difficult.

These diminutive territories, unable to contribute much to the federal union, were most insistent in their demands on it and least willing to contribute what they could. Eager to get as much from and sacrifice as little as possible to the national government, some proclaimed their refusal to exchange rule by Britain for control by a strong West Indies federation. Their suspicion that the larger islands were likely to be less sympathetic to their needs and less generous than the Colonial Office was well founded. Yet their intense desire for self-government hampered achievement of any effective national union and thwarted development of any genuine sense of community.

Every territory, primarily concerned with its own pressing problems, distrusted the others. The insularity of each diminished the prospects of all. Trinidad and Jamaica were alarmed at the prospect of having to support the small islands, which in turn feared domination by those larger and wealthier. All were internally divided by cleavages of race, class, and colour, as well as by the yawning gulf between the rich and the poor. Under such circumstances it was difficult to develop a real sense of community even within a single island and much more difficult throughout the whole region. The Federation of the West Indies, as Sir Hugh Wooding wisely observed, 'was conceived in fear, lived throughout its brief existence with fear, and finally perished through fear'.[80]

In a revealing comment at the Montego Bay Conference Sir Alexander Bustamante remarked, 'To me Jamaica and Jamaica's interests come first. It must be so'. Federations, added Mr. Manley, are born of social, economic, and moral necessity.[81] Once it became clear that the larger islands could achieve autonomy alone, their leaders saw no need for union, dreaded its financial obligations, and conveniently forgot what Mr. Manley had described in 1957 as their 'tremendous responsibility' to assist the development of the whole British West Indies.[82]

In the British Caribbean fear of outside aggression did not, as in most federations, provide an argument for co-operative action. No external threat required pooling West Indian resources. Only the smaller islands could confidently expect from union clear economic advantages. The striking imbalances among the territories in size, wealth, and population, and consequently in power, were other major reasons for the Federation's failure.

National leadership was never strong enough to impose solutions acceptable to the large islands. Sir Grantley Adams and his cabinet received more criticism than appreciation of their singularly thankless task. Although the federal House of Representatives, like legislatures elsewhere, on occasion resembled a beer-garden, it is worth preserving a tribute to it by Morris Cargill of Jamaica. While acknowledging that he had spent many hours of excruciating boredom in the national parliament, he yet recalled that the debates were sometimes 'of a very high standard. Ashford Sinanan, Florence Daysh, and one or two other federal members of parliament were debaters of the highest skill: witty, penetrating and civilized; far in advance of anyone we've ever had in our Jamaica House with the exception of Mr. Manley when he puts his mind to it. The Speaker, Erskine Ward, was an outstanding man as well as ... remarkably good at his job ... fair, well-informed and courageous.[83]

A stronger, more efficient, and more tactful Prime Minister might have made a greater impact but probably could not have held together the Federation unless he had been a Jamaican or Trinidadian and thus able to attract from these two islands the support always essential but never forthcoming. Although the Premier of Jamaica led the West Indies Federal Labour Party of which the Premier of Trinidad was an outstanding member, the two men were soon at odds and rapidly became the Federation's major opponents. The national government's profoundly difficult position was made even more difficult by local journalists who, like their colleagues elsewhere, found disputes and recrimination better copy than patient efforts to secure agreement. Discussions on the most contentious issues were almost always conducted in a blaze of publicity.

The Federation won many friends abroad, but failed in the arts of conciliation and co-operation at home. It neither managed to reconcile the two largest islands nor to achieve their prestige. It was never successfully popularized among its own citizens and no one seemed to consider it his business to try to achieve this. 'The root cause of failure', declared the Trinidadian Minister for External Affairs four years after the Federation's collapse, 'was lack of adequate preparation designed to get the people of the Caribbean to know and understand each other'.[84] Neither before the West Indies came into being nor during its brief life was any serious effort made by anyone to explain its rationale to its scattered citizens or to solicit their loyalty to the new nation.

On various matters rifts always apparent among the islands widened instead of narrowed during the life of the Federation. As a Conservative member of the British Commons remarked during the debate at Westminster on the West Indies Bill: 'there was always local island patriotism, but there was never, unfortunately, a wider West Indian patriotism . . . There was, to be perfectly honest, a sad failure of human relationships'.[85] This assessment should, however, be qualified by recognition of the intense West Indianism of many distinguished civil servants and professional people, who devoted years of hard work to building a nation, only to find it brought down about their heads. Most British Caribbean students at universities in the United Kingdom, Canada, and the United States were also convinced West Indians. Hence the saying that the Federation and West Indian nationhood were conceived in London and Toronto rather than in the Caribbean.[86]

Regional nationalism was always liveliest, not in attitudes towards federation, wherein insular sentiment usually dominated, but in a common enthusiasm for calypsos and cricket, ready pride in the work of Caribbean writers, and practical concern for territories afflicted by such natural disasters as hurricanes and tidal waves. A warm-hearted response to neighbours in need can invariably be relied on from even the poorest West Indian island. This generous sympathy in the face of others' misfortunes unfortunately did not carry over into the political sphere.

Ultimately the Federation failed because insularity triumphed over national loyalties. This outcome seems in retrospect almost inevitable in an atmosphere where attacks on an effective federal government became synonymous with local patriotism, and each constitutional conference, from 1948 to 1961, allocated less power and less revenue to the centre. For centuries the British Caribbean islands had been isolated, with their main lines of communication to the United Kingdom, not to each other. The development of air transport, which finally made union feasible, did little to break down the parochialism of the average West Indian who could not afford air fares, even to the next island.

The small white communities which for generations had formed the ruling élites had far more opportunities for education and travel than the vast majority of their darker compatriots. They might have been expected to exhibit more vision. Most, however, were primarily concerned with their own declining status and with maintaining their preferred economic position. Few chose to associate themselves whole-heartedly, or at all, with goals represented by the Federation. Very few were willing to work as partners and fellow West Indians with their black and brown countrymen to build a new state. Had they tried to do so they might have been rebuffed. On the other hand, their support and influence might have been significant.

An able Trinidadian commented that no one would have been 'more impressed and pleased than the black masses at a powerful, independent entry of the white people into the federation discussion. A politically sophisticated leadership, confident of itself and thinking of the nation, would have gone out of its way to encourage such a manifestation, however faintly it first appeared'.[87] The position of the whites was difficult and their attachment to the old colonial order understandable. Yet if posterity is likely to condemn the part played by leading West Indians in destroying their Federation, the sins of omission of the privileged white enclaves throughout the islands must be included.

The very receptiveness of the Colonial Office towards aspirations for a united West Indies also detracted from the liveliness of British Caribbean nationhood. 'In this rarefied atmosphere of benevolent co-operation', it was aptly remarked, 'the flame . . . was bound to flicker and burn low . . . There was no cause left to keep West Indian nationalism fresh, and it quietly withered'.[88] As a Trinidadian observed, 'it is our loyalty to the parish pump that has brought us to the present sorry pass'.[89] Although some West Indians realized that the Federation provided their best hope of preserving civil liberties and democratic government, after four troubled years the islands abandoned what Mr. Manley had once described as 'the greatest adventure of our people in all time'.[90]

Since the mid-twentieth century, to abolish colonialism and achieve independence has proved relatively easy. To create and sustain a new nation firmly based on informed public opinion is singularly difficult. Without a sense of community they labour in vain who build a federal state.

The union was no sooner disbanded than its peoples demonstrated a lively desire to preserve some regional co-operation. 'The case for a West Indian federation', Sir Arthur Lewis maintained in 1967, 'is as strong as ever'.[91] This view he based on the common cultural and political heritage of the British Caribbean peoples and on their need jointly to tackle common economic problems, to ensure competent administration, and to preserve political and civil freedoms.

Norman Manley once described federation as 'a dream and a hope and a promise of salvation'.[92] Belief in a comprehensive West Indianism was always an act of faith: the substance of things hoped for by men of vision. It may again quicken the peoples of the Commonwealth Caribbean. In Sir Arthur's words, another generation of West Indians 'may once more face their destiny, which is to come together as a nation'.[93]

Notes

1. 'Referendum a Fight for Life', *Sunday Gleaner* (Kingston), 6 Aug. 1961.
2. *Daily Gleaner*, 28 July, 22 Aug., 17 Sept. 1961.
3. *Federation: What It Will Really Cost Jamaica* (Kingston, 1961): Rex Nettleford, ed., *Manley and the New Jamaica* (London, 1971), p. 175.
4. *Daily Gleaner*, 17, 19, 29 Aug., 16, 19 Sept. 1961.
5. 'The End of the Federation: Some Constitutional Implications', *West Indian Economist*, IV (March 1962), 16.
6. *Sunday Guardian* (Port-of-Spain), 17 Sept. 1961.
7. *Daily Gleaner*, 10 Oct. 1961.
8. J.B. Kelly, 'The Jamaica Independence Constitution', *West Indian Economist*, IV (Christmas 1962), 9–20, and (March 1962), 11–26.
9. *West Indian Economist*, III (Oct. 1961), 3.
10. Weekly Gleaner, 23 Aug. 1967; Sir John Mordecai, *The West Indies: The Federal Negotiations* (London, 1968), p. 311; *Daily Gleaner*, 25 Aug. 1967.
11. *The Times* (London), 21, 22 Sept. 1961; *Daily Gleaner*, 2 Oct. 1961. A thoughtful analysis of the significance of the

referendum is given by Brian Chapman, 'Jamaica's Future in Doubt', *Manchester Guardian Weekly*, 28 Sept. 1961.
12. *The Times* (London), 21 Sept. 1961.
13. *The Torchlight* (Grenada), 22 Sept. 1961; *The Voice of St Lucia* (Castries), 30 Sept. 1961; *Daily Gleaner*, 14 Oct., 4 Nov. 1961.
14. *Commonwealth Survey*, VII (10 Oct. 1961), 1035; Sir Algernon Aspinall, *The British West Indies* (London, 1912), p. 415.
15. *The Times* (London), 30 Sept., 6 Oct. 1961; *Daily Gleaner*, 6 Oct. 1961; *Chronicle of the West Indies Committee*, LXXVI (Oct.-Nov. 1961), 248.
16. *Sunday Guardian*, 1, 8 Oct. 1961; *Daily Gleaner*, 9 Oct. 1961.
17. Address to a press conference on 4 Nov. 1961; *Weekly Gleaner*, 6 Nov. 1961.
18. *The Times* (London), 25 Sept. 1961; *Sunday Guardian*, 5 Nov. 1961.
19. 'Thomas Wright', *Daily Gleaner*, 11 Nov. 1961.
20. Broadcast on 15 Oct. 1961, published in the *West Indies Federal Review*, II (Oct. 1961), 2–15.
21. *West Indies Federal Review*, II (Oct. 1961), 2–15.
22. The West Indies Federal Information Service, Press Release, 29 Oct., 21 Dec. 1961.
23. *Sunday Guardian*, 24 Sept., 1, 20, 22 Oct. 1961; *Daily Gleaner*, 20 Oct. 1961.
24. *Eastern Caribbean Federation*, Report to the Prime Minister by Professor Arthur Lewis (Port-of-Spain, 1961). In Feb. 1962 Professor Lewis presented a second report, *Proposals for an Eastern Caribbean Federation of Eight Territories* (Port-of-Spain, 1962), embodying minor alterations in his original recommendations. See also his *The Agony of the Eight* (Bridgetown, n.d.).
25. *Sunday Guardian*, 5 Nov. 1961; *Daily Gleaner*, 13 Nov. 1961.
26. *Sunday Guardian*, 12 Nov. 1961.
27. *Daily Gleaner*, 12, 19 Oct. 1961.
28. 'Behind the Curtain', *Sunday Guardian*, 8, 22, 29 Oct., 12, 19 Nov., 17 Dec. 1961, 7 Jan. 1962.
29. *Weekly Gleaner*, 9 Dec. 1961, 9 Feb. 1962.
30. *The Nation* (People's National Movement party organ), IV, 15 Jan. 1962.
31. Trinidad and Tobago House of Representatives, *Debates* (12 Jan. 1962), cols. 27, 50.
32. Leading editorial on 'Fixing our Day of Destiny', *Sunday Guardian*, 27 May 1962.
33. Henry Paul, *Sunday Guardian*, 13 May 1962.
34. *Sunday Guardian*, 18, 27 March 1962.
35. Albert Gomes and David J. Chin, *Sunday Guardian*, 21, 22 Jan., 4 Feb. 1962.
36. *Weekly Gleaner*, 19 Jan. 1962.
37. Leigh Richardson, 'Disruption and Confusion in the West Indies', *Sunday Guardian*, 28 Jan. 1962.
38. *Weekly Gleaner*, 2 Feb. 1962.
39. *Sunday Guardian*, 21, 28 Jan., 4, 11, 25 Feb. 1962.
40. *Weekly Gleaner*, 9 Feb. 1962.
41. *Voice of St. Lucia*, 3 Feb. 1962.
42. *The Times* (London), 13 Dec. 1962; *Weekly Gleaner*, 2 Feb. 1962.
43. *Daily Gleaner*, 31 Jan. 1962.
44. *West Indian Economist*, IV (May 1962), 6–7.
45. *Weekly Gleaner*, 2 Feb. 1962.
46. *Ibid.*
47. Great Britain, *Report of the Jamaica Independence Conference, 1962*, Cmmd. 1638 (London, 1962), 5–14.
48. Leading editorial on 'Jamaica Alone?', *Chronicle of the West India Committee*, LXXVII (March 1962), 111–16.
49. Great Britain, House of Commons, *Parliamentary Debates*, vol. 643, no. 49 (6 Feb. 1962), cols. 230–5; Mordecai, *The West Indies*, p. 448.

50. Great Britain, House of Lords, *Parliamentary Debates,* vol. 237 (6 March 1962), cols. 1158–90.

51. Great Britain, House of Commons, *Parliamentary Debates,* vol. 656 (26 March 1962), cols. 849–941. This long and able debate examined in detail the various reasons for the collapse of the West Indies Federation.

52. *Weekly Gleaner,* 9 Feb. 1962.

53. The West Indies, House of Representatives, *Parliamentary Debates,* V (14–22 Feb. 1962), cols. 763–1336.

54. Ibid, V (22 Feb. 1962), cols. 1369–80.

55. *The Times* (London), 15, 21, 26 March 1962.

56. *Sunday Guardian,* 3 June 1962.

57. Derek Walcott, 'Spiritual Purpose Lacking', *Sunday Guardian,* 5 Jan. 1964.

58. Great Britain, *Report of the Trinidad and Tobago Independence Conference, 1962,* Cmmd. 1757 (London, 1962).

59. *Weekly Gleaner,* 9 Feb. 1962.

60. *Sunday Guardian,* 1 April, 27 May 1962.

61. Kenneth Hill, 'Trinidad's Need for Tolerance', *Sunday Guardian,* 3 June 1962.

62. *Anti-Slavery Monthly Reporter* (Aug. 1828), pp 284–5, cited by D.J. Murray, *The West Indies and the Development of Colonial Government, 1801–34* (Oxford, 1965), p. 155.

63. Grenada Legislative Council, *Debates,* 21 June 1960, p. 7. The extent to which West Indians participated, at each step of the way, in deciding to federate and in determining the shape of their national constitution is carefully traced in an illuminating article by Jesse H. Proctor, Jr, 'The Framing of the West Indian Federal Constitution: an Adventure in National Self-Determination', *Revista de Historia de América,* LVII-LVIII (Dec. 1964), 51–119.

64. Barbados House of Assembly, *Debates,* 10 Feb. 1948, p. 255; 19 Jan. 1956, p. 1957.

65. Jamaica House of Representatives, *Proceedings,* 30 Nov. 1955; *Daily Gleaner,* 2 Nov. 1958.

66. The West Indies, Federal Information Service Press Release, 31 May 1961.

67. *Daily Gleaner,* 22 May 1962.

68. Ibid, 17 April 1961.

69. *The Times* (London), 9 May 1962.

70. The West Indies, House of Representatives, *Debates,* V (19 July 1961), cols. 250–1. See also 'Britain, Europe and The West Indies', *West Indian Economist,* III (June 1961), 10–16.

71. *Weekly Gleaner,* 14 Sept. 1962.

72. Ibid, 1 Feb. 1963.

73. 'Is Jamaica Awakening?', *West Indian Economist,* IV (April 1962), 5.

74. Albert Gomes, 'Behind the Headlines', *Sunday Guardian,* 17 Dec. 1961.

75. C.L.R. James, *Party Politics in the West Indies* (San Juan, Trinidad, 1962), p. 143.

76. *Sunday Guardian,* 4 Feb. 1962.

77. *Weekly Gleaner,* 2 Feb. 1962.

78. The West Indies, House of Representatives, *Debates,* II (25 May 1960), col. 1945; J.H. Proctor, Jr, 'Constitutional Defects and the Collapse of the West Indian Federation', *Public Law* (Summer 1964), 131; Sir Arthur Lewis, 'Epilogue' in Mordecai, *The West Indies,* p. 461.

79. 'Overcoming Insularity in Jamaica', *Weekly Gleaner,* 11 Nov. 1970.

80. 'Death of a Federation — Epilogue', *Sunday Advocate,* 2 April 1967.

81. Great Britain, Colonial Office, No. 218, *Proceedings* of the Conference on the Closer Association of the British West Indian Colonies, part II (London, 1948), pp. 25, 57–62.

82. 'The West Indian Experience and Hopes', in P.A. Lockwood, ed., *Canada and the West Indies,* Allison University Publication No. 2 (Sackville, New Brunswick 1957), p. 28.

83. 'Thomas Wright', *Weekly Gleaner,* 2 March 1962.

84. Dr. Patrick Solomon, in an address to the Caribbean Commonwealth Parliamentary Association, *Weekly Gleaner,* 18 May 1966.

85. Great Britain, House of Commons, *Parliamentary Debates,* vol. 656, No. 83 (26 March 1962), col 883. Nigel Fisher was the speaker.

86. Brian Chapman, 'Jamaica's Future in Doubt', *Manchester Guardian Weekly,* 28 Sept. 1961.

87. James, *Party Politics in the West Indies,* p. 156.

88. Hugh W. Springer, *Reflections on the Failure of the First West Indian Federation,* Occasional Papers in International Affairs No. 4 (Cambridge, 1962), pp. 41–2.

89. Albert Gomes, 'Behind the Curtain', *Sunday Guardian,* 11 March 1962.

90. 'The West Indian Experience and Hopes', in Lockwood, p. 28.

91. Epilogue to Mordecai's *The West Indies.*

92. Radio broadcast on 9 June 1960, announcing his intention to hold a referendum, Nettleford, ed., *Manley and the New Jamaica,* p. 175.

93. Epilogue to Mordecai, p. 461.

From Carifta to Caricom: Deepening Caribbean Integration

W. Andrew Axline

Although the conception of regional integration that emerged in the resolutions of the 1967 Georgetown Conference was a comprehensive one (albeit essentially *laissez-faire* in nature), when CARIFTA finally came into operation in 1968 it was essentially a type I integration scheme involving the elimination of tariffs and quantitative measures on intra-regional trade. Costs of participation for the LDCs were reduced somewhat by means of the reserve list and less stringent application of some of the other obligations. The distributive aspects of the bargain between the MDCs and LDCs, the Caribbean Development Bank (CDB) was still in the discussion stage. The agreement establishing the CDB was not signed until October 18, 1969, and the Bank was not formally established until January 1970. According to the CARIFTA Secretariat from the very beginning some 90% of intra-regional trade was freed.[1]

The essentially expansive nature of CARIFTA was characterized in the following way by ECLA's office for the Caribbean in Port of Spain.

Since its inception the CARIFTA has been regarded as a process for accelerating trade between its members and stimulating production, although other aspects of regional integration might be considered equally important. At the end of 1972 it is still essentially a Free Trade Area, and progress must be assessed primarily in terms of the acceleration of intra-area trade.[2]

Thus, the limited type II integration scheme that had been negotiated in 1968 was yet to be realized, and the LDCs were faced with certain real costs of integration, with the benefits of integration still being in the realm of promises. Even after its formal establishment in 1970 the Caribbean Development Bank failed to live up to the exceptions of the LDCs as a major corrective mechanism. In 1970 one project for hotel development was approved[3] and in 1971 twenty projects totalling $6,009.160.000 (EC) were approved.[4] The major problem with the Bank, however, was the delay in disbursing funds. As in all under-developed areas there was a shortage of administrative skills. Applications for funds were required to satisfy stringent criteria often beyond the capacity of those applicants most in need of development capital. Also, since the CDB will finance only part of the funds required the applicant must find other sources of finance, which is usually very difficult, and for which the applicant usually waits until he receives a response from the CDB as a means to establish a credit rating. These factors explain the long delay between the approval of a request and the actual payment of funds, exemplified by the fact that in 1972 funds for projects totalling $6,050.000.00 (EC) was approved, while only $446,463.00 was paid out.[5]

The cumbersome nature of this process was partly due to the conception of the CDB as a sort of International Bank for Reconstruction and Development (IBRD) on a regional scale, with its relatively rigorous lending criteria, rather than as an integration bank whose major purpose is as a corrective measure primarily benefitting the LDCs. Steps were taken to correct partially this situation by the MDCs who agreed to make no requests to the 'soft loan' window, leaving this entirely to the LDCs. More recently, William Demas, successor to Sir Arthur Lewis as President of the Caribbean Development Bank, has manifested a conception of the institution which is more along the lines of an integration bank.[6]

At the same time the LDCs were experiencing frustration over the ineffectiveness of the CDB the gains from liberalizing trade were following the expected pattern of mainly benefitting the MDCs. From 1967 to 1971 total CARIFTA Intra-regional imports rose from EC $95 million to an estimated EC $188 million, an increase of 98% for the period, or an average of 19% a year. Prior to CARIFTA the average annual growth rate was less than 6%.[7] The growth of intra-regional trade continued to $260 million for 1972, $298 million for 1973,[8] and $510 million in 1974.[9]

Trade between the MDCs of Barbados, Guyana, Jamaica and Trinidad and Tobago accounted for over 60% of this regional trade in 1967 and 69% in 1971 as well as for all of the growth in trade, with the relative share of intra-CARIFTA trade accounted for by the LDCs declining from 1967–71. During this same period intra-area trade between the LDCs declined form 1.9% to 1.4% of total regional trade.[10]

As a result of the shifting trade patterns in the region, a number of disputes rose among the MDCs over alleged violations of the CARIFTA Treaty. Among the most notable of these were the textile war between Jamaica and Trinidad and Tobago, 1968–72, the 'onion row' over exports of onions from Barbados to Guyana and Trinidad and Tobago in 1971, and the conflict between Jamaica and Guyana over the latter's imposition of a 5% handling charge on imports. These conflicts are further indication that the creation of a free trade area was having an important impact on regional trade.

In sum, this pattern of trade was clearly one of polarization, with Jamaica and Trinidad and Tobago reaping the biggest gains, followed by Barbados, while Guyana's exports remained relatively stable. The LDCs, on the other hand, experienced no appreciable increase in exports to other CARIFTA countries.[11] Thus, the Associated States and Belize witnessed a relative loss in gains from integration as compared to the MDCs at the same time that promised corrective measures were not forthcoming. This feeling of increased costs of integration was exacerbated by growing inflation, one of the causes of which was seen to be CARIFTA, even though as yet there was no common external tariff.

The Agricultural Marketing Protocol (AMP), which had been created as the basis for rationalizing agricultural production in the region, reducing dependence on imports of food-stuffs from third countries, and providing benefits for the more agricultural LDCs, was also contributing to polarization within the region. The LDCs, in addition to being less industrialized, were less competitive in agricultural production, and the guaranteed minimum regional price of the AMP stimulated greater production in the MDCs, further weakening the position of the LDCs. To offset this and to build real compensatory aspects into the regional agricultural system, the Guaranteed Market Scheme (GMS) was devised to provide protected access to MDC markets for agricultural products from the LDCs.[12] For the ECCM countries, however, the AMP did not respond to their claims for a share of regional development through structural transformation by creating an industrial base in their countries. They were not willing to remain primary producers in an industrializing Caribbean. Allocation

of industries within the region did represent the kind of corrective measure which would respond to these claims, but had remained a dead letter since it had been incorporated in the resolutions of the 1967 Georgetown Conference.

The member governments of the region were acutely aware of this pattern of unequal distribution of benefits, particularly the LDCs, which individually and collectively expressed the feeling that they were not receiving equitable treatment. A Barbados trade mission touring the CARIFTA territories in 1969 found a generalized feeling of dissatisfaction among the smaller territories, who felt themselves dominated by the MDCs. The business community of the LDCs was found to be pessimistic, and an official of the St. Lucia Marketing Board specifically mentioned agricultural competition from Trinidad and Tobago's oranges.[13] Mr. James Fitzallen Mitchell, Minister of Trade for St. Vincent, while admitting that the AMP had stimulated sales of sweet potatoes to Trinidad and Tobago, accused that country of trying to exploit the limited agricultural benefits of the region as well as the industrial benefits, which was seen as unfair.[14] Mr. Coulthard, president of the Chamber of Commerce of Dominica, in his address to the annual meeting in January 1970, made one of the most comprehensive statements of the position of the LDCs. He accused CARIFTA of having caused a sudden increase in prices through consumption taxes and profiteering by manufacturers in the big four, and declared that the LDCs had gained little and suffered considerable disadvantages from integration. Along with this he pointed out that proposals for some kind of allocation of industry had not been implemented, that the people of the Associated States felt abandoned and that for them CARIFTA was a dead loss.[15]

i. The Common External Tariff: An Expansive Policy

It was within this setting of actual and perceived polarization that the next stage of regional negotiations was being prepared. Steps were being taken to implement another principle agreed upon at the 1967 Georgetown Conference, the erection of a common external tariff, a measure that was expansive rather than distributive in nature in that it would create regional economic benefits through trade diversion and/or creation while the benefits would be likely to reinforce the disparity among the MDCs and the LDCs.[16]

It is at this point in the Caribbean integration process that the negotiating strategies began to approximate more closely the theoretically posited pattern, with MDC-LDC lines drawn along expansive-distributive issues, and with the business sector playing a major role in reinforcing the *laissez-faire* nature of the Caribbean integration scheme.

The move to establish a common external tariff within CARIFTA was the most contentious policy issue of the Caribbean integration movement to date, and the period from 1971–73 took on characteristics of a permanent crisis until agreement was finally reached on a linked expansive-distributive policy which created a package of integration measures acceptable to all the governments of the region.

Pursuant to the commitment to study the feasibility of a Common External Tariff (CET) in the 1967 resolutions of the Georgetown Conference (Annex A of the CARIFTA Accord) the Carifta Council of Ministers in 1970 appointed a committee under the leadership of Secretary-General William Demas. The report of this committee was handed over to the member governments early in 1971.[17] This event served as the stimulus for the taking of positions on the issue. The MDCs strongly supported the CET, with Jamaica's position evolving away from the reticence of 1967–68, while the LDCs manifested great resistance. The private sector showed some ambivalence on the issue, but eventually played a major role in the ultimate compromise. The intellectuals of the region remained critical of the continued phased freeing of trade approach to integration, and labour remained relatively insignificant in the negotiations.

The question of harmonization of fiscal incentives had earlier been raised at the 1967 Conference of governmental representatives, and ECLA had been asked to study the question. The adoption of a regional policy of uniform 'tax holidays' was seen as complementary to the common external tariff, and the two measures were treated as part of a single package. As was the case in 1968, Trinidad and Tobago and Guyana were the most eager to 'deepen' the integration movement. In 1970 the government of Trinidad and Tobago expressed hope that a CET would be adopted by early in 1971.[18] Earlier that same year Guyana's Prime Minister, Forbes Burnham, called on the regional governments to implement the 1967 decisions calling for harmonization of fiscal incentives and a common external tariff.[19] This support provided a favourable political base for the active efforts of the Secretariat to move to the next stage of integration. Barbados, seeking a protected regional market for her fledgling light industry supported the idea of a common external tariff, although the relatively low national tariff meant that there was likely to be an increase in prices. In Barbados, as in Jamaica the eventual support for the CET reflected a policy advocated by the manufacturing sector as opposed to commercial interests, a division which was reflected in the regional business organization, the Caribbean Association of Industry and Commerce (CAIC).[20]

Jamaica was the only country of the region in which a major debate took place over the move to a common external tariff. During this period the Jamaican position evolved to one of support from the earlier position expressed by the Jamaican High Commission in Trinidad in 1968.

Participation (in Carifta) would be in respect of a free trade agreement within the Caribbean area and not in a Common Market involving uniformity of external tariffs or full economic integration involving the first two aspects plus free movement of peoples among other important factors.[21]

In 1972, however the Jamaican Prime Minister, Mr. Michael Manley, declared that the harmonization of fiscal incentives and the establishment of a common external tariff were very important steps which followed logically from the existence of CARIFTA.[22] This change in position followed the change in government in 1972 which brought the PNP to power under the leadership of Norman Manley's son, and reflected the ambivalence of Jamaica's policy toward CARIFTA during this period. This ambivalence flowed from the contradiction between the gains from trade which Jamaica had realized and the potential benefits to Jamaican manufacturing from a protected regional market on one hand, and continuing fear of being involved in a regional political union along with the sacrifice of possible unilateral arrangements with the U.S., the U.K. and Canada on the other hand. Robert Lightbourne, Jamaican Minister of Trade and leader of a CARIFTA mission to Europe and Great Britain in 1969, specifically referred to the Jamaican referendum on federation in stating his reticence to CARIFTA's having any political objective, and cited the alternative possibility of integration with the U.S., Canada, or even England.[23] Later, as an independent member of Parliament Lightbourne said of Caribbean integration that it 'appears to be growing into a federation in everything but name'.[24] The new government, however, was in favour of the move to a common external tariff, and the private sector was supportive of this. The Jamaica Manufacturers Association (JMA) was in the vanguard of this support, and remained active in its promotion throughout the period, with JMA President, Charles Henderson-Davis, citing Jamaica's benefits from expanding markets and declaring:

The urgently needed introduction of a common external tariff and of a standardization of harmonization of industrial incentives are two subjects that require immediate attention.[25]

The shift in the position of the Jamaican government on the deepening of the integration movement which put her in agreement with the other MDCs was a key element in the eventual establishment of CARICOM.

Similarly, the LDCs were coalescing around a position opposed to the adoption of a common external tariff. For them the move was seen as a step which would exacerbate the unfavourable situation which had resulted from the creation of CARIFTA. At the ninth Council of Ministers meeting the LDCs expressed their objection to the CET.[26] While expressing their support for the principle of further integration they felt that the new tariff would lead to further socio-economic problems in the countries that depended heavily on customs for public revenue.[27] The government of Dominica was reticent with regard to the establishment of a common external tariff, feeling that it would create artificial barriers within which higher prices and low quality would result,[28] and the government of Montserrat, which was to become the most outspoken of the LDCs, stated that since the country was not benefitting from CARIFTA they would never agree on the harmonization of fiscal incentives or a CET.[29]

The differences in the positions of the MDCs and LDCs came directly into confrontation when the common external tariff was discussed at the tenth Council of Ministers Meeting in Roseau, Dominica, in July, 1972 and this conflict continued through the negotiations of the eleventh (October 1972) and twelfth (April 1973) Council Meetings and the seventh and eight Heads of Government Conferences, culminating in the signing of the Georgetown Accord at the last of these in April 1973.

At the tenth and eleventh Council Meetings the major issues of advancing the integration movement took the form of a linked expansive-distributive negotiation, with the LDCs insisting on the allocation of industries within CARIFTA as the *sine qua non* of their acceptance of the harmonization of fiscal incentives and the common external tariff. Although the proposal for harmonizing fiscal incentives allowed the LDCs to grant more general tax concessions than the MDCs, it was still looked on as a cost in that it might deter potential foreign investment in the region. The LDCs originally asked for a 95 to 5 distribution of industries in their favour. At the tenth Council Meeting in July 1972 it was agreed that a package of measures including

the CET, harmonization of fiscal incentives, allocation of industries and a common regional approach to negotiations with the European Economic Community would be discussed at the eleventh Council of Ministers Meeting and seventh Heads of Government Conference in Port of Spain in October 1972.[30] The Secretariat Committee appointed to study these questions was to have its report ready at that time.

At the October meeting in Trinidad the deadlock between the MDCs and the LDCs was apparent from the beginning. At the Council meeting which immediately preceded the Heads of Government Conference the LDCs made it clear that they were not prepared to take any further steps toward deepening integration unless the MDCs committed themselves to make 'tangible manifestation of the ways in which development is going to come to the Less Developed Countries'.[31] Their demand for concrete benefits of industrialization from CARIFTA was central to the issue, as made by John Mitchell, Premier of St. Vincent and chairman of the LDC caucus.

We of the less developed territories share the desire of other Carifta members for meaningful economic integration. But, our people want to see factories — they want to see visible benefits of Carifta.[32]

At the Heads of Government Conference there were angry verbal exchanges over the demands of the LDCs, with Kamaluddin Mohammed, Trinidad and Tobago's Minister of West Indian Affairs, stating

we cannot give blood as some of the representatives of the LDCs want. But it is in our interest and in theirs to find a reasonable compromise.[33]

At one point Trinidad and Tobago expressed its willingness to set up as a compromise, at the government level if necessary, one industry in any of the LDCs, and proposed that Jamaica and Guyana do the same. At another point, S. S. Ramphal, Guyana's Minister of External Affairs, proposed a compromise in the form of a resolution that the Eastern Caribbean countries and the MDCs set about the task of 'accelerating' their economic growth through industrial development to coincide with the fifth anniversary of CARIFTA, May 1, the following year.[34] Michael Manley of Jamaica proposed a compromise whereby a number of articles of the CARIFTA Agreement, namely Articles 5, 17, 18 and 39 would be amended to give the LDCs more favourable treatment.[35] In effect, this proposal would simply involve enlarging the 'opting out' type of solution whereby LDC costs of integration would be further lowered, rather than the benefits of integration being more equitably redistributed. The proposed amendments would lower the local value added criterion for area tariff treatment to 40% (from 50%) for the LDCs, give them five more years to phase out the reserve list, allow them to grant income tax allowances for intra-regional imports, permit discrimination in favour of local producers in governmental purchases, and allow the imposition of duties on imports from the MDCs which directly threatened LDC production. None of these articles was to be permitted to the MDCs.

Although these proposed measures would in effect lower the short term costs of participation for the LDCs, presumably until some benefits of industrialization could be realized, it did not satisfy the demand for concrete steps to allocate industries to the LDCs. The measure which finally did represent a step in this direction did not come from one of the member governments,however, but from a joint proposal of the CARIFTA Secretariat and the Caribbean Association of Industry and Commerce (CAIC).

The question of allocation of industries had been included in Annex A of CARIFTA, along with the CET and harmonization of fiscal incentives as one of the principles adopted at the Georgetown Conference in 1967 and subsequently by the Heads of Government Conference. Indeed, allocation of industries within the region had been perhaps the most studied of the principles involved in the deepening of regional integration. Articles 4 and 7 of Annex A state:

4. The principle should be accepted that certain industries may require for their economic operation the whole or a large part of the entire regional market protected by a common external tariff or other suitable instrument. The location of such industries and the criteria to be applied in respect thereof, as well as the implementation of the principle accepted above, should be the subject of immediate study — such study to have special regard to the situation of the relatively Less-developed countries. . .

7. The principle of seeking to establish more industries in the Less-Developed Countries should be accepted and the ECLA Secretariat should be asked to undertake feasibility studies immediately with a view to identifying industries which should be located in the Less-Developed Countries and to devising special measures for securing the establishment of such industries in these countries. These studies should be submitted to governments no less than one year after the commencement of free trade.[36]

A number of studies were undertaken including ones by the Economic Commission for Latin America (ECLA) and the United Nations Industrial Development Organization (UNIDO) on four sectors, submitted in 1969, by a special committee appointed by the CARIFTA Council of Ministers, and by ECLA on the Development of Small and Medium-Scale Industries and Industrial Estates in Grenada, St. Lucia, Dominica and St. Vincent. All this activity culminated in the resolution of the tenth Council of Ministers Meeting establishing the Location of Industry Task Force headed by the Secretary-General William Demas. This Task Force saw as its objective the promotion of industrial development in the LDCs, partly as an end in itself and partly as a means toward achieving a more equitable distribution of benefits within CARIFTA. The Task Force was advised by the Caribbean Development Bank that a report by the Economist Intelligence Unit (EIU) had identified a number of industries already existing in the LDCs that were capable of being expanded by the time of the seventh Heads of Government Conference in October 1972. However, no concrete steps had been taken to locate industries in the LDCs, and the smaller islands were exercising concerted pressure, co-ordinated through the ECCM, to extract commitment for such steps on the part of the MDCs as a price for their going along with the common external tariff and the harmonization of fiscal activities.

ii. The Caribbean Investment Corporation: A Distributive Policy

The outcome of the insistence by the LDCs on the inclusion of a distributive policy to offset their losses from deepening integration was the proposal of a corrective measure designed to enhance their chances of industrialization. The proposed measure was a regional investment company to provide equity capital for the establishment of industry in the LDCs. The idea for this regional investment company had come out of a joint Secretariat-CAIC mission to the LDCs in September 1972 whose purpose was to find a compromise which would allow the adoption of a CET. In a meeting between the CAIC Committee and the CARIFTA Location of Industry Task Force on September 14, 1972, it was decided that the main points to be discussed would be the development of an operational plan for the location of industries in the LDCs and the adoption of a common regional position with respect to negotiation of associated status with the EEC, for which a common external tariff was considered to be an important bargaining strength.[37]

The joint mission visited the seven member countries of the East Caribbean Common Market, discussing with government officials and members of the private sector the common external tariff and the harmonization of fiscal incentives. During the trip it became apparent that the LDCs were not willing to accept these further steps in integration without some measures to increase the benefits to them. The report of the mission provided a summary of seven observations, including:

6. The government representatives the mission met, all displayed a determination to bring about quickly some industrial development in their countries, and most displayed a conviction of the rightness of their approach. . .
7. All the government representatives seem to accept the vital necessity to strengthen the integration grouping at the same time as the benefits are more equitably distributed.[38]

This last observation, to the degree that it recognizes that progress in pursuing development through integration is not likely to succeed if it continues to be based on compromises which simply provide exceptions to the less development members, is an important indication of the kind of attitude necessary for adopting linked expansive-distributive policies.

The CAIC report contained six recommendations, the first and the last of which provided the basis for the ultimate compromise on the adoption of a CET.

1. The Mission urges regional governments to adopt as soon as possible the following measures:
   (a) The EECM and the CARIFTA Common External Tariffs and Protective Policy.
   (b) The scheme for the Harmonization of Fiscal Incentives to Industry.
   (c) The establishment of double taxation agreements with proper provisions for tax sharing allowances, among CARIFTA territories.
   (d) The strengthening of Article 39 of the CARIFTA Agreement making sure, however, that in so doing the MDCs, as CARIFTA partners, should retain their advantage over third countries.
   (e) The lower value-added requirement for products from the LDCs to qualify for area tariff treatment.
   (f) The lengthening of the period with respect to the LDCs for removing duties from items on the Reserve List.
   (g) To allow for the movement of funds between the MDCs and the LDCs, so long as machinery is in force in the LDCs to avoid the subsequent outflow of such funds to outside the region.
   (h) To provide for the easy movement of persons among CARIFTA countries for training as well as servicing joint MDC/LDC industrial ventures.
   (i) To bring about harmonization of standards in the productive process.
   (j) To bring about the harmonization of company law in the region.
   (k) To remove the alien status now suffered by CARIFTA citizens in other CARIFTA territories than their own.
   (l) With respect to all these measures, the Mission strongly recommends that the governments agree to the adoption of a set time-table for their implementation.

6. The Mission recommends that:
   An intensive study of the feasibility of an Investment Company as conceived and developed in discussions with both the Public and Private Sectors during the tour, should be vigorously pursued by the CARIFTA Secretariat.[39]

The last point, which was added after the other recommendations had been drafted, was the key element in the package of measures agreed upon at the seventh Heads of Government Conference as the basis of moving from CARIFTA to CARICOM. An agreement on a joint common approach to negotiations with the European Economic Community was ratified, and the final communiqué of the Conference included the major points of the package. It was agreed that the Caribbean Free Trade Association would become the Caribbean Common Market on May 1, 1973, and that there would be a series of measures designed to promote the economic development of the LDCs, particularly their industrial development. There were proposals for the harmonization of fiscal incentives, the establishment of a common external tariff, a common protective policy, rationalization of agriculture, greater monetary and financial co-operation and measures for location of industry in the LDCs. On this last point proposals were accepted on the establishment of a Caribbean multinational investment company, an export credit insurance scheme to be operated by the CDB, private and public technical assistance, and the use of technical research facilities in the MDCs by the LDCs.[40]

These proposals, along with the amendments to Articles 5, 17, 18, and 39 of the CARIFTA Agreement defined the nature of the new Caribbean integration scheme to be adopted. Between October 1972 and the next (eighth) Heads of Government Conference in Georgetown, Guyana, in April 1973, however, specific details of the package had to be worked out. During the period a joint Secretariat-CAIC committee under the co-direction of William Demas and Aaron Matalon, a leading Jamaican businessman, worked on the details of the regional investment company. At the twelfth Council of Ministers Meeting in December 1972, the LDCs continued their insistence on concrete steps being taken to help them, with Antigua's Minister of Trade Selwyn Walter declaring that there are still 'burning issues to be settled'.

In March 1973, William Demas characterized the compromise in the following manner:

In my assessment, the package of instruments agreed to by the last Heads of Government Conference for giving opportunities for development to the LDCs in the Caribbean goes beyond anything I have found in any other grouping among developing states.[41]

That same month CARIFTA officials meeting in Antigua settled some of the most controversial questions, including the common external tariff and the harmonization of fiscal incentives, and completed a draft agreement on the avoidance of double taxation as a means of encouraging the flow of private capital from the MDCs to the LDCs, particularly in the form of joint ventures.[42]

iii. The Georgetown Accord: Negotiating a Linked Expansive-Distributive Policy

There was a general feeling that much progress had been made toward the ratification of an agreement which would allow all twelve CARIFTA member countries to move to the common market. Final negotiations were to be settled at the thirteenth Council of Ministers Meeting immediately preceding the eighth Heads of Government Conference where the agreement would be ratified. At the Council meeting the Demas-Matalon Report was received outlining the establishment of the Caribbean Investment Corporation (CIC). The report proposed the establishment of an investment company whose funds would be contributed by both governments and the private sector and would be used to provide equity investment for agricultural and industrial projects in the LDCs.

Rather than being a simple exercise in ironing out the final points of negotiation over the compromise to be ratified by the Heads of Government Conference, however, the Council Meeting found itself in deadlock when late in the first day of its meeting the government of Montserrat placed a 'surprise' document before the Council demanding specific distributive concessions from the MDCs. The 'Montserrat paper' as the document came to be called, contained the most comprehensive statement of the need for compensatory and corrective mechanisms of a 'positive' or *dirigiste* nature, including the direct transfer of funds from the MDCs to the LDCs.[43] The Document, although submitted by the government of Montserrat, had been prepared in collaboration with the ECCM Secretariat, and thus represented a broader LDC position. The Montserrat paper began with a comprehensive survey of the problems and prospects of Caribbean integration, including a sophisticated analysis of the nature and causes of polarization, and criticism of the inadequacy of existing measures to counter the problem.

The Government of Montserrat is not yet persuaded that current regional economic integration programmes proposed for the Commonwealth Caribbean give anything like adequate recognition to the dangers of polarization in the Commonwealth Caribbean context. It is simply not creditable that the proposed amendments to the CARIFTA Agreement, the harmonization of fiscaL incentives to industry, the establishment of a Caribbean Investment Corporation and the activities of the Caribbean Development Bank will, by themselves, arrest, let alone reverse current trends towards polarization.[44]

Following this extensive analysis, a series of twelve proposals was made for taking action to realize the long-term aspirations of integration, including:[45]

1. The drafting and implementation of precise development objectives, plans and programmes for the integration movement.
2. The allocation and reservation of production of specific commodities to the LDCs.
3. A fund to provide competitive salaries for the specialist posts of the Industrial Evaluation and Promotion unit in the ECCM Secretariat and the Industrial Development Corporation in the LDCs.
4. A technical committee to prepare a regional perspective plan.
5. Provisions for periodic replenishment of CIC resources.
6. The CIC should be required to work to agreed performance and time targets.
7. A commission to guard the rights of Caribbean consumers.
8. A provision to give effect to articles 2 and 3 of the CARIFTA agreement calling for an equitable sharing of benefits, requiring that MDC countries enjoying trade surpluses with LDCs pay each LDC annually a sum equal to 10 per cent of the F.O.B. value of the surplus on trade in industrial products for the preceding year. The LDC would be allowed to use the money for economic development.

The paper concluded with the request that Montserrat be accorded a special position amongst the LDCs parallel to Barbados's special position among the MDCs, with concessionary measures being applied for the benefit of Montserrat.[46]

The discussion of the Montserrat paper and related questions of the distribution of benefits from integration occupied virtually all the discussion at the thirteenth Council Meeting, which ended in deadlock after five days of deliberation without resolving the issues. The discussion carried over into the eighth Heads of Government Conference with a sharp division still existing between MDCs and LDCs, and with some delegates threatening that they might have to go to a common market without the LDCs.[47] One delegate was quoted as saying of the LDCs 'They want to see smoke coming from the factories before signing the agreement for the common market'.[48] To a Jamaican delegate was attributed the comment that 'The man who coined the term MDCs should be assassinated'.[49]

The governments of the MDCs were not willing to go beyond the concessions that had been discussed, and there was some feeling that the LDCs were asking too much. The Prime Minister of Barbados, Errol Barrow, rejected the arguments by the LDCs that they were receiving no benefits from integration, and accused them of failing to mobilize their manpower resources to take advantage of loans from the Caribbean Development Bank.[50] In Jamaica and in Trinidad and Tobago there was also some resentment of the demands of the Associated States. A signed editorial in the *Daily Gleaner* stated that

The small islands need a real federation. . . they only have one view in relation to the four larger territories: How much do we have to give them?[51]

Writing in the Trinidad *Guardian*, Richard Toby, a private consultant and former fiscal adviser to the Prime Minister, said

The unemployment and other problems of Tobago and the outlying areas of Trinidad ought not to be underestimated. A country with an unemployment problem of between 15 percent and 20 percent could not seriously consider making fiscal concessions to other countries at the price of retarding its own development or of pursuing measures for facilitating the development of other countries while restricting its own economic growth on the ground of regional economic cooperation.[52]

These statements provide a clear expression of the tension between nationalist forces and the requirements of regionalism among underdeveloped countries.

On the basis of the existing proposals, and with the realization that a crucial stage in the development of Caribbean integration was at hand the member countries did arrive at a compromise permitting the establishment of the Caribbean Common Market and Community. This compromise was embodied in the Georgetown Accord, which was signed April 12, 1973. The Georgetown Accord provided for the signing of the Caribbean Community Treaty July 4, 1973, to come into effect on August 1, 1973, for the four independent territories of Barbados, Guyana, Jamaica and Trinidad and Tobago. The LDCs were to join the Community and Common Market by May 1,1973. The Georgetown Accord also provided for the coming into force on June 1, 1973, of three agreements of special interest to the LDCs, the Agreement on the Harmonization of Fiscal Incentives to Industry, the Agreement on the Avoidance of Double Taxation, and the Agreement on the Establishment of the Caribbean Investment Corporation, as well as other special measures allowing exceptions to the LDCs.[53] Montserrat was given special consideration among the LDCs. In effect the Georgetown Accord was an agreement to proceed to CARICOM in two stages, with the MDCs joining in August 1973, and the LDCs in May 1974, after the formal establishment of concrete measures to help the LDCs in June 1973.

Ten of twelve CARIFTA members signed the Georgetown Accord, with Antigua and Montserrat remaining outside, not satisfied that they would receive adequate benefits. A special ministerial team from the MDCs led by the Secretary-General visited Montserrat on May 3 and 4, 1973, to work out special measures to allow Montserrat's participation in CARICOM. Out of this visit came an agreement based on ten specific proposals which were the conditions under which Montserrat would join CARICOM.[54] They were the following:

1. MDC governments provide maximum assistance to the formulation of a National Development plan.
2. An industrial planner be assigned to Montserrat from an MDC for at least a year.
3. Funds be made available under the Commonwealth Caribbean Technical Assistance Programme to hire an Industrial Development Officer for three years.
4. The MDCs undertake to absorb the exportable production of Montserrat's industrial enterprise.
5. Some areas of industrial enterprise be established as joint project with the MDCs.
6. The MDCs urge that special priority be given to Montserrat in the financing of CIC projects and that a substantial sum of CIC funds be earmarked for projects in Montserrat.
7. Appropriate personnel from the MDCs be made available to Montserrat to help in preparing a Port Development Project.
8. Appropriate staff of the CARICOM Secretariat initiate studies on the rationalization of sea and air cargo transport to Montserrat.
9. The MDCs continue to assist Montserrat in agriculture through provision of personnel and

training facilities under the Commonwealth Caribbean Technical Assistance Programme.

10. The MDCs continue to provide personnel and training facilities in all other fields of Public Administration under the Commonwealth Caribbean Technical Assistance Programme.

On the basis of these concessions the government of Montserrat announced that it would join CARICOM on May 1, 1974,[55] and the Montserrat legislature unanimously passed a resolution to that effect.[56]

Antigua, in July 1974, after several months of hesitation joined CARICOM, following study of the question by a governmental committee, the visit of an opposition delegation to Georgetown to pledge their support of integration, and a call for LDC unity on matters of integration.

The MDCs signed the Treaty of Chaguaramas establishing CARICOM on July 4, 1973. In April 1974, Grenada, Belize, Dominica, Montserrat, St. Vincent and St. Lucia adhered. On July 26, 1974, St. Kitts-Nevis-Anguilla, which had been blocked from signing over the question of Anguilla became the final member to join the Caribbean Community and Common Market. At that time Caribbean integration moved to a customs union combined with a series of other measures to comprise a more advanced type II integration scheme.

iv. The Pattern of Negotiations in Caribbean Integration: The Second Phase

With the coming into force of the Treaty of Chaguaramas for all the member states of CARICOM, the countries of the Commonwealth Caribbean succeeded in advancing the integration movement to a form which was better adapted to contribute to the goal of economic development of the region. The crisis surrounding this move bears witness to the difficulty of the task, and analysis of the negotiating process sheds light on the nature of Third World regional integration.

The establishment of CARICOM represented the creation of a more advanced (although still limited) type II integration scheme based on a customs union accompanied by measures to more equitably distribute the costs and benefits of integration through cost-lowering measures for the LDCs and corrective measures, the Caribbean Development Bank and the Caribbean Investment Corporation. The negotiations preceding the agreement on this scheme in the Georgetown Accord found a dichotomy of bargaining positions with the more developed independent countries of the region advocating expansive policies and resisting distributive policies, and with the lesser developed countries of

the East Caribbean and Belize insisting on distributive measures as a price for their support of the expansive policy of a common external tariff. The outcome, as found in the Georgetown Accord and in amendments to CARIFTA policies and practices, was based on a package of measures which represented a linked expansive-distributive policy.

As in the case of the establishment of CARIFTA in 1968, a strong external stimulus was provided by the United Kingdom's application for entry into the European Economic Community, which confronted them with the prospect of losing, or at least having to renegotiate their preferential export markets. This external factor played a continuing and important role in CARICOM negotiations as the Commonwealth Caribbean countries joined the other African, Caribbean and Pacific (ACP) countries to bargain over their relationship with the EEC. The independent territories were anxious to enter these negotiations with the united front of a single Caribbean negotiating position which depended very much on maintaining unity among all CARIFTA members in moving to CARICOM.

The eventual linked expansive-distributive policy outcome was achieved only because the LDCs were able to act in a concerted manner to bargain for the truly distributive measures rather than settle for 'opting out' provisions or avoidance mechanisms. This represented an evolution from the earlier negotiations where the LDCs had pursued a foot-dragging strategy of avoiding or delaying the costs of integration. In 1972, however, when the MDCs attempted to gain their support by providing even more liberal obligations for the LDCs, the latter were not content with these concessions and demanded measures for the allocation of industries. Their position was made more effective by a co-ordination of their efforts through the ECCM Secretariat and the CARIFTA Secretariat whose efforts to bring about his more comprehensive conception of integration were pursued with relentless energy both in the initiation of proposals and in personal diplomacy with individual governments. The Secretariat represented the vanguard of the integration movement, pushing to advance the cause while delicately remaining within the limits accepted by the governments.

The governments of the MDCs also found themselves supporting a common position arising from the desire to create a protected regional market for their products through the creation of a common external tariff. The change of a government in Jamaica, and the resulting change in the Jamaican position toward the creation of a customs union was perhaps the most crucial factor in the eventual adoption of CARICOM. If Jamaica, one of the most important of the MDCs, had retained her earlier opposition to the establishment of a CET, this opposition in conjunction with the opposition of the LDCs would have been difficult to overcome. The domestic political opposition in Jamaica remained vocally critical of the move to CARICOM, mainly by evoking the spectre of a revived federation, but the concrete gains perceived by the manufacturing sector provided important support to the government's desire to support the customs union.

The other MDCs also supported the common external tariff, with Trinidad and Tobago and Guyana being the most supportive of even deeper integration. During the period of negotiations, 1971–73, Guyana became more and more outspoken in favor of some form of political integration. Barbados, as the least well-off of the MDCs, was again accorded certain opting-out provisions of the CET and harmonization of fiscal incentives which lowered the cost of further integration and which placed her in a special category among the MDCs.

Apart from measures adopted to make the Caribbean Development Bank an institution more adapted to the needs of the LDCs, the only truly distributive measure embodied in the move from CARIFTA to CARICOM was the Caribbean Investment Corporation. The CIC is an institution which is designed to transfer development benefits from the MDCs to the LDCs in the form of equity-capital investment. Although the governments and private sectors of all member countries are contributors, the major part of the funds are provided by MDCs, and the capital is destined for projects only in the LDCs. Even though 60% of the capital is from public sources the institution is essentially *laissez-faire* in nature, and its establishment did not really satisfy the LDC demand for allocation of industry in their territories. The CIC, however, is the only institution through which free movement of capital from MDCs to LDCs is permitted in the region, because of foreign exchange restrictions in the MDCs who fear a flight of capital through the LDCs whose currency is freely convertible.

The EECM countries have undertaken to allocate among themselves 35 industries identified by the Economist Intelligence Unit (EIU) report as being suitable for establishment in their territories, but the MDCs are not barred from establishing these same industries, some of which already exist in their countries. The MDCs have agreed not to· offer fiscal incentives to these industries, but since other external economies such as developed infrastructure and lower cost inputs are often more important than tax holidays in influencing location decisions, CARICOM still lacks any adequate policy of industrial allocation which is likely to effectively counter the problem of polarization. For the same reasons the more generous fiscal incentives allowed the LDCs within the provisions of the Agreement on the Harmonization of Fiscal Incentives are not likely to have a major influence on attracting industry.

Another 'permissive' element of the Georgetown Accord is the agreement to eliminate double taxation among the MDCs and LDCs, which, again, simply eliminates a minor obstacle to MDC investment in LDCs by assuring the investor he will not be taxed in both places, but which takes no positive action to provide investment.

In sum, the negotiated package of measures although comprising elements of a corrective mechanism represents a minimal step toward the LDC demand for allocation of industry. This again reflects the fact that the LDCs are in a very weak negotiating position *vis-à-vis* the MDCs. The MDCs have increased exports to the LDCs, but these markets remain very limited. The fact that the LDCs succeeded in getting the CIC as part of the bargain is attributable to their common front and the strong desire to keep them in the organization to present a single negotiating position to the EEC on the part of the MDCs. Thus this external political factor played a key role in the outcome. There clearly was a limit to what the MDCs were willing to concede, however, and direct allocation of industry or transfer of funds was beyond that limit.

The Caribbean Investment Corporation as a *laissez-faire* gesture toward allocation of industry owned much to the role of the private sector in the region, and its nature reflects very much their conception of integration. Just as the ICCC had played a major role in the phased freeing of trade approach to integration in 1967, its successor organization, the CAIC played a major role in the key element of the CARICOM negotiations, the Caribbean Investment Corporation. The CIC proposal emanated from the joint CAIC-Secretariat mission the LDCs in 1972, and the participation of the private sector in the form of contribution of 40% of the funds was based on the desire to avoid the adoption of very *dirigiste* corrective measures and to preserve the free enterprise nature of the integration movement by preempting total state control. This position came from the realization on the part of the business community that some distributive measures were necessary to succeed in getting total regional support for the common external tariff, and that if the private sector was not involved the state would make major inroads into regional economic activity. The promotion and support of the Caribbean Investment Corporation as a policy of the CAIC was the culmination of politics within the CAIC which included members from the

MDCs and the LDCs, both from Chambers of Commerce and Manufacturers Associations, thus regrouping elements from both the commercial and industrial sectors. The ultimate position of the CAIC represented an understanding of the problem of polarization and a consequent realization of the need for distributive measures to accompany the CET. It also reflected the domination of the manufacturers 'produce and sell' position over the importers 'buy and sell' position on the Common External Tariff. Even though the latter were numerous in the region, the importance of the manufacturers associations, particularly in Jamaica and Trinidad and Tobago, plus increasing investment on the part of the commercial sector in industrial enterprise provided the basis of support for a policy which eventually led to adoption of the CIC. The private sector was also aware of the very strong commitment on the part of the governments to encouraging industrial production and the possibility of state action to achieve this goal. The mission to the LDCs demonstrated what was required as a compromise for the LDCs, and the Demas-Matalon Report which resulted from collaboration between the CAIC committee and the Secretarial Task force provided the basis for creation of the Caribbean Investment Corporation.

A real limit to the degree to which *dirigiste* measures could be adopted was also imposed by the fact that the dominant economic doctrine of the region is free enterprise. Even St. Lucia, the most committed country to political integration among the LDCs was hesitant about a real system of industrial allocation. According to the CAIC mission report, Premier John Compton. . . 'expressed a preference for the competitive attraction of industries among the LDCs rather than any administrative system of allocation and reservation'.[53] This reluctance to adopt any 'direct' transfer of benefits, even through compensatory mechanisms, was manifest in the unwillingness to adopt the proposal of the Montserrat paper to transfer 10% of trade surpluses from MDCs to LDCs. Trinidad and Tobago's contribution to a special fund to aid the LDCs in obtaining counterpart funds through the CDB and her balance of payments support to central banks of the MDCs are the closest to direct transfers that has occurred, and this was undertaken on an *ad hoc* basis.

The nature of the negotiations surrounding the movement from CARIFTA to CARICOM indicates the limits imposed on the degree to which a *dirigiste* approach to integration was possible. Within these constraints, however, the Georgetown Accord and subsequent Treaty of Chaguaramas represented a linked expansive-distributive policy outcome which even more closely reflected the the-

oretical pattern suggested than did the initial negotiation of the CARIFTA Agreement. As in the earlier stage of negotiations political considerations and external factors influenced the degree to which the policy positions of the relevant actors followed the pattern suggested by the perceived opportunity costs based on economic integration theory. This general pattern was reinforced in the third stage of negotiation of Caribbean integration, the proposed move to a type III integration scheme with the consideration of a policy to regulate direct foreign investment and the transfer of technology into the region.

Abbreviations

CARIFTA:	Caribbean Free Trade Association
LDCs:	Less Developed Countries
MDCs:	More Developed Countries
ECLA:	Economic Commission of Latin America
EC:	Eastern Caribbean (currency)
AMP:	Agricultural Markets Protocol
ECCM:	East Caribbean Common Market
CARICOM:	Caribbean Community
CAIC:	Caribbean Association of Industry & Commerce
EEC:	European Economic Community
F.O.B.	Free on Board
ICCC:	Incorporated Caribbean Chambers of Industry and Commerce

Notes

1. Commonwealth Caribbean Regional Secretariat, *From Carifta to Caribbean Community* (Georgetown, Guyana, 1972), p. 35.
2. Economic Commission for Latin America, Office for the Caribbean, *The Caribbean Integration Programme (1968–1972)*, POS/INT 72/8 COPR. 1, Port of Spain, 1973 (Draft), p. 17.
3. Caribbean Development Bank, *Annual Report, 1970* (Bridgetown, Barbados), 1971.
4. Caribbean Development Bank, *Annual Report, 1971* (Bridgetown, Barbados), 1972.
5. Caribbean Development Bank, *Annual Report, 1973* (Bridgetown, Barbados), 1974, p. 11.
6. William G. Demas, Statement at the Sixteenth Session of the Economic Commission for Latin America, Port of Spain, May 6–14, 1975, *Speeches and Resolutions*, p. 13. See also William G. Demas, *Address to the Fifth Annual Meeting of the Board of Governors*, May 26, 27, 1975 (Bridgetown, Barbados).
7. ECLA, *The Caribbean Integration Programme (1968–1972)*, p. 17.
8. Economic Commission for Latin America Office for the Caribbean, *Economic Activity. Caribbean Community Countries — 1973* (Port of Spain, 1974), ECLA/POS 74/10.

9. Economic Commission for Latin America, Office for the Caribbean, *Economic Activity Caribbean Community Countries, 1974* (Port of Spain, 1975), ECLA/POS 75/4.
10. ECLA, *The Caribbean Integration Programme (1968–1972)*, p. 19.
11. Commonwealth Caribbean Regional Secretariat (CCRS), *From Carifta to Caribbean Community*, p. 36.
12. A discussion and critical evaluation of the Agricultural Market Protocol and Guaranteed Market Scheme is provided by agricultural economist Louis L. Smith, *Critical Evaluation of the Performance of the ECCM countries under the Agricultural Marketing Protocol (AMP) and the Guaranteed Market Scheme (GMS)* (Port of Spain: ECLA: Office for the Caribbean, 1974), ECLA/POS 74/16. The World Bank undertook an extensive analysis of the agricultural situation in its regional study, including an analysis of the impact of integration on agriculture. International Bank for Reconstruction and Development (IBRD), *Caribbean Regional Study,* volume III, *Agriculture,* Report No. 566a (Washington, D.C., 1975). See also K. L. Roache, 'Prospects for Agricultural Growth in the Commonwealth Caribbean for the next ten years', in *Development Prospects and Options in the Commonwealth Caribbean,* ed. by Edith Hodgkinson (London: Overseas Development Institute,1976), pp. 21–9.
13. Barbados *Advocate-News,* May 12, 1969.
14. *Ibid.,* June 27, 1970, and October 4, 1970.
15. Trinidad *Express,* June 6, 1970.
16. Although we have argued that in general integration among developing countries is likely to result in trade diversion,the World Bank study finds that CARICOM has probably had a net trade creating effect. IBRD, *op. cit.*
17. Jamaica *Daily Gleaner,* February 25, 1971.
18. Trinidad *Express,* supplement, July 19, 1970.
19. Guyana *Graphic,* April 15, 1970.
20. As early as 1969 the Barbados Manufacturers Association called for protection from third-country imports. Barbados *Advocate-News,* December 28, 1969.
21. Trinidad *Guardian,* February 21, 1968.
22. *Ibid.,* October 8, 1972.
23. Barbados *Advocate-News,* October 5, 1969.
24. Jamaica *Daily Gleaner,* April 27, 1973.
25. *Ibid.,* March 30, 1972.
26. Barbados *Advocate-News,* October 8, 1971.
27. *Ibid.,* October 8, 1971.
28. Trinidad *Guardian,* October 4, 1971.
29. Barbados *Advocate-News,* June 18, 1970.
30. Guyana *Graphic,* July 13, 1972.
31. Trinidad *Guardian,* October 11, 1972.
32. Guyana *Graphic,* October 8, 1972.
33. *Ibid.*
34. *Ibid.,* October 9, 1972.
35. *Ibid.,* October 13, 1972.
36. CCRS, *From Carifta to Caribbean Community,* p. 44.
37. *Report of a Meeting Between CAIC's Special Committee and the CARIFTA Task Force held in the Office of the Barbados Chamber of Commerce,* September 14, 1972, pp. 39–40.
38. The Caribbean Association of Industry and Commerce, Inc., *Report of the Mission Undertaken by the Caribbean Association of Industry and Commerce (CAIC) to the LDCs of CARIFTA to Discuss and Stimulate the Establishment of Industrial Ventures in the LDCs,* October 1972, p. 1.
39. *Ibid.,* pp. 2, 3.
40. Guyana *Graphic,* October 17, 1972.
41. *Ibid.,* March 4, 1973.
42. Trinidad *Express,* March 3, 1973.
43. Barbados *Advocate-News,* April 7, 1973.
44. Commonwealth Caribbean Regional Secretariat, Eight Conference of Heads of Government of Commonwealth Caribbean Countries, Georgetown, Guyana, April 9–12, 1973, *Montserrat's Proposals on the Caribbean Common Market* (submitted by Montserrat), HGC 18/73, March 30, 1973, p. 2.
45. *Ibid.,* pp. 4–5.
46. *Ibid.,* p. 6.
47. Jamaica *Daily Gleaner,* April 12, 1973.
48. Trinidad *Express,* April 11, 1973.
49. *Ibid.*
50. Guyana *Graphic,* April 26, 1974.
51. Thomas Wright, Jamaica *Daily Gleaner,* April 24, 1973.
52. Trinidad *Guardian,* March 5, 1973.
53. The Georgetown Accord; Commonwealth Caribbean Regional Secretariat, *The Caribbean Community — A Guide* (Georgetown), Guyana, 1973, Appendix A, pp. 93–6.
54. Memorandum, Chief Ministers Office, Government of Montserrat, n.d., pp. 4–5.
55. Barbados *Advocate-News,* October 18, 1973.
56. *Ibid.,* March 2, 1974.
57. CAIC, *Report of Mission. . . . ,* p. 16.

American Colonial Integration of Puerto Rico

G. K. Lewis

In the decade that has passed since the publication of my earlier book, *Puerto Rico: Freedom and Power in the Caribbean,* in 1963, the Puerto Rican tragedy has deepened and become more severe, both in quantitative measurement and in qualitative character. While other colonial territories in the Caribbean became independent during that period — Barbados and Guyana in 1966, the Bahamas in 1973, Grenada in 1974 — Puerto Rico remains even more deeply in thrall to the American superpower. As, too, the internal contradictions of American corporate capitalism in its imperialist phase have become increasingly acute, sharpened immeasurably by the prolonged Southeast Asian war, these contradictions have made themselves felt more and more in the subordinate colonial society. The growing pressure of these contradictions has given a new and brutalizing edge to the twin properties of the American dominion: (1) colonialism in its purest form, exemplified by military occupation, juridical control, economic exploitation, and a process of deculturation almost amounting to deliberate ethnocide; and (2) neocolonialism in the form of the growth of intermediary island elites that have co-opted the local government machinery in San Juan, but whose capacity to innovate in the realm of territorial public policy is severely limited by the ultimate and awesome power of the federal government in Washington. These two phenomena constitute two sides of the same coin: a highly organized structure of imperialist domination, perfected to a degree never before seen in the history of the Caribbean.

If this sounds like revolutionary rhetoric rather than sober analysis, even a brief glance at what has taken place during the last ten years will establish its essential verity. Every seminal problem has changed only in degree, not in kind. There is, in the first place, the continuing Puerto Rican obsession with status politics which, like the slavery issue in pre-Civil War America, or the church-state issue in the Third French Republic, is a cancer that infects every tissue of the body politic. Nor is that accidental; it is related, with inexorable logic, to the continuing politico-administrative control of the island territory by the Washington politicians and bureaucrats. Some 85% of the basic areas of government that constitute national sovereignty in any generally understood definition of that term remain under the jurisdiction of the U.S. Congress: immigration, transportation, tariff policy and trade, financial laws, environment, citizenship, juridical appeals, communications, minimum wages and other labour matters, navigable waters, planning, transfer of federal lands, and military use of the island territory under the guise of 'common defense'. The government of Puerto Rico, in effect, governs practically nothing. The juridico-constitutional status of the island still stands on the base of the curious 'unincorporated territory' theory of the old *Insular* cases, with its denial of certain 'nonfundamental' rights to the U.S. citizen who happens to be Puerto Rican, despite the fact that, as many Puerto Rican constitutional experts have pointed out, the distinction between 'fundamental' and 'nonfundamental' rights has been rejected in U.S. Supreme Court decisions in the last decade, in a constitutional revolution that has immeasurably extended the area of individual freedoms and protections deemed to be 'fundamental'. Correspondingly, the Federal Relations Act of 1952, which failed to challenge the old 'limited citizenship' theory, is so utterly archaic that not only does its language signify the extension of rights granted by a sovereign power to a subordinate possession but also, even more important, it leaves untouched, and therefore inferentially disposed in favour of federal interests, all of those relationships in which the very survival of Puerto Rico as a society is at stake: military bases situated in heavily populated civilian areas, sugar quotas, foreign relations, international representation, declaration of war, and final judicial review. And in all of this, as if to add insult to injury, the U.S. connection requires Puerto Ricans to obey the commanding mandate of an alien constitution in the continuing operation of which, either by means of a shared presidential vote or an elected congressional delegation, they do not share.

This basic, fundamental inequity of citizenship runs through the entire apparatus of the Puerto Rican-United States relationship. Nothing illustrates it so starkly — to take only a single example — as the application of the U.S. Selective Service Act. The central issue of American politics throughout the last decade has been the Vietnamese war. In the figure of the young American war dissenter, it has given new popularity both to Thoreau's doctrine of legitimate disobedience and to the old medieval doctrine of the 'unjust war'. Yet that dissenter can appeal to his congressman, vote against the President in his capacity as commander-in-chief, of the armed forces, and even appeal to the old doctrine of states' rights. His Puerto Rican counterpart can resort to none of these measures. He is subject to a regime of obligatory military service over which, quite literally, he has no control even though he is an American citizen. As a U.S. Virgin Islands newspaper editorial has put it, speaking of the young male Virgin Islander who is in the same boat, he can be compelled to bear arms, to be maimed and crippled, even to die for his country, without any right to cast a vote for the person of his choice, who, in addition to becoming President, will become his commander-in-chief and, holding both positions, can send him into war without even the consent of Congress. Judge Hiram Cancio's bold decision, in *United States of America v. Edwin Feliciano Grafals* (1970), speaking for the San Juan District Court, supported that argument. Although accepting the constitutionality of the applicability of Selective Service legislation to the island, Judge Cancio emphatically impugned its justice. He did so on the grounds, first, that there exists in Puerto Rico no express and specific consent on the part of the Puerto Rican people to the legislation because the so-called generic consent supposedly given in the consultations via referenda between 1950 and 1952 does not constitute such a consent; and, second, that so long as Puerto Rico is neither a state of the union nor an independent sovereign state, and at the same time is a 'Commonwealth' not clearly defined in its terms by Congress, many 'respectable and intelligent' Puerto Ricans may in fact reasonably argue that such unilateral application of congressional legislation to the 'commonwealth' is unjust. It only remains to add to that historic judgment two items: first, that Congress has so far failed to yield to Judge Cancio's suggestion that the issue be resolved by agreement that the penal provisions of the Selective Service Act and similar legislation should not apply to Puerto Rico unless expressly approved by its own legislature and governor; and, second, that during the entire period of the shameful Vietnamese adventure not a single leading voice of either of the Puerto Rican Establishment political parties dared whisper a murmur of criticism against its perpetra-

tors. It is small wonder that the University of Puerto Rico crisis of 1969–1971 centred around the effort, finally successful, of the radical *independentista* student forces to eject the ROTC program from the campus.

Puerto Rico, in brief, remains a province subordinate to American power. That this is so is testified to by the intriguing fact that all of the various elements on the local political scene agree to that dictum, although naturally enough they arrive at it from different ideological perspectives. The *incondicionales* of the Partido Nuevo Progresista (PNP), seeing commonwealth status as an unsatisfactory halfway house, want full statehood. The various centrist parties including the reigning Partido Popular Democrático (PPD), want a new 'pact of association' with the United States. The various *independentista* factions want sovereign independence, some of them by means of outright revolt, some of them by means of mutual accord with Washington. To read their respective platforms in the 1972 elections is to perceive that all of them, in one way or another, conceive the present relationship to be juridically ambiguous, politically disadvantageous, and economically one-sided.

There is general agreement — to take, as an example, another irritating bone of contention — on the matter of immigration control and policy. 'The lack of power on the part of the colonial government of Puerto Rico to control the entry of foreigners into the country, in accordance with our needs and aspirations', wrote the Partido Independentista Puertorriqueño (PIP) in 1971, 'constitutes one of the gravest problems that we confront today. While thousands of our fellow countrymen have been obliged to leave the island in search of work opportunities and better conditions of life, a large number of foreigners, both North Americans and Cubans have established themselves here, displacing Puerto Rican workers. Something like 30,000 persons who are not Puerto Rican vote in our elections. A large sector of these immigrants control a high proportion of the country's communications media, thus directly influencing public opinion'. 'We must recognize', wrote the *autonomista* wing of the Partido Popular in its famous *Pronunciamento de Aguas Buenas* in 1970, 'that this is a densely populated island, scarcely able to produce enough to maintain its almost 3 million inhabitants. As a consequence, Puerto Ricans have become involuntary actors in one of the most dramatic migratory episodes of modern times. Something like 1 million Puerto Ricans have been forced to seek out a better life in the United States during the last twenty five years ... Correspondingly, along with this phenomenon, there has taken place in recent times a massive immigration of foreigners which has cancelled out the differential between Puerto Ricans leaving and entering the island. We are faced with the serious problem of the growing displacement of our population with another of foreign origin. This is a grave problem that could acquire an alarming magnitude'. 'A new pact of association', wrote the liberal breakaway party, Partido del Pueblo, in 1972, 'would require that the people of Puerto Rico possess the authority to determine its own policy and procedures respecting the admission and expulsion of foreigners within the territorial limits of its jurisdiction'.

The professional student of colonialism will immediately recognize here two traditional trademarks of colonial society. The first is that this society, unable to shape its own public policy, is compelled, in effect, to export its unemployment problem; in the Puerto Rican issue, literally one-third of the population has been forced into more or less involuntary exile, to live in the ghettos of the North American* cities. The second is that it is obliged to receive, in return, the future of the expatriate who has played such a large role in the history of Caribbean colonialism generally: in the Puerto Rican case, this has meant both the North American, who generally brings with him a characteristic racial prejudice against Puerto Ricans, and the Cuban political exile, who brings with him a cultural prejudice against Puerto Ricans. Increasingly, the Puerto Rican, like the native Virgin Islander in St. Thomas and St. Croix begins to feel like a stranger in his own society. It is not surprising, then, that many of them, irrespective of ideological preferences, begin to resent the situation. Nor must this be seen as an expression of xenophobic chauvinism, for Puerto Ricans have traditionally been a hospitable people. There are few *independentistas* who will not acknowledge, in the true spirit of international camaraderie, that one of the leaders of the 1868 revolt against Spain was Matías Brugman, a *yanqui,* or that the father of the Puerto Rican labour movement, Santiago Iglesias, was a Spaniard. It is, rather, that today they feel inundated by an invasion of whole alien ethnic blocs who share little with them. The resentment flares up every so often in the disputes in the local newspaper correspondence columns around the theme 'Who is a Puerto Rican?' How deeply the intergroup animosities are felt can be gauged from the fact that whenever a local journalist suggests in an article that a *norte-americano* or a *cubano* can never hope to be accepted as a Puerto Rican (one journalist, in an unfortunate moment, termed the

Cubans 'the Jews of the Caribbean'), he is met with a response of fury truly paranoid in its expression.

Puerto Rico, then, is still governed through the instrumentality of an unchanged Federal Relations Act and by 'congressional government', a system of government whose grievous defects have not basically changed since Woodrow Wilson dissected them in 1885 in his *Congressional Government A Study in America Politics.* What has changed at every point of the political-ideological spectrum is the Puerto Rican attitude to the system. The national mood — no matter what indices are used to measure it — has undergone a profound transformation. The earlier euphoria of the 1950s and early 1960s, when the Popular architects could declaim the Estado Libre Asociado as a bold new experiment pregnant with creative energies that could transform American federalism, has been replaced by a mood of growing doubt, dismay, and disillusionment. It would be difficult today to find even the most sanguine of Commonwealth theoreticians (who flourish like the green bay tree in the colonial climate of opinion) who would dare use the extravagant language of the earlier period.

A number of factors have contributed to this metamorphosis. In part, of course, it is the change from one generation to another. The political class of the classic Popular era was shaped by the Puerto Rico of the 1930s, a mainly agricultural economy trapped in colonial poverty; its successors have been shaped by a new Puerto Rico, urban, industrialized, and more educated, in which over 65% of the population lives in the four major districts of the huge San Juan megalopolis. In the very nature of things, since time and tide wait for no man, this has precipitated a new style in the sociology of insular politics. The old type of political leader, who imposed a unipersonal rule on both party machine and followers, has been replaced by the consensus-seeking, committee-room technocratic leader, so that there is a world of difference, for instance, between Luis Muñoz Marín, who governed his party as a *cacique* would govern an Indian tribe, and his successor to the governorship, Rafael Hernández Colón, who prefers the anonymous style of behind-the-scenes consultation with all groups of the party *familia.* Negotiation and consensus replace heroic histrionics; conformity gives way to legitimate dissent; legislative chieftains assert themselves boldly against the Governor in the Casa Blanca; a more sophisticated electorate, as the famous 1968 election showed, learns the art of the split vote or even the absentee ballot; and,

---

*Since the term *American* refers, properly speaking, to inhabitants of all the Americas, the term *North American* is used throughout this essay to refer to the people and the institutions of the United States.

ironically, the only contemporary political leader who still manages a charismatic style, thereby making the rational also emotionally palatable, is Rubén Berríos, the new leader of the reinvigorated Partido Independentista Puertorriqueño, in which the process of high ideological and structural change has been the most pronounced of all. Both individual voter and individual party member have begun to revolt against the traditional *personalismo* of insular politics, where trust was more important than belief, face-to-face encounter securing the person's *dignidad* through the ritual approval of others was more important than open dissent, which might expose the person to the terror of ridicule, and, finally, personal fealty to the *jefe* was equated with party loyalty.

It is important to note how this profound change in political psychology has affected the status issue. Up to 1964, the date of his abdication, Muñoz was able to impose successfully his slogan 'status is not an issue' upon party and electorate alike because he was undisputed master of the monolithic Popular organization and because there existed no real, viable opposition. After 1964 both these conditions disappeared. Kenneth Farr's book, *Personalism and Politics: Institutionalization of the Popular Democratic Party of Puerto Rico,* has effectively described the democratizing process that took place between 1964 and 1970 in the Popular machine. It was a process precipitated by a series of events: the growing rift between Muñoz and Roberto Sánchez Vilella, his hand-picked successor; the open struggle after 1965 between the 'old guard' and the 'new generation' on the vexing issue of the university reform law; the formation of the 'jíbaros de Negrón' in response to the organization of the younger liberal elements; Muñoz's return to leadership; the fratricidal 1968 campaign for nominations; the debacle of the party convention in July 1968, ending as it did with Sánchez Vilella's 'bolt' from the party and the founding of his own Partido del Pueblo, or People's Party; and all of this culminating in the trauma of the Popular defeat in the 1968 election by the rising Partido Nuevo Progresista (PNP), successor to the old Statehood Republican Party. Much of this was a struggle between the *muñozcista* traditionalists and the group of 'young Turks', many of them university faculty members, who revolted against a tradition in which ideological conformity was imposed under the dubious doctrine of 'majority mandate' and 'party discipline'.

The end result has been to give some degree of institutionalization to the party, after the manner of institutionalized parties like the PRI in Mexico and the Congress Party in India; and, more, to make it possible for party 'mavericks' like Severo Colberg

and Roberto Rexach Benítez to act as a new 'ginger group' without having their dissidence identified, as in the old days, with treason. It is too early to say, of course, that the disease of orthodoxy has completely disappeared from insular politics, as the successive withdrawal of dissidents like Bennie Frankie Cerezo and Justo Méndez from the PNP and the perennial secessions from the PIP sufficiently illustrate. But the lesson secreted in the recent history of the PPD is plain for the high mandarins of all parties to see. And it is worth adding, as a Caribbean comparison, that the calamitous decline of the People's National Movement in Trinidad dramatically underlines the lesson, for it was a decline directly traceable to the fact that the party from its beginning in 1955 was based upon the single rock of the legendary intellectual brilliance of its leader, Dr. Eric Williams.

The second factor that made possible the reemergence of the status issue in Puerto Rico is the growth of a viable multi-party system, replacing the one-party oligarchy of the Populares. It is a cardinal law of politics that prolonged stay in power corrupts even the most idealistic of parties. By the mid–1960s the Popular leadership had almost completely lost touch with the changing class character of the electorate. It was in a period of transitional ideology; having lost its early neo-socialist agrarian radicalism, it had yet fully to discover the urban, middle-class liberalism to which now, in 1974, it is committed. And since politics, like nature, abhors a vacuum, the gap was filled by new groupings. On the Right it was the PNP, pursuing an aggressive statehood strategy and appealing to all of the elements disillusioned with Muñoz and his vague rhetoric about 'social justice' — the poor, the new middle class of the *urbanización* villas, the new motorized salariat, the teachers, and the police. As elements, moreover, that had been taught a new acquisitive instinct by the industrialization program that the Populares themselves had initiated, these elements were by no means prepared to accept the specious arguments of Popular bogus radicalism, the argument, for example, that the PNP gubernatorial candidate, Luis Ferré, a Ponce cement millionaire, was unfit to be governor simply because he was a millionaire; on the contrary, they saw in Ferré's capitalist wealth everything that fulfilled their daydreams about rapid upward social mobility. Correspondingly, the gap created by the Popular decline was filled on the Left by the revamped PIP, pursuing an aggressive independence strategy with the added element of socialist ideology, and appealing, with its militant slogan, *arriba los de abajo,* to the 40 to 45% or more Puerto Ricans who still live in poverty or near-poverty.

That combination of demands for full sovereign independence and a socialist commonwealth thus challenged the curious Popular assumption that the issues of status and social organization could be artificially separated from each other, almost as if they were possessed of separate and independent lives of their own, instead of being inextricably interwoven. It is the exaggerated dependency on the North American political order that perpetuates and intensifies the insular poverty, and it is in this sense, interestingly enough, that the wheel of Puerto Rican politics has come full cycle. The great achievement of the young Muñoz after 1938 was to introduce a new style of political address, replacing the florid and empty oratory of the old-style politicians, with its fulsome references to the beauty of Puerto Rican nature and of Puerto Rican women, with a new attention to the bread-and-butter issues of *jíbaro* life, combined with an *independentista* stand on political status. The new orators of the radical nationalist sectors of the present period have gone back, albeit with a sharper ideological frame of reference, to that earlier innovative manner.

These two factors, of course, have been part cause, part result of a correspondingly important change that has taken place in the character of the Puerto rican electorate. Yesterday it was an electorate too timid to challenge the rule of the politicians. Today it has become far more independently minded, far more skeptical of bland promises, far more ready to examine the record of those it has elected to office. Groups that were once taken for granted by the politicians — public school teachers, for example — have become pressure groups of their own, as the recent Teachers' Association strike demonstrates. The churches, in their turn, are to be reckoned with as a separate force. In 1960 Muñoz could afford to attack the Catholic bishops who sought to organize a vote against him. In 1974 it would have been far more difficult for the government of his successors to ignore, let alone to criticize, the Pentecostal and Evangelical churches, which were able to bring an estimated 100,000 faithful into the streets to demonstrate against the Commonwealth Supreme Court's controversial judgment on the so-called church noise issue. In sum, a variety of factors — the new complexity of the social structure, the growth of the professions, the new social impatience of the poor — have combined to end the old monopoly of the politicians. The politicians must now court a public opinion which before they would almost take for granted. The silent electorate has become an assertive electorate. The old type of political boss has been replaced by the new type of political aspirant, like José Enrique Arraras of the Populares and Carlos Romero Barceló of the Statehood Republicans, who must learn to talk and argue his way into office. That new type is also beginning to write books of social and political commentary, a thing unheard of among the practitioners of the old style; Romero Barceló's booklet *La Estadidad es para los pobres* is a case in point.

Taking all these factors into account, it is true that far from status not being an issue, the issue has taken on new status. Political Puerto Rico, like Caesar's Gaul, is still divided into three parts: the protagonists, respectively, of Commonwealth, statehood, and independence. Commonwealth status has declined because it has shown itself powerless to deal effectively with the social and economic ills, old and new, of the society. It has been jokingly said that the 1787 Constitution was founded on the assumption of the immortality of George Washington; in similar fashion, the 1952 Puerto Rican Constitution was founded on the assumption of the immorality of Muñoz. His retirement has left a leadership vacuum, for no successor has been able to defend Commonwealth with any of his brilliancy, intellectual virtuosity, wit, and verbal dexterity. It is true that the concept of polarization enunciated by PIP theoreticians — that Commonwealth would disappear, to be replaced by an open confrontation between statehood and independence — has proven to be an empty hope; yet there has undeniably taken place a decline in the intellectual quality of the argumentative defenses of Commonwealth. The statehood ideal, at the same time, showed that it would pass the ultimate and crucial test of electoral appeal when it proved in 1968 that it had the capacity to win an election and constitute a government. The remarkable revitalization for the *independentista* forces also shows that they can garner significant segments of electoral support, notwithstanding their socialist label, once naively supposed to be alien to the local political tradition. So much is all of this so that the U.S.-Puerto Rico Status Commission of 1965 felt obliged to report that all of the three status alternatives possessed social and cultural viability within the framework of the operating normative values of the society. This explains why it is possible to meet people of all three ideological persuasions at most local social gatherings; although, at the same time, there has been a noticeable tendency toward ideological segregation at the social level and an equally noticeable tendency toward accentuated ideological intolerance.

SECTION TWELVE
Independence, Nationhood, and Identity

Shortly after the onset of their imperialist establishment, Caribbean Societies began to create and nourish elements that sought to push them away from their colonial scaffold. As the process of creolization accelerated during the eighteenth century, most societies were already having intense political discussion about the degree of 'independence' necessary to ventilate their nativist consciousness and interests. Invariably, however, popular opinion in colonial societies was divided on questions of autonomy, independence, and identity.

A general trend, nonetheless, was the strengthening over time of the case of those who insisted that Caribbean societies were more than mercantile outposts, but social formations with their own internal logic, cultural features, and ontological legitimacy. Associated with this process was the tendency of inhabitants, mostly creoles, to see themselves as 'citizens' rather than colonials who desired nation-status in order to rationalize the relationship between their consciousness and reality.

The demand for nationhood by Caribbean inhabitants, therefore, emerged from the cauldron of centuries of colonial domination. The nature of their relationships with corresponding metropoles, and the time at which the demand for political freedom was made, determined the nature of the outcome; that is, whether there would be constitutional reforms, or wars of liberation. These essays provide the insights necessary for a full understanding of the political and ideological circumstances facing different parts of the Caribbean at different times as they came to terms with the independence option.

In 'Divided to the Vein' Beckles examines the ideology and political vision of the founding fathers of the first Caribbean nation. It is clear that, on the one hand, Haiti constituted a powerful example of one possible way of breaking away from the colonial scaffold; but on the other hand, the article reveals that there were internal and external factors which were to prove intractable obstacles in the process of nation-building, not least being inter-ethnic political rivalry. Suchlicki's analysis of the philosophical writings and political articulations of José Martí, seen as the principal ideologue of Cuban independence, illustrates the continuity of thought between the Haitian episode and the Cuban experience at the end of the nineteenth century. Gordon Lewis illustrates the way in which independence politics emerged in the English-speaking Caribbean, and indicates the contradictions inherent in a 'negotiated' independence in which issues of form rather than substance attained autonomy. Nettleford and Beckles discuss the logical internal, social consequences of the Lewis thesis for Jamaica and Barbados respectively. They both show that independence did not resolve, in a favourable manner, many fundamental issues for the black majority especially those concerning the legitimacy of their heritage, identity, and role within the 'free' formation. Many things of African origins remain suppressed and devoid of instinctive official blessing at independence, sending signals to the social majority that the value structure and social culture of the colonizing minority, their descendants, and their imperial support groups, remain at the centre of important matters. This condition raises questions on the ground about the meaning of independence and the end of colonial rule for the social majority.

Divided to the Vein: The Problem of Race, Colour and Class Conflict in Haitian Nation-Building, 1804–1820

Hilary Beckles

No other event in the history of the Americas demonstrates in the way the Haitian Revolution does the tragic and heroic feature of the concomitant struggles against slavery and colonization. In ideological terms, its magnitude embraced the entire colonized world and its anti-slavery political successes were unprecedented. A generation earlier, revolutionaries in the North America colonies fought and won a war against British colonial rule, but kept slavery as the socioeconomic basis of their 'independent' dispensation.[1] They were forced to return to the battlefield a century later in order to resolve the problem of slavery with the politics of nation-building.

The retreat from the politics of universal social liberation by mainland Americans ultimately tainted the moral and philosophical integrity of their revolution, and suggests its corruption by sponsors of racist and elitist ideology. Blacks and coloureds in the French colony of St. Dominigue, then, were chosen by circumstances to lead the anti-colonial movement of the Americas to its highest level by insisting upon the inseparable unity of political freedom and social liberty. Between 1791 and 1804 they took the Atlantic slave-based, colonial complex and turned it upside down in search of fundamental human rights, and in so doing established a political and social conjuncture that significantly shaped the history of the Atlantic World.[2]

The stakes were high. Saint Dominigue was the Caribbean's most populous and economically prosperous colony; the relation between 'capitalism and slavery' was in good shape, as had been the case with Jamaica in the first half of the century. The social structure under which black slaves lived and died as the 'natally' disenfranchised was cast in centuries of anti-black social custom and ideology. The plantations of Saint Dominigue symbolized the wealth and class/caste power of whites. It was the showpiece of the European colonial enterprise, as Barbados had been in the mid-seventeenth century. Armies under the leadership of Toussaint L'Ouverture could not have chosen a more significant monument with which to make their point.

Having smashed the prized mercantile edifice, rebels had little time in which to pick up the pieces and begin the task of constructing a national order within which to display concepts of liberty and popular freedom. For them, it was a new world for the brave — a frontier to be conquered. The legacies of the old order, as expected, continued to dwell among those whose interest were better served by the displaced system, while the many anxieties of facing the future characterized the thinking of those responsible for charting the new way. The world was revolutionized and freedom, once again, was born in a bloodbath.[3]

From the beginning Toussaint the Liberator seemed prepared to accommodate his revolutionary anti-slavery position within the constitutional framework of a restructured French colonial authority. He was an irretrievable emancipationist, but he was no 'independista'. It was only following his arrest and deportation to France in June 1802 by imperial forces, and the subsequent spread of rumours throughout Saint Dominigue that emperor Napoleon had decreed the re-enslavement of all colonial blacks, that conditions were established for the waging of a full scale anti-colonial war. By the end of September, black and coloured rebels, under their separate military commanders, constituted an informal revolutionary army whose intention was to drive French imperial forces from the colony and declare its political sovereignty.[4]

Within less than a year of Toussaint's removal from the political arena of Saint Dominigue, military commanders, many of whom had participated in the circumstances leading up to his arrest, were making plans to transform what was essentially an anti-slavery, civil rights struggle, into a war of national liberation. In mid May, 1803, black and coloured generals, recognizing the need to establish a central command, met at Archaie to finalize plans for the coordination of military strategies. Of the black generals, Henri Christophe had consolidated his position in the north, while Jean Jacques Dessalines had entrenched himself in the Artibonite region. The mulatto generals, Alexandre Pétion and Nicholas Geffrard, were considered rulers of the West and South respectively.[5] The goal of these generals, David Nicholls suggests, was 'complete independence' since at this stage of the struggle they were convinced that whites were the 'common enemy, and that they must at all costs be defeated.'[6]

At the Archaie meeting General Jean Jacques Dessalines, a former field commander of Toussaint, well known for his distrust of the French, was chosen Chief of Military Operations, and invested with the task if leading the troops against the Imperial army under the command of General Rochambeau. After six months of bloody warfare, the French army, recognizing the impossibility of defeating the indigenous forces, surrendered on November 17, 1803 and agreed to terms set by Dessalines. Rochambeau's army, decimated and humiliated, was given ten days to remove itself from St. Domingue; Dessalines took the opportunity to impress upon departing troops that should they return to attempt a retake of the colony none of them would be spared to settle an agreement or to tell the tale.

The war of national liberation was the final stage in a wider struggle for freedom which was fashioned in its early stages under Toussaint's leadership. Under Dessalines, the struggle for sovereignty took the shape of an anti-colonial war that culminated in a unilateral declaration of independence. The state of Haiti was proclaimed at Gonalves on January 1, 1804. It was the second society in colonial America to successfully throw off the yoke of colonial subjection; it was the first to build a new dispensation upon the basis of universal citizenry. Slavery was declared banished forever. The Act of Independence was signed by Dessalines, Commander-in-Chief, and generals Christophe, Pétion, Cherveaux, Geffrard, Vernet and Gabard. Of these six Generals of Divisions, there were two blacks and four mulattos.[7] As will be demonstrated later, this ethnic distribution represented forces endemic to the country's ideological makeup that would soon assume determining political characteristics.

Assessments of post-independence realities in Haiti, Nicholls states, should recognize at the outset that the country had its birth within the context of a very bloody 'war of national liberation'.[8] The cost of independence, according to Alex Dupuy, if measured in terms of human lives and material

destruction, was extraordinary; he states, in relation to human costs:

It is estimated that the total number of dead following the [French] expedition and the subsequent war of independence neared 150,000. Those permanently disabled were between 50,000 and 55,000 on the French side, and 100,000 and 130,000 on the Haitian side.[9]

With respect to material damage, he adds:

The war of independence also left the economy in shambles. Le Cap, Port-de-Paix, Gonaives, and Saint-Marc were burned to the ground, and throughout the island plantations, sugar mills, ships, irrigation networks, wharfs, and domesticated and draft animals were destroyed. Though it is not possible to calculate the precise financial cost of the war, some put it at 1,144,258,948 Francs. Haiti, in other words, inherited a shattered economy.[10]

Against this background, then, the creation of the State of Haiti entailed at once acts of physical reconstruction as well as socio-ideological transformation.

The independence struggle, however, produced more than the debilitating circumstances of ruined infrastructure and economy. There were other internal and external features that were to prove intractable obstacles in the process of nation-building. Lyonel Paguin lists some of these as international ill-will, hostility and suspicion, unrest among the revolutionized labourers, dislocated concepts of productivity, and the presence of two rival elites — black and mulatto — jostling for political and economic supremacy.[11] The validity of Paqauin's assessment is reinforced when it is recognized that the principal difficulties of nation-building experienced by Haitians in the areas of foreign relations and domestic politics resulted from these characteristic features of the revolutionary process. These features overlapped and coalesced, and in so doing generated forces that tended toward endemic economic inefficiency, social instability and political disorder — circumstances that proved antithetical to the process of socio-economic development.

From the outset, then, Haiti's attempt at nation-building seemed to contradict forces germane to the colonial enterprise. At one level explanations are to be found in the fact that the revolutionary process incurred powerful trans-imperial ideological, economic, political and military opposition. At another level, the peculiar endogenous circumstances of inter-ethnic political rivalry that haunted the process of institution formation and growth should not be minimized. The twin elements of anti-colonialism and anti-slavery within the revolution dictated ultimately that too many important matters be settled immediately. Issues of national sovereignty, social and economic justice, black economic enfranchisement, and cultural redemption, for example,had to be tackled without delay. The viability and popularity of the revolution would depend upon the extent to which achievements were made in these areas. Nation-building would be effective only when the correct balances were struck and held between contending social groups with respect to their expectations and aspirations. This was the task of Dessalines' administration.

By way of settling the matter of his constitutional authority Dessalines bestowed upon himself the title of Emperor in very much the same manner that Napoleon (whose army he had conquered) had done. Then he chose his ministers in accordance with his perception of their attitudes toward the French. The French army, though driven from Haiti, remained garrisoned at neighbouring Spanish Santo Domingo; also, the country remained inhabited by a substantial community of French citizens who had supported Generals LeClerc and Rochambeau in their effort to turn back the revolution. The political climate, not surprisingly, was charged with fear of counter-revolution and invasion. Tensions ran high, and Dessalines' government reacted by giving preference to military preparedness above the need for urgent socio-economic reconstruction.

The oppressive sense of national insecurity that pervaded all aspects of life during the first year of independence, therefore, fashioned to a considerable degree socio-economic politics, as well as constitutional provisions. While it is correct to note that this environment assisted in legitimizing the continued rule of the Generals, and specifically the establishment of Dessalines' dictatorship, emphasis should also be placed on the fact that after thirteen years of fighting (defeating French, English and Spanish troops) there was no logical reason to expect political and military complacency. In addition to being named emperor, Dessalines was also proclaimed governor-general for life with the right to name his successor. His military officers ran all departments of government, including the judiciary and civil administration.[12]

Deep-seated political animosity toward the French, derived in large measure from the massacres associated with the war of liberation, was immediately fuelled by French diplomatic efforts to destabilize the infant regime. Emissaries were dispatched to the United States, Great Britain, Spain and Holland — the principal slave-owning nations — in order to secure their suspension of commercial and diplomatic relations with the independent state. France demanded that the least these nations could do in order to illustrate their disgust at rebel slaves constituting themselves into a nation was to refuse them any official recognition. In this regard, the French Ambassador to the United States, M. Talleyrand, informed General Louis Turreau in Washington:

The existence of an armed negro people, occupying places that they have despoiled by the most criminal acts, is a horrible spectacle for all white nations; all of them should feel that; by allowing them to continue in that state, they are sparing incendiaries and assassins.[13]

It was not difficult to reach an agreement on this issue; all slave-owning nations were of the opinion that M. Talleyrand was preaching to the converted.

Before his death, General LeClerc had expressed doubt as to whether European military power was capable of breaking the will of Haitians in order to conquer their land. Consequently, imperial efforts were directed at bringing the regime to its knees by means of the systematic application of political and economic pressures. It was within the context of this military stand-off that Haitian governments developed their foreign policies. While the French feared the victorious army, and dared not invade, Haitian governments recognized their weaknesses and limitations, and sought to minimize conflict with France and other slave-owning powers. Unable to export their revolution and hit France once again where it really hurt, Haitian policy reflected a determined pragmatism that spoke of a form of blockade deeper than economic embargoes. Dessalines exposed this crisis when he informed enslaved blacks in Martinique: 'Unfortunately, . . . I am not able to fly to your assistance and break your chains. Alas, an invincible obstacle separates us . . . But perhaps a spark from the fire which we have kindled will spring forth in your soul'.[14]

In subsequent speeches, Dessalines developed in detail a hands-off policy with respect to the slave colonies of France and England. In 1805, in order to give political firmness and certainty to this policy, he cast it within the constitution with the following clause: 'The emperor will not undertake any enterprise with a view to making conquest or to trouble the peace and internal regime of foreign colonies'.[15] This policy, however, did not protect neighbouring Spanish Santo Domingo which at this time was under French control. His unsuccessful invasion of 1805 echoed Toussaint's earlier design to bring the island under Haitian rule in order to abolish slavery throughout and to secure national borders. The emperor explained that his invasion constituted no breach of the non-intervention edict since he recognized as 'borders only those traced by nature and the sea'.[16]

Dessalines' policy of non-intervention in the internal affairs of neighbouring colonies was conceived in terms of the need to prevent the mobilization of a European military coalition against his state. The French did succeed in achieving among the slave-owning powers a general policy of non-recognition of Haiti, but the securing of a total economic blockade proved more problematic. The emperor seemed less concerned about the possibility of an effective economic blockade, and boasted that merchants would never forego economic gain in support of the nebulous ideologies of their governments.[17]

The United States emerged as Haiti's principal trading partner during the first year. English merchants, operating mainly out of Jamaica, jostled with the Americans for the larger share of Haitian trade. The Americans, however, in an effort to gain French support during the negotiation with Spain over the purchase of Louisiana, agreed to suspend commercial negotiations with Haiti in February, 1806. Dessalines, in response, encouraged the English and Dutch to take up the American trade in order to secure critical foreign exchange and army supplies for his military regime.

As the French government tightened its diplomatic grip around the throat of the young nation, the position of whites in the country, mostly French citizens, became increasingly precarious. Under Dessalines' rule, they assumed the image of a political target against whom revengeful blacks and coloureds would vent their anger. Everywhere in Haiti, argued Robin Blackburn, there were expressions of a strong anti-French orientation'.[18] The French, Dessalines suggests, unlike the British, were the principal defenders of Caribbean slavery. Against this background, according to Blackburn, Dessalines launched a 'bloodthirsty vendetta against the French'.[19]

Considering himself politically justified on account of French inhabitants continuous counter-revolutionary activity, within six weeks of independence Dessalines took over their estates, and those found guilty before military tribunals of aiding Generals LeClerc and Rochambeau were executed. The name of France, and the treachery of its citizens, the emperor surmised, 'darkened' the plains of Haiti; everywhere, he continued, they plot to re-enslave blacks.[20] By the end of April 1, 1804, hundreds of French citizens were accused of treason, tried, and found guilty and put to death. This policy proved popular with the army and civilians alike. It was the turning tide of war and revolution and those who misread the currents found themselves drawn under.

As far as Dessalines was concerned it was necessary that Haiti purge itself of French influences as a precondition for nation-building. Psychological and cultural decolonization, he declared, could be achieved by the systematic eradication of things French from the new order. The revolution would not be completed, and the young nation weaned, he insisted, until the 'last vestiges of the European idol' were removed.[21] In this way, according to Dupuy, Dessalines 'made the question of race paramount ideologically and politically. It was on grounds of 'avenging the crimes committed against the black race by the white'. Dupuy states, 'that Dessalines justified his massacre of the French'.[22] In one of many speeches, the emperor provided rationalizations for his policy as follows:

It is not enough tho have driven from our country the barbarians who, for ages, have stained it with blood; it is not enough to have repressed the successive factions which, by turns, sported with a phantom of liberty which France placed before their eyes. It has become necessary to ensure by a last act of national authority, the permanent empire of liberty in the country which has given us birth. It is necessary to deprive an inhuman government, which has hitherto held our minds in a state of most humiliating torpor, of every hope of enslaving us again . . . The French name still darkens our plains; everything reminds us of the cruelties of that barbarous people . . . When shall we be tired of breathing the same air with them? What have we in common with that bloody-minded people? Their cruelties compared to our moderation — their colour to ours — the extension of seas which separate us — our avenging climate — all plainly tell us they are not our brethren; that they never will become so; and if they find an asylum among us, they will still be the instigators of troubles and divisions.[23]

The independence constitution of 1805, Dessalines' ideological charter for the new state, outlined clearly in uncompromising language the kind of society that was considered just, progressive and cohesive. At its core were two principal concepts; first, the need to render honourable the black race that had been dishonoured by slavery; second, the desire to achieve social stability and economic progress within a programme of economic enfranchisement for blacks and coloureds. Under the circumstances of revolutionary independence, the only form of government that seemed likely to attain these objectives, Dessalines indicated, was a military dictatorship in which the power to choose all top ranking military, judicial and civil personnel resided with the Commander-in-Chief.[24]

The militarization of government, however, imposed its own form of constraints on the nature of political praxis and created circumstances that inhibited the legitimization of democratic impulses. Blackburn was correct to assert that the politics of black emancipation 'predated the declaration of independence'.[25] This suggests that the aspirations of the labouring classes for autonomy and living space had vintage qualities, and now required a generalized political programme that would inform the entire fabric of administrative arrangements. The constitution, then, was required to guarantee the civic liberty of all inhabitants in addition to outlining the ideological course of redressing historical imbalances by means of the economic enfranchisement of blacks.

Such political demands seemed immediately contradictory within a revolutionary environment. Suspicion and fear of different groups surrounded government policy at all levels, though blacks and mulattoes seemed in agreement that their economic empowerment should take place at the expense of whites, and with government support. Boisrond Tonnerre, we are told, on hearing Chapéron read the first draft of the constitution he had written, replied: 'All that which has been formulated is not in accordance with our real feelings; to draw up the Act of Independence, we need the skin of a whiteman for parchment, his skull for a writing desk, his blood for ink, and a bayonet for pen'.[26] Commander-in-Chief, Dessalines, apparently in agreement with his sentiment, called upon Tonnerre, a mulatto like his colleague Charéron, to fine tune the draft and present a final document.

It is instructive to note that Dessalines placed the responsibility for producing the independence constitution in the hands of the mulatto core within his administration. He understood as clearly the role they had played in strengthening his military command as their longstanding social and ideological antipathy to blacks. The constitution, he insisted, should reflect the passion involved in the rejection of the French colonial ethos as much as the colourism and racism that separated the various shades of black people. For him, there were two contending races — black and white. Coloureds, in his sociological understanding, were part of the black race and should be encouraged to see themselves as such.

On the eve of the public presentation of the independence constitution reports of the daily execution of French citizens in Haiti appeared throughout the European press. The praise that Toussaint had earlier received in sections of this press for his alleged moderation, sympathy with the French Empire, and willingness to negotiate the peace, paled against the background of the new militancy. Its provisions were explicit on the question of race, colour, identity, and nationhood. It declared that all citizens irrespective of colour or race, be classified under the generic category of black.

In terms of the country's history, the constitution was bold and ideologically confrontationist. It was rooted within the development of race relations and the sociology of miscegenation in Saint Dominigue. Dessalines, unlike Toussaint, was attempting to come to terms in a legalistic sort of way with the ideological superstructure of race and colour that had survived the war of liberation.[27] Toussaint's prior constitution of 1801 had stipulated that all individuals regardless of race or colour were equal, and that discrimination based upon such characteristics was illegal. General Moise, of course, had broken with Toussaint on the matter of his equivocation with respect to black economic empowerment and wide-ranging concessions to whites. Moise charged that Toussaint was prepared to accept whites owning and managing property to the detriment of blacks who had fought so bloody a war for their liberty. He is reported as having said: 'Toussaint always reproaches me in the name of the metropole, but his interests are those of the whites, and I will like the whites only when they give me back my eyes that they took from me in battle'.[28]

Dessalines' position should therefore be assessed against the background of the crisis of Toussaint's policy. Toussaint's critical error was that he allowed a political rift to grow between himself and the class of labouring poor. It resulted in his execution of General Moise whose ideological position was legitimate and popular within the context of revolution. According to C.L.R. James:

It was in method, and not in principle, that Toussaint failed. The race question is subsidiary to the class question in politics, and to think of imperialism in terms of race is disastrous. But to neglect the racial factor as merely incidental is an error only less grave than to make it fundamental. There were Jacobin workmen in Paris who would have fought for the blacks against Bonaparte's troops. But the international movement was not then what it is today, and there were none in San Domingo. The black labourers saw only the old slave-owning whites. These would accept the new regime, but never to the extent of fighting for it against a French army, and the masses knew this. Toussaint of course knew this also. He never trusted Age, his Chief of Staff who was a Frenchman, and asked Age's junior Lamartiniere, to keep an eye on him. Toussaint explained nothing, and allowed the masses to think that their old enemies were being favoured at their expense. In allowing himself to be looked upon as taking the side of the whites against the blacks, Toussaint committed the unpardonable crime in the eyes of the community where the whites stood for so much evil. That they should get back their property was bad enough. That they should be privileged was intolerable. And to shoot Moise, the black, for the sake of the white was more than an error, it was a crime.[29]

Toussaint had argued his case for the partial reconstitution of the white propertied class within the context of a development model based upon world trade and the normalization of diplomatic relations with Europe — France in particular. His pragmatic understanding of the economics and politics of liberation and reconstruction, however, did not always take into consideration the sociological and ideological factors 'on the ground', and it was here that he misread or ignored the power of popular opinion.

Like Toussaint, Dessalines was most concerned with the serious socio-political divisions between the coloureds and the blacks. He was, however, less charitable and accommodating. Whites, he insists, had never accepted fully kinship relations with their coloured offsprings. As a result, he believed that blacks should have the conceptual power to impose a new set of guidelines for the governance of these relations. All citizens were black, and that included coloureds. By redefining the coloureds as black Dessalines sought to reject whites' traditional definition of them as separate and distinct from the black community and race. This way he hoped the racialism/colourism that divided blacks and coloureds would subside, and that they would see themselves merely as different shades of the black race — and more importantly, as one nation.

At the same time, to round things off politically, Article 12 of the 1805 Constitution denied whites the right to own property. Whites sought to circumvent this provision by transferring their property to politically supportive and biologically related mulattoes. Dessalines responded by annulling such property transfers and conducted procedures for the verification of property rights throughout the nation. This was his way of ensuring that the newly acquired political power of blacks was not compromised by a resurgence of white and/or mulatto economic centres within the national policy. He was determined to confront the relationship between race and economic power. The question of land ownership was the key to all discussions. Landlessness was long associated with unfreedom, while political and economic power were rooted socially with the ownership of land and other forms of property. During the closing years of slavery white colonists and the mulatto Affranchis had frequently clashed on this matter; the effect of the revolution was to propel blacks to the fore of the traditional discussion.

Dessalines, then, had little choice but to attempt to reconcile for the masses of former slaves the continuing relationship between freedom, landlessness, harsh discipline and persistent white-mulatto property dominance. Toussaint's 1801 constitution represented a mild attempt in this direction. In fact, Toussaint made much of the apparent moderation

of ex-slaves in their demands for the redress of historical wrongs. In a letter to the Directory dated 28th October, 1791, he stated:

If it were true that the blacks were so wrong to think that the properties on St. Dominigue belonged to them, why wouldn't they make themselves masters by driving off men of other colours, whom they could easily master by their numerical superiority? If they had sworn a fierce hatred against the whites, how is it that at this moment the white population of Le Cap equals that of the blacks and men of colour? How is it that more than half of the sugar planters of the Le Cap plain are white? If union and fraternity didn't reign among men of all classes, would whites, reds, and blacks be seen living in perfect equality?[30]

His politics, James reminds us, tended to run ahead of the political reality facing the populace. Statements such as this indicate the extent to which he conducted his diplomacy with much vision but against the grain of political consciousness.

The main effect of Toussaint's constitution upon property relations and distribution was that the mulattoes filled the ownership vacuum left by the fleeing French. This development antagonized the blacks and drove General Moise to arms. Against this background Dessalines sought to disenfranchise this group of coloured inheritors by replacing them with a new black aristocracy comprising mainly military men. In order to achieve this end he declared all appropriated lands the property of the state, and provided that the state retained the right to allocate, lease, or sell lands as it saw fit. While Dessalines sought to use land allocation policies as instruments to achieve equality between blacks and mulattoes and thereby remove the colour bar that separated them, tension between these groups continued to increase. Frustrated by the intractable nature of mulatto-black colourism, he proclaimed, in an effort to ease the tension: 'Be on your guard, negroes and mulattoes, we have all fought against the whites: the properties which we have conquered by the spilling of our blood belong to us all: I intend that they be divided with equity.[31]

The mulattoes, of course, continued to claim that Dessalines' constitution represented an attempt to impose a black Nationalist ethos upon a country whose racial mixture could not sustain it. The reasons for their objections were put in the following terms: first, that racial differences exist and constitute an important factor in social life and ought to be accepted as endemic to the national reality; second, that they were better placed than blacks to resume the task of economic reconstruction on the basis of their longer association with metropolitan financial/commercial institutions; third, that greater goodwill existed towards them within the slave-owning world that surrounded their country; and finally, that they constituted the educated and administrative elite without whom nation-building was not possible.

The political reasoning of mulattoes, however, strengthened suspicion among the blacks that they could be easily used by the French in an effort to restore the *ancien regime*. Their principal leader, Rigaud, had been used in this way when he rallied large numbers of mulattoes in support of LeClerc's attempt to restore slavery. DeVastey, a prominent mulatto intellectual, considered it necessary to dedicate much time lecturing mulattoes on the importance of resisting negrophobic anti-nationalist posturing. He urged them to recognize that their future resided in a meaningful political integration with blacks.[32]

The complex nature of vested interests within the independent dispensation, then, meant that Dessalines' policy of black enfranchisement would create opposition as the basis of race and colour considerations, as well as on class and ideological grounds. As black officers of his regime accumulated substantial landholdings across the country and accusations of their appropriation of public funds for personal utilization increased, the disenchantment of the revolutionary rank and file grew in direct proportions. Thus, while Dessalines sought to keep race equality at the centre of state policy, the politics of class interest emerged paramount and released a wide range of destabilizing political forces.

Nowhere was the class issue more clearly expressed than in the agricultural sector. Privileged blacks sought to secure their class position by land appropriation which mulattoes perceived as being at their expense. At the same time the rise of the black and mulatto elite, both committed to high productivity from cheap labour, encountered persistent resistance from the labouring poor. Meanwhile, the traditional mulatto landed elite, in addition to those mulattoes like Pétion and Geffrard, who wielded power within the military, considered their seizure of the state an inevitable act of class and ethnic expression. Rumours of an alleged attempt to invite General Rigaud, exiled in Paris since his defeat by Toussaint, to return as President circulated in town and country. It seemed only a matter of time before Dessalines' regime collapsed under the weight of one or more of these pressures.

Nicholls contends that the Dessalines state floundered on the shores of his policy to remove the conditions of social injustice from the life experience of the black population.[33] For Dupuy, the crisis had its roots as much within the corruption that characterized civil administration and military excess. While there is ample evidence to support

both contentions, it should be emphasized that all indicators point toward the mulattoes as the principal socio-political force behind the weakening and discrediting of Dessalines' regime. Certainly, by the end of 1805, they were prepared to attempt his removal as Head of State. While it is true that Christophe, General-in-Chief of the army, also played a part in fomenting anti-Dessalines sentiments, it was Pétion whose political opinion constituted the catalyst. On October 17, 1806, after the outbreak of insurrection in the south and west of the country, encouraged by Pétion's supporters, Dessalines was ambushed at Pont Rouge, outside of Port-au-Prince in Pétion's territory, and assassinated.[34]

Dessalines' death plunged the young nation into further political chaos. The antagonism of race and class bitterness intensified in such a manner as to confirm that it had remained a part of the institutional fabric of society. In one respect, Dessalines' demise was symbolic of his weakness in the face of endemic race and class forces in much the same way that Toussaint's removal indicated his acquiescence to colonial ideology. In this regard, Haiti was a young nation with very old and enduring problems.

On immediate result of the murder of Dessalines was that the mulatto elite considered itself better placed to restore its ideological and economic authority. Skilful political play was clearly evident when the Constituent Assembly met in Port-au-Prince on November 30, 1806 to elect a new President. Pétion's hand in this event was hardly concealed; it was his decision not to come forward as the new President, but to support Christophe's nomination on the ground that he would prove an easy leader to manipulate. Christophe, it was alleged, had played much the same role in Dessalines' downfall as Dessalines had played in Toussaint's. He was elected President with much fanfare and celebration, but only for a term of four years, and with little executive powers; these powers were decisively shifted to the mulatto dominated Senate.

Toussaint and Dessalines had taken for themselves indefinite tenure with respect to governance; Christophe supporters wasted no time in assuring him that his authority would be compromised so long as Pétion remained in control of Port-au-Prince and of the Constituent Assembly. They knew, of course, that within Pétion's political and military power resided elements that came together in order to discredit Dessalines' administration. It was therefore no surprise to those within ruling circles when Christophe sent his army into combat against Pétion.

It was a failed mission. Heavy losses were sustained on both sides, but the mulatto forces won the day. Christophe's army of blacks returned to Cap Haiten in full recognition that mulattoes now constituted an effective, autonomous military power. The ideological forces of colourism were once again as clear as they were during the slavery period. Blacks and mulattoes represented two rival factions whose mutual distrust and dislike represented the principal destabilizing political force within the new state. The two groups squared off to control their separate spaces, and the nation splintered after less than five years.

As expected, Christophe consolidated his position in the north and Artibonite region where he established his rule as President for life as a mini-state he chose to call Haiti. Meanwhile, the Senate in Port-au-Prince, still supportive of Pétion, elected him President of a new state called the Republic of Haiti that comprised the west and south of the country. The two states declared mutual political hostility resulting in a civil war that lasted until 1818 when Pétion died. It was in 1820, following the death of Christophe, who in 1811 had proclaimed himself King Henry I, that the country was united — this time under the Presidency of Jean-Pierre Boyer.

In spite of the persistent tension between Republic and Monarchy, their common ideological posture with respect to national liberation created the context for a convergence in many aspects of policy. Both remained firmly committed to anti-slavery and Haitian Independence. Both declared themselves to the concept of 'blackness' in a revivalist sort of way. Yet, they were at war, and living with intense fear and anxiety about a possible French military invasion. In addition, both states sought to base their economic development plans upon the subjection of the labouring poor to harsh regimes of enforced plantation labour — a process that ensured popular resistance and revolt.

The dialectical unfolding of race and class relationships within the two states was influenced considerably by the external pressures exerted by regional slave-owning powers. In order to counter these pressures, Christophe went to great lengths in order to appease the British. On becoming king he adopted the regalia of the St. James Court, brought in their educators, scientists and other consultants and advisors. Both the King and Pétion, after consultation with British officials, opened their national markets to British commerce by significantly lowering tariffs and duties on their goods. Pétion, however, favoured the Americans and courted their good relations in an effort to weaken the French continuing claim to their former colony.

The French, of course, persisted with their successful bid to prevent any slave-owning power from officially recognizing Haitian independence. The Treaty of Paris signed by the British in 1814 was in some respects a critical development. It provided that England would return the captured colonies of Martinique and Guadeloupe to France, and the diplomatic undertaking was upheld that 'St. Domingue' still existed as a French colony.

France's continued claim to Haiti created the ideological context for both Christophe and Pétion to increase military preparedness, and to issue statements of nationalistic defiance. While they both experienced problems in meeting the economic aspirations and social objectives of the labouring classes, there clearly was a popular understanding that the return to French colonial rule was highly undesirable. In spite of draconian plantation labour laws, police and magisterial abuse of state power, workers' abhorrence for French rule provided scope for leaders to maintain an aggressive diplomacy with respect to sovereignty.

A small proportion of the labouring class under Christophe's regime was able to concretize their freedom within the ownership of land, and only after the Goman Rebellion in the south between 1807 and 1819 did labourers gain the opportunity to become secure peasants (*plquets*) under Pétion's regime. According to Michel-Rolph Trouillot, 'The mulâtres who dominated the west and south after Christophe's death could not afford to alienate the masses of cultivators on the issues of land and labour without seeing the colour question revived by the most ambitious nouveaux libres'.[35] In addition, noted Trouillot, increasing French diplomatic hostility 'forced the mulâtres to court a majority, which they would need in the case of a French invasion'. These circumstances, he concluded, for political as well as economic reasons, meant that 'both Pétion and Boyer ended up selling or granting to many blacks more land than they would have wished.[36] That Christophe considered it necessary to close his border in order to prevent workers fleeing to Pétion's republic was indicative of the widespread view that the black masses fared better with respect to landowning under mulatto rule in the south, and hence might have concluded that the opportunity for real freedom and independence was greater there.

The general experience for labourers, however, is not to be found in the formation of a valley peasantry, but in the flight to the mountains where a subsistence agriculture was fashioned to deliver semblance of a genuine freedom. Coffee farming made possible a cash economy which though rooted in the hills was linked directly to the established mercantile networks. The masses of Haiti came to perceive independence within the context of a flight from the plantations — and state authority — in much the same way that maroons had perceived it during slavery. Haiti, then, had retained many of the structural and ideological features of the slavery period within its agriculture, and a general withdrawal of enthusiasm by the workers had been the inevitable result. Furthermore, it has been suggested that whereas Christophe's peasants had taken up residence in the hills, and Pétion's on the plains, the common result was that both states declined economically and were left with empty treasuries.

In 1818, following Pétion's death, Boyer became President of the republic. It was then that popular consciousness within the monarchy gained its clearest expression within the decade. Workers and soldiers alike rose up against their king and offered their allegiance to Boyer. This was the end of the civil war, the divided nation, and of Christophe. He committed suicide on October 8, 1820, and Boyer seized the opportunity to reunite the one million Haitians under a single republic. Five years later, he settled the matter of France's official recognition of Haiti by agreeing to pay France an indemnity of 150 million francs for former slave owners — a penalty described by Paguin as 'an insane price to ask, let alone pay'.[37] This debt, generally described as a burdensome levy on the economy, added considerably to the further productive decay of Haiti by draining away foreign exchange earnings. It was not fully paid until 1922. The historic nation, then, resurrected by Boyer after twelve years of division, started its noble journey encumbered by the immense weight of the cross of western recognition.

The task of nation-building, then, seemed an impossible one given the circumstances of the time. Persons outside of Haiti had no reason to believe that Haitians could make a success of it, especially those who recognized the immense hostility with which the rebel state had been greeted. For slave-owning European nations Haiti constituted the worst possible nightmare, and they eagerly awaited the restoration of a reality determined exclusively by an uncompromised white over black matrix. The slave-owning, but revolutionary, republican Americans were clearly embarrassed by Haiti's unilateral claim to be their progeny — a paternal recognition that brought neither comfort nor conciliation. All were in agreement that Haiti should be recaptured and returned to imperial rule.

Likewise, persons within the country found it difficult to reject ideological lines that were drawn during the long colonial periods, and which

remained indelibly etched within the national consciousness. Divided to the vein, blacks and mulattoes tore their country apart in search of an ethnic advantage that would prove elusive and mutually self-destructive. Though they found themselves in a sea of troubles they fought themselves for command of the vessel. Under these circumstances, it proved impossible to travel in a chartered and agreed upon direction.

Notes

1. See Benjamin Quaries, *The Negro in the American Revolution,* (Chapel Hill, 1961), pp. 19–30, 111–128. Arthur Zilversmit, *The First Emancipation: The Abolition of Slavery in the North* (Chicago, 1967), pp. 124–130. Ira Berlin, *Slaves Without Masters: The Free Negro in the Antebellum South* (Oxford, 1974), pp. 80–100. Staughton Lynd, *Class Struggle, Slavery and the United States Constitution,* (New York, 1967), pp. 159–201. Eugene Genovese, *From Rebellion to Revolution: Afro-American Slave Revolts in the Making of the Modern World* (Baton Rouge, 1979); G.K. Lewis, *Main Currents in Caribbean Thought* (Baltimore, 1983), pp. 171–239. Hilary Beckles, 'Caribbean Anti-Slavery: The Self-Liberation Ethos of Enslaved Blacks', *Journal of Caribbean History,* vol. 22, nos. 1–2, 1988, pp. 1–19; Robert Paquette, 'The Economics, Politics and Ideology of Anti-Slavery', *Nieuwe Westindische Gids,* vol. 63, 1989, pp 242–50.
2. Robin Blackburn, *The Overthrow of Colonial Slavery, 1776–1848* (London, 1988), pp. 213–265; C.L.R. James, *The Black Jacobins: Toussaint L'Ouverture and the San Domingo Revolution* (London, 1938). Carolyn Fick, 'Black Peasants and Soldiers in the Saint Domingue Revolution' in Frederick Krantz, (ed.) *History From Below* (Montreal, 1985), pp. 243–60. David Geggus, 'From his Most Catholic Majesty to the Godless Republic: The Volte Face of Toussaint L'Ouverture and the Ending of Slavery in Saint Domingue', *Revue Francaise d'Histoire d'Outer Mer,* 241, 1978, pp. 480–90; and 'The French and Haitian Revolutions, and the Resistance to Slavery in the Americas: An Overview', *Revue Francaise d'Histoire d'Outer Mer,* LXXVI, 1989, pp. 107–24; 'Slave Resistance Studies and the Saint-Domingue Slave Revolt: Some Preliminary Considerations', University of Florida Occasional Papers, 4, 1983.
3. Alex Dupuy, *Haiti in the World Economy: Class, Race and Underdevelopment since 1700* (London, 1989), p. 74; Claude Auguste and Marcel Auguste, *L'Expedition LeClerc, 1801–1803* (Port-au-Prince, 1985), pp. 313–318.
4. James, *The Black Jacobins,* pp.289–300.
5. See Lyonel Paquin, *The Haitians: Class and Colour Politics* (New York, 1983), p. 25.
6. David Nicholls, *From Dessalines to Duvalier: Race, Colour and National Independence in Haiti* (Cambridge, 1979), p. 33.
7. Paquin, p. 24.
8. David Nicholls, 'Rural Protest and Peasant Revolt in Haiti, 1804–1869' in Malcolm Cross and Arnaud Marks, *Peasants, Plantations and Rural Communities in the Caribbean* (Leiden, 1979), p. 31.
9. Dupuy, p. 74.
10. *Ibid.*
11. Paquin, pp. 20–26.
12. Dupuy, p. 75.
13. Cited in Donald Robinson, *Slavery in the Structure of American Politics, 1765–1820* (New York, 1979), p. 371.

14. Nicholls, *From Dessalines to Duvalier,* p. 35.
15. *Ibid.,* p. 36.
16. *Ibid.,* p. 35.
17. *Ibid.,* p. 37.
18. Blackburn, pp. 253–54.
19. *Ibid.*
20. Dupuy, p. 75.
21. Nicholls, *From Dessalines to Duvalier,* p. 35.
22. Dupuy, p. 75.
23. *Ibid.,* pp. 75–76.
24. *Ibid.,* p. 79.
25. Blackburn, pp. 258–260.
26. Nicholls, *From Dessalines to Duvalier,* p. 36.
27. Henock Trouillot, *Dessalines ou la Tragedie Post-Coloniale* (Port-au-Prince, 1966), pp. 33–34; M. Lubin, 'Les premiers rapports de la nation Latienne avec L'etranger', *Journal of Interamerican Studies,* Vol. 10, 1968, pp. 277–278.
28. Cited in Francois Lacroix, *Memoires pour servir a L'Histoire de la revolution de Saint-Domingue* (Paris, 1820) Vol. 2, p. 48; Pauleus Sannon, *Histoire de Toussaint L'Ouverture* (Port-au-Prince, 1933), Vol. 3, p. 25.
29. James, *The Black Jacobins,* pp. 283–84; see also, Herbert Cole, *Christophe, King of Haiti* (New York, 1967), pp.

46–54; Gabriel Debien, 'L'Esprit d'independence chez les colons de Saint Domingue au XVille siecies', *Notes d'Histoire Coloniale,* No. 13, 1947.
30. Cited in George Tyson Jr., (ed.) *Toussaint L'Ouverture: Great Lives Observed* (Englewood Cliffs, 1973), pp. 40–41.
31. Nicholls, *From Dessalines to Duvalier,* p. 38.
32. *Ibid.,* p. 36.
33. *Ibid.,* p. 38.
34. Dupuy, p. 81; Paquin, p. 29.
35. Michel-Rolph Trouillot, 'The inconvenience of Freedom: Free People of Colour and the Political Aftermath of Slavery in Dominica and Saint Domingue/Haiti', in Frank McGlynn and Seymour Drescher (eds.) *The Meaning of Freedom: Economics, Politics and Culture after Slavery* (Pittsburgh, 1992), p. 163; see also Trouillot's *Haiti: State Against Nation: The Origins and Legacies of Duvalierism* (New York, 1990).
36. *Ibid.,* 'The inconvenience of Freedom', p. 163.
37. Paquin, p. 38; Jean Fouchard, *The Haitian Maroons: Liberty or Death* (New York, 1981); Yvan Debbasch, 'The Border Maroons of Saint Domingue: Le Maniel', in Richard Prince (ed.) *Maroon Societies: Rebel Slave Communities in the Americas* (Baltimore, 1979), pp. 135–143.

The Political Ideology of José Marti

Jaime Suchlicki

From the ideological and organizational points of view, the Cuban War of Independence represented Marti's revolution. His ideas formed the foundation on which the revolution rested, and his knocking on the conscience of the Cubans awakened the feeling that brought about the war.

The purpose of this paper is to trace the ideas of Marti regarding that war, and to probe into his mind in order to explain his political ideology; but before undertaking this task, something should be said about the history and intellectual conditions existing in Cuba during the nineteenth century.

In Cuba during the first half of the nineteenth century there was little thought of independence from Spain. Nevertheless, the revolutionary spirit of the French and American revolutions, and the struggles for independence in Spanish America inspired the minds of the Cubans with the desire for freedom. The writings and ideas of Feliz Varela, Jose de la Luz y Caballero, Jose A. Saco, Domingo del Monte and others helped to create the necessary conditions conducive to revolution. Cuba had, in addition to these political and social thinkers, a tradition of poets and literary writers. Jose Maria Heredia, Jose Jacinto Milanes, Gabriel de la Concepcion Valdes (Placido), Cirilo Villaverde, Gertrudis Gomez de Avellaneda, Juan Clemente Zenea, and others, awakened in the Cuban people, with their verse and prose, a romantic love for their island and a nationalistic urge to liberate her from the Spanish yoke.

The Cubans looked to Spain for the needed reforms that would change the status quo of their oppressed island. They turned their eyes to a Spain, fighting against Jose Bonaparte; enacting, through the Constitution of 1812, liberal reforms; and experiencing the revolutionary era of 1820. They hoped for the extension of this liberalism to Cuba. Only when they sadly realized that the mistakes of Spanish rule in America had not been a sufficient lesson to Spain, they turned to the idea of independence.

Throughout the nineteenth century, sporadic conspiracies and revolutionary attempts were discovered by Spain, but it was not until 1868 that the first great effort was made to liberate the ever faithful island from Spanish rule. Thousands of lives were sacrificed on both sides, as Cuba was plunged into a Ten Year War. Spain, realizing that subjugation by force was impossible, agreed on granting reforms and in 1878 an armistice was reached. The Spanish generals met the insurgent leaders at Zanjon, Cuba, where a treaty was arranged, liberal reforms were granted, and the Cubans laid down their arms in good faith. Once the island was pacified, there was a reversion to the old policy and the treaty was shamelessly repudiated.

The failure of Spain to live up to its promises caused much dissatisfaction. The Cubans came to realize that the Spanish government would not honour its commitments and that the only solution was to continue fighting. Actually the war had never ceased. Since October 1878, a Cuban Revolutionary Committee was functioning in New York under the direction of General Calizto Garcia, one of the military leaders of the Ten Year War. This organization, aided by war veterans still living in Cuba, began to prepare for the resumption of hostilities against Spain. On August 6, 1879, a new revolt broke out in Cuba. This premature movement, known as *La Guerra Chiquita,* ended a year later with the surrender of the Cuban patriots.

The years that followed were characterized by schism among the Cubans. The enthusiasm and prestige of the Cuban patriots and military leaders were not sufficient to coordinate and direct the revolutionary efforts. The need was for a figure that would inspire, with leadership and stature, the union of all the Cubans, both in exile and on the island.

This vacuum was filled by a young poet and revolutionist, whose devotion and faith in the righteousness of the cause of Cuban independence made him rise above his contemporaries to unite and lead them. José Marti was born in La Habana on January 28, 1853, of Spanish parents. His environment, teachers and friends helped arouse in him a devotion to the cause of freedom, and the tradition of Cuban political writings influenced his embryonic mind. At the age of seventeen he was sent to jail for political reasons, an event which left a lasting moral and physical impression upon him. Soon thereafter he was deported to Spain, where at the age of twenty-one he received his degree in philosophy and law from the University of Zaragoza.

Marti travelled from Spain to various capitals of Europe, and in 1875 he went to Mexico. The two years he spent in the Aztec nation were maturing years. Mexico was going through a period of intellectual ferment, and Marti was exposed to the ideas of Gabino Barreda, Justo Sierra, Ignacio Altamirano and others. The coming into power of Porfirio Diaz promoted his departure from Mexico to Guatemala, where he taught literature and philosophy. After the Peace of Zanjon in 1878, he returned to Cuba and began practicing law. His revolutionary activities were soon discovered by the Spanish authorities, and again he was deported to Spain, from where he escaped to France. Finally in 1880, Marti arrived in the United States and made New York the centre of his activities for the next decade. Nevertheless, he continued to travel throughout America and to observe the many problems of the Latin American nations.

While the years in exile strengthened his character and prepared him for his martyrdom, his travels exposed him to the ideas of the old and new continent. In Spain Marti came in to contact with the ideas of the German philosopher Krause. The Krausist ideas, imported to Spain from Germany by J. Sanz del Rio, were uppermost in the Spanish thought of that time. In France Marti met Victor Hugo, whose humanism and love for the poor made a lasting impression on him. From Baltasar Gracian, he took his literary style, his liking for philosophical essays and for commentaries on ethics and politics; from Francisco de Goya, kindliness toward the humble and the penetration that unveiled men's souls; from his contemporary, Joaquin Costa, his love for agriculture, his friendliness for rural workers and his uncompromising repugnance for the evils of politics or expedient dissimulation.[1] The years spent in exile and the persecution and imprisonment, did not make Marti resentful. He never lost faith in the inner goodness of man. 'Man is organized and good', he wrote, 'and in the end always saves himself'.[2]

What distinguished Marti and made him, above all, a leader of people, was his quality to organize and to harmonize. His mark of leadership was to take man's passions, beliefs and ideas, and mould them for a common cause. His oratory inspired his listeners, his honesty and sincerity, demonstrated by his actions, inspired faith, and his conviction in the ideas he was pursuing, gained for him the respect and loyalty of all who knew him.

Marti relied not only on the physical strength of man, but on his spiritual powers. When he had to call on virtues that men did not appear to have, he helped them bring those virtues out. Many times he said that man was not what he seemed to be, but rather what he was inside. 'What mattered was not man as he was, but as he should be'.[3]

Marti's great undertaking was to liberate Cuba. He always felt that America would not be free as long as parts of it were not. He wanted a country fought for and won by the efforts of the Cubans — one that could respect itself and demand respect from others. He rejected the idea of a country obtained through the benevolence of a foreign power.

Marti realized very early that independence from Spain was the only solution for Cuba, and that this could only be achieved through war as no concession could be expected from Spain. Furthermore, the annexationist ideas had been taking shape in the minds of many Cubans and North Americans, and the danger of Cuba becoming a possession of the United States, convinced him that a fast and decisive war was necessary. In 1882 he referred to the advocates of annexationism in Cuba as: 'An important group of cautious men, proud enough to despise Spanish domination, but too timid to risk their welfare fighting against it'.[4] Throughout the next decade, the annexationist ideas remained as an impending threat to the independence movement and a main concern to Marti: 'The annexationists are a grave and constant factor in Cuba politics', he wrote in 1892, 'and the duty of the Cubans . . . is to follow the more popular and historic solution, the more unavoidable and natural solution: the War for Independence'.[5]

Marti did not desire the war he was destined to organize. He fully understood the horrors of war, but he saw some positive and concrete achievements that would come out of it. 'In a new and heterogeneous country', he said, 'the benefits of war, for the development and unification of the national character, are greater than the partial disaster produced to the repairable wealth'.[6]

Marti's wisdom concerning the war resided in his understanding of the reasons that produced the failure of the Ten Year War and on his analysis of the existing conditions. In the Ten Year War indefinite prolongation, internal dissension and regionalism were vicious circles which the insurgents could not break through. Furthermore, lack of support and organization had been a definite factor in the outcome of the war. Marti realized that the triumph of the revolutionary forces was not dependent on the existence of military leaders, not even on oppressive conditions inside the island, but on popular support for the war. What was needed was to create the necessary conditions so the Cuban people would want the war and be willing to organize in pursuing its objectives. 'A group of men pushed by its people', he wrote, 'can obtain what Bolivar did; but a group of heroes abandoned by its people might look like bandits'.[7]

The popular character that Marti wanted the struggle for independence to have, and his fear of a military dictatorship after the expulsion of Spain were expressed in a letter to Maximo Gomez in 1884. Gomez and Antonio Maceo, two generals of the last war, were at the time engaged in conspiratory activities. Marti had participated in them, but his fear and doubts regarding the authoritarian attitudes of Gomez prompted his break with the movement. In that letter he wrote:

A nation cannot be founded, General, in the same manner as an army camp is commanded. When in the preliminary works for a revolution there is no showing of sincere desire to compromise, what guarantees could there be that public liberties will be respected tomorrow? What are we General? The modest and heroic servants of an idea or the brave and lucky *caudillos* that are getting ready to take the war to a people for the purpose of later subjugating then?. . .

The fatherland belongs to no one, but if it did, it belongs, and only in spirit, to the one who serves it with the greatest unselfishness and intelligence.[8]

Marti had no faith in those incomplete and rootless attempts which appeared sporadically and were born, he felt, from the desire for personal glory. He was interested in keeping watch over the awakening of Cuban feeling in order to direct it along the road for independence. To organize the war it was necessary to revive the faith of the people, and to combine all efforts so they would culminate in victory. This, Marti thought, could only be accomplished through the organization of a party. 'If a revolutionary party does not exist', he wrote, 'to inspire sufficient trust or channel the aspirations of the country, to whom will the people turn, but to the men of the annexationist party'.[9]

Marti directed all of his efforts to this end after 1884. His speeches and writings earned him respect and admiration, and his name took root in the hearts of the Cubans. Years of propaganda and constant activity had their result. By the end of 1891, the union of all the Cubans in exile was beginning to take place, and Marti was recognized as the undisputed leader and dynamic force behind the independence movement.

On JaNuary 5, 1892, Martí attended a meeting in Key West, where the representatives of the different political groups in exile approved a set of resolutions previously drawn up by Martí. These resolutions, called *Bases,* constituted the foundation of the Cuban Revolutionary Party. On April 10, 1892, the *Bases* were unanimously proclaimed

by all the Cubans and Puerto Rican emigrees in the United States.[10]

Marti brought out in the *Bases* the ideas that had been ripening within him during the previous decade. They represented a pragmatic approach to the Cuban situation, appealed to all classes and races, and touched upon some essential political problems, on international relations, and on the organization of the war. The *Bases* were not aimed at defining any political philosophy to be adopted after independence, nor at creating a document that would become a source of controversy. It should, however, be noted that they were drawn with special consideration for the international situation of Cuba.

Article I contemplated complete independence for Cuba and Puerto Rico. Article II defined the character of the war as 'generous and short, aimed at assuring, in peace and work, the happiness of the inhabitants of the island'. Article III defined the future task of Cuba as: 'fulfilling, in the historic life of the continent, the difficult duties assigned to her by her geographic position'. Article IV spoke of 'founding a new people, and of establishing democracy capable of defeating, through real work and the equilibrium of social forces, the dangers of sudden freedom in a society reared for slavery'. Article V stated the aim of the war as 'the decorum and well-being of all the Cubans and the rendering of the free fatherland to all the people'. Article VI expressed 'the intention to substitute for the economic chaos reigning in Cuba a system of public fiscal administration, which shall immediately open the country to the diverse activities of its inhabitants'. Article VII mentioned the desire of the party 'not to alienate the peoples with whom prudence of affection suggested or imposed the maintenance of cordial relations'. Article VIII enumerated five concrete objectives; the third of these objectives showed Marti's concern with the danger involved to Cuban lives when organizing a war based on popular support. He mentioned the desire of the Party 'to disseminate the knowledge of the spirit and method of the revolution in Cuba, and to create in the inhabitants of the island a favourable disposition toward a revolutionary victory, which would not place Cuban lives in unnecessary jeopardy'.[11]

Marti gave to the party a democratic organization based on the supremacy of the civilian command over the military. The direction of the activities was placed in the hands of a delegate elected annually. From the formation of the party until its disappearance, three years later, Marti occupied that position. 'The articles of the party', Marti wrote, were established to remedy past mistakes

. . . and to assure the continuous intervention of the Cuban people in the control of its own affairs'.[12]

From 1892 on, Marti's efforts were directed toward the realization of his dream: the independence of Cuba. So well had he organized the revolution, that when he gave the order for the uprising early in 1895, the ultimate expulsion of Spain from the island was assured.

In Santo Domingo, on the eve of his departure for Cuba, Marti reiterated, in what was later known as the Manifesto of Montecristi, the reasons for the war. In this document, signed also by Gomez and issued on March 25, 1895, Marti reaffirmed the right of Cuba to obtain through self-sacrifice and determination, its freedom and independence from Spain. He advocated a war without hate, with mutual respect for the honest Spaniard, pious with those who repented, but inflexible with vice, crime or inhuman actions.[13]

The same day the Manifesto was made public, Marti wrote a letter to his friend, Federico Henriquez Carvajal, which has been considered by most Cuban historians as his political testament. Marti had become quite concerned with the expansionist activities of the United States, and he viewed them as a threat to the independence of Latin America. Conscious of his destiny and of his duty toward Cuba and toward the entire American Continent, he wrote the following:

I called forth the war; my responsibility begins rather than ends with it. For me the Fatherland will never be triumph but agony and duty . . . The person who thinks of himself does not love his country; and the ills of nations reside, however subtly they may at times be disguised, in the barriers or hasty actions with which the self-interest of their representatives regard or accelerate the natural course of events . . . The Antillas will save the independence of our America, and the now dubious and battered honour of English America, and perhaps hasten to stabilize the world. . . .[14]

Soon after, Marti landed in Cuba to participate in the war, but a Spanish bullet cut his life short on May 19, 1895. Marti's death represented a tremendous blow to the morale of the revolution; his voice was not to be heard again, but his writings and ideas remained to be studied by the following generations.

Marti can only be understood if we think of him as a student of social problems, rather than a purely political doctrinaire. He did not have a preconceived scheme for the organization of society, nor did he accept prefabricated moulds that would impose a rigid political philosophy upon society. This, together with the fragmentary nature of his writings, makes the study of his political ideology difficult.

Marti approached the problems of society with idealism and optimism. He regarded his time as an age of progress in which man walked the earth, inspired by sentiments of love and humanity. It was the optimistic chant of a happy era when man, on his way upward, rose from his knees to dominate the world. Marti had seen man on the threshold of that world, ready for the leap that would make him the master of himself and his future greatness. To achieve this, it was man's task to develop his capabilities to the maximum.[15]

For Marti, man could never be sacrificed for the aggrandizement of society. He thought of man not only as an individual, but as a member of society. By fulfilling his destiny, man was to realize his place of duty and influence in the larger organism of society. The belief that a better man was destined to live in a better world is present in most of his writings.

Two ideas underlie the whole of Marti's political ideology: the idea of liberty and the idea of justice. Again and again he spoke of them as the supreme aim of human life. Marti thought of man as belonging to two groups: those who loved freedom because they only wanted it for themselves, and those who loved freedom because they wanted it for every man.[16] Freedom was for him a right that entailed the obligation to extend it and respect the freedom of other men; freedom based on sacrifice and hard work. 'Man', he said, 'should not expect others to give him freedom, but work hard in its pursuit'.[17] The type of freedom that Marti advocated had to be based on custom and law, on individual rights and on the mutual respect of all classes.[18]

The second idea was that of justice. 'Justice', he wrote, is the adaptation of positive law to natural law'.[19] But how was justice to be achieved in society? He felt that to create a just society it wasn't enough to give political liberty, it was also necessary to distribute the wealth. The accumulation of wealth in the hands of a few was conducive to injustices. 'Exclusive wealth is unjust', he wrote. 'In political economy and good government to distribute is to make happiness'.[20] He believed that the greatness of nations was dependent on the economic independence of its individuals. Therefore, it was necessary that everyone should possess and cultivate a piece of land.[21] 'The distribution of land', he explained, 'if given to those who are working for low wages, would draw them away from low salary jobs'.[22] He did not advocate the taking of the land away from the large land holders, but the distribution of the land that the government possessed. 'Cuba had', according to Marti, 'an abundance of fertile land'.[23]

Marti's political ideology pointed to the suppression of the Spanish colonial system and to the establishment of a Republican type of government in Cuba. That new order, generated through revolution, would enact laws according to the needs of society. He felt that after the liberation from Spain, Cuba had to be liberated from Spanish customs and its legacy of social vices. This was to come slowly, as a process of political maturity, of education, which, without hate, would establish the foundation of a healthy Republic. The new nation was to be based on the close collaboration of all social classes, and not on the struggle of one class against the other. It would be the fatherland where everyone could live in peace with freedom and justice — a nation based on law, order and the hard work of its inhabitants.[24]

The task of the government was to put an end to the injustices of society. Government was to act as the equilibrating force, active and ready to participate in the shaping of society. 'The government', he wrote, 'is a moderating and guiding force, ready to intervene to solve existing conflicts'.[25] he wanted a government born out of and in accord with the needs of the country — a government that, without creating dissatisfaction among the intellectual aristocracy, would allow for the development of the more numerous and uneducated elements of the population.[26]

For the type of government Marti advocated, there was a need for an unselfish and dedicated ruler. These, he felt, were the moral qualities necessary to govern. The ruler should be, in addition, a man of culture and love. A necessary quality for the man in power was to be able to see ahead of his own times. 'To govern', he wrote, 'is to foresee'.[27]

Marti was a firm believer in democracy and in periodic elections. He thought that the natural environment for the development of democracy was in a Republican type of regime. He did not envision the possibility of democracy flourishing in any other type of political system. He felt that elections were fundamental for the preservation of democracy and warned against ambitious men, who wanted, through flattery and empty promises to the voters, to perpetuate, themselves in power. Votes were sacred and men had not only the right, but also the duty, to vote. 'A careless vote', he wrote, 'is a lost right, and indifference toward elections, the forerunner of the tyrant'.[28]

Politics was a delicate and complex art for Marti. It was not a matter of form or ideologies, but the art of guiding and combining through pacific means the different elements in society.[29] Politics could not be borrowed from other nations, but had to be indigenous to the country. 'With the knowledge of the natural elements', he concluded, compromise could be agreed upon and conflicts would be prevented'.[30]

Marti believed in the concept of the State as expressed in the ideas of the French Revolution: a State based on natural law, with a written constitution and a division of powers. He felt that man made laws were just, only if they were based on natural law. Constitutions had to be the product of the true needs of the nation. It was impossible to make constitutions with ideological elements alone. 'A constitution', he explained, 'is a live and practical law'.[31]

Much has been written regarding Marti's attitude toward the United States. His writings have been slanted to show him as being strongly anti-Yankee, or to portray him as the advocate of a Latin America in the image of the United States. The truth lies, perhaps, somewhere between the two extremes. Marti admired the accomplishments of the United States, while at the same time he saw the evils of a society in which, according to him, man placed too much emphasis on material wealth and on his selfish interest. 'The Cubans', he wrote, 'admire this nation, the greatest ever built by freedom, but they distrust the evil conditions that, like worms in the blood, have begun their work of destruction in this mighty Republic ... They cannot honestly believe that excess individualism and reverence for wealth are preparing the United States to be the typical nation of liberty.. We love the country of Lincoln as much as we fear the country of Cutting'.[32]

Marti was a firm believer in individual initiative, private property and honest profit. He saw two evils in the United States capitalistic society: monopoly that limited the free flow of products in the national market, and protectionism, which caused the same result in international trade. For Marti, the injustices of capitalism were only temporary defects and abuses that could be remedied. He did not advocate the suppression of free enterprise. He was anti-capitalistic because of his humanitarian approach to economics and his desire for justice for the poor and the working class. '... the rich capitalist', he wrote, 'forces the worker to work for the lowest wages ... It is the duty of the State to put an end to unnecessary misery'.[33]

Marti understood the influence that economics exerted on politics. Therefore, he advocated that nations should sell to different nations, and not become dependent on any one market. 'Whoever says economic union', he wrote, 'says political union. The people who buy command; the people who sell obey'.[34] Marti viewed with alarm the economic ties Cuba had with the United States, and the danger involved in any closer commercial relations with their neighbour to the North. Realizing the economic importance of the United States and the geographical situation of Cuba, Marti advocated friendlier relations but without any political or economic dependence. He saw the impossibility of maintaining Cuban independence against the will of the United States. 'We are firmly resolved', he said, 'to deserve, request and obtain its (United States) sympathy, without which independence would be very difficult to obtain and maintain'.[35]

Marti looked at the Western Hemisphere and saw it divided into two peoples with different origins and customs. This did not mean that their relation should be based on animosity; on the contrary, he felt that with mutual understanding and respect for the sovereignty of every nation, it was possible to be friends.

People devoted to the liberation of their country are often so absorbed in the task that they become narrow-minded and lose touch with events surrounding them. Not so Marti. He was a citizen of America. Like Bolivar, he thought in terms of a continent, he looked at the events of his homeland, but never lost sight of America. He thought of himself as a son of America, and as such, he felt indebted to her.[36] For Marti, America began in the Rio Grande and ended in the Patagonia. 'The Americans', he explained, 'are one in origin, hope and danger'.[37] He considered it a magnificent spectacle to see a continent made up of so many factors, emerging into compact nations. What was needed was the union of all the Latin Americans. 'The spiritual union', he said, 'is indispensable to the salvation and happiness of the peoples of America'.[38]

Marti was an advocate of everything that was American. American ideas and institutions had to be the foundation on which the future would be built. American men were needed to eradicate the vices inherited from colonial times and the American past had to be studied carefully. 'The history of America', he wrote, 'from the Incas on up to today, should be taught very conscientiously'.[39]

Marti had seen the political chaos and confusion of the emerging Latin American nations and the ambitions of *caudillos,* who sacrificed the interest of the people in their desire to remain in power. He had witnessed the political confusion and foreseen the difficulties which Cuba were to face. His writings were not a mere rhetorical exercise, but a lively lesson for his contemporaries and future generations.

Each one of his ideas encompassed a moral teaching, directed toward making a better man. Marti fulfilled the concept of the man he had advocated. His dedication to the cause of Cuban independence, his love and faith in humanity, and his honest and sincere life, rank him very high among the founders of America.

Notes

1. Pedro de Alba: 'Martí and His Pilgrimage', *Pan American Union Bulletin.* May 1945; p. 267.
2. 'Generoso Deseo', Article in *Patria.* April 30, 1982. Gonzalo de Quesada, ed., *Obras Completas de Martí,* La Habana, Editorial Trópico, 1937; Vol. 3, p. 39. *Patria,* founded in 1892, was the official newspaper of the Cuban Revolutionary Party, and continued to be published until the end of Spanish domination in Cuba. Through its pages, Martí was able to communicate his ideas to the Cuban exiles. *Patria* was, from the progaganda point of view, the most important vehicle to promote the war against Spain. The *Obras* is the most complete collection of the writings of Martí. They contained almost everything that he ever wrote. The volumes are organized in chronological order and the *Guia* (Guide), which comprises one volume, is of extraordinary usefulness).
3. Article in the newspaper *El Partido Liberal,* México, January 30, 1891. *Obras Completas,* Vol. 19, p. 21.
4. Letter to Gómez, July 20, 1882. *Obras Completas,* Vol. 1, p. 201.
5. 'The Annexationist Remedy', *Patria,* July 2, '1892. *Obras Completas,* Vol. 3.
6. 'La Guerra', *Patria,* July 9, 1892. *Obras Completas,* Vol. 3; p. 187.
7. Letter to Emilio Núñez, October 13, 1880; Félix Lizaso, ed., *Epistolario de José Martí.* La Habana, Cultural, S.A., 1930; Vol. 1, p. 69. The Epistolario is a three volume collection of Martí's letters. Although not complete, its chronological order allows for the study of some of Martí's ideas as they evolved with the passage of time, and for an approach and understanding of Martí, not only as a political and social writer, but also as a man.
8. Letter to Gómez, October 20, 1884. *Obras Completas,* Vol. 1; pp. 215–219.
9. *Obras Completas,* Vol. 1, p. 207, are quoted in Emilio Roig de Leuchsenring, ed., *Vida y Pensamiento de Martí.* La Habana, Municipio de La Habana, 1942; Vol. 1, p. 89.
10. Nestor Carbonell: *Martí, carne y espíritu.* La Habana, 1952; p. 158.
11. The full text of the *Bases* can be found in: Emilio Roig de Leuchsenring, ed., 'La Revolución de Martí', *Cuadernos de Historia Habanera.* La Habana, 1941; Vol. 19, pp. 57–58.
12. Letter to the President of the Club of Kingston, Jamaica, May 25, 1892. *Obras Completas,* Vol. 3, p. 75.
13. The full text of the Manifesto can be found in *Obras Completas,* Vol. 8, pp. 159–176.
14. Letter to Federico Henríquez Carvajal, March 25, 1895. *Obras Completas,* Vol. 8, pp. 187–190.
15. Article in the Magazine: *La Opinión Nacional.* Caracas, March 22, 1881. Lilia Castro de Morales, ed., *Diccionario del pensamiento de José Martí.* La Habana, Editorial Selecta, 1953; p. 180. The *Diccionario* is a one volume summary of Martí's thoughts; it contains short paragraphs of his writings, organized by topics, with their corresponding citations. The *Diccionario* gives the reader a quick reference fore many of Martí's ideas, while at the same time it serves as a guide to his major works.
16. 'Sobre mariano Balaguer', *Patria,* April 16, 1892. *Diccionario,* p. 212.
17. Lecture in Steck Hall, January 24, 1880. *Obras Completas,* Vol. 9, p. 15.

18. Article in the Magazine: *La América*. New York, November 1883. *Diccionario*, p. 211.
19. Letter to Joaquín. Macal, Minister of Foreign Relations of Guatemala, April 11, 1877. *Obras Completas*, Vol. 19, p. 47.
20. *Guatemala*, Monograph published by Martí in Mexico in 1878. *Obras Completas*, Vol. 19, p. 87.
21. Ibid., p. 71.
22. 'El Partido Revolucionario a Cuba', *Patria*, May 27, 1893. *Obras Completas*, Vol. 5, p. 78.
23. Ibid.
24. Speech in the Cuban Lyceum, Tampa, November 26, 1891. *Obras Completas*, Vol. 9, pp. 151–170.
25. Article in the *Revista Universal*. México, August 14, 1875. *Obras Completas*, Vol. 49, p. 65.
26. Letter to Federico Henríquez Carvajal: *Obras Completas*.
27. 'La Conferencia Monetaria', *La Revista Ilustrada*. New York, May 1891. *Obras Completas*, Vol. 22, p. 28.
28. 'Las Elecciones del 10 de abril', *Patria*, April 16, 1893. *Obras Completas*, Vol. 5, p. 11.
29. 'El tercer año del Partido Revolucionario Cubano', *Patria*, April 17, 1894. *Obras Completas*, Vol. 6, p. 203.
30. 'Ciegos y desleales', *Patria*, January 28, 1893. *Obras Completas*, Vol. 4, p. 150.
31. Article in *La Opinión nacional,* May 23, 1882. *Diccionario*, p. 110.
32. 'Cuba and the United States', March 1889. *Obras Completas*, Vol. 2, p. 53. This essay was Martí's answer to two editorials, regarding the purchase of Cuba by the U.S. that had appeared in *The Manufacturer of Philadelphia* and the *New York Evening Post*. These newspapers showed extreme contempt for the people of the island. Martí denounced with passion and courage their animosity and the offense to the dignity of his countrymen.
33. Philip S. Forner: *A History of Cuba.* New York, International Publishers, 1963; Vol. II, p. 335.
34. 'La conferencia monetaria', *Op. cit.*
35. Letter to Gerardo Castellanos, August 4, 1892, *Epistolario*, Vol. 2, p. 120, as quoted in Manuel I. Méndez: *Martí: Estudio crítico-biográfico.* La Habana, 1941; p. 145.
36. Letter to Fausto Teodore de Aldrey, July 1881, *Epistolario*, Vol. 1, pp. 71–73.
37. Letter to Pío Vázquez, July 1893. *Obras Completas*, Vol. 19, p. 201.
38. Speech about Bolivar, New York, 1893. *Diccionario*, p. 67.
39. Article in *El Partido Liberal*. México, January 1891. *Diccionario*, p. 65.

The Challenge of Independence in the British Caribbean

Gordon Lewis

With independence the West Indian society faces, after the discovery and emancipation, its third seminal period. The discovery set the original pattern of the society as a slave-based sugar monoculture producing massive profits for absentee owners. Emancipation laid the foundations of a changing Creole society of limited commercial capitalism and peasant individualism. The first period, because of its indiscriminate use of imported slave labour, left behind it a legacy of excessive population in relation to the economy's resources. The second period, because of its use of indentured labour, left behind it a legacy of a low-wage economy with living standards artificially kept low by the maintenance of a reservoir of unemployed and underemployed persons. Independence — which, unlike emancipation, is merely a redefinition of the legal status of the society not necessarily bringing in its wake a profound social metamorphosis such as characterized post-emancipation society — inherits those problems created by the slave and Creole societies. It is true to say, in essence, that the central reality of independence is the need to convert the patterns set by those earlier social systems into an independent national society run primarily in the interests of its independent citizens.

It is, of course, easy to see what independence, on the surface, means. The new nation takes over the paraphernalia of sovereignty. There are the conventional decisions to join the United Nations and, in the West Indian case, to remain within the Commonwealth; the latter being a decision not made so much out of sentimental regard as out of the need to be represented in a vital trading and finance area. For the crass difference between London's treatment of the Guiana government in 1953 and of the Rhodesian secessionist revolt in 1966 was proof, if it were needed, of the double standard of United Kingdom attitudes to the white and coloured members of the Commonwealth. 'Commonwealth alignment', in any case, must be a meaningless phrase when countries like Trinidad and Jamaica have more in common, speaking now of their basic problems, with countries like Yugosla-

via or the United Arab Republic than with Canada or Australia. There is the need for the new nation to set up missions abroad; while, internally, it has to take over the responsibilities of defence and public order by means of new defence forces and control over the police, the last powers yielded up by the imperialist agents. New constitutions must be written, mostly following the Westminster model. The popularly elected minister takes over from the expatriate official. The mass party replaces the individual legislator in the task of organizing and reflecting public opinion. The machinery of government, in brief, becomes adjusted to the new national requirements. Not the least symbolic expression of the change is the final removal of the Colonial Secretary from the colonial arena, thus ending the ridiculous pretension that a whole empire could be effectively governed by a single department in London. That had been seen more than a century ago by the Utilitarian critics of the Colonial Office. 'The Secretary of State for the colonies', observed Sir William Molesworth in the period after 1832, 'traverses and retraverses, in his imagination, the terraqueous globe; flying from the Arctic to the Antarctic pole; hurrying from the snows of North America to the burning regions of the tropics; rushing across from the fertile islands of the West Indies to the arid deserts of South Africa and Australia; like nothing on earth, or in romance, save the Wandering Jew'. Independence puts an end at least to that particular absurdity in a society that has been full of absurdities, of ossified institutions existing like so many Egyptian-style mummies in the hospitable colonial climate of opinion.

But all these are the obvious surface phenomena of independence. They indicate little of the more profound metamorphosis of social structure and social attitudes that the traumatic transition from the colonial status to freedom ought to mean if it is to mean anything at all. New problems will demand new perspectives, new plans, new mental assumptions about the underlying fundamentals of life. A new sense of urgency will have to make itself felt, for one of the crippling handicaps of West Indian life has been the deceptive sense of security engendered by colonial rule. West Indians have been made to feel, frequently to their own satisfaction, that with paramount responsibility resting with London, Britain would always look after things, would always guarantee their safety. So, West Indians have been, like Mr Micawber, incurable optimists waiting for something to turn up. Their capacity for positive action rooted in a frank appraisal of the reality of things was thus seriously undermined. There was lacking the one single incentive, the knowledge that they were on their own in an uncertain and frequently hostile world, calculated to nurture that capacity. That incentive is now there. The real problem of independence is whether the West Indian society can respond creatively to that challenge or will react negatively, seeking in typical colonial fashion to find alibis for inaction or even deliberate evasion of responsibility.

The challenge means a great number of things. It means a new inner strength, both for the individual and the society, the readiness to look inwards, not outwards, for solutions to problems. It means the creation of new institutions, cultural and social as well as political and economic. It means, in brief, the growth of a new positive citizenship, what Rousseau termed in a famous chapter 'a new civil religion'. A new type of public opinion must be organized as the popular base of that citizenship. Equally, a new sense of personal responsibility, of personal involvement, must grow up, for much of what passes for a new national spirit is frequently a sterile anti-colonial prejudice. Even a critic of Caribbean colonialism as left-wing as Daniel Guerin has referred to the temptation, especially in Caribbean politicians, to make the United States into a scapegoat for whatever goes wrong in the area.[1] The game of blaming the ex-colonial power for everything, however historically justifiable it may be, becomes increasingly anachronistic with the passage of time. For it is not enough, with independence, to be merely against something, however justifiably. One must be for something. The social energies of newly liberated peoples, hitherto unutilized in the colonial system, now await the invention of new institutions and new purposes to fulfill themselves. The West Indies, after some early false starts, are thus clearly on the move. The basic questions of their future revolve not around the movement itself but around the direction in which it will propel itself.

Independence, then, means a national stock-taking of heroic proportions. Literally every institution of the society comes in for close re-examination by the new nationalist ethic. Both the political

party and the trade union are under pressure to provide answers to the main problems of high unemployment, illiteracy, a dying sugar industry, a high-cost import structure combined with a low-paid and relatively unskilled labour force, a vulnerable production structure dependent on metropolitan references, an archaic wages-incomes-profits-prices complex that badly needs rationalization, as the acrimonious Trinidadian debate over the 1965 Industrial Stabilization Bill shows; and so on. The trade union movement, in particular, must face the possibility of new tactics in the industrial struggle as they replace the old tactics; thus, a Trinidadian leader, quoting the United States union leader George Meany, has noted that American unions are now active in politics because they have found that, although the company spy and the professional strike-breaker have just about passed from the scene and although unions have certain protections under the law, the employer has decided that the place to curb the union movement is in the legislative field; with the implication that the West Indian scene is likely to witness a similar development. That is undoubtedly true; and it is interesting to note that the time period during which the West Indian trade union has passed from the status of a social pariah to that of a 'sacred cow' more or less exactly corresponds to the time period, that is to say the period since the 1937 passage of the Wagner Act, during which the American movement has undergone the same metamorphosis.[2] Both political party and union also face the problem of bridging the gulf between their middle class professional leadership and their rank and file. For much of what passes for political 'stability' in the self-congratulatory literature is in reality only a reflection of the traditional apathy of the West Indian masses. The West Indian union leader, in particular, is rarely a proletarian either by birth or inclination and in general knows little more about the proletariat of his locals than a good sepoy colonel of 1856 would have known about the Indian villages from which his recruits came.[3]

The West Indian churches, in turn, face a similar challenge. Their humanitarian record of slavery reform is well known. But for a century or more they have tended to live on the memory of that record. It is suggestive, then, that they are already beginning to take a larger view of their social responsibilities, whether it is in the form of their campaign, as in Antigua and Jamaica, against the introduction of legalized casino gambling as an adjunct to the tourist industry, or their plea, as with the Caribbean Roman Catholic bishops, for the application of Catholic social justice to the problem of mass subnormal living standards, or even, as with the case of the 1962 resolution of the

Jamaican Presbyterian Church on foreign policy matters, their concern for a Christian foreign policy for independent nations.[4] There is, even more than that, the question, peculiarly urgent with the advent of a new political status, of the West Indianization of the churches, for, as an Anglican canon of the Trinidad diocese has put it, it would be incongruous in any developing nationalism to insist on natives serving in the state while surrendering the churches to the oversight of foreigners.[5] The civil services, likewise, face the transition from being a colonial power group to becoming a representative bureaucracy under national political control. The readjustment of attitudes that will require in the individual officer has been noted, for the Jamaican service, in Mr B. St J. Hamilton's book.[6] The ideal of what the civil servant under the independence regime should strive to be has likewise been sketched for the Trinidadian case by the exhaustive Lewis Report.[7] The adjustment will be exacting enough, for the definition of an able civil servant under the colonial regime, as the Lewis report points out, was that he attain skills in the art of 'paper passing' to expatriate officers, thus inhibiting the growth of a positive attitude to the decision-making process;[8] while no less a person than the Premier of Barbados has noted, with reference to the privileged status of civil servants under the same colonial regime, that they have traditionally regarded themselves as some army of occupation sent down to the area by the Colonial Office.[9] The new and important subgroup, finally, of the resident West Indian university faculties, as well as the annual flow of graduate students now sent down into the national life, will have to face the challenge of (1) reshaping an inherited aristocratic concept of education into a democratic one for new social purposes and (2) rewriting West Indian history to counterbalance the hitherto existing academic work by either American-oriented students of West Indian affairs or European scholars who have considered Caribbean colonialism as most significant because it reflects the economic and political struggles of the Old World. The adjustment of values and behaviour patterns that all of these groups, as well as others, must meet reflects, in brief, the claimant demands of a new citizenship rooted in the obligation to serve the national community. That citizenship is thus seen as a new social solvent absorbing all groups on a basis of equality in what the Guyanese journalist-essayist P. H. Daly has aptly termed the 'assimilative state'.

The search for a new national interest, it becomes obvious, is the search for a new cultural identity. All newly independent societies seek a positive philosophy to replace the habits of colonial dependency. For, with independence, the society belongs to the resident groups; so, the West Indian society is no longer what Adolphe Roberts once called a semi-barbarous preserve for a small privileged caste of expatriate Englishmen. The logical accompaniment of that, so it seems to the new nation-builders, must be the growth of a new cultural nationalism, a new pride in the hitherto repressed Creole culture fixed upon Captain Cipriani's *dictum* that 'The Englishman has taught us that his home is his castle'. The overpowering cultural image of Britain, reinforced by the West Indian mimetic process, and which permeates nearly every nook and cranny of West Indian social psychology, must give way to new concepts of national and even personal identity rooted in West Indian experience itself. Nor is this merely an academic exercise, needful just for the sake of doing it. It is of immediate urgency, for without that new unifying force the independent Antilles, like independent Haiti earlier on, may be destroyed on the rocks of cultural schizophrenia. Much of West Indian opinion already sees this, perceiving clearly that independence goes far beyond questions of a national flag, a national anthem and a national emblem and becomes a question of psychological survival.

West Indians, as persons, this is to say, have to emancipate themselves in their innermost selves from the English psycho-complex. It will not be an easy task. It cannot be seen, as some writers on the area have seen it, as an act of national choice, as if things like social structure, even national character, are commodities, as it were, that new nations can select like so many customers in a food market. It is always easier to give up ideas than to surrender feelings. It will be the task, obviously, of a generation or more, working through education and experience. No one who has seen how difficult it has been for Puerto Ricans to rid themselves of an American psycho-complex will be likely to underestimate the magnitude of this challenge.

For, frankly, West Indians start out on this road with massive, even frightening handicaps. There is little left of the original culture in which to take pride, save for a few scattered artifacts. The Carib Queen of Arima and the Carib reserve villages in St Vincent and Dominica are about all that is left of the original populations. The cultural amalgam of the slave society was no doubt a real thing. But what it was in detail is a closed book, if only because both white planter and mulatto middle class looked on it with contempt. Later Caribbean scholarship, again, has so far done nothing comparable to the tremendous work of American historians on slavery as a social institution. Nor was there, before slavery, a pre-colonial civilization that could serve as the historical base of a rejuvenated nationalism. It would be difficult, certainly, to write for the West Indies the kind of book, like Basil Davidson's *Rediscovery of Africa,* which describes flourishing feudal civilizations pre-dating the arrival of Europeans; and that fact perhaps accounts for the ambivalence and indecisiveness of the West Indian attitude to things African. The West African nationalist can feel himself the inheritor of the great kingdoms of Ghana and Dahomey. The West Indian nationalist has no such refuge. His collective tragedy is that he is, in his cultural self, a schizoid person. He is, in the Martiniquan phrase, *peau noir, masque blanc,* the possessor of a pseudo-European culture in an Afro-Asian environment. It is for that reason that the regional political-constitutional story has seemed at times something of a farcical drama in which the Colonial Office has seemed more eager to give than West Indians have been to receive. There is no first principle of reference, no great martyrology to inspire the new generations. When, therefore, the West Indian playwright is asked, as in the Federal Festival of 1958, to produce a pageant-play on the region's history he has no one great single event, like the Haitian war of liberation or the Cuban Ten Years War, to use as the central *motif* of his production.

Present day attitudes have been shaped by this legacy. There is little conception of government in the national sense. Government, for most people, is something from which to extract special privileges denied to others. Authority is either laughed at, as in Trinidad, or passively deferred to, as in Barbados. There is little understanding of the idea of creative partnership between citizen and state. The pursuit of individual happiness, of the famous Trinidadian 'freeness', makes itself felt in spendthrift habits and a tradition of gluttony, as can be seen in any Christmas in the West Indies. Those habits, in turn, angrily resist any national fiscal policy that calls for their curtailment, as the frequency of successive austerity budget crisis demonstrates. Above all, this is a society deeply impregnated with anti–intellectual attitudes. For, as Père Labat complained bitterly, at the beginning of the eighteenth century, everything was imported into the West Indies except books. Hence the sorry catalogue of general attitudes to things intellectual, only slowly giving way to new and more ideal pressures: the belief in the West Indian student that higher education means education abroad, the low status, financial and social, of the teaching profession, the amusing credulous belief of the West Indian crowd that an 'intellectual' is anybody who writes letters to the local newspaper or possesses a 'certificate' from some third-rate commercial institute run by profit-hungry managers. 'Here, then,'

Dr Williams has written with justifiable asperity, 'is the reality of Independence — seeking to deal with our problems on a national scale and in an international context with a mentality conceived in slavery, cradled in indenture, and nurtured in colonialism. The dominant result is the confusion of anti–intellectualism. The slave society had no use for books, the indentured society built jails instead of schools, the colonial system inflicted on us a Director of Education without qualifications. So we, the products of this evil trinity, run all over the place despising qualifications, seeking a special position which has no relevance to our economic realities, aping the customs and attitudes of absentee planters and expatriate officials'.[10]

Nothing, then, is easier than to laugh at the spectacle of the nation-builders of the newly-independent states attempting to reconstruct something out of this dismal heritage. The literature on the region is full of the jaundiced English writer making fun of West Indian follies, without seeing that the joke is on him since they are the reflection of English follies. A critic writing recently from the University of Puerto Rico has managed to dismiss it all, in a piece of entertaining satire, as nothing more than a 'riot of nonsense' and 'fiery irrationalities'.[11] There is much, without doubt, to justify the structure. To read the discussions in the West Indian press on the need for a distinctive national costume, or to note the bathos of the new national anthems, or to view the passions capable of being worked up over the question as to whether the new Jamaican Governor-General should wear a uniform on ceremonial occasions, is to be made painfully aware of the comedy involved in the effort to set up national rituals and symbols overnight. The same is true of the sort of undignified squabbling that goes on as various groups and individuals seek to claim credit for having been in 'on the ground floor' of the early national struggles, as if there were not 'glory enough for all'; the exchange of correspondence in the Jamaican press between W. A. Domingo and others concerning the genesis of the Jamaican nationalist movement after 1936 is typical.[12] But before all this is seen as raw material for satire two things ought to be remembered. The first is that to expect a growing national consciousness based solely on 'reason' and 'moderation' is to ignore the emotional aspects of human nature in politics. Men are rarely satisfied with merely abstract symbols of a new freedom. They need something more exciting, more tangible, more immediately recognizable. They are, true enough, members of the general army of humanity. But they are, first and foremost, members of their small platoon, through which they experience, as a part, the sense of belonging to the whole. And that this is a generally universal truth of human nature is evident enough from the fact that Kohr has to draw most of his examples of the 'insanity' of nationalism from the established and presumably more 'mature' European countries. If, then, Germans feel that their famous Shakespearian translations are superior to the English original, Puerto Ricans, as a Caribbean example, are surely entitled to compare Rafael Hernandez's patriotic hymn *Lamento Borincano* to Beethoven's Fifth Symphony; and the one as much as the other is an amiable fault easily forgiven.

The second point to make concerns the socio-psychological background of the contemporary efforts of cultural nationalism. For the new nationalism is not simply a mental error or a political mistake. It has real roots in historical experience, being, in fact, the response to the old colonialism. It goes back, in its origins, to the deep sense of shame, humiliation and basic loss of self-respect involved in being ruled by others even when, as with the English Antillean case, it has been a comparatively benign rule. In this sense, as Sekou Toure has put it, nationalism is psychologically inevitable for the liberated colonial peoples. To overlook all this is to be guilty of gross historical naïveté. It is true that symbols may come to be accepted, dangerously, as substitutes for, instead of merely being aides to the solid feelings of national community arising out of common social experience. West Indians themselves, however, are aware of the danger. As Dr Williams has remarked of the Trinidadian case, it takes more than a national anthem, however stirring, a national coat of arms however distinctive, a national flag however appropriate, a national flower however beautiful, to make a nation.[13] There is little evidence that West Indians, who possess the saving grace, in any case, of a pronounced sense of wry humour, are ready to elevate those symbols to the status of the grotesque identity-building absurdities Kohr is concerned to pillory. Yet there is a real critique to be made of contemporary West Indian nationalism, although it is not the one that critics like Kohr make. It has to do, essentially, with the particular road to social growth and economic development that West Indian governments in the new era have elected to take. For independence is the beginning only. It is not the end. In one way, it merely replaces the national struggle against the external metropolitan power with an internal struggle between the various social and ethnic groups of the new national society, to determine who will inherit the vacuum of power left behind by the departing imperialists. There is nothing in the act of independence that minimizes the fact that the society continues to be a class society in which the Creole

commercial and professional groups retain a halo of merit over them and sustain the pose by a sort of psychological confidence trick played by the communications media on the traditionally deferential West Indian masses. The general outcome of the transfer of power from the old empires to the new successor-states thus means little more, in social power terms, than the consolidation of the ruling class hold of (1) a nascent middle class using independence as a ladder to governmental, civil service and diplomatic appointments and (2) a growing business class seeking a new role in the world context of international capitalism. For the West Indian populace as a whole that means simply a change of masters only, and possible, too, a change in some ways for the worse, for since the bourgeois groups understand them better, psychologically, than did the English officialdom their exploitation by those groups may be made that much easier.

In retrospect, that outcome takes on a certain air of historical inevitability. For after 1938 the potentially revolutionary *élan vital* of the masses was anaesthetized by being canalized into institutions — trade unions, political parties, co-operative societies — controlled by the bourgeois groups. The leadership elements that resisted that process — whether because of a radical racial perspective, as with Garveyism, or because of a radical political perspective, as with individuals like Lennox Pierre and John La Rose in Trinidad and Richard Moore and Reginald Pierrepointe in Barbados — were either pushed aside or purged by the dominant right-wing forces. Others, like George Padmore, who might have fought the process, elected to concentrate on the more promising African scene, not being excited by a West Indian 'revolution' led by a political leadership whose ideas of political emancipation hardly went further than the replacement of the Crown Colony system run by English personnel by a domestic class system run by a native-born *élite*. Others, again, like C.L.R. James, saw clearly enough, in sporadic writing, that no 'revolution' was worthwhile in which peasant and worker did not remain the primary agents, the leading properties of the experiment, for only the submerged classes were capable of genuinely revolutionary activity. But James, in any case, was personally isolated from the West Indian scene, not returning until 1958 (by which time the damage, from the revolutionary viewpoint, had been done) and in any case spoiled his capacity to help by an exaggerated sense of personal importance and, more generally, by his failure to appreciate that far from being a pure revolutionary class the West Indian ordinary people, by the time of independence, had become themselves seriously tainted with colonial bourgeois impurities. All of this, added up, facilitated the bloodless victory of the bourgeois spirit, whether in conservative or reformist garb, in the majority political parties that carried through the passage to independence. That was what took place in all of the West Indian societies, a truth only obscured in the Guyanese case by the Jaganite habit of retaining the orthodox terminology of the traditional Marxist literature.

The result, in the West Indian society of the present day, is the rule of the many by the few. A new vocabulary of nationalist respectability appears in which the fashionable slogan of 'citizenship' really amounts to the general acceptance of goals set by the new governing oligarchy. Ceremonial speech-making does little but play variations on the theme. A rhetorical passage out of the contribution of the University of the West Indies — 'We as citizens must be aware of that thing called political philosophy, as well as be prepared to formulate a particular philosophy to match the political needs and realities . . . . of the Caribbean. Do we ever sit and ask ourselves the question, where are we coming from, where are we going, and what do we want now? What body of coherent ideas and principles are our public servants, both politicians and senior civil servants, formulating for the future of this country? And if there are these ideas, have they been passed on to the general populace for acceptance and comment?'[14] — is typical , taking for granted as it does that the role of the masses in the new dispensation is 'acceptance' of ideas made for them by the *élite*. The search for a national interest and a cultural identity, legitimate and desirable as they are, too easily becomes the private game of that same *élite*, so that the important truth — that neither national interest nor identity of any genuine character can be achieved save as they rest on the foundation of social equality and economic justice — is persistently obscured.

Nationalism is thus reduced to a tragic farce in which it is identified with the receipt of empty honorific titles in the British honours award system, solidifying as that does the disease of West Indian social snobbishness; or with the governmental elevation of beauty queens and (as in Jamaica) of vulgarized forms of folk music like the 'Ska' dance into national symbols; or with the official patronage of Decolonization Institutes that preach the lesson of national self-reliance while every other aspect of the official government programme negates the lesson. In every territory, more or less, the population is organized, politically, in 'safe' political parties, the most glaring example being the organization of the *lumpenproletariat* of the

West Kingston slums into semi-military political gangs directed by the leaders of both of the Jamaican political groupings. Even the entry of the masses into the national politics, after universal suffrage, can be seen not as the great civic advance West Indian liberals make it out to be but as a process of essentially conservative politicization, since it helped create the new popular belief that politics held the key to all problems and the panacea to every social ill. Hence the West Indian political passion, the amazing fury of the West Indian political partisan, the conviction that 'politics' will cure all. This could only lead to a dead end, since politics is a result, not a first cause. But it was a delusion naturally encouraged by the new class of political office holders who thereby at one and the same time diverted mass energy into a safe outlet and obtained a veneer of legitimacy of their own new status within the West Indian power structure.

The social question, to put this in another way, is thus subordinated to the national question. That subordination, perhaps necessary in the pre-independence era, becomes a tactic of evasion in the post-independence era. The slogans of the national struggle, mostly attacking colonialism, are perpetuated, more and more anachronistically, in the new situation, so that an argument that certainly possesses a manifest degree of historical validity — that the British imperialists are responsible for the legacy they have left behind — is converted into a scapegoat for the frustrations generated by the continuing class-relations of the society. It is tempting to see this, as some indignant English left-wing ideologues in the region see it, as the fruits of a greedy and selfish middle class that lacks a social conscience.[15] But this is to attribute motives to the governing classes (a thoroughly un-Marxian procedure) instead of recognizing that their behaviour is the simple and logical consequence of the system they represent. Or it is possible to see it all, as the Jamaican commentator Frank Hill has seen it, in more optimistic terms, as the outcome of a process in which there has come into power in Jamaica a true governing class in the form of the JLP-PNP political administrators whose full-time energies are devoted to maintaining the state power; who constitute, therefore, a 'natural' governing class in a way that neither the group of mercantile-industrial capitalists nor of the intellectuals constitutes one.[16]

But this second line of argument is hardly convincing unless an unrealistic separation is made between a 'governing' class in the sense of a group of professional politicians exercising the art of statecraft, and a 'ruling' class in the fuller sociological sense of a group controlling the means of production in the economy. To assume such a separation, speaking now of the Jamaican situation, is untenable for two reasons. First, it is so because although the new class of JLP-PNP political leaders were more alike in both educational background and colour distribution to the general population than were the long-established economic élite, this did not prevent the acceptance in both political parties of programmes that left untouched the basic principle of the private ownership of production means; the Federation struggle, as already seen, converted the PNP into the declared defendant of the Jamaican protectionist-minded business interests which the JLP, in any case, always had been. Secondly, there took place in Jamaica, as Bell notes, a process of co-optation of the new political leadership into the social and associational life of the older economic *élites*, thereby facilitating, if only partially, a tendency to leave inarticulate or unattended the discontents of the lower classes.[17] In the light of these facts it is difficult to accept Hill's defence of the political 'governing' class as an entity of more or less pure Platonic statesmen-administrators whose 'restraint' and 'sense of responsibility' were the main factors for the advance of Jamaican independence. If that in fact were so it would be difficult to find reasons to explain why Jamaica today remains a society deeply divided along both social and racial lines.

Clearly enough, there are limits to the social utility of nationalism. There is much to be said, as already noted, in defence of it. Yet in and of itself it cannot engineer the radical reconstruction of the social order. Like emancipation before it, it is the necessary condition of such reconstruction. But it is not the reconstruction itself. At its best, it promises an end to the colonial psychology of self-contempt. At its worst, it confers a badge of plausible ideological respectability on the identification of the national interest with the sectional interests of the Creole ruling groups. It is true that West Indian nationalism has not done all that it might have done because it has lacked the solidifying unguent of a war of colonial liberation. Writers like Fanon, as in his eulogy of the Algerian Revolution, have argued that the mere experience of violent anti-colonial combat becomes a moral purgative cleansing the colonial spirit with a lasting restorative power. But the decline, after victory, of the Algerian Revolution itself suggests that the memory of colonial comradeship in arms, however evocatively splendid, cannot in itself play that role. The new national society stands in need of more permanent ideas that relate to the continuing experience of its members in the present. That, on any showing, means a socialist ideology so that the nationalist ethic may be married to the planned

organization of social equality. Until that ideology emerges, based on the class consciousness of the masses, the West Indian societies will remain the complacent and apathetic communities they have become, lacking the intangible feeling of expectancy, the eagerness to see what the future will bring and the readiness to act to bring the future more rapidly to fruition.[18]

Notes

1. Daniel Guérin, *The West Indies and Their Future* (London, Denis Dobson, 1961), p. 172.
2. John Rojas, in *Evening News* (Port of Spain, Trinidad, 27 November 1961).
3. See, for example, Rawle Farley (ed.), *Labour Education in the British Caribbean* (Extra-Mural Department, University College of the West Indies, 1960). See also the concluding remarks in Francis X. Mark, *The History of the Barbados Workers' Union* (Bridgetown, Advocate Commercial Printing, N.D.), pp. 167–68. The remark in the text about a sepoy colonel of 1856 is taken from the review of the Farley volume by H. P. Jacobs, *Daily Gleaner*, 20 December 1961.
4. Statement of the Jamaica Christian Council on gambling, *Daily Gleaner*, 10 October 1962; exchange of correspondence between Sir Alexander Bustamante and Moderator of the Presbyterian Church of Jamaica, *Daily Gleaner*, 5 November 1962; Statement of the Roman Catholic Caribbean Bishops, *Antigua Star*, 16 February 1962.
5. Canon Farquhar, 'Candid Comments', *Trinidad Guardian*, 23 December 1956.
6. B. L. St John Hamilton, *Problems of Administration in an Emergent Nation. A Case Study of Jamaica* (New York, Frederick A. Praegar, Inc., Special Studies, 1964).
7. Trinidad and Tobago, *First Report of the Working Party on the Role and Status of the Civil Service in the Age of Independence* (St Ann's, Port of Spain, September 1964).
8. *Ibid.*, para. 32.
9. Hon. Errol Barrow, Barbados, *House of Assembly. Debates*, Official Report, 11 June 1963, p. 22.
10. Eric Williams, 'The Reality of Independence', *The Nation*, Vol. 7, No. 15, 22 January 1965.
11. Leopold Kohr, 'Is Reason Treason? Does economic development signal the end of a country's uniqueness?', *San Juan Review*, May 1965.
12. *Public Opinion* (Kingston, Jamaica), 3 February 1962, 28 July 1962, 20 October 1962.
13. Eric Williams, *History of the People of Trinidad and Tobago* (Port of Spain, PNM Publishing Co., 1962), p. 280.
14. Rex Nettleford, Staff Tutor, University of the West Indies, in *The Torchlight* (St George's, Grenada), 10 June 1962.
15. See, for example, W. I. Carr, speech to Life Underwriters' Conference, in *Spotlight* (Kingston, Jamaica), February 1964.
16. Frank Hill, 'Need for a Governing Class', reprinted, *Caribbean Quarterly*, in 'Editorial Comments and Notes', Vol. 8, No. 3 (September 1962).
17. Wendell Bell, *Jamaican Leaders. Political Attitudes in a New Nation* (Berkeley and Los Angeles, University of California Press, 1964), pp. 74–75. See also M. G. Smith, 'The Plural Framework of Jamaican Society', *The Plural Society in the British West Indies* (Berkeley and Los Angeles, University of California Press, 1965).
18. The emphasis of the nationalist philosophy upon a national consensus framework of reference leads to a dan-

gerous underestimation of its internal contradictions. Thus a recent West Indian Statement can write of Eric Williams and C. L. R. James without perceiving that their different ideological ways of looking at West Indian society makes it somewhat misleading to write about them as if they were merely West Indian nationalist ideologues, Philip

Sherlock, *West Indies* (London, Thames and Hudson, 1966), pp. 155–58. It is sometimes easier for the outside observer, who is free of local pressures, to see this, for example, Ivar Oxaal, 'C. L. R. James vs. Eric Williams: The Formative Years', *Trinidad and Tobago Index* (The University, Hull, England), No. 2, Fall. 1965.

Race, Identity and Independence in Jamaica

Rex Nettleford

In focusing attention on the need for Jamaican blacks to assume economic as well as political control of their country, the phenomenon of Black Power can lay some of its strongest claims to relevance. Jamaicans did seek the political Kingdom first but all things have not followed in the interest of the blacks and so many are now stronger in the view that *economic independence is a necessary pre-condition of any real political independence.*[1] The concern is not exclusive to Black Power advocacy. In fact there is universal outrage at the control of our destiny by foreign exploiters and this is to be found among a wide cross-section of Jamaicans, some of whom are not black. Yet the Chinese and Lebanese (Syrian) Jamaicans are particularly vulnerable in the face of Black Power attacks because they are dominant at levels of economic activity where it is thought blacks should be in control.[2] The dilemma that surrounds any attempt to blacken the distributive trades and other branches of commerce is, however, nowhere examined in the literature of Jamaican Black Power. Instead, a listing is made (from *Who's Who in Jamaica*) of what the advocates call 'intensified white economic power in Jamaica'. Over one hundred commercial businesses are controlled says the information sheet by 'four white families.* In most cases they are outright owners. For the rest they are either Managing Director, Chairman of the Board of Directors or Directors of these Companies.[3] The information sheet ends with an apocalyptic injunction from the Old Testament — 'Riches profit not in the day of wrath; but righteousness delivereth from death. Proverbs II, verse 4'. The question is still worth asking as to what is to happen to the Chinese** and the Syrians and the

Jamaican Jews who between them command much wealth and material comfort compared with the blacks. Is their property to be expropriated so as to accommodate control by the 90–odd per cent black Jamaicans? The blacks in Jamaica have not displayed until recently much interest in commercial life. This was no doubt due partly to cultural conditioning and partly to lack of facilities to finance businesses. The understandable preoccupation of blacks with respectability and status professions probably kept them out of occupations of profit. But it is said that money in Jamaica produces power; and without money, say the Black Power advocates, the blacks are powerless. But it may be that the Jamaican black man will have to rid himself of the cultural cocoon in respect of his dislike of manual work at home and be now concerned with consciously acquiring the skills, other than white-collar ones, that will make him economically independent. He will probably have to be prepared to make sacrifices in the way many of his Chinese and Syrian countrymen did a generation or two ago, without fear of humiliation. It may be that the black man will have to stop littering the countryside with illegitimate children, dull the memory of his proverbial castration by slavery and face the responsibility of fathering a family unit as a base from which to build his social and economic security. It may even be that what is being demanded of the Jamaican black is impossible, since it requires a complete break with a past which has left too big and deep and permanent a scar on his consciousness.

This may be one instinctive reason for Black Power advocates' concentration on the bigger problems of the black collectivity — on the

---

*Two Jewish and two Lebanese (Syrians) families are named. They are again named by Blackman in his Column 'Time Now' who describes them as 'parasites who rise or fall with American fortunes'. (See *Abeng,* Vol. I, No. 33, September 11, 1969.)
**In 1854 the first group of Chinese came to Jamaica via Colon, Panama, where they had gone to work on the railway. This was a private scheme which failed. From 1884, however, Chinese immigration received official blessing and in that year 696 Chinese arrived from Hong Kong to work as indentured labourers on the estates. Some 109 women were among them, 508 men, 59 boys, 17 girls and one baby. The Chinese who came after this left the estates and entered the grocery business which they still dominate in the island's townships. Resentment against the 'Chinese invasion' developed as far back as 1911–12. This had disappeared with the integration of a new generation of Chinese into the society. (See 'Chinese in the Caribbean', v.p. Oswald Hoston, Kingston, 1941, esp. pp. 27, 29, 81, 83, 97.).

national aspects of economic life. The focus tends to be on the big industries such as sugar, tourism and bauxite, which all have the common feature of being foreign owned and foreign directed.* The entire policy of foreign investment and the exploitation of Jamaican resources become then the target of attack. It has been the paradox of national development that the optimism indicated by the statistics of the annual *Economic Survey of Jamaica* bears little relation to the facts of life among the majority of the people. The information that the gross domestic product increased by 9.1% in 1968 as compared with 5.5% in 1967 remains more a discussion point for professional economists than a reason for jubilation among the perpetual poor.[4] Factors such as the increase in general price level and a rise in population are likely to reduce considerably the per capita increase of the GDP in any case. But this in itself is more a matter for attack and counter-attack between Government and Opposition. Problems of unemployment and the maldistribution of income remain realities. The Gleaner editorialized a further problem after the 1969 Budget Debate. 'Government claims that unemployment is being reduced. The Opposition claims unemployment is rising. Who is right? Government claims the income gap is being bridged; while the Opposition claims that the income gap is widening. Who is right?' The editorial, in conclusion, agreed with the Leader of the Opposition, Michael Manley, that 'signs of discontent which have become manifest over past months indicate that many Jamaicans are not participating sufficiently in the development process'.[5] Although Mr. Manley reportedly disapproved of what the editorial called 'trouble-making instigating', his views on non-participation would be endorsed by Black Power advocates. The Jamaican economy, then, despite its brilliant recorded statistical performance over the past decade and a half, has not lived up to the expectations of an ex-slave society struggling to give full meaning to emancipation and freedom. As the *New World* article on 'Sugar, Our Life or Death' puts it, 'The period which elapsed since Emancipation can . . . best be understood in terms of two interdependent processes; the one leading legal equality to its logical conclusion in full popular political representation (adult suffrage) and self-determination (independence) the other *involving attempts to secure an economic structure which would bring political and economic relations into equilibrium'*[6] [my emphasis].

It is the consistent thwarting of this latter process which angers the Black Power advocates most as it does the entire range of young intellectual thinking in the Caribbean today. It is this which made the economist Havelock Brewster invite readers to take a long hard look at the sugar industry. High production cost, low profits and low wages plague the industry despite the protection it gets by 'unusually high' negotiated price and quota provisions. The call for mechanization has been heeded by the Government but the British investors are loathe to invest the kind of money needed to resuscitate the 160,000 acres of very arable land now planted out in what is often described as a dying industry.

'Surprising as it may seem', read a letter to the *Gleaner* from the Manager of the Sugar Manufacturers' Association of Jamaica Limited, 'for the four years 1965 to 1968, the earnings of the sugar estates as a whole, after offsetting the losses, have been of the order of twenty thousand pounds per annum on a capital employed of over twenty-two million pounds — *an average annual rate of earnings of less than one-tenth of one per cent for the four year period'* [my emphasis].[7] The experience with sugar is indelibly imprinted on the consciousness of black West Indians. Even in its dormant state the slave product remains the ghost that haunts the mind of the aware Jamaican. Such intangible considerations which turn on its slave connexions are too often ignored in assessments by government officials and management alike. Instead workers are blamed for being perverse and workers in turn, not infrequently, expect the worst of the heirs of slavemasters. To make matters worse it is not profitable though it still serves as one of the largest sources of employment in the country.** Sugar's connexion with the past is the surest link with the still unrewarding present in the minds of many critics of the society. As the Cuban journalist-historian Ramiro Guerra y Sanchez said, the final goal of the sugar economy was to 'produce at minimum cost a basic commodity or luxury article for a distant market at a profit, even though that policy will in the long run ruin the producing country economically, socially and politically.[8]

It is not difficult to see why some analysts see this logic of exploitation working itself through in the more recent bauxite industry which produces another basic commodity for the distant North American market at immense profit. The instruments of exploitation are still cheap labour and foreign capital in search of profit. This results, inter

---

*Black Power advocates' strongest case. See 'The New Imperialism' by Blackman in *Abeng,* Vol. I, No. 33, especially paragraphs 3–6.
**In 1967 the sugar industry employed some 63,244 persons in croptime or 8.8 per cent of the workforce. (*Economy Survey of Jamaica,* 1968.)

alia, in the loss of land. And if the land is lost, all shall have been lost, including liberty and honour according to the Caribbean historian of sugar. It is in this spirit that Black Power advocates assault the fact of foreign domination and what is seen (and not without some just fears) as the industrial annexation of Jamaica by North America.

So sugar remains a special problem to Jamaicans. After all it did bring slavery and indentureship, the plantation system and colonial dependence. It now brings little returns in terms of living wage for the vast majority of the workers. It remains, despite the rationalization of the labour force (by some 25%) a symbol of servitude for social-conscious advocates of change and many Black Power adherents are among these. The anger is exacerbated by the fact that a suitable substitute seems to elude political decision-takers as it has academic analysts. Meanwhile, sugar remains king in its capacity to employ labour in a country burdened with chronic unemployment. Attempts at mechanization would seem at this point to be a last ditch to resuscitate it if not to its pristine glory, at least to a tolerable position.

Less tolerable is the tourist industry which the Black Power militants see as the curse to end all curses. This, in their eyes, is the direct 'sell-out' of the country by black politicians to the 'white devils' of North America. This attitude is said to have an adverse effect on the industry, particularly in Canada where 'for some time now we've been getting a bad press — inaccurate and exaggerated stories about the imminence of revolution and the influence here of the Black Power boys. In consequence we are losing a lot of tourist business, and even Jamaicans in Canada are writing home in alarm. . . .'[9] The statistical surveys show an impressive increase from some £10,000,000 sterling (20 million Jamaican dollars*) in 1959 to just under £40,000,000 sterling or 80 million Jamaican dollars in 1969. Though some of this is attributed to transfer of visitors from a Cuba that went under Castro, tourist promotion has intensified in its hard-sell of sun, beach and old-world ambience.[10] Probably the most apt Black Power comment on the industry is to be seen on the front page of an early issue of *Abeng* which carried a picture culled from a Holiday Magazine dated November, 1968. It shows a black beach boy with shining teeth supporting on his shoulders a middle-aged white female tourist clad in bathsuit cov-

ering an unmistakably unbecomingly obese figure but grinning away at the unusual piece of sporting. The *Abeng* caption read 'Tourism on top, we underneath'.[11] This attitude betrays what has been a longstanding dislike of tourism particularly among the Jamaican middle classes. The northern littoral between Port Maria and Montego Bay, a distance of about seventy miles, is still regarded as 'foreign country' by many Jamaicans and the reports of discrimination against local inhabitants have not endeared the industry to many. It remains, however, a big money earner for the country and is even regarded in some quarters as a way of making quick hard currency for more meaningful and long-term development. The fact that the vast majority of tourists are white and North American would naturally go against the grain of Black Power advocates.

he distrust of North America comes out strongest, however, in attitudes to the bauxite-alumina industry. In this Black Power advocates have some of their firmest allies. For many Jamaicans see this as the 'colonial industry' *par excellence,* controlled as it is from multinational bases situated outside of the country.** They know that decision-taking does not rest with Jamaicans and seldom with the white functionaries who reside in the island. The subtle discriminatory practices against native Jamaicans in the matter of appointments and job responsibility are abhorred. While many of the local executives are paid enormous salaries they are said to have no real responsibility and job satisfaction is seldom realized. Pockets of colonial-type housing compounds are all but reserved for white expatriates of the management class and the break-through by a black or brown Jamaican into the haven is often regarded as a major feat. Labour may be well paid, but only after strong trade union pressure, and even then the entire wage differentials in the economy at large.

'Why', the question is asked, 'the concentration on mining — the stealing of our earth and the raping of the hillsides?' the manufacture of alumina goes further, it is conceded, but not far enough, it is frequently argued. 'Why such small royalties when the situation has changed so radically since 1950 when the first "sell-out" took place?' The unions, it is also argued, are, in any case, in collusion with the United Steelworkers of America who have a vested interest in Jamaica remaining a primary source of supply so that North American

---

*Jamaica converted its currency to dollars and cents in September, 1969.
**Six companies now operate in Jamaica: Aluminium Company of America (Alcoa) in the parish of Clarendon; Aluminium Canada (Alcan) Jamaica Ltd., in Manchester, St. Ann and St. Catherine; Aluminium Partners (Alpart) consortium of Anaconda, Kaiser and Reynolds in St. Elizabeth; Kaiser in St. Ann; Reynolds Jamaica Mines in St. Ann; and Revere Copper and Brass in St. Elizabeth.

workers can enjoy job security. Some militants favour nationalization but this has less support than would be supposed. There is, however, support for an aluminium smelter so that Jamaicans can participate in the full range of the aluminium industry from mining to smelting. Why should Jamaica not negotiate one as Puerto Rico has done?* One point of view insists that a successful lobby could be organized in Washington to obtain from the United States the undertaking to guarantee Jamaica a market of, say, 100,000 tons of ingot annually. Cost factors notwithstanding, this point of view insists that Jamaica could produce competitive ingots. Another point of view holds that Jamaica should emulate Guinea by obtaining controlling shares in the Bauxite alumina companies operating in Jamaica.[12] Even if it means financing the shareholding by a loan, the industry is profitable enough to make the debt self-liquidating within a generation. There has, however, been no Black Power comment on the corresponding sacrifices (e.g. an austere lifestyle and higher personal taxes) that would have to be made. Yet another point of view sees bauxite-alumina firms being charged a very high surtax which could be ploughed back into development projects that could generate more income and provide more jobs. This would be essentially a government matter but since the government, in the eyes of Black Power advocates, is a 'stooge of white power', it is unlikely that this point of view would win their support.

At least one of the bauxite owners is optimistic about Black Power and bauxite in Jamaica. Appearing before the Canadian Senate's Standing Committee on Foreign Affairs, Mr. Nathaniel V. Davis, President of Alcan Aluminium Ltd., replied to a question about the rise of Black Power in the Caribbean as follows: '. . . we are alert to some of these developments which are occurring. We believe that areas such as Jamaica and Guyana — the lesser developed areas that are basically short of capital — can use their capital to better advantage in areas other than those in which we may be operating. We believe that, effectively, the governments and the people of Jamaica and Guyana are partners with us in this profitability of our enterprises in the two countries, although the entire risk capital has been invested by us. These forces are at work in many parts of the world, but we believe basic economic sense should prevail and that these countries would use their resources in areas that they can develop better themselves'. The speaker added his belief 'that the equity participation which has come into these countries from Canada has brought not only profits and income and foreign exchange to the countries, but technological and managerial skills as well'. Senator Connolly the questioner from Ottawa West obliged with 'And taxes', and the President of Alcan Aluminium concurred.**

It could be argued by management interests in bauxite that the cost structure of the industry of the industry is nowhere realistically discussed by Black Power advocates. But it is doubtful whether in the absence of investment exposure by exploiting firms many of these advocates could be aware of the implications of their demands in terms of national ownership of the industry. Sterling Brubaker in his book *Aluminium Industry* has this to say: 'There is no transport advantage to be had from moving fuel to the bauxite source for smelting ore to metal, for, in addition to the carbon and fluoride used in reduction and the soda and fuel used in the alumina stage, about 4–5 tons of coal would be required to produce enough power to smelt a ton of metal and the metal would still have to be shipped to market. Thus the advantage lies with moving the bauxite or, far better, the alumina.[13] Persons who inhabit exploited economies would hardly expect otherwise since the advantage lies with the white owners of the smelting plants. But Brubaker seems to be saying that the advantage lies also with the primary producers such as Jamaica, when he further writes 'Apart from questions of prestige then, an aluminium smelting industry is not essential to a country for reasons of defence, industrial progress, or employment. It may help conserve foreign exchange through import substitution, but usually at the cost of more expensive metal; it may earn exchange with only a minimal diversion of domestic resources if it is commercially viable and able to attract foreign capital; or it may permit collateral benefits from river development projects'.[14] Brubaker admits that he understands the desire on the part of developing countries to claim any economic rent arising through exploitation of their resources. But in the same paragraph he expresses summary doubt as to whether 'there is much rent to be claimed in the aluminium industry. *Bauxite supplies are so large and widespread that they have limited scarcity value'* [my emphasis].

---

*Prompted by Reports in the Jamaican press that Alcoa planned to build a 2 million-dollar smelter in Puerto Rico that would benefit some 1,000 workers to the tune of 5 million dollars annually. (See *Star*, April 21, 1969. Also letter to Editor, 'Jamaica Bypassed', *Daily Gleaner*, May 19, 1969).
**See *Proceedings of the Standing Committee on Foreign Affairs*, p. 19, Senate of Canada, Second Session, 28th Parl., Tues., Nov. 25, 1969.

Brubaker's work may well be based on the best principles of scholarship and hard-headed statistical analysis, but Black Power advocates would see him as the apostle of exploitation and the defender of white power interests against defenseless Third World countries like Jamaica. The inevitable distrust ensures, then, the perpetuation among Jamaican cynics (black and otherwise) of the grave doubts they harbour about bauxite-alumina and its long-term effect on the economic strength of their country.

Implied in the persistent view that the bauxite-alumina industry ought to be rationalized into a nationally-determined enterprise, is a confidence in the force of the political power which Jamaicans have acquired, but which they have allowed to become frozen informal institutions. It can indeed be reasonably argued that the elected representatives of the Jamaican people (the majority of whom are black) ought to have enough confidence in their constituents to use their political leverage to the advantage of the people of Jamaica. Even if economics were to dictate otherwise, the power of politics could indeed force a foreign company to accede to the demands of Jamaicans who, at least potentially, own the land from which the rich ore is mined. But then Black Power advocates would counter this with the view that Jamaicans do not really own the land, have no power and never will until they have *complete economic control.*

The advocates share with others the deep fear that the economic aspects of Jamaican life are likely to remain the province of outsiders while Jamaicans are barely allowed to get on with the political and the 'harmless' cultural aspects. This division of labour is grossly unrealistic and unhealthy. For it merely allows decisions about the destiny of the Jamaican people to be taken elsewhere rather than through the democratic process in which many Jamaicans seem to take great price. The one-man-one-vote principle, the claims for workers' right to strike, the conduct of public affairs through rank,open, free, parliamentary debate would all be meaningless. Some Black Power advocates feel that this is exactly the situation as it now is in Jamaica. In their eyes the gains of political independence are all but negated by the economic satellization of the country by North America (the United States and Canada). This has prompted the declaration that Jamaican politicians have no power and that they are black masks of authority shielding the white faces of power. Yet although neat distinctions between 'authority' and 'power' are necessary intellectual preoccupations[15] they must also be prepared to stand the test of real political experience. Authority begets power and *vice versa.* What is not unreasonable to ask is that the Prime Minister of Jamaica with the authority of office must find the myriad ways of using his office and authority to acquire power. But to deny him and his ministers this capacity is to absolve them from all responsibility and therefore from all blame for the decisions they take. And this Black Power advocates, or any one else, would not be willing to do.

A politician without power may be a politician without respect, to parody a famous Garvey saying. But he also becomes an official without the burden of public moral responsibility. One way out of the intellectual dilemma would be to write off the politicians as public vegetables (and some Black Power advocates do). This, however, does not always relate to realities. Many of these would-be 'public vegetables' are themselves talking the language of Jamaicanization, of self-respect and of the need for Jamaican ownership of economic resources. They do, however, speak in Establishment jargon which blurs the substance with repetitious clichés of rhetoric and it is this which in turn rouses the impatience of the militant and progressive who desire action and quick change. It pleases less those Black Power advocates who do not in any case equate Jamaicanization with black ownership. What may be more usefully examined, however, is the question of whether black Jamaican politicians are not too sensitive to the constraints within which they work and whether they should not muster their creative drive to burst through man-made barriers in dealing with big brother countries and rich international trading partners.* It may be that our black politicians lack the skill to achieve objectives and the vision to perceive the needs. Perhaps these politicians underestimate the strength of the small nation in the world today and over-value the power that supposedly inheres in military might and technological achievement. It may even be that Jamaican politicians do not appreciate, sufficiently, the twentieth century demands for teamwork and organization. Perhaps old attitudes and prejudices and their very conditioning in the ways of the white man's world, preclude them from grasping, fully, the need for a society like Jamaica to cultivate its intellectual capacities through its university and other educational institutions so that its resources can be maximized — both material, however limited, and human which can be limitless.

---

*The view of a young black West Indian intellectual is that 'there are no vast, impersonal forces *constraining* Jamaican or any other West Indian country to accept as given the continued dependence of these territories. The solution lies in our hands'. (James Milette in article, 'Exit Norman', *Moko,* No. 3, Port-of-Spain, Trinidad).

Black Awareness and Self-knowledge

Black Power advocacy declares unerring faith in the human resources. The power that seemingly inheres in a certain type of human knowledge is regarded as limitless by many Black Power advocates. Garvey had enjoined the Negroes of his time to know themselves, to become aware of the great potential of their blackness and to enjoy the pride that flows from this awareness.[16] His *Philosophy and Opinions* is full of such injunctions. The Black Power Movement in the United States has aggressively declaimed that black is beautiful in defiance of white arrogance and in support of the new discovery. The Jamaican Black Power advocates also put the striving of a black image through a 're-evaluation of ourselves as blacks'[17] as a necessary precondition of attainment of power. Some share with other Jamaicans the view that this must be the result of a social process. Others settle in the thought that black awareness and black pride are essentially a psychological state of mind. The Jamaican society lends itself to both points of view. It is still a society that needs to liberated from a strong white bias.*

The value-system is Western which is understandable. But weighting in favour of European habits, mores and idiosyncracies at the expense of the contribution of peoples other than Europeans is well known to be the bane of black existence in the New World. Too many Jamaicans (black and otherwise) have for too long believed the myth of white European superiority and black African backwardness. For most it is now second-nature to think in terms which serve to negate the very fact of their own existence. Yet for a long time, Jamaicans have fought against the persistence of the white bias in the society. Not least among these was Marcus Garvey himself and many who campaigned for self-government in the thirties. The antidote was the positive swing of the pendulum over to the side of Africa so as to redress the balance. The Rastafarians later committed themselves fully and adopted outward signs of the inward grace.

Black Power advocates now follow in the same pattern and so do others with less vociferous attachment to the cause. A major symbol of 'belonging' on this level is the wearing of the dashiki — an American adaptation of the loose Hausa shirt, and this has been imported into Jamaica. Its functional and aesthetic virtues aside, it acts as a piece of ideological protective clothing for many.** It is doubtful whether the dashiki, in fact, achieves all this in the Jamaican situation but the garment has succeeded as a symbol of emancipation from the strictures of formal European dress.) It has been referred to by a Jamaican citizen writing to the press as a piece of 'black stupidity'.[18] Others, however, find the newly developed practice in Jamaica quite valid. 'Wearing an African dress', a letter in reply read, 'is a silent and dignified "statement" by a Jamaican of African origin that he belongs to one of the clearly defined, and I should like to think, *great* races of the world. Jamaica has many racial origins, and those who wish to indicate dignity of the African heritage should feel free to do so by way of haircuts, dashikis or what have you'.[19] The so-called Afro hair style now popular among American black women has also found its place among Jamaican Black Power advocates as well as among others who are either in the fashion or have discovered the style's flattering potential. The Rastafarians had gone much further two or three decades before wearing their hair in long and matted braids. They also adopted sandals and knitted woollen caps and sashes of red, green and gold — the colours of the flag of Ethiopia. Like some of them, many Black Power advocates mistake the form for the substance and betray much misunderstanding in what Africa is about. The late Tom Mboya's article written for the *New York Times* magazine was reprinted in the Jamaican leading newspaper. In this he revealed that New World blacks would find it extremely difficult to become Africans. 'Some think', he wrote, 'that to identify with Africa one should wear a shaggy beard or a piece of cloth on one's head or a cheap garment on one's body . . . An African walks barefoot or wears sandals made of old tyres not because it is his culture but because he lives in poverty . . . White people have often confused the symbols of our poverty with our culture: I would hope that black people would not make the same error'.[20] Many Jamaican black people have made the same error.

It is such people who will have to understand with Tom Mboya that the culture of the black peoples of Africa is 'something much deeper'.[21] It is in this context that one must understand the Black Power call for the teaching of African History, like that of the Garveyites and Rastafarians before this.

---

*See my Essays 'National Identity and Attitudes to Race' (p. 17) and 'The Melody of Europe, The Rhythm of Africa...' (p. 171).

**Black Power advocates find ideological support in Frantz Fanon's analysis of the use of the veil by women in revolutionary Algeria in the sense that it 'protects, reassures, isolates'. (See Fanon's 'Algeria Unveiled' in *A Dying Colonialism*, Grove Press Inc., New York, 1967, pp. 35–67.

The tendency in the past has been to look almost exclusively for what one writer calls 'the elements of unquestioned grandeur in the African past'.[22] But Mboya in the article cited above seems to give priority to what he called the 'basic qualities' such as the 'extended family ties and the codes governing relations between old and young, our concept of mutual social responsibility and communal activities, our sense of humour, our belief in a supreme being and our ceremonies for birth, marriage and death'.[23]

This was the emphasis placed on the value of African History by historian Walter Rodney who emphasized in his article in the Black Power Journal *Bongo Man* the fact that ordinary African life had meaning and value. In other words, concern about the indisputable grandeur of African antiquity should give place to questions about the actual historical position of the ordinary African before his enforced 'exile'. Did he live in a kind of Hobbesian state of nature, driven by unbridled passions, lacking in any sense of personal security and with a life devoid of compassion and reason? Did he, in fact, live like the proverbial beast without moral awareness and relying utterly on force for his self-preservation, therefore justifying his being encaged in slavery for a period of *taming?* Or, did he inhabit communities which were structured on his proven capacity to abstract from his experience principles which he in turn ordered into maxims of prudence serving as guide for his actions and for his working relationships with others with whom he came into contact? Was he in fact some noble savage? That one-time fashionable image of the pre-Bondage African with his innocence intact may have been useful for disciples of negritude romanticizing the purity of the original and authentic African before his Fall into slavery. But this child-of-nature image also suggests a Man without a capacity to grasp the complexities, obligations, rights and moral implications of social relationship and therefore without the faculty to think (though he apparently feels) or the skill to organize and perceive of himself as a member of society. The reconstruction of African History, if Black Power at all requires it, must as a matter of priority concern itself with establishing for the benefit of human knowledge, basic and undisputed facts about the essential *humanity* of the ordinary pre-Bondage African. 'That is one of the weakest aspects of our perception of the African past' it is said.

It is not surprising since concepts of power and achievement are based on European canons of historiography with emphasis on crusades, conquests, kings and emperors, political infighting and imperial annexations. Garvey's very sense of grandeur betrayed the conscious creation of black parallels of certain white trappings of office. Like others after him, he felt the need to emphasize what have come to be generally regarded as some of the real achievements of his forbears. There *were* early Sudanic empires — complex in organization and enveloping wide expanses of territory. The Benin bronzes are the essence of creativity, craftsmanship and sophistication and it is yet to be proven that these were the work of the Portuguese. Nor were the brilliant Ife heads the creation of Egyptians as some Europeans would have it. The Zimbabwe ruins of Central Africa betray townships, civilization and capacities for sophisticated social organization and Nkrumah's claims of an earlier kingdom of Ghana when Europeans were slaughtering each other are all now documented and accepted as major contributions to human history. Before this, as the West African historian K. O Dike once wrote, 'Many statements on Africa rested not on the evidence of history or the ascertained fact, but on preconceived notions which in other contexts the scholars responsible would dismiss with appropriate academic detachment'.[24]

Jamaicans should be acquainted by now with this approach for the same thing can be said about the early writing of Jamaican and West Indian history. The works of West Indian historians and sociologists over the pat twenty years have been to correct much of this wrong. This in itself gives the Jamaican Black Power advocates the responsibility to place West Indian history in the service of their cause. The fact of slavery is too often passed over in an attempt to learn what happened before slavery when both are, in fact, important. The basic humanity of the people, brought as slaves, in terms of their civilization and especially the intrinsic meaning and value of their ordinary life will indeed deepen one's understanding of the sustained rebellion by the African slave against his involuntary servitude in the West Indies. Black Power advocates are right then in asking that this be taught in schools and not just at the University level where a course in African History had been introduced.* But their emphasis on African History even at the expense of West Indian and Jamaican History betrays a basic dilemma. It is what Mboya called the *contradiction between black nationalism and, in this case, Jamaican nationalism.* It is a contradiction because complete identification with Africa

---

*Paradoxically the banning by the Jamaican Government of Walter Rodney who was hired to teach this has put a temporary halt to the programme.

(or countries of Africa) is difficult in a world of nation states. Yet it is reasonable for New World blacks to be concerned with the reconstruction of an African past that can serve their interests of identity wherever they may find themselves. Their very identity, wherever they are, is thwarted by an attitude born of the very assumption by a ruling white ethos that the blacks have no past beyond that of slavery and degradation. African achievement therefore has a place not so much for the sake of the past but for the present and the future; and African nationals, as any African leader would aver, are deeply committed to the use of their history as a function of modernization. The call for teaching an African language in Jamaican schools is, in this sense, an unnecessary relic of the past. Language is an organic device for meaningful communication for doing things practical. That is how the hundreds of African tongues are used, not as museum pieces for nostalgic viewers. Many of the new African countries find English and French practical and use them despite their strong cultural commitment to the 'African personality'. Black Power advocates may not agree but the future of their identity — black, Jamaican, or Jamaican black seems tied up with the use of English.

This is the measure of the subtle connexions with which Jamaican Black Power advocates, like all fellow-West Indians, must learn to cope. Echoing Wilson Harris, the Guyanese novelist-philosopher, a West Indian economist betrayed welcome sensibilities. 'What is remarkable about the West Indian' he wrote, 'is a sense of subtle links, the series of subtle and nebulous links which are latent within him, the latent ground of old and new personalties'.[25]

The perspective is indeed poetic but this is precisely the problem of the Jamaican black. Pedestrian polemics, statistical growth rate and national income columns, as well as broad sociological categories, are techniques that are unlikely to bring ready solutions in the matter of race relations in this part of the world. The dimensions of probing become deeply personal and individual, just as the humiliation of suffering has been, and still is, for many. This is not to underestimate the importance of the collective, but one is not talking simply of tactics and strategy, one is also concerned with final fulfillment. One must indeed take seriously a Black Power sympathizer's warning against confusing 'personal emancipation with collective liberation', but black awareness must turn on self-knowledge. Lloyd Best is probably right in his view that a 'grasp of the cold facts and *knowledge of self* are the true sources of compassion'.[26] Perhaps the Jamaican or West Indian black has advantages he is failing to exploit. He has always had to operate as an *individual* in his struggle for survival. Perhaps greater reflection on this aspect of his past could point some directions without betraying the cause of unity.

Much of what is expressed here would contradict one of Black Power's main tenets — namely the unity of the cause of all black men. But to deny persons who are black some form of individual uniqueness is in itself a kind of injustice. It is true that, although the blacks have been scattered, slavery, the plantation system and colonialism have thrown up a common framework of suffering and humiliation. Yet factors of time, place and circumstances have produced differences of lifestyle, of orientations and even of aspirations among people though they may look alike. The blocking of black creative wellsprings by the tyranny of dependence may now be perpetuated by the tyranny of a 'black culturalism' which sets goals without due concern for the feelings of the people involved and the objective factors that might go contrary to those goals. The richest cultures of black Africa, as of other peoples, are the fruits of cross-fertilization. Black Power militants may well exploit the creative potential of their black brothers in the West for they are the very expression of this continuing process of cross-fertilization. One God, one aim, one destiny in some things perhaps but not in all and to further deprive the black man of the agony of individual choice may be to deprive him of his humanity. One need hardly worry that European commentators interpret contemporary tribal conflict in some countries of Africa as manifestations of pure atavism. The Africans, as human beings, presumably have it in their nature to make choices and among the choices open to them, as to people everywhere, is good or evil, peace or violence.

Notes

1. Ramiro Guerra y Sanchez: *Sugar and Society in the Caribbean,* Yale University Press, 19654, p. 86.
2. *Bongo Man,* Journal of African Youth, No. 1, December, 1968, p. 27, and No. 2, January-February, 1969, p. 8. N.B. This is a cyclostyled predecessor of *Abeng* and emerged from the spate of protest pamphlets which followed on the events of October 16, 1968.
3. 'Intensified White Power in Jamaica', cyclostyled broadsheet (anonymous).
4. *Economic Survey of Jamaica,* 1968 (Central Planning Unit, Jamaica).
5. *Daily Gleaner,* June 7, 1969.
6. Editorial in *New World* Pamphlet No. 4, December, 1967, and Article following entitled *The Sugar Industry — Our Life or Death,* by Havelock Brewster.
7. *Daily Gleaner,* August 29, 1969 (Letter to the Editor); see also *New World* Pamphlet, *op. cit.;* Daily Gleaner, January to August, 1969, *passim,* esp. (Report 'Desperate State of the Sugar Industry', June 11); Feature article, 'Decline in the Sugar Crop', by Farm Reporter in *Sunday Gleaner,*

June 22; Feature article, 'Sugar — Two Major Crises rubbing cheek by jowl' by Farm Reporter, *Sunday Gleaner*, August 31.

8. R. Guerra y Sanchez, *op. cit.*, p. 97.

9. *Daily Gleaner*, September 2, 1969, 'Candidly Yours' — Column by Thomas Wright which is the pen-name of a well-known Jamaican journalist and radio-television commentator of Caucasian stock.

10. Annual Reports Jamaica Tourist Board, also Article 'Jamaica . . . 1973?' in *International Business*, May, 1969, by Frank E. Block.

11. *Abeng*, Vol. I, No. 6, March 8, 1969, and *Moko*, No. 4 (Article) 'Bauxite: Guinea will own her own' by Norman Girvan in which he says 'Guinea's new bauxite deal . . . shows that countries like ours can attract capital and skills from outside to develop their bauxite resources without giving these away to the larger international corporations'.

13. Sterling Brubaker: *Aluminium Industry*, Johns Hopkins University Press, 1967, pp. 156–7.

14. *Ibid.*, p. 245.

15. For a stimulating study of Power see *The Active Society* (A Theory of Social and Political Processes by Amitai Etzioni, Collier-Macmillan, London, The Free Press, N.Y., 1968, esp. Chaps. 13, 14.

16. See *e.g. No More Apologizing*, Speech made on visit to Montego Bay in 1921. Reported in *Daily Gleaner*, April 4, 1921, reproduced in full in *Bongo Man*, No. I, December, 1968. See also Amy Jacques Garvey (ed.) *Philosophy and Opinions of Marcus Garvey, Philosophy and Opinions*, Part I.

17. Walter Rodney, 'Why Black Power in the West Indies', *Bongo Man*, Vol. 2, pp. 3–13.

18. Letter to the Editor, *Daily Gleaner*, June 7, 1969.

19. Letter to the Editor, *Daily Gleaner*, June 16, 1969.

20. Tom Mboya (Article): 'Back to Africa Desire Unrealistic', *Sunday Gleaner*, August 10, 1969.

21. *Ibid.*

22. W. Rodney: 'African History in the Service of the Black Evolution', *Bongo Man*, No. I, p. 4.

23. T. Mboya: *op. cit.*

24. K.O. Dike: 'African History and Self Government', *West Africa*, March 14, 1953.

25. Lloyd Best: 'Black Power and the Afro-American in Trinidad and Tobago', *Sunday Gleaner*, April 6, 1969.

26. *Ibid.*

Independence and the Social Crisis of Nationalism in Barbados

Hilary Beckles

Independence in Historical Perspective

It is no longer contentious to argue that the principal socio-economic relations of Caribbean societies — created, shaped, and matured in the context of an iniquitous slave-based colonial culture — have been resistant to the formal procedures of liberal constitutional decolonization. Scholars have shown that within the dialectics of historical change and continuity, post-independent dispensations remain characterized essentially by divisive colonial legacies still held forth as normative ideals. In the indicative case of Barbados, importance should be attached to the political decision to appoint the last colonial governor as the first head of state (Governor-General) of the 'independent' regime. Indeed, as Mr. Errol Barrow, the champion of the so-called 'parting of ways' event and first Prime Minister of Barbados, was fond of saying 'the Lord giveth and the Lord taketh'. For some analysts, independence as a constitutional development was conceived precisely in such ambivalent terms,[1] and therefore lacked the political will necessary for propulsion away from the colonial scaffold.

It is within the context of this psycho-political inertia, compromise or refusal, that Lawrence Fisher's recent book, 'Colonial Madness: Mental Health in Barbadian Social Order', exposes fully the fundamental contradiction that haunts the still maturing nationalist consciousness.[2] For Fisher, the black community remains psychologically kidnapped by social relations, economic structures, and ideologies that have their origins within the ancient plantation regime which began to disintegrate as early as the late eighteenth century. The overt display and articulation of these still virulent forces within contemporary society represent for many nothing short of an open attack upon the relevance and legitimacy of the African derived mindscape, and symbolize the unashamed promotion and institutionalization of minority eurocentricism. For many persons, including those not prepared to contribute to a discourse on race, power, and politics, such a state of affairs raises certain questions about the social location of socio-economic authority, and the more serious pathological concerns that surround the issues of national identity and personality.

Fisher's argument that long term resource marginalization, political impotence and dependency, have impacted negatively on blacks, points to Professor Gordon Lewis' thesis that in modern Barbados, more so than in any other independent West Indian state, the 'racial bullying and economic intimidation' of the black population has ensured that white power remains 'pretty much the order of the day'.[3] This reality represents, at least as far as Lewis is concerned, a severe indictment of independence if perceived in transformative socio-economic terms, hence his call for caution in associating it with the term 'progress'.

The politics of the post-independence order, however, should be located within a systematic periodization of the struggle to dismantle, or render impotent, the structures and ideas that informed the colonial ethos. It can be argued, even if in general terms, that the primary socio-political agitation within the country in the last 300 years has been that waged by the oppressed black majority against the white and coloured property owning elite for a 'moral' share of resource ownership, institutional participation, social honour, and economic security. Consequently, the tripartite inter-relation of white economic power, black political protest, and social progress in the process of decolonization, can be used as a guide in the search for evidence supportive of the Lewis paradigm which posits that an alliance of white capital and black politics constituted the ideological basis of a problematic social contract in the post-independence period.

The intellectual coherence of such an argument can be strengthened by the admission of evidence presented by Hilbourne Watson, Trevor Marshall, Cecilia Karch, P.I Gomes, George Belle, Christine Barrow, and others, which shows that whites in contemporary society, who constitute less than 5%

of the island's population 'enjoy a life of privilege, ease, and comfort' based upon their dominant control of the corporate economy.[4] For these scholars the ownership and control of economic resources is so decisively related to the acquisition and use of socio-political power, that the economic hegemony of whites guarantees them the ability to gain a 'larger share of the decision-making process' and set for the country a 'development policy favourable to their interests'.[5] The widespread perception that such is indeed the case, is currently at the fore of the social consciousness of the post-independence generation. For this 'new breed', who should not have experienced colonialism first hand, there has been some remodelling of the ancient structure — more doors opened and ceilings raised — but the ideological and economic foundations remain clearly recognizable, and most rooms with a view to, and at, the top are still believed to be reserved for persons who cannot be visibly identified as having 'African blood flowing in their veins'.[6]

Independence, then, as an important political stage in the development of the civil rights movement, should be critically assessed in historical terms. Logically, there is no better place to start than with the origins of the English colonizing mission in 1627. Since then, evidence shows that non-whites, integrated into the system as unfree labourers, resisted in all ways possible the hegemonic plantation regime, and sought its reform and overthrow, largely because of the brutal racial nature of its social repression and its general inhumanity. In 1803, John Poyer, Barbadian historian and ruling class ideologue, outlined in an open letter to the Governor Seaforth what for whites was the 'natural' basis of black subjection and racial inferiority. Poyer's ideas assisted in shaping the general world view of a slaveowning elite that held social power over white popular consciousness. He stated:

In every well constituted society, a state of subordination necessarily arises from the nature of civil government. Without this no political union can long subsist. To maintain this fundamental principle, it becomes absolutely necessary to preserve the distinctions which naturally exist or are accidentally introduced into the community. With us, two grand distinctions exist resulting from the nature of our society. First, between the white inhabitants and free people of colour, and secondly, between masters and slaves. Nature has strongly defined the differences [not] only in complexion, but in the mental, intellectual and corporal faculties of the different species. Our colonial code has acknowledged and adopted the distinction. . . .

In Poyer's time, and after, the oppressed, whether slaves, wage labourers, or peasants opposed this world view. As a result, popular agitators from Bussa to Samuel Prescod, Duncan O'Neale to Barrow, sought political enfranchisement, social equality, economic betterment, and the institutionalization of non-racial ideologies.

The typology (see Table 2) of civil rights struggles, then, identifies independence as a major act of democratic self-affirmation, the legitimization of popular ideology and culture, and the consummation of phase two of the black struggle — the

Table 1. Barbados Population by Race, 1970

Race	%
Blacks	91
Whites	4
Coloureds/Mixed	4
East Indian	0.4
Others	0.6

SOURCE: Population Census, 1970

Table 2. Typology of the Civil Rights Struggle in Barbados

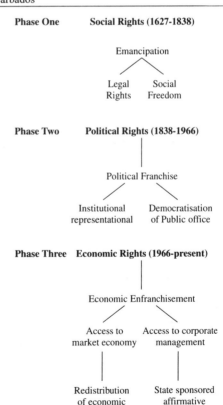

seizing of the state by the majority. The attainment of universal adult suffrage in 1950, sixteen years before independence, made possible the emergence of democratic government and the creation of the context and foundations for phase three of the struggle — the dismantlement of traditional forms of resource monopoly and the attainment of a democratic economic culture.

The ideology and actualization of independence, therefore, with all its political rationalizations, cannot be separated from the general forces mobilized by, and through, the civil rights movement. Though as an historic event it ritualized at one level the triumph of natives over imperialists, it also symbolized in real terms the formal political reduction of the social white elite and the institutionalization of labour-based black political authority. But, as Raymond Mack observed, whites soon realized that the 'only way' to 'protect their economic power' was to 'accommodate to black political power' within the irretrieval context of popular democracy'.[7]

It was, however, a politically problematic and socially uncomfortable realization and adjustment. Powerful elements within the white economic elite resisted independence with all the might they could muster, and intimated that in the event of their failure an economic strike or withdrawal of enthusiasm could result. In general, the forces they mobilized against the movement were considerable, but insufficient to deter the ruling Democratic Labour Party. Their political lobbies argued that independence would sever links with imperial authority, which were vital to the maintenance of their class and race dominance. In addition, their racist ideology was expressed, according to Ronald Mapp, a veteran black labour politician, in their generally discreet utterances that 'the coloured boys' could not 'run anything'.[8]

A mixture of anti-black racism and perceptions of social and economic interest, therefore, accounted for the white elite's opposition to the independence process, which meant that as a political and constitutional concept, nationhood was born within the context of racial fear and hostility. Many within the white elite could not politically celebrate the event, and some wished it a short life, hoping that the country would plunge into the constitutional chaos that had engulfed British Guiana in the previous decade. Those developments, noted Karch, had serious implications for the country in the future, and ensured that race was to remain 'a salient factor in Barbadian class relations'.[9]

Origins of the Crisis

Such developments, however, should not have surprised anyone familiar with the political history of the colony since the end of the nineteenth century. As the civil right struggle intensified before and after the First World War, the white elite took measures to strengthen its control over economic resources. In spite of a history of internal strife and competition, planters and merchants recognized the implication of a growing black political movement which was designed to break, in the short term, their political hegemony, and ultimately loosen their control over the national economy. In 1917, elements within the traditional planter class, that still firmly controlled the colonial state, established a large corporation, Plantations Company Limited, with the intention of increasing the size of capital funds available to the industry, and to enable them to purchase and retain plantations, thus minimizing the land engrossment tendency of the Bridgetown merchant houses. In addition, the company was designed to pilot the planters' entry into the commercial sector, thereby taking competition to the merchant class, and to capitalize on investment funds being accumulated in the non-sugar sectors.

In 1920, the merchant class, realizing the effectiveness of the planters' corporate innovation, responded by forming their own large-scale firm — Barbados Shipping and Trading Company Limited. This company became known as the 'Big Six' since it resulted from the amalgamation of the six largest commercial companies operative in the island at that time: Manning, Gardiner Austin, DaCosta, Musson, R. And G. Challenor, and Wilkinson and Haynes. The formation of this company was both a response to planter consolidation, and the inevitable response to the threat to accumulation posed by the depression. The presence of these two corporations — Plantations Company Limited, and Barbados Shipping and Trading Company Limited — signalled the origins of white corporate monopoly capitalism in Barbados, and a further stage in the successful economic domination of the colony by a white elite.[10]

During the 1920s, these two companies competed for trade, arable land and control of government policy. But the threat of black political agitation that had emerged after the mid–1920s, forced their directorates to consider strategies for the consolidation of their political power. The development of organized radicalism in the workplace following the defeated dockworkers' action in 1927, presented the context for the abandonment of outright competition between the two companies. In 1934, they established jointly the Barbados Produce Exporters Association (BPEA) which, at least symbolically, represented the consummation of the planter-merchant economic alliance, and the entrenchment of corporate capitalism. It was against this economic background that the workers' movement had risen during the 1920s and early 1930s. Consolidated corporate economic power now sought to define the political boundaries in which blacks were preparing to struggle for a more democratic order; it was this corporate organizational force that was confronted by Duncan O'Neale, Clennell Wickham, Clement Payne, Herbert Seale, Wynter Crawford, and the Garveyites.

On July 26, 1937, the working class of Barbados, ideologically mobilized by Clement Payne's organization, rose up against over 300 years of white power. Armed with stones, bottles, sticks and a host of other such inefficient instruments, workers attacked the new centre of ruling-class power — the commercial district of the city. It was a war on the corporate symbols of white power. They smashed office fronts and store windows and overturned vehicles on Broad Street; they shouted to the 'marooned' white employees in the notorious Barbados Mutual Insurance Company building, which also housed the 'whites only' Bridgetown Club, 'you blasted sons of white bitches', and attempted to burn the building.[11] While the building was being drenched in kerosene, rebels were attacked by a police detachment who fired blank volleys form their rifles. Properties were also damaged in Bay Street, Probyn Street and other peripheral commercial districts. The rebels did not attack residential homes. In the 1816 rebellion, they burnt the sugar plantations; in 1937, they were smashing the financial and commercial plantations.

By midday, the police had been instructed to use all possible means to restrain and subdue the rebels. They reported being informed that some rebels had been in possession of firearms and were prepared to use them. With bayonets fixed to their rifles, which were now loaded with live rounds of ammunition, police detachments confronted blacks in Bridgetown and killed several. This display of military might threw unarmed rebels on the defensive; groups broke up, as individuals fled in fear of their lives.

Meanwhile, news of the morning affair had spread to the countryside, and hungry workers there responded by seizing property and capital; they looted potato fields and plantation stocks, and threatened white plantation personnel. In St. Lucy and St. Andrew, workers were most determined to appropriate as much goods from the plantation as possible. In these parishes planters enlisted specially armed constables who added to the list of fatalities by shooting persons suspected of appropriating estate property. By the morning of 30th July, the revolt was crushed by these various armed forces, and calm was restored to both town and country. No whites were killed, while fourteen blacks were reported to have lost their lives and forty-seven injured. Over 500 were arrested and approximately 260 tried and convicted after receiving, in many cases, severe beatings from the police and special constables.

Under such circumstances, the context for the crisis of nationhood was established. Labour leaders soon rejected the ideas of 1937 and Clement Payne as hero; their subservience to white economic power emerged as the order to the day; the logical consequence was the fragmentation of national consciousness. Grantley Adams emerged in the post-rebellion period as the leading parliamentary representative of the civil rights movement, and orchestrated a personally successful political campaign in which he projected himself as a socialist committed to an equitable distribution of economic resources and political liberalization. In full awareness that the sugar plantation system represented the historical basis of merchant-planter oligarchical conservatism and racism, Adams initially focussed upon the need to restructure the ownership of the sugar industry as the key to sociopolitical and economic democratization. He argued for the partial nationalization of the industry as a prerequisite for economic and social reform. Lord Moyne, Chairman of the Imperial Commission of Inquiry into the 1937 rebellion, recognizing the economic revolution implicit within Adam's proposal, moved quickly for a fuller explanation: The exchange was as follows:

ADAMS: I suggest that the plantation system is basically the cause of our trouble, and I think that the system which has survived in Barbados for three hundred years, of having a small narrow, wealthy class and a mass of cheap labour on the other side, should be abolished ... As I have pointed My Lord, even such social legislation as we have had in the last ten years or so has been rather the result of fear, than of a real sense of social justice...

LORD MOYNE: Well then, you recommend the nationalization of the sugar industry. Do you really think you could get a greater efficiency in that way?

ADAMS: When we use the term nationalization, perhaps it connotes more than we intended, that is to say — not in the English sense a complete nationalization; we are really suggesting government ownership of sugar factories, cooperative production, and marketing.

LORD MOYNE: Provided that your scheme remains in the realms of practical politics and that you are content with making the best of the present system and seeing that there is a fair distribution of the resources of the industry, I think you are on rather safe ground.[12]

Adams, as leader of the Barbados Labour Party that emerged after the rebellion, was soon to reverse his ideas about containing planter-merchant oligarchical power by undermining their monopolistic ownership of productive land and the sugar industry. He had taken Lord Moyne's signal about nationalization and land reform not being within 'the realms of practical politics'. This was the first major setback of the contemporary civil rights movement. The political culture thereafter has been reaping the bitter fruit of national discord on the question of race, economic power, and nationalism. In accounting for Adams' backing away from structural economic change during the 1950s, Professor Gordon Lewis argued that his leadership accepted the widespread Barbadian belief that a radical stance on the sugar question destroys a political career; it also fell victim of the idea, sedulously spread by the plantocracy, that a nationalization policy would lead to economic disaster and social chaos.

Political struggles in the decade after 1937 that sought to break through Adams' capitulation were centred on the Congress Party. Indeed, the 1944 election was fought over many of the issues that surfaced during the workers' rebellion, and the investigation thereafter. Led by Wynter Crawford, Congress was incisive, and at times acerbic, in its evaluation of political events, and its campaign revived memories of Clement Payne's movement. It made no compromises in its self-assertion as the radical wing of the labour movement, and Crawford in particular suggested that both Adams' Labour Party and the planter-merchant party, the Electors Association, were involved in a conspiracy to undermine the workers' search for economic power and to deflect the march towards socialism. Throughout the country, the Congress Party called for adult suffrage, government nationalization programmes, land reform, industrialization, state ownership of important parts of the agricultural sector, and the disestablishment of the still influential white dominated Anglican Church. Its manifesto called upon workers to 'vote for a new Barbados', and the *Barbados Observer*, the Party newspaper edited by Crawford, carried the messages: 'Forward to a People's Victory' and 'Bring Socialism to Barbados'.

The *Barbados Advocate* carried the programme of the Electors' Association, while the *Barbados*

Table 3. Population of Barbados by Race, 1946

White	9,839
Black	148,923
East Indian	100
Syrian/Chinese	36
Coloureds	33,828
Not Specified	74

SOURCE: Digest of Colonial Statistics, No. 36 Jan-March, 1958, p. 67

Observer, was particularly venomous in its attack upon the planters' party. The *Barbados Observer* of Saturday, 4th November 1944 carried an article which illustrated what the radicals thought of the Electors Association:

... Throughout the history of this island, it has been dominated by a small and selfish clique and it is indeed remarkable that now, this clan senses that it has reached a crisis, it has actually had the shamelessness and the temerity to publicly appeal to the people of this island and ask them to help them consolidate their weakening position ... for sheer presumptuous impudence it is unparalleled. It is an absolute insult to the intelligence of the people. Only the congenital idiots among the masses will vote for the candidates of the Electors' Association on November 27th.

Two weeks later the *Observer*, by way of deepening its political critique of the planter-merchant class, carried a column which stated:

Barbados is in revolt against the status quo. Throughout the country thousands of middle and working class men and women are voicing the most determined protests against poverty and unemployment. These thousands are resolved to put more of the wealth in the colony at the service of the people; these thousands are in deadly earnest, this spirit may well be called NEW DEMOCRACY ... No longer are the people of this island prepared to entrust their destinies to the representatives of big business.

When the votes were counted on 27th November, the Congress Party had won eight seats, the Labour Party seven seats, and the Electors' Association eight seats. The coalition of the two labour parties seemed natural in the circumstance in order to break the political power of the white elite. These electoral results, represented, at least in theory, a resounding victory for the labour movement over the traditional planter-merchant political forces. Crawford spoke of the end of the planter-government and the triumph of the progressive democratic forces, while the leadership of the Electors' Association began to prepare a strategy for the protection of its members' economic and social interests.

The strategy adopted by the politically defeated planter-merchant elite, especially after the 1951 election, was two-fold. First, to regroup and examine what role, if any, they could play, in shaping and controlling the politics of the successful labour parties. The Barbados Labour Party was triumphant in 1951, and the Democratic Labour Party, formed in 1955 by elements that had broken away from the formal political engagements, chose to finance the labour parties, demand positions on the boards of statutory corporations, and manipulate economic policy in such a manner as to convince government of the still effective political power of big business. They also impressed upon government that any discussion about economic development should involve their members, and more importantly, that the social and political climate of the country should favour them if their economic cooperation was to be assured. Not surprisingly, the economic aspects of the Democratic Labour Party's manifesto in the 1961 election suggested that it was a moderate, compromising party.

Barrow's policy on land reform and nationalization, was cautious and limited to minimum government ownership of public utilities and bankrupt estates. He stressed government partnership with the white elite, rather than confront them with reform, or state ownership. On the social aspects of reform policies, his party agreed that there had been significant legislation in the previous two decades, and its only attempts of transforming race and managerial relations in the work place, were confined to the need for black tellers in the Bridgetown commercial banks. No campaign was launched to address or redress unequal resource ownership. This was the second major betrayal of the civil rights movement — capitulation in the face of consolidated mercantile power.

When Barrow's government approached the British government with its independence plan, therefore, it was doing so after having tied itself to the planter-merchant view that resource redistribution policies, such as land reforms and nationalization, that would have transferred economic resources to the black majority for its development, were not necessary for the building of a new order; as Lord Moyne had said, such policies were outside 'the realm of practical politics'. Barrow, then, like Adams before, sought to modernize, not revolutionize the country's economic structure. His government was attracted to the 'Puerto Rican model' of industrialization as outlined by the eminent St. Lucian economist Arthur lewis, which emphasized the relations between local capital and foreign investment. As a result, at no time, other than at elections, were serious discussions held about the redistribution of wealth and economic power in favour of the black majority. It was a leadership that showed openly its policy dependent on the cooperation of the white mercantile elite.

Government wasted no time in going about the task of revising and expanding previous legislative provisions for the encouragement of tourism and agriculture. Tourism was promoted as a major industrial sector during the first four years of the regime, and government revenues earned from this sector increased at a remarkable rate. A hotel construction boom assisted in stimulating the local manufacturing sector and contributed to reduced unemployment levels. In general, the Democratic Labour Party had launched a backdoor and unpoliticized assault upon the sugar industry's dominance of the economy, a process which earned Barrow the image of being socio-politically opposed to planter interests. But it was not a 'real' image. By 1966 the planter class had already completed its metamorphosis, and had emerged as a mercantile force since it was obvious that wealth accumulation was greater and easier in the distributive trades. Barrow, then, was pursuing the 'elusive pimpernel'; the same men in new clothing were sitting on statutory boards and advising his government.

Though the tourist industry was manipulated as an employment generator for the youth, and a major foreign exchange earner, industrialization by invitation was the policy instrument designed for economic takeoff. Light manufacturing industries were encouraged, especially those with a labour-intensive bias and an import substitution potential. More liberal tax holidays and duty-free incentives on raw materials were offered to the foreign private sector in order to promote industrialization. This policy was implemented alongside direct government action, through the Industrial Development Act and the Export Industries Act of 1963. Within three years of these legislations some forty-four industrial plants were established, providing more than 2,000 jobs.

Early success in significantly increasing the annual rate of growth of the gross domestic product distinguished the government's economic performance from that of its predecessor. There had also been marked expansion in non-sugar agriculture, especially livestock, poultry and vegetables. Sugar, nonetheless, still dominated the economy, earning $37 million in 1963 compared with $26 million in 1960. These upward economic indicators gave the government much confidence in its programme. No policy efforts were made, however, to restructure the distribution of economic resources, though occasionally mention was made of the need to nationalize the sugar industry. In general, the planter-merchant elite remained firmly in economic control, and corporations such as Plantations Company Limited and the Barbados Shipping and Trading Company Limited expanded rapidly. The Democratic Labour Party, therefore, prepared itself for an era of peaceful co-existence with the Bridgetown mercantile community.

The black community, meanwhile appeared more confident in expressing its hitherto stultified racial consciousness. The rapidly expanding professional and intellectual group, in particular, emerged as advocates of a revived political ideology that demanded government's imposition of pressure upon the white corporate elite in order to desegregate the workplace. In addition, black power activists, alienated from political office, urged government to use its fiscal and legislative authority in order to democratize the ownership of economic resources.

In general, there was widespread feeling within the country by 1964 that society was poised for a push away from its colonial foundations, and that the Democratic Labour Party regime had the potential, and support, to chart a new and independent path. Meanwhile, sections of the traditional merchant-planter community feared that the social and economic basis of their elitism was under ideological attack, and began to express their opposition to what seemed inevitable — the move towards political decolonization. For them, any constitutional break with Britain would be an act of revolution given the 300 years of mercantilism from which they could not disengage their political and economic vision.

The entrenchment of Westminster-style government in the post-independence period was perhaps inevitable given the refusal of the ruling Democratic Labour Party, and the opposition Barbados Labour Party, to distance the island from the ideological and socio-economic framework inherited during the colonial era. Independence within the confines of the imperial Commonwealth system was what the Democratic Labour Party government had proposed and attained in 1966, and the rejection of republicanism, in itself a popular measure, was also another obvious indicator of the limits which would be placed upon nationalist transformation thereafter.

With the planter-merchant's political party discredited and removed from the political arena it was obvious that its members would seek protection for their vested economic interests within one or both of the dominant labour parties. Both parties had cultivated traditions of criticism of the oligarchical political attitudes and practices of the planter-merchant elite, but both had also sought to court its economic power and managerial expertise within their political strategies. For labour leaders, these positions were not considered contradictory; as a result a conciliatory arrangement between white corporate power and black political administrations emerged as the dominant political equation of the post-independence period.

The Democratic Labour Party, which had grown up alongside the anti-colonial nationalist surge of the cold-war years, while being supportive of liberation causes in Africa and Asia, for example, remained cautious on the question of white economic and racial domination in Barbados. Indeed, its all-black government in 1970 found it necessary to prevent Trinidadian-born, American black-power activist, Stokeley Carmichael, from addressing public audiences in Barbados during his short and well-policed visit on the pretence of government commitment to non-racialist politics and the defence of white minority rights. The 1970 Public Order Act not only sought to suppress the black power movement, but also to escalate police surveillance of known black-consciousness radicals. Nonetheless, the Party won the 1971 general election with a handsome majority, including strong support from the grateful white community.

The leadership of the Barbados Labour Party, with its political image becoming increasingly associated with the interest of the corporate sector, remained skeptical, if not critical, of black radicalism. The economic crisis of the mid–1970s, which followed the escalation of oil prices, resulted in a premium being placed upon financial and managerial acumen within regional politics, rather than black economic empowerment; this context was effectively exploited by the Barbados Labour Party in the 1976 general election. Now led by Tom Adams, son of Sir Grantley Adams, the Barbados Labour Party, with an undoubtedly private-sector image, was able to defeat the Democratic Labour Party and restore the sagging confidences of the white corporate elite within the country.

It remains difficult to assess the extent to which the independent state was constrained, in terms of socio-economic transformation, without looking closely at the political ideology of Errol Barrow, popularly considered as the father of independence even though the Congress Party under Crawford had carried independence as a major issue during the 1940s. Both Lewis and Belle have offered political judgements on the Democratic Labour Party administration under Barrow's leadership between 1961 and 1976. For Lewis, it was the politics of modernization and not social transformation, while for Belle it was the politics of factionalism and populism. Lewis argues that Barrow sought less to integrate blacks into the economy than to modernize whites control of it. For example, he stated that successive debates on, and investigation into, the sugar industry under the Barrow regime degenerated into questions about management and organization, rather than ownership and control. Also, to questions of economic development answers were sought not in black economic enfranchisement, but in tourism expansion, labour emigration, and sugar subsidies. As such, the Independence issue in 1966 was not associated with ideologies of internal transformation.

In order to loosen the white commercial elite's hold over policy, Barrow's strategy was to modernize the economy away from sugar and the distributive trades by expanding tourism and manufacturing. These sectors, he suggested, would give government a sufficient revenue flow in order to reduce dependency on the merchant-planter alliance, and at the same time, give him sufficient elbow room to challenge archaic and regressive socio-economic attitudes. He was successful in the diversification of the country's economic base, but did not achieve a corresponding weakening of the merchant-planter control over development policy. In fact, during the 1960s, the economic base of the white elite increased substantially, and by 1976 they were still strong enough to participate in the defeat of his party and the reinstatement of the Barbados Labour Party. According to Belle, the planter-merchant class continued to monopolize the best agricultural land, the sugar industry, and dominate tourism and the distributive sector. Also, an examination of the centre of its economic power, the conglomerate Barbados Shipping and Trading Company Limited, simply confirms that this class had grown from strength to strength.

Unable to implement structural changes in the ownership of productive resources, Barrow resorted to a wide range of social politics designed to create the potential for long-term transformations. These included free secondary and university education, national insurance schemes, incentives to small black businesses, and a comprehensive health policy. These policies, however, represented a retreat to Fabian socialism and the politics of gradual reform, both of which were considered respectable and unproblematic from the ideological viewpoint of the dominant class and race.

With these policy developments in mind, and the subsequent passing of anti-black protest legislation in the form of the May 1970 Public Order Act, Barrow's conservatism surfaced in a manner that struck at the very roots of the independence concept. By pandering to undemocratic white entrepreneurs, and repressing black activism, and conceiving these policies to be in the interest of the country in the context of a dying colonization, must surely be considered part of the basis of his

defeat in 1976. Certainly, by that time his image as 'father of the nation' took a significant hammering, especially since the populace were referring to his apparent arrogance and double standards on the questions of race, class, and power.

During the period 1976 to 1986, the swing to the right of the Barbados Labour Party, especially under the leadership of Tom Adams, led to the formidable entrenchment of 'white power' in Barbados, while the Public Order Act continued to exist as a deterrent to 'Black Power' hopefuls. The psychological profile of the Tom Adams' regime was certainly one which confronted the black masses with big capital and high finance. Fear of victimization of black radicals was commonplace and the belief that government would use security forces against radical activists was widespread.

With the election in 1986, the black population defeated the Barbados Labour Party regime and returned Barrow to power in a 'silent revolutionary' fashion which restored his credibility as representing the nationalist conscience. For many, he was offered a second chance to carry out radical changes in the country. He was expected to crush the arrogant manipulative offensive of the white business community. He was also expected to return Barbados' foreign policy to a more independent path. His death on June 1, 1987, meant that all these expectations were never fulfilled. Many people believed he had a plan to assert nationalist sovereignty in a more aggressive manner, as was the case between 1966 and 1976. Some, however, believed that he would have much of the same — a populist on domestic policies and a vigorous radical on foreign issues — both of which would fall short of a radical transformation of the country's socio-economic structures.

The political articulation of the black civil rights movement since independence, however, came mainly from minority elements within both labour parties. All failed, however, to mobilize forces for meaningful democratization of economic resource ownership. In spite of the alienation of the planter-merchant elite from political office, its political influence has increased considerably since 1966. During the 1986 general election, for example, a major argument levelled against the Barbados Labour Party government by Dr. Don Blackman, a former cabinet minister who crossed the floor and joined the Democratic Labour Party, was that its leadership was manipulated by the corporate elite to such an extent that it had become a mercantile puppet administration.

If labour governments of the 1940s and 1950s seemed unprepared to confront planter interests, then since independence they have been equally unprepared to tackle the manipulative might of the mercantile elite. As a result, a fundamental national division of labour, what for some amounts to a post-colonial political form of Hobbesian social contract, emerged in independent Barbados having as its principal parties, whites dominating the economy, and blacks dominating the state. Within this 'alliance for progress' were two assumptions, both buried deep in the culture of colonial racism. First, that since the whites, with few exceptions, had opposed the rise of popular democracy and independence, they had in effect disqualified themselves from public service in the new governmental order. Whites, then, were either rejected as candidates by the labour parties, or took the view that they had no moral authority in relation to the praxis of representative democracy. Second, whites mobilized their ideological argument that blacks had no propensity towards big business, and implemented policies designed to keep them out of the market economy. Blacks were effectively kept away from the centres of economic power in the private sector; they were rarely invited to sit as directors of corporate boards, or to serve as managers.

Institutional anti-black racism in the private sector grew up alongside anti-white prejudice in the public sector, and by the 1980s references to discrimination against blacks in the corporate economy became the centre of popular social discourse. To some extent, the post-independence emergent black middle class, politically impotent in terms of its relation to white capital, capitulated in the face of its historical role as a transformative force. Unwilling to challenge the merchant aristocracy in the market place, it developed a dependency ideology and consciousness which compromised its position as the formal guardians of state power. According to Karch:

The black middle class embraced the prevailing ideological system; many were proponents of Empire. The majority sought access to the system; they did not seek to destroy it. Status as a middle class and their dependency on the paternalism of the oligarchy, and the colonial system, blunted the nationalist revolutionary spirit of black middle income groups and go a long way in explaining the recent political history of the island. Individuals from this class, not the class as a class, became political leaders and spokesmen for the majority population. It was the massive unrest of the black working class which propelled them into the limelight. Where leadership emerged from the ranks of the working class, it was repressed.[13]

The origins of their subordinate relation can be traced, in part, to the Grantley Adams refusal to challenge the plantocracy's monopoly of land during the post-rebellion decade when the nationalization of the sugar industry and land reform policies appeared as policy objectives of the labour movement.

Resolving the Crisis

The crisis of the race relations in the market place relates, then, to the systematic political suppression of democratization policies, and the deep-seated dependency of the neo-conservative black professional middle class. Both these developments in turn are rooted in the structure of economic power and its attendant ideological package. Indeed, it is commonly articulated that the white elite, in spite of its opposition to the independence process, has emerged as its principal beneficiaries, in social as well as economic terms. National 'Poet of the People', Bruce St. John, saw this clearly when he wrote in a poem entitled 'Political Progress':

We got democracy!
Man shut you mout.
We en got democracy?

Who in de assembly now?
Who sheltering who now?
Backra telling we wuh to eat,
Backra telling we wuh to wear,
Backra telling we wuh to live in,
Backra telling we when.
Backra out o' de assembly
But backra mekkin' 'e money!

Slave got government,
Slave got opposition,
Slave defending labour,
Slave opposing slave,
Who defending backra?
Backra making money!
Money without Assembly?
Slave making joke.

The ownership pattern and the control mechanism of major businesses are no guarded secrets. It is immediately obvious that the commanding heights of the corporate economy are controlled and manipulated by merchants and executives drawn from a white community. These persons constitute a commercial and financial (though not an industrial) elite which wields levels of power (social and political) far in excess of what their demographic proportion suggests. They control the large locally-owned corporations in all economic sectors; the largest local life insurance company; and the most prestigious accounting, auditing and financial services companies.

By virtue of sitting on the boards of these corporations, and dominating their top management executive positions, these groups are placed in a position to direct the destiny, not only of the corporate sector, but of the overall national economy. After 1950, when adult suffrage was achieved, Labour governments, elected mostly by blacks, and administered totally by blacks, have found it necessary to pander to these 'interest groups', to the extent that these groups now perceive their interests and the national interests as one and the same. They constitute, furthermore, a silent and hidden force that successfully manipulated elements of the political directorate to its own end. The corporate power of these groups has never been challenged by an organized political force. Indeed, some analysts say that their policy has been to kidnap the state and use it to discredit, alienate, and remove potential and actual critics of their dominance. Over the years, critics of all kinds have been labelled as 'undesirables' and 'misfits' by these groups,through supporters in the state structures, and elements within the mass media which they control directly through stock ownership, and indirectly through advertising power. The collective economic control of this elite is also expressed in terms of its ability to determine the number and nature of black executives who occupy high level managerial positions in local corporations.

Blacks admitted to the corporate boardrooms generally feel a deep sense of either gratitude or resentment; neither of which emotions is healthy in terms of building a market culture for national mobilization and development. They are made to feel as outsiders since, by and large, they work for, or under, the 'white man'. They all know where their ceiling is located; they all know on which doors they cannot knock. The odd black who slips through the crack in the structure, is either very good, and hence indispensable, or a beneficiary of white paternalism. Either way, they have no strong foundation on which to rest, and survive on the fragile goodwill of suspicious bosses. This state of affairs, though as yet not measured by the economists, is believed to be having its toll on the corporate economy in terms of low productivity. It has been said that an instinctive withdrawal of enthusiasm (and hence productivity crisis at the management level) is their common response to the institutional racism they experienced in corporate management. As in slavery, whites see this as evidence of laziness and ineptitude. Recently, the *Economist* magazine, [July 8, 1989] looking at the crisis of race relations in corporate Barbados, made the following observations:

In a family firm, family members naturally get promoted, so young whites sometimes get promotion over experienced blacks. Work sometimes gets contracted out to a second cousin or a classmate from primary school; there, too, whites may sometimes give jobs to whites. There are plenty of black jockeys at the races these days, not many black owners. It is easy for blacks to feel powerless, and for whites to feel they are under siege in their own country. A tiff between a white manger and a black employee can be brooded on in private as a racial squabble. Some of the suspicions are real, some imaginary, some a bit of both. Given the history, perhaps the surprise is how little racial tension there is in Barbados today.

The refusal of successive governments to address corporate institutional racism has led to the open display of race ideologies within the economy that is clearly harmful from the point of view of national efficiency. Many persons have debated at length the basis of the crisis, and have raised it in the context of continuing racial injustice against blacks. Dr. Waldo Waldron-Ramsey, former Barbados ambassador to the United Nations, and a popular newspaper columnist, articulated the historical basis of white racism in an excellent article published in the Barbados *Daily Nation*, July 6, 1989. Entitled 'De-mystification of the legend', the column reads:

There is a legend, of a sort, that in Barbados only Euro-Barbadians or caucasoid Barbadians can manage and run business enterprises here. That they are better at it than any other race. That they have had many years in the experience of management, and so, almost as a group, they are now, ipso facto, experts at business.

On the other hand, people of African origin have no such tradition and acquired expertise to rely upon. That Africans or people of the black race have other strengths and expertise as a people. But managing big business is not one of them. Our colonial education and experience have been so contrived and devised, that they lend a certain credence to that myth. And worst still, many of the Africans in Barbados, would seem to have been seduced by this facile, weak, and unsubstantiated argument. There is no truth in it at all. But this had been part of the colonial plot to weaken the sinews of the majority in the colonial population, and to render the imperium infinitely more secure by augmenting the faith of that section of the population which could more readily identify with imperial masters.

Since the general election of 1986 in which the Democratic Labour Party was returned to office after ten years of opposition, with a crushing 24–3 defeat of the ruling Barbados Labour Party, the question of democratization of economic resources and open market opportunities have hung in the air, lacking focus and organizational direction. Dr. Don Blackman, Democratic Labour Party Member of Parliament for St. Michael East, had waged an ideological war against the government of the Barbados Labour Party, of which he was a former minister, for its subservient relationship with the white mercantile elite, and had made a tremendous impact upon popular consciousness with his speeches on black economic alienation. Dr. Blackman's charge was that these commercial groups, by virtue of monopolizing corporate power, had functioned as the real Cabinet of the country, with power to overturn decisions made at the highest levels by the People's Parliamentary representatives. In several talks he referred to the merchants and money lenders as 'white shadows', a force not to be seen but always to be felt. These 'white shadows', Blackman argued, were the real government of Barbados since they had the power to manipulate the state machinery for their own interests, and had forced government into accepting the view that corporate interests and those of the nation were one and the same.

Against this background, discussions about the ownership of resources and the control of financial institutions developed; sometimes debates were serious, other times just reflective of the empty political emotionalism that party politics can encourage. In any event, the public was being encouraged to look at the way in which corporate power was undermining the fabric and spirit of political democracy, and to consider the significance of this development for social and race relations within the society.

The transfer of power from colony to self government, then, as Karch has noted 'was not accompanied by a challenge to the control of the economy by a small, cohesive, white elite'.[14] Though class relations and race relations were modified with black political administration since the 1950s, Karch noted, 'the basic division within the society continues to be a dichotomy between black and white'. Even in tourism, the plank of the post-independence economy, the leading instrument of modernization according to state policy, where 'control is local, it is white'.[15] In fact, according to Karch, 'it is the white section of the population that has benefitted from diversification in much the same manner that the transformation to the corporate plantation economy favoured them earlier in the century'.[16] With these conclusions, Karch emphasized that 'the persistence of the racial factor in inequitable structures of ownership and control alerts us to the necessity of examining the importance of race in the maintenance of the economic order'.[17]

Current debates about the relations between white economic power and black politics which have now become endemic, suggest that the only way forward towards a non-racial democracy is to address the question of economic and ideological relations within the market economy. On this matter the weight of history is great, but the late Professor Elsa Goveia warns us of the danger inherent in not honestly confronting historical legacies as a prerequisite for positive policy formulation:

Ever since the time of emancipation we have been trying to combine opposite principles in our social system. But sooner or later we shall have to face the fact that we are courting defeat when we attempt to build a new heritage of freedom upon a structure of society which binds us all too closely to the old heritage of slavery. Liberty and equality are good consorts, for, though their claims sometimes conflict, they rest upon a common basis of ideas which makes them reconcilable. But a most profound incompatibility necessarily results from the uneasy union which joins democracy with the accumulated remains of enslavement.[18]

That blacks need to attain their economic franchise through economic democratization is undoubtedly a matter of national importance at this time. If there is an inevitability about this process then one might add that the correct position to take is to abandon the politics of economic democracy and allow history to take its course; this way the reconstruction of blacks' economic culture, devastated in part by slavery and post-slavery conditions, would certainly be achieved. This position, however, illustrates a certain disregard for the forces and logic of history and an undeveloped understanding of institutional evolution.

Notes

1. See Hilary Beckles, *A History of Barbados: From Amerindian Society to Nation State* (Cambridge University Press, Cambridge, 1990), pp. 198–210. Also 'Radicalism and Errol Barrow in the Political Tradition of Barbados, *Caribbean Affairs*, April-June, 1989, Vol. 2, No. 2, pp. 107–113; also *Corporate Power in Barbados: The Mutual Affair* (Bridgetown, Lighthouse Publications, 1989), pp. 1–56.

2. Lawrence Fisher, *Colonial Madness: Mental Health in Barbadian Social Order* (Rutgers University Press, New Brunswick, 1985), p. 9–64.

3. Gordon Lewis, *The Growth of the Modern West Indies* (London, MacGibbon and Kee, 1968), pp. 43–44. See also, Philip Curtin, 'The Black Experience of Colonialism and Imperialism', in S. Mintz, ed., *Slavery, Colonialism and Racism*, (New York, 1974), pp. 19–20.

4. Quote from Trevor Marshall, 'The Whites in Perspective', *The New Bajan*, July 1990, pp. 42–43. See also by the same author, 'The Riots of 1937', in *The New Bajan*, October 1989, pp. 17–18. Cecilia Karch, 'Changes in Barbadian Social Structure, 1860–1937', *I.S.E.R.*, Cave Hill, 1977; also, 'The Growth of the Corporate Economy in Barbados: Class/Race Factors, 1890–1977' in Susan Craig, ed., *Contemporary Caribbean: A Sociological Reader*, Vol. 1 (Port of Spain, The College Press), pp. 213–241. Christine Barrow and J.E. Greene, *Small Business in Barbados: A Case of Survival* (Cave Hill, I.S.E.R.) 1979; George Belle, 'The Political Economy of Barbados, 1937–1946; 1966–1972', MSc Thesis, U.W.I., 1974. P.I. Gomes, 'Barbados: The Post Independence Period, 1966–1976',

Working Papers on Caribbean Society, Series A, No. 3, October 1980. See for comparison with Jamaica, Stanley Reid, 'An Introductory Approach to the Concentration of Power in the Jamaican Corporate Economy and Notes on its Origin', in Carl Stone and Aggrey Brown, eds., *Essays on Power and Change in Jamaica* (I.S.E.R., Kingston, 1977). Hilbourne Watson, 'Attempts at Industrial Restructuring in Barbados', Department of Political Science, Howard University; mimeo, 1986. _____ 'The 1986 General Elections and Political Economy in Contemporary Barbados', ibid; mimeo, 1986.

5. Karch, 'Growth of the Corporate Economy', p. 228.

6. See Fisher, *Colonial Madness,* p. 18. Also Jerome Handler, *The Unappropriated People: Freedmen in the Slave Society of Barbados,* (Baltimore, The Johns Hopkins University Press, 1974), p. 190. See also, Raymond T. Smith, 'Race and Class in Post-Emancipation Caribbean', in Robert Ross ed., *Racism and Colonialism: Essays on Ideology and Social Structure* (Leiden University Press, The Hague), pp. 93–100.

7. Raymond W. Mack, 'Race, Class, and Power in Barbados' in Wendell Bell, ed., *The Democratic Revolution in the West Indies* (Cambridge, Schenkman Publishing Co., 1967), pp. 158–159.

8. Ibid, p. 156. See also, Francis Mark, *The History of the Barbados Workers Union* (Bridgetown, 1966), pp. 3–19.

9. Karch, 'The Growth of the Corporate Economy', pp. 215–216.

10. Ibid. See also Michael Sleeman, 'The Agri-Business Bourgeoisie of Barbados and Martinique' in P.I. Gomes, ed., *Rural Development in the Caribbean* (Kingston, Heinemann, 1985); Cecilia Karch, 'The Role of the Barbados Mutual Life Assurance Society during the International Sugar Crisis of the late 19th Century', Paper presented at the 12th Annual Conference of Caribbean Historians, *Trinidad,* U.W.I., 1980. Hilary Beckles, *Corporate Power in Barbados*, pp. 19–56.

11. Cited in Bonham Richardson, *Panama Money in Barbados, 1900–1920* (Tennessee University Press, Knoxville, 1985), p. 241. See also, Beckles, *Corporate Power in Barbados,* pp. 42–43.

12. See Beckles, *A History of Barbados,* p. 176. See also Evidence from the Moyne Commission report; also W. Martin Will, 'Political Development in the Mini-State Caribbean: A Focus on Barbados', Ph.D. Dissertation, The University of Missouri, 1972, pp. 91–95.

13. Karch, 'The Growth of the Corporate Economy, p. 224.

14. Ibid., p. 228.

15. Ibid., p. 231.

16. Ibid.

17. Ibid., p. 237.

18. Elsa Goveia, *Slave Society in the British Leeward Islands,* (Yale University Press, New Haven, 1965), p. 338.

SECTION THIRTEEN
Protest, Socialism and Revolution

The completion of the independence process in many Caribbean regions did not always challenge the deep-seated structural and ideological forces which had matured during slavery and its immediate aftermath. Independent societies, therefore, inherited much of the institutional and ideological legacies of the old colonial regime, and struggles had to be initiated to rid them of the neo-colonial baggage.

The regurgitation experience in many places engendered serious political and social crises. The anti-black racism of old proved difficult to exorcize and eradicate, while the compromise made between imperialist hegemonic economic interest and the new political leaders proved unacceptable to the first generation born within the nation-state. Everywhere, the socially and economically disadvantaged questioned the meaning of their political enfranchisement and adopted militant methods in their search for progress.

Ruiz's explanation for the origins of the Cuban Revolution indicates the persistence of certain objective conditions, legacies of the period before the War of Independence, that problematized popular notions of freedom, and which could only be resolved by armed struggle. The Castro revolutionary leadership that toppled the American supported Batista dictatorship had popular approval precisely because it offered the opportunity to restore to prominence the values of liberty and freedom within creole consciousness.

The conceptual relationship between the Cuban experience, the 'Black-Power' movement of the 1960s and 1970s, and the Grenada Revolution of 1979, can be identified in these essays. National independence in Trinidad and Tobago, argues Bennett, left in place the traditional ruling economic elite whose ideological posterings continued to be unaccommodating to blacks who remained economically marginalized in spite of their control of the state. The call for Black Power, he argues, constituted a demand for the unification of economic and political enfranchisement processes.

The short-lived Grenada Revolution has received, to date, many subjective examinations. Heine brings the freshness of an objective analysis to bear upon what must be considered one of the most important developments of the post-independence period in the English-speaking Caribbean. His account of the collapse of the revolution is stimulating, and illustrates the characteristic features of neo-colonialism within the country and the region.

Perhaps the fundamental crisis of the post-independence Caribbean resided in the extent to which they have succumbed to the dictates of financial and monetary institutions that constitute the hegemonic agencies of global Euro-American imperialism. The World Bank and the International Monetary Fund (IMF) are two such institutions that have forced their way into the policy-making corridors of Caribbean governments, and thereby enhancing their dependency. Ferguson outlines one consequence of this process, namely the anti-IMF mass riot in the Dominican Republic in 1984. By revolt, the people sought to encourage government to withdraw the austerity measures imposed, the result of an IMF-government agreement. These essays illustrate part of the current crisis of the Caribbean world, and suggest that the historical quest for freedom by inhabitants remain a powerful historical force.

Cuba: The Making of the 1959 Revolution

Ramon Eduardo Ruiz

A society split by wide income differences, in which rich and poor lived in separate worlds, where a pervasive spirit of mistrust set individuals and groups against each other, provided shaky foundations for its institutions. In reality, the infant Republic never developed institutions of its own. The laws, the courts, and the government rested on a colonial experience that left the Cubans unprepared to rule themselves, and on foreign models ill-suited to domestic conditions. The institutions were victimized by public apathy, corruption, and self-interest.

No institution mirrored more accurately the native scene than the political parties. In the beginning, three factions battled for supremacy on the local political scene: the Conservative, Moderate, and Liberal parties. Until the late twenties, they divided the public coffers among themselves and joined forces to prevent a successful attack on their monopoly. In the 1930s the Conservatives renamed themselves the Democratic Party; the more status-quo minded among them formed the Republican Party in the forties. In the meantime, the Liberals became allies of Gerardo Machado, a stigma that virtually destroyed them as a potent political force after his downfall. All were conservative parties of wealthy Cubans with little mass support. Their program eulogized private enterprise, 'democratic and honest' government, and opposed Communism. Their platforms expressed regret for the passing of the 'good old days' and when the chips were down, they preferred dictatorship to 'chaos and disorder'.

Opposed to the Liberals and Conservatives were the reform 'parties' of the middle sectors. From the early thirties until the late forties, Grau's Auténticos headed the list of these parties. He and his followers challenged proponents of the status quo only briefly, and when they fell into line after accepting an accommodation with the older parties, Grau won the presidency in 1944 with the support of reactionary Republicans. Embittered by the turn of events, reformers organized the Party of the Cuban People, the Ortodoxos, who claimed the mantle of Martí for themselves. By 1958 the Ortodoxos had split into moderates and radicals. Apparently a rule of thumb dictated the course of Cuban politics: conservatives remained faithful to their banner, but reformers, both individuals and parties, eventually joined the enemy camp.

The protest of the fifties was against all parties for, as Leslie Dewart states, all parties were totally discredited. When Batista seized power in 1952, middle-sector government was in a state of virtual political bankruptcy. Party goals were the spoils of office and the public treasury, for distribution among party hacks and leaders. The parties functioned in a world of their own, independent of public demands and aspirations, where loyalty to the party, its members and its leadership, dictated decisions and the outline of political philosophy. No one, explained J. González Lanuza, more resembled a Conservative than a Liberal. Party leaders with whom members identified, and who had welded them together, enjoyed immense stature, for the parties were personalist organizations, directed and controlled by one man: if successful at the polls, by the President of the Republic; if not, by the man who aspired to succeed him. At the local level, the boss on his way up the political ladder or the *jefe político* dispensed favours granted him by his superiors in return for his support. Cuba's political history had been the story of such men: the Menocals, Machados, Batistas, and Graus. The *caudillo* ruled, the chieftain who put personal and party needs above political principles and ideology, who served the foreign investor and the affluent. In the history of the island, wrote Carlos Márquez Sterling, 'the point that stood out was the reliance on the *caudillo* as an expression of the Cuban intellect.' Not surprisingly, therefore, Cuba, with the exception of the Auténticos in the 1930s, had no party of truly national or popular scope. Fidel Castro stepped out of that setting.

On the political front, violence characterized almost a third of the Republic's history: the first decade of the twentieth century, the late twenties until 1936 and, again, after 1953. In the countryside the Cuban had turned to the guerilla warfare he had utilized against the Spaniards in the Ten Years' War, in the period from 1895 to 1898, and against Machado and Batista. Rich and poor alike indulged themselves in the national pastime of terror.

The ABC, one of the island's legendary protest groups, was a case in point. Organized in December 1931 to battle the Machado tyranny, it employed terror to combat terror. Composed mainly of young men from intellectual and professional ranks, the ABC won national acclaim for its ability to intimidate Machado and his gang of hired thugs. All members belonged to one of three alphabetical cells, from which the society took its name. During its heyday, the ABC had 2,000 members who, in the words of Ruby Hart Phillips, Havana correspondent of the New York *Times,* were 'pleasant-mannered, well-educated youths, despite the fact they were certainly murderers'. Sick of the cynical generation of 1895 veterans who had run Cuba since independence, the ABC resorted to violence to combat political ills, meanwhile urging abrogation of the Platt Amendment and a gradual break-up of the extensive American-owned plantations. On the fall of Machado, the ABC dominated the short-lived Céspedes administration and, after Grau toppled Céspedes, focused its terror tactics on Grau and his allies, openly supporting the unsuccessful revolt against them in November 1933. The ABC, however, was not alone in its use of violence. After Batista's thugs shot Antonio Guiteras in May 1935, members of 'Young Cuba', which had been headed by Guiteras, sought revenge by killing every man who had participated in the murder of their leader. Eddie Chibás, idol of Cuban idealists in the late forties, won his spurs as a young man by throwing a bomb at a streetcar in the days of Machado. Mobs in Havana looted stores and wantonly killed Machado's backers after the dictator abandoned the city.

Without an effective political apparatus, Cuba was left at the mercy of the army; its two national chieftains, Machado and Batista, had controlled more than half the Republic's history. Unlike the military in other Spanish American countries, where the army's ties with the élite often fostered an 'unholy trinity' with church and landlord, the Cuban army had an unconventional background. It was of recent origin — a twentieth-century phenomenon dating back less than five decades — the progeny of American policy architects who, having watched a motley band of malcontents oust Cuba's first president in 1906, decided to build an army to prevent a similar occurrence in the future. In one of his last acts, therefore, Charles E. Magoon had provided for a permanent army. However, the rebels of 1906 had been veterans of the struggle for independence and members of the Liberal party which had popular sympathy. Thus, from the beginning the army was a foreign institution and,

in the eyes of countless citizens of the island, an enemy of true patriots as well as the tool of vested interests.

Magoon further muddied the situation by appointing as the army's commander-in-chief 'Pino' Guerra, the very man who had captained the organized revolt against Estrada Palma. When Estrada Palma announced his re-election, so legend has it, Guerra, then a Liberal representative in congress, walked out, threatening to 'seek justice somewhere else'. To train him and to build a modern army, Magoon dispatched Guerra to France and the United States to study military organization and tactics, to make impossible a repetition of the kind of revolt Guerra had engineered.

Although a foreign institution, the military took on local characteristics. As the servant of successive administrations from 1909 to 1933, the army had cloaked itself in the mantle of its sister institutions from Mexico to Argentina. The 'Hispanization' of the army began with Guerra. In 1912 President José Miguel Gómez had decided that his re-election alone could save Cuba from chaos, but he feared the army, for Guerra was a vocal supporter of Gómez' rival, Alfredo Zayas. To rid himself of Guerra, Gómez offered him a special mission to Europe and a lucrative reward. When Guerra adamantly declined, Gómez had him shot. Fortunately for Guerra, the would-be assassins proved inept and he escaped with a wounded leg. Not one to repeat a mistake, Guerra resigned, leaving his post in the hands of Gómez' closest friend. Later, Guerra embraced Gómez, and the two helped to thwart Zayas' presidential ambitions. Yet not until the advent of Machado did the army become the personalist body native to Spanish American politics. A military man himself, Machado transformed the army into his personal tool and, in the process, into the spokesman for the rich and well-born. Ironically, it was this pampered military that overthrew him in 1933.

When Batista and his sergeants, men of humble antecedents, ousted a clique of officers from control of the army, they created a wholly new military situation. As army boss, Batista granted commissions to 527 enlisted men; only 116 of the former 500 officers, those willing to accept a mulatto commander, kept their commissions. By deposing the officer clique whose background identified it with ruling groups, Batista divorced the military from the traditional power structure; by race and social position, Batista and his men belonged to the lower classes. Yet Batista's betrayal of the revolutionaries in 1934, who undoubtedly had majority sentiment behind them, destroyed what mass popularity the army had won in its earlier coup. Born of mutiny and betrayal, the post-Machado army became the puppet of Batista, a military establishment shorn of traditional ties with the élite, an opportunist, predatory army of professional soldiers of the lower class but devoid of any class loyalties, distrusted alike by the populace and the affluent.

Thus Batista's army found itself in an anomalous situation. It was not popular, yet its personnel by race and class had close ties with the poor. The army had a high percentage of Afro-Cuban officers, approximately one out of three. General Querejeta, a Negro, commanded the army in 1949. Such a military had few staunch defenders in the ruling cliques; nonetheless, the army had consolidated its position by siding with the vested interests, the enemies of reform. The plebeian army, therefore, was caught between spokesmen for the status quo who decried change in any form, and the populace, with which the army had bonds and which demanded change.

To keep his hard-won victory, Batista walked a tightrope: to placate his men, he increased the size of the army, raised the pay of its officers, and allotted to it a larger share of the national budget. He limited opportunities for graft but never cut them off entirely, gave the army a more active role in political affairs, and employed soldiers to carry out social reforms, even asking them to build schools. In this manner, Batista's army achieved a new image by the late thirties. But the *caudillo* never strayed far from the premise that led him to betray Grau. His army maintained the status quo, which placated native and foreign interests, and, in return, the plutocracy learned to live with the mulatto sergeant turned officer-politician.

After 1944 the Auténticos attempted to purge the army of Batista's cronies, but ultimately failed. Grau began the shake up, replacing Batista's chief-of-staff with an officer of his own choosing and shifting or retiring the military commanders of the six provinces. When Grau and Prío Socarrás quarrelled, Prío launched his housecleaning of the armed forces, ousting Grau's men and substituting his own. Prío had doubtful success, for army officers twice plotted his overthrow before 1952. The Auténtico purge of the military, obviously, had not paid dividends, for the coup that returned Batista to power was the work of the army. Yet the coup alienated the army even more from responsible public opinion. Hence, in 1958, its position remained unchanged; it was a personalist military force lacking close links with either the wealthy or the poor, without strong roots in the socio-economic structure of the island or in the life of the people. The strength of the army rested on arms supplied by the United States,

which stamped the military as an alien force in the minds of nationalists.

The Catholic church occupied an analogous position, because it had failed to act as a cohesive element, or to unite, as it so often did on the Spanish American mainland, the conservative, traditional forces in society. In Cuba it was merely another feeble institution with only superficial strength. True, the church enjoyed a wide popular base in the 80% of the people who were nominally Catholic. Approximately a tenth of them practiced their religion, however. Compared to Peruvians, Colombians, or even Mexicans, Cubans were not a religious people. Thousands of them — including women, who tended to be more 'Catholic' than their menfolk — had embraced the materialistic doctrine of Communism. In his study of the churches in the island, J. Merle Davis claimed that the Cuban, though raised in the Roman Catholic fold, was 'outwardly an agnostic'; and according to Leslie Dewart, a Catholic philosopher who spent long years on the island, 'The Church and any organized, institutional practices are to most Cubans . . . ridiculous and beneath contempt'. Of the Spanish American people, then, the Cuban was the least Catholic in his practices and attitudes, in terms of his devotion to the Church, his support of it, and his aesthetic and social life.

Institutionally, the Church was especially weak in rural areas. The Spanish colonial clergy had never built a large number of churches in the villages and towns, and nothing was done to shift the emphasis after independence. Without churches, there was no substantial rural clergy, which left contact between priest, cane-cutter, and farmer to happen-stance. Even on a national level, Cuba had just 725 priests for a population of six million, one for every 7850 inhabitants. In the end, observed Lowry Nelson, as an established, functioning institution the Church was 'virtually nonexistent' in rural Cuba. In large measure, therefore, the farmer, *colono,* and field-worker had no major stake in the fortunes of the Church.

Racial questions helped isolate the Church even more from rural people. Much of the countryside, and certainly heavily populated Oriente, was of Afro-Cuban stock, but more than three-fourths of the clergy was Spanish, including nearly all of the hierarchy. The alien priests, therefore, failed to establish much contact with the Afro-Cuban population or to minister to its spiritual needs. Davis reported 'no religious life' among Afro-Cubans. The inability of the Church to respond or communicate helped to explain, at least in part, the survival of crude forms of African spiritualism in small Afro-Cuban communities. Thus the Church could not claim a rural army of the faithful, nor call upon the rural people either to defend the Church's institutional position or that of society as a whole.

Nor was the Church a national pillar of strength. Except for a small, loyal band of largely urban and upper-income faithful, the Church had no mass following. Unlike the Church in other Spanish American republics, where it successfully resisted lay criticism, the Cuban Church had lost its special standing. Church and state were separated in 1900 and, less than two decades afterward, divorce was legalized. Nor had the divorce law simply languished on the statute books. Thousands of Cubans had taken advantage of it. In the twenties Machado signed a decree liberalizing the divorce law on the pattern of Nevada legislation, hoping in this manner to attract divorce business to the island. Batista's own divorce in 1944 touched off a wave of divorces among army officers and politicians. A law enacted in 1900 had made marriage a civil contract, though the Cuban clergy had eventually prevailed on American occupation authorities to permit marriage in either the Church or civil courts. However, of the 107 municipalities polled on this change, 80 opposed it, as did three of the six provincial governors and all but one of the magistrates in courts of first instance. In relation to other Latin American countries, a surprisingly large number of Cubans belonged to Protestant congregations. The Masonic lodges in Cuba were the largest in all of Latin America; every major town had its lodge, while their membership, which included such famous names as José Martí and Antonio Maceo, invariably played leading roles in the political and economic life of their communities.

Historical factors underlay this picture. The quality of the colonial clergy had been poor; too often the hierarchy had staffed Cuban churches with ecclesiastical offenders from the mainland colonies. Since Church and state were united under Spain, the clergy had opposed independence, incurring the wrath of the patriot fathers and alienating majority sentiment on the island. Nor had the Church indicated any deep concern for the plight of the poor. As a Spanish institution, the Church was a bond between colony and mother country, a bond that must be severed if Cuba was to be free. No wonder, then, that debates over the Church question were among the most acrimonious at the 1901 Constitutional Convention, which abolished the state-supported Church and decreed freedom for all religious sects and, in so doing, liberated the island from the clerical issue that haunts much of Spanish America.

In summary, the Church, loosely allied with upper-income groups, its national position weak and virtually absent in rural Cuba, particularly among Afro-Cubans, was an institution with little vitality or inclination to support reformers. Only a minority of lay Catholics opposed Batista; while one of the cardinals of the Church, Manuel Arteaga, travelled to the National Palace to congratulate the *caudillo* on his coup. The Church could not hold society together or rally public opinion, either in self-interest or on behalf of the status quo.

Despite the splintered nature of society, unity existed, a unity reflecting growing awareness of what it meant to be Cuban, and of Cuba's destiny as a people. In the 1920s a wave of nationalism engulfed the island; subdued in the forties, nationalism was on the move again by 1958, with a militancy of its own among the intelligentsia and the youth of Cuba. The result of years of frustration, of hopes dashed before they were reality, the new nationalism voiced popular aspirations for a society free of the old evils and the foreigner. The new nationalism advocated the return of the land to its native owners, diversification of agriculture, and industrialization. Believers dreamt of liberating the people from the foreign yoke, on which they placed the burden of responsibility for past failures. And the yoke, in their minds, wa the United States.

This, then, was the structure of Cuban society in 1958. Cuba was a country with an affluent layer closely identified with American capital at the top and, at the bottom of the social scale, a large working mass, often exploited but better off than its counterparts in Spanish America. In between, amorphous middle groups existed, all striving to keep up appearances with the rich and equally dependent on foreign markets and imports. Neither the army nor the Church played its accustomed Spanish American role, though both were loosely tied to the status quo. Of the political parties none, with the exception of the Communists, had managed to build a tough, disciplined organization; none had survived the rigours of the Batista dictatorship of the fifties. Organized labour, in the interim, had succumbed to the venality of the times, which were increasingly difficult for hundreds of thousands of workers whose livelihood depended on the fickle sugar industry.

Why, in summary, did Cuba experience a successful revolution in 1959?

It seems probable that the Cuban Revolution developed because a number of the conditions were present that have almost always characterized pre-revolutionary societies. In terms of Crane Brinton's famous study of the revolutionary process, Cuban society shared certain 'uniformities' with old regimes in England, the United States, France, and Russia, that had suffered revolutions.

To use Brinton's first of five 'uniformities', these societies were not unprosperous but, on the contrary, upward-bound societies, where revolutionary elements were more annoyed or restrained than oppressed. The revolutions did not emerge from hungry and miserable people without hope of change. In comparison with other Spanish American peoples, Cubans were well off, particularly the middle sectors, which were among the largest in Latin America. However, although middle-sector politicians had wielded political power since the forties, the majority of individuals in the middle sectors had no voice in government during the Batista years. Revolutions, to cite Chalmers Johnson, occur in societies that have suffered change, but still demand further change.

Moreover, sharp class conflict characterized Cuba's pre-revolutionary society, though not in simplistic Marxist terms. Discontent centred in the middle sectors which, to employ Brinton's analysis, had 'made money, or at least . . . have enough to live on, and who contemplate bitterly the imperfections of . . . [the] socially privileged'. As he puts it, 'Revolution seems more likely when social classes are close together than when they are far apart'. But not only were the middle sectors restless; organized labour, a large and potent political force since the late 1930s, claimed a long history of violent struggles against both foreign and domestic employers.

Further, the dependent sugar economy had given a special character to Cuban society which made it vulnerable to the attack of a militant and committed minority. The welfare of nearly every segment of the population rested precariously on the production of sugar or, indirectly, on the importation for resale of American manufactured goods purchased almost entirely with the profits from sugar sales in the United States. For the great majority of workers, sugar dictated a predictable seasonal pattern, cycles of jobs and of unemployment based on sugar sales abroad. When harvests were good and markets abundant, there were well-paid jobs for the workers, but when sugar prices fell on evil days, wages dropped. Insecurity and discontent, therefore, were salient features of the worker's life in Cuba.

Nor did the old regime have a strong set of 'native' values with which to defend itself. To use David Riesman's terminology, the island's society was 'other directed'; social, economic, and value patterns were derived from outsiders. The middle sectors were particularly dependent and imitative. No independent middle class existed with a consciousness of class or an identity of its own. Instead of a national bourgeoisie, there were 'international' middle sectors economically and even culturally dependent upon the United States for survival. Because infant Cuban industries employed only a fraction of the population, only a small minority of 'middle class' Cubans engaged in activities dissociated from American interests.

Meanwhile, the old rulers of Cuba, essentially the sugar men, had become ineffectual politically, accepting passively the Batista coup of 1952 and later — some of them at least — supporting the anti-Batista protest largely out of inability to propose solutions of their own. In Brinton's terms, the old rulers of Cuba had lost faith in their ability to rule and the moral vigour required to control political life on the island. Many of the old class had become dissolute, succumbing to immoral ways in their personal lives, and consequently were politically inept.

Like the middle sectors, the plutocracy had little coherence as a class, being utterly dependent on foreign interests. Sugar, the lifeblood of the plutocracy, had almost no future outside the American orbit. Largely a phenomenon of the post-independence era, the plutocracy possessed few roots in the colonial past to equate it with the powerful and traditional ruling élites of the South American republics. National welfare for the plutocracy had narrow limits, circumscribed by the needs of the domestic sugar industry and the demands of American foreign policy. These needs of the plutocracy frequently clashed with the aspirations of youth and the aims of nationalistic intellectuals.

Furthermore, governmental machinery had broken down, partly because the old institutions had never fully achieved stability and partly because they were unresponsive to the economic problems posed by a declining sugar economy, problems which had bred dissatisfaction at almost every level of Cuban society. A governmental apparatus which had responded to the reality of politically primitive conditions during the first three decades of the Republic's life proved ineffectual in dealing with the demands of social classes eager to implant both political and economic reforms. One reason revolution takes place, Chalmers Johnson reminds us, is that 'non-revolutionary change' has failed.

Politically, Cuba was an immature society, with weak and unstable institutions and political parties that represented the will of *caudillos* or political cliques. Local government was conspicuous by its absence, while at every level party politics commanded decisions. Honesty in public life was a rare virtue as liberals, moderates, and conservatives vied with each other for an opportunity to plunder the national exchequer. Middle-sector rule — that panacea of many political scientists — had proved an illusion, for middle-sector government in Cuba was inefficient, corrupt, and nonrepresentative.

Nonpolitical institutions fell into the familiar mould. All had failed to provide a basis for unity for Cuba's fragmented society. The Catholic Church, largely urban and Spanish, had a tenuous hold on the population; rural dwellers and Afro-Cubans especially played only a marginal role in the Church. Except for a privileged minority, most Cubans paid no more than lip-service to the Church. Labour unions were essentially government-run and government-controlled, responsive not to the demands of their membership but to politicians. The army was the personal tool of Batista, with little or no support in the population at large or in the monied classes.

The intelligentsia, moreover, formed a bitter, restless, and alienated minority in society. Denied a voice in government and hostile to the values of the money-oriented middle sectors, to which most of them originally belonged, they voiced an increasingly negative view of Cuban society, much of which embodied their denunciations of the sugar economy and its ties with the United States. The intelligentsia's attack on the political structure of Cuba revealed not merely a discontent with Batistianos, Auténticos, and old *politicos* alike, but general disenchantment with the political principles of the old regime.

One by-product of this alienation was the participation of intellectuals in the ranks of the Communist party. Partly out of a sense of despair and partly because of the promise of socialism to provide a more equitable and moral society for the future which, says Denis W. Brogan, was 'the great emotional strength of socialism, the force that won it so many supporters of the first rank in the last century', Cuban intellectuals helped to build an efficient Communist party apparatus and a unified labour movement. In the history of Cuban party politics only the Auténticos of the thirties managed to win a more genuinely popular following than the Communists and their intellectual allies. Ultimately, the Communist party provided Fidel Castro with the political organization, discipline, and goals he sorely needed when his loosely knit and heterogeneous 26th of July Movement began to disintegrate after the victory of 1959.

But in addition to the 'uniformities' that it shared with the pre-revolutionary societies of England, the United States, France, and Russia, Cuban society displayed revolutionary symptoms of its own. After all, as Chalmers Johnson stresses, a particular revolution must be studied within the context of the social system in which it develops.

For one, the Revolution of 1959 was made possible by Cuba's own revolutionary tradition. Since the middle of the nineteenth century every generation of Cubans had experienced revolution. Political and social turmoil had engulfed the island approximately every twenty-five years; the Ten Years' War of 1868 to 1878, the struggle for independence that began in 1895, and the revolution of 1933. Between 1902 and 1920 the island suffered at least two political revolutions which, though limited in objectives, disrupted peace and order. On the basis of Cuban history, the Cubans could rightly claim the right — indeed the obligation — to revolt in order to eliminate old grievances.

Second, a strident nationalism that placed the blame for many of Cuba's troubles on United States foreign policy, and on a sugar industry that relied on American capital and markets, provided a rallying cry around which Cubans of diverse backgrounds could be united. Nationalism offered Castro the means by which to win popular backing, endorsement of his drastic reforms, and support in his battle against the allies of the United States on the island. Anti-American nationalism thrived especially among intellectuals who were convinced that to achieve true freedom — an increasingly popular aspiration — Cuba must drastically modify or sever its traditional relations with the United States.

Finally, in Fidel Castro the Cubans discovered an extraordinarily gifted political prophet and leader who, with his bold challenge to Batista, not only captured the imagination and loyalty of the young but in the process managed to clothe himself with the mantle of José Martí, first of the great Cuban revolutionary figures. Undoubtedly the political and economic conditions in Cuba paved the way for Castro's surprising success, but the Revolution would have been vastly different without the leadership of this quixotic and charismatic man.

The Black Power February (1970) Revolution in Trinidad

Herman L. Bennett

The post-colonial history of the anglophone Caribbean lends itself to a fruitful analysis of the process of decolonization and the challenges that the new states confronted. During the first decades of their independence, Jamaica in 1968 and Trinidad in 1970 experienced social disturbances that took on a seemingly revolutionary character. In addition, several groups and individuals throughout the area issued demands for the elimination of colonial ties, habits, and institutions, as well as the redistribution of national wealth.

At the forefront of these demands were radical intellectuals and university students who criticized independence as a 'flawed achievement'. Many of these critics noted that a transformation in the social, political, and economic systems had not been effected in the post-colonial period. Criticism of the post-colonial order was not limited to university students and radical intellectuals, however. Among individuals in the general population who had hoped that independence would lead to improved material conditions, frustration prevailed when promised reforms and better socio-economic conditions remained elusive goals. This frustration led to sporadic social unrest, anti-government protests, and politically motivated violence directed against the expatriate as well as the indigenous elite. Yet, failed expectations alone cannot explain that Jamaicans in 1968 and Trinidadians in 1970 took to the streets to express their grievances.

By the mid–1960s, critics such as the university-based intellectuals who belonged to the New World Group, as well as an amorphous group of students, workers, the urban unemployed, and middle-class exponents of Trinidadian nationalism and Black Power who constituted the National Joint Action Committee (NJAC), concluded that decolonization had only initiated another phase of colonialism. Their criticisms, along with those of the noted Guyanese historian and Black Power advocate, Walter Rodney, were undoubtedly influential in shaping the character of the social disturbances that occurred in Trinidad. It can be maintained that the critics were also enormously effective in questioning the legitimacy of West Indian independence in general and in raising questions that the new leaders had to confront.

Primarily concerned with the issue of West Indian dependency on foreign capital, the radical intellectuals who comprised the New World Group were prominent critics of post-colonial development strategies. Trinidad's small size and dependence on preferential markets had convinced the ruling political elite that economic self-reliance was not feasible.[1] The inheritors of the colonial state were, consequently, persuaded to adopt the dependent development strategy advocated by the Saint Lucian economist, Sir Arthur Lewis. The Puerto Rican model, or 'Industrialization by Invitation' as it was called, saw the government grant pioneer status to incoming firms, enabling them to enjoy tax holidays, accelerated deprecation, duty free imports, and other concessions. The government, in turn, hoped that industrialization would secure employment for the local population and that the local business elite would eventually acquire the capital and expertise to take over the industries. But members of the New World Group viewed the reliance on foreign capital as evidence that the West Indies remained economically dependent and underdeveloped, and that states such as Trinidad served the interests of the local and metropolitan elite.

The New World Group, therefore, concluded that the development of national economic and political structures was impeded by foreign capital and that unless ownership and investment patterns were changed colonial relations would persist. Seeking to eradicate the colonial legacy, the New World Group proposed an effective break with imperialism, the rise to power by the black masses, and the formulation of an indigenous political philosophy and culture. It also proposed a solution to underdevelopment and dependency. In the group's opinion, West Indian nations should 'disengage' from international capitalism while initiating domestic capital accumulation. In the transition process, the state would play an active role by imposing import restrictions and other limitations on foreign capital. The state, moreover, would utilize local resources (labour, capital, and natural resources) to support the national bourgeoisie who, in turn, would foster independent development and ensure that West Indian economies operated from a position of strength and self-reliance in their interaction with international capitalism. Interestingly, the New World Group's alternative parallels the dependent development strategy of Sir Arthur Lewis which also emphasized the necessity to generate local capital for development. Unlike Lewis's model, however, the New World Group rejected an alliance with foreign capital during the transition to economic self-reliance. It argued that precisely because Lewis's strategy relied on foreign capital, West Indian economies would remain structurally dependent on international capitalism.

Although they criticized the dependence on foreign capital and proposed solutions, members of the New World Group stressed the importance of intellectuals staying above active politics.[2] Lloyd Best, a spokesman for the group, summarized the members' objectives as eschewing established ideologies, providing an examination of Caribbean societies in their specificities, committing themselves to theorizing, and finally avoiding the political fray. Critics of the New World Group have suggested that its tactical stance reflected the organization's class composition and that this orientation eventually led to its demise.[3] Although its influence remained primarily academic, the New World Group, by criticizing the prevailing development strategies and proposing to transform the dependent West Indian economies into independent ones, posed an important challenge to the post-colonial order.

Not all intellectuals in the Caribbean avoided political activism, however. Walter Rodney, for example, bridged the divisions between radical intellectuals, university students, and the urban poor of West Kingston. Rodney's analysis of the post-colonial period in the Caribbean extended beyond the political and economic systems to include questions of identity, social classes, the role of intellectuals, the importance of African history, the Afro-Indian debate, and, most importantly, the deplorable socio-economic conditions of the masses. As one of the more prominent Black Power proponents in the Caribbean, Walter Rodney brought 'together class and racial issues precisely the way' the West Indian political systems 'sought to prevent and to which [they were] most vulnerable'.[4] Inspired by Rodney's ideas, many young radicals throughout the Caribbean embraced Black Power and raised probing questions about the political order. To the surprise of most observers, the most sustained expression of Black Power emerged in Trinidad where the ruling People's National Movement (PNM) had been characterized as the best example of black majority rule. James Millette, however, was most perspicacious when he noted that 'black men in power do not connote Black Power'. Black people in the West Indies, Millette maintained, were frustrated and felt 'betrayed' by those blacks who claimed to rule in their name. Failed expectations, he suggested, was the primary reason why the confrontation emerged as a Black Power movement.[5]

At the forefront of the Trinidadian Black Power movement was the National Joint Action Committee. The organization first gained prominence in 1969 when its members barred the Canadian governor general from entering the University of the West Indies' Saint Augustine campus. NJAC's action was an expression of solidarity with the West Indian students arrested in Canada for their participation in the Sir George Williams University Affair.[6] Following the incident involving the Canadian governor general, NJAC broadened its appeal by concerning itself with community issues confronting workers, the unemployed, the poor, and other dispossessed elements in Trinidadian society.

In their political tracts, 'Slavery to Slavery' and 'Conventional Politics or Revolution', as well as in their news journal, *Liberation,* NJAC members established their reputation as critics of the post-colonial order. Between 1969 and 1970, the organization repeatedly addressed the linkage between the political order and the economy.[7] NJAC portrayed the economic system as being subservient to international capitalism. Its members argued that since the 'white power structure' controlled the economy, it followed that black people were oppressed because they were victims of economic exploitation. Consequently, independence merely changed 'imperial masters, the Maple, and the Stars and Stripes for the Union Jack. The decay of colonialism had heralded the dawn of neo-colonialism'.[8] Thus, the destiny of the West Indies was still being determined by an external elite.

The indigenous elite, however, was held responsible for maintaining metropolitan interests, thereby ensuring that the exploitation of black people would continue. The so-called 'Afro-Saxons', NJAC members argued, were cultural reflections of Europeans in terms of values, education, and orientation. NJAC, therefore, rejected independence as being an act of deception and suggested that no significant change would be forthcoming until the 'black whites' were removed from political power.

Apparently, NJAC was not concerned with conventional politics or any goal short of revolutionary change. The organization's radicalism was evident in its proposal for economic reconstruction, which called for public ownership and control of the land, national ownership and control of the entire sugar industry, establishing a land use plan, linking both sectors of the economy to generate local capital, diversifying trade links to reduce dependency, eliminating unemployment in five years, and allowing trade unions to have strike privileges.[9] As one NJAC spokesman stated about the new order: 'It is no point talking in terms of reform . . .we have always to think in terms of total rejection of the system which has so dehumanized and oppressed black people'.[10]

Contrary to popular opinion, however, NJAC's programme was not grounded in an Afro-Marxist framework. Within the leadership ranks there was open hostility to Marxism of any sort. The Workers Educational Association, a Marxist-Leninist organization, for example,which had joined the NJAC coalition at its inception, was later expelled for allegedly not understanding the problems of black people.[11] Although NJAC maintained ties with individual Marxists, the organization's main ideological thrust was an anti–imperialism fused with ethnic nationalism. Responding to critics who charged that NJAC's appeal was overly racial, a spokesman remarked that the 'emphasis on blackness . . . was a necessary prerequisite for the first phase of the Black Movement'.[12]

NJAC's Black Power emphasis was somewhat injudicious in a racially heterogeneous society like Trinidad. Given the shrewd manipulation of hostilities between Afro- and East Indian Trinidadians (who respectively comprised 42% and 37% of the population), Black Power only exacerbated a potentially explosive relationship. During the events of 1970, NJAC grossly underestimated the level of hostility existing between both groups. Although both shared similar socio-economic conditions, the years of racial tension and conflict in addition to cultural differences effectively prevented Afro-Indian unity.[13]

Despite the failure to incorporate East Indians into the Black Power movement, members of NJAC were outspoken ideological critics of the post-colonial state. Their analysis and solutions to the problems of dependency reflected a degree of political sophistication similar to that of the New World Group and Walter Rodney. It also appears that NJAC was able to raise the level of consciousness among the poor by arguing that independence had provided little or no change in the lives of most people. In the final analysis, however the revolutionary objectives of NJAC frightened participants in the February revolt, causing some to reembrace the conventional political system.

The critics of the nature of independence agreed that colonial attitudes still prevailed everywhere in the West Indies. They charged, for example, that the substitution of a national flag, anthem, and motto was at best 'symbol manipulation' initiated by the indigenous elite.[14] This elite, Rodney and NJAC pointed out, could not envision a self-reliant existence. Dependency, on the other hand, delayed societal reconstruction which would ensure popular and indigenous control; political, economic, and cultural autonomy; and a more equitable distribution of the nation's resources. Given the extent to which the West Indies were still dominated by foreign elements, the nature of this criticism can be described as nationalist. For as Norman Girvan observed, 'a reaction against imperialism assumes a nationalist character'.[15]

By the late 1960s, the nationalist ideologies, especially Black Power, appealed increasingly to the urban dispossessed. The source of this appeal was the deteriorating socio-economic conditions that Black Power proponents addressed. The 'black massa', it was argued, 'pays greater attention to the representation of foreign investors and their domestic allies than to the needs of oppressed blacks'.[16] Because of its racial and somewhat xenophobic dimensions, Black Power attracted the urban poor whose conditions were in part determined by their race and relation to foreign capital.

Yet to suggest that the ideological currents espoused by the New World Group, Rodney, or NJAC inspired the events of 1970 is to ignore the other causes of the disturbances in Trinidad. Whereas radical intellectuals and university students sought to eradicate dependent relations, the urban dispossessed wanted to improve their material conditions. The prevailing ideology of Black Power was important to the urban poor but employed only insofar as it articulated their social grievances. Commitment to changes beyond the redress of social grievances was essentially confined to organizations like NJAC and the New World Group in addition to individuals like Rodney. Limited in their demands, the majority of demonstrators placed restrictions on the content, the nature, and the eventual outcome of the social disturbances that occurred in Trinidad.

Popular Mobilization

Inspired by the anniversary of the Sir George Williams University Affair, a group of two hundred students and their supporters participated in a protest demonstration denouncing Canadian imperialism and racism. Within days, the events of February 26, 1970, had escalated into a massive Black Power demonstration that paralyzed Trinidad and

Tobago. The disturbances lasted until the declaration of a 'State of Emergency' on April 21 when the authorities brought the situation under control, leaving the Trinidadian political system more or less intact.

The bitter confrontation between militant blacks and the post-colonial government of Trinidad was a surprise to most Caribbean observers. Even among Trinidadians aware of the growing political temper and an emerging black consciousness, surprise was expressed at the massive support Black Power advocates, especially NJAC, gained between February and April 1970. Although the disturbances did not constitute an incipient revolution, as many Trinidadians feared, they profoundly challenged the foundations of conventional Trinidadian politics. The events were initially a nationalist expression on the part of radical university students and intellectuals who demanded an end to metropolitan dominance over Trinidadian society. In order to attract supporters, however, the activists had to address issues relevant to the average Trinidadian, in particular unemployment, racism, and material dispossession. These considerations at once defined and limited the goals, content, and nature of the disturbances.

Given its limitations, it is more appropriate to characterize the events between February and April somewhat loosely as a 'revolt'. For revolts are basically angry or violent expressions by individuals or groups who refuse to continue in their present condition. Symbolizing reform for its participants, a revolt embraces various sectors of the population including the youth, the unemployed, and the dispossessed. The lack of a coherent ideology, moreover, places constraints on the objectives and outcome of a revolt. Mark Hagopian suggests that 'the lack or weakness of ideology helps to explain why many revolts hesitate and then disintegrate after having [confronted] the forces of order. The revolt simply does not know what to do'. In view of their limited objectives, revolts are basically 'conservative or even retrograde' in nature since most participants only seek to better their socio-economic condition. Thus the possibility of effecting fundamental changes does not exist.[17]

Between February and April, for example, NJAC failed to articulate a coherent ideological position or programme. The ambiguities surrounding Black Power also suggest that the so-called 'February Revolution' lacked the basis for fundamental change. If the conditions for a revolution were in fact present, what explains the apparent lack of participation by the industrial and agricultural workers who comprised a significant proportion of the population? The lack of interest among members of the population in general can be explained partly in terms of their ideological reservations about Black Power and what it appeared to represent. Most people were unwilling to support a movement that could jeopardize their existing status. Among industrial workers, 'Industrialization by Invitation' had created a small 'relatively well-paid unionized working-class elite' which was unwilling to support any radical departure from conventional politics.[18]

The same case can be made for the majority of the protesters, many of whom were primarily interested in improving their material conditions. When looting, burning, and bombing of businesses occurred, many of the marchers were appalled by the lack of discipline and abandoned the 'revolutionary' movement. If the objective of most participants was to reform the political system in order to improve their socio-economic conditions, the leadership of the February Revolution overestimated the importance of symbolic gestures pertaining to black pride and consciousness. In fact, the level of commitment among the demonstrators was misinterpreted. If the majority of protesters had been committed to revolution, the demonstrations would have maintained their intensity beyond the declaration of the State of Emergency. This was not the case. Yet the implications of the disturbances cannot be easily dismissed. The events between February 26 and April 21 strongly suggest that a fundamental dissatisfaction with the post-colonial order existed among young urban blacks, who were overrepresented among the unemployed and dispossessed. Black Power attracted young urban blacks because it spoke to their immediate needs.

The first portent of the challenge to the existing order occurred on the first day of Carnival, February 9, 1970, when Black Power themes and protest bands appeared alongside the traditional fantasy and historical costumes.[19] The political overtones were apparent, for example, in a depiction of the black experience, entitled 'The Truth about Blacks — Past and Present', which portrayed slaves and indentured servants in addition to 'massas' and the 'stooges of the massas'.[20]

Within seventeen days, the situation reached crisis proportions when NJAC set in motion the February revolt. Although it was viewed as a spontaneous Black Power demonstration in support of the West Indian students arrested in connection with the Sir George Williams University Affair, the events that followed were an outgrowth of the sociopolitical tensions permeating Trinidad. Motivated by the anniversary of the Canadian incident, demonstrators under the direction of NJAC directed their venom at Canadian authorities and Canadian-owned businesses in Trinidad's capital, Port of Spain. As the day proceeded, the focus of the demonstrators broadened to include the Roman Catholic church when a number of the demonstrators entered the Cathedral of the Immaculate Conception, gave speeches, and engaged in sharp exchanges with the priests. The crowd then proceeded to Woodford Square where demonstrators listened.to speeches until 7:00 p.m.[21]

After the initial demonstration,the Sir George Williams University Affair became insignificant in relation to the events that followed. The affair was only important in that it enabled NJAC and other organizations to link racism in Canada to the realities in Trinidad. Organizational leaders like Geddes Granger, Dave D'Abreau, Alwdyn Primus, and Carl Blackwood repeatedly emphasized how racism and foreign capital were related to the systemic problems confronting Trinidad. For the majority of the participants, mainly university students, the linkage was made explicit by the fact that Canada was the largest foreign investor in Trinidad. One can, therefore, conclude that the initial demonstrators were inspired by anti–imperialist sentiments.

The government reacted swiftly to the demonstration by arresting nine NJAC members for 'unlawful assembling in the vicinity and within the Cathedral of the Immaculate Conception'.[22] Instead of decapitating the movement with the arrests, however, the government's response served to exacerbate the situation. Intrigued by the events of February 26 and issues raised by NJAC, an estimated 10,000 people paralyzed Trinidad's capital when they gathered to greet the nine arrested NJAC spokesmen on March 4. Members of Black Power organizations from throughout Trinidad, including the Black Panthers, the African Unity Brothers, the African Cultural Association, the Afro-Turf Limers ('limers' refer to people who gather on street corners, generally unemployed), the Pinetoppers, the Southern Liberation Movement, and the National Freedom Organization, joined the assemblage on March 4 to express their solidarity with NJAC.[23]

Led by NJAC leader Geddes Granger, the demonstrators marched into Shanty Town, an urban ghetto in Port of Spain. In Shanty Town, the protesters asked the residents to join them. According to the *Guardian* reporter Raoul Pantin, 'They came. Asked to talk, one did. She gave a very brief talk, attacking the government for the fact of Shanty Town'.[24] NJAC spokesmen then criticized the 'white racist power structure' and its 'black tools' for oppressing black people.[25] The need for black unity was also repeatedly emphasized, while

the mostly young demonstrators shouted 'Power' accompanied by clenched-fist, Black Power salutes.

The March 4 demonstration marked a critical point in the revolt. NJAC leaders realized almost immediately that the crowd was only receptive to ideas that pertained to such local issues as unemployment, poverty, and racial discrimination. At this point, NJAC members altered their interpretation of Black Power so that it would focus specifically on local issues thereby de-emphasizing its initial anti–imperialist and nationalist orientation. Throughout the two-month revolt, the central ideological content of Black Power would remain limited to practical issues relevant to the majority of the demonstrators.

The mood among protesters grew increasingly militant after the March 4 demonstration. In response to the shooting of John Gomez, an innocent bystander, an angry crowd, consisting of school children, young men and women, hurled objects at stores and the police. In the following days, the demonstration continued with an added dimension. Molotov cocktails were thrown into the home of the minister of education and culture, while the Bank of Nova Scotia, Kirpalanis (an East Indian-owned dry goods store), the Modern Wear Garment factory, and other businesses were victims of similar attacks.[26] Thus by March 8, police assaults, retaliatory violence, and the increasing militancy of the demonstrators had intensified the situation.

At this point, it is possible that Geddes Granger, the NJAC leader, began to sense the possibilities for more drastic action. Granger stated that 'we are prepared to take over the country'.[27] The government, in turn, felt threatened by the demonstrations and sporadic violence. The minister of industry, commerce, and petroleum claimed that the current crisis was being 'engineered by communist agitators trained and paid by Fidel Castro' who 'were using the Sir George Williams affair as a red herring in their revolutionary move aimed at the overthrowing of the ruling PNM government'.[28] In contrast, members of the East Indian-based parliamentary opposition, the Democratic Labour Party (DLP), feeling less threatened, provided a more trenchant analysis: '[T]he protesters have taken to the streets to express . . . their disappointment and disenchantment with the present state of affairs . . . Everyone knows that unemployment is compounding the economic as well as social ills of the country'.[29] Although perceptive in its critique, the DLP — along with other observers — saw the February revolt simply as black pride manifesting itself in wanton violence against East Indians, whites, and private property.[30]

In response to claims that the Black Power movement was anti-East Indian, Geddes Granger announced that the demonstrators would proceed to the sugar cane areas populated largely by East Indians to express their solidarity with them. Aware of Trinidad's racially plural nature and the underlying tension that existed between blacks and East Indians, the NJAC leadership realized the boost the movement would receive if disillusioned East Indians united with Afro-Trinidadians. Granger stated that this symbolic march would give the demonstrators (who were primarily young, unemployed black youths) 'an opportunity to share the work experience of the Indians and to witness the suffering of the people and the way they are exploited'. 'The experience', Granger argued, 'would help us develop a new understanding that would further strengthen the bond, of brotherhood between black people — Indians and blacks'.[31] In addition, the NJAC leader issued a formal statement inviting the Roman Catholic archbishop of Port of Spain to join the marchers on their historic trek into Caroni. On the morning of March 26, over 6,000 Afro-Trinidadians marched the twenty-six miles into the heart of the Indian belt, Caroni, to express solidarity with their Indian brothers and sisters.

Despite strong opposition from Bhadase Maraj, head of the All Trinidad Sugar Estates and Factory Workers Trade Union and the Democratic Labour Party, who had threatened the marchers with violence if they entered the sugar belt, the march took place without incident.[32] While the march had shown that no conflict between the two races would materialize, it also demonstrated that the protesters could not expect substantial East Indian support. Suspicion between the two groups was widespread, and it would take more than a march to alleviate the tension that existed. The Black Power leaders underestimated the importance of these divisions, and failed to provide the necessary ground work within the Indian community.[33]

The term 'black', moreover, generally referred to persons of predominantly African descent. Most Indians did not regard themselves as being black. In a letter to the editor, for example, an Indian writer responded negatively to having been categorized as such by the Black Power movement: 'I object to being called black . . . Indians belong to the Caucasian or 'white' race . . . why then call Indians black?'[34] D. Jugmohan, in a more dispassionate letter, wrote, 'You, the Black Power members are asking us to join you in your march for power . . . Your sudden interest in the East Indian sugar workers is viewed with suspicion . . . We are not prepared to support you'.[35] Overall, the concept of Black Power had little appeal for the Indian pop-

ulation and throughout the period of unrest the majority of participants were of African descent.[36]

Opposition to Black Power was not limited to East Indians, however. A number of Afro-Trinidadians questioned the relevance of Black Power in a multiracial society like Trinidad. In a letter to the editor, Dr. R. K. Richardson observed that 'Black Power seems unsuitable for application to the requirements of this multiracial, multi-coloured society because the term suggests a racist content'. 'Majority Power', he argued, was more applicable since it would facilitate the 'elimination of unemployment and the achievement of rapid socio-economic re-orientation'.[37] Another writer, Dr. T. K. Agbie, expressed contempt for a concept that would 'spoil our peaceful and prosperous island'. Rejecting Black Power on the grounds that it was incompatible with the existing 'racial harmony, progressive government and standard of living', he expressed hope that the government would 'crush this ugly rebellion'.[38] Similarly, Violent Purplint (a pseudonym) abstained from embracing Black Power. 'It is dangerous', she wrote, 'to sympathize with Black Power. The ideas they are propagating are much more dangerous than the violence'.[39] Some letters were characterized by racial self-hatred in their criticism of Black Power. That of Charles Williams stated, 'I am a dark Negro through no fault of mine . . . In my opinion black is an ugly word to describe a person'. 'Black Power', he continued, 'is no compliment'.[40]

In general, the reactions to Black Power varied. Certain generalizations can be made, however. More affluent members of Trinidad society, especially blacks, felt threatened by the concept of Black Power and the aims of the February revolt. The poor, on the other hand, particularly urban blacks, were sympathetic to the goals of the movement as long as it promised material improvement. This attitude among the urban poor reflected their limited interests and was ultimately responsible for the reformist nature and eventual disintegration of the February revolt.

Evidence of divisions within the movement first emerged on March 18 when the Black Panthers withdrew their support from the February revolt.[41] The division between the Panthers and NJAC arose out of ideological differences. Brian Meeks suggests that while 'objectively the massive demonstrators stood for revolution, large sections of the demonstrators had hoped for reform from the PNM'.[42] Ideologically, the Black Panthers stood with the reform-oriented demonstrators. At most, they saw the role of the demonstrations as a way of forcing the People's National Movement to democratize the society. The Panthers' departure, however, did not seriously affect the movement for at no point in their history had they been able to organize and recruit a large number of Trinidadians.

On March 23, sensing a moment of weakness in the revolt, Prime Minister Eric Williams addressed the nation. Attempting to regain his progressive image, Dr. Williams announced that several changes were taking place in the government. For one thing, he had fired the minister of industry, commerce, and petroleum, the same person who had charged that the Black Power demonstrations were Communist-inspired plots. Next, he stated that a 5% special tax would be levied on companies and the revenue used to combat unemployment. In addition, the prime minister warned the business community 'to set its house in order with respect to discrimination in employment'. He also mentioned that further government intervention in the private sector was being planned, including a proposal to purchase a 51% interest in the largest sugar producer, Caroni Ltd.[43]

To the surprise of many Trinidadians, the prime minister expressed his support for Black Power. 'The fundamental feature of the demonstrators was the insistence on Black Dignity, the manifestation of Black consciousness and the demand for Black economic power. The entire population must understand the demand for Black economic power. The entire population must understand that these demands are perfectly legitimate and are entirely in the interest of the community as a whole. If this is Black Power then I am for Black Power'.[44]

Although all of these proposals were quite radical in the context of the PNM's official platform, they were incapable of pacifying the revolutionary movement. The next day, in fact, the police in an attempt to disperse angry protesters from the commercial district, where some were involved in the destruction of private property, released tear gas which only served to exacerbate an already tense situation. Thus, the expectation that government-initiated reforms would heal the division between the demonstrators and the ruling elite appeared to have been unfulfilled.

Several observers have concluded that March 24 was the critical point of the revolutionary movement, because many of the reform-oriented demonstrators were now looking for 'a confrontation to bring the regime down as quickly as possible'.[45] This interpretation is misleading, however, given the events that occurred between March 25 and April 21. Although the numerical strength of the protesters continued to increase, the reformist nature of the movement remained apparent, as reflected in the NJAC manifesto entitled 'What the NJAC Wants Is What Any Poor Man in the Community Wants'. Its demands included 'food, shel-

ter, employment, dignity to regain his manhood, having a place in the political structure; to be able to play some part in the economy and be able to contribute meaningfully to his family and community'.[46]

The manifesto condemned 'the evil society' that was oppressing poor black people. As such, the movement was 'prepared to take any action in order to bring about the important changes'.[47] Elaborating on the manifesto, Granger told a crowd in Woodford Square that 'we are in the midst of a revolution' and that 'it was a confrontation between the poor and the rich, the haves and the havenots'.[48] Although Granger's rhetoric suggests the application of a class analysis, participants in the revolutionary movement and members of the NJAC shunned any references to Marxism. For example, when George Weekes, president of the Oil-field Workers Trade Union, addressed the demonstrators as 'Comrades', the crowd shouted 'None ah dat . . . We are brothers and sisters'.[49]

The final stage of the revolutionary movement began on April 9 with the funeral of Basil Davis, a twenty-two-year old NJAC supporter who had been shot and killed by the police. In a spectacular display of strength, between 30,000 and 100,000 people joined the movement's procession for its first martyr.[50] In the aftermath of the funeral, A.N.R. Robinson, minister of external affairs and a likely successor to Eric Williams, announced his resignation from the cabinet. Explaining his move, Robinson stated that he did not feel that a 'sufficiently serious attempt [has been] made by the government to remove the underlying causes of the present situation in the country'.[51]

Following the funeral, the situation became increasingly explosive. The Black Power leaders were beginning to enhance their strength by forming loose alliances with various organizations and individuals who had traditionally supported the PNM, such as the National Association of Steelbandsmen, the Oil-field Workers Trade Union, the Trinidad and Tobago Electricity Commission Workers, and several progressive labour leaders from the transportation and sugar unions. Previously, Michael Als, leader of the Young Power Organization, expressed his organization's support for the February revolt by issuing a statement calling on the government to stop granting pioneer status to foreign companies, to drop all charges against NJAC, and to lift the ban on the Trinidadian-born Black Power advocate, Stokely Carmichael.[52] The Young Power Organization also called for a radical transformation of the political, economic, and educational structure.[53]

Collectively, the various organizations announced plans for a general strike that would take place on April 21 and 22. The significance of this alliance cannot be overstated. The organizations, especially the steelband movement and the Young Power organization, had been cultural and political outlets for a large section of the black population. The PNM, which in the past had derived its strength from a coalition of progressive intellectuals, students, workers, and unemployed, now found itself opposed by precisely those sectors.

In response to the impending strike, Prime Minister Williams declared a State of Emergency on April 21. The declaration imposed a dawn-to-dusk curfew and led to the arrest of fifteen Black Power leaders. In contrast to its past behaviour, the government decapitated the revolutionary movement by arresting its leaders. Thus, after April 21 protest activities almost ceased. On April 21, however, one more incident occurred that paralyzed Trinidad. A section of the 750–man Defence Force, when called up to reinforce the State of Emergency, revolted against its superiors. While it is now clear that the linkage between the army's revolt and the Black Power movement was superficial, the event triggered the fear of a military coup. Fortunately for the government, the Coast Guard was able to contain the 'mutineers' who were eventually arrested.[54]

The historical record surrounding the February revolt is in many respects incomplete. Even today, one can only speculate about the central objectives of the revolutionary movement. Although NJAC spoke emphatically about the 'new man', the 'new society', and the need to 'regain black manhood', the pronouncements remained vague and ambiguous. The February revolt was not characterized by a coherent ideology, specific strategy, or definite objectives. Critics and supporters alike, for example, repeatedly questioned the aims of the Black Power Movement. An editorial in the *Trinidad Guardian* on March 11, 1970, stated that 'the dissenters have so far not been able to articulate quite properly the precise causes of their discontent'.[55] Several days later, the *Guardian* reiterated its criticism in addition to questioning the viability of constant demonstrations: 'Further demonstrations would only tire out the demonstrators themselves and make protest seem pointless. It is necessary for the demonstrators to articulate their demands'.[56] NJAC responded by rejecting suggestions to introduce specific demands into the movement, maintaining that the people wanted more demonstrations.

NJAC's Jacobinism and reluctance to organize the demonstrators around specific objectives, plus the fact that the majority of the demonstrators were narrowly focused on reforms within the conventional political system, were in part responsible for

the February revolt's failure to effect change in Trinidad. Yet, the larger responsibility for the movement's failure rests with the fact that the revolt involved only a small segment of the population. The lack of participation suggests that discontent was not as pervasive or as intense as some observers argued. Moreover, even if NJAC had had a more coherent ideology, structure, and programme of action, it is doubtful that the revolt could have brought the government down. Throughout the rebellion, the government forces were never seriously challenged. Nevertheless, the movement awakened the Trinidadian elite to the plight of young urban blacks who out of frustration embraced Black Power as a viable alternative to their deplorable predicament.

The urban unemployed, however, did more than just embrace Black Power. Whereas before the February revolt Black Power's orientation provided a far-reaching analysis and program of action (which included a dependency analysis conditioned by West Indian realities, explored the causes of underdevelopment, and emphasized a racial and class analysis in the context of the West Indian political economy), the objectives of the urban poor limited its demands to a redress of socio-economic grievances.

NJAC members were, in turn, confronted with the option of making their analysis relevant to local conditions or being bypassed altogether. Out of political necessity, NJAC opted for the former despite its limited appeal. The reformist nature of the February revolt was illustrated, for example, at a rally several days before the State of Emergency at which NJAC recounted the movement's victories: 'Pay increases for the police regiment, Coast Guard and allocations for the "improvement" of the steelband movement . . . because of the Black Power Movement'.[57] Although there was no mention of ameliorating the deplorable socio-economic conditions, the abovementioned gains give credence to the revolt's reformist orientation.

Finally, despite its limitations during the February revolt, Black Power called attention to the alarming socio-economic conditions in Trinidad in addition to representing a nationalist expression on the part of radical intellectuals and students. In the Trinidadian context, social grievances and nationalist aspirations were not mutually exclusive. The class/colour correlation and its connection to foreign capital provided NJAC with sufficient fuel to link both causes under the rubric of Black Power. Moreover, the various dimensions of Black Power served to raise questions about the social order and the role of foreign capital, and most importantly reminded the nation of its failure to alleviate, as promised, the deplorable socio-economic conditions of most Trinidadians. When it was perceived that the People's National Movement had failed to transform Trinidad, radical intellectuals, students, and the urban dispossessed concluded that 'Massa Day No Dun Yet'.

Notes

1. Ryan, *Race and Nationalism,* p. 384.
2. Gray, 'State Power', pp. 347–52.
3. *Ibid.,* p. 347.
4. Payne, 'The Rodney Riots', p. 165.
5. James Millette, 'The Black Revolution', Port of Spain (n.d.), pp. 6–9.
6. On February 11, 1969, a group of West Indian students attending Sir George Williams University began to complain about racist practices by a biology professor. Hoping to have their case heard, the students took their grievances to a university board. This was to no avail. Finally the students staged a sit-in at the university's $1.6 million computer centre, after which followed a ten-hour battle with police resulting in the destruction of the computer centre, school cafeteria, and faculty lounge. Consequently, the students were arrested and charged with conspiracy to commit arson and felonious mischief. See 'Students Riot in Canada', *Trinidad Guardian,* February 13, 1969, p. 1.
7. Riviere, *Black Power,* p. 23.
8. *Ibid.,* p. 14.
9. Ryan, *Race and Nationalism,* pp. 427–28.
10. Riviere, *Black Power,* p. 27.
11. Meeks, 'The Development of the 1970 Revolution', p. 251.
12. Riviere, *Black Power,* p. 4.
13. David Nicholls suggests that throughout the Black Power movement less than one percent of the participants were of East Indian origin. 'East Indians and Black Power', p. 447.
14. Carl Stone develops this concept in *Class, Race and Political Behaviour,* p. 98.
15. Girvan, *The Political Economy of Race,* p. 1.
16. Riviere, *Black Power,* p. 27.
17. Hagopian, *The Phenomenon of Revolution,* pp. 11–12, 317.
18. Ryan, *Race and Nationalism,* p. 363.
19. Meeks, 'The Development of the 1970 Revolution', p. 194.
20. 'Jour Ouvert 1970', *Trinidad Guardian,* February 10, 1970, p. 1.
21. Raoul Pantin and Hollis Boisselle, 'Black Power March in City: Demonstrators Take Over Roman Catholic Cathedral', *Trinidad Guardian,* February 27, 1970, p. 1.
22. Raoul Pantin, 'Bail Refused 8 Charged under Riot Ordinance', *Trinidad Guardian,* February 28, 1970, p. 1.
23. Raoul Pantin, 'Marchers Go to Shanty Town — Groups Come to Town to Join Demonstrations', *Trinidad Guardian,* March 5, 1970, p. 1.
24. *Ibid.*
25. *Ibid.*
26. Raoul Pantin, 'Black Power March to San Juan — 14,000 at Cruisee Meeting', *Trinidad Guardian,* March 7, 1970, p. 1.

27. John Babb and Raoul Pantin, 'Minister Blames Red Agitators', *Trinidad Guardian,* March 10, 1970, p. 1.
28. *Ibid.*
29. John Babb, 'DLP Calls on Government to Break Silence', *Trinidad Guardian,* March 7, 1970, p. 1.
30. This was the general impression conveyed by the *Trinidad Guardian* between February and April 1970.
31. Raoul Pantin, 'Archbishop Invited to Join 'Power' March to Caroni' *Trinidad Guardian,* March 11, 1970, p. 1.
32. Raoul Pantin, 'March to Caroni Incident-Free', *Trinidad Guardian,* March 13, 1970, p. 1.
33. Nicholls, 'East Indians and Black Power', p. 446.
34. Gasesh Hall, 'Indians Are Not Black', Letter to the Editor, *Trinidad Guardian,* April 8, 1970, p. 10.
35. D. Jugmohan, 'We Do Not Intend to Support You', Letter to the Editor, *Trinidad Guardian,* April 8, 1970, p. 8.
36. Nicholls, 'East Indians and Black Power', p. 447.
37. R. K. Richardson, 'Majority Power' Would Be Better', Letter to the Editor, *Trinidad Guardian,* March 26, 1970.
38. T. K. Agbie, 'We Do Not Need Black Power', Letter to the Editor, *Trinidad Guardian,* April 4, 1970, p. 8.
39. Violent Purplint, 'Let's Have Poor Power, Not Black Power', Letter to the Editor, *Trinidad Guardian,* April 2, 1970, p. 8.
40. Charles Williams, 'Black Power — Ridiculous Misnomer', Letter to the Editor, *Trinidad Guardian,* April 26, 1970, p. 10.
41. 'Panthers Take Back Seat at Black Power Meeting', *Trinidad Guardian,* March 18, 1970, p. 1.
42. Meeks, 'The Development of the 1970 Revolution', p. 212.
43. Eric Williams, 'Prime Minister's Television Broadcast', *Trinidad Guardian,* March 23, 1970, pp. 3–10.
44. *Ibid.*
45. Lloyd Best, 'The February Revolution', *Tapia,* December 1970, p. 1.
46. 'Black Power: The Stirrings of an Integrative Society', *Trinidad Guardian,* March 21, 1970, p. 6.
47. 'Black Power Goes West', *Trinidad Guardian,* March 26, 1970, p. 1.
48. *Ibid.*
49. John Babb, 'Police Use Tear Gas on Crowd', *Trinidad Guardian,* March 25, 1970, p. 1.
50. 'Power Funeral for Shot Youth', *Trinidad Guardian,* April 8, 1970, p. 1.
51. 'Talk of War by NJAC', *Trinidad Guardian,* April 14, 1970, p. 1.
52. 'Young Power March in the South', *Trinidad Guardian,* May 26, 1968, p. 3.
53. 'Black Power Goes West', *Trinidad Guardian,* Mach 26, 1970, p. 1.
54. For a detailed discussion of the Trinidad mutiny, see 'Peace Talks Going on at Chag.: Dissidence in Army Confirmed', *Trinidad Guardian,* April 23, 1970, p. 1, and 'Situation Very Much under Control', *Trinidad Guardian,* March 11, 1970, p. 10.
55. 'And Now to the Constructive Phase', *Trinidad Guardian,* March 11, 1970, p. 10.
56. 'Showing Solidarity', *Trinidad Guardian,* March 14, 1970, p. 6.
57. 'Gov't Planning Snap Elections, NJAC Claims', *Trinidad Guardian,* April 4, 1970, p. 1.

Grenada: A Revolution Aborted

Jorge Heine

'THE REVO killed our children' read the graffiti in St. George's after the execution of Maurice Bishop and his supporters, in the crucial turning point of those 'two weeks that shook the Caribbean' — from Bishop's arrest to the landing of U.S. troops on Grand Anse beach on 25 October 1983. Indeed, in Fort Rupert the revolution had not only killed its own children, it had killed itself.

The 13 March 1979 uprising that toppled Prime Minister Eric Gairy in Grenada was the first unconstitutional transfer of power to take place in the Commonwealth Caribbean. In turn, the 1983 invasion of Grenada by U.S. forces was the first time an English-speaking Caribbean territory was occupied by U.S. troops, and the first occupation of a Caribbean nation-state by the United States since 1965. Events on this small island (133 square miles, population 90,000) located at the southern tip of the Eastern Caribbean have thus had a remarkable impact on hemispheric and even global affairs.

As the single most advanced effort to bring socialism to the English-speaking Caribbean, regionally the Grenadian Revolution stands only after the Haitian Revolution of 1804 and the Cuban Revolution of 1959 in the scope and degree of change brought to political institutions (albeit obviously on a much smaller scale). Over and beyond this significance within the broader sweep of Caribbean history, the People's Revolutionary Government (PRG) also embodies an important effort at bringing about a transition to socialism in a small, underdeveloped country. Although since the end of World War II the locus of revolution has shifted to the Third World, and although there are now over twenty cases of such transitions in Asia, Africa, and Latin America (from Vietnam to Mozambique, from Angola to Nicaragua), relatively few efforts to develop some empirically based generalizations on that experience have been made.[1] What made the Grenadian Revolution and its tragic denouement possible? Were Grenadian events a harbinger of things to come in the Caribbean, or were they unique, the product of a special combination of circumstances unlikely to be replicated elsewhere? Had the revolution reached a dead end by mid–1983, and was the Fort Rupert massacre of 19 October only the sub-product of a social and political process that had exhausted itself? Or rather, was it the case of a successful effort at social and political change that was ultimately aborted because of a failure of statecraft and the unlimited ambition of one man, Bernard Coard?

Over and beyond the specific features of the revolution, the Grenada experience has also raised a number of central theoretical and policy questions that go to the heart of the dilemmas faced by many small developing societies today. To what extent were some of the PRG's criticisms of the Westminster model of parliamentary democracy as applied to the Commonwealth Caribbean valid? Did the various mechanisms of grassroots democracy established by the PRG effectively deepen popular participation in the island's governance? What is the role of the vanguard party in the transition to socialism, and how can any emerging tensions between the party and the mass organizations be creatively harnessed? Which social sectors are likely to support a vanguard party committed to socialism in a society in which an urban working class is almost non-existent?

The Grendadian Case

As the smallest and most densely populated of the Windward Islands, Grenada shares in the legacy of plantation society that is one of the defining features of the Caribbean region. The overwhelming majority of the population is of African descent, reflecting the massive importation of African slaves by British colonies in the seventeenth and eighteenth centuries to work on the sugar estates, which until the mid-nineteenth century provided the core of the island's economic activity. As elsewhere in the West Indies, a small part of the population is also of East Indian and Portuguese descent, the offspring of the indentured labourers from India and Madiera brought in to replace the slave labour lost in the wake of Emancipation.

Like all Caribbean societies, Grenada is an artificial society, in the sense that the social fabric was created anew by the European colonizers after the eradication of the indigenous Carib population. As M. G. Smith observed in his pioneering study *Social Stratification in Grenada,* an important social cleavage separates the Grenadian folk from the elite. While the former tend to be dark skinned, to have relatively little education, and to live in the countryside, the latter tend to be light skinned, to be better educated, and to live in the city — mostly in St. George's.[2] Unlike, say, Mexicans or Nigerians, Grenadians have no traditional culture to fall back on. Theirs is a Creole society, marked both by the imprint of the British colonizer and the African heritage kept alive by the common folk and ultimately defining its identity by the peculiar admixture of both elements in its Caribbean setting. In this, as in much else, Grenada is not too different from the rest of the West Indies. But there are a number of features specific to Grenada. One of them is the legacy of the French presence on the island, reflected in the French patois spoken until some years ago by the peasantry. Another, perhaps more important one is the strong influence of Catholicism; some two-thirds of the population is Catholic.

Grenada is also unique in two additional (and interrelated) aspects. It was among the earliest islands to move away from the cultivation of sugar as the mainstay of the economy. As early as 1870 sugar ceased to be the island's main economic crop, as cocoa, nutmeg, and bananas emerged as the planters' and the farmers' preferred crops. This has allowed Grenada to develop a more diversified economic base than many of the other islands. The inability of many of the larger estates to recruit enough labour after Emancipation also led to the breakup of many of them and the development of a small peasantry, which is perhaps the single most significant element of Grenadian social structure.[3] The rugged terrain, which did not lend itself easily to mechanized agriculture, the relatively high quality of the soil, and the ensuing sharecropping system, or *metayage,* all contributed to the emergence of a rather unique land-tenure pattern in which a relatively small number of estate owners, who controlled a considerable amount of land, co-existed with a large number of peasants owning small and often highly fragmented parcels of land. One result of this is what Singham has referred to as an agroproletariat, a social grouping marked both by the ownership of land and by the need to engage in wage labour.[4]

It is against this background that we have to analyze the emerging pattern of crown politics, the successful challenge to it of Gairyism, and the ultimate displacement of Eric Matthew Gairy by the New Jewel Movement (NJM) in 1979.

The New Jewel Movement Diagnosis

Gairy, of course, was not only instrumental in bringing about universal suffrage to Grenada, he also played a key role in Grenada's gradual constitutional development — to associated statehood in 1967 and to full independence in 1974. The island was the first of the Windward and Leeward islands to accede to full sovereignty. But in the process of augmenting the powers of his office as chief (later prime) minister, Gairy seemed less and less prepared to engage in the power sharing, tolerance for dissent, and respect for the opposition that are supposed to be associated with parliamentary democracy. The former champion of Grenada's estate workers rights clamped down with a heavy hand on the demonstrations of an increasingly radicalized urban petty bourgeoisie and a younger generation of Grenadians. To these people Gairy's earlier triumphs meant little, his eccentricities (like his involvement with UFOs) seemed a national embarrassment, and the stagnation and poverty of the island offered only a dim future.

A number of young Grenadian professionals trained abroad, radicalized by their exposure to the plight of the West Indian communities in Britain and in the United States, and deeply affected by the black power 'February revolution' that took place in Trinidad in 1970, started to organize a variety of groups to challenge Gairy. Maurice Bishop, Kendrick Radix, and the other leading members of Forum, MACE, and MAP quickly moved from the seeming sterility of black power ideology to a grassroots democracy perspective, inspired by such notions as Tanzania's *ujamaa* socialism and economic cooperativism.[5] Despite their interest in a wide variety of Third World currents of social and political thought, the JEWEL boys, as they would later come to be known, had no intention of limiting themselves to sitting around a table in a rum shop spinning theories of revolution. After getting involved in a variety of protest movements from 1970 to 1973, they founded the New Jewel Movement in March 1973 and rapidly started to make a name for themselves as the most active and effective opponents of Gairyism.

A good proof of the down-to-earth approach to politics and how attuned to Grenadian realities the NJM leadership was is the New Jewel Movement Manifesto. Despite isolated digressions into academic jargon, the manifesto provides a vivid listing of the many difficulties faced by Grenada's common folk, including high inflation and unemployment rates, lack of educational facilities, and deficiencies in the health service and the transportation system. It then sets forth an extremely detailed program of social, economic, and political reconstruction of Grenada (going even into such matters as the court dress of lawyers and judges), anticipating many of the measures to be enacted later by the PRG.

It proposes the nationalism of the tourist, banking, and insurance sectors of the economy and ends on a note quite self-consciously modelled after the Communist Manifesto ('People of Grenada, you have nothing to lose but your continued exploitation'), but it is not a socialist program. Rather, it calls for developing Grenada with a much greater emphasis on self-reliance, making appropriate use of Grenada's own human and material resources. On the economic front, it stresses the development of what it calls the new tourism, owned and managed by Grenadians and using local products, as well as the development of the agricultural and fisheries sectors. Politically, its most startling and original proposal is its radical rejection of the existing Westminster system ('it fails to involve the people except for a few seconds once in every five years') and its proposed substitution by an elaborate system of people's assemblies (at the village, parish, and national levels) and a national government based on collective leadership (there would be no premier) elected by the National Assembly.

Implicit in many of the proposed measures is a strong critique of the Grenadian economic system as it had operated until then (as well as its insertion into the world economy). But there is no denunciation of capitalism per se or any effort to identify the underlying reasons for Grenada's poverty, over and beyond the incompetence of the politicians who ruled the country. More than anything, it is a call for action and a blueprint for change, inviting Grenadians to take their destiny into their own hands and to start to define their own, still somewhat blurred, national identity.

In finding their identity and political vocation while studying abroad, young men like Maurice Bishop, Unison Whiteman, and Bernard Coard were hardly alone. Many other West Indian radical politicians in the making underwent the same process in the late sixties and early seventies. What is unique about the NJM group is that they did not remain in the political wilderness, as many of their counterparts in the Eastern Caribbean do to this day. And the reasons for their success in reaching political power a scant six years after the formal founding of the NJM have as much to do with the complex changes Grenadian society underwent from the fifties to the seventies as with the strategy and tactics used by the JEWEL boys.

Sociologically, perhaps one of the most significant phenomena to occur in Grenada from the fifties onward was the gradual but steady expansion of the petty bourgeoisie. Based on the growth of the educational system, as well as on the emergence of tourism in the late fifties as an increasingly important economic activity, the numerically very small middle sectors in Grenadian society, located between the elite and the folk, started to become more and more a force to be reckoned with in Grenadian politics, particularly in and around St. George's. Gairy himself, in expanding the civil service (which he finally managed to get under his control with the advent of associated statehood in 1967), also contributed to the growth of this social class.[6]

The spark that ignited the growing resentment against Gairy in 1970 was a nurses' strike, and it is also indicative of the source of NJM support in the mid-seventies that the only two organizations that actively sympathized with the NJM within the Committee of Twenty-Two (the most important anti-Gairy front) were two teachers' unions, and that the first union actually organized from scratch by the NJM was the Bank Workers Union. Voting data from the 1976 elections and 1984 survey data indicate beyond doubt that support for the NJM (and later the PRG) was considerably higher among the younger, better educated, urban sectors of the population than among the older, poorer, less educated rural dwellers — which had been the bedrock of Gairy's support ever since he successfully defended the rights of estate workers in the early fifties.[7]

And this leads to the basic nature of the appeal exercised by the NJM and the reasons for its political success. For a variety of reasons, Grenadian nationalism had, until the seventies, been an extremely fragile and vulnerable sentiment. As a small island marked by heavy out-migration, Grenadians found themselves pulled in many directions. In addition to being Grenadian citizens, at one point or other they had been part of the British Empire, members of the West Indies Federation, and there was even one election (in 1962) largely fought on the issue of annexation to Trinidad and Tobago ("Go Trinidad"), a step then apparently favoured by a majority of the electorate.

The black power movement, the emergence into nationhood of other West Indian territories in the sixties, and the militancy of the civil rights struggle in the United States all had a strong impact in the Eastern Caribbean, and particularly in Grenada, as more and more West Indians started to look for ways to find and affirm their personal and national identity. Though Gairy could have tried to tap into this burgeoning (albeit still undefined) search for a national identity, he was unable to do so. In fact, he was so reluctant to submit the issue of independence to the people's will that he bypassed the referendum he was supposed to hold on the subject. He argued that the issue of independence had been settled in the 1972 general elections (where he introduced the issue vaguely and at the last minute) and asked the United Kingdom to grant independence without further ado. The way he phrased the whole affair ('Grenada does not have to support independence; independence will support Grenada') accurately reflects his rather uninspiring approach to the issue of national self-affirmation.

The root of the NJM's appeal to this still small but increasingly visible and powerful petty bourgeoisie — the teachers, bank clerks, nurses, high school students, and young professionals — was precisely its ability to tap into this search for a national identity. And the NJM's way of approaching it was just the opposite from the pompous and self-aggrandizing style used by Gairy (with expensive extravaganzas like the Eastern Caribbean Water Festival held in 1975) or his grotesque efforts to convince the United Nations to set up a centre for the observation of unidentified flying objects in Grenada.

If the New Jewel Movement Manifesto started with a detailed inventory of the many unmet needs of Grenadians of all walks of life, it ended with an appeal to build a society in which questions such as Who are we? What is the nature of our condition? Why are we in that condition? would be at the centre of the national agenda. They were the sorts of questions that the Grenada National Party (which had campaigned in 1962 under the banner of annexing Grenada to Trinidad) or Gairy's GULP were simply unable to ask, let alone attempt to answer.

The NJM's Strategy and Tactics

It is only in the context of that powerful nationalist appeal tied to the immediate material needs of the people that the NJM's rapidly growing support can be understood and appreciated. If organizationally the NJM evolved into a vanguard party, programmatically and operationally it remained a highly flexible and undogmatic, nationalist, anti-dictatorial movement. Its appeal cut across all segments of the Grenadian community but struck a particularly responsive chord in the younger generation and among the emerging petty bourgeoisie.

This willingness to challenge Gairyism on all fronts had already become evident before the formal founding of the party. For example, Unison Whiteman and Selwyn Strachan, both of the JEWEL, ran under the banner of the Grenada National Party in the 1972 elections, albeit losing badly. But this flexible approach to the political struggle would soon bloom and come into its own

as Gairy clumsily clamped down on the swelling forces of the opposition to his rule.

From such seemingly minor (but symbolically powerful) issues as fighting for the public's access to a beach surrounded by the estate of an absentee landlord to the very issue of Grenadian independence, the NJM was quick to seize on issues that would command wide public attention. Although supporting Grenadian independence in principle, it strongly opposed and denounced the manner in which Gairy brought independence to Grenada; indeed the very independence celebrations were marred by strikes and demonstrations across the island against what was largely seen as a scheme by Gairy to augment his own powers.

Bishop and his colleagues also proved as adept in the wheeling and dealing with the far more senior leaders of the Grenada National Party as they were at stirring up the crowds at market square. Gearing up for the 1975 general elections, they outmaneuvered former Chief Minister Herbert Blaize in the negotiations for the formation of the Popular Alliance coalition. At the end of the day, the NJM secured three (versus the GNP's two) seats in the Grenadian Parliament. This still left Gairy with an absolute majority but catapulted Bishop into the position of leader of the Opposition.

It was to be neither in the streets nor at York House, however, that the Gairy era would ultimately come to an end. It was in the barracks, in the valley of True Blue, where on 13 March 1979 the armed wing of the NJM overpowered Gairy's army while the Prime Minister was on his way to New York for a United Nations meeting.

And the NJM seizure of power cannot be understood as a Blanquist *coup de main* led by a small group of conspirators. If that had been the case, the enormous outpouring of support that followed Maurice Bishop's radio address announcing the establishment of the PRG would be incomprehensible. The uprising, rather, was simply the culmination of six years of political struggle in which Bishop and his colleagues had effectively managed to generate a considerable amount of support — in marked contrast with the listless and feeble opposition to Gairy exercised by the Grenada National Party. And it was this same flexibility, willingness to try what works (rather than whatever happened to be prescribed by ideology) that characterized the PRG in most of its programs and public policies.

It was in the educational sphere where this flexibility came particularly to the fore, leading to some of the government's most significant achievements. Quite apart from the establishment of free secondary education and the enormous expansion of opportunities for Grenadians to pursue university studies, this also involved a new approach to linguistic policy, enhancing the role of Grenadian Creole, innovative teacher training programmes, and a wide-ranging literacy campaign. Perhaps surprisingly in a government led by a man educated in Catholic schools, no such flexibility obtained in the policy followed toward the established churches. The rather dogmatic approach taken occasionally by the PRG on church-state relations created unnecessary obstacles and difficulties for the government in what is, after all, a profoundly religious society.

Mobilization, Participation, and the Nature of the State

The most far-reaching changes brought about by the PRG were in the political sphere. The very establishment of a new government based on its revolutionary legitimacy rather than on elections was of course the first and most important of these changes. Directed by Prime Minister Maurice Bishop and seconded by Minister of Finance (later Deputy Prime Minister) Bernard Coard, the PRG was formed by a cabinet composed predominantly, though not exclusively, of NJM members. The government also established a new Supreme Court for Grenada and legislated, through cabinet-approved decrees, the people's laws.

The army was also dissolved and a new armed force was established, the People's Revolutionary Army (PRA), led by Commander Hudson Austin and staffed by many close associates of Bernard Coard. In addition, a people's militia was developed, in which civilians were trained to support the PRA in the case of an attack on the island.

The most original of the changes introduced, though, were those related to the new mechanisms of popular participation established at the village and parish level. In keeping with the grassroots democracy notions advanced in the NJM Manifesto in 1973, councils and assemblies were set up. The idea was that people would discuss their needs and aspirations at the community level and then transmit them to the leadership for appropriate action. The zonal and parish councils, open to all members of the community, were, in principle, to meet at least once a month.

As one former PRG cabinet member put it, 'Prior to the revolution, once a year the minister of finance would present the budget in Parliament to fifteen people: there might have been another ten or twenty in the gallery. And that was it. The people have now changed all that. Now people know what a budget is. In every single village, technicians from the ministry would go to make the national presentation of the budget'.[8] And these

were not simple well-rehearsed exercises in public relations but important mechanisms of popular participation, which gave rise to some of the most important public policy initiatives of the PRG:

The concept of the national transportation system, for example, did not originate with the PRG; it came from the people. It was mentioned at one meeting by the participants. The technicians mentioned it at other meetings, and there was a tremendous upsurge of support for the idea; it just caught like fire. We were talking about productivity, and people started to say 'we are being late for work, children are late for schools', etc. We had been to OPEC and received some balance of payments support. We were going to use it for asphalt to repair roads, but decided to buy twenty-six buses from Japan, instead.[9]

As with any innovative political structure, there were problems in the implementation of the village and zonal councils. The fact of the matter is, however, that the experience of the councils should remain as one of the most important experiments in grassroots democracy to have taken place in the Caribbean.

In addition to these participatory mechanisms, a number of mass organizations were also created to mobilize the Grenadian population, most prominently the National Women's Organization (NWO) and the National Youth Organization (NYO). Finally, Grenadian trade unionism also received a strong measure of support from the PRG through a variety of laws that effectively increased the number of unionized workers to some 10,000 by 1983, close to a third of the active labour force.

Rather than framing its politics within the logic and discourse of the Westminster system — as even West Indian governments ostensibly committed to socialism, as the Manley regime in Jamaica (1972–1980) and the Burnham regime in Guyana (1964–1985), have done — the PRG thus framed its political project within a radically different approach, one based on the principles of what Maurice Bishop referred to as 'revolutionary democracy'. As a perceptive Trinidadian commentator has observed: 'In effect, the emphasis placed on the existence of free and fair elections as a measure of democratic freedoms serves to obscure the fact that elections ought to be merely the end of a complicated social process, and that in the Caribbean it is these crucial preconditions which are all too often missing'.[10]

In mobilizing the people and actively involving them in the enormous task of national reconstruction, the PRG managed to start to build those very preconditions and develop that sense of national belonging that had so sorely been missing in the past. As one visiting Barbadian journalist put it on the first anniversary of the revolution:

Every home was also spik and span, rubbish and garbage neatly tucked away, trash removed and the roads cleaner than any I have seen in any other Caribbean island, including our own. Even as one drove off the beaten track, one saw continuing evidence of this enthusiasm and pride in the country.

For those who do not know Grenada, this may not be very important, but for those who have travelled there over the years, the destitution which is still there always had an air of abject helplessness about it which was most depressing. Today, the small and fragile houses of the poor are still evident, but their occupants now convey an air of expectancy, of feeling that better days are coming and that it will indeed be all right in the morning.[11]

The Political Economy of the Transition

In marked contrast with other instances of transition to socialism in the Western Hemisphere, such as in Jamaica and Chile, the economy was not the Achilles' heel of the Grenadian Revolution. In fact, in the summer of 1983, only a few months before the public emergence of the factional struggle between Bishop and Coard, the World Bank and the International Monetary Fund had given their ringing endorsement to the policies followed by the PRG in the economic arena — a far cry from what such organizations would have voiced about the situation in Jamaica in 1980 or in Chile in the winter of 1973.

The relative success of the PRG in putting Grenada's economic house in order while moving toward socialism is particularly remarkable in view of the disastrous state of the public sector it encountered upon coming to power; the openness and vulnerability of the Grenadian economy; its tenure during a period (1979–1983) that started with the second oil shock and was marked by one of the biggest recessions experienced by the industrialized capitalist countries since the 1930s; and the damages suffered by the island's agriculture as a result of Hurricane Allen.

During the second half of the 1970s the Grenadian economy had started to recover somewhat from the serious difficulties it had undergone in the earlier part of the decade. But it was still an economy characterized by low investment rates, high unemployment, inflation, and a per capita income that in real terms was lower in 1979 than in 1970. One major problem was Grenada's extremely low absorptive capacity. As one study put it in 1979, 'Actual development expenditures have fallen far short of the budgeted amount each year largely as a consequence of difficulties in project preparation, implementation and monitoring'.[12]

It was in this context that the PRG attempted to steer a new course. Identifying agriculture, tourism, and fisheries as the three pillars of the island's

economy, the PRG launched an ambitious programme of economic reconstruction. The basic purpose of the programme was to 'shift the distribution of power and resources ... so that the national economy (as opposed to the externally controlled sector) would become the primary source of growth and accumulation'.[13]

Investment increased dramatically, from E.C.$9 million in 1979, to $110 million in 1982, reaching 50.2% of Grenada's gross domestic product, most of it public investment for infrastructural purposes (of which about 40% went to the international airport). Services, particularly in health and education but also in other areas, were drastically improved. Unemployment was reduced from an estimated 50% in 1979 to 15% in 1983. Perhaps most significantly, when compared to the Chilean, Jamaican, and Nicaraguan experiences, these vastly increased spending programmes did not lead to the runaway inflation that has become almost a trademark of other Third World transitions to socialism. From 21.2% in 1980 and 18.8% in 1981, inflation actually declined to 7.8% in 1982 and 6.1% in 1983.

According to the Caribbean Development Bank, the average growth rate of Grenada for 1981–1983 (2.2%) was the third highest of all of the English-speaking Caribbean. There were no shortages of consumer goods in Grenada from 1979 to 1983, either; if anything, shortages that had existed in previous years of such basic staples as rice, for example, ceased to exist with the establishment of the National Market and Import Board (NMIB) established by the PRG. All of this does not mean that there weren't problems or that the PRG's economic policy didn't create difficulties of its own. What it does mean is that, during a particularly difficult period in the international economy, a small, extremely open (and therefore very vulnerable) economy like Grenada's was able to do quite well even as it pressed forth with major changes.

What was the key behind the considerable economic achievements of the PRG? Foreign aid was undoubtedly a vital tool to achieve the government's objectives, but this still begs the question as to what was done to obtain such a considerable amount of external assistance in the first place and, no less important, what lay behind the extremely effective and efficient utilization of such resources.

Three aspects are particularly worth underscoring in this regard. The first is the ability shown by the PRG leadership to identify the main bottleneck hampering the development of the Grenadian economy and to act to remove it with great determination and boldness. The 'can do' attitude that permeated the PRG was nowhere as evident as in its relentless determination to construct the international airport and thus overcome what the World Bank described in 1979 as 'the most limiting single factor in achieving the island's growth possibilities'.[14] Revealingly, the World Bank itself opposed the immediate construction of the airport, arguing that further studies were needed and that construction of the airport had to go hand in hand with expansion of Grenada's hotel capacity. Various international agencies also sought to limit the length of the runway, offering support if it was kept to 7,000 feet — insufficient to receive jumbo jets. None of this sidetracked the PRG's determination to build a full-length international airport.[15]

The second aspect relates to the very tight control that was exercised over public spending. Government agencies had to submit monthly expenditure reports to the Ministry of Finance, where they were checked as to whether they were in line with projected spending. No purchases could be made without a voucher countersigned by the Ministry of Finance. It was this tight fiscal management that allowed the PRG to increase social services and capital expenditures considerably and to get inflation under control. By not giving in to the populist temptation of untrammeled government spending that has been a hallmark of socialist transitions elsewhere, the PRG showed that efficient and successful economic management is by no means incompatible with a commitment to socialism. In fact, as the cases of Chile and Jamaica clearly demonstrate, such management may be becoming more and more a prerequisite for avoiding the failure of such transitions. With slogans such as 'You can only take out what you put in', its emphasis on matters like productivity and output, and its involvement of the people in the discussion of the national budget, the PRG effectively linked the Grenadian people's heightened expectations with their own abilities to make possible a higher standard of living for all.

The third element of the PRG's economic policy that stands out is the acute consciousness among the leadership about the very real limits of the regulatory capacities of the state in peripheral societies. As Maurice Bishop put it in November 1979,

We are not in the least bit interested as a government in attempting to run all sectors of the economy. That would be an impossibility. The massive problems we already have with storage space, with qualified personnel, and that kind of thing in the few areas we have moved into, like the National Commercial Bank and the National Importing Board, shows very clearly to us that it would be a massive nightmare for us if, for example, we were to go and try to sell cloth or rice and saltfish or even operate a Coke factory.[16]

This pragmatism came not by a painful trial and error method but as a result of an examination of

the experience of other developing societies undergoing socialist transitions; and it was applied from the very beginning of the PRG. It resulted in a policy that paid handsome dividends in many areas. Contrary to the advice of visiting Bank of Guyana officers, for example, the PRG never established foreign exchange controls. As a result, hard currency remittances from abroad into Grenada not only never dried up but tripled from E.C.$16 million in 1978 to E.C.$42 million in 1980 and stayed in that range for the duration of the revolution.

International Affairs

Much more radical than the controlled and incremental changes brought about in domestic economic policy by the PRG were those implemented in Grenada's foreign relations. Diplomatic relations with Cuba were quickly established, and a movement toward a relatively close alignment with the Soviet Union as well as with militant Third Worldism in a variety of international fora also took place. This was part of the reason for Washington's unremitting hostility toward the revolution. This seeming mismatch between domestic policies marked, in general, by pragmatism and accommodation and a foreign policy so daring in its defiance of the United States is one of the puzzles about the Grenadian Revolution.

Some writers argue that the basis for this approach can be found in the theory of the non-capitalist path, predicated as it is on anti–imperialist solidarity in ever closer connection with the world socialist system. The strong anti-imperialist posture adopted by the PRG ever since Maurice Bishop's 13 April 1979, 'In nobody's backyard' speech — far from being a mere exercise in rhetoric seemingly divorced from Bishop's conciliatory approach to domestic politics — performed two important functions. On the one hand, it was a tool to mobilize support for the PRG, tapping again into that reservoir of nationalist appeal that had for long been one of the NJM's strong suits. 'I have never felt as much a Grenadian as I do today', was the way noted Grenadian journalist Alister Hughes put it in May 1981, two years into the revolution.[18] On the other hand, the PRG's anti–imperialist foreign policy allowed it to gain access to the sort of international funding for its projects it was interested in, not only from Cuba, but also from countries such as North Korea, Libya, and Iraq, not to mention the Soviet Union itself.

There is little doubt that, in terms of both objectives, the policy paid handsome dividends for quite some time. It also contributed to a steady deterioration in relations between Washington and St.

George's, a deterioration that culminated in the October 1983 invasion of Grenada by U.S. troops.

In the end, perhaps the most striking thing about Grenada's foreign relations was the high price the PRG paid for its strong support of the Soviet Union and how little it got in return from the Soviets (as opposed to the Cubans and other foreign donors). The Soviet Union took almost four years to establish a fully manned embassy in St. George's and provided no major economic aid, although treaties for substantial amounts of military aid were signed in 1983.

Charisma, Class, and Crisis

As Grenadian political scientist Patrick Emmanuel has observed, most West Indian political parties have been 'one-man shows'. But the essential condition for such domination has been the overwhelming personal popularity of the leader, who could use this resource to deal with the threat of 'independent-minded men' within his organization.[19] This is valid from Alexander Bustamante's Jamaican Labour Party to Eric Williams's People's National Movement, from Vere Bird's Antigua Labour Party to Eric Gairy's GULP. Such leaders have fallen into one of two categories: they have been either trade union organizers who have risen up through the ranks, using their trade union base to build up their political following (and their political party), or middle-class professionals (often lawyers or scholars) trained abroad who at some point return to their homeland and are able to translate their educational credentials and eloquence into considerable political capital — 'middle-class heroes', as Singham put it. Eric Gairy and Maurice Bishop clearly embody these two very different types of leaders. But whereas Gairy found it difficult to reach beyond his fundamentally rural trade union base and exercise a genuine national appeal, Bishop's charisma was such that it allowed him to reach Grenadians from all backgrounds and social classes. Even people who had become hostile to the revolution retained their faith in Bishop's leadership.

Although much ink has been spilled on the internal crisis of the revolution and the increasingly personalized conflict between Bernard Coard and Maurice Bishop, most of it has tended to focus on the ideological dimensions of this conflict rather than on its psychological roots. Using psychoanalytic tools, and going beyond the relatively static analysis that has emerged from the reductionist casting of Coard and Bishop as two different political 'types' bound to come into conflict with each other, it is necessary to explore in some depth the personal and political background of the *dramatis personae* in the revolution's final crisis. This way, by the interweaving of Bishop's and Coard's psychological profiles with a detailed examination of their behaviour during the crisis emerges a new interpretation of the revolution's abortion.

Abbreviations

EC:	Eastern Caribbean
GULP:	Grenada United Labour Party
MACE:	Movement for the Advancement of Community Effort
MAP:	Movement of the Assemblies of the People
NJM:	New Jewel Movement
OPEC:	Organization of Petroleum Exporting Countries
PRG:	Peoples Revolutionary Government

Notes

1. Among the very few books dealing with the subject systematically is Richard R. Fagen, Carmen Diana Deere, and Joe Luis Caraggio, eds., *Transition and Development: Problems of Third World Socialism* (New York: Monthly Review Press, 1986).
2. See M. G. Smith, *Social Stratification in Grenada* (Berkeley: University of California Press, 1965).
3. See George I. Brizan, *The Grenadian Peasantry and Social Revolution 1931–1951,* ISER Working Paper 21 (Mona, Jamaica: University of the West Indies, 1974); and John Brierly, *Small Farming in Grenada, W.I.* (Manitoba: University of Manitoba Press, 1974).
4. See Archie W. Singham, *The Hero and the Crowd in a Colonial Polity* (New Haven: Yale University Press, 1968).
5. The only person quoted by name in the long New Jewel Movement Manifesto is Julius Nyerere.
6. Whereas in 1946 there were only 75 secondary school students in Grenada, this number had reached 4,967 by 1970. The Jacobses estimate that in the late sixties there were 500 Grenadians enrolled at Universities abroad. Tourism expanded steadily through the sixties and early seventies; tourist arrivals peaked at 37,933 in 1973 and dropped sharply after independence. See R. Jacobs and I. Jacobs, *Grenada: The Route to Revolution* (Havana: Casa de las Americas, 1980), p. 94.
7. The three NJM candidates elected on the ticket of the Popular Alliance in 1976 were elected in the St. George's area — Bernard Coard, Unison Whiteman, and Maurice Bishop. For the 1984 survey data, see Patrick Emmanuel, Farley Brathwaite, and Eudine Barriteau, *Political Change and Public Opinion in Grenada 1979–1984,* ISER Occasional Paper 19, (Cave Hill, Barbados: University of the West Indies, 1986).
8. Personal interview with Lyden Ramdhanny, PRG deputy minister of finance and minister of tourism, Grenville, 30 Aug. 1987.
9. *Ibid.*
10. Allan Harris, 'The Road to Coup d'Etat', *Trinidad Guardian,* 8 Apr. 1979.
11. Harold Hoyte, 'The Popular Revolutionary Government', the *Nation* (Barbados), 19 Mar. 1980.
12. World Bank, 'Current Economic Position and Prospects of Grenada', Report 2439–GRD, 19 Apr. 1979.

13. Paget Henry, 'Grenada and the Theory of Peripheral Transformation', paper delivered at the Ninth Annual Conference of the Caribbean Studies Association, St. Kitts, 30 May–2 June 1984.

14. World Bank, 'Current Economic Position'.

15. Interview with Ramdhanny.

16. Maurice Bishop, the *Nation* (Barbados), 21 Nov. 1979.

17. Bernard Coard, statement from the dock, in Friends for Jamaica, 'The Side You Haven't Heard: The Maurice Bishop Murder Trial' (New York: mimeo, 1987), p. 11.

18. Comments made to the author, May 1981, Barbados.

19. P. Emmanuel, *Crown Colony Politics in Grenada, 1917–1951* (ISER: Occasional Paper 7; U.W.I., Cave Hill, Barbados, 1978).

Pain and Protest: The 1984 Anti-IMF Revolt in the Dominican Republic

James Ferguson

On Monday 23 April 1984 Santo Domingo erupted. Following the relative tranquility of the Easter weekend, a sudden wave of popular protest and fury shook the capital. Its immediate cause was a series of dramatic price rises, announced by the government the previous Thursday and introduced that morning in the country's shops. Medicines went up by 200%; rice, milk and cooking oil all doubled in price.

In the poverty-stricken *barrio* of Capotillo, 100 neighbourhood organizations had agreed a common programme of demands to President Jorge Blanco and the PRD government. They wanted the withdrawal of the price increases, a minimum monthly salary of 200 *pesos,* the provision of electricity and water to Capotillo residents and the abrogation of the agreement recently signed between the Dominican government and the International Monetary Fund. The organizers planned a twelve-hour strike, and shops, businesses and transport duly closed down altogether. As crowds gathered on the streets to demonstrate against the price rises the military went into action with batons and tear gas. The crowds fought back, erecting burning barricades and looting the local INESPRE distribution centre.

As riots spread throughout the capital and thirty other towns and villages, the troops opened fire. By 25 April, 112 Dominican civilians were dead (of whom 27 were women and 5 children), 500 more were wounded and 5,000 were under arrest. Of the dead and wounded nearly all were shot by the security forces. That day President Jorge Blanco publicly praised the military for its efforts.

The armed forces and the National Police have given an example of restraint [*ecuanimidad*], displaying their high degree of professionalism, elevated human feeling and respect for life . . . they have kept their reactions within the limits of reasonable prudence and displayed excellent training.

The riots of April 1984 finally destroyed the already flagging popularity of the PRD government and brought to the world's attention the social cost of the so-called stabilization programmes which the IMF imposes upon indebted Third World countries. They also galvanized the Dominican popular movement which since the early 1980s has posed the most fundamental challenge to the country's old political order.

Condemned to Debt

By early 1983 the Dominican economy had reached the point of no return. Like almost every other country in Latin America, it was hopelessly in debt and unable to meet repayment obligations on existing loans. From a figure of US$600 million in 1973 the external debt had escalated to US$2,400 million ten years later. The debt crisis was in many ways the hangover which followed the euphoria of the short-lived 'Dominican miracle'. During the boom years of the early 1970s credit had been all too easily available. Encouraged by high commodity prices and a buoyant US economy, domestic businesses borrowed freely from the state-controlled Central Bank, often at subsidized rates. The Central Bank, in return, borrowed from US and European banks keen to recycle the so-called 'petrodollars' which the 1973–4 oil price rise had brought into the world banking system. Partly buffered against the first oil shock by the high sugar price of 1974 and foreign investment, the Dominican economy, with its rapid industrialization and construction boom, grew dramatically — but on credit.

The Balaguer government of 1966–78 was profligate, pushing up the debt from US$158 million in 1966 to US$1,100 million in 1977. Not only did it borrow heavily to complete its ambitious public works programme, but it also took large amounts of food from the US on credit which it distributed on subsidized terms to the poorest social sectors while at the same time holding down their wages. Between 1973 and 1983, over US$358 million of food was imported on mostly 20–year repayment

566

schedules (Plant 1987:142). At the same time, Balaguer allowed the decentralized state corporations to contract their own loans from any available source. The economic elite did well out of these policies. Middle-class Santo Domingo was largely built during this period, while the elite spirited US$368 million out of the country and deposited it in private bank accounts abroad.

By the mid–1970s, the miracle was already running out of steam. Commodity prices dropped after the high point of 1974, the first oil price rise began to be felt in the state-sector industries and Balaguer's policy of holding down wages depressed those industries which catered to the domestic market. Meanwhile, the foreign companies which invested so spectacularly in the early 1970s withdrew their profits as the boom subsided. Between 1975 and 1978 for every dollar of new foreign investment, US$1.60 left the Dominican Republic as repatriated profit.

The PRD government which took power in 1978 inherited a sick economy. It also ran into a series of external shocks which exacerbated the crisis. World market prices for sugar, coffee and nickel were all in decline. Then, in August 1979, Hurricane David destroyed large areas of the Dominican Republic, killing some 1,000 people and causing approximately US$1,000 million in damage. It came one month after the second worldwide rise in oil prices which inflated the country's import bill and precipitated recession in the US and a resulting rise in world interest rates. As exports dropped and interest rates rose, debt servicing climbed from US$87 million in 1978 to US$250 million in 1982. That year, the world sugar price stood at a mere five cents per pound, as opposed to 76 cents per pound in 1975.

Squeezed by external forces, the Guzman administration tried to honour its election pledge to reduce unemployment by resorting to the time-honoured strategy of massive public-sector recruitment. Within two years it created 60,000 jobs, mostly for PRD loyalists. Guzman also raised the minimum wage and decreed a ten per cent wage rise to public-sector workers, the first for several years. To increase its popularity further, the PRD government encouraged the CDE and INESPRE to provide the urban poor with cheap electricity and subsidized food. To finance these measures, Guzman was forced to borrow more and to print money, thereby fuelling inflation.

Following Guzman's suicide in July 1982, Jorge Blanco took office for a further four-year PRD term and found the state coffers empty. The balance of payments deficit for that year stood at US$560 million in overdue debt repayments. The new PRD government promised an 'economic democracy'; it introduced a programme of moderate tax increases and banned some luxury imports to preserve hard currency. But confidence in the PRD's economic management was fading fast. Guzman's nationalization of a single US enterprise, the Rosario Dominicano goldmine, in 1979 had already disturbed US investors. The *peso*, although officially worth one dollar, was losing its value as Dominicans preferred to put their trust in dollars, and by 1982 the dollar had risen to 1.35 *pesos* on the parallel market.

Jorge Blanco had to face the inevitable. Only an agreement with the IMF would give the Dominican government access to new funds. But these new funds were only available at a heavy social cost.

The IMF

On 21 January 1983 the PRD administration reached agreement with the IMF on a three-year extended loan facility, worth US$466 million. The first US$195.8 million was to be made available that year, with the next installment to be renegotiated the following January. The agreement's importance to the Dominican government went beyond the actual money involved, since the IMF's seal of approval for the government's policies was a precondition for renegotiating existing debts and gaining access to fresh loans. The conditions attached to the IMF's support, however, were stringent. As elsewhere in the Third World, the multilateral agency insisted on a sweeping 'stabilization' programme, aiming to cut government spending and increase export earnings as a way of paying back the debt. In the first year the IMF insisted that the government honour overdue debt repayments, reduce Central Bank loans to the public sector, freeze state-sector salaries and remove most import restrictions. Most importantly, it stipulated that the Dominican *peso* — which since 1947 had been officially fixed at par with the dollar — should be devalued by officially recognizing the existing parallel or black market exchange rate and creating a single rate based on the *peso*'s real value.

Devaluation of the *peso* involved more than a psychological blow to Dominican national pride. It meant that the price of imports, held down by an artificially high *peso,* would rise dramatically, while exports would become much more competitive. For the PRD government, it was a choice between hurting domestic consumers and boosting exports by devaluation or protecting domestic consumption and stifling exports by maintaining an overvalued *peso.* The IMF favoured the former as a way of redressing the balance of payments imbalance; the government realized, however, that to raise the price of imported goods too steeply would spell political disaster. This was especially the case since so many basic items — food, oil, medicines — are imported into the Dominican Republic.

Jorge Blanco tried to compromise. The government maintained dollar-*peso* parity for imports of oil and medicines (thereby effectively subsidizing these items) but allowed basic foods to rise according to free-market pressures. Protests broke out at once, as milk, eggs, wheat and other staples rose in price. The IMF, however, was not satisfied, and at the end of the first year insisted that the parallel exchange rate would have to be eliminated altogether as a precondition for receiving the second installment. In the meantime, it refused to pay any more to the Dominican Republic and effectively blocked loans and grants from other quarters.

The PRD government now blamed the IMF for all its economic woes and appealed in an open letter to President Reagan to intercede on its behalf. Reagan advised the Dominicans to bow to the IMF's demands and USAID froze the 1984 US$80 million aid package until this was done. After a series of desperate meetings, Jorge Blanco was forced to capitulate. On 19 April he announced that food and medicine prices would be liberalized. Four days later the riots began. Far from signalling the end of the IMF 'stabilization' programme, the 1984 unrest was followed by further, more sweeping economic reforms. By mid–1985, after yet another package of austerity measures, the *peso* was floating at a market rate of 3.30 to the dollar, with all imports being paid for at that rate. The IMF had also forced Jorge Blanco to reduce the government subsidy on imported oil, thereby passing on price increases to consumers. By the beginning of 1985, food prices had already increased by an average of 50 to 100% over the previous year. As a result, *Caribbean Insight* reported in June 1985, poor families in Santo Domingo could no longer afford meat, milk or even plantains — normally a cheap Caribbean staple.

Moreover, as it decreed price rises, the government systematically held down wages and repressed popular protest. In February 1985 the government responded to protests and a general strike by arresting hundreds of trade unionists and shooting four demonstrators. Armed soldiers surrounded the house of Juan Bosch.

Despite the enormous cost to poor Dominicans, it is debatable whether the IMF-approved policies really improved the Dominican economy. Certain sectors certainly profited handsomely from the devaluation, most notably foreign and domestic entrepreneurs with interests in export-led industries and tourism. For them, the devaluation meant dramatically reduced labour costs in dollar terms and a hugh increase in their *peso* earnings from exports abroad. But of the ailing state-sector industries such as sugar, power and basic foods, the austerity programme was disastrous, exposing them to sudden price rises in imported fuel and machinery. The outcome, predictably, was inflation — from 4.8% in 1983 to 37.5% in 1985. Between 1980 and 1985 the real value of the minimum wage fell by 20%. As Deere *et al* (1990:43) point out:

rather than the stability promised by IMF technicians, the Dominican Republic has seen increased inflation and unemployment and negative GDP growth rates. Measured unemployment increased from 21% in 1981 to 27% in 1985. Even though foreign investment in the export-processing zones boomed in the 1980s, gross domestic investment was negative between 1980 and 1985, recovering only in 1986. The main accomplishment of this austerity programme was that the Dominican Republic was able to meet its debt-servicing commitments — $571 million, amounting to 76% of export earnings, was repaid in 1985 — and the country's external debt was rescheduled thanks to the 'good offices' of the IMF.

The Crisis Continues

The IMF played a large part in the PRD's electoral defeat of 1986 and in the return of Joaquín Balaguer. Balaguer had witnessed what the IMF had done to the PRD's popularity and at first distanced himself from dealings with the agency. In any case, his initial economic plans were hardly compatible with the IMF prescription of budgetary restrain and austerity. Instead, Balaguer proposed to revitalize the economy through a massive programme of public works, aimed at creating jobs and boosting related economic sectors. In 1988 and 1989, the Balaguer regime spent more in capital expenditure (in other words, the building programme) than on current expenditure such as salaries. As a result, wages were further cut back, while imports related to the construction boom forced up inflation. In 1989 inflation stood at 45%; in 1990 it approached 100% before recessionary policies forced it down again.

In 1990 Balaguer adopted a radically different economic approach, cutting back public spending and capital investment by almost 50%. The attempt to stop inflation appeared to have succeeded by the end of 1991, when the rate fell from 100% to single figures. But this was achieved at the cost of a severe recession, with GDP falling by 5.1% in 1990 and a forecast 5% again in 1991. The construction industry which had boomed in the previous four years was particularly badly hit, with widescale job losses.

The *peso*, meanwhile, steadily lost its value, slipping from the official rate of 3.30 to the dollar in 1985 to a parallel market rate of 7.90 in June 1988. In August the government forcibly closed down the private *casas de cambio* and insisted that all foreign exchange transactions be conducted through commercial banks under Central Bank supervision at a single 6.35 rate. The pressure to devalue further and a booming black market took *peso* to 10.20 per dollar in 1990 and 12.67 by the end of 1991.

Nor did the Dominican debt crisis improve with Balaguer's return. Although Jorge Blanco's austerity programme had persuaded commercial banks to reschedule US$765 million of debt in 1986, by early 1987 the debt had risen to US$4,200 million. In 1990, the US embassy in Santo Domingo reported that the Dominican government had interest arrears of more than US$700 million and owed a total sum equivalent to 75% of GDP. Of this, it owed 22% to commercial banks, 34% to the so-called Paris Club of developed country government leaders, 15% to other bilateral lenders (chiefly Mexico and Venezuela for oil supplies), 26% to international institutions (the IMF, World Bank, IADB) and 3% to short-term suppliers.

Another agreement with the IMF seemed increasingly inevitable, despite Balaguer's repeated refusals to follow the PRD's example. After several years of rumour and counter-rumour, Balaguer finally announced in June 1991 that the IMF would provide an 18–month standby facility of US$113 million. More importantly, the pact provided for the renegotiation of US$926 million in debt to the Paris Club. The IMF's conditions were as follows: market-led adjustment of the dollar-*peso* exchange rate, the payment of debt arrears, an end to subsidies to state corporations and the elimination of price controls. The agreement signalled an important change in Balaguer's attitude towards the debt problem, and the government began to catch up with the payment of arrears. Again it was a recipe that would do most harm to the poor.

Growing Poverty

Inflation, devaluation and tough income policies have made the Dominican poor much poorer in the course of the 1980s. The Central Bank estimates that in that decade the real value of average wages fell by 32.5%. In October 1989, for example, the minimum monthly salary was established at 650 *pesos.* At the prevailing dollar exchange rate of 6.28 *pesos,* this was worth US$103.50. Yet although the minimum wage was raised in September 1990 to 1,040 *pesos,* devaluation had reduced

the *peso* to 10.20 to the dollar, giving a real monthly salary of only US$101.96. According to the Economic Research Centre, 57% of Dominicans now live in poverty, up from 47% in 1984, while 30% live in absolute poverty, compared to 16% in 1984. The gap between rich and poor has also widened; in 1991 20% of households accounted for 61% of income, while the poorest 20% shared less than 3%.

Fiscal policy particularly benefits the wealthy and hurts the poor. Income tax is extremely low and is often simply avoided by the rich through political favouritism, special exemptions and fraud. Excise tax on alcoholic beverages actually raises more revenue than total national income tax (Cuddington and Asilis 1990:349). The main source of revenue, however, is import and export taxes. The former push up the price of many imported staple foods and domestic goods, while the latter take a large cut from the income of small peasant producers who cultivate such export crops as coffee, tobacco and cocoa. The multinational export industries which operate outside the IFZs, however, rarely pay any tax whatsoever, enjoying exemptions from both import and export taxation. Attempts to introduce a redistributive system of income and property taxation have met with predictable hostility from the economic elite. Juan Bosch's proposals for moderate fiscal reform played an important role in his downfall.

The government's recurring fiscal deficit, caused largely by inadequate tax collection, as well as the debt crisis, means that social services, theoretically provided by right in the Dominican Constitution, are increasingly under strain. Spending on education, for instance, fell from 13.3% of the government budget in 1983 to 6.7% in 1988. This halving of resources means larger classes, fewer qualified teachers, dilapidated buildings and massive levels of non-attendance among children from poor families. An estimated 80% of teachers receive less than the national minimum wage. Although education is nominally free and compulsory for all children between seven and 14, it is estimated that 66% of children attending primary school do not complete their education. With a rapidly rising birthrate (official government figures suggest that 39% of the population is under 15), the crisis in education is doing long-term damage to the country's future. But for the part played by various Church organizations in teaching at all levels, the situation would be even worse. Meanwhile, private establishments cater for the children of the wealthy in Santo Domingo, preparing them for training at North American universities.

Health services, which underwent considerable expansion and improvement in the 1960s and

1970s are also chronically under-resourced and inadequate. Preventable illnesses such as tuberculosis and typhoid, spread through poor sanitation, polluted water and substandard housing, have begun to increase in the late 1980s and early 1990s, with significant outbreaks of typhoid in the Santo Domingo slum area of La Ciénaga ('the swamp') in the summers of 1990 and 1991. In the second epidemic an estimated 30 children died. Public hospitals lack the most basic drugs and equipment, while continual power cuts add to the difficulties of providing treatment. Vaccination programmes are inadequate; in 1991 only 51% of children under the age of one were vaccinated against preventable diseases. Like teachers, medical staff are underpaid, leading to massive emigration among qualified doctors and nurses and general demoralization. In the first part of 1991, medical workers were among the most militant in their opposition to Balaguer's austerity policies. In August, 7,000 doctors finally ended a 12–week strike after the government agreed to raise their salaries by 50%.

Despite the seemingly endless construction activity around Santo Domingo, most Dominicans face poor housing conditions and basic services. In 1989, for instance, 63% of the population had no access to electricity. According to the daily newspaper, *Listín Diario,* in 1990 seven out of ten families had no sanitary facilities in their homes; eight out of ten had no piped water, while 40% of water consumed was believed polluted. According to UNICEF, almost 60,000 Dominican children live permanently on the streets. Refuse collection in many urban areas is almost non-existent, forcing people to dump rubbish in populated areas, increasing the risk of disease. Even the elegant middle-class districts of Santo Domingo are blighted by foul-smelling heaps of rubbish left uncollected in the streets.

The Popular Movement

In the shantytown *barrio* of La Ciénaga the shacks of wood and corrugated iron tumble down to the dirty water of the Ozama river. When it rains and the river rises, houses are flooded or even swept away. Because there is no refuse collection,people have thrown their rubbish into gulleys and pathways. A damaged wall in the *barrio*'s main drainage channel has made the problem worse, threatening the inhabitants with sudden flooding when tropical storms send torrents of water down the steep hillside.

With the financial help of international aid agencies, the Neighbourhood Rights Defence Committee (COPADEBA) is reconstructing the broken wall. Local people do the work. At the same time, COPADEBA is setting up a number of 'popular shops' in the most deprived urban areas, where basic foods will be bought in bulk and sold at no profit to local people. But the organization's main task is to campaign against the forced eviction of slum dwellers who stand in the way of the Balaguer government's 'beautification' scheme.

Founded in 1979 as a response to the power of large landowners in the growing slum areas, COPADEBA is now the biggest popular organization in Santo Domingo. Its roots lie within the radical Catholic Church, but its rank-and-file membership is overwhelmingly made up of ordinary inhabitants of the slum districts. A series of local committees, regularly elected, sends delegates to a regional committee which coordinates policy and action. An estimated 87% of COPADEBA's membership is made up of women.

The Dominican popular movement, like its equivalent in other Latin American countries, grew in strength due to the economic crisis of the 1980s and the resulting deterioration in social conditions. It also reflects the same region-wide disenchantment with traditional party politics as a means of achieving concrete improvements in everyday living conditions. Through their experience of the corruption, clientelism and incompetence attached to the party political system, many Dominicans are alienated from the electoral process and expect little from politicians. As a result, popular protest often takes alternative forms, even though political parties attempt to harness such protest to their own objectives.

It was the PRD governments of 1978–86 and their relative liberalization of Dominican society which allowed political activity, and the popular organizations, to grow more freely after the repression of the 1966–78 Balaguer regime. During that period there had been influential organizations such as mothers' clubs and youth and sports' associations, but their militancy had been much curtailed by the persecution of political activists. When the PRD came to power in 1978, however, as during the ephemeral Bosch presidency, trade unions, peasant groups, Church-led organizations, student bodies, left-wing parties and neighbourhood committees proliferated. The trade union movement, in particular, experienced a new sense of freedom after the coercion and restrictive legislation of the Balaguer years. New unions and confederations appeared, while the political parties, the PRD, the PLD, the Communist Party and far-left groups struggled for influence within them. At the same time, the schism between the highly conservative hierarchy of the Dominican Catholic Church and its radical grassroots activists widened. In   slum   districts   and   impoverished   rural backwaters, a new generation of priests was instrumental in forming *comunidades de base* (base communities) which combined liberation theology with practical economic development projects.

From these various currents within Dominican society emerged a heterogeneous popular movement. To some extent, it owed its existence, character and strategies to the weaknesses of other organizations. The trade unions, for example, were hopelessly fragmented and open to political cooption; they also represented a small percentage of Dominican workers (today only 12% of the workforce is unionized) and had neither the strength nor resources to carry out effective industrial action. Left-wing parties, with their tendency towards sectarian divisions and splits, also failed to create a credible opposition to the main parties.

More importantly, the popular movement was, and is, made up primarily of people traditionally excluded from conventional political organizations: women, youth, the unemployed, the marginalized workers of the so-called informal sector. These workers, who earn a living as domestic servants, street sellers or in thousands of small workshops and small businesses, belong to no trade union and may have little day-to-day contact with the established political parties. The movement has no single national leadership or structure (although attempts have been made to create these), but is based on communities and neighbourhoods. Its objectives are consequently local in form and concrete: access to piped water or electricity, the construction of a school or medical clinic, the creation of a communal credit system or neighbourhood shop.

The Santo Domingo-based research centre, CEDEE, records and analyses the actions undertaken by the popular movement and its different objectives on a six–monthly basis. Between January and June 1990, for instance, CEDEE monitored 102 different actions. Of these 20 were in support of increased wages, 20 for land titles, nine for improvements to local health services and nine for the provision of housing. The rest covered such issues as increased flour prices, a community made homeless by a mining scheme and general working conditions.

Objectives such as these invariably bring popular organizations into conflict with the state. Sometimes, popular pressure can bring results, especially around election time when political parties are more inclined to listen to their potential voters. But more often than not, demands for improved social services are ignored. The traditional strategy of the popular movement, the neighbourhood strike, often leads to physical confrontation with the police and other security forces as protestors try to block roads in order to bring a neighbourhood literally to a standstill. But over the years, organizers of such strikes have grown adept at avoiding head-on clashes with the police. Coordination between different neighbourhoods and regions also means that the security forces are faced with many simultaneous demonstrations. According to CEDEE, the range of popular actions includes local stoppages, workplace strikes, land seizures, demonstrations, pickets and the occupation of local government buildings.

The IMF riots of 1984 marked the areas where the popular movement was to be most active in the following years. The most militant organizations have grown up in slum areas of Santo Domingo such as Capotillo and La Ciénaga and in other cities such as San Pedro Macorís and Santiago. These are the urban districts which have grown disproportionately through migration from the countryside since the 1960s. As a result, they suffer a critical shortage of basic services and amenities. Since 1984, these and other districts have witnessed a succession of actions in support of specific local demands.

In the rural areas there is less of a tradition of militancy, although a strong sense of community solidarity often exists. This has led sociologists to contrast urban unrest with the *probeza tranquila* (peaceful poverty) of the countryside. Yet, the late 1970s witnessed an increase in peasant organization and activity, particularly centred around the fight for agrarian reform. In 1979 the Independent Peasant Movement (MCI) was founded, which by 1985 claimed a membership of 75,000. Radical in its campaigns for land redistribution and improved prices and services, the MCI has also raised more general political issues such as the debt crisis and the government's relationship with the IMF.

Beyond local strikes, demonstrations and land occupations, the popular organizations have regularly come together to carry out nationwide protests. In March 1988, for instance, the National Conference of Popular Organizations, a national network of local groups, called for a 48–hour general strike in protest at food price rises. The strike was only partly successful and was abandoned after one day. In June 1989, however, a better organized 48–hour strike, supported by 307 trade union and popular groups, completely stopped all activities in the country. Its demands, ignored by the Balaguer government, were explicitly national and political: an increased minimum wage, an end to debt repayments and specific economic and agrarian reforms.

The 'New Actors'

The popular organizations have succeeded because they are different from the established political parties. Whereas these are hierarchial, authoritarian and male-dominated, the popular movement is characterized by democratic participation and the widescale involvement of women. The National Confederation of Peasant Women (CONA-MUCA), for example, has a membership of 8,000 drawn from 21 regional federations. It works alongside the MCI, but at the same time retains its independence from what it sees as a machismo-dominated organization. A survey of women's participation in Santo Domingo in 1989 revealed that 17 intermediate organizations and 39 base groups were exclusively involved with women's popular education and action (Ianni 1990:88). For many women the popular organizations offer a way to address the problems they encounter on a daily basis.

But this emphasis on local problems has brought criticism, notably from the traditional left-wing parties, that the popular organizations have no coherent long-term strategy. Critics have also accused *barrio* organizations of relieving the state of its social responsibilities, of establishing a parallel structure of social services which replaces what the state fails to provide. When political activists have tried to take over the popular organizations there has been considerable friction. After the spectacular militancy of 1984, for instance, a series of Popular Struggle Committees (CLPs) were established in order to coordinate protest action nationally. Attempts by political groups to take control of the CLPs led to disagreements and splits, with the formation of rival and parallel organizations. In late 1991 there were two main coordinating bodies: the CLPs and the more powerful Collective of Popular Organizations (COP). The COP led a number of local disputes in 1991 and organized a two-day national strike in July.

The popular movement is capable of mobilizing large numbers of Dominicans to protest against government policy. However, it seems incapable of sustaining a united front and is prone to schisms and splits. Its very diversity and spontaneity work against a long-term political programme, while attempts to forge such a programme lead to divisions and leadership crises. As the sociologist Vanna Ianni (1990:91) concludes:

The mass of the poor is not just the sum total of millions of isolated, atomized, alienated individuals. Instead, a dense network of interrelations binds together their daily lives; it unites and mixes kinship relationships with those between neighbours, work relationships with those built on common interests. Primary loyalties are interwoven with ties of mutual aid and become mixed up with the relations connected with various forms of *asociacionismo*. Neighbourhood committees, base Christian communities, housewives' committees, cultural and religious

groups, sport clubs, parents' and school associations, environmental groups and, at an intermediate level, a plethora of different organizations and institutions feed the permanent ebb and flow of interrelationships in town and countryside.

This is what determines popular feelings and perceptions; this network collects experiences and lived realities, links people's expectations and makes sense of their anxieties, fears and hopes. The unfolding of this web of interrelationships explains how the crisis of April 1984 came about and the events which followed. It also explains the repeated and deep difficulties which beset attempts to establish coordination of the different organizations, either at a national level or throughout the capital.

The central paradox of the popular movement is that it wields enormous political power but has so far been unwilling and unable to use that power within the established political system. It has no electoral ambitions, nor does it envisage a revolutionary seizure of power. Instead, it articulates the daily needs and aspirations of those who have been most clearly failed by the political system.

Conscious of these self-imposed limitations, some organizations within the popular movement have tried to formulate an explicitly political programme which goes beyond short-term single issues. The Research Group for Community Action (GRIPAC), for example, published a pamphlet in 1990 which called for the formation of a 'political, social and popular front'. According to GRIPAC:

As regards its *programme*, the political, social and popular front must take up those demands which have not yet been met in the last 499 years. Among these we can emphasize:

1. An end to the government's current economic policy and the resignation of Balaguer.
2. An increase in democracy, through political, constitutional, institutional, economic and social reforms.
3. The promotion of our cultural identity against foreign penetration.
4. The struggle for full national sovereignty and independence.
5. A coherent policy of national development which protects the world's environment.
6. The non-payment of the external debt rejecting the IMF's stabilization policies and supporting the establishment of a new international economic order.
7. A sovereign foreign policy which, recognizing the right of peoples to self-determination, promotes solidarity and integration in the Caribbean, Latin America, and among the oppressed in all parts of the world.
8. The establishment of a democratic and popular government (GRIPAC 1990:21–2).

Alongside the organizations of the *barrios* and rural districts, professional associations, representing workers in the field of education, medicine, law and science, have also emerged in protest at declining social conditions. These qualified, middle-class professionals have been hit both by public-sector wage austerity and by spending cuts in schools, universities and hospitals. As a result, organizations such as the Dominican Medical Association (AMD) and the Dominican Teachers' Association (ADP) have come into bitter conflict with the government. The ADP, for instance, claiming that most state school teachers were earning only 550 *pesos* (US$44) per month, went on strike for three months in the summer of 1991. This action took place at the same time as doctors and nurses operated a go-slow in public hospitals.

The Dominican trade union movement, traditionally weak and divided, also underwent a process of revitalization in the course of 1991. In May of that year, unions affiliated to the PLD, PRD and left-wing parties came together to form the United Confederation of Workers (CUT). Although still numerically weak, the CUT nevertheless marked a new departure for the Dominican labour movement. Its first confrontation with the Balaguer government came in July 1991, when it called a three-day general strike to demand a doubling of the minimum wage. The strike was abandoned on the second day, however, despite support from the two main opposition parties.

The almost permanent series of strikes against government economic policy produced only isolated concessions during the course of 1991. The new agreement with the IMF steered the Balaguer administration away from the reflationary policies it had pursued from 1986 onwards and towards further cuts in public spending. This could only result in continued conflict with state-sector workers.

Beyond the Lighthouse

The year 1992 marks a watershed for the Dominican Republic. Using the Colombus quincentennial as a pretext for a massive public relations campaign, the country is seeking to project an international image as a stable democracy with thriving new industries and investment potential.

1992 also sees the creation of the Single European Market, and the Dominican government is hoping that its membership of the Lomé Convention will allow it to diversify exports away from over-dependence on the US. Speaking in Santo Domingo in October 1991, the EEC representative predicted that the Dominican Republic could become a bridge for trade between Europe and the Americas, since it enjoys the preferential access accorded by both Lomé and the Caribbean Basin Initiative. As moves towards greater Caribbean integration and cooperation gradually materialize, the country has the opportunity to lessen its historic isolation from the non-Spanish speaking Caribbean. Yet, relations with Haiti remain a stumbling-block to its acceptance into the non-Spanish Caribbean community and full membership of CARICOM.

The year is likely to be a turning-point in another sense as the Balaguer era draws to a close. Already the struggle for succession is underway within the ruling party, while the PRD believes itself ready to return to power after years of marginalization. The popular movement will play a central role in the process of post-Balaguer political change, even if the precise form it takes remains unpredictable. As long as the poor of the *barrios* and countryside remain excluded from the political system, the future will be one of continued conflict and economic decline. If, on the other hand, a more participatory political culture evolves, escaping from the traditions of *caudillos* and clientilism, a generation of grassroots activists and organizers can offer the impetus for real change.

Observers and participants alike are undecided as to how the popular movement can best influence the course of political change. Some argue that the movement should continue to act primarily as a pressure group on the government, pushing for specific reforms to the benefit of the poor. Others, however, envisage a more direct role for the popular movement, encompassing participation in some form of broad based government. Most are agreed that the movement's most significant contribution to Dominican politics lies in its sense of grassroots democracy, divorced from the cynicism of the conventional party system.

The Dominican Republic has little experience of democracy. The ephemeral Bosch presidency of 1963, marred by indecision and uncertainty, was the closest approximation to a democratic regime in the country's history. In the thirty years since the end of the Trujillo dictatorship, authoritarianism and corruption have dominated political life. But these conditions have not prevented the growth of popular organizations whose potential, if not actual achievements, is enormous. Ultimately the future of Dominican democracy lies with the poor of the shantytowns and rural communities who make up these organizations. Only with their inclusion in the developing political process can the Dominican Republic hope to move forward from its seemingly endless crisis.

Acronyms

ADP	*Asociación Dominicana de Profesores* Dominican Teachers' Association
AMD	*Asociación Médica Dominicana* Dominican Medical Association
CARICOM	Caribbean Common Market
CDE	*Corporación Dominicana de Electricidad* Dominican Electricity Corporation
CEDEE	*Centro Dominicano de Estudios de la Educación* Dominican Centre of Education Studies
CLP	*Comité de Lucha Popular* Popular Struggle Committee
CONAMUCA	*Confederación Nacional de Mujeres Campesinas* National Confederation of Peasant Women
COP	*Colectivo de Organizaciones Populares* Collective of Popular Organizations
COPADEBA	*Comités para la Defensa de los Derechos Barriales* Neighbourhood Rights Defence Committees
CUT	*Central Unitaria de Trabajadores* United Confederation of Workers
EEC	European Economic Community
GRIPAC	*Grupo de Investigación para la Acción Comunitaria* Research Group for Community Action
IADB	Inter American Development Bank
IFZ	Industrial Free Zone
IMF	International Monetary Fund
INESPRE	*Instituto para la Estabilización de los Precios* Institute for Price Stabilization
MCI	*Movimiento Campesino Independiente* Independent Peasant Movement
PLD	*Partido de la Liberación Dominicana* Dominican Liberation Party
PRD	*Partido Revolucionario Dominicano* Dominican Revolutionary Party
UNICEF	United Nations International Children's Emergency Fund
USAID	United States Agency for International Development

References

John T. Cuddington and Carlos Asilis (1990), 'Fiscal Policy, the Current Account and the External Debt Problem in the Dominican Republic'. *Journal of Latin American Studies*, Cambridge, vol 20, part 2.

Carmen Diana Deere *et al* (1990), *In the Shadows of the Sun: Caribbean Development Alternatives and US Policy*. Boulder CO, Westview Press.

GRIPAC (1990), *Por un movimiento social y popular alternativo*. Santo Domingo, GRIPAC.

Vanna Ianni (1990), 'De la democracía dominicana'. *Ciencia y Sociedad*, Santo Domingo, vol 15, no 1.

Select Bibliography

The following is a list of additional secondary works which should serve as a guide for more detailed reading on the themes covered in the book. Some sources appear more than once as they fall under several themes. Full publication details are given at the *first* listing of each reference. Thereafter, only a shortened version is provided.

SECTION ONE: *Expectations of a New Beginning*

Aimes, H.S., The Transition from Slave to Free Labor in Cuba', *The Yale Review*, 15 (May 1906)

Bell, K.N. & Morrell, W.P., *Select Documents on British Colonial Policy 1830–60*. Oxford, 1968

Bolland, O.N., 'The Politics of Freedom in the British Caribbean', in F. McGlynn & S. Drescher (eds.) *The Meaning of Freedom: Economics, Politics and Culture after Slavery*. Pittsburgh and London, 1992

Burn, W.L., *Emancipation and Apprenticeship in the British West Indies*. London, 1937

Curtin, P., 'The "Free System" in Theory and Practice' in Curtin, *Two Jamaicas: The Role of Ideas in a Tropical Colony, 1830–1865*. New York, 1970

Davy, J. *The West Indies Before and Since Slave Emancipation*, London, 1971 edn.

Holt, T. C., *The Problem of Freedom: Race, Labor and Politics in Jamaica and Britain, 1832–1938*. Baltimore: Kingston 1992

Leyburn, J., *The Haitian People*. New Haven, 1966

Marshall, W.K. 'Emancipation and Labour Relations in four Windward Islands', in D. Richardson (ed.), *Abolition and its Aftermath*, London, 1985

Matheison, W.L., *British Slavery and its Abolition, 1823–38*. New York, 1967

Phillippo, J.M., *Jamaica: Its Past and Present State*. London, 1843

Thome, J.A. & Kimball, J.H., *Emancipation in the West Indies*. New York, 1838

Wilmot, S., 'Not "Full Free": The Ex-Slaves and the Apprenticeship System in Jamaica, 1834–38", *Jamaica Journal*, 17:3 (1984)

Wright, J.M., *History of the Bahama Islands with a Special Study of the Abolition of Slavery in the Colony*. Baltimore, 1905

SECTION TWO: *Emancipation in Action*

Adamson, A., *Sugar Without Slaves: The Political Economy of British Guiana*. New Haven, 1972

Aimes, H.S., 'The Transition from Slave to Free Labor . . .'.

Besson, J. 'Land Tenure in the Free Villages of Trelawny, Jamaica: A Case Study in the Caribbean Peasant Response to Emancipation' *Slavery & Abolition*, 5 (May 1984)

Bigelow, J. *Jamaica in 1850*. London: New York, 1851

Bolland, O.N., *The Formation of a Colonial Society: Belize from Conquest to Crown Colony*. Baltimore, 1977

———, 'Reply to William Green's The Perils of Comparative History', *Comparative Studies in Society and History*, 26:1 (1984)

Burn, W.L., *Emancipation and Apprenticeship*

Curtin. P.D., 'The Free System . . .'

Davy, J., *The West Indies before and since Slave Emancipation*.

Eltis, D., 'Abolitionists Perceptions of Society after Slavery' in J. Walvin (ed). *Slavery and British Society, 1776–1846*. London, 1982

Fraginals, M.M., Pons, F.M. & Engerman, S., *Between Slavery and Free Labor: The Spanish Speaking Caribbean in the 19th Century* Baltimore, 1985

Green, W.A., 'Emancipation'. In *British Slave Emancipation: The Sugar Colonies and the Great Experiment, 1830–1865*. Oxford, 1976

———, 'The Perils of Comparative History: Belize and the Sugar Colonies after Slavery', *Comparative Studies in Society and History*, 26:1 (1984)

Hall, D.G., *Free Jamaica 1838–65: An Economic History*. New Haven, 1959

———, *Five of the Leewards, 1834–70: The Major Problems of the Post-emancipation Period in Antigua, Barbuda, Montserrat, Nevis and St. Kitts*. Barbados, 1971

Higman, B.W., 'Slavery Remembered: The Celebrations of Emancipation in Jamaica', *Journal of Caribbean Geography*, 2 (1986)

Holt, T.C., *The Problem of Freedom*

Johnson, H., *The Bahamas in Slavery and Freedom*. Kingston: London, 1991

Levy, C., *Emancipation, Sugar and Federalism: Barbados and the West Indies, 1833–1876*. Gainsville, 1980

Leyburn, J., *The Haitian People*

Marshall, T., 'Post-emancipation Adjustments in Barbados, 1838–76', in A. Thompson, (ed.), *Emancipation 1*, Barbados, 1986.

Marshall, W.K., 'Emancipation and Labour Relations . . .'.

McLewin, P., *Power and Economic Change: The Response to Emancipation in Jamaica and British Guiana, 1840–65*. New York, 1987.

Phillippo, J.M., *Jamaica: Its Past and Present State*

Shepherd, V.A., 'The Apprenticeship Experience on Jamaican Livestock Farms', *Jamaica Journal*, 22:1 (1989)

———, The Effects of the Abolition of Slavery on Jamaican Livestock Farms', *Slavery and Abolition* 10, 2 (1989)

Sires, R.V., Negro Labour in Jamaica in the Years Following Emancipation', *Journal of Negro History*, XXV:4 (1940)

The Narrative of Nancy Prince: A Black Woman's Odyssey through Russia and Jamaica. New York, 1990

Wilmot, S. (ed.), *Adjustments to Emancipation in Jamaica*, Social History Project Publication, Department of History, UWI, Mona, 1988

Wood, D., *Trinidad in Transition: The Years After Slavery*. London, 1968

SECTION THREE: *Peasants and Planters*

Beckles, H., *A History of Barbados: From Amerindian Settlement to Nation State.* Cambridge, 1990

Chamberlain, M., 'Renters and Farmers: The Barbadian Plantation Tenantry System, 1917–1937', *Journal of Caribbean History* 24:2 (1990)

Cross, M. & Marks, A., *Peasants, Plantations and Rural Communities in the Caribbean* Guildford, England, 1979

Eisner, G., *Jamaica 1830–1930: A Study in Economic Growth* Connecticut, 1961

Farley, R., 'The Rise of a Peasantry in British Guiana', *Social and Economic Studies* 2:4 (1954)

———, 'The Rise of Village Settlements in British Guiana', *Caribbean Quarterly*, 3:2 (1953)

Gomes, P., (ed.), *Rural Development in the Caribbean.* Kingston: London 1985

Handler, J., 'The History of Arrowroot and the Origin of the Peasantries in the British West Indies'. *Journal of Caribbean History*, 2 (1971)

Johnson, H., 'Post-emancipation Labour systems (in the Bahamas),' in Johnson, *The Bahamas in Slavery and Freedom* Kingston: London, 1991

———, 'The Origins and Early Development of Cane-Farming in Trinidad', *Journal of Caribbean History*, 54 (1972)

Knox, A.J., 'Opportunities and Opposition: The Rise of Jamaica's Black Peasantry and the Nature of Planter Resistance', *Canadian Review of Sociology and Anthropology*, 4 (1977)

Lobdell, R.A., 'British Officials and the West Indian Peasantry, 1842–1838', in M. Cross & G. Heuman (eds). *Labour in the Caribbean.* (London, 1988)

Lundhal, M., *Peasants and Poverty: a Study of Haiti.* New York, 1979

Mandle, J., *The Plantation Economy: Population and Economic Change in Guyana* Philadelphia, 1973.

Mintz, S., 'From Plantations to Peasantries in the Caribbean', in S. Mintz and S. Price (eds.), *Caribbean Contours*, Baltimore, 1985

———, 'The Question of Caribbean Peasantries: A Comment'. *Caribbean Studies* 1, 3 (1961)

———, *Caribbean Transformations.* Chicago, 1974

———, 'Slavery and the Rise of Peasantries', *Historical Reflections*, 6:1 (1979)

———, 'A Note on the Definition of Peasantries', *Journal of Peasant Studies*, 1 (1973)

Moore, B., *Race, Class and Social Segmentation in British Guiana.* New York, 1987

Paget, H., 'The Free Village System in Jamaica', *Caribbean Quarterly*, 1:4 (1954)

Satchell, V., *From Plots to Plantations: Land Transactions in Jamaica, 1866–1900.* UWI, Mona, 1990

Trouillot, M.R., *Peasants and Capital: Dominica in the World Economy.* Baltimore, 1988

SECTION FOUR: *Immigrants and Indentured Labourers*

Adamson, A., *Sugar Without Slaves*

———, 'The Reconstruction of Plantation Labour After Emancipation: The Case of British Guiana', in S. Engerman & E. Genovese, (eds.), *Race and Slavery in the Western Hemisphere.* Princeton, 1975

Birbalsingh, F. (ed.)., *Indenture and Exile: The Indo-Caribbean Experience.* Toronto, 1989

Bolland, O.N., *The Formation of a Colonial Society: Belize from Conquest to Crown Colony.*

———, 'Reply to William Green's The Perils of Comparative History'.

Bryan, P., 'The Question of Labor in the Sugar Industry of the Dominican Republic in the late 19th and early 20th Century', in Fraginals et al, *Between Slavery and Free Labor.*

Corbitt, D.C., 'Immigration in Cuba', *Hispanic American Historical Review*, 22 (May 1942)

Cross, M. & Heuman, G., (eds.). *Labour in the Caribbean.*

Cumper, G.E., 'Labour Demand and Supply in the Jamaican Sugar Industry, 1830–1950', *Social and Economic Studies* 2 (March 1954)

Dabydeen, D. & Samaroo, B. (eds.) *India in the Caribbean* Hansib/University of Warwick, 1987

Engerman, S. 'Economic Change and Contract Labour in the British Caribbean: The End of Slavery and the Adjustment to Emancipation', in Richardson (ed.), *Abolition and its Aftermath*

Espinal, R., 'The Dominican Working Class: Labour Control Under Trujillo and After', in Heuman & Cross, *Labour in the Caribbean*

Fraser, P.D., 'The Immigration Issue in British Guiana, 1903–1913, *Journal of Caribbean History*, 14 (1981)

Green, W.A., *British Slave Emancipation*

Hoefte, R., 'The Quest for Labour in a Plantation Economy: Indentured Immigration to Suriname, 1863–1939', *Latinoamercanist*, 18:1 (1982)

———, 'Female Indentured Labour in Suriname: For Better or Worse?', *Boletin de Estudios Latinoamericanos y del Caribe*, 42 (1987)

———, 'The Position of Female British Indian and Javanese Contract Labourers in Suriname: A Last Word', *Boletin de Estudios Latinoamericanos y del Caribe*, 43, (1987)

Johnson, H., ed., *After the Crossing: Immigrants and Minorities in Caribbean Creole Society.* London, 1988

———, 'Immigration and the Sugar Industry of Trinidad at the end of the 19th Century', *Journal of Caribbean History*, 3 (1971)

———, 'The Anti-Chinese Riots of 1918 in Jamaica', *Caribbean Quarterly*, 28 (1982)

Kloosterboer, W., *Involuntary Labour since the Abolition of Slavery.* Reprint, Westport, Connec., 1976

Laurence, K.0., *Immigration Into the West Indies in the 19th Century.* Chapters in Caribbean History Series, Bridgetown, 1971.

Leyburn, J., *The Haitian People* 1941. New Haven, 1966 edn.

Lundhal, M., 'The Rise and Fall of the Haitian Labour Movement', in Cross & Heuman, *Labour in the Caribbean.*

Mangru, B., *Benevolent Neutrality: Indian Government Policy and Labour Migration to British Guyana, 1854–1884.* Hansib: London, 1987

Marshall, W.K., *The Postslavery Labour Problem Revisited.* Elsa Goveia Memorial Lecture, Dept. of History, UWI, Mona, 1991

Moore, B., *Race, Class and Social Segmentation in British Guiana*

Moutoussamy, E., *La Guadeloupe et son Indianite.* Paris, 1987

Riviere, W.E., 'Labour Shortage in the BWI after Emancipation'. *Journal of Caribbean History*, 4 (May 1972) 1–30.

Rodney, W., *A History of the Guyanese Working People 1881–1905.* London, 1981

Schuler, M., 'Working slave'. in *Alas, Alas, Kongo: A Social History of Indentured African Immigration into Jamaica, 1841–1865.* Baltimore, 1980

———, *Liberated Africans in 19th Century Guyana*, U.W.I., Mona, 1991

Scott, R., 'Labour control in Cuba after emancipation,' in Cross & Heuman *Labour in the Caribbean*

Senior, H.C., 'German Immigrants in Jamaica, 1834–38'. *Journal of Caribbean History*, 10 & 11 (1978), 25–53

Sewell, W.G., *The Ordeal of Free Labour in the British West Indies*. London, 1968

Shepherd, V., 'From Rural Plantations to Urban Slums: The Economic Status and Problems of "East" Indians in Kingston Jamaica in the late 19th and early 20th century', *Immigrants & Minorities*, 5:2 (1986)

———, 'Indian Women in Jamaica, 1845–1945', in Birbalsingh, ed, *Indenture and Exile*.

———, Transients to Citizens: The Development of a Settled Indian Community in Jamaica', *Jamaica Journal,* 18 (1985)

Thomas, M.E., *Jamaica and Involuntary Laborers from Africa, 1840–1865*. Gainsville, 1974

Thompson, A., 'Historical Writing on Migration into the Commonwealth Caribbean: A Bibliographical Review of the Period c. 1838 — c. 1938', *Immigrants and Minorities*, 5:2 (1986)

Tinker, H., 'The Origins of Indian Migration to the West Indies', in Birbalsingh, *Indenture and Exile*.

Trouillot, M.R., 'Labour and Emancipation in Dominica: Contribution to a Debate', *Caribbean Quarterly*, 30: 3&4 (1984)

Wood, D., *Trinidad in Transition: The Years after Slavery* (London, 1968)

SECTION FIVE: *Government, Political Control and Popular Revolt*

Ayearst, M., *The British West Indies: The Search for Self Government*. Washington Square, New York, 1960

Bakan, A., *Ideology and Class Conflict in Jamaica: The Politics of Rebellion*, Montreal, 1990

Baud, M., 'Peasant Resistance in the Dominican Republic, 1870–1924', in Cross & Heuman *Labour in the Caribbean*

Burt, A., 'The First Installment of Representative Government in Jamaica, 1884', *Social and Economic Studies*, 11 (Sept., 1962)

Chan, V.O., 'The Riots of 1856 in British Guiana', *Caribbean Quarterly,* 16 (1970)

Chase, R., 'Protest in Post-emancipation Dominica: The Guerre Negre of 1844', *Journal of Caribbean History*, 23:2 (1989)

Currey, H.F., 'British Honduras: From Public Meeting to Crown Colony'. *The Americas*, 13 (1956)

Curtin, P.D., *Two Jamaicas*

Dupuy, A., 'Spanish Colonialism and the Origin of Underdevelopment in Haiti', *Latin American Perspectives*, 3:2 (1970)

Dutton, G., *In Search of Governor Eyre*. New York: South Melbourne, 1982

———, *The Hero as Murderer: the Life of Edward John Eyre*. London, 1967

Hall, D.G., *Free Jamaica*

———, *Five of the Leewards*

Heuman, G., *Between Black and White: Race, Politics and the Free Coloureds in Jamaica, 1792–1865*. Westport, Conn., 1981

———, 'The Struggle for the Settler Vote: Politics and the Franchise of Post-emancipation Jamaica', in Cross & Marks, *Peasants, Plantations and Rural Communities in the Caribbean*

Hoefte, R., 'Control and Resistance: Indentured Labour in Suriname', *Nieuwe West Indische Gids (New West Indian Guide)*, 61:1, 2 (1987)

Hoetink, H., *The Dominican People, 1850–1900*. Baltimore: London, 1983

Knox, B., 'The Queen's letter of 1865 and British Policy towards Emancipation and Indentured Labour in the West Indies 1830–65', *Historical Journal*, 29 (June 1986)

———, 'The British Government and the Governor Eyre Controversy, 1865–1875', *Historical Journal*, 19 (1976)

Manning, H., *British Colonial Government after the Revolution*. New Haven, 1933

Mintz, S.W., 'The Rural Proletariat and the Problem of Rural Proletarian Consciousness', *Journal of Peasant Studies*, 1:3 (1974)

Moore, B.L., *Race, Class and Social Segmentation*

Nicholls. D., *Haiti in Caribbean Context: Ethnicity, Economy and Revolt*. London, 1985

Olivier, Lord S., *The Myth of Governor Eyre*. London, 1933.

Pim, B.C.T., *The Negro and Jamaica*. London, 1866

Ramos Mattei, A., 'The Rise of a Sugar Proletariat Labour Force and the Emergence of Strikes in the Puerto Rican Sugar Industry, 1873–1905', in Cross & Heuman, *Labour in the Caribbean*

Roberts, S., *The History of French Colonial Policy*. (London, 1963)

Robotham, D., 'The "Notorious Riots": The Socio-economic and Political Bases of Paul Bogle's Revolt', UWI, Mona, 1981

Rodney, W., *History of the Guyanese Working People*

Schuler, M., *Alas, Alas, Kongo*

Semmel, B., *The Governor Eyre Controversy*. London, 1962

Singh, K., *Bloodstained Tombs: The Muharram Massacre, 1884*. London, 1988

Turton, P., *Jose Marti: Architect of Cuba's Freedom*. London, 1986

Ward, S.R., *Reflections upon the Gordon Rebellion*. n.p., 1866

Will, H.A., *Constitutional Change in the British West Indies, 1880–1903*. Oxford, 1970

Williams, N., *A History of the Cayman Islands*. Grand Cayman, 1970

Wilmot, S., 'Race, Electoral Violence and Constitutional Reform in Jamaica, 1830–54', *Journal of Caribbean History*, 17 (1982), 1–13

Wrong, H., *Government of the West Indies*. Oxford, 1923

SECTION SIX: *Women and Gender*

Brereton, B., 'General Problems and Issues in Studying the History of Women', in P. Mohammed and C. Shepherd, (eds.), *Gender in Caribbean Development*. UWI, 1988

Brodber, E., 'Afro-Jamaican Women at the Turn of the Century', *Social & Economic Studies*, 35 (1986)

French, J., 'Colonial Policy Towards Women after the 1938 Uprising: The Case of Jamaica', *Caribbean Quarterly*, 34:3,4 (1988)

Haniff, N.Z., *Blaze a Fire*

Hart, K. (ed.), *Women and the Sexual Division of Labour in the Caribbean*. Kingston, 1989

Higman, B.W., 'Domestic Service in Jamaica since 1750', in Higman (ed.), *Trade, Government and Society in Caribbean History*. Kingston, 1983

Hoefte, R., 'Female Indentured Labour in Suriname'

———, 'The Position of Female British Indian and Javanese Contract Labourers in Suriname: A Last Word'.

Kelley, D., 'St. Lucia's Female Electronics Factory Workers: Key Components in an Export-oriented Industrialization Strategy', *World Development*, 14 (1986)

Lobdell, R., 'Women in the Jamaican Labour Force, 1881–1921', *Social and Economic Studies*, 37 (1988)

Massiah, J. (ed.), 'Women in the Caribbean', Vols 1 & 2. *Social and Economic Studies*, 35:2, 3 (1986)

Mohammed, P. & Shepherd, C., (eds.), *Gender in Caribbean Development*. UWI, 1988

Reddock, R., *Elma Francois: The NWCSA and the Workers' Struggle for Change in the Caribbean*. London, 1988

Safa, H., 'Economic Autonomy and Sexual Equality in Caribbean Society', *Social and Economic Studies*, 35 (1986)

Senior, O., *Working Miracles: Women's Lives in the English-Speaking Caribbean*. London: Indiana, 1991

Shepherd, V., ———, 'Indian Women in Jamaica'.

Wiltshire-Brodber, R., 'Gender, Race and Class in the Caribbean', in Mohammed & Shepherd, *Gender in Caribbean Development*

SECTION SEVEN: *Social Policy and Class Formation*

Beckles, H., *A History of Barbados*

Bellegarde-Smith, P., 'Haitian Social Thought in the 19th Century: Class Formation and Westernization', *Caribbean Studies*, 20:1 (1980)

Bolt, C., *Victorian Attitudes to Race*. Toronto, 1971

Brereton, B., 'Society and Culture in the Caribbean', in F. Knight and M. Cross (eds)., *The Modern Caribbean*: North Carolina, 1989

———, *Race Relations in Colonial Trinidad* Cambridge, 1979.

———, *A History of Modern Trinidad*. Kingston, 1991

Bryan, P., *The Jamaican People* McMillan Caribbean, 1991

Campbell, C., *Colony and Nation: A Short History of Education in Trinidad and Tobago*. Kingston, 1992

Eisner, G., *Jamaica, 1830–1930*

Gordon, S., *A Century of West Indian Education*. London, 1963

Green, W.A., *British Slave Emancipation*

Greenfield, S. M., *English Rustics in Black Skin: A Study of Modern Family Forms in a Pre-industrialized Society*. New Haven, 1967

Henriques, F., *Family and Colour in Jamaica*. London, 1953

Holt, T.C., *The Problem of Freedom: Race, Labor and Politics in Jamaica and Britain, 1932–1938*

Lowenthal, D., *West Indian Societies*. New York, 1972

Moore, B., *Race, Class and Social Segmentation*

Roberts, G., *The Population of Jamaica*. Cambridge, 1957.

Smith, R.T., 'Family, Social Change and Social Policy in the West Indies', *New West Indian Guide*, 56:3, 4 (1982)

SECTION EIGHT: *The Sugar Industry: Crisis and Adjustments*

Albert, B. & Graves, A., *Crisis and Change in the International Sugar Economy, 1860–1914*. Norwich, 1984

Beachy, R.W., *The British West Indies Sugar Industry in the late 19th Century*. Oxford, 1957

Brown, D.R., 'The Response of the Banking Sector to the General Crisis Trinidad, 1836–56', *Journal of Caribbean History*, 24, 1 (1990)

Castillo, Jose del, 'The Formation of the Dominican Sugar Industry in Fraginals et al, *Between Slavery and Free Labor*

Curtin, P.D., 'The British Sugar Duties and West Indian Prosperity', *Journal of Economic History*, xiv, (1954)

———, *Two Jamaicas*

Cust, R., *A Treatise on the West Indian Incumbered Estates Act*. London, 1865

Davy, J., *The West Indies Before and Since Slave Emancipation*. London, 1854

Eisner, G., *Jamaica 1830–1930*

Feuer, C.H., 'Better must come: Sugar and Jamaica in the 20th century', *Social and Economic Studies*, 33 (1984)

Garcia, Fe Iglesias, 'The Development of Capitalism in Cuban Sugar Production, 1860–1900', in Fraginals, et al. *Between Slavery and Free Labor*

Green, W.A., *British Slave Emancipation*

———, 'The Planter Class and British West Indian Sugar Production before and after Emancipation', *Economic History Review*, 26 (1973)

Hall, D.G., *Free Jamaica*

———, *Five of the Leewards*

Higman, B.W., 'The Internal Economy of the Jamaican Pens, 1760–1890'. *Social and Economic Studies*, 38: 1 (1989)

Hoernel, R.B., 'Sugar and Social Change in Oriente, Cuba 1898–1946', *Journal of Latin American Studies* 8 (1976)

Karch, C., 'The Role of the Barbados Mutual Life Assurance Society During the International Sugar Crisis of the late 19th century', in K.O. Laurence, ed., Papers from the 12th Association of Caribbean Historians' Conference, Barbados, 1984

Knight, F., 'Jamaican Migrants and the Cuban Sugar Industry, 1900–34', in Fraginals, et al., *Between Slavery and Free Labor*

Levy, C., *Emancipation, Sugar and Federalism*

Mandle, J., *The Plantation Economy: Population and Economic Change in Guyana*

Ramos Mattei, A., 'Technical Innovations and Social Change in the Sugar Industry of Puerto Rico, 1870–1880, in Fraginals et al., *Between Slavery and Free Labor*

Rodney, W., *A History of the Guyanese Working People*

Satchell, V., *From Plots to Plantations*

Sewell, W., *The Ordeal of Free Labour*

Trouillot, M.R., *Peasants and Capital*

Wills, J., 'Colonial Policy and Economic Development in the B.W.I. 1895–1903', *Economic History Review*, 23 (1970)

SECTION NINE: *The Labour Movement: Decolonization and Democracy*

Beckles, H., *A History of Barbados*

Bell, W., The Democratic Revolution in the West Indies Cambridge, Mass., 1967

Bolland, O.N., 'The Labour Movement and the Genesis of Modern Politics in Belize', in Cross & Heuman, *Labour in the Caribbean*

———, *Colonialism and Resistance in Belize: Essays in Historical Sociology*. Belize, 1988

Breakthrough from Colonialism: An Interdisciplinary Study of Statehood. Rio Piedras, Puerto Rico, 1984

Brereton, B., *A History of Modern Trinidad*

Burton, R.D., *Assimilation or Independence?: Prospects from Martinique*. Montreal, 1978

Cacho, C.P., 'British Honduras: A Case of Deviation in Commonwealth Caribbean Decolonization', *New World Quarterly*, 3:3 (1967)

Campbell, E., *Trade Unions and Modernization: The Case of Suriname*. Eindhoven: [s.n.] 1988

Campbell, H., *Rasta and Resistance: From Marcus Garvey to Walter Rodney*. New Jersey, 1987

Carnegie, J., *Some Aspects of Jamaican Politics, 1918–1938* Kingston, 1969

Chase, A., *A History of Trade Unionism In Guyana, 1900–61*. Georgetown, 1964

Craig, S., *Smiles and Blood: The Ruling Class Response to the Workers' Rebellion of 1937 in Trinidad and Tobago*. London, 1988

Craton, M., *A History of the Bahamas*. London, 1968

Cordova, E., *Castro and the Cuban Labour Movement: Statecraft and Society in a Revolutionary Period, 1959–1961*. Lanham, Maryland, 1987

Cronin, E.D., *Black Moses: The Story of Marcus Garvey and the UNIA*. Madison, 1955

Cross, M., 'The Political Representation of Organized Labour in Trinidad and Guyana: A Comparative Puzzle', in Cross & Heuman, *Labour in the Caribbean*.

Eaton, G., *Alexander Bustamante and Modern Jamaica*. Kingston, 1975

Elkins, W.F., *Black Power in the Caribbean: The Beginnings of the Modern National Movement*. New York, 1977

Emmanuel, P., *Crown Colony Politics in Grenada, 1917–51*. Bridgetown, 1978

Erskine, N.L., *Decolonizing Theology*. New York, 1981

Fernandez, J.A., *Belize: A Case Study for Democracy in Central America*. Hants., England, 1989

French, J., 'Colonial Policy Towards Women after the 1938 Uprising. . . .'.

Galvin, M., 'The Early Development of the Organized Labor Movement in Puerto Rico', *Latin American Perspectives*, 3 (1976)

Hamilton, B., 'Marcus Garvey: Cultural Activist', *Jamaica Journal*, 20:3 (1987)

———, 'Trade Unionism in the English-Speaking Caribbean: The Formative Years and the Caribbean Labour Congress', in S. Craig (ed.), *The Contemporary Caribbean: A Sociological Reader*. Port of Spain, 1982

Hennessey, A., 'The Imperatives and Complexities of the Cuban Labour Movement', in Cross & Heuman, *Labour in the Caribbean*

Henry, Z., *Labour Relations and Industrial Conflict in the Commonwealth Caribbean*. Port of Spain, 1972

Hoyos, F.A., *Grantley Adams and the Social Revolution* London, 1974

Hunte, K., 'Duncan O'Neale: Apostle of Freedom', *New World Quarterly*, 3:1, 2 (1966)

Jacobs, W.R., 'The Politics of Protest in Trinidad: The Strikes and Disturbances of 1937', *Caribbean Studies*, 17:1, 2 (1977)

Jacques-Garvey, A., (ed.), *Philosophy and Opinions of Marcus Garvey*. New York, 1986

———, & Essien-Udom, E.U., (eds.), *More Philosophy and Opinions of Marcus Garvey*. London, 1987

James, C.L.R., *The Life of Captain Cipriani: The Case for West Indian Self-Government*. London, 1932

Johnson, H., 'Oil, Imperial Policy and the Trinidad Disturbances, 1937', *Journal of Imperial and Commonwealth History*, 4:1 (1975)

Kambon, K., *For Bread, Justice and Freedom: A Political Biography of George Weekes*. London, 1988

Knowles, W.H., *Trade Union Development and Industrial Relation in the British West Indies*. Berkeley, 1959

Lewis, G.K., *Notes on the Puerto Rican Revolution: An Essay on American Dominance and Caribbean Resistance*. New York, 1974

Lewis, R. & Bryan, P., *Garvey: His Work and Impact* I.S.E.R., UWI, Mona, 1988

Lewis, R., 'Garvey's Forerunners: Love and Bedward', *Race and Class*, 28 (Winter 1987)

Lewis, W.A., *Labour in the West Indies: The Birth of a Workers Movement*. London, 1939

Lundhal, M., 'The Rise and Fall of the Haitian Labour Movement'.

Manley, M., *A Voice at the Workplace*. Washington, 1991

Mark, F., *The History of the Barbados Worker's Union*. Barbados, 1965.

Martin, A., *Race First: The Ideological and Organizational Struggles of Marcus Garvey and the U.N.I.A.* Westport, Connec. 1976

Martin, T., 'Revolutionary Upheaval in Trinidad, 1919', *Journal of Negro History*, LVIII, 3 (1973)

Munroe, T., *The Politics of Constitutional Decolonization in Jamaica, 1944–62*. I.S.E.R., Mona, 1972

——— & Robotham, D., *Struggles of the Jamaican People*. Kingston, 1977

Nicholls, D., *From Dessalines to Duvalier: Race, Colour and National Independence in Haiti*. Cambridge, 1976

Obika, N., *An Introduction to the Life and Times of T.U.B. Butler: The Father of the Nation*. Trinidad, 1983

O'Gorman, P., 'On Reggae and Rastafarianism — and a Garvey Prophecy', *Jamaica Journal*, 20:3 (1987)

Oxaal, I., *Race and Revolutionary Consciousness: A Documentary Interpretation of the 1970 Black Power Revolt in Trinidad*. Cambridge, Mass., 1971

Palmer, C., 'Identity, Race and Black Power in Independent Jamaica', in Knight and Palmer, eds., *The Modern Caribbean*

Perez, L.A., *Cuba Between Empires*. Pittsburgh, 1982

Phelps. O., 'Rise of the Labour Movement in Jamaica', *Social and Economic Studies*, 18:4 (1960)

Post, K., 'The Politics of Protest in Jamaica', *Social and Economic Studies*, 18:4 (1960)

———, *Arise Ye Starvelings: The Jamaican Labour Rebellion of 1938*. The Hague, 1978.

———, *Strike the Iron: A Colony at War: Jamaica 1939–45* 2 Vols., The Hague, 1981

Reddock, R., *Elma Francois*

Rich, P., 'Sydney Olivier, Jamaica and the Debate on British Colonial Policy in the West Indies', in Cross & Heuman, *Labour in the Caribbean*

Rodney, W., *A History of the Guyanese Working People*

Ryan, S., *Race and Nationalism in Trinidad and Tobago: A Study of Decolonization in a Multiracial Society*. Toronto, 1972

Samaroo, B., 'The Trinidad Workingmen's Association and the Origin of Popular Protest in a Crown Colony', *Social and Economic Studies*, 21:2 (1972)

Singham, A., *The Hero and the Crowd in a Colonial Policy*. New Haven, 1968

Stone, C. & Brown, A., (eds.), *Essays in Power and Change in Jamaica*. Kingston, 1977

St. Pierre, M., 'The 1938 Jamaica Disturbances: A Portrait of Mass Reaction against Colonialism', *Social and Economic Studies*, 27 (1978)

Stubbs, J., *Tobacco on the Periphery: A Case Study of Cuban Labour History, 1860–1958*. Cambridge, 1985

Thomas, R., *The Trinidad Labor Riots of 1937*

Turton, P., *Jose Marti*

SECTION TEN: *Economic Diversification and Transformation*

Andie, F.M., *Fiscal Survey of the French Caribbean*. Puerto Rico, 1965

Beckford, G., *Persistent Poverty: Underdevelopment in Plantation Economies in the Third World*. New York, 1972

———, *Readings in Caribbean Economy*. I.S.E.R., 1975

Bergad, L.W., *Coffee and the Growth of Agrarian Capitalism in 19th century Puerto Rico*. Princeton, 1983

Bernal, R., 'The Great Depression, Colonial Policy and Industrialization in Jamaica', *Social and Economic Studies*, 37 (1988)

Best, L. & Levitt, K., *Externally Propelled Industrialization and Growth in the Caribbean*. Montreal, 1968

Burton, R.D., *Assimilation or Independence?: Prospects for Martinique*. Montreal, 1978

Campos, R. & Bonilla, F., 'Bootstraps and Enterprize Zones: The Underside of Late Capitalism in Puerto Rico and the United States', *Review*, 4 (1982)

Cross & Marks, *Peasants, Plantations and Rural Communities in the Caribbean*

de Kadt, E., (ed)., *Patterns of Foreign Influence in the Caribbean*. Oxford, 1972

Dietz, J.L., *Economic History of Puerto Rico: Institutional Change and Capitalist Development.* New Jersey, 1986

Eisner, G., *Jamaica 1830–1930*

Farrell, T., 'Arthur Lewis, and the Case for Caribbean Industrialization', *Social and Economic Studies*, 29 (1980)

Girvan, N., *Corporate Imperialism.* New York, 1976

——, *Foreign Capital and Economic Underdevelopment in Jamaica* , Kingston , 1971

——, *The Caribbean Bauxite Industry.* I.S.E.R., Mona, 1967

—— & *Readings in the Political Economy of the*
Jefferson, O., *Caribbean.* Kingston, 1971

Goslinga, C.C., *The Dutch in the Caribbean and in Suriname, 1791–1942.* Van Gorcum, 1990

Handler, J., 'The History of Arrowroot and the Origin of Peasantries'. Journal of Caribbean History, II (1971)

Hart, A., 'The Banana in Jamaica: Export Trade', *Social and Economic Studies*, 3:2 (1954)

Higman, B.W., 'Domestic Service in Jamaica since 1750', in Higman, (ed.), *Trade, Government and Society in Caribbean History.*

——, 'The Internal Economy of the Jamaican Pens'.

Hope, K., *Economic Development in the Caribbean.* New York, 1986

Jefferson, O., *The Post War Economic Development of Jamaica* Mona, Jamaica, 1972

Kelley, D., 'St. Lucia's Female Electronics Factory Workers:

Lewis, W.A., 'Industrialization of the British West Indies', *Caribbean Economic Review*, 2 (1950)

Mandle, J., *The Plantation Economy*

——, *Patterns of Caribbean Development: An Interpretive Essay on Economic Change.* New York, 1982

McKee, D.L., *Developmental Issues in Small Island Economies.* New York, 1990

Moohr, M., 'The Discovery of Gold and the Development of Peasant Industries in Guyana, 1884–1914', *Caribbean Studies*, 15:2

Newton, V., *The Silver Men: West Indian Labour Migration to Panama, 1850–1914.* Kingston, 1984

O'Loughlin, C., *Economic and Political Change.* New Haven, 1968.

Rampersad, F.B., *Growth and Structural Change in the Economy of Trinidad and Tobago, 1951–61.* Mona, 1963

Richardson, B., *Panama Money in Barbados, 1900–20.* Tennessee, 1985

Satchell, V., *From Plots to Plantations*

Sleeman, M., 'The Agri-business Bourgeoise in Barbados and Martinique', in Gomes (ed.), *Rural Development in the Caribbean*

Thompson, R., *Green Gold: Bananas and Dependency in the Eastern Caribbean.* Connec., 1987

Ward, J.R., *Poverty and Progress in the Caribbean, 1800–1960.* Basingstoke, 1985

Brewster, H., 'Economic Dependence: A Quantitative Interpretation', *Social and Economic Studies* 22 (1973)

Burton, R.D., *Assimilation or Independence?: Prospects for Martinique.* Montreal, 1978

Chernick, S.E., *The Commonwealth Caribbean: The Integration Experience.* Baltimore, 1978

Demas, W., *Essays on Caribbean Integration and Development.* Kingston, 1976

Dietz, J.L., 'Imperialism and Underdevelopment: A Theoretical Perspective and a Case Study of Puerto Rico', *Review of Radical Political Economics*, 11 (1979)

Douglas, P.H., 'The American Occupation of Haiti', *Political Science Quarterly*, 42 (1927)

Erisman, H.M., *The Caribbean Challenge: US Policy in a Volatile Region.* Boulder, Colorado, 1984

Foner, P.S., *The Spanish-Cuban-American War and the Birth of American Imperialism.* 2 vols. New York, 1972

Hatch, J.C., *Dwell Together in Unity.* London, 1958

Hawkins, I., *The Changing Face of the Caribbean.* Bridgetown, 1976

Heine, J., 'Beyond bootstrap: Puerto Rico's Development Experiences and the Third World in the 1980s'. *Trans Africa Forum*, 1:3 (1983)

Langley, L., *The U.S. and the Caribbean, 1900–1970.* Georgia, 1980

Joseph, C.L., 'The strategic importance of the British West Indies, 1882–1932', *Journal of Caribbean History*, 7 (1973)

Lowenthal, D., (ed.), *The West Indies Federation.* New York, 1961

Meikle, L.S., *Confederation of the British West Indies versus Annexation to the United States of America: A Political Discourse on the West Indies.* New York, 1969

Montaque, L.L., *Haiti and the US, 1714–1938.* New York, 1966

Mordecai, J., *The West Indies: The Federal Negotiations* London, 1968

Murch, A., *Black Frenchmen: The Political Integration of the French Antilles.* Cam:, Mass., 1971

Palmer, R.W., *Caribbean Dependency on the United States Economy.* New York, 1979

Perloff, H.S., *Puerto Rico's Economic Future: A Study in Planned Development.* Chicago, 1950

Poner, P., *History of Cuba and its Relations with the United States*

Proudfoot, M., *Britain and the United States in the Caribbean: A Comparative Study in Methods of Development.* New York, 1954

Schmidt, H., *The U.S. Occupation of Haiti, 1915–1934* New Brunswick, 1971

Wallace, E., *The British Caribbean from the Decline of Colonialism to the end of Federation.* Toronto, 1977

SECTION ELEVEN: *Political and Economic Integration*

Axline, W., *Caribbean Integration: The Politics of Regionalism.* New York, 1979

Balassa, B., *The Theory of Economic Integration.* Illinois, 1961

Barry, T., Wood, B., & Preusch, D., *The Other Side of Paradise: Foreign Control in the Caribbean.* New York, 1984

Beckford, G. ed., *Caribbean Economy.* I.S.E.R., 1975

Benjamin, J. R., *The United States and Cuba: Hegemony and Dependent Development, 1880–1934.* Pittsburgh, 1977

Brewster, H., *The Dynamics of West Indian Economic Integration* & Thomas, C., I.S.E.R., Mona, 1967

SECTION TWELVE: *Independence, Nationhood and Identity*

Ashcraft, N., *Colonialism and Underdevelopment: Processes of Political Economic Change in British Honduras.* New York, 1973

Bakan, A. *Ideology and Class Conflict*

Beckles, H., 'From Colony to State', in Beckles, *History of Barbados*

Bell, W., *Jamaican Leaders: Political Attitudes in a New Nation.* Berkeley, 1984

Black, J.K., *The Dominican Republic: Politics and Development in an Unsovereign State.* Boston, 1986

Burton, R.D., *Assimilation or Independence?*

Cacho, C.P., 'British Honduras: A Case of Deviation in Commonwealth Caribbean Decolonization', *New World Quarterly*, 3:3 (1967)

Chin, H. & Buddingh, H., *Suriname: Politics, Economics and Society*. London, 1987

Craton, M., *A History of the Bahamas*

Creque, D.D., *The U.S. Virgin Islands and the Eastern Caribbean*. Philadelphia, 1968

Despres, L., *Cultural Pluralism and Nationalist Politics in British Guiana*. Chicago, 1967

Dookhan, I., 'Military-Civilian Conflicts in the Virgin Islands During World War 2', *Journal of Caribbean History*, 24:1 (1990)

Edie, C.J., *Democracy by Default: Dependency and Clientelism in Jamaica*. Boulder, Colorado, Kingston, 1990

Glissant, E., *Caribbean Discourse: Selected Essays*. Virginia, 1989

Grant, C.H., *The Making of Modern Belize: Politics, Society and British Colonialism in Central America*. Cambridge, 1976

Gray, O., *Radicalism and Social Change in Jamaica, 1960–72* Tennessee, 1991

Hughes, C.A., *Race and Politics in the Bahamas*. St. Lucia, 1981

Ince, B.A., *Decolonization and Conflict in the United Nations: Guyana's Struggle for Independence*. Cam: Mass., 1974

James, C.L.R., *The Future in the Present*. London, 1977

Johnson, R.A., *Puerto Rico: Commonwealth or Colony?* New York, 1980

Knight, F., *The Caribbean: Genesis of a Fragmented Nationalism*. New York, 1990 edn.

Lewis, G.K., *Growth of the Modern West Indies*. New York, 1968

———, *Puerto Rico: Freedom and Power in the Caribbean*. New York, 1963

Lidin, H.J., *History of the Puerto Rican Independence Movement*. New Jersey, 1981

Lowenthal, D., *The Aftermath of Sovereignty: West Indian Perspectives*. New York, 1973

Magid, A., *Urban Nationalism: A Study of Political Development in Trinidad*. Gainsville: Florida, 1988

Manley, N.W., *Norman Washington Manley and the New Jamaica: Selected Speeches and Writing*. Longman, Caribbean, 1971

Marable, M., *African and Caribbean Politics from Kwame Nkrumah to the Grenada Revolution*. London, 1987

Moen, A.M., 'Curacao 1969: Crisis and Change', in Craig, *Sociological Reader*

Munroe, T., *The Politics of Constitutional Decolonization*

Murch, A., *Black Frenchmen: The Political Integration of the French Antilles*

Nettleford, R., et al., *The Rastafarians in Jamaica*

O'Loughlin, C., *Economic and Political Change in the Leeward and Windward Islands*.

Oxaal. I., *Black Intellectuals Come to Power* Cambridge: Mass., 1968

Premdas, R., *Party Politics and Racial Division in Guyana* Denver, 1973

Roberts, S., *The History of French Colonial Policy, 1870–1925* London, 1963

Rodney, W., *Groundings with my Brother*. London, 1969

Ryan, S., *Race and Nationalism in Trinidad and Tobago* Toronto, 1872

Samoiloff, L.C., *The Spanish Caribbean from Columbus to Castro* Boston, 1979

Shoman, A., 'Birth of the Nationalist Movement in Belize, 1950–54', *Journal of Belizean Affairs*, 2 (1973)

Stone, C. *Power in the Caribbean Basin: A Comparative Study of Political Economy*. Philadelphia, 1986

———, *Democracy and Clientelism in Jamaica*. New Brunswick, 1980

The Intellectual Roots of Independence: An Anthology of Puerto Rican Political essays. New York, 1980

Thomas, H., *Cuba*. London, 1971

Williams, E., 'The Colonial Nationalist Movement', in E. Williams, *From Columbus to Castro: The History of the Caribbean, 1492–1969*. Andre Deutsch: London, 1970

Witter, M. et al, *Small Garden, Bitter Weed*. London, 1982

Young, A., *Approaches to Local Self-Government in British Guiana*. London, 1958

SECTION THIRTEEN: *Protest, Socialism and Revolution*

Ameringer, C.D., *The Democratic Left in Exile: The Anti-dictatorial Struggle in the Caribbean, 1945–59*. Florida, 1974

Blerald, P.A., 'Guadeloupe-Martinique: A System of Colonial Domination in Crisis', in F. Ambursley and R. Cohen (eds.), *Crisis in the Caribbean*. New York, 1983

Bennett, H., *The Modern Caribbean*. Chapel Hill, 1989

Bishop, M., *In Nobody's Backyard: Maurice Bishop's 1979–1983*. London, 1984

Castro, F., *History Will Absolve Me*. Havana, 1967

———, *Revolutionary Struggle, 1947–58*. Cam: M.I.T., 1972

Corbitt, D., 'Cuban Revisionist Interpretations of Cuba's Struggle for Independence', *Hispanic American Historical Review*, 43 (1963)

Dietz, J.L., 'Imperialism and Underdevelopment. . .'.

Ferguson, J., *Dominican Republic: Beyond the Lighthouse*. London, 1992

Heine, J., *A Revolution Aborted: The Lessons of Grenada*. Pittsburgh, 1991

Hooker, J.R., *Black Revolutionary: George Padmore's Path from Communism to Panafricanism*. London, 1967

Hoyos, F.A., *Grantley Adams and the Social Revolution*.

Jagan, C., *The Caribbean: Whose Backyard?* s.i., s.n., 1984

———, *A West Indian State: Pro-imperialist or Anti-imperialist?*

Kaufman, M., *Jamaica Under Manley: Dilemmas of Socialism and Democracy*. Connecticut, 1985

Lewis, G.K., *Puerto Rico: Freedom and Power*

Lidin, H.J., *History of the Puerto Rican Independence Movement*.

Liss, S., *Roots of Radicalism: Radical Thought in Cuba*. Nebraska, 1987

Manley, M., *The Politics of Change: A Jamaican Testament*. London, 1974

———, *Struggle in the Periphery*. London, 1982

Medin, T., *Cuba: The Shaping of Revolutionary Consciousness* Boulder: Colorado, 1990

Nettleford, R., *Identity, Race and Protest*. New York, 1972

Oxaal, I., *Race and Revolutionary Consciousness*

Payne, A., 'From Michael with Love: The Nature of Socialism in Jamaica', *Journal of Commonwealth and Comparative Politics*, X1V (1976)

Ruiz, R., *Cuba: The Making of a Revolution*. Massachusetts, 1968

Stephens, E.H & Stephens, J.D., *Democratic Socialism in Jamaica: The Political Movement and Social Transformation in Dependent Capitalism*. Princeton, 1986

Thomas, C.Y., *Dependence and Transformation: The Economics of the Transition to Socialism*. New York, 1974